Solutions Manual for

Calculus

with Trigonometry and Analytic Geometry

Second Edition

John H. Saxon Jr.

Frank Y. H. Wang

Revised by:

Bret L. Crock

James A. Sellers

Calculus with Trigonometry and Analytic Geometry
Second Edition

Solutions Manual

Printed in the United States of America.

ISBN: 1-56577-148-6

Editorial staff: Brian Rice, Clint Keele, Matt Maloney, Eric Scaia

Copyediting staff: Chris Davey, Susan Toth

Production staff: Angela Johnson, Carrie Brown, Eric Atkins, Brenda Bell, Jane Claunch, David LeBlanc, Chad Morris, Tonea Morrow, Lucas Peters, Nancy Rimassa, Debra Sullivan, Darlene Terry, Jason Vredenburg

15 16 17 0607 18 17 16
4500606962

Reaching us via the Internet

www.saxonpublishers.com

E-mail: info@saxonpublishers.com

Preface

This manual contains solutions to every problem in the *Calculus,* Second Edition, textbook. Early solutions of problems of a particular type contain every step. Later solutions omit steps considered unnecessary. We have attempted to stay as close as possible to the methods and procedures outlined in the textbook. Please keep in mind that many problems have more than one correct solution. While these solutions are designed to be representative of a student's work, students who submit alternative solutions should not necessarily lose credit. For ease of grading, the answer to each problem is usually set in boldface type to make it more noticeable. When a solution contains no boldface type, the entire solution is the answer to the problem.

The following people were instrumental in the development of this solutions manual, and we gratefully acknowledge their contributions: Bret Crock for writing and revising the solutions; Clint Keele, Matt Maloney, and Eric Scaia for editing the solutions; Tyler Akagi, Carmen Lemoine, and Kelli Robinson for working the problems and checking the answers; Eric Atkins, Brenda Bell, Jane Claunch, David LeBlanc, Tonea Morrow, Lucas Peters, Nancy Rimassa, Debra Sullivan, and Jason Vredenburg for typesetting the manual and creating the graphics; Chad Morris and Darlene Terry for proofreading the manual; Chris Davey and Susan Toth for copyediting the manual; and Carrie Brown and Brian Rice for supervising the project.

Problem Set 1

1. A. $7\frac{1}{4}\text{ ft}^2 = 7.25\text{ ft}^2$

   B. $0.8\text{ yd}^2 \times \frac{3^2\text{ ft}^2}{1\text{ yd}^2} = 7.2\text{ ft}^2$

   Quantity A is greater: **A**

2. A. $7(2t - 2t) = 7(0) = 0$

   B. $-6(3t - 3t) = -6(0) = 0$

   Quantities A and B are equal: **C**

3. If $x = 8$ and $y = 3$, then quantity A is greater.
   If $x = 5$ and $y = 13$, then quantity B is greater.
   If $x = 6$ and $y = 6$, then the quantities are equal.

   Insufficient information: **D**

4. $a = \frac{3 + 6}{2} = 4.5$

   A. $3a = 13.5$

   B. $a + 6 = 10.5$

   Quantity A is greater: **A**

5.
$$\frac{m}{x} = y\left(\frac{1}{R_1} + \frac{a}{R_2}\right)$$
$$\frac{m}{x} = \frac{y}{R_1} + \frac{ay}{R_2}$$
$$mR_1R_2 = R_2xy + R_1axy$$
$$mR_1R_2 - R_1axy = R_2xy$$
$$R_1(mR_2 - axy) = R_2xy$$
$$R_1 = \boldsymbol{\frac{R_2xy}{mR_2 - axy}}$$

6. $$a + \frac{1}{a + \frac{1}{a}} = a + \frac{1}{\frac{a^2 + 1}{a}} = a + \frac{a}{a^2 + 1}$$
$$= \boldsymbol{\frac{a^3 + 2a}{a^2 + 1}}$$

7. $$\frac{1}{a + \frac{1}{x + \frac{1}{m}}} = \frac{1}{a + \frac{1}{\frac{mx + 1}{m}}} = \frac{1}{a + \frac{m}{mx + 1}}$$
$$= \frac{1}{\frac{amx + a + m}{mx + 1}} = \boldsymbol{\frac{mx + 1}{amx + a + m}}$$

8. $$\frac{x^2y}{1 + m^2} + \frac{x}{y} = \frac{x^2y^2}{y(1 + m^2)} + \frac{x(1 + m^2)}{y(1 + m^2)}$$
$$= \boldsymbol{\frac{x^2y^2 + x + m^2x}{y + m^2y}}$$

9. $$\frac{4 - 3\sqrt{2}}{8 - \sqrt{2}} = \frac{4 - 3\sqrt{2}}{8 - \sqrt{2}}\left(\frac{8 + \sqrt{2}}{8 + \sqrt{2}}\right)$$
$$= \frac{32 + 4\sqrt{2} - 24\sqrt{2} - 6}{64 - 2} = \frac{26 - 20\sqrt{2}}{62}$$
$$= \boldsymbol{\frac{13 - 10\sqrt{2}}{31}}$$

10. $$\frac{x^a y^{a+b}}{x^{-a/2}y^{b-1}} = x^a x^{a/2} y^{a+b} y^{-b+1} = \boldsymbol{x^{3a/2}y^{a+1}}$$

11. $$\frac{m^{x+2}b^{x-2}}{m^{2x/3}b^{-3x/2}} = m^{x+2}m^{-2x/3}b^{x-2}b^{3x/2}$$
$$= \boldsymbol{m^{x/3+2}b^{5x/2-2}}$$

12. $$\sqrt{xy}\,x^{2/3}y^{-3/2} = x^{1/2}x^{2/3}y^{1/2}y^{-3/2} = \boldsymbol{x^{7/6}y^{-1}}$$

13. $$\begin{cases} 2x + 3y = -4 \\ x - 2z = -3 \\ 2y - z = -6 \end{cases}$$
$$z = 2y + 6$$
$$x - 2(2y + 6) = -3$$
$$x - 4y = 9$$
$$x = 4y + 9$$
$$2(4y + 9) + 3y = -4$$
$$8y + 18 + 3y = -4$$
$$11y = -22$$
$$y = -2$$
$$x = 4(-2) + 9 = 1$$
$$z = 2(-2) + 6 = 2$$
(1, −2, 2)

14. $a^2x - a^2 - 4b^2x + 4b^2$
$= a^2(x - 1) - 4b^2(x - 1)$
$= (a^2 - 4b^2)(x - 1)$
$= \boldsymbol{(a - 2b)(a + 2b)(x - 1)}$

15. $16a^{4m+3} - 8a^{2m+3} = \boldsymbol{8a^{2m+3}(2a^{2m} - 1)}$

16. $a^2b^{2x+2} - ab^{2x+1} = \boldsymbol{ab^{2x+1}(ab - 1)}$

17. $9x^2 - y^4 = (3x)^2 - (y^2)^2 = \boldsymbol{(3x + y^2)(3x - y^2)}$

18. $a^6 - 27b^3c^3 = (a^2)^3 - (3bc)^3$
$= \mathbf{(a^2 - 3bc)(a^4 + 3a^2bc + 9b^2c^2)}$

19. $x^3y^6 + 8m^{12} = (xy^2)^3 + (2m^4)^3$
$= \mathbf{(xy^2 + 2m^4)(x^2y^4 - 2m^4xy^2 + 4m^8)}$

20. $\frac{12!}{8!\,4!} = \frac{12 \cdot 11 \cdot 10 \cdot 9 \cdot 8!}{8!\,4!} = \frac{12 \cdot 11 \cdot 10 \cdot 9}{4 \cdot 3 \cdot 2}$
$= 11 \cdot 5 \cdot 9 = \mathbf{495}$

21. $\frac{n \cdot (n!)}{(n+1)!} = \frac{n \cdot n!}{(n+1) \cdot n!} = \mathbf{\frac{n}{n+1}}$

22. $\sum_{i=1}^{3} 4 = 4 + 4 + 4 = \mathbf{12}$

23. $\sum_{m=0}^{3} \frac{3^m}{m+1} = 1 + \frac{3}{2} + 3 + \frac{27}{4} = \mathbf{\frac{49}{4}}$

24.
$$V = \frac{4}{3}\pi r^3$$
$$\frac{4}{3}\pi = \frac{4}{3}\pi r^3$$
$$r = 1$$
$$A = 4\pi r^2$$
$$= 4\pi(1)^2$$
$$= \mathbf{4\pi\ m^2}$$

25.
$$A = \pi r^2$$
$$4\pi = \pi r^2$$
$$r = 2$$
$$V = \frac{1}{3}\pi r^2 h = \frac{1}{3}\pi\, 2^2(4)$$
$$= \mathbf{\frac{16}{3}}\pi\ \mathbf{cm^3}$$

Problem Set 2

1. Midpoint $= \left(\frac{4+10}{2}, \frac{2-2}{2}\right) = (7, 0)$
$$d = \sqrt{(7-6)^2 + (0-8)^2}$$
$$= \sqrt{1+64} = \mathbf{\sqrt{65}}$$

2.
$$(5\sqrt{2})^2 = y^2 + 5^2$$
$$50 = y^2 + 25$$
$$y^2 = 25$$
$$y = \mathbf{5}$$

3.
$$2x - 3y + 2 = 0$$
$$3y = 2x + 2$$
$$y = \mathbf{\frac{2}{3}x + \frac{2}{3}}$$

4.
$$4y = -3x + 2$$
$$y = -\frac{3}{4}x + \frac{1}{2}$$
$$\text{slope} = -\frac{3}{4} \qquad \perp\text{slope} = \frac{4}{3}$$
$$y + 1 = \frac{4}{3}(x - 1)$$
$$\mathbf{y = \frac{4}{3}x - \frac{7}{3}}$$

5.
$$x^2 - 3x - 4 = 0$$
$$x^2 - 3x = 4$$
$$x^2 - 3x + \frac{9}{4} = 4 + \frac{9}{4}$$
$$\left(x - \frac{3}{2}\right)^2 = \frac{25}{4}$$
$$x = \frac{3}{2} \pm \frac{5}{2}$$
$$x = \mathbf{4, -1}$$

6.
$$2x^2 = x + 3$$
$$2x^2 - x = 3$$
$$x^2 - \frac{1}{2}x = \frac{3}{2}$$
$$x^2 - \frac{1}{2}x + \frac{1}{16} = \frac{3}{2} + \frac{1}{16}$$
$$\left(x - \frac{1}{4}\right)^2 = \frac{25}{16}$$
$$x = \frac{1}{4} \pm \frac{5}{4}$$
$$x = \mathbf{\frac{3}{2}, -1}$$

7.
$$3x^2 - x - 7 = 0$$
$$x = \frac{1 \pm \sqrt{1 - 4(3)(-7)}}{6}$$
$$x = \mathbf{\frac{1}{6} \pm \frac{\sqrt{85}}{6}}$$

8.
$$\begin{array}{r} 2x^2 + 6x + 15 \\ x - 3\overline{)2x^3 + 0x^2 - 3x + 5} \\ \underline{2x^3 - 6x^2} \\ 6x^2 - 3x \\ \underline{6x^2 - 18x} \\ 15x + 5 \\ \underline{15x - 45} \\ 50 \end{array}$$

$$\mathbf{2x^2 + 6x + 15 + \frac{50}{x - 3}}$$

9. $\begin{cases} xy = -4 \\ y = -x - 2 \end{cases}$

$$x(-x - 2) = -4$$
$$-x^2 - 2x = -4$$
$$x^2 + 2x - 4 = 0$$
$$x = \frac{-2 \pm \sqrt{4 - 4(1)(-4)}}{2}$$
$$x = -1 \pm \sqrt{5}$$

$\mathbf{(-1 + \sqrt{5}, -1 - \sqrt{5}), (-1 - \sqrt{5}, -1 + \sqrt{5})}$

10.

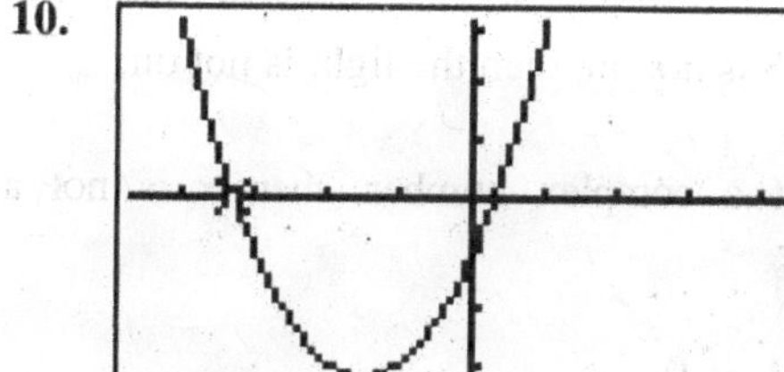

$x \approx$ **−3.302776**

Zero
X=.30277564 Y=0

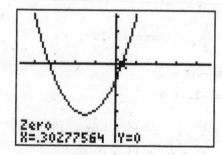

$x \approx$ **0.30277564**

11.

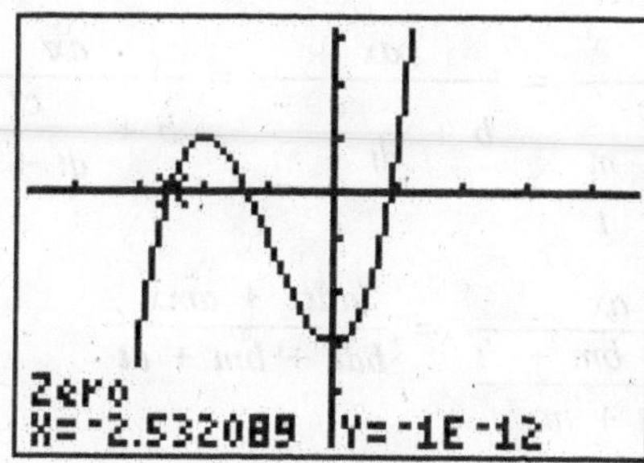

$x \approx$ **−2.532089**

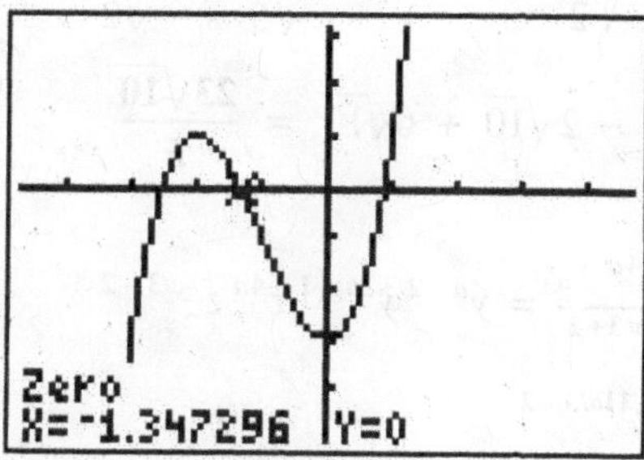

$x \approx$ **−1.347296**

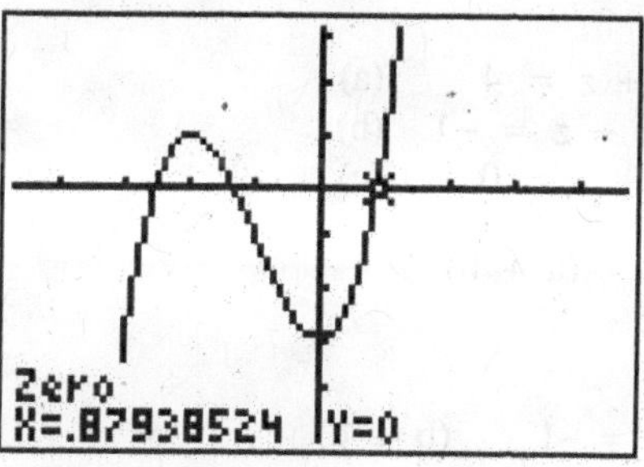

$x \approx$ **0.87938524**

12. Let Y1=X²−3X+1 and Y2=X³+3X²−3.

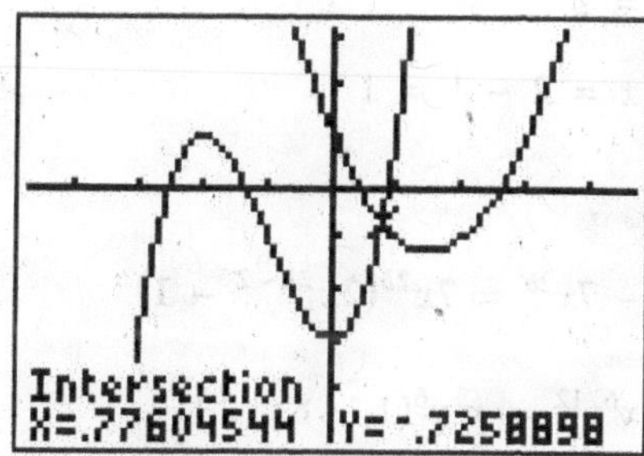

(0.77604544, −0.7258898)

13.
$$k^2 = \frac{1}{bc}\left(\frac{x}{3} - \frac{6y}{d}\right)$$
$$k^2 = \frac{x}{3bc} - \frac{6y}{bcd}$$
$$3bcdk^2 = dx - 18y$$
$$dx = 3bcdk^2 + 18y$$
$$x = \mathbf{\frac{3bcdk^2 + 18y}{d}}$$

14. $$\frac{ax}{b + \dfrac{c}{d + \dfrac{m}{t}}} = \frac{ax}{b + \dfrac{c}{\dfrac{dt + m}{t}}} = \frac{ax}{b + \dfrac{ct}{dt + m}}$$

$$= \frac{ax}{\dfrac{bdt + bm + ct}{dt + m}} = \mathbf{\frac{adtx + amx}{bdt + bm + ct}}$$

15. $$3\sqrt{\frac{2}{5}} - 4\sqrt{\frac{5}{2}} + 3\sqrt{40} = \frac{3\sqrt{2}}{\sqrt{5}} - \frac{4\sqrt{5}}{\sqrt{2}} + 6\sqrt{10}$$

$$= \frac{3\sqrt{10}}{5} - 2\sqrt{10} + 6\sqrt{10} = \mathbf{\frac{23\sqrt{10}}{5}}$$

16. $$\frac{y^{a-2}z^{4a}}{y^{-2a-1}z^{a/3+2}} = y^{a-2}y^{2a+1}z^{4a}z^{-a/3-2}$$

$$= \mathbf{y^{3a-1}z^{11a/3-2}}$$

17. $$\sqrt{x^3y^3}\,y^{1/3}x^{2/3} = x^{3/2}x^{2/3}y^{3/2}y^{1/3} = \mathbf{x^{13/6}y^{11/6}}$$

18. $$\begin{cases} x + y + z = 4 & \text{(a)} \\ 2x - y - z = -1 & \text{(b)} \\ x - y + z = 0 & \text{(c)} \end{cases}$$

$3x = 3 \quad$ (a + b)

$x = 1$

$3x - 2y = -1 \quad$ (b + c)

$3 - 2y = -1$

$-2y = -4$

$y = 2$

$z = y - x = 2 - 1 = 1$

(1, 2, 1)

19. $$14x^{4b-2} - 7x^{2b} = \mathbf{7x^{2b}(2x^{2b-2} - 1)}$$

20. $$x^3y^6 - 8x^6y^{12} = x^3y^6(1 - 8x^3y^6)$$
$$= x^3y^6[(1)^3 - (2xy^2)^3]$$
$$= \mathbf{x^3y^6(1 - 2xy^2)(1 + 2xy^2 + 4x^2y^4)}$$

21. $$\frac{n!}{(n-1)!} = \frac{n \cdot (n-1)!}{(n-1)!} = \mathbf{n}$$

22. $$\sum_{n=1}^{3}(n^2 - 2) = -1 + 2 + 7 = \mathbf{8}$$

23. $$\sum_{j=-2}^{1}\frac{2j - 3}{3} = -\frac{7}{3} - \frac{5}{3} - 1 - \frac{1}{3} = \mathbf{-\frac{16}{3}}$$

24.

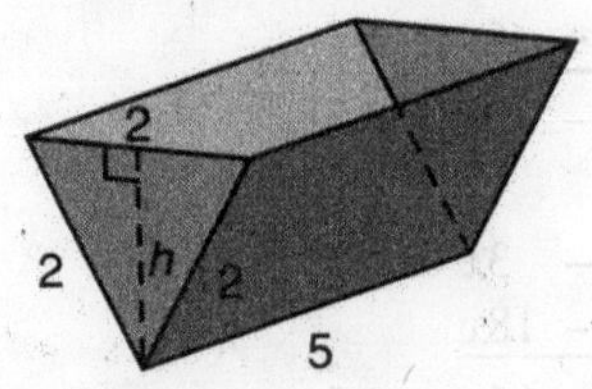

$h = \sqrt{3}$

$V = (\text{Area}_{\text{Triangle}})(\text{Length})$

$= \frac{1}{2}(2)(\sqrt{3})(5)$

$= \mathbf{5\sqrt{3}\ m^3 \approx 8.6603\ m^3}$

25. If $x^2 = y^2$, then $x = \pm y$.

Insufficient information: **D**

PROBLEM SET 3

1. If the switch is on, then the light is on.

2. If the light is not on, then the switch is not on.

3. If the switch is not on, then the light is not on.

4. If x is not a complex number, then x is not a real number.

5. $2y - x - 1 = 0$

$2y = x + 1$

$y = \frac{1}{2}x + \frac{1}{2}$

slope $= \frac{1}{2} \qquad \perp$slope $= -2$

$y - 2 = -2(x - 2)$

$\mathbf{y = -2x + 6}$

6. $$x^2 = -6x - 13$$
$$x^2 + 6x + 13 = 0$$
$$x^2 + 6x + 9 + 13 - 9 = 0$$
$$\mathbf{(x + 3)^2 + 4 = 0}$$

7. $x^2 - 3x - 7 = 0$

$$x = \frac{3 \pm \sqrt{9 - 4(1)(-7)}}{2}$$

$$= \mathbf{\frac{3}{2} \pm \frac{\sqrt{37}}{2}}$$

8. $\begin{cases} 2y^2 - x^2 = 1 \\ y + 1 = x \end{cases}$

$$2y^2 - (y + 1)^2 = 1$$
$$2y^2 - y^2 - 2y - 1 = 1$$
$$y^2 - 2y - 2 = 0$$
$$y = \frac{2 \pm \sqrt{4 - 4(1)(-2)}}{2}$$
$$y = 1 \pm \sqrt{3}$$

$x = y + 1 = 2 \pm \sqrt{3}y$

$\mathbf{(2 + \sqrt{3}, 1 + \sqrt{3}), (2 - \sqrt{3}, 1 - \sqrt{3})}$

9.
$$\begin{array}{r} x^2 - 12x - 2 \\ x - 1\overline{\big)\,x^3 - 13x^2 + 10x - 8} \\ \underline{x^3 - x^2} \\ -12x^2 + 10x \\ \underline{-12x^2 + 12x} \\ -2x - 8 \\ \underline{-2x + 2} \\ -10 \end{array}$$

$$\mathbf{x^2 - 12x - 2 - \frac{10}{x - 1}}$$

10.

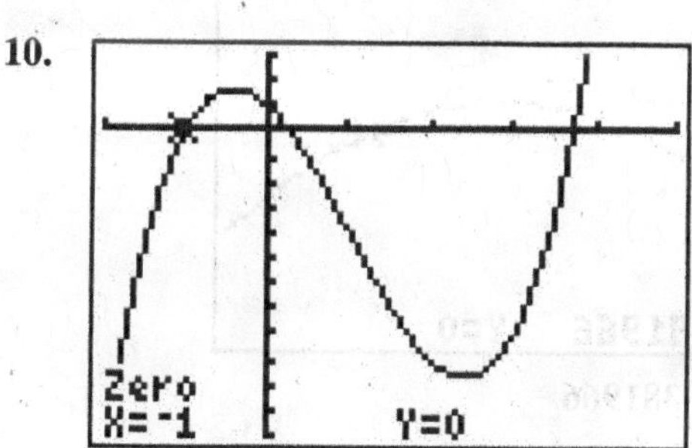

$x = \mathbf{-1}$

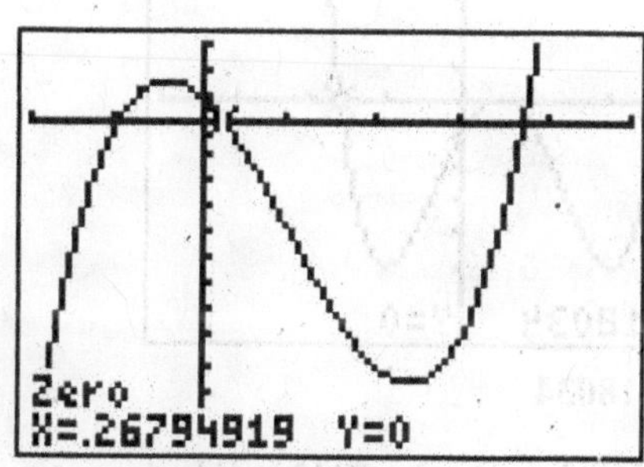

$x \approx$ **0.26794919**

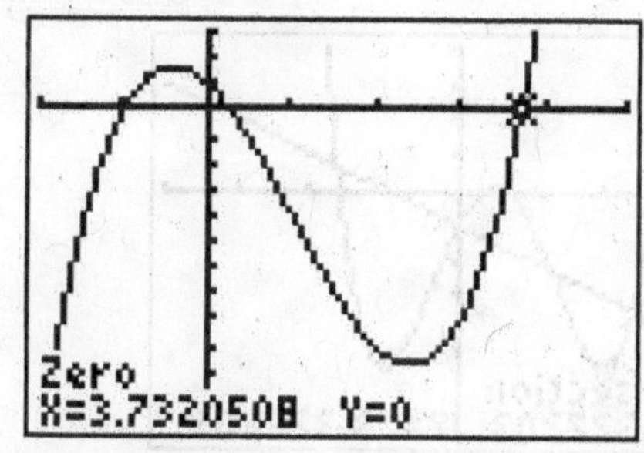

$x \approx$ **3.7320508**

11. 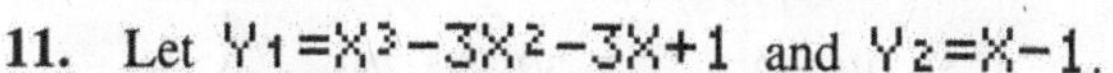
Let Y1=X³-3X²-3X+1 and Y2=X-1.

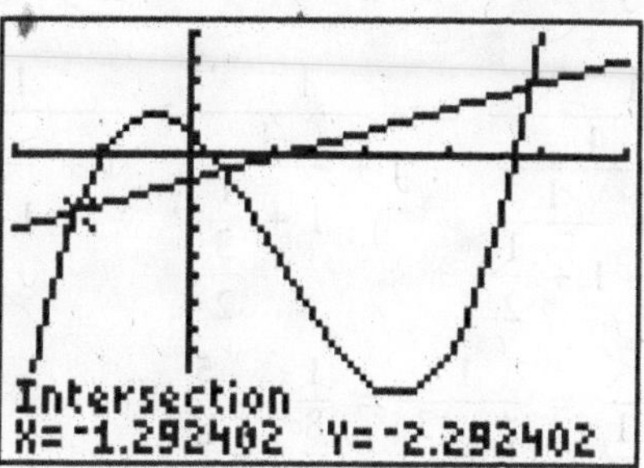

(–1.292402, –2.292402)

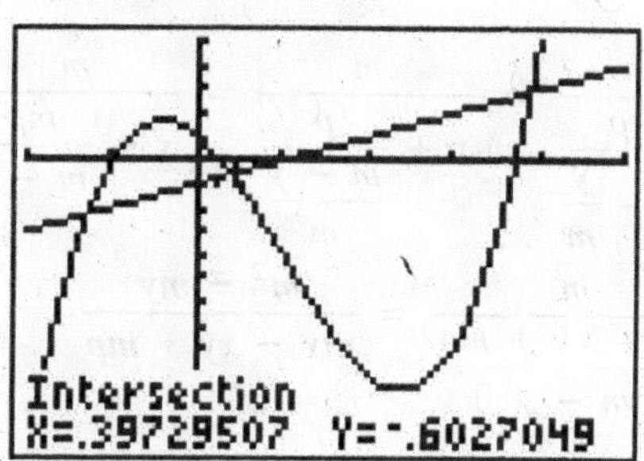

(0.39729507, –0.6027049)

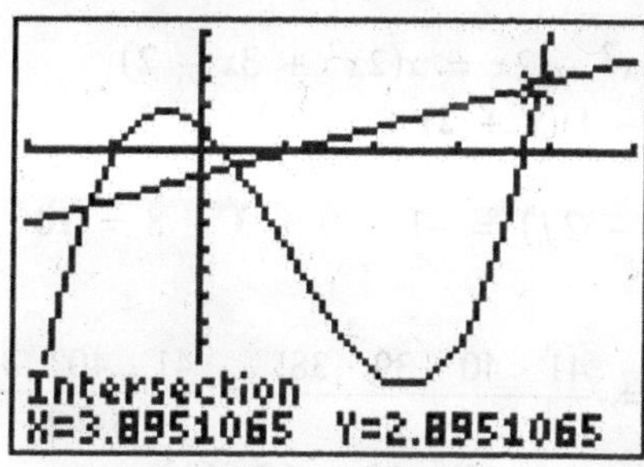

(3.8951065, 2.8951065)

12.
$$\frac{m + b}{c} = \frac{1}{k}\left(\frac{a}{R_1} + \frac{b}{R_2}\right)$$
$$\frac{m + b}{c} = \frac{a}{kR_1} + \frac{b}{kR_2}$$
$$kR_1R_2(m + b) = acR_2 + bcR_1$$
$$kmR_1R_2 + bkR_1R_2 = acR_2 + bcR_1$$
$$kmR_1R_2 + bkR_1R_2 - bcR_1 = acR_2$$
$$R_1(kmR_2 + bkR_2 - bc) = acR_2$$
$$\mathbf{\frac{acR_2}{kmR_2 + bkR_2 - bc}} = R_1$$

13. $\dfrac{4 - 2\sqrt{3}}{2 - \sqrt{3}} = \dfrac{2(2 - \sqrt{3})}{2 - \sqrt{3}} = \mathbf{2}$

14. $5\sqrt{\dfrac{3}{7}} - 2\sqrt{\dfrac{7}{3}} + \sqrt{84} = \dfrac{5\sqrt{21}}{7} - \dfrac{2\sqrt{21}}{3} + 2\sqrt{21}$

$= \mathbf{\dfrac{43\sqrt{21}}{21}}$

15. $\sqrt{x^3y^5}\; y^{1/4}x^{3/2} = x^{3/2}x^{3/2}y^{5/2}y^{1/4} = \mathbf{x^3y^{11/4}}$

16. $\dfrac{1}{1+\dfrac{1}{1+\dfrac{1}{1+\dfrac{1}{2}}}} = \dfrac{1}{1+\dfrac{1}{1+\dfrac{1}{\frac{3}{2}}}} = \dfrac{1}{1+\dfrac{1}{1+\dfrac{2}{3}}}$

$= \dfrac{1}{1+\dfrac{1}{\frac{5}{3}}} = \dfrac{1}{1+\frac{3}{5}} = \dfrac{1}{\frac{8}{5}} = \mathbf{\dfrac{5}{8}}$

17. $\dfrac{m}{x+\dfrac{p}{1-\dfrac{y}{m}}} = \dfrac{m}{x+\dfrac{p}{\frac{m-y}{m}}} = \dfrac{m}{x+\dfrac{mp}{m-y}}$

$= \dfrac{m}{\dfrac{mx-xy+mp}{m-y}} = \mathbf{\dfrac{m^2-my}{mx-xy+mp}}$

18. $a^3b^3 - 8x^6y^9 = (ab)^3 - (2x^2y^3)^3$
$= \mathbf{(ab - 2x^2y^3)(a^2b^2 + 2abx^2y^3 + 4x^4y^6)}$

19. $2x^3 + 3x^2 - 2x = x(2x^2 + 3x - 2)$
$= \mathbf{x(2x - 1)(x + 2)}$

20. $\sum_{j=1}^{4} (j^2 - 2j) = -1 + 0 + 3 + 8 = \mathbf{10}$

21. $\dfrac{41!}{38!\,3!} = \dfrac{41\cdot 40\cdot 39\cdot 38!}{38!\,3!} = \dfrac{41\cdot 40\cdot 39}{3\cdot 2}$
$= 41\cdot 20\cdot 13 = \mathbf{10{,}660}$

22. $\dfrac{a^2-b^2}{a+b} = \dfrac{(a+b)(a-b)}{(a+b)} = \mathbf{a-b}$

23. $\dfrac{n!\,(n+1)!}{(n+2)!} = \dfrac{n!\,(n+1)!}{(n+2)(n+1)!} = \mathbf{\dfrac{n!}{n+2}}$

24. $\dfrac{r}{h} = \dfrac{r}{h}$

$\dfrac{2}{6} = \dfrac{r}{2}$

$r = \dfrac{2(2)}{6} = \dfrac{2}{3}$

$V = \dfrac{1}{3}\pi r^2 h = \dfrac{1}{3}\pi\left(\dfrac{2}{3}\right)^2(2)$

$= \mathbf{\dfrac{8}{27}\pi\ cm^3 \approx 0.9308\ cm^3}$

25. If x and y are both positive or both negative and $x > y$, then $\frac{1}{y} > \frac{1}{x}$. If x is positive and y is negative, then $\frac{1}{x} > \frac{1}{y}$.

Insufficient information: **D**

Problem Set 4

1.

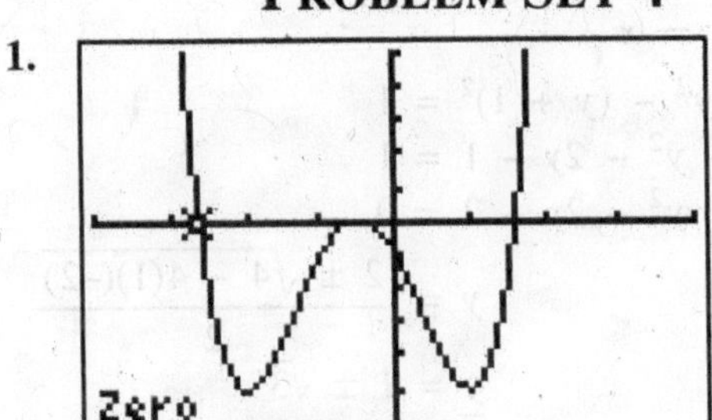

$x \approx \mathbf{-2.618034}$

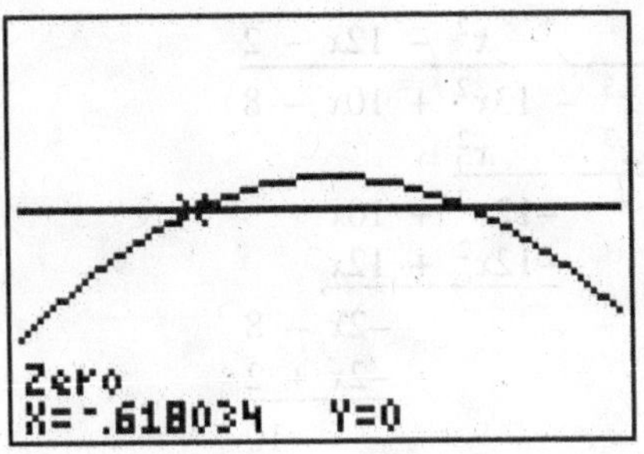

$x \approx \mathbf{-0.618034}$

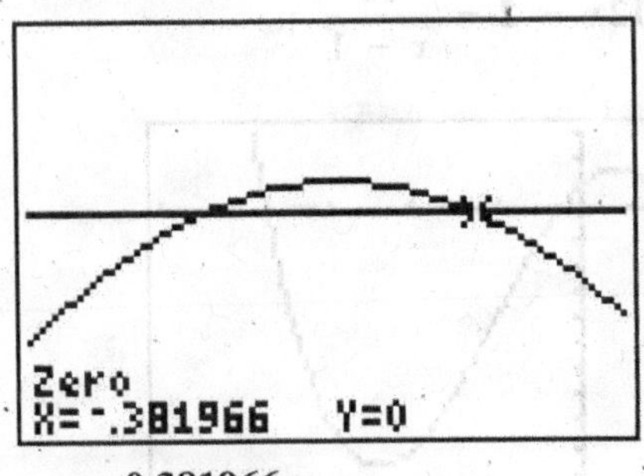

$x \approx \mathbf{-0.381966}$

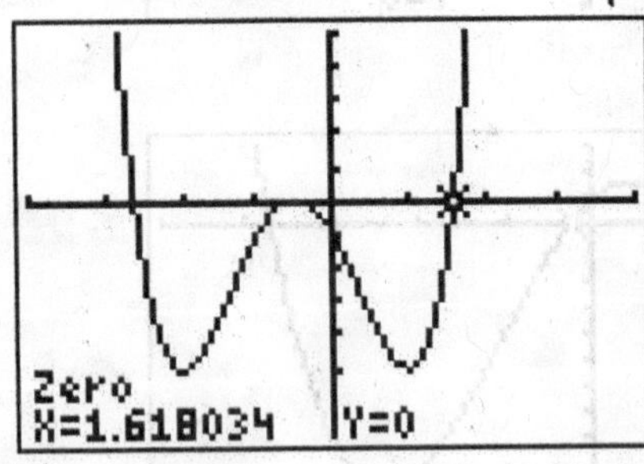

$x \approx \mathbf{1.618034}$

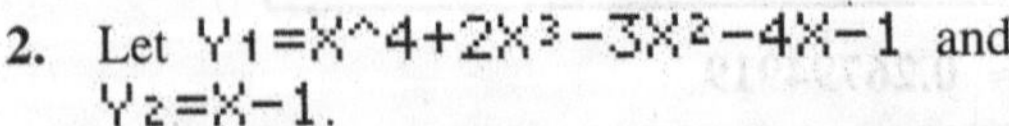

2. Let Y1=X^4+2X³−3X²−4X−1 and Y2=X−1.

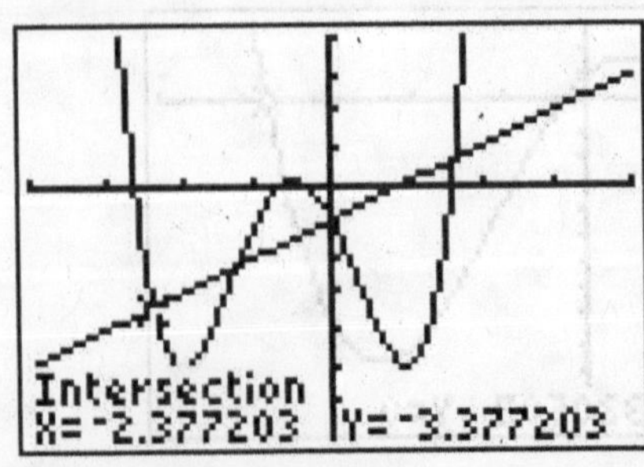

(−2.377203, −3.377203)

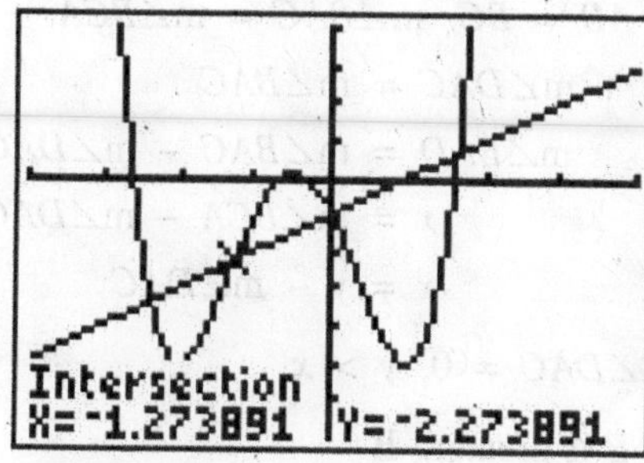

(–1.273891, –2.273891)

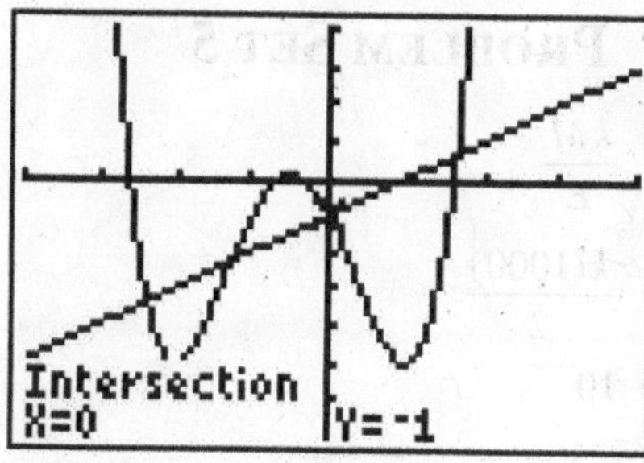

(0, –1)

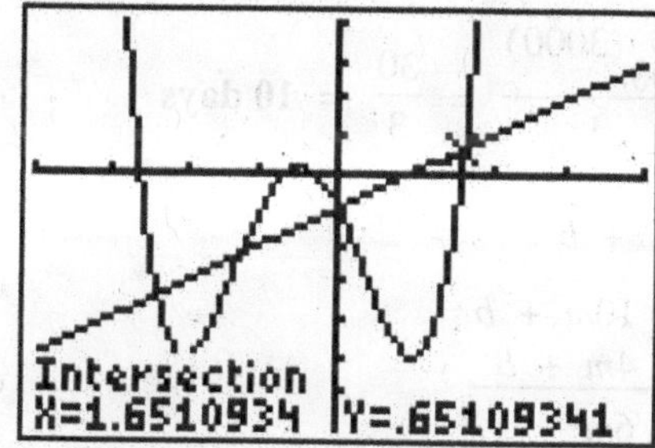

(1.6510934, 0.65109341)

3. $\cos^2 \frac{\pi}{3} - \cot \frac{\pi}{4} + \sin \frac{\pi}{6} = \left(\frac{1}{2}\right)^2 - 1 + \frac{1}{2}$

$= \mathbf{-\frac{1}{4}}$

4. $\sec 60° + \csc^2 \frac{\pi}{3} = 2 + \left(\frac{2}{\sqrt{3}}\right)^2 = \mathbf{\frac{10}{3}}$

5. $3 \cos \frac{17\pi}{6} + 2 \cos -\frac{5\pi}{3} = 3 \cos \frac{5\pi}{6} + 2 \cos \frac{\pi}{3}$

$= 3\left(-\frac{\sqrt{3}}{2}\right) + 2\left(\frac{1}{2}\right) = \mathbf{-\frac{3\sqrt{3}}{2} + 1}$

6. $4 \tan -\frac{3\pi}{4} + \sin -\frac{\pi}{4} = 4(1) + \left(-\frac{\sqrt{2}}{2}\right)$

$= \mathbf{4 - \frac{\sqrt{2}}{2}}$

7. $(\sin^2 \theta)(\csc \theta)(\cot \theta) = \left(\frac{\sin^2 \theta}{1}\right)\left(\frac{1}{\sin \theta}\right)\left(\frac{\cos \theta}{\sin \theta}\right)$

$= \mathbf{\cos \theta}$

8. $\frac{\tan \theta \sin \theta}{\sec \theta} = \frac{\sin \theta}{\cos \theta} \sin \theta \cos \theta = \mathbf{\sin^2 \theta}$

9. If a function is one-to-one, then it is not both increasing and decreasing.

10. Contrapositive: If your thumb does not hurt, then you did not hit your thumb with a hammer.

Converse: If your thumb hurts, then you hit your thumb with a hammer.

Inverse: If you did not hit your thumb with a hammer, then your thumb does not hurt.

11. $-3y = \frac{x}{3} + 2$

$y = -\frac{1}{9}x - \frac{2}{3}$

$\text{slope} = -\frac{1}{9}$

$\mathbf{y + 3 = -\frac{1}{9}(x + 9)}$

$-9y - 27 = x + 9$

$\mathbf{x + 9y + 36 = 0}$

12. $2x^2 + 7x - 15 = 0$

$(2x - 3)(x + 5) = 0$

$x = \mathbf{\frac{3}{2}, -5}$

13. $x^2 + x - 1 = 0$

$x = \frac{-1 \pm \sqrt{1 - 4(1)(-1)}}{2}$

$x = \mathbf{-\frac{1}{2} \pm \frac{\sqrt{5}}{2}}$

14. $(3x^2 - 4x + 5)(2x - 1)$

$= 6x^3 - 3x^2 - 8x^2 + 4x + 10x - 5$

$= \mathbf{6x^3 - 11x^2 + 14x - 5}$

15. $\begin{cases} x^2 + y^2 = 8 \\ x + y = 0 \end{cases}$

$y = -x$

$x^2 + (-x)^2 = 8$

$2x^2 = 8$

$x = \pm 2$

(2, –2), (–2, 2)

16. $\frac{1}{r} = v\left(\frac{1}{r_1} + \frac{1}{r_2}\right)$

$\frac{1}{r} = \frac{v}{r_1} + \frac{v}{r_2}$

$r_1 r_2 = r(r_2 v + r_1 v)$

$r = \frac{r_1 r_2}{v(r_1 + r_2)}$

17. $\frac{(n-1)!\,n!}{(n-2)!} = \frac{(n-1)(n-2)!\,n!}{(n-2)!} = \mathbf{(n-1)n!}$

18. $5\sqrt{\frac{1}{5}} - 3\sqrt{5} + \sqrt{50} = \sqrt{5} - 3\sqrt{5} + 5\sqrt{2}$

$= \mathbf{5\sqrt{2} - 2\sqrt{5}}$

19. $\frac{x^3 - y^3}{x^2 + xy + y^2} = \frac{(x-y)(x^2 + xy + y^2)}{x^2 + xy + y^2}$

$= \mathbf{x - y}$

20. $\sum_{i=-1}^{1} (2^i + i) = -\frac{1}{2} + 1 + 3 = \mathbf{\frac{7}{2}}$

21. $\frac{1}{1 + \frac{1}{1 + \frac{1}{3}}} = \frac{1}{1 + \frac{1}{\frac{4}{3}}} = \frac{1}{1 + \frac{3}{4}} = \frac{1}{\frac{7}{4}} = \mathbf{\frac{4}{7}}$

22. $SA = \text{Perimeter}_{\text{Base}} \cdot \text{Height} + 2\text{Area}_{\text{Base}}$

$= 2(w + l)(h) + 2(wl)$

$= 2(hw + hl) + 2(wl)$

$= \mathbf{2(hw + hl + lw)\ units^2}$

23.

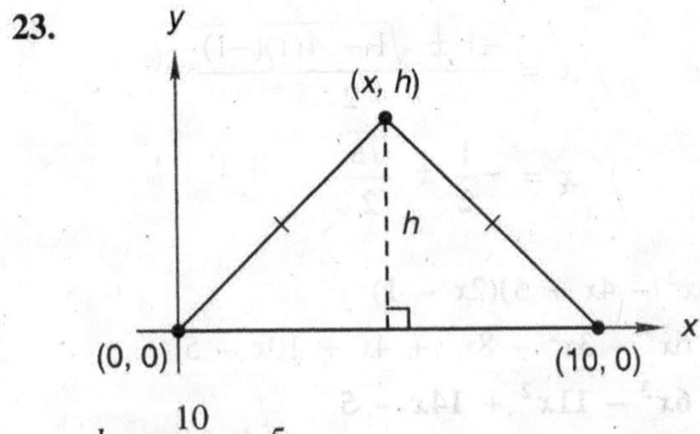

$h = \frac{10}{2} = 5$

(5, 5)

24. If $0 < x < 1$, then $x > x^{10}$ and quantity A is greater.

If $x = 1$, then $x = x^{10}$ so A and B are equal.

If $x > 1$, then $x < x^{10}$ and B is greater.

Insufficient information: **D**

25. Because $AB = BC$, $m\angle BAC = m\angle BCA$.

$m\angle BAD + m\angle DAC = m\angle BAC$

$m\angle BAD = m\angle BAC - m\angle DAC$

$x = m\angle BCA - m\angle DAC$

$x = y - m\angle DAC$

Since $m\angle DAC \neq 0$, $y > x$.

Quantity B is greater: **B**

PROBLEM SET 5

1. $T = \frac{kM}{E}$

$5 = \frac{k(1000)}{2}$

$1000k = 10$

$k = \frac{1}{100}$

$T = \frac{\frac{1}{100}(3000)}{3} = \frac{30}{3} = \mathbf{10\ days}$

2. $C = mF + b$

$12 = 10m + b$

$-\ \ 6 = 4m + b$

$6 = 6m$

$m = 1$

$b = 2$

$C = F + 2$

$C = 9$

\$9 million

3.

River

$100\ m^2$

W

L

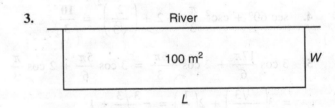

$LW = 100$

$W = \frac{100}{L}$

$F = L + 2W$

$F = L + 2\left(\frac{100}{L}\right)$

$F = \mathbf{\left(L + \frac{200}{L}\right)\ m}$

4. 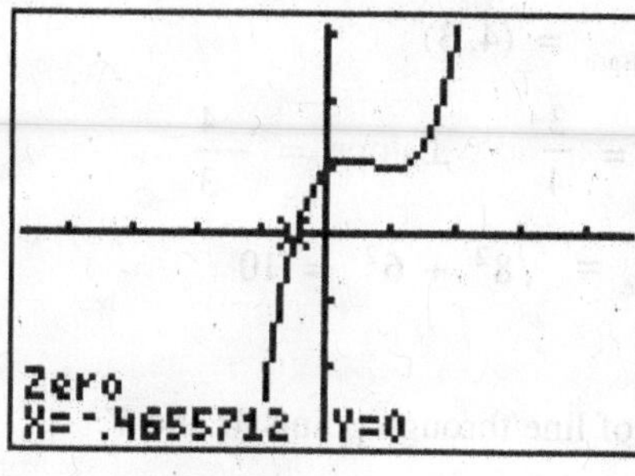

$x \approx \mathbf{-0.4655712}$

5. Let `Y1=X³-2X²+X+1` and `Y2=X²-2`.

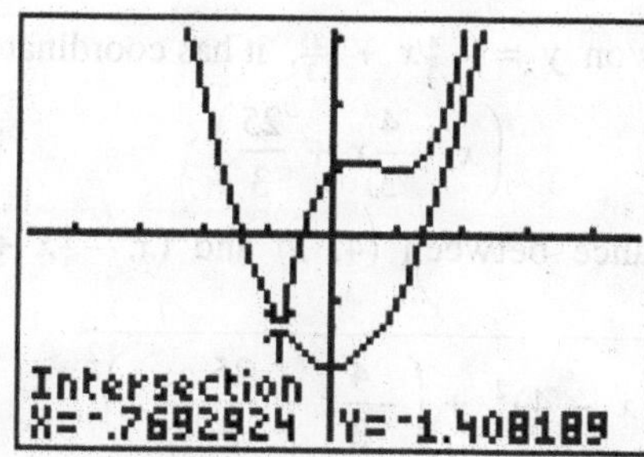

(−0.7692924, −1.408189)

6. $50° \times \dfrac{\pi}{180°} \approx \mathbf{0.8727}$

7. $2\cos\dfrac{5\pi}{4} - \sec\dfrac{\pi}{4} = 2\left(-\dfrac{\sqrt{2}}{2}\right) - \dfrac{2}{\sqrt{2}}$

$= -\sqrt{2} - \sqrt{2} = \mathbf{-2\sqrt{2}}$

8. $\tan^2\dfrac{\pi}{3} - \cot^2\dfrac{\pi}{3} = (\sqrt{3})^2 - \left(\dfrac{1}{\sqrt{3}}\right)^2 = 3 - \dfrac{1}{3}$

$= \mathbf{\dfrac{8}{3}}$

9. $\sin^2\dfrac{2\pi}{3} - \csc\dfrac{\pi}{2} = \left(\dfrac{-\sqrt{3}}{2}\right)^2 - (-1)$

$= \dfrac{3}{4} + 1 = \mathbf{\dfrac{7}{4}}$

10. $(\sin^2 x)(\csc x)(\cos x) = \sin^2 x\left(\dfrac{1}{\sin x}\right)(\cos x)$

$= \mathbf{\sin x \cos x}$

11. $\dfrac{\cos\alpha\sec\alpha}{\csc\alpha} = \dfrac{\cos\alpha\left(\dfrac{1}{\cos\alpha}\right)}{\dfrac{1}{\sin\alpha}} = \dfrac{1}{\dfrac{1}{\sin\alpha}}$

$= \mathbf{\sin\alpha}$

12. **If the polygon does not have four sides, then the polygon is not a triangle.**

13. $2x^2 - 3x + 1 = 0$

$$x = \frac{3 \pm \sqrt{9 - 4(2)(1)}}{4}$$

$$x = \mathbf{1, \frac{1}{2}}$$

14. Parallel to the y-axis implies a vertical line. Vertical lines have equations of the form $x = c$, where c is some constant. The vertical line through the point (2, 3) must be $x = 2$, or in general form $\mathbf{x - 2 = 0}$.

15. $\begin{cases} y = x^2 + 1 \\ y = 2x \end{cases}$

$x^2 + 1 = 2x$

$x^2 - 2x + 1 = 0$

$$x = \frac{2 \pm \sqrt{4 - 4(1)(1)}}{2}$$

$$x = 1$$

$y = 2(1) = 2$

(1, 2)

16. $x^2 = \sqrt{y + 1}$

$x^4 = y + 1$

$\mathbf{y = x^4 - 1}$

17. $\dfrac{x^3 - a^3}{x - a} = \dfrac{(x - a)(x^2 + ax + a^2)}{x - a}$

$= \mathbf{x^2 + ax + a^2}$

18. $\dfrac{\sqrt{3} + \sqrt{2}}{\sqrt{3} - \sqrt{2}} = \dfrac{\sqrt{3} + \sqrt{2}}{\sqrt{3} - \sqrt{2}}\left(\dfrac{\sqrt{3} + \sqrt{2}}{\sqrt{3} + \sqrt{2}}\right)$

$= \dfrac{3 + 2\sqrt{6} + 2}{3 - 2} = \mathbf{5 + 2\sqrt{6}}$

19. $\dfrac{4}{m + \dfrac{a}{x - 1}} = \dfrac{4}{\dfrac{mx - m + a}{x - 1}} = \mathbf{\dfrac{4x - 4}{mx - m + a}}$

20. $\dfrac{18!}{16!\,2!} = \dfrac{18 \cdot 17 \cdot 16!}{16! \cdot 2} = 9 \cdot 17 = \mathbf{153}$

21. $\displaystyle\sum_{n=1}^{4} [(-2)^n + 1] = -1 + 5 - 7 + 17 = \mathbf{14}$

22. $A = \pi r^2$

$9\pi = \pi r^2$

$r = 3 \text{ cm}$

$V = \frac{1}{3}\pi r^2 h$

$12\pi = \frac{1}{3}\pi(9)h$

$h = 4 \text{ cm}$

$l^2 = r^2 + h^2$

$l^2 = 9 + 16$

$l = 5 \text{ cm}$

$SA = \pi r^2 + \pi rl = 9\pi + 15\pi$

$= \mathbf{24\pi\ cm^2} \approx \mathbf{75.3982\ cm^2}$

23. (a) $y = -\frac{4}{3}x + \frac{25}{3}$

slope $= -\frac{4}{3}$ $\quad \perp$slope $= \frac{3}{4}$

(b) $y + 4 = \frac{3}{4}(x - 3)$

$y = \frac{3}{4}x - \frac{9}{4} - 4$

$\mathbf{y = \frac{3}{4}x - \frac{25}{4}}$

(c) $-\frac{4}{3}x + \frac{25}{3} = \frac{3}{4}x - \frac{25}{4}$

$\frac{175}{12} = \frac{25}{12}x$

$x = 7$

$y = \frac{3}{4}(7) - \frac{25}{4} = \frac{21}{4} - \frac{25}{4} = -1$

(7, –1)

(d) $d = \sqrt{(7-3)^2 + (-1+4)^2} = \sqrt{4^2 + 3^2}$

$= \sqrt{16 + 9} = \sqrt{25} = \mathbf{5\ units}$

24. 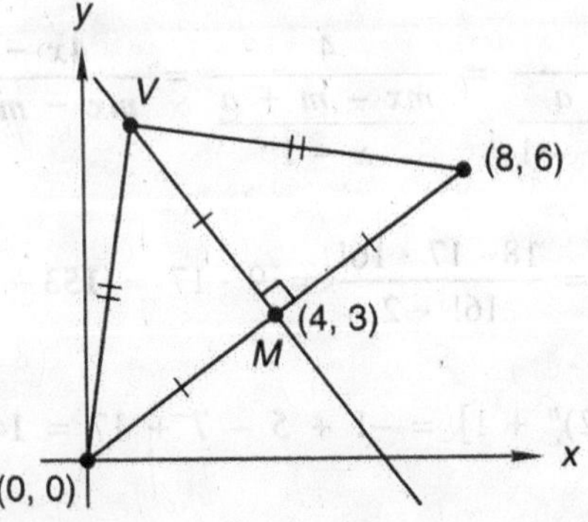

$\text{Midpoint}_{\text{Base}} = (4, 3)$

$\text{Slope}_{\text{Base}} = \frac{3}{4}$ $\quad \perp\text{slope} = -\frac{4}{3}$

$\text{Length}_{\text{Base}} = \sqrt{8^2 + 6^2} = 10$

$MV = 5$

Equation of line through points M and V:

$y - 3 = -\frac{4}{3}(x - 4)$

$y = -\frac{4}{3}x + \frac{25}{3}$

Since V is on $y = -\frac{4}{3}x + \frac{25}{3}$, it has coordinates

$$\left(x, -\frac{4}{3}x + \frac{25}{3}\right)$$

The distance between (4, 3) and $(x, -\frac{4}{3}x + \frac{25}{3})$ equals 5.

$5 = \sqrt{(x-4)^2 + \left(-\frac{4}{3}x + \frac{25}{3} - 3\right)^2}$

$25 = (x-4)^2 + \left(-\frac{4}{3}x + \frac{16}{3}\right)^2$

$25 = x^2 - 8x + 16 + \frac{16}{9}x^2 - \frac{128}{9}x + \frac{256}{9}$

$25 = \frac{25}{9}x^2 - \frac{200}{9}x + \frac{400}{9}$

$0 = \frac{25}{9}x^2 - \frac{200}{9}x + \frac{175}{9}$

$0 = 25x^2 - 200x + 175$

$0 = x^2 - 8x + 7$

$0 = (x-7)(x-1)$

$x = 7, 1$

If $x = 7$, then $y = -1$, which is in the fourth quadrant. If $x = 1$, then $y = 7$. The coordinates of the third vertex are **(1, 7).**

25. If $x < y$, $x < 0$, and $y < 0$, then $-x > -y$.

Quantity A is greater: **A**

PROBLEM SET 6

1. $\frac{PV}{T} = \frac{PV}{T}$

$\frac{5(5)}{100} = \frac{4P}{1000}$

$400P = 25{,}000$

$P =$ **62.5 newtons per square meter**

2.

$$A = 2x^2 + 4xh$$
$$100 = 2x^2 + 4xh$$
$$100 - 2x^2 = 4xh$$
$$h = \frac{100 - 2x^2}{4x}$$
$$h = 25x^{-1} - \frac{1}{2}x$$

$$V = x^2h$$
$$V = x^2\left(25x^{-1} - \frac{1}{2}x\right)$$
$$V = 25x - \frac{1}{2}x^3$$

3.

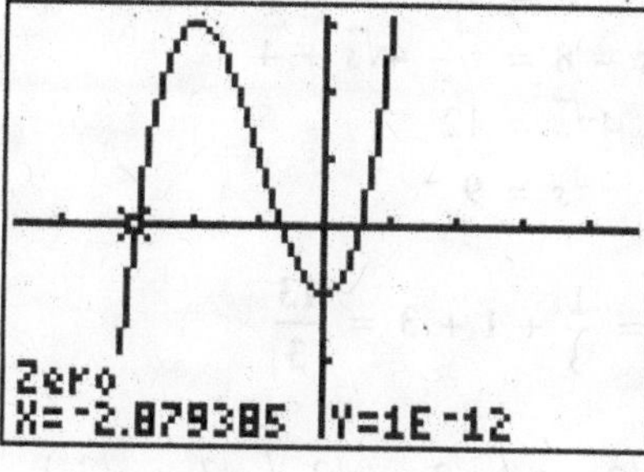

$x \approx -2.879385$

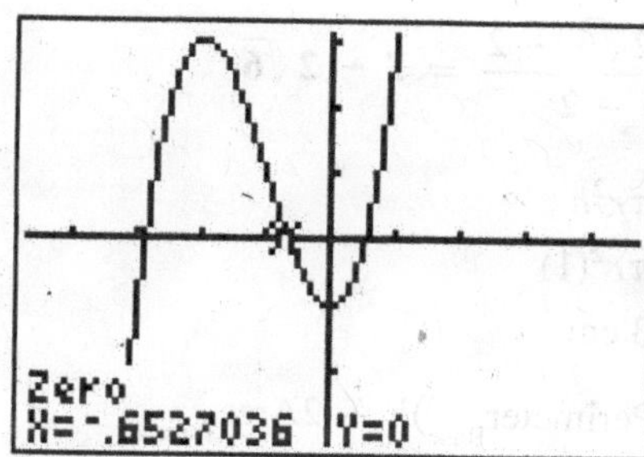

$x \approx$ **−0.6527036**

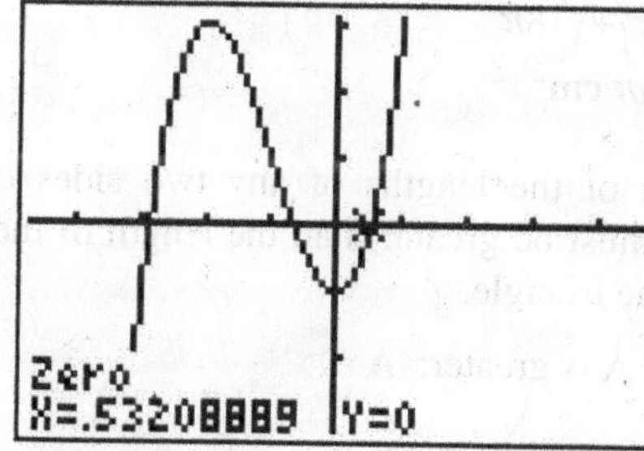

$x \approx$ **0.53208889**

4. Let Y1=X³+3X²−1 and Y2=e^(X).

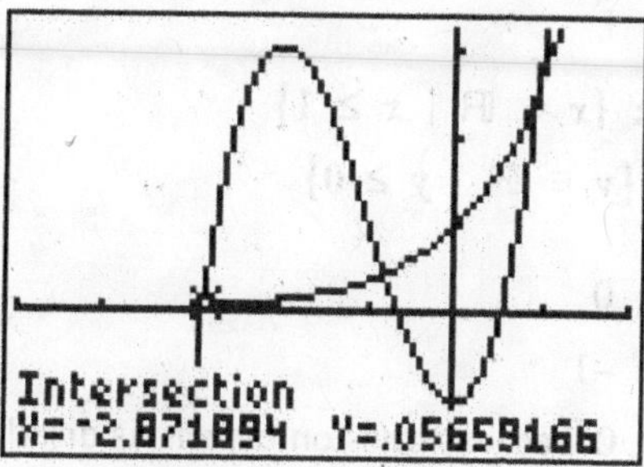

(−2.871894, 0.05659166)

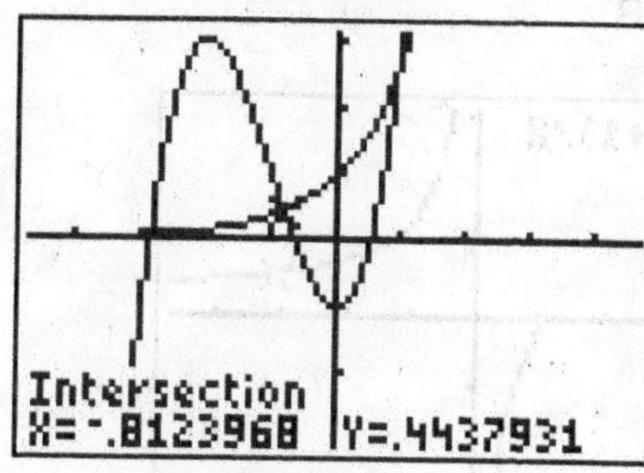

(−0.8123968, 0.4437931)

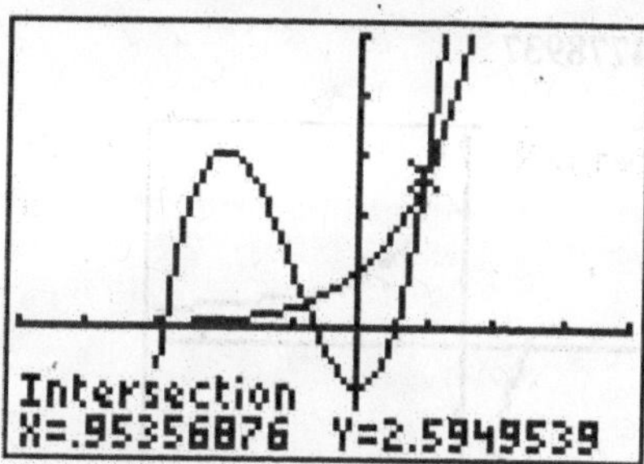

(0.95356876, 2.5949539)

5. $1.570796327 \times \frac{180°}{\pi} = \mathbf{90°}$

6. Choice **B** is correct because every x-value is mapped to exactly one y-value.

7. (a) $\psi(1) \approx \mathbf{3}$

(b) $\psi(-1) \approx \mathbf{0}$

(c) $\psi(-2) \approx \mathbf{1}$

8. When $f(x) = x^2 + 1$, appropriate y-values are obtained for the given x-values.

The correct choice is **C**.

9.
$$f(x) = 2x^2 - 1$$
$$f(x + \Delta x) = 2(x + \Delta x)^2 - 1$$
$$f(x + \Delta x) = 2[x^2 + 2x(\Delta x) + (\Delta x)^2] - 1$$
$$f(x + \Delta x) = \mathbf{2x^2 + 4x(\Delta x) + 2(\Delta x)^2 - 1}$$

10. $x - 1 \geq 0$

$x \geq 1$

Domain: $\{x \in \mathbb{R} \mid x \geq 1\}$

Range: $\{y \in \mathbb{R} \mid y \geq 0\}$

11. $x + 1 \geq 0$

$x \geq -1$

But $x \neq 0$ because division by zero is disallowed.

Domain: $\{x \in \mathbb{R} \mid x \geq -1, x \neq 0\}$

Range: $\mathbb{R}$

12. 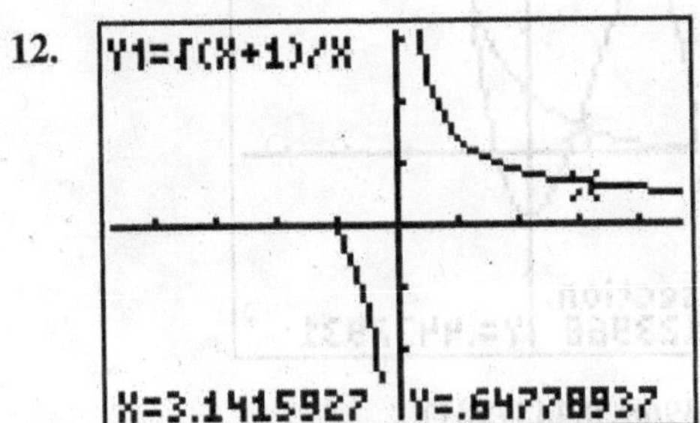

$y \approx$ **0.64778937**

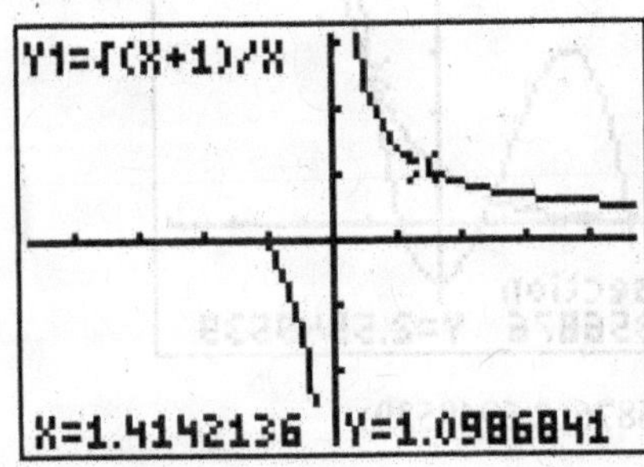

$y \approx$ **1.0986841**

13. $2\cos^2\frac{5\pi}{4} - \sec^2\frac{\pi}{4} = 2\left(-\frac{\sqrt{2}}{2}\right)^2 - \sqrt{2}^2$

$= 2\left(\frac{1}{2}\right) - 2 = \mathbf{-1}$

14. $\cot\frac{\pi}{6} + \sin -\frac{\pi}{3} = \frac{3}{\sqrt{3}} + \left(-\frac{\sqrt{3}}{2}\right)$

$= \sqrt{3} - \frac{\sqrt{3}}{2} = \mathbf{\frac{\sqrt{3}}{2}}$

15. $\sin\frac{\pi}{6}\cos -\frac{\pi}{3} = \frac{1}{2}\left(\frac{1}{2}\right) = \mathbf{\frac{1}{4}}$

16. $(\cot^2 x)(\sec^2 x)(\sin x)$

$= \frac{\cos^2 x}{\sin^2 x} \cdot \frac{1}{\cos^2 x} \cdot \sin x = \frac{1}{\sin x} = \mathbf{\csc x}$

17. $\frac{(\cot\theta)(\sec\theta)}{(\csc\theta)} = \frac{\frac{\cos\theta}{\sin\theta}\left(\frac{1}{\cos\theta}\right)}{\csc\theta} = \frac{\csc\theta}{\csc\theta} = \mathbf{1}$

18. Converse: If I live in Oklahoma, then I live in Norman.

Inverse: If I do not live in Norman, then I do not live in Oklahoma.

19. The product of the slopes of perpendicular lines is always -1 because perpendicular slopes are opposite reciprocals. Therefore $mn = \mathbf{-1}$.

20. $\sqrt{s} - \sqrt{s - 8} = 2$

$\sqrt{s - 8} = \sqrt{s} - 2$

$s - 8 = s - 4\sqrt{s} + 4$

$4\sqrt{s} = 12$

$\mathbf{s = 9}$

21. $\sum_{i=-1}^{1} 3^i = \frac{1}{3} + 1 + 3 = \mathbf{\frac{13}{3}}$

22. $\frac{\sqrt{3} - \sqrt{2}}{\sqrt{3} + \sqrt{2}} = \left(\frac{\sqrt{3} - \sqrt{2}}{\sqrt{3} + \sqrt{2}}\right)\left(\frac{\sqrt{3} - \sqrt{2}}{\sqrt{3} - \sqrt{2}}\right)$

$= \frac{3 - 2\sqrt{6} + 2}{3 - 2} = \mathbf{5 - 2\sqrt{6}}$

23. $V = \pi r^2 h$

$9\pi = \pi r^2(1)$

$r = 3$ cm

$SA = (\text{Perimeter}_{\text{Base}})h + 2\text{Area}_{\text{Base}}$

$= 2\pi rh + 2\pi r^2$

$= 2\pi(3)(1) + 2\pi(9)$

$= 6\pi + 18\pi$

$= \mathbf{24\pi\ cm^2}$

24. The sum of the lengths of any two sides of any triangle must be greater than the length of the third side of the triangle.

Quantity A is greater: **A**

25. $2(5x - 10) = x^2 - 20$

$10x - 20 = x^2 - 20$

$x^2 - 10x = 0$

$x(x - 10) = 0$

$x = 0, 10$

If $x = 0$ then both the angle and the arc have negative measures, therefore the only acceptable answer is $x = \mathbf{10}$.

PROBLEM SET 7

1. $A = \dfrac{kE}{T}$

$5 = \dfrac{k(20)}{8}$

$k = 2$

$A = \dfrac{2(12)}{6} = \mathbf{4}$

2. $W = mF + b$

$170 = 10m + b$

$170 - 95 = (10m + b) - (5m + b)$

$75 = 5m$

$m = 15$

$b = 20$

$W = 15F + 20$

$50 = 15F + 20$

$30 = 15F$

$F = \mathbf{2}$

3. 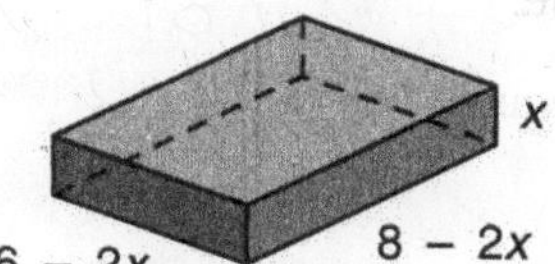

$V = lwh$

$V = (8 - 2x)(6 - 2x)x$

$V = (48 - 16x - 12x + 4x^2)x$

$V = (4x^2 - 28x + 48)x$

$\mathbf{V = 4x^3 - 28x^2 + 48x}$

4. This problem is equivalent to finding the zeros of the given quartic equation.

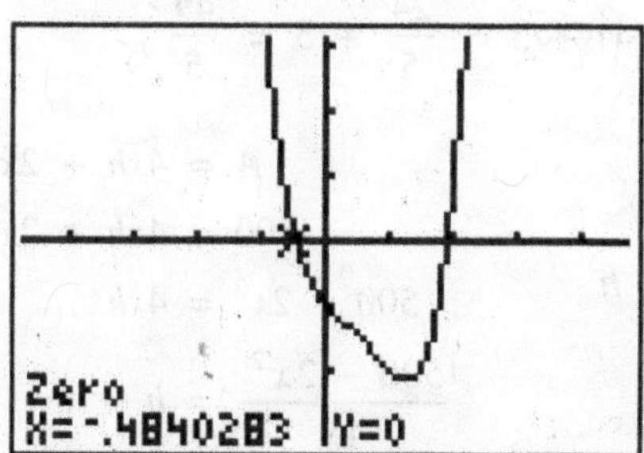

$x \approx \mathbf{-0.4840283}$

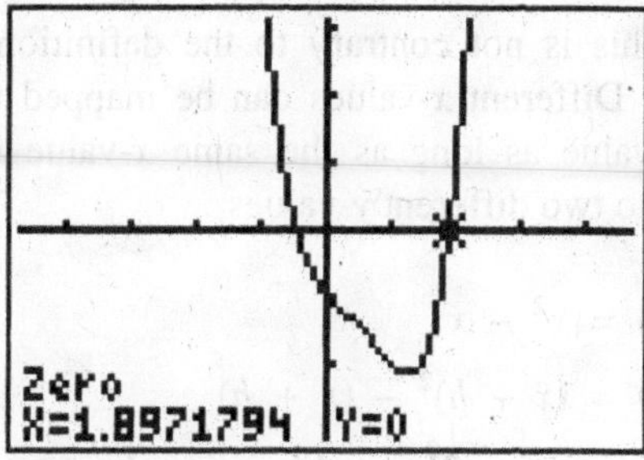

$x \approx \mathbf{1.8971794}$

5. $P_1 = \left(\cos\dfrac{\pi}{6}, \sin\dfrac{\pi}{6}\right) = \left(\dfrac{\sqrt{3}}{2}, \dfrac{1}{2}\right)$

$P_2 = \left(\cos\dfrac{2\pi}{3}, \sin\dfrac{2\pi}{3}\right) = \left(-\dfrac{1}{2}, -\dfrac{\sqrt{3}}{2}\right)$

6. 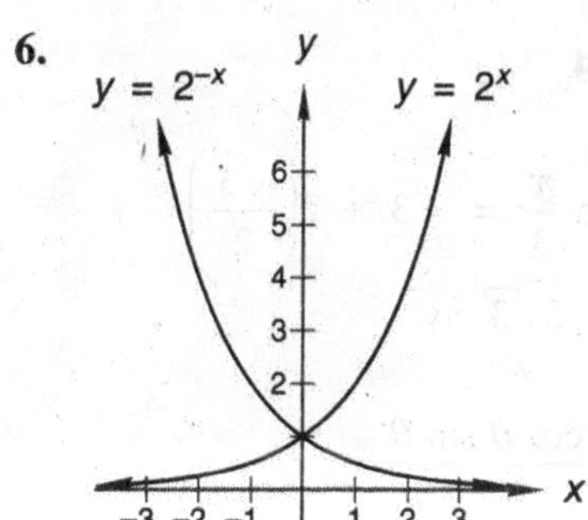

7. 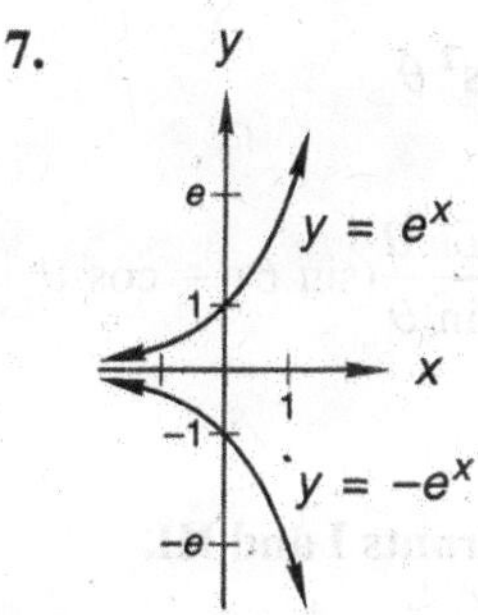

8. 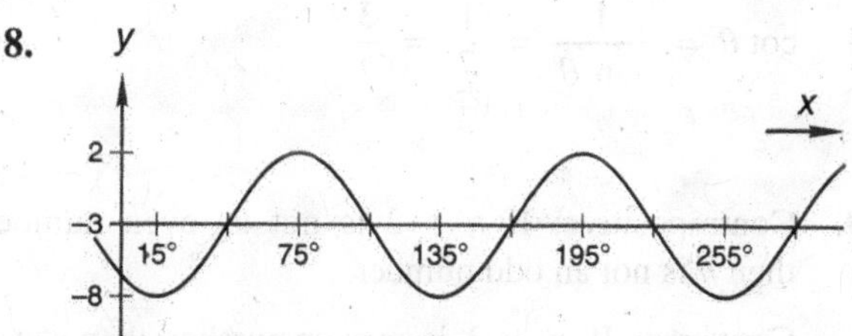

9. Centerline: 2 Phase: $-\dfrac{\pi}{2}$ or $\dfrac{\pi}{2}$

Amplitude: 3 Period: 2π

$\mathbf{y = 2 + 3\cos\left(x + \dfrac{\pi}{2}\right)}$ or

$\mathbf{y = 2 - 3\cos\left(x - \dfrac{\pi}{2}\right)}$

10. **False.** This is not contrary to the definition of a function. Different x-values can be mapped to the same y-value as long as the same x-value is not mapped to two different y-values.

11. $$f(x) = x^2 - x$$
$$f(x + h) = (x + h)^2 - (x + h)$$
$$\mathbf{f(x + h) = x^2 + 2hx + h^2 - x - h}$$

12. **Domain:** $\mathbb{R}$

Range: $\{y \in \mathbb{R} \mid -1 \le y \le 1\}$

13. $$\sin^2 \frac{\pi}{4} \cos^2 \frac{3\pi}{4} = \left(-\frac{\sqrt{2}}{2}\right)^2 \left(-\frac{\sqrt{2}}{2}\right)^2 = \left(\frac{1}{2}\right)\left(\frac{1}{2}\right) = \mathbf{\frac{1}{4}}$$

14. $$\tan \frac{2\pi}{3} + 2 \sin \frac{\pi}{3} = \sqrt{3} + 2\left(\frac{\sqrt{3}}{2}\right) = \sqrt{3} + \sqrt{3} = \mathbf{2\sqrt{3}}$$

15. $$\frac{\cos\theta \sin\theta}{\tan\theta} = \frac{\cos\theta \sin\theta}{\frac{\sin\theta}{\cos\theta}} = \frac{\cos\theta \sin\theta \cos\theta}{\sin\theta} = \mathbf{\cos^2\theta}$$

16. $$(\cot\theta)(\sin\theta) - \cos\theta = \frac{\cos\theta}{\sin\theta}(\sin\theta) - \cos\theta = \cos\theta - \cos\theta = \mathbf{0}$$

17. Tangent is positive in **quadrants I and III.**

18. $$\cot\theta = \frac{1}{\tan\theta} = \frac{1}{\frac{7}{3}} = \mathbf{\frac{3}{7}}$$

19. Contrapositive: If $n + 2$ is not an even number, then n is not an odd number.

Converse: If $n + 2$ is an even number, then n is an odd number.

Inverse: If n is not an odd number, then $n + 2$ is not an even number.

20. $$x^2 + y^2 = 9$$
$$1 + y^2 = 9$$
$$y^2 = 8$$
$$\mathbf{y = \pm 2\sqrt{2}}$$

21. $$\frac{\frac{1}{x + h} - \frac{1}{x}}{h} = \frac{\frac{x}{x(x + h)} - \frac{x + h}{x(x + h)}}{h} = \frac{\frac{-h}{x(x + h)}}{h} = \mathbf{-\frac{1}{x(x + h)}}$$

22. Both e and π are irrational, so they cannot be represented as a ratio of whole numbers.

Choice **B** is correct.

23. **No.** The input value of 1 is mapped to two different output values.

24.

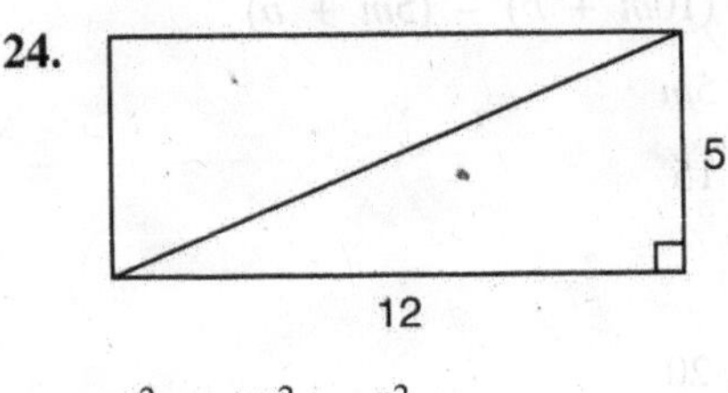

$$d^2 = 12^2 + 5^2$$
$$d = \mathbf{13}$$

25. The sum of the measures of any two angles of any triangle is equal to the exterior angle of the triangle's third angle.

The quantities are equal: **C**

PROBLEM SET 8

1. $$D = mx + b$$
$$5 = 0m + b$$
$$b = 5$$
$$17 = 10m + 5$$
$$12 = 10m$$
$$m = \frac{6}{5}$$
$$D = \frac{6}{5}(4) + 5 = \frac{24}{5} + 5 = \mathbf{\frac{49}{5}}$$

2.

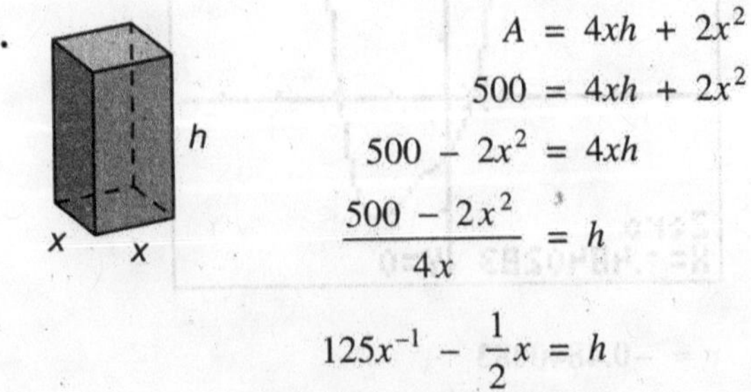

$$A = 4xh + 2x^2$$
$$500 = 4xh + 2x^2$$
$$500 - 2x^2 = 4xh$$
$$\frac{500 - 2x^2}{4x} = h$$
$$125x^{-1} - \frac{1}{2}x = h$$

$V = x^2h$

$V = x^2\left(125x^{-1} - \frac{1}{2}x\right)$

$\mathbf{V = 125x - \frac{1}{2}x^3}$

3. (a) $y = x^2 + 2x - 3$

$y = (x^2 + 2x + 1) - 3 - 1$

$\mathbf{y = (x + 1)^2 - 4}$

(b)

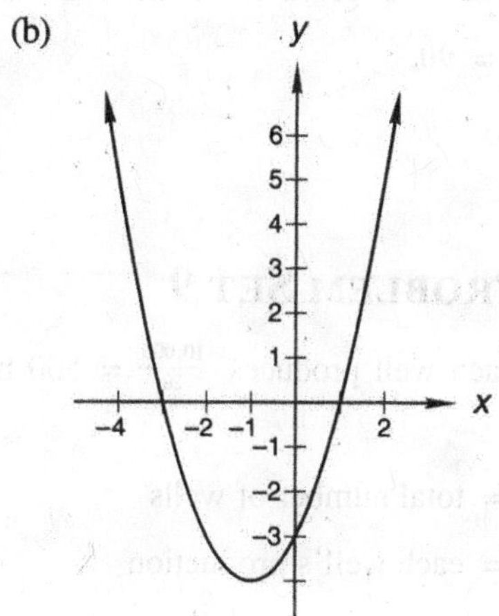

(c) The parabola opens **upward.**

(d) $\mathbf{x = -1}$

(e) **(–1, –4)**

4.

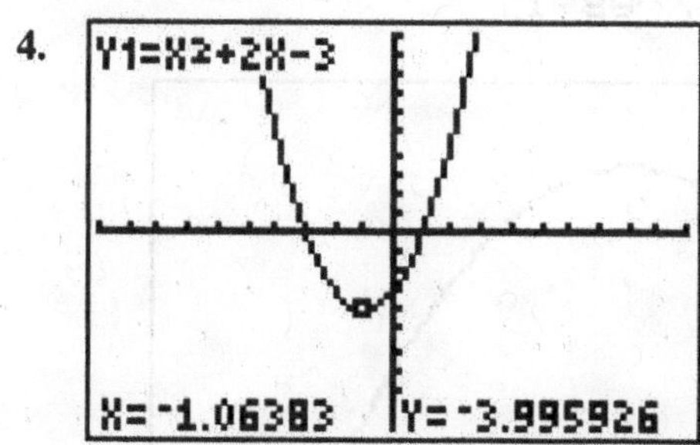

(–1.0638, –3.9959) in ZStandard

Answers may vary.

5. (a) $\sin^2\theta + \cos^2\theta = 1$

$$\frac{\sin^2\theta}{\sin^2\theta} + \frac{\cos^2\theta}{\sin^2\theta} = \frac{1}{\sin^2\theta}$$

$$\mathbf{1 + \cot^2\theta = \csc^2\theta}$$

(b) $\sin^2\theta + \cos^2\theta = 1$

$$\frac{\sin^2\theta}{\cos^2\theta} + \frac{\cos^2\theta}{\cos^2\theta} = \frac{1}{\cos^2\theta}$$

$$\mathbf{\tan^2\theta + 1 = \sec^2\theta}$$

6. $\sin^2\frac{\pi}{7} + \cos^2\frac{\pi}{7} = \mathbf{1}$

7. $\sec^2\frac{5\pi}{4} + 2\tan -\frac{\pi}{4} = \sqrt{2}^2 + 2(-1)$

$= 2 - 2 = \mathbf{0}$

8. $\sin -\theta = -\sin\theta = \mathbf{\frac{4}{5}}$

9. $\cos\left(\frac{\pi}{2} - \theta\right) = \sin\theta = \mathbf{-\frac{4}{5}}$

10. $\sec\left(\frac{\pi}{2} - \theta\right) = \csc\theta = \frac{1}{\sin\theta} = \mathbf{-\frac{5}{4}}$

11. $\frac{\sin^2 x + 2 + \cos^2 x}{3\csc^2 -x} = \frac{\sin^2 x + \cos^2 x + 2}{3(-\csc x)^2}$

$= \frac{1 + 2}{3\csc^2 x} = \frac{1}{\csc^2 x} = \mathbf{\sin^2 x}$

12. $\left[\sec\left(\frac{\pi}{2} - x\right)\right](\sin -x) = \csc x(-\sin x)$

$= \frac{-\sin x}{\sin x} = \mathbf{-1}$

13. $(\sin x)\left[\cos\left(\frac{\pi}{2} - x\right)\right] + (\cos -x)(\cos x)$

$= (\sin x)(\sin x) + (\cos x)(\cos x)$

$= \sin^2 x + \cos^2 x = \mathbf{1}$

14. $x^2 - 3x + 2 = 0$

$(x - 2)(x - 1) = 0$

$\mathbf{x = 2, 1}$

15. $\frac{3}{x} = \frac{7}{x + L}$

$7x = 3x + 3L$

$4x = 3L$

$\mathbf{x = \frac{3}{4}L}$

16. $\frac{a}{h} = \frac{4}{x + h}$

$4h = ax + ah$

$4h - ah = ax$

$h(4 - a) = ax$

$\mathbf{h = \frac{ax}{4 - a}}$

17. $\left(\cos -\frac{\pi}{3}, \sin -\frac{\pi}{3}\right) = \left(\frac{1}{2}, -\frac{\sqrt{3}}{2}\right)$

18.

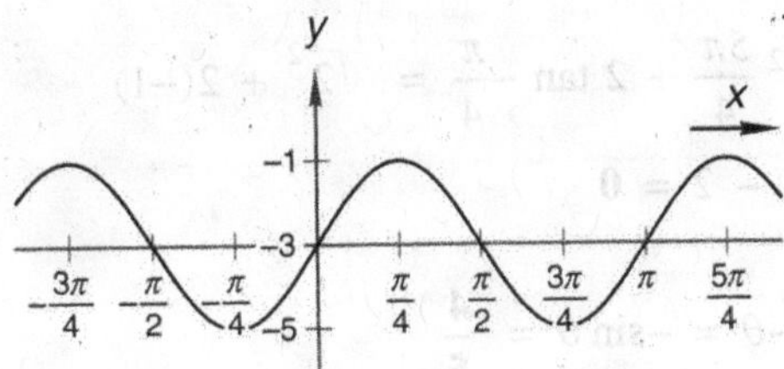

19. Centerline: –1 Period: 2π

Amplitude: 11 Phase: $\frac{\pi}{2}$ or $-\frac{\pi}{2}$

$\mathbf{y = 1 + 11 \sin\left(\theta - \frac{\pi}{2}\right)}$ or

$\mathbf{y = 1 - 11 \sin\left(\theta + \frac{\pi}{2}\right)}$

20. In both B and D each x-value is mapped to exactly one y-value.

Choices **B** and **D** are correct.

21. $\frac{(x+h)^2 - x^2}{h} = \frac{x^2 + 2hx + h^2 - x^2}{h}$

$= \frac{2hx + h^2}{h} = \frac{h(2x + h)}{h} = \mathbf{2x + h}$

22. Let `Y1=cos(X³)` and `Y2=X²`.

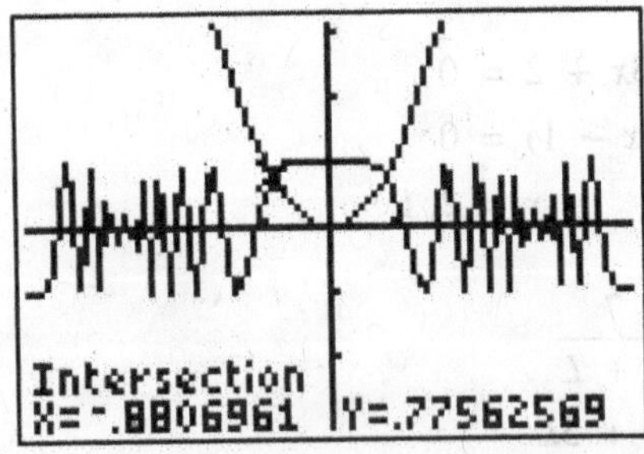

(–0.8806961, 0.77562569)

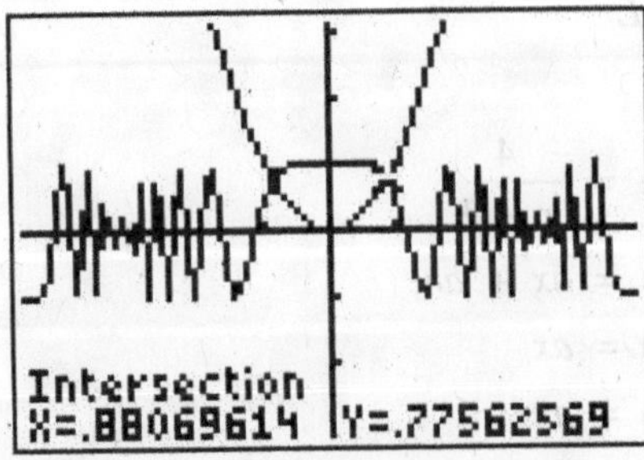

(0.88069614, 0.77562569)

23. $f(x) = 2(x + 3)(x + 2)$

$f(x) = 2(x^2 + 5x + 6)$

$\mathbf{f(x) = 2x^2 + 10x + 12}$

24. If $y > 0$, then $x > z$. If $y < 0$, then $x < z$.

Insufficient information: **D**

25. If $a + b = 10$, then $a^2 + 2ab + b^2 = 100$.

Substituting $ab = 5$ gives $a^2 + 10 + b^2 = 100$ or $\mathbf{a^2 + b^2 = 90}$.

Problem Set 9

1. Originally, each well produces $\frac{10{,}000}{20} = 500$ barrels per day.

$20 + x =$ total number of wells

$500 - 10x =$ each well's production

$V = (20 + x)(500 - 10x)$

$\mathbf{V = 10{,}000 + 300x - 10x^2}$

2. (a) Set `Xmin=0, Xmax=70, Xscl=10, Ymin=0, Ymax=15000, Yscl=1000,` and `Xres=1`.

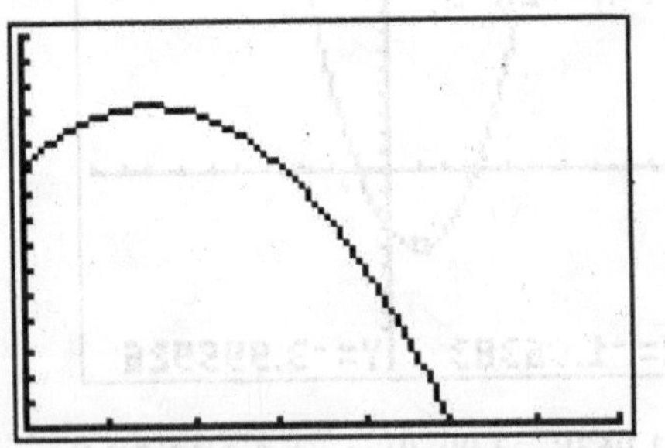

(b)

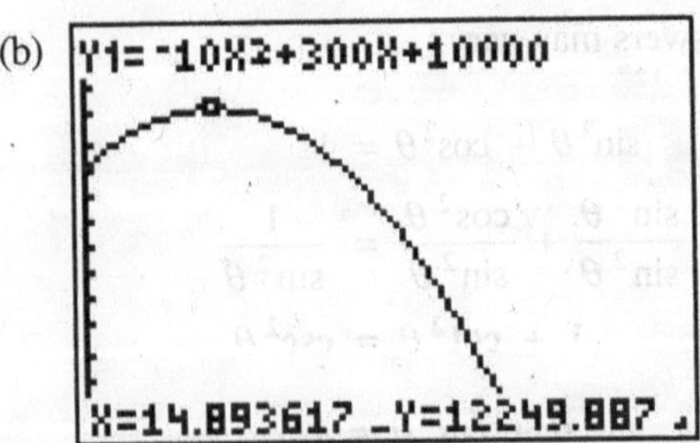

(c) **15 additional wells**

(d) **12,250 barrels of oil per day**

3. 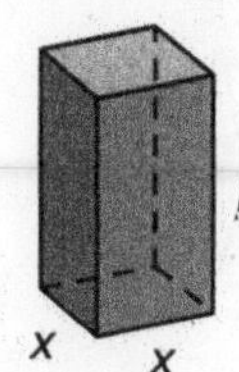

$$V = x^2h$$
$$125 = x^2h$$
$$h = \frac{125}{x^2}$$
$$h = 125x^{-2}$$

$$A = x^2 + x^2 + 4xh$$
$$C = 5x^2 + 2x^2 + 2(4xh)$$
$$C = 7x^2 + 8xh$$
$$C = 7x^2 + 8x(125x^{-2})$$
$$\mathbf{C = 7x^2 + 1000x^{-1}}$$

4. $y = x^2 - 3x + 4$

$$y = \left(x^2 - 3x + \frac{9}{4}\right) + 4 - \frac{9}{4}$$
$$y = \left(x - \frac{3}{2}\right)^2 + \frac{7}{4}$$

Vertex: $\left(\mathbf{\frac{3}{2}, \frac{7}{4}}\right)$

Axis of symmetry: $x = \mathbf{\frac{3}{2}}$

5. $x_m = \dfrac{-5 + 0}{2} = -2.5$ $\qquad y_m = \dfrac{-8 + 4}{2} = -2$

(−2.5, −2)

6. (a) $7.3 = 10^L$

$$L = \log 7.3 \approx 0.8633$$
$$7.3 = 10^{\log 7.3} \approx \mathbf{10^{0.8633}}$$

(b) $7.3 = e^L$

$$L = \ln 7.3 \approx 1.9879$$
$$7.3 = e^{\ln 7.3} \approx \mathbf{e^{1.9879}}$$

7. If $3^y = 4$, then $\log_3 4 = y$.

Choice **B** is correct.

8. $\dfrac{y^3 y^{3/4-2} z^2}{y^{(3-2)/3} z^{(3-2)/6}} = y^{3+3/4-2-1/3} z^{2-1/6}$

$= \mathbf{y^{17/12} z^{11/6}}$

9. (a) If $10^x = 3$, then $x = \mathbf{\log 3 \approx 0.4771.}$

(b) If $e^x = 5$, then $x = \mathbf{\ln 5 \approx 1.6094.}$

10. $\log_3 27 = 2b + 1$

$$3^{2b+1} = 27$$
$$3^{2b+1} = 3^3$$
$$2b + 1 = 3$$
$$2b = 2$$
$$\mathbf{b = 1}$$

11. $\log_x (3x - 2) = 2$

$$x^2 = 3x - 2$$
$$x^2 - 3x + 2 = 0$$
$$(x - 2)(x - 1) = 0$$
$$x = \mathbf{2, 1}$$

12. (a)

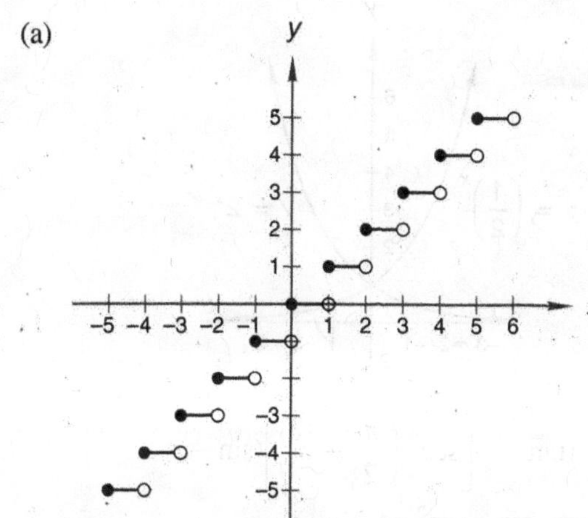

(b) $\mathbf{f(1.2) = 1;\ f(-1.2) = -2}$

13.

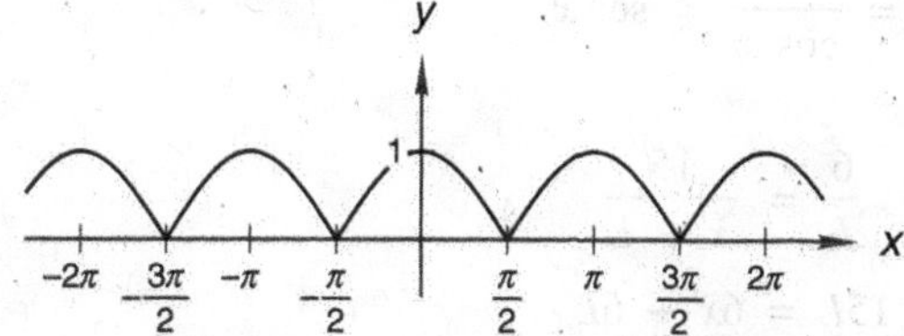

14.

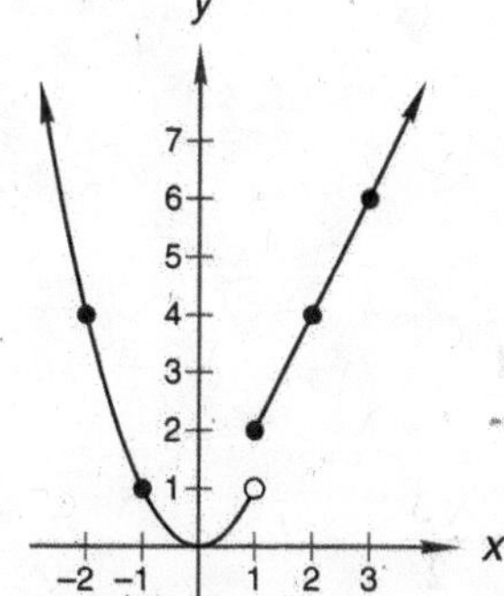

15. "x is less than 0.001 away from 3."

$\mathbf{\{x \in \mathbb{R} \mid 2.999 < x < 3.001\}}$

16. $f(x) = \begin{cases} -2 & \text{when } x < 0 \\ x - 1 & \text{when } 0 \le x \le 3 \\ 1 & \text{when } x > 3 \end{cases}$

17. Centerline: -5 Period: 3π $C = \frac{2}{3}$

Amplitude: 4 Phase: $-\frac{5\pi}{4}, \frac{\pi}{4}$

$$y = -5 + 4 \sin\left[\frac{2}{3}\left(x + \frac{5\pi}{4}\right)\right] \text{ or}$$

$$y = -5 - 4 \sin\left[\frac{2}{3}\left(x - \frac{\pi}{4}\right)\right]$$

18.

19. $(\tan -x)\left[\sec^2\left(\frac{\pi}{2} - x\right)\right](\sin -x)$

$= -\tan x \csc^2 x\,(-\sin x)$

$= \frac{\sin x}{\cos x} \cdot \frac{1}{\sin^2 x} \cdot \sin x$

$= \frac{1}{\cos x} = \mathbf{\sec x}$

20. $\frac{6}{L} = \frac{15}{x + L}$

$15L = 6x + 6L$

$9L = 6x$

$\mathbf{L = \frac{2}{3}x}$

21. $y_1 = \sin \frac{\pi}{6} = \mathbf{\frac{1}{2}}$

$y_2 = \sin 210° = \mathbf{-\frac{1}{2}}$

$y_3 = \sin\left(-\frac{\pi}{3}\right) = \mathbf{-\frac{\sqrt{3}}{2}}$

22. The mapping of f **is not a function.** Each value of x is mapped to two different values: the positive and negative square root of x.

23. $f(x + h) - f(x) = (x + h)^2 - x^2$

$= x^2 + 2hx + h^2 - x^2$

$= \mathbf{2hx + h^2}$

24. $\frac{\sum_{i=1}^{10} i}{10} = \frac{55}{10} = \mathbf{5.5}$

25. This is a geometric representation of the Pythagorean Theorem; the sum of the squares of the lengths of the legs of a right triangle is equal to the square of the length of the hypotenuse of the triangle.

The quantities are equal: **C**

Problem Set 10

1.

$d^2 = 60^2 + 80^2$

$d^2 = 10{,}000$

$d = \mathbf{100 \text{ miles}}$

2. (a)

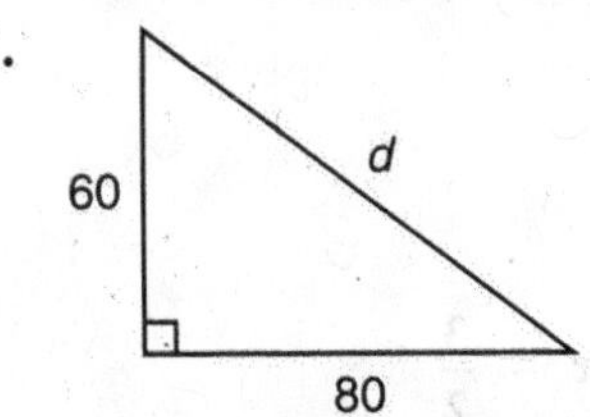

$V = x^2h$

$100 = x^2h$

$h = \frac{100}{x^2}$

$h = 100x^{-2}$

$A = 2x^2 + 4xh$

$A = 2x^2 + 4x(100x^{-2})$

$\mathbf{A = 2x^2 + 400x^{-1}}$

(b) x must be greater than zero because it is the length of a side.

$\{x \in \mathbb{R} \mid x > 0\}$

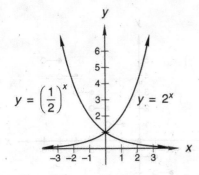

3.

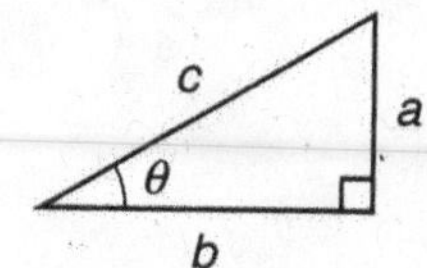

$$\sin^2\theta + \cos^2\theta = \left(\frac{a}{c}\right)^2 + \left(\frac{b}{c}\right)^2$$

$$= \frac{a^2 + b^2}{c^2} = \frac{c^2}{c^2} = 1$$

Therefore, $\mathbf{\sin^2\theta + \cos^2\theta = 1.}$

$$\sin^2\theta + \cos^2\theta = 1$$

$$\frac{\sin^2\theta}{\sin^2\theta} + \frac{\cos^2\theta}{\sin^2\theta} = \frac{1}{\sin^2\theta}$$

$$\mathbf{1 + \cot^2\theta = \csc^2\theta}$$

$$\sin^2\theta + \cos^2\theta = 1$$

$$\frac{\sin^2\theta}{\cos^2\theta} + \frac{\cos^2\theta}{\cos^2\theta} = \frac{1}{\cos^2\theta}$$

$$\mathbf{\tan^2\theta + 1 = \sec^2\theta}$$

4.

$$F = 3x + 2L$$

$$100 = 3x + 2L$$

$$100 - 3x = 2L$$

$$L = 50 - \frac{3}{2}x$$

$$A = xL$$

$$A = x\left(50 - \frac{3}{2}x\right)$$

$$\mathbf{A = 50x - \frac{3}{2}x^2}$$

5. According to the Remainder Theorem $f(1)$ is the value of the remainder when the polynomial is divided by $x - 1$.

$f(x) = x^5 - 2x^4 + x^3 - x^2 + 3x + 1$

$f(1) = 1 - 2 + 1 - 1 + 3 + 1 = 3$

The remainder is **3**.

6. (a)

$$\begin{array}{r|rrrrr} -1 & 1 & 0 & -2 & 2 & 1 \\ & \downarrow & -1 & 1 & 1 & -3 \\ \hline & 1 & -1 & -1 & 3 & \boxed{-2} \end{array}$$

$f(-1) = \mathbf{-2}$

(b)

$$\begin{array}{r|rrrrr} 1 & 1 & 0 & -2 & 2 & 1 \\ & \downarrow & 1 & 1 & -1 & 1 \\ \hline & 1 & 1 & -1 & 1 & \boxed{2} \end{array}$$

$f(1) = \mathbf{2}$

(c)

$$\begin{array}{r|rrrrr} 3 & 1 & 0 & -2 & 2 & 1 \\ & \downarrow & 3 & 9 & 21 & 69 \\ \hline & 1 & 3 & 7 & 23 & \boxed{70} \end{array}$$

$f(3) = \mathbf{70}$

7. Possible rational zeros:

$$\frac{\pm1, \pm2, \pm4}{\pm1} = \mathbf{\pm1, \pm2, \pm4}$$

8.

$$\begin{array}{r|rrrr} 1 & 1 & -1 & -4 & 4 \\ & \downarrow & 1 & 0 & -4 \\ \hline & 1 & 0 & -4 & \boxed{0} \end{array}$$

$$f(x) = (x - 1)(x^2 - 4)$$

$$= (x - 1)(x + 2)(x - 2)$$

Roots: **1, 2, –2**

9. Set `Y1=X^4-22X³+πX²-X+√(2)` and then use the `1:value` feature in the `CALCULATE` menu.

(a) If $x = \frac{1}{3}$, then $y \approx \mathbf{0.6275}$

(b) If $x = \sqrt{3}$, then $y \approx \mathbf{-96.2084}$

(c) If $x = \frac{\pi}{2}$, then $y \approx \mathbf{-71.5842}$

10. $47° \times \frac{\pi}{180°} \approx \mathbf{0.8203}$

11. (a)

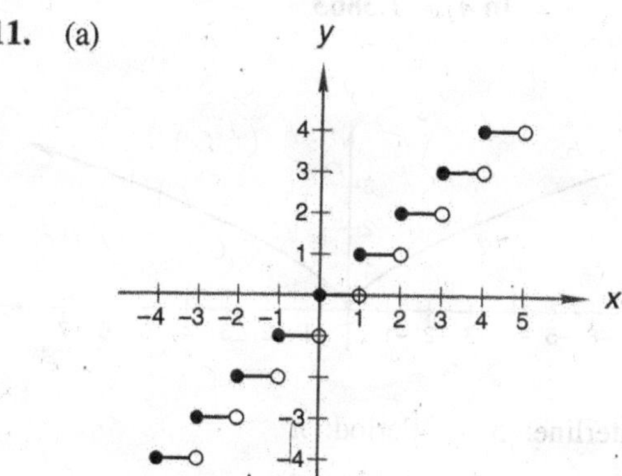

(b) $y = |x^2 + x - 2|$

$y = |(x + 2)(x - 1)|$

Zeros: –2, 1

y-intercept: $y = 2$

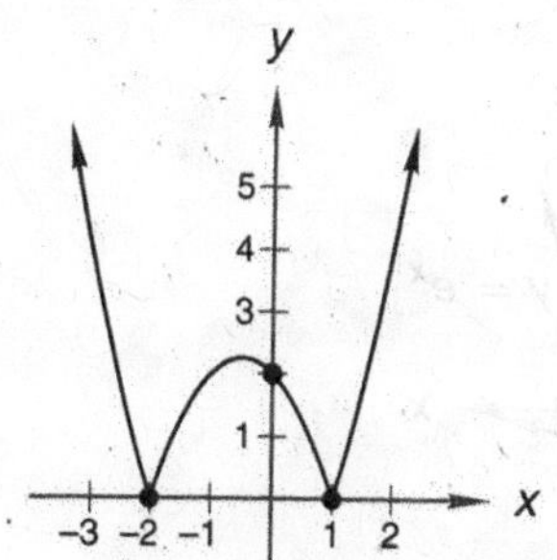

12. $2x + 1 = \log_{1/3} 9$

$$\left(\frac{1}{3}\right)^{2x+1} = 9$$

$$(3^{-1})^{2x+1} = 3^2$$

$$3^{-2x-1} = 3^2$$

$$-2x - 1 = 2$$

$$-2x = 3$$

$$x = -\frac{3}{2}$$

13. $\ln b^3 = 2$

$$b^3 = e^2$$

$$(b^3)^{1/3} = (e^2)^{1/3}$$

$$b = e^{2/3} \approx \mathbf{1.9477}$$

14. (a) $10^x = 4$

$$\log 10^x = \log 4$$

$$x = \log 4 \approx \mathbf{0.6021}$$

(b) $e^x = 4$

$$\ln e^x = \ln 4$$

$$x = \ln 4 \approx \mathbf{1.3863}$$

15.

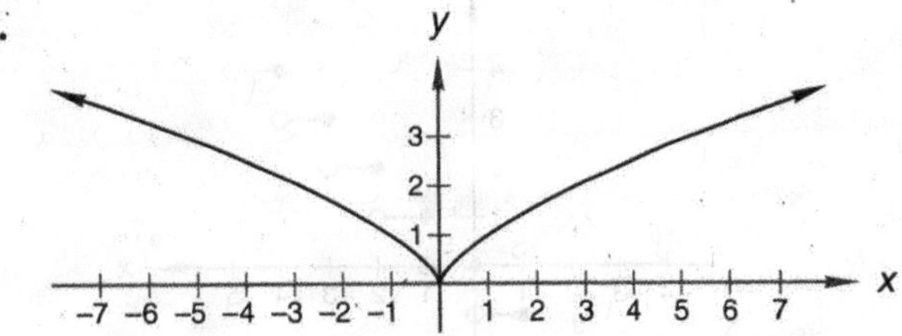

16. Centerline: 5 Period: π

Amplitude: 4 Phase: $\frac{3\pi}{8}, -\frac{\pi}{8}$

$$y = 5 + 4\sin\left[2\left(x - \frac{3\pi}{8}\right)\right] \text{ or}$$

$$y = 5 - 4\sin\left[2\left(x + \frac{\pi}{8}\right)\right]$$

17.

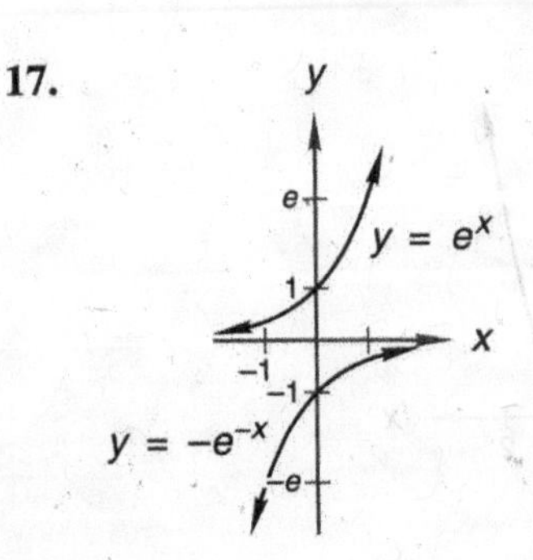

18. $|2x - 3| < 4$

$$\left|2\left(x - \frac{3}{2}\right)\right| < 4$$

$$2\left|x - \frac{3}{2}\right| < 4$$

$$\left|x - \frac{3}{2}\right| < 2$$

"x is less than 2 away from $\frac{3}{2}$."

-1 0 1 2 3 4

19. $\sec\alpha = \dfrac{\sqrt{a^2 + b^2}}{b}$

20. $\dfrac{\sin^2 -\theta + \cos^2 -\theta + 2}{3\tan -\theta} = \dfrac{1 + 2}{3\tan -\theta}$

$$= \frac{1}{\tan -\theta} = \frac{1}{-\tan\theta} = -\cot\theta$$

21. $\sin x - \sin x\cos^2 x = \sin x\,(1 - \cos^2 x)$

$$= \sin x\,(\sin^2 x) = \sin^3 x$$

22. $f(x) = c(x - 2)(x + 3)$

$$6 = c(3 - 2)(3 + 3)$$

$$6 = 6c$$

$$c = 1$$

$$f(x) = (x - 2)(x + 3)$$

$$\mathbf{f(x) = x^2 + x - 6}$$

23. $\dfrac{f(x + \Delta x) - f(x)}{\Delta x} = \dfrac{(x + \Delta x)^2 - x^2}{\Delta x}$

$$= \frac{x^2 + 2x(\Delta x) + (\Delta x)^2 - x^2}{\Delta x}$$

$$= \frac{2x(\Delta x) + (\Delta x)^2}{\Delta x} = \frac{\Delta x(2x + \Delta x)}{\Delta x}$$

$$= \mathbf{2x + \Delta x}$$

24.

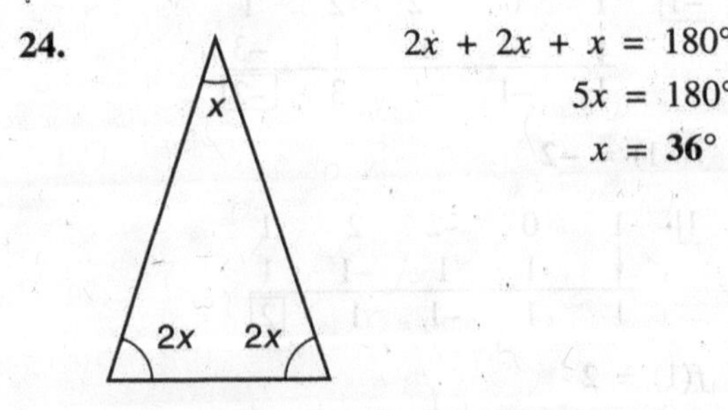

$$2x + 2x + x = 180°$$

$$5x = 180°$$

$$x = \mathbf{36°}$$

25. $4x + 60 = (5x - 40) + 3x$

$$4x + 60 = 8x - 40$$

$$100 = 4x$$

$$x = \mathbf{25}$$

PROBLEM SET 11

1. $S = \dfrac{k}{X^2}$

$8 = \dfrac{k}{5^2}$

$k = 200$

$S = \dfrac{200}{X^2} = \dfrac{200}{2^2} = \mathbf{50}$

2.

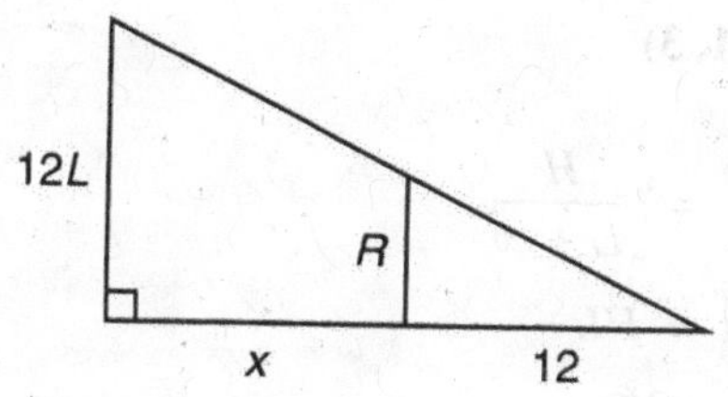

$\dfrac{R}{12} = \dfrac{12L}{x + 12}$

$144L = Rx + 12R$

$Rx = 144L - 12R$

$x = \dfrac{144L - 12R}{R}$

$x = 144LR^{-1} - 12$

Shadow $= x + 12 = (144LR^{-1} - 12) + 12$

$= \mathbf{144LR^{-1}}$ **in.**

3. (a) $\lim_{x\to 0^+} f(x) = \mathbf{2}$ (b) $\lim_{x\to 0^-} f(x) = \mathbf{1}$

(c) $\lim_{x\to -1^-} f(x) = \mathbf{-1}$ (d) $\lim_{x\to -1^+} f(x) = \mathbf{0}$

4.

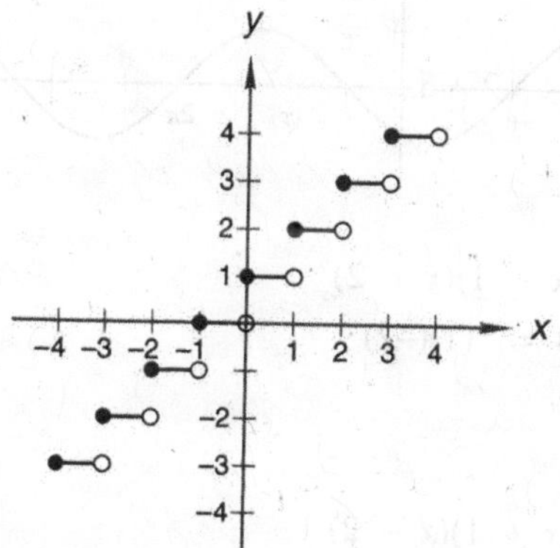

(a) $\lim_{x\to 1^+} g(x) = \mathbf{2}$ (b) $\lim_{x\to 1^-} g(x) = \mathbf{1}$

5. (a)

$\underline{-1\rfloor}$	2	−4	3	−2	1	−1
	↓	−2	6	−9	11	−12
	2	−6	9	−11	12	$\boxed{-13}$

$f(-1) = \mathbf{-13}$

(b)

$\underline{2\rfloor}$	2	−4	3	−2	1	−1
	↓	4	0	6	8	18
	2	0	3	4	9	$\boxed{17}$

$f(2) = \mathbf{17}$

(c)

$\underline{-2\rfloor}$	2	−4	3	−2	1	−1
	↓	−4	16	−38	80	−162
	2	−8	19	−40	81	$\boxed{-163}$

$f(-2) = \mathbf{-163}$

6. (a) Possible rational roots: $\dfrac{\pm 1, \pm 3}{\pm 1, \pm 2, \pm 3, \pm 6}$

$= \mathbf{\pm 1, \pm\frac{1}{2}, \pm\frac{1}{3}, \pm\frac{1}{6}, \pm 3, \pm\frac{3}{2}}$

(b)

$\underline{3\rfloor}$	6	−19	2	3
	↓	18	−3	−3
	6	−1	−1	$\boxed{0}$

$h(x) = (x - 3)(6x^2 - x - 1)$

$= (x - 3)(3x + 1)(2x - 1)$

Rational zeros: $\mathbf{3, -\frac{1}{3}, \frac{1}{2}}$

7.

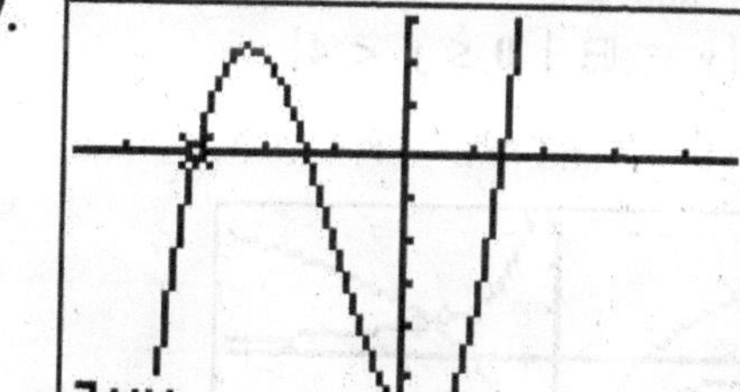

$x = \mathbf{-3}$

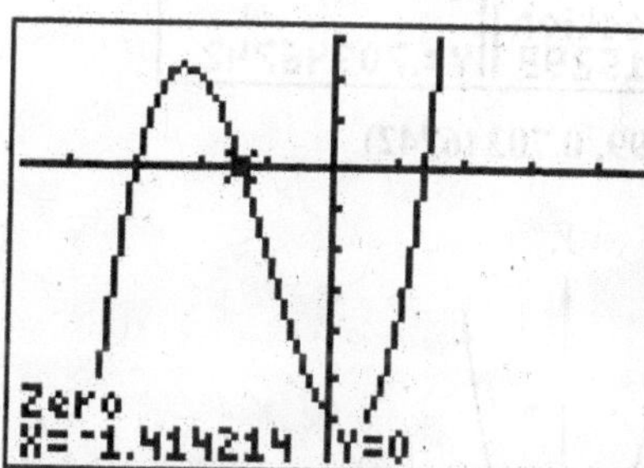

$x \approx \mathbf{-1.414214}$

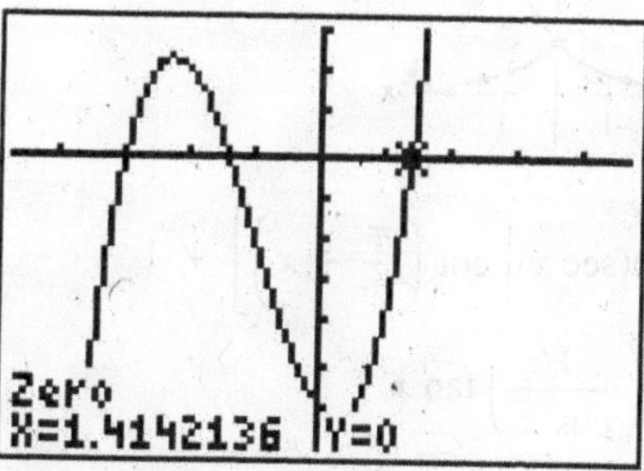

$x \approx \mathbf{1.4142136}$

8. $1 = \log_x (2x - 7)$
$x^1 = 2x - 7$
$x = \mathbf{7}$

9. $e^x = 10$
$x = \mathbf{\ln 10} \approx \mathbf{2.3025}$

10.

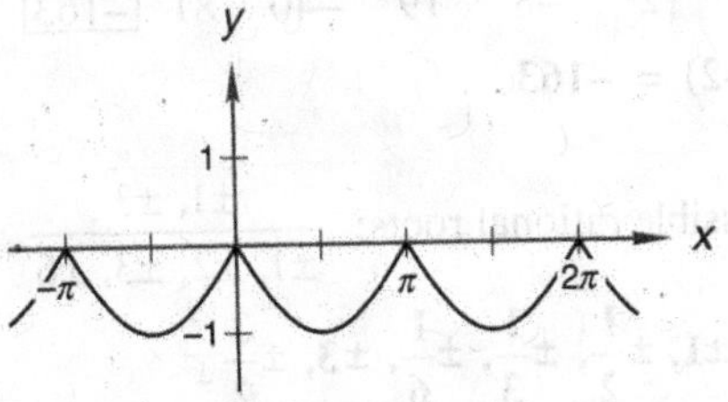

11. $r^2 = (-2 - 1)^2 + (6 - 2)^2$
$r^2 = (-3)^2 + 4^2$
$r^2 = 9 + 16$
$r^2 = 25$
$r = 5$
$\mathbf{5^2 = (x - 1)^2 + (y - 2)^2}$

12. If $y = x^2$ and $|x| < 2$, then $0 \le y < 4$.
Range: $\{y \in \mathbb{R} \mid 0 \le y < 4\}$

13. Let Y1=1/X and Y2=ln(X²).

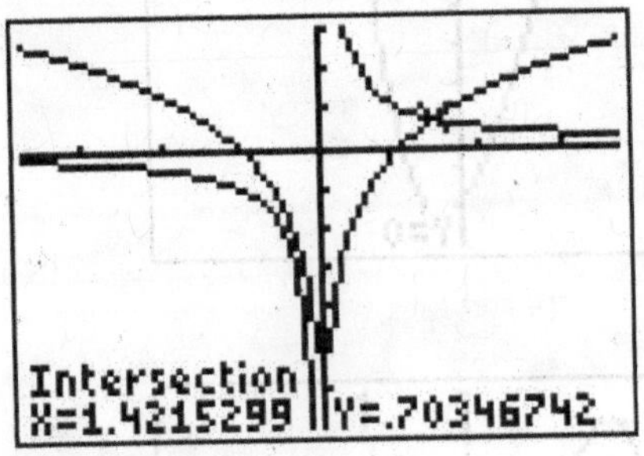

(1.4215299, 0.70346742)

14.

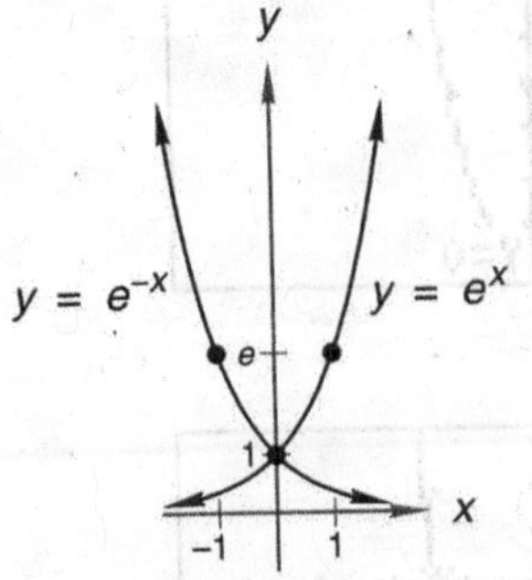

15. $-(\sin -x)(\sec x)\left[\cot\left(\frac{\pi}{2} - x\right)\right] + 1$

$= \sin x \left(\frac{1}{\cos x}\right) \tan x + 1$

$= \left(\frac{\sin x}{\cos x}\right) \tan x + 1 = \tan^2 x + 1 = \sec^2 x$

16. $\dfrac{\sin x - \sin x \cos^2 x}{\sec^2 x - 1} = \dfrac{\sin x (1 - \cos^2 x)}{\tan^2 x}$

$= \dfrac{\sin x \sin^2 x}{\tan^2 x} = \dfrac{\sin^3 x \cos^2 x}{\sin^2 x}$

$= \mathbf{\sin x \cos^2 x}$

17. $y = x^2 - 2x + 4$
$y = (x^2 - 2x + 1) + 4 - 1$
$y = (x - 1)^2 + 3$

Vertex: **(1, 3)**

18. $\dfrac{6}{L} = \dfrac{H}{L + x}$

$6L + 6x = HL$
$HL - 6L = 6x$
$L(H - 6) = 6x$

$\mathbf{L = \dfrac{6x}{H - 6}}$

19. $|3x + 6| < 15$
$|x + 2| < 5$

"x is less than 5 away from -2."

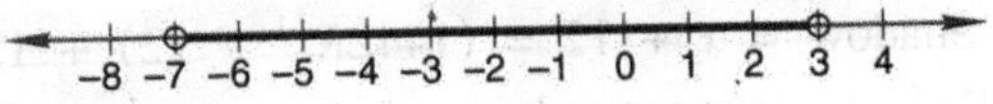

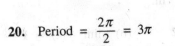

20. Period $= \dfrac{2\pi}{\frac{2}{3}} = 3\pi$

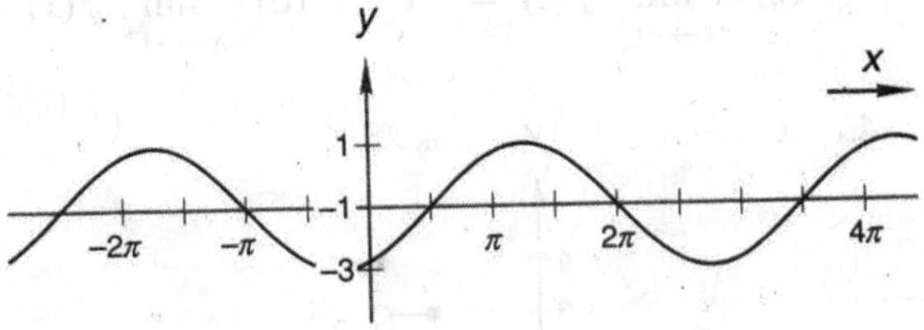

21. $f(x) = c(x + 1)(x - 2)$
$f(0) = -4 = c(1)(-2)$
$-4 = -2c$
$c = 2$

$f(x) = 2(x + 1)(x - 2)$
$\mathbf{f(x) = 2x^2 - 2x - 4}$

22. $x^2 - 1 \ge 0$
$x^2 \ge 1$
$|x| \ge 1$

Domain: $\{x \in \mathbb{R} \mid |x| \ge 1\}$
Range: $\{y \in \mathbb{R} \mid y \ge 0\}$

23. $$\frac{f(x + \Delta x) - f(x)}{\Delta x} = \frac{\frac{1}{x + \Delta x} - \frac{1}{x}}{\Delta x}$$

$$= \frac{\frac{x - (x + \Delta x)}{x(x + \Delta x)}}{\Delta x} = \frac{\frac{-\Delta x}{x(x + \Delta x)}}{\Delta x}$$

$$= \mathbf{\frac{-1}{x(x + \Delta x)}}$$

24. $s = \frac{1}{2}(5 + 6 + 7) = \frac{1}{2}(18) = 9$

$$A = \sqrt{9(9 - 5)(9 - 6)(9 - 7)}$$

$$= \sqrt{216} = \mathbf{6\sqrt{6}\ units^2} \approx \mathbf{14.6969\ units^2}$$

25. The sum of the lengths of any two sides of any triangle must be greater than the length of the third side of the triangle.

Quantity B is greater: **B**

PROBLEM SET 12

1. Let s = side of square and h = height of rectangle.

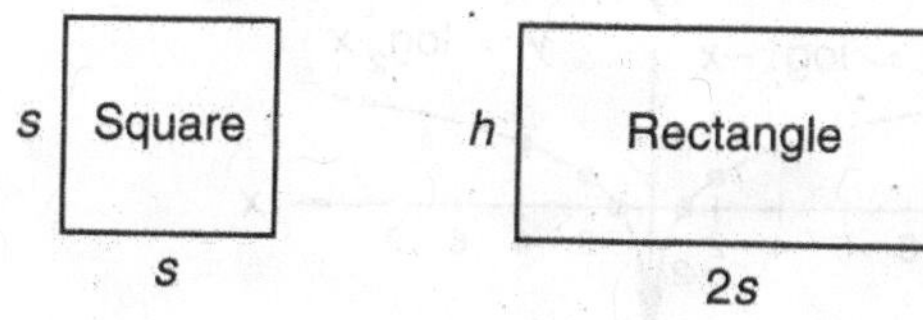

Area:

$$8s^2 = 2sh$$
$$8s^2 = 2s(8)$$
$$s^2 = 2s$$
$$s^2 - 2s = 0$$
$$s(s - 2) = 0$$
$$s = 0, 2$$

Perimeter:

$$4s + 16 = 2(2s + h)$$
$$2s + 8 = 2s + h$$
$$h = 8$$

Square: 2 × 2

Rectangle: 4 × 8

2. h 10 x

$$10^2 = h^2 + x^2$$
$$h^2 = 100 - x^2$$
$$\mathbf{h = \sqrt{100 - x^2}\ feet}$$

3. For the key trigonometric identities, see section 12.A in the textbook.

$$\sin(A + B) = \sin A \cos B + \cos A \sin B$$
$$\sin(A + A) = \sin A \cos A + \cos A \sin A$$
$$\mathbf{\sin(2A) = 2 \sin A \cos A}$$

$$\cos(A + B) = \cos A \cos B - \sin A \sin B$$
$$\cos(A + A) = \cos A \cos A - \sin A \sin A$$
$$\mathbf{\cos(2A) = \cos^2 A - \sin^2 A}$$

$$\cos(2A) = \cos^2 A - (1 - \cos^2 A)$$
$$\mathbf{\cos(2A) = 2\cos^2 A - 1}$$

$$\cos(2A) = (1 - \sin^2 A) - \sin^2 A$$
$$\mathbf{\cos(2A) = 1 - 2\sin^2 A}$$

4. $\cos \alpha = \frac{1}{5}$

$$\cos(2\alpha) = 2\cos^2 \alpha - 1 = 2\left(\frac{1}{5}\right)^2 - 1$$

$$= \frac{2}{25} - 1 = \mathbf{-\frac{23}{25}}$$

5. (a) $$\tan(A + B) = \frac{\sin(A + B)}{\cos(A + B)}$$

$$\tan(A + B) = \frac{\sin A \cos B + \cos A \sin B}{\cos A \cos B - \sin A \sin B}$$

$$\tan(A + B) = \frac{\frac{\sin A \cos B}{\cos A \cos B} + \frac{\cos A \sin B}{\cos A \cos B}}{\frac{\cos A \cos B}{\cos A \cos B} - \frac{\sin A \sin B}{\cos A \cos B}}$$

$$\mathbf{\tan(A + B) = \frac{\tan A + \tan B}{1 - \tan A \tan B}}$$

(b) $$\tan(A - B) = \frac{\sin(A - B)}{\cos(A - B)}$$

$$\tan(A - B) = \frac{\sin A \cos B - \cos A \sin B}{\cos A \cos B + \sin A \sin B}$$

$$\tan(A - B) = \frac{\frac{\sin A \cos B}{\cos A \cos B} - \frac{\cos A \sin B}{\cos A \cos B}}{\frac{\cos A \cos B}{\cos A \cos B} + \frac{\sin A \sin B}{\cos A \cos B}}$$

$$\mathbf{\tan(A - B) = \frac{\tan A - \tan B}{1 + \tan A \tan B}}$$

6. $\tan 75° = \tan (45° + 30°)$

$$= \frac{\tan 45° + \tan 30°}{1 - \tan 45° \tan 30°}$$

$$= \frac{1 + \frac{\sqrt{3}}{3}}{1 - 1\left(\frac{\sqrt{3}}{3}\right)} = \frac{\frac{3 + \sqrt{3}}{3}}{\frac{3 - \sqrt{3}}{3}}$$

$$= \frac{3 + \sqrt{3}}{3 - \sqrt{3}} = \frac{3 + \sqrt{3}}{3 - \sqrt{3}}\left(\frac{3 + \sqrt{3}}{3 + \sqrt{3}}\right)$$

$$= \frac{9 + 6\sqrt{3} + 3}{9 - 3} = \frac{12 + 6\sqrt{3}}{6} = \mathbf{2 + \sqrt{3}}$$

7. $(\sin x + \cos x)^2 = \sin^2 x + 2 \sin x \cos x + \cos^2 x$

$= (\sin^2 x + \cos^2 x) + 2 \sin x \cos x = 1 + \sin (2x)$

8.

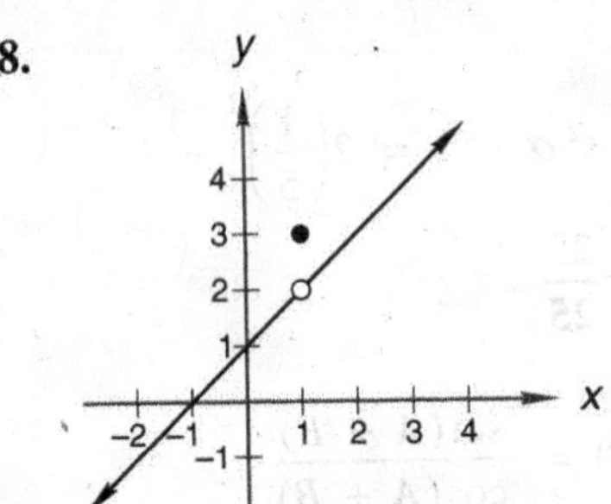

9. (a) $\lim\limits_{x \to 1^+} f(x) = \mathbf{2}$

(b) $\lim\limits_{x \to 1^-} f(x) = \mathbf{2}$

10. Possible rational roots:

$$\frac{\pm 1, \pm 2, \pm 4}{\pm 1, \pm 2} = \pm 1, \pm \frac{1}{2}, \pm 2, \pm 4$$

$$\begin{array}{r|rrrr} \underline{-1} & 2 & -7 & -5 & 4 \\ & \downarrow & -2 & 9 & -4 \\ \hline & 2 & -9 & 4 & \boxed{0} \end{array}$$

$y = 2x^3 - 7x^2 - 5x + 4$

$= (x + 1)(2x^2 - 9x + 4)$

$= (x + 1)(2x - 1)(x - 4)$

Roots: $\mathbf{-1, \frac{1}{2}, 4}$

11. $\log_4 (3x + 1) = \frac{1}{2}$

$3x + 1 = 4^{1/2}$

$3x + 1 = 2$

$3x = 1$

$x = \mathbf{\frac{1}{3}}$

12.

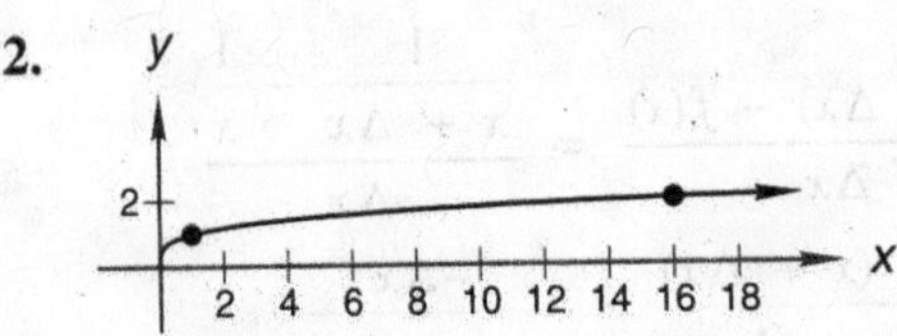

13.

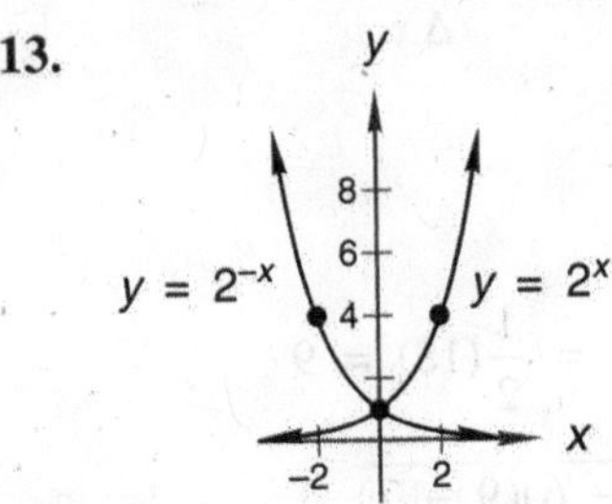

14.

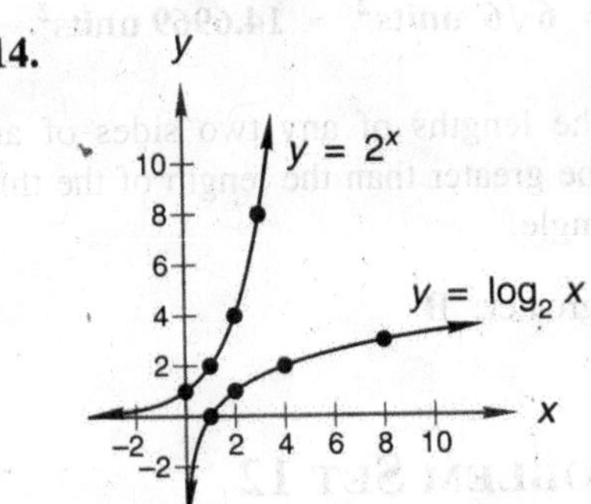

15.

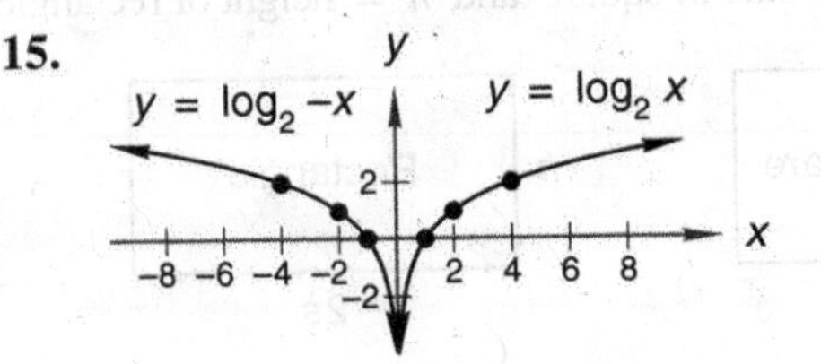

16. $\left[\sin\left(\frac{\pi}{2} - x\right)\right](\csc -x)(\sin x)(\cos -x)$

$= \cos x (-\csc x) \sin x \cos x = \cos x (-1) \cos x$

$= \mathbf{-\cos^2 x}$ or $\mathbf{\sin^2 x - 1}$

17. $f(x) = c(x + 1)(x - 2)$

$f(0) = -2 = c(1)(-2)$

$-2 = -2c$

$c = 1$

$f(x) = (x + 1)(x - 2)$

$\mathbf{f(x) = x^2 - x - 2}$

18. $\frac{y}{10 - x} = \frac{5}{10}$

$10y = 5(10 - x)$

$2y = 10 - x$

$\mathbf{y = 5 - \frac{1}{2}x}$

19. Period $= \frac{2\pi}{3}$

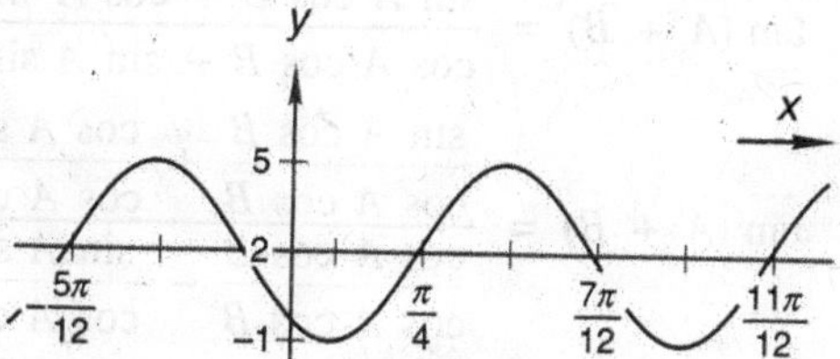

20. $\frac{f(x + h) - f(x)}{h} = \frac{2(x + h)^2 - 2x^2}{h}$

$= \frac{2(x^2 + 2hx + h^2) - 2x^2}{h}$

$= \frac{2x^2 + 4hx + 2h^2 - 2x^2}{h} = \frac{h(4x + 2h)}{h}$

$= \mathbf{4x + 2h}$

21. (a) $\cos(2A) = 2\cos^2 A - 1$

$2\cos^2 A = 1 + \cos(2A)$

$\cos^2 A = \frac{1}{2} + \frac{1}{2}\cos(2A)$

Let $A = \frac{x}{2}$.

$\cos^2 \frac{x}{2} = \frac{1}{2} + \frac{1}{2}\cos x$

$\mathbf{\cos \frac{x}{2} = \pm\sqrt{\frac{1}{2} + \frac{1}{2}\cos x}}$

(b) $\cos(2A) = 1 - 2\sin^2 A$

$2\sin^2 A = 1 - \cos(2A)$

$\sin^2 A = \frac{1}{2} - \frac{1}{2}\cos(2A)$

Let $A = \frac{x}{2}$.

$\sin^2 \frac{x}{2} = \frac{1}{2} - \frac{1}{2}\cos x$

$\mathbf{\sin \frac{x}{2} = \pm\sqrt{\frac{1}{2} - \frac{1}{2}\cos x}}$

22. $1 - x \geq 0$

$1 \geq x$

$\mathbf{\{x \in \mathbb{R} \mid x \leq 1\}}$

23. If the sides opposite two angles of a triangle do not have equal lengths, then the two angles do not have equal measures.

24. $\frac{1}{2}x = 75$

$\mathbf{x = 150°}$

$\frac{1}{2}z = 35$

$\mathbf{z = 70°}$

$x + y + z = 360°$

$y = 360° - 150° - 70°$

$\mathbf{y = 140°}$

25.

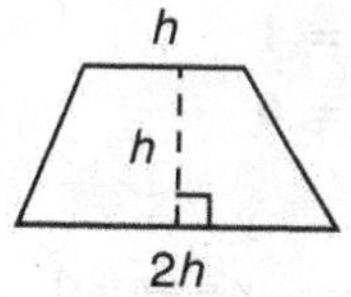

$A = \left(\frac{B_1 + B_2}{2}\right)h$

$12 = \left(\frac{h + 2h}{2}\right)h$

$12 = \frac{3}{2}h^2$

$h^2 = 8$

$h = \mathbf{2\sqrt{2}\ units} \approx \mathbf{2.8284\ units}$

Problem Set 13

1. $\frac{S}{D^2W} = \frac{S}{D^2W}$

$\frac{40}{M^2P} = \frac{S}{3^2 A}$

$S(M^2 P) = 40(9A)$

$\mathbf{S = \frac{360A}{M^2P}}$

2.

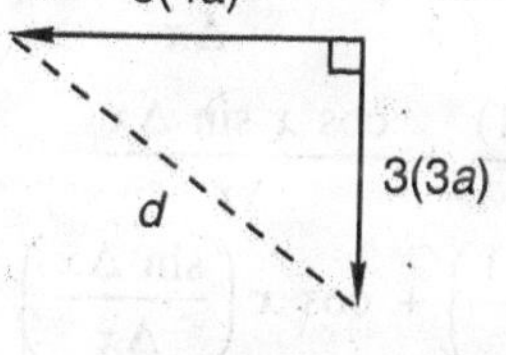

$d^2 = [3(4a)]^2 + [3(3a)]^2$

$d^2 = 144a^2 + 81a^2$

$d^2 = 225a^2$

$d = \mathbf{15a\ miles}$

3. $\sin^{-1} -\frac{\sqrt{2}}{2} = \mathbf{-\frac{\pi}{4}}$

4. $\cos^{-1} \frac{\sqrt{3}}{2} = \mathbf{\frac{\pi}{6}}$

5. $\csc x = -2$

$\sin x = -\frac{1}{2}$

$x = \mathbf{210°, 330°}$

6. $\cos^2 x = 1$

$\cos x = \pm 1$

$x = \mathbf{0, \pi}$

7.
$$\sin^2 x + 2\cos x - 2 = 0$$
$$(1 - \cos^2 x) + 2\cos x - 2 = 0$$
$$\cos^2 x - 2\cos x + 1 = 0$$
$$(\cos x - 1)(\cos x - 1) = 0$$
$$\cos x = 1$$
$$x = \mathbf{0}$$

8.

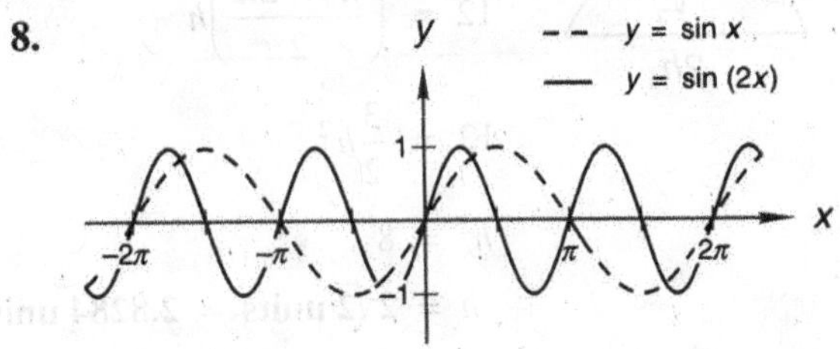

9.

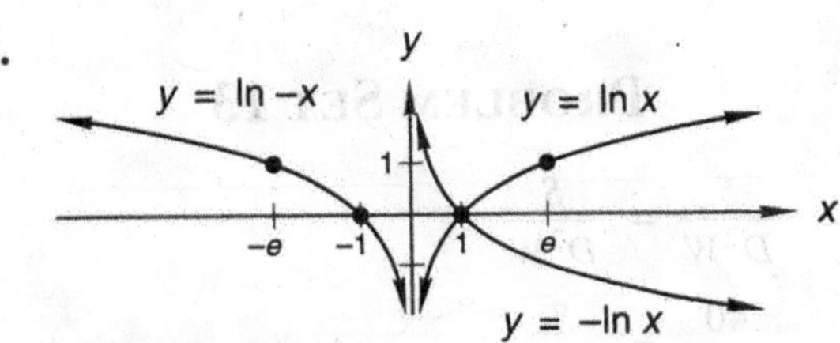

10. $\dfrac{\sin(x + \Delta x) - \sin x}{\Delta x}$

$= \dfrac{\sin x \cos \Delta x + \cos x \sin \Delta x - \sin x}{\Delta x}$

$= \dfrac{\sin x \cos \Delta x - \sin x}{\Delta x} + \dfrac{\cos x \sin \Delta x}{\Delta x}$

$= \dfrac{\sin x (\cos \Delta x - 1)}{\Delta x} + \dfrac{\cos x \sin \Delta x}{\Delta x}$

$= \sin x \left(\dfrac{\cos \Delta x - 1}{\Delta x}\right) + \cos x \left(\dfrac{\sin \Delta x}{\Delta x}\right)$

11. For the key trigonometric identities, see section 12.A in the textbook.

$\cos(A + B) = \cos A \cos B - \sin A \sin B$

$\cos(A + A) = \cos A \cos A - \sin A \sin A$

$\mathbf{\cos(2A) = \cos^2 A - \sin^2 A}$

$\cos(2A) = \cos^2 A - (1 - \cos^2 A)$

$\mathbf{\cos(2A) = 2\cos^2 A - 1}$

$\cos(2A) = (1 - \sin^2 A) - \sin^2 A$

$\mathbf{\cos(2A) = 1 - 2\sin^2 A}$

12. (a) $\tan(A + B) = \dfrac{\sin(A + B)}{\cos(A + B)}$

$\tan(A + B) = \dfrac{\sin A \cos B + \cos A \sin B}{\cos A \cos B - \sin A \sin B}$

$\tan(A + B) = \dfrac{\dfrac{\sin A \cos B}{\cos A \cos B} + \dfrac{\cos A \sin B}{\cos A \cos B}}{\dfrac{\cos A \cos B}{\cos A \cos B} - \dfrac{\sin A \sin B}{\cos A \cos B}}$

$\tan(A + B) = \dfrac{\tan A + \tan B}{1 - \tan A \tan B}$

(b) $\tan(2A) = \tan(A + A)$

$= \dfrac{\tan A + \tan A}{1 - \tan A \tan A} = \dfrac{2\tan A}{1 - \tan^2 A}$

Since $\tan A = \dfrac{1}{2}$

$\tan(2A) = \dfrac{2\left(\frac{1}{2}\right)}{1 - \left(\frac{1}{2}\right)^2} = \dfrac{1}{1 - \frac{1}{4}} = \mathbf{\dfrac{4}{3}}$

13.

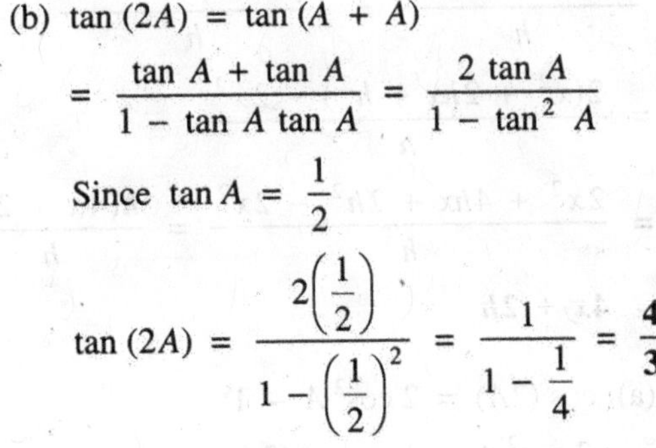

14. (a) $\lim_{x \to 1^+} f(x) = \mathbf{1}$ (b) $\lim_{x \to 1^-} f(x) = \mathbf{1}$

(c) $f(1) = \mathbf{3}$

15. (a)

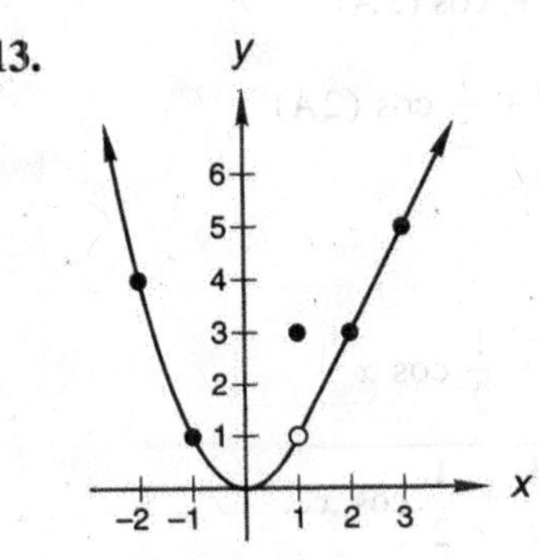

(b) $y = \sqrt{9 - x^2}$ describes only the positive square root, which coincides with the portions of the graph of a circle of radius 3 that lie on or above the x-axis.

(c) To graph a complete circle on a graphing calculator we need to graph it in two parts:
`Y1=√(9−X²)` and `Y2=−√(9−X²)`

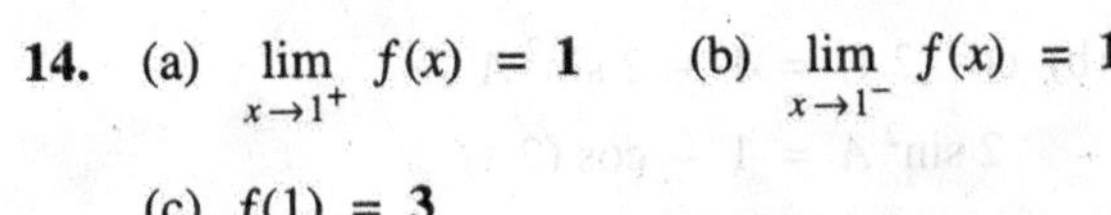

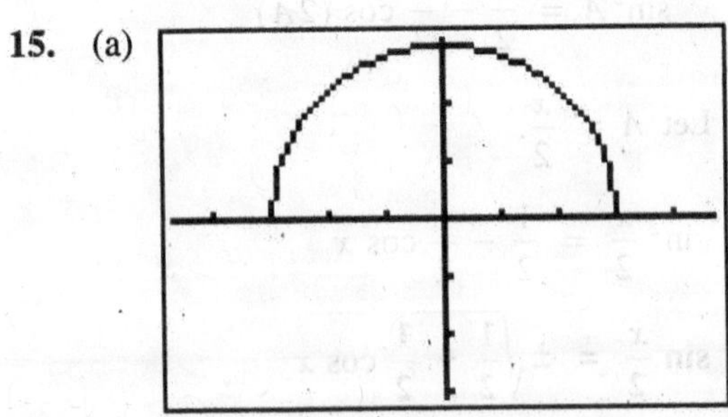

16. The axis of symmetry is halfway between the roots.

$$x = \frac{2 + (-6)}{2} = -2$$

17. $A = \pi r^2$

$4\pi = \pi r^2$

$r = 2$

$(x - 1)^2 + (y + 2)^2 = 2^2$

18. $$\frac{f(x + \Delta x) - f(x)}{\Delta x} = \frac{\frac{2}{x + \Delta x} - \frac{2}{x}}{\Delta x}$$

$$= \frac{\frac{2x - 2(x + \Delta x)}{x(x + \Delta x)}}{\Delta x} = \frac{\frac{-2\Delta x}{x(x + \Delta x)}}{\Delta x}$$

$$= \frac{-2}{x(x + \Delta x)}$$

19. 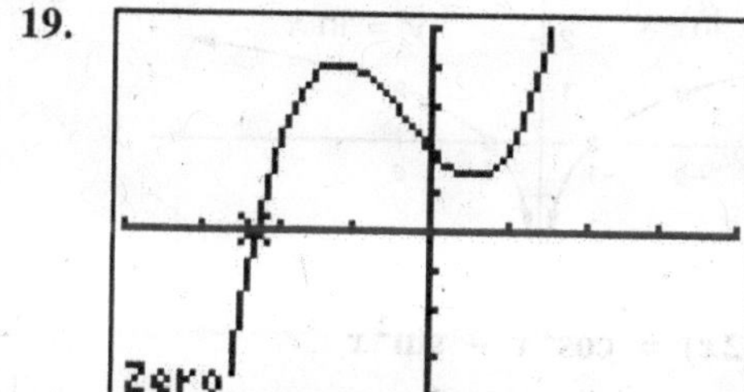

$x \approx -2.269531$

20. Let Y1=5 and Y2=e^(X).

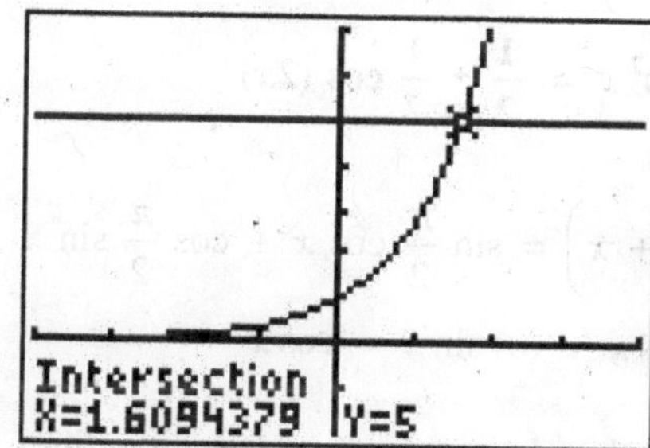

(a) **(1.609, 5)**

(b) $e^x = 5$

$x = \ln 5$

Point of intersection: **(ln 5, 5)**

21. $y = \frac{\sqrt{x - 2}}{x}$

$x - 2 \geq 0$

$x \geq 2$ and division by zero is not allowed.

$\{x \in \mathbb{R} \mid x \geq 2\}$

22. Draw an auxillary line segment.

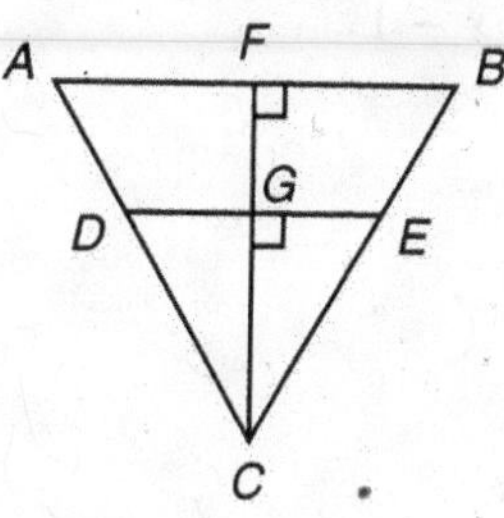

ΔCEG is a 30-60-90 right triangle.

Since $GC = h$, $GE = \frac{h}{\sqrt{3}}$ and $DE = \frac{2h}{\sqrt{3}}$

$DE = \frac{2\sqrt{3}h}{3} \approx \mathbf{1.1547h}$

23. $$\frac{1}{4}\sum_{n=1}^{4} f(1) = \frac{1}{4}[f(1) + f(1) + f(1) + f(1)]$$

$$= \frac{1}{4}(1 + 1 + 1 + 1) = \mathbf{1}$$

24. Since side CB is opposite $\angle A$ it must be greater than side AC which is opposite $\angle B$.

Quantity A is greater: **A**

25. $x^4 - y^4 = (x^2 + y^2)(x^2 - y^2) = 3(4) = \mathbf{12}$

PROBLEM SET 14

1. 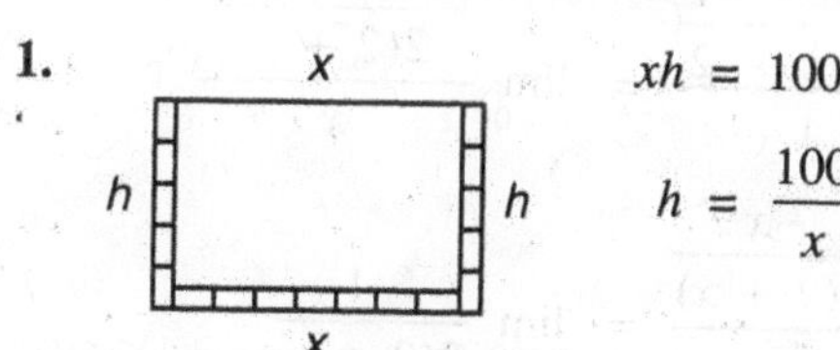

$xh = 100$

$h = \frac{100}{x}$

Perimeter $= 2x + 2h$

Cost $= 50(2h) + 50x + 20x$

$C = 100h + 70x$

$C = 100\left(\frac{100}{x}\right) + 70x$

$\mathbf{C = 10{,}000x^{-1} + 70x}$

2. $d = mh = rt$

$mh = r(h - 2)$

$r = \frac{mh}{h - 2}$ **miles per hour**

3. $y = \dfrac{x^2 - 1}{x - 1} = \dfrac{(x + 1)(x - 1)}{x - 1}$

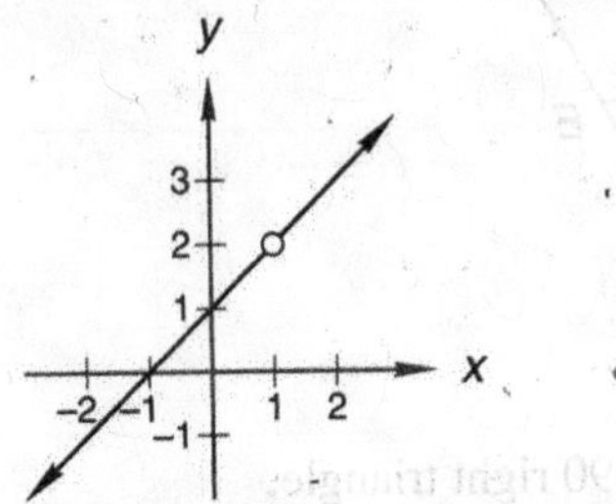

4. $\lim\limits_{x\to 3} \dfrac{x^2 + 2x}{x + 2} = \dfrac{9 + 6}{5} = \dfrac{15}{5} = \mathbf{3}$

5. $\lim\limits_{x\to 2} \dfrac{x^2 + x - 6}{x - 2} = \lim\limits_{x\to 2} \dfrac{(x + 3)(x - 2)}{x - 2}$

$= \lim\limits_{x\to 2} (x + 3) = 2 + 3 = \mathbf{5}$

6. $\lim\limits_{x\to a} \dfrac{x^2 - a^2}{x - a} = \lim\limits_{x\to a} \dfrac{(x + a)(x - a)}{x - a}$

$= \lim\limits_{x\to a} (x + a) = a + a = \mathbf{2a}$

7. $\lim\limits_{x\to 0} \dfrac{(2 + x)^2 - 2^2}{x} = \lim\limits_{x\to 0} \dfrac{4 + 4x + x^2 - 4}{x}$

$= \lim\limits_{x\to 0} \dfrac{4x + x^2}{x} = \lim\limits_{x\to 0} (4 + x) = 4 + 0 = \mathbf{4}$

8. $\lim\limits_{x\to 0} \dfrac{\dfrac{1}{2 + x} - \dfrac{1}{2}}{x} = \lim\limits_{x\to 0} \dfrac{\dfrac{2 - (2 + x)}{2(2 + x)}}{x}$

$= \lim\limits_{x\to 0} \dfrac{\dfrac{-x}{2(2 + x)}}{x} = \lim\limits_{x\to 0} \dfrac{-1}{2(2 + x)}$

$= \dfrac{-1}{2(2 + 0)} = -\dfrac{\mathbf{1}}{\mathbf{4}}$

9. $2 \sin^2 x - 3 \cos x = 3$

$2(1 - \cos^2 x) - 3 \cos x = 3$

$2 \cos^2 x + 3 \cos x + 1 = 0$

$(2 \cos x + 1)(\cos x + 1) = 0$

$2 \cos x + 1 = 0$ or $\cos x + 1 = 0$

$\cos x = -\dfrac{1}{2}$ $\qquad \cos x = -1$

$\mathbf{x = 120°, 180°, 240°}$

10. $y = 4 - 2 \sin (3x)$

Amplitude: 2 **Period:** $\dfrac{2\pi}{3}$

Centerline: $\mathbf{y = 4}$

11.

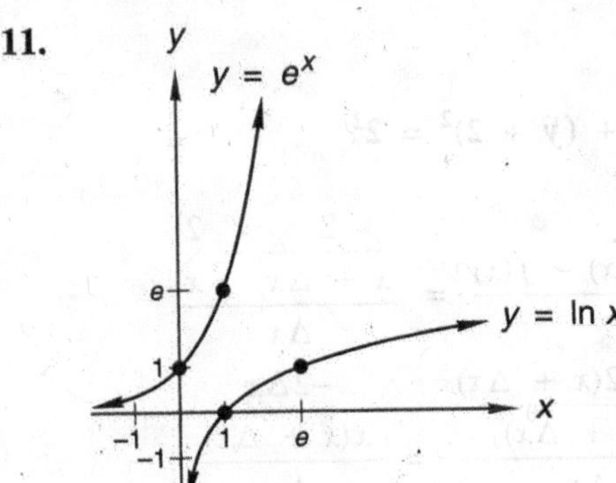

12.

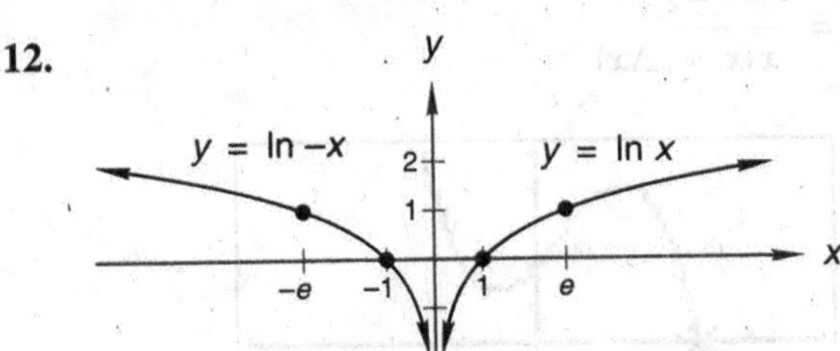

13. (a) $\mathbf{\cos (2x) = \cos^2 x - \sin^2 x}$

$\mathbf{\cos (2x) = 1 - 2 \sin^2 x}$

$\mathbf{\cos (2x) = 2 \cos^2 x - 1}$

(b) $\cos (2x) = 2 \cos^2 x - 1$

$2 \cos^2 x = 1 + \cos (2x)$

$\mathbf{\cos^2 x = \dfrac{1}{2} + \dfrac{1}{2} \cos (2x)}$

14. $\sin \left(\dfrac{\pi}{2} + x\right) = \sin \dfrac{\pi}{2} \cos x + \cos \dfrac{\pi}{2} \sin x$

$= (1) \cos x + (0) \sin x = \mathbf{\cos x}$

15. (a) For the key trigonometric identities, see section 12.A in the textbook.

$\tan (A - B) = \dfrac{\sin (A - B)}{\cos (A - B)}$

$\tan (A - B) = \dfrac{\sin A \cos B - \cos A \sin B}{\cos A \cos B + \sin A \sin B}$

$\tan (A - B) = \dfrac{\dfrac{\sin A \cos B}{\cos A \cos B} - \dfrac{\cos A \sin B}{\cos A \cos B}}{\dfrac{\cos A \cos B}{\cos A \cos B} + \dfrac{\sin A \sin B}{\cos A \cos B}}$

$\tan (A - B) = \mathbf{\dfrac{\tan A - \tan B}{1 + \tan A \tan B}}$

(b) $\tan 15° = \tan (60 - 45)°$

$$= \frac{\tan 60° - \tan 45°}{1 + \tan 60° \tan 45°} = \frac{\sqrt{3} - 1}{1 + \sqrt{3}(1)}$$

$$= \frac{\sqrt{3} - 1}{1 + \sqrt{3}}\left(\frac{1 - \sqrt{3}}{1 - \sqrt{3}}\right) = \frac{\sqrt{3} - 3 - 1 + \sqrt{3}}{1 - 3}$$

$$= \frac{-4 + 2\sqrt{3}}{-2} = \mathbf{2 - \sqrt{3}}$$

16. $y - 1 = \ln x$

$$e^{y-1} = e^{\ln x}$$

$$\mathbf{x = e^{y-1}}$$

17. $y = -|x^2 - 3x - 4|$

$y = -|(x - 4)(x + 1)|$

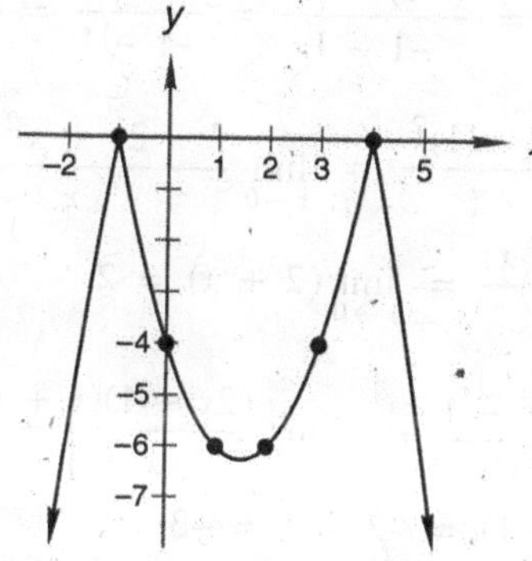

18. Choices B, C, and D will fail the vertical line test.

Only choice **A** is correct.

19. $|x - 1| < 2$ "x is less than 2 away from 1"

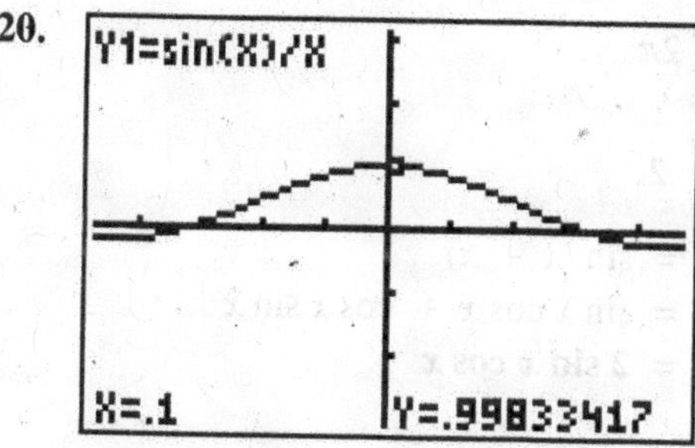

20.

Y1=sin(X)/X

X=.1 Y=.99833417

Guess: $\lim_{x \to 0} \frac{\sin x}{x} = \mathbf{1}$

21. $(\sec -x)\left[\sin\left(\frac{\pi}{2} - x\right)\right]$

$+ (\sin -x)\left[\cos\left(\frac{\pi}{2} - x\right)\right]$

$= \sec x \cos x + (-\sin x) \sin x$

$= 1 - \sin^2 x = \mathbf{\cos^2 x}$

22. A. A circle is not a function.

B. A vertically opening parabola IS a function.

C. A horizontally opening parabola is not a function.

D. Same graph as choice C.

The correct choice is **B**.

23. $\left(\frac{\sqrt{x + h} - \sqrt{x}}{h}\right)\left(\frac{\sqrt{x + h} + \sqrt{x}}{\sqrt{x + h} + \sqrt{x}}\right)$

$$= \frac{x + h - x}{h(\sqrt{x + h} + \sqrt{x})} = \mathbf{\frac{1}{\sqrt{x + h} + \sqrt{x}}}$$

24. $\sum_{x=1}^{4} \frac{1}{x} = \frac{1}{1} + \frac{1}{2} + \frac{1}{3} + \frac{1}{4} = \mathbf{\frac{25}{12}}$

25. Regardless of whether x is positive, negative, or zero, $\sqrt{x^2} = |x|$.

The quantities are equal: **C**

Problem Set 15

1. $R_1 = \frac{1}{2}$; $R_2 = \frac{1}{6}$

$T(R_1 + R_2) = 1$

$T\left(\frac{1}{2} + \frac{1}{6}\right) = 1$

$T\left(\frac{2}{3}\right) = 1$

$T = \mathbf{\frac{3}{2}\ hr}$

2. $S + L = 40$

$S = 40 - L$

$P = SL$

$\mathbf{P = 40L - L^2}$

3. (a) $\mathbf{(-\infty, -2)}$ **and** $\mathbf{(2, \infty)}$

(b) $\mathbf{(-2, 2)}$

(c) $\mathbf{(0, \infty)}$

(d) $\mathbf{(-\infty, 0)}$

4. Possible rational roots: ±1, ±2, ±4

$$\begin{array}{r|rrrr} -2 & 1 & 0 & -6 & -4 \\ & \downarrow & -2 & 4 & 4 \\ \hline & 1 & -2 & -2 & \boxed{0} \end{array}$$

$$x^3 - 6x - 4 = 0$$

$$(x + 2)(x^2 - 2x - 2) = 0$$

$$\mathbf{x = -2, 1 \pm \sqrt{3}}$$

5. – – – | + + + | – – | + + + +

–5 –4 –3 –2 –1 0 1 2 3 4

Zeros: **–3, 0, 2**

6.

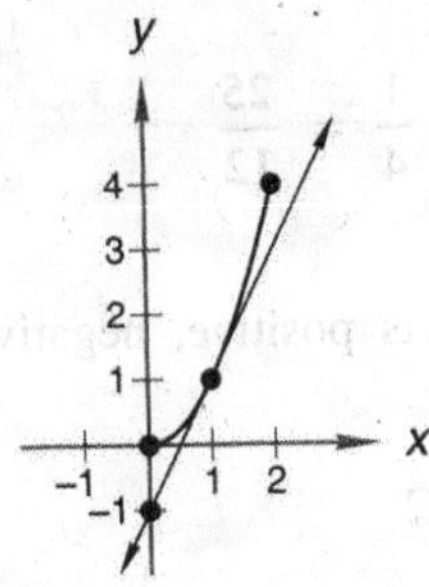

Answers may vary: (1, 1), (0, –1)

$$\text{slope} \approx \frac{1 - (-1)}{1 - 0} = \frac{2}{1} = \mathbf{2}$$

7. $\tan^2 x = 1$

$\tan x = \pm 1$

$$x = \boldsymbol{\frac{\pi}{4}, \frac{3\pi}{4}, \frac{5\pi}{4}, \frac{7\pi}{4}}$$

8.

$$\sin^2 x - \sin x + \frac{1}{4} = 0$$

$$\left(\sin x - \frac{1}{2}\right)\left(\sin x - \frac{1}{2}\right) = 0$$

$$\sin x = \frac{1}{2}$$

$$x = \boldsymbol{\frac{\pi}{6}, \frac{5\pi}{6}}$$

9. $\arcsin x = y$

$\mathbf{x = \sin y}$

10. (a) $x^2 - 8y - 4x + 20 = 0$

$$8y = x^2 - 4x + 20$$

$$y = \boldsymbol{\frac{1}{8}x^2 - \frac{1}{2}x + \frac{5}{2}}$$

(b)

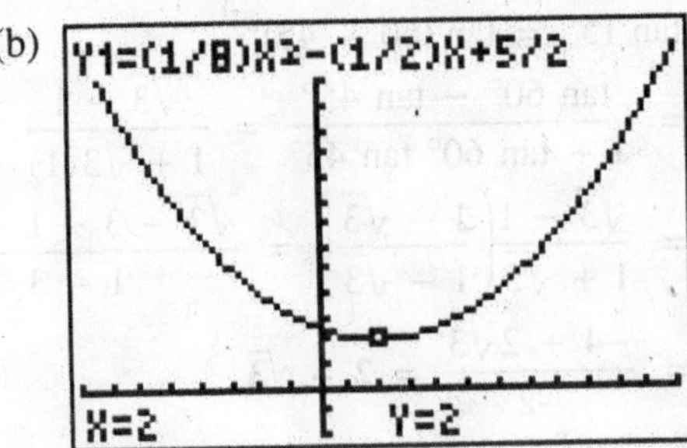

(c) **(2, 2)**

11. $\lim_{x\to 1} \frac{x^2 - 1}{x - 1} = \lim_{x\to 1} \frac{(x + 1)(x - 1)}{x - 1}$

$= \lim_{x\to 1} (x + 1) = 1 + 1 = \mathbf{2}$

12. $\lim_{x\to -1} \frac{x^2 + 1}{x - 1} = \frac{(-1)^2 + 1}{-1 - 1} = \frac{1 + 1}{-1 - 1} = \mathbf{-1}$

13. $\lim_{x\to 0} \frac{(1 + x)^2 - (1)^2}{x} = \lim_{x\to 0} \frac{1 + 2x + x^2 - 1}{x}$

$= \lim_{x\to 0} \frac{x(2 + x)}{x} = \lim_{x\to 0} (2 + x) = \mathbf{2}$

14. $\lim_{x\to -1} \frac{2x^2 + x - 1}{x + 1} = \lim_{x\to -1} \frac{(2x - 1)(x + 1)}{x + 1}$

$= \lim_{x\to -1} (2x - 1) = -2 - 1 = \mathbf{-3}$

15. $\frac{[2(x + \Delta x) + 3] - (2x + 3)}{\Delta x}$

$= \frac{2x + 2(\Delta x) + 3 - 2x - 3}{\Delta x} = \frac{2(\Delta x)}{\Delta x} = \mathbf{2}$

16. If $y = \frac{1}{k}\sin(kx)$ is to have a period of 4π, then $\frac{2\pi}{k} = 4\pi$.

$4\pi(k) = 2\pi$

$k = \boldsymbol{\frac{1}{2}}$

17. $\sin(2x) = \sin(x + x)$

$\sin(2x) = \sin x \cos x + \cos x \sin x$

$\mathbf{\sin(2x) = 2\sin x \cos x}$

18.

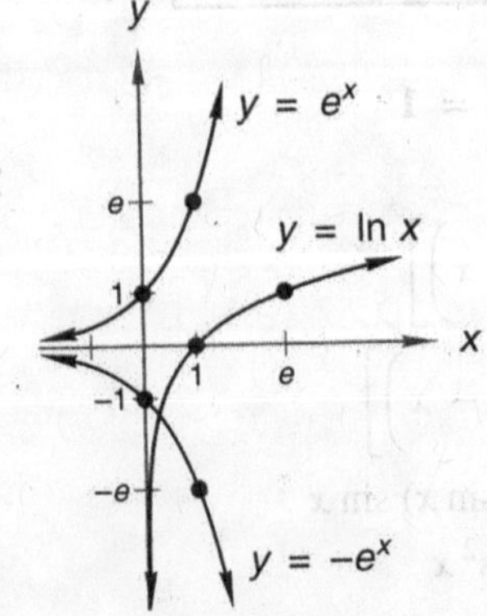

19. $\cos(2A) = 1 - 2\sin^2 A = 1 - 2\left(\frac{1}{7}\right)$

$= 1 - \frac{2}{7} = \mathbf{\frac{5}{7}}$

20. $\log_2\left(\frac{x-1}{x+1}\right) = 3$

$$\frac{x-1}{x+1} = 2^3$$

$$8x + 8 = x - 1$$

$$7x = -9$$

$$x = \mathbf{-\frac{9}{7}}$$

21. The equation of the origin-centered unit circle is $x^2 + y^2 = 1$. If (x, y) is a point on this circle, then $x^2 + y^2$ is equal to **1**.

22. "y is less than 0.01 away from 3."
$\{y \in \mathbb{R} \mid 2.99 < y < 3.01\}$

23.

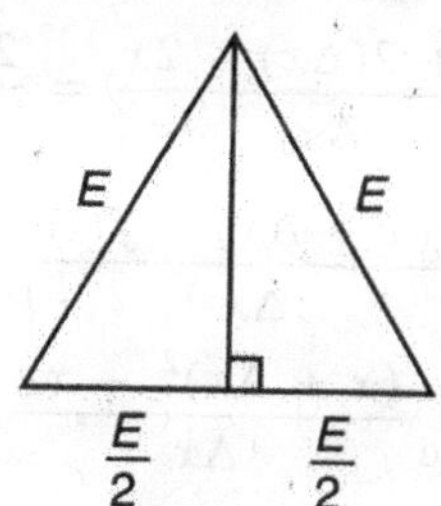

$V = A_{\text{Base}} H_{\text{Prism}}$

$V = \frac{1}{2}(E)\left(\frac{\sqrt{3}E}{2}\right)L$

$V = \mathbf{\frac{\sqrt{3}}{4}E^2L\ \text{cm}^3}$

24. 1, 4, 9, 16, ...
$1^2, 2^2, 3^2, 4^2, 5^2, \ldots$
The next term is **25**.

25. $x + y + z = 180°$ and $t + s + v = 180°$

$x + y + z + t + s + v = 180° + 180° = \mathbf{360°}$

Problem Set 16

1.
$$25 = 100m + b$$
$$-(29 = 120m + b)$$
$$-4 = -20m$$

$$m = \frac{1}{5}$$

$$25 = 100\left(\frac{1}{5}\right) + b$$

$$b = 5$$

$$s = \left(\frac{1}{5}\right)c + 5$$

$$30 = \left(\frac{1}{5}\right)c + 5$$

$$25 = \left(\frac{1}{5}\right)c$$

$$c = \textbf{125 cars}$$

2.
$$p = 2(l + w)$$

$$\frac{p}{2} = l + w$$

$$l = \frac{p}{2} - w$$

$$A = l \cdot w$$

$$A = \left(\frac{p}{2} - w\right)w$$

$$A = \mathbf{\frac{1}{2}pw - w^2}$$

3. $\ln(x + 2) - \ln(x - 1) = \ln 5$

$$\ln\left(\frac{x+2}{x-1}\right) = \ln 5$$

$$\frac{x+2}{x-1} = 5$$

$$5x - 5 = x + 2$$

$$4x = 7$$

$$x = \mathbf{\frac{7}{4}}$$

4. $2\log_3 x - \log_3 4 = 2$

$$\log_3 x^2 - \log_3 4 = 2$$

$$\log_3\left(\frac{x^2}{4}\right) = 2$$

$$3^2 = \frac{x^2}{4}$$

$$36 = x^2$$

$$x = \mathbf{6}$$

5.
$$27^{2x+1} = 9$$
$$(3^3)^{2x+1} = 3^2$$
$$3^{6x+3} = 3^2$$
$$6x + 3 = 2$$
$$x = \mathbf{-\frac{1}{6}}$$

6.
$$10^{x+1} = e^{2x}$$
$$(x + 1)\ln 10 = 2x$$
$$x \ln 10 + \ln 10 = 2x$$
$$x \ln 10 - 2x = -\ln 10$$
$$x(\ln 10 - 2) = -\ln 10$$
$$x = \frac{-\ln 10}{\ln 10 - 2}$$
$$x = \mathbf{\frac{\ln 10}{2 - \ln 10}}$$

7.
$$3^{-x+1} = 4^{x+2}$$
$$(-x + 1)\ln 3 = (x + 2)\ln 4$$
$$-x \ln 3 + \ln 3 = x \ln 4 + 2 \ln 4$$
$$\ln 3 - \ln 16 = x \ln 4 + x \ln 3$$
$$\ln\left(\frac{3}{16}\right) = x(\ln 4 + \ln 3)$$
$$x = \mathbf{\frac{\ln\left(\frac{3}{16}\right)}{\ln 12}}$$

8. $f(x) = |x^2 - 1| = |(x + 1)(x - 1)|$

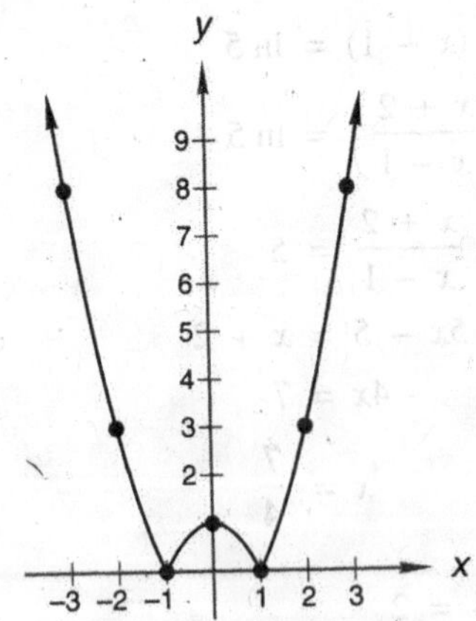

9. **Increasing: (–1, 0), (1, ∞)**
Decreasing: (–∞, –1), (0, 1)

10. $x = \mathbf{0}$

11. + + + | – – | + | – – | + + +

–3 –2 –1 0 1 2 3 4

12. (a)

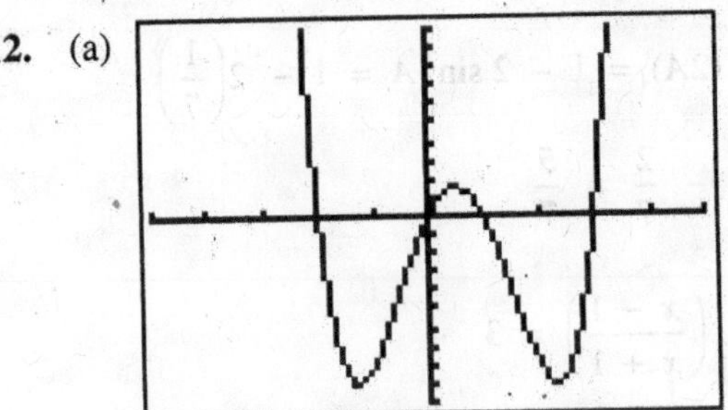

(b) Using `4:maximum` in the `CALCULATE` menu, the high point is **(0.5, 1.5625).**

13.
$$4 \sin^2 x - 3 = 0$$
$$\sin^2 x = \frac{3}{4}$$
$$\sin x = \pm\frac{\sqrt{3}}{2}$$
$$x = \mathbf{\frac{\pi}{3}, \frac{2\pi}{3}, \frac{4\pi}{3}, \frac{5\pi}{3}}$$

14.
$$\frac{f(x + \Delta x) - f(x)}{\Delta x} = \frac{2(x + \Delta x) - 2x}{\Delta x}$$
$$= \frac{2x + 2(\Delta x) - 2x}{\Delta x} = \frac{2(\Delta x)}{\Delta x} = \mathbf{2}$$

15.
$$\lim_{\Delta x \to 0} \frac{f(x + \Delta x) - f(x)}{\Delta x}$$
$$= \lim_{\Delta x \to 0} \frac{(x + \Delta x)^2 - x^2}{\Delta x}$$
$$= \lim_{\Delta x \to 0} \frac{x^2 + 2x(\Delta x) + (\Delta x)^2 - x^2}{\Delta x}$$
$$= \lim_{\Delta x \to 0} \frac{\Delta x(2x + \Delta x)}{\Delta x} = \lim_{\Delta x \to 0} (2x + \Delta x) = \mathbf{2x}$$

16.
$$\lim_{t \to 1} \frac{t^2 - 2t + 1}{t - 1} = \lim_{t \to 1} \frac{(t - 1)(t - 1)}{t - 1}$$
$$= \lim_{t \to 1} (t - 1) = 1 - 1 = \mathbf{0}$$

17.
$$\lim_{s \to 1} \frac{s - 1}{s^2 + 1} = \frac{1 - 1}{1 + 1} = \frac{0}{2} = \mathbf{0}$$

18. (a) $\lim_{x \to 0} (e^x + 1) = e^0 + 1 = 1 + 1 = \mathbf{2}$

(b)

X	Y1
-.03	1.9704
-.02	1.9802
-.01	1.99
0	2
.01	2.0101
.02	2.0202
.03	2.0305

X=0

As x approaches 0, y approaches **2.**

19. Centerline: $y = 35$ Amplitude: 40

Period: $\frac{\pi}{2}$ $C = \frac{2\pi}{\frac{\pi}{2}} = 4$ Phase: $\frac{5\pi}{8}$ or $\frac{7\pi}{8}$

$$\mathbf{y = 35 + 40 \sin \left[4\left(\theta - \frac{5\pi}{8}\right)\right]} \text{ or}$$

$$\mathbf{y = 35 - 40 \sin \left[4\left(\theta - \frac{7\pi}{8}\right)\right]}$$

20.

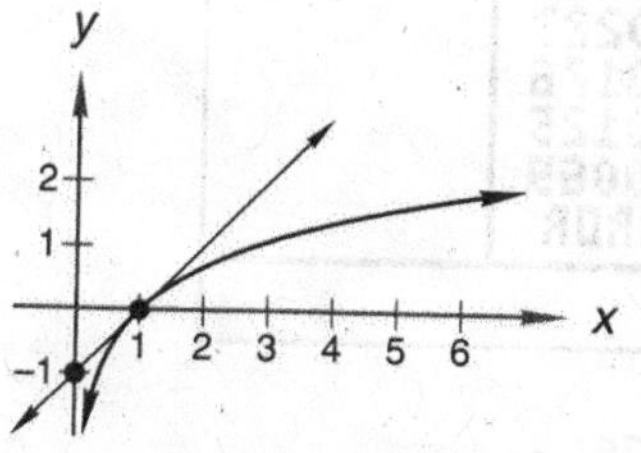

Answers may vary: (1, 0), (0, −1)

$$\text{slope} \approx \frac{0 - (-1)}{1 - 0} = \frac{1}{1} = \mathbf{1}$$

21. The argument of a logarithm must be positive, so $-x > 0$, or $x < 0$.

Domain: $\{x \in \mathbb{R} \mid x < 0\}$

Range: $\mathbb{R}$

22. $\sin^2 x + \cos^2 x = 1$

$\sin^2 43° + \cos^2 43° = \mathbf{1}$

23. (a) $\tan(2A) = \frac{\sin(2A)}{\cos(2A)} = \frac{2 \sin A \cos A}{\cos^2 A - \sin^2 A}$

$$= \frac{\frac{2 \sin A \cos A}{\cos^2 A}}{\frac{\cos^2 A}{\cos^2 A} - \frac{\sin^2 A}{\cos^2 A}} = \frac{2 \tan A}{1 - \tan^2 A}$$

(b) $\tan(2A) = \frac{2 \tan A}{1 - \tan^2 A} = \frac{2(2)}{1 - (2)^2}$

$$= \frac{4}{1 - 4} = -\frac{\mathbf{4}}{\mathbf{3}}$$

24. $\frac{1}{\sqrt[3]{x^2}} = \frac{1}{(x^2)^{1/3}} = \frac{1}{x^{2/3}} = x^{-2/3}$

$\sqrt[3]{x^{-2}} = (x^{-2})^{1/3} = x^{-2/3}$

With $x > 0$ the quantities are equal: **C**

25. By drawing a diagonal and "triangulating" the quadrilateral, the quadrilateral is split into two triangles each having a sum of interior angles of 180°. Therefore, $x + y + z + t = \mathbf{360°}$

PROBLEM SET 17

1. $\text{Average rate} = \mathbf{\frac{40M + 60B}{M + B}}$ **mph**

2. [400 sq. ft rectangle with sides l and w]

$lw = 400$

$l = \frac{400}{w}$

$$P = 2(l + w) = 2\left(\frac{400}{w} + w\right)$$

$$= \mathbf{800w^{-1} + 2w}$$

3. $\lim_{x \to \infty} \frac{3x^3 - 2x + 4}{1 - 2x^3} = \lim_{x \to \infty} \frac{3 - \frac{2}{x^2} + \frac{4}{x^3}}{\frac{1}{x^3} - 2}$

$$= \frac{3 - 0 + 0}{0 - 2} = -\frac{\mathbf{3}}{\mathbf{2}}$$

4. $\lim_{x \to -\infty} \frac{x^3 - 6x}{5x + x^2} = \lim_{x \to -\infty} \frac{x - \frac{6}{x}}{\frac{5}{x} + 1} = \frac{-\infty - 0}{0 + 1}$

$$= \mathbf{-\infty}$$

5. $\lim_{x \to a} \frac{x^2 - a^2}{x - a} = \lim_{x \to a} \frac{(x + a)(x - a)}{x - a}$

$$= \lim_{x \to a} (x + a) = a + a = \mathbf{2a}$$

6. $\lim_{x \to a} \frac{x - a}{x^2 + a^2} = \frac{a - a}{a^2 + a^2} = \frac{0}{2a^2} = \mathbf{0}$

7. $\lim_{x \to -1} f(x) = \mathbf{\infty}$

8. $\lim_{x \to 1^-} f(x) = \mathbf{-\infty}$

9. $\lim_{x \to 1^+} f(x) = \mathbf{\infty}$

10. The $\lim_{x \to 1} f(x)$ is **undefined** because the limit from the left does not equal the limit from the right.

11. **Increasing: $(-\infty, -1)$**

Decreasing: $(-1, 1)$, $(1, \infty)$

12.
$$\sin^2 x + 2\cos x - 2 = 0$$
$$(1 - \cos^2 x) + 2\cos x - 2 = 0$$
$$\cos^2 x - 2\cos x + 1 = 0$$
$$(\cos x - 1)(\cos x - 1) = 0$$
$$\cos x = 1$$
$$\mathbf{x = 0}$$

13.
$$2\ln x = \ln(x - 1) + \ln(x - 2)$$
$$\ln x^2 = \ln(x^2 - 3x + 2)$$
$$x^2 = x^2 - 3x + 2$$
$$3x = 2$$
$$x = \frac{2}{3}$$

Since this gives a negative argument there is **no solution.**

14.
$$4^{2x} = 16^{1-x}$$
$$4^{2x} = (4^2)^{1-x}$$
$$4^{2x} = 4^{2-2x}$$
$$2x = 2 - 2x$$
$$4x = 2$$
$$x = \mathbf{\frac{1}{2}}$$

15.
$$y = e^x$$
$$\ln y = \ln(e^x)$$
$$x = \mathbf{\ln y}$$

16. $y = -2 + 3\sin(4x)$

Amplitude: 3 **Period:** $\frac{2\pi}{4} = \mathbf{\frac{\pi}{2}}$

Centerline: $\mathbf{y = -2}$

17. For the key trigonometric identities, see section 12.A in the textbook.
$$\cos(2A) = \cos(A + A)$$
$$\cos(2A) = \cos A\cos A - \sin A\sin A$$
$$\cos(2A) = \cos^2 A - \sin^2 A$$
$$\cos(2A) = \cos^2 A - (1 - \cos^2 A)$$
$$\cos(2A) = 2\cos^2 A - 1$$
$$2\cos^2 A = 1 + \cos(2A)$$
$$\mathbf{\cos^2 A = \frac{1}{2} + \frac{1}{2}\cos(2A)}$$

18.
$$2\sin\left(\frac{\pi}{2} - x\right)\frac{1}{\sec -x} - 1$$
$$= 2\cos x\left(\frac{1}{\sec x}\right) - 1 = 2\cos x(\cos x) - 1$$
$$= 2\cos^2 x - 1 = \mathbf{\cos(2x)}$$

19.

X	Y1
.006	1.0312
.005	1.0269
.004	1.0223
.003	1.0176
.002	1.0125
.001	1.0069
0	ERROR

X=0

$$f(0.003) = \mathbf{1.0176}$$
$$f(0.002) = \mathbf{1.0125}$$
$$f(0.001) = \mathbf{1.0069}$$
$$\lim_{x\to 0^+} f(x) = \mathbf{1}$$

20. Find the slope perpendicular to the given line.
$$2y - x + 3 = 6$$
$$2y = x + 3$$
$$y = \frac{1}{2}x + \frac{3}{2}$$
$$\perp \text{ slope} = -2$$

Find a perpendicular line through (1, –1).
$$y + 1 = -2(x - 1)$$
$$y = -2x + 1$$

Find the intersection of 2 lines.
$$\frac{1}{2}x + \frac{3}{2} = -2x + 1$$
$$\frac{5}{2}x = -\frac{1}{2}$$
$$x = -\frac{1}{5}$$

Intersection: $\left(-\frac{1}{5}, \frac{7}{5}\right)$

Find the distance between 2 points.
$$d = \sqrt{\left(\frac{7}{5} + 1\right)^2 + \left(-\frac{1}{5} - 1\right)^2}$$
$$= \sqrt{\left(\frac{12}{5}\right)^2 + \left(\frac{-6}{5}\right)^2} = \sqrt{\frac{180}{25}} = \mathbf{\frac{6\sqrt{5}}{5}}$$

21.
$$4^{2p-5} = 7^{3p+2}$$
$$(2p - 5)\ln 4 = (3p + 2)\ln 7$$
$$2p\ln 4 - 5\ln 4 = 3p\ln 7 + 2\ln 7$$
$$2p\ln 4 - 3p\ln 7 = 2\ln 7 + 5\ln 4$$
$$p(2\ln 4 - 3\ln 7) = \ln 49 + \ln 1024$$
$$p = \mathbf{\frac{\ln 50{,}176}{\ln 16 - \ln 343}}$$

22.

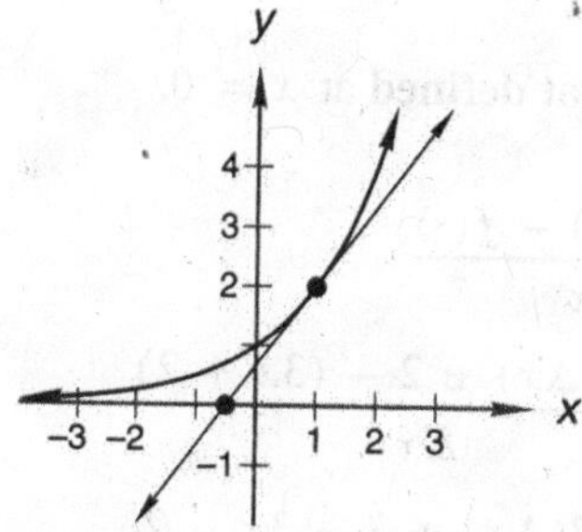

Answers may vary: (1, 2), (−0.5, 0)

$$\text{slope} \approx \frac{2 - 0}{1 - (-0.5)} = \frac{2}{1.5} = \mathbf{1.\overline{3}}$$

23.
$$\lim_{h\to 0} \frac{f(x + h) - f(x)}{h}$$
$$= \lim_{h\to 0} \frac{2(x + h)^2 - 2x^2}{h}$$
$$= \lim_{h\to 0} \frac{2(x^2 + 2xh + h^2) - 2x^2}{h}$$
$$= \lim_{h\to 0} \frac{2x^2 + 4xh + 2h^2 - 2x^2}{h}$$
$$= \lim_{h\to 0} \frac{h(4x + 2h)}{h}$$
$$= \lim_{h\to 0} (4x + 2h) = 4x + 2(0) = \mathbf{4x}$$

24. $x + y + z = 180°$ (straight angle)

$y + a + b = 180°$ (sum of interior angles)

The quantities are equal: **C**

25.
$$(x + y)^2 = x^2 + 2xy + y^2$$
$$= (x^2 + y^2) + 2xy$$
$$= (20) + 2(8)$$
$$= 36$$

If $(x + y)^2 = 36$ then $x + y = \pm 6$. Since x and y are both positive $x + y = \mathbf{6}$.

PROBLEM SET 18

1. $R_A = \frac{1}{6} \qquad R_B = \frac{1}{3}$
$$\left(\frac{1}{6} + \frac{1}{3}\right)T = 1$$
$$\frac{1}{2}T = 1$$
$$T = \mathbf{2\ hr}$$

2.

20,000 sq. meters

H

P

$PH = 20{,}000$

$$H = \frac{20{,}000}{P}$$

$$F = 2H + P$$
$$= 2\left(\frac{20{,}000}{P}\right) + P$$
$$= \mathbf{40{,}000P^{-1} + P}$$

3. $(f + g)(x) = x^2 + 1 + \sqrt{x - 1}$

$(f + g)(5) = 5^2 + 1 + \sqrt{5 - 1} = \mathbf{28}$

4. $(fg)(x) = (x^2 + 1)\sqrt{x - 1}$

$(fg)(5) = (5^2 + 1)\sqrt{5 - 1} = \mathbf{52}$

5.
$$\left(\frac{f}{g}\right)(x) = \frac{x^2 + 1}{\sqrt{x - 1}}$$
$$\left(\frac{f}{g}\right)(5) = \frac{5^2 + 1}{\sqrt{5 - 1}} = \mathbf{13}$$

6. $x - 1 > 0$

$x > 1$

$\mathbf{\{x \in \mathbb{R} \mid x > 1\}}$

7. $(f \circ g)(x) = f(\sqrt{x - 1}) = (\sqrt{x - 1})^2 + 1$

$= x - 1 + 1 = x$

$(f \circ g)(3) = \mathbf{3}$

8. $x - 1 \geq 0$

$x \geq 1$

Domain: $\mathbf{\{x \in \mathbb{R} \mid x \geq 1\}}$

Range: $\mathbf{\{y \in \mathbb{R} \mid y \geq 1\}}$

9.

$g(x) = 2x - \pi$

$x \longrightarrow$ [g] $\longrightarrow (2x - \pi)$

$f(x) = \cos x$

$(2x - \pi) \longrightarrow$ [f] $\longrightarrow \cos(2x - \pi)$

10. $\lim_{x\to\infty} \dfrac{1 - x^2}{3x^2 + 2x - 4} = \lim_{x\to\infty} \dfrac{\frac{1}{x^2} - 1}{3 + \frac{2}{x} - \frac{4}{x^2}}$

$= \dfrac{0 - 1}{3 + 0 - 0} = -\mathbf{\dfrac{1}{3}}$

11. $\lim_{x\to\infty} \dfrac{3x^2}{x^3 - 4x + 1} = \lim_{x\to\infty} \dfrac{\frac{3}{x}}{1 - \frac{4}{x^2} + \frac{1}{x^3}}$

$= \dfrac{0}{1 - 0 + 0} = \mathbf{0}$

12. (a) $\lim_{x\to -2} f(x) = \infty$

(b) The $\lim_{x\to 1} f(x)$ is **undefined.**

13. $\dfrac{\pi}{2} = \arcsin x$

$x = \sin \dfrac{\pi}{2}$

$\mathbf{x = 1}$

14. $\ln x - \ln(x + 1) = \ln 2$

$\ln\left(\dfrac{x}{x + 1}\right) = \ln 2$

$\dfrac{x}{x + 1} = 2$

$2x + 2 = x$

$x = -2$

This value gives a negative argument, so there is **no solution.**

15. – – – | + + + + | – – | + + +

–4 –3 –2 –1 0 1 2 3

Above: (–3, 0), (2, ∞)

Below: (–∞, –3), (0, 2)

16.

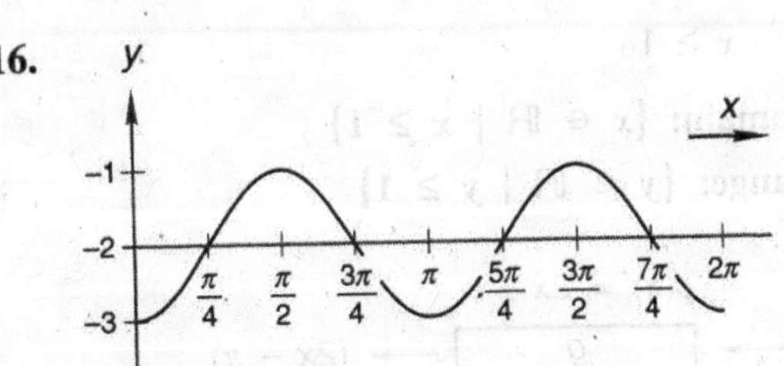

17. $\left(\mathbf{0, \dfrac{\pi}{2}}\right)$ and $\left(\boldsymbol{\pi}, \mathbf{\dfrac{3\pi}{2}}\right)$

18.

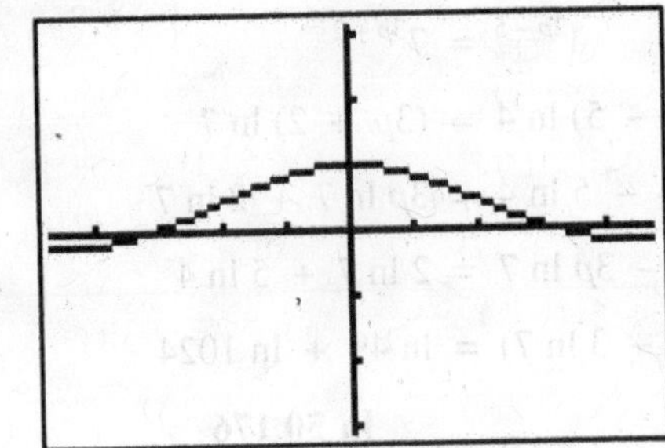

Guess: $\lim_{x\to 0} \dfrac{\sin x}{x} = \mathbf{1}.$

The function is **not defined** at $x = 0$.

19. $\lim_{\Delta x\to 0} \dfrac{f(x + \Delta x) - f(x)}{\Delta x}$

$= \lim_{\Delta x\to 0} \dfrac{3(x + \Delta x) + 2 - (3x + 2)}{\Delta x}$

$= \lim_{\Delta x\to 0} \dfrac{3x + 3(\Delta x) + 2 - 3x - 2}{\Delta x}$

$= \lim_{\Delta x\to 0} \dfrac{3(\Delta x)}{\Delta x} = \lim_{\Delta x\to 0} 3 = \mathbf{3}$

20. If x^2 does not equal 4, then x does not equal 2.

21. $\dfrac{(\sec^2 x - 1)(\cos -x)}{(1 - \cos^2 x)(\tan^2 x + 1)} = \dfrac{\tan^2 x \cos x}{\sin^2 x \sec^2 x}$

$= \dfrac{\tan^2 x \cos x}{\tan^2 x} = \cos x$

22. $7^{3x-2} = 13^{x+1}$

$(3x - 2)\ln 7 = (x + 1)\ln 13$

$3x \ln 7 - 2\ln 7 = x\ln 13 + \ln 13$

$3x\ln 7 - x\ln 13 = \ln 13 + 2\ln 7$

$x(3\ln 7 - \ln 13) = \ln 13 + \ln 49$

$x = \dfrac{\mathbf{\ln(637)}}{\mathbf{\ln\left(\frac{343}{13}\right)}} \approx \mathbf{1.9729}$

23.

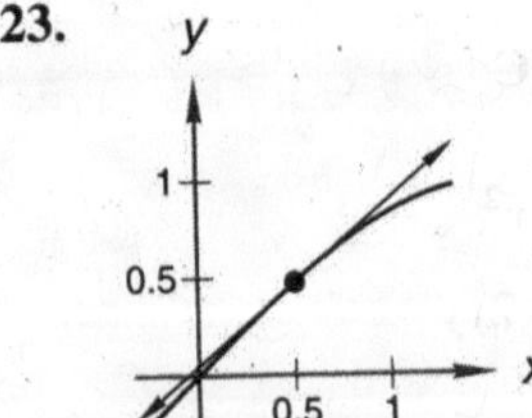

Answers may vary: (0.5, sin (0.5)), (0, 0.05)

slope $= \dfrac{\sin(0.5) - 0.05}{0.5} \approx \mathbf{0.8589}$

24.

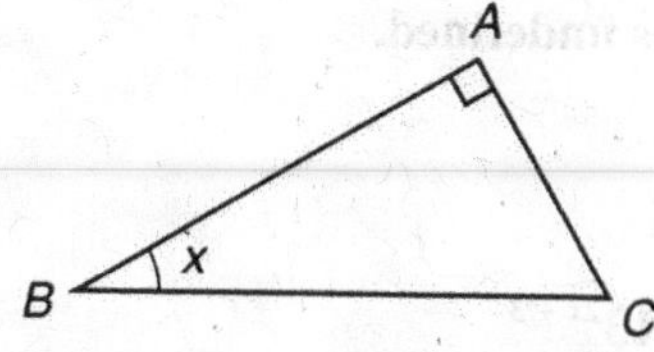

$BC = 2$ (diameter of circle)

$\angle A = 90°$ (intersects diameter of circle)

$$\sin x = \frac{AC}{BC} \qquad \cos x = \frac{AB}{BC}$$

$$\sin x = \frac{AC}{2} \qquad \cos x = \frac{AB}{2}$$

$$AC = 2 \sin x \qquad AB = 2 \cos x$$

$$\text{Area } \Delta ABC = \frac{1}{2}\text{base} \cdot \text{height}$$
$$= \frac{1}{2}(AC)(AB)$$
$$= \frac{1}{2}(2 \sin x)(2 \cos x)$$
$$= 2 \sin x \cos x$$
$$= \mathbf{\sin (2x)}$$

25. Beginning with 1, each succeeding term of the given sequence is found by adding the next whole number to the preceeding term of the sequence.

1, 1 + 0, 1 + 1, 2 + 2, 4 + 3, 7 + 4, 11 + 5, 16 + 6, ...

1, 1, 2, 4, 7, 11, **16**, ...

PROBLEM SET 19

1. $Id^2 = Id^2$

$N5^2 = IM^2$

$$I = \frac{25N}{M^2}$$

2. $$f'(x) = \lim_{\Delta x \to 0} \frac{f(x + \Delta x) - f(x)}{\Delta x}$$
$$= \lim_{\Delta x \to 0} \frac{3(x + \Delta x) + 2 - (3x + 2)}{\Delta x}$$
$$= \lim_{\Delta x \to 0} \frac{3x + 3(\Delta x) + 2 - 3x - 2}{\Delta x}$$
$$= \lim_{\Delta x \to 0} \frac{3(\Delta x)}{\Delta x} = \lim_{\Delta x \to 0} 3 = \mathbf{3}$$

3. $$f'(x) = \lim_{\Delta x \to 0} \frac{f(x + \Delta x) - f(x)}{\Delta x}$$
$$= \lim_{\Delta x \to 0} \frac{(x + \Delta x)^3 - x^3}{\Delta x}$$
$$= \lim_{\Delta x \to 0} \left[\frac{x^3 + 3x^2(\Delta x) + 3x(\Delta x)^2}{\Delta x} + \frac{(\Delta x)^3 - x^3}{\Delta x} \right]$$
$$= \lim_{\Delta x \to 0} \frac{\Delta x[3x^2 + 3x(\Delta x) + (\Delta x)^2]}{\Delta x}$$
$$= \lim_{\Delta x \to 0} [3x^2 + 3x(\Delta x) + (\Delta x)^2] = \mathbf{3x^2}$$

4. $$f'(x) = \lim_{\Delta x \to 0} \frac{f(x + \Delta x) - f(x)}{\Delta x}$$
$$= \lim_{\Delta x \to 0} \frac{[(x + \Delta x)^2 + (x + \Delta x)] - (x^2 + x)}{\Delta x}$$
$$= \lim_{\Delta x \to 0} \left[\frac{x^2 + 2x(\Delta x) + (\Delta x)^2 + x + \Delta x}{\Delta x} + \frac{-x^2 - x}{\Delta x} \right]$$
$$= \lim_{\Delta x \to 0} \frac{\Delta x[2x + \Delta x + 1]}{\Delta x}$$
$$= \lim_{\Delta x \to 0} (2x + \Delta x + 1) = \mathbf{2x + 1}$$

5. $$f'(x) = \lim_{\Delta x \to 0} \frac{f(x + \Delta x) - f(x)}{\Delta x}$$
$$= \lim_{\Delta x \to 0} \frac{\frac{2}{x + \Delta x} - \frac{2}{x}}{\Delta x}$$
$$= \lim_{\Delta x \to 0} \frac{\frac{2x - 2x - 2\Delta x}{x(x + \Delta x)}}{\Delta x}$$
$$= \lim_{\Delta x \to 0} \frac{-2\Delta x}{(\Delta x)(x)(x + \Delta x)}$$
$$= \lim_{\Delta x \to 0} \frac{-2}{x(x + \Delta x)} = -\frac{2}{x^2}$$

$$f'(5) = -\frac{2}{5^2} = \mathbf{-\frac{2}{25}}$$

6. Let Y1=((2+X)²−2²)/X.

X	Y1	
-.03	3.97	
-.02	3.98	
-.01	3.99	
0	ERROR	
.01	4.01	
.02	4.02	
.03	4.03	

X=0

$$\lim_{x\to 0}\frac{(2+x)^2-2^2}{x} = \mathbf{4}$$

7. $(f\circ g) = f\left(\frac{1}{x}\right)$

$(f\circ g)(x) = \ln\frac{1}{x}$

Domain: $\{x \in \mathbb{R} \mid x > 0\}$

Range: $\mathbb{R}$

8. (a) **±1, ±3, ±5, ±15**

(b)

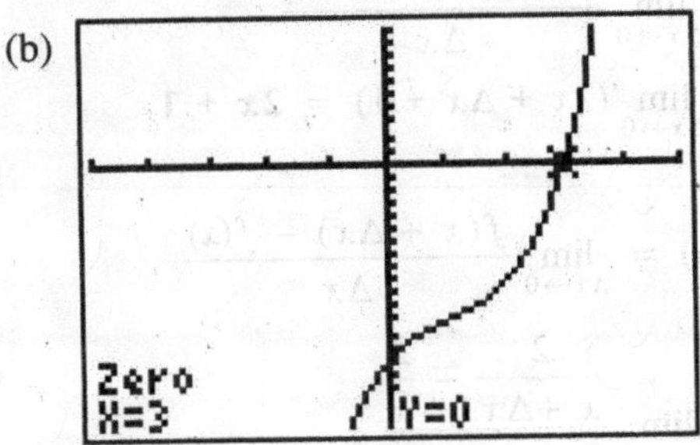

Yes, **3** is one of its roots.

9. $$\lim_{x\to-\infty}\frac{2x-15x^3}{14x^2-13x} = \lim_{x\to-\infty}\frac{\frac{2}{x}-15x}{14-\frac{13}{x}}$$

$$= \frac{0+\infty}{14-0} = \infty$$

10. $$\lim_{x\to-\infty}\frac{3-14x^5+2x^3}{x^4-x^5+1}$$

$$= \lim_{x\to-\infty}\frac{\frac{3}{x^5}-14+\frac{2}{x^2}}{\frac{1}{x}-1+\frac{1}{x^5}}$$

$$= \frac{0-14+0}{0-1+0} = \mathbf{14}$$

11. $\lim_{x\to 2} f(x) = \infty$

12. The $\lim_{x\to-2} f(x)$ is **undefined.**

13. **(0, 2) and (4, ∞)**

14. $$\begin{aligned} e^{-x+5} &= 13^{2x+3} \\ -x+5 &= (2x+3)\ln 13 \\ -x+5 &= 2x\ln 13 + 3\ln 13 \\ 5-3\ln 13 &= 2x\ln 13 + x \\ 5-3\ln 13 &= x(2\ln 13+1) \\ x &= \mathbf{\frac{5-3\ln 13}{2\ln 13+1}} \end{aligned}$$

15. $$\begin{aligned} \log_2 x + \log_2 (x-2) &= \log_2 3 \\ \log_2 (x^2-2x) &= \log_2 3 \\ x^2-2x &= 3 \\ x^2-2x-3 &= 0 \\ (x-3)(x+1) &= 0 \\ x &= 3, -1 \\ x &= \mathbf{3} \end{aligned}$$

16. $$\begin{aligned} \sin x &= \cos x \\ \frac{\sin x}{\cos x} &= 1 \\ \tan x &= 1 \\ x &= \mathbf{\frac{\pi}{4}, \frac{5\pi}{4}} \end{aligned}$$

17. $$\begin{aligned} \frac{5}{5} &= \frac{AB}{x} \\ 5x &= 5\,AB \\ AB &= x \end{aligned}$$

$$\text{Area } \Delta ABC = \frac{1}{2}(AB)x = \mathbf{\frac{1}{2}x^2}$$

18. "x is less than ε away from 4"

$\{x \in \mathbb{R} \mid 4-\varepsilon < x < 4+\varepsilon\}$

19. $\sin(A+B) = \sin A\cos B + \cos A\sin B$

$$= \frac{3}{5}\left(\frac{5}{13}\right) + \frac{4}{5}\left(\frac{12}{13}\right) = \frac{3}{13} + \frac{48}{65} = \mathbf{\frac{63}{65}}$$

20. Let `Y1=X³+X²-5X-5` and `Y2=X²-7`.

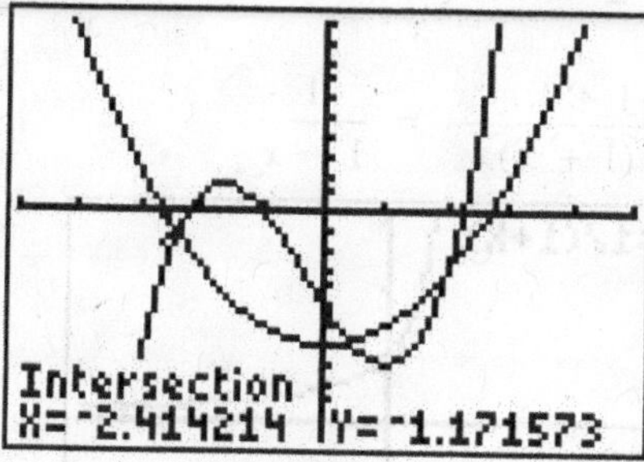

(–2.414214, –1.171573)

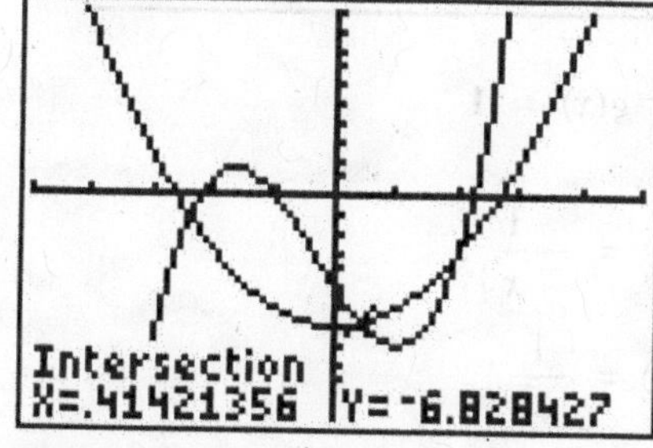

(0.41421356, –6.828427)

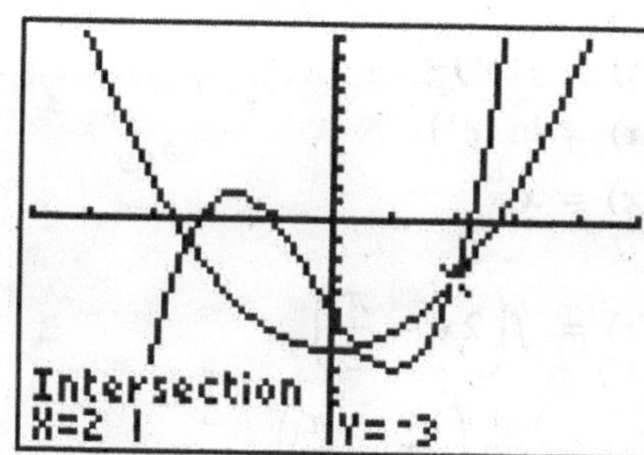

(2, –3)

21. For the key trigonometric identities, see section 12.A in the textbook.

$$\cos(2x) = \cos(x + x)$$
$$\cos(2x) = \cos x \cos x - \sin x \sin x$$
$$\cos(2x) = \cos^2 x - \sin^2 x$$
$$\cos(2x) = (1 - \sin^2 x) - \sin^2 x$$
$$\cos(2x) = 1 - 2\sin^2 x$$
$$2\sin^2 x = 1 - \cos(2x)$$
$$\mathbf{\sin^2 x = \frac{1}{2} - \frac{1}{2}\cos(2x)}$$

22. `nDeriv(sin(X),X,0.5)` ≈ **0.8776**

23. `nDeriv(2^X,X,1)` ≈ **1.3863**

24.

$$s = \frac{6}{\sqrt{2}} = 3\sqrt{2} \approx \mathbf{4.2426}$$

25. If the three points are colinear and A and C are the endpoints, then $AC = AB + BC$. If A and C are not the endpoints, then $AB + BC > AC$. If the three points are not colinear, then $AB + BC > AC$.

Insufficient information: **D**

Problem Set 20

1.
$$d = \sqrt{(x-2)^2 + (y-3)^2}$$
$$= \sqrt{(x-2)^2 + [(2x+1) - 3]^2}$$
$$= \sqrt{(x-2)^2 + (2x-2)^2}$$
$$= \sqrt{x^2 - 4x + 4 + 4x^2 - 8x + 4}$$
$$= \mathbf{\sqrt{5x^2 - 12x + 8}}$$

2. $\log_{10} x = \mathbf{\dfrac{\ln x}{\ln 10}}$

3. $\log_4 15 = \dfrac{\ln 15}{\ln 4} \approx \mathbf{1.9534}$

4.
$$\frac{d}{dx}(5x - 3)$$
$$= \lim_{\Delta x \to 0} \frac{5(x + \Delta x) - 3 - (5x - 3)}{\Delta x}$$
$$= \lim_{\Delta x \to 0} \frac{5x + 5(\Delta x) - 3 - 5x + 3}{\Delta x}$$
$$= \lim_{\Delta x \to 0} \frac{5(\Delta x)}{\Delta x} = \lim_{\Delta x \to 0} 5 = \mathbf{5}$$

5.
$$\frac{d}{dx}(3x^2) = \lim_{\Delta x \to 0} \frac{3(x + \Delta x)^2 - 3x^2}{\Delta x}$$
$$= \lim_{\Delta x \to 0} \frac{3(x^2 + 2x(\Delta x) + (\Delta x)^2) - 3x^2}{\Delta x}$$
$$= \lim_{\Delta x \to 0} \frac{3x^2 + 6x(\Delta x) + 3(\Delta x)^2 - 3x^2}{\Delta x}$$
$$= \lim_{\Delta x \to 0} \frac{\Delta x[6x + 3(\Delta x)]}{\Delta x}$$
$$= \lim_{\Delta x \to 0} [6x + 3(\Delta x)] = \mathbf{6x}$$

6. $D_x\left(\frac{-1}{x}\right) = \lim_{\Delta x\to 0} \frac{\frac{-1}{x+\Delta x} - \left(\frac{-1}{x}\right)}{\Delta x}$

$= \lim_{\Delta x\to 0} \frac{\frac{-x + (x + \Delta x)}{x(x+\Delta x)}}{\Delta x}$

$= \lim_{\Delta x\to 0} \frac{\Delta x}{x(x+\Delta x)\Delta x}$

$= \lim_{\Delta x\to 0} \frac{1}{x(x+\Delta x)} = \frac{1}{x^2}$

7. Let $Y_1=\sqrt{(9-X^2)}$ and $Y_2=-Y_1$.

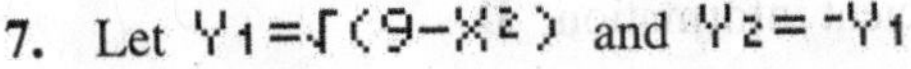

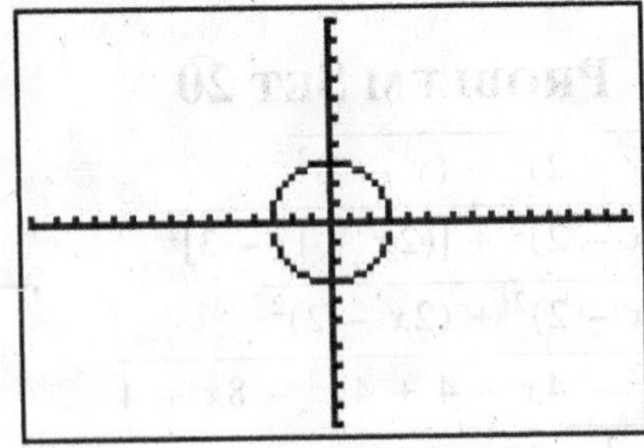

The graph does not look like a circle unless it is graphed in the ZSquare mode on a symmetric axis.

8. $\frac{x^2}{9} + \frac{y^2}{4} = 1$

$\frac{4}{9}x^2 + y^2 = 4$

$y^2 = 4 - \frac{4}{9}x^2$

$y = \pm\sqrt{4 - \frac{4}{9}x^2}$

Let $Y_1=\sqrt{(4-4X^2/9)}$ and $Y_2=-Y_1$.

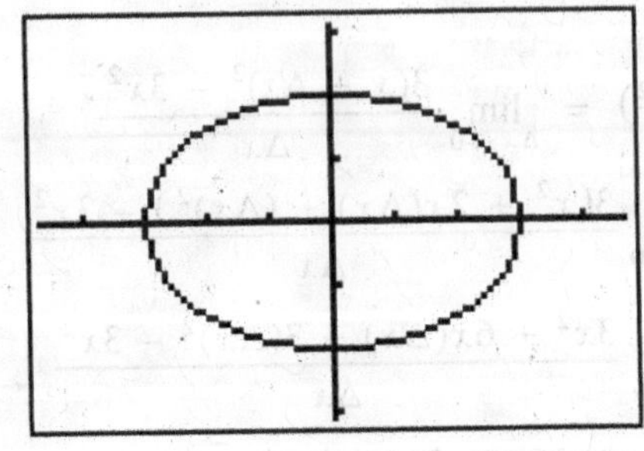

9. (a) $g(x) = \frac{f(1+x) - f(1)}{x} = \frac{\frac{-1}{1+x} + 1}{x}$

$= \frac{-1 + 1 + x}{(1+x)x} = \frac{1}{1+x}$

Y1=1/(1+X)

X=-.1 Y=1.1111111

(b) $\lim_{x\to 0} g(x) = \mathbf{1}$

(c) $f(x) = -\frac{1}{x}$

$f'(x) = \frac{1}{x^2}$

$f'(1) = \mathbf{1}$

They are equal.

10. $(f \circ g)(x) = f(e^x)$

$(f \circ g)(x) = \ln(e^x)$

$\boldsymbol{(f \circ g)(x) = x}$

11. $(f \circ g)(x) = f\left(2x - \frac{\pi}{2}\right)$

$(f \circ g)(x) = \sin\left(2x - \frac{\pi}{2}\right)$

$\boldsymbol{(f \circ g)(x) = \sin\left[2\left(x - \frac{\pi}{4}\right)\right]}$

12. $3\log_2 12 + \log_{16} 92$

$= 3\frac{\ln 12}{\ln 2} + \frac{\ln 92}{\ln 16} \approx \mathbf{12.3858}$

13. $\lim_{x\to 2^+} \frac{2 - \frac{2}{x}}{4 - x^2} = \frac{2 - 1^-}{4 - 4^+} = \frac{1^+}{0^-} = -\infty$

$\lim_{x\to 2^-} \frac{2 - \frac{2}{x}}{4 - x^2} = \frac{2 - 1^+}{4 - 4^-} = \frac{1^-}{0^-} = \infty$

The limit is **undefined.**

14. $\lim_{x\to 3} \frac{2x^2 - 2x - 12}{x - 3} = \lim_{x\to 3} \frac{2(x-3)(x+2)}{x-3}$

$= \lim_{x\to 3} 2(x+2) = 2(5) = \mathbf{10}$

15. $\lim_{x\to\infty} \frac{x^2 + 3x}{x^3} = \lim_{x\to\infty} \frac{\frac{1}{x} + \frac{3}{x^2}}{1} = \frac{0+0}{1} = \mathbf{0}$

16. $- - - \mid + + + + + \mid - - - \mid + + +$

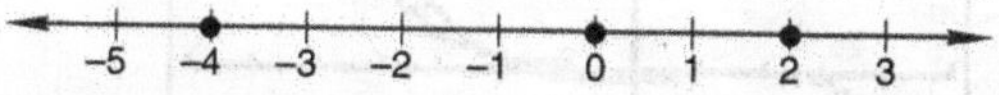

(–4, 0) and (2, ∞)

17. $y = \arcsin \frac{x}{2}$

$\sin y = \frac{x}{2}$

$x = \mathbf{2 \sin y}$

18. $\sin^2 x - 1 = 0$

$\sin^2 x = 1$

$\sin x = \pm 1$

$x = \boldsymbol{\frac{\pi}{2}, \frac{3\pi}{2}}$

19.
$$\begin{array}{r|rrrr} -1 & 1 & 2 & 3 & k \\ & \downarrow & -1 & -1 & -2 \\ \hline & 1 & -1 & 2 & \boxed{0} \end{array}$$

$k - 2 = 0$

$k = \mathbf{2}$

20. $[(\sec -x) - 1](\sec x + 1)$

$= (\sec x - 1)(\sec x + 1) = \sec^2 x - 1 = \mathbf{\tan^2 x}$

21. $\frac{1 + \sqrt{3}}{2 - \sqrt{3}} = \left(\frac{1 + \sqrt{3}}{2 - \sqrt{3}}\right)\left(\frac{2 + \sqrt{3}}{2 + \sqrt{3}}\right)$

$= \frac{2 + \sqrt{3} + 2\sqrt{3} + 3}{4 - 3} = \mathbf{5 + 3\sqrt{3}}$

22. For the key trigonometric identities, see section 12.A in the textbook.

$\cos(2A) = \cos(A + A)$

$\cos(2A) = \cos A \cos A - \sin A \sin A$

$\cos(2A) = \cos^2 A - \sin^2 A$

$\cos(2A) = \cos^2 A - (1 - \cos^2 A)$

$\cos(2A) = 2\cos^2 A - 1$

$2\cos^2 A = 1 + \cos(2A)$

$\cos^2 A = \frac{1}{2} + \frac{1}{2}\cos(2A)$

With $A = \frac{x}{2}$, $\cos^2 \frac{x}{2} = \frac{1}{2} + \frac{1}{2}\cos x$

$\boldsymbol{\cos \frac{x}{2} = \pm\sqrt{\frac{1}{2} + \frac{1}{2}\cos x}}$

23. `nDeriv(cosX,X,0)` = **0**

24. Area $\Delta AEB = \frac{1}{2}(AB)(CB)$

Area $\Delta ACB = \frac{1}{2}(AB)(CB)$

The quantites are equal: **C**

25. $a = 1,\ r = 2;\ t_6 = ar^5 = (1)(2)^5 = \mathbf{32}$

PROBLEM SET 21

1.

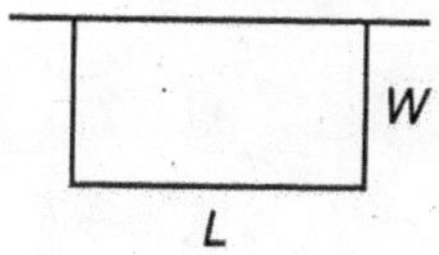

$2W + L = 100$

$2W = 100 - L$

$W = 50 - \frac{1}{2}L$

$A = LW$

$A = L\left(50 - \frac{1}{2}L\right)$

$\boldsymbol{A = 50L - \frac{1}{2}L^2}$

2. (a)

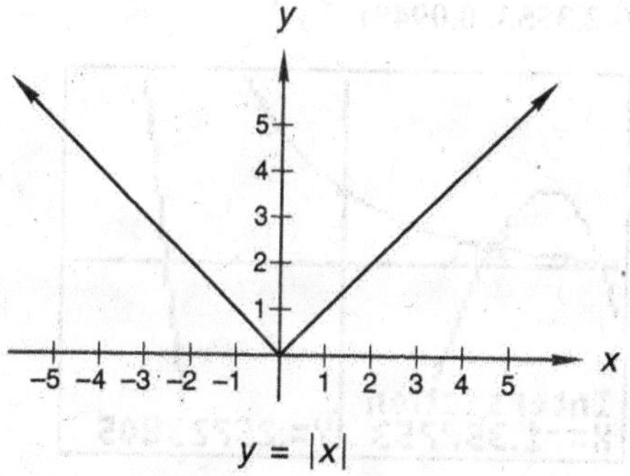

(b) $\boldsymbol{y = |x + 2| - 1}$

3.

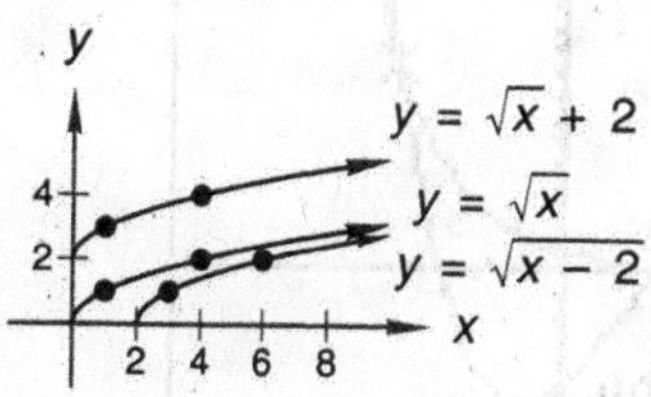

4. $g(x) = \dfrac{1}{x + 3}$

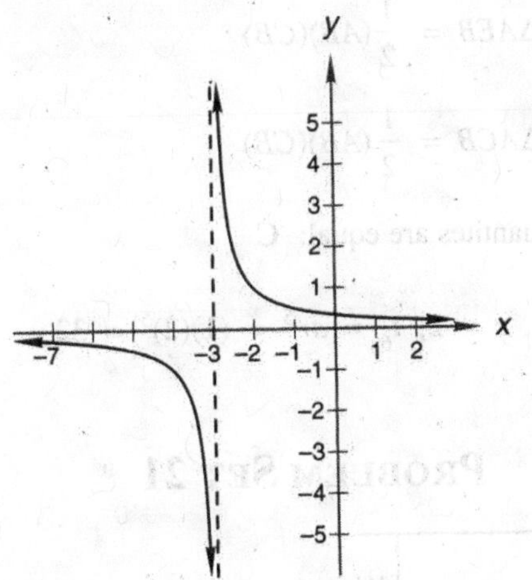

5. $\log_{10} x = \dfrac{\ln x}{\ln 10}$

6. $\log_3 x = \dfrac{\ln x}{\ln 3}$

7. Let `Y1=X³+2X²-3X-5` and `Y2=e^(X)`.

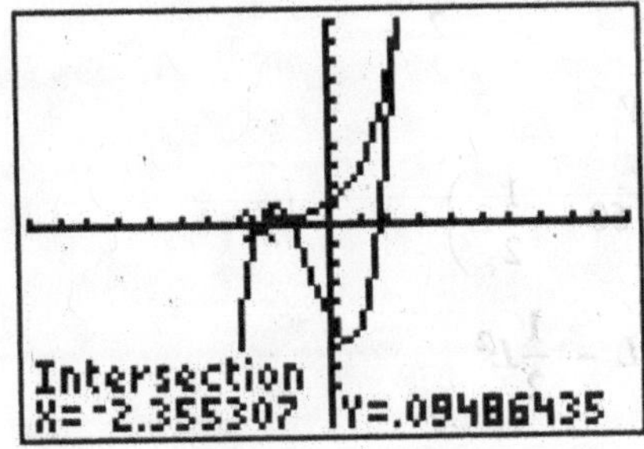

(−2.3553, 0.0949)

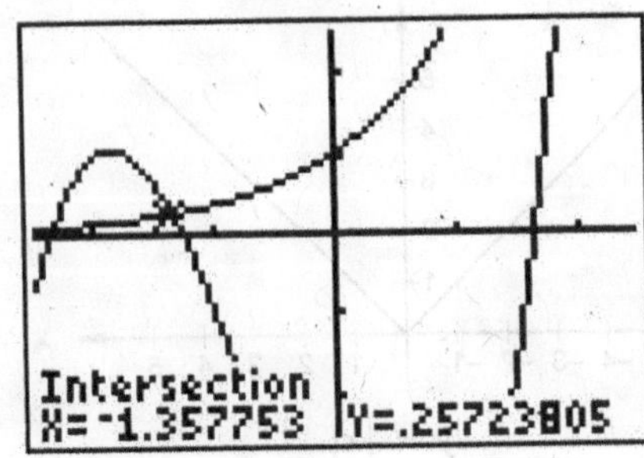

(−1.3578, 0.2572)

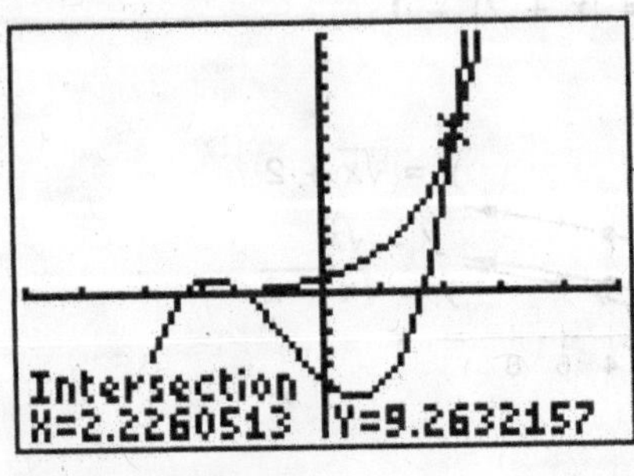

(2.2261, 9.2632)

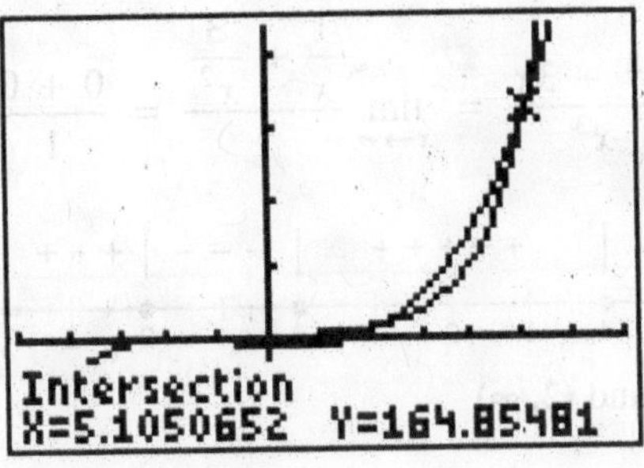

(5.1051, 164.8548)

8. $$\frac{dy}{dx} = \lim_{\Delta x \to 0} \frac{-(x + \Delta x)^2 + x^2}{\Delta x}$$
$$= \lim_{\Delta x \to 0} \frac{-[x^2 + 2x(\Delta x) + (\Delta x)^2] + x^2}{\Delta x}$$
$$= \lim_{\Delta x \to 0} \frac{-2x(\Delta x) - (\Delta x)^2}{\Delta x}$$
$$= \lim_{\Delta x \to 0} (-2x - \Delta x) = \mathbf{-2x}$$

9. $$\lim_{\Delta x \to 0} \frac{(x + \Delta x)^2 + 2(x + \Delta x) - (x^2 + 2x)}{\Delta x}$$
$$= \lim_{\Delta x \to 0} \frac{x^2 + 2x(\Delta x) + (\Delta x)^2}{\Delta x} + \lim_{\Delta x \to 0} \frac{2x + 2(\Delta x) - x^2 - 2x}{\Delta x}$$
$$= \lim_{\Delta x \to 0} \frac{\Delta x(2x + \Delta x + 2)}{\Delta x}$$
$$= \lim_{\Delta x \to 0} (2x + \Delta x + 2) = \mathbf{2x + 2}$$

10. $$\frac{x^2}{4} + y^2 = 1$$
$$y^2 = 1 - \frac{x^2}{4}$$
$$y = \pm\sqrt{1 - \frac{x^2}{4}}$$

```
Y1=√(1-(X²/4))
Y2=-Y1
```

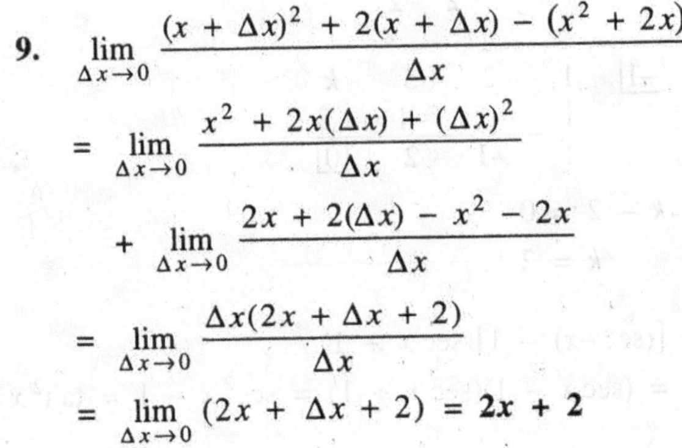

11. $g(x) = \dfrac{-(2 + x)^2 + 4}{x}$

(a) 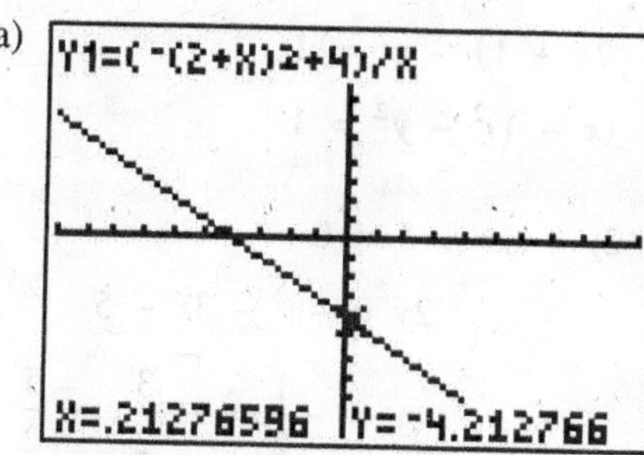

$\lim_{x \to 0} g(x) = -4$

(b) $D_x f(x) = -2x$

$-2(2) = \mathbf{-4}$; **they are the same.**

12. $(g \circ f)(x) = g(x^2)$

$(\boldsymbol{g} \circ \boldsymbol{f})(\boldsymbol{x}) = \boldsymbol{e^{x^2}}$

13.

Function	Domain	Range
f	$\mathbb{R}$	$\{y \in \mathbb{R} \mid y \geq 0\}$
g	$\mathbb{R}$	$\{y \in \mathbb{R} \mid y > 0\}$
$g \circ f$	$\mathbb{R}$	$\{y \in \mathbb{R} \mid y \geq 1\}$

14. $\lim_{x \to 0^+} -\dfrac{1}{x} = -\dfrac{1}{0^+} = -\infty$

$\lim_{x \to 0^-} -\dfrac{1}{x} = -\dfrac{1}{0^-} = \infty$

The limit is **undefined.**

15. $\lim_{x \to 0^+} \dfrac{1}{x^2} = \dfrac{1}{0^+} = \infty$

$\lim_{x \to 0^-} \dfrac{1}{x^2} = \dfrac{1}{0^+} = \infty$

$\lim_{x \to 0} \dfrac{1}{x^2} = \infty$

16. $\lim_{x \to \infty} \dfrac{3x^3 - 14x^2 + 5}{1 - 2x^3} = \lim_{x \to \infty} \dfrac{3 - \frac{14}{x} + \frac{5}{x^3}}{\frac{1}{x^3} - 2}$

$= \dfrac{3 - 0 + 0}{0 - 2} = \mathbf{-\dfrac{3}{2}}$

17. $10^{-2x} = 5$

$-2x = \log 5$

$x = \dfrac{\mathbf{\log 5}}{\mathbf{-2}} \approx \mathbf{-0.3495}$

18. $f(x) = |x^2 - 3x + 2|$

$f(x) = |(x - 2)(x - 1)|$

(a) 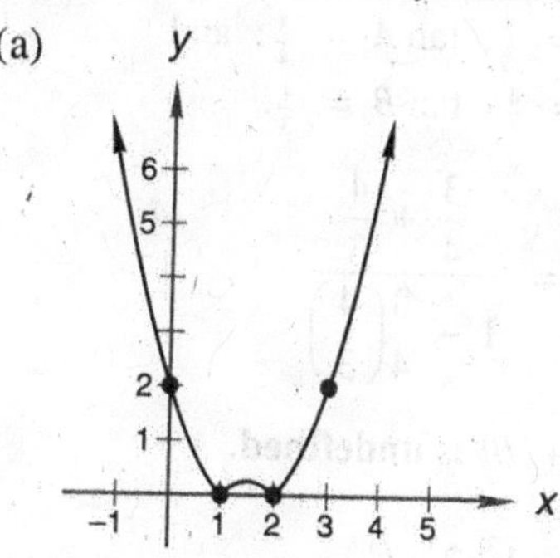

(b) $\left(\mathbf{1, \dfrac{3}{2}}\right)$, $\mathbf{(2, \infty)}$

19. $\sin x - \sin x \cos^2 x = \sin x\,(1 - \cos^2 x)$

$= \sin x\,(\sin^2 x) = \sin^3 x$

20. 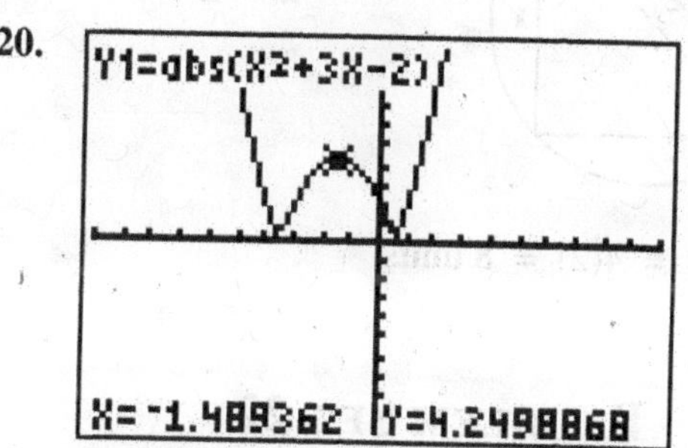

(–1.5, 4.2)

21. For the key trigonometric identities, see section 12.A in the textbook.

$\cos(2x) = \cos(x + x)$

$\cos(2x) = \cos x \cos x - \sin x \sin x$

$\cos(2x) = \cos^2 x - \sin^2 x$

$\cos(2x) = \cos^2 x - (1 - \cos^2 x)$

$\cos(2x) = 2\cos^2 x - 1$

$2\cos^2 x = 1 + \cos(2x)$

$\mathbf{\cos^2 x = \dfrac{1}{2} + \dfrac{1}{2}\cos(2x)}$

22. 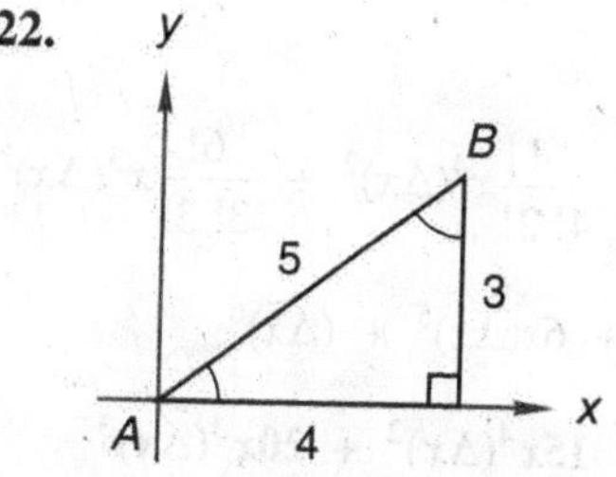

If $\sin A = \dfrac{3}{5}$, then $\mathbf{\cos A = \dfrac{4}{5}}$.

If $\sin B = \dfrac{4}{5}$, then $\mathbf{\cos B = \dfrac{3}{5}}$.

23. $\tan(A + B) = \dfrac{\tan A + \tan B}{1 - \tan A \tan B}$

Since $\sin A = \frac{3}{5}$, $\tan A = \frac{3}{4}$; and since $\sin B = \frac{4}{5}$, $\tan B = \frac{4}{3}$.

$$\tan(A + B) = \frac{\frac{3}{4} + \frac{4}{3}}{1 - \frac{3}{4}\left(\frac{4}{3}\right)}$$

Thus $\tan(A + B)$ is **undefined.**

24. $1, 8, 27, \ldots = 1^3, 2^3, 3^3, \ldots$

Fourth term $= 4^3 =$ **64**

25.

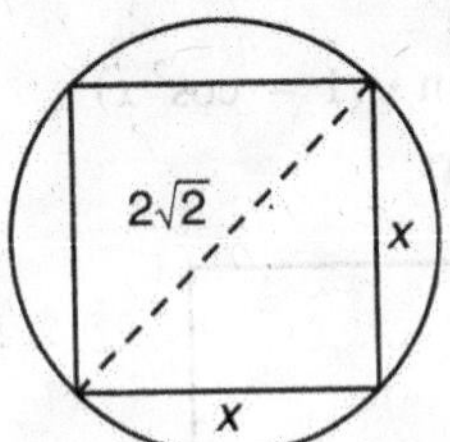

$$x^2 + x^2 = (2\sqrt{2})^2$$
$$2x^2 = 8$$
$$x = 2$$

$P = 4x = 4(2) =$ **8 units**

PROBLEM SET 22

1. $V = hlw$

$V = x(10 - 2x)(12 - 2x)$

$V = x(120 - 44x + 4x^2)$

$\mathbf{V = 120x - 44x^2 + 4x^3}$

2. $\dfrac{6!}{3!\,3!}(2y)^3(-3x^5)^3$

$= \dfrac{6 \cdot 5 \cdot 4}{3 \cdot 2}(2^3 y^3)[(-3)^3(x^5)^3]$

$= 20(8y^3)(-27x^{15}) = -4320x^{15}y^3$

Coefficient: **−4320**

3. $(x + \Delta x)^6$

$= x^6 + 6x^5(\Delta x) + \dfrac{6!}{4!\,2!}x^4(\Delta x)^2 + \dfrac{6!}{3!\,3!}x^3(\Delta x)^3$

$+ \dfrac{6!}{2!\,4!}x^2(\Delta x)^4 + 6x(\Delta x)^5 + (\Delta x)^6$

$\mathbf{= x^6 + 6x^5(\Delta x) + 15x^4(\Delta x)^2 + 20x^3(\Delta x)^3}$

$\mathbf{+ 15x^2(\Delta x)^4 + 6x(\Delta x)^5 + (\Delta x)^6}$

4. (a) **Parabola** (b) **Circle**

(c) **Hyperbola** (d) **Ellipse**

5. **Hyperbola**

$$x^2 - 2x - y^2 = 0$$
$$(x^2 - 2x + 1) - y^2 = 1$$
$$\mathbf{(x - 1)^2 - y^2 = 1}$$

6. $x^2 + 2y + 3x + 5 = 0$

$$2y = -x^2 - 3x - 5$$
$$y = -\frac{1}{2}x^2 - \frac{3}{2}x - \frac{5}{2}$$

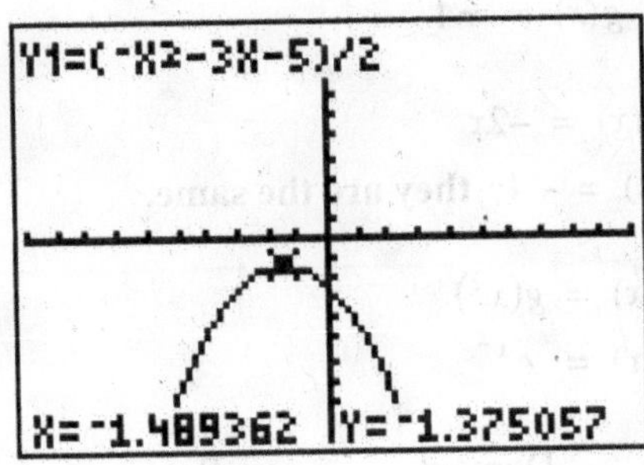

(−1.5, −1.4)

7. $f(x) = |x^2 - 1|$

$f(x) = |(x + 1)(x - 1)|$

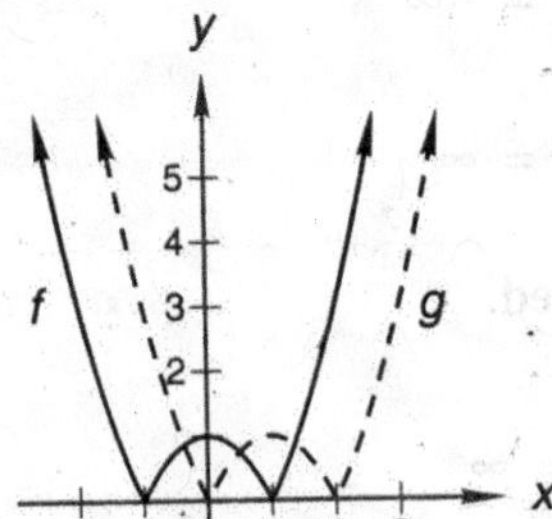

8.

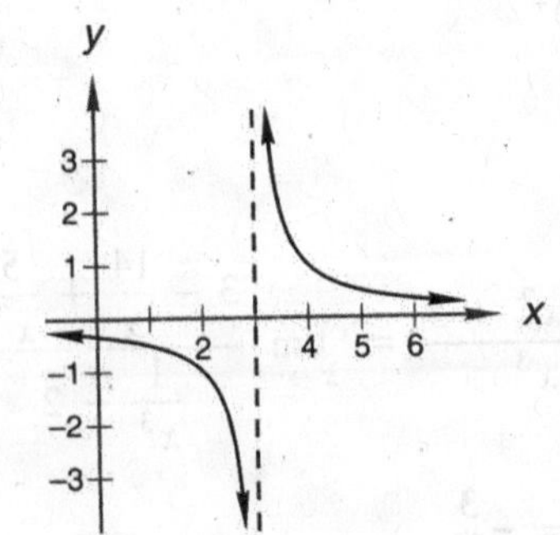

Vertical: $\mathbf{x = 3}$

Horizontal: $\mathbf{y = 0}$

9. $\log_3 x = \dfrac{\ln x}{\ln 3}$

10. Let Y1=√(16−X²)
Y2=−Y1, and
Y3=−2X+1.

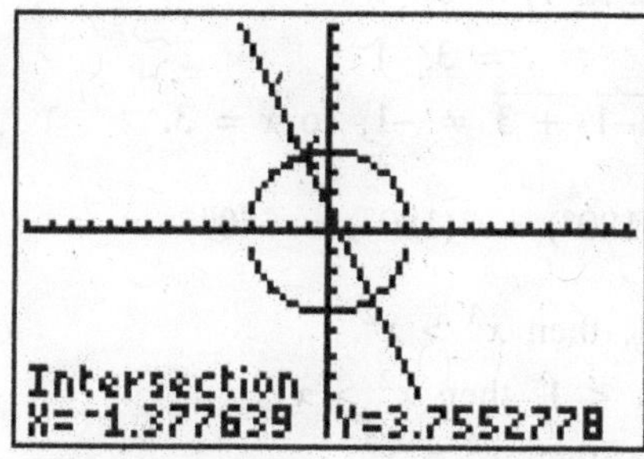

(−1.3776, 3.7553)

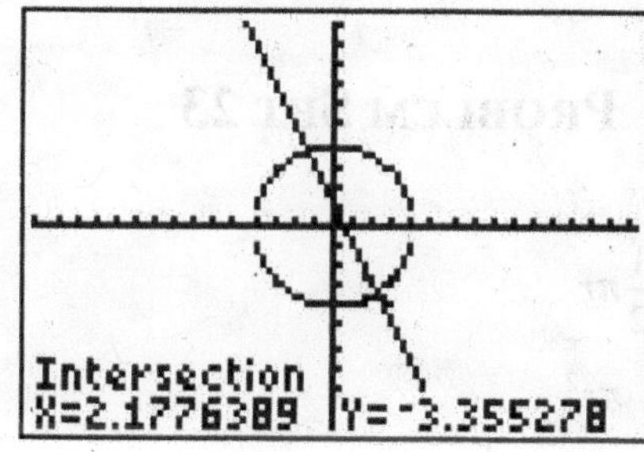

(2.1776, −3.3553)

11. $$\frac{d}{dx}f(x) = \lim_{\Delta x \to 0} \frac{3(x + \Delta x) + 5 - (3x + 5)}{\Delta x}$$
$$= \lim_{\Delta x \to 0} \frac{3x + 3(\Delta x) + 5 - 3x - 5}{\Delta x}$$
$$= \lim_{\Delta x \to 0} \frac{3(\Delta x)}{\Delta x}$$
$$= \mathbf{3}$$

12. $$\frac{dy}{dx} = \lim_{\Delta x \to 0} \frac{\frac{-2}{x + \Delta x} + \frac{2}{x}}{\Delta x}$$
$$= \lim_{\Delta x \to 0} \frac{\frac{-2x + 2(x + \Delta x)}{x(x + \Delta x)}}{\Delta x}$$
$$= \lim_{\Delta x \to 0} \frac{-2x + 2x + 2(\Delta x)}{x(x + \Delta x)\Delta x}$$
$$= \lim_{\Delta x \to 0} \frac{2}{x(x + \Delta x)} = \mathbf{\frac{2}{x^2}}$$

13. Domain of f: $\{x \in \mathbb{R} \mid x > 0\}$
Domain of g: $\mathbb{R}$

14. $$y = a(x - 2)(x + 1)$$
$$-4 = a(0 - 2)(0 + 1)$$
$$2 = a$$
$$y = 2(x^2 - x - 2)$$
$$\frac{y}{2} = x^2 - x + \frac{1}{4} - \frac{1}{4} - 2$$
$$\frac{y}{2} = \left(x - \frac{1}{2}\right)^2 - \frac{1}{4} - 2$$
$$y = 2\left(x - \frac{1}{2}\right)^2 - \frac{9}{2}$$

The axis of symmetry is $\mathbf{x = \frac{1}{2}}$.

15. $$\lim_{x \to \infty} \frac{3 - 2x + x^3}{2 + 14x^3} = \lim_{x \to \infty} \frac{\frac{3}{x^3} - \frac{2}{x^2} + 1}{\frac{2}{x^3} + 14}$$
$$= \frac{0 - 0 + 1}{0 + 14} = \mathbf{\frac{1}{14}}$$

16. $\sin^{-1}(\sin 270°) = \sin^{-1}(-1) = \mathbf{-90°}$

17. $\sec x = -2 \qquad (180° \le x < 360°)$
$$\cos x = -\frac{1}{2}$$
$$x = \mathbf{240°}$$

18.

5, B, 60°, $5\sqrt{3}$, 10, C

$$\frac{x}{10} = \frac{h}{5\sqrt{3}}$$
$$x = \mathbf{\frac{2h}{\sqrt{3}}}$$

19. $|2x - 3| < \varepsilon$
$$\left|x - \frac{3}{2}\right| < \frac{\varepsilon}{2}$$

"x is less than $\frac{\varepsilon}{2}$ away from $\frac{3}{2}$."

$$\left\{x \in \mathbb{R} \;\middle|\; \frac{3}{2} - \frac{\varepsilon}{2} < x < \frac{3}{2} + \frac{\varepsilon}{2}\right\}$$

20. 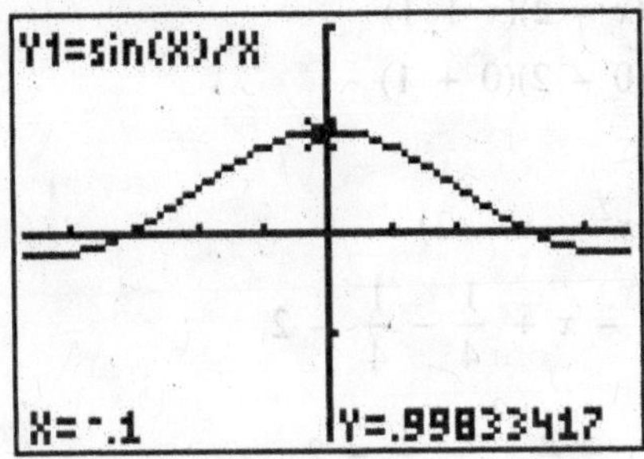

$\lim_{x \to 0} \frac{\sin x}{x} = \mathbf{1}$

21. 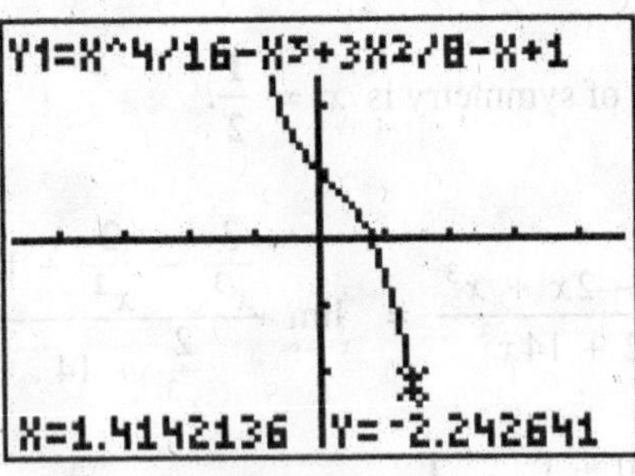

$f(\sqrt{2}) \approx \mathbf{-2.242641}$

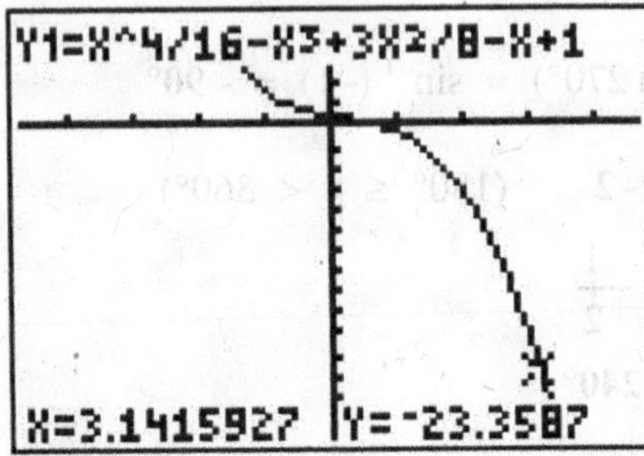

Window: $x[-4.7, 4.7]$, $y[-30, 10]$, Yscl=2

$f(\pi) \approx \mathbf{-23.3587}$

22.
$$9^2 + 12^2 = (y + z)^2$$
$$225 = (y + z)^2$$
$$y + z = 15$$
$$y = 15 - z$$

$$x^2 + y^2 = 81 \qquad x^2 + z^2 = 144$$
$$x^2 = 81 - y^2 \qquad x^2 = 144 - z^2$$

$$81 - y^2 = 144 - z^2$$
$$z^2 - y^2 = 63$$
$$z^2 - (15 - z)^2 = 63$$
$$z^2 - (225 - 30z + z^2) = 63$$
$$30z = 288$$
$$z = \mathbf{\frac{48}{5}}$$

$$y = 15 - \frac{48}{5} = \mathbf{\frac{27}{5}}$$

$$x^2 = 81 - \left(\frac{27}{5}\right)^2 = \frac{1296}{25}$$

$$x = \mathbf{\frac{36}{5}}$$

23.
$$\sqrt{2 + 3} = x$$
$$2x + 3 = x^2$$
$$x^2 - 2x - 3 = 0$$
$$(x - 3)(x + 1) = 0$$
$$x = 3, -1$$

But $\sqrt{2(-1) + 3} \neq -1$, so $x = \mathbf{3}$.

24. $(5 - 2)(180°) = 3(180°) = \mathbf{540°}$

25. If $x > 1$, then $x^3 > x^2$.
If $0 < x < 1$, then $x^2 > x^3$.
If $x = 0$, then $x^2 = x^3$.
Insufficient information: **D**

PROBLEM SET 23

1.
$$2\pi r = 4s$$
$$s = \frac{1}{2}\pi r$$
$$A_{\text{Circle}} = \pi r^2$$
$$A_{\text{Square}} = s^2 = \frac{1}{4}\pi^2 r^2 \approx 0.785\pi r^2$$

The circle has the greater area.

2. If $0 \le x < 2\pi$, then $0 \le 3x < 6\pi$.

$$\sin(3x) = -\frac{1}{2}$$
$$3x = \frac{7\pi}{6}, \frac{11\pi}{6}, \frac{19\pi}{6}, \frac{23\pi}{6}, \frac{31\pi}{6}, \frac{35\pi}{6}$$
$$x = \mathbf{\frac{7\pi}{18}, \frac{11\pi}{18}, \frac{19\pi}{18}, \frac{23\pi}{18}, \frac{31\pi}{18}, \frac{35\pi}{18}}$$

3. If $0 \le x < 2\pi$, then $0 \le 4x < 8\pi$.

$$\tan(4x) = -\frac{\sqrt{3}}{3}$$
$$4x = \frac{5\pi}{6}, \frac{11\pi}{6}, \frac{17\pi}{6}, \frac{23\pi}{6}, \frac{29\pi}{6}, \frac{35\pi}{6}, \frac{41\pi}{6}, \frac{47\pi}{6}$$
$$x = \mathbf{\frac{5\pi}{24}, \frac{11\pi}{24}, \frac{17\pi}{24}, \frac{23\pi}{24}, \frac{29\pi}{24}, \frac{35\pi}{24}, \frac{41\pi}{24}, \frac{47\pi}{24}}$$

4. **Ellipse**

5. $x^2 + 4y^2 - 16y + 12 = 0$

$$4y^2 - 16y = -x^2 - 12$$

$$y^2 - 4y = -\frac{1}{4}x^2 - 3$$

$$y^2 - 4y + 4 = -\frac{1}{4}x^2 + 1$$

$$(y - 2)^2 = -\frac{1}{4}x^2 + 1$$

$$y = 2 \pm \sqrt{-\frac{1}{4}x^2 + 1}$$

```
Y1=2+√(-(1/4)X²+1)
Y2=2-√(-(1/4)X²+1)
```

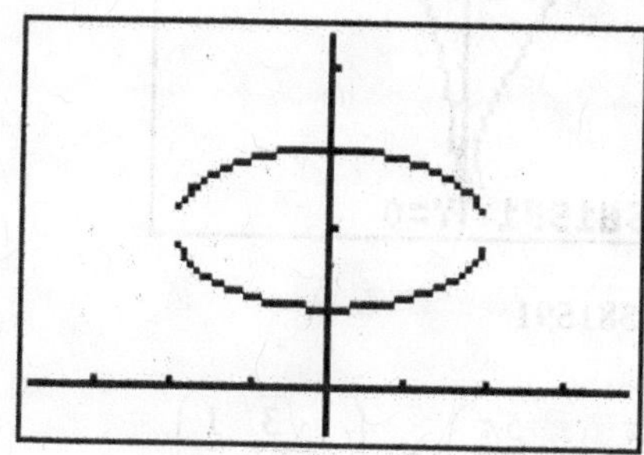

6. $(x + \Delta x)^8$

$$= x^8 + 8x^7(\Delta x) + \frac{8!}{6!\,2!}x^6(\Delta x)^2 + \frac{8!}{5!\,3!}x^5(\Delta x)^3 + \frac{8!}{4!\,4!}x^4(\Delta x)^4 + \frac{8!}{3!\,5!}x^3(\Delta x)^5 + \frac{8!}{2!\,6!}x^2(\Delta x)^6 + 8x(\Delta x)^7 + (\Delta x)^8$$

$$= \mathbf{x^8 + 8x^7(\Delta x) + 28x^6(\Delta x)^2 + 56x^5(\Delta x)^3 + 70x^4(\Delta x)^4 + 56x^3(\Delta x)^5 + 28x^2(\Delta x)^6 + 8x(\Delta x)^7 + (\Delta x)^8}$$

7. $g(x) = 2 + 3f\left(x - \frac{\pi}{2}\right)$

$$g(x) = 2 + 3\sin\left(x - \frac{\pi}{2}\right)$$

Centerline: $y = 2$ Phase: $\frac{\pi}{2}$

Amplitude: 3 Period: 2π

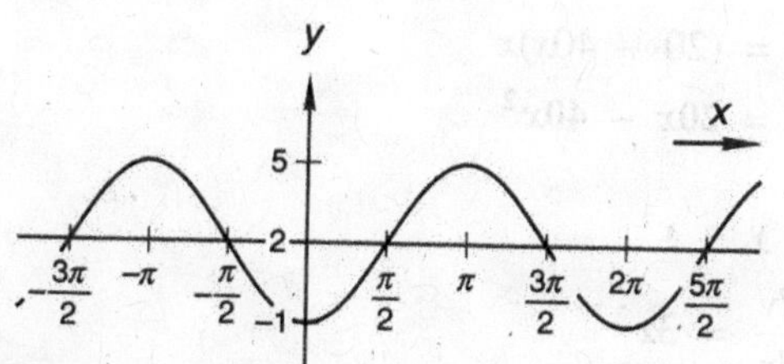

8. $y = \frac{1}{x + 2} + 3$

9. $4^x = 17$

$$x \ln 4 = \ln 17$$

$$x = \mathbf{\frac{\ln 17}{\ln 4}} \text{ or } \mathbf{\frac{\log 17}{\log 4}} \text{ or } \mathbf{\log_4 17}$$

10. $\frac{d}{dx}f(x) = \lim_{\Delta x \to 0} \frac{-4(x + \Delta x) + 5 - (-4x + 5)}{\Delta x}$

$$= \lim_{\Delta x \to 0} \frac{-4x - 4(\Delta x) + 5 + 4x - 5}{\Delta x}$$

$$= \lim_{\Delta x \to 0} \frac{-4(\Delta x)}{\Delta x} = \mathbf{-4}$$

11. $D_x y = \lim_{\Delta x \to 0} \frac{(x + \Delta x)^3 - x^3}{\Delta x}$

$$= \lim_{\Delta x \to 0} \frac{x^3 + 3x^2(\Delta x) + 3x(\Delta x)^2}{\Delta x} + \lim_{\Delta x \to 0} \frac{(\Delta x)^3 - x^3}{\Delta x}$$

$$= \lim_{\Delta x \to 0} \frac{\Delta x[3x^2 + 3x(\Delta x) + (\Delta x)^2]}{\Delta x}$$

$$= \lim_{\Delta x \to 0} [3x^2 + 3x(\Delta x) + (\Delta x)^2] = \mathbf{3x^2}$$

12.

	Domain	Range
f:	$\mathbb{R}$	$\{y \in \mathbb{R} \mid -1 \le y \le 1\}$
g:	$\mathbb{R}$	$\{y \in \mathbb{R} \mid y \ge 0\}$

13. $(f \circ g)(x) = f(x^2)$

$$\mathbf{(f \circ g)(x) = \sin(x^2)}$$

Domain: $\mathbb{R}$

Range: $\{y \in \mathbb{R} \mid -1 \le y \le 1\}$

14. $\lim_{x \to \infty} \frac{x^2 - 3x^3 + 14}{4x^3 - 7x^2 - 5} = \lim_{x \to \infty} \frac{\frac{1}{x} - 3 + \frac{14}{x^3}}{4 - \frac{7}{x} - \frac{5}{x^3}}$

$$= \frac{0 - 3 + 0}{4 - 0 - 0} = -\frac{3}{4}$$

15. $\lim_{x \to 1} \frac{x^2 + x - 2}{x^2 - 1} = \lim_{x \to 1} \frac{(x + 2)(x - 1)}{(x + 1)(x - 1)}$

$$= \lim_{x \to 1} \frac{x + 2}{x + 1} = \frac{3}{2}$$

16. $\lim_{x\to\infty} \frac{x^2 + 6x - 4}{x^3 + 4x^2 - 1} = \lim_{x\to\infty} \frac{\frac{1}{x} + \frac{6}{x^2} - \frac{4}{x^3}}{1 + \frac{4}{x} - \frac{1}{x^3}}$

$= \frac{0 + 0 - 0}{1 + 0 - 0} = \frac{0}{1} = \mathbf{0}$

17. $y = x^2 + x - 2$

$y = (x + 2)(x - 1)$

The graph of $y = x^2 + x - 2$ is a parabola with zeros at $x = -2$ and $x = 1$. The vertex is thus at $x = -\frac{1}{2}$, $y = -\frac{9}{4}$, and y is increasing on the interval $\left(-\frac{1}{2}, \infty\right)$.

18.

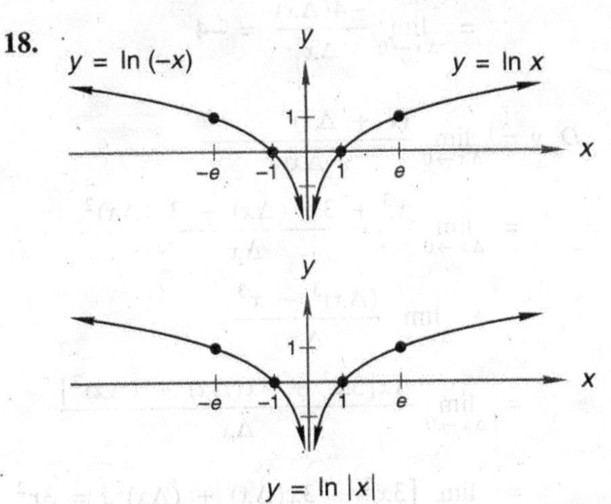

19. $(\cot^2 x + 1)(\sin^2 -x) + \left[\cos\left(\frac{\pi}{2} - x\right)\right](\sin -x)$

$= \csc^2 x \sin^2 x + \sin x(-\sin x)$

$= 1 - \sin^2 x = \cos^2 x$

20.

1⌋	1	−3	4	k
	↓	1	−2	2
	1	−2	2	$\boxed{k + 2}$

$k + 2 = 0$

$k = \mathbf{-2}$

21. (a) $\cos^2 x = \frac{1}{2} + \frac{1}{2}\cos(2x)$

(b) $\cos^2(15°) = \frac{1}{2} + \frac{1}{2}\cos 30°$

$= \frac{1}{2} + \frac{1}{2}\left(\frac{\sqrt{3}}{2}\right)$

$= \frac{1}{2} + \frac{\sqrt{3}}{4}$

$\cos^2(15°) = \frac{2 + \sqrt{3}}{4}$

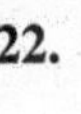

22.

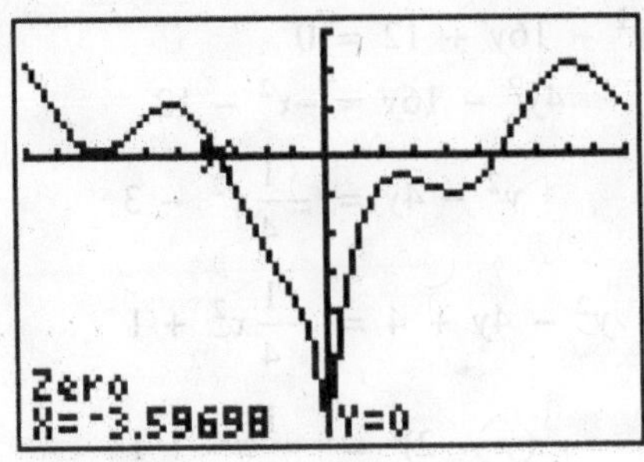

$x \approx \mathbf{-3.59698}$

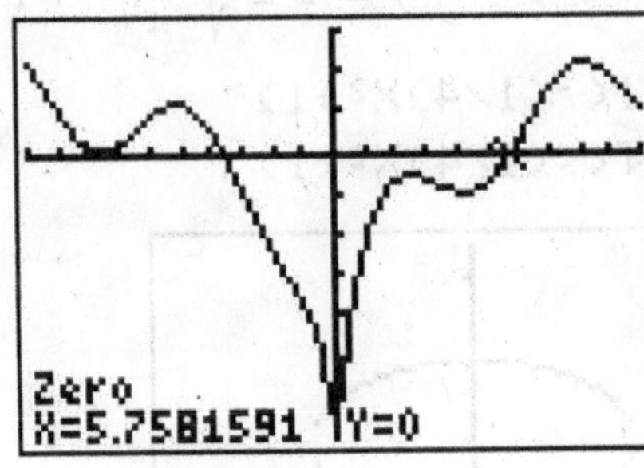

$x \approx \mathbf{5.7581591}$

23. $\left(\cos\frac{5\pi}{6}, \sin\frac{5\pi}{6}\right) = \left(-\frac{\sqrt{3}}{2}, \frac{1}{2}\right)$

24.

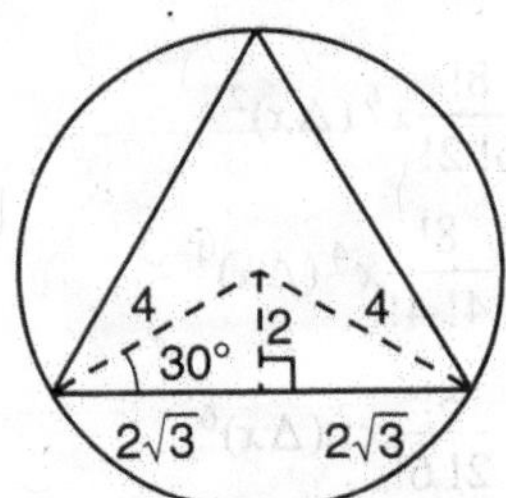

$\mathbf{4\sqrt{3}}$ **units**

25. x percent of $y = \frac{x}{100}(y) = \frac{xy}{100}$

y percent of $x = \frac{y}{100}(x) = \frac{xy}{100}$

The quantities are equal: **C**

Problem Set 24

1. $V = 20(1 - 2x)x$

$V = (20 - 40x)x$

$V = \mathbf{20x - 40x^2}$

2. $y = x^3$

$\frac{dy}{dx} = \mathbf{3x^2}$

3. $f(x) = \sqrt[3]{x} = x^{1/3}$

$f'(x) = \frac{1}{3}x^{-2/3} = \mathbf{\frac{1}{3\sqrt[3]{x^2}}}$

4. $s = \frac{1}{t^3} = t^{-3}$

$\frac{ds}{dt} = -3t^{-4} = \mathbf{-\frac{3}{t^4}}$

5. $y = \sqrt[4]{x^3} = x^{3/4}$

$D_x y = \frac{3}{4}x^{-1/4} = \mathbf{\frac{3}{4\sqrt[4]{x}}}$

6. $y = \frac{1}{x^2} = x^{-2}$

$\frac{dy}{dx} = -2x^{-3} = \mathbf{-\frac{2}{x^3}}$

7. (a)

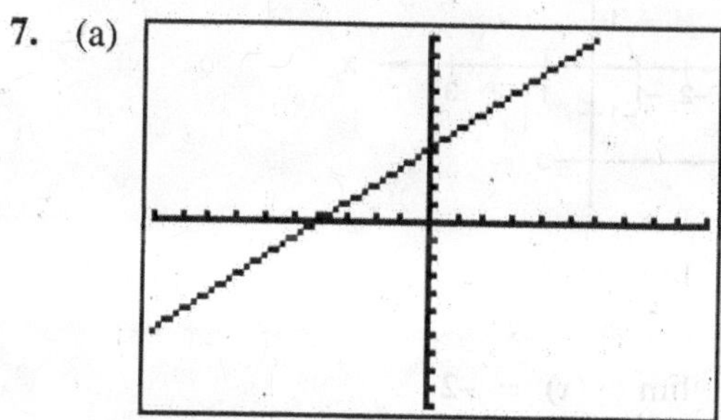

(b) $\lim_{x \to 0} g(x) = \mathbf{4}$

(c) $f'(x) = 2x$; $f'(2) = 2(2) = \mathbf{4}$

(d) **They are the same.**

8. If $0 \le \theta < 2\pi$, then $0 \le 3\theta < 6\pi$.

$\cos(3\theta) = -\frac{1}{2}$

$3\theta = \frac{2\pi}{3}, \frac{4\pi}{3}, \frac{8\pi}{3}, \frac{10\pi}{3}, \frac{14\pi}{3}, \frac{16\pi}{3}$

$\theta = \mathbf{\frac{2\pi}{9}, \frac{4\pi}{9}, \frac{8\pi}{9}, \frac{10\pi}{9}, \frac{14\pi}{9}, \frac{16\pi}{9}}$

9. $4y^2 + 8y - x + 5 = 0$

$4y^2 + 8y = x - 5$

$y^2 + 2y = \frac{1}{4}x - \frac{5}{4}$

$y^2 + 2y + 1 = \frac{1}{4}x - \frac{1}{4}$

$(y + 1)^2 = \frac{1}{4}(x - 1)$

$y = -1 \pm \frac{1}{2}\sqrt{x - 1}$

```
Y1=-1+0.5√(X-1)
Y2=-1-0.5√(X-1)
```

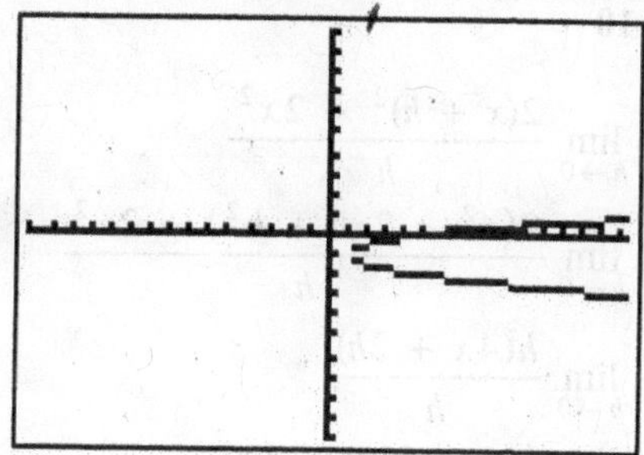

10. $\frac{7!}{4!\,3!}x^4(-2y)^3 = 35x^4(-8y^3) = -280x^4y^3$

Coefficient: **−280**

11. $g(x) = f(-x) = e^{-x}$

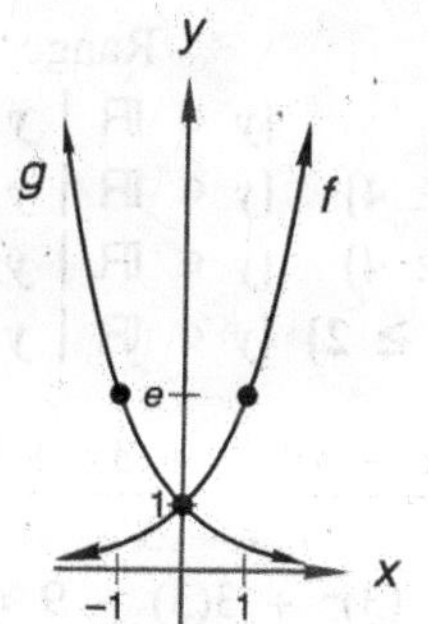

12. $h(x) = 1 + f\left(x - \frac{\pi}{4}\right)$

$h(x) = 1 + \cos\left(x - \frac{\pi}{4}\right)$

Centerline: $y = 1$ Phase: $\frac{\pi}{4}$

Amplitude: 1 Period: 2π

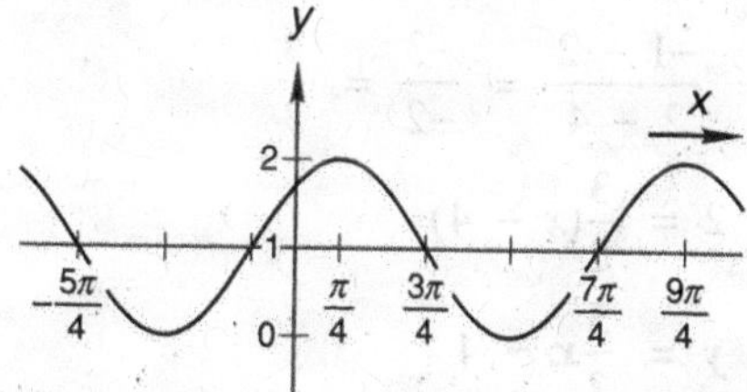

13.

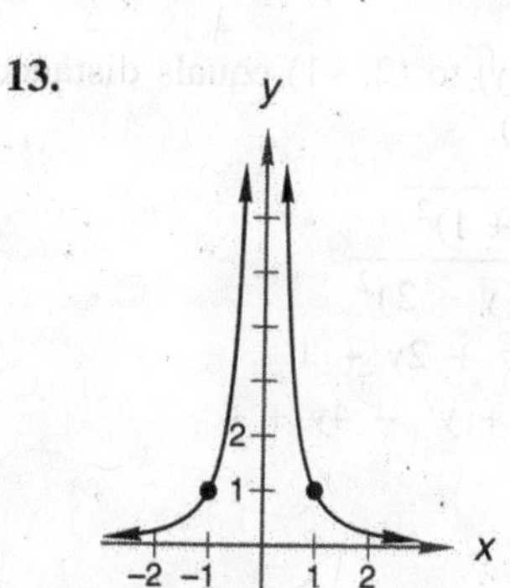

14. $y = \log x$

$y = \dfrac{\ln x}{\ln 10}$

15. $f'(x) = \lim_{h\to 0} \dfrac{2(x+h)^2 - 2x^2}{h}$

$= \lim_{h\to 0} \dfrac{2(x^2 + 2xh + h^2) - 2x^2}{h}$

$= \lim_{h\to 0} \dfrac{h(4x + 2h)}{h}$

$= \lim_{h\to 0} (4x + 2h) = \mathbf{4x}$

16. (a) $(f \circ g)(x) = f(\sqrt{x - 4})$

$\mathbf{(f \circ g)(x) = x - 4}$

$(g \circ f)(x) = g(x^2)$

$\mathbf{(g \circ f)(x) = \sqrt{x^2 - 4}}$

(b)

	Domain	Range
f	$\mathbb{R}$	$\{y \in \mathbb{R} \mid y \geq 0\}$
g	$\{x \in \mathbb{R} \mid x \geq 4\}$	$\{y \in \mathbb{R} \mid y \geq 0\}$
$f \circ g$	$\{x \in \mathbb{R} \mid x \geq 4\}$	$\{y \in \mathbb{R} \mid y \geq 0\}$
$g \circ f$	$\{x \in \mathbb{R} \mid \lvert x\rvert \geq 2\}$	$\{y \in \mathbb{R} \mid y \geq 0\}$

17. $\lim_{x\to 3} \dfrac{x^3 - 27}{x - 3} = \lim_{x\to 3} \dfrac{(x-3)(x^2 + 3x + 9)}{x - 3}$

$= \lim_{x\to 3} x^2 + 3x + 9 = (3)^2 + 3(3) + 9 = \mathbf{27}$

18. $\lim_{x\to\infty} \dfrac{2x^3 - x^4}{2x^2 - 1} = \lim_{x\to\infty} \dfrac{2x - x^2}{2 - \frac{1}{x^2}}$

$= \dfrac{\infty - \infty^2}{2 - 0} = \dfrac{-\infty}{2} = \mathbf{-\infty}$

19. (a) $\left(\dfrac{2+4}{2}, \dfrac{-1+2}{2}\right) = \mathbf{\left(3, \dfrac{1}{2}\right)}$

(b) $m = \dfrac{-1-2}{2-4} = \dfrac{-3}{-2} = \dfrac{3}{2}$

$y - 2 = \dfrac{3}{2}(x - 4)$

$\mathbf{y = \dfrac{3}{2}x - 4}$

(c) Distance from (x, y) to $(2, -1)$ equals distance from (x, y) to $(4, 2)$.

$\sqrt{(x-2)^2 + (y+1)^2}$

$= \sqrt{(x-4)^2 + (y-2)^2}$

$x^2 - 4x + 4 + y^2 + 2y + 1$

$= x^2 - 8x + 16 + y^2 - 4y + 4$

$6y = -4x + 15$

$\mathbf{y = -\dfrac{2}{3}x + \dfrac{5}{2}}$

20. $-y = \log_6 x$

$6^{-y} = x$

y	1	0	−1
x	$\frac{1}{6}$	1	6

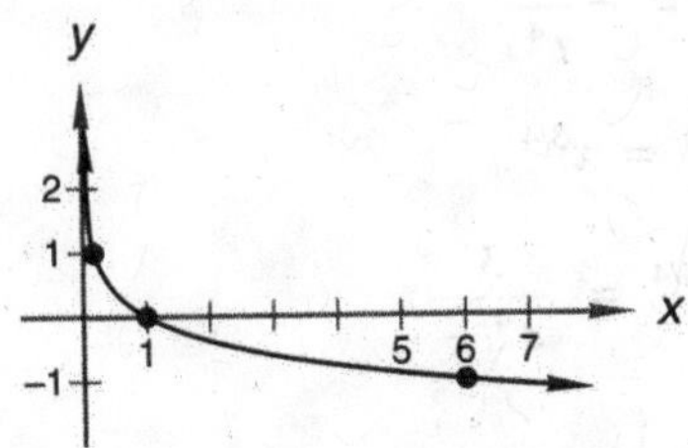

21.

(a) $\lim_{x\to 1^+} f(x) = \mathbf{2}$

(b) $\lim_{x\to 1^-} f(x) = \mathbf{-2}$

22. "y is less than 0.001 away from L"

$\mathbf{(L - 0.001, L + 0.001)}$

23. $(1 - \cos^2 x)\csc^2 x + \tan^2 x$

$= \sin^2 x \csc^2 x + \tan^2 x$

$= 1 + \tan^2 x = \sec^2 x$

24. $3\tan^2 \dfrac{\pi}{6} + 2\sin^2 -\dfrac{\pi}{4}$

$= 3\left(\dfrac{\sqrt{3}}{3}\right)^2 + 2\left(-\dfrac{\sqrt{2}}{2}\right)^2$

$= 3\left(\dfrac{3}{9}\right) + 2\left(\dfrac{2}{4}\right) = 1 + 1 = \mathbf{2}$

25. $m\angle ADC = \mathbf{40°}$; $\angle ABC$ and $\angle ADC$ are inscribed angles that intercept the same arc, therefore they have the same measure.

Problem Set 25

1. $d = \sqrt{(x-3)^2 + (x^2-4)^2}$

$d = \sqrt{x^2 - 6x + 9 + x^4 - 8x^2 + 16}$

$d = \mathbf{\sqrt{x^4 - 7x^2 - 6x + 25}}$

2. $\frac{P_1V_1}{T_1} = \frac{P_2V_2}{T_2}$

$\frac{NL}{K} = \frac{P_2 4}{1000}$

$4KP_2 = 1000\,NL$

$P_2 = \frac{1000\,NL}{4K}$

$P_2 = \mathbf{250\,NLK^{-1}}$ **newtons per square meter**

3. $f'(x) = \lim_{h\to 0} \frac{f(x+h) - f(x)}{h}$

$= \lim_{h\to 0} \frac{\sqrt{x+h} - \sqrt{x}}{h}$

$= \lim_{h\to 0} \left(\frac{\sqrt{x+h} - \sqrt{x}}{h}\right)\left(\frac{\sqrt{x+h} + \sqrt{x}}{\sqrt{x+h} + \sqrt{x}}\right)$

$= \lim_{h\to 0} \frac{x+h-x}{h(\sqrt{x+h} + \sqrt{x})}$

$= \lim_{h\to 0} \frac{1}{\sqrt{x+h} + \sqrt{x}} = \frac{1}{\sqrt{x} + \sqrt{x}} = \mathbf{\frac{1}{2\sqrt{x}}}$

4. $y = x^{14}$ $\qquad D_x y = \mathbf{14x^{13}}$

5. $y = \frac{1}{x^3} = x^{-3}$ $\qquad \frac{dy}{dx} = -3x^{-4} = \mathbf{-\frac{3}{x^4}}$

6. $f(x) = \sqrt{x^3} = x^{3/2}$

$f'(x) = \frac{3}{2}x^{1/2} = \mathbf{\frac{3\sqrt{x}}{2}}$

7. $s(t) = \frac{1}{\sqrt{t}} = \frac{1}{t^{1/2}} = t^{-1/2}$

$\frac{ds}{dt} = -\frac{1}{2}t^{-3/2} = \mathbf{-\frac{1}{2\sqrt{t^3}}}$

8. $f(x) = \frac{1}{5}x^5 + 5x^{-2} + 6x^4 + 3$

$f'(x) = \mathbf{x^4 - 10x^{-3} + 24x^3}$

9. $y = \frac{4}{u^2} - 3\sqrt{u}$ or $y = 4u^{-2} - 3u^{1/2}$

$y = 4u^{-2} - 3u^{1/2}$

$\frac{dy}{du} = -8u^{-3} - \frac{3}{2}u^{-1/2}$

$\frac{dy}{du} = \mathbf{-\frac{8}{u^3} - \frac{3}{2\sqrt{u}}}$

10. $s(t) = v_0 t + \frac{1}{2}at^2$

$s'(t) = \mathbf{v_0 + at}$

11. (a)

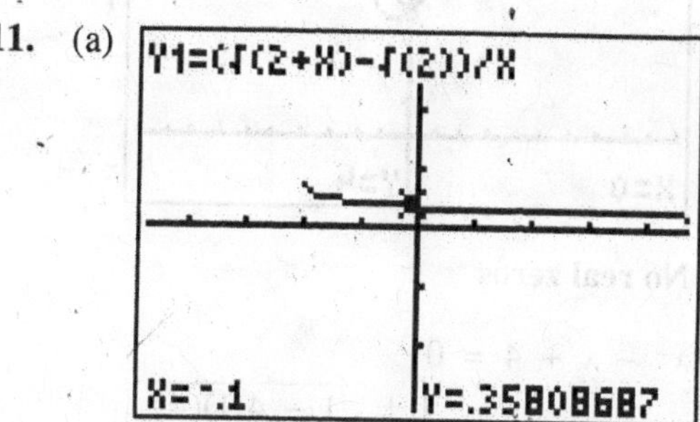

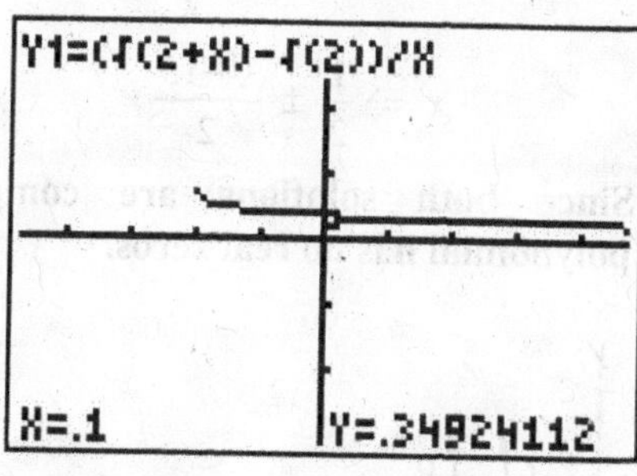

$y(0) \approx \mathbf{0.35}$

(b) $f(x) = \sqrt{x} = x^{1/2}$

$f'(x) = \frac{1}{2}x^{-1/2} = \mathbf{\frac{1}{2\sqrt{x}}}$

(c) $f'(2) = \frac{1}{2\sqrt{2}} \approx \mathbf{0.35}$

(d) **They are the same.**

12. $\cos(3\theta) = -1$

$3\theta = \pi, 3\pi, 5\pi$

$\theta = \mathbf{\frac{\pi}{3}, \pi, \frac{5\pi}{3}}$

13. $y^2 = x^2 - 4x$

$y = \pm\sqrt{x^2 - 4x}$

Let Y1=√(X²-4X) and Y2=-Y1.

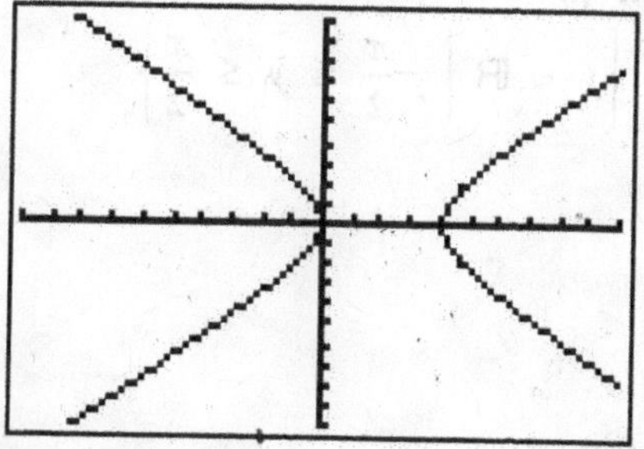

14. (a)

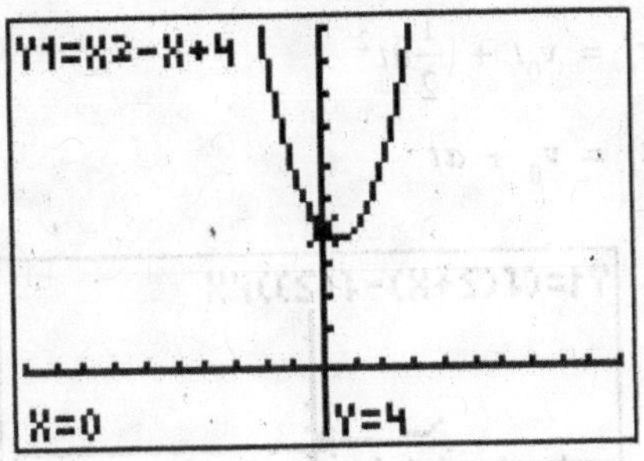

No real zeros

(b) $x^2 - x + 4 = 0$

$$x = \frac{1 \pm \sqrt{1 - 4(1)(4)}}{2}$$

$$x = \frac{1}{2} \pm \frac{\sqrt{-15}}{2}$$

Since both solutions are complex, the polynomial has no real zeros.

15.

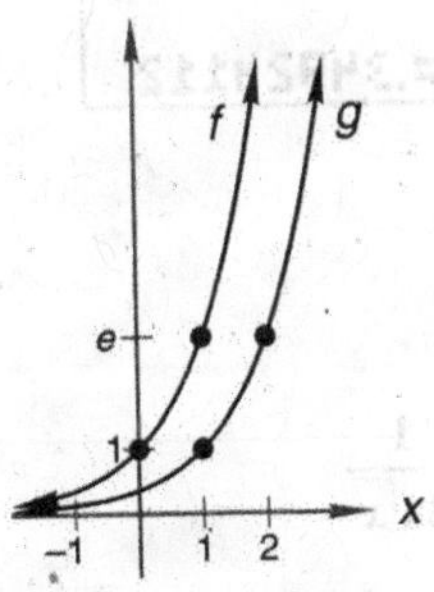

16. The graph of f is the graph of $y = \frac{1}{x}$ shifted 2 units up and 3 units to the right. The graph of $y = \frac{1}{x}$ is never increasing, therefore the graph of f **is never increasing.**

17.

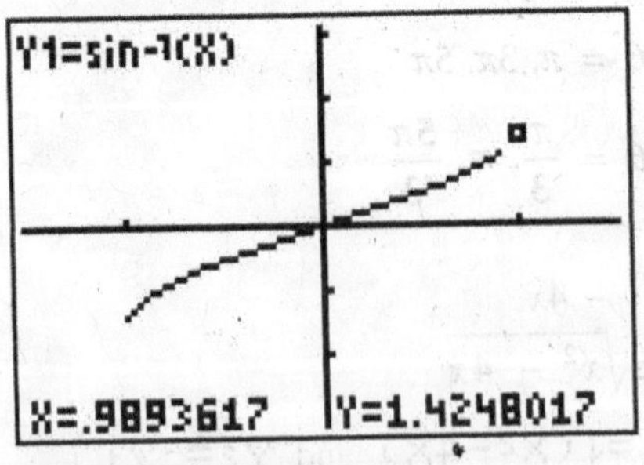

Domain: $\{x \in \mathbb{R} \mid -1 \leq x \leq 1\}$

Range: $\left\{y \in \mathbb{R} \,\middle|\, -\frac{\pi}{2} \leq y \leq \frac{\pi}{2}\right\}$

18. $\ln(3x + 2) - \ln(2x - 1) = \ln 5$

$$\ln\left(\frac{3x + 2}{2x - 1}\right) = \ln 5$$

$$\frac{3x + 2}{2x - 1} = 5$$

$$10x - 5 = 3x + 2$$

$$7x = 7$$

$$x = \mathbf{1}$$

19.

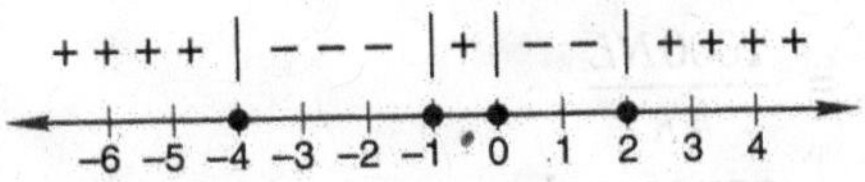

20. $\dfrac{2\cos x}{\sin(2x)} \csc -x = \dfrac{2\cos x}{2\sin x \cos x}\left(\dfrac{1}{\sin -x}\right)$

$$= \frac{1}{\sin x}\left(\frac{1}{-\sin x}\right) = -\frac{1}{\sin^2 x} = -\csc^2 x$$

21. $e^{9k} = 2$

$$9k = \ln 2$$

$$k = \mathbf{\frac{\ln 2}{9}}$$

22. $\dfrac{5!}{3!\,2!}(x^3)(-2y)^2 = 40x^3y^2$

Coefficient: **40**

23. **Domain:** $\{x \in \mathbb{R} \mid x \geq 0\}$

Range: $\{y \in \mathbb{R} \mid y \geq 1\}$

24.

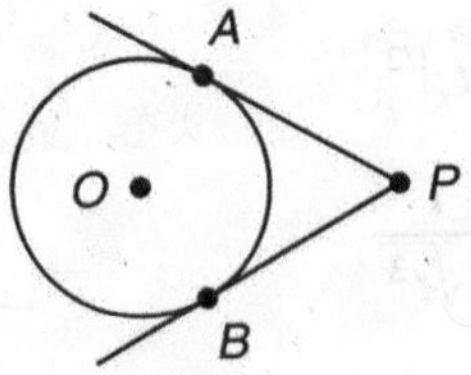

$\overline{PA} \cong \overline{PB}$

The quantities are equal: **C**

25. $\dfrac{AB}{AD} = \dfrac{BC}{DC}$

$$\frac{x}{c} = \frac{a}{a + b}$$

$$x = \mathbf{\frac{ac}{a + b}}$$

PROBLEM SET 26

1. $W(t) = W_0e^{kt}$

$200 = 150e^k$

$\frac{4}{3} = e^k$

$\ln\left(\frac{4}{3}\right) = k$

$\mathbf{W(t) = 150e^{\ln(4/3)t}}$

$W(3) = 150e^{3\ln(4/3)} = 150e^{\ln(4/3)^3}$

$= 150\left(\frac{4}{3}\right)^3 = \mathbf{355.5556\ g}$

2. $A(t) = A_0e^{kt}$

$0.8 = 1e^{2k}$

$\ln 0.8 = 2k$

$k = \frac{\ln 0.8}{2}$

$0.5 = e^{\ln 0.8/2\, t}$

$\ln 0.5 = \frac{\ln 0.8}{2}t$

$t = \frac{2\ln 0.5}{\ln 0.8}$

$t \approx 6.2126$ hr past midnight

$t \approx$ **6:12:45.a.m.**

3. $V(t) = V_0e^{kt}$

$300 = 100e^{2k}$

$3 = e^{2k}$

$\ln 3 = 2k$

$k = \frac{\ln 3}{2}$

$400 = 100e^{(\ln 3)t/2}$

$4 = e^{(\ln 3)t/2}$

$\ln 4 = \frac{\ln 3}{2}t$

$t = \frac{2\ln 4}{\ln 3}$

$t \approx 2.5237$ hr past 1 p.m.

$t \approx$ **3:31:25 p.m.**

4. $f(t) = \sqrt{2}\,t^{-2} + 3t^{-3}$

$\mathbf{f'(t) = -2\sqrt{2}\,t^{-3} - 9t^{-4}}$

5. $y = 3x^4 - 2x^{-1/2} + 2$

$\mathbf{\frac{dy}{dx} = 12x^3 + x^{-3/2}}$

6. $f(x) = e^x + \ln|x| - \sin x + \cos x$

$\mathbf{f'(x) = e^x + \frac{1}{x} - \cos x - \sin x}$

7. $y = \ln u - 2e^u + u^{1/2}$

$\mathbf{\frac{dy}{du} = \frac{1}{u} - 2e^u + \frac{1}{2}u^{-1/2}}$

8. $y = 2\sin x + 14e^x - 14x^{-1}$

$\mathbf{D_xy = 2\cos x + 14e^x + 14x^{-2}}$

9. $s(t) = x_0 + v_0t + \frac{1}{2}at^2$

$\mathbf{s'(t) = v_0 + at}$

10. $f(x) = 3e^x - 4\cos x - \frac{1}{4}\ln|x|$

$\mathbf{f'(x) = 3e^x + 4\sin x - \frac{1}{4x}}$

11. $D_xy = \lim_{h\to 0}\frac{f(x+h) - f(x)}{h}$

$= \lim_{h\to 0}\frac{-3(x+h)^2 + 3x^2}{h}$

$= \lim_{h\to 0}\frac{-3(x^2 + 2xh + h^2) + 3x^2}{h}$

$= \lim_{h\to 0}\frac{-6xh - 3h^2}{h}$

$= \lim_{h\to 0}(-6x - 3h) = \mathbf{-6x}$

12. $y^2 + 4y + 4 = x^2 - 2x$

$(y+2)^2 = x^2 - 2x$

$y + 2 = \pm\sqrt{x^2 - 2x}$

$y = -2 \pm \sqrt{x^2 - 2x}$

Y1=-2+√(X²-2X)

Y2=-2-√(X²-2X)

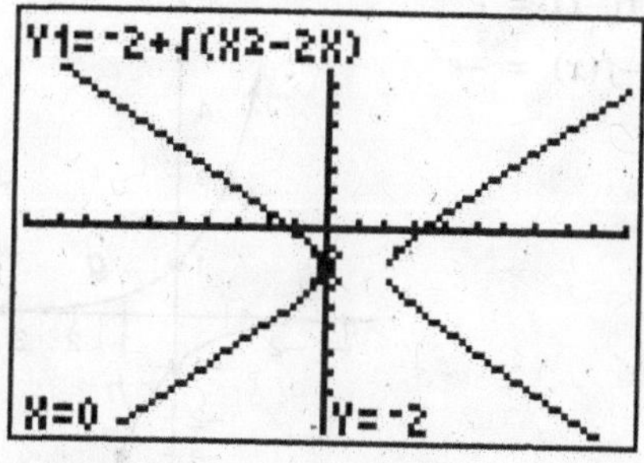

Vertices: **(0, –2), (2, –2)**

13. $y = \sin(x - 3) + 2$

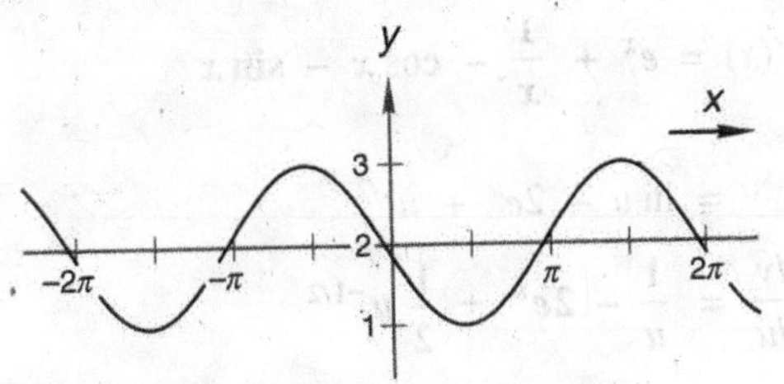

14.
$$\sin^2 x + 2\cos x - 2 = 0$$
$$(1 - \cos^2 x) + 2\cos x - 2 = 0$$
$$\cos^2 x - 2\cos x + 1 = 0$$
$$(\cos x - 1)^2 = 0$$
$$\cos x - 1 = 0$$
$$\cos x = 1$$
$$\mathbf{x = 0}$$

15.

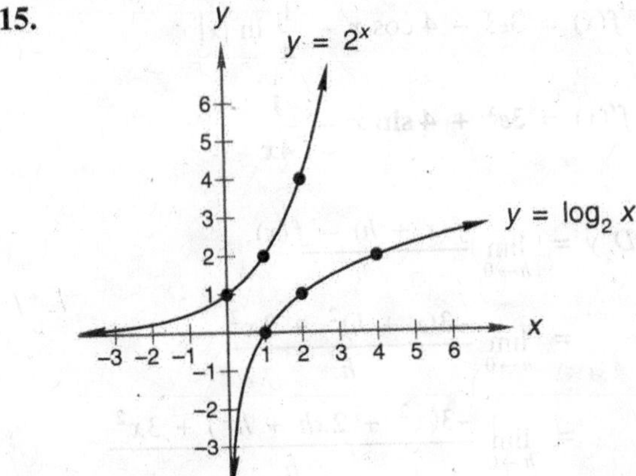

16. $$\lim_{x\to\infty} \frac{2x - 3x^2 + 4}{2x^2 + 14} = \lim_{x\to\infty} \frac{\frac{2}{x} - 3 + \frac{4}{x^2}}{2 + \frac{14}{x^2}}$$

$$= \frac{0 - 3 + 0}{2 + 0} = \mathbf{-\frac{3}{2}}$$

17.
$$4 = 3^x$$
$$\ln 4 = x \ln 3$$
$$x = \mathbf{\frac{\ln 4}{\ln 3}}$$

18. $g(x) = f(-x) = e^{-x}$

$h(x) = -f(x) = -e^x$

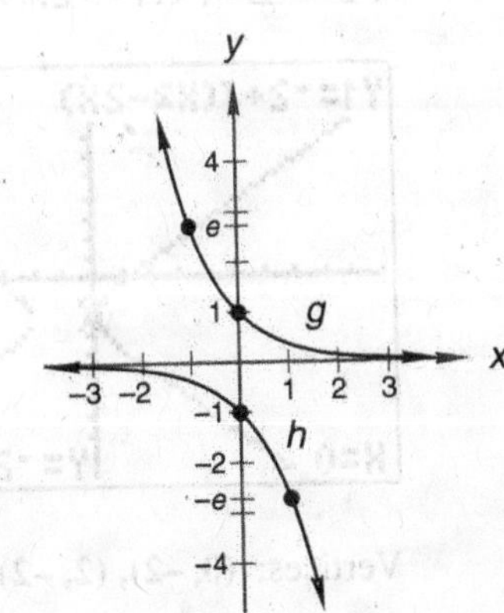

19.
$$\log_5(x + 3) + \log_5 10 = 3$$
$$\log_5(10x + 30) = 3$$
$$10x + 30 = 5^3$$
$$10x = 95$$
$$\mathbf{x = 9.5}$$

20. If a function is continuous at $x = a$, then the function has a derivative at $x = a$.

21. $\tan(3\theta) = 1$

If $0 \le \theta < 2\pi$, then $0 \le 3\theta < 6\pi$.

$$3\theta = \frac{\pi}{4}, \frac{5\pi}{4}, \frac{9\pi}{4}, \frac{13\pi}{4}, \frac{17\pi}{4}, \frac{21\pi}{4}$$

$$\theta = \mathbf{\frac{\pi}{12}, \frac{5\pi}{12}, \frac{3\pi}{4}, \frac{13\pi}{12}, \frac{17\pi}{12}, \frac{7\pi}{4}}$$

22.

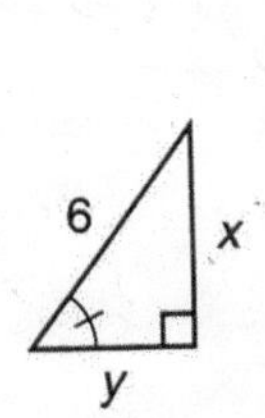

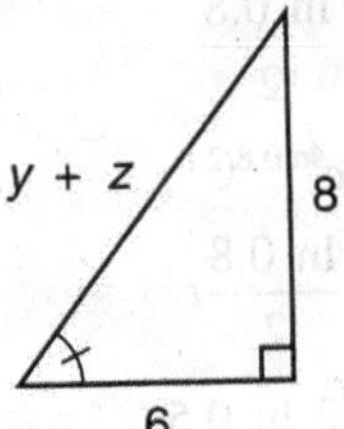

$$y + z = 10$$

$$\frac{6}{10} = \frac{x}{8} \qquad \frac{6}{10} = \frac{y}{6}$$
$$10x = 48 \qquad 10y = 36$$
$$\mathbf{x = 4.8} \qquad \mathbf{y = 3.6}$$
$$y + z = 10$$
$$3.6 + z = 10$$
$$\mathbf{z = 6.4}$$

23.
$$2a = 4 \qquad 2b = 2$$
$$a = 2 \qquad b = 1$$
$$\mathbf{\frac{(x + 2)^2}{1} + \frac{(y - 3)^2}{4} = 1}$$

24.
$$s = \frac{1}{2}(5 + 7 + 10) = 11$$
$$A = \sqrt{11(11 - 5)(11 - 7)(11 - 10)}$$
$$A = \sqrt{11(6)(4)(1)}$$
$$A = \mathbf{2\sqrt{66} \text{ units}^2}$$

25. $$\mathbf{\left(\frac{a + b}{2}, \frac{c}{2}\right)}$$

The diagonals of a parallelogram bisect one another.

PROBLEM SET 27

1. $A(t) = A_0 e^{kt}$

$A(1) = A_0 e^k$

$1{,}530{,}000 = A_0 e^k$

$A_0 = 1{,}530{,}000e^{-k}$

$A(3) = A_0 e^{3k}$

$3{,}000{,}000 = (1{,}530{,}000e^{-k})e^{3k}$

$e^{2k} = \frac{100}{51}$

$2k = \ln \frac{100}{51}$

$k = \frac{1}{2} \ln \frac{100}{51}$

$A_0 = 1{,}530{,}000\, e^{-\ln\sqrt{\frac{100}{51}}} = 1{,}530{,}000\sqrt{0.51}$

$\mathbf{A(t) = 1{,}530{,}000\sqrt{0.51}e^{-t \ln \sqrt{0.51}}}$

$A(7) = 1{,}530{,}000\sqrt{0.51}e^{-7 \ln \sqrt{0.51}}$

$A(7) \approx$ **\$11,534,025.37**

2. $y = x^{-3/2} - \frac{1}{3}e^x + 4 \cos x$

$\frac{dy}{dx} = \mathbf{-\frac{3}{2}x^{-5/2} - \frac{1}{3}e^x - 4 \sin x}$

3. $f(x) = x^{-1} + 2 \ln |x| - 3 \sin x$

$f'(x) = \mathbf{-x^{-2} + \frac{2}{x} - 3 \cos x}$

4. $y = 2u^2 - \frac{1}{3}u^{1/3} + c$

$D_u y = \mathbf{4u - \frac{1}{9}u^{-2/3}}$

5. $f'(x) = \lim_{h \to 0} \frac{f(x + h) - f(x)}{h}$

$= \lim_{h \to 0} \frac{-\frac{1}{x + h} + \frac{1}{x}}{h} = \lim_{h \to 0} \frac{\frac{-x + x + h}{x(x + h)}}{h}$

$= \lim_{h \to 0} \frac{1}{x(x + h)} = \mathbf{\frac{1}{x^2}}$

6. $y = 3e^x - 2x^3$

$\frac{dy}{dx} = 3e^x - 6x^2$

$\frac{d^2y}{dx^2} = 3e^x - 12x$

$\frac{d^3y}{dx^3} = \mathbf{3e^x - 12}$

7. $f(t) = 3 \sin t + \ln t$

$f'(t) = 3 \cos t + t^{-1}$

$f''(t) = \mathbf{-3 \sin t - t^{-2}}$

8. $f(x) = \ln |x|$

$f'(x) = \frac{1}{x} = x^{-1}$

$f''(x) = -x^{-2} = -\frac{1}{x^2}$

$f''(-14) = -\frac{1}{(-14)^2} = \mathbf{-\frac{1}{196}}$

9. $y = x^2 + 3$

$\frac{dy}{dx} = 2x$

$\left.\frac{dy}{dx}\right|_{-1} = -2$

$y - 4 = -2(x + 1)$

$\mathbf{y = -2x + 2}$

10. $y = \sin x - \cos x$

$\frac{dy}{dx} = \cos x + \sin x$

$\left.\frac{dy}{dx}\right|_{-1} = \cos(-1) + \sin(-1) = \mathbf{-0.3012}$

11. $y = 2e^x$

$\frac{dy}{dx} = 2e^x$

$\left.\frac{dy}{dx}\right|_{2} = 2e^2$

$y - 2e^2 = 2e^2(x - 2)$

$\mathbf{y = 2e^2x - 2e^2}$

12. For the key trigonometric identities, see section 12.A in the textbook.

$\cos(2\theta) = \cos(\theta + \theta)$

$\cos(2\theta) = \cos\theta \cos\theta - \sin\theta \sin\theta$

$\cos(2\theta) = \cos^2\theta - \sin^2\theta$

$\cos(2\theta) = \cos^2\theta - (1 - \cos^2\theta)$

$\cos(2\theta) = 2\cos^2\theta - 1$

$2\cos^2\theta = 1 + \cos(2\theta)$

$\mathbf{\cos^2\theta = \frac{1}{2} + \frac{1}{2}\cos(2\theta)}$

13. If $0 \le x < 360°$ then $0 \le 4x < 1440°$.

$$\sin(4x) + 1 = 0$$
$$\sin(4x) = -1$$
$$4x = 270°, 630°, 990°, 1350°$$
$$x = \mathbf{67.5°, 157.5°, 247.5°, 337.5°}$$

14.
$$4y^2 - 8y = 9x^2 + 32$$
$$y^2 - 2y = \frac{9}{4}x^2 + 8$$
$$y^2 - 2y + 1 = \frac{9}{4}x^2 + 9$$
$$(y-1)^2 = \frac{9}{4}x^2 + 9$$
$$y = 1 \pm \sqrt{\frac{9}{4}x^2 + 9}$$

```
Y1=1+√(9/4X²+9)
Y2=1-√(9/4X²+9)
```

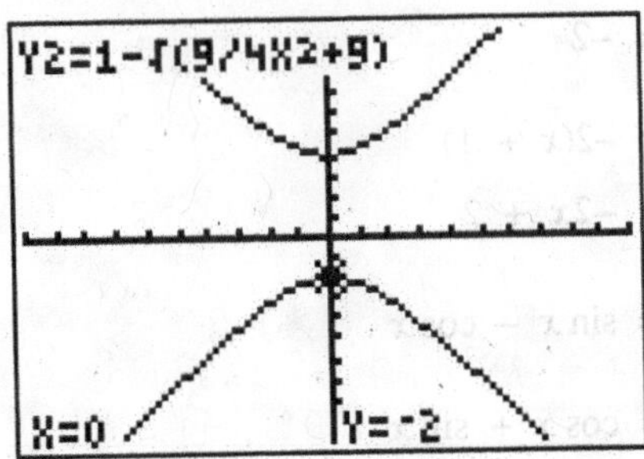

Vertices: **(0, 4), (0, –2)**

15. (a) $m(x) = \dfrac{y - 1}{x - \frac{\pi}{2}}$

$$\mathbf{m(x) = \frac{\sin x - 1}{x - \frac{\pi}{2}}}$$

(b)

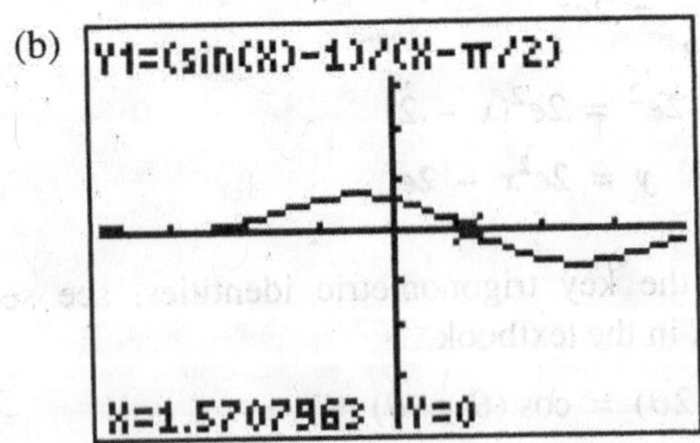

(c) $\displaystyle\lim_{x\to\pi/2} \frac{\sin x - 1}{x - \frac{\pi}{2}} = \mathbf{0}$

(d) If $y = \sin x$, then $y' = \cos x$.

$$\left.\frac{dy}{dx}\right|_{\pi/2} = \cos\left(\frac{\pi}{2}\right) = \mathbf{0}$$

(e) **They are the same.**

16. $\log_3 5 = \dfrac{\ln 5}{\ln 3} \approx \mathbf{1.4650}$

17. (a) f: **Domain: $\{x \in \mathbb{R} \mid x \ge 1\}$**

Range: $\{y \in \mathbb{R} \mid y \ge 0\}$

g: **Domain: $\mathbb{R}$**

Range: $\{y \in \mathbb{R} \mid y \ge 0\}$

(b) $(f \circ g)(x) = f(x^2)$

$\mathbf{(f \circ g)(x) = \sqrt{x^2 - 1}}$

Domain: $\{x \in \mathbb{R} \mid |x| \ge 1\}$

Range: $\{y \in \mathbb{R} \mid y \ge 0\}$

18.
$$\frac{21!\,4!}{5!\,7!\,18!} = \frac{21 \cdot 20 \cdot 19 \cdot 18! \cdot 4!}{5 \cdot 4! \cdot 7! \cdot 18!}$$
$$= \frac{21 \cdot 20 \cdot 19}{5 \cdot 7 \cdot 6 \cdot 5 \cdot 4 \cdot 3 \cdot 2} = \mathbf{\frac{19}{60}}$$

19.

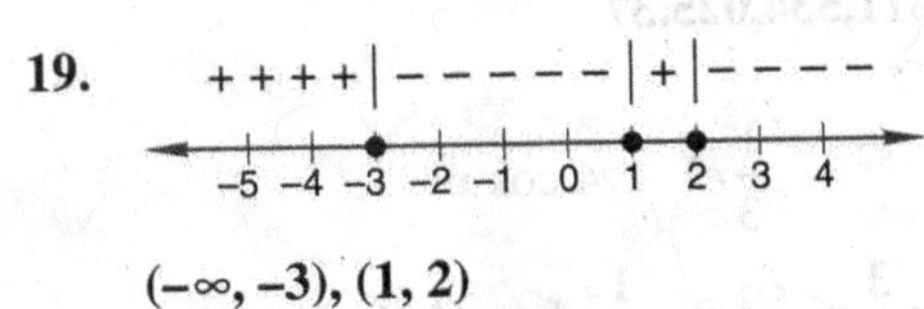

(–∞, –3), (1, 2)

20. $y = \dfrac{x^2 - 1}{x - 1} = \dfrac{(x+1)(x-1)}{x-1}$

$$\lim_{x\to 1} \frac{x^2 - 1}{x - 1} = \lim_{x\to 1}(x + 1) = \mathbf{2}$$

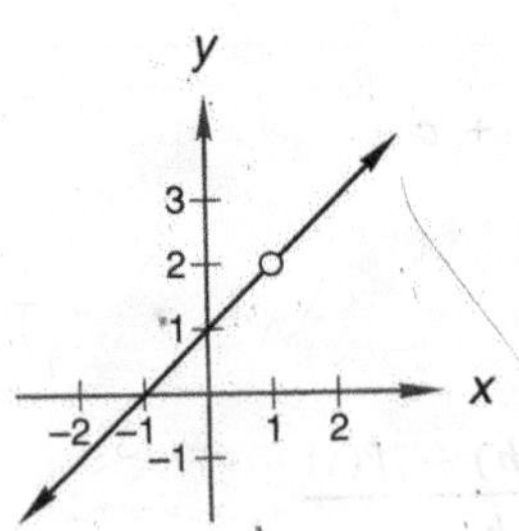

21. $f(2) = \mathbf{7}$

22. Possible zeros: $x = \dfrac{\pm 1, \pm 2, \pm 3, \pm 6}{\pm 1}$

$= \pm 1, \pm 2, \pm 3\ \pm 6$

```
1| 1   -2   -5    6
   ↓    1   -1   -6
   1   -1   -6   [0]
```

$f(x) = (x - 1)(x^2 - x - 6)$

$f(x) = (x - 1)(x - 3)(x + 2)$

Zeros: $x = \mathbf{-2, 1, 3}$

23.
$$y = a(x-1)(x+2)$$
$$-4 = a(0-1)(0+2)$$
$$-4 = -2a$$
$$a = 2$$
$$y = 2(x-1)(x+2)$$
$$y = 2(x^2 + x - 2)$$
$$\mathbf{y = 2x^2 + 2x - 4}$$

24.
$$x(a+x) = (x-1)(x-1+6)$$
$$x(a+x) = (x-1)(x+5)$$
$$ax + x^2 = x^2 + 4x - 5$$
$$ax = 4x - 5$$
$$x(a-4) = -5$$
$$x = \frac{-5}{a-4}$$
$$\mathbf{x = \frac{5}{4-a}}$$

25.
$$x - y = 4$$
$$(x-y)^2 = 4^2$$
$$x^2 - 2xy + y^2 = 16$$
$$x^2 - 2(3) + y^2 = 16$$
$$\mathbf{x^2 + y^2 = 22}$$

PROBLEM SET 28

1.
$$A(t) = A_0 e^{kt}$$
$$100 = 2{,}000{,}000e^{29k}$$
$$0.00005 = e^{29k}$$
$$\ln 0.00005 = 29k$$
$$k = \frac{\ln 0.00005}{29}$$
$$500{,}000 = 2{,}000{,}000e^{(\ln(0.00005)/29)t}$$
$$0.25 = e^{(\ln(0.00005)/29)t}$$
$$\ln 0.25 = \frac{\ln 0.00005}{29}t$$
$$t = \frac{29 \ln 0.25}{\ln 0.00005}$$
$$t \approx 4.0594$$

On the fifth of the month

2.

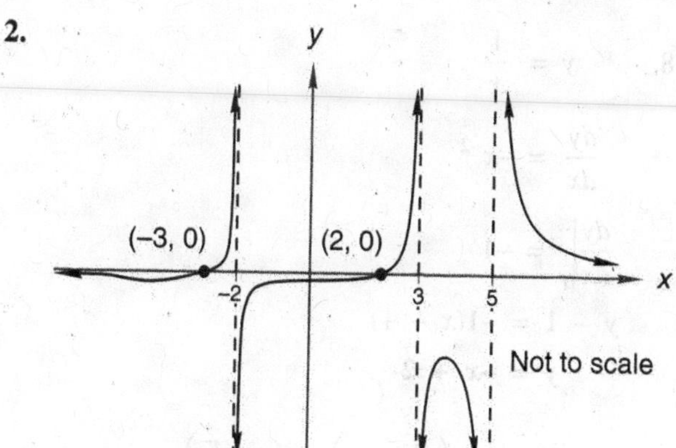

3.

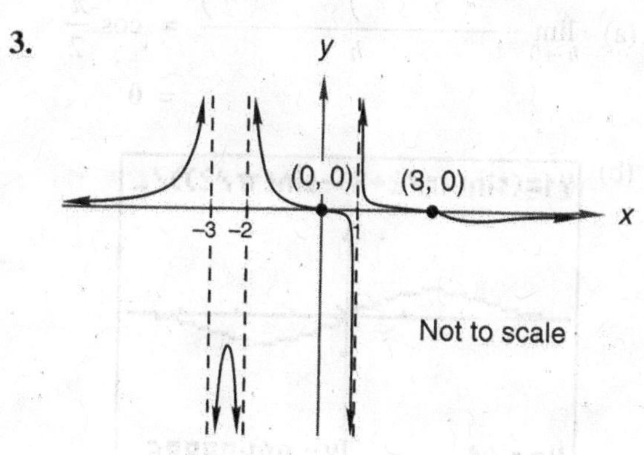

4.
$$s(t) = x_0 + v_0 t + \frac{1}{2}gt^2$$
$$s'(t) = v_0 + gt$$
$$s''(t) = \mathbf{g}$$

5.
$$y = \frac{1}{u}$$
$$\frac{dy}{du} = -u^{-2}$$
$$\frac{d^2y}{du^2} = 2u^{-3}$$
$$\left.\frac{d^2y}{du^2}\right|_2 = 2(2)^{-3} = \mathbf{\frac{1}{4}}$$

6.
$$y = \frac{1}{5}e^x - 2\cos x + 3\ln|x|$$
$$\frac{dy}{dx} = \frac{1}{5}e^x + 2\sin x + \frac{3}{x}$$
$$\left.\frac{dy}{dx}\right|_2 = \frac{1}{5}e^2 + 2\sin 2 + \frac{3}{2} \approx \mathbf{4.7964}$$

7.
$$y = 2\sin x + \cos x$$
$$\frac{dy}{dx} = 2\cos x - \sin x$$
$$\left.\frac{dy}{dx}\right|_{4.2} = 2\cos(4.2) - \sin(4.2) \approx \mathbf{-0.1089}$$

8. $y = \frac{1}{x}$

$\frac{dy}{dx} = -x^{-2}$

$\left.\frac{dy}{dx}\right|_1 = -1$

$y - 1 = -1(x - 1)$

$\mathbf{y = -x + 2}$

9. (a) $\lim_{h\to 0} \frac{\sin\left(\frac{\pi}{2} + h\right) - \sin\left(\frac{\pi}{2}\right)}{h} = \cos\frac{\pi}{2}$

$= \mathbf{0}$

(b) 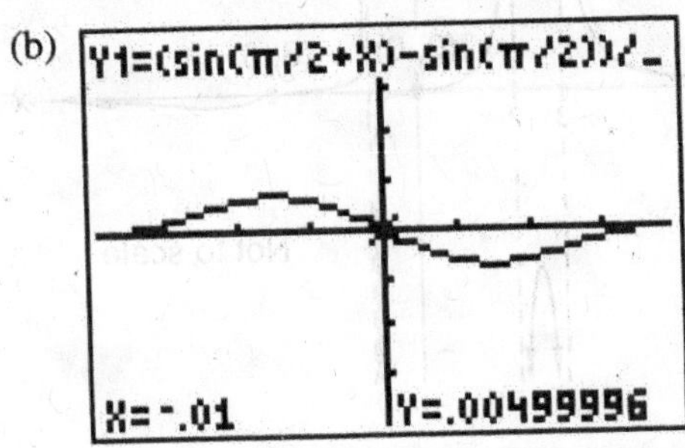

$\lim_{x\to 0} y = \mathbf{0}$

y	−0.05	0.05	−0.005	0.005
x	0.1	−0.1	0.01	−0.01

10. $(x^2 - 2x) + (y^2 + 12y) = -6$

$(x^2 - 2x + 1) + (y^2 + 12y + 36)$

$= -6 + 1 + 36$

$(x - 1)^2 + (y + 6)^2 = 31$

$(y + 6)^2 = 31 - (x - 1)^2$

$-6 \pm \sqrt{31 - (x - 1)^2} = y$

```
Y1=-6+√(31-(X-1)²)
Y2=-6-√(31-(X-1)²)
```

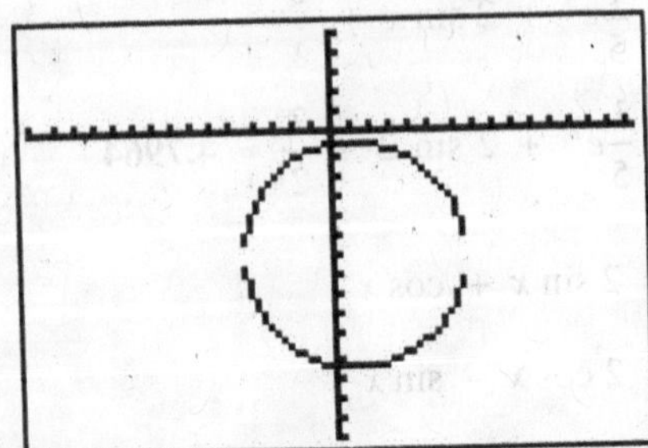

Center: **(1, −6)**

11.

$$\begin{array}{r|rrrr} -1 & 1 & 1 & -2 & -2 \\ & \downarrow & -1 & 0 & 2 \\ \hline & 1 & 0 & -2 & \boxed{0} \end{array}$$

$x^3 + x^2 - 2x - 2 = (x + 1)(x^2 - 2)$

$= (x + 1)(x + \sqrt{2})(x - \sqrt{2})$

$\mathbf{(x + \sqrt{2}), (x - \sqrt{2})}$

12. $f(x) = \sqrt{x} \qquad g(x) = 1 + \sqrt{x - 2}$

The graph of *g* is the graph of *f* shifted two units to the right and one unit up.

13. $f(4) = \mathbf{5}$

14. $-2 \ln 2 + \ln (x - 2) = \ln (2x - 4)$

$\ln (x - 2) = \ln (2x - 4) + \ln 2^2$

$\ln (x - 2) = \ln [4(2x - 4)]$

$x - 2 = 8x - 16$

$14 = 7x$

$2 = x$

However, $\ln (x - 2)$ is not defined for $x = 2$, so there is **no solution.**

15. (a) $f(x) = \frac{x^2 + x - 6}{x + 3} = \frac{(x + 3)(x - 2)}{x + 3}$

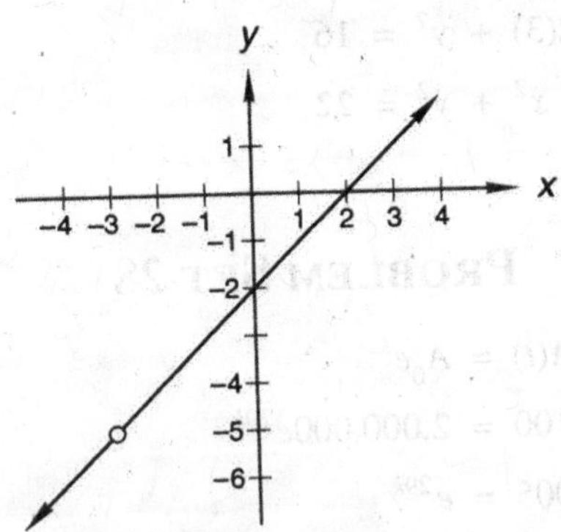

(b) 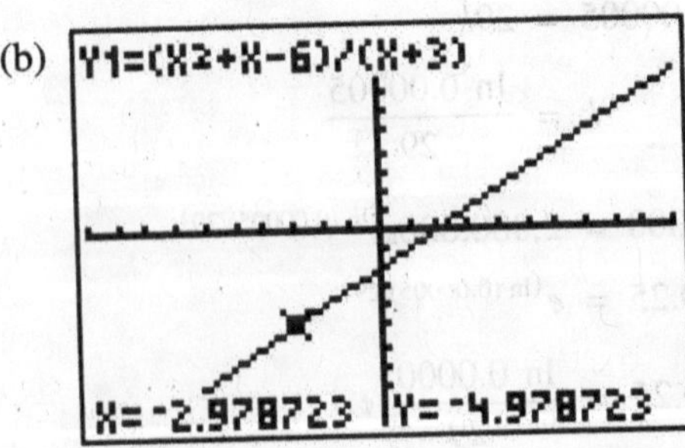

$\lim_{x\to -3} f(x) = \mathbf{-5}$

(c) $\lim_{x\to -3} f(x) = \lim_{x\to -3} (x - 2) = \mathbf{-5}$

The answers are the same.

16. $\log_b 53 = 31$

$$b^{31} = 53$$

$$b = \sqrt[31]{53}$$

17. $y = x^2$

$$\frac{dy}{dx} = 2x$$

The correct choice is **C.**

18. $|3x - 1| < 16$

$$\left|x - \frac{1}{3}\right| < \frac{16}{3}$$

$$\{x \in \mathbf{Z} \mid -4 \leq x \leq 5\}$$

19. $\dfrac{(\sin x + \cos x)^2 - 1}{2 \sin -x}$

$$= \frac{\sin^2 x + 2 \sin x \cos x + \cos^2 x - 1}{-2 \sin x}$$

$$= \frac{2 \sin x \cos x}{-2 \sin x} = -\cos x$$

20. $\cos\left(-\dfrac{13\pi}{3}\right) \sin^2 \dfrac{\pi}{4} = \cos\left(-\dfrac{\pi}{3}\right) \sin^2 \dfrac{\pi}{4}$

$$= \frac{1}{2}\left(\frac{\sqrt{2}}{2}\right)^2 = \frac{1}{4}$$

21. $\dfrac{2 - \sqrt{3}}{1 - \sqrt{2}}\left(\dfrac{1 + \sqrt{2}}{1 + \sqrt{2}}\right) = \dfrac{2 + 2\sqrt{2} - \sqrt{3} - \sqrt{6}}{1 - 2}$

$$= \mathbf{-2 - 2\sqrt{2} + \sqrt{3} + \sqrt{6}}$$

22. $\sqrt{x^2 + (y - 1)^2} = \sqrt{(x - x)^2 + (y + 1)^2}$

$$x^2 + y^2 - 2y + 1 = y^2 + 2y + 1$$

$$\mathbf{x^2 = 4y}$$

23. $x^2 = 4y$

$$\mathbf{y = \frac{1}{4}x^2}$$

24. Midpoints: $\left(\dfrac{c}{2}, \dfrac{d}{2}\right), \left(\dfrac{a + c}{2}, \dfrac{d}{2}\right)$

Because the two y-coordinates are the same, the line is horizontal: $y = \frac{d}{2}$

The line that bisects any two sides is parallel to the third side.

25. Number of diagonals $= \dfrac{(n - 3)n}{2}$

$$\frac{(6 - 3)(6)}{2} = \mathbf{9}$$

PROBLEM SET 29

1. $A(t) = A_0 e^{kt}$

$$50 = 20e^{2k}$$

$$2.5 = e^{2k}$$

$$\ln 2.5 = 2k$$

$$k = \frac{1}{2} \ln 2.5$$

$$A(t) = 20e^{(\ln 2.5)t/2}$$

$$A(5) = 20e^{2.5 \ln 2.5}$$

$$= 20(2.5)^{2.5} \approx \mathbf{197.6424\ cm^2}$$

2. $y = 3x^{-2} + 2 \sin x + 2e^x$

$$dy = \mathbf{-6x^{-3}\,dx + 2 \cos x\,dx + 2e^x\,dx}$$

3. $y = 2 \ln |u| - 4u^{-1/2}$

$$dy = \mathbf{2u^{-1}\,du + 2u^{-3/2}\,du}$$

4. $y = t^{1/3} + 2$

$$dy = \mathbf{\frac{1}{3}t^{-2/3}\,dt}$$

5.

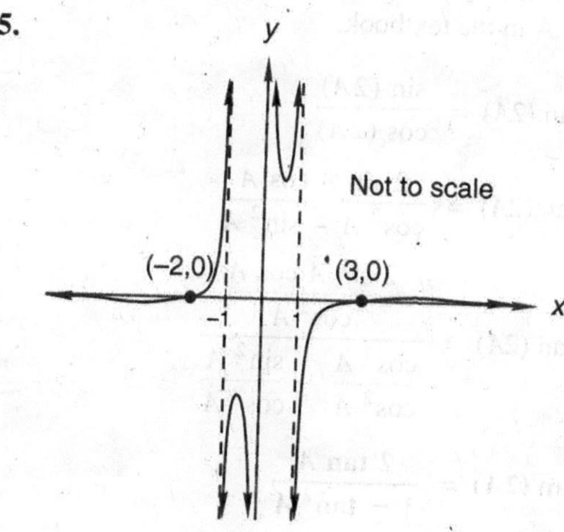

6. $y = x^{1/2}$

$$\frac{dy}{dx} = \frac{1}{2}x^{-1/2} = \frac{1}{2\sqrt{x}}$$

$$\left.\frac{dy}{dx}\right|_4 = \frac{1}{2(2)} = \frac{1}{4}$$

When $x = 4$, $y = 2$.

$$y - 2 = \frac{1}{4}(x - 4)$$

$$\mathbf{y = \frac{1}{4}x + 1}$$

7. 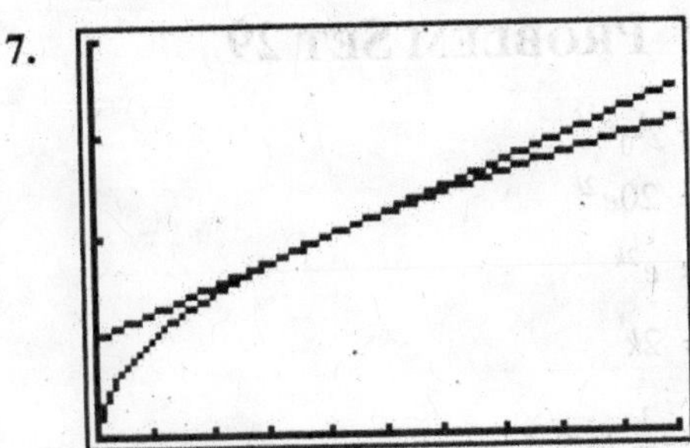

8.
$$y = \sin x$$
$$\frac{dy}{dx} = \cos x$$
$$\frac{d^2y}{dx^2} = -\sin x$$
$$\frac{d^3y}{dx^3} = -\cos x$$
$$\left.\frac{d^3y}{dx^3}\right|_{3.5} = \mathbf{-\cos 3.5 \approx -0.9365}$$

9. `nDeriv(4ln(abs(X))+2e^(X)-cos(X),X,-1.78)` $\approx$ **−2.8881**

10. For the key trigonometric identities, see section 12.A in the textbook.

$$\tan(2A) = \frac{\sin(2A)}{\cos(2A)}$$
$$\tan(2A) = \frac{2\sin A\cos A}{\cos^2 A - \sin^2 A}$$
$$\tan(2A) = \frac{\dfrac{2\sin A\cos A}{\cos^2 A}}{\dfrac{\cos^2 A}{\cos^2 A} - \dfrac{\sin^2 A}{\cos^2 A}}$$
$$\mathbf{\tan(2A) = \frac{2\tan A}{1-\tan^2 A}}$$
$$\tan(2A) = \frac{2\left(-\frac{1}{4}\right)}{1-\left(-\frac{1}{4}\right)^2} = \frac{-\frac{1}{2}}{\frac{15}{16}} = \mathbf{-\frac{8}{15}}$$

11.
$$4^{x^2-4x+7} = 64$$
$$4^{x^2-4x+7} = 4^3$$
$$x^2 - 4x + 7 = 3$$
$$x^2 - 4x + 4 = 0$$
$$(x-2)^2 = 0$$
$$\mathbf{x = 2}$$

12. If $0 \le x < \pi$, then $0 \le 4x < 4\pi$.

$$\sin(4x) = -\frac{1}{2}$$
$$4x = \frac{7\pi}{6}, \frac{11\pi}{6}, \frac{19\pi}{6}, \frac{23\pi}{6}$$
$$x = \mathbf{\frac{7\pi}{24}, \frac{11\pi}{24}, \frac{19\pi}{24}, \frac{23\pi}{24}}$$

13.

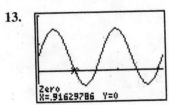

Zero X=.91629786 Y=0

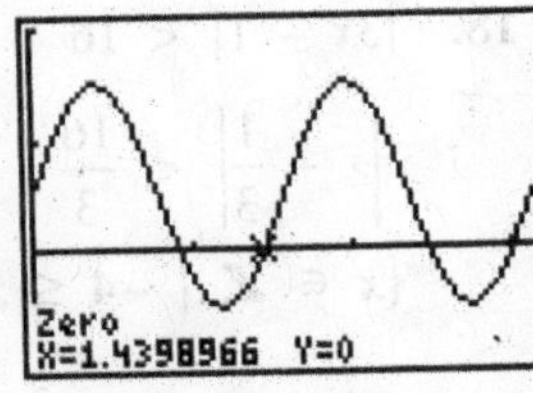

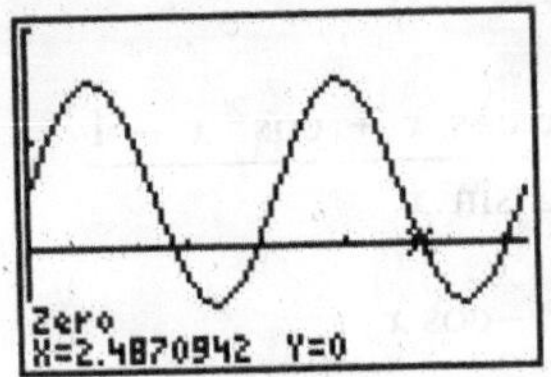

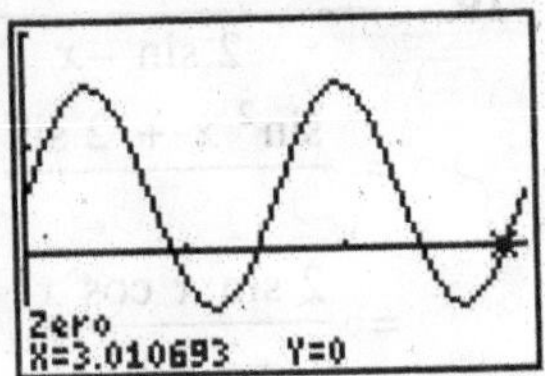

The zeros of $y = \sin(4x) + 0.5$ are $x =$ **0.9163, 1.4399, 2.4871,** and **3.0107.**

These x-values are the same as those in problem 12.

14.
$$4y^2 - 8y - (9x^2 - 36x) = 68$$
$$4(y^2 - 2y + 1) - 9(x^2 - 4x + 4) = 36$$
$$4(y-1)^2 - 9(x-2)^2 = 36$$
$$9 + \frac{9}{4}(x-2)^2 = (y-1)^2$$
$$\pm\sqrt{9 + \frac{9}{4}(x-2)^2} = y - 1$$

```
Y1=1+√(9+2.25(X-2)²)
Y2=1-√(9+2.25(X-2)²)
```

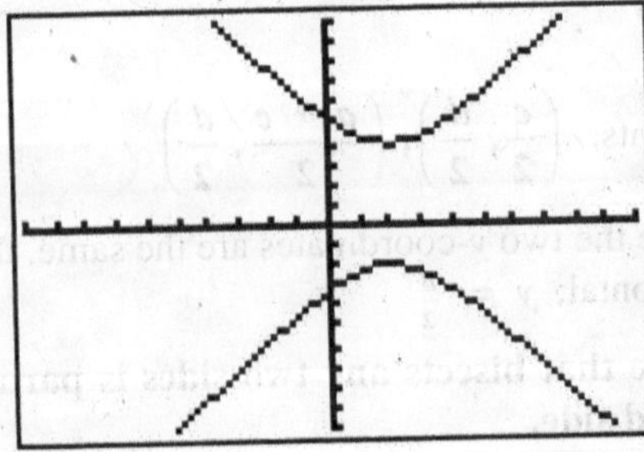

Center: **(2, 1)**

15. $$\lim_{\Delta x \to 0} \frac{\ln(x+\Delta x) - \ln x}{\Delta x} = \frac{d}{dx}\ln x = \mathbf{\frac{1}{x}}$$

16. 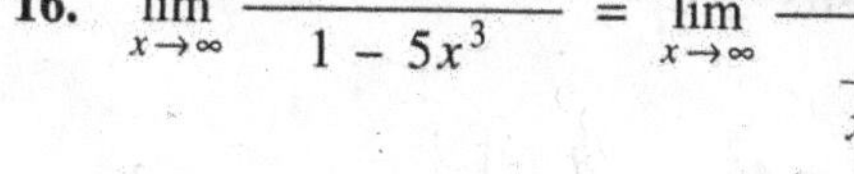

$$\lim_{x\to\infty} \frac{2x^3 - x^2 + 1}{1 - 5x^3} = \lim_{x\to\infty} \frac{2 - \frac{1}{x} + \frac{1}{x^3}}{\frac{1}{x^3} - 5} = -\frac{2}{5}$$

17.

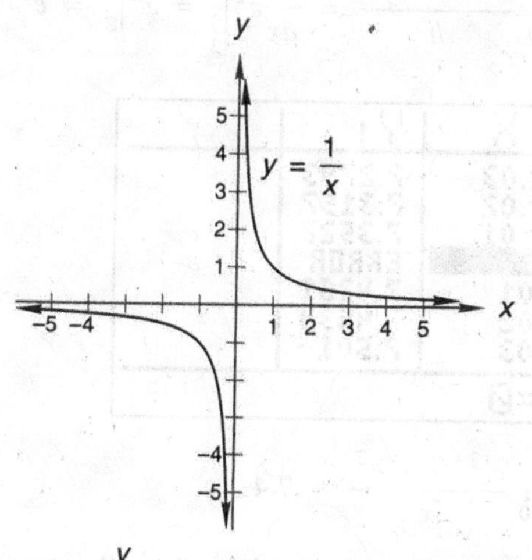

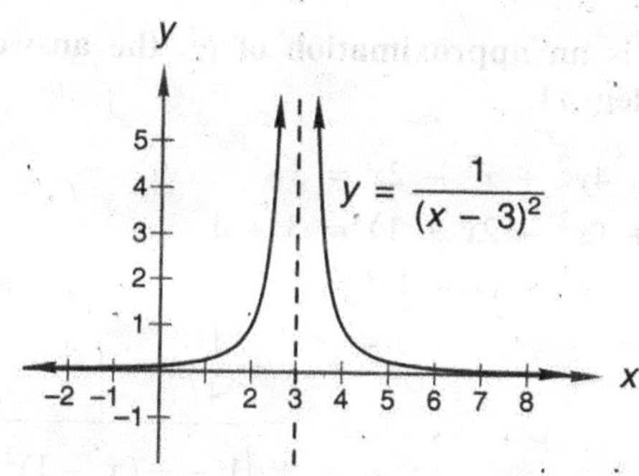

18. (a) $\sin^{-1}\frac{1}{2} = \frac{\pi}{6}$ (b) $\sin x = \frac{1}{2}$

$$x = \frac{\pi}{6}, \frac{5\pi}{6}$$

19. $f(x) = e^{5x^2 + x - 2}$

$h(x) = 5x^2 + x - 2$

$x \longrightarrow$ [h] $\longrightarrow 5x^2 + x - 2$

$g(x) = e^x$

$\longrightarrow$ [g] $\longrightarrow e^{5x^2 + x - 2}$

20.

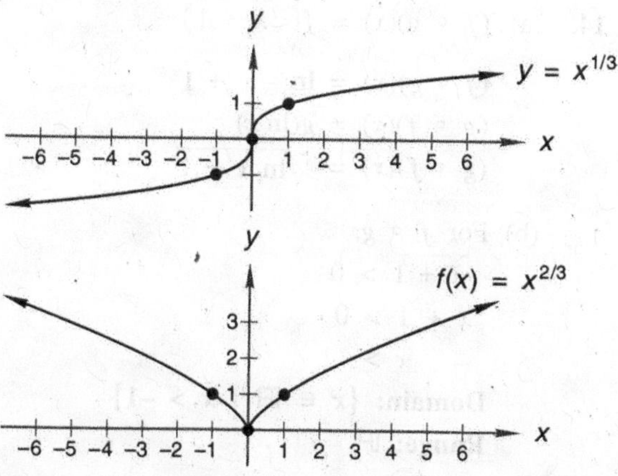

21. **Domain:** $\mathbb{R}$

Range: $\{y \in \mathbb{R} \mid -1 \le y \le 3\}$

22.

$$2^x = 5$$
$$x \ln 2 = \ln 5$$
$$x = \frac{\ln 5}{\ln 2} \approx 2.3219$$

23. If $f(x) = 2^x$, then $f(-1) = \frac{1}{2}$, $f(0) = 1$, and $f(1) = 2$.

The correct choice is **C.**

24. Length of hypotenuse $= \sqrt{a^2 + b^2}$

Midpoint of hypotenuse: $\left(\frac{a}{2}, \frac{b}{2}\right)$

Length of median $= \sqrt{\frac{a^2}{4} + \frac{b^2}{4}}$

$$= \frac{1}{2}\sqrt{a^2 + b^2}$$

The length of the median is half the length of the hypotenuse.

25. $1 + 2 + 3 + \cdots + 98 + 99 + 100$

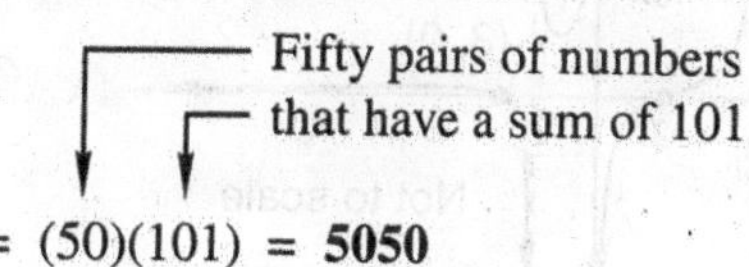

Fifty pairs of numbers that have a sum of 101

$= (50)(101) = \mathbf{5050}$

PROBLEM SET 30

1. Rate · Time = Distance

$$MH = D$$

Time should be $H - 2$.

$$R = \frac{D}{T} = \frac{MH}{H-2} \text{ mph}$$

2.

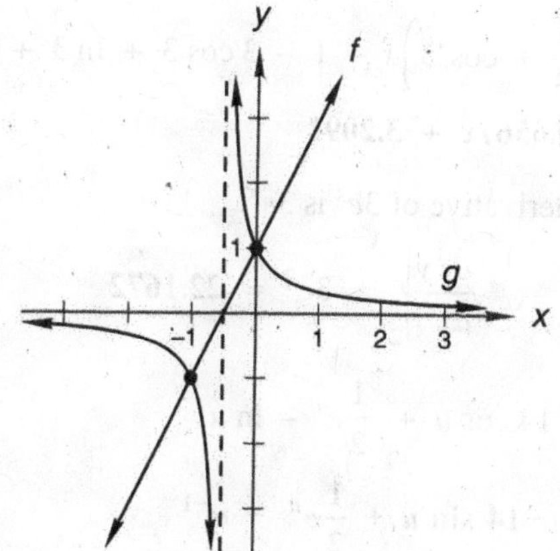

3.

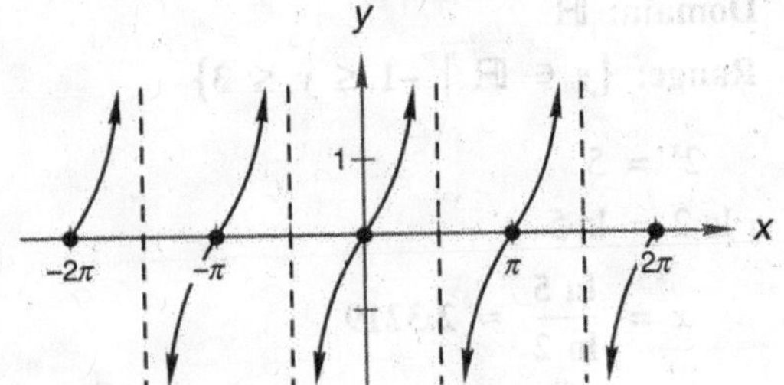

4.

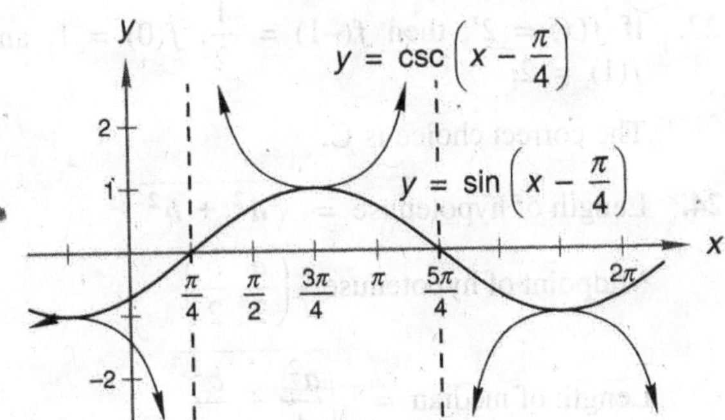

5. $y = 3 \sin t - \sqrt{2}e^t + \frac{1}{3} \ln |t|$

$dy = \mathbf{3 \cos t \, dt - \sqrt{2}\, e^t \, dt + \frac{1}{3} t^{-1} \, dt}$

6.

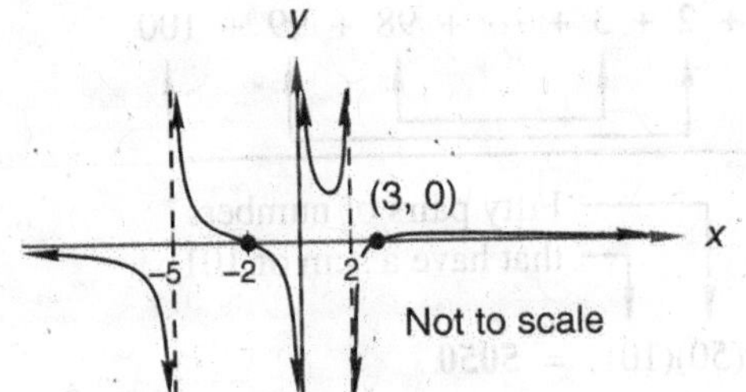

7.
$$y = \ln x + \sin x$$
$$\frac{dy}{dx} = \frac{1}{x} + \cos x$$
$$\left.\frac{dy}{dx}\right|_3 = \frac{1}{3} + \cos 3$$
$$y - (\ln 3 + \sin 3) = \left(\frac{1}{3} + \cos 3\right)(x - 3)$$
$$y = \left(\frac{1}{3} + \cos 3\right)x - 1 - 3\cos 3 + \ln 3 + \sin 3$$
$$y \approx \mathbf{-0.6567x + 3.2097}$$

8. Every derivative of $3e^x$ is $3e^x$:
$$\left.\frac{d^5y}{dx^5}\right|_2 = 3e^2 \approx \mathbf{22.1672}$$

9.
$$y = 14 \cos u + \frac{1}{2}e^u - \ln u$$
$$\frac{dy}{du} = \mathbf{-14 \sin u + \frac{1}{2}e^u - u^{-1}}$$

10.
$$y = t^{2/3} - 3t^{-1}$$
$$\frac{dy}{dt} = \mathbf{\frac{2}{3}t^{-1/3} + 3t^{-2}}$$

11.
$$\lim_{h \to 0} \frac{e^{(2+h)} - e^2}{h} = \left.\frac{d}{dx}e^x\right|_2 = \left.e^x\right|_2 = \mathbf{e^2}$$

12.

X	Y1
-.03	7.2793
-.02	7.3157
-.01	7.3522
0	ERROR
.01	7.4261
.02	7.4634
.03	7.501

X=0

$$\lim_{x \to 0} \frac{e^{(2+x)} - e^2}{x} \approx \mathbf{7.4}$$

This is an approximation of e^2, the answer to problem 11.

13.
$$4y^2 + x^2 - 2x = 3$$
$$4y^2 + (x^2 - 2x + 1) = 3 + 1$$
$$4y^2 + (x - 1)^2 = 4$$
$$y^2 = 1 - \frac{1}{4}(x - 1)^2$$
$$y = \pm\sqrt{1 - \frac{1}{4}(x - 1)^2}$$

Y1=√(1−0.25(X−1)²) Y2=−Y1

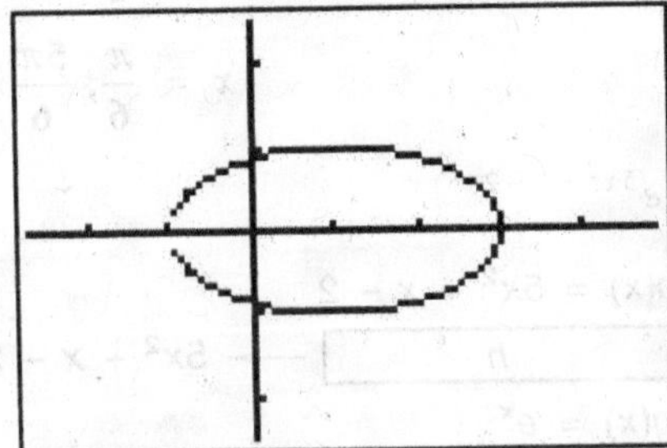

Center: **(1, 0)**

14. (a) $(f \circ g)(x) = f(\sqrt{x + 1})$

$\mathbf{(f \circ g)(x) = \ln \sqrt{x + 1}}$

$(g \circ f)(x) = g(\ln x)$

$\mathbf{(g \circ f)(x) = \sqrt{\ln x + 1}}$

(b) For $f \circ g$:
$$\sqrt{x + 1} > 0$$
$$x + 1 > 0$$
$$x > -1$$

Domain: $\{x \in \mathbb{R} \mid x > -1\}$

Range: $\mathbb{R}$

For $g \circ f$:

$$\ln x + 1 \geq 0$$
$$\ln x \geq -1$$
$$x \geq e^{-1}$$

Domain: $\left\{x \in \mathbb{R} \mid x \geq \dfrac{1}{e}\right\}$

Range: $\{y \in \mathbb{R} \mid y \geq 0\}$

15. For the key trigonometric identities, see section 12.A in the textbook.

$$\cos(2A) = \cos(A + A)$$
$$\cos(2A) = \cos A \cos A - \sin A \sin A$$
$$\cos(2A) = \cos^2 A - \sin^2 A$$
$$\cos(2A) = \cos^2 A - (1 - \cos^2 A)$$
$$\cos(2A) = 2\cos^2 A - 1$$
$$2\cos^2 A = 1 + \cos(2A)$$
$$\cos^2 A = \frac{1}{2} + \frac{1}{2}\cos(2A)$$
$$\cos A = \pm\sqrt{\frac{1}{2} + \frac{1}{2}\cos(2A)}$$
$$\boldsymbol{\cos\frac{x}{2} = \pm\sqrt{\frac{1}{2} + \frac{1}{2}\cos x}}$$

16. - - - -|+ + +|-|+|- - - -

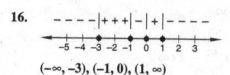

–5 –4 –3 –2 –1 0 1 2 3

(–∞, –3), (–1, 0), (1, ∞)

17.

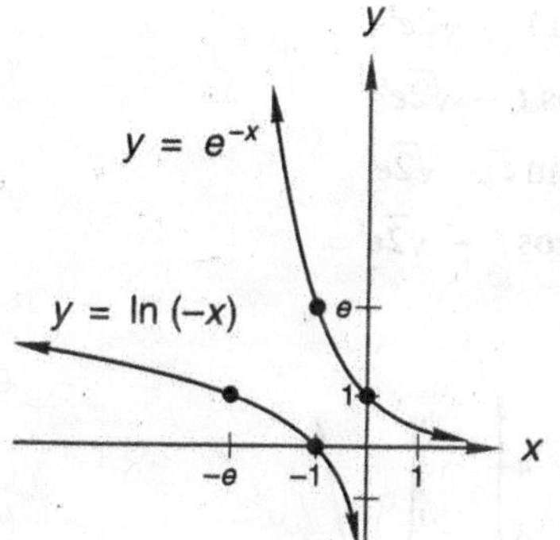

18.

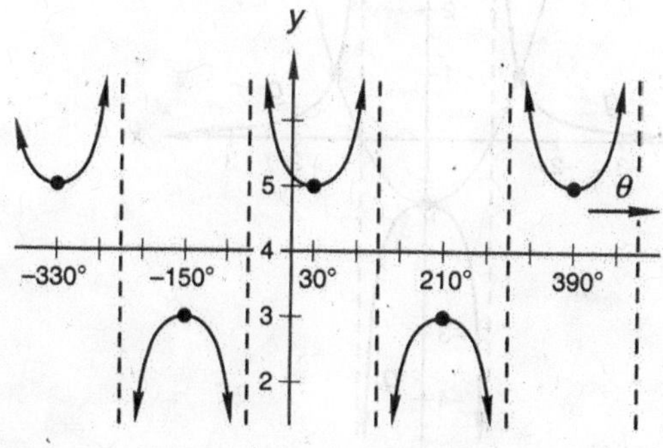

19. $f(3) = 4$

20. $P_1 = \left(\cos\dfrac{5\pi}{6}, \sin\dfrac{5\pi}{6}\right) = \left(-\dfrac{\sqrt{3}}{2}, \dfrac{1}{2}\right)$

$P_2 = \left(\cos\dfrac{-5\pi}{6}, \sin\dfrac{-5\pi}{6}\right) = \left(-\dfrac{\sqrt{3}}{2}, -\dfrac{1}{2}\right)$

21.

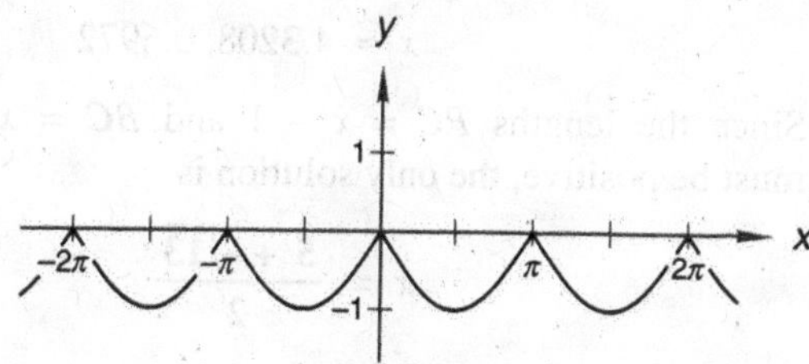

22. $g(x) = f\left(x - \dfrac{\pi}{4}\right) = 2 + \sin\left(x - \dfrac{\pi}{4}\right)$

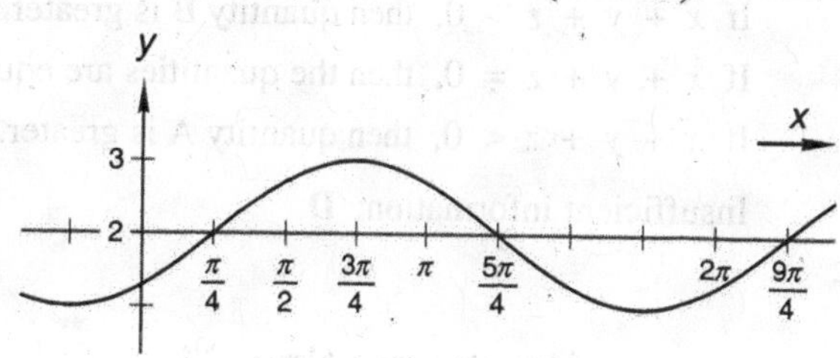

23. $x^2 + y^2 = 8$

$$y^2 = 8 - x^2$$
$$y = \pm\sqrt{8 - x^2}$$

Y₁=√(8–X²) Y₂=–Y₁ Y₃=ln(X)

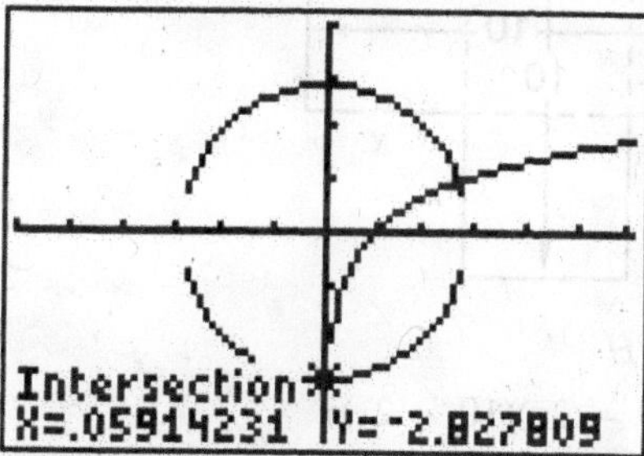

(0.0591, –2.8278)

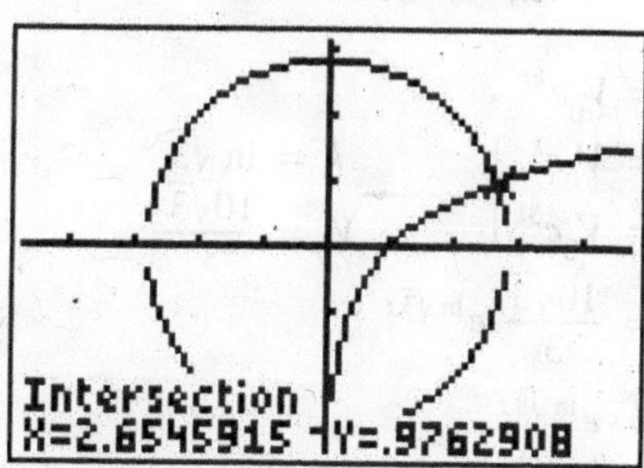

(2.6546, 0.9763)

24.
$$x^2 = (x-1)(x-1+x-2)$$
$$x^2 = (x-1)(2x-3)$$
$$x^2 = 2x^2 - 5x + 3$$
$$x^2 - 5x + 3 = 0$$
$$x = \frac{5 \pm \sqrt{13}}{2}$$
$$x \approx 4.3208, 0.6972$$

Since the lengths $PC = x - 1$ and $BC = x - 2$ must be positive, the only solution is

$$x = \mathbf{\frac{5 + \sqrt{13}}{2}}$$

25. Average of x, y, and z: $\dfrac{x+y+z}{3}$

If $x + y + z > 0$, then quantity B is greater.

If $x + y + z = 0$, then the quantities are equal.

If $x + y + z < 0$, then quantity A is greater.

Insufficient information: **D**

PROBLEM SET 31

1.

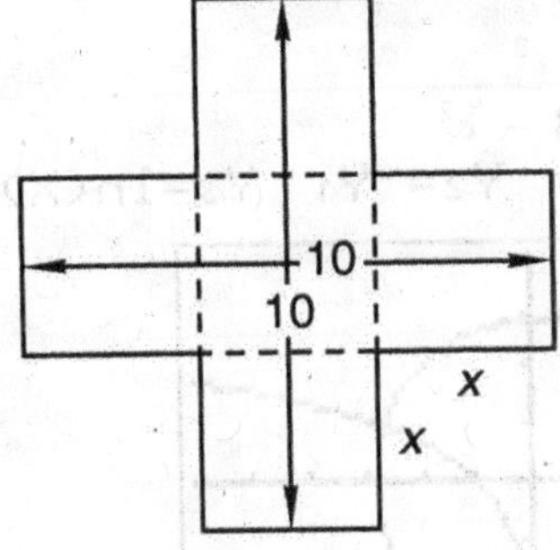

$$V = LWH$$
$$V = (10-2x)(10-2x)x$$
$$V = (100 - 40x + 4x^2)x$$
$$\mathbf{V = 4x^3 - 40x^2 + 100x}$$

2.
$$V_t = V_0 e^{kt}$$
$$\left.\begin{aligned} 10 &= V_0 e^k \\ 30 &= V_0 e^{3k} \end{aligned}\right\} \longrightarrow k = \ln\sqrt{3}, \quad V_0 = \frac{10\sqrt{3}}{3}$$
$$60 = \frac{10\sqrt{3}}{3} e^{\ln\sqrt{3}\,t}$$
$$6\sqrt{3} = e^{\ln\sqrt{3}\,t}$$
$$\ln 6\sqrt{3} = \ln\sqrt{3}\,t$$
$$t = \frac{\ln 6\sqrt{3}}{\ln\sqrt{3}} \approx \mathbf{4.2619\ minutes}$$

3.
$$y = x^3 e^x$$
$$y' = x^3 e^x + e^x(3x^2)$$
$$\mathbf{y' = x^2 e^x (x + 3)}$$

4.
$$y = -3t\cos t$$
$$\frac{dy}{dt} = -3t(-\sin t) + \cos t\,(-3)$$
$$\frac{dy}{dt} = \mathbf{3(t\sin t - \cos t)}$$

5.
$$f(x) = x^2 \ln|x|$$
$$f'(x) = x^2\left(\frac{1}{x}\right) + \ln|x|\,(2x)$$
$$f'(x) = x + 2x\ln|x|$$
$$f'(-2) = -2 - 4\ln 2$$
$$f'(-2) = \mathbf{-2 - \ln 16 \approx -4.7726}$$

6.
$$s = 2x^2 y$$
$$ds = 2x^2\,dy + y(4x)\,dx$$
$$ds = \mathbf{2x^2\,dy + 4xy\,dx}$$

7.
$$s = -x^{-1/2} + 2\cos x$$
$$s' = \frac{1}{2}x^{-3/2} - 2\sin x$$
$$s'' = \mathbf{-\frac{3}{4}x^{-5/2} - 2\cos x}$$

8.
$$f(t) = 3\sin t - \sqrt{2}e^t$$
$$f'(t) = 3\cos t - \sqrt{2}e^t$$
$$f''(t) = -3\sin t - \sqrt{2}e^t$$
$$f'''(t) = \mathbf{-3\cos t - \sqrt{2}e^t}$$

9.

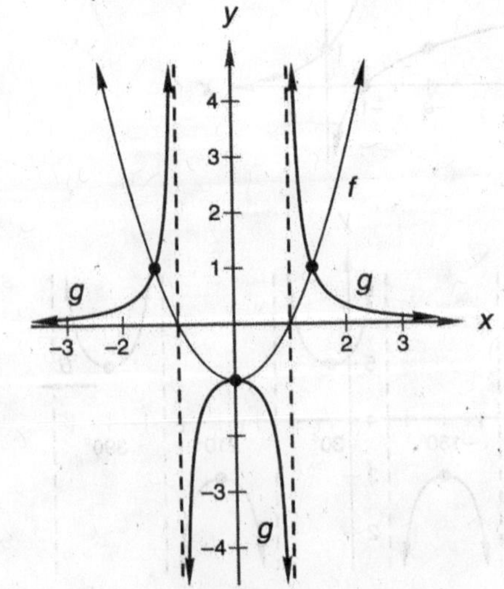

10.

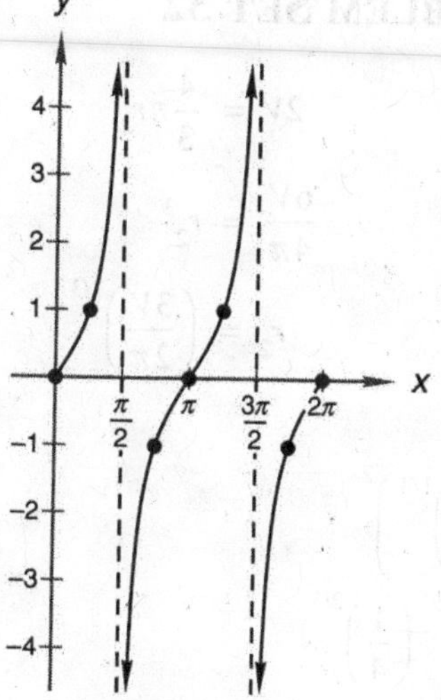

11.

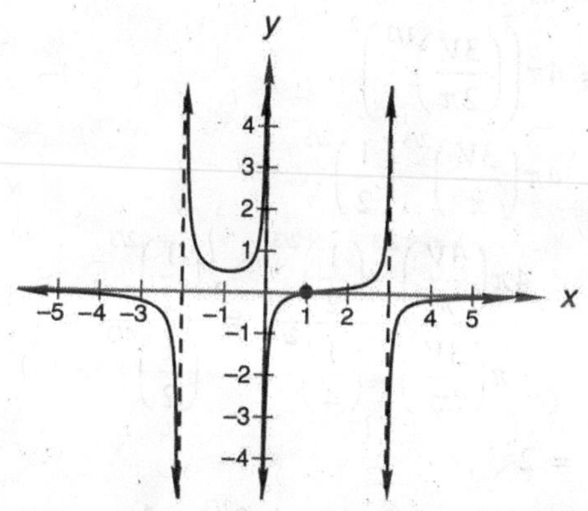

12.
$$y = x^{2/3}$$
$$y' = \frac{2}{3}x^{-1/3}$$
$$y'(8) = \frac{2}{3\sqrt[3]{8}} = \frac{1}{3}$$
$$y - 4 = \frac{1}{3}(x - 8)$$
$$y = \mathbf{\frac{1}{3}x + \frac{4}{3}}$$

13. Let `Y1=3√(X²)` and `Y2=(1/3)X+4/3`.

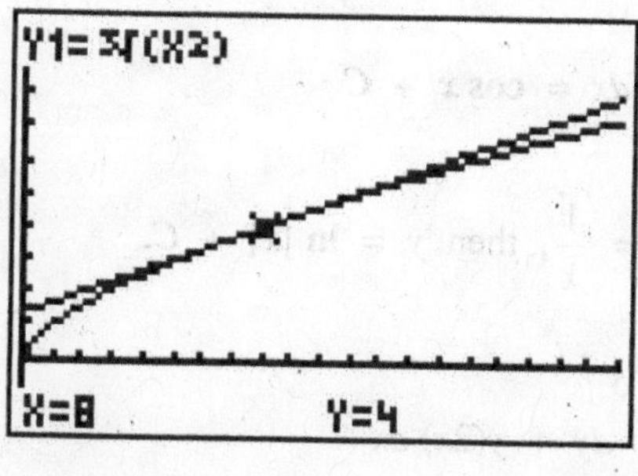

14. $\tan(A + B) = \dfrac{\tan A + \tan B}{1 - \tan A \tan B}$
$$= \frac{\frac{1}{2} + 4}{1 - \frac{1}{2}(4)} = \frac{\frac{9}{2}}{-1} = \mathbf{-\frac{9}{2}}$$

15. $\dfrac{3}{8} = \dfrac{r}{4}$
$$8r = 12$$
$$r = \frac{3}{2} \text{ cm}$$
$$V = \frac{1}{3}\pi r^2 h = \frac{1}{3}\pi\left(\frac{9}{4}\right)(4) = \mathbf{3\pi \text{ cm}^3}$$

16. If $0 < x < 2\pi$, then $0 < 3x < 6\pi$.
$$\sin(3x) = -\frac{\sqrt{2}}{2}$$
$$3x = \frac{5\pi}{4}, \frac{7\pi}{4}, \frac{13\pi}{4}, \frac{15\pi}{4}, \frac{21\pi}{4}, \frac{23\pi}{4}$$
$$x = \mathbf{\frac{5\pi}{12}, \frac{7\pi}{12}, \frac{13\pi}{12}, \frac{5\pi}{4}, \frac{7\pi}{4}, \frac{23\pi}{12}}$$

17. $y = f(x - 1) = |x - 1|$

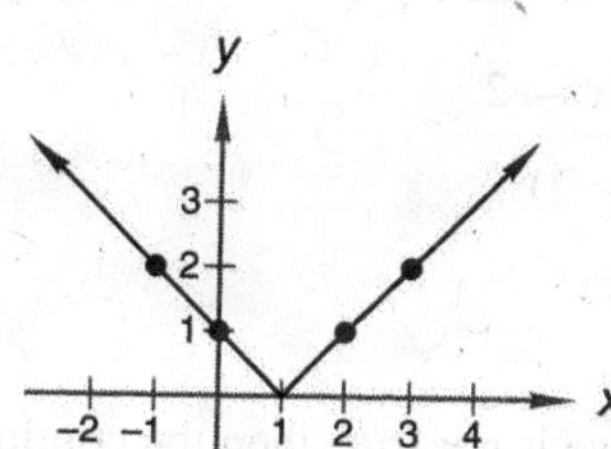

18.
$$4x^2 + y^2 - 2y = 3$$
$$4x^2 + (y^2 - 2y + 1) = 3 + 1$$
$$4x^2 + (y - 1)^2 = 4$$
$$x^2 + \frac{(y - 1)^2}{2^2} = 1$$

The equation represents an **ellipse** with its center at **(0, 1)**.

$$(y - 1)^2 = 4 - 4x^2$$
$$y - 1 = \pm\sqrt{4 - 4x^2}$$

`Y1=1+√(4-4X²)`   `Y2=1-√(4-4X²)`

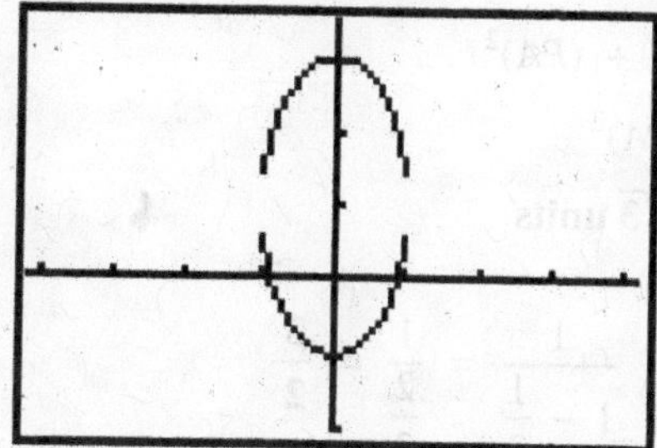

19. $2 \ln x - \ln\left(x + \frac{1}{2}\right) = \ln 2$

$$\ln x^2 - \ln\left(x + \frac{1}{2}\right) = \ln 2$$

$$\ln\left(\frac{x^2}{x + \frac{1}{2}}\right) = \ln 2$$

$$2x + 1 = x^2$$

$$x^2 - 2x - 1 = 0$$

$$x = \frac{2 \pm \sqrt{4 - 4(1)(-1)}}{2}$$

$$x = 1 + \sqrt{2} \approx \mathbf{2.4142}$$

20. $\lim_{x \to -2} \frac{2x^2 + 3x - 2}{x^2 + 4} = \frac{8 - 6 - 2}{8} = \mathbf{0}$

21. Possible zeros: $x = \frac{\pm 1, \pm 2}{\pm 1} = \pm 1, \pm 2$

1⌋	1	−1	2	−2
	↓	1	0	2
	1	0	2	[0]

$$y = x^3 - x^2 + 2x - 2$$

$$y = (x - 1)(x^2 + 2)$$

Zero: **1**

22. If the contrapositive is not true, then the conditional statement is not true.

23. The absolute value of any number is greater than −1. $\mathbb{Z}$

24. 

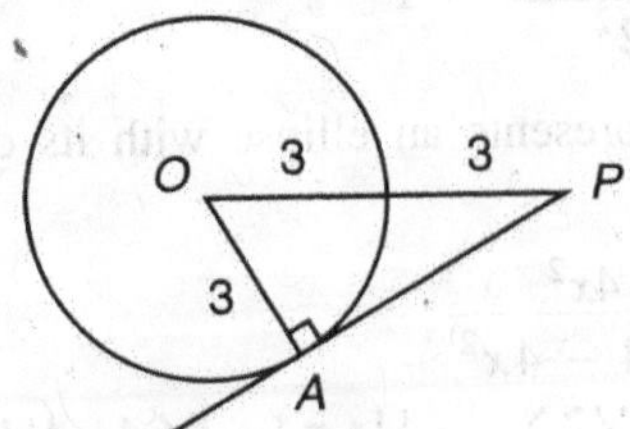

$$6^2 = 3^2 + (PA)^2$$

$$27 = (PA)^2$$

$$PA = \mathbf{3\sqrt{3}\ units}$$

25. $\frac{a}{1 - r} = \frac{1}{1 - \frac{1}{3}} = \frac{1}{\frac{2}{3}} = \mathbf{\frac{3}{2}}$

PROBLEM SET 32

1. $V = \frac{4}{3}\pi r_1^3$ $\qquad$ $2V = \frac{4}{3}\pi r_2^3$

$\frac{3V}{4\pi} = r_1^3$ $\qquad$ $\frac{6V}{4\pi} = r_2^3$

$r_1 = \left(\frac{3V}{4\pi}\right)^{1/3}$ $\qquad$ $r_2 = \left(\frac{3V}{2\pi}\right)^{1/3}$

$$A_1 = 4\pi r_1^2$$

$$= 4\pi\left(\left(\frac{3V}{4\pi}\right)^{1/3}\right)^2$$

$$= 4\pi\left(\frac{3V}{\pi}\right)^{2/3}\left(\frac{1}{4}\right)^{2/3}$$

$$A_2 = 4\pi r_2^2$$

$$= 4\pi\left(\left(\frac{3V}{2\pi}\right)^{1/3}\right)^2$$

$$= 4\pi\left(\frac{3V}{\pi}\right)^{2/3}\left(\frac{1}{2}\right)^{2/3}$$

$$\frac{A_2}{A_1} = \frac{4\pi\left(\frac{3V}{\pi}\right)^{2/3}\left(\frac{1}{2}\right)^{2/3}}{4\pi\left(\frac{3V}{\pi}\right)^{2/3}\left(\frac{1}{4}\right)^{2/3}} = \frac{\left(\frac{1}{2}\right)^{2/3}}{\left(\frac{1}{2}\right)^{4/3}} = \left(\frac{1}{2}\right)^{-2/3}$$

$$= 2^{2/3}$$

The ratio of surface areas is $\mathbf{2^{2/3} : 1}$.

2. (a) $\mathbf{(y + 4)^2 + (x + 4)^2 = 12^2}$

(b) $\mathbf{\frac{y}{4} = \frac{4}{x}}$

3. $\mathbf{x^5 + C}$

4. $\mathbf{t^3 + C}$

5. $\int \cos x\, dx = \mathbf{\sin x + C}$

6. $\int e^t\, dt = \mathbf{e^t + C}$

7. $\int -\sin x\, dx = \mathbf{\cos x + C}$

8. If $\frac{dy}{dx} = \frac{1}{x}$, then $y = \mathbf{\ln |x| + C}$.

9. $u = x^2 y$

$$du = x^2\, dy + y(2x)\, dx$$

$$du = \mathbf{x(x\, dy + 2y\, dx)}$$

10. $h(x) = e^x \sin x$

$h'(x) = e^x \cos x + \sin x\,(e^x)$

$h'(x) = e^x(\cos x + \sin x)$

11. $y = x \ln x$

$\frac{dy}{dx} = x\left(\frac{1}{x}\right) + \ln x = 1 + \ln x$

$\left.\frac{dy}{dx}\right|_{2.5} = 1 + \ln 2.5 \approx 1.9163$

12. $f(x) = x^2 + x - 2$

$f(x) = (x + 2)(x - 1)$

$f\left(-\frac{1}{2}\right) = \frac{1}{4} - \frac{1}{2} - 2$

$f\left(-\frac{1}{2}\right) = -\frac{9}{4}$

Vertex: $\left(-\frac{1}{2}, -\frac{9}{4}\right)$

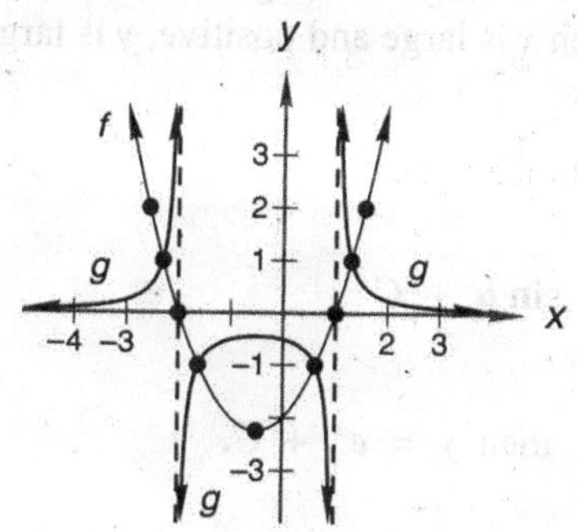

13.

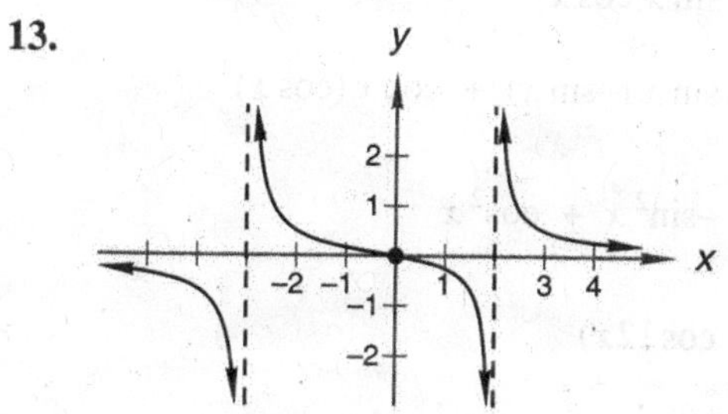

14. $y = 2x^{3/4} - 4x^{-1}$

$\frac{dy}{dx} = \frac{3}{2}x^{-1/4} + 4x^{-2}$

15. $x^2 - (y^2 - 2y) = 5$

$x^2 - (y^2 - 2y + 1) = 5 - 1$

$x^2 - (y - 1)^2 = 4$

$\frac{x^2}{2^2} - \frac{(y - 1)^2}{2^2} = 1$

The equation represents a hyperbola with its center at **(0, 1)**.

$(y - 1)^2 = x^2 - 4$

$y - 1 = \pm\sqrt{x^2 - 4}$

```
Y1=1+√(X² - 4)
Y2=1-√(X² - 4)
```

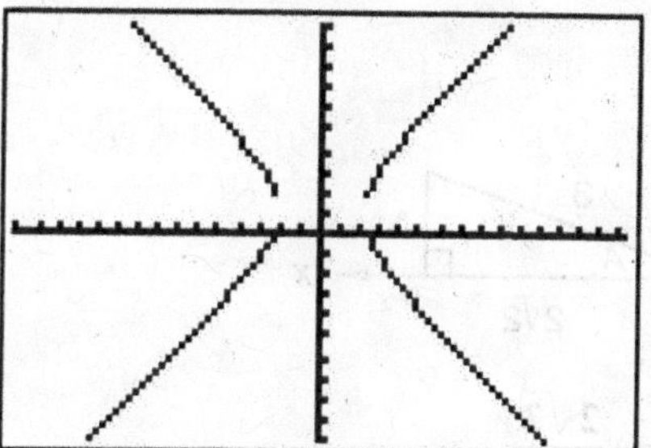

16. $\cos(2A) = 1 - 2\sin^2 A$

$2\sin^2 A = 1 - \cos(2A)$

$\sin^2 A = \frac{1}{2} - \frac{1}{2}\cos(2A)$

$\sin A = \pm\sqrt{\frac{1}{2} - \frac{1}{2}\cos(2A)}$

$\sin\frac{x}{2} = \pm\sqrt{\frac{1}{2} - \frac{1}{2}\cos x}$

$\cos(2A) = 2\cos^2 A - 1$

$2\cos^2 A = 1 + \cos(2A)$

$\cos^2 A = \frac{1}{2} + \frac{1}{2}\cos(2A)$

$\cos A = \pm\sqrt{\frac{1}{2} + \frac{1}{2}\cos(2A)}$

$\cos\frac{x}{2} = \pm\sqrt{\frac{1}{2} + \frac{1}{2}\cos x}$

17. $\lim_{x\to\infty} \frac{3x - \frac{5}{x^2}}{\frac{1}{x^2} - 1} = \frac{\infty - 0}{0 - 1} = \frac{\infty}{-1} = -\infty$

18. $f(3) = 5$

19.

$\lim_{x\to 0^+} f(x) = 1 \qquad \lim_{x\to 0^-} f(x) = 0$

20. $|x - 1| < 0.4$

"x is less than 0.4 away from 1"

$\{x \in \mathbb{R} \mid \mathbf{0.6 < x < 1.4}\}$

21. Since $\sin A$ and $\cos A$ are both positive, A must be a first quadrant angle.

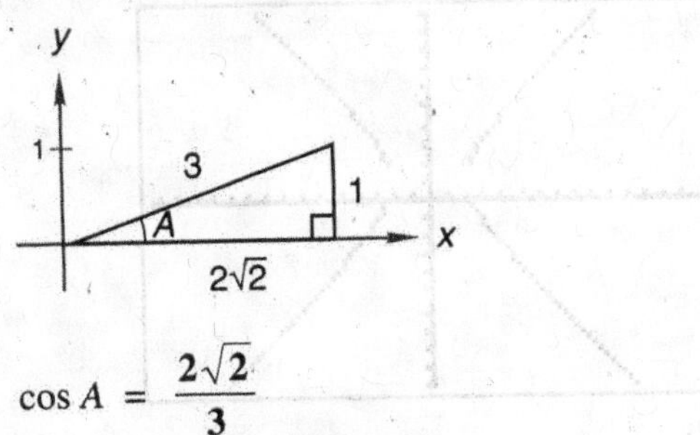

$$\cos A = \frac{\mathbf{2\sqrt{2}}}{\mathbf{3}}$$

22. $(\sin -A)\left[\cos\left(\frac{\pi}{2} - A\right)\right](\cos A)$

$$= (-\sin A)(\sin A)(\cos A)$$

$$= -\left(\frac{1}{3}\right)^2 \frac{2\sqrt{2}}{3} = -\frac{\mathbf{2\sqrt{2}}}{\mathbf{27}}$$

23.

$$2\log_2 x + \log_2 9 = 1$$
$$\log_2 x^2 + \log_2 9 = 1$$
$$\log_2 (9x^2) = 1$$
$$9x^2 = 2$$
$$x = \frac{\mathbf{\sqrt{2}}}{\mathbf{3}}$$

24.

$$m_1 = \frac{a - 0}{a - 0} = \frac{a}{a} = \mathbf{1}$$

$$m_2 = \frac{a - 0}{0 - a} = \frac{a}{-a} = \mathbf{-1}$$

Since the slopes are negative reciprocals of each other, the diagonals are perpendicular.

25. $\dfrac{a}{1 - r} = \dfrac{1}{1 - \frac{1}{2}} = \dfrac{1}{\frac{1}{2}} = \mathbf{2}$

Problem Set 33

1. $A = \frac{1}{2}bh = \frac{1}{2}(2)(y) = \mathbf{y\ units^2}$

2.

$$I_t = I_0 e^{kt}$$
$$20 = 10e^k$$
$$2 = e^k$$
$$k = \ln 2$$
$$I_5 = 10e^{(\ln 2)5} = 10e^{\ln 2^5} = 10(2^5) = \mathbf{320}$$

3.

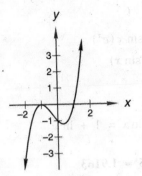

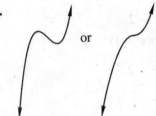

4. or

5. $y = -x(x - 2)^2$ is a negative cubic which crosses the x-axis at $x = 0$ and touches the x-axis at $x = 2$. When x is large and negative, y is large and positive. When x is large and positive, y is large and negative.

The correct choice is **C**.

6. $\int \cos u\, du = \mathbf{\sin u + C}$

7. If $\frac{dy}{dx} = e^x$, then $\mathbf{y = e^x + C}$.

8.

$$y = \sin x \cos x$$
$$\frac{dy}{dx} = \sin x(-\sin x) + \cos x(\cos x)$$
$$\frac{dy}{dx} = -\sin^2 x + \cos^2 x$$
$$\frac{dy}{dx} = \mathbf{\cos(2x)}$$

9.

$$f(t) = 3e^t \cos t$$
$$f'(t) = 3e^t(-\sin t) + \cos t\,(3e^t)$$
$$f'(t) = 3e^t(\cos t - \sin t)$$
$$f'(6) = 3e^6(\cos 6 - \sin 6) \approx \mathbf{1500.2538}$$

10.

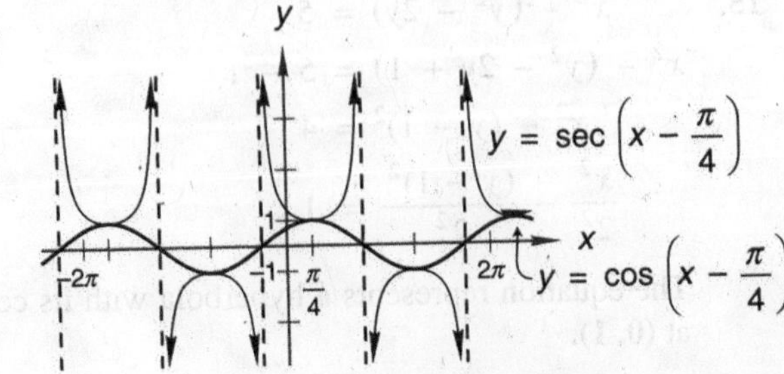

11. $y = 2e^x - \ln u + 4 \sin t$

$$dy = \mathbf{2e^x\,dx - \frac{1}{u}\,du + 4 \cos t\,dt}$$

12.

$$y = \sin x$$
$$y' = \cos x$$
$$y'(16.3) = \cos 16.3$$
$$y - \sin 16.3 = (\cos 16.3)(x - 16.3)$$
$$\mathbf{y \approx -0.8298x + 12.9678}$$

13.

$$f(x) = 2 \sin x$$
$$f'(x) = \mathbf{2 \cos x}$$
$$f''(x) = \mathbf{-2 \sin x}$$
$$f'''(x) = \mathbf{-2 \cos x}$$

14. (a) $(x + 4)^2 + (y + 4)^2 = 12^2$

$$(y + 4)^2 = 144 - (x + 4)^2$$
$$y + 4 = \sqrt{144 - (x + 4)^2}$$

Y1=-4+√(144-(X+4)²)

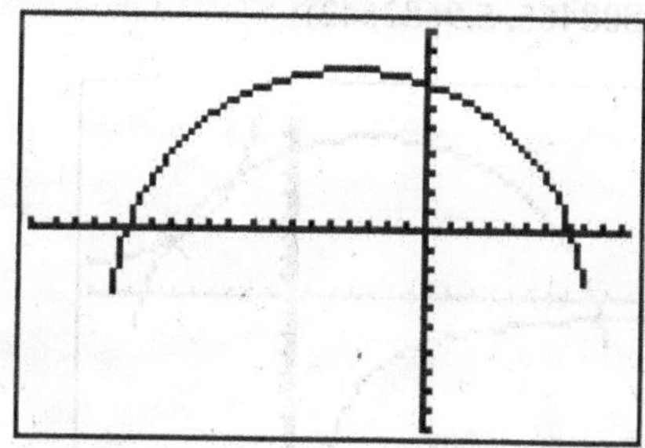

(b) Y2=16/X

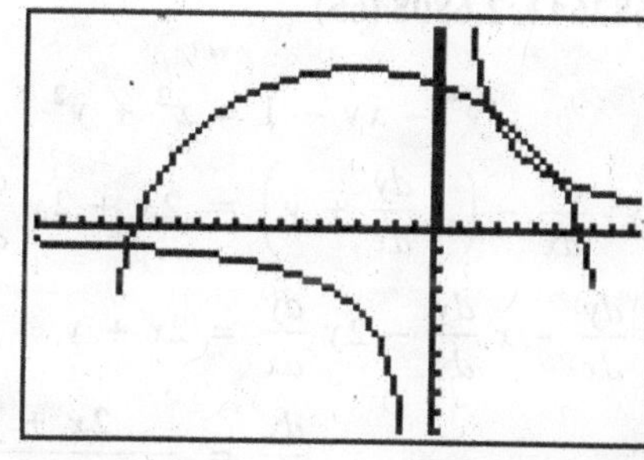

(c)

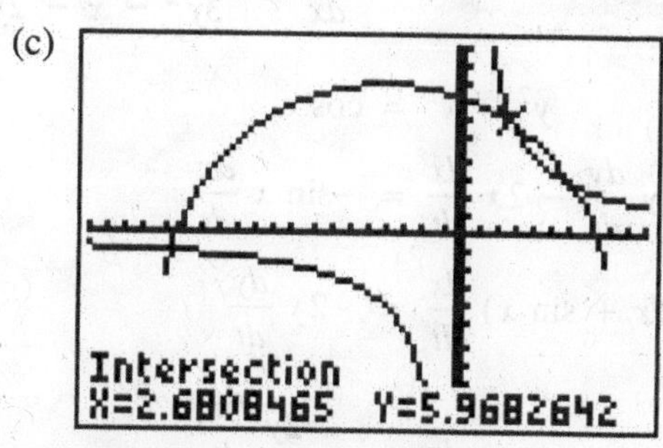

(2.6808465, 5.9682642)

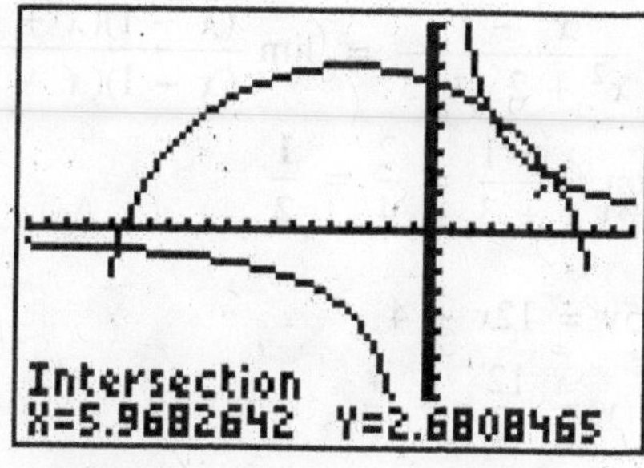

(5.9682642, 2.6808465)

15. $\displaystyle\lim_{h\to 0} \frac{e^{e+h} - e^e}{h} = \frac{d}{dx}e^x\bigg|_e = \mathbf{e^e}$

16. $\log_3 10 = \dfrac{\ln 10}{\ln 3} \approx \mathbf{2.0959}$

17.

$$\tan(2A) = \frac{\sin(2A)}{\cos(2A)}$$
$$\tan(2A) = \frac{2 \sin A \cos A}{\cos^2 A - \sin^2 A}$$
$$\tan(2A) = \frac{\dfrac{2 \sin A \cos A}{\cos^2 A}}{\dfrac{\cos^2 A}{\cos^2 A} - \dfrac{\sin^2 A}{\cos^2 A}}$$
$$\mathbf{\tan(2A) = \frac{2 \tan A}{1 - \tan^2 A}}$$

18.

$$y = \arcsin x$$
$$\mathbf{x = \sin y}$$

19. $h(x) = g(2 \sin x) = |2 \sin x|$

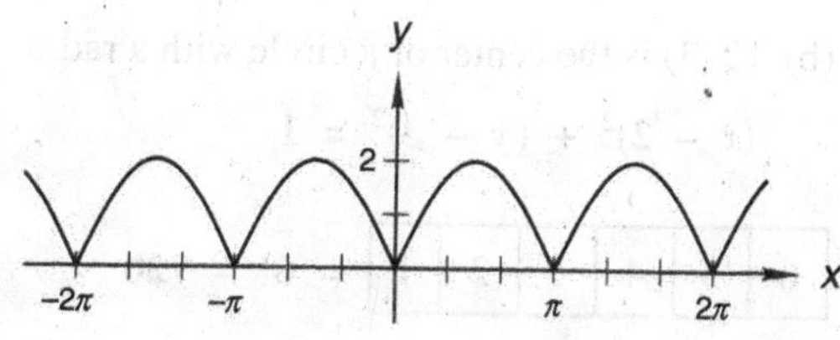

20. $1 + 2(\sin -x)\left[\cos\left(\dfrac{\pi}{2} - x\right)\right] = 1 - 2 \sin x \sin x$

$$= 1 - 2\sin^2 x$$
$$= \cos(2x)$$

21. If $0 < x < 2\pi$, then $0 < 3x < 6\pi$.

$$\cos(3x) = \frac{1}{2}$$
$$3x = \frac{\pi}{3}, \frac{5\pi}{3}, \frac{7\pi}{3}, \frac{11\pi}{3}, \frac{13\pi}{3}, \frac{17\pi}{3}$$
$$x = \mathbf{\frac{\pi}{9}, \frac{5\pi}{9}, \frac{7\pi}{9}, \frac{11\pi}{9}, \frac{13\pi}{9}, \frac{17\pi}{9}}$$

22. $\lim_{x\to 1} \frac{x^2 - 1}{x^2 + 2x - 3} = \lim_{x\to 1} \frac{(x-1)(x+1)}{(x-1)(x+3)}$

$= \lim_{x\to 1} \frac{x+1}{x+3} = \frac{2}{4} = \mathbf{\frac{1}{2}}$

23. (a) $5y = 12x + 4$

$y = \frac{12}{5}x + \frac{4}{5}$

$m = \frac{12}{5}, \perp m = -\frac{5}{12}$

$y - 3 = -\frac{5}{12}(x - 2)$

$y = -\frac{5}{12}x + \frac{23}{6}$

$\frac{12}{5}x + \frac{4}{5} = -\frac{5}{12}x + \frac{23}{6}$

$\frac{169}{60}x = \frac{91}{30}$

$x = \frac{182}{169} = \frac{14}{13}$

Intersection: $\left(\frac{14}{13}, \frac{44}{13}\right)$

$d = \sqrt{\left(2 - \frac{14}{13}\right)^2 + \left(3 - \frac{44}{13}\right)^2}$

$= \sqrt{\left(\frac{12}{13}\right)^2 + \left(-\frac{5}{13}\right)^2}$

$= \sqrt{\frac{144 + 25}{169}} = \mathbf{1\ unit}$

(b) (2, 3) is the center of a circle with a radius of 1.

$\mathbf{(x - 2)^2 + (y - 3)^2 = 1}$

24.

6	5	4	3	2	1

$= 6! = \mathbf{720}$

25. This is an independent event: $\mathbf{\frac{1}{2}}$

PROBLEM SET 34

1. (a) $\mathbf{(x + 4)^2 + (y + 4)^2 = 144}$

(b) $\frac{y}{4} = \frac{4}{x}$

$xy = 16$

$\mathbf{y = \frac{16}{x}}$

(c) $(y + 4)^2 = 144 - (x + 4)^2$

$y = -4 \pm \sqrt{144 - (x + 4)^2}$

Y1=-4+√(144-(X+4)²) Y2=16/X

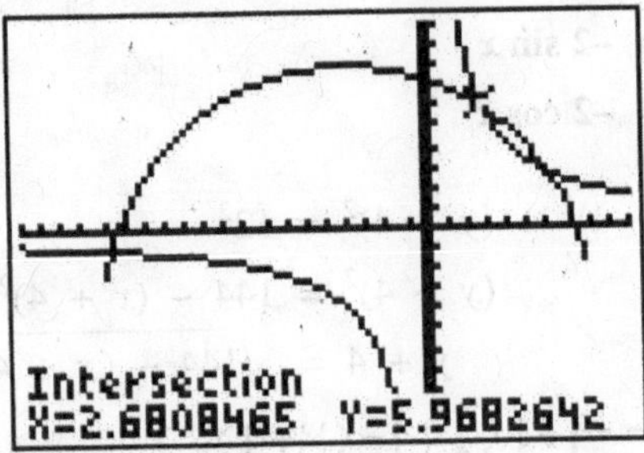

(2.6808465, 5.9682642)

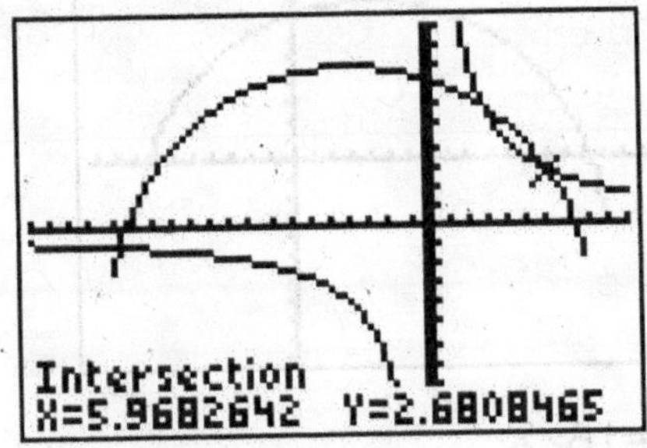

(5.9682642, 2.6808465)

2. $y^3 - xy - 1 = x^2 + y^2$

$3y^2 \frac{dy}{dx} - \left(x\frac{dy}{dx} + y\right) = 2x + 2y\frac{dy}{dx}$

$3y^2 \frac{dy}{dx} - x\frac{dy}{dx} - 2y\frac{dy}{dx} = 2x + y$

$\frac{dy}{dx} = \mathbf{\frac{2x + y}{3y^2 - x - 2y}}$

3. $y^2 - x^2 = \cos x$

$2y\frac{dy}{dt} - 2x\frac{dx}{dt} = -\sin x\frac{dx}{dt}$

$(-2x + \sin x)\frac{dx}{dt} = -2y\frac{dy}{dt}$

$\frac{dx}{dt} = \mathbf{\frac{2y\frac{dy}{dt}}{2x - \sin x}}$

4. $x^2 + y^2 = 1$

$$2x + 2y\frac{dy}{dx} = 0$$

$$\frac{dy}{dx} = \frac{-x}{y}$$

$$\text{slope} = \frac{\frac{\sqrt{2}}{2}}{\frac{\sqrt{2}}{2}} = \mathbf{1}$$

5.

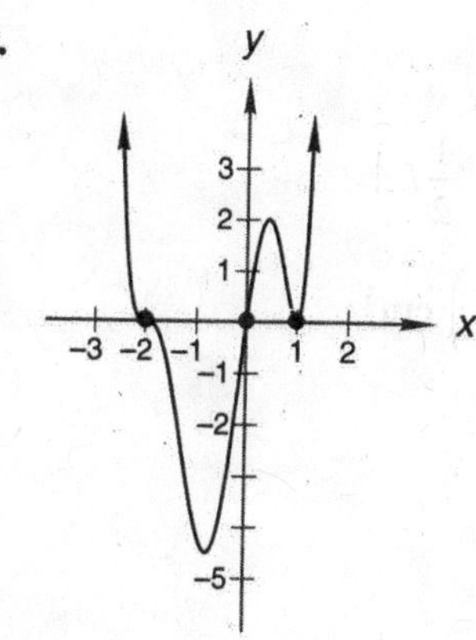

6. $\bar{x} = \frac{-b}{na} = \frac{-1}{3(-2)} = \frac{1}{6}$

Inflection point: $\left(\frac{1}{6}, 1\frac{5}{27}\right)$

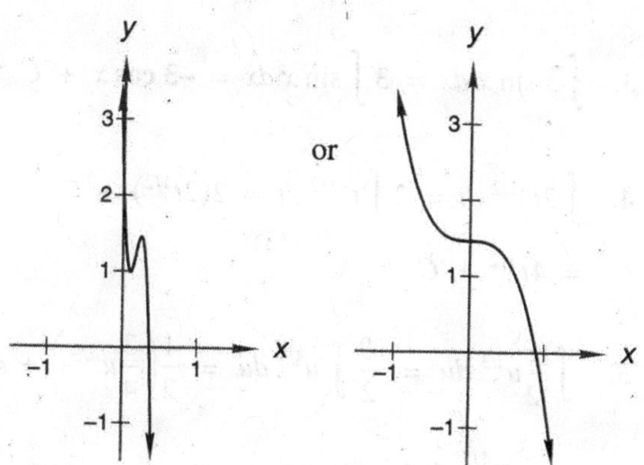

7. $\mathbf{F(x) = x^3 + C}$

8. $\int 5x^4\,dx = \mathbf{x^5 + C}$

9. $\int e^t\,dt = \mathbf{e^t + C}$

10. $\int -\sin u\,du = \mathbf{\cos u + C}$

11. $y = x^3 \cos x$

$y' = x^3(-\sin x) + \cos x\,(3x^2)$

$\mathbf{y' = x^2(-x \sin x + 3 \cos x)}$

12. $s = -3u^2v$

$ds = (-3u^2)\,dv + v(-6u\,du)$

$\mathbf{ds = -3u(u\,dv + 2v\,du)}$

13. $y = 2\ln x + 4x^{2/3} - \frac{1}{3}e^x$

$$\frac{dy}{dx} = \mathbf{\frac{2}{x} + \frac{8}{3}x^{-1/3} - \frac{1}{3}e^x}$$

14. $s(t) = s_0 + v_0t + \frac{1}{2}gt^2$

$s'(t) = v_0 + gt$

$s''(t) = \mathbf{g}$

15. $f(x) = x^2 - 2x - 1$

$= (x^2 - 2x + 1) - 1 - 1$

$= (x - 1)^2 - 2$

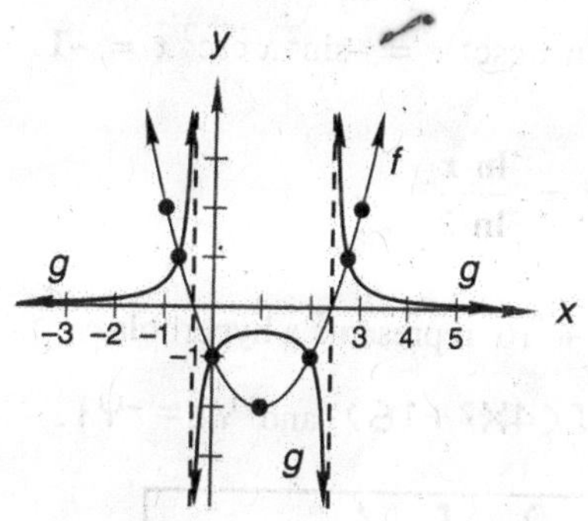

16.

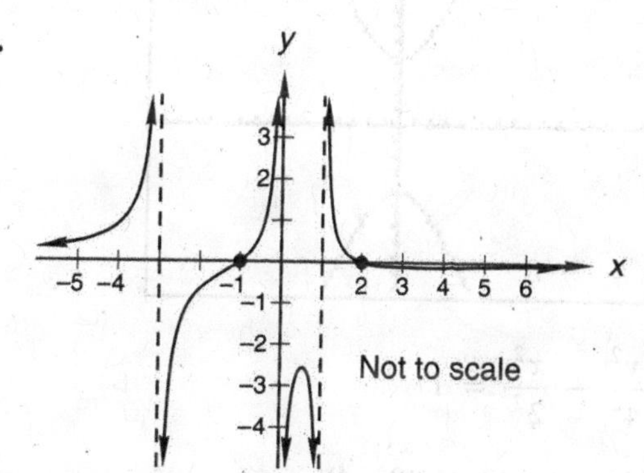

17. $f(3) = \mathbf{4}$

18. $g(x) = f(2x) = \sin(2x)$

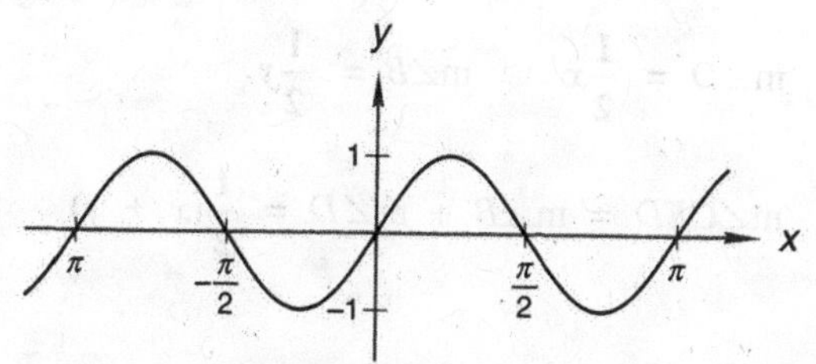

19. Let `Y1=X²sin(1/X)`.

X	Y1
-.03	-8E-4
-.02	1E-4
-.01	5.1E-5
0	ERROR
.01	-5E-5
.02	-1E-4
.03	8.5E-4

X=0

$$\lim_{x\to 0}\left[x^2 \sin\left(\frac{1}{x}\right)\right] = \mathbf{0}$$

20. $e^x = y$

$$\mathbf{x = \ln y}$$

21. $(\sin -x)\left[\cos\left(\frac{\pi}{2} - x\right)\right]\left[\sec^2\left(\frac{\pi}{2} - x\right)\right]$

$$= -\sin x \sin x \csc^2 x = -\sin^2 x \csc^2 x = \mathbf{-1}$$

22. $y = \log_2 x = \mathbf{\dfrac{\ln x}{\ln 2}}$

23. $y^2 = 4x^2 + 16$ represents a hyperbola.

Let `Y1=√(4X²+16)` and `Y2=-Y1`.

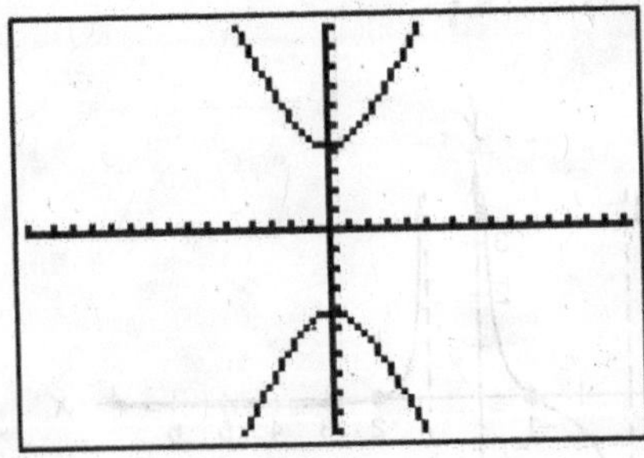

$$\frac{y^2}{4^2} - \frac{x^2}{2^2} = 1$$

Vertices: **(0, 4), (0, −4)**

24. $\dfrac{7!}{4!\,3!} = 7 \cdot 5 = \mathbf{35}$ **ways**

25. $m\angle D = \mathbf{\frac{1}{2}x}$ $\qquad m\angle B = \mathbf{\frac{1}{2}y}$

$$m\angle CED = m\angle B + m\angle D = \mathbf{\frac{1}{2}(x + y)}$$

PROBLEM SET 35

1. $L = w$

$$SA = 2Lw + 2wH + 2LH$$
$$100 = 2L^2 + 2LH + 2LH$$
$$100 = 2L^2 + 4LH$$
$$4LH = 100 - 2L^2$$
$$H = 25L^{-1} - \frac{1}{2}L$$

$$V = LwH$$
$$= L(L)\left(25L^{-1} - \frac{1}{2}L\right)$$
$$= \mathbf{\left(25L - \frac{1}{2}L^3\right)\ cm^3}$$

2. $S_t = S_0 e^{kt}$

$$60 = 50e^k$$
$$\frac{6}{5} = e^k$$
$$k = \ln 1.2$$
$$S_6 = 50e^{(\ln 1.2)(6)}$$
$$= 50(1.2)^6 = \mathbf{149.2992\ fathoms/s}$$

3. $\int 3 \sin x\, dx = 3\int \sin x\, dx = \mathbf{-3\cos x + C}$

4. $\int 2t^{-1/2}\, dt = 2\int t^{-1/2}\, dt = 2(2t^{1/2}) + C$

$$= \mathbf{4t^{1/2} + C}$$

5. $\int \frac{1}{2}u^{1/3}\, du = \frac{1}{2}\int u^{1/3}\, du = \frac{1}{2}\left(\frac{3}{4}u^{4/3}\right) + C$

$$= \mathbf{\frac{3}{8}u^{4/3} + C}$$

6. $\int 3x\, dx = 3\int x\, dx = 3\left(\frac{1}{2}x^2\right) + C = \mathbf{\frac{3}{2}x^2 + C}$

7. $$2x^2y + y^2 = \cos x$$

$$(2x^2)\frac{dy}{dx} + y(4x) + 2y\frac{dy}{dx} = -\sin x$$
$$\frac{dy}{dx}(2x^2 + 2y) = -\sin x - 4xy$$
$$\frac{dy}{dx} = \mathbf{\frac{-\sin x - 4xy}{2x^2 + 2y}}$$

8. $$u^2 + v^2 = 2uv$$
$$2u\frac{du}{dt} + 2v\frac{dv}{dt} = 2u\frac{dv}{dt} + 2v\frac{du}{dt}$$
$$\frac{du}{dt}(2u - 2v) = 2u\frac{dv}{dt} - 2v\frac{dv}{dt}$$
$$\frac{du}{dt} = \frac{2(u - v)\frac{dv}{dt}}{2(u - v)}$$
$$\frac{du}{dt} = \frac{dv}{dt}$$

9. $$y^2 - x^2 = 1$$
$$2y\frac{dy}{dx} - 2x = 0$$
$$\frac{dy}{dx} = \frac{x}{y}$$
$$\left.\frac{dy}{dx}\right|_{(0,1)} = \frac{0}{1} = 0$$
$$\mathbf{y = 1}$$

10. The graph of $y = x^3(x + 2)^2$ crosses the x-axis at $x = 0$ and touches the x-axis at $x = -2$. When x is large and positive, y is large and positive. When x is large and negative, y is large and negative.

The correct choice is **A**.

11. or or or

12. $$s(t) = t^{1/3} - 2t^{1/2} + 3t^{-1}$$
$$s'(t) = \frac{1}{3}t^{-2/3} - t^{-1/2} - 3t^{-2}$$
$$s''(t) = -\frac{2}{9}t^{-5/3} + \frac{1}{2}t^{-3/2} + 6t^{-3}$$
$$s''(2) = -\frac{2}{9}(2)^{-5/3} + \frac{1}{2}(2)^{-3/2} + 6(2)^{-3}$$
$$s''(2) \approx \mathbf{0.8568}$$

13. $$\lim_{\Delta x \to 0} \frac{e^{x+\Delta x} - e^x}{\Delta x} = \frac{d}{dx}e^x = \mathbf{e^x}$$

14. $$\lim_{x \to 2} \frac{x^2 + x - 6}{x - 2} = \lim_{x \to 2} \frac{(x + 3)(x - 2)}{x - 2}$$
$$= \lim_{x \to 2} (x + 3) = \mathbf{5}$$

15. $$\lim_{x \to \infty} \frac{x + 1}{x} = \lim_{x \to \infty} \frac{1 + \frac{1}{x}}{1} = \frac{1 + 0}{1} = \mathbf{1}$$

16.

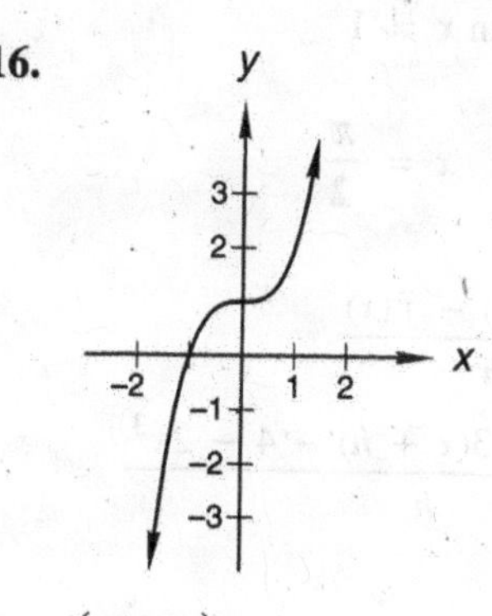

$(-\infty, \infty)$

17. $$8^{2x-1} = 4$$
$$(2^3)^{2x-1} = 2^2$$
$$2^{6x-3} = 2^2$$
$$6x - 3 = 2$$
$$x = \mathbf{\frac{5}{6}}$$

18.

$\underline{-1}|$	2	0	1	k
	↓	−2	2	−3
	2	−2	3	$\boxed{0}$

$$k - 3 = 0$$
$$\mathbf{k = 3}$$

19.

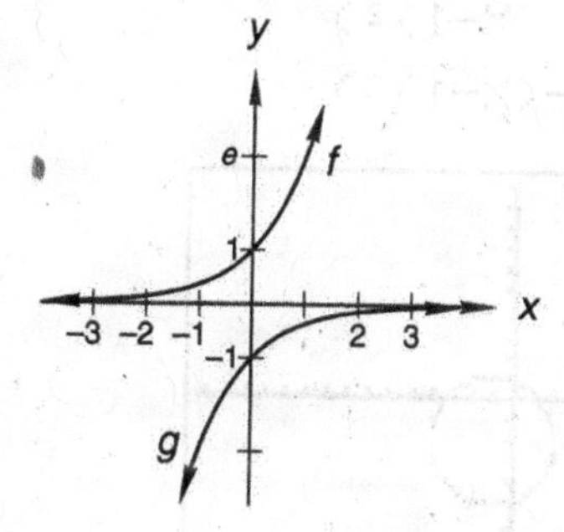

20. $$g(x) = -3 + 2f\left(x - \frac{\pi}{3}\right)$$
$$= \mathbf{-3 + 2\sin\left(x - \frac{\pi}{3}\right)}$$

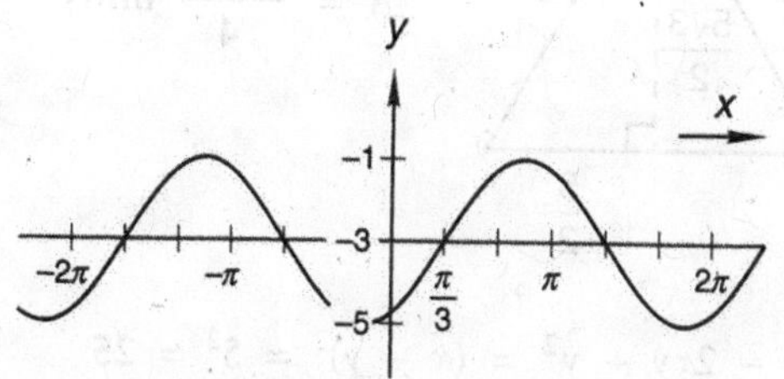

21. $2\sin^2 x - 3\sin x + 1 = 0$

$(2\sin x - 1)(\sin x - 1) = 0$

$\sin x = \frac{1}{2}$ $\quad\quad$ $\sin x = 1$

$x = \frac{\pi}{6}, \frac{5\pi}{6}$ $\quad\quad$ $x = \frac{\pi}{2}$

22. $f'(x) = \lim_{h\to 0} \frac{f(x+h) - f(x)}{h}$

$= \lim_{h\to 0}\left[\frac{2(x+h)^3 + 3(x+h) - 4 - 2x^3}{h} + \frac{-3x+4}{h}\right]$

$= \lim_{h\to 0}\left[\frac{2x^3 + 6x^2h + 6xh^2 + 2h^3 + 3x + 3h}{h} + \frac{-4 - 2x^3 - 3x + 4}{h}\right]$

$= \lim_{h\to 0} \frac{6x^2h + 6xh^2 + 2h^3 + 3h}{h}$

$= \lim_{h\to 0} (6x^2 + 6xh + 2h^2 + 3) = \mathbf{6x^2 + 3}$

23. $x^2 - 2x + y^2 + 4y = 4$

$(x-1)^2 - 1 + (y+2)^2 - 4 = 4$

$(x-1)^2 + (y+2)^2 = 9$

This represents a circle centered at **(1, –2).**

```
Y1=-2+√(9-(X-1)²)
Y2=-2-√(9-(X-1)²)
```

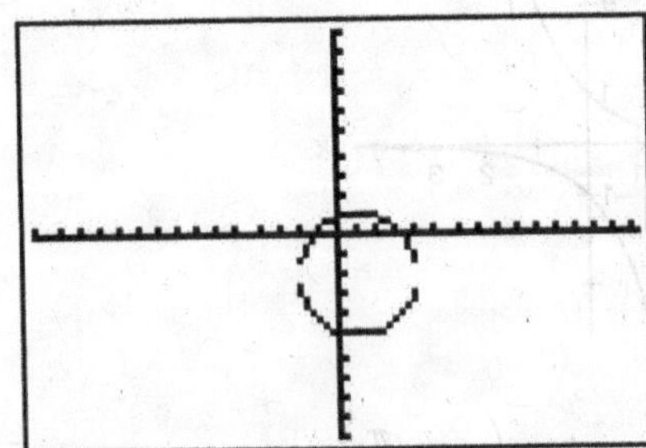

24.

$A = \frac{1}{2}(5)\left(\frac{5\sqrt{3}}{2}\right)$

$A = \mathbf{\frac{25\sqrt{3}}{4}}$ **units²**

25. $x^2 - 2xy + y^2 = (x-y)^2 = 5^2 = \mathbf{25}$

PROBLEM SET 36

1. Circumference of circle:

$C = 2\pi r = 20\pi$ cm

Circumference of cone:

$\frac{2\pi - x}{2\pi}(20\pi) = \mathbf{10(2\pi - x)}$ **cm**

Radius of cone:

$2r\pi = 10(2\pi - x)$

$r\pi = 5(2\pi - x)$

$r = \frac{10\pi - 5x}{\pi}$

$r = \left(\mathbf{10 - \frac{5}{\pi}x}\right)$ **cm**

2. $y = \frac{1}{3}x^3 - x$

$y' = x^2 - 1$

$0 = x^2 - 1$

$0 = (x+1)(x-1)$

Critical numbers: $x = \mathbf{-1, 1}$

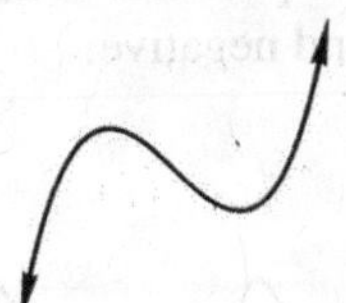

Local maximum: $\left(\mathbf{-1, \frac{2}{3}}\right)$

Local minimum: $\left(\mathbf{1, -\frac{2}{3}}\right)$

3. $f(x) = x^3 - \frac{9}{2}x^2 + 6x + 3$

$f'(x) = 3x^2 - 9x + 6$

$0 = 3(x^2 - 3x + 2)$

$0 = (x-2)(x-1)$

Critical numbers: $x = \mathbf{1, 2}$

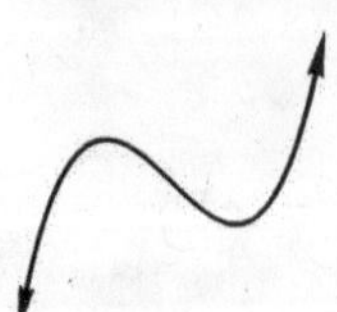

Local maximum: $\left(\mathbf{1, \frac{11}{2}}\right)$

Local minimum: (2, 5)

4. $\int \frac{1}{20} u^{1/2}\, du = \frac{1}{20} \int u^{1/2}\, du$

$= \frac{1}{20}\left(\frac{2}{3} u^{3/2}\right) + C = \mathbf{\frac{1}{30} u^{3/2} + C}$

5. $\int 2 \cos t\, dt = 2 \int \cos t\, dt = \mathbf{2 \sin t + C}$

6. $\int 3\, dx = 3 \int dx = \mathbf{3x + C}$

7. $y^3 + xy = e^x$

$3y^2 \frac{dy}{dx} + x \frac{dy}{dx} + y = e^x$

$\frac{dy}{dx}(x + 3y^2) = e^x - y$

$\frac{dy}{dx} = \mathbf{\frac{e^x - y}{x + 3y^2}}$

8. $x = \sin y$

$1 = \cos y \frac{dy}{dx}$

$\frac{dy}{dx} = \mathbf{\sec y}$

9. $2x - y^2 = \ln x$

$2 \frac{dx}{dt} - 2y \frac{dy}{dt} = x^{-1} \frac{dx}{dt}$

$\frac{dx}{dt}(2 - x^{-1}) = 2y \frac{dy}{dt}$

$\frac{dx}{dt} = \frac{2y \frac{dy}{dt}}{\frac{2x - 1}{x}}$

$\frac{dx}{dt} = \mathbf{\frac{2xy \frac{dy}{dt}}{2x - 1}}$

10. $f(x) = x \sin x$

$f'(x) = x \cos x + \sin x$

$f'(-1) = -\cos(-1) + \sin(-1) \approx \mathbf{-1.3818}$

11. $y = 2x^2 + 3 \sin x - 4 \cos x + \ln x$

$\frac{dy}{dx} = \mathbf{4x + 3 \cos x + 4 \sin x + x^{-1}}$

12.

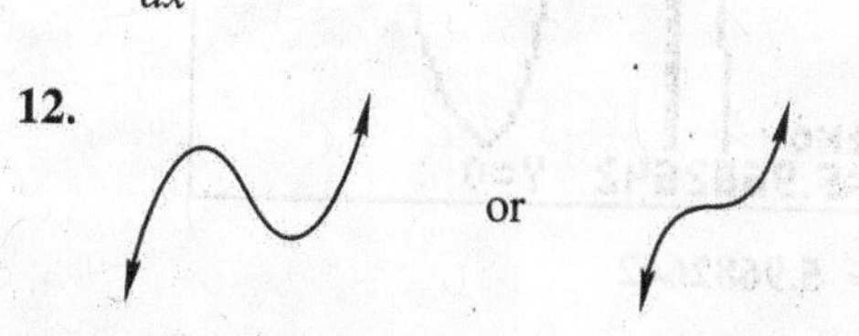

13.

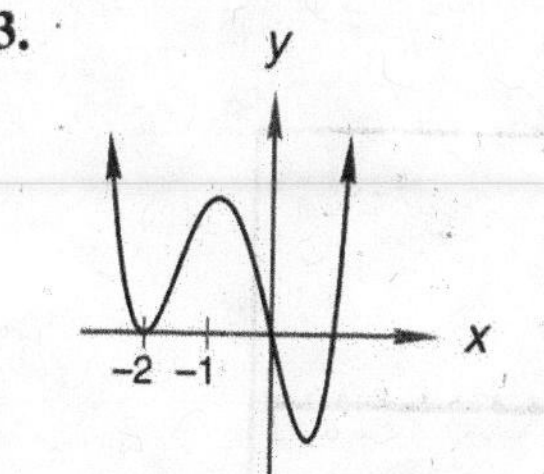

14.

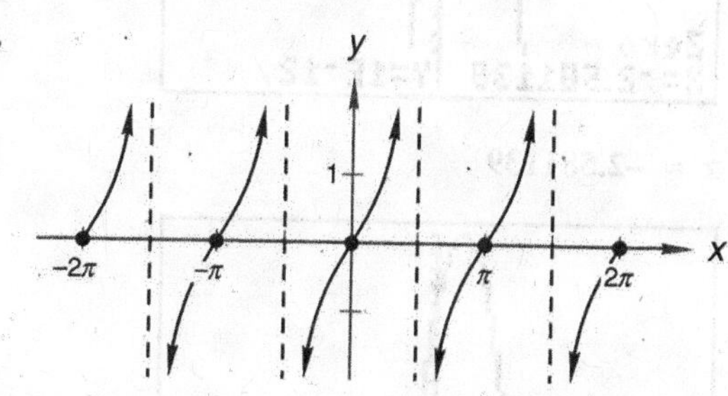

15.

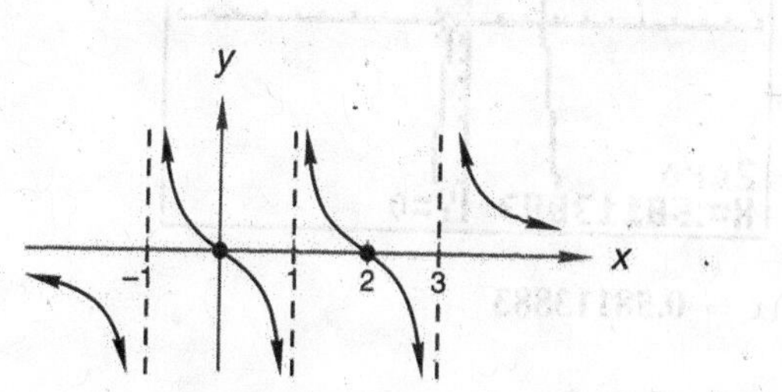

16. $\tan(A + B) = \frac{\tan A + \tan B}{1 - \tan A \tan B}$

$\tan(A + A) = \frac{\tan A + \tan A}{1 - \tan A \tan A}$

$\mathbf{\tan(2A) = \frac{2 \tan A}{1 - \tan^2 A}}$

17. (a) Let

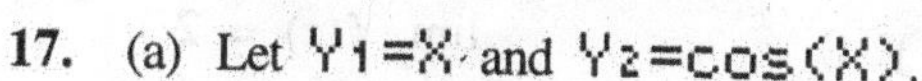

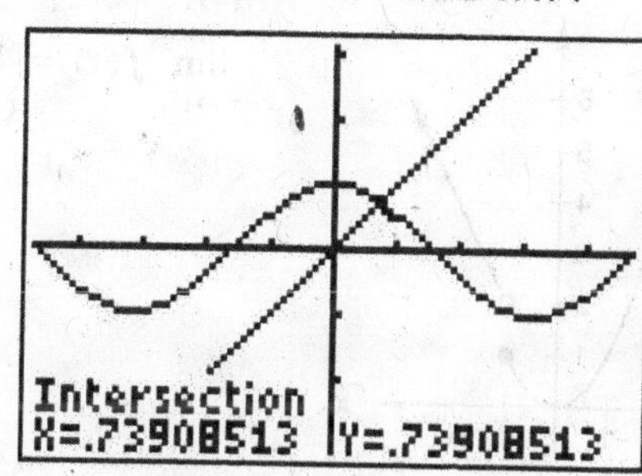

$x \approx \mathbf{0.73908513}$

(b)

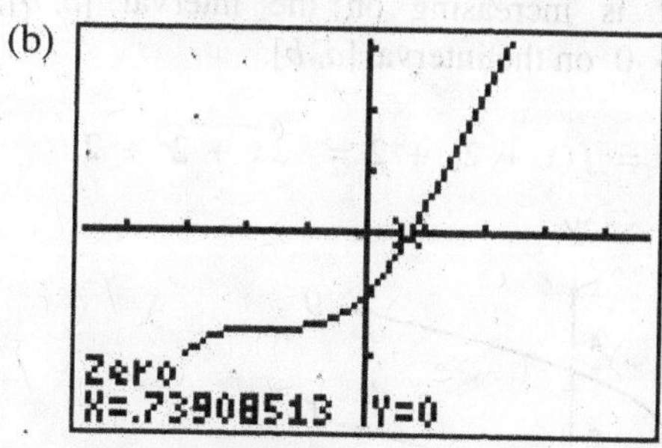

$x \approx \mathbf{0.73908513}$

They are the same.

18. Y1=-4X²-8X+6

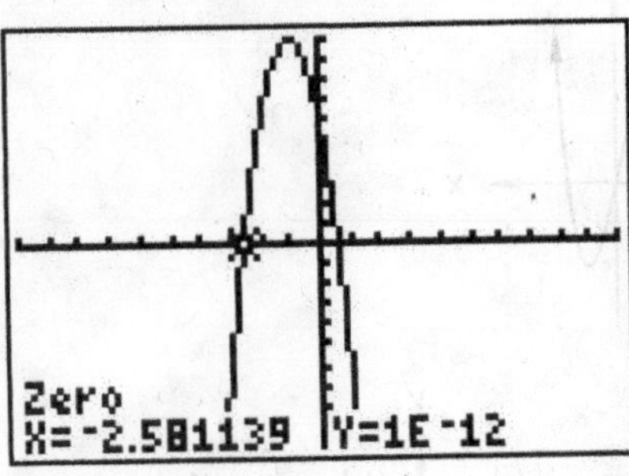

$x \approx$ **−2.581139**

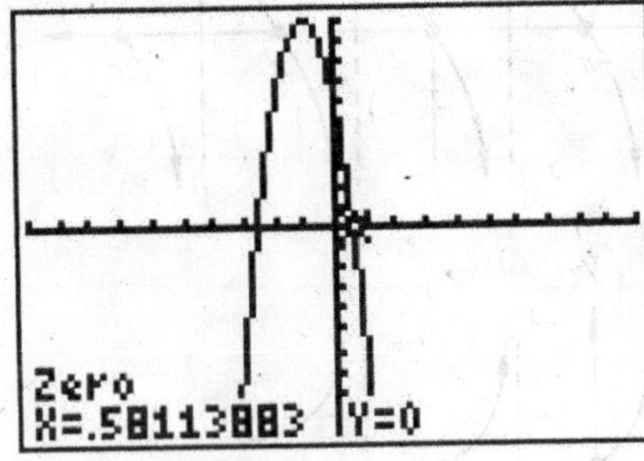

$x \approx$ **0.58113883**

19. $\log_b 27 = 3$
$b^3 = 27$
$b = \mathbf{3}$

20. $\displaystyle\lim_{t\to\infty} \frac{2t^2 + 3}{4 - 5t^2} = \mathbf{-\frac{2}{5}}$

21.
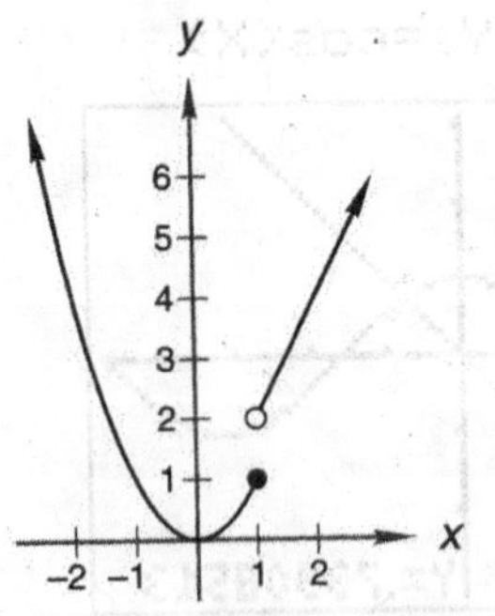

$\displaystyle\lim_{x\to 1^+} f(x) = \mathbf{2}$

$\displaystyle\lim_{x\to 1^-} f(x) = \mathbf{1}$

22. **If f is increasing on the interval $[a, b]$, then $f' > 0$ on the interval $[a, b]$.**

23. $g(x) = f(x + 2) + 2 = \mathbf{\sqrt{x + 2} + 2}$

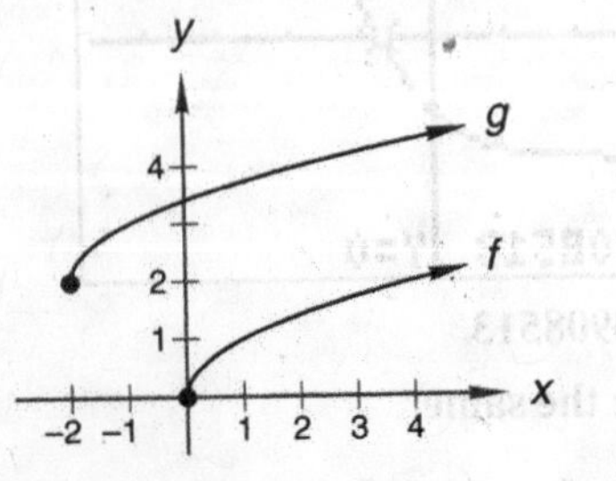

24.
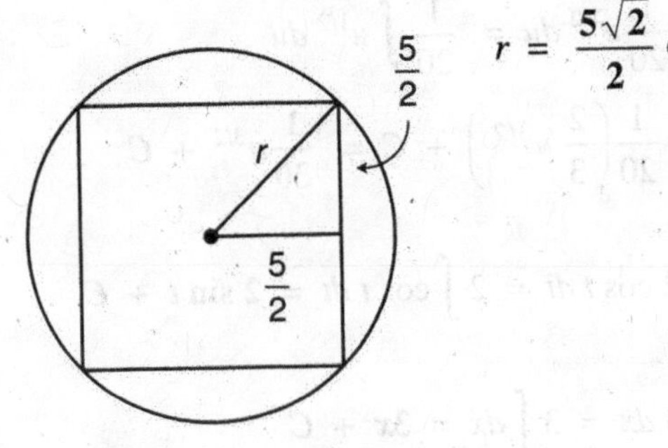

$r = \mathbf{\dfrac{5\sqrt{2}}{2}}$ **cm**

25. $x - y > 0$
$x > y$
$x^2 - 2xy + y^2 = (x - y)^2$
$x^2 + 2xy + y^2 = (x + y)^2$

If x and y are both positive or both negative, B is greater. Otherwise A is greater.

Insufficient information: **D**

PROBLEM SET 37

1. (a) $\mathbf{(y + 4)^2 + (x + 4)^2 = 144}$

(b) $\mathbf{\dfrac{y}{4} = \dfrac{4}{x}}$

(c) $y = \dfrac{16}{x}$

$\mathbf{\left(\dfrac{16}{x} + 4\right)^2 + (x + 4)^2 = 144}$

(d) Only positive roots make sense.

Y1=(16/X+4)²+(X+4)²−144

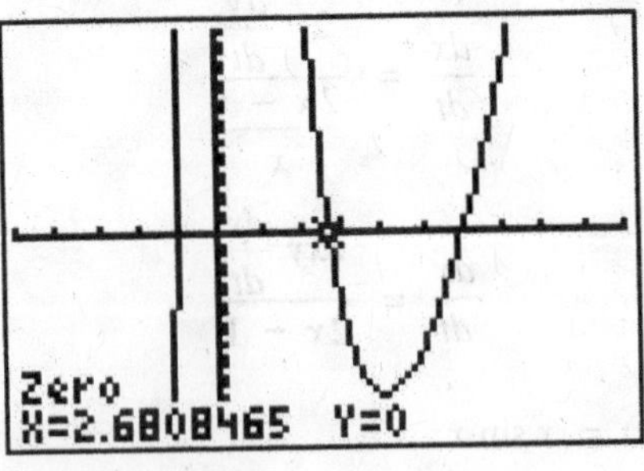

$x \approx$ **2.6808465**

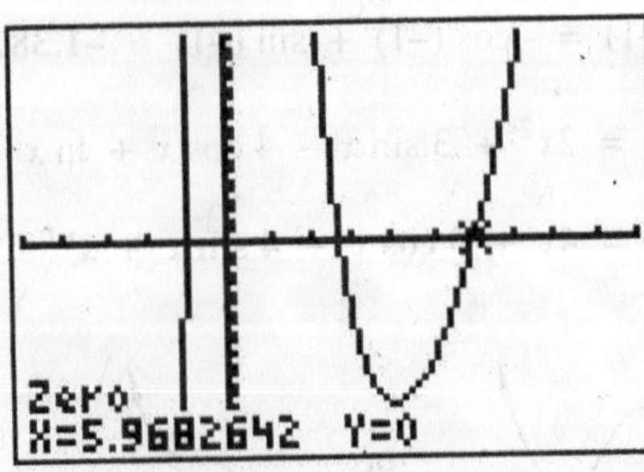

$x \approx$ **5.9682642**

2. $u = x^3 - 3x^2 + 1 \qquad du = (3x^2 - 6x)\,dx$
$y = u^{20}$
$dy = 20u^{19}\,du$
$dy = 20(x^3 - 3x^2 + 1)^{19}(3x^2 - 6x)\,dx$
$\frac{dy}{dx} = 20(x^3 - 3x^2 + 1)^{19}(3x^2 - 6x)$
$\frac{dy}{dx} = \mathbf{60x(x - 2)(x^3 - 3x^2 + 1)^{19}}$

3. $u = t^3 + 1 \qquad du = 3t^2\,dt$
$y = \sin u$
$dy = \cos u\,du$
$dy = \cos(t^3 + 1)(3t^2)\,dt$
$\frac{dy}{dt} = \mathbf{3t^2 \cos(t^3 + 1)}$

4. $u = \cos x \qquad du = -\sin x\,dx$
$y = u^3$
$dy = 3u^2\,du$
$dy = 3(\cos x)^2(-\sin x)\,dx$
$\frac{dy}{dx} = \mathbf{-3\cos^2 x \sin x}$

5. $u = x^2 + 1 \qquad du = 2x\,dx$
$y = \ln u$
$dy = \frac{1}{u}\,du$
$dy = \frac{1}{x^2 + 1}(2x)\,dx$
$\frac{dy}{dx} = \mathbf{\frac{2x}{x^2 + 1}}$

6. $u = x^3 + 2x - 1 \qquad du = (3x^2 + 2)\,dx$
$y = u^{1/3}$
$dy = \frac{1}{3}u^{-2/3}\,du$
$dy = \frac{1}{3}(x^3 + 2x - 1)^{-2/3}(3x^2 + 2)\,dx$
$\frac{dy}{dx} = \mathbf{\frac{1}{3}(x^3 + 2x - 1)^{-2/3}(3x^2 + 2)}$

7. $u = x^2 - 1 \qquad du = 2x\,dx$
$y = u^{-1/2}$
$dy = -\frac{1}{2}u^{-3/2}\,du$
$dy = -\frac{1}{2}(x^2 - 1)^{-3/2}(2x)\,dx$
$\frac{dy}{dx} = \mathbf{-x(x^2 - 1)^{-3/2}}$

8. (a) $f(x) = -3x^4 - 4x^3 + 12x^2 - 12$
$f'(x) = -12x^3 - 12x^2 + 24x$
$0 = -12x(x^2 + x - 2)$
$0 = -12x(x + 2)(x - 1)$
Critical numbers: $x = \mathbf{-2, 0, 1}$

(b) 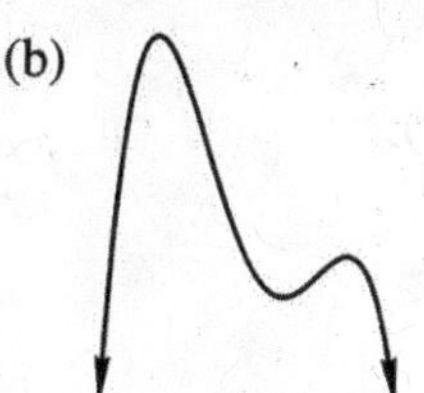

Local maxima: (–2, 20), (1, –7)
Local minimum: (0, –12)

9. $\int 3u^{-1/2}\,du = 3\int u^{-1/2}\,du$
$= 3(2u^{1/2}) + C = \mathbf{6u^{1/2} + C}$

10. $\int -4t^{2/3}\,dt = -4\int t^{2/3}\,dt$
$= -4\left(\frac{3}{5}t^{5/3}\right) + C = \mathbf{-\frac{12}{5}t^{5/3} + C}$

11. $\int x \cdot x^{1/2}\,dx = \int x^{3/2}\,dx = \mathbf{\frac{2}{5}x^{5/2} + C}$

12. $xy^2 - 2y = e^x$
$x(2y)\frac{dy}{dx} + y^2 - 2\frac{dy}{dx} = e^x$
$\frac{dy}{dx}(2xy - 2) = e^x - y^2$
$\frac{dy}{dx} = \mathbf{\frac{e^x - y^2}{2(xy - 1)}}$

13. $x^2 - 4y^2 = 0$
$2x - 8y\frac{dy}{dx} = 0$
$\frac{dy}{dx} = \frac{x}{4y}$
$\text{slope} = \frac{4}{4(2)} = \frac{1}{2}$
$y - 2 = \frac{1}{2}(x - 4)$
$\mathbf{y = \frac{1}{2}x}$

14. $f'(x) = \lim_{h \to 0} \frac{f(x+h) - f(x)}{h}$

$= \lim_{h \to 0} \frac{\sqrt{x+h} - \sqrt{x}}{h}$

$= \lim_{h \to 0} \left(\frac{\sqrt{x+h} - \sqrt{x}}{h}\right)\left(\frac{\sqrt{x+h} + \sqrt{x}}{\sqrt{x+h} + \sqrt{x}}\right)$

$= \lim_{h \to 0} \frac{x + h - x}{h(\sqrt{x+h} + \sqrt{x})}$

$= \lim_{h \to 0} \frac{1}{\sqrt{x+h} + \sqrt{x}}$

$= \frac{1}{\sqrt{x} + \sqrt{x}} = \mathbf{\frac{1}{2\sqrt{x}}}$

15. 

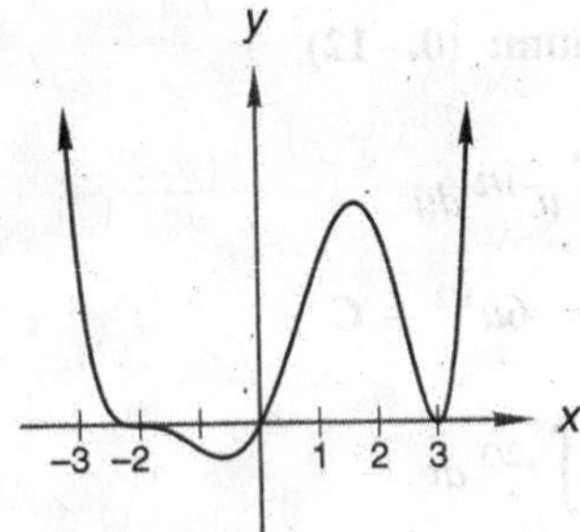

16. f: **Domain:** $\{x \in \mathbb{R} \mid x > 0\}$

Range: $\mathbb{R}$

g: **Domain:** $\{x \in \mathbb{R} \mid x \geq 1\}$

Range: $\{y \in \mathbb{R} \mid y \geq 0\}$

17. $(f \circ g)(x) = f(\sqrt{x-1})$

$(f \circ g)(x) = \ln \sqrt{x - 1}$

Domain: $\{x \in \mathbb{R} \mid x > 1\}$

18. If $0 \leq \theta < \pi$ then $0 \leq 3\theta < 3\pi$.

$2 \tan 3\theta = \sqrt{3}$

$\tan 3\theta = \frac{\sqrt{3}}{2}$

$3\theta \approx 0.7137, 3.8553, 6.9969$

$\theta \approx$ **0.2379, 1.2851, 2.3323**

19.

X	Y1
10000	2.7181
20000	2.7182
30000	2.7182
40000	2.7182
50000	2.7182
60000	2.7183
70000	2.7183

X=70000

$\lim_{x \to \infty} \left(1 + \frac{1}{x}\right)^x = e \approx$ **2.7183**

20. $\cos(2x) = \cos^2 x - \sin^2 x$

$\cos(2x) = (1 - \sin^2 x) - \sin^2 x$

$\cos(2x) = 1 - 2\sin^2 x$

$2\sin^2 x = 1 - \cos(2x)$

$\mathbf{\sin^2 x = \frac{1}{2} - \frac{1}{2}\cos(2x)}$

21. $y = A(x + 1)(x - 2)$

$-4 = A(1)(-2)$

$A = 2$

$y = 2(x + 1)(x - 2)$

$\mathbf{y = 2x^2 - 2x - 4}$

22. $(\sin -x)\left[\csc\left(\frac{\pi}{2} - x\right)\right] = -\sin x \sec x$

$= -\frac{\sin x}{\cos x} = \mathbf{-\tan x}$

23. $\lim_{n \to \infty} \frac{n^2 - 2n - 3}{2 - n^2} = \frac{1}{-1} = \mathbf{-1}$

24. $\begin{vmatrix} 2 & 3 \\ -1 & d \end{vmatrix} = 4$

$2d - (-1)(3) = 4$

$2d + 3 = 4$

$\mathbf{d = \frac{1}{2}}$

25. If $x = 3$ and $y = 2$, then $x^y > y^x$.

If $x = 4$ and $y = 2$, then $x^y = y^x$.

If $x = 5$ and $y = 3$, then $x^y < y^x$.

Insufficient information: **D**

PROBLEM SET 38

1. $V_t = V_0 e^{kt}$

$15 = 10e^{2k}$

$1.5 = e^{2k}$

$\ln 1.5 = 2k$

$k = \frac{1}{2} \ln 1.5$

$k = \ln \sqrt{1.5}$

$30 = 10e^{\ln \sqrt{1.5}\, t}$

$3 = e^{\ln \sqrt{1.5}\, t}$

$\ln 3 = \ln \sqrt{1.5}\, t$

$t = \frac{\ln 3}{\ln \sqrt{1.5}} \approx 5.4190$

5:25:08 a.m.

2. 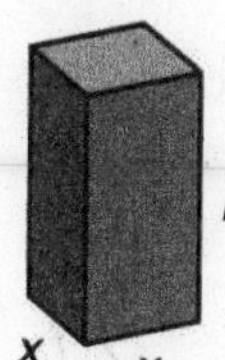

$$x^2h = 64$$
$$h = 64x^{-2}$$

$$A = 4xh + 2x^2$$
$$= 4x(64x^{-2}) + 2x^2$$
$$= \mathbf{(256x^{-1} + 2x^2)\ in.^2}$$

3. $\int (2x^2 - 3x^{-1/2} + 3)\,dx$

$$= \mathbf{\frac{2}{3}x^3 - 6x^{1/2} + 3x + C}$$

4. $\int \left(2\cos u - \frac{2}{u} + 3\sin u\right) du$

$$= \mathbf{2\sin u - 2\ln|u| - 3\cos u + C}$$

5. $u = x^3 + 2x + 1 \qquad du = (3x^2 + 2)\,dx$

$$y = \cos u$$
$$dy = -\sin u\,du$$
$$dy = -\sin(x^3 + 2x + 1)(3x^2 + 2)\,dx$$
$$\frac{dy}{dx} = \mathbf{-\sin(x^3 + 2x + 1)(3x^2 + 2)}$$

6. $u = \sin x \qquad du = \cos x\,dx$

$$y = \ln|u|$$
$$dy = \frac{1}{u}\,du$$
$$dy = \frac{1}{\sin x}(\cos x)\,dx$$
$$\frac{dy}{dx} = \mathbf{\cot x}$$

7. $u = x^2 + 2x + 1 \qquad du = (2x + 2)\,dx$

$$y = u^{-1/2}$$
$$dy = -\frac{1}{2}u^{-3/2}\,du$$
$$dy = -\frac{1}{2}(x^2 + 2x + 1)^{-3/2}(2x + 2)\,dx$$
$$dy = -\frac{1}{2}[(x + 1)^2]^{-3/2}[2(x + 1)]\,dx$$
$$\frac{dy}{dx} = \mathbf{-(x + 1)^{-2}}$$

8. $u = \sin t + 2e^t \qquad du = (\cos t + 2e^t)\,dt$

$$s = 2\ln|u|$$
$$ds = \frac{2}{u}\,du$$
$$ds = \frac{2}{\sin t + 2e^t}(\cos t + 2e^t)\,dt$$
$$\frac{ds}{dt} = \mathbf{\frac{2(\cos t + 2e^t)}{\sin t + 2e^t}}$$

9. (a) $f(x) = 3x^4 - 8x^3 - 6x^2 + 24x - 1$

$$f'(x) = 12x^3 - 24x^2 - 12x + 24$$
$$0 = 12x^2(x - 2) - 12(x - 2)$$
$$0 = (x - 2)(12x^2 - 12)$$
$$0 = 12(x - 2)(x^2 - 1)$$
$$0 = 12(x - 2)(x + 1)(x - 1)$$

Critical numbers: $x = \mathbf{-1, 1, 2}$

(b) 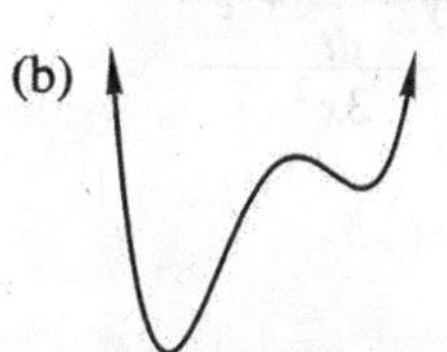

Local minima: (–1, –20), (2, 7)
Local maximum: (1, 12)

10. 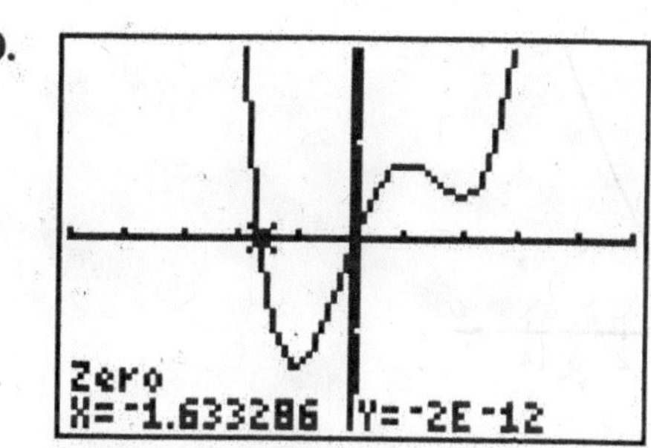

$x \approx \mathbf{-1.633286}$

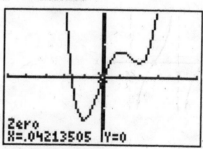

Zero
X=.04213505 Y=0

$x \approx \mathbf{0.04213505}$

11. $xy - y^3 = \sin x$

$$x\frac{dy}{dx} + y - 3y^2\frac{dy}{dx} = \cos x$$
$$\frac{dy}{dx}(x - 3y^2) = \cos x - y$$
$$\frac{dy}{dx} = \mathbf{\frac{\cos x - y}{x - 3y^2}}$$

12. $$y^2 - 2xy = e^x$$

$$2y\frac{dy}{dx} - \left(2x\frac{dy}{dx} + 2y\right) = e^x$$

$$\frac{dy}{dx}(2y - 2x) = e^x + 2y$$

$$\frac{dy}{dx} = \mathbf{\frac{e^x + 2y}{2(y - x)}}$$

13. $$x^3 - y^3 = e^t$$

$$3x^2\frac{dx}{dt} - 3y^2\frac{dy}{dt} = e^t$$

$$3x^2\frac{dx}{dt} = 3y^2\frac{dy}{dt} + e^t$$

$$\frac{dx}{dt} = \mathbf{\frac{3y^2\frac{dy}{dt} + e^t}{3x^2}}$$

14.

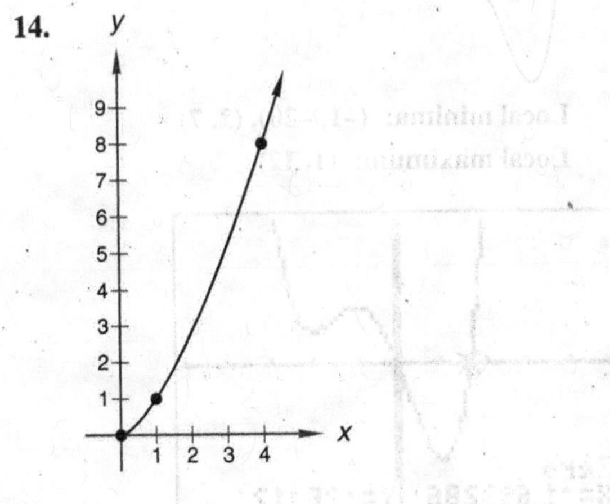

15.

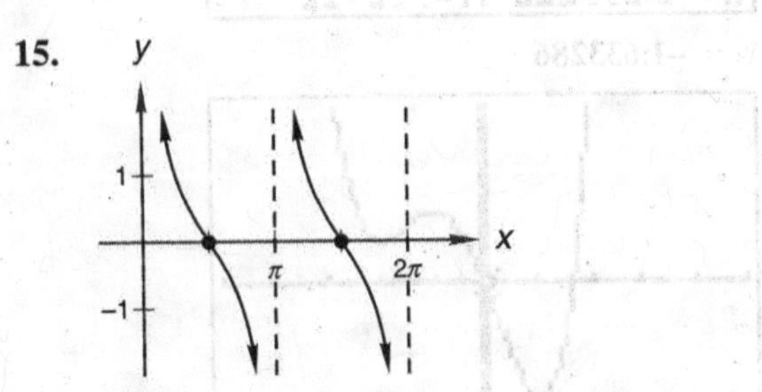

16.

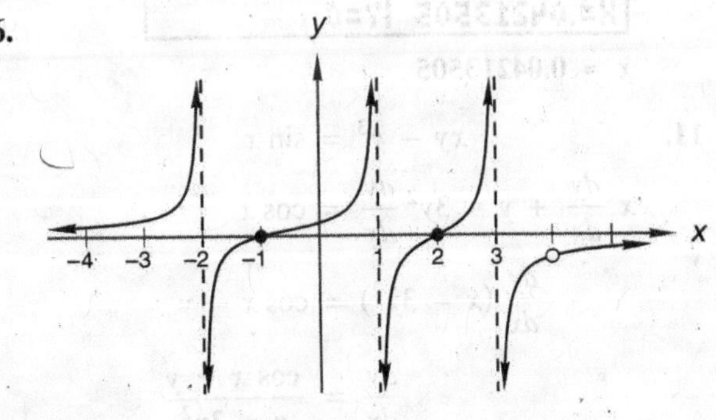

17.

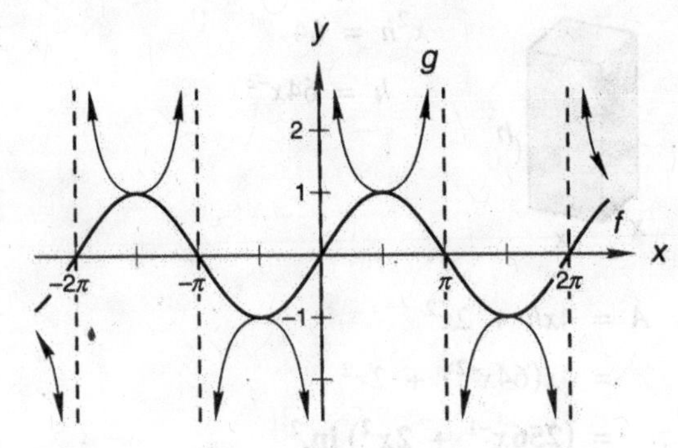

18.

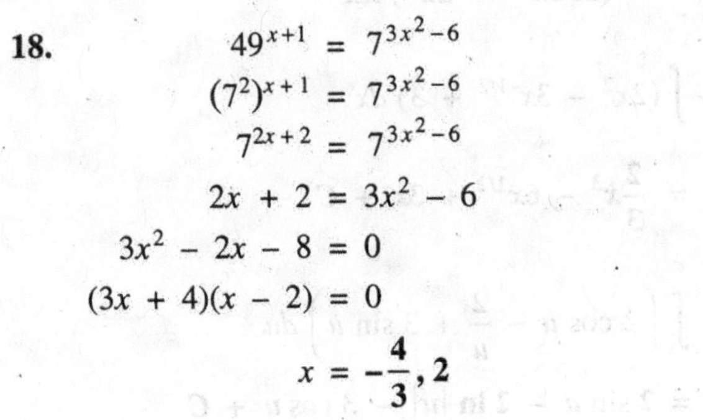

$$49^{x+1} = 7^{3x^2-6}$$

$$(7^2)^{x+1} = 7^{3x^2-6}$$

$$7^{2x+2} = 7^{3x^2-6}$$

$$2x + 2 = 3x^2 - 6$$

$$3x^2 - 2x - 8 = 0$$

$$(3x + 4)(x - 2) = 0$$

$$x = \mathbf{-\frac{4}{3}, 2}$$

19.

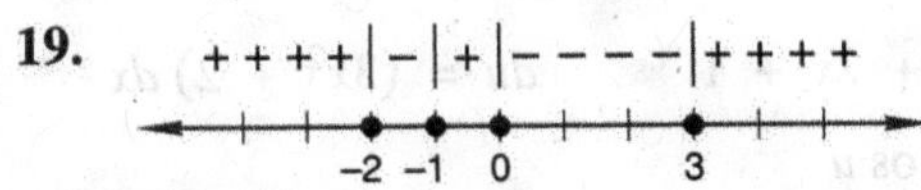

20. **Centerline: $y = -2$**

$C = \frac{2\pi}{4}$ **Period: $\frac{\pi}{2}$**

Amplitude: 3

21. $1 + 2 + 3 + \cdots + 38 + 39 + 40$

$= 41(20) = \mathbf{820}$

22. $\tan^2\frac{\pi}{15} - \sec^2\frac{\pi}{15} = \mathbf{-1}$

23. $\left[\sin\left(\frac{\pi}{2} - \theta\right)\right](\tan\theta)(\sin -\theta)$

$= \cos\theta\tan\theta(-\sin\theta)$

$= \cos\theta\left(\frac{\sin\theta}{\cos\theta}\right)(-\sin\theta) = \mathbf{-\sin^2\theta}$

24.

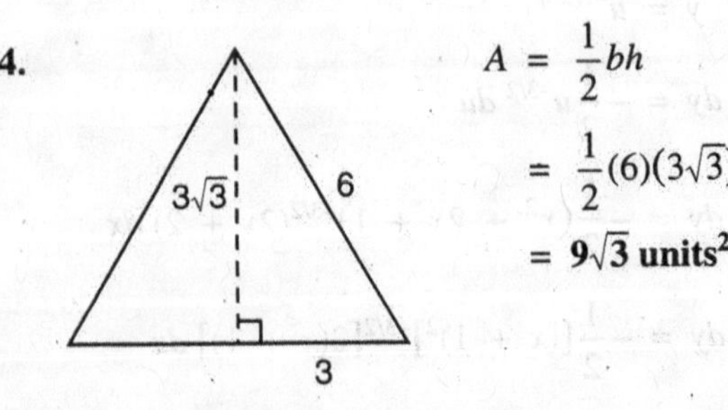

$$A = \frac{1}{2}bh$$

$$= \frac{1}{2}(6)(3\sqrt{3})$$

$$= \mathbf{9\sqrt{3}\text{ units}^2}$$

25. $x - y = 3$

$x^2 - 2xy + y^2 = 9$

$x^2 + y^2 = 2xy + 9$

The quantities are equal: **C**

PROBLEM SET 39

1.

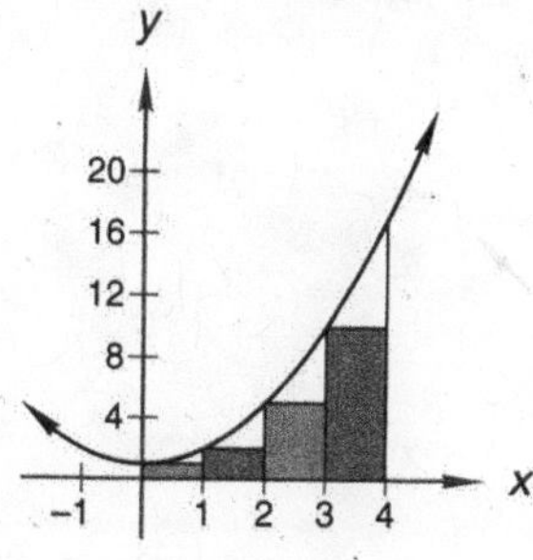

$$S_L = \frac{4}{4}[f(0) + f(1) + f(2) + f(3)]$$

$$= 1 + 2 + 5 + 10 = \mathbf{18\ units^2}$$

2.

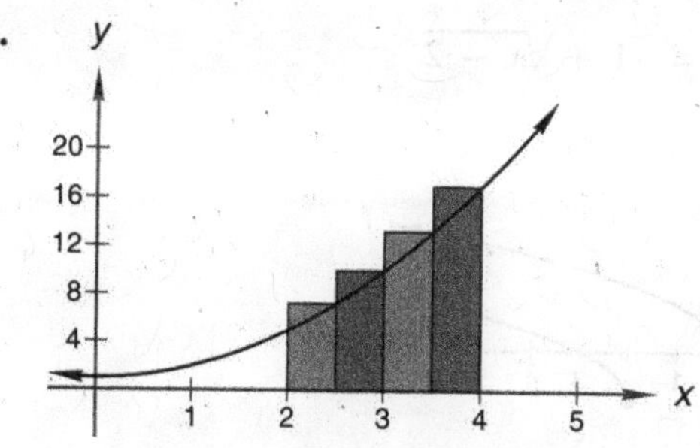

$$S_U = \frac{2}{4}\left[f\left(\frac{5}{2}\right) + f(3) + f\left(\frac{7}{2}\right) + f(4)\right]$$

$$= \frac{1}{2}\left(\frac{29}{4} + 10 + \frac{53}{4} + 17\right)$$

$$= \frac{1}{2}\left(\frac{95}{2}\right) = \mathbf{\frac{95}{4}\ units^2}$$

3.

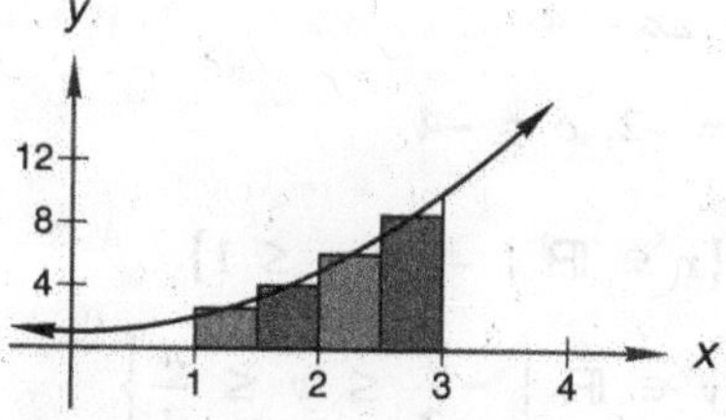

$$S_M = \frac{2}{4}\left[f\left(\frac{5}{4}\right) + f\left(\frac{7}{4}\right) + f\left(\frac{9}{4}\right) + f\left(\frac{11}{4}\right)\right]$$

$$= \frac{1}{2}\left(\frac{41}{16} + \frac{65}{16} + \frac{97}{16} + \frac{137}{16}\right)$$

$$= \frac{1}{2}\left(\frac{340}{16}\right) = \mathbf{\frac{85}{8}\ units^2}$$

4. $\int (4e^x - x^{-1/2} + 6)\, dx$

$$= \mathbf{4e^x - 2x^{1/2} + 6x + C}$$

5. $\int \left(3e^x - \frac{2}{x} + \sin x - \cos x\right) dx$

$$+ \int (-4x^{-1/2} + 2x^5)\, dx$$

$$= \mathbf{3e^x - 2\ln|x| - \cos x - \sin x - 8x^{1/2}}$$

$$\mathbf{+ \frac{1}{3}x^6 + C}$$

6. $u = \cos x \qquad du = -\sin x\, dx$

$y = e^u$

$dy = e^u\, du$

$dy = e^{\cos x}(-\sin x)\, dx$

$\frac{dy}{dx} = \mathbf{-e^{\cos x} \sin x}$

7. $u = x^3 - 4x^2 + 2x - 5$

$du = (3x^2 - 8x + 2)\, dx$

$y = \sin u$

$dy = \cos u\, du$

$\frac{dy}{dx} = \mathbf{\cos(x^3 - 4x^2 + 2x - 5)(3x^2 - 8x + 2)}$

8. $u = \sin x \qquad du = \cos x\, dx$

$y = u^3$

$dy = 3u^2\, du$

$dy = 3(\sin x)^2 \cos x\, dx$

$\frac{dy}{dx} = \mathbf{3\sin^2 x \cos x}$

9. (a) $y = \frac{1}{4}x^4 + \frac{2}{3}x^3 - \frac{1}{2}x^2 - 2x + 5$

$y' = x^3 + 2x^2 - x - 2$

$0 = x^2(x + 2) - (x + 2)$

$0 = (x + 2)(x^2 - 1)$

$0 = (x + 2)(x + 1)(x - 1)$

Critical numbers: $x = \mathbf{-2, -1, 1}$

(b)

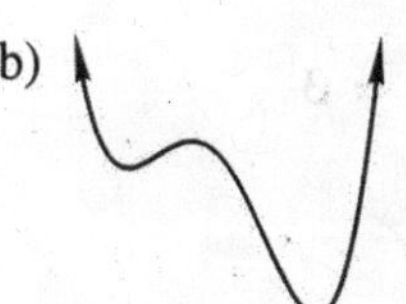

Local minimums: $\left(\mathbf{-2, \frac{17}{3}}\right), \left(\mathbf{1, \frac{41}{12}}\right)$

Local maximum: $\left(\mathbf{-1, \frac{73}{12}}\right)$

10. $$x^2 + y^2 = 9$$

$$2x\frac{dx}{dt} + 2y\frac{dy}{dt} = 0$$

$$\frac{dx}{dt} = \frac{-2y\frac{dy}{dt}}{2x}$$

$$\frac{dx}{dt} = -\frac{y}{x}\frac{dy}{dt}$$

11. `nDeriv(ln(abs(X))+e^X,X,-2)`
$\approx$ **−0.3647**

12.
$$f(x) = -3\cos x$$
$$f'(x) = 3\sin x$$
$$f''(x) = 3\cos x$$
$$f'''(x) = -3\sin x$$
$$f'''(3) = -3\sin 3 \approx \mathbf{-0.4234}$$

13.
$$f(x) = 12\ln|x|\sin x$$
$$f'(x) = 12\left(\ln|x|\cos x + \frac{\sin x}{x}\right)$$
$$f'(0.5) = 12\left(\ln 0.5\cos 0.5 + \frac{\sin 0.5}{0.5}\right)$$
$$f'(0.5) \approx \mathbf{4.2067}$$

14. (a)

X	Y1
1.97	.50379
1.98	.50252
1.99	.50125
2	ERROR
2.01	.49875
2.02	.49752
2.03	.49629

X=2

Guess: **0.5**

(b) $f(x) = \ln x$

$$f'(x) = \frac{1}{x}$$

$$f'(2) = \mathbf{\frac{1}{2}}$$

15. $$\lim_{n\to\infty}\frac{3n^2}{1000n + n^2} = \frac{3}{1} = \mathbf{3}$$

16. $$\lim_{x\to 0^-}\frac{x+1}{x} = -\infty$$

$$\lim_{x\to 0^+}\frac{x+1}{x} = \infty$$

$\lim_{x\to 0}\frac{x+1}{x}$ **does not exist.**

17. $$\lim_{n\to\infty}\frac{3n^3 - 4n^2}{n^2 - 5n} = \lim_{n\to\infty}\frac{3n - 4}{1 - \frac{5}{n}} = \frac{3(\infty) - 4}{1 - 0}$$

$$= \mathbf{\infty}$$

18. **False.** The function may not exist at $x = 1$ but the limits still could. Such would be the case with a function like $f(x) = \frac{(x+2)(x-1)}{x-1}$ whose graph is shown here:

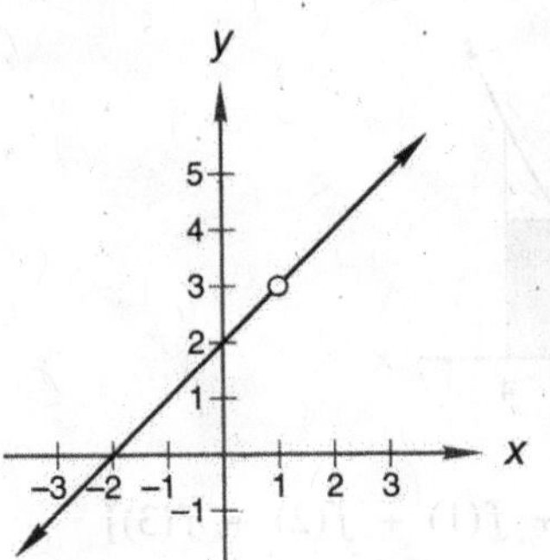

19. $f(x) = \sqrt{x}$

$g(x) = -1 + \sqrt{x - 2}$

20.
$$y = a(x + 1)(x - 2)$$
$$y = a(x^2 - x - 2)$$
$$-4 = a(0 - 0 - 2)$$
$$a = 2$$
$$y = 2(x^2 - x - 2)$$
$$y = 2x^2 - 2x - 4$$
$$\mathbf{a = 2,\ b = -2,\ c = -4}$$

21. **Domain:** $\{x \in \mathbb{R} \mid -1 \le x \le 1\}$

Range: $\left\{y \in \mathbb{R} \mid -\frac{\pi}{2} \le y \le \frac{\pi}{2}\right\}$

22. $1^2 + 2^2 + 3^2 + 4^2 = 30$

$$S_4 = \frac{4(5)(9)}{6} = \frac{180}{6} = 30$$

$$S_{40} = \frac{40(41)(81)}{6} = \mathbf{22{,}140}$$

23. $\displaystyle\sum_{i=-1}^{1} -\left(\frac{1}{2}\right)^i = -\left(\frac{1}{2}\right)^{-1} - \left(\frac{1}{2}\right)^0 - \left(\frac{1}{2}\right)^1$

$= -2 - 1 - \frac{1}{2} = -\frac{7}{2}$

24. $(\sin x)\left[\cos\left(\frac{\pi}{2} - x\right)\right] + (\cos -x)\left[\sin\left(\frac{\pi}{2} - x\right)\right]$

$= \sin x \sin x + \cos x \cos x$

$= \sin^2 x + \cos^2 x = 1$

25.

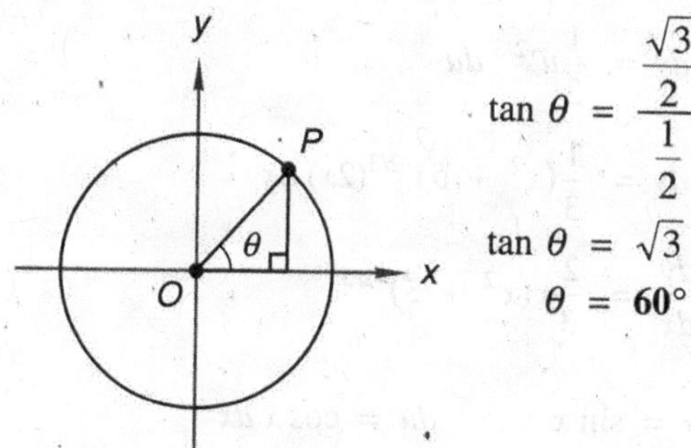

$\tan\theta = \dfrac{\frac{\sqrt{3}}{2}}{\frac{1}{2}}$

$\tan\theta = \sqrt{3}$

$\theta = \mathbf{60°}$

Problem Set 40

1. $V(t) = 20e^t$

$V'(t) = 20e^t$

$V'(3) = \mathbf{20e^3\,\frac{cm^3}{s}} \approx \mathbf{401.7107\,\frac{cm^3}{s}}$

2. $s(t) = -2t^2 + t^3$

$v(t) = -4t + 3t^2$

$v(1) = -4 + 3 = \mathbf{-1\,\frac{unit}{s}}$

3. $y = -3\ln|x| \qquad y' = -\frac{3}{x}$

$m = \frac{-3}{-3} = 1 \qquad \perp m = -1$

$y - \ln\frac{1}{27} = -(x + 3)$

$\mathbf{y = -x - 3 + \ln\frac{1}{27}}$

4. (a) $f(x) = x^3 + \frac{3}{2}x^2 - 6x + 2$

$f'(x) = 3x^2 + 3x - 6$

$0 = 3(x^2 + x - 2)$

$0 = 3(x + 2)(x - 1)$

Critical numbers: $x = \mathbf{-2, 1}$

(b)

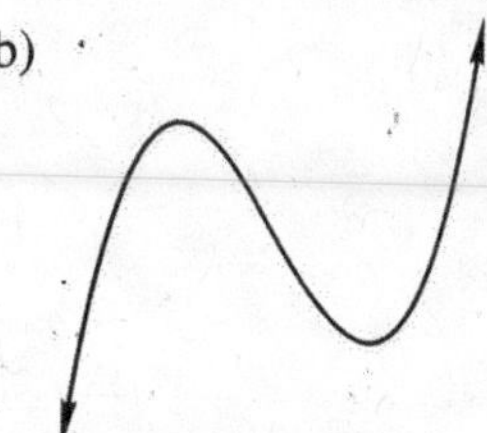

Local maximum: (−2, 12)

Local minimum: $\mathbf{\left(1, -\frac{3}{2}\right)}$

5.

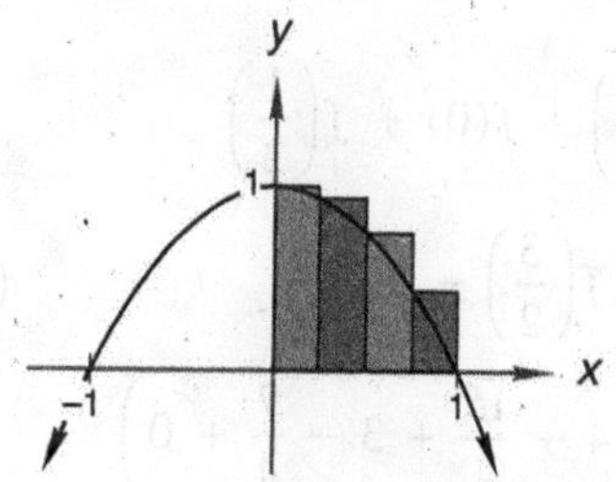

$S_U = \frac{1}{4}\left[f(0) + f\left(\frac{1}{4}\right) + f\left(\frac{1}{2}\right) + f\left(\frac{3}{4}\right)\right]$

$= \frac{1}{4}\left(1 + \frac{15}{16} + \frac{3}{4} + \frac{7}{16}\right)$

$= \frac{1}{4}\left(\frac{25}{8}\right) = \mathbf{\frac{25}{32}\ units^2}$

6.

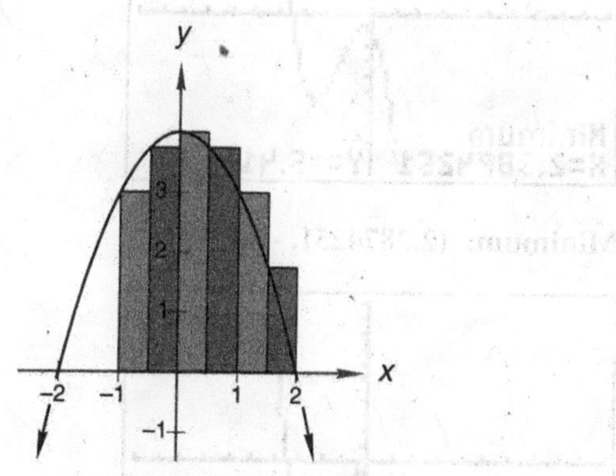

$S_L = \frac{3}{6}\left[f(-1) + f\left(-\frac{1}{2}\right) + f(0)\right.$

$\left.+ f\left(\frac{1}{2}\right) + f(1) + f\left(\frac{3}{2}\right)\right]$

$= \frac{1}{2}\left(3 + \frac{15}{4} + 4 + \frac{15}{4} + 3 + \frac{7}{4}\right)$

$= \frac{1}{2}\left(\frac{77}{4}\right) = \mathbf{\frac{77}{8}\ units^2}$

7.

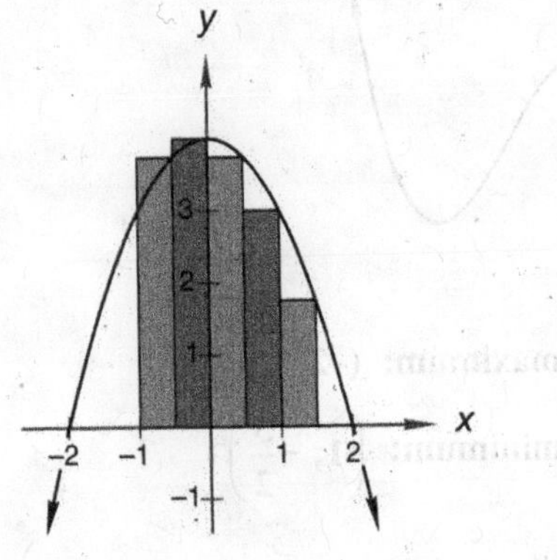

$$S_R = \frac{3}{6}\left[f\left(-\frac{1}{2}\right) + f(0) + f\left(\frac{1}{2}\right) + f(1) + f\left(\frac{3}{2}\right) + f(2)\right]$$

$$= \frac{1}{2}\left(\frac{15}{4} + 4 + \frac{15}{4} + 3 + \frac{7}{4} + 0\right)$$

$$= \frac{1}{2}\left(\frac{65}{4}\right) = \mathbf{\frac{65}{8}\ units^2}$$

8.

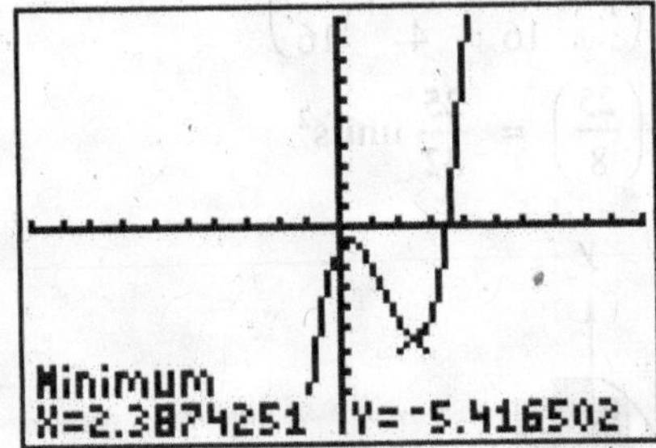

Minimum: (2.3874251, −5.416502)

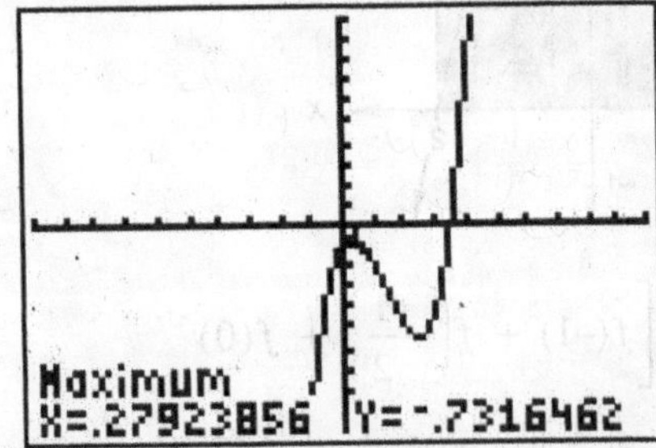

Maximum: (0.27923856, −0.7316462)

9. nDeriv(X³,X,2) = **12.000001**

$y = x^3$

$y' = 3x^2$

$y'|_2 = 3(2)^2 = \mathbf{12}$

10. $\int\left(2\sin x - 4x - \frac{3}{2}x^{1/2} - 3\right)dx$

$= \mathbf{-2\cos x - 2x^2 - x^{3/2} - 3x + C}$

11. $\int\left(\frac{\sqrt{2}}{t} + 3\cos t + 1\right)dt$

$= \mathbf{\sqrt{2}\ln|t| + 3\sin t + t + C}$

12. $\int\left(\frac{x+1}{x}\right)dx = \int\left(1 + \frac{1}{x}\right)dx$

$= \mathbf{x + \ln|x| + C}$

13. $u = x^2 + 5 \qquad du = 2x\,dx$

$y = u^{1/3}$

$dy = \frac{1}{3}u^{-2/3}\,du$

$dy = \frac{1}{3}(x^2 + 5)^{-2/3}(2x)\,dx$

$\frac{dy}{dx} = \mathbf{\frac{2}{3}x(x^2 + 5)^{-2/3}}$

14. $u = \sin x \qquad du = \cos x\,dx$

$s = \ln|u|$

$ds = \frac{1}{u}du$

$ds = \frac{1}{\sin x}(\cos x\,dx)$

$\frac{ds}{dx} = \mathbf{\cot x}$

15. $u = \sin x \qquad du = \cos x\,dx$

$y = -u^4$

$dy = -4u^3\,du$

$dy = -4(\sin x)^3\cos x\,dx$

$\frac{dy}{dx} = \mathbf{-4\sin^3 x\cos x}$

16. $\sin x + \cos y = xy$

$\cos x - \sin y\frac{dy}{dx} = x\frac{dy}{dx} + y$

$\frac{dy}{dx}(x + \sin y) = \cos x - y$

$\frac{dy}{dx} = \mathbf{\frac{\cos x - y}{x + \sin y}}$

17. $A = \frac{4}{3}\pi r^3$

$dA = 4\pi r^2\,dr$

$\frac{dA}{dt} = \mathbf{4\pi r^2\frac{dr}{dt}}$

18. $f(x) = 2\ln|x|$

$$f'(x) = 2x^{-1}$$
$$f''(x) = -2x^{-2}$$
$$f'''(x) = 4x^{-3}$$
$$f'''(-2) = 4(-2)^{-3}$$
$$f'''(-2) = -\frac{1}{2}$$

19. $y = e^x \ln|x|$

$$\frac{dy}{dx} = \frac{e^x}{x} + \ln|x|\,(e^x)$$
$$\frac{dy}{dx} = e^x(x^{-1} + \ln|x|)$$

20. $f(x) = x^2 + x - 2 = \left(x + \frac{1}{2}\right)^2 - \frac{9}{4}$

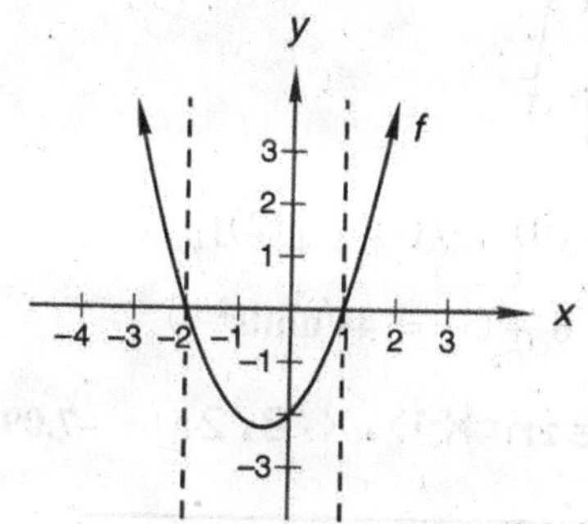

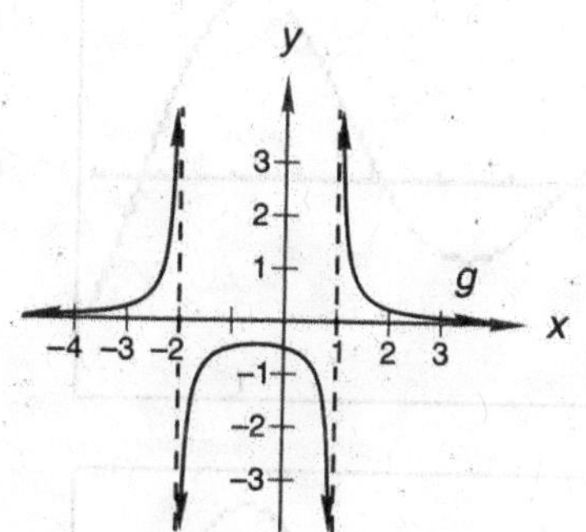

21. $\log_3 5 = \frac{\ln 5}{\ln 3} \approx \mathbf{1.4650}$

22. $\lim_{x\to\infty} \frac{x^3 - 4x + 5}{1 - 2x^3} = -\frac{1}{2}$

23. $\frac{1 - \sin^2\theta}{\cos^2\left(\frac{\pi}{2} - \theta\right)} = \frac{\cos^2\theta}{\sin^2\theta} = \mathbf{\cot^2\theta}$

24. $1^3 + 2^3 + 3^3 = 36$

$$S_3 = \left[\frac{3(4)}{2}\right]^2 = 6^2 = 36$$
$$S_{40} = \left[\frac{40(41)}{2}\right]^2 = 820^2 = \mathbf{672{,}400}$$

25. $x = 2y$

$$x^2 = 4y^2$$
$$\frac{1}{4}x^2 = y^2$$

The quantities are equal: **C**

Problem Set 41

1. $V_t = V_0 e^{kt}$

$$1 = 3e^{k(1)}$$
$$\frac{1}{3} = e^k$$
$$\ln\frac{1}{3} = k$$
$$V_7 = 3e^{7\ln(1/3)}$$
$$= 3e^{\ln(1/3)^7}$$
$$= 3\left(\frac{1}{3}\right)^7$$
$$= \frac{1}{3^6}\textbf{ liter} \approx \textbf{0.0014 liter}$$

2.

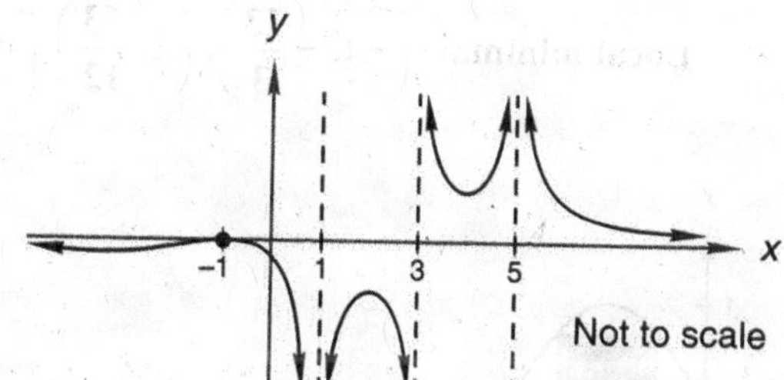

3.

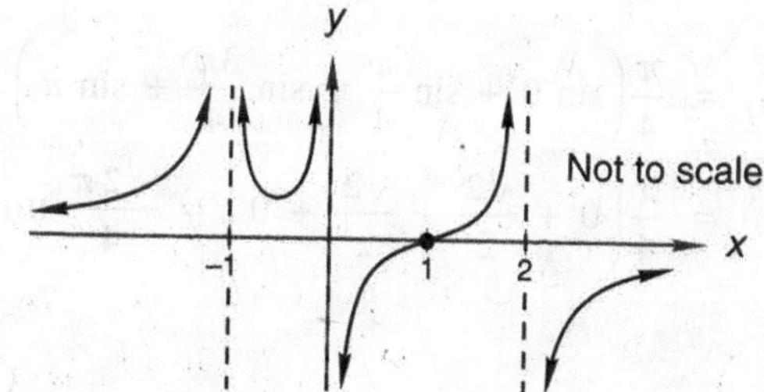

4. $P(t) = 20{,}000e^t$

$$P'(t) = 20{,}000e^t$$
$$P'(3) = \mathbf{20{,}000e^3} \approx \mathbf{401{,}711}$$

5. $V = \frac{4}{3}\pi r^3$

$\frac{dV}{dt} = \mathbf{4\pi r^2 \frac{dr}{dt}}$

6. $y = x + \ln x$

$y' = 1 + \frac{1}{x}$

$y'|_1 = 2 \qquad \perp \text{slope} = -\frac{1}{2}$

$y - 1 = -\frac{1}{2}(x - 1)$

$\mathbf{y = -\frac{1}{2}x + \frac{3}{2}}$

7. (a) $y = \frac{1}{4}x^4 + \frac{4}{3}x^3 - \frac{1}{2}x^2 - 4x + 9$

$y' = x^3 + 4x^2 - x - 4$

$y' = (x + 4)(x^2 - 1)$

$0 = (x + 4)(x + 1)(x - 1)$

Critical numbers: $x = \mathbf{-4, -1, 1}$

(b)

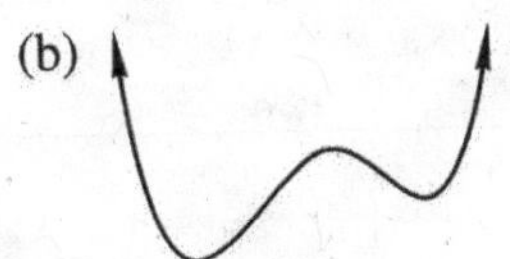

Local maximum: $\left(\mathbf{-1, \frac{137}{12}}\right)$

Local minima: $\left(\mathbf{-4, -\frac{13}{3}}\right), \left(\mathbf{1, \frac{73}{12}}\right)$

8.

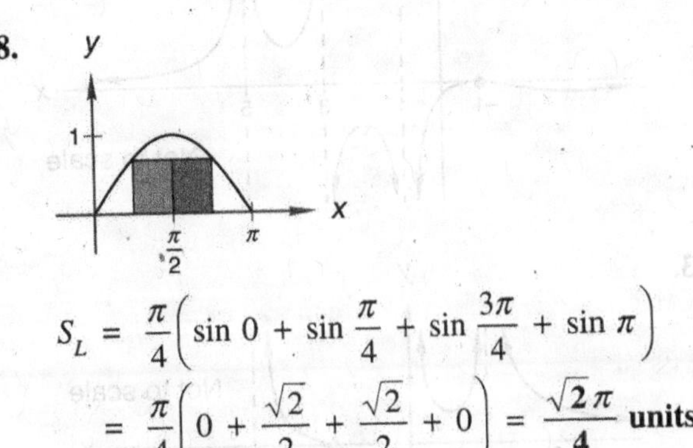

$S_L = \frac{\pi}{4}\left(\sin 0 + \sin\frac{\pi}{4} + \sin\frac{3\pi}{4} + \sin\pi\right)$

$= \frac{\pi}{4}\left(0 + \frac{\sqrt{2}}{2} + \frac{\sqrt{2}}{2} + 0\right) = \mathbf{\frac{\sqrt{2}\pi}{4}\ \textbf{units}^2}$

9.

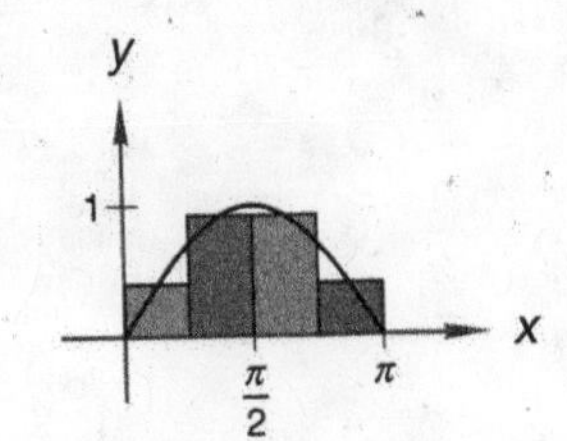

$S_M = \frac{\pi}{4}\left(\sin\frac{\pi}{8} + \sin\frac{3\pi}{8} + \sin\frac{5\pi}{8} + \sin\frac{7\pi}{8}\right)$

$\approx$ **2.0523 units²**

10.

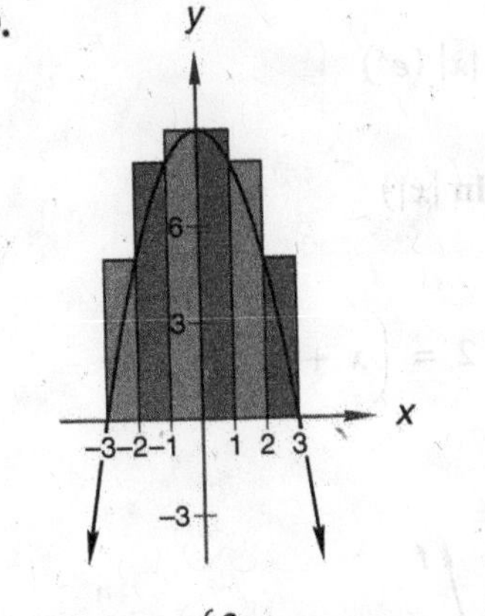

$S_U = 2\left\{\frac{3}{3}[f(0) + f(1) + f(2)]\right\}$

$= 2(9 + 8 + 5) =$ **44 units²**

11. `nDeriv(sin(X⁻¹),X,0.2)` $\approx$ **−7.0940**

12. (a)

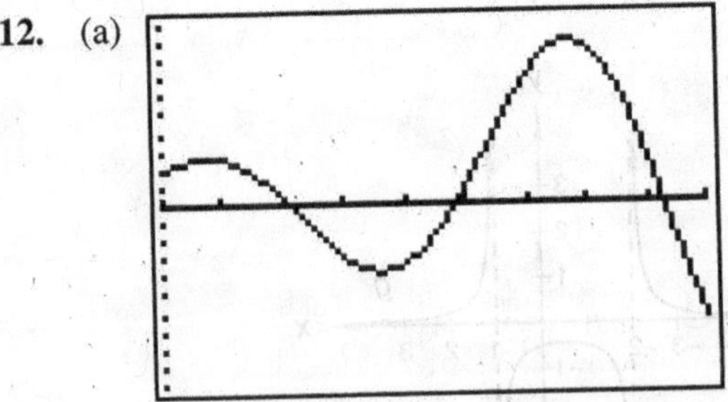

(b)

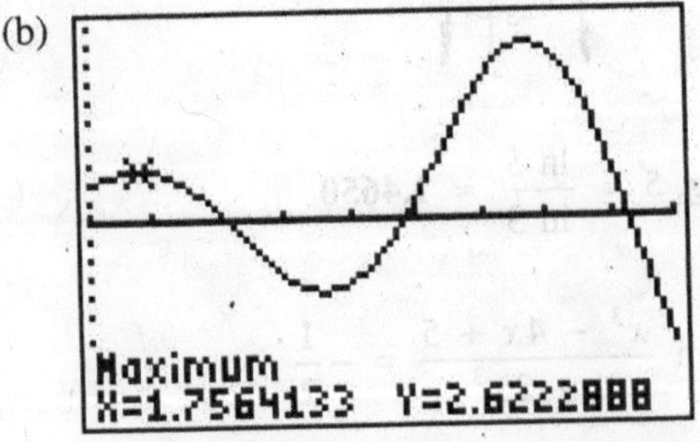

Local maximum: (1.7564133, 2.6222888)

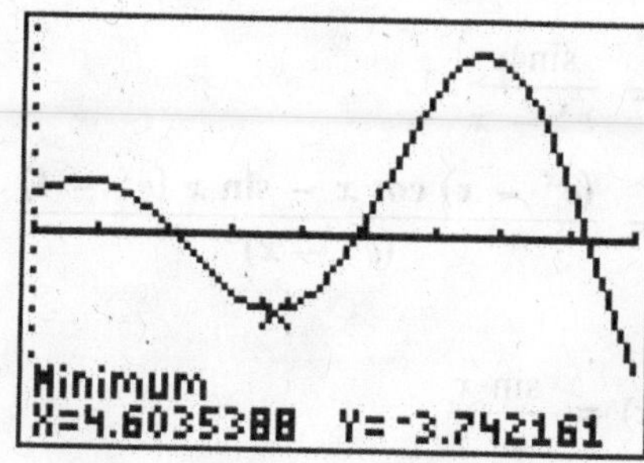

Local minimum: **(4.6035388, –3.742161)**

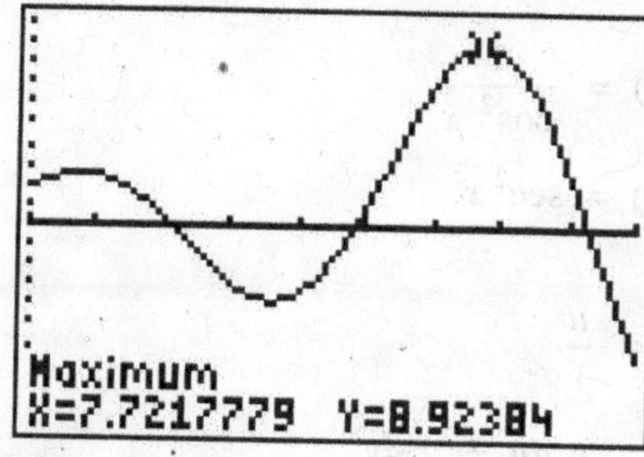

Local maximum: **(7.7217779, 8.92384)**

(c)

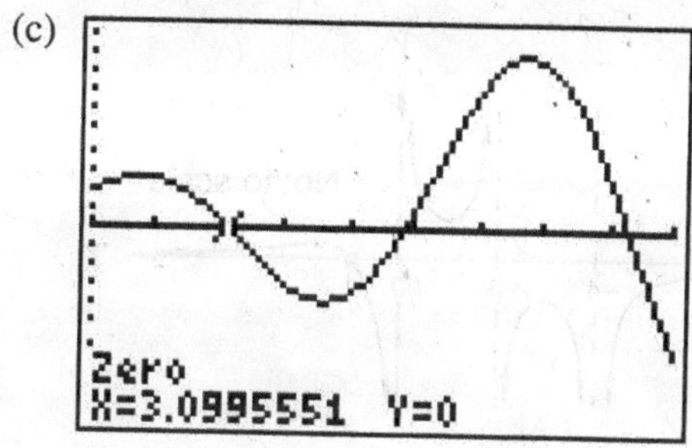

$x \approx$ **3.0995551**

13. $\int (2 \sin u - 3u^{-3})\, du = \mathbf{-2 \cos u + \frac{3}{2}u^{-2} + C}$

14. $\int -\frac{3}{t}\, dt = \mathbf{-3 \ln |t| + C}$

15. $\int (2x^{-1/2} - 4)\, dx = \mathbf{4x^{1/2} - 4x + C}$

16. $u = x^2 + 1 \qquad du = 2x\, dx$

$y = u^{-1/2}$

$dy = -\frac{1}{2}u^{-3/2}\, du$

$dy = -\frac{1}{2}(x^2 + 1)^{-3/2}\, 2x\, dx$

$\frac{dy}{dx} = \mathbf{-x(x^2 + 1)^{-3/2}}$

17. $u = x^2 + 1 \qquad du = 2x\, dx$

$y = \ln |u|$

$dy = \frac{1}{u}\, du$

$dy = \frac{1}{x^2 + 1} 2x\, dx$

$\frac{dy}{dx} = \mathbf{\frac{2x}{x^2 + 1}}$

18. $u = \sin x \qquad du = \cos x\, dx$

$y = \ln |u|$

$dy = \frac{1}{u}\, du$

$dy = \frac{1}{\sin x} \cos x\, dx$

$\frac{dy}{dx} = \mathbf{\cot x}$

19. $y = x^2 e^x$

$y' = x^2 e^x + e^x(2x)$

$y' = \mathbf{xe^x(x + 2)}$

20. $y = x \ln |x|$

$y' = \frac{x}{x} + \ln |x|$

$y' = \mathbf{1 + \ln |x|}$

21.

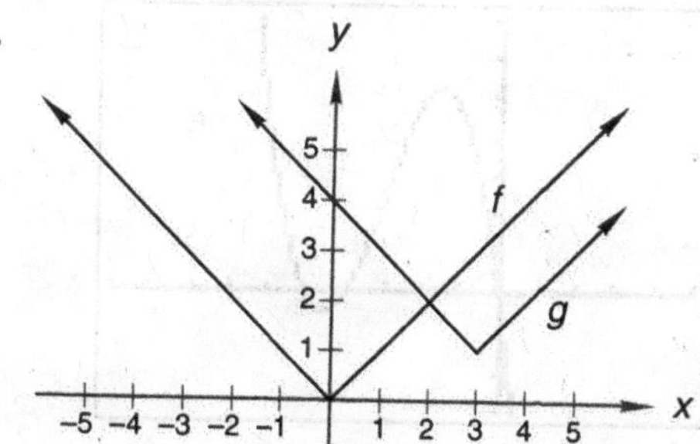

22. $fg(x) = f(x)\, g(x) = \ln x \left(\frac{1}{x}\right)$

$fg(x) = \mathbf{\frac{\ln x}{x}}$

Domain: $\{x \in \mathbb{R} \mid x > 0\}$

23.

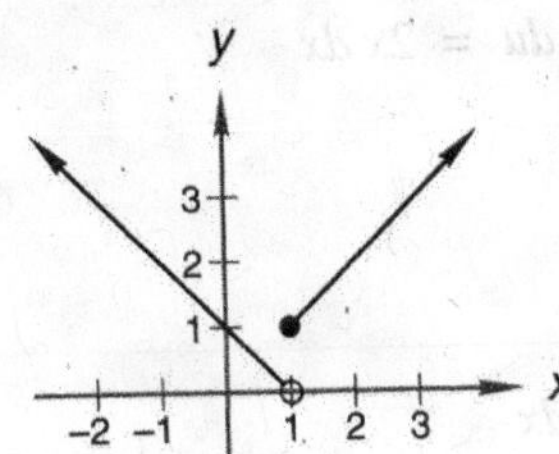

$\lim_{x \to 1^-} f(x) = \mathbf{0}$

$\lim_{x \to 1^+} f(x) = \mathbf{1}$

24. $\dfrac{6}{r} = \dfrac{10}{h}$

$$10r = 6h$$

$$r = \frac{6h}{10}$$

$$r = \mathbf{\frac{3}{5}h}$$

25. $S_n = \dfrac{n(n+1)}{2}$

$$S_{200} = \frac{200(201)}{2}$$

$$S_{200} = \mathbf{20{,}100}$$

PROBLEM SET 42

1. (a) $\mathbf{V = x(10 - 2x)(8 - 2x)}$

(b)

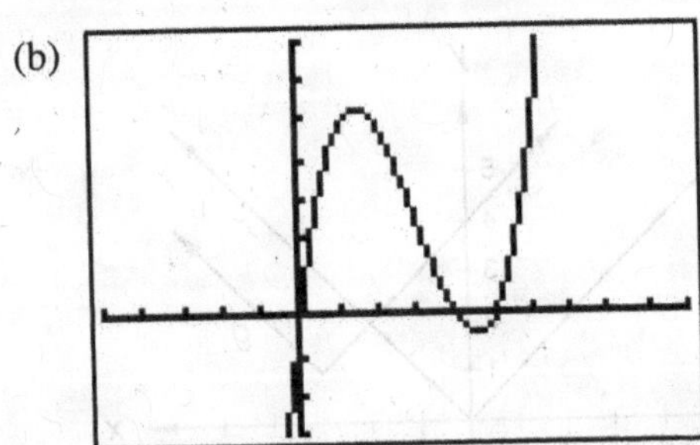

(c)

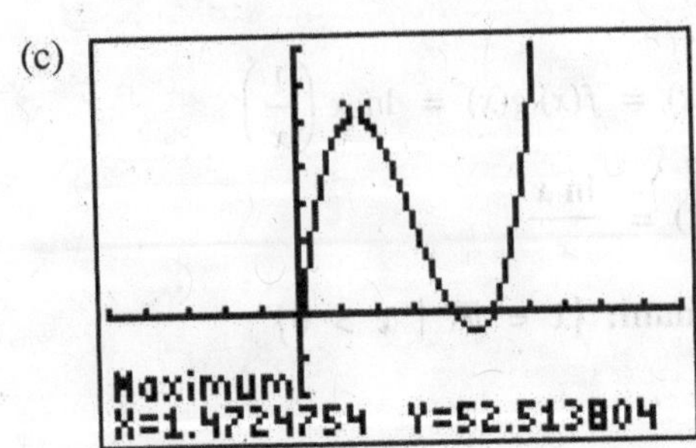

$x \approx \mathbf{1.4724754}$

$V \approx \mathbf{52.513804\ in.^3}$

(d) $\mathbf{\{x \in \mathbb{R} \mid 0 < x < 4\}}$

2. $y = \dfrac{\sin x}{e^x - x}$

$$y' = \mathbf{\frac{(e^x - x)\cos x - \sin x\,(e^x - 1)}{(e^x - x)^2}}$$

3. $f(x) = \dfrac{\sin x}{\cos x}$

$$f'(x) = \frac{\cos x \cos x + \sin x \sin x}{\cos^2 x}$$

$$f'(x) = \frac{1}{\cos^2 x}$$

$$f'(x) = \mathbf{\sec^2 x}$$

4. $y = \dfrac{u}{v}$

$$dy = \mathbf{\frac{v\,du - u\,dv}{v^2}}$$

5.

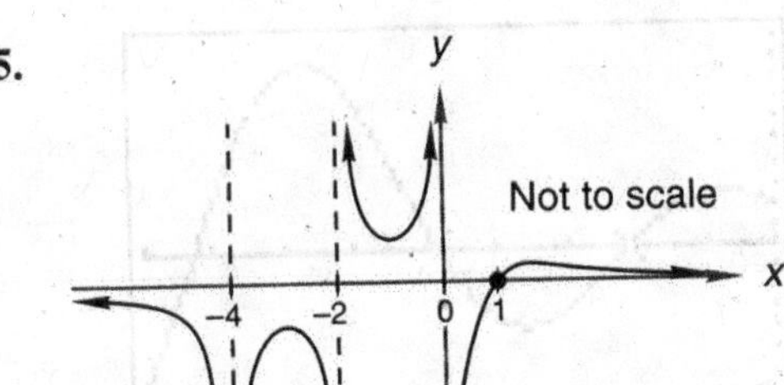

6. $V = \dfrac{1}{3}\pi r^2 h$

$$\frac{dV}{dt} = \frac{1}{3}\pi r^2 \frac{dh}{dt} + \frac{2}{3}\pi r h \frac{dr}{dt}$$

$$\frac{dV}{dt} = \mathbf{\frac{1}{3}\pi r\left(r\frac{dh}{dt} + 2h\frac{dr}{dt}\right)}$$

7.

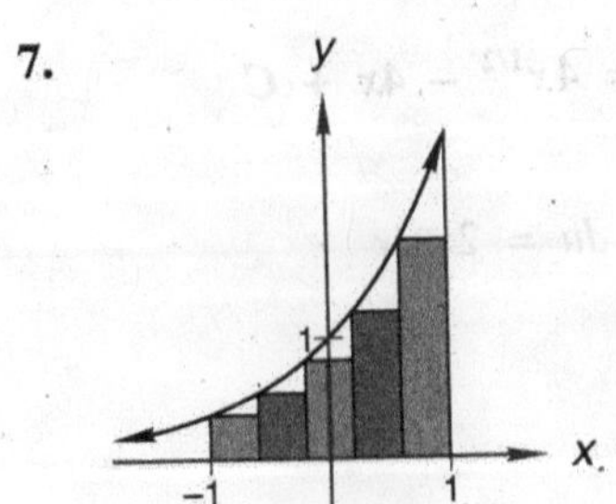

$$S_L = \frac{2}{5}\left(e^{-1} + e^{-3/5} + e^{-1/5} + e^{1/5} + e^{3/5}\right)$$

$$\approx \mathbf{1.9116\ units^2}$$

8.

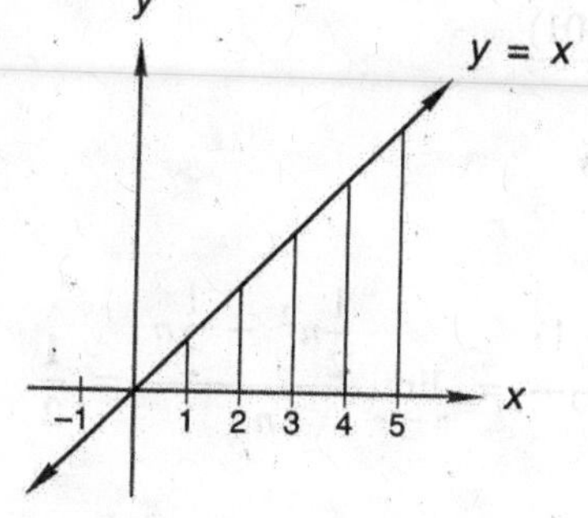

(a) $S_U = 1(1 + 2 + 3 + 4 + 5) = \mathbf{15\ units^2}$

(b) $S_L = 1(0 + 1 + 2 + 3 + 4) = \mathbf{10\ units^2}$

(c) $A = \frac{1}{2}bh = \frac{1}{2}(5)(5) = \mathbf{\frac{25}{2}\ units^2}$

(d) $S_U = \frac{5}{n}\left(\frac{5}{n} + \frac{10}{n} + \frac{15}{n} + \cdots + \frac{5n}{n}\right)$

$= \frac{5}{n}\left[\frac{5}{n}(1 + 2 + 3 + \cdots + n)\right]$

$= \frac{25}{n^2}\left[\frac{n(n+1)}{2}\right]$

$= \mathbf{\frac{25(n+1)}{2n}\ units^2}$

9. $y = \cos x$

$\frac{dy}{dx} = -\sin x$

$\left.\frac{dy}{dx}\right|_{\pi} = 0 \qquad \perp$ slope is undefined

$\mathbf{x = \pi}$

10. (a) $f(x) = -\frac{1}{4}x^4 + \frac{1}{2}x^2 - 3$

$f'(x) = -x^3 + x$

$0 = -x(x^2 - 1)$

$0 = -x(x + 1)(x - 1)$

Critical numbers: $\mathbf{x = -1, 0, 1}$

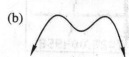

(b)

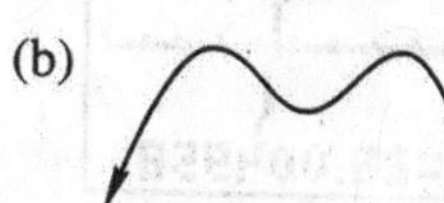

Local maxima: $\mathbf{\left(-1, -\frac{11}{4}\right), \left(1, -\frac{11}{4}\right)}$

Local minimum: $\mathbf{(0, -3)}$

11. $\int \left(2x^2 - x^{-1/2} + e^x + \frac{1}{x} - \sin x\right) dx$

$= \mathbf{\frac{2}{3}x^3 - 2x^{1/2} + e^x + \ln|x| + \cos x + C}$

12. $\int -4u^{1/2}\, du = \mathbf{-\frac{8}{3}u^{3/2} + C}$

13. $u = x^2 + \sin x \qquad du = (2x + \cos x)\, dx$

$y = \ln|u|$

$dy = \frac{1}{u}\, du$

$dy = \frac{(2x + \cos x)\, dx}{x^2 + \sin x}$

$\frac{dy}{dx} = \mathbf{\frac{2x + \cos x}{x^2 + \sin x}}$

14. $u = x^3 + 3 \qquad du = 3x^2\, dx$

$y = u^{-1/2}$

$dy = -\frac{1}{2}u^{-3/2}\, du$

$dy = -\frac{1}{2}(x^3 + 3)^{-3/2}(3x^2)\, dx$

$\frac{dy}{dx} = \mathbf{-\frac{3}{2}x^2(x^3 + 3)^{-3/2}}$

15. $P(t) = 16e^{-4t}$

$P'(t) = -64e^{-4t}$

$P'(4) = \mathbf{-64e^{-16}}$

16. $s(t) = 2t^{-1/2} + \ln|t|$

$s'(t) = -t^{-3/2} + t^{-1}$

$s'(t) = \mathbf{t^{-3/2}(t^{1/2} - 1)}$

17. $y = 2u^3e^u$

$\frac{dy}{du} = 2u^3e^u + e^u(6u^2)$

$\frac{dy}{du} = \mathbf{2u^2e^u(u + 3)}$

18.

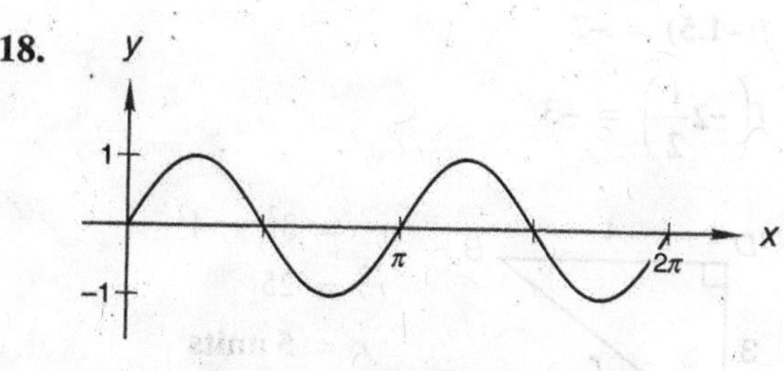

$\mathbf{\left[0, \frac{\pi}{4}\right), \left(\frac{3\pi}{4}, \frac{5\pi}{4}\right), \left(\frac{7\pi}{4}, 2\pi\right]}$

19. $V = \frac{1}{3}\pi r^2 h = \frac{1}{3}\pi\, 3^2(6) = \mathbf{18\pi\ cm^3}$

20.
$$\cos(2A) = \cos^2 A - \sin^2 A$$
$$\cos(2A) = \cos^2 A - (1 - \cos^2 A)$$
$$\cos(2A) = 2\cos^2 A - 1$$
$$2\cos^2 A = 1 + \cos(2A)$$
$$\cos^2 A = \frac{1}{2} + \frac{1}{2}\cos(2A)$$
$$\cos A = \pm\sqrt{\frac{1}{2} + \frac{1}{2}\cos(2A)}$$
$$\mathbf{\cos\frac{x}{2} = \pm\sqrt{\frac{1}{2} + \frac{1}{2}\cos x}}$$
$$\cos(2A) = \cos^2 A - \sin^2 A$$
$$\cos(2A) = (1 - \sin^2 A) - \sin^2 A$$
$$\cos(2A) = 1 - 2\sin^2 A$$
$$2\sin^2 A = 1 - \cos(2A)$$
$$\sin^2 A = \frac{1}{2} - \frac{1}{2}\cos(2A)$$
$$\sin A = \pm\sqrt{\frac{1}{2} - \frac{1}{2}\cos(2A)}$$
$$\mathbf{\sin\frac{x}{2} = \pm\sqrt{\frac{1}{2} - \frac{1}{2}\cos x}}$$

21. $|x - 1| < 0.01$

"x is less than 0.01 away from 1"

(0.99, 1.01)

22.

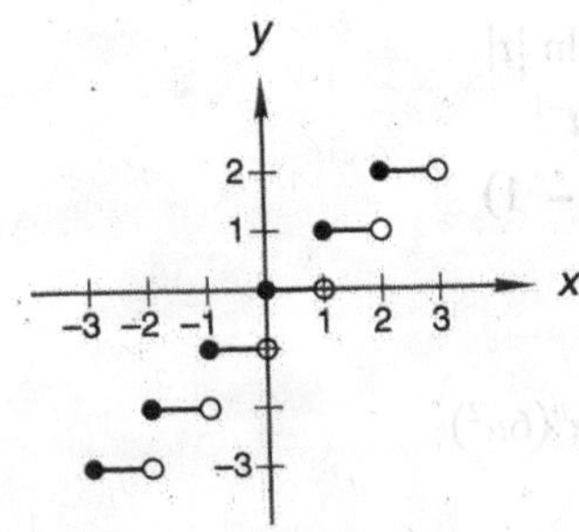

$f(1.2) = \mathbf{1}$

$f(-1.5) = \mathbf{-2}$

$f\left(-2\frac{1}{2}\right) = \mathbf{-3}$

23. D, 4, B, 3, r, O

$$r^2 = 3^2 + 4^2$$
$$r^2 = 25$$
$$r = \mathbf{5\ units}$$

24.
$$S_{300} = \frac{300(301)}{2}$$
$$S_{300} = \mathbf{45{,}150}$$

25.
$$\lim_{n\to\infty} \frac{\frac{1}{2}n(n+1)}{n^2} = \lim_{n\to\infty} \frac{\frac{1}{2}n^2 + \frac{1}{2}n}{n^2} = \mathbf{\frac{1}{2}}$$

PROBLEM SET 43

1. (a)
$$2h + 2r + \pi r = 20$$
$$2h = 20 - 2r - \pi r$$
$$\mathbf{h = 10 - r - \frac{1}{2}\pi r}$$

(b)
$$A = 2rh + \frac{1}{2}\pi r^2$$
$$A = 2r\left(10 - r - \frac{1}{2}\pi r\right) + \frac{1}{2}\pi r^2$$
$$A = 20r - 2r^2 - \pi r^2 + \frac{1}{2}\pi r^2$$
$$\mathbf{A = \left(-2 - \frac{1}{2}\pi\right)r^2 + 20r}$$

(c)

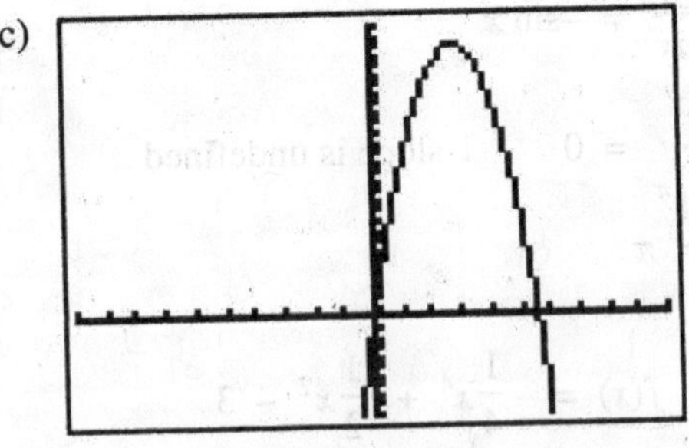

(d)

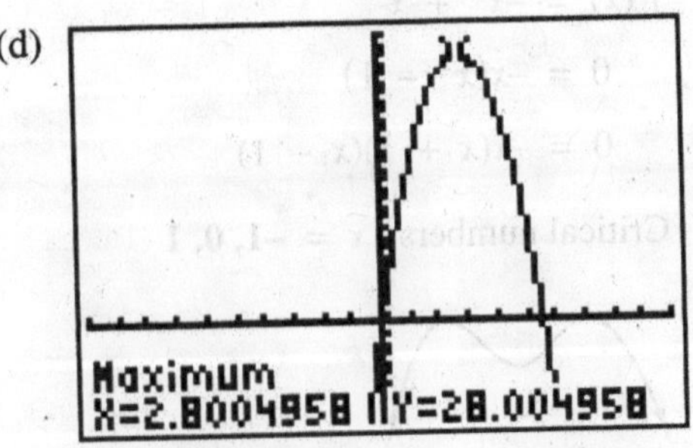

$r \approx$ **2.8004958 units**

$A \approx$ **28.004958 units²**

2.

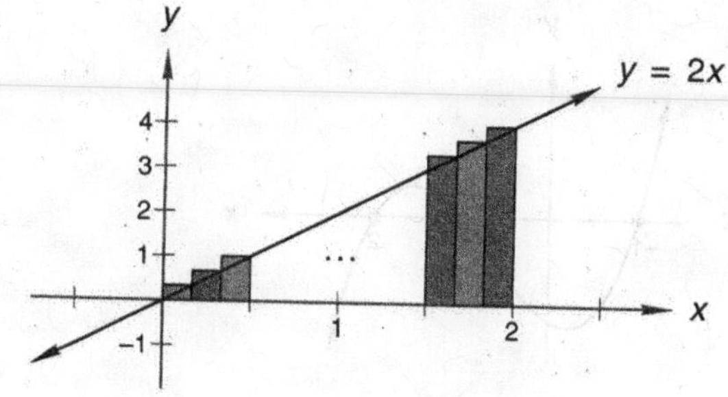

$$\Delta x = \frac{2}{n}$$

$$x_1 = \Delta x,\ x_2 = 2\,\Delta x,\ x_3 = 3\,\Delta x,\ \ldots,\ x_n = n\,\Delta x$$

$$\begin{aligned}
S_U &= \Delta x[2(\Delta x) + 2(2\,\Delta x) + 2(3\,\Delta x) + \cdots \\
&\quad + 2(n\Delta x)] \\
&= \Delta x(2\,\Delta x)(1 + 2 + 3 + \cdots + n) \\
&= 2(\Delta x)^2(1 + 2 + 3 + \cdots + n) \\
&= 2\left(\frac{2}{n}\right)^2\left[\frac{n(n+1)}{2}\right] \\
&= \frac{8}{n^2}\left[\frac{n(n+1)}{2}\right] = \frac{4(n+1)}{n}
\end{aligned}$$

$$A = \lim_{n\to\infty} S_U = \lim_{n\to\infty} 4\left(\frac{n+1}{n}\right) = \mathbf{4\ units^2}$$

$$A = \frac{1}{2}bh = \frac{1}{2}(2)(4) = 4\text{ units}^2$$

3.

$$\Delta x = \frac{2}{n}$$

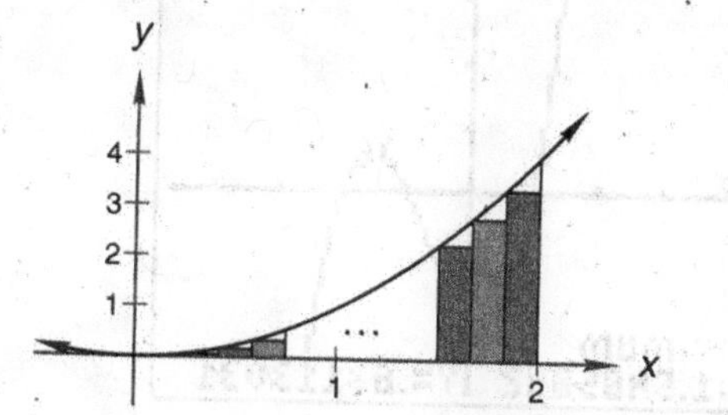

$$x_0 = 0,\ x_1 = \Delta x,\ x_2 = 2\,\Delta x,\ x_3 = 3\,\Delta x,\ \ldots,$$
$$x_{n-1} = (n-1)\,\Delta x$$

$$\begin{aligned}
S_L &= \Delta x\left\{0^2 + (\Delta x)^2 + (2\Delta x)^2 + (3\Delta x)^2 + \cdots \right. \\
&\quad \left. + [(n-1)\,\Delta x]^2\right\} \\
&= \Delta x[(\Delta x)^2 + 2^2(\Delta x)^2 + 3^2(\Delta x)^2 + \cdots \\
&\quad + (n-1)^2(\Delta x)^2] \\
&= \Delta x(\Delta x)^2[1 + 2^2 + 3^2 + \cdots + (n-1)^2] \\
&= (\Delta x)^3[1 + 2^2 + 3^2 + \cdots + (n-1)^2] \\
&= \left(\frac{2}{n}\right)^3\left(\frac{(n-1)(n-1+1)(2(n-1)+1)}{6}\right) \\
&= \frac{8}{n^3}\left[\frac{(n-1)n(2n-1)}{6}\right] \\
&= \frac{4(n-1)(2n-1)}{3n^2}
\end{aligned}$$

$$\begin{aligned}
A &= \lim_{n\to\infty} S_L = \lim_{n\to\infty} \frac{4}{3}\left[\frac{(n-1)(2n-1)}{n^2}\right] \\
&= \frac{4}{3}(2) = \mathbf{\frac{8}{3}\ units^2}
\end{aligned}$$

4.

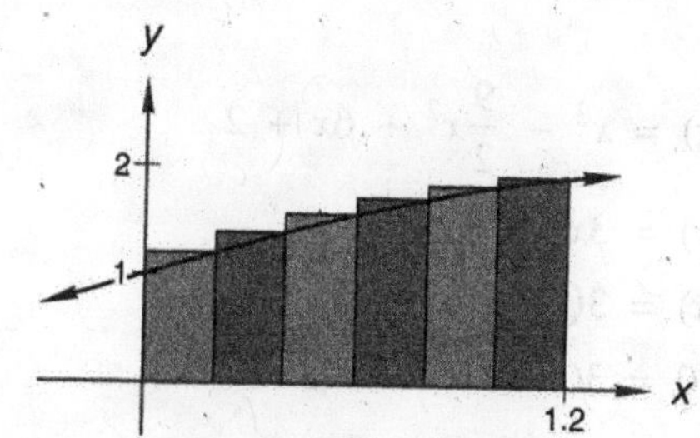

$$\Delta x = \frac{1.2}{6} = 0.2$$

$$\begin{aligned}
S_R &= 0.2(\sin 0.2 + 1 + \sin 0.4 + 1 + \sin 0.6 \\
&\quad + 1 + \sin 0.8 + 1 + \sin 1 + 1 \\
&\quad + \sin 1.2 + 1) \\
&= 0.2(6 + \sin 0.2 + \sin 0.4 + \sin 0.6 \\
&\quad + \sin 0.8 + \sin 1 + \sin 1.2) \\
&\approx \mathbf{1.9287\ units^2}
\end{aligned}$$

5. $S_R = \displaystyle\sum_{i=0}^{9} \mathbf{0.12[\sin(0.12i) + 1]}$

6.
$$y = \frac{e^x + x}{\cos x}$$

$$\frac{dy}{dx} = \frac{\cos x\,(e^x + 1) + (e^x + x)\sin x}{\cos^2 x}$$

$$\frac{dy}{dx} = \mathbf{\sec x\,(e^x + 1) + \tan x \sec x\,(e^x + x)}$$

7.
$$y = \frac{x^2 + 3}{x^3 - 2x}$$

$$\frac{dy}{dx} = \frac{(x^3 - 2x)(2x) - (x^2 + 3)(3x^2 - 2)}{(x^3 - 2x)^2}$$

$$\frac{dy}{dx} = \frac{2x^2(x^2 - 2) - (x^2 + 3)(3x^2 - 2)}{x^2(x^2 - 2)^2}$$

$$\frac{dy}{dx} = \mathbf{\frac{2}{x^2 - 2} - \frac{(x^2 + 3)(3x^2 - 2)}{x^2(x^2 - 2)^2}}$$

8. $d\left(\dfrac{u}{v}\right) = \dfrac{v\,du - u\,dv}{v^2} = \mathbf{\dfrac{du}{v} - \dfrac{u\,dv}{v^2}}$

9.

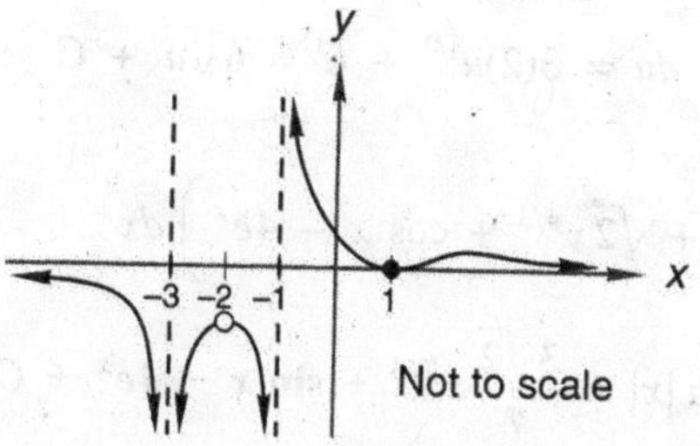

y

−3 −2 −1 1 x

Not to scale

10. $s(t) = \sin t$
$v(t) = \cos t$
$v(\pi) = \cos \pi$
$v(\pi) = $ **−1 unit/s**

11. (a) $f(x) = x^3 - \frac{9}{2}x^2 + 6x + 2$
$f'(x) = 3x^2 - 9x + 6$
$f'(x) = 3(x^2 - 3x + 2)$
$0 = 3(x - 2)(x - 1)$
Critical numbers: $x = $ **1, 2**

(b)
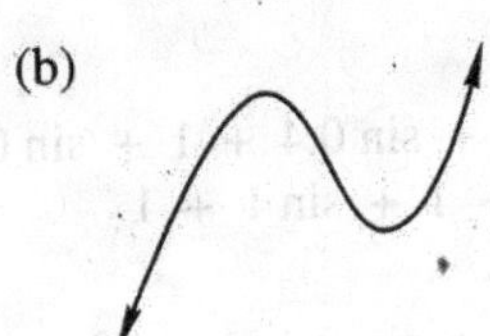

Local maximum: $\left(\mathbf{1, \frac{9}{2}}\right)$

Local minimum: (2, 4)

12. $u = e^x - 1 \qquad du = e^x\,dx$
$y = u^{1/2}$
$dy = \frac{1}{2}u^{-1/2}\,du$
$dy = \frac{1}{2}(e^x - 1)^{-1/2}e^x\,dx$
$$\frac{dy}{dx} = \mathbf{\frac{e^x}{2\sqrt{e^x - 1}}}$$

13. $u = x^2 - 1 \qquad du = 2x\,dx$
$y = u^{-1/3}$
$dy = -\frac{1}{3}u^{-4/3}\,du$
$dy = -\frac{1}{3}(x^2 - 1)^{-4/3}(2x)\,dx$
$$\frac{dy}{dx} = \mathbf{-\frac{2}{3}x(x^2 - 1)^{-4/3}}$$

14. $\int 3u^{-1/2}\,du = 3(2)u^{1/2} + C = \mathbf{6\sqrt{u} + C}$

15. $\int\left(\frac{3}{x} + \sqrt{2}x^{4/3} + \cos x - 4e^x\right)dx$
$= \mathbf{3\ln|x| + \frac{3\sqrt{2}}{7}x^{7/3} + \sin x - 4e^x + C}$

16.
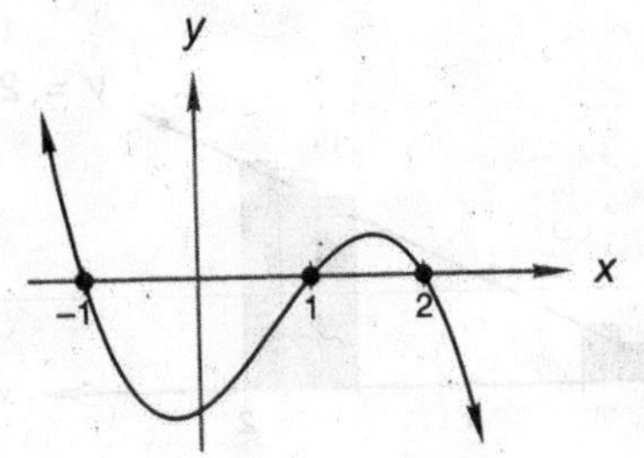

17.
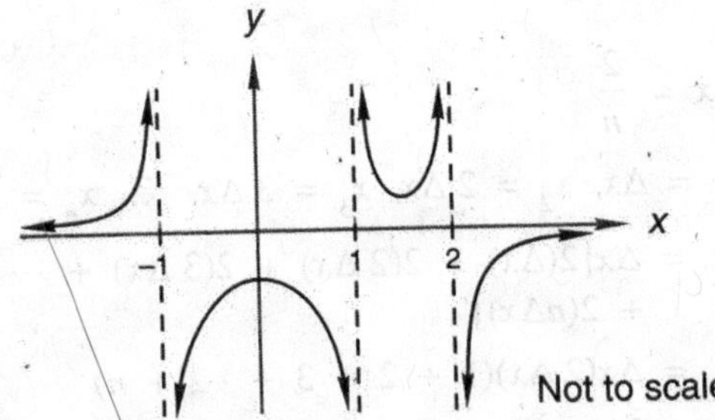

18.
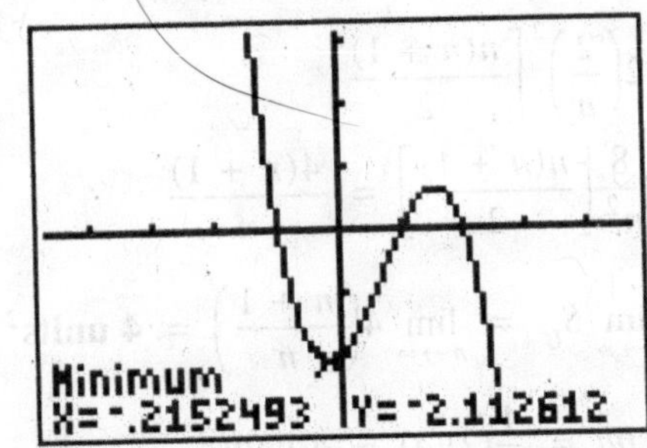

Local minimum: (−0.2152493, −2.112612)

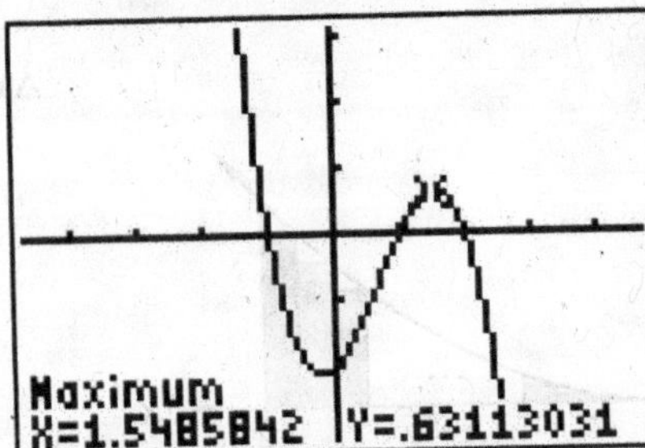

Local maximum: (1.5485842, 0.63113031)

19.
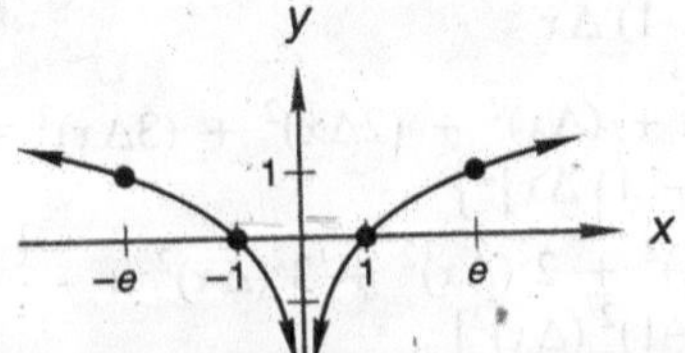

20. $\lim_{x \to 0^+} \ln|x| = \mathbf{-\infty}$

21. (a) $2x + 2y = 50$
$2y = 50 - 2x$
$y = 25 - x$
$A = xy$
$A = x(25 - x)$
$A = \mathbf{25x - x^2}$

(b) $\{x \in \mathbb{R} \mid 0 \le x \le 25\}$

(c)

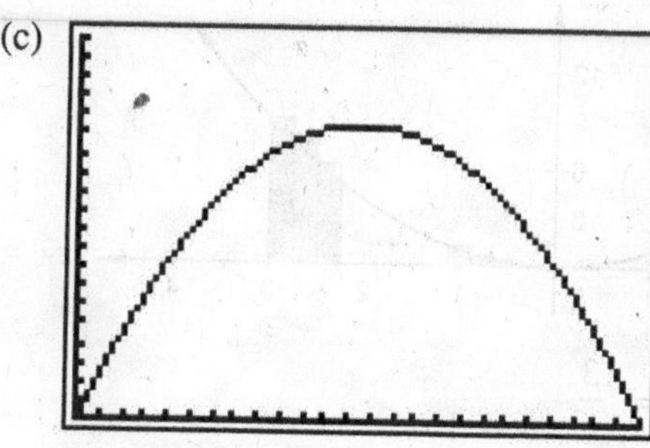

(d)

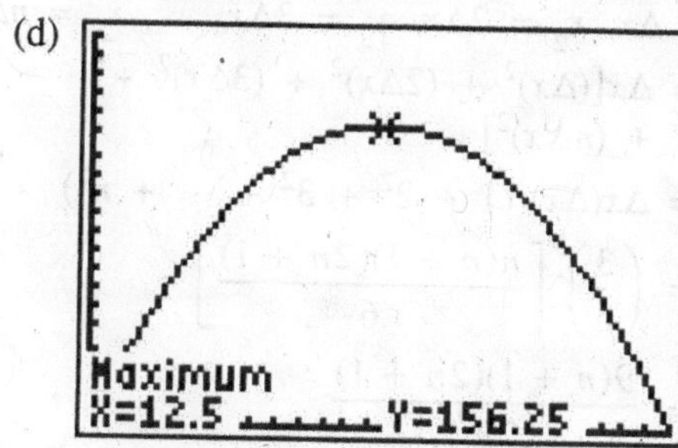

Maximum: **(12.5, 156.25)**

22. $f(x) = a(x - b)(x - c)$
$f(x) = a(x - 1)(x + 2)$
$f(0) = a(-1)(2)$
$-4 = -2a$
$a = 2$
$\mathbf{f(x) = 2(x - 1)(x + 2)}$

23. (a) The equation represents a **circle** of radius 2 centered at the origin.

(b) $x^2 + y^2 = 4$
$y^2 = 4 - x^2$
$y = \pm\sqrt{4 - x^2}$

```
Y1=√(4-X²)  Y2=-√(4-X²)
```

24. $\left[-\sin\left(\frac{\pi}{2} - x\right)\right](\cos -x) + 1 = -\cos x \cos x + 1$
$= 1 - \cos^2 x = \sin^2 x$

25. $a - b = 2$
$a = b + 2$
$a^2 = b^2 + 4b + 4$
$a^2 > b^2 + 4b + 3$
Quantity A is greater: **A**

PROBLEM SET 44

1. $T_t = T_0 e^{kt}$
$48 = 6e^{3k}$
$8 = e^{3k}$
$3k = \ln 8$
$k = \frac{1}{3}\ln 8$
$k = \ln 2$
$T_{14} = 6e^{14 \ln 2}$
$= 6e^{\ln 2^{14}}$
$= 6(2^{14})$
$=$ **98,304 troubles**

2. (a) $\mathbf{x^2y = 27}$

(b) $\mathbf{A = 2x^2 + 4xy}$

(c) $y = 27x^{-2}$ $\quad A = 2x^2 + 4x(27x^{-2})$
$\mathbf{A = 2x^2 + 108x^{-1}}$

(d) $\{x \in \mathbb{R} \mid x > 0\}$

(e)

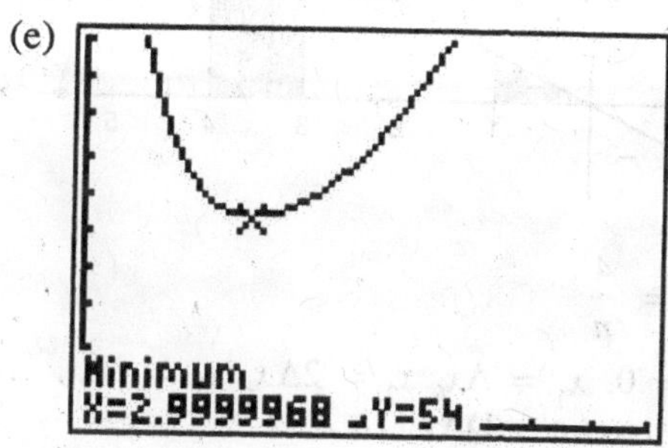

$x \approx$ **2.9999968**
$A =$ **54 units²**

3. $y = \sin u \qquad u = 5x^3$
$\frac{dy}{dx} = \frac{dy}{du} \cdot \frac{du}{dx}$
$\frac{dy}{dx} = \cos u \cdot 15x^2$
$\frac{dy}{dx} = \mathbf{15x^2 \cos(5x^3)}$

4. $y = \ln|u| \qquad u = x^3 + e^x$
$\frac{dy}{dx} = \frac{dy}{du} \cdot \frac{du}{dx}$
$\frac{dy}{dx} = \left(\frac{1}{u}\right)(3x^2 + e^x)$
$\frac{dy}{dx} = \mathbf{\frac{3x^2 + e^x}{x^3 + e^x}}$

5. $f'(x) = \lim_{h \to 0} \dfrac{f(x+h) - f(x-h)}{2h}$

$= \lim_{h \to 0} \dfrac{-3(x+h) + 2 - [-3(x-h) + 2]}{2h}$

$= \lim_{h \to 0} \dfrac{-3x - 3h + 2 + 3x - 3h - 2}{2h}$

$= \lim_{h \to 0} \dfrac{-6h}{2h} = \mathbf{-3}$

6. $f'(1) = \lim_{x \to 1} \dfrac{f(x) - f(1)}{x - 1}$

$= \lim_{x \to 1} \dfrac{-x^2 + 1}{x - 1}$

$= \lim_{x \to 1} \dfrac{-(x+1)(x-1)}{x-1}$

$= \lim_{x \to 1} -(x+1) = \mathbf{-2}$

7.

$\Delta x = \dfrac{4}{n}$

$x_0 = 0,\ x_1 = \Delta x,\ x_2 = 2\Delta x,\ x_3 = 3\Delta x,\ \ldots,$
$x_{n-1} = (n-1)\Delta x$

$S_L = \Delta x\{3\Delta x + 3(2\Delta x) + 3(3\Delta x) + \cdots + 3[(n-1)\Delta x]\}$

$= 3\Delta x(\Delta x)[1 + 2 + 3 + \cdots + (n-1)]$

$= 3(\Delta x)^2\left[\dfrac{(n-1)n}{2}\right]$

$= 3\left(\dfrac{4}{n}\right)^2\left[\dfrac{(n-1)n}{2}\right]$

$= \dfrac{24(n-1)}{n}$

$A = \lim_{n \to \infty} \dfrac{24(n-1)}{n} = \mathbf{24\ units^2}$

$A = \dfrac{1}{2}bh = \dfrac{1}{2}(4)(12) = 24 \text{ units}^2$

8.

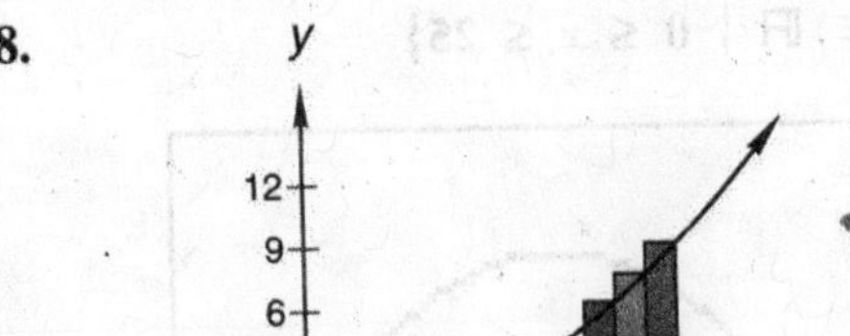

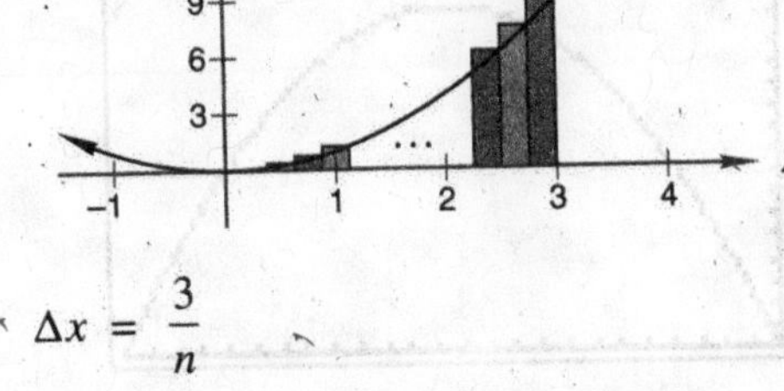

$\Delta x = \dfrac{3}{n}$

$x_1 = \Delta x,\ x_2 = 2\Delta x,\ x_3 = 3\Delta x,\ \ldots,\ x_n = n\Delta x$

$S_U = \Delta x[(\Delta x)^2 + (2\Delta x)^2 + (3\Delta x)^2 + \cdots + (n\Delta x)^2]$

$= \Delta x(\Delta x)^2(1 + 2^2 + 3^2 + \cdots + n^2)$

$= \left(\dfrac{3}{n}\right)^3\left[\dfrac{n(n+1)(2n+1)}{6}\right]$

$= \dfrac{9(n+1)(2n+1)}{2n^2}$

$A = \lim_{n \to \infty} \dfrac{9(n+1)(2n+1)}{2n^2} = \mathbf{9\ units^2}$

9. $f(x) = \dfrac{\sin x}{e^x + x^2}$

$f'(x) = \dfrac{(e^x + x^2)(\cos x) - \sin x\,(e^x + 2x)}{(e^x + x^2)^2}$

$f'(x) = \mathbf{\dfrac{\cos x}{e^x + x^2} - \dfrac{\sin x\,(e^x + 2x)}{(e^x + x^2)^2}}$

10. $y = \dfrac{\ln x}{\sin x + \cos x}$

$y' = \dfrac{(\sin x + \cos x)\frac{1}{x} - \ln x\,(\cos x - \sin x)}{(\sin x + \cos x)^2}$

$y' = \mathbf{\dfrac{1}{x(\sin x + \cos x)} - \dfrac{\ln x\,(\cos x - \sin x)}{1 + \sin(2x)}}$

11.

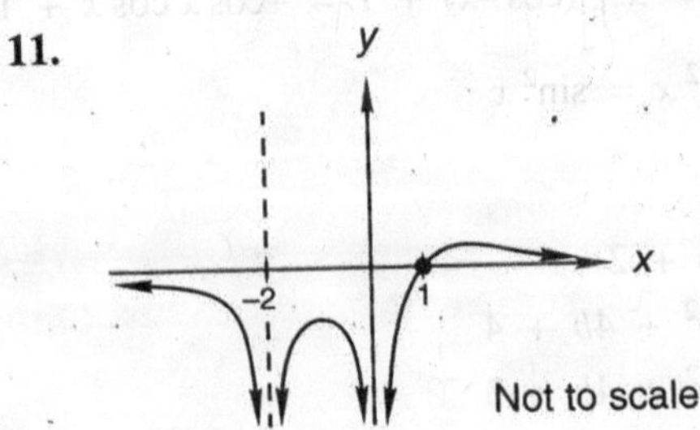

12. $s(t) = -2\ln(t+1)$

$v(t) = \dfrac{-2}{t+1}$

$v(2) = \dfrac{-2}{2+1} = \mathbf{-\dfrac{2}{3}\ \dfrac{unit}{s}}$

13. $y = \sin x \qquad \frac{dy}{dx} = \cos x$

$\left.\frac{dy}{dx}\right|_{\pi/2} = 0 \qquad \perp$ slope is undefined

$x = \frac{\pi}{2}$

14. $\int (3t^{-1/2} + 4 \cos t + 6t^2 + 6)\, dt$

$= \mathbf{6t^{1/2} + 4 \sin t + 2t^3 + 6t + C}$

15. $\int \left(\frac{3}{x} + 4 \sin x + 5e^x + x^{-6}\right) dx$

$= \mathbf{3 \ln |x| - 4 \cos x + 5e^x - \frac{1}{5}x^{-5} + C}$

16. $(fg)(x) = 3e^x(4 \sin x)$
$(fg)(x) = 12e^x \sin x$
$(fg)'(x) = 12e^x \cos x + \sin x\, (12e^x)$
$(fg)'(x) = \mathbf{12e^x(\cos x + \sin x)}$

17. $y = 2x^{-1} + 3x \ln |x| - 6$

$\frac{dy}{dx} = -2x^{-2} + 3x\left(\frac{1}{x}\right) + 3 \ln |x|$

$\frac{dy}{dx} = \mathbf{-2x^{-2} + 3 \ln |x| + 3}$

18. $u = x^2 - 4 \qquad du = 2x\, dx$

$h(x) = u^{-1/2}$

$dh(x) = -\frac{1}{2}u^{-3/2}\, du$

$dh(x) = -\frac{1}{2}(x^2 - 4)^{-3/2}\, (2x)\, dx$

$h'(x) = \mathbf{-x(x^2 - 4)^{-3/2}}$

19. $\frac{10}{L + x} = \frac{5}{L}$

$10L = 5L + 5x$

$5L = 5x$

$L = x$

$\frac{dL}{dt} = \mathbf{\frac{dx}{dt}}$

20. $\lim_{t\to\infty} \frac{2t - t^3}{14t^3 - 4t^4} = \lim_{t\to\infty} \frac{\frac{2}{t^3} - \frac{1}{t}}{\frac{14}{t} - 4} = \frac{0}{-4} = \mathbf{0}$

21. $\lim_{x\to-1} \frac{2x + 2}{x^2 + 2x + 1} = \lim_{x\to-1} \frac{2(x + 1)}{(x + 1)(x + 1)}$

$= \lim_{x\to-1} \frac{2}{x + 1}$

The limit does not exist.

22.

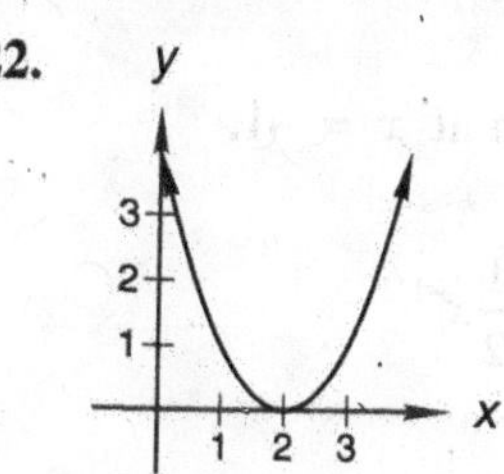

23. 

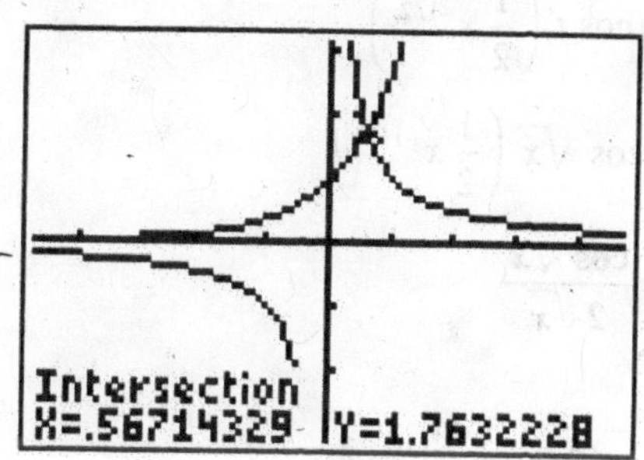

(0.56714329, 1.7632228)

24. For any y between 0 and 1 $y^2 > y^3$, so $\frac{1}{y^2} < \frac{1}{y^3}$.
Quantity B is greater: **B**

25. $S_{200} = \left[\frac{200(201)}{2}\right]^2 = \mathbf{404{,}010{,}000}$

Problem Set 45

1.

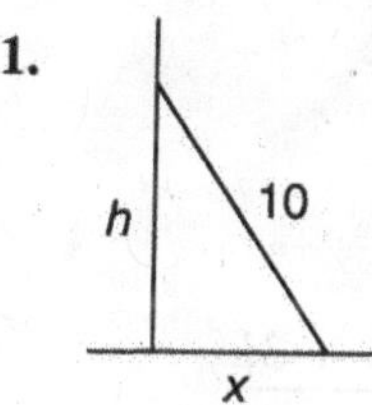

$h^2 + x^2 = 10^2$

$h^2 = 100 - x^2$

$h = \mathbf{\sqrt{100 - x^2}}$ **feet**

2. If f' is positive the function has positive slope. This occurs at points **B** and **D.**

3.

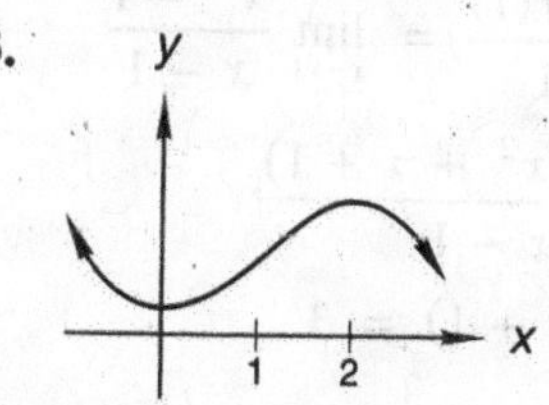

4.

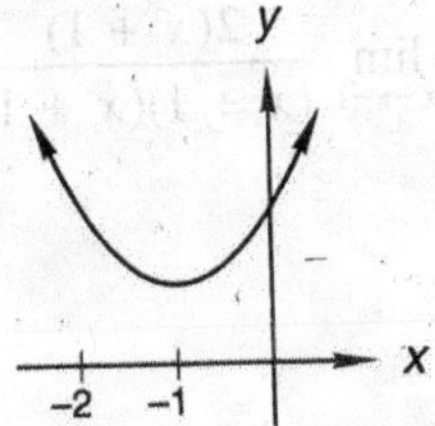

f attains a **local minimum at $x = -1$.**

5. $\dfrac{dy}{dt} = \cos t \qquad \dfrac{dt}{dx} = \dfrac{1}{2}x^{-1/2}$

$$\frac{dy}{dx} = \frac{dy}{dt} \cdot \frac{dt}{dx}$$
$$= (\cos t)\left(\frac{1}{2}x^{-1/2}\right)$$
$$= \cos\sqrt{x}\left(\frac{1}{2}x^{-1/2}\right)$$
$$= \boldsymbol{\frac{\cos\sqrt{x}}{2\sqrt{x}}}$$

6. $\dfrac{dy}{du} = -u^{-2} \qquad \dfrac{du}{dx} = 2x$

$$\frac{dy}{dx} = \frac{dy}{du} \cdot \frac{du}{dx}$$
$$= -u^{-2}(2x)$$
$$= \boldsymbol{\frac{-2x}{(x^2+1)^2}}$$

7. $$f'(x) = \lim_{h\to 0} \frac{f(x+h) - f(x-h)}{2h}$$
$$= \lim_{h\to 0}\left[\frac{(x+h)^2 + 3(x+h)}{2h} - \frac{(x-h)^2 + 3(x-h)}{2h}\right]$$
$$= \lim_{h\to 0}\left[\frac{x^2 + 2xh + h^2 + 3x + 3h}{2h} + \frac{-x^2 + 2xh - h^2 - 3x + 3h}{2h}\right]$$
$$= \lim_{h\to 0} \frac{4xh + 6h}{2h} = \lim_{h\to 0}(2x+3) = \mathbf{2x + 3}$$

8. $$f'(1) = \lim_{x\to 1} \frac{f(x) - f(1)}{x - 1} = \lim_{x\to 1} \frac{x^3 - 1}{x - 1}$$
$$= \lim_{x\to 1} \frac{(x-1)(x^2 + x + 1)}{x - 1}$$
$$= \lim_{x\to 1}(x^2 + x + 1) = \mathbf{3}$$

9. $$S_L = \frac{\pi}{4}\left(\sin 0 + \sin\frac{\pi}{4} + \sin\frac{3\pi}{4} + \sin\pi\right)$$
$$= \frac{\pi}{4}\left(0 + \frac{\sqrt{2}}{2} + \frac{\sqrt{2}}{2} + 0\right)$$
$$= \frac{\pi}{4}(\sqrt{2})$$
$$= \boldsymbol{\frac{\sqrt{2}\pi}{4}}\ \textbf{units}^2$$

10. $$S_M = \frac{\pi}{4}\left(2\sin\frac{\pi}{8} + 2\sin\frac{3\pi}{8}\right)$$
$$= \frac{\pi}{2}\left(\sin\frac{\pi}{8} + \sin\frac{3\pi}{8}\right)$$
$$= \textbf{2.0523 units}^2$$

11. $\Delta x = \dfrac{4}{n}$

$x_0 = 0,\ x_1 = \Delta x,\ x_2 = 2\Delta x,\ \ldots,$

$x_{n-1} = (n-1)\Delta x$

$$A = \lim_{n\to\infty} \Delta x\{0^3 + (\Delta x)^3 + (2\Delta x)^3 + \cdots + [(n-1)\Delta x]^3\}$$
$$= \lim_{n\to\infty} \Delta x[(\Delta x)^3 + 2^3(\Delta x)^3 + \cdots + (n-1)^3(\Delta x)^3]$$
$$= \lim_{n\to\infty} (\Delta x)^4[1^3 + 2^3 + \cdots + (n-1)^3]$$
$$= \lim_{n\to\infty} \left(\frac{4}{n}\right)^4\left[\frac{(n-1)n}{2}\right]^2$$
$$= \lim_{n\to\infty} \frac{4^3(n-1)^2}{n^2} = \textbf{64 units}^2$$

12. $y = \dfrac{\cos x}{\sin x}$

$y' = \dfrac{\sin x\,(-\sin x) - \cos x \cos x}{\sin^2 x}$

$y' = \dfrac{-\sin^2 x - \cos^2 x}{\sin^2 x}$

$y' = \mathbf{-\csc^2 x}$

13. $f(x) = \dfrac{e^x}{1 + x^2}$

$f'(x) = \dfrac{(1 + x^2)e^x - e^x(2x)}{(1 + x^2)^2}$

$f'(x) = \mathbf{\dfrac{e^x}{1 + x^2} - \dfrac{2xe^x}{(1 + x^2)^2}}$

14. (a) $f(x) = \dfrac{1}{3}x^3 + \dfrac{3}{2}x^2 + 2x + 2$

$f'(x) = x^2 + 3x + 2$

$0 = x^2 + 3x + 2$

$0 = (x + 2)(x + 1)$

Critical numbers: $x = \mathbf{-2, -1}$

(b) 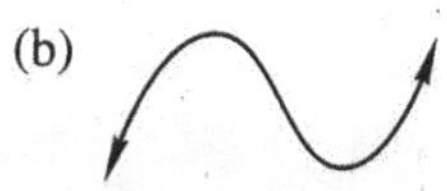

Local maximum: $\mathbf{\left(-2, \dfrac{4}{3}\right)}$

Local minimum: $\mathbf{\left(-1, \dfrac{7}{6}\right)}$

15. (a) 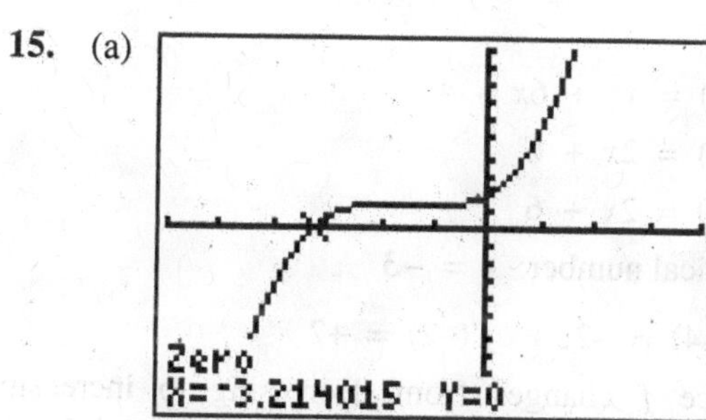

$x \approx \mathbf{-3.214015}$

(b) 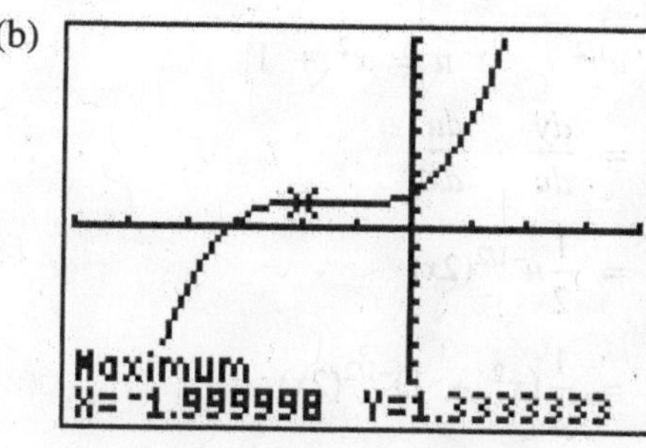

Local maximum: (–1.999998, 1.3333333)

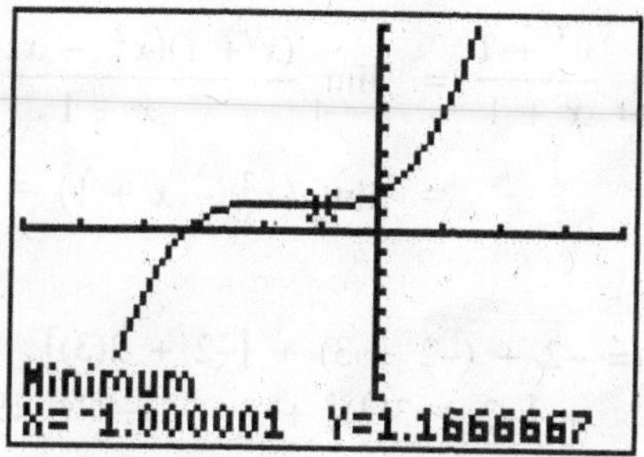

Local minimum: (–1.000001, 1.1666667)

(c) **They are approximately the same.**

16. $u = x^3 + 5 \qquad du = 3x^2\,dx$

$y = u^{-1/2}$

$dy = -\dfrac{1}{2}u^{-3/2}\,du$

$dy = -\dfrac{1}{2}(x^3 + 5)^{-3/2}(3x^2)\,dx$

$\mathbf{\dfrac{dy}{dx} = -\dfrac{3}{2}x^2(x^3 + 5)^{-3/2}}$

17. $f(x) = x - x \ln|x|$

$f'(x) = 1 - \left(x\dfrac{1}{x} + \ln|x|\right)$

$f'(x) = 1 - 1 - \ln|x|$

$f'(x) = \mathbf{-\ln|x|}$

18. $s(t) = s_0 + v_0t + \dfrac{1}{2}gt^2$

$s'(t) = \mathbf{v_0 + gt}$

19. $\int(\pi e^t - 2\sin t + 1)\,dt = \mathbf{\pi e^t + 2\cos t + t + C}$

20. $\int\left(\dfrac{4}{u} + 3u^{-15}\right)du = \mathbf{4\ln|u| - \dfrac{3}{14}u^{-14} + C}$

21. $(f \circ g)(x) = f(g(x))$

$(f \circ g)(x) = f(x^2 - 1)$

$\mathbf{(f \circ g)(x) = \sqrt{x^2 - 1}}$

22. $x^2 - 1 \ge 0$

$x^2 \ge 1$

$|x| \ge 1$

Domain: $\mathbf{\{x \in \mathbb{R} \mid |x| \ge 1\}}$

Range: $\mathbf{\{y \in \mathbb{R} \mid y \ge 0\}}$

23. $\lim_{x\to-1} \dfrac{x^3+1}{x+1} = \lim_{x\to-1} \dfrac{(x+1)(x^2-x+1)}{x+1}$

$= \lim_{x\to-1} (x^2 - x + 1) = \mathbf{3}$

24. $S_{20} = -2 + (-2+3) + [-2+2(3)] + [-2+3(3)] + \cdots + [-2+19(3)]$

$= -2(20) + [3 + 2(3) + 3(3) + \cdots + 19(3)]$

$= -2(20) + 3(1 + 2 + 3 + \cdots + 19)$

$= -2(20) + 3\left[\dfrac{19(20)}{2}\right]$

$= -40 + 3(190) = \mathbf{530}$

25.

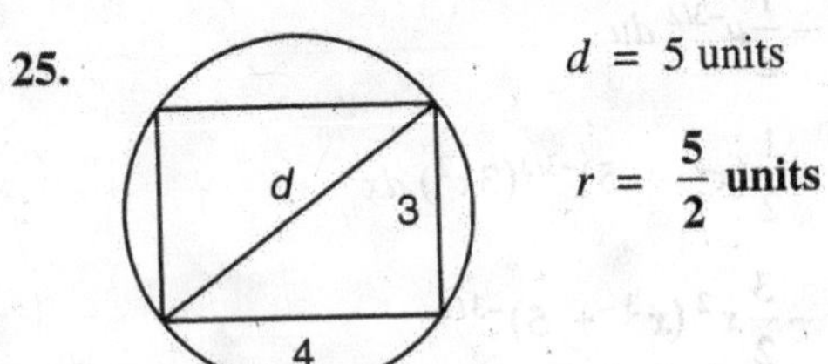

$d = 5$ units

$r = \dfrac{5}{2}$ **units**

3.

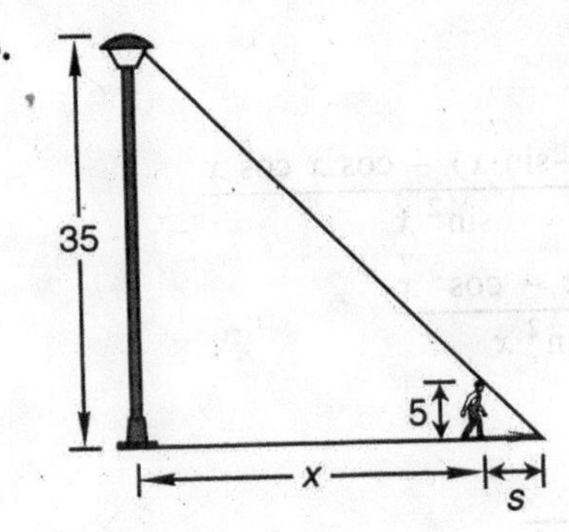

$\dfrac{s}{5} = \dfrac{x+s}{35}$

$35s = 5x + 5s$

$30s = 5x$

$6s = x$

$6\dfrac{ds}{dt} = \dfrac{dx}{dt}$

$\dfrac{ds}{dt} = \dfrac{3}{6}$

$\dfrac{ds}{dt} = \mathbf{\dfrac{1}{2}\dfrac{ft}{s}}$

4.

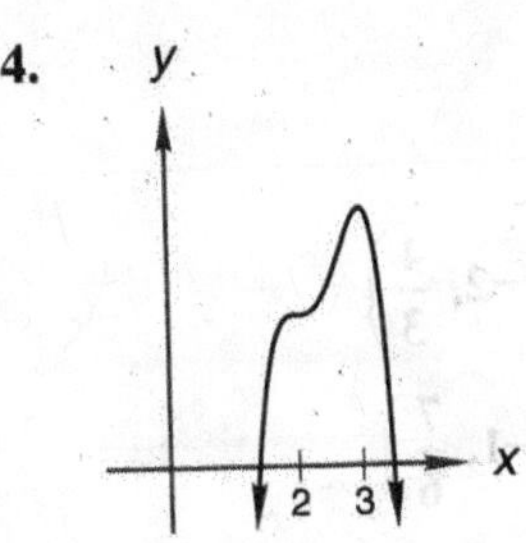

PROBLEM SET 46

1. $P = \dfrac{K}{I}$

$K = PI$

$x = \dfrac{PI}{J}$ **people**

2. When $x = 4$, $h = 2\sqrt{21}$.

$h^2 + x^2 = 10^2$

$2h\dfrac{dh}{dt} + 2x\dfrac{dx}{dt} = 0$

$\dfrac{dh}{dt} = \dfrac{-2x\dfrac{dx}{dt}}{2h}$

$\dfrac{dh}{dt} = \dfrac{-x}{h}\dfrac{dx}{dt}$

$\dfrac{dh}{dt} = \dfrac{-4}{2\sqrt{21}}(1)$

$\dfrac{dh}{dt} = \mathbf{-\dfrac{2\sqrt{21}}{21}\dfrac{m}{s}}$

5. $f(x) = x^2 + 6x - 4$

$f'(x) = 2x + 6$

$0 = 2x + 6$

Critical number: $x = \mathbf{-3}$

$f'(-4) = -2 \qquad f'(-2) = +2$

Since f changes from decreasing to increasing at $x = -3$, there is an **absolute minimum at $x = -3$.**

6. $y = u^{1/2} \qquad u = x^2 + 1$

$\dfrac{dy}{dx} = \dfrac{dy}{du} \cdot \dfrac{du}{dx}$

$= \dfrac{1}{2}u^{-1/2}(2x)$

$= \dfrac{1}{2}(x^2+1)^{-1/2}(2x)$

$= \mathbf{x(x^2+1)^{-1/2}}$

7. $y = e^u \qquad u = \sin x$

$$\frac{dy}{dx} = \frac{dy}{du} \cdot \frac{du}{dx}$$
$$= e^u \cos x$$
$$= \mathbf{e^{\sin x} \cos x}$$

8. $$f'(1) = \lim_{x\to 1} \frac{f(x) - f(1)}{x - 1} = \lim_{x\to 1} \frac{\sqrt{x} - 1}{x - 1}$$
$$= \lim_{x\to 1} \frac{\sqrt{x} - 1}{(\sqrt{x} + 1)(\sqrt{x} - 1)}$$
$$= \lim_{x\to 1} \frac{1}{\sqrt{x} + 1} = \frac{1}{1 + 1} = \mathbf{\frac{1}{2}}$$

9. $$f'(x) = \lim_{h\to 0} \frac{f(x + h) - f(x - h)}{2h}$$
$$= \lim_{h\to 0} \frac{(x + h)^2 + 3 - [(x - h)^2 + 3]}{2h}$$
$$= \lim_{h\to 0} \left(\frac{x^2 + 2xh + h^2 + 3 - x^2}{2h} + \frac{2xh - h^2 - 3}{2h} \right)$$
$$= \lim_{h\to 0} \frac{4xh}{2h} = \lim_{h\to 0} 2x = \mathbf{2x}$$

10.

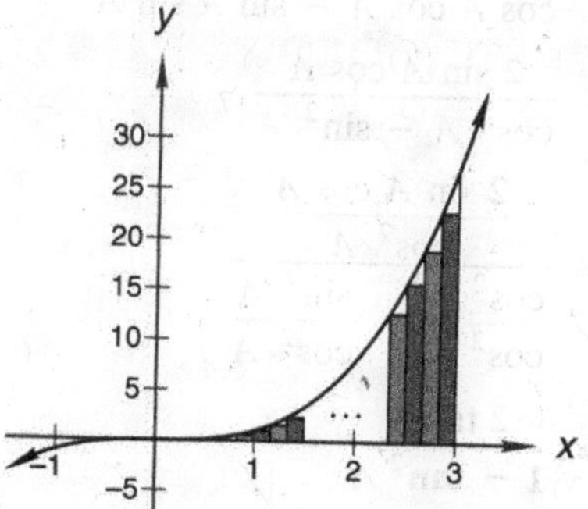

$$\Delta x = \frac{3}{n}$$

$x_0 = 0,\ x_1 = \Delta x,\ x_2 = 2\Delta x,\ \ldots,$
$x_{n-1} = (n - 1)\Delta x$

$$A = \lim_{n\to\infty} \Delta x\{0^3 + (\Delta x)^3 + (2\Delta x)^3 + \cdots + [(n - 1)\Delta x]^3\}$$
$$= \lim_{n\to\infty} \Delta x\{(\Delta x)^3[1^3 + 2^3 + \cdots + (n - 1)^3]\}$$
$$= \lim_{n\to\infty} (\Delta x)^4[1^3 + 2^3 + \cdots + (n - 1)^3]$$
$$= \lim_{n\to\infty} \left(\frac{3}{n}\right)^4 \left[\frac{(n - 1)n}{2}\right]^2$$
$$= \lim_{n\to\infty} \frac{3^4 (n - 1)^2}{2^2 n^2} = \mathbf{\frac{81}{4}}\ \textbf{units}^2$$

11. $$f(x) = \frac{\sin x}{\cos x + \sin x}$$
$$f'(x) = \frac{(\cos x + \sin x) \cos x}{(\cos x + \sin x)^2} - \frac{\sin x (- \sin x + \cos x)}{(\cos x + \sin x)^2}$$
$$f'(x) = \frac{\cos^2 x + \sin x \cos x}{\cos^2 x + 2 \sin x \cos x + \sin^2 x} + \frac{\sin^2 x - \sin x \cos x}{\cos^2 x + 2 \sin x \cos x + \sin^2 x}$$
$$f'(x) = \mathbf{\frac{1}{1 + \sin (2x)}}$$

12. $$y = 2x \ln |x| + 5$$
$$y' = 2x\left(\frac{1}{x}\right) + \ln |x|\ (2)$$
$$y' = \mathbf{2 + \ln x^2}$$

13. $u = x^2 + 1 \qquad du = 2x\,dx$

$$y = (x^2 + 1)^{1/2}$$
$$y = u^{1/2}$$
$$dy = \frac{1}{2}u^{-1/2}\,du$$
$$dy = \frac{1}{2}(x^2 + 1)^{-1/2}(2x)\,dx$$
$$\frac{dy}{dx} = \mathbf{x(x^2 + 1)^{-1/2}}$$

14. $u = \sin x \qquad du = \cos x\,dx$

$$y = e^{\sin x}$$
$$y = e^u$$
$$dy = e^u\,du$$
$$dy = e^{\sin x} \cos x\,dx$$
$$\frac{dy}{dx} = \mathbf{e^{\sin x} \cos x}$$

15.
$$x^2 + 2y^2 + 6y - 8 = 0$$
$$x^2 + 2(y^2 + 3y) = 8$$
$$x^2 + 2\left(y^2 + 3y + \frac{9}{4}\right) = 8 + \frac{9}{2}$$
$$x^2 + 2\left(y + \frac{3}{2}\right)^2 = \frac{25}{2}$$
$$2\left(y + \frac{3}{2}\right)^2 = \frac{25}{2} - x^2$$
$$\left(y + \frac{3}{2}\right)^2 = \frac{25}{4} - \frac{x^2}{2}$$
$$y = -\frac{3}{2} \pm \sqrt{\frac{25}{4} - \frac{x^2}{2}}$$

```
Y1=-1.5+√(6.25-0.5X²)
Y2=-1.5-√(6.25-0.5X²)
```

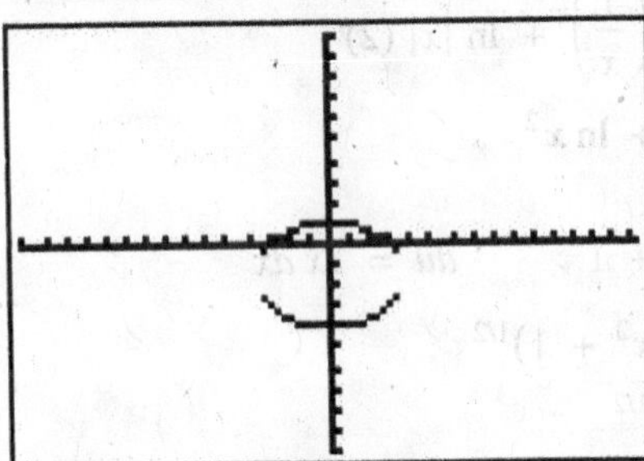

$$x^2 + 2\left(y + \frac{3}{2}\right)^2 = \frac{25}{2}$$
$$\frac{x^2}{\frac{25}{2}} + \frac{\left(y + \frac{3}{2}\right)^2}{\frac{25}{4}} = 1$$

Center: $\left(\mathbf{0}, -\frac{\mathbf{3}}{\mathbf{2}}\right)$

16. (a) $f(x) = 3x^4 + 4x^3 - 12x^2 + 5$
$$f'(x) = 12x^3 + 12x^2 - 24x$$
$$0 = 12x(x^2 + x - 2)$$
$$0 = 12x(x + 2)(x - 1)$$

Critical numbers: $x =$ **−2, 0, 1**

(b) 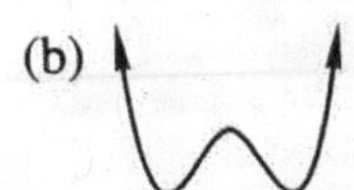

Local maximum: (0, 5)

Local minima: (−2, −27), (1, 0)

17. $\int \left(3x + e^x - x^{-1/2} + \frac{1}{3}\right) dx$
$$= \frac{3}{2}x^2 + e^x - 2x^{1/2} + \frac{1}{3}x + C$$

18. $\int \left(t + \frac{1}{t} - 3 + t^5 + t^{-5} - \sin t\right) dt$
$$= \frac{1}{2}t^2 + \ln|t| - 3t + \frac{1}{6}t^6 - \frac{1}{4}t^{-4} + \cos t + C$$

19.

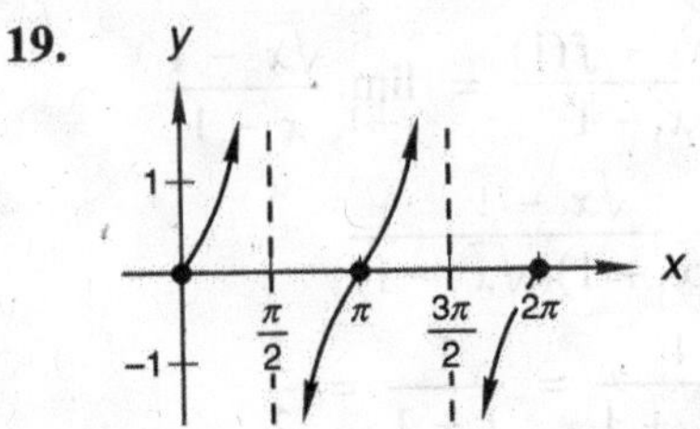

20.
$$f(x) = 2\sin x$$
$$f'(x) = 2\cos x$$
$$f''(x) = -2\sin x$$
$$f'''(x) = -2\cos x$$
$$f'''(2) = -2\cos 2 \approx \mathbf{0.8323}$$

21.
$$\tan(2A) = \frac{\sin(2A)}{\cos(2A)}$$
$$\tan(2A) = \frac{\sin(A + A)}{\cos(A + A)}$$
$$\tan(2A) = \frac{\sin A\cos A + \cos A\sin A}{\cos A\cos A - \sin A\sin A}$$
$$\tan(2A) = \frac{2\sin A\cos A}{\cos^2 A - \sin^2 A}$$
$$\tan(2A) = \frac{\frac{2\sin A\cos A}{\cos^2 A}}{\frac{\cos^2 A}{\cos^2 A} - \frac{\sin^2 A}{\cos^2 A}}$$
$$\tan(2A) = \frac{2\tan A}{1 - \tan^2 A}$$

22. (a) $f'(2) =$ `nDeriv(e^(X²),X,2)`

$f(2) \approx$ **218.3934**

(b) $f'(2) = e^4$

$g'(x) = 2x,\ g'(2) = 4$

$f(2) \cdot g'(2) \approx$ **218.3926**

(c) **They are approximately the same.**

23.

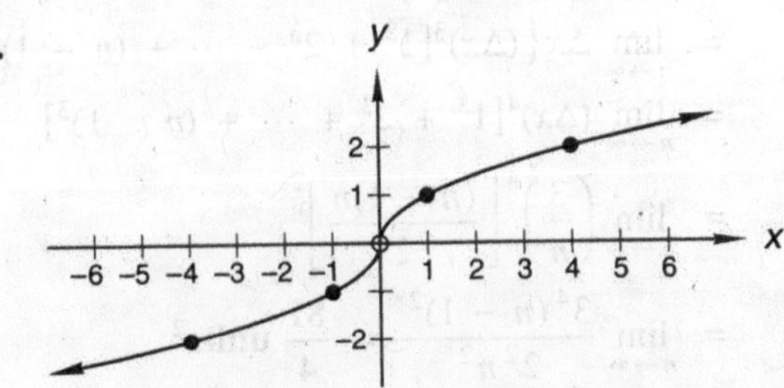

24. (a) $\lim_{x\to 0^+} f(x) = \mathbf{0}$ (b) $\lim_{x\to 0^-} f(x) = \mathbf{0}$

25.
$$a - b = 2$$
$$a^2 - 2ab + b^2 = 4$$
$$a^2 + b^2 = 4 + 2ab$$

The quantities are equal: **C**

PROBLEM SET 47

1.

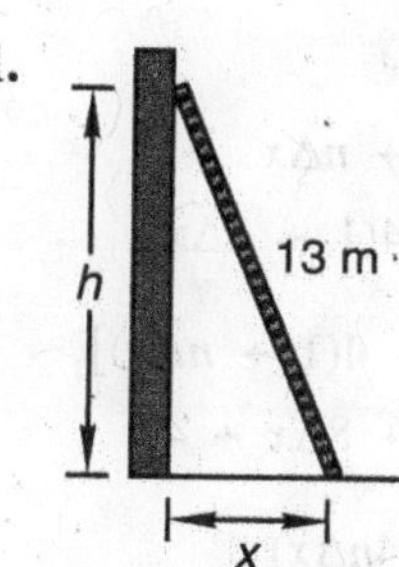

$$h^2 + 5^2 = 13^2$$
$$h = 12$$

$$x^2 + h^2 = 13^2$$
$$2x\frac{dx}{dt} + 2h\frac{dh}{dt} = 0$$
$$\frac{dh}{dt} = \frac{-x}{h}\frac{dx}{dt}$$
$$\frac{dh}{dt} = \frac{-(5)}{(12)}(2)$$
$$\frac{dh}{dt} = -\frac{5}{6}$$

The ladder is **falling at $\frac{5}{6}\frac{\text{m}}{\text{s}}$**.

2. $V = \frac{4}{3}\pi r^3$

$$\frac{dV}{dt} = 4\pi r^2\frac{dr}{dt}$$
$$\frac{dr}{dt} = \frac{\frac{dV}{dt}}{4\pi r^2}$$
$$\frac{dr}{dt} = \frac{(1)}{4\pi(100)}$$
$$\frac{dr}{dt} = \mathbf{\frac{1}{400\pi}\frac{cm}{s}}$$

3. $A = \int_{-1}^{2} x^2\,dx = \frac{1}{3}[x^3]_{-1}^{2}$

$$= \frac{8}{3} - \left(-\frac{1}{3}\right)$$
$$= \mathbf{3\ units^2}$$

4. $A = \int_{-1}^{0.5} 2e^x\,dx = 2[e^x]_{-1}^{0.5}$

$$= \mathbf{2\left(\sqrt{e} - \frac{1}{e}\right)\ units^2 \approx 2.5617\ units^2}$$

5. $A = \int_{1}^{3} \frac{1}{x}\,dx = [\ln x]_1^3$

$$= \mathbf{\ln 3\ units^2 \approx 1.0986\ units^2}$$

6. $A = \int_{1}^{3} x^{1/3}\,dx = \frac{3}{4}[x^{4/3}]_1^3$

$$= \mathbf{\frac{3}{4}(3\sqrt[3]{3} - 1)\ units^2 \approx 2.4951\ units^2}$$

7. (a) $f(x) = -2x^3 - 3x^2 - 4$
$$f'(x) = -6x^2 - 6x$$
$$0 = -6x(x + 1)$$

Critical numbers: $x = \mathbf{-1, 0}$

(b)

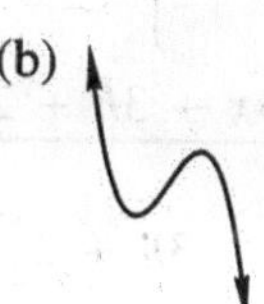

Local maximum: (0, –4)

Local minimum: (–1, –5)

8. $f'(x) = -6x^2 - 6x$
$$f'(-2) = -24 + 12 < 0$$
$$f'\left(-\frac{1}{2}\right) = -\frac{3}{2} + 3 > 0$$
$$f'(1) = -6 - 6 < 0$$

- - - - | + | - - - -

−1 0 $f'(x)$

Since f has negative slope to the left of $x = -1$ and positive slope to the right of $x = -1$, $x = \mathbf{-1}$ **is a relative minimum.** Since f has positive slope to the left of $x = 0$ and negative slope to the right of $x = 0$, $x = \mathbf{0}$ **is a relative maximum.**

9. $y = e^u \qquad u = x + \cos x$

$$\frac{dy}{dx} = \frac{dy}{du}\cdot\frac{du}{dx}$$
$$\frac{dy}{dx} = e^u(1 - \sin x)$$
$$\frac{dy}{dx} = \mathbf{e^{x+\cos x}(1 - \sin x)}$$

10. $y = u^{-1/2} \qquad u = e^x + 1$

$$\frac{dy}{dx} = \frac{dy}{du} \cdot \frac{du}{dx}$$

$$\frac{dy}{dx} = -\frac{1}{2}u^{-3/2}(e^x)$$

$$\frac{dy}{dx} = \mathbf{-\frac{e^x}{2}(e^x + 1)^{-3/2}}$$

11. $$f'(2) = \lim_{x\to 2} \frac{f(x) - f(2)}{x - 2}$$

$$= \lim_{x\to 2} \frac{(x^2 + 1) - 5}{x - 2} = \lim_{x\to 2} \frac{x^2 - 4}{x - 2}$$

$$= \lim_{x\to 2} \frac{(x + 2)(x - 2)}{x - 2} = \lim_{x\to 2} (x + 2) = \mathbf{4}$$

12. $$f'(x) = \lim_{h\to 0} \frac{f(x + h) - f(x - h)}{2h}$$

$$= \lim_{h\to 0} \left\{ \frac{2(x + h)^2 + 3(x + h) + 2}{2h} - \frac{[2(x - h)^2 + 3(x - h) + 2]}{2h} \right\}$$

$$= \lim_{h\to 0} \left(\frac{2x^2 + 4xh + 2h^2 + 3x + 3h + 2}{2h} - \frac{[2x^2 - 4xh + 2h^2 + 3x - 3h + 2]}{2h} \right)$$

$$= \lim_{h\to 0} \frac{8xh + 6h}{2h} = \lim_{h\to 0} 4x + 3 = \mathbf{4x + 3}$$

13. $u = x + \sin x \qquad du = (1 + \cos x)\,dx$

$$y = 3e^u$$

$$dy = 3e^u\,du$$

$$dy = 3e^{x + \sin x}(1 + \cos x)\,dx$$

$$\frac{dy}{dx} = \mathbf{3e^{x + \sin x}(1 + \cos x)}$$

14. $y = 4t^3 \ln t$

$$\frac{dy}{dt} = 4t^3\left(\frac{1}{t}\right) + \ln t\,(12t^2)$$

$$\frac{dy}{dt} = 4t^2 + 12t^2 \ln t$$

$$\frac{dy}{dt} = \mathbf{4t^2(1 + 3\ln t)}$$

15. $y = 6u - u^{-1/2}$

$$\frac{dy}{dx} = \mathbf{6 + \frac{1}{2}u^{-3/2}}$$

16. $$y = \frac{\sin x}{x^2 + 1}$$

$$\frac{dy}{dx} = \frac{(x^2 + 1)\cos x - \sin x\,(2x)}{(x^2 + 1)^2}$$

$$\frac{dy}{dx} = \mathbf{\frac{\cos x}{x^2 + 1} - \frac{2x \sin x}{(x^2 + 1)^2}}$$

17. $\Delta x = \dfrac{4}{n}$

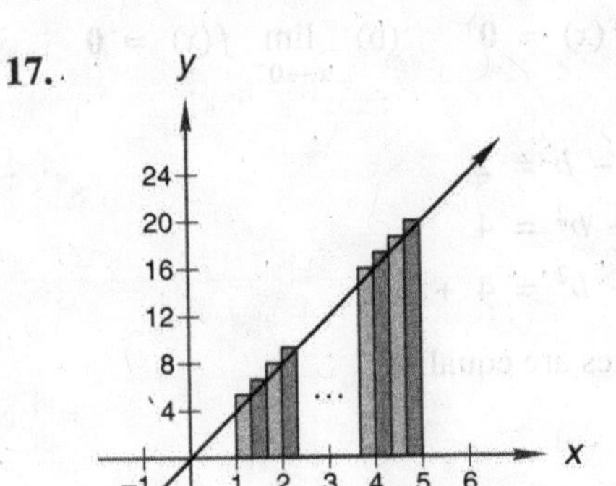

$x_1 = 1 + \Delta x,\ x_2 = 1 + 2\Delta x,$

$x_3 = 1 + 3\Delta x,\ \ldots,\ x_n = 1 + n\Delta x$

$$A = \lim_{n\to\infty} \Delta x[4(1 + \Delta x) + 4(1 + 2\Delta x) + 4(1 + 3\Delta x) + \cdots + 4(1 + n\Delta x)]$$

$$= \lim_{n\to\infty} \Delta x(4 + 4\Delta x + 4 + 8\Delta x + 4 + 12\Delta x + \cdots + 4 + 4n\Delta x)$$

$$= \lim_{n\to\infty} \Delta x[4n + 4\Delta x(1 + 2 + 3 + \cdots + n)]$$

$$= \lim_{n\to\infty} \frac{4}{n}\left[4n + 4\left(\frac{4}{n}\right)\frac{n(n + 1)}{2}\right]$$

$$= \lim_{n\to\infty} \frac{4}{n}[4n + 8(n + 1)]$$

$$= \lim_{n\to\infty} \left[16 + \frac{32(n + 1)}{n}\right]$$

$$= 16 + 32 = \mathbf{48\ units^2}$$

$$A_{Trap} = \frac{(4 + 20)4}{2} = 48\ \text{units}^2$$

18.

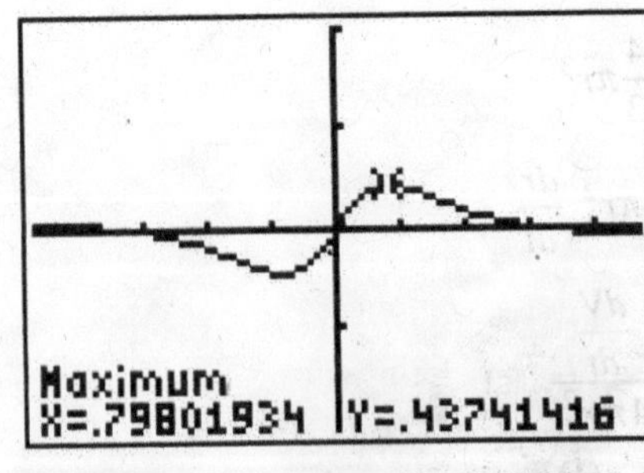

Relative maximum: (0.79801934, 0.43741416)

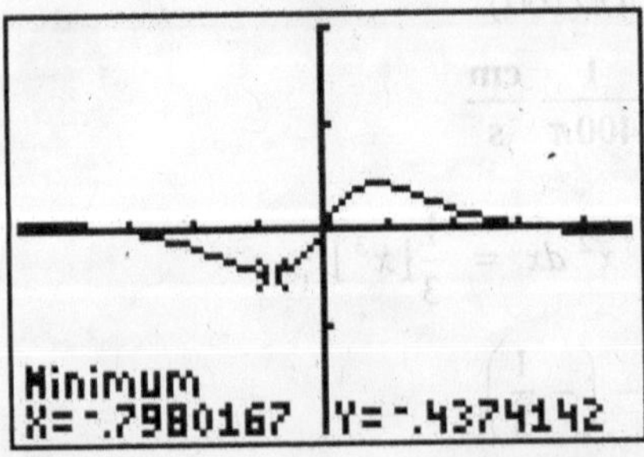

Relative minimum: (−0.7980167, −0.4374142)

19.

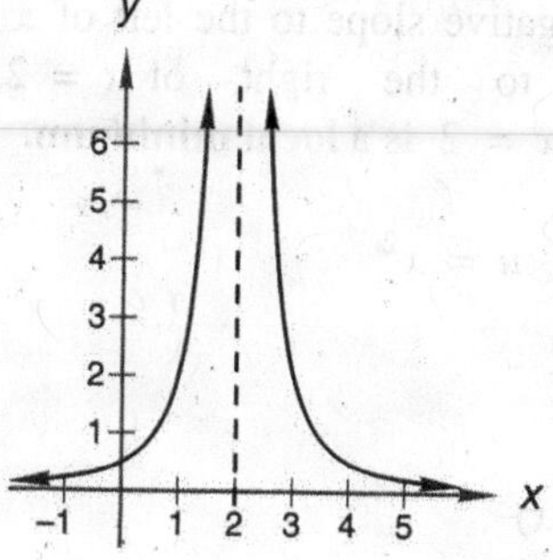

20.

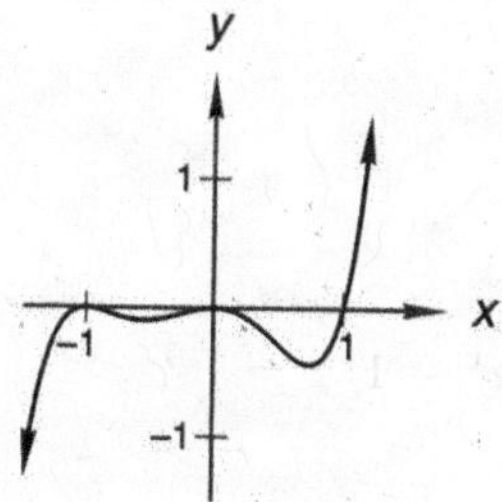

21. Domain: $\{x \in \mathbb{R} \mid -1 \le x \le 1\}$
Range: $\{y \in \mathbb{R} \mid 0 \le y \le \pi\}$

22.
$$\cos(2x) = 1 - 2\sin^2 x$$
$$2\sin^2 x = 1 - \cos(2x)$$
$$\sin^2 x = \frac{1}{2} - \frac{1}{2}\cos(2x)$$

23.
$$\int \left(4e^x + 2\cos x + x^{-5} + \frac{1}{x} + x^{1/2}\right) dx$$
$$= 4e^x + 2\sin x - \frac{1}{4}x^{-4} + \ln|x| + \frac{2}{3}x^{3/2} + C$$

24. $(x + y)^2 = x^2 + 2xy + y^2$
If x and y are both positive, then A is greater.
If x and y have opposite signs, then B is greater.
Insufficient information: **D**

25. $f(1) \approx$ **0.8414709848**
$\sin(1) \approx$ **0.8414709848**
They are the same.

PROBLEM SET 48

1.
$$V = \frac{1}{3}\pi r^2 h = \frac{(10)}{3}\pi r^2$$
$$\frac{dV}{dt} = \frac{20}{3}\pi r\frac{dr}{dt}$$
$$\frac{dV}{dt} = \frac{20}{3}\pi(24)(1)$$
$$\frac{dV}{dt} = 160\pi\ \frac{\text{cm}^3}{\text{s}}$$

2.
$$V = \frac{4}{3}\pi r^3$$
$$\frac{dV}{dt} = 4\pi r^2\frac{dr}{dt}$$
$$(2) = 4\pi(7)^2\frac{dr}{dt}$$
$$\frac{dr}{dt} = \frac{1}{98\pi}$$
$$A = 4\pi r^2$$
$$\frac{dA}{dt} = 8\pi r\frac{dr}{dt}$$
$$\frac{dA}{dt} = 8\pi(7)\left(\frac{1}{98\pi}\right)$$
$$\frac{dA}{dt} = \frac{4}{7}\ \frac{\text{cm}^2}{\text{s}}$$

3.
$$y = \cos x$$
$$y = \sin\left(\frac{\pi}{2} - x\right)$$
$$y = \sin u$$
$$dy = \cos u\, du$$
$$dy = \cos\left(\frac{\pi}{2} - x\right)(-dx)$$
$$\frac{dy}{dx} = -\sin x$$

4.
$$\frac{d}{dx}\cot x = \frac{d}{dx}\left(\frac{\cos x}{\sin x}\right)$$
$$= \frac{\sin x(-\sin x) - \cos x\cos x}{\sin^2 x}$$
$$= \frac{-1}{\sin^2 x} = -\csc^2 x$$

5. $y = \csc x = \dfrac{1}{\sin x} = (\sin x)^{-1}$

$u = \sin x \qquad du = \cos x\, dx$

$y = u^{-1}$

$dy = -u^{-2}\, du$

$dy = -(\sin x)^{-2} \cos x\, dx$

$\dfrac{dy}{dx} = \dfrac{-\cos x}{\sin^2 x}$

$\dfrac{dy}{dx} = \mathbf{-\csc x \cot x}$

6. $y = e^x \csc x$

$\dfrac{dy}{dx} = e^x(-\csc x \cot x) + \csc x\,(e^x)$

$\dfrac{dy}{dx} = \mathbf{e^x \csc x\,(1 - \cot x)}$

7. $y = x^2 \sec x$

$\dfrac{dy}{dx} = x^2 \sec x \tan x + \sec x\,(2x)$

$\dfrac{dy}{dx} = \mathbf{x \sec x\,(x \tan x + 2)}$

8. $A = \int_{0.5}^{2} \left(e^x + \dfrac{1}{x}\right) dx = [e^x + \ln|x|]_{0.5}^{2}$

$= e^2 + \ln 2 - (e^{0.5} + \ln 0.5)$

$= e^2 - e^{0.5} + \ln 2 - \ln 0.5$

$= \mathbf{(e^2 - \sqrt{e} + \ln 4)\ units^2}$

9. $A = \int_{0.5}^{2.5} x^{2/3}\, dx = \dfrac{3}{5}[x^{5/3}]_{0.5}^{2.5}$

$= \mathbf{\dfrac{3}{5}(2.5^{5/3} - 0.5^{5/3})\ units^2}$

10. $A = \int_{-3}^{-1} -\dfrac{1}{x}\, dx = -[\ln|x|]_{-3}^{-1}$

$= \mathbf{\ln 3\ units^2}$

11. $A = \int_{-\pi/2}^{\pi/2} \cos\theta\, d\theta = \sin\theta\Big]_{-\pi/2}^{\pi/2}$

$= \mathbf{2\ units^2}$

12. $f(x) = x^2 + bx + c$

$f'(x) = 2x + b$

$0 = 2x + b$

$2x = -b$

$x = \mathbf{-\dfrac{b}{2}}$

13. Since there is negative slope to the left of $x = 2$, positive slope to the right of $x = 2$, and $g'(2) = 0$, then $x = 2$ is a **local minimum.**

14. $y = 4 \sin u \qquad u = x^2$

$\dfrac{dy}{dx} = \dfrac{dy}{du} \cdot \dfrac{du}{dx}$

$\dfrac{dy}{dx} = 4 \cos u\,(2x)$

$\dfrac{dy}{dx} = 4 \cos(x^2)\,(2x)$

$\dfrac{dy}{dx} = \mathbf{8x \cos(x^2)}$

15. $y = -u^{-1/2} \qquad u = e^x - 1$

$\dfrac{dy}{dx} = \dfrac{dy}{du} \cdot \dfrac{du}{dx}$

$\dfrac{dy}{dx} = \dfrac{1}{2}u^{-3/2}(e^x)$

$\dfrac{dy}{dx} = \dfrac{1}{2}(e^x - 1)^{-3/2}e^x$

$\dfrac{dy}{dx} = \mathbf{\dfrac{e^x}{2}(e^x - 1)^{-3/2}}$

16. $s(t) = t^3 - t^2 - 12$

$v(t) = 3t^2 - 2t$

$v(3) = 3(3)^2 - 2(3)$

$v(3) = \mathbf{21}$

17. $\int (-u^{-1/2} + 2u^2 - 1 + 3u^{1/2} + 2 \sin u - \cos u + u^{-5} - 4e^u)\, du$

$= \mathbf{-2u^{1/2} + \dfrac{2}{3}u^3 - u + 2u^{3/2} - 2 \cos u - \sin u - \dfrac{1}{4}u^{-4} - 4e^u + C}$

18. $\int \dfrac{x^2 + x + 1}{x}\, dx = \int \left(x + 1 + \dfrac{1}{x}\right) dx$

$= \mathbf{\dfrac{1}{2}x^2 + x + \ln|x| + C}$

19. $\log_x 3 = 5$

$x^5 = 3$

$x = \mathbf{3^{1/5} \approx 1.2457}$

20. $y = \log_2 x = \mathbf{\dfrac{\ln x}{\ln 2} \approx 1.4427 \ln x}$

21. (a) $g(h) = \dfrac{(1+h)^3 - (1-h)^3}{2h}$

X	Y1
-.3	3.09
-.2	3.04
-.1	3.01
0	ERROR
.1	3.01
.2	3.04
.3	3.09

X=0

$\lim_{h \to 0} g(h) = \mathbf{3}$

(b) $f(x) = x^3$
$f'(x) = 3x^2$
$f'(1) = \mathbf{3}$

(c) **They are the same.**

22.

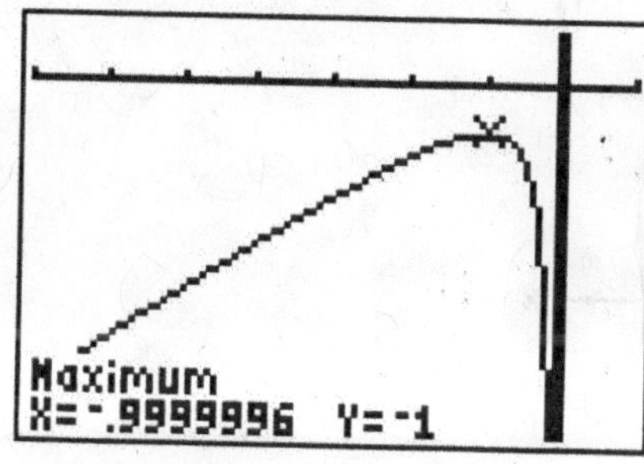

Relative maximum: **(–1, –1)**

23. (a) nDeriv((2X+1)/(X²+1),X,2)
$\approx \mathbf{-0.4}$

(b) $\dfrac{h(2)g'(2) - g(2)h'(2)}{[h(2)]^2}$

$= \dfrac{5(2) - 5(4)}{25}$

$= -\dfrac{10}{25} = \mathbf{-0.4}$

(c) **They are the same.**

24. $|2x - 3| < 4$

$\left|x - \dfrac{3}{2}\right| < 2$

"x is less than 2 away from $\dfrac{3}{2}$"

–2 –1 0 1 2 3 4 5

25. $xy = 1$

$x = \dfrac{1}{y}$

$-x = -\dfrac{1}{y}$

The quantities are equal: **C**

PROBLEM SET 49

1. $\dfrac{r}{h} = \dfrac{5}{10}$

$10r = 5h$

$r = \dfrac{h}{2}$

$V = \dfrac{1}{3}\pi r^2 h$

$V = \dfrac{1}{12}\pi h^3$

$\dfrac{dV}{dt} = \dfrac{1}{4}\pi h^2 \dfrac{dh}{dt}$

$-1 = \dfrac{1}{4}\pi(25)\dfrac{dh}{dt}$

$\dfrac{dh}{dt} = \mathbf{-\dfrac{4}{25\pi}\ \dfrac{cm}{s}}$

2.

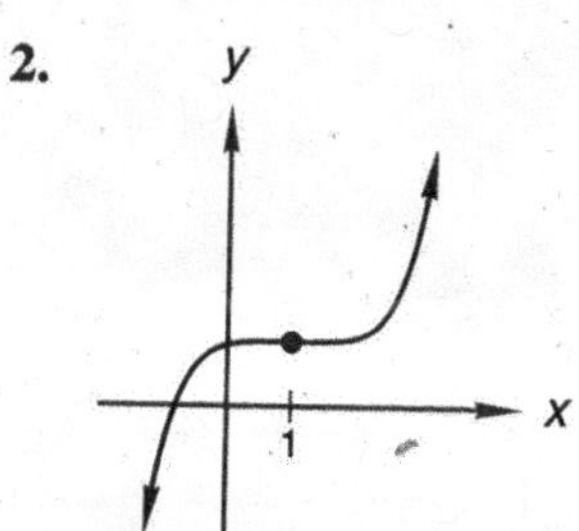

3. (a) $f(x) = x^4 - 2x^2$
$f'(x) = 4x^3 - 4x$
$0 = 4x(x^2 - 1)$
$0 = 4x(x + 1)(x - 1)$
Critical numbers: $x = \mathbf{-1, 0, 1}$

(b)

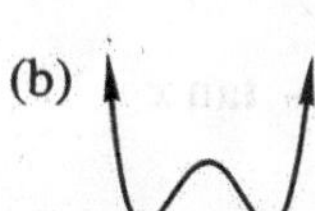

Relative maximum: (0, 0)
Relative minima: (–1, –1), (1, –1)

4. $f(x) = x^4 - 2x^2$
$f'(x) = 4x^3 - 4x$
$f''(x) = 12x^2 - 4$
$f''(-1) = 12 - 4 > 0$ **Minimum at $x = -1$**
$f''(0) = 0 - 4 < 0$ **Maximum at $x = 0$**
$f''(1) = 12 - 4 > 0$ **Minimum at $x = 1$**

5. $A = \displaystyle\int_0^3 x^{1/2}\,dx = \frac{2}{3}[x^{3/2}]_0^3 = \frac{2}{3}(3^{3/2})$

$= \mathbf{2\sqrt{3}\ units^2 \approx 3.4641\ units^2}$

6. $A = \int_0^{\pi} 2\sin\theta\, d\theta = 2[-\cos\theta]_0^{\pi} = \mathbf{4\ units^2}$

7. $A = \int_{-1}^{2} (x^3 - x + 2)\, dx$

$= \left[\frac{1}{4}x^4 - \frac{1}{2}x^2 + 2x\right]_{-1}^{2}$

$= 4 - 2 + 4 - \left(\frac{1}{4} - \frac{1}{2} - 2\right)$

$= \mathbf{\frac{33}{4}\ units^2}$

8. $A = \int_0^{2\pi} (4 + 2\sin\theta)\, d\theta$

$= [4\theta - 2\cos\theta]_0^{2\pi}$

$= 8\pi - 2 - (0 - 2)$

$= \mathbf{8\pi\ units^2}$

9.

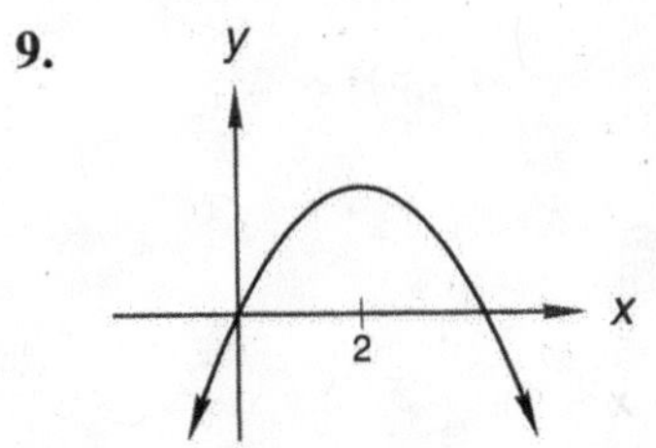

10. $y = 4x \csc x$

$y' = 4x(-\csc x \cot x) + \csc x\,(4)$

$y' = \mathbf{4 \csc x\,(1 - x \cot x)}$

11. $g(x) = x \ln|x| - x \tan x$

$g'(x) = x\left(\frac{1}{x}\right) + \ln|x| - (x \sec^2 x + \tan x)$

$g'(x) = \mathbf{1 + \ln|x| - x\sec^2 x - \tan x}$

12. $u = \sin x + \cos x \qquad du = (\cos x - \sin x)\, dx$

$y = 13u^{22}$

$dy = 13(22)u^{21}\, du$

$dy = 286(\sin x + \cos x)^{21}(\cos x - \sin x)\, dx$

$\frac{dy}{dx} = \mathbf{286(\sin x + \cos x)^{21}(\cos x - \sin x)}$

13. $y = 6u^4 \qquad u = \sin x + \cos x$

$\frac{dy}{dx} = \frac{dy}{du} \cdot \frac{du}{dx}$

$= 24u^3(\cos x - \sin x)$

$= 24(\sin x + \cos x)^3(\cos x - \sin x)$

$= 24(\sin x + \cos x)^2(\cos^2 x - \sin^2 x)$

$= \mathbf{24[1 + \sin(2x)]\cos(2x)}$

14. $f(x) = 2\ln|x| + 3$

$f'(x) = \frac{2}{x} = 2x^{-1}$

$f''(x) = -2x^{-2}$

$f'''(x) = 4x^{-3}$

$f'''(-2) = 4(-2)^{-3}$

$f'''(-2) = \mathbf{-\frac{1}{2}}$

15.

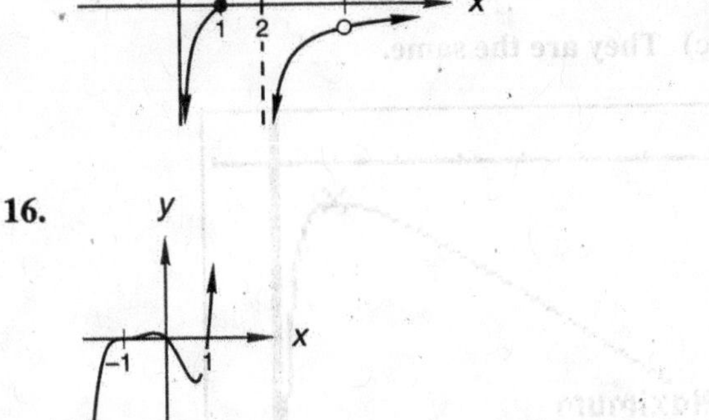

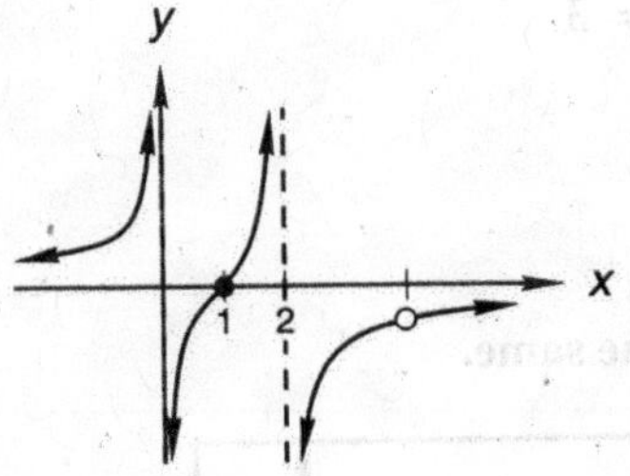

16. (graph)

17. $y = \cos x$

$y = \sin\left(\frac{\pi}{2} - x\right)$

$y = \sin u$

$dy = \cos u\, du$

$dy = \cos\left(\frac{\pi}{2} - x\right)(-dx)$

$\frac{dy}{dx} = -\sin x$

18. $y = 2e^x - \cos x + 14\sin x$

$y' = \mathbf{2e^x + \sin x + 14\cos x}$

19.

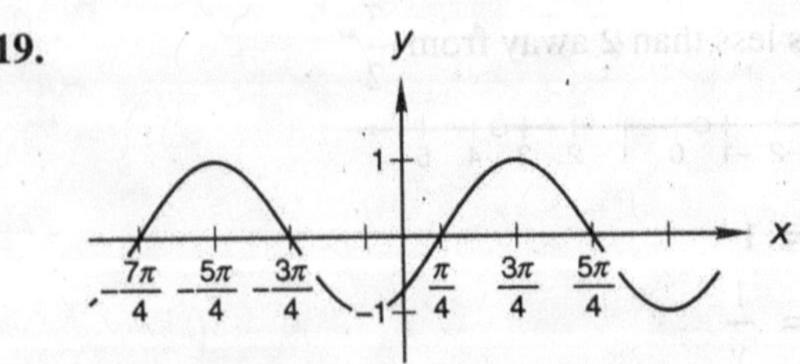

20. $\lim_{h\to 0} \frac{3xh - 4h^2}{h} = \lim_{h\to 0} (3x - 4h) = \mathbf{3x}$

21. (a)

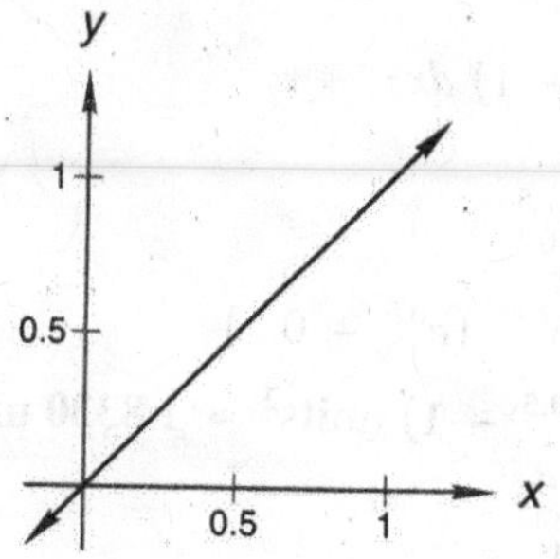

(b) $\mathbf{\frac{1}{n}}$

(c) $\mathbf{\frac{1}{n}, \frac{3}{n}, \frac{6}{n}, \frac{n}{n} = 1}$

(d) $A = \lim_{n\to\infty} \frac{1}{n}\left(\frac{1}{n} + \frac{2}{n} + \frac{3}{n} + \cdots + \frac{n}{n}\right)$

$= \lim_{n\to\infty} \left(\frac{1}{n}\right)^2 (1 + 2 + 3 + \cdots + n)$

$= \lim_{n\to\infty} \frac{1}{n^2}\left[\frac{n(n+1)}{2}\right]$

$= \mathbf{\lim_{n\to\infty} \frac{n+1}{2n}}$

22. $\int (4x^{-1/2} - 3x^{1/2} - x^{\pi} + x^{-\pi} - 3\sin x + \cos x - 2e^x)\,dx$

$= \mathbf{8x^{1/2} - 2x^{3/2} - \frac{x^{\pi+1}}{\pi+1} + \frac{x^{1-\pi}}{1-\pi} + 3\cos x + \sin x - 2e^x + C}$

23. $\frac{d}{dx}\tan x = \frac{d}{dx}\left(\frac{\sin x}{\cos x}\right)$

$= \frac{\cos x \cos x - \sin x(-\sin x)}{\cos^2 x}$

$= \frac{1}{\cos^2 x} = \sec^2 x$

24. $|x - 3| < 4$

"x is less than 4 away from 3"

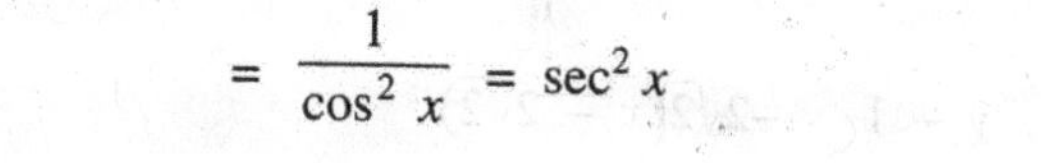

25. (a) `nDeriv((X+ln(X))/(sin(X)+cos(X)),X,1)`

$\approx$ **1.6052**

(b) $f(1) = \mathbf{1}$; $g(1) \approx \mathbf{1.3818}$

(c) $f'(x) = \mathbf{1 + \frac{1}{x}}$; $g'(x) = \mathbf{\cos x - \sin x}$

(d) $f'(1) = \mathbf{2}$; $g'(1) \approx \mathbf{-0.3012}$

(e) $\frac{g(1)f'(1) - f(1)g'(1)}{[g(1)]^2}$

$\approx \frac{(1.3818)(2) - (1)(-0.3012)}{(1.3818)^2}$

$\approx$ **1.6051**

(f) **They are approximately the same.**

PROBLEM SET 50

1. $x^2 + y^2 = 9$

$2x\frac{dx}{dt} + 2y\frac{dy}{dt} = 0$

$\frac{dx}{dt} = -\frac{y}{x}\frac{dy}{dt}$

$\frac{dx}{dt} = \frac{-1}{2\sqrt{2}}(-2)$

$\frac{dx}{dt} = \mathbf{\frac{\sqrt{2}}{2}\ \frac{units}{s}}$

2.

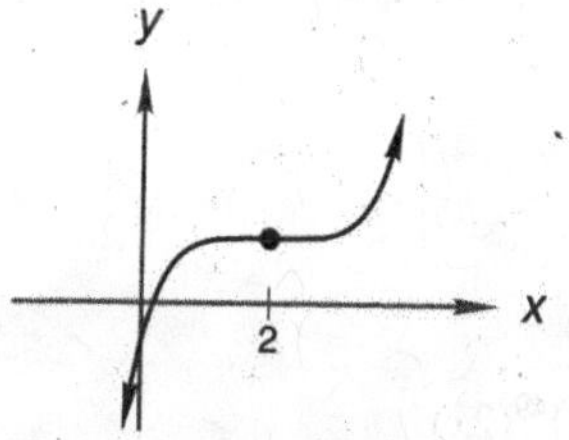

3. (a) $f(x) = -12x^4 + 4x^3 + 12x^2 - 1$

$f'(x) = -48x^3 + 12x^2 + 24x$

$0 = -12x(4x^2 - x - 2)$

Critical numbers: $x = \mathbf{-0.5931, 0, 0.8431}$

(b)

Relative maxima: (−0.5931, 0.9018)
(0.8431, 3.8638)

Relative minimum: (0, −1)

4. (a) $f'(x) = -12x^4 + 4x^3 + 12x^2 - 1$

$f'(x) = -48x^3 + 12x^2 + 24x$

$f''(x) = -144x^2 + 24x + 24$

$0 = -24(6x^2 - x - 1)$

$0 = -24(3x + 1)(2x - 1)$

Inflection points: $x = -\frac{1}{3}, \frac{1}{2}$

(b)

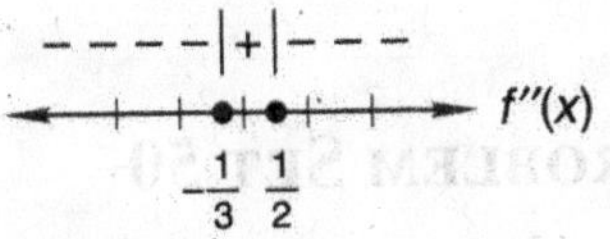

Concave up: $\left(-\frac{1}{3}, \frac{1}{2}\right)$

Concave down: $\left(-\infty, -\frac{1}{3}\right)$ and $\left(\frac{1}{2}, \infty\right)$

5. $f(x) = \tan(3x^2 - 4x + 1)$

$f'(x) = \sec^2(3x^2 - 4x + 1)(6x - 4)$

$f'(x) = \mathbf{2\sec^2(3x^2 - 4x + 1)(3x - 2)}$

6. $y = \ln(\sec x)$

$y' = \dfrac{\sec x \tan x}{\sec x}$

$y' = \mathbf{\tan x}$

7. $h(x) = (x^2 - 4)^{50}$

$h'(x) = 50(x^2 - 4)^{49}(2x)$

$h'(x) = \mathbf{100x(x^2 - 4)^{49}}$

8. $y = e^x(x^2 + 4)^{50}$

$y' = e^x(50)(x^2 + 4)^{49}(2x) + (x^2 + 4)^{50}e^x$

$y' = \mathbf{e^x(x^2 + 4)^{49}(x^2 + 100x + 4)}$

9. $g(t) = \dfrac{\sin(2t)}{\cos^2 t}$

$g(t) = \dfrac{2\sin t\cos t}{\cos^2 t}$

$g(t) = 2\tan t$

$g'(t) = \mathbf{2\sec^2 t}$

10. $A = \int_{-1}^{2}(-x^2 + x + 2)\,dx$

$= \left[-\frac{1}{3}x^3 + \frac{1}{2}x^2 + 2x\right]_{-1}^{2}$

$= -\frac{8}{3} + 2 + 4 - \left(\frac{1}{3} + \frac{1}{2} - 2\right)$

$= \mathbf{\frac{9}{2}}$ **units²**

11. $A = \int_{0.5}^{1.5}(e^x - 1)\,dx$

$= [e^x - x]_{0.5}^{1.5}$

$= e^{1.5} - 1.5 - (e^{0.5} - 0.5)$

$= \mathbf{(e^{1.5} - e^{0.5} - 1)}$ **units² ≈ 1.8330 units²**

12. $A = \int_1^2 \frac{x + 1}{x}\,dx$

$= \int_1^2\left(1 + \frac{1}{x}\right)dx$

$= [x + \ln|x|]_1^2$

$= 2 + \ln 2 - (1 + 0)$

$= \mathbf{(1 + \ln 2)}$ **units² ≈ 1.6932 units²**

13. $\int\sqrt{x}(x - 2)\,dx = \int(x^{3/2} - 2x^{1/2})\,dx$

$= \mathbf{\frac{2}{5}x^{5/2} - \frac{4}{3}x^{3/2} + C}$

14. $\int(x - 2)^2\,dx = \int(x^2 - 4x + 4)\,dx$

$= \mathbf{\frac{1}{3}x^3 - 2x^2 + 4x + C}$

15. $x^2 + y^2 = 9$

$2x + 2y\dfrac{dy}{dx} = 0$

$\dfrac{dy}{dx} = -\dfrac{x}{y}$

$m = \dfrac{-2\sqrt{2}}{1}$

$y - 1 = -2\sqrt{2}(x - 2\sqrt{2})$

$\mathbf{y = -2\sqrt{2}x + 9}$

16. $y = -2\cos x$

$\dfrac{dy}{dx} = 2\sin x$

$\dfrac{d^2y}{dx^2} = 2\cos x$

$\left.\dfrac{d^2y}{dx^2}\right|_2 = 2\cos 2 \approx \mathbf{-0.8323}$

17. $\lim_{h\to 0}\dfrac{e^{x+h} - e^x}{h} + \lim_{n\to\infty}\dfrac{1}{1 - n^2} = e^x + 0 = e^x$

18. $\int \left(3x^{1/2} - 4x^{-1/3} + \sin x - 2x^{-4} - \frac{7}{x} - 3e^x \right) dx$

$= \mathbf{2x^{3/2} - 6x^{2/3} - \cos x + \frac{2}{3}x^{-3} - 7 \ln |x| - 3e^x + C}$

19.

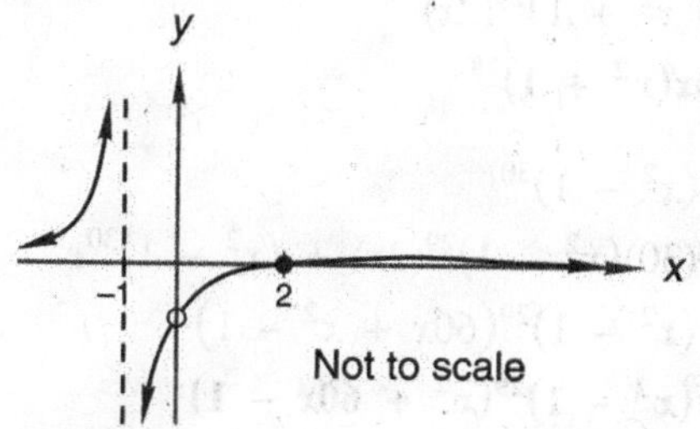

20.

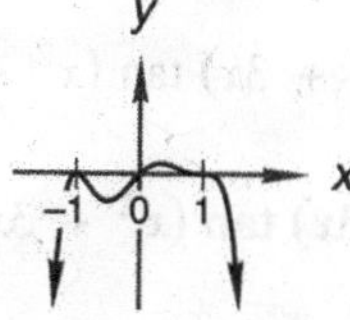

21. (a) $\Delta x = \frac{1 - 0}{n} = \frac{1}{n}$

i	x_i	$f(x_i)$
1	$\left(\frac{1}{n}\right)$	$\left(\frac{1}{n}\right)$
2	$2\left(\frac{1}{n}\right)$	$2\left(\frac{1}{n}\right)$
3	$3\left(\frac{1}{n}\right)$	$3\left(\frac{1}{n}\right)$
$\vdots$	$\vdots$	$\vdots$
n	$n\left(\frac{1}{n}\right)$	$n\left(\frac{1}{n}\right)$

$\lim_{n\to\infty} \frac{1}{n}\left[\frac{1}{n} + \frac{2}{n} + \frac{3}{n} + \cdots + 1\right]$

$= \lim_{n\to\infty} \sum_{i=1}^{n} f(x_i)\frac{b - a}{n}$

$= \mathbf{\int_0^1 x\, dx}$

(b) $\int_0^1 x\, dx = \frac{1}{2}x^2 \Big]_0^1 = \mathbf{\frac{1}{2}}$

22. $e^x = 21$

$x = \mathbf{\ln 21 \approx 3.0445}$

23. $\log_x (4x) = 2$

$x^2 = 4x$

$x^2 - 4x = 0$

$x(x - 4) = 0$

$x = 0, 4$

$x = \mathbf{4}$

24. $g(x) = [f(x)]^2$

$g'(x) = 2f(x)\, f'(x)$

$g'(0) = 2f(0)f'(0) = \mathbf{2}$

25. (a)

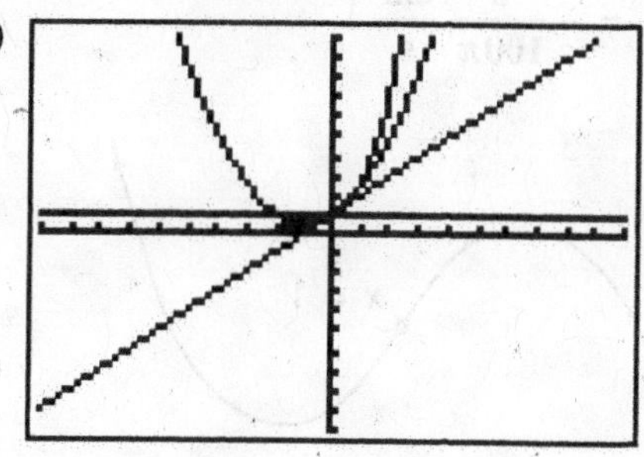

(b)

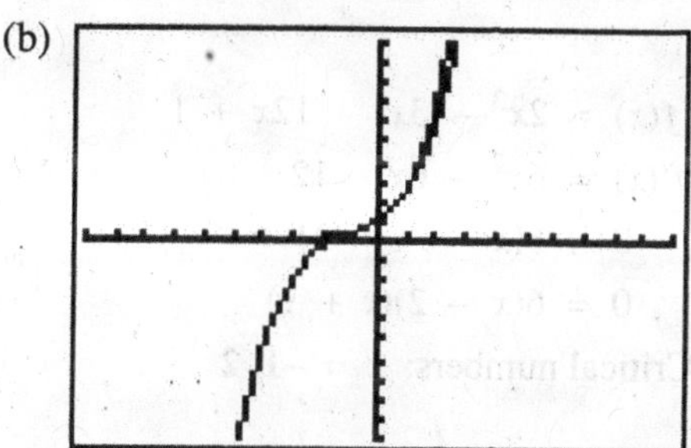

(c)

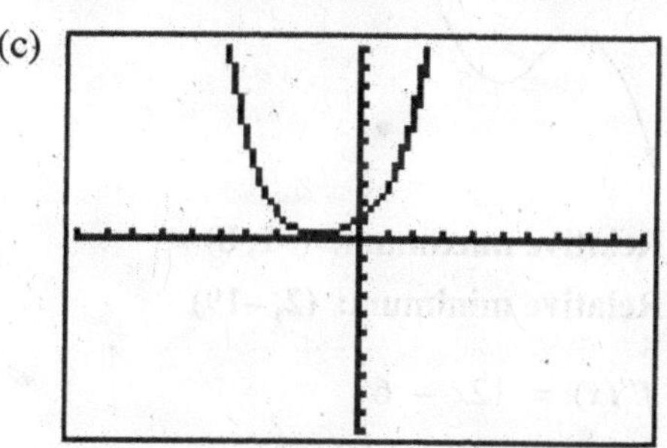

PROBLEM SET 51

1. $\frac{dV}{dt} = -3\frac{\text{cm}^3}{\text{s}}$ $r = 5 \text{ cm}$

$V = \frac{4}{3}\pi r^3$

$\frac{dV}{dt} = 4\pi r^2 \frac{dr}{dt}$

$(-3) = 4\pi(25)\frac{dr}{dt}$

$\frac{dr}{dt} = -\mathbf{\frac{3}{100\pi}\frac{cm}{s}}$

2.

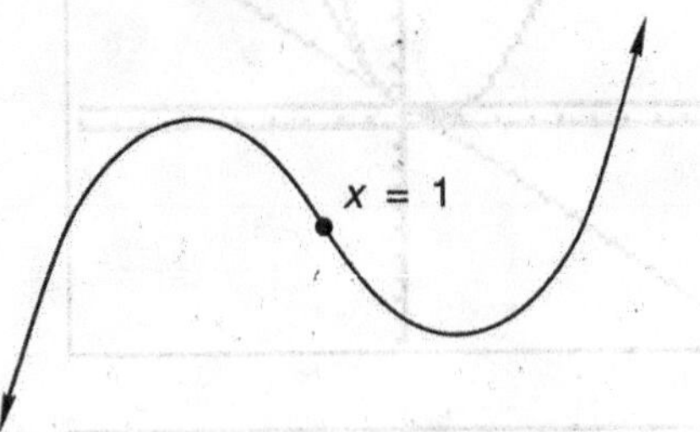

3. (a) $f(x) = 2x^3 - 3x^2 - 12x + 1$

$f'(x) = 6x^2 - 6x - 12$

$0 = 6(x^2 - x - 2)$

$0 = 6(x - 2)(x + 1)$

Critical numbers: $x = \mathbf{-1, 2}$

(b)

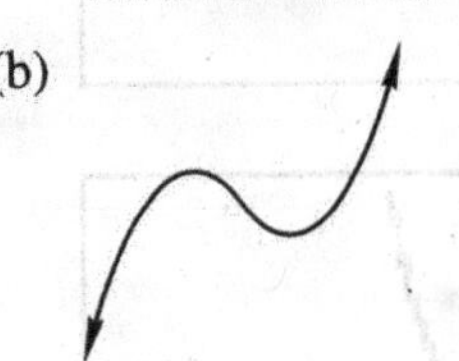

Relative maximum: (–1, 8)
Relative minimum: (2, –19)

4. (a) $f''(x) = 12x - 6$

$0 = 6(2x - 1)$

Inflection point at $x = \mathbf{\frac{1}{2}}$

(b) $f''(0) = -6$ and $f''(1) = 6$

Concave up: $\left(\mathbf{\frac{1}{2}, \infty}\right)$

5. $\int 12x(x^2 + 4)^5\, dx = \mathbf{(x^2 + 4)^6 + C}$

6. $\int 6(\sin t)^5 \cos t\, dt = \mathbf{\sin^6 t + C}$

7. $\int (x^2 + 4)^{-1/2} x\, dx = \mathbf{\sqrt{x^2 + 4} + C}$

8. $\int 4x e^{2x^2}\, dx = \mathbf{e^{2x^2} + C}$

9. $\int \frac{6x + 1}{3x^2 + x}\, dx = \mathbf{\ln|3x^2 + x| + C}$

10. $\int 4e^{4\sin x}\cos x\, dx = \mathbf{e^{4\sin x} + C}$

11. $y = (x^2 + 1)^{30}$

$y' = 30(x^2 + 1)^{29}(2x)$

$y' = \mathbf{60x(x^2 + 1)^{29}}$

12. $y = e^x(x^2 - 1)^{30}$

$y' = e^x(30)(x^2 - 1)^{29}(2x) + (x^2 - 1)^{30}e^x$

$y' = e^x(x^2 - 1)^{29}(60x + x^2 - 1)$

$y' = \mathbf{e^x(x^2 - 1)^{29}(x^2 + 60x - 1)}$

13. $y = [\sec(x^2 + 3x)]^2$

$y' = 2\sec(x^2 + 3x)\sec(x^2 + 3x)\tan(x^2 + 3x) \times (2x + 3)$

$y' = \mathbf{2(2x + 3)\sec^2(x^2 + 3x)\tan(x^2 + 3x)}$

14. $f(x) = \frac{\sin x}{(x^2 + 1)^{10}}$

$f'(x) = \frac{(x^2 + 1)^{10}\cos x}{(x^2 + 1)^{20}} - \frac{\sin x(10)(x^2 + 1)^9(2x)}{(x^2 + 1)^{20}}$

$f'(x) = \mathbf{\frac{(x^2 + 1)\cos x - 20x\sin x}{(x^2 + 1)^{11}}}$

15. $g(x) = 3\ln|\cos x|$

$g'(x) = \frac{-3\sin x}{\cos x}$

$g'(x) = \mathbf{-3\tan x}$

16. $y = e^{\tan(\sin x)}$

$y' = \mathbf{e^{\tan(\sin x)}\sec^2(\sin x)\cos x}$

17. $A = \int_{-2}^{1} e^x\, dx = [e^x]_{-2}^{1} = \mathbf{(e - e^{-2})\ units^2}$

18. $A = \int_1^2 \frac{x + 2}{x}\, dx = \int_1^2 \left(1 + \frac{2}{x}\right) dx$

$= [x + 2\ln x]_1^2$

$= 2 + 2\ln 2 - (1 + 0)$

$= \mathbf{1 + \ln 4\ units^2}$

$\approx \mathbf{2.3863\ units^2}$

19. $\lim_{x\to1}\frac{e^x - e^1}{x - 1} = \frac{d}{dx}e^x\Big|_1 = e^1 = \mathbf{e}$

20. (a) $\Delta x = \frac{5-0}{n} = \frac{5}{n}$

i	x_i	$f(x_i)$
1	$\left(\frac{5}{n}\right)$	$\left(\frac{5}{n}\right)$
2	$2\left(\frac{5}{n}\right)$	$2\left(\frac{5}{n}\right)$
3	$3\left(\frac{5}{n}\right)$	$3\left(\frac{5}{n}\right)$
⋮	⋮	⋮
n	$n\left(\frac{5}{n}\right)$	$n\left(\frac{5}{n}\right)$

$$\lim_{n\to\infty}\frac{5}{n}\left[\frac{5}{n} + \frac{10}{n} + \frac{15}{n} + \cdots 5\right]$$

$$= \lim_{n\to\infty}\sum_{i=1}^{n} f(x_i)\frac{b-a}{n}$$

$$= \mathbf{\int_0^5 x\,dx}$$

(b) $\int_0^5 x\,dx = \left[\frac{1}{2}x^2\right]_0^5 = \mathbf{\frac{25}{2}}$

21. (a)
$$x^2 = x$$
$$x^2 - x = 0$$
$$x(x-1) = 0$$

Fixed points: **(0, 0), (1, 1)**

(b)
$$4x^2 + 4x - 1 = x$$
$$4x^2 + 3x - 1 = 0$$
$$(4x-1)(x+1) = 0$$

Fixed points: $\mathbf{\left(\frac{1}{4}, \frac{1}{4}\right), (-1, -1)}$

(c)
$$\frac{1}{x+1} = x$$
$$x^2 + x = 1$$
$$x^2 + x - 1 = 0$$
$$x = \frac{-1 \pm \sqrt{1 - 4(1)(-1)}}{2}$$

Fixed points: $\mathbf{\left(\frac{-1+\sqrt{5}}{2}, \frac{-1+\sqrt{5}}{2}\right)}$, $\mathbf{\left(\frac{-1-\sqrt{5}}{2}, \frac{-1-\sqrt{5}}{2}\right)}$

22. Let `Y1=1+sin(X)` and `Y2=X`.

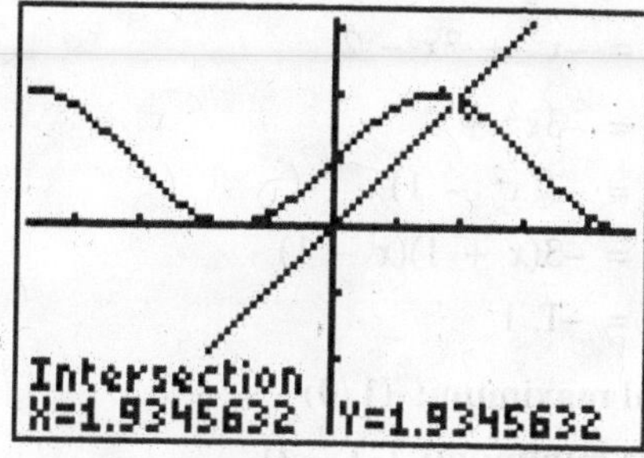

(1.9345632, 1.9345632)

23. Let `Y1=-1+tan(X)` and `Y2=X`.

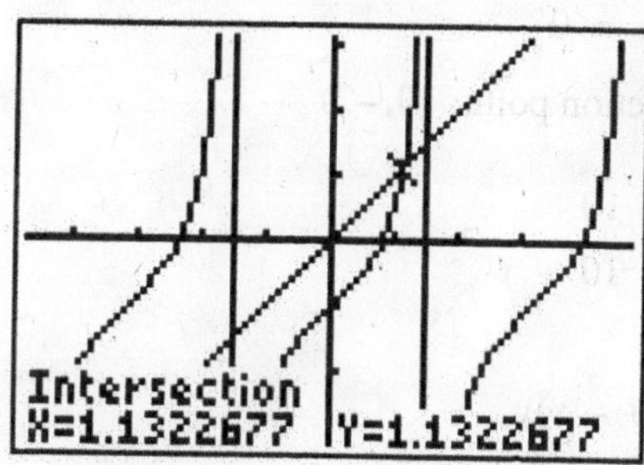

(1.1322677, 1.1322677)

24. A. $e^{x_1} + e^{x_2} \neq e^{x_1 + x_2}$

B. $\ln x_1 + \ln x_2 \neq \ln(x_1 + x_2)$

C. $3x_1 + 3x_2 = 3(x_1 + x_2)$

D. $x_1^2 + x_2^2 \neq (x_1 + x_2)^2$

The correct choice is **C.**

25.
$$\left(\frac{e^{bx}}{e^{ax}}\right)' = \frac{be^{bx}}{ae^{ax}}$$
$$(e^{bx-ax})' = \frac{b}{a}e^{bx-ax}$$
$$(e^{(b-a)x})' = \frac{b}{a}e^{(b-a)x}$$
$$e^{(b-a)x}(b-a) = \frac{b}{a}e^{(b-a)x}$$
$$b - a = \frac{b}{a}$$
$$ab - a^2 = b$$
$$ab - b = a^2$$
$$b = \mathbf{\frac{a^2}{a-1}}$$

Problem Set 52

1. (a) $f(x) = -x^3 + 3x - 2$

$$f'(x) = -3x^2 + 3$$
$$0 = -3(x^2 - 1)$$
$$0 = -3(x + 1)(x - 1)$$
$$x = -1, 1$$

Local maximum: (1, 0)
Local minimum: (–1, –4)

(b) $f''(x) = -6x$

$$0 = -6x$$
$$x = 0$$

Inflection point: **(0, –2)**

2. $x + y = 10$

$$x = 10 - y$$

$$P = xy$$
$$P = (10 - y)y$$
$$P = 10y - y^2$$
$$P' = 10 - 2y$$
$$0 = 10 - 2y$$

$y =$ **5** and $x =$ **5**

3.

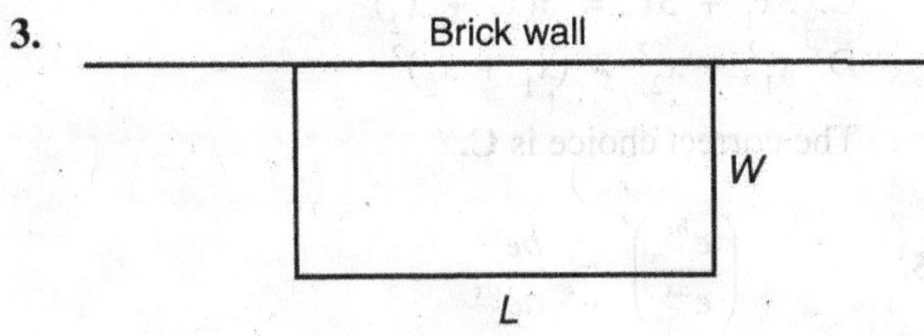

$$2W + L = 200$$
$$L = 200 - 2W$$

$$A = LW$$
$$A = (200 - 2W)W$$
$$A = 200W - 2W^2$$
$$A' = 200 - 4W$$
$$0 = 200 - 4W$$

W = 50 yards, L = 100 yards

4.

$20 - 2x$

$10 - 2x$

$0 < x < 5$

$$V = x(10 - 2x)(20 - 2x)$$
$$V = x(200 - 60x + 4x^2)$$
$$V = 200x - 60x^2 + 4x^3$$
$$V' = 200 - 120x + 12x^2$$
$$0 = 200 - 120x + 12x^2$$
$$x \approx 2.1133$$

Dimensions: 15.7735 cm × 5.7735 cm × 2.1133 cm

$V_{max} = V(2.1133) \approx$ **192.4501 cm³**

5. $\int 5 \cos x \sin^4 x\, dx = \mathbf{\sin^5 x + C}$

6. $\int (2x)\left(\frac{3}{2}\right)(x^2 + 3)^{1/2}\, dx = \mathbf{(x^2 + 3)^{3/2} + C}$

7. $\int 2xe^{x^2}\, dx = \mathbf{e^{x^2} + C}$

8. $\int \frac{2x\, dx}{x^2 - 1} = \mathbf{\ln|x^2 - 1| + C}$

9. $\int 2x \sin(x^2 + 3)\, dx = \mathbf{-\cos(x^2 + 3) + C}$

10. $\int (x - 1)\sqrt{x}\, dx = \int (x^{3/2} - x^{1/2})\, dx$

$$= \mathbf{\frac{2}{5}x^{5/2} - \frac{2}{3}x^{3/2} + C}$$

11. $\int (x^{-3} + 1)^2\, dx = \int (x^{-6} + 2x^{-3} + 1)\, dx$

$$= \mathbf{-\frac{1}{5}x^{-5} - x^{-2} + x + C}$$

12. $y = \frac{\sqrt{x + 1}}{\sqrt{x - 1}} = \left(\frac{x + 1}{x - 1}\right)^{1/2}$

$$y' = \frac{1}{2}\left(\frac{x + 1}{x - 1}\right)^{-1/2}\left[\frac{x - 1 - (x + 1)}{(x - 1)^2}\right]$$

$$y' = \frac{1}{2}\left(\frac{x \pm 1}{x + 1}\right)^{1/2}\left[\frac{-2}{(x - 1)^2}\right]$$

$$y' = \mathbf{-(x + 1)^{-1/2}(x - 1)^{-3/2}}$$

13. $y = (x^2 + 3)^4 \sin x$

$$y' = (x^2 + 3)^4 \cos x + (\sin x)(4)(x^2 + 3)^3(2x)$$
$$y' = \mathbf{(x^2 + 3)^3[\cos x\,(x^2 + 3) + 8x \sin x]}$$

14. $y = xe^{x^2+1}$

$$y' = xe^{x^2+1}(2x) + e^{x^2+1} = \mathbf{e^{x^2+1}(2x^2 + 1)}$$

15. $y = \sec^2 x$

$y' = 2 \sec x \sec x \tan x = \mathbf{2 \sec^2 x \tan x}$

16. $A = \int_{-1}^{1} (e^x + 1)\, dx = \left[e^x + x\right]_{-1}^{1}$

$= e + 1 - (e^{-1} - 1)$

$= \mathbf{(e - e^{-1} + 2)\ units^2 \approx 4.3504\ units^2}$

17. $A = \int_0^{\pi} \sin x\, dx = -\cos x\big|_0^{\pi} = 1 - (-1)$

$= \mathbf{2\ units^2}$

18. $\lim_{h \to 0} \frac{e^{x+h} - e^x}{h} = \mathbf{e^x}$

19.

x	$1 + x + \frac{x^2}{2}$	e^x
0.1	1.105	1.1052
0.2	1.220	1.2214
0.3	1.345	1.3499

20. $\mathbf{\{x \in \mathbb{R} \mid x \geq 0,\ x \neq 1\}}$

21. $V = \pi r^2 h$

$300 = \pi r^2 h$

$h = \frac{300}{\pi r^2}$

$A = 2\pi r^2 + 2\pi r h$

$A = 2\pi r^2 + 2\pi r\left(\frac{300}{\pi r^2}\right)$

$A = 2\pi r^2 + 600 r^{-1}$

A_m when $\mathbf{r = 3.6278\ cm,\ h = 7.2557\ cm}$

22. Let `Y1=X³+2X-1` and `Y2=X`.

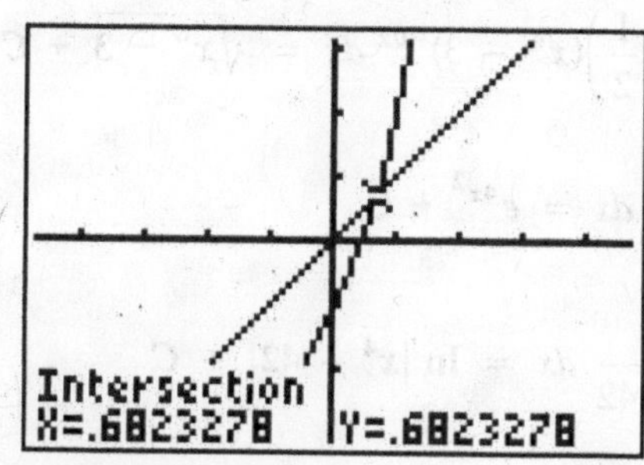

(0.6823278, 0.6823278)

23. Let `Y1=3X³+sin(X)-1` and `Y2=X`.

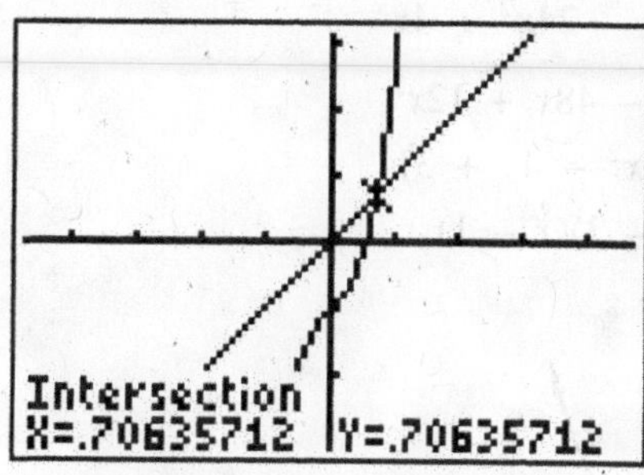

(0.70635712, 0.70635712)

24. A. $\ln(x_1 x_2) = \ln x_1 + \ln x_2$

B. $\frac{1}{x_1 x_2} \neq \frac{1}{x_1} + \frac{1}{x_2}$

C. $(x_1 x_2)^2 \neq x_1^2 + x_2^2$

D. $\sin(x_1 x_2) \neq \sin x_1 + \sin x_2$

The correct choice is **A.**

25. $g'(x) = \lim_{h \to 0} \frac{g(x + h) - g(x)}{h}$

$= \lim_{h \to 0} \frac{3xh + \frac{3}{2}h^2}{h}$

$= \lim_{h \to 0} \left(3x + \frac{3}{2}h\right)$

$= \mathbf{3x}$

PROBLEM SET 53

1. $A = lw = 200$

$l = 200w^{-1}$

$F = 2l + 2w = 400w^{-1} + 2w$

$F' = -400w^{-2} + 2$

$0 = -\frac{400}{w^2} + 2$

$\frac{400}{w^2} = 2$

$w = 10\sqrt{2}$

$F = \frac{400}{10\sqrt{2}} + 2(10\sqrt{2})$

$= 20\sqrt{2} + 20\sqrt{2}$

$= \mathbf{40\sqrt{2}\ yd}$

2. $V = x(6 - 2x)(6 - 2x)$

$V = 36x - 24x^2 + 4x^3$

$V' = 36 - 48x + 12x^2$

$0 = 12(x^2 - 4x + 3)$

$0 = (x - 3)(x - 1)$

$x = 1, 3$

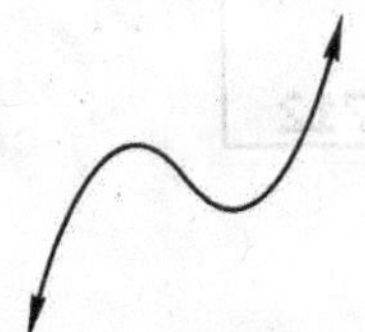

Maximum at $x = 1$ Minimum at $x = 3$

Dimensions: 1 in. × 4 in. × 4 in.; $V = 16$ in.^{3}

3. $A = s^2$ $P = 4s$

$\frac{dA}{dt} = 2s\frac{ds}{dt}$ $\frac{dP}{dt} = 4\frac{ds}{dt}$

$\frac{dA}{dt} = 2(6)(2)$ $\frac{dP}{dt} = 4(2)$

$\mathbf{\frac{dA}{dt} = 24\,\frac{cm^2}{s}}$ $\mathbf{\frac{dP}{dt} = 8\,\frac{cm}{s}}$

4. $\int_0^{3\pi/2} \cos x\,dx = [\sin x]_0^{3\pi/2} = -1 - (0) = \mathbf{-1}$

5. $\int_1^3 (x^3 - e^x)\,dx = \left[\frac{1}{4}x^4 - e^x\right]_1^3$

$= \frac{81}{4} - e^3 - \left(\frac{1}{4} - e\right)$

$= \mathbf{20 - e^3 + e \approx 2.6327}$

6. $\int_{\pi/2}^{\pi} (\sin x - \cos x)\,dx = [-\cos x - \sin x]_{\pi/2}^{\pi}$

$= 1 - 0 - (0 - 1) = \mathbf{2}$

7. (a) $A = \int_1^5 \frac{1}{x}\,dx \approx$ `fnInt(1/X,X,1,5)`

$\approx$ **1.6094 units^2**

(b) $\ln 5 \approx$ **1.6094**

(c) **They are the same.**

8.

(a) $A = \int_1^8 x^{1/2}\,dx = \left[\frac{2}{3}x^{3/2}\right]_1^8$

$= \frac{32\sqrt{2}}{3} - \frac{2}{3} = \mathbf{\frac{32\sqrt{2} - 2}{3}\ units^2}$

(b) $A = \int_1^3 x^{1/2}\,dx = \left[\frac{2}{3}x^{3/2}\right]_1^3$

$= \frac{6\sqrt{3}}{3} - \frac{2}{3} = \mathbf{\frac{6\sqrt{3} - 2}{3}\ units^2}$

(c) $A = \int_3^8 x^{1/2}\,dx = \left[\frac{2}{3}x^{3/2}\right]_3^8$

$= \frac{32\sqrt{2}}{3} - \frac{6\sqrt{3}}{3} = \mathbf{\frac{32\sqrt{2} - 6\sqrt{3}}{3}\ units^2}$

(d) $\frac{6\sqrt{3} - 2}{3} + \frac{32\sqrt{2} - 6\sqrt{3}}{3}$

$= \frac{32\sqrt{2} - 2}{3}$ units^2

They are equal.

9. $\int_e^{\pi} 2^x\,dx \approx$ `fnInt(2^X,X,e^(1),π)`

$\approx$ **3.2375**

10. $\int_{\sqrt{2}}^{9.5} \log x\,dx$

$\approx$ `fnInt(log(X),X,√(2),9.5)`

$\approx$ **5.5639**

11. (a) $\lim_{n\to\infty} \frac{10}{n}\sum_{i=1}^{n}\left(\frac{10i}{n}\right)^2 = \mathbf{\int_0^{10} x^2\,dx}$

(b) $\int_0^{10} x^2\,dx = \frac{1}{3}x^3\Big]_0^{10} = \mathbf{\frac{1000}{3}}$

12. $\int 8\sin^7 x\cos x\,dx = \mathbf{\sin^8 x + C}$

13. $\int (4x^3)\left(\frac{1}{2}\right)(x^4 - 3)^{-1/2}\,dx = \mathbf{\sqrt{x^4 - 3} + C}$

14. $\int 8xe^{4x^2}\,dx = \mathbf{e^{4x^2} + C}$

15. $\int \frac{4x^3}{x^4 - 42}\,dx = \mathbf{\ln|x^4 - 42| + C}$

16. $\int \cos(\sin^2 x)\sin(2x)\,dx = \mathbf{\sin(\sin^2 x) + C}$

17. $y = 2x \ln (x^2 + 1) + 4 \tan x$

$$y' = 2x\left(\frac{2x}{x^2 + 1}\right) + 2 \ln (x^2 + 1) + 4 \sec^2 x$$

$$\mathbf{y' = \frac{4x^2}{x^2 + 1} + 2 \ln (x^2 + 1) + 4 \sec^2 x}$$

18. $y = \dfrac{-e^x}{\cot^2 x + x}$

$$y' = \frac{(\cot^2 x + x)(-e^x)}{(\cot^2 x + x)^2} + \frac{e^x[2 \cot x (-\csc^2 x) + 1]}{(\cot^2 x + x)^2}$$

$$\mathbf{y' = -\frac{e^x}{\cot^2 x + x} + \frac{e^x(-2 \cot x \csc^2 x + 1)}{(\cot^2 x + x)^2}}$$

19. $y = \sec (\tan x^2)$

$$y' = \sec (\tan x^2) \tan (\tan x^2) \sec^2 x^2 (2x)$$

$$\mathbf{y' = 2x \sec^2 x^2 \sec (\tan x^2) \tan (\tan x^2)}$$

20. f has positive slope on $(-\infty, -2)$, negative slope on $(-2, 0)$, and positive slope on $(0, \infty)$.

Only choice **A** has positive value on $(-\infty, -2)$ and $(0, \infty)$ and negative value on $(-2, 0)$, which matches the description of f.

21.

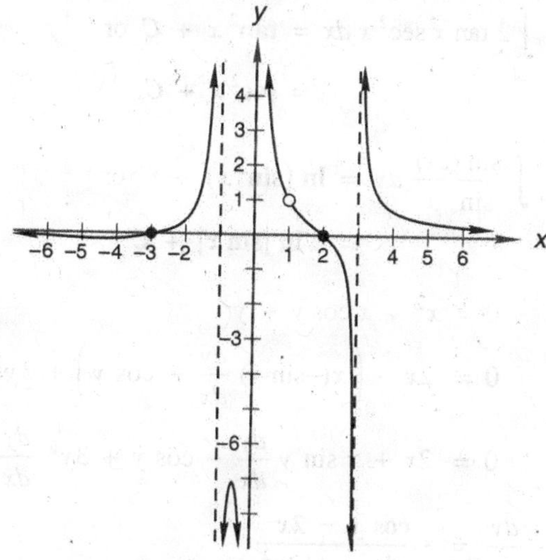

22.

x	$1 - \frac{x^2}{2!} + \frac{x^4}{4!}$	$\cos x$
0.1	0.9950	0.9950
0.2	0.9801	0.9801
0.3	0.9553	0.9553

23. $\displaystyle\lim_{x\to 2} \frac{f(x) - f(2)}{x - 2} = \lim_{x\to 2} \frac{x^2 - 2 - 2}{x - 2}$

$$= \lim_{x\to 2} \frac{x^2 - 4}{x - 2} = \lim_{x\to 2} \frac{(x + 2)(x - 2)}{x - 2}$$

$$= \lim_{x\to 2} (x + 2) = \mathbf{4}$$

24. $m = \dfrac{0 + \cos 26°}{\sin 26° - 0} = \dfrac{\cos 26°}{\sin 26°} = \cot 26°$

The correct choice is **C.**

25. Adding 3 to each value of x has the effect of shifting the graph of f three units to the left.

The correct choice is **B.**

PROBLEM SET 54

1. (a) $A = lw$

$$3600 = lw$$

$$l = 3600w^{-1}$$

$$P = 2l + 2w$$

$$P = 2(3600w^{-1}) + 2w$$

$$P = 7200w^{-1} + 2w$$

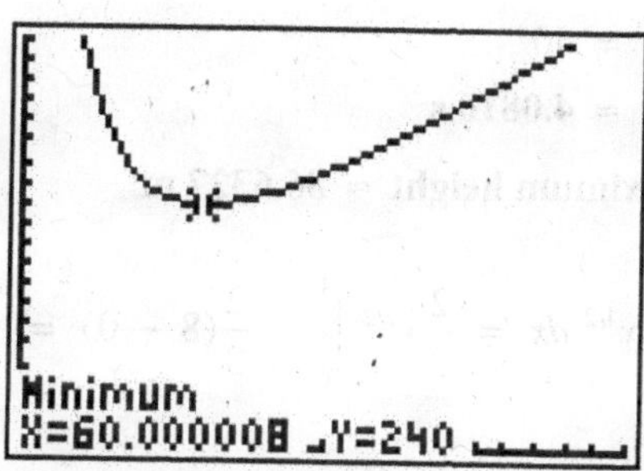

Window: Xmin=0, Xmax=200, Xscl=10, Ymin=0, Ymax=400, Yscl=200

Dimensions: 60 m × 60 m

$\mathbf{P_{min} = 240\ m}$

(b) $P = 7200w^{-1} + 2w$

$$P' = \frac{-7200}{w^2} + 2$$

$$\frac{7200}{w^2} = 2$$

$$w^2 = 3600$$

$$w = 60 \text{ m}, \; l = 60 \text{ m}, \; P = 240 \text{ m}$$

Dimensions: 60 m × 60 m

$\mathbf{P_{min} = 240\ m}$

2. $x(t) = -4t^2 + 2t - 1$
   $v(t) = -8t + 2$
   $a(t) = -8$
   $x(2) = -16 + 4 - 1$
   $\mathbf{x(2) = -13}$ **units**
   $\mathbf{v(2) = -14}$ **units/s**
   $\mathbf{a(2) = -8}$ **units/s²**

3. $x(t) = t^2 + t - 2$
   $v(t) = 2t + 1$
   $0 = 2t + 1$
   $t = -\frac{1}{2}$
   $a(t) = 2$

   At rest when $t = -\frac{1}{2}$

   Moving right when $t > -\frac{1}{2}$

   Always accelerating, never decelerating

4. $h(t) = -4.9t^2 + 40t + 5$
   $v(t) = -9.8t + 40$
   $9.8t = 40$
   $t \approx$ **4.0816 s**

   Maximum height $\approx$ **86.6327 m**

5. $\int_0^4 x^{1/2}\,dx = \frac{2}{3}x^{3/2}\Big]_0^4 = \frac{2}{3}(8 - 0) = \mathbf{\frac{16}{3}}$

6. $\int_1^3 \frac{1}{x}\,dx = \ln|x|\Big]_1^3 = \ln 3 - \ln 1 = \mathbf{\ln 3}$

7. $\int_{\pi/6}^{\pi/2} \cos x\,dx = \sin x\Big]_{\pi/6}^{\pi/2} = 1 - \frac{1}{2} = \mathbf{\frac{1}{2}}$

8. $\int_1^2 x^{-2}\,dx = \mathbf{\frac{1}{2}}$

9. $\int_{\ln 3}^{e^2} \sqrt{e^x}\,dx =$ `fnInt(√(e^X),X,`
   `ln(3),e^2)`
   $\approx$ **76.9891**

10. $\int_{-1}^{1} 2\sqrt{1 - x^2}\,dx$
    $\approx$ `fnInt(2√(1-X²),X,-1,1)`
    $\approx$ **3.1416**

11. 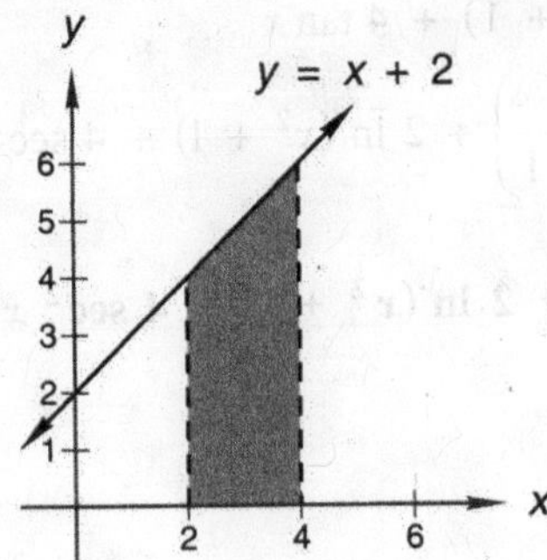

$$A_{Trap} = \frac{2[f(2) + f(4)]}{2} = 4 + 6 = \mathbf{10\ units^2}$$

$$A = \int_2^4 (x + 2)\,dx$$
$$= \left[\frac{1}{2}x^2 + 2\right]_2^4$$
$$= 8 + 8 - (2 + 4)$$
$$= \mathbf{10\ units^2}$$

12. $\int 2x\left(\frac{3}{2}\right)\sqrt{x^2 + 1}\,dx = \mathbf{(x^2 + 1)^{3/2} + C}$

13. $\int (\cos x)e^{\sin x}\,dx = \mathbf{e^{\sin x} + C}$

14. $\int \left(\frac{1}{x}\right)(4)(\ln x)^3\,dx = \mathbf{(\ln x)^4 + C}$

15. $\int 2\tan x \sec^2 x\,dx = \mathbf{\tan^2 x + C}$ or
    $= \mathbf{\sec^2 x + C}$

16. $\int \frac{\sin(2x)}{\sin^2 x}\,dx = \mathbf{\ln(\sin^2 x) + C}$ or
    $= \mathbf{2\ln|\sin x| + C}$

17. $0 = x^2 - x\cos y + y^3$
    $0 = 2x - \left(x(-\sin y)\frac{dy}{dx} + \cos y\right) + 3y^2\frac{dy}{dx}$
    $0 = 2x + x\sin y\frac{dy}{dx} - \cos y + 3y^2\frac{dy}{dx}$
    $\frac{dy}{dx} = \mathbf{\frac{\cos y - 2x}{x\sin y + 3y^2}}$

18. $y = \dfrac{e^{x^2}}{x^2 + 1}\cos^2 x + e^x \csc x$

$$\frac{dy}{dx} = \frac{(x^2 + 1)(2x)e^{x^2} - (2x)e^{x^2}}{(x^2 + 1)^2}\cos^2 x + 2\cos x\,(-\sin x)\frac{e^{x^2}}{x^2 + 1} + e^x \csc x - \csc x \cot x\, e^x$$

$$\frac{dy}{dx} = \mathbf{\frac{2x^3 e^{x^2}}{(x^2 + 1)^2}\cos^2 x - \frac{e^{x^2}\sin(2x)}{x^2 + 1} + \frac{e^x}{\sin x}(1 - \cot x)}$$

19. $y = \ln\left(\dfrac{x}{3}\right) = \ln x - \ln 3$

$y(e) = \ln e - \ln 3 = 1 - \ln 3$

$y' = \dfrac{1}{x}$

$y'(e) = \dfrac{1}{e}$

$y - (1 - \ln 3) = \dfrac{1}{e}(x - e)$

$y = \dfrac{1}{e}x - 1 + 1 - \ln 3$

$\mathbf{y = \dfrac{1}{e}x - \ln 3}$

20. $\dfrac{dy}{dx} = \sin(2x)$

$y = \displaystyle\int \sin(2x)\,dx$

$y = -\dfrac{1}{2}\cos(2x) + C$

The correct choice is **C.**

21. $\displaystyle\lim_{n\to\infty} \frac{5n^2}{10{,}000n + n^3} = \mathbf{0}$

22. $\displaystyle\lim_{h\to 0} \frac{e^{e+h} - e^e}{h} = \frac{d}{dx}e^x\Big|_e = e^x\Big|_e = \mathbf{e^e}$

23.

x	$x - \dfrac{x^3}{3!} + \dfrac{x^5}{5!}$	$\sin x$
0.1	0.0998	0.0998
0.2	0.1987	0.1987
0.3	0.2955	0.2955

24.

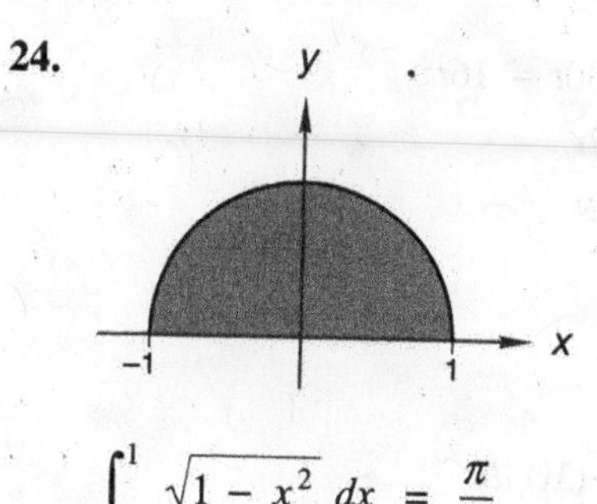

$$\int_{-1}^{1} \sqrt{1 - x^2}\,dx = \mathbf{\frac{\pi}{2}}$$

25. $x + y = 20$

$x = 20 - y$

$P = xy$

$P = (20 - y)y$

$P = 20y - y^2$

$P' = 20 - 2y$

$2y = 20$

$\mathbf{y = 10,\ x = 10}$

Problem Set 55

1.

n	$f^{(n)}(x)$	$f^{(n)}(0)$
0	$3x^2 + 4x - 3$	-3
1	$6x + 4$	4
2	6	6
3	0	0

$p(x) = -3 + 4x + \dfrac{6x^2}{2}$

$\mathbf{p(x) = -3 + 4x + 3x^2}$

2.

n	$f^{(n)}(x)$	$f^{(n)}(0)$
0	$\sin x$	0
1	$\cos x$	1
2	$-\sin x$	0
3	$-\cos x$	-1
4	$\sin x$	0
⋮	⋮	⋮

$p(x) = x - \dfrac{x^3}{3!} + \dfrac{x^5}{5!} - \dfrac{x^7}{7!} + \cdots$

$$\sin x = p(x) = \mathbf{\sum_{n=0}^{\infty} (-1)^n \frac{x^{2n+1}}{(2n+1)!}}$$

3.
$$h(t) = 100 + 30t - 16t^2$$
$$v(t) = 30 - 32t$$
$$-46 = 30 - 32t$$
$$-76 = -32t$$
$$t = \mathbf{2.375\ s}$$

4.
$$A = \int_0^{\pi/3} 3\sin(3x)\,dx$$
$$= -\cos(3x)\Big]_0^{\pi/3}$$
$$= -(-1) - (-1)$$
$$= \mathbf{2\ units^2}$$

5.
$$A = \int_1^e \frac{1}{x}\,dx = \ln|x|\Big]_1^e = \ln e - \ln 1 = \mathbf{1\ unit^2}$$

6.
$$\int \frac{1}{2}(2x + 1)(x^2 + x + 1)^{-1/2}\,dx$$
$$= \boldsymbol{\sqrt{x^2 + x + 1} + C}$$

7.
$$\int 4\tan^3 x \sec^2 x\,dx = \mathbf{\tan^4 x + C}$$

8.
$$\int 3(\sec^2 x)(\sec x \tan x)\,dx = \mathbf{\sec^3 x + C}$$

9.
$$\int \frac{x + 1}{x}\,dx = \int \left(1 + \frac{1}{x}\right) dx = \mathbf{x + \ln|x| + C}$$

10.
$$y = e^{2x}\tan^2 x$$
$$y' = e^{2x}(2)\tan x \sec^2 x + \tan^2 x\, e^{2x}(2)$$
$$y' = \mathbf{2e^{2x}\tan x\,(\sec^2 x + \tan x)}$$

11.
$$y = \frac{(x^2 + 1)^{1/2}}{x + \sin x}$$
$$y' = \frac{(x + \sin x)\left(\frac{1}{2}\right)(x^2 + 1)^{-1/2}(2x)}{(x + \sin x)^2} - \frac{(x^2 + 1)^{1/2}(1 + \cos x)}{(x + \sin x)^2}$$
$$y' = \mathbf{\frac{x(x^2 + 1)^{-1/2}}{x + \sin x} - \frac{(x^2 + 1)^{1/2}(1 + \cos x)}{(x + \sin x)^2}}$$

12. (a)

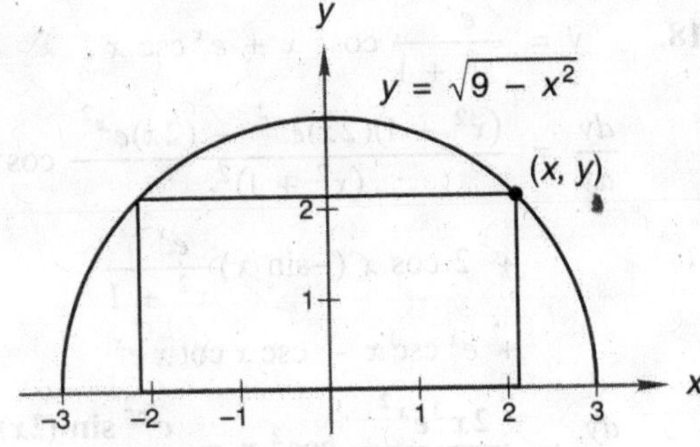

$$A = 2xy = 2x(9 - x^2)^{1/2}$$

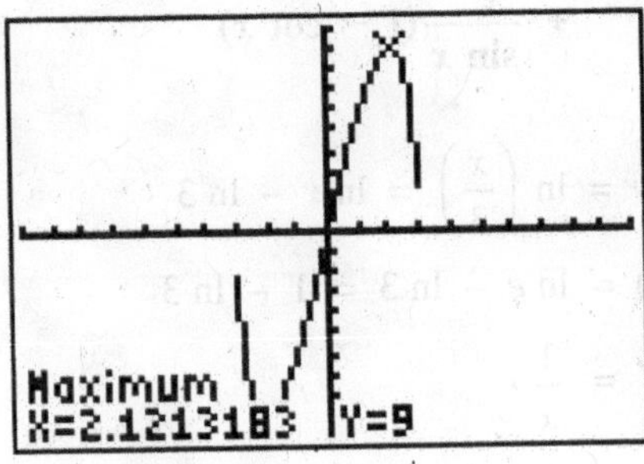

$$A_{max} = \mathbf{9\ cm^2}$$

Dimensions: 4.2426 cm × 2.1213 cm

(b)
$$A = 2x(9 - x^2)^{1/2}$$
$$A' = 2x\left(\frac{1}{2}\right)(9 - x^2)^{-1/2}(-2x) + 2(9 - x^2)^{1/2}$$
$$A' = -2x^2(9 - x^2)^{-1/2} + 2(9 - x^2)^{1/2}$$
$$A' = -2(9 - x^2)^{-1/2}\left[x^2 - (9 - x^2)\right]$$
$$0 = -2(9 - x^2)^{-1/2}(2x^2 - 9)$$
$$0 = 2x^2 - 9$$
$$x^2 = \frac{9}{2}$$
$$x = \frac{3\sqrt{2}}{2}$$
$$A_{max} = \mathbf{9\ cm^2}$$

Dimensions: $\mathbf{3\sqrt{2}\ cm \times \frac{3\sqrt{2}}{2}\ cm}$

13.
$$y = x\ln x$$
$$\frac{dy}{dx} = x\left(\frac{1}{x}\right) + \ln x$$
$$\frac{dy}{dx} = 1 + \ln x$$
$$\frac{d^2y}{dx^2} = \frac{1}{x}$$
$$\left.\frac{d^2y}{dx^2}\right|_{e^2} = \frac{1}{e^2}$$ implies **positive concavity**

14. $\frac{dr}{dt} = 3\ \frac{\text{cm}}{\text{s}} \qquad r = 10\text{ cm}$

$A = 4\pi r^2$

$\frac{dA}{dt} = 8\pi r\ \frac{dr}{dt}$

$\frac{dA}{dt} = 8\pi(10)(3)$

$\frac{dA}{dt} = \mathbf{240\pi\ \frac{cm^2}{s}}$

15. $\lim_{x\to\infty} \frac{x^3 - 2x^2}{1 - x^4} = \mathbf{0}$

16. $\lim_{x\to 2} \frac{e^x - e^2}{x - 2} = \frac{d}{dx}e^x\Big|_2 = \mathbf{e^2}$

17. $\lim_{\Delta x\to 0} \frac{\cos(\pi + \Delta x) - \cos\pi}{\Delta x} = \frac{d}{dx}\cos x\Big|_\pi$

$= -\sin\pi = \mathbf{0}$

18. $\lim_{n\to\infty} \frac{3}{n}\sum_{i=1}^{n} \ln(x_i) = \int_1^4 \ln x\,dx \text{ for } 1 \le x_i \le 4$

The interval must be 3 units long, beginning at 1 and ending at 4. The function is ln (x), not 3 ln (x).

The correct choice is **C.**

19. $y = \ln x^2$

$y' = \frac{2x}{x^2}$

$y' = \frac{2}{x}$

$m = 2 \quad (1, 0)$

$y - 0 = 2(x - 1)$

$\mathbf{y = 2x - 2}$

20. $y = 2\sin x$

$\frac{dy}{dx} = 2\cos x$

$\frac{d^2y}{dx^2} = -2\sin x$

$\frac{d^3y}{dx^3} = -2\cos x$

$\frac{d^4y}{dx^4} = 2\sin x$

$\frac{d^4y}{dx^4}\Big|_{\pi/2} = \mathbf{2}$

21. $\frac{dy}{dx} = 2x$

$y = x^2 + C$

$1 = 1 + C$

$C = 0$

$\mathbf{f(x) = x^2}$

22.

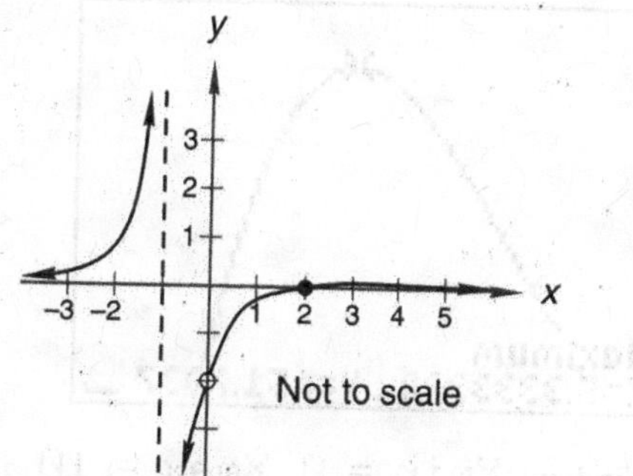

23. $f(x) = ax^3 + bx$

$-1 = a + b$

$b = -1 - a$

$f'(x) = 3ax^2 + b$

$3 = 3a + b$

$3 = 3a - 1 - a$

$4 = 2a$

$\mathbf{a = 2,\ b = -3}$

24. $\int g'(f(x))\,f'(x)\,dx = \mathbf{g(f(x)) + C}$

25. $x^2 + y^2 = 200$

$y = \sqrt{200 - x^2}$

$P = xy$

$P = x(200 - x^2)^{1/2}$

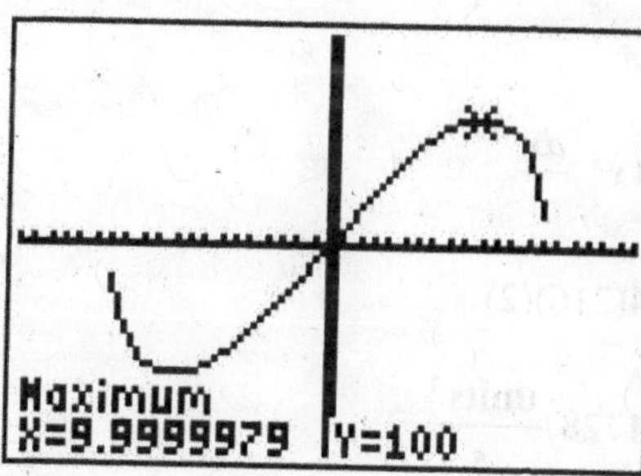

Window: Xmin=-20, Xmax=20,

Ymin=-190, Ymax=190

The graph of function P has a maximum value of 100, but no minimum.

The correct choice is **E.**

PROBLEM SET 56

1. (a) $2x + y = 16$

$y = 16 - 2x$

$V = x^2y$

$V = x^2(16 - 2x)$

$V = 16x^2 - 2x^3$

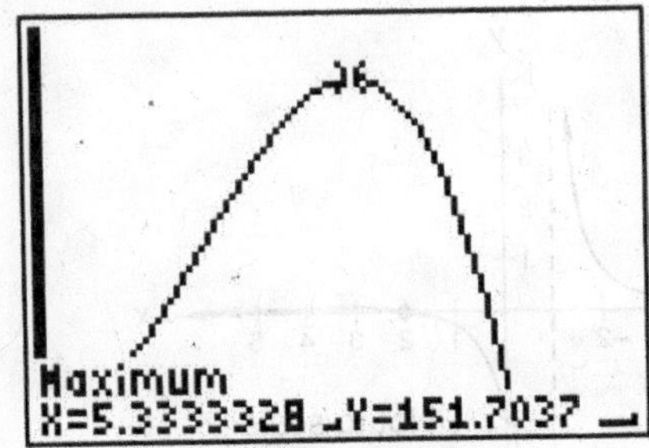

Window: Xmin = 0, Xmax = 10
Ymin = 0, Ymax = 200

$V_{max} \approx$ **151.7037 ft³**

Dimensions: $\frac{16}{3}$ **ft** $\times$ $\frac{16}{3}$ **ft** $\times$ $\frac{16}{3}$ **ft**

(b) $V' = 32x - 6x^2$

$0 = 2x(16 - 3x)$

$x = 0, \frac{16}{3}$

$V'' = 32 - 12x$

$V''\left(\frac{16}{3}\right) < 0$

Thus $x = \frac{16}{3}$ is a maximum.

$V_{max} \approx$ **151.7037 ft³**

Dimensions: $\frac{16}{3}$ **ft** $\times$ $\frac{16}{3}$ **ft** $\times$ $\frac{16}{3}$ **ft**

2. $y = x^4$

$\frac{dy}{dt} = 4x^3 \frac{dx}{dt}$

$\frac{dy}{dt} = 4(216)(2)$

$\frac{dy}{dt} = \mathbf{1728 \frac{units^4}{s}}$

3. $x(t) = t^3 + 2t^2 - 7t + 4$

$v(t) = 3t^2 + 4t - 7$

$0 = 3t^2 + 4t - 7$

$0 = (3t + 7)(t - 1)$

$t = -\frac{7}{3}, 1$

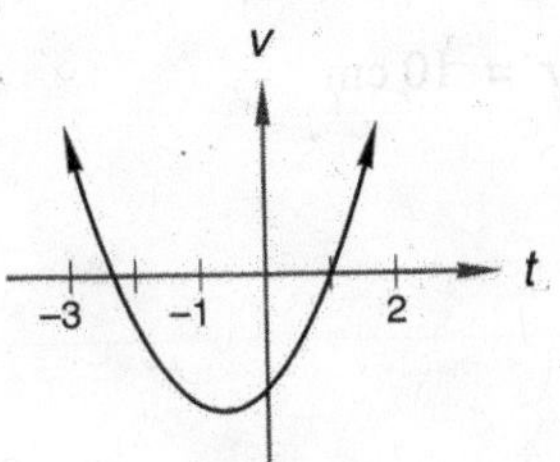

At rest when $t = -\frac{7}{3}, 1$

Moving left when $-\frac{7}{3} < t < 1$

Moving right when $t > 1$ **and when** $t < -\frac{7}{3}$

4. $h(t) = -16t^2 + 40t + 100$

$v(t) = -32t + 40$

$0 = -32t + 40$

$t = 1.25$ s

Maximum height at $h(1.25)$ = **125 ft**

5. $\int_{-\pi/2}^{\pi} 2 \sin x \, dx = -2 \cos x\Big]_{-\pi/2}^{\pi} = \mathbf{2}$

6. $\int_1^4 x^{1/2}\, dx = \frac{2}{3}x^{3/2}\Big]_1^4 = \frac{16}{3} - \frac{2}{3} = \mathbf{\frac{14}{3}}$

7. $\int 4xe^{x^2}\, dx = 2\int 2xe^{x^2}\, dx = \mathbf{2e^{x^2} + C}$

8. $\int \frac{1}{4} \sin^6 t \cos t \, dt = \mathbf{\frac{1}{28} \sin^7 t + C}$

9. $\int \frac{x\,dx}{2x^2 + 1} = \frac{1}{4}\int \frac{4x\,dx}{2x^2 + 1}$

$= \mathbf{\frac{1}{4} \ln (2x^2 + 1) + C}$

10. $\int 3x^2(x^3 - 2)^{1/2}\, dx = \mathbf{\frac{2}{3}(x^3 - 2)^{3/2} + C}$

11. $\int 4 \cos (3t) \sin^2 (3t)\, dt = \frac{4}{3}\int 3 \cos (3t) \sin^2 (3t)\, dt$

$= \mathbf{\frac{4}{9} \sin^3 (3t) + C}$

12. $\int \frac{\cos (ax)}{\sqrt{1 + \sin (ax)}}\, dx$

$= \frac{1}{a}\int a \cos (ax)\, [1 + \sin (ax)]^{-1/2}\, dx$

$= \mathbf{\frac{2}{a}[1 + \sin (ax)]^{1/2} + C}$

13. $y = \dfrac{\sin(2x+1)}{x^2+2} + 2\tan x$

$y' = \dfrac{(x^2+2)\cos(2x+1)(2)}{(x^2+2)^2}$

$\quad - \dfrac{\sin(2x+1)(2x)}{(x^2+2)^2} + 2\sec^2 x$

$y' = \mathbf{\dfrac{2\cos(2x+1)}{x^2+2} - \dfrac{2x\sin(2x+1)}{(x^2+2)^2}}$

$\mathbf{+\ 2\sec^2 x}$

14. $y = \ln|\sin x + x| + \csc(2x)$

$y' = \mathbf{\dfrac{\cos x + 1}{\sin x + x} - 2\csc(2x)\cot(2x)}$

15.

n	$f^{(n)}(x)$	$f^{(n)}(0)$
0	$-2x^2 - 7x + 2$	2
1	$-4x - 7$	-7
2	-4	-4
3	0	0

$p(x) = 2 - 7x - \dfrac{4x^2}{2}$

$p(x) = \mathbf{2 - 7x - 2x^2}$

16.

n	$f^{(n)}(x)$	$f^{(n)}(0)$
0	$\cos x$	1
1	$-\sin x$	0
2	$-\cos x$	-1
3	$\sin x$	0
4	$\cos x$	1
5	$-\sin x$	0
6	$-\cos x$	-1
$\vdots$	$\vdots$	$\vdots$

$p(x) = 1 - \dfrac{x^2}{2!} + \dfrac{x^4}{4!} - \dfrac{x^6}{6!} + \cdots$

$\cos x = p(x) = \mathbf{\displaystyle\sum_{n=0}^{\infty} (-1)^n \frac{x^{2n}}{(2n)!}}$

17. $\dfrac{1}{9}x^2 - \dfrac{1}{4}y^2 = 1$

$\dfrac{2}{9}x - \dfrac{1}{2}y\dfrac{dy}{dx} = 0$

$\dfrac{dy}{dx} = \dfrac{\frac{2}{9}x}{\frac{1}{2}y}$

$\dfrac{dy}{dx} = \dfrac{4x}{9y}$

$m = \dfrac{4\left(\frac{9}{2}\right)}{9\sqrt{5}} = \dfrac{18}{9\sqrt{5}} = \mathbf{\dfrac{2\sqrt{5}}{5}}$

18.

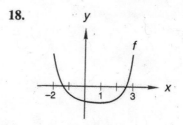

y

f

x

−2 1 3

19.

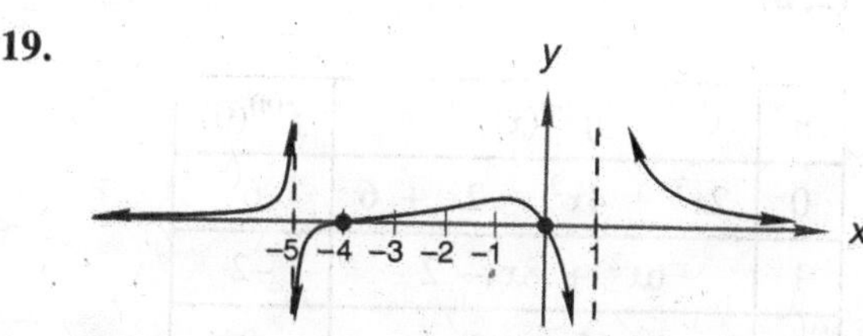

20. $f'(\sqrt{13}) \approx$ `nDeriv(3^sin(X)+sin(cos(X)),X,√(13))`

$\approx \mathbf{-0.3208}$

21. $\dfrac{1}{2}\displaystyle\int_{-2}^{2} \sqrt{4 - x^2}\, dx$

$\approx$ `0.5fnInt(√(4-X²),X,-2,2)`

$\approx \mathbf{3.1416}$

22. $\displaystyle\int_{\sqrt{3}}^{e^{\pi}} \sqrt{3^x + \cos x}\, dx$

$\approx$ `fnInt(√(3^X+cos(X)),X,√(3),e^π)`

$\approx \mathbf{603{,}448.4645}$

23. $\displaystyle\lim_{x\to3} f(x) = \lim_{x\to3}\frac{x^2-9}{x-3} = \lim_{x\to3}\frac{(x+3)(x-3)}{x-3}$

$= \displaystyle\lim_{x\to3}(x+3) = \mathbf{6}$

24. $\log_3 x = \dfrac{\ln x}{\ln 3}$

25. **90°** The diameter does not matter, the measure of an inscribed angle is always half the measure of the intercepted arc.

PROBLEM SET 57

1. $m = -\dfrac{3}{2}$ $\quad y = -\dfrac{3}{2}x + 6$

$$A = xy$$
$$A = x\left(-\frac{3}{2}x + 6\right)$$
$$A = -\frac{3}{2}x^2 + 6x$$
$$A' = -3x + 6$$
$$3x = 6$$
$$x = 2$$

(2, 3)

2.

n	$f^{(n)}(x)$	$f^{(n)}(0)$
0	$2x^3 + 4x^2 - 2x + 6$	6
1	$6x^2 + 8x - 2$	−2
2	$12x + 8$	8
3	12	12
4	0	0

$$p(x) = 6 - 2x + \frac{8x^2}{2!} + \frac{12x^3}{3!}$$
$$\mathbf{p(x) = 6 - 2x + 4x^2 + 2x^3}$$

3.

n	$f^{(n)}(x)$	$f^{(n)}(0)$
0	e^x	1
1	e^x	1
2	e^x	1
3	e^x	1
⋮	⋮	⋮

$$p(x) = 1 + x + \frac{x^2}{2!} + \frac{x^3}{3!} + \cdots$$
$$e^x = \sum_{n=0}^{\infty} \frac{x^n}{n!}$$

4.
$$x^2 + y^2 = 25$$
$$2x\frac{dx}{dt} + 2y\frac{dy}{dt} = 0$$
$$\frac{dx}{dt} = \frac{-y}{x}\frac{dy}{dt}$$
$$\frac{dx}{dt} = \frac{-3}{4}(-3)$$
$$\frac{dx}{dt} = \mathbf{\frac{9}{4}\ \frac{units}{s}}$$

5. (a) $V = x(0.3 - 2x)^2$

Maximum
X=.05000237 Y=.002

Window: Xmin = 0, Xmax = 0.15,
Ymin = 0, Ymax = 0.005

Size of square = 0.05 m

V_{max} **= 0.002 m³**

(b)
$$V = x(0.09 - 1.2x + 4x^2)$$
$$V = 0.09x - 1.2x^2 + 4x^3$$
$$V' = 0.09 - 2.4x + 12x^2$$
$$0 = 12x^2 - 2.4x + 0.09$$
$$x = \frac{2.4 \pm \sqrt{5.76 - 4.32}}{24}$$
$$x = 0.15, 0.05$$

$x = 0.15$ is a minimum.
$x = 0.05$ is a maximum.

Size of square = 0.05 m

V_{max} **= 0.002 m³**

6.
$$s(t) = -12t + t^3$$
$$v(t) = -12 + 3t^2$$
$$3t^2 = 12$$
$$t^2 = 4$$
$$t = -2, 2$$

7. $\int_{-1}^{5} f(x)\,dx = \int_{-1}^{4} f(x)\,dx + \int_{4}^{5} f(x)\,dx$
$= -3 + 2 = \mathbf{-1}$

8. $\int_{1}^{3} [-3f(x) + 2g(x)]\,dx$
$= -3\int_{1}^{3} f(x)\,dx + 2\int_{1}^{3} g(x)\,dx$
$= 6 + 8 = \mathbf{14}$

9. Maximum value of $\int_{-1}^{3} f(x)\,dx$ is
$[3 - (-1)](4) = 16$ so $\int_{-1}^{3} f(x)\,dx \le 16$
The correct choice is **A.**

10. $\int_{1}^{9} x^{-1/2}\,dx = 2x^{1/2}\Big|_{1}^{9} = 2(3 - 1) = \mathbf{4}$

11. $\int_{-\pi/2}^{3\pi} \cos x\,dx = \sin x\Big|_{-\pi/2}^{3\pi} = 0 - (-1) = \mathbf{1}$

12. $\int \frac{3x + 1}{3x^2 + 2x}\,dx = \frac{1}{2}\int \frac{2(3x + 1)}{3x^2 + 2x}\,dx$
$= \mathbf{\ln\sqrt{3x^2 + 2x} + C}$

13. $\int (4x + 2)e^{x^2+x}\,dx = 2\int (2x + 1)e^{x^2+x}\,dx$
$= \mathbf{2e^{x^2+x} + C}$

14. $\int (2x + 1)(x^2 + x + 1)^{-1/2}\,dx$
$= \mathbf{2\sqrt{x^2 + x + 1} + C}$

15. $\int \tan^3 x \sec^2 x\,dx = \mathbf{\frac{1}{4}\tan^4 x + C}$

16.

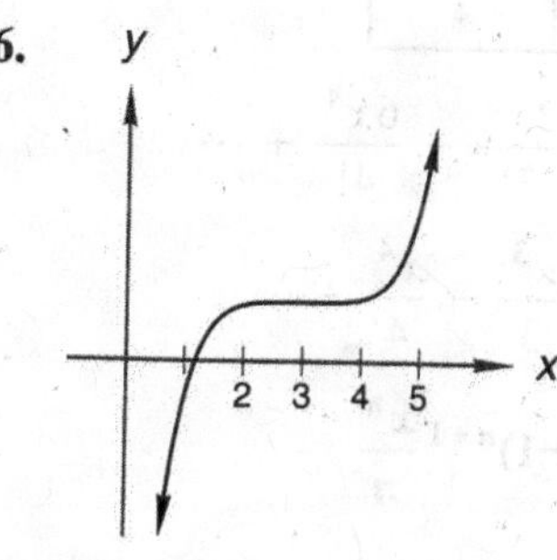

17. $\int_{1}^{k} \frac{1}{x}\,dx = 1$ or $\int_{k}^{1} \frac{1}{x}\,dx = 1$

$\ln|x|\Big]_{1}^{k} = 1$ $\qquad$ $\ln|x|\Big]_{k}^{1} = 1$

$\ln k - \ln 1 = 1$ $\qquad$ $\ln 1 - \ln k = 1$

$\ln k = 1$ $\qquad$ $-\ln k = 1$

$k = e$ $\qquad$ $\ln k = -1$

$k = e^{-1}$

18. f is probably cubic and its slope from left to right must change from positive to negative to positive.
The correct choice is **D.**

19.

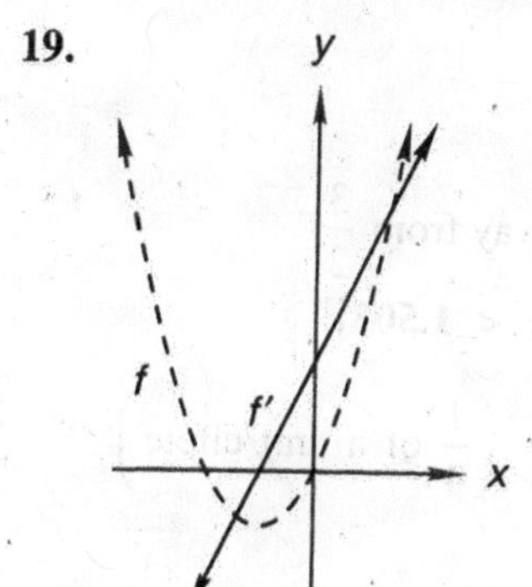

20. $y = \frac{e^{x^2} + x}{x^2 + 2x} + \sec^3(2x) + \csc^3(4x)$

$\frac{dy}{dx} = \frac{(x^2 + 2x)(2xe^{x^2} + 1)}{(x^2 + 2x)^2}$
$- \frac{(e^{x^2} + x)(2x + 2)}{(x^2 + 2x)^2}$
$+ 3\sec^2(2x)\sec(2x)\tan(2x)(2)$
$+ 3\csc^2(4x)[-\csc(4x)]\cot(4x)(4)$

$\frac{dy}{dx} = \mathbf{\frac{2xe^{x^2} + 1}{x^2 + 2x} - \frac{2(e^{x^2} + x)(x + 1)}{(x^2 + 2x)^2}}$
$\mathbf{+\ 6\sec^3(2x)\tan(2x)}$
$\mathbf{-\ 12\csc^3(4x)\cot(4x)}$

21. $y = \frac{(x + 2)^{1/2}}{x}$

$y' = \frac{x\left(\frac{1}{2}\right)(x + 2)^{-1/2} - (x + 2)^{1/2}}{x^2}$

$y'(2) = \frac{\frac{1}{2} - 2}{4} = -\frac{3}{8}$ $\qquad$ $\perp$ slope $= \frac{8}{3}$

$y - 1 = \frac{8}{3}(x - 2)$

$\mathbf{y = \frac{8}{3}x - \frac{13}{3}}$

22.

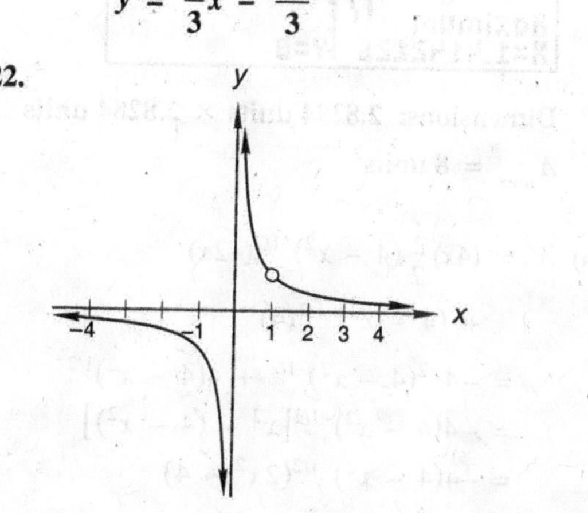

23. $|2x - 3| < 0.01$

$$2\left|x - \frac{3}{2}\right| < 0.01$$

$$\left|x - \frac{3}{2}\right| < 0.005$$

"x is less than 0.005 away from $\frac{3}{2}$"

$\{x \in \mathbb{R} \mid 1.495 < x < 1.505\}$

24. $\int_0^1 \sqrt{1 - x^2}\, dx = \frac{\pi}{4}$ $\left(\frac{1}{4}\text{ of a unit circle}\right)$

25. $d = x - x^3$

$d' = 1 - 3x^2$

$3x^2 = 1$

$x^2 = \frac{1}{3}$

$x = \frac{\sqrt{3}}{3}$

PROBLEM SET 58

1. (a) $A = 2x(2y)$

$= 4xy$

$= 4x(4 - x^2)^{1/2}$

$x^2 + y^2 = 4$

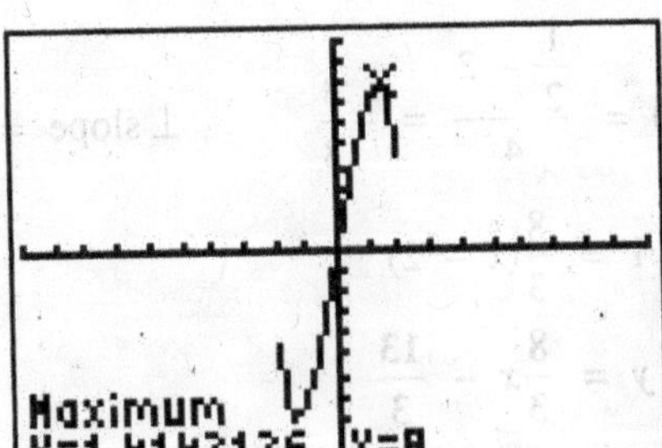

Dimensions: 2.8284 units × 2.8284 units

$A_{max} = 8 \text{ units}^2$

(b) $A' = (4x)\frac{1}{2}(4 - x^2)^{-1/2}(-2x)$

$+ (4 - x^2)^{-1/2}(4)$

$= -4x^2(4 - x^2)^{-1/2} + 4(4 - x^2)^{1/2}$

$= -4(4 - x^2)^{-1/2}[x^2 - (4 - x^2)]$

$= -4(4 - x^2)^{-1/2}(2x^2 - 4)$

$2x^2 - 4 = 0$

$x^2 = 2$

$x = \sqrt{2}$

Dimensions: $2\sqrt{2}$ units × $2\sqrt{2}$ units

$A_{max} = 8 \text{ units}^2$

2.

n	$f^{(n)}(x)$	$f^{(n)}(0)$
0	$\sin x$	0
1	$\cos x$	1
2	$-\sin x$	0
3	$-\cos x$	-1
4	$\sin x$	0
5	$\cos x$	1
6	$-\sin x$	0
⋮	⋮	⋮

$$p(x) = x - \frac{x^3}{3!} + \frac{x^5}{5!} - \frac{x^7}{7!} + \cdots$$

$$\sin x = \sum_{n=0}^{\infty} (-1)^n \frac{x^{2n+1}}{(2n+1)!}$$

3.

n	$f^{(n)}(x)$	$f^{(n)}(0)$
0	$\ln(1 + x)$	0
1	$(1 + x)^{-1}$	1
2	$-(1 + x)^{-2}$	-1
3	$2(1 + x)^{-3}$	2
4	$-6(1 + x)^{-4}$	-6
⋮	⋮	⋮

$$p(x) = x - \frac{x^2}{2!} + \frac{2x^3}{3!} - \frac{6x^4}{4!} + \cdots$$

$$p(x) = x - \frac{x^2}{2} + \frac{x^3}{3} - \frac{x^4}{4} + \cdots$$

$$\ln(1 + x) = \sum_{n=1}^{\infty} (-1)^{n+1} \frac{x^n}{n}$$

4. $A = 4\pi r^2$

$\frac{dA}{dt} = 8\pi r \frac{dr}{dt}$

$\frac{dA}{dt} = 8\pi(10)(3)$

$\frac{dA}{dt} = 240\pi \frac{\text{cm}^2}{\text{s}}$

5. $h(t) = 100 + 50t - 16t^2$

$v(t) = 50 - 32t$

$-75 = 50 - 32t$

$32t = 125$

$t \approx$ **3.9063 s**

6.
$$y = 4x - 3$$
$$x = 4y - 3$$
$$4y = x + 3$$
$$y = \frac{1}{4}x + \frac{3}{4}$$
$$\mathbf{f^{-1}(x) = \frac{1}{4}x + \frac{3}{4}}$$
$$(f \circ f^{-1})(x) = f(f^{-1}(x)) = f\left(\frac{1}{4}x + \frac{3}{4}\right) = 4\left(\frac{1}{4}x + \frac{3}{4}\right) - 3 = x + 3 - 3$$
$$\mathbf{(f \circ f^{-1})(x) = x}$$
$$(f^{-1} \circ f)(x) = f^{-1}(f(x)) = f^{-1}(4x - 3) = \frac{1}{4}(4x - 3) + \frac{3}{4} = x - \frac{3}{4} + \frac{3}{4}$$
$$\mathbf{(f^{-1} \circ f)(x) = x}$$

7.
$$y = 2 \ln x$$
$$x = 2 \ln y$$
$$\frac{x}{2} = \ln y$$
$$y = e^{x/2} = f^{-1}(x)$$
$$f^{-1}(3) = \mathbf{e^{3/2}}$$

8.
$$y = \sin x \cos y$$
$$x = \sin y \cos x$$
$$\mathbf{\sin y = \frac{x}{\cos x}}$$

9.
$$\int_{-1}^{3} [3f(x) - g(x)]\, dx$$
$$= 3\int_{-1}^{3} f(x)\, dx - \int_{-1}^{3} g(x)\, dx$$
$$= 3(4) - (-2) = \mathbf{14}$$

10. Maximum value of $\int_{-1}^{2} f(x)\, dx$ is $[2 - (-1)](10) = 30$

Minimum value of $\int_{-1}^{2} f(x)\, dx$ is $[2 - (-1)](-5) = -15$

$$-15 \le \int_{-1}^{2} f(x)\, dx \le 30$$

The correct choice is **A**.

11.
$$\int_{1}^{2} f(x)\, dx + \int_{2}^{4} f(x)\, dx = \int_{1}^{4} f(x)\, dx$$
$$\int_{1}^{2} f(x)\, dx + 6 = 10$$
$$\int_{1}^{2} f(x)\, dx = \mathbf{4}$$

12.
$$\sin(xy) = x$$
$$\cos(xy)\left(x\frac{dy}{dx} + y\right) = 1$$
$$x\frac{dy}{dx} + y = \sec(xy)$$
$$\mathbf{\frac{dy}{dx} = \frac{\sec(xy) - y}{x}}$$

13.
$$x^3 + y^2 = y$$
$$3x^2 + 2y\frac{dy}{dx} = \frac{dy}{dx}$$
$$\frac{dy}{dx} - 2y\frac{dy}{dx} = 3x^2$$
$$\frac{dy}{dx} = \frac{3x^2}{1 - 2y}$$
$$\left.\frac{dy}{dx}\right|_{(0,1)} = \frac{3(0)}{1 - 2(1)} = 0$$

Only a horizontal line has a slope of 0, so $\mathbf{y = 1}$.

14.
$$y = (2x)^{1/2}$$
$$y' = \frac{1}{2}(2x)^{-1/2}(2) = \frac{1}{\sqrt{2x}}$$
$$y'(4) = \frac{1}{2\sqrt{2}}$$
$$\perp \text{ slope} = -2\sqrt{2}$$
$$y - 2\sqrt{2} = -2\sqrt{2}(x - 4)$$
$$\mathbf{y = -2\sqrt{2}x + 10\sqrt{2}}$$

15. $y = \dfrac{e^{2x} + e^{-x^2}}{x^3 + 1} - 3 \cot x$

$y' = \dfrac{(x^3 + 1)(2e^{2x} - 2xe^{-x^2})}{(x^3 + 1)^2}$

$- \dfrac{(e^{2x} + e^{-x^2})(3x^2)}{(x^3 + 1)^2} + 3 \csc^2 x$

$\boldsymbol{y' = \dfrac{2(e^{2x} - xe^{-x^2})}{x^3 + 1} - \dfrac{3x^2(e^{2x} + e^{-x^2})}{(x^3 + 1)^2}}$

$\boldsymbol{+ 3 \csc^2 x}$

16. $y = \dfrac{1}{\ln 2} \ln (x^2 + 3x - 1) - \dfrac{\sin x}{\cos (ax)}$

$y' = \dfrac{2x + 3}{(\ln 2)(x^2 + 3x - 1)}$

$- \dfrac{\cos (ax) \cos x + \sin x \sin (ax) (a)}{\cos^2 (ax)}$

$y' = \dfrac{2x + 3}{(\ln 2)(x^2 + 3x - 1)} - \dfrac{\cos x}{\cos (ax)}$

$- \dfrac{a \sin x \sin (ax)}{\cos^2 (ax)}$

$\boldsymbol{y' = \dfrac{2x + 3}{(\ln 2)(x^2 + 3x - 1)} - \cos x \sec'(ax)}$

$\boldsymbol{- a \sin x \tan (ax) \sec (ax)}$

17. $\int (3x^2 + 2)(2x^3 + 4x)^{-1/2}\, dx$

$= \dfrac{1}{2} \int 2(3x^2 + 2)(2x^3 + 4x)^{-1/2}\, dx$

$= \boldsymbol{\sqrt{2x^3 + 4x} + C}$

18. $\int (\cos x - 1)e^{\sin x - x}\, dx = \boldsymbol{e^{\sin x - x} + C}$

19. $\int \cos (ax) \sin^4 (ax)\, dx$

$= \dfrac{1}{a} \int a \cos (ax) \sin^4 (ax)\, dy$

$= \boldsymbol{\dfrac{1}{5a} \sin^5 (ax) + C}$

20. $\lim_{x\to\infty} \dfrac{x^2 - 3}{3 + x - 5x^2} = \boldsymbol{-\dfrac{1}{5}}$

21. A. $y = \sin x$

$\dfrac{dy}{dx} = \cos x$

$\dfrac{d^2y}{dx^2} = -\sin x$

$\dfrac{d^3y}{dx^3} = -\cos x$

B. $y = 2e^x$

$\dfrac{dy}{dx} = 2e^x$

$\dfrac{d^2y}{dx^2} = 2e^x$

$\dfrac{d^3y}{dx^3} = 2e^x$

C. $y = x^3$

$\dfrac{dy}{dx} = 3x^2$

$\dfrac{d^2y}{dx^2} = 6x$

$\dfrac{d^3y}{dx^3} = 6$

D. $y = \cos x$

$\dfrac{dy}{dx} = -\sin x$

$\dfrac{d^2y}{dx^2} = -\cos x$

$\dfrac{d^3y}{dx^3} = \sin x$

The correct choice is **B.**

22. $\int_0^3 \sqrt{9 - x^2}\, dx$ is $\frac{1}{4}$ of a circle with a radius of 3, which equals $\frac{9\pi}{4}$.

$\dfrac{4}{9} \int_0^3 \sqrt{9 - x^2}\, dx = \dfrac{4}{9}\left(\dfrac{9\pi}{4}\right) = \pi$

23. $\sec^2 (2\theta) = \dfrac{1}{\cos^2 (2\theta)} = \dfrac{1}{(\cos^2 \theta - \sin^2 \theta)^2}$

$= \dfrac{1}{\left[\left(\dfrac{6}{10}\right)^2 - \left(\dfrac{8}{10}\right)^2\right]^2} = \dfrac{1}{\left(\dfrac{36}{100} - \dfrac{64}{100}\right)^2}$

$= \dfrac{1}{\left(-\dfrac{28}{100}\right)^2} = \left(-\dfrac{25}{7}\right)^2 = \boldsymbol{\dfrac{625}{49}}$

24. $\tan \theta = \dfrac{h}{6}$

$\boldsymbol{\sec^2 \theta \dfrac{d\theta}{dt} = \dfrac{1}{6} \dfrac{dh}{dt}}$

25. $\int_0^k e^x\, dx = 3$

$e^x\Big]_0^k = 3$

$e^k - e^0 = 3$

$e^k = 4$

$\boldsymbol{k = \ln 4}$

Problem Set 59

1. (a) $V = (4 - x)(4 - 2x)x$

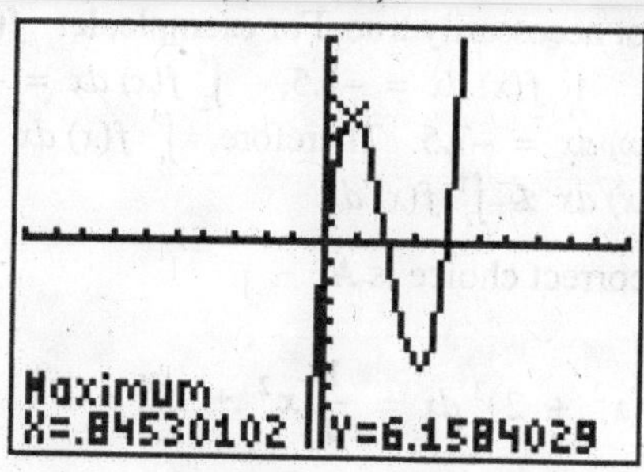

$V_{max} \approx$ **6.1584 m³** when $x \approx$ **0.8453 m**

(b) $V = (16 - 12x + 2x^2)x$

$V = 16x - 12x^2 + 2x^3$

$V' = 16 - 24x + 6x^2$

$0 = 3x^2 - 12x + 8$

$x = \dfrac{12 \pm \sqrt{144 - 96}}{6}$

$x = 2 \pm \dfrac{4\sqrt{3}}{6} = 2 \pm \dfrac{2\sqrt{3}}{3}$

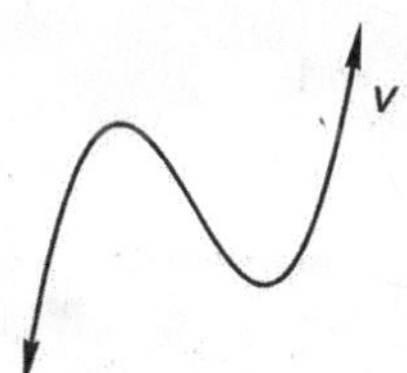

Maximum when $x = 2 - \dfrac{2\sqrt{3}}{3}$

$$V = 16\left(2 - \frac{2\sqrt{3}}{3}\right) - 12\left(2 - \frac{2\sqrt{3}}{3}\right)^2 + 2\left(2 - \frac{2\sqrt{3}}{3}\right)^3$$

$$V = 32 - \frac{32\sqrt{3}}{3} - 12\left(4 - \frac{8\sqrt{3}}{3} + \frac{4}{3}\right) + \left(8 - \frac{16\sqrt{3}}{3} + \frac{8}{3}\right)\left(2 - \frac{2\sqrt{3}}{3}\right)$$

$$V = 32 - \frac{32\sqrt{3}}{3} - 48 + 32\sqrt{3} - 16 + \left(\frac{32}{3} - \frac{16\sqrt{3}}{3}\right)\left(2 - \frac{2\sqrt{3}}{3}\right)$$

$$V = -32 + \frac{64\sqrt{3}}{3} + \frac{64}{3} - \frac{64\sqrt{3}}{9} - \frac{32\sqrt{3}}{3} + \frac{32}{3}$$

$V_{max} = \dfrac{32\sqrt{3}}{9}$ **m³ when** $x = \left(2 - \dfrac{2\sqrt{3}}{3}\right)$ **m**

2.

n	$f^{(n)}(x)$	$f^{(n)}(0)$
0	$\cos x$	1
1	$-\sin x$	0
2	$-\cos x$	-1
3	$\sin x$	0
4	$\cos x$	1
5	$-\sin x$	0
6	$-\cos x$	-1
⋮	⋮	⋮

$$p(x) = 1 - \frac{x^2}{2!} + \frac{x^4}{4!} - \frac{x^6}{6!} + \cdots$$

$$\cos x = \sum_{n=0}^{\infty} (-1)^n \frac{x^{2n}}{(2n)!}$$

3.

n	$f^{(n)}(x)$	$f^{(n)}(0)$
0	$(x + 1)^{-1}$	1
1	$-(x + 1)^{-2}$	-1
2	$2(x + 1)^{-3}$	2
3	$-6(x + 1)^{-4}$	-6
4	$24(x + 1)^{-5}$	24
⋮	⋮	⋮

$$p(x) = 1 - x + \frac{2x^2}{2!} - \frac{6x^3}{3!} + \frac{24x^4}{4!} + \cdots$$

$$p(x) = 1 - x + x^2 - x^3 + x^4 - \cdots$$

$$\frac{1}{x + 1} = \sum_{n=0}^{\infty} (-1)^n x^n$$

4.

$$\tan\theta = \frac{h}{6}$$

$$\sec^2\theta \frac{d\theta}{dt} = \frac{1}{6}\frac{dh}{dt}$$

$$\frac{d\theta}{dt} = \cos^2\theta \, \frac{1}{6}\frac{dh}{dt}$$

$$\frac{d\theta}{dt} = \left(\frac{6}{10}\right)^2 \frac{1}{6}(1)$$

$$\frac{d\theta}{dt} = \frac{3}{50}\ \frac{\text{rad}}{\text{s}}$$

5. $\displaystyle\int_a^d f(x)\,dx = 6\frac{5}{12} - \frac{23}{6} - 4\frac{1}{3} = -\frac{7}{4}$

6. $A = 4\int_0^{\pi/2} \cos x\, dx = 4 \sin x\Big]_0^{\pi/2} = \mathbf{4\ units^2}$

7.

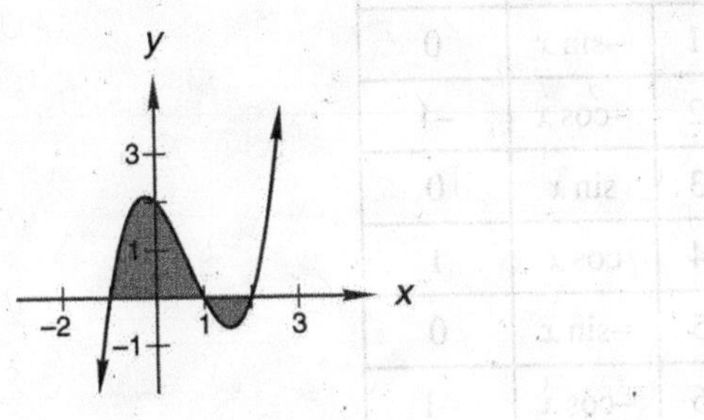

$$A = \int_{-1}^{1} (x - 1)(x + 1)(x - 2)\, dx$$
$$+ \int_{2}^{1} (x - 1)(x + 1)(x - 2)\, dx$$

8. Area

≈ `fnInt(Xe^sin(x-1),X,π/9,π/4)`

≈ **0.6180 units²**

9.
$$y = 3x + 2$$
$$x = 3y + 2$$
$$3y = x - 2$$
$$y = \frac{1}{3}x - \frac{2}{3}$$
$$f^{-1}(x) = \frac{1}{3}x - \frac{2}{3}$$
$$f^{-1}(4) = \frac{2}{3}$$

$$(f \circ f^{-1})(x) = f\left(\frac{1}{3}x - \frac{2}{3}\right)$$
$$(f \circ f^{-1})(x) = 3\left(\frac{1}{3}x - \frac{2}{3}\right) + 2$$
$$(f \circ f^{-1})(x) = x$$
$$(f^{-1} \circ f)(x) = f^{-1}(3x + 2)$$
$$(f^{-1} \circ f)(x) = \frac{1}{3}(3x + 2) - \frac{2}{3}$$
$$(f^{-1} \circ f)(x) = x$$

10.
$$y = \frac{1}{x}$$
$$x = \frac{1}{y}$$
$$y = \frac{1}{x}$$
$$g(x) = \frac{1}{x}$$

11.
$$y = \tan x$$
$$x = \tan y$$

12. Choice A is a specific case of one of the general properties discussed in Lesson 52. Choices B and C are not necessarily true. For example, let $f(x) = -x$. Then $\int_1^2 f(x)\, dx = -1.5$, $\int_2^4 f(x)\, dx = -6$, and $\int_2^4 f(x)\, dx = -7.5$. Therefore, $\int_1^4 f(x)\, dx \not\geq 0$ and $\int_1^2 f(x)\, dx \not\leq \int_2^4 f(x)\, dx$.

The correct choice is **A**.

13. $\int 2x(x^2 + 2)^3\, dx = \mathbf{\frac{1}{4}(x^2 + 2)^4 + C}$

14. $\int (2x - 1)(x^2 - x + 1)^{-1/2}\, dx$

$= \mathbf{2\sqrt{x^2 - x + 1} + C}$

15. $\pi \int \cos^2 (2x) \sin (2x)\, dx$

$= -\frac{\pi}{2} \int -2 \cos^2 (2x) \sin (2x)\, dx$

$= \mathbf{-\frac{\pi}{6} \cos^3 (2x) + C}$

16.
$$y = 2x^3 - 3x^2 + 12x + 1$$
$$y' = 6x^2 - 6x + 12$$
$$y'' = 12x - 6$$
$$0 < 12x - 6$$
$$12x > 6$$
$$\mathbf{x > \frac{1}{2}}$$

17.
$$y = \frac{\cos (3x)}{x^2 + 2} + \tan (2x)$$
$$y' = \frac{(x^2 + 2)[(-\sin (3x)](3) - \cos (3x)(2x)}{(x^2 + 2)^2} + \sec^2 (2x)(2)$$
$$y' = \mathbf{\frac{-3 \sin (3x)}{x^2 + 2} - \frac{2x \cos (3x)}{(x^2 + 2)^2} + 2 \sec^2 (2x)}$$

18.
$$y = \frac{1}{2}e^{\pi - x}$$
$$y' = -\frac{1}{2}e^{\pi - x}$$

At $\left(2, \frac{1}{2}e^{\pi - 2}\right)$, slope $= -\frac{1}{2}e^{\pi - 2}$

$\perp$ slope $= \frac{2}{e^{\pi - 2}}$

$$y - \frac{1}{2}e^{\pi - 2} = \frac{2}{e^{\pi - 2}}(x - 2)$$
$$\mathbf{y = \frac{2}{e^{\pi - 2}}x - \frac{4}{e^{\pi - 2}} + \frac{e^{\pi - 2}}{2}}$$

19. $x = \sin(xy)$

$$1 = \cos(xy)\left(x\frac{dy}{dx} + y\right)$$

$$\sec(xy) = x\frac{dy}{dx} + y$$

$$\frac{dy}{dx} = \frac{\sec(xy) - y}{x}$$

20.

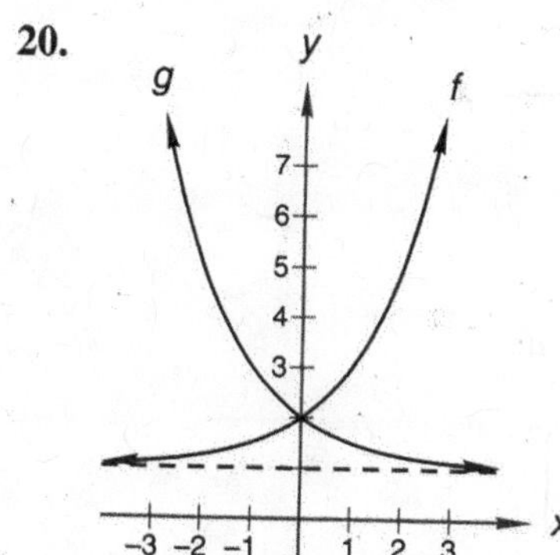

21. $(x - 2)^2 + (y - 3)^2 = 9$

The equation describes a **circle** with a radius of 3 whose center is the point (2, 3).

22. **Domain:** $\mathbb{R}$

Range: $\{y \in \mathbb{R} \mid 1 \le y \le 3\}$

23. $y = -x - 1$

24. Find the point of intersection.

$$\frac{1}{2}x^2 = 1 - \frac{1}{2}x^2$$

$$x^2 = 1$$

$$x = 1$$

Intersection: $\left(1, \frac{1}{2}\right)$

Determine the two slopes at $\left(1, \frac{1}{2}\right)$.

$y_1 = \frac{1}{2}x^2 \qquad y_2 = 1 - \frac{1}{2}x^2$

$y_1' = x \qquad y_2' = -x$

$y_1'(1) = 1 \qquad y_2'(1) = -1$

Calculate the angle of intersection.

$$\theta = \tan^{-1}\left(\frac{m_1 - m_2}{1 + m_1m_2}\right) = \tan^{-1}\left(\frac{1-(-1)}{1-1}\right)$$

$$\theta = \tan^{-1}\left(\frac{2}{0}\right) = 90°$$

25. $f(x) = \dfrac{x^2 + 2x - 3}{x^2 + bx + 4}$ is continuous if $x^2 + bx + 4 \ne 0$. If $x^2 + bx + 4 = 0$, then

$$x = \frac{-b \pm \sqrt{b^2 - 4(1)(4)}}{2(1)}.$$

This has no solution if $b^2 - 16 < 0$

$$b^2 < 16$$

$$|b| < 4$$

The correct choice is **C.**

Problem Set 60

1. (a) $x^2h = 1000$

$$h = 1000x^{-2}$$

$$A = 2x^2 + 4xh$$

$$A = 2x^2 + 4x(1000x^{-2})$$

$$A = 2x^2 + 4000x^{-1}$$

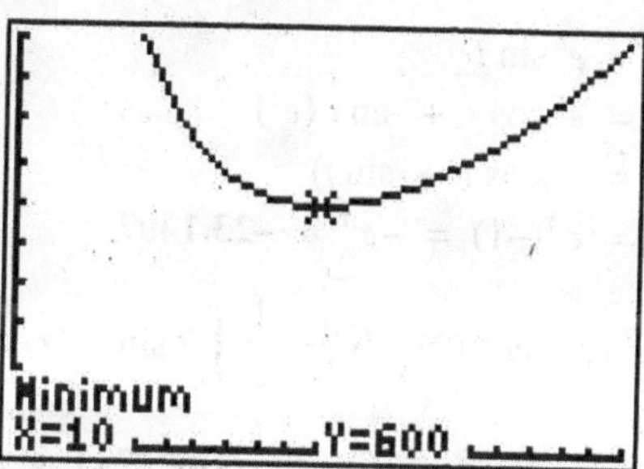

Window: Xmin = 0, Xmax = 20, Ymin = 0, Ymax = 1000, Yscl = 100

Dimensions: 10 in. × 10 in. × 10 in.

(b) $A' = 4x - 4000x^{-2} = 0$

$$\frac{4000}{x^2} = 4x$$

$$4x^3 = 4000$$

$$x^3 = 1000$$

$$x = 10 \text{ in.}$$

Dimensions: 10 in. × 10 in. × 10 in.

2.

n	$f^{(n)}(x)$	$f^{(n)}(0)$
0	e^x	1
1	e^x	1
2	e^x	1
3	e^x	1
⋮	⋮	⋮

$$p(x) = 1 + x + \frac{x^2}{2!} + \frac{x^3}{3!} + \cdots$$

$$e^x = \sum_{n=0}^{\infty} \frac{x^n}{n!}$$

3.

n	$f^{(n)}(x)$	$f^{(n)}(0)$
0	$\ln(1 - x)$	0
1	$-(1 - x)^{-1}$	-1
2	$-(1 - x)^{-2}$	-1
3	$-2(1 - x)^{-3}$	-2
4	$-6(1 - x)^{-4}$	-6
$\vdots$	$\vdots$	$\vdots$

$$p(x) = -x - \frac{x^2}{2!} - \frac{2x^3}{3!} - \frac{6x^4}{4!} - \cdots$$

$$p(x) = -x - \frac{x^2}{2} - \frac{x^3}{3} - \frac{x^4}{4} - \cdots$$

$$\ln(1 - x) = \sum_{n=1}^{\infty} -\frac{\boldsymbol{x^n}}{\boldsymbol{n}}$$

4.
$$\begin{aligned} s(t) &= e^t \sin t \\ v(t) &= e^t \cos t + \sin t\,(e^t) \\ v(t) &= e^t(\cos t + \sin t) \\ v(\pi) &= e^{\pi}(-1) = -e^{\pi} \approx \mathbf{-23.1407} \end{aligned}$$

5.
$$\int \sin^3(2x)\cos(2x)\,dx = \frac{1}{2}\int 2\sin^3(2x)\cos(2x)\,dx = \boldsymbol{\frac{1}{8}\sin^4(2x) + C}$$

6.
$$\begin{aligned} &\int (1 + \cos x)^{-1/2}\sin x\,dx \\ &= -\int (1 + \cos x)^{-1/2}(-\sin x)\,dx \\ &= \boldsymbol{-2\sqrt{1 + \cos x} + C} \end{aligned}$$

7.
$$\int \left(x + 1 + \frac{2}{x}\right)dx = \frac{1}{2}x^2 + x + 2\ln|x| + C = \boldsymbol{\frac{1}{2}x^2 + x + \ln x^2 + C}$$

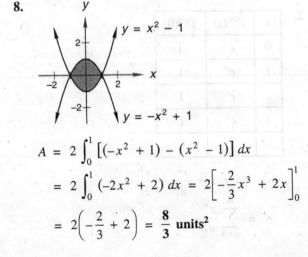

8.

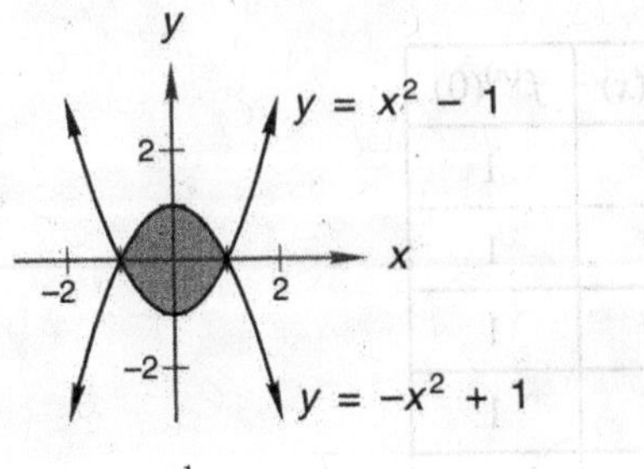

$$\begin{aligned} A &= 2\int_0^1 [(-x^2 + 1) - (x^2 - 1)]\,dx \\ &= 2\int_0^1 (-2x^2 + 2)\,dx = 2\left[-\frac{2}{3}x^3 + 2x\right]_0^1 \\ &= 2\left(-\frac{2}{3} + 2\right) = \boldsymbol{\frac{8}{3}\ \text{units}^2} \end{aligned}$$

9.

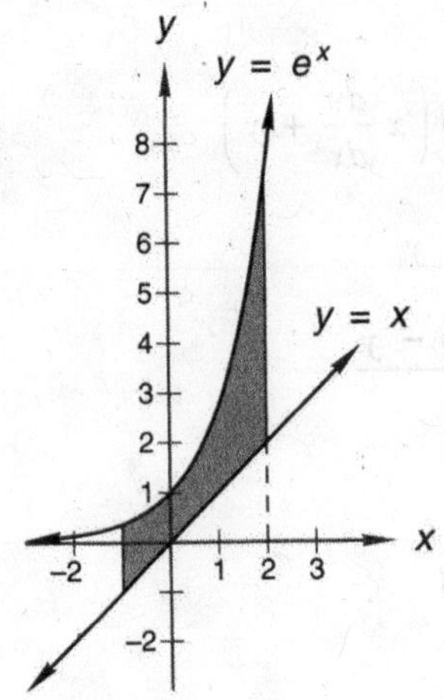

$$\begin{aligned} A &= \int_{-1}^{2} (e^x - x)\,dx \\ &= \left[e^x - \frac{1}{2}x^2\right]_{-1}^{2} \\ &= e^2 - 2 - \left(e^{-1} - \frac{1}{2}\right) \\ &= \boldsymbol{\left(e^2 - e^{-1} - \frac{3}{2}\right)\ \text{units}^2 \approx 5.5212\ \text{units}^2} \end{aligned}$$

10.

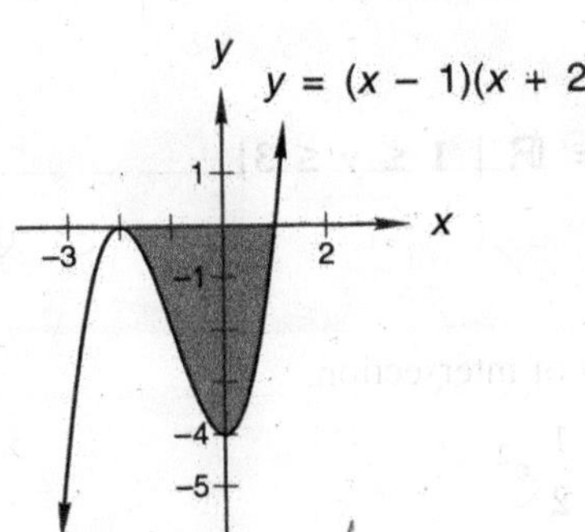

$$\begin{aligned} A &= \int_1^{-2} (x - 1)(x + 2)^2\,dx \\ &= \int_1^{-2} (x - 1)(x^2 + 4x + 4)\,dx \\ &= \int_1^{-2} (x^3 + 3x^2 - 4)\,dx \\ &= \left[\frac{1}{4}x^4 + x^3 - 4x\right]_1^{-2} \\ &= 4 - 8 + 8 - \left(\frac{1}{4} + 1 - 4\right) \\ &= 7 - \frac{1}{4} = \boldsymbol{\frac{27}{4}\ \text{units}^2} \end{aligned}$$

11.

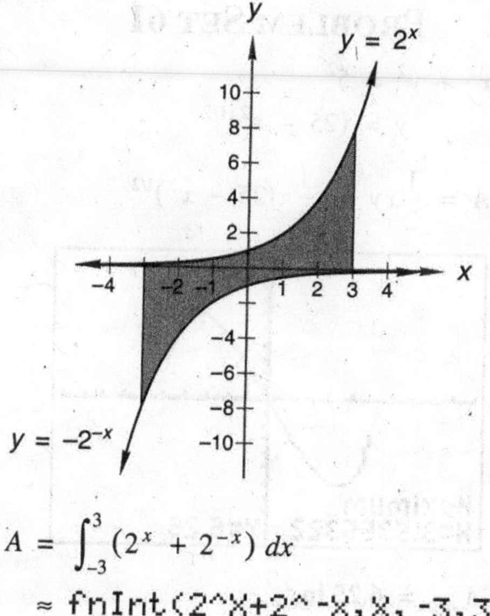

$A = \int_{-3}^{3} (2^x + 2^{-x})\,dx$

$\approx$ fnInt(2^X+2^-X,X,-3,3)

$\approx$ **22.7224 units²**

12. $\int_a^d f(x)\,dx = -A + B - C = B - (A + C)$

The correct choice is **D.**

13.
$$y = 2 \ln x$$
$$x = 2 \ln y$$
$$\frac{x}{2} = \ln y$$
$$y = e^{x/2} = f^{-1}(x)$$
$$f^{-1}(2) = \mathbf{e}$$

14.
$$y = \sin x$$
$$x = \sin y$$
$$y = \mathbf{\arcsin x}$$

15.
$$y = e^{(\ln 2)(x^2+1)}$$
$$y' = e^{(\ln 2)(x^2+1)}(\ln 2)(2x)$$
$$y' = \mathbf{e^{(\ln 2)(x^2+1)} x \ln 4}$$

16.
$$y = \frac{\ln|\sin x|}{x^2 - 1}$$
$$y' = \frac{(x^2 - 1)\dfrac{\cos x}{\sin x} - \ln|\sin x|\,(2x)}{(x^2 - 1)^2}$$
$$y' = \mathbf{\frac{\cot x}{x^2 - 1} - \frac{2x \ln|\sin x|}{(x^2 - 1)^2}}$$

17.
$$y = e^{x^2+2x}(\cot x)^2$$
$$y' = e^{x^2+2x}2(\cot x)(-\csc^2 x) + \cot^2 x\, e^{x^2+2x}(2x + 2)$$
$$y' = \mathbf{2 \cot x\, e^{x^2+2x}[-\csc^2 x + (x + 1)\cot x]}$$

18.
$$y = x \ln x - x$$
$$\frac{dy}{dx} = x\left(\frac{1}{x}\right) + \ln x - 1$$
$$\frac{dy}{dx} = \ln x$$
$$\frac{d^2y}{dx^2} = \frac{1}{x}$$
$$\left.\frac{d^2y}{dx^2}\right|_1 = \mathbf{1}$$

19.
$$\frac{1}{4}x^2 + \frac{1}{9}y^2 = 1$$
$$\frac{1}{2}x + \frac{2}{9}y\frac{dy}{dx} = 0$$
$$\frac{dy}{dx} = -\frac{9x}{4y}$$
$$\left.\frac{dy}{dx}\right|_{\left(\sqrt{3},\frac{3}{2}\right)} = \frac{-9\sqrt{3}}{4\left(\frac{3}{2}\right)} = \mathbf{-\frac{3\sqrt{3}}{2}}$$

20. Positive slope and positive concavity occur at point **C.**

21.

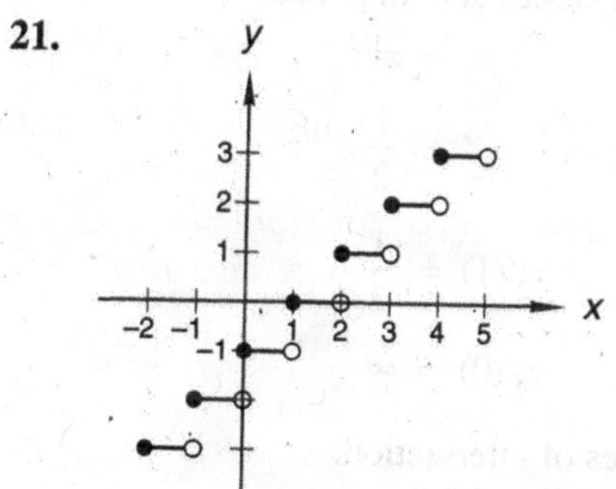

22. $(\tan -\theta)(\cos -\theta)\left[\sec\left(\frac{\pi}{2} - \theta\right)\right]$

$= -\tan\theta \cos\theta \csc\theta = -\sin\theta \csc\theta = \mathbf{-1}$

23. $y = 3 + 2 \sin[3(x - 15°)]$

Amplitude: 2 **Phase angle: 15°**

Period: 120°

24. (a) Let `Y1=(10^X-10^-X)/2` and `Y2=8`.

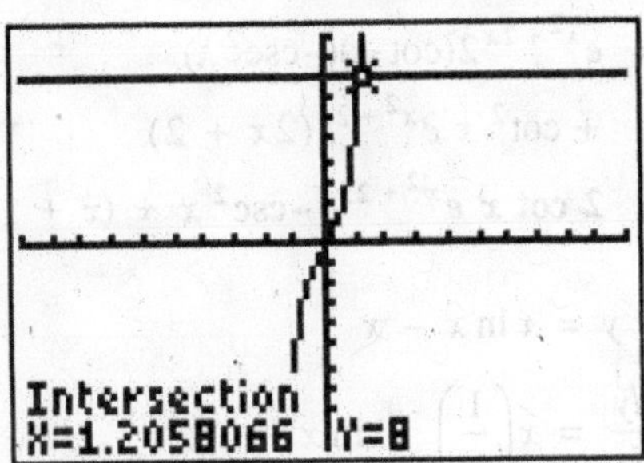

$x \approx$ **1.2058066**

(b)
$$\frac{10^x - 10^{-x}}{2} = 8$$
$$10^x - 10^{-x} = 16$$
$$10^{2x} - 1 = 16(10^x)$$
$$(10^x)^2 - 16(10^x) - 1 = 0$$
$$10^x = \frac{16 \pm \sqrt{256 - 4(1)(-1)}}{2}$$
$$10^x = 8 \pm \frac{\sqrt{260}}{2}$$
$$10^x = 8 \pm \sqrt{65}$$
$$x = \mathbf{\log(8 + \sqrt{65}) \approx 1.205806591}$$

25. Find the points of intersection.

$$x^3 = \sqrt{x}$$
$$x^3 - \sqrt{x} = 0$$
$$\sqrt{x}(x^{5/2} - 1) = 0$$
$$x = 0, 1$$

Intersection: (0, 0) and (1, 1)

Determine the slopes at both points.

$$y_1 = x^3 \qquad y_2 = x^{1/2}$$
$$y_1' = 3x^2 \qquad y_2' = \frac{1}{2}x^{-1/2}$$
$$y_1'(1) = 3 \qquad y_2'(1) = \frac{1}{2}$$
$$y_1'(0) = 0 \qquad y_2'(0) = \infty$$

Find the angles of intersection.

At (0, 0), $\theta =$ **90°** because one tangent line is vertical while the other is horizontal. At the point (1, 1),

$$\theta = \tan^{-1}\left(\frac{m_1 - m_2}{1 + m_1 m_2}\right) = \tan^{-1}\left(\frac{3 - \frac{1}{2}}{1 + \frac{3}{2}}\right)$$
$$= \tan^{-1}\left(\frac{\frac{5}{2}}{\frac{5}{2}}\right) = \mathbf{45°}$$

Problem Set 61

1. (a) $x^2 + y^2 = 5^2$
$$y = (25 - x^2)^{1/2}$$
$$A = \frac{1}{2}xy = \frac{1}{2}x(25 - x^2)^{1/2}$$

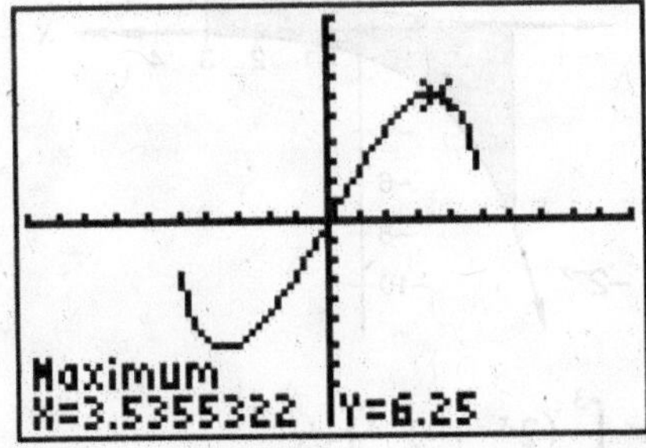

$$A_{max} = \mathbf{6.25\ in.^2}$$

(b)
$$A' = \left(\frac{1}{2}x\right)\frac{1}{2}(25 - x^2)^{-1/2}(-2x) + (25 - x^2)^{1/2}\left(\frac{1}{2}\right)$$
$$A' = -\frac{1}{2}x^2(25 - x^2)^{-1/2} + \frac{1}{2}(25 - x^2)^{1/2}$$
$$A' = \frac{1}{2}(25 - x^2)^{-1/2}\left[-x^2 + (25 - x^2)\right]$$
$$A' = \frac{1}{2}(25 - x^2)^{-1/2}(-2x^2 + 25)$$
$$0 = -2x^2 + 25$$
$$2x^2 = 25$$
$$x^2 = \frac{25}{2}$$
$$x = \frac{5\sqrt{2}}{2}$$
$$A_{max} = \frac{1}{2}\left(\frac{5\sqrt{2}}{2}\right)\left(25 - \frac{25}{2}\right)^{1/2}$$
$$= \frac{5\sqrt{2}}{4} \cdot \frac{5\sqrt{2}}{2}$$
$$= \mathbf{\frac{25}{4}\ in.^2 = 6.25\ in.^2}$$

2. $e^x = \mathbf{1 + x + \frac{x^2}{2} + \frac{x^3}{3!} + \cdots}$

3. (a)

n	$f^{(n)}(x)$	$f^{(n)}(0)$
0	e^{-x}	1
1	$-e^{-x}$	-1
2	e^{-x}	1
3	$-e^{-x}$	-1
⋮	⋮	⋮

$$p(x) = \mathbf{1 - x + \frac{x^2}{2} - \frac{x^3}{3!} + \cdots}$$

(b) $e^x = 1 + x + \frac{x^2}{2} + \frac{x^3}{3!} + \cdots$

$$e^{-x} = 1 + (-x) + \frac{(-x)^2}{2} + \frac{(-x)^3}{3!} + \cdots$$

$$e^{-x} = 1 - x + \frac{x^2}{2} - \frac{x^3}{3!} + \cdots$$

They are the same.

4. $V = \pi r h^2 - \frac{1}{3}\pi h^3$

$$\frac{dV}{dt} = 2\pi r h \frac{dh}{dt} - \pi h^2 \frac{dh}{dt}$$

$$1 = \frac{dh}{dt}[2\pi(7)(4) - \pi(4)^2]$$

$$\frac{dh}{dt} = \mathbf{\frac{1}{40\pi} \frac{in.}{s}}$$

5. $f(x) = ax^3 + b$

$5 = a + b$

$5 = 1 + b$

$\mathbf{b = 4}$

$f'(x) = 3ax^2$

$12 = 12a$

$\mathbf{a = 1}$

6. $f(x) = ax^2 + bx + c$

$5 = a + b + c$

$-(-1 = a - b + c)$

$6 = 2b$

$b = 3$

$f'(x) = 2ax + b$

$5 = 2a + b$

$2 = 2a$

$a = 1$

$(1) + (3) + c = 5$

$c = 1$

$\mathbf{f(x) = x^2 + 3x + 1}$

7. Since f'' is linear, f must be cubic.

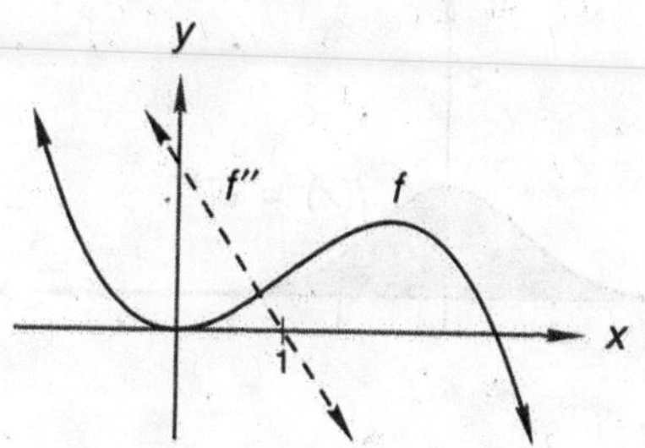

8. $f''(x) = 6$

$f'(x) = 6x + b$

$4 = 6 + b$

$b = -2$

$f'(x) = 6x - 2$

$f(x) = 3x^2 - 2x + c$

$4 = 3 - 2 + c$

$c = 3$

$\mathbf{f(x) = 3x^2 - 2x + 3}$

9. $\int \sin(3x)\,dx = \frac{1}{3}\int 3\sin(3x)\,dx$

$$= \mathbf{-\frac{1}{3}\cos(3x) + C}$$

10. $\int (\sin x)^{-2}\cos x\,dx = -(\sin x)^{-1} + C$

$$= \mathbf{-\csc x + C}$$

11. $\int e^{-x}\,dx = -\int -e^{-x}\,dx = \mathbf{-e^{-x} + C}$

12.

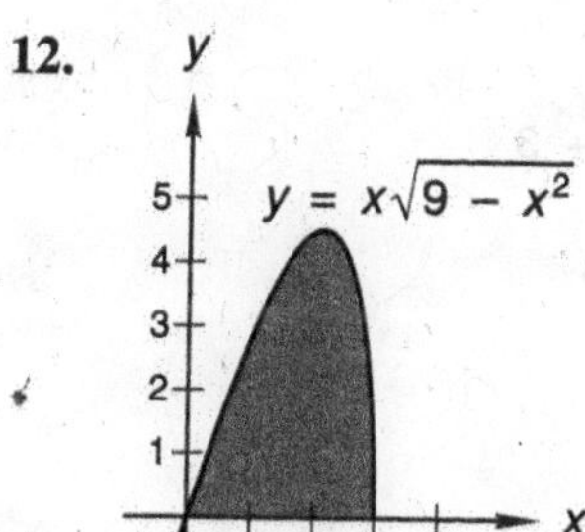

$$A = \int_0^3 x(9 - x^2)^{1/2}\,dx$$

$$= -\frac{1}{2}\int_0^3 -2x(9 - x^2)^{1/2}\,dx$$

$$= -\frac{1}{3}\left[(9 - x^2)^{3/2}\right]_0^3$$

$$= -\frac{1}{3}(0 - 27) = \mathbf{9\ units^2}$$

13.

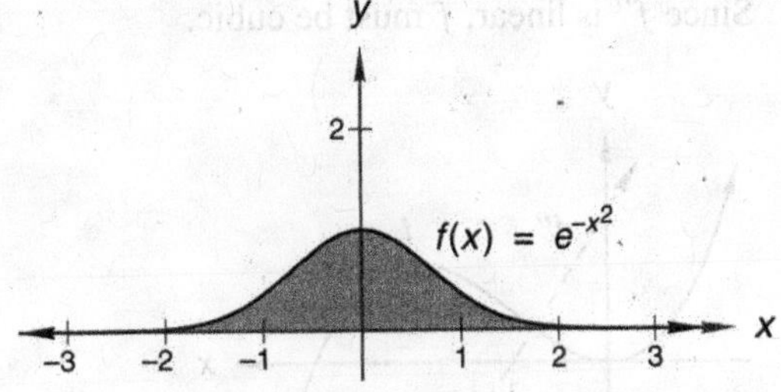

$$A = 2\int_0^2 e^{-x^2}\,dx$$

≈ `2fnInt(e^(-X²),X,0,2)`

$\approx$ **1.7642 units²**

14.

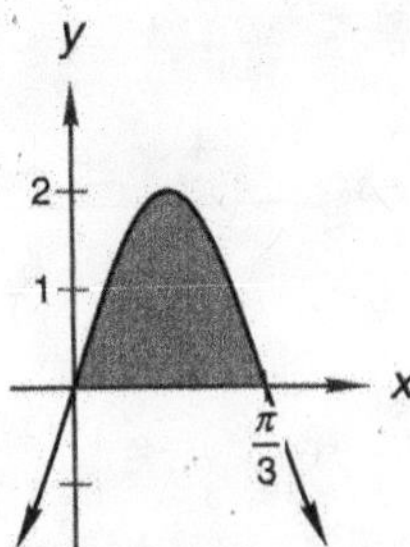

$$A = \int_0^{\pi/3} 2\sin(3x)\,dx$$

$$= -\frac{2}{3}\int_0^{\pi/3} -3\sin(3x)\,dx$$

$$= -\frac{2}{3}[\cos(3x)]_0^{\pi/3}$$

$$= -\frac{2}{3}(-1-1) = \mathbf{\frac{4}{3}\ units^2}$$

15.

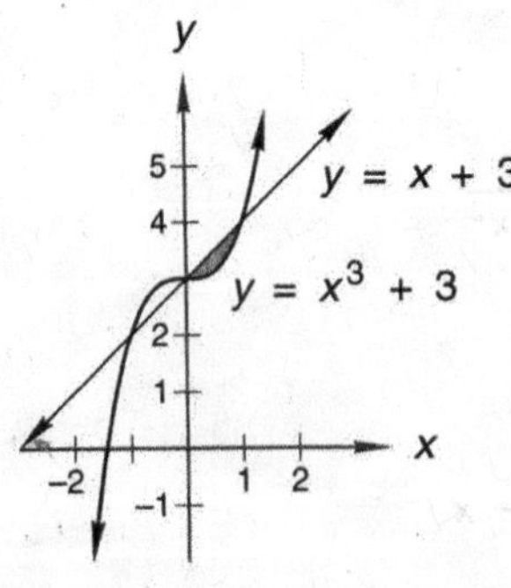

$$A = \int_0^1 [(x+3) - (x^3+3)]\,dx$$

$$= \int_0^1 (x - x^3)\,dx$$

$$= \left[\frac{1}{2}x^2 - \frac{1}{4}x^4\right]_0^1$$

$$= \frac{1}{2} - \frac{1}{4} = \mathbf{\frac{1}{4}\ unit^2}$$

16.

$$\int_{-2}^{2}(4x^3 + k)\,dx = 15$$

$$[x^4 + kx]_{-2}^{2} = 15$$

$$16 + 2k - (16 - 2k) = 15$$

$$4k = 15$$

$$k = \mathbf{\frac{15}{4}}$$

17.

$$\int_1^k \frac{1}{x}\,dx = 2 \quad \text{or} \quad \int_k^1 \frac{1}{x}\,dx = 2$$

$$[\ln|x|]_1^k = 2 \qquad [\ln|x|]_1^k = 2$$

$$\ln k - \ln 1 = 2 \qquad \ln 1 - \ln k = 2$$

$$\ln k = 2 \qquad \ln k = -2$$

$$k = \mathbf{e^2} \qquad k = \mathbf{e^{-2}}$$

18.

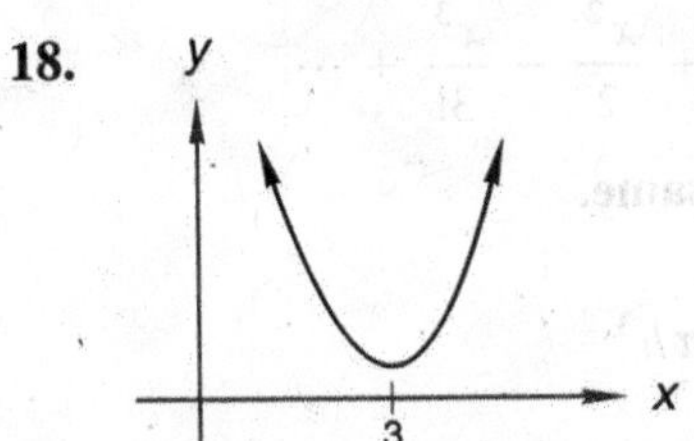

19. f'' is a negative constant.

f' is negative and linear.

f is a negative quadratic.

The graph of f is a **parabola that opens downward.**

20.

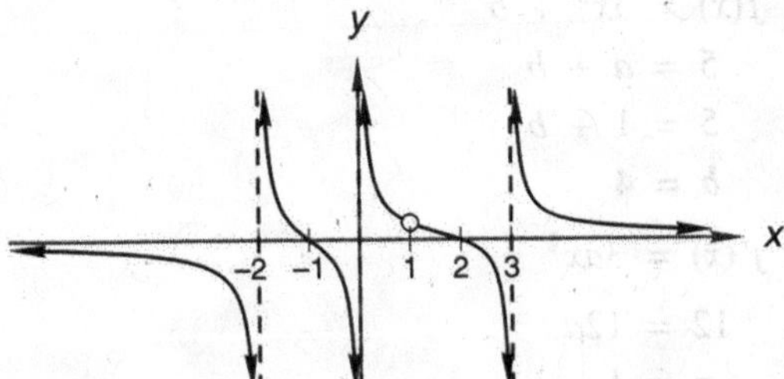

21.

$$f'(x) = \lim_{h\to 0}\frac{\frac{1}{x+h} - \frac{1}{x}}{h} = \lim_{h\to 0}\frac{\frac{x-(x+h)}{x(x+h)}}{h}$$

$$= \lim_{h\to 0}\frac{-1}{x(x+h)} = \mathbf{-\frac{1}{x^2}}$$

22.

$$y = (x^3 + x + 1)^{-1/2} + e^{4x-3}\tan(\pi x)$$

$$y' = -\frac{1}{2}(x^3 + x + 1)^{-3/2}(3x^2 + 1)$$

$$+ e^{4x-3}\sec^2(\pi x)(\pi) + \tan(\pi x)\,e^{4x-3}(4)$$

$$\mathbf{y' = -\frac{1}{2}(3x^2 + 1)(x^3 + x + 1)^{-3/2}}$$

$$\mathbf{+ e^{4x-3}[\pi\sec^2(\pi x) + 4\tan(\pi x)]}$$

23. $\{x \in \mathbb{R} \mid -1 \leq x \leq 1\}$

24. The graph of $g(x)$ is the same as the graph of $f(x)$, except that it is translated 2 units to the right. If $f(x)$ is continuous on $[1, 3]$, then $g(x)$ must be continuous on **[3, 5]**.

25. The graphs must intersect: $mx = \ln x$

They must have the same slope: $m = \frac{1}{x}$

$$\left(\frac{1}{x}\right)x = \ln x$$

$$1 = \ln x$$

$$x = e$$

$$m = \frac{\mathbf{1}}{\boldsymbol{e}}$$

PROBLEM SET 62

1.

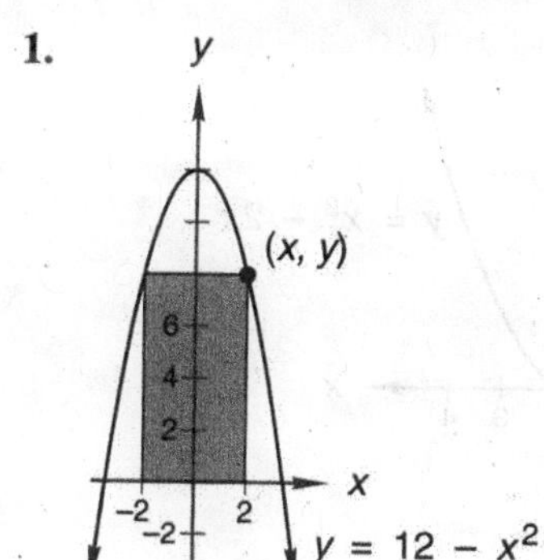

$$A = 2xy$$
$$= 2x(12 - x^2)$$
$$= 24x - 2x^3$$

(a)

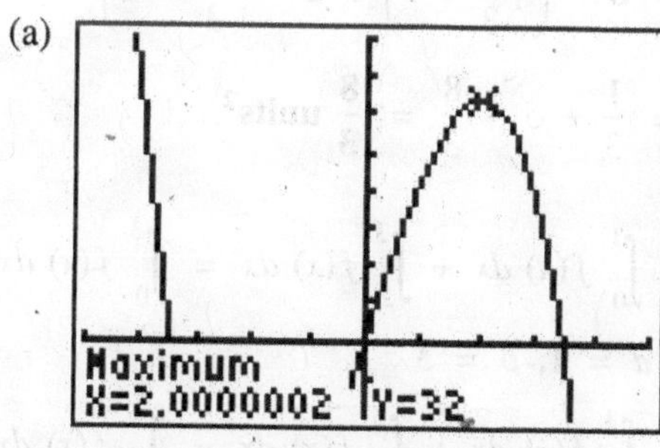

Window: Xmin=-5, Xmax=5, Ymin=-10, Ymax=40, Yscl=5

$A_{max} = \mathbf{32\ units^2}$

(b) $A' = 24 - 6x^2$

$$6x^2 = 24$$
$$x^2 = 4$$
$$x = 2$$

$A|_2 = 48 - 16 = \mathbf{32\ units^2}$

2.

n	$f^{(n)}(x)$	$f^{(n)}(0)$
0	$(1 + x)^{-1}$	1
1	$-(1 + x)^{-2}$	−1
2	$2(1 + x)^{-3}$	2
3	$-6(1 + x)^{-4}$	−6
4	$24(1 + x)^{-5}$	24
⋮	⋮	⋮

$$p(x) = 1 - x + \frac{2x^2}{2!} - \frac{6x^3}{3!} + \frac{24x^4}{4!} - \cdots$$

$$p(x) = \mathbf{1 - x + x^2 - x^3 + x^4 - \cdots}$$

3. (a)

n	$f^{(n)}(x)$	$f^{(n)}(0)$
0	$(1 - x)^{-1}$	1
1	$(1 - x)^{-2}$	1
2	$2(1 - x)^{-3}$	2
3	$6(1 - x)^{-4}$	6
⋮	⋮	⋮

$$p(x) = 1 + x + \frac{2x^2}{2!} + \frac{6x^3}{3!} + \cdots$$

$$p(x) = \mathbf{1 + x + x^2 + x^3 + \cdots}$$

(b) $\frac{1}{1 + (-x)} = 1 - (-x) + (-x)^2 - (-x)^3 + \cdots$

$$\frac{1}{1 - x} = 1 + x + x^2 + x^3 + \cdots$$

They are the same.

4. $W = F \cdot d = 20\text{ N} \cdot 30\text{ m} = \mathbf{600\ joules}$

5. $W = \int_0^3 \left(\frac{1}{2}x^3 + x\right) dx$

$$= \left[\frac{1}{8}x^4 + \frac{1}{2}x^2\right]_0^3$$

$$= \frac{81}{8} + \frac{9}{2} = \frac{\mathbf{117}}{\mathbf{8}}\ \textbf{joules}$$

6. $W = \int_2^4 3x\,dx$

$= \left[\frac{3}{2}x^2\right]_2^4$

$= 24 - 6 =$ **18 joules**

7. $\text{Au} = \int_3^6 \frac{7}{t}\,dt$

$= [7 \ln t]_3^6$

$= 7(\ln 6 - \ln 3)$

$=$ **7 ln 2 ounces** $\approx$ **4.8520 ounces**

8. $f(x) = ax^2 + bx$

$f'(x) = 2ax + b$

$$\begin{aligned} 2 &= a + b \\ -(-1 &= 4a + b) \\ \hline 3 &= -3a \end{aligned}$$

$\boldsymbol{a = -1,\ b = 3}$

9. $\frac{dy}{dx} = 2x$

$y = x^2 + C$

$5 = 4 + C$

$C = 1$

$\boldsymbol{f(x) = x^2 + 1}$

10. $\int \cos\left(2x - \frac{\pi}{2}\right) dx = \frac{1}{2}\int 2\cos\left(2x - \frac{\pi}{2}\right) dx$

$= \boldsymbol{\frac{1}{2}\sin\left(2x - \frac{\pi}{2}\right) + C}$

11. $\int (2x^{3/2} - 3x^{1/2} + 4x^{-1/2})\,dx$

$= \boldsymbol{\frac{4}{5}x^{5/2} - 2x^{3/2} + 8x^{1/2} + C}$

12. $\int (\sin t)^{1/2} \cos t\,dt = \boldsymbol{\frac{2}{3}\sin^{3/2} t + C}$

13. $\int \tan^3 x \sec^2 x\,dx = \boldsymbol{\frac{1}{4}\tan^4 x + C}$

14.

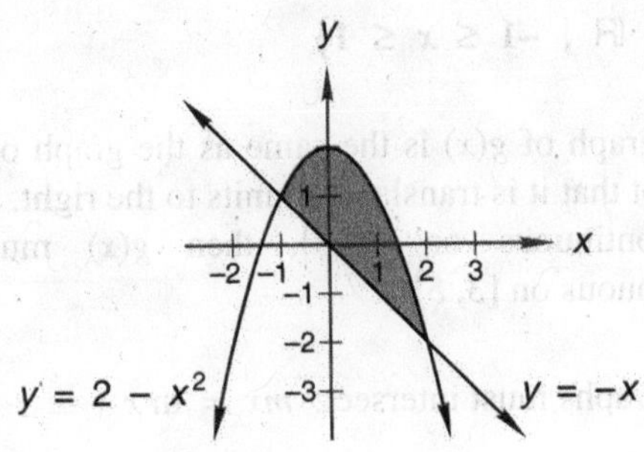

$A = \int_{-1}^{2} [(2 - x^2) - (-x)]\,dx$

$= \int_{-1}^{2} (-x^2 + x + 2)\,dx$

$= \left[-\frac{1}{3}x^3 + \frac{1}{2}x^2 + 2x\right]_{-1}^{2}$

$= -\frac{8}{3} + 2 + 4 - \left(\frac{1}{3} + \frac{1}{2} - 2\right)$

$= -3 + 8 - \frac{1}{2} = \boldsymbol{\frac{9}{2}}$ **units²**

15.

$A = \int_{-1}^{0} (x^2 - 2x)\,dx + \int_{2}^{0} (x^2 - 2x)\,dx$

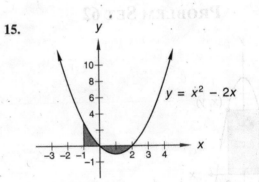

$= \left[\frac{1}{3}x^3 - x^2\right]_{-1}^{0} + \left[\frac{1}{3}x^3 - x^2\right]_{2}^{0}$

$= 0 - \left(-\frac{1}{3} - 1\right) + 0 - \left(\frac{8}{3} - 4\right)$

$= \frac{1}{3} + 5 - \frac{8}{3} = \boldsymbol{\frac{8}{3}}$ **units²**

16. (a) $\int_0^1 f(x)\,dx + \int_2^3 f(x)\,dx = \int_0^3 f(x)\,dx$

$\boldsymbol{a = 1,\ b = 3}$

(b) $\int_0^3 f(x)\,dx + \int_3^5 f(x)\,dx = \int_0^5 f(x)\,dx$

$\boldsymbol{a = 3,\ b = 5}$

17. $y = x^3 + x$

$\boldsymbol{x = y^3 + y}$

18. $y = \ln x$

$x = \ln y$

$y = e^x$

$f^{-1}(1) = e$

19. $h(t) = 200t - 16t^2$

$v(t) = 200 - 32t$

$32t = 200$

$t = 6.25$

$h(6.25) = 200(6.25) - 16(6.25)^2 = \mathbf{625\ ft}$

20. $y = e^{\sin x}(2x - 1)^{-1/2} + \ln(2x)$

$$y' = e^{\sin x}\left[-\frac{1}{2}(2x - 1)^{-3/2}(2)\right] + (2x - 1)^{-1/2}e^{\sin x}\cos x + \frac{1}{x}$$

$$= e^{\sin x}\left[-(2x - 1)^{-3/2}\right] + (2x - 1)^{-1/2}e^{\sin x}\cos x + \frac{1}{x}$$

$$= \mathbf{e^{\sin x}(2x - 1)^{-3/2}[-1 + (2x - 1)\cos x] + \frac{1}{x}}$$

21. $y = 2e^{\sin x}$

$$\frac{dy}{dx} = 2\cos x\, e^{\sin x}$$

$$\frac{d^2y}{dx^2} = 2\cos x \cos x\, e^{\sin x} + e^{\sin x}(-2\sin x)$$

$$\frac{d^2y}{dx^2} = \mathbf{2e^{\sin x}(\cos^2 x - \sin x)}$$

22. If $f(x) = \ln(\cos x)$, then $\cos x > 0$.

The correct choice is **D**.

23.

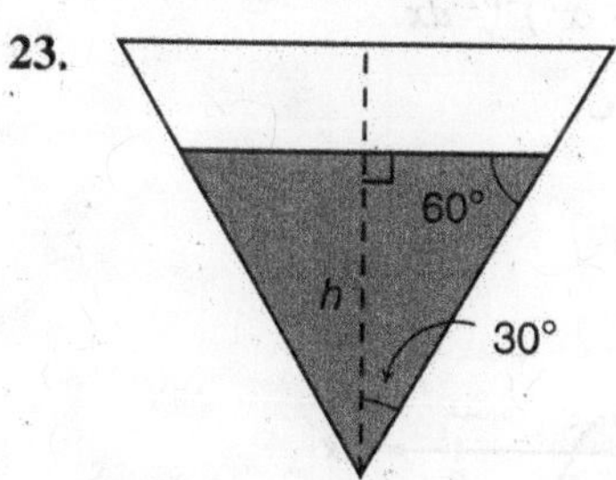

$V =$ Area of triangle · Length

$$= \frac{1}{2}bh \cdot 4$$

$$= \frac{1}{2}(2)\left(\frac{h}{\sqrt{3}}\right)h \cdot 4$$

$$= \mathbf{\frac{4\sqrt{3}}{3}h^2\ ft^3}$$

24. $f(g(x)) = \ln\sqrt{x^2 + 1}$

$g(x) = \mathbf{\sqrt{x^2 + 1}}$

25. (a) Let Y1=(e^(X)-e^(-X))/2 and Y2=7.

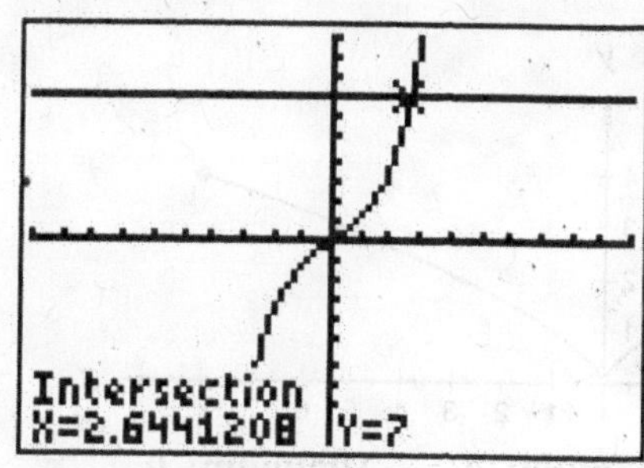

$x \approx \mathbf{2.6441208}$

(b) $14 = e^x - e^{-x}$

$14e^x = (e^x)^2 - 1$

$0 = (e^x)^2 - 14e^x - 1$

$$e^x = \frac{14 \pm \sqrt{196 - 4(1)(-1)}}{2}$$

$e^x = 7 \pm 5\sqrt{2}$

$x = \mathbf{\ln(7 + 5\sqrt{2}) \approx 2.6441}$

Problem Set 63

1.

$2\frac{h}{\sqrt{3}}$

60°

h

30°

$$V = \frac{1}{2}\left(2\frac{h}{\sqrt{3}}\right)h \cdot 4$$

$$V = \frac{4}{\sqrt{3}}h^2$$

$$\frac{dV}{dt} = \frac{8}{\sqrt{3}}h\frac{dh}{dt}$$

$$(1) = \frac{8}{\sqrt{3}}(\sqrt{3})\frac{dh}{dt}$$

$$\frac{dh}{dt} = \mathbf{\frac{1}{8}\frac{ft}{min}}$$

2. $f(x) = 2x^3 + 3x^2 - 12x + 1$
$f'(x) = 6x^2 + 6x - 12$
$0 = 6(x^2 + x - 2)$
$0 = 6(x + 2)(x - 1)$
$f(-3) = 10 \qquad f(-2) = 21 \qquad f(1) = -6$
Maximum: 21 Minimum: −6

3. 

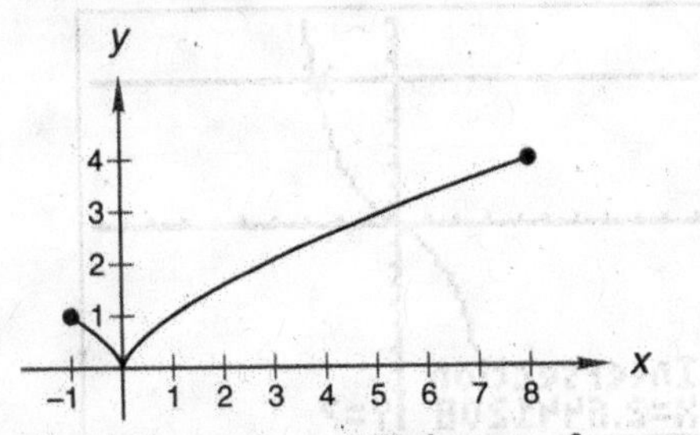

Maximum: 4 Minimum: 0

4. 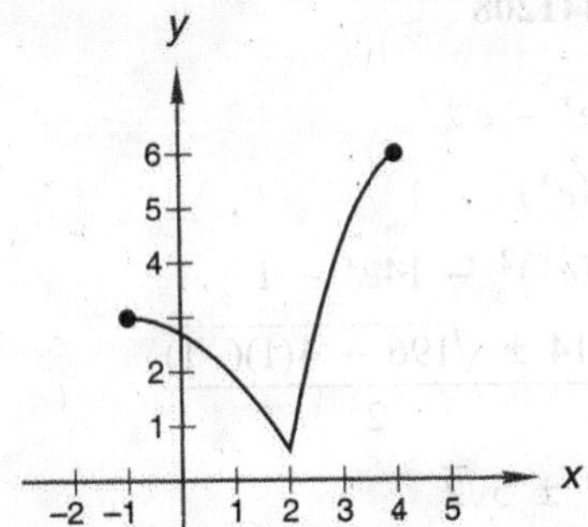

Maximum at $x = 4$ Minimum at $x = 2$

5. (a) The line segment in the first quadrant passes through the points (0, 3) and (3, 0), and so has equation $\boldsymbol{y = -x + 3}$.

(b) $A = bh = (2x)(-x + 3) = \boldsymbol{-2x^2 + 6x}$

(c) $A' = -4x + 6$
$4x = 6$
$x = \frac{3}{2}$
$A_{\max} = -2\left(\frac{3}{2}\right)^2 + 6\left(\frac{3}{2}\right)$
$= -\frac{9}{2} + 9 = \boldsymbol{\frac{9}{2}\ \text{cm}^2}$

6. $W = \int_1^3 2x\,dx$
$= [x^2]_1^3$
$= 9 - 1 =$ **8 joules**

7. $d = \int_0^2 (3t^2 + 1)\,dt = [t^3 + t]_0^2$
$= 8 + 2 =$ **10 meters**

8. $f(x) = ae^x + b$
$f'(x) = ae^x$
$3 = a + b$ and $3 = a$ $\qquad \boldsymbol{a = 3,\ b = 0}$

9. $y = \ln x$
$y' = \frac{1}{x} = x^{-1}$
$y'' = -x^{-2} = -\frac{1}{x^2}$
y'' is concave up when $-\frac{1}{x^2} > 0$
$\frac{1}{x^2} < 0$

x^2 is always positive, as is $\frac{1}{x^2}$.

Since $\frac{1}{x^2}$ can never be less than 0, the graph of $y = \ln x$ is **never** concave upward.

10. $\int_1^3 \frac{x^2 - 1}{x + 1}\,dx = \int_1^3 \frac{(x + 1)(x - 1)}{x + 1}\,dx$
$= \int_1^3 (x - 1)\,dx$
$= \left[\frac{1}{2}x^2 - x\right]_1^3$
$= \frac{9}{2} - 3 - \left(\frac{1}{2} - 1\right)$
$= \mathbf{2}$

11. $\int \cos(2x)\, e^{\sin(2x)}\,dx = \frac{1}{2}\int 2\cos(2x)\, e^{\sin(2x)}\,dx$
$= \boldsymbol{\frac{1}{2}e^{\sin(2x)} + C}$

12. $\int e^{-2x}\,dx = -\frac{1}{2}\int -2e^{-2x}\,dx$
$= \boldsymbol{-\frac{1}{2}e^{-2x} + C}$

13. $\int (3x^2 + 2x)(x^3 + x^2)^{-1/2}\,dx$
$= \boldsymbol{2\sqrt{x^3 + x^2} + C}$

14. 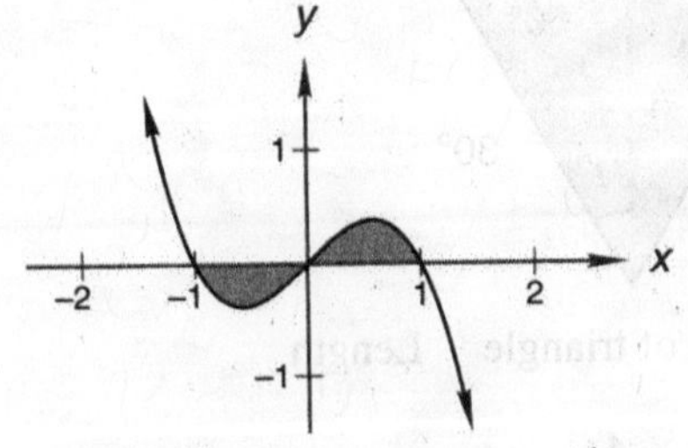

$A = \int_0^{-1} (-x^3 + x)\,dx + \int_0^1 (-x^3 + x)\,dx$
$= \left[-\frac{1}{4}x^4 + \frac{1}{2}x^2\right]_0^{-1} + \left[-\frac{1}{4}x^4 + \frac{1}{2}x^2\right]_0^1$
$= -\frac{1}{4} + \frac{1}{2} - \frac{1}{4} + \frac{1}{2} = \boldsymbol{\frac{1}{2}\ \text{units}^2}$

15. $a = -1, b = 5$

16. $a = -5, b = -3$

17. $\int_b^a 2f(x)\,dx = -2\int_a^b f(x)\,dx = -2(-4) = \mathbf{8}$

18.
$$y = e^{2x}\tan^2 x$$
$$y' = e^{2x}(2\tan x\sec^2 x) + \tan^2 x\,(2e^{2x})$$
$$y' = \mathbf{2e^{2x}\tan x\,(\sec^2 x + \tan x)}$$

19.
$$y = \frac{(x^2+1)^{1/2}}{x + \sin x}$$
$$y' = \frac{(x+\sin x)\frac{1}{2}(x^2+1)^{-1/2}(2x)}{(x+\sin x)^2} - \frac{(x^2+1)^{1/2}(1+\cos x)}{(x+\sin x)^2}$$
$$y' = \mathbf{\frac{x(x^2+1)^{-1/2}}{x+\sin x} - \frac{(x^2+1)^{1/2}(1+\cos x)}{(x+\sin x)^2}}$$

20.
$$f(x) = x\ln x$$
$$f'(x) = x\left(\frac{1}{x}\right) + \ln x$$
$$f'(x) = 1 + \ln x$$
Increasing when: $1 + \ln x > 0$
$$\ln x > -1$$
$$x > e^{-1}$$

The correct choice is **C**.

21.

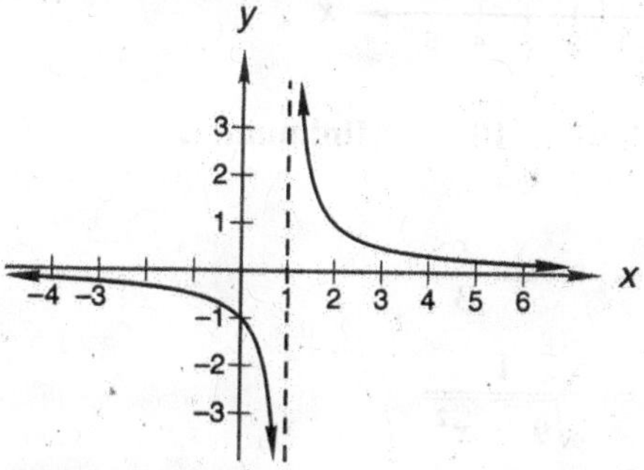

$\lim\limits_{x\to 1^+} f(x) = \infty$ $\qquad$ $\lim\limits_{x\to 1^-} f(x) = -\infty$

22. $\lim\limits_{x\to 2}\dfrac{\ln x - \ln 2}{x - 2} = \dfrac{d}{dx}\ln x\Big|_2 = \mathbf{\dfrac{1}{2}}$

23.

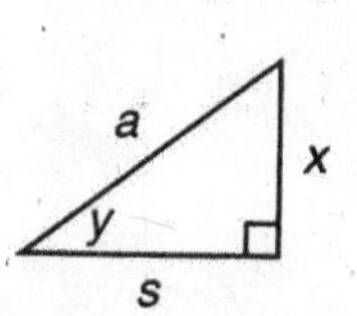

$$a^2 = x^2 + s^2$$
$$s^2 = a^2 - x^2$$
$$s = \sqrt{a^2 - x^2}$$

$$\cos y = \frac{s}{a}$$
$$\mathbf{\cos y = \frac{\sqrt{a^2 - x^2}}{a}}$$

24.
$$x^2 + y^2 = 1 \qquad (x-1)^2 + y^2 = 1$$
$$y^2 = 1 - x^2 \qquad 1 - (x-1)^2 = y^2$$

Find the point of intersection.
$$1 - x^2 = 1 - (x-1)^2$$
$$1 - x^2 = 1 - (x^2 - 2x + 1)$$
$$1 - x^2 = 1 - x^2 + 2x - 1$$
$$2x = 1$$
$$x = \frac{1}{2}$$

Intersection: $\left(\frac{1}{2}, \frac{3}{4}\right)$

Determine the two slopes at $\left(\frac{1}{2}, \frac{3}{4}\right)$.
$$y_1^2 = 1 - x^2$$
$$y_1 = (1 - x^2)^{1/2}$$
$$y_1' = \frac{1}{2}(1 - x^2)^{-1/2}(-2x)$$
$$y_1' = -x(1 - x^2)^{-1/2}$$
$$y_1'\left(\frac{1}{2}\right) = -\frac{1}{2}\left(\frac{3}{4}\right)^{-1/2} = -\frac{1}{\sqrt{3}}$$

$$y_2^2 = 1 - (x-1)^2$$
$$y_2 = (-x^2 + 2x)^{1/2}$$
$$y_2' = \frac{1}{2}(-x^2 + 2x)^{-1/2}(-2x + 2)$$
$$y_2' = (-x + 1)(-x^2 + 2x)^{-1/2}$$
$$y_2'\left(\frac{1}{2}\right) = \frac{1}{2}\left(\frac{3}{4}\right)^{-1/2} = \frac{1}{\sqrt{3}}$$

Calculate the angle of intersection.
$$\tan\theta = \frac{m_1 - m_2}{1 + m_1 m_2}$$
$$\theta = \tan^{-1}\left(\frac{-\frac{1}{\sqrt{3}} - \frac{1}{\sqrt{3}}}{1 - \frac{1}{3}}\right)$$
$$= \tan^{-1}\left(\frac{-\frac{2}{\sqrt{3}}}{\frac{2}{3}}\right)$$
$$= \tan^{-1} -\sqrt{3} = -60° = \mathbf{60°}$$

25.
$$Q(p) = 10{,}000 - 50(p - 20)$$
$$Q(p) = 11{,}000 - 50p$$
$$R(p) = p(11{,}000 - 50p)$$
$$\mathbf{R(p) = 11{,}000p - 50p^2}$$

Problem Set 64

1. $Q(p) = 4000 - 100(p - 16)$

$Q(p) = 5600 - 100p$

$R(p) = 5600p - 100p^2$

$R'(p) = 5600 - 200p$

$200p = 5600$

$p = \mathbf{\$28}$

2. (a) $A = bh = 2xy = \mathbf{2x\sqrt{9 - x^2}}$

(b) $A' = (2x)\frac{1}{2}(9 - x^2)^{-1/2}(-2x) + 2(9 - x^2)^{1/2}$

$A' = -2x^2(9 - x^2)^{-1/2} + 2(9 - x^2)^{1/2}$

$A' = 2(9 - x^2)^{-1/2}[-x^2 + (9 - x^2)]$

$A' = 2(9 - x^2)^{-1/2}(-2x^2 + 9)$

$A' = 0$ when $-2x^2 + 9 = 0$

$x^2 = \frac{9}{2}$

$x = \frac{3\sqrt{2}}{2}$

Dimensions: $\mathbf{3\sqrt{2}}$ **units** $\times$ $\mathbf{\frac{3\sqrt{2}}{2}}$ **units**

3.

n	$f^{(n)}(x)$	$f^{(n)}(0)$
0	$(1 - x)^{-2}$	1
1	$2(1 - x)^{-3}$	2
2	$6(1 - x)^{-4}$	6
3	$24(1 - x)^{-5}$	24
⋮	⋮	⋮

$p(x) = 1 + 2x + \frac{6x^2}{2!} + \frac{24x^3}{3!} + \cdots$

$p(x) = \mathbf{1 + 2x + 3x^2 + 4x^3 + \cdots}$

4. $f(x) = x^3 - 6x^2 + 2$

$f'(x) = 3x^2 - 12x$

$0 = 3x(x - 4)$

$x = 0, 4$

Critical numbers: $x = -1, 0, 4, 5$

$f(-1) = -5$; $f(0) = 2$; $f(4) = -30$; $f(5) = -23$

Maximum: 2 **Minimum: –30**

5. $f(x) = x^{3/2} - x$

$f'(x) = \frac{3}{2}x^{1/2} - 1$

$0 = \frac{3}{2}x^{1/2} - 1$

$x^{1/2} = \frac{2}{3}$

$x = \frac{4}{9}$

Critical numbers: $x = 0, \frac{4}{9}, 2$

$f(0) = 0$; $f\left(\frac{4}{9}\right) = -\frac{4}{27}$

$f(2) = 2\sqrt{2} - 2$

Maximum: $\mathbf{2\sqrt{2} - 2}$

Minimum: $\mathbf{-\frac{4}{27}}$

6.

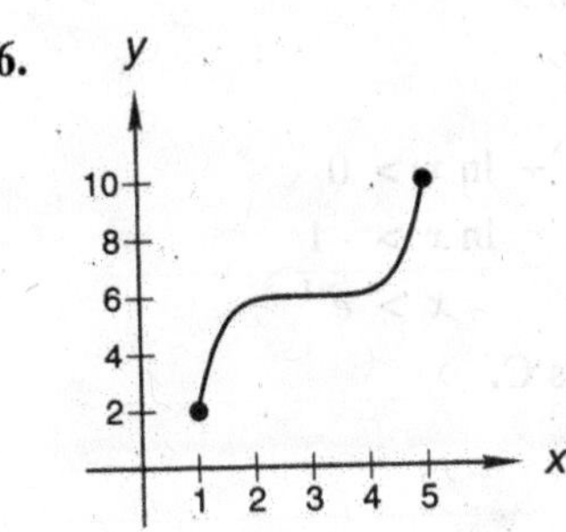

Maximum: 10 **Minimum: 2**

7. $y = \arcsin\frac{x}{3}$

$\frac{dy}{dx} = \mathbf{\frac{1}{\sqrt{9 - x^2}}}$

8. $y = \cos^{-1}\frac{x}{5}$

$y' = \mathbf{\frac{-1}{\sqrt{25 - x^2}}}$

9. $y = \tan^{-1}\frac{x}{2}$

$\frac{dy}{dx} = \mathbf{\frac{2}{x^2 + 4}}$

10. $\int \frac{1}{\sqrt{1 - x^2}}\,dx = \mathbf{\arcsin x + C}$

11. $W = \int_2^4 2x\,dx$
$= [x^2]_2^4$
$= 16 - 4$
$= \mathbf{12\ joules}$

12. $f(x) = a \sin x + b$
$f'(x) = a \cos x$
$5 = a + b$ and $3 = a$
$\mathbf{a = 3,\ b = 2}$

13.

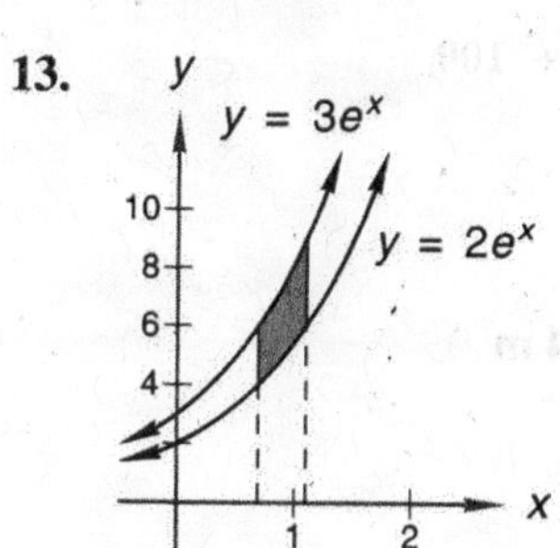

$A = \int_{\ln 2}^{\ln 3} (3e^x - 2e^x)\,dx$
$= \int_{\ln 2}^{\ln 3} e^x\,dx$
$= [e^x]_{\ln 2}^{\ln 3}$
$= 3 - 2 = \mathbf{1\ unit^2}$

14.

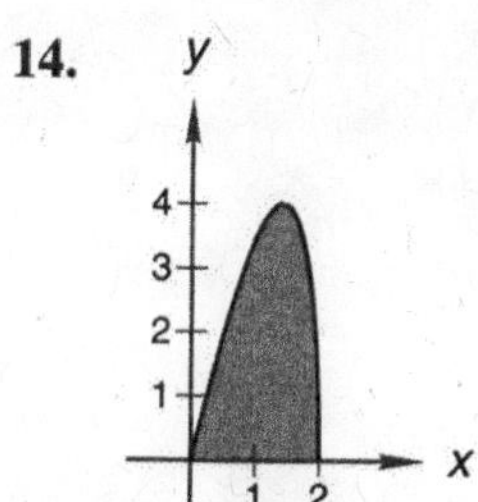

$A = \int_0^2 2x(4 - x^2)^{1/2}\,dx$
$= -\frac{2}{3}[(4 - x^2)^{3/2}]_0^2$
$= -\frac{2}{3}(0 - 8) = \mathbf{\frac{16}{3}\ units^2}$

15. $A \approx$ `fnInt(e^(X²),X,-1,1)`
$\approx \mathbf{2.9253\ units^2}$

16. $\int_1^7 f(x)\,dx = \int_1^3 f(x)\,dx + \int_3^7 f(x)\,dx$
$= -5 + 6 = \mathbf{1}$

17. $\int_7^1 -5f(x)\,dx = 5\int_1^7 f(x)\,dx = 5(1) = \mathbf{5}$

18. $y = x^{1/2}$
$\frac{dy}{dx} = \frac{1}{2}x^{-1/2}$
$\frac{d^2y}{dx^2} = -\frac{1}{4}x^{-3/2}$
$\left.\frac{d^2y}{dx^2}\right|_1 = \mathbf{-\frac{1}{4}}$

19. $y = \sin(\cos x)$
$y' = \cos(\cos x)(-\sin x)$
slope $= y'|_{\pi/2} = \cos(0)(-1) = -1$
At $\left(\frac{\pi}{2}, 0\right)$, $y - 0 = -\left(x - \frac{\pi}{2}\right)$
$\mathbf{y = -x + \frac{\pi}{2}}$

20. $y = [\sin(2x) + x]^{1/3} + \frac{\csc(3x)}{x^3 + 1}$
$y' = \frac{1}{3}[\sin(2x) + x]^{-2/3}[2\cos(2x) + 1]$
$+ \frac{(x^3 + 1)[-3\csc(3x)\cot(3x)]}{(x^3 + 1)^2}$
$- \frac{\csc(3x)(3x^2)}{(x^3 + 1)^2}$
$\mathbf{y' = \frac{2\cos(2x) + 1}{3\sqrt[3]{[\sin(2x) + x]^2}} - \frac{3\csc(3x)\cot(3x)}{x^3 + 1}}$
$\mathbf{- \frac{3x^2\csc(3x)}{(x^3 + 1)^2}}$

21. $\int (3x^2 + 2x + 1)(x^3 + x^2 + x)^{1/2}\,dx$
$= \mathbf{\frac{2}{3}(x^3 + x^2 + x)^{3/2} + C}$

22. $\lim_{x\to\infty} \frac{x^3 - 2x^2}{1 - x^4} = \mathbf{0}$

23. $\lim_{\Delta x\to 0} \frac{\cos(\pi + \Delta x) - \cos\pi}{\Delta x} = \left.\frac{d}{dx}\cos x\right|_\pi$
$= -\sin\pi = \mathbf{0}$

24. (a) $$\frac{x^2}{a^2} + \frac{y^2}{b^2} = 1$$

$$\frac{y^2}{b^2} = 1 - \frac{x^2}{a^2}$$

$$y^2 = b^2 - \left(\frac{b}{a}\right)^2 x^2$$

$$y = \sqrt{b^2 - \left(\frac{b}{a}\right)^2 x^2}, \quad x > 0$$

(b) $$\int_0^a \sqrt{b^2 - \left(\frac{b}{a}\right)^2 x^2}\, dx$$

25. From problem 24 in Problem Set 63, these curves intersect when $x = \frac{1}{2}$. In the same problem, $y_1 = (1 - x^2)^{1/2}$ and $y_2 = (-x^2 + 2x)^{1/2}$. In the fourth quadrant,

$$y_1 = -(1 - x^2)^{1/2}$$
$$y_1' = x(1 - x^2)^{-1/2}$$
$$y_2 = -(-x^2 + 2x)^{1/2}$$
$$y_2' = (x - 1)(-x^2 + 2x)^{-1/2}$$

$$m_1 = y_1'|_{1/2} = \frac{1}{\sqrt{3}}$$

$$m_2 = y_2'|_{1/2} = -\frac{1}{\sqrt{3}}$$

$$\tan\theta = \frac{m_1 - m_2}{1 + m_1 m_2}$$

$$\theta = \tan^{-1}\left(\frac{\frac{1}{\sqrt{3}} + \frac{1}{\sqrt{3}}}{1 - \frac{1}{3}}\right)$$

$$\theta = \tan^{-1} -\sqrt{3} = \mathbf{60^\circ}$$

PROBLEM SET 65

1. $$\frac{dx}{dt} = -100\ \frac{\text{m}}{\text{s}} \qquad x = 2000\text{ m}$$

$$\cot\theta = \frac{x}{1000}$$

$$x = 1000\cot\theta$$

$$\frac{dx}{dt} = -1000\csc^2\theta\,\frac{d\theta}{dt}$$

$$(-100) = -1000\left(\frac{1000\sqrt{5}}{1000}\right)^2 \frac{d\theta}{dt}$$

$$\frac{1}{10} = 5\,\frac{d\theta}{dt}$$

$$\frac{d\theta}{dt} = \mathbf{\frac{1}{50}\ \frac{rad}{s}}$$

2. $$a(t) = -9.8$$
$$v(t) = -9.8t$$
$$\mathbf{h(t) = -4.9t^2 + 500}$$
$$\mathbf{h(3) = 455.9\ m}$$
$$\mathbf{v(3) = -29.4\ m/s}$$
$$\mathbf{a(3) = -9.8\ m/s^2}$$

3. $$a(t) = -9.8$$
$$v(t) = -9.8t + 30$$
$$\mathbf{h(t) = -4.9t^2 + 30t + 100}$$
$$0 = -9.8t + 30$$
$$t \approx 3.0612\text{ s}$$
$$h(3.0612) \approx \mathbf{145.9184\ m}$$

4. $$y = \cos x$$
$$\mathbf{x = \cos y}$$

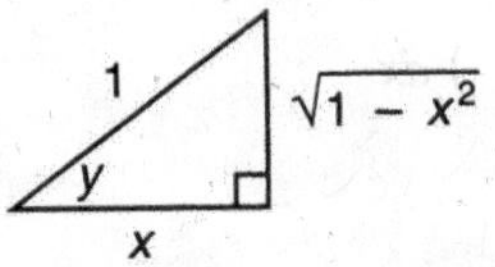

$$1 = -\sin y\,\frac{dy}{dx}$$

$$\frac{dy}{dx} = -\csc y$$

$$\frac{dy}{dx} = -\frac{1}{\sqrt{1 - x^2}}$$

$$\mathbf{\frac{d}{dx} f^{-1}(x) = -\frac{1}{\sqrt{1 - x^2}}}$$

$$(f^{-1})'(0.2) \approx \mathbf{-1.0206}$$

5. $$y = \arcsin\frac{x}{3}$$

$$\frac{dy}{dx} = \frac{1}{\sqrt{9 - x^2}}$$

$$\left.\frac{dy}{dx}\right|_2 = \frac{1}{\sqrt{9 - 4}} = \mathbf{\frac{\sqrt{5}}{5}}$$

6. $$y = \arctan\frac{x}{2}$$

$$\frac{dy}{dx} = \mathbf{\frac{2}{x^2 + 4}}$$

7. $f(x) = 2x^3 - 3x^2 - 12x + 7$

$f'(x) = 6x^2 - 6x - 12$

$0 = 6(x - 2)(x + 1)$

Critical numbers: $x = -2, -1, 2, 3$

$f(-2) = 3;\ f(-1) = 14;\ f(2) = -13;\ f(3) = -2$

Maximum: 14 **Minimum: −13**

8. Critical numbers: $x = -1, 1, 3$

$f(-1) = 2 \qquad f(1) = 0 \qquad f(3) = 2$

Maximum of 2 at $x = -1$ and $x = 3$.

Minimum of 0 at $x = 1$.

9. 

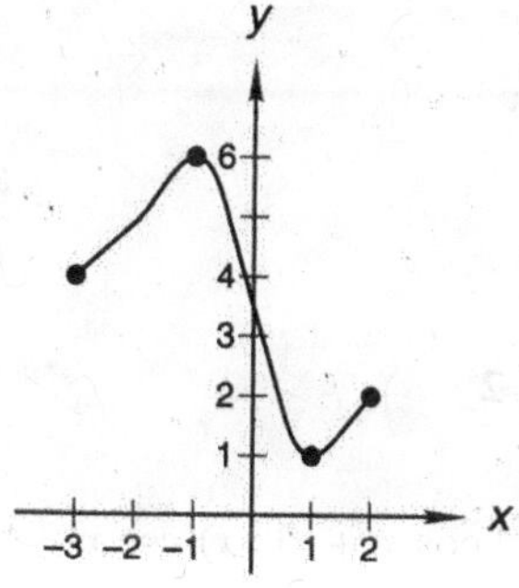

Maximum: 6 **Minimum: 1**

10. (a) $A = \frac{1}{2}bh$

$= \frac{1}{2}(2x)\left(3 - \frac{1}{12}x^2\right)$

$= \mathbf{3x - \frac{1}{12}x^3}$

(b) $A' = 3 - \frac{1}{4}x^2$

$0 = 3 - \frac{1}{4}x^2$

$\frac{1}{4}x^2 = 3$

$x^2 = 12$

$x = 2\sqrt{3}$

$A_{max} = 3(2\sqrt{3}) - \frac{1}{12}(24\sqrt{3})$

$= 6\sqrt{3} - 2\sqrt{3}$

$= \mathbf{4\sqrt{3}\ units^2}$

11. $W = \int_1^2 2x\,dx$

$= [x^2]_1^2$

$= 4 - 1$

$=$ **3 joules**

12. $f(x) = ax^2 + b \qquad g(x) = x^2 + ax$

$f'(x) = 2ax \qquad g'(x) = 2x + a$

$f'(2) = g'(2)$

$4a = 4 + a$

$\mathbf{a = \frac{4}{3}}$

With $f(1) = 5,\ a + b = 5$

$\frac{4}{3} + b = 5$

$\mathbf{b = \frac{11}{3}}$

13. $\int \cos(2x)\,[1 + \sin(2x)]^{-1/2}\,dx$

$= \frac{1}{2}\int 2\cos(2x)\,[1 + \sin(2x)]^{-1/2}\,dx$

$= \mathbf{\sqrt{1 + \sin(2x)} + C}$

14. $\int xe^{x^2+\pi}\,dx = \frac{1}{2}\int 2xe^{x^2+\pi}\,dx$

$= \mathbf{\frac{1}{2}e^{x^2+\pi} + C}$

15. 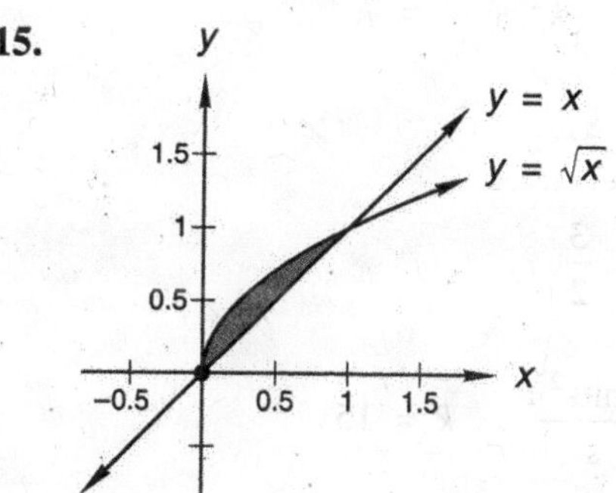

$A = \int_0^1 (x^{1/2} - x)\,dx$

$= \left[\frac{2}{3}x^{3/2} - \frac{1}{2}x^2\right]_0^1$

$= \frac{2}{3} - \frac{1}{2} = \mathbf{\frac{1}{6}\ unit^2}$

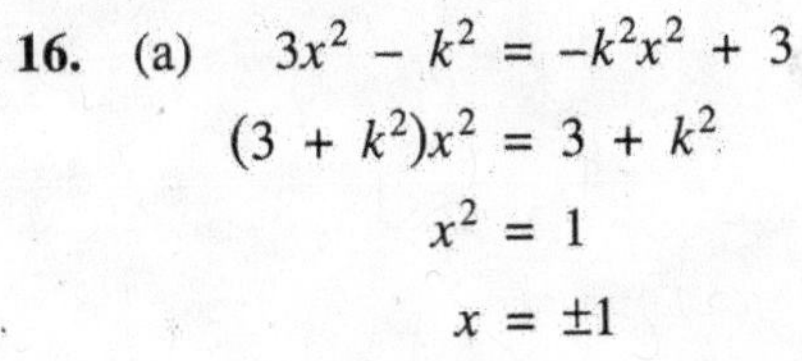

16. (a)
$$3x^2 - k^2 = -k^2x^2 + 3$$
$$(3 + k^2)x^2 = 3 + k^2$$
$$x^2 = 1$$
$$x = \pm 1$$

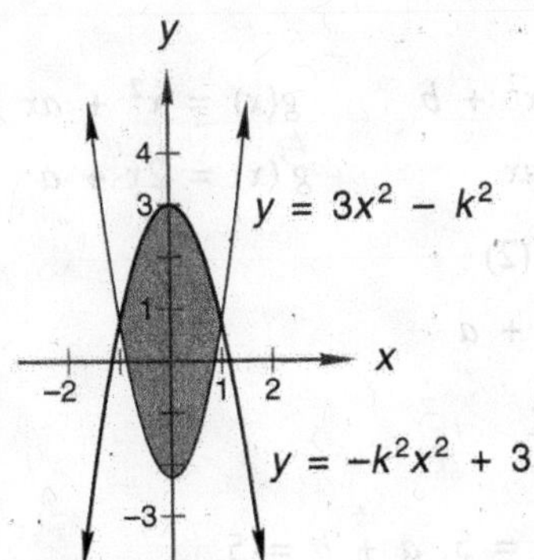

$$A(k) = \int_{x=-1}^{x=1} \left[(-k^2x^2 + 3) - (3x^2 - k^2)\right] dx$$
$$= \left[-\frac{k^2}{3}x^3 + 3x - x^3 + k^2x\right]_{x=-1}^{x=1}$$
$$= \left(-\frac{k^2}{3} + 3 - 1 + k^2\right) - \left(\frac{k^2}{3} - 3 + 1 - k^2\right)$$
$$= \left(\frac{2}{3}k^2 + 2\right) - \left(-\frac{2}{3}k^2 - 2\right)$$
$$= \left(\mathbf{\frac{4}{3}k^2 + 4}\right) \textbf{units}^2$$

(b)
$$A(k) = \frac{4}{3}k^2 + 4 = 7$$
$$\frac{4}{3}k^2 = 3$$
$$k = \mathbf{\frac{3}{2}}$$

17.
$$\frac{dA}{dt} = 5\,\frac{\text{units}^2}{\text{s}} \qquad k = 15$$
$$A = \frac{4}{3}k^2 + 4$$
$$\frac{dA}{dt} = \frac{8}{3}k\frac{dk}{dt}$$
$$(5) = \frac{8}{3}(15)\frac{dk}{dt}$$
$$\frac{dk}{dt} = \mathbf{\frac{1}{8}\,\frac{unit}{s}}$$

18.
$$\int_1^c f(x)\,dx + \int_c^5 f(x)\,dx = \int_1^5 f(x)\,dx$$
$$\int_1^c f(x)\,dx + (-2) = 10$$
$$\int_1^c f(x)\,dx = \mathbf{12}$$

19.
$$\int_1^e \frac{1}{x}\,dx = [\ln x]_1^e = 1 - 0 = \mathbf{1}$$

20.
$$y = 2\sin x$$
$$\frac{dy}{dx} = 2\cos x$$
$$\frac{d^2y}{dx^2} = -2\sin x$$
$$\frac{d^3y}{dx^3} = -2\cos x$$
$$\frac{d^4y}{dx^4} = 2\sin x$$
$$\left.\frac{d^4y}{dx^4}\right|_{\pi/2} = 2(1) = \mathbf{2}$$

21.
$$y = (\sin x)^{1/2} + e^{2x}\cos x + (\ln x)(\csc x)$$
$$y' = \frac{1}{2}(\sin x)^{-1/2}\cos x + e^{2x}(-\sin x) + 2\cos x\, e^{2x} + (\ln x)(-\csc x\cot x) + (\csc x)\left(\frac{1}{x}\right)$$
$$y' = \mathbf{\frac{\cos x}{2\sqrt{\sin x}} + e^{2x}(2\cos x - \sin x) + \csc x\left(\frac{1}{x} - \ln x\cot x\right)}$$

22.

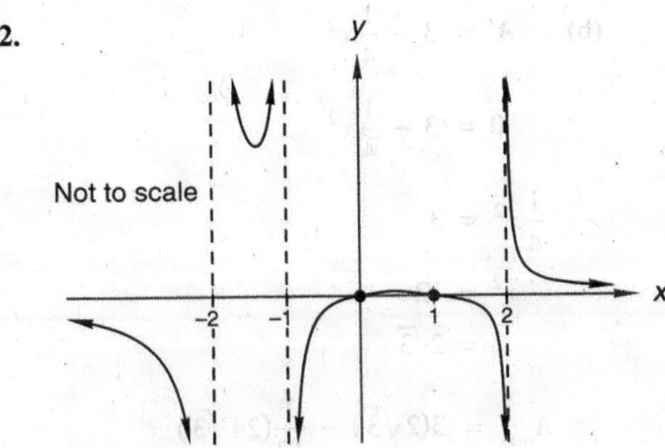

Concave up: (−2, −1), (2, ∞)
Concave down: (−∞, −2), (−1, 2)

23.
$$\lim_{x\to 2}\frac{e^x - e^2}{x - 2} = \left.\frac{d}{dx}e^x\right|_2 = \mathbf{e^2}$$

24. A. $f\left(\frac{x_1}{x_2}\right) = \frac{x_2}{x_1} \neq \frac{1}{x_1} - \frac{1}{x_2}$

B. $f\left(\frac{x_1}{x_2}\right) = \ln \frac{x_1}{x_2} = \ln x_1 - \ln x_2$

C. $f\left(\frac{x_1}{x_2}\right) = \left(\frac{x_1}{x_2}\right)^2 \neq x_1^2 - x_2^2$

D. $f\left(\frac{x_1}{x_2}\right) = \sin \frac{x_1}{x_2} \neq \sin x_1 - \sin x_2$

The correct choice is **B.**

25. $y = 2x + b$

$y^2 = 4x^2 + 4bx + b^2 \qquad y^2 = 4x$

The curves intersect when

$$4x = 4x^2 + 4bx + b^2$$
$$0 = 4x^2 - 4x + 4bx + b^2$$
$$0 = 4x^2 + (-4 + 4b)x + b^2$$
$$x = \frac{4 - 4b}{8} \pm \frac{\sqrt{16 - 32b + 16b^2 - 4(4)(b^2)}}{8}$$

For 2 distinct roots, or points of intersection:

$$16 - 32b + 16b^2 - 16b^2 > 0$$
$$32b < 16$$
$$\mathbf{b < \frac{1}{2}}$$

PROBLEM SET 66

1. $W = \int_1^5 (x^2 - 3x)\,dx$

$$= \left[\frac{1}{3}x^3 - \frac{3}{2}x^2\right]_1^5$$
$$= \frac{125}{3} - \frac{75}{2} - \left(\frac{1}{3} - \frac{3}{2}\right)$$
$$= \mathbf{\frac{16}{3}\ joules}$$

2. Acceleration due to gravity is always **-9.8 m/s²**.

3. $a(t) = -9.8$

$v(t) = -9.8t + 20$

$\mathbf{h(t) = -4.9t^2 + 20t + 160}$

$\mathbf{h(2) = 180.4\ m}$

$\mathbf{v(2) = 0.4\ m/s}$

$\mathbf{a(2) = -9.8\ m/s^2}$

4. $u = \pi x^2 \qquad du = 2\pi x\,dx$

$$\int_0^1 x\cos(\pi x^2)\,dx$$
$$= \frac{1}{2\pi}\int_0^\pi \cos u\,du$$
$$= \frac{1}{2\pi}[\sin u]_0^\pi = \mathbf{0}$$

5. $u = \cos(5x) \qquad du = -5\sin(5x)\,dx$

$$\int_0^\pi [\sin(5x)]e^{\cos(5x)}\,dx$$
$$= -\frac{1}{5}\int_1^{-1} e^u\,du = \frac{1}{5}\int_{-1}^1 e^u\,du$$
$$= \frac{1}{5}\left[e^u\right]_{-1}^1 = \mathbf{\frac{1}{5}\left(e - \frac{1}{e}\right)}$$

6.

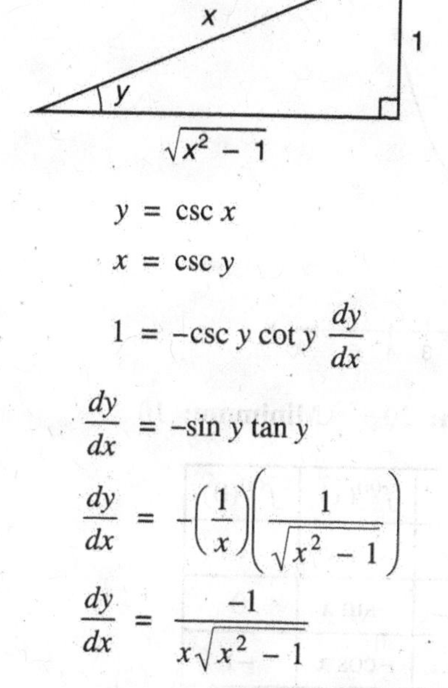

$$y = \csc x$$
$$x = \csc y$$
$$1 = -\csc y \cot y \frac{dy}{dx}$$
$$\frac{dy}{dx} = -\sin y \tan y$$
$$\frac{dy}{dx} = -\left(\frac{1}{x}\right)\left(\frac{1}{\sqrt{x^2 - 1}}\right)$$
$$\frac{dy}{dx} = \frac{-1}{x\sqrt{x^2 - 1}}$$
$$\mathbf{(f^{-1})'(x) = \frac{-1}{x\sqrt{x^2 - 1}}}$$

7. $y = \arcsin \frac{x}{3}$

$$\frac{dy}{dx} = \frac{1}{\sqrt{9 - x^2}}$$
$$\left.\frac{dy}{dx}\right|_{3/2} = \frac{1}{\sqrt{9 - \frac{9}{4}}} = \frac{1}{\sqrt{\frac{27}{4}}} = \mathbf{\frac{2\sqrt{3}}{9}}$$

8. $y = \arctan(\sin x)$

$$\frac{dy}{dx} = \mathbf{\frac{\cos x}{\sin^2 x + 1}}$$

9. $f(x) = \frac{4}{3}x^3 - 2x^2 - 15x$

$f'(x) = 4x^2 - 4x - 15$

$0 = (2x - 5)(2x + 3)$

$x = \frac{5}{2}, -\frac{3}{2}$

Critical numbers: $x = -3, -\frac{3}{2}, \frac{5}{2}, 4$

$f(-3) = -9;\quad f\left(-\frac{3}{2}\right) = 13\frac{1}{2}$

$f\left(\frac{5}{2}\right) = -29\frac{1}{6};\quad f(4) = -6\frac{2}{3}$

Maximum: $\mathbf{13\frac{1}{2}}$ **Minimum:** $\mathbf{-29\frac{1}{6}}$

10.

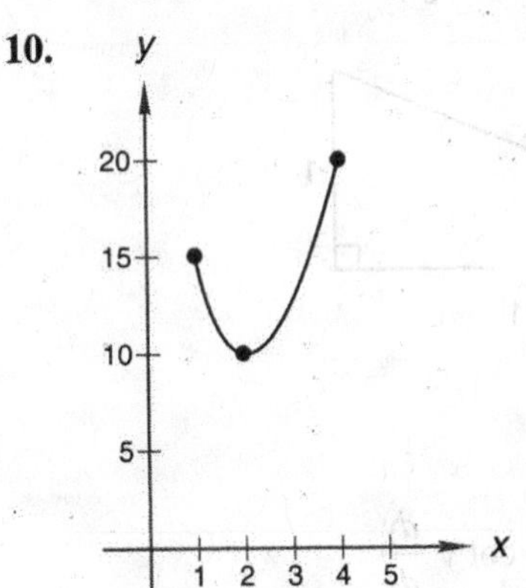

Maximum: 20 **Minimum: 10**

11.

n	$f^{(n)}(x)$	$f^{(n)}(0)$
0, 4, 8...	$\cos x$	1
1, 5, 9...	$-\sin x$	0
2, 6, 10...	$-\cos x$	-1
3, 7, 11...	$\sin x$	0

$\cos x = \mathbf{1 - \frac{x^2}{2} + \frac{x^4}{4!} - \frac{x^6}{6!} + \cdots}$

12. (a)

n	$f^{(n)}(x)$	$f^{(n)}(0)$
0	$\cos(2x)$	1
1	$-2\sin(2x)$	0
2	$-4\cos(2x)$	-4
3	$8\sin(2x)$	0
4	$16\cos(2x)$	16
5	$-32\sin(2x)$	0
6	$-64\cos(2x)$	-64

$\cos(2x) = 1 - \frac{4x^2}{2!} + \frac{16x^4}{4!} - \frac{64x^6}{6!} + \cdots$

$= \mathbf{1 - \frac{(2x)^2}{2} + \frac{(2x)^4}{4!} - \frac{(2x)^6}{6!} + \cdots}$

(b) $\cos x = 1 - \frac{x^2}{2!} + \frac{x^4}{4!} - \frac{x^6}{6!} + \cdots$

$\cos(2x)$

$= 1 - \frac{(2x)^2}{2!} + \frac{(2x)^4}{4!} - \frac{(2x)^6}{6!} + \cdots$

They are the same.

13. $f(x) = a\sin x + b\cos x$

$f'(x) = a\cos x - b\sin x$

$f'(\pi) = 2 = -a$

$f'\left(\frac{\pi}{2}\right) = 4 = -b$

$\mathbf{a = -2,\ b = -4}$

14. $u = x + 1 \qquad du = dx$

$\int x(x + 1)^{1/2}\,dx$

$= \int (u - 1)u^{1/2}\,du$

$= \int (u^{3/2} - u^{1/2})\,du$

$= \frac{2}{5}u^{5/2} - \frac{2}{3}u^{3/2} + C$

$= \frac{2}{15}u^{3/2}(3u - 5) + C$

$= \frac{2}{15}(x + 1)^{3/2}[3(x + 1) - 5] + C$

$= \mathbf{\frac{2}{15}(x + 1)^{3/2}(3x - 2) + C}$

15. $\int (1 + \cos x)(x + \sin x)^3\,dx$

$= \mathbf{\frac{1}{4}(x + \sin x)^4 + C}$

16. $\int \frac{x^2 + 1}{x}\,dx = \int \left(x + \frac{1}{x}\right)dx$

$= \mathbf{\frac{1}{2}x^2 + \ln|x| + C}$

17. $\int \frac{x}{x^2 + 1}\,dx = \frac{1}{2}\int \frac{2x}{x^2 + 1}\,dx$

$= \frac{1}{2}\ln(x^2 + 1) + C$

$= \mathbf{\ln\sqrt{x^2 + 1} + C}$

18. $\int \frac{1}{x^2 + 1}\, dx = \mathbf{arctan}\ \boldsymbol{x} + \boldsymbol{C}$

19. $\int \frac{x}{x^2 + 4}\, dx = \frac{1}{2}\int \frac{2x}{x^2 + 4}\, dx$

$= \mathbf{ln}\ \sqrt{\boldsymbol{x}^2 + 4} + \boldsymbol{C}$

20. $y = \frac{\tan(x^3 - 1)}{e^2 + e^x}$

$y' = \frac{(e^2 + e^x)\sec^2(x^3 - 1)(3x^2)}{(e^2 + e^x)^2} - \frac{\tan(x^3 - 1)(e^x)}{(e^2 + e^x)^2}$

$y' = \boldsymbol{\frac{3x^2 \sec^2(x^3 - 1)}{e^2 + e^x} - \frac{e^x \tan(x^3 - 1)}{(e^2 + e^x)^2}}$

21. $y = e^{2x}\sec(\pi x)$

$y' = e^{2x}\sec(\pi x)\tan(\pi x)(\pi) + \sec(\pi x)(2e^{2x})$

$y' = \boldsymbol{e^{2x}\sec(\pi x)[\pi\tan(\pi x) + 2]}$

22. $y = \frac{x}{x^2 + 1}$

$\frac{dy}{dx} = \frac{(x^2 + 1) - x(2x)}{(x^2 + 1)^2}$

$\frac{dy}{dx} = \frac{-x^2 + 1}{(x^2 + 1)^2}$

$\left.\frac{dy}{dx}\right|_1 = \frac{0}{4} = 0$

$y - \frac{1}{2} = 0(x - 1)$

$\boldsymbol{y = \frac{1}{2}}$

23. The simple example $y = x^2 + 1$ can be used to exclude choices A, B, and D. Polynomial functions are continuous for all x, so the correct choice is **C.**

24. $\int_0^a \sqrt{a^2 - x^2}\, dx$ represents the first quadrant area of an origin-centered circle with a radius of a.

$\int_0^a \frac{b}{a}\sqrt{a^2 - x^2}\, dx = \frac{b}{a}\int_0^a \sqrt{a^2 - x^2}\, dx$

$= \frac{b}{a}\left(\frac{a^2\pi}{4}\right) = \boldsymbol{\frac{ab\pi}{4}}$

25. $\tan\theta = \frac{x}{10}$

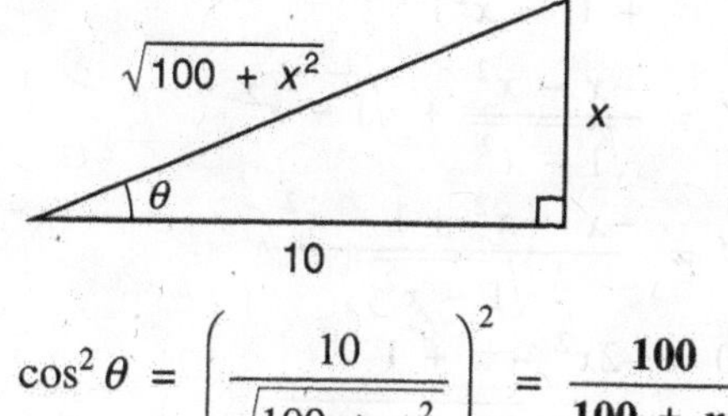

$\cos^2\theta = \left(\frac{10}{\sqrt{100 + x^2}}\right)^2 = \boldsymbol{\frac{100}{100 + x^2}}$

PROBLEM SET 67

1.

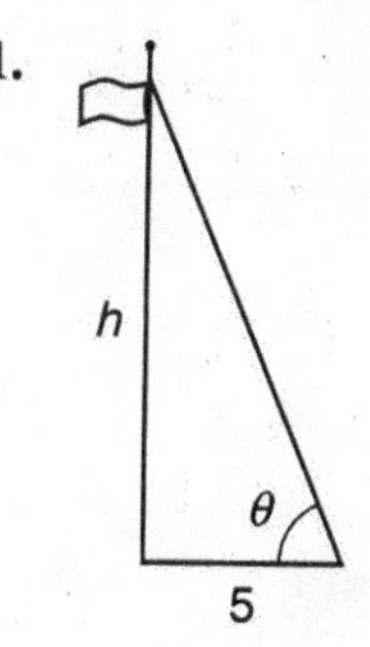

$\tan\theta = \frac{h}{5}$

$h = 5\tan\theta$

$\frac{dh}{dt} = 5\sec^2\theta\,\frac{d\theta}{dt}$

$(1) = 5\left(\frac{13}{5}\right)^2\frac{d\theta}{dt}$

$1 = \frac{169}{5}\frac{d\theta}{dt}$

$\frac{d\theta}{dt} = \boldsymbol{\frac{5}{169}\,\frac{\text{rad}}{\text{s}}}$

2. $a(t) = -9.8$

$\boldsymbol{v(t) = -9.8t - 20}$

$\boldsymbol{h(t) = -4.9t^2 - 20t + 160}$

$0 = -4.9t^2 - 20t + 160$

$t = \frac{20 - \sqrt{400 - 4(-4.9)(160)}}{-9.8}$

$t \approx \mathbf{4.0270\ s}$

3. (a) $A = \frac{(b_1 + b_2)h}{2}$

$= \frac{(2 + 2x)y}{2}$

$= \boldsymbol{(1 + x)\sqrt{1 - x^2}}$

(b) $A' = (1 + x)\left(\frac{1}{2}\right)(1 - x^2)^{-1/2}(-2x)$

$+ (1 - x^2)^{1/2}$

$A' = \dfrac{-x - x^2}{\sqrt{1 - x^2}} + \sqrt{1 - x^2}$

$A' = \dfrac{-x - x^2 + 1 - x^2}{\sqrt{1 - x^2}}$

$0 = -2x^2 - x + 1$

$x = \dfrac{1 \pm \sqrt{1 - 4(-2)(1)}}{-4}$

$x = \dfrac{1}{2}$

$A_{max} = \dfrac{3\sqrt{3}}{4}$ **units²**

4. $f(x) = \frac{2}{3}x^3 - \frac{1}{2}x^2 - 10x - 1$

$f'(x) = 2x^2 - x - 10$

$0 = (2x - 5)(x + 2)$

$x = \frac{5}{2}, -2$

Critical numbers: $x = -3, -2, \frac{5}{2}, 5$

$f(-3) = 6\frac{1}{2}$; $f(-2) = 11\frac{2}{3}$

$f\left(\frac{5}{2}\right) = -18\frac{17}{24}$; $f(5) = 19\frac{5}{6}$

Maximum: $19\frac{5}{6}$ **Minimum: $-18\frac{17}{24}$**

5. $\mathbf{A = 2\int_0^2 (4 - y^2)\,dy}$

6. $4 - y^2 = 3y$

$y^2 + 3y - 4 = 0$

$(y + 4)(y - 1) = 0$

$y = -4, 1$

$A = \int_{-4}^{1} [(4 - y^2) - 3y]\,dy$

$= \left[-\frac{1}{3}y^3 - \frac{3}{2}y^2 + 4y\right]_{-4}^{1}$

$= -\frac{1}{3} - \frac{3}{2} + 4 - \left(\frac{64}{3} - 24 - 16\right)$

$= 44 - \frac{65}{3} - \frac{3}{2} = \mathbf{\frac{125}{6}}$ **units²**

7.

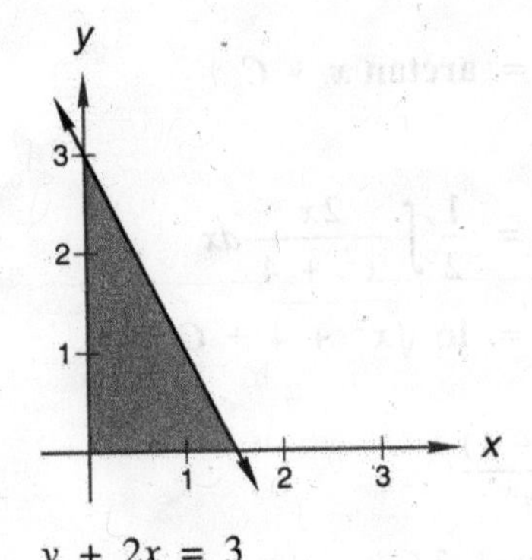

$y + 2x = 3$

$2x = -y + 3$

$x = -\frac{1}{2}y + \frac{3}{2}$

$\mathbf{A = \int_0^3 \left(-\frac{1}{2}y + \frac{3}{2}\right) dy}$

8. $u = 2x - 1$ $du = 2\,dx$

$\int_1^5 2x(2x - 1)^{1/2}\,dx$

$= \int_1^9 \frac{1}{2}(u + 1)u^{1/2}\,du$

$= \int_1^9 \left(\frac{1}{2}u^{3/2} + \frac{1}{2}u^{1/2}\right) du$

$= \left[\frac{1}{5}u^{5/2} + \frac{1}{3}u^{3/2}\right]_1^9$

$= \frac{243}{5} + 9 - \left(\frac{1}{5} + \frac{1}{3}\right) = \mathbf{\frac{856}{15}}$

9. `fnInt(2X√(2X-1),X,1,5)` ≈ **57.0667**

They are the same.

10. (a)

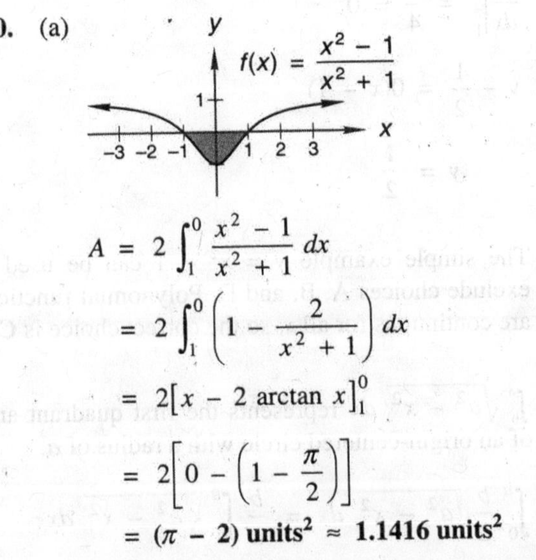

$A = 2\int_1^0 \frac{x^2 - 1}{x^2 + 1}\,dx$

$= 2\int_1^0 \left(1 - \frac{2}{x^2 + 1}\right) dx$

$= 2[x - 2\arctan x]_1^0$

$= 2\left[0 - \left(1 - \frac{\pi}{2}\right)\right]$

$= \mathbf{(\pi - 2)}$ **units²** ≈ **1.1416 units²**

(b) `fnInt((X²-1)/(X²+1),X,1,-1)`

≈ **1.1416**

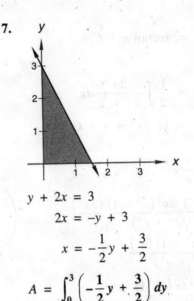

11. $u = \dfrac{\pi x^2}{2} \qquad du = \pi x\,dx$

$$\int_0^1 x \sin \frac{\pi x^2}{2}\,dx = \int_0^{\pi/2} \frac{1}{\pi} \sin u\,du$$

The correct choice is **B.**

12. $f(x) = \arcsin \dfrac{x}{2}$

$$f'(x) = \frac{1}{\sqrt{4 - x^2}}$$

$$f'(1) = \frac{1}{\sqrt{3}} = \frac{\sqrt{3}}{3}$$

13. $y = \arctan x$

$$\frac{dy}{dx} = \frac{1}{x^2 + 1}$$

$$\left.\frac{dy}{dx}\right|_{\sqrt{3}/2} = \frac{1}{\frac{3}{4} + 1} = \mathbf{\frac{4}{7}}$$

14. $d = \displaystyle\int_{\sqrt{10}}^{\sqrt{26}} t(t^2 - 1)^{1/2}\,dt$

$$= \frac{1}{2}\int_{\sqrt{10}}^{\sqrt{26}} 2t(t^2 - 1)^{1/2}\,dt$$

$$= \frac{1}{3}\left[(t^2 - 1)^{3/2}\right]_{\sqrt{10}}^{\sqrt{26}}$$

$$= \frac{1}{3}(125 - 27) = \mathbf{\frac{98}{3}\ units}$$

15. $\displaystyle\int \sin^3 x \cos x\,dx = \mathbf{\frac{1}{4}\sin^4 x + C}$

16. $\displaystyle\int \cos x\,(\sin x)^{-2}\,dx = -(\sin x)^{-1} + C$

$$= \mathbf{-\csc x + C}$$

17. $\displaystyle\int \frac{3}{\sqrt{9 - x^2}}\,dx = \mathbf{3 \arcsin \frac{x}{3} + C}$

18. $\displaystyle\int 3x(9 - x^2)^{-1/2}\,dx$

$$= 3\left(-\frac{1}{2}\right)\int -2x(9 - x^2)^{-1/2}\,dx$$

$$= \mathbf{-3\sqrt{9 - x^2} + C}$$

19.

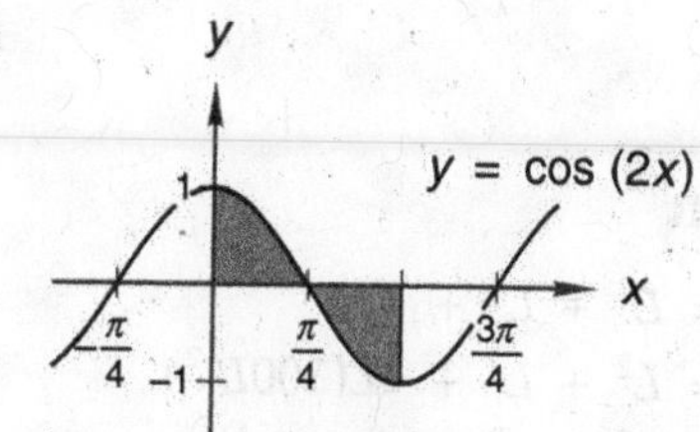

$$A = 2\int_0^{\pi/4} \cos(2x)\,dx = \int_0^{\pi/4} 2\cos(2x)\,dx$$

$$= \sin(2x)\Big]_0^{\pi/4}$$

$$= \mathbf{1\ unit^2}$$

20. If $f(x)$ is greater than or equal to zero on the interval $[2, 4]$, then $\int_2^4 f(x)\,dx$ must be greater than or equal to zero. Thus $\int_4^2 f(x)\,dx$ would have to be less than or equal to zero.

The correct choice is **B.** Choices A, C, and D cannot be validated with the given information.

21. $f(x) = Ce^{kx}$

$$f'(x) = Cke^{kx}$$

$$f(0) = \mathbf{4} = C$$

$$f'(0) = 2 = Ck$$

$$2 = 4k$$

$$k = \mathbf{\frac{1}{2}}$$

22. $y = \dfrac{e^{-x} + e^{\cos x}}{2x^{1/2} + 1}$

$$y' = \frac{(2x^{1/2} + 1)(-e^{-x} - \sin x\, e^{\cos x})}{(2x^{1/2} + 1)^2} - \frac{(e^{-x} + e^{\cos x})(x^{-1/2})}{(2x^{1/2} + 1)^2}$$

$$y' = \mathbf{\frac{-e^{-x} - \sin x\, e^{\cos x}}{2\sqrt{x} + 1} - \frac{e^{-x} + e^{\cos x}}{\sqrt{x}(2\sqrt{x} + 1)^2}}$$

23. $f'(2) = \displaystyle\lim_{h\to 0} \frac{f(2 + h) - f(2)}{h}$

$$f(x) = \sin x$$

$$f'(x) = \cos x$$

$$f'(2) = \mathbf{\cos 2}$$

24. $V = L^2h$

$300 = L^2h$

$\mathbf{h = 300L^{-2}}$ **ft**

$$\text{Surface Area} = L^2 + L^2 + 4Lh = L^2 + L^2 + 4L(300L^{-2}) = L^2 + L^2 + 1200L^{-1}$$

$$\text{Cost} = 8L^2 + 4L^2 + 15(1200L^{-1})$$

$$\textbf{Cost} = \mathbf{(12L^2 + 18{,}000L^{-1})} \textbf{ dollars}$$

25. $f(x) = x^3 - x^2 - 4x + 4$

$b = a^3 - a^2 - 4a + 4$

$f'(x) = 3x^2 - 2x - 4$

$f'(a) = 3a^2 - 2a - 4$

Slope of line through the 2 points is $3a^2 - 2a - 4$

Slope of tangent is $\dfrac{b - (-8)}{a - 0} = \dfrac{b + 8}{a}$

$$3a^2 - 2a - 4 = \frac{b + 8}{a}$$

$$3a^3 - 2a^2 - 4a = b + 8$$

$$b = 3a^3 - 2a^2 - 4a - 8$$

$$a^3 - a^2 - 4a + 4 = 3a^3 - 2a^2 - 4a - 8$$

$$2a^3 - a^2 - 12 = 0$$

$$a = 2$$

$\mathbf{a = 2, b = 0}$

PROBLEM SET 68

1. (a) $V = x^2y = 300$

$$y = 300x^{-2}$$

$$A = x^2 + x^2 + 4xy = x^2 + x^2 + 4x(300x^{-2}) = x^2 + x^2 + 1200x^{-1}$$

$$\text{Cost} = 8x^2 + 4x^2 + 15(1200x^{-1})$$

$$\textbf{Cost} = \mathbf{(12x^2 + 18{,}000x^{-1})} \textbf{ dollars}$$

(b) $C' = 24x - 18{,}000x^{-2}$

$$\frac{18{,}000}{x^2} = 24x$$

$$24x^3 = 18{,}000$$

$$x^3 = 750$$

$$x = \sqrt[3]{750} = 5\sqrt[3]{6}$$

$$y = \frac{300}{(5\sqrt[3]{6})^2}$$

$$y = \frac{300}{25 \cdot 6^{2/3}} = \frac{12 \cdot 6^{1/3}}{6} = 2\sqrt[3]{6}$$

Dimensions: $\mathbf{5\sqrt[3]{6}\,m \times 5\sqrt[3]{6}\,m \times 2\sqrt[3]{6}\,m}$

(c) From (b) $x = 5\sqrt[3]{6} \approx 9.0856$

and $y = 2\sqrt[3]{6} \approx 3.6342.$

Let `Y1=12X²+18000/X` and adjust the window settings as follows:

`Xmin=-2, Xmax=20, Ymin=-3000, Ymax=10000, Yscl=1000`

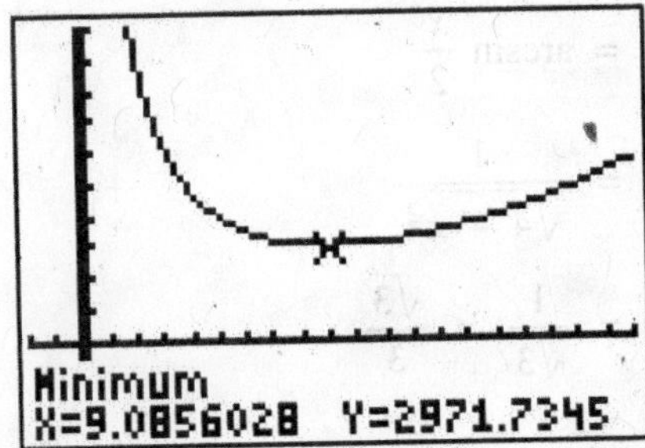

$x \approx \mathbf{9.0856}$

$$y = 300x^{-2} \approx \frac{300}{(9.0856)^2} \approx \mathbf{3.6342}$$

2. $a(t) = -32$

$v(t) = -32t$

$\mathbf{h(t) = -16t^2 + 400}$

3. $f(x) = x^6 - x^2 + 5$

$f(-x) = (-x)^6 - (-x)^2 + 5$

$f(-x) = x^6 - x^2 + 5$

$f(-x) = f(x)$ **Even**

4. $g(x) = x^3 - 2x$

$g(-x) = (-x)^3 - 2(-x)$

$g(-x) = -x^3 + 2x$

$g(-x) = -g(x)$ **Odd**

5. $h(x) = e^x$

$h(-x) = e^{-x}$

$h(-x) \neq h(x),\ h(-x) \neq -h(x)$ **Neither**

6. $F(x) = e^{-\pi x^2}$

$F(-x) = e^{-\pi(-x)^2}$

$F(-x) = e^{-\pi x^2}$

$F(-x) = F(x)$ **Even**

7. $G(x) = \dfrac{x + \sin x}{\cos x}$

$$G(-x) = \frac{-x + \sin(-x)}{\cos(-x)}$$

$$G(-x) = \frac{-x - \sin x}{\cos x}$$

$G(-x) = -G(x)$ **Odd**

8. $H(x) = x^2 + \cos x$
$H(-x) = (-x)^2 + \cos(-x)$
$H(-x) = x^2 + \cos x$
$H(-x) = H(x)$ **Even**

9. $u = \cos x \qquad du = -\sin x\, dx$

$$\int_0^{\pi} (\sin x)e^{\cos x}\, dx = \int_1^{-1} -e^u\, du = \int_{-1}^{1} e^u\, du$$

The correct choice is **C.**

10.

n	$f^{(n)}(x)$	$f^{(n)}(0)$
0	$\frac{1}{2} - \frac{1}{2}\cos(2x)$	0
1	$\sin(2x)$	0
2	$2\cos(2x)$	2
3	$-4\sin(2x)$	0
4	$-8\cos(2x)$	-8
5	$16\sin(2x)$	0
6	$32\cos(2x)$	32
⋮	⋮	⋮

$$\sin^2 x = \frac{2x^2}{2!} - \frac{8x^4}{4!} + \frac{32x^6}{6!} - \frac{128x^8}{8!} + \cdots$$

$$\sin^2 x = \boldsymbol{\frac{2^1x^2}{2!} - \frac{2^3x^4}{4!} + \frac{2^5x^6}{6!} - \frac{2^7x^8}{8!} + \cdots}$$

11. $$\frac{d}{dx}\left[\frac{2(x+1)^{1/2}}{x^2 + \sin^3(2x)}\right]$$

$$= \frac{[x^2 + \sin^3(2x)](x+1)^{-1/2}}{[x^2 + \sin^3(2x)]^2} - \frac{2(x+1)^{1/2}[2x + 3\sin^2(2x)\, 2\cos(2x)]}{[x^2 + \sin^3(2x)]^2}$$

$$= \boldsymbol{\frac{1}{\sqrt{x+1}[x^2 + \sin^3(2x)]} - \frac{4\sqrt{x+1}[x + 3\sin^2(2x)\cos(2x)]}{[x^2 + \sin^3(2x)]^2}}$$

12. $$\frac{d}{dx}\left[\arcsin(3x) - \frac{1}{4}\sin^4(3x)\right]$$

$$= \frac{3}{\sqrt{1-9x^2}} - 3\sin^3(3x)\cos(3x)$$

$$= \boldsymbol{3\left[\frac{1}{\sqrt{1-9x^2}} - \sin^3(3x)\cos(3x)\right]}$$

13. $$\int \cos(3x)\sin^3(3x)\, dx = \frac{1}{3}\int 3\cos(3x)\sin^3(3x)\, dx$$

$$= \boldsymbol{\frac{1}{12}\sin^4(3x) + C}$$

14. $$\int x(x^3+1)\, dx = \int (x^4 + x)\, dx$$

$$= \boldsymbol{\frac{1}{5}x^5 + \frac{1}{2}x^2 + C}$$

15. $$\int \frac{6}{4 + 9x^2}\, dx = \int \frac{2(3)}{2^2 + (3x)^2}$$

$$= \boldsymbol{\arctan\frac{3x}{2} + C}$$

16. $$1 - y = -1 + y^2$$
$$y^2 + y - 2 = 0$$
$$(y+2)(y-1) = 0$$
$$y = -2, 1$$

$$A = \int_{-2}^{1} [(1-y) - (-1+y^2)]\, dy$$
$$= \int_{-2}^{1} (-y^2 - y + 2)\, dy$$
$$= \left[-\frac{1}{3}y^3 - \frac{1}{2}y^2 + 2y\right]_{-2}^{1}$$
$$= -\frac{1}{3} - \frac{1}{2} + 2 - \left(\frac{8}{3} - 2 - 4\right)$$
$$= \boldsymbol{\frac{9}{2}\ \textbf{units}^2}$$

17. (a) $\int_a^b f(x)\, dx + \int_1^3 f(x)\, dx = \int_0^3 f(x)\, dx$

$\boldsymbol{a = 0,\ b = 1}$

(b) $\boldsymbol{a = 0,\ b = 2}$

18. $f(x) = x^3 - 7x^2 + 10x$
$f'(x) = 3x^2 - 14x + 10$
$0 = 3x^2 - 14x + 10$
$$x = \frac{14 \pm \sqrt{196 - 4(3)(10)}}{6}$$
$$x = \frac{7 \pm \sqrt{19}}{3}$$

Critical numbers: $x = 0, \frac{7 \pm \sqrt{19}}{3}, 5$

$f(0) = 0 \qquad f\left(\frac{7 - \sqrt{19}}{3}\right) \approx 4.0607$

$f\left(\frac{7 + \sqrt{19}}{3}\right) \approx -8.2088 \qquad f(5) = 0$

Maximum: 4.0607 **Minimum: –8.2088**

19. 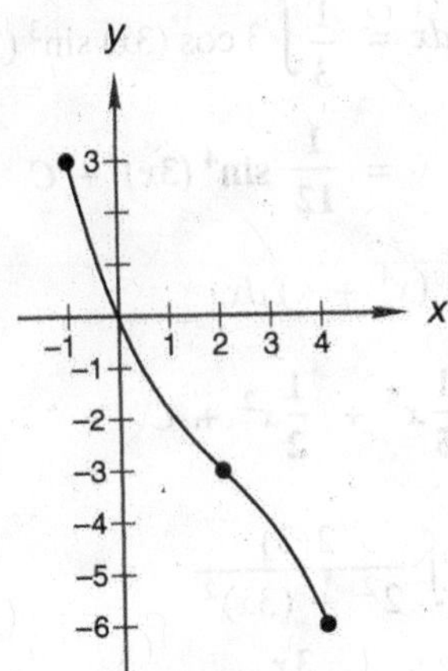

Maximum: 3
Minimum: −6

20. $f(t) = Ae^t + B$
$f'(t) = Ae^t$
$f'(0) = \mathbf{10} = \mathbf{A}$
$f(0) = 5 = A + B$
$\mathbf{B = 5}$

21. $\mathbf{A = \int_1^4 [f(x) - g(x)]\,dx}$

22. With $y = x^3 + x$, $y = 2$ when $x = 1$. Since a function and its inverse are one-to-one, $\mathbf{f^{-1}(2) = 1.}$

23. (a) $A = WL = 200$
$L = 200W^{-1}$
$200 = WL$
$$0 = W\frac{dL}{dt} + L\frac{dW}{dt}$$
$$\mathbf{0 = W\frac{dL}{dt} + 200W^{-1}\frac{dW}{dt}}$$
(b) $$0 = (10)(15) + \frac{200}{(10)}\frac{dW}{dt}$$
$$-150 = 20\frac{dW}{dt}$$
$$\frac{dW}{dt} = \mathbf{-\frac{15}{2}\frac{\text{units}}{\text{s}}}$$

24. $y = 2^x$
$\ln y = x\ln 2$
$\mathbf{y = e^{x\ln 2}}$ or $\mathbf{y = e^{\ln 2^x}}$

25. $y_1 = \ln x \qquad y_2 = 2x^2$
$y_1' = \frac{1}{x} \qquad y_2' = 4x$
$\frac{1}{x} = 4x$
$4x^2 = 1$
$x = \frac{1}{2}$

PROBLEM SET 69

1. (a) $A = LW = 1000$
$W = 1000L^{-1}$
$1000 = LW$
$$0 = L\frac{dW}{dt} + W\frac{dL}{dt}$$
$$\mathbf{0 = L\frac{dW}{dt} + 1000L^{-1}\frac{dL}{dt}}$$
(b) $0 = L(-1) + 1000L^{-1}(10)$
$L = 10{,}000L^{-1}$
$L^2 = 10{,}000$
$L = \mathbf{100\ m}$

2. $B_t = B_0e^{kt}$
$1100 = 1000e^{k(1)}$
$1.1 = e^k$
$k = \ln 1.1$
$B_{10} = 1000e^{(\ln 1.1)10}$
$= 1000e^{\ln(1.1)^{10}}$
$= 1000(1.1)^{10}$
$= \mathbf{\$2593.74}$

3. $u = x \quad du = dx \quad v = e^x \quad dv = e^x\,dx$
$$\int xe^x\,dx = xe^x - \int e^x\,dx$$
$$= xe^x - e^x + C$$
$$= \mathbf{e^x(x - 1) + C}$$

4. $u = \ln x \quad du = \frac{1}{x}\,dx \quad v = x \quad dv = dx$
$$\int \ln x\,dx = x\ln x - \int dx$$
$$= x\ln x - x + C$$
$$= \mathbf{x(\ln x - 1) + C}$$

5. $u = \ln x \quad du = \frac{1}{x}\,dx \quad v = \frac{1}{2}x^2 \quad dv = x\,dx$
$$\int x\ln x\,dx = \frac{1}{2}x^2\ln x - \int\frac{1}{2}x\,dx$$
$$= \frac{1}{2}x^2\ln x - \frac{1}{4}x^2 + C$$
$$= \frac{1}{4}x^2(2\ln x - 1) + C$$
$$= \mathbf{\frac{1}{4}x^2(\ln x^2 - 1) + C}$$

6. $u = 2x \quad du = 2\,dx \quad v = \sin x \quad dv = \cos x\,dx$

$$\int 2x \cos x\,dx = 2x \sin x - \int 2 \sin x\,dx$$

$$= 2x \sin x + 2 \cos x + C$$

$$= \mathbf{2(x \sin x + \cos x) + C}$$

7. $u = x \quad du = dx \quad v = -\cos x \quad dv = \sin x\,dx$

$$\int x \sin x\,dx = -x \cos x + \int \cos x\,dx$$

$$= \mathbf{-x \cos x + \sin x + C}$$

8. $f(x) = \dfrac{\sin x \cos x}{x^2}$

$$f(-x) = \frac{\sin(-x) \cos(-x)}{(-x)^2}$$

$$f(-x) = \frac{-\sin x \cos x}{x^2}$$

$f(-x) = -f(x)$ **Odd**

9. $f(x) = x^2 + \cos x$

$$f(-x) = (-x)^2 + \cos(-x)$$

$$f(-x) = x^2 + \cos x$$

$f(-x) = f(x)$ **y-axis symmetry**

10. $\dfrac{d}{dx}\left(\dfrac{xe^{\cos(3x)}}{x^3 + 1}\right)$

$$= \frac{(x^3 + 1)[-3xe^{\cos(3x)} \sin(3x) + e^{\cos(3x)}]}{(x^3 + 1)^2} - \frac{xe^{\cos(3x)}(3x^2)}{(x^3 + 1)^2}$$

$$= \mathbf{\frac{e^{\cos(3x)}[-3x \sin(3x) + 1]}{x^3 + 1} - \frac{3x^3 e^{\cos(3x)}}{(x^3 + 1)^2}}$$

11. $y = \arcsin x^2$

$$y' = \mathbf{\frac{2x}{\sqrt{1 - x^4}}}$$

12. $\displaystyle\int \cos x (\sin x + 1)^{-1/2}\,dx + \int x^{-5}\,dx$

$$+ \frac{1}{2} \int \frac{2x}{\sqrt{1 - (x^2)^2}}\,dx$$

$$= \mathbf{2\sqrt{\sin x + 1} - \frac{1}{4}x^{-4} + \frac{1}{2} \arcsin x^2 + C}$$

13. $u = \sin(2x) \qquad du = 2 \cos(2x)\,dx$

$$\int_0^{\pi/4} [\cos(2x)][e^{\sin(2x)}]\,dx$$

$$= \int_0^1 \frac{1}{2} e^u\,du$$

$$= \frac{1}{2}\left[e^u\right]_0^1$$

$$= \mathbf{\frac{1}{2}(e - 1) \approx 0.8591}$$

14. `fnInt(cos(2X)e^(sin(2X)),X,0,π/4)` $\approx$ **0.8591**

They are the same.

15.

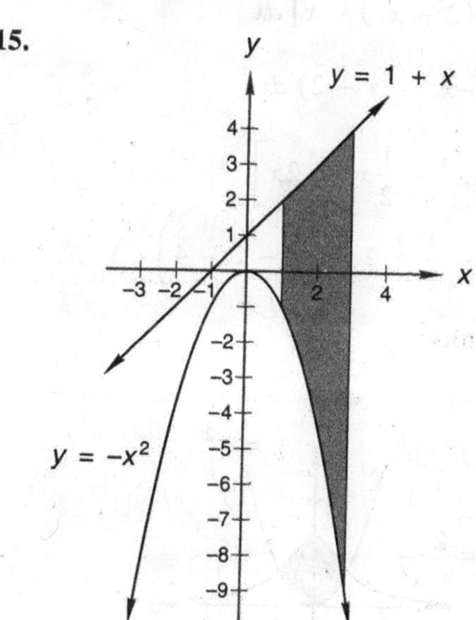

$$A = \int_1^3 [(1 + x) - (-x^2)]\,dx$$

$$= \int_1^3 (x^2 + x + 1)\,dx$$

$$= \left[\frac{1}{3}x^3 + \frac{1}{2}x^2 + x\right]_1^3$$

$$= 9 + \frac{9}{2} + 3 - \left(\frac{1}{3} + \frac{1}{2} + 1\right)$$

$$= \mathbf{\frac{44}{3}\ \text{units}^2}$$

16.

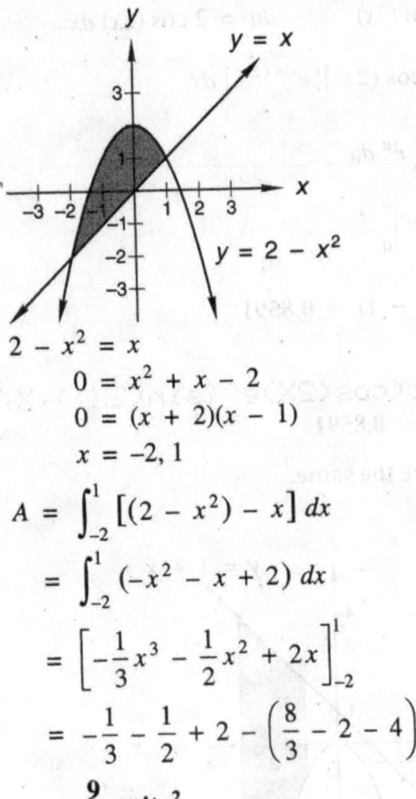

$$2 - x^2 = x$$
$$0 = x^2 + x - 2$$
$$0 = (x + 2)(x - 1)$$
$$x = -2, 1$$

$$A = \int_{-2}^{1} [(2 - x^2) - x]\,dx$$
$$= \int_{-2}^{1} (-x^2 - x + 2)\,dx$$
$$= \left[-\frac{1}{3}x^3 - \frac{1}{2}x^2 + 2x\right]_{-2}^{1}$$
$$= -\frac{1}{3} - \frac{1}{2} + 2 - \left(\frac{8}{3} - 2 - 4\right)$$
$$= \mathbf{\frac{9}{2}\ units^2}$$

17. (a)

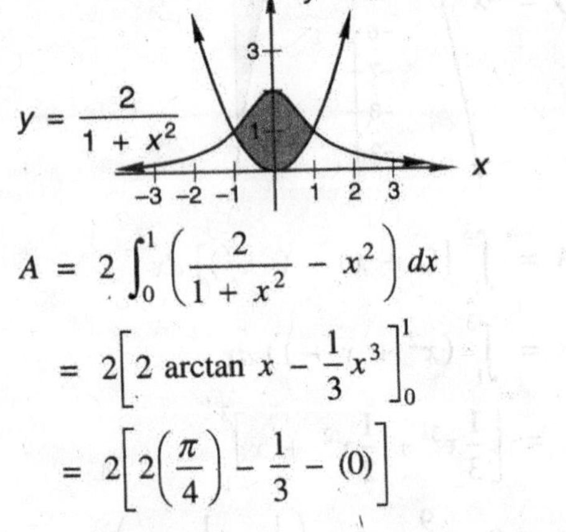

$$A = 2\int_0^1 \left(\frac{2}{1 + x^2} - x^2\right) dx$$
$$= 2\left[2 \arctan x - \frac{1}{3}x^3\right]_0^1$$
$$= 2\left[2\left(\frac{\pi}{4}\right) - \frac{1}{3} - (0)\right]$$
$$= \left(\pi - \frac{2}{3}\right) \mathbf{units^2} \approx \mathbf{2.4749\ units^2}$$

(b)
```
fnInt(2/(1+X²)-X²,X,-1,1)
```
$\approx$ **2.4749 units²**

18.

$$A = \int_{-2}^{0} y(y - 1)(y + 2)\,dy$$

19.

n	$f^{(n)}(x)$	$f^{(n)}(0)$
0	$\frac{1}{2} + \frac{1}{2}\cos(2x)$	1
1	$-\sin(2x)$	0
2	$-2\cos(2x)$	-2
3	$4\sin(2x)$	0
4	$8\cos(2x)$	8
5	$-16\sin(2x)$	0
6	$-32\cos(2x)$	-32
⋮	⋮	⋮

$$\cos^2 x = 1 - \frac{2x^2}{2!} + \frac{8x^4}{4!} - \frac{32x^6}{6!} + \cdots$$
$$\cos^2 x = \mathbf{1 - x^2 + \frac{2^3x^4}{4!} - \frac{2^5x^6}{6!} + \cdots}$$

20.
$$y = 4x - 12$$
$$3 = 4x - 12$$
$$x = \frac{15}{4}$$

Since f and f^{-1} are one-to-one,

$$f^{-1}(3) = \mathbf{\frac{15}{4}}$$

21. (a)

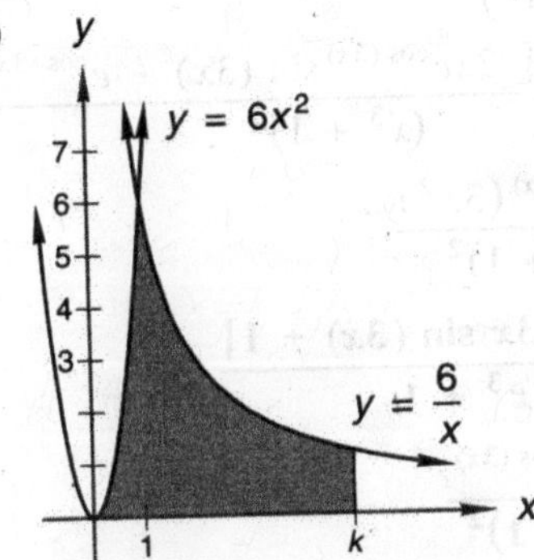

$$A = \int_0^1 6x^2\,dx + \int_1^k \frac{6}{x}\,dx$$
$$= [2x^3]_0^1 + [6 \ln x]_1^k$$
$$= 2 - 0 + 6 \ln k - 0$$
$$= \mathbf{(2 + 6 \ln k)\ units^2}$$

(b)
$$2 + 6 \ln k = 20$$
$$6 \ln k = 18$$
$$\ln k = 3$$
$$k = e^3$$

(c) $A = 2 + 6 \ln k$

$$\frac{dA}{dt} = \frac{6}{k}\frac{dk}{dt}$$

$$(8) = \frac{6}{(27)}\frac{dk}{dt}$$

$$\frac{dk}{dt} = \mathbf{36\ \frac{units}{s}}$$

22. (a) $\int_{-1}^{3} f(x)\,dx + \int_{3}^{5} f(x)\,dx = \int_{-1}^{5} f(x)\,dx$

$$\int_{3}^{5} f(x)\,dx = 7 - (-3)$$

$$\int_{3}^{5} f(x)\,dx = \mathbf{10}$$

(b) $\int_{5}^{-1} f(x)\,dx - \int_{5}^{3} f(x)\,dx$

$= -7 + 10 = \mathbf{3}$

23. If $f(x) = \ln(\cos x)$, then $\cos x > 0$.

$\cos x > 0$ when $-\frac{\pi}{2} < x < \frac{\pi}{2}$.

The correct choice is **A**.

24. Having the point $(-x, -y)$ on the same curve as the point (x, y) means the curve is odd, or has origin symmetry. This is true for any origin centered circle.

The correct choice is **B**.

25. (a) $f(x) = \ln(x^2 - 9)$

$f(-x) = \ln[(-x)^2 - 9]$

$f(-x) = \ln(x^2 - 9)$

$f(-x) = f(x)$ **y-axis symmetry**

(b) $x^2 - 9 > 0$

$x^2 > 9$

$|x| > 3$

$\{\mathbf{x \in \mathbb{R} \mid |x| > 3}\}$

(c) $\ln(x^2 - 9) = 0$

$x^2 - 9 = 1$

$x^2 = 10$

$x = \mathbf{\pm\sqrt{10}}$

(d) $y = \ln(x^2 - 9)$

$x = \ln(y^2 - 9)$

$e^x = y^2 - 9$

$y^2 = e^x + 9$

$y = \sqrt{e^x + 9}$

$\mathbf{f^{-1}(x) = \sqrt{e^x + 9}}$

PROBLEM SET 70

1. (a)

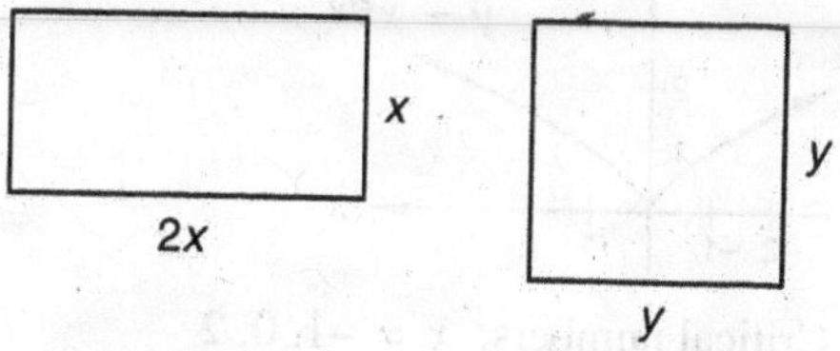

$2x(x) \ge 800$ $\qquad$ $y^2 \ge 100$

$x^2 \ge 400$ $\qquad$ $y \ge 10$ m

$\mathbf{x \ge 20}$ **m**

$6x + 4y = 340$

$3x + 2y = 170$

$y = -\frac{3}{2}x + 85$

$-\frac{3}{2}x + 85 \ge 10$

$-\frac{3}{2}x \ge -75$

$\mathbf{x \le 50}$ **m**

(b) $A = 2x^2 + y^2$

$A = 2x^2 + \left(-\frac{3}{2}x + 85\right)^2$

$A = 2x^2 + \frac{9}{4}x^2 - 255x + 7225$

$\mathbf{A = \frac{17}{4}x^2 - 255x + 7225}$

(c) $A' = \frac{17}{2}x - 255$

$\frac{17}{2}x = 255$

$x = 30$

Critical numbers: $x = 20, 30, 50$

$A(20) = 3825$

$A(30) = 3400$

$A(50) = 5100$

$\mathbf{A_{max} = 5100\ m^2}$

2. (a) $a(t) = -9.8$

$v(t) = -9.8t + 10$

$\mathbf{h(t) = -4.9t^2 + 10t + 100}$

$\mathbf{h(3) = 85.9}$ **m**

(b) $0 = -4.9t^2 + 10t + 100$

$$t = \frac{-10 \pm \sqrt{100 - 4(-4.9)(100)}}{-9.8}$$

$t \approx \mathbf{5.6512\ s}$

3. 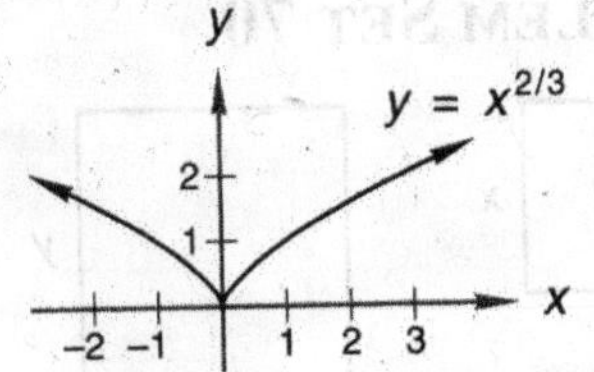

Critical numbers: $x = -1, 0, 2$

$y(-1) = 1 \qquad y(0) = 0$

$y(2) = \sqrt[3]{4} \approx 1.5874$

Maximum: $\sqrt[3]{4}$ Minimum: 0

4. $f(x) = ax^2 + bx + C$

$f(0) = 2 = C$

$f'(x) = 2ax + b$

$$\begin{aligned} 5 &= 2a + b \\ +\ (-1 &= -2a + b) \\ \hline 4 &= 2b \end{aligned}$$

$b = 2,\ a = \dfrac{3}{2}$

$\mathbf{f(x) = \dfrac{3}{2}x^2 + 2x + 2}$

5. $\lim_{x\to 0} \sin \dfrac{1}{x}$ **does not exist**

6. $\lim_{x\to 0^+} \dfrac{|x|}{x} = \mathbf{1}$ because when $x > 0$, $\dfrac{|x|}{x} = 1$

7. $\lim_{x\to 0^+} \frac{1}{x} = +\infty \qquad \lim_{x\to 0^-} \frac{1}{x} = -\infty$

$\lim_{x\to 0} \frac{1}{x}$ **does not exist**

8. $\lim_{x\to 0} \dfrac{1}{x^2} = \infty$

9. $\lim_{x\to 2} f(x)g(x) = 3(-2) = \mathbf{-6}$

10. $\lim_{x\to 1} 2[f(x)]^2 = 2(\pi)^2 = \mathbf{2\pi^2}$

11. $\lim_{x\to 2} \dfrac{f(x) + g(x)}{f(x)g(x)} = \dfrac{3 + (-2)}{3(-2)} = \mathbf{-\dfrac{1}{6}}$

12. $\lim_{x\to 0} (-x^2 + 1) = \lim_{x\to 0} (x^2 + 1) = 1$

$\lim_{x\to 0} f(x) = \mathbf{1}$

13. **Not necessarily.** If g is a continuous function this would be true, but g could have a removable discontinuity (a hole) at $x = 2$.

14. $u = 3x \quad du = 3\,dx \quad v = -\cos x \quad dv = \sin x\,dx$

$$\begin{aligned} \int 3x \sin x\,dx &= -3x \cos x + \int 3 \cos x\,dx \\ &= -3x \cos x + 3 \sin x + C \\ &= \mathbf{-3(x \cos x - \sin x) + C} \end{aligned}$$

15. $u = 2x \quad du = 2\,dx \quad v = \dfrac{1}{2}e^{2x} \quad dv = e^{2x}\,dx$

$$\begin{aligned} \int 2xe^{2x}\,dx &= xe^{2x} - \int e^{2x}\,dx \\ &= xe^{2x} - \frac{1}{2}e^{2x} + C \\ &= \mathbf{e^{2x}\left(x - \frac{1}{2}\right) + C} \end{aligned}$$

16. $u = \ln x \quad du = \dfrac{1}{x}\,dx \quad v = x \quad dv = dx$

$$\begin{aligned} \int \ln x\,dx &= x \ln x - \int dx \\ &= x \ln x - x + C \\ &= \mathbf{x(\ln x - 1) + C} \end{aligned}$$

17. $$\begin{aligned} \int \frac{e^x}{9 + e^{2x}}\,dx &= \frac{1}{3}\int \frac{3e^x}{3^2 + (e^x)^2}\,dx \\ &= \mathbf{\frac{1}{3} \arctan \frac{e^x}{3} + C} \end{aligned}$$

18. Only in A is it true that $f(-x) = f(x)$

$$e^{(-x)^2} = e^{x^2}$$

So choice **A** is an even function and, thus, has y-axis symmetry.

19. 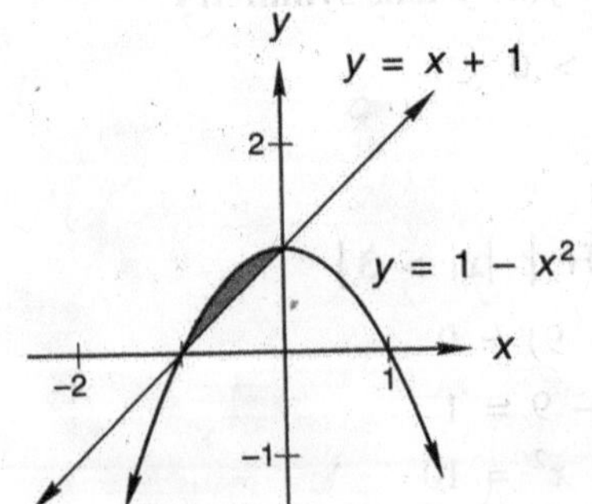

$$\begin{aligned} A &= \int_{-1}^{0} [(1 - x^2) - (x + 1)]\,dx \\ &= \int_{-1}^{0} (-x^2 - x)\,dx \\ &= \left[-\frac{1}{3}x^3 - \frac{1}{2}x^2\right]_{-1}^{0} \\ &= 0 - \left(\frac{1}{3} - \frac{1}{2}\right) = \mathbf{\frac{1}{6}\ unit^2} \end{aligned}$$

20. (a) $y = \arctan x$

$$y' = \frac{1}{1 + x^2}$$

$$y - \frac{\pi}{4} = \frac{1}{2}(x - 1)$$

$$y = \frac{1}{2}x - \frac{1}{2} + \frac{\pi}{4}$$

$$\mathbf{y = \frac{1}{2}x + \frac{\pi - 2}{4}}$$

(b) $y + \frac{\pi}{4} = \frac{1}{2}(x + 1)$

$$y = \frac{1}{2}x + \frac{1}{2} - \frac{\pi}{4}$$

$$\mathbf{y = \frac{1}{2}x + \frac{2 - \pi}{4}}$$

21. $y = \dfrac{e^{\cos x} \sin x}{\ln (2x)} - \arctan (2x)$

$$y' = \frac{\ln (2x)\,(e^{\cos x} \cos x - \sin x\, e^{\cos x} \sin x)}{[\ln (2x)]^2}$$

$$- \frac{e^{\cos x} \sin x \left(\frac{1}{x}\right)}{[\ln (2x)]^2} - \frac{2}{4x^2 + 1}$$

$$\mathbf{y' = \frac{e^{\cos x}(\cos x - \sin^2 x)}{\ln (2x)} - \frac{e^{\cos x} \sin x}{x[\ln (2x)]^2}}$$

$$\mathbf{- \frac{2}{4x^2 + 1}}$$

22. $\int (x + 1)e^{x^2 + 2x}\, dx$

$$= \frac{1}{2}\int (2x + 2)e^{x^2 + 2x}\, dx$$

$$\mathbf{= \frac{1}{2}e^{x^2 + 2x} + C}$$

23. $\int x \sin (x^2 + \pi)\, dx$

$$= \frac{1}{2}\int 2x \sin (x^2 + \pi)\, dx$$

$$\mathbf{= -\frac{1}{2} \cos (x^2 + \pi) + C}$$

24.

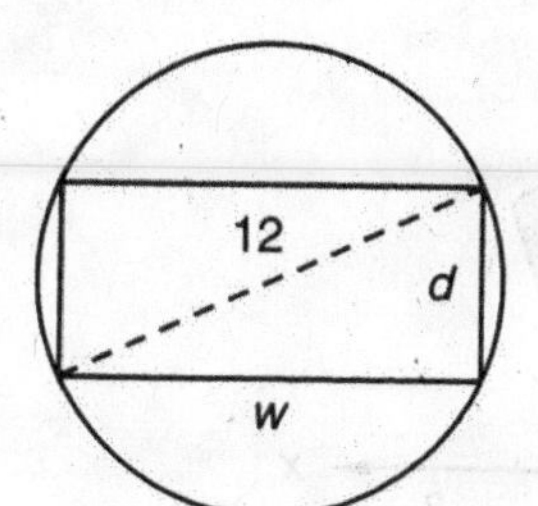

$$w^2 + d^2 = 12^2$$

$$d^2 = 144 - w^2$$

$$wd^2 = w(144 - w^2)$$

$$\mathbf{wd^2 = 144w - w^3}$$

25. $y = \log_3 x$

$$\mathbf{y = \frac{\ln x}{\ln 3}}$$

Problem Set 71

1. $w^2 + d^2 = 12^2$

$$d^2 = 144 - w^2$$

$$s = kwd^2$$

$$s = kw(144 - w^2)$$

$$s = k(144w - w^3)$$

$$s' = k(144 - 3w^2)$$

$$0 = 3k(48 - w^2)$$

$$w^2 = 48$$

$$\mathbf{w = 4\sqrt{3}\ units}$$

2. $W = \int_1^3 \frac{1}{2}x^2\, dx$

$$= \left[\frac{1}{6}x^3\right]_1^3$$

$$= \frac{27}{6} - \frac{1}{6}$$

$$\mathbf{= \frac{13}{3}\ joules}$$

3.

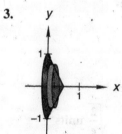

$$V = \int_0^{1/2} \pi r^2\, dx$$

$$= -\frac{\pi}{2}\int_0^{1/2} -2(-2x + 1)^2\, dx$$

$$= -\frac{\pi}{6}\left[(-2x + 1)^3\right]_0^{1/2}$$

$$= -\frac{\pi}{6}(0 - 1) = \mathbf{\frac{\pi}{6}\ units^3}$$

4.

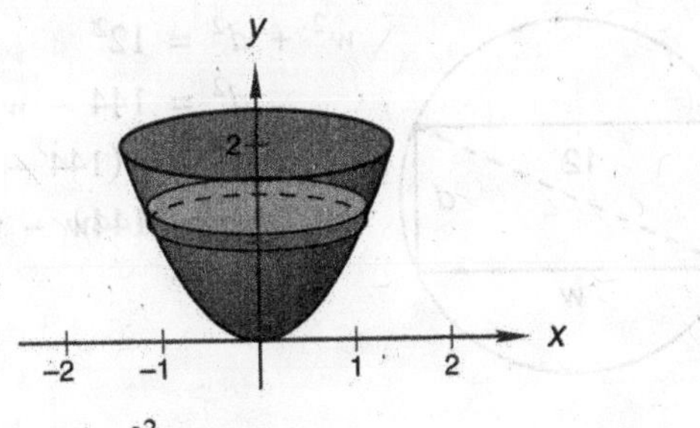

$$V = \int_0^2 \pi r^2\,dy$$
$$= \pi \int_0^2 y\,dy$$
$$= \frac{\pi}{2}[y^2]_0^2$$
$$= \frac{\pi}{2}(4 - 0) = \mathbf{2\pi\ units^3}$$

5.

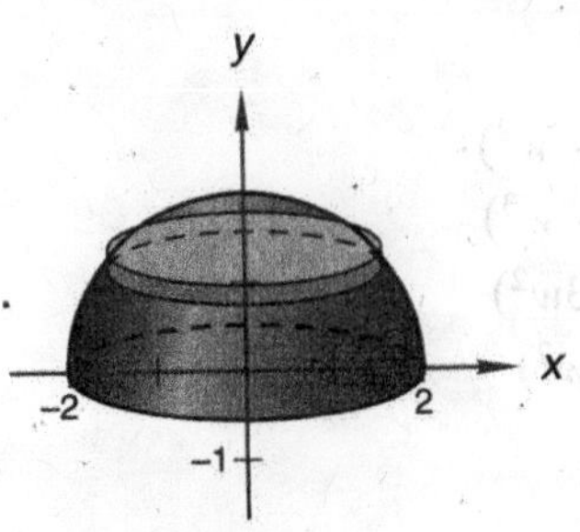

$$x^2 + y^2 = 4$$
$$x^2 = 4 - y^2$$
$$V = \int_0^2 \pi r^2\,dy$$
$$V = \pi \int_0^2 (4 - y^2)\,dy$$

6. (a) $A = 2xy = \mathbf{2xe^{-x^2}}$

(b) $A' = 2xe^{-x^2}(-2x) + 2e^{-x^2}$
$$0 = 2e^{-x^2}(-2x^2 + 1)$$
$$x^2 = \frac{1}{2}$$
$$x = \frac{\sqrt{2}}{2}$$
$$A_{max} = 2\left(\frac{\sqrt{2}}{2}\right)e^{-1/2} = \sqrt{\frac{2}{e}}\ \textbf{units}^2$$

7. $\lim_{x\to\pi} \frac{2f(x)}{g(x)} = \frac{2(2)}{\frac{1}{3}} = \mathbf{12}$

8. $\lim_{x\to-\pi} \pi[f(x)]^2 = \pi(-2)^2 = \mathbf{4\pi}$

9. $\lim_{x\to\pi} [3f(x) - g(x)] = 3(2) - \frac{1}{3} = \mathbf{\frac{17}{3}}$

10. (a) By the sandwich theorem, $\lim_{x\to0} g(x) = \mathbf{0}$ because $f(x) \le g(x) \le h(x)$, $\lim_{x\to0} f(x) = 0$, and $\lim_{x\to0} h(x) = 0$.

(b)

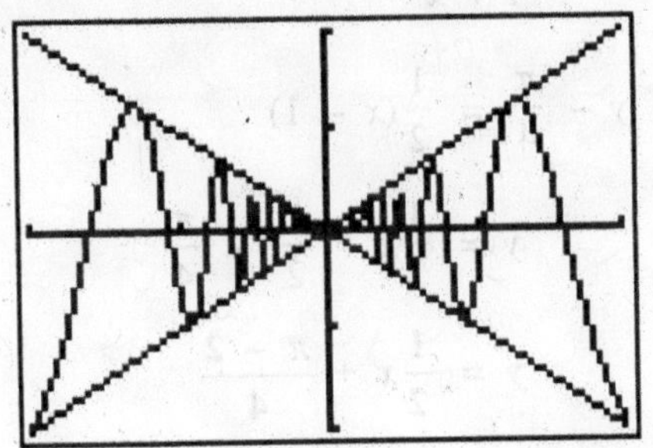

(c) It appears that $\lim_{x\to0} x \sin\frac{1}{x} = \mathbf{0}$ by the sandwich theorem.

11. $$\int \frac{3x}{\sqrt{25 - 9x^4}}\,dx = \frac{1}{2}\int \frac{6x}{\sqrt{5^2 - (3x^2)^2}}\,dx$$
$$= \mathbf{\frac{1}{2}\arcsin\frac{3x^2}{5} + C}$$

12. $u = x \quad du = dx \quad v = \frac{1}{2}e^{2x} \quad dv = e^{2x}\,dx$
$$\int xe^{2x}\,dx = \frac{1}{2}xe^{2x} - \int \frac{1}{2}e^{2x}\,dx$$
$$= \frac{1}{2}xe^{2x} - \frac{1}{4}e^{2x} + C$$
$$= \mathbf{\frac{1}{4}e^{2x}(2x - 1) + C}$$

13. $u = 3x \quad du = 3\,dx \quad v = -\cos x \quad dv = \sin x\,dx$
$$\int 3x\sin x\,dx = -3x\cos x + \int 3\cos x\,dx$$
$$= -3x\cos x + 3\sin x + C$$
$$= \mathbf{-3(x\cos x - \sin x) + C}$$

14. $u = \ln x \quad du = \frac{1}{x}\,dx \quad v = x^2 \quad dv = 2x\,dx$
$$\int 2x\ln x\,dx = x^2\ln x - \int x\,dx$$
$$= x^2\ln x - \frac{1}{2}x^2 + C$$
$$= \mathbf{x^2\left(\ln x - \frac{1}{2}\right) + C}$$

15.

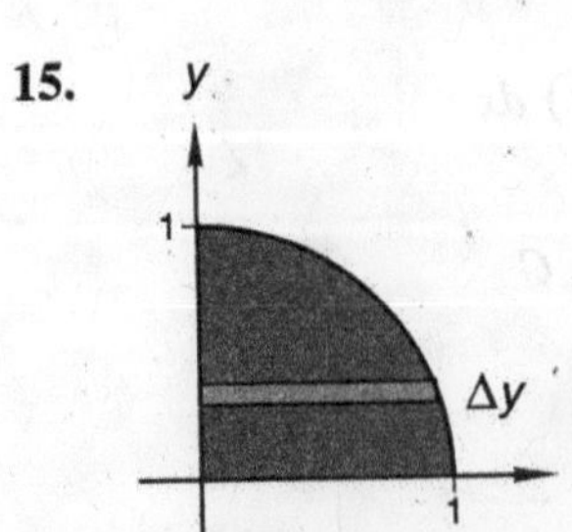

$$x^2 + y^2 = 1$$
$$x^2 = 1 - y^2$$
$$x = \sqrt{1 - y^2}$$
$$A = \mathbf{\int_0^1 \sqrt{1 - y^2}\,dy}$$

16. $h(x) = x^3(x^2 + 1)$
$h(x) = x^5 + x^3$
$h(-x) = (-x)^5 + (-x)^3$
$h(-x) = -x^5 - x^3$
$h(-x) = -h(x)$ odd
origin symmetry

17. $A = 2\int_0^1 \left(4 - \frac{4}{1 + x^2}\right) dx$
$= 2[4x - 4 \arctan x]_0^1$
$= 2[4 - \pi - (0)]$
$= \mathbf{2(4 - \pi)\ units^2}$

18. $y = \operatorname{arccsc} \frac{x}{4}$
$y' = \dfrac{-4}{x\sqrt{x^2 - 16}}$

19. $y = \arctan(e^x) + \dfrac{(2x + 1)^{1/2}}{\sin x - x}$
$y' = \dfrac{e^x}{e^{2x} + 1} + \dfrac{(\sin x - x)\frac{1}{2}(2x + 1)^{-1/2}(2)}{(\sin x - x)^2}$
$- \dfrac{(2x + 1)^{1/2}(\cos x - 1)}{(\sin x - x)^2}$
$y' = \dfrac{e^x}{e^{2x} + 1} + \dfrac{1}{\sqrt{2x + 1}(\sin x - x)}$
$- \dfrac{\sqrt{2x + 1}(\cos x - 1)}{(\sin x - x)^2}$

20. $\int x^2 e^{x^3}\, dx = \frac{1}{3}\int 3x^2 e^{x^3}\, dx$
$= \frac{1}{3}e^{x^3} + C$

21. $\int (\cos x)(\sin^3 x + 1)\, dx$
$= \int (\sin^3 x \cos x + \cos x)\, dx$
$= \frac{1}{4}\sin^4 x + \sin x + C$

22. $u = x^2 + 1 \qquad du = 2x\, dx \qquad x\, dx = \frac{1}{2}\, du$
$\int_1^2 x \ln(x^2 + 1)\, dx = \frac{1}{2}\int_2^5 \ln u\, du$
The correct choice is **C**.

23. $y = 4x - 5$
$x = 4y - 5$
$4y = x + 5$
$y = \frac{1}{4}x + \frac{5}{4}$
$f^{-1}(x) = \frac{1}{4}x + \frac{5}{4}$

24. The remainder theorem states that if a polynomial is divided by $(x - c)$, then the remainder is equal to $f(c)$. Thus if a polynomial is divided by $(x - 3)$, the remainder must be $f(3)$.
The correct choice is **A**.

25. If a function has origin symmetry, then it must be odd, which implies $f(-x) = -f(x)$.
If $f(x) = 2 \sin x$, then $f(-x) = -2 \sin x = -f(x)$.
The correct choice is **D**.
(*Note:* Changing the amplitude of a sine curve does not change its origin symmetry.)

PROBLEM SET 72

1. $r = 4 \text{ cm} \qquad \frac{dr}{dt} = 2\ \frac{\text{cm}}{\text{s}}$
$h = 6 \text{ cm} \qquad \frac{dh}{dt} = 2\ \frac{\text{cm}}{\text{s}}$
$V = \frac{1}{3}\pi r^2 h$
$\frac{dV}{dt} = \frac{1}{3}\pi r^2 \frac{dh}{dt} + \frac{2}{3}\pi rh \frac{dr}{dt}$
$\frac{dV}{dt} = \frac{1}{3}\pi(16)(2) + \frac{2}{3}\pi(4)(6)(2)$
$\frac{dV}{dt} = \frac{32}{3}\pi + 32\pi$
$\frac{dV}{dt} = \mathbf{\frac{128\pi}{3}\ \frac{cm^3}{s}}$

2. (a) $a(t) = -9.8$
$v(t) = \mathbf{-9.8t - 48}$
$h(t) = \mathbf{-4.9t^2 - 48t + 160}$

(b) $0 = -4.9t^2 - 48t + 160$
$t = \dfrac{48 - \sqrt{48^2 - 4(-4.9)(160)}}{-9.8}$
$t \approx \mathbf{2.6282\ s}$

(c) $v(2.6282) \approx \mathbf{-73.7564\ m/s}$

3. (a)

$$x^2 + 2xy + 7y^2 = 8$$

$$2x\,dx + 2x\,dy + 2y\,dx + 14y\,dy = 0$$

$$\mathbf{2(x + y)\frac{dx}{dt} + 2(x + 7y)\frac{dy}{dt} = 0}$$

(b)

$$2(x + y)\frac{dx}{dt} + 2(x + 7y)\frac{dy}{dt} = 0$$

$$2(3 + 2)\frac{dx}{dt} + 2[3 + 7(2)]\left(\frac{5}{17}\right) = 0$$

$$10\frac{dx}{dt} + 10 = 0$$

$$\mathbf{\frac{dx}{dt} = -1}$$

4. $y = \log_2 x$

$$y' = \frac{1}{x \ln 2}$$

$$\text{slope} = y'|_3 = \frac{1}{3 \ln 2} = \frac{1}{\ln 8}$$

$\perp$ slope $= \mathbf{-\ln 8}$

5. $y = 3^x$

$y' = 3^x \ln 3$

slope $= y'|_4 = 3^4 \ln 3$

$= \mathbf{81 \ln 3 \approx 88.9876}$

$y - 81 = 81 \ln 3\,(x - 4)$

$y = 81(\ln 3)x - 324 \ln 3 + 81$

$\mathbf{y \approx 88.9876x - 274.9504}$

6. $y = 43^x + 3^x + \log_3 x - \log_{43} x$

$$\frac{dy}{dx} = \mathbf{43^x \ln 43 + 3^x \ln 3 + \frac{1}{x \ln 3} - \frac{1}{x \ln 43}}$$

7.

n	$f^{(n)}(x)$	$f^{(n)}(0)$
0	2^x	1
1	$2^x \ln 2$	$\ln 2$
2	$2^x(\ln 2)^2$	$(\ln 2)^2$
3	$2^x(\ln 2)^3$	$(\ln 2)^3$
$\vdots$	$\vdots$	$\vdots$

$$2^x = \mathbf{1 + (\ln 2)x + \frac{(\ln 2)^2 x^2}{2!} + \frac{(\ln 2)^3 x^3}{3!} + \cdots}$$

8. (a) $f(x) = x^3 - 3x^2 - 9x + 5$

$f'(x) = 3x^2 - 6x - 9$

$0 = 3(x^2 - 2x - 3)$

$0 = 3(x - 3)(x + 1)$

Critical numbers: $x = -2, -1, 3, 4$

$f(-2) = 3$

$f(-1) = 10$

$f(3) = -22$

$f(4) = -15$

Maximum: 10 Minimum: −22

(b)

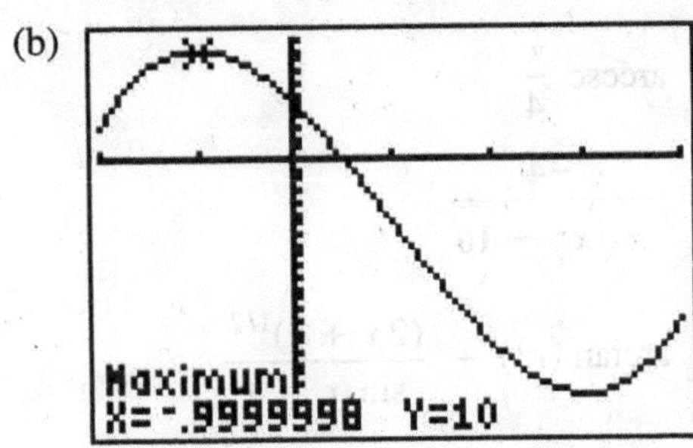

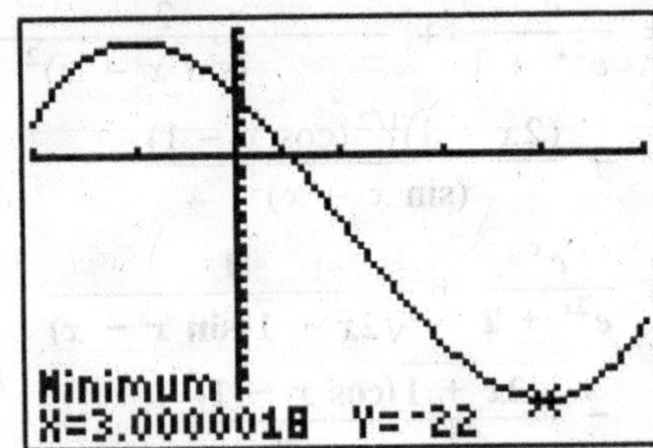

9.

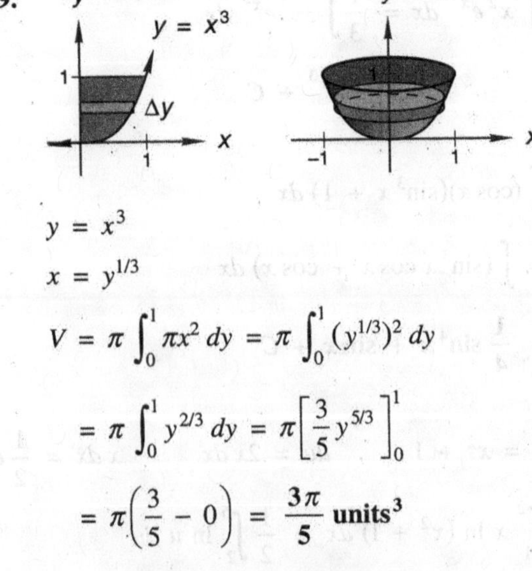

$y = x^3$

$x = y^{1/3}$

$$V = \pi \int_0^1 \pi x^2\,dy = \pi \int_0^1 (y^{1/3})^2\,dy$$

$$= \pi \int_0^1 y^{2/3}\,dy = \pi\left[\frac{3}{5}y^{5/3}\right]_0^1$$

$$= \pi\left(\frac{3}{5} - 0\right) = \mathbf{\frac{3\pi}{5}\ \text{units}^3}$$

10.

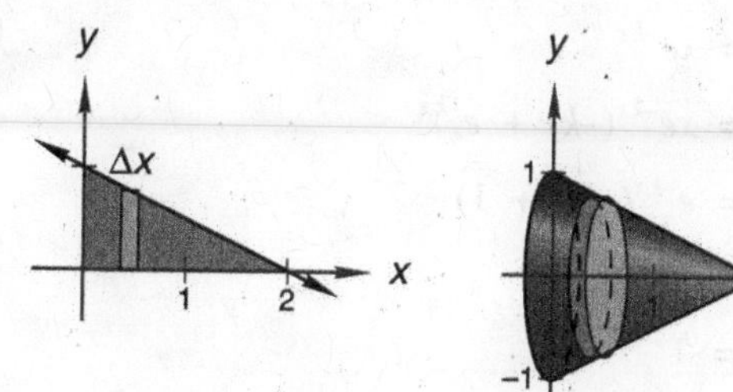

$$y = -\frac{1}{2}x + 1$$

$$V = \pi \int_0^2 \pi y^2\, dx = \pi \int_0^2 \left(-\frac{1}{2}x + 1\right)^2 dx$$

11.

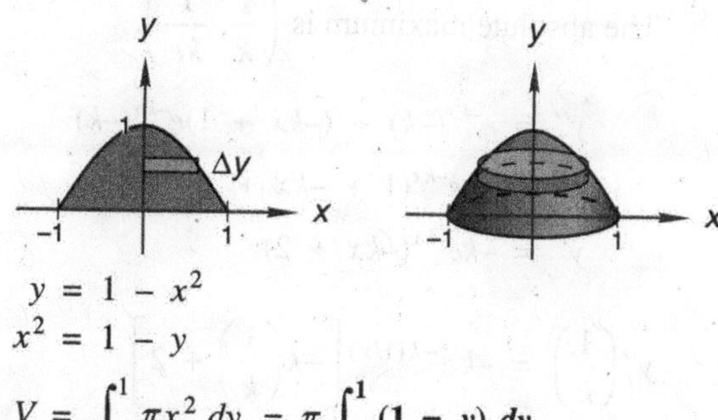

$$y = 1 - x^2$$
$$x^2 = 1 - y$$
$$V = \int_0^1 \pi x^2\, dy = \pi \int_0^1 (1 - y)\, dy$$

12. $u = x \quad du = dx \quad v = e^{3x} \quad dv = 3e^{3x}\, dx$

$$\int 3xe^{3x}\, dx = xe^{3x} - \int e^{3x}\, dx$$
$$= xe^{3x} - \frac{1}{3}e^{3x} + C$$
$$= e^{3x}\left(x - \frac{1}{3}\right) + C$$

13. $\int \pi \sin(\pi x)\, dx = \mathbf{-\cos(\pi x) + C}$

14. $u = x + 1 \qquad du = dx \qquad x = u - 1$

$$\int_0^3 x\sqrt{x+1}\, dx = \int_1^4 (u-1)u^{1/2}\, du$$
$$= \int_1^4 (u^{3/2} - u^{1/2})\, du$$
$$= \left[\frac{2}{5}u^{5/2} - \frac{2}{3}u^{3/2}\right]_1^4$$
$$= \frac{64}{5} - \frac{16}{3} - \left(\frac{2}{5} - \frac{2}{3}\right)$$
$$= \mathbf{\frac{116}{15}}$$

15. $h(x) = f(x)g(x)$

$$g(x) = \frac{h(x)}{f(x)}$$

$$\lim_{x\to\pi} g(x) = \lim_{x\to\pi} \frac{h(x)}{f(x)} = \frac{\frac{1}{\pi}}{3} = \frac{1}{3\pi}$$

16. (a) By the sandwich theorem, $\lim_{x\to 0} g(x) = \mathbf{1}$ because $f(x) \le g(x) \le h(x)$, $\lim_{x\to 0} f(x) = 1$, and $\lim_{x\to 0} h(x) = 1$.

(b)

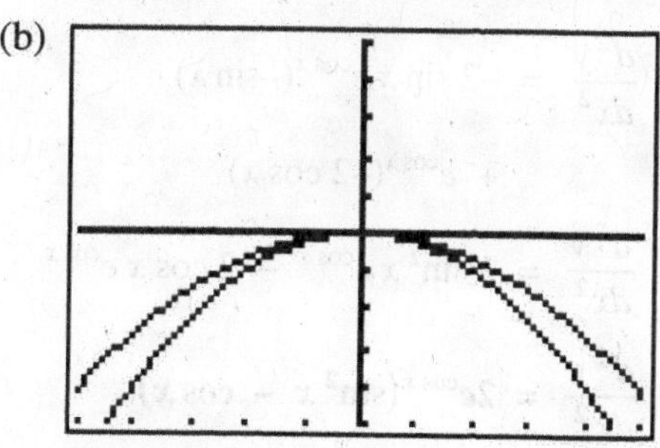

(c) It appears that $\lim_{x\to 0} \frac{\sin x}{x} = \mathbf{1}$ by the sandwich theorem.

17.
$$h(x) = x \sin x$$
$$h(-x) = -x \sin(-x)$$
$$h(-x) = x \sin x$$
$$h(-x) = h(x)$$

Even

18. (a) $\int_0^2 f(x)\, dx + \int_2^5 f(x)\, dx = \int_a^b f(x)\, dx$

$\mathbf{a = 0,\ b = 5}$

(b) $-\int_4^6 f(x)\, dx + \int_1^6 f(x)\, dx = \int_a^b f(x)\, dx$

$\int_a^b f(x)\, dx + \int_4^6 f(x)\, dx = \int_1^6 f(x)\, dx$

$\mathbf{a = 1,\ b = 4}$

19. $y = 2\cos^2 x + \arctan(2x) + \dfrac{2(2x+1)^{1/2}}{x^2 + 1}$

$$y' = -4\cos x \sin x + \frac{2}{4x^2 + 1} + \frac{(x^2+1)(2x+1)^{-1/2}(2)}{(x^2+1)^2} - \frac{2(2x+1)^{1/2}(2x)}{(x^2+1)^2}$$

$$y' = \mathbf{-2\sin(2x) + \frac{2}{4x^2+1} + \frac{2}{\sqrt{2x+1}(x^2+1)} - \frac{4x\sqrt{2x+1}}{(x^2+1)^2}}$$

20. (a) $y = 2e^{\cos x}$

$$\frac{dy}{dx} = \mathbf{-2 \sin x\, e^{\cos x}}$$

$$\frac{d^2y}{dx^2} = -2 \sin x\, e^{\cos x}(-\sin x) + e^{\cos x}(-2 \cos x)$$

$$\frac{d^2y}{dx^2} = 2 \sin^2 x\, e^{\cos x} - 2 \cos x\, e^{\cos x}$$

$$\frac{d^2y}{dx^2} = \mathbf{2e^{\cos x}(\sin^2 x - \cos x)}$$

(b) $\frac{dy}{dt} = \frac{dy}{dx}\frac{dx}{dt}$

$$\frac{dy}{dt} = -2 \sin x\, e^{\cos x}\frac{dx}{dt}$$

$$5 = -2(1)(1)\frac{dx}{dt}$$

$$\frac{dx}{dt} = \mathbf{-\frac{5}{2}\frac{units}{s}}$$

21. $\int (x + 1)e^{-x^2 - 2x}\, dx$

$$= -\frac{1}{2}\int (-2x - 2)e^{-x^2 - 2x}\, dx$$

$$= \mathbf{-\frac{1}{2}e^{-x^2 - 2x} + C}$$

22. $\int \frac{x}{x^2 + 1}\, dx = \frac{1}{2}\int \frac{2x}{x^2 + 1}\, dx$

$$= \frac{1}{2}\ln(x^2 + 1) + C$$

$$= \mathbf{\ln\sqrt{x^2 + 1} + C}$$

23. $\int \frac{1}{4x^2 + 1}\, dx = \frac{1}{2}\int \frac{2}{(2x)^2 + 1}\, dx$

$$= \mathbf{\frac{1}{2}\arctan(2x) + C}$$

24. $PV = k$

$$5(1000) = k$$

$$k = 5000$$

$$15V = 5000$$

$$V = \mathbf{\frac{1000}{3}\ m^3}$$

25. $y = xe^{-kx}$

$$y' = xe^{-kx}(-k) + e^{-kx}$$

$$y' = e^{-kx}(-kx + 1)$$

$$0 = -kx + 1$$

$$kx = 1$$

$$x = \frac{1}{k}$$

$$y\left(\frac{1}{k}\right) = \frac{1}{k}e^{-k(1/k)} = \frac{1}{ke}$$

The absolute maximum is $\left(\mathbf{\frac{1}{k}, \frac{1}{ke}}\right)$.

$$y'' = e^{-kx}(-k) + (-kx + 1)e^{-kx}(-k)$$

$$y'' = -ke^{-kx}(1 + -kx + 1)$$

$$y'' = -ke^{-kx}(-kx + 2)$$

$$y''\left(\frac{1}{k}\right) = -ke^{-k(1/k)}\left[-k\left(\frac{1}{k}\right) + 2\right]$$

$$= -ke^{-1}$$

$$= -\frac{k}{e}$$

Since k is a positive constant, $-\frac{k}{e}$ is negative. The second derivative having a negative value at a critical number means that the critical number is a maximum.

PROBLEM SET 73

1. (a) $V = \pi r^2 h$

$$432\pi = \pi x^2 y$$

$$y = 432x^{-2}$$

$$\text{Cost} = 8(2\pi x^2) + 2\pi xy$$

$$= 8(2\pi x^2) + 2\pi x(432x^{-2})$$

$$= \mathbf{(16\pi x^2 + 864\pi x^{-1})\ dollars}$$

(b) $0 = 32\pi x - 864\pi x^{-2}$

$$\frac{864\pi}{x^2} = 32\pi x$$

$$32\pi x^3 = 864\pi$$

$$x^3 = 27$$

$$\mathbf{x = 3\ cm,\ y = 48\ cm}$$

(c)

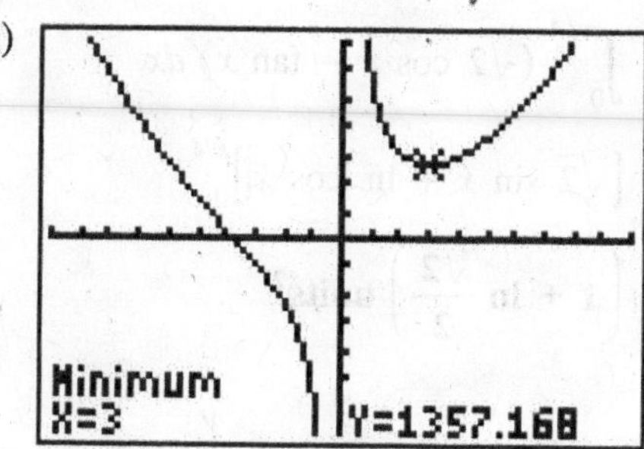

$\text{Cost}_{\text{min}} = \mathbf{\$1357.17}$

2. $W = \int_{1/\sqrt{3}}^{\sqrt{3}} \frac{3}{1 + x^2}\,dx$

$= 3[\arctan x]_{1/\sqrt{3}}^{\sqrt{3}}$

$= 3\left(\frac{\pi}{3} - \frac{\pi}{6}\right)$

$= \mathbf{\frac{\pi}{2}\ joules}$

3. $a(t) = -32$

$v(t) = -32t + 20$

$\mathbf{h(t) = -16t^2 + 20t + 500}$

$0 = -16t^2 + 20t + 500$

$t = \mathbf{6.25\ s}$

4. $y = \log_3 x$

$y' = \frac{1}{x \ln 3}$

$\text{slope} = \mathbf{\frac{1}{9 \ln 3}}$

$y(9) = \log_3 9 = 2$

$y - 2 = \frac{1}{9 \ln 3}(x - 9)$

$\mathbf{y = \frac{1}{9 \ln 3}x - \frac{1}{\ln 3} + 2}$

5. $y = 5^x$

$y' = 5^x \ln 5$

$\text{slope} = 5^2 \ln 5$

$\perp \text{slope} = \mathbf{-\frac{1}{25 \ln 5}}$

6. $y = \log_2 x + 4^x - \log_6 x$

$y' = \mathbf{\frac{1}{x \ln 2} + 4^x \ln 4 - \frac{1}{x \ln 6}}$

7. $y = 2 \cdot 5^x + 3 \log_7 x$

$y' = 2 \cdot 5^x \ln 5 + \frac{3}{x \ln 7}$

$y' = \mathbf{5^x \ln 25 + \frac{3}{x \ln 7}}$

8. $y = 24^{(x^2 + 3x)}$

$y' = \mathbf{(\ln 24)(2x + 3)24^{(x^2 + 3x)}}$

9. $y = |x + 1|$

$y = \begin{cases} x + 1 \text{ when } x \geq -1 \\ -x - 1 \text{ when } x < -1 \end{cases}$

$y' = \begin{cases} \mathbf{1 \text{ when } x > -1} \\ \mathbf{-1 \text{ when } x < -1} \end{cases}$

10. $y = \left|\sqrt{x^2 - 9}\right|$

$y = \sqrt{x^2 - 9}$

$y = (x^2 - 9)^{1/2}$

$y' = \frac{1}{2}(x^2 - 9)^{-1/2}(2x)$

$y' = \mathbf{\frac{x}{\sqrt{x^2 - 9}}, \text{ when } |x| > 3}$

11. $\int 13^x\,dx = \mathbf{\frac{13^x}{\ln 13} + C}$

12. $\int \log_3 x\,dx = \int \frac{\ln x}{\ln 3}\,dx$

$= \frac{1}{\ln 3}\int \ln x\,dx$

$= \mathbf{\frac{1}{\ln 3}(x \ln x - x) + C}$

$= \mathbf{x \log_3 x - \frac{x}{\ln 3} + C}$

13. $\int x \cdot 2^{x^2 + 4}\,dx = \frac{1}{2 \ln 2}\int 2x \cdot 2^{x^2 + 4} \ln 2\,dx$

$= \mathbf{\frac{2^{x^2 + 4}}{\ln 4} + C}$

14. $\int \tan x\,dx = \int \frac{\sin x}{\cos x}\,dx$

$= -\int \frac{-\sin x}{\cos x}\,dx$

$= \mathbf{-\ln|\cos x| + C}$ or $\mathbf{\ln|\sec x| + C}$

15. $\int (\sin x)(\cos^3 x + 1)\,dx$

$= \int (\cos^3 x \sin x + \sin x)\,dx$

$= -\frac{1}{4}\cos^4 x - \cos x + C$

16.

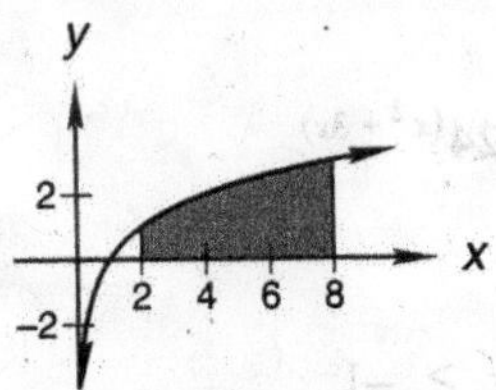

$A = \int_2^8 \log_2 x\,dx = \frac{1}{\ln 2}\int_2^8 \ln x\,dx$

17.

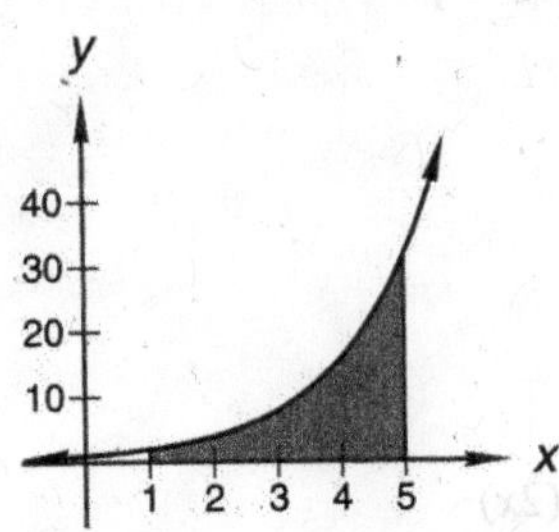

$A = \int_1^5 2^x\,dx = \frac{1}{\ln 2}\int_1^5 2^x \ln 2\,dx$

$= \frac{1}{\ln 2}\left[2^x\right]_1^5 = \frac{1}{\ln 2}(32 - 2)$

$= \frac{30}{\ln 2}$ **units²**

18.

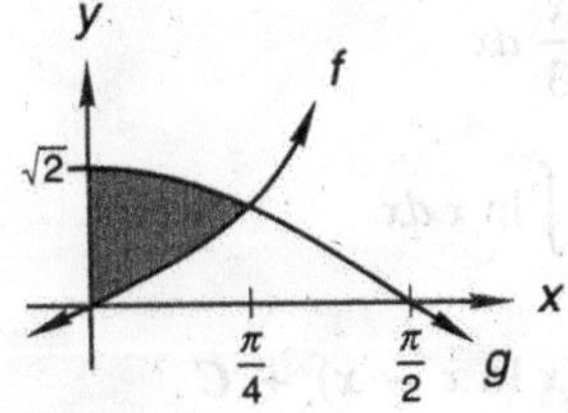

$\tan x = \sqrt{2}\cos x$

$\frac{\sin x}{\cos x} = \sqrt{2}\cos x$

$\sin x = \sqrt{2}\cos^2 x$

$\sin x = \sqrt{2}(1 - \sin^2 x)$

$\sqrt{2}\sin^2 x + \sin x - \sqrt{2} = 0$

$(\sin x + \sqrt{2})(\sqrt{2}\sin x - 1) = 0$

$\sin x = -\sqrt{2}$ $\quad$ $\sin x = \frac{1}{\sqrt{2}}$

No Solution $\quad$ $x = \frac{\pi}{4}$

$\left(\frac{\pi}{4}, 1\right)$

19. $A = \int_0^{\pi/4} (\sqrt{2}\cos x - \tan x)\,dx$

$= \left[\sqrt{2}\sin x + \ln|\cos x|\right]_0^{\pi/4}$

$= \left(1 + \ln\frac{\sqrt{2}}{2}\right)$ **units²**

20.

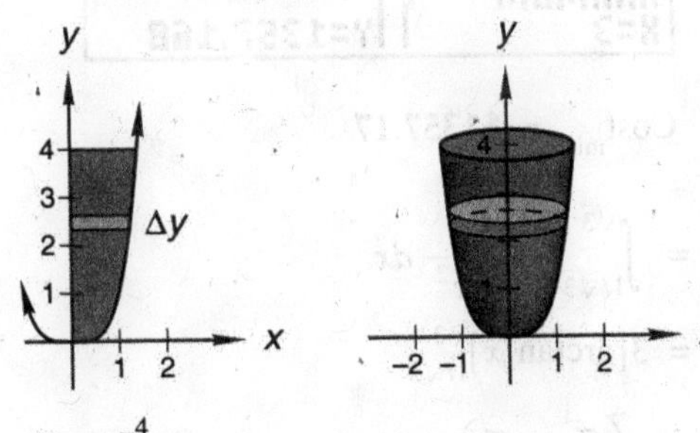

$y = x^4$

$x^2 = \sqrt{y}$

$V = \int_0^4 \pi x^2\,dy$

$= \pi\int_0^4 \sqrt{y}\,dy$

$= \frac{2\pi}{3}\left[y^{3/2}\right]_0^4$

$= \frac{2\pi}{3}(8 - 0) = \frac{16\pi}{3}$ **units³**

21. If $x < 0$, $\frac{|x|}{x} = -1$.

$\lim_{x \to 0^-} \frac{|x|}{x} = -1$

22. $\lim_{x \to 1} \frac{1}{(x-1)^2} = \infty$

23. $h(x) = f(x^3 + \sin x)$

$h(x) = (x^3 + \sin x)^2$

$h(-x) = [(-x)^3 + \sin(-x)]^2$

$h(-x) = (-x^3 - \sin x)^2$

$h(-x) = [-1(x^3 + \sin x)]^2$

$h(-x) = (x^3 + \sin x)^2$

$h(-x) = h(x)$ **y-axis symmetry**

24. $f(x) = x^3 + ax^2 + bx + c$

$f(0) = -2$

$\mathbf{c = -2}$

$f(-1) = 0$

$0 = -1 + a - b - 2$

$a - b = 3$

$f'(x) = 3x^2 + 2ax + b$

$f''(x) = 6x + 2a$

$f''(0) = 0$

$2a = 0$

$\mathbf{a = 0}$

$0 - b = 3$

$\mathbf{b = -3}$

$\mathbf{f(x) = x^3 - 3x - 2}$

25. (a) $f(x) = x^4 - 3x^2 + 2$

$f'(x) = 4x^3 - 6x$

$f'(1) = 4 - 6 = -2$

$y = -2(x - 1)$

$\mathbf{y = -2x + 2}$

(b) $4x^3 - 6x = -2$

$4x^3 - 6x + 2 = 0$

$\mathbf{x = -1.3660,\ 0.3660,\ 1}$

PROBLEM SET 74

1. $PV = k$

$5(1000) = k$

$k = 5000$

$PV = 5000$

$10V = 5000$

$V = 500$

$PV = 5000$

$$P\frac{dV}{dt} + V\frac{dP}{dt} = 0$$

$$10\frac{dV}{dt} + 500(0.05) = 0$$

$$\frac{dV}{dt} = \mathbf{-2.5\ \frac{m^3}{s}}$$

2. $$W = \int_1^4 (x + 2)\,dx = \left[\frac{1}{2}x^2 + 2x\right]_1^4$$

$$= 8 + 8 - \left(\frac{1}{2} + 2\right) = \mathbf{\frac{27}{2}\ joules}$$

3. $F = \int$ weight density · depth · area

$$= \int_0^3 1000(3 - y)(6)\,dy$$

$$= 6000\int_0^3 (3 - y)\,dy$$

$$= 6000\left[3y - \frac{1}{2}y^2\right]_0^3$$

$$= 6000\left[9 - \frac{9}{2} - (0)\right]$$

$$= 6000\left(\frac{9}{2}\right)$$

$= \mathbf{27{,}000\ newtons}$

4. $F = \int$ weight density · depth · area

$$= \int_0^3 3000(3 - y)y\,dy$$

$$= 3000\int_0^3 (3y - y^2)\,dy$$

$$= 3000\left[\frac{3}{2}y^2 - \frac{1}{3}y^3\right]_0^3$$

$$= 3000\left(\frac{27}{2} - 9 - 0\right)$$

$= \mathbf{13{,}500\ newtons}$

5. $F = \int$ weight density · depth · area

$$= \int_{-3}^0 1000(-y)2x\,dy$$

$y = -\sqrt{9 - x^2}$

$y^2 = 9 - x^2$

$x^2 = 9 - y^2$

$x = \sqrt{9 - y^2}$

$$F = \mathbf{2000\int_{-3}^{0} -y\sqrt{9 - y^2}\,dy}$$

Entering `fnInt(2000(-X)√(9-X²),X,-3,0)` gives the result **18,000 newtons.**

6.

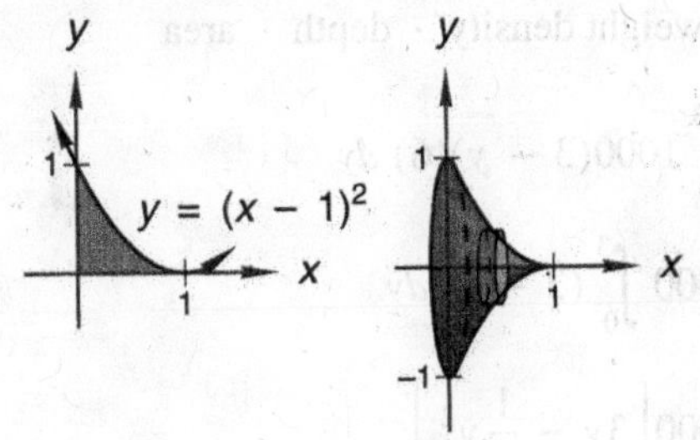

$$V = \int_0^1 \pi y^2\,dx = \pi\int_0^1 (x-1)^4\,dx$$
$$= \frac{\pi}{5}\left[(x-1)^5\right]_0^1 = \frac{\pi}{5}[0-(-1)] = \mathbf{\frac{\pi}{5}\ unit^3}$$

7.

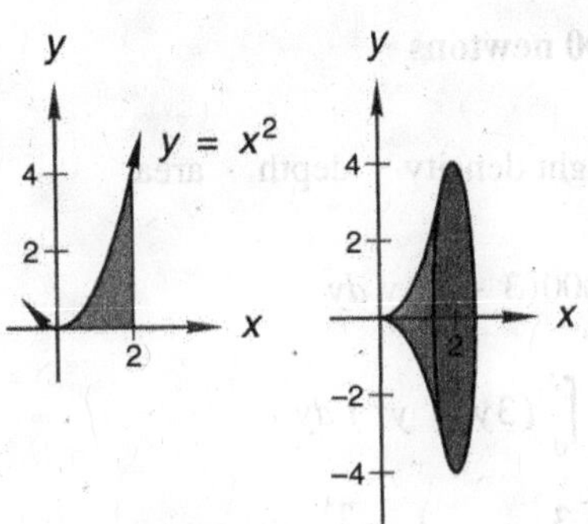

$$V = \int_0^2 \pi y^2\,dx = \pi\int_0^2 x^4\,dx$$
$$= \frac{\pi}{5}\left[x^5\right]_0^2 = \frac{\pi}{5}(32-0) = \mathbf{\frac{32}{5}\pi\ units^3}$$

8.

n	$f^{(n)}(x)$	$f^{(n)}(0)$
0	3^x	1
1	$3^x \ln 3$	$\ln 3$
2	$3^x(\ln 3)^2$	$(\ln 3)^2$
3	$3^x(\ln 3)^3$	$(\ln 3)^3$
⋮	⋮	⋮

$$3^x = 1 + x\ln 3 + \frac{(\ln 3)^2x^2}{2!} + \frac{(\ln 3)^3x^3}{3!} + \cdots$$

$$3^x = \mathbf{\sum_{n=0}^{\infty}\frac{(\ln 3)^n x^n}{n!}}$$

9. $y = \log_5 x + 7^x + \log_8 x$

$$y' = \mathbf{\frac{1}{x\ln 5} + 7^x\ln 7 + \frac{1}{x\ln 8}}$$

10. $y = 3.5^x - 2\log_3 x$

$$y' = \mathbf{3.5^x\ln 3.5 - \frac{2}{x\ln 3}}$$

11. $y = \operatorname{arcsec}\dfrac{x}{a}$

$$y' = \mathbf{\frac{a}{x\sqrt{x^2-a^2}}}$$

12. $y = \arcsin(3x) + \dfrac{(1-x)^{1/2}}{x\sin x}$

$$y' = \frac{3}{\sqrt{1-9x^2}} + \frac{(x\sin x)\frac{1}{2}(1-x)^{-1/2}(-1)}{(x\sin x)^2} - \frac{(1-x)^{1/2}(x\cos x+\sin x)}{(x\sin x)^2}$$

$$y' = \mathbf{\frac{3}{\sqrt{1-9x^2}} - \frac{1}{2\sqrt{1-x}(x\sin x)} - \frac{\sqrt{1-x}(x\cos x+\sin x)}{(x\sin x)^2}}$$

13. $\displaystyle\int \log_5 x\,dx = \int\frac{\ln x}{\ln 5}\,dx$

$$= \mathbf{\frac{1}{\ln 5}(x\ln x - x) + C}$$
$$= \mathbf{x\log_5 x - \frac{x}{\ln 5} + C}$$

14. $u = 2x \quad du = 2\,dx \quad v = e^{2x} \quad dv = 2e^{2x}\,dx$

$$\int 4xe^{2x}\,dx = 2xe^{2x} - \int 2e^{2x}\,dx$$
$$= 2xe^{2x} - e^{2x} + C$$
$$= \mathbf{e^{2x}(2x-1) + C}$$

15. $u = x \qquad v = -\dfrac{1}{2}\cos(2x)$

$du = dx \qquad dv = \sin(2x)\,dx$

$$\int x\sin(2x)\,dx = -\frac{1}{2}x\cos(2x) + \int\frac{1}{2}\cos(2x)\,dx$$
$$= \mathbf{-\frac{1}{2}x\cos(2x) + \frac{1}{4}\sin(2x) + C}$$

16. $\displaystyle\int 3\tan x\,dx = 3\int\frac{\sin x}{\cos x}\,dx$

$$= \mathbf{-3\ln|\cos x| + C}$$
$$= \mathbf{3\ln|\sec x| + C}$$

17. $\displaystyle\int x(x^2+\pi)^{-1/2}\,dx = \frac{1}{2}\int 2x(x^2+\pi)^{-1/2}\,dx$

$$= (x^2+\pi)^{1/2} + C$$
$$= \mathbf{\sqrt{x^2+\pi} + C}$$

18. $\int (\sin x)(1 + 2\cos x)^{1/2}\,dx$

$= -\frac{1}{2}\int -2\sin x\,(1 + 2\cos x)^{1/2}\,dx$

$= \mathbf{-\frac{1}{3}(1 + 2\cos x)^{3/2} + C}$

19. (a) $|\sin x| = 0 \quad -\pi \le x \le 2\pi$

$\mathbf{x = -\pi, 0, \pi, 2\pi}$

(b)

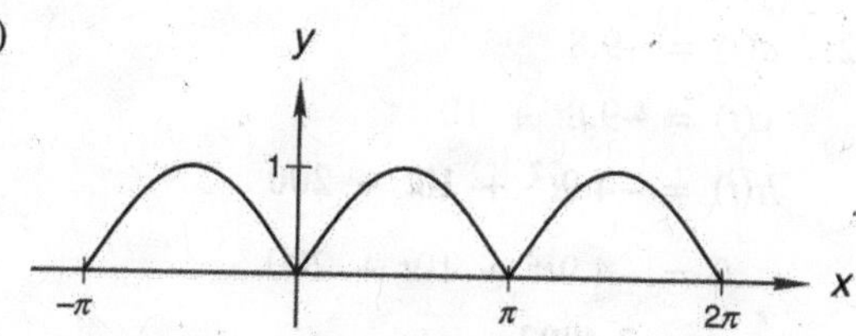

(c) $f(x) = \begin{cases} \sin x & \text{when } 0 \le x \le \pi \\ -\sin x & \text{when } -\pi \le x < 0 \\ & \text{or } \pi < x \le 2\pi \end{cases}$

$\mathbf{f'(x) = \begin{cases} \cos x & \text{when } 0 < x < \pi \\ -\cos x & \text{when } -\pi < x < 0 \\ & \text{or } \pi < x < 2\pi \end{cases}}$

20. (a) $h(x) = g(|\sin x|) = \mathbf{\sin^2 x}$

(b) $\sin^2 x = 0 \quad -\pi \le x \le \pi$

$\mathbf{x = -\pi, 0, \pi}$

(c)

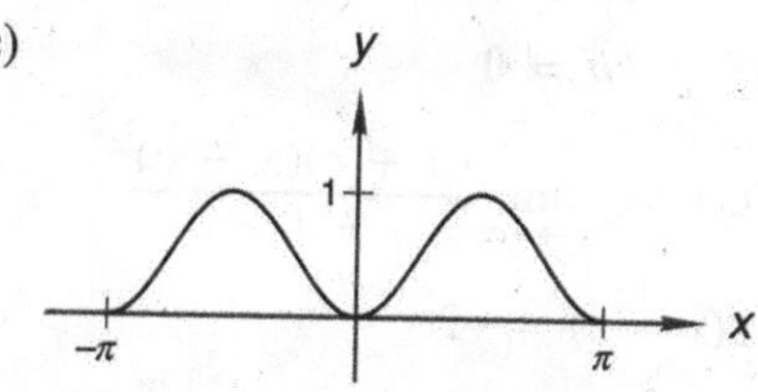

(d) **Domain:** $\mathbf{\{x \in \mathbb{R} \mid -\pi \le x \le \pi\}}$

Range: $\mathbf{\{y \in \mathbb{R} \mid 0 \le y \le 1\}}$

(e) $h'(x) = 2\sin x\cos x$

$h'(x) = \sin(2x)$

$h'\left(\frac{\pi}{4}\right) = 1$

$h\left(\frac{\pi}{4}\right) = \left(\frac{\sqrt{2}}{2}\right)^2 = \frac{1}{2}$

$y - \frac{1}{2} = 1\left(x - \frac{\pi}{4}\right)$

$y = x - \frac{\pi}{4} + \frac{1}{2}$

$\mathbf{y = x + \frac{2 - \pi}{4}}$

21. (a) $\lim_{x\to 1} \frac{x^3 - 1}{x - 1} = \lim_{x\to 1} \frac{(x - 1)(x^2 + x + 1)}{x - 1}$

$= \lim_{x\to 1}(x^2 + x + 1)$

$= \mathbf{3}$

(b) If $x > 0$, $\frac{|x|}{x} = 1$.

$\lim_{x\to 0^+} \frac{|x|}{x} = \mathbf{1}$

(c) $\lim_{x\to 0} \sin\frac{1}{x}$ **does not exist**

(d) $\lim_{x\to 0^-} x\sin x = \mathbf{0}$

22. $f(x) = \frac{x - 1}{x + 1} \qquad f(1) = 0$

$f'(x) = \frac{(x + 1) - (x - 1)}{(x + 1)^2}$

$f'(x) = \frac{2}{(x + 1)^2}$

$f'(1) = \frac{1}{2}$

$y - 0 = \frac{1}{2}(x - 1)$

$\mathbf{y = \frac{1}{2}x - \frac{1}{2}}$

23. $Q(p) = 1000 - \frac{100(p - 100)}{20}$

$Q(p) = 1000 - 5(p - 100)$

$Q(p) = 1000 - 5p + 500$

$\mathbf{Q(p) = 1500 - 5p}$

$R(p) = p(1500 - 5p)$

$\mathbf{R(p) = 1500p - 5p^2}$

24. In order for a function to have an inverse that is a function, the original function must be one-to-one, which means it is strictly increasing or strictly decreasing.

The correct choice is **A**.

25. (a)
$$x + xy + 2y^2 = 6$$
$$1 + x\frac{dy}{dx} + y + 4y\frac{dy}{dx} = 0$$
$$\frac{dy}{dx}(x + 4y) = -y - 1$$
$$\frac{dy}{dx} = \mathbf{\frac{-y - 1}{x + 4y}}$$

(b)
$$\left.\frac{dy}{dx}\right|_{(2,1)} = \frac{-1 - 1}{2 + 4} = \frac{-2}{6} = -\frac{1}{3}$$
$$y - 1 = -\frac{1}{3}(x - 2)$$
$$y = -\frac{1}{3}x + \frac{2}{3} + 1$$
$$\mathbf{y = -\frac{1}{3}x + \frac{5}{3}}$$

(c)
$$\frac{-y - 1}{x + 4y} = -\frac{1}{3}$$
$$3y + 3 = x + 4y$$
$$x = -y + 3$$
$$x + xy + 2y^2 = 6$$
$$(-y + 3) + (-y + 3)y + 2y^2 = 6$$
$$-y + 3 - y^2 + 3y + 2y^2 = 6$$
$$y^2 + 2y - 3 = 0$$
$$(y + 3)(y - 1) = 0$$
$$y = -3, 1$$

(6, –3)

(d)
$$2y^2 + xy + (x - 6) = 0$$
$$y = \frac{-x \pm \sqrt{x^2 - 4(2)(x - 6)}}{4}$$
$$\mathbf{y = \frac{-x \pm \sqrt{x^2 - 8x + 48}}{4}}$$

```
Y1=(-X+√(X²-8X+48))/4
Y2=(-X-√(X²-8X+48))/4
```

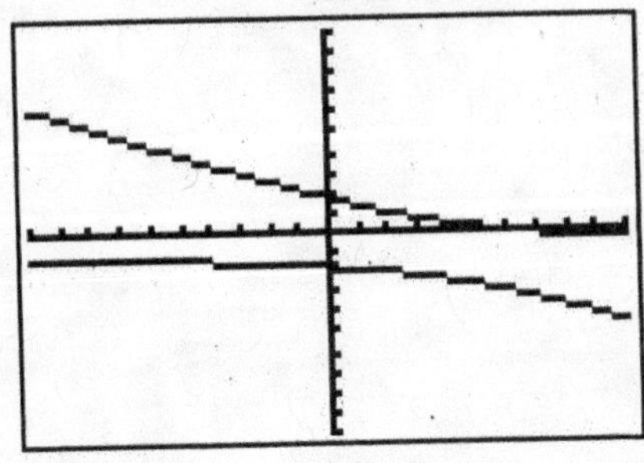

PROBLEM SET 75

1. $Q(p) = 1500 - 5p$
$R(p) = 1500p - 5p^2$
$R'(p) = 1500 - 10p$
$10p = 1500$
$p = 150$

\$1.50

2. $a(t) = -9.8$
$v(t) = -9.8t + 10$
$\mathbf{h(t) = -4.9t^2 + 10t + 200}$
$0 = -4.9t^2 + 10t + 200$
$\mathbf{t = 7.4902 \text{ s}}$

3. This statement must be true if f is continuous on [1, 4]. Since we are not sure that f is continuous the statement is **not necessarily true.**

4. Both $f(-1)$ and $f(4)$ must be defined.
The correct choice is **D.**

5. $\lim_{x\to 2^-} (|x| + 2) = f(2)$
$4 = 4 + 2b$
$2b = 0$
$\mathbf{b = 0}$

6. $\lim_{x\to -c} f(x) = \lim_{x\to -c} \frac{(x + c)(x - c)}{x + c}$
$= \lim_{x\to -c} (x - c) = -2c$
$f(-c) = 2c$
$\mathbf{(-\infty, -c), (-c, \infty)}$

7.

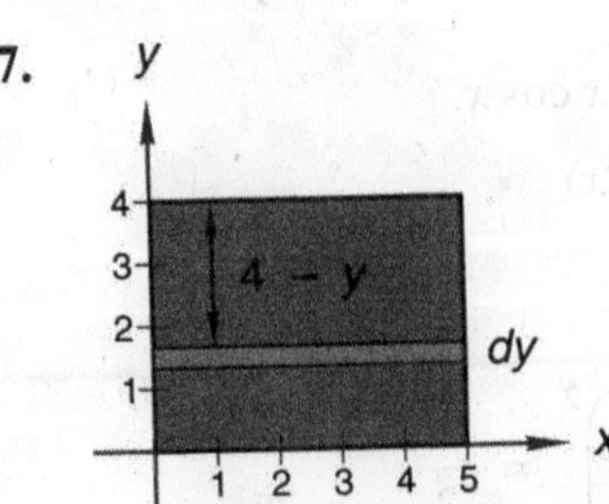

$$F = \int \text{weight density} \cdot \text{depth} \cdot \text{area}$$
$$= \int_0^4 5000(4 - y)(5)\,dy$$
$$= \mathbf{25{,}000 \int_0^4 (4 - y)\,dy}$$

8. $y = x - 2$
$x = y + 2$

$$F = \int \text{weight density} \cdot \text{depth} \cdot \text{area}$$
$$= \int_{-2}^{0} 9000(-y)(y + 2)\,dy$$
$$= 9000 \int_{-2}^{0} (-y^2 - 2y)\,dy$$
$$= 9000\left[-\frac{1}{3}y^3 - y^2\right]_{-2}^{0}$$
$$= 9000\left[0 - \left(\frac{8}{3} - 4\right)\right]$$
$$= 9000\left(\frac{4}{3}\right) = \mathbf{12{,}000\ newtons}$$

9. (a) $|x^2 - 9| = 0$
$x^2 = 9$
$x = \mathbf{3, -3}$

(b)

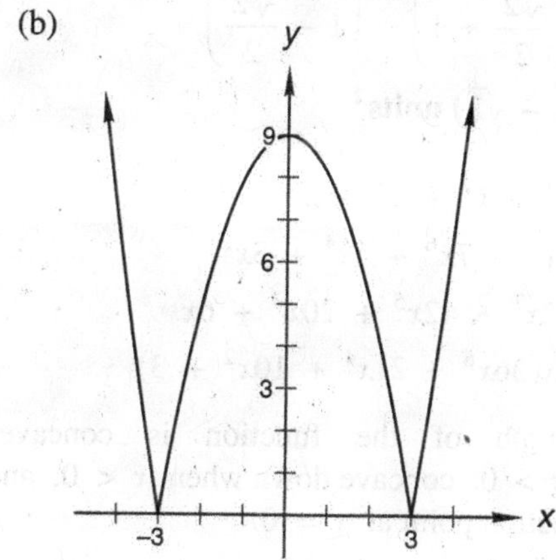

(c) $f'(x) = \begin{cases} \mathbf{2x} & \textbf{when } |x| > 3 \\ \mathbf{-2x} & \textbf{when } |x| < 3 \end{cases}$

10. $f(x) = |x^2 - 2x|$
$x^2 - 2x = 0$
$x(x - 2) = 0$
$x = 0, 2$

$$f(x) = \begin{cases} x^2 - 2x & \text{when } x \le 0 \text{ or } x \ge 2 \\ -x^2 + 2x & \text{when } 0 < x < 2 \end{cases}$$

$$f'(x) = \begin{cases} 2x - 2 & \text{when } x < 0 \text{ or } x > 2 \\ -2x + 2 & \text{when } 0 < x < 2 \end{cases}$$

$f'(x)$ is undefined when $x = 0, 2$
$f'(x) = 0$ when $x = 1$
Critical numbers: $-2, 0, 1, 2, 3$
$f(-2) = 8$ $f(0) = 0$ $f(1) = 1$
$f(2) = 0$ $f(3) = 3$
Maximum: 8 **Minimum: 0**

11.

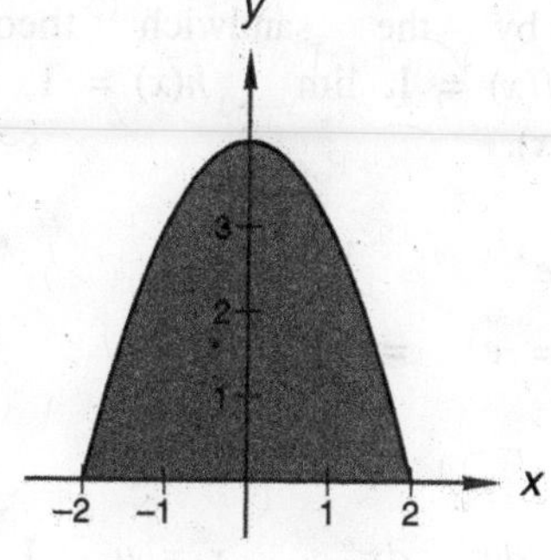

$y = 4 - x^2$
$x^2 = 4 - y$

$$V = \int \pi r^2\,dy$$
$$= \pi \int_0^4 x^2\,dy$$
$$= \boldsymbol{\pi \int_0^4 (4 - y)\,dy}$$

12. $y = 5^{x^2+1} + \dfrac{2x}{(x + 1)^{1/2}}$

$$y' = 5^{x^2+1}(2x)\ln 5 + \frac{(x + 1)^{1/2}(2) - (2x)\frac{1}{2}(x + 1)^{-1/2}}{x + 1}$$
$$y' = 5^{x^2+1}x\ln 25 + \frac{2}{\sqrt{x + 1}} - \frac{x}{(x + 1)^{3/2}}$$
$$\boldsymbol{y' = 5^{x^2+1}x\ln 25 + \frac{x + 2}{(x + 1)^{3/2}}}$$

13. $\int [2^x + (x + 1)^{-1/2}]\,dx$

$$= \frac{2^x}{\ln 2} + 2(x + 1)^{1/2} + C$$
$$= \boldsymbol{\frac{2^x}{\ln 2} + 2\sqrt{x + 1} + C}$$

14. $u = x \quad du = dx \quad v = e^{-x} \quad dv = -e^{-x}\,dx$

$$\int -xe^{-x}\,dx = xe^{-x} - \int e^{-x}\,dx$$
$$= xe^{-x} + e^{-x} + C$$
$$= \boldsymbol{e^{-x}(x + 1) + C}$$

15. $$\int \frac{9x^2}{9 + 49x^6}\,dx = 9\int \frac{x^2}{3^2 + (7x^3)^2}\,dx$$
$$= \frac{9}{63}\int \frac{3(21)x^2}{3^2 + (7x^3)^2}\,dx$$
$$= \boldsymbol{\frac{1}{7}\arctan\frac{7x^3}{3} + C}$$

16. $\lim_{x\to 0} g(x) = \mathbf{1}$ by the sandwich theorem because $\lim_{x\to 0} f(x) = 1$, $\lim_{x\to 0} h(x) = 1$, and $f(x) \le g(x) \le h(x)$.

17. $h(x) = g(x^2) = e^{x^2}$

$h(-x) = e^{(-x)^2} = e^{x^2} = h(x)$

Even

18. $u = x + 1 \qquad du = dx \qquad x = u - 1$

$$\int_1^4 x(x+1)^{1/2}\,dx = \int_2^5 (u-1)u^{1/2}\,du$$

$$= \int_2^5 (u^{3/2} - u^{1/2})\,du$$

The correct choice is **C**.

19. $y = \arcsin(2x)$

$$y' = \frac{2}{\sqrt{1-4x^2}}$$

$$m = \frac{2}{\sqrt{1-\frac{1}{4}}} = \frac{4\sqrt{3}}{3}$$

$$y - \frac{\pi}{6} = \frac{4\sqrt{3}}{3}\left(x - \frac{1}{4}\right)$$

$$y = \frac{4\sqrt{3}}{3}x - \frac{\sqrt{3}}{3} + \frac{\pi}{6}$$

$$\mathbf{y = \frac{4\sqrt{3}}{3}x + \frac{\pi - 2\sqrt{3}}{6}}$$

20.

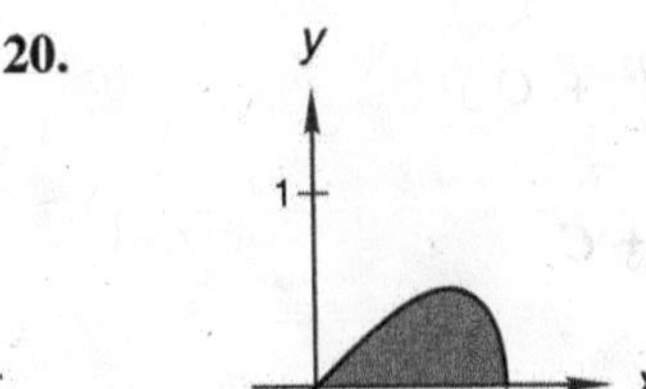

$$A = \int_0^1 x(1-x^2)^{1/2}\,dx$$

$$= -\frac{1}{2}\int_0^1 -2x(1-x^2)^{1/2}\,dx$$

$$= -\frac{1}{3}\left[(1-x^2)^{3/2}\right]_0^1$$

$$= -\frac{1}{3}(0-1) = \mathbf{\frac{1}{3}\ unit^2}$$

21.

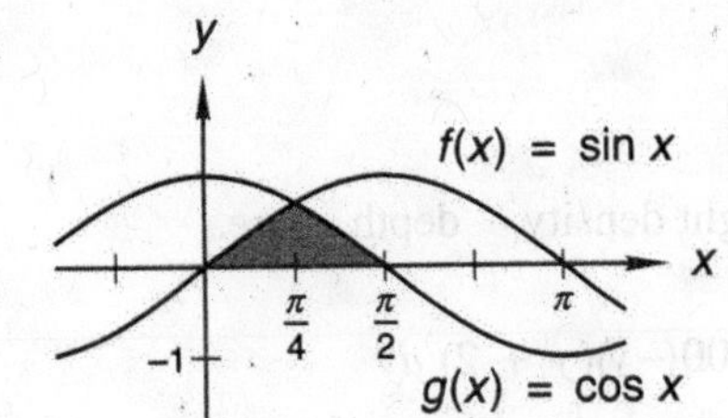

$\sin x = \cos x$

$\tan x = 1$

$x = \dfrac{\pi}{4}$

$$\left(\frac{\pi}{4}, \frac{\sqrt{2}}{2}\right)$$

22. $A = \displaystyle\int_0^{\pi/4} \sin x\,dx + \int_{\pi/4}^{\pi/2} \cos x\,dx$

$$= [-\cos x]_0^{\pi/4} + [\sin x]_{\pi/4}^{\pi/2}$$

$$= -\left(\frac{\sqrt{2}}{2} + 1\right) + \left(1 - \frac{\sqrt{2}}{2}\right)$$

$$= \mathbf{(2 - \sqrt{2})\ units^2}$$

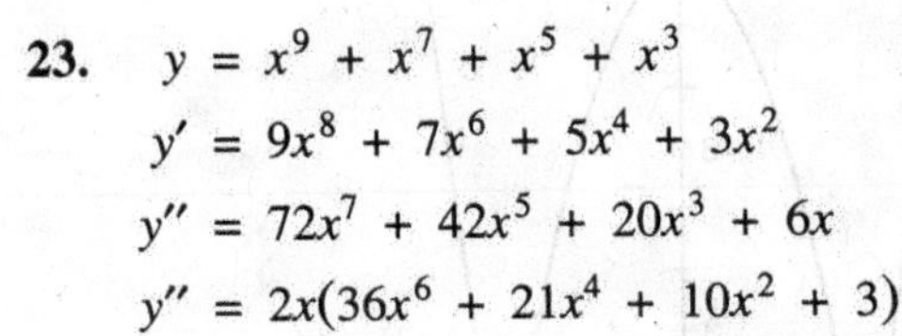

23. $y = x^9 + x^7 + x^5 + x^3$

$y' = 9x^8 + 7x^6 + 5x^4 + 3x^2$

$y'' = 72x^7 + 42x^5 + 20x^3 + 6x$

$y'' = 2x(36x^6 + 21x^4 + 10x^2 + 3)$

The graph of the function is concave up when $x > 0$, concave down when $x < 0$, and has an inflection point at $x = 0$.

The correct choice is **D**.

24. (a)

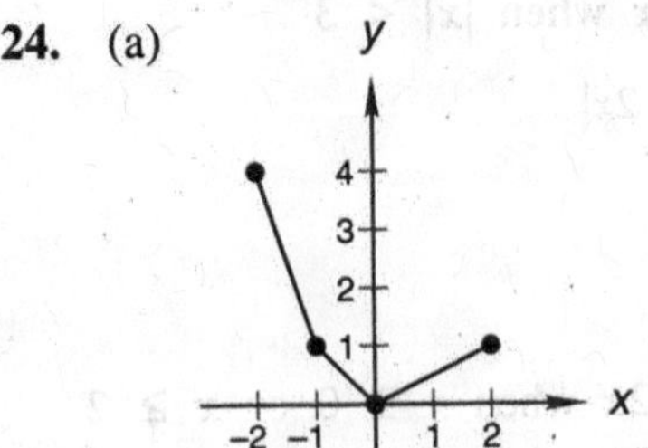

(b)

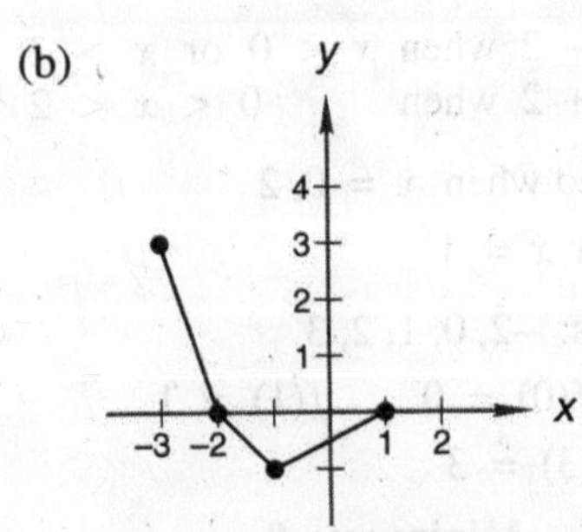

(c)

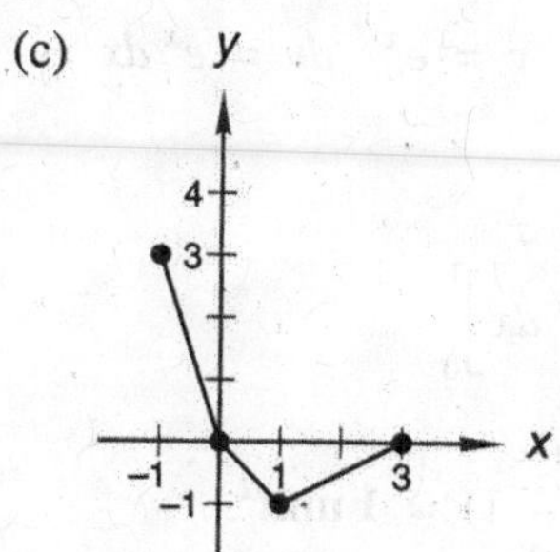

25.

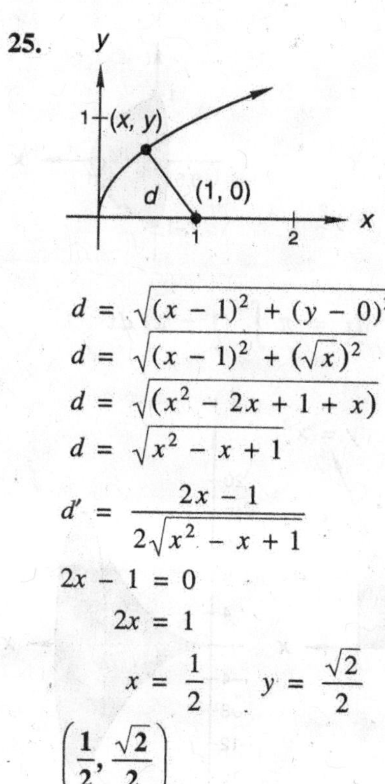

$$d = \sqrt{(x-1)^2 + (y-0)^2}$$
$$d = \sqrt{(x-1)^2 + (\sqrt{x})^2}$$
$$d = \sqrt{(x^2 - 2x + 1 + x)}$$
$$d = \sqrt{x^2 - x + 1}$$
$$d' = \frac{2x-1}{2\sqrt{x^2 - x + 1}}$$
$$2x - 1 = 0$$
$$2x = 1$$
$$x = \frac{1}{2} \qquad y = \frac{\sqrt{2}}{2}$$
$$\left(\frac{1}{2}, \frac{\sqrt{2}}{2}\right)$$

Problem Set 76

1. $$A(t) = A_0e^{kt}$$
$$17{,}000 = 10{,}000e^{3k}$$
$$1.7 = e^{3k}$$
$$\ln 1.7 = 3k$$
$$k = \frac{\ln 1.7}{3}$$
$$A(4) = 10{,}000e^{4 \ln 1.7/3} = \mathbf{\$20{,}289.21}$$

2. $$y = 3x - 6$$
$$y + 6 = 3x$$
$$x = \frac{1}{3}y + 2$$
$$F = \int \text{weight density} \cdot \text{depth} \cdot \text{area}$$
$$= \int_0^3 9800(3-y)\left(\frac{1}{3}y + 2\right) dy$$
$$= \mathbf{9800 \int_0^3 (3-y)\left(\frac{1}{3}y + 2\right) dy}$$

3. $$\int \sin^3 x\,dx = \int \sin x\,(1 - \cos^2 x)\,dx$$
$$= \int (\sin x - \cos^2 x \sin x)\,dx$$
$$= \mathbf{-\cos x + \frac{1}{3}\cos^3 x + C}$$

4. $$\int \sin^2 x \cos^3 x\,dx$$
$$= \int \sin^2 x \cos x\,(1 - \sin^2 x)\,dx$$
$$= \int (\sin^2 x \cos x - \sin^4 x \cos x)\,dx$$
$$= \mathbf{\frac{1}{3}\sin^3 x - \frac{1}{5}\sin^5 x + C}$$

5. $$\int \sin^3 x \cos^2 x\,dx$$
$$= \int \sin x\,(1 - \cos^2 x)\cos^2 x\,dx$$
$$= \int (\cos^2 x \sin x - \cos^4 x \sin x)\,dx$$
$$= \mathbf{-\frac{1}{3}\cos^3 x + \frac{1}{5}\cos^5 x + C}$$

6. $$\int (\sin^2 x + \cos^2 x)\,dx = \int 1\,dx = \mathbf{x + C}$$

7. $$\lim_{x\to 0^+} (-2x + b) = f(0)$$
$$\mathbf{b = 1}$$

8. $$\lim_{x\to 2} f(x) = \lim_{x\to 2} \frac{x^3 - 8}{x - 2}$$
$$= \lim_{x\to 2} \frac{(x-2)(x^2 + 2x + 4)}{x-2}$$
$$= \lim_{x\to 2} (x^2 + 2x + 4)$$
$$= 12 \neq 16 = f(2)$$
Since $\lim_{x\to 2} f(x) \neq f(2)$, f is **not continuous** at $x = 2$.

9. $f(x) = x^3 + ax^2 + bx + c$

$f'(x) = 3x^2 + 2ax + b$

$f''(x) = 6x + 2a$

Since the graph of f passes through (0, 1), $\mathbf{c = 1.}$

Since the graph has a relative minimum at $x = 0$,

$$f'(0) = 0$$
$$3(0)^2 + 2a(0) + b = 0$$
$$\mathbf{b = 0}$$

Since the graph has an inflection point at $x = -\frac{2}{3}$,

$$f''\left(-\frac{2}{3}\right) = 0$$
$$6\left(-\frac{2}{3}\right) + 2a = 0$$
$$\mathbf{a = 2}$$

10.

n	$f^{(n)}(x)$	$f^{(n)}(0)$
0	$(1 + e^x)^2$	4
1	$2e^x(1 + e^x)$ $= 2e^x + 2e^{2x}$	$4 = 2 + 2^1$
2	$2e^x + 2(2e^{2x})$ $= 2e^x + 4e^{2x}$	$6 = 2 + 2^2$
3	$2e^x + 4(2e^{2x})$ $= 2e^x + 8e^{2x}$	$10 = 2 + 2^3$
⋮	⋮	⋮

$$(1 + e^x)^2 = \frac{f(0)}{0!} + \frac{f'(0)}{1!}x + \frac{f''(0)}{2!}x^2 + \frac{f'''(0)}{3!}x^3 + \cdots$$

$$(1 + e^x)^2 = \mathbf{4 + 4x + 3x^2 + \frac{5}{3}x^3 + \cdots + \frac{2 + 2^i}{i!}x^i + \cdots}$$

11. (a)

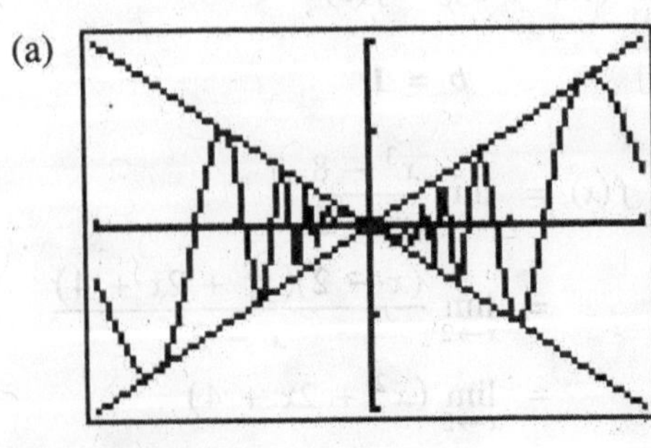

(b) $\lim_{x\to 0} x \cos \frac{1}{x} = \mathbf{0}$ by the sandwich theorem, because $-|x| \le x \cos\left(\frac{1}{x}\right) \le |x|$ and $\lim_{x\to 0} -|x| = 0$ and $\lim_{x\to 0} |x| = 0$.

12. $u = x \quad du = dx \quad v = e^x \quad dv = e^x\, dx$

$$A = \int_0^1 xe^x\, dx$$
$$= \left[xe^x - \int e^x\, dx\right]_0^1$$
$$= \left[xe^x - e^x\right]_0^1$$
$$= e - e - (0 - 1) = \mathbf{1\ unit^2}$$

13.

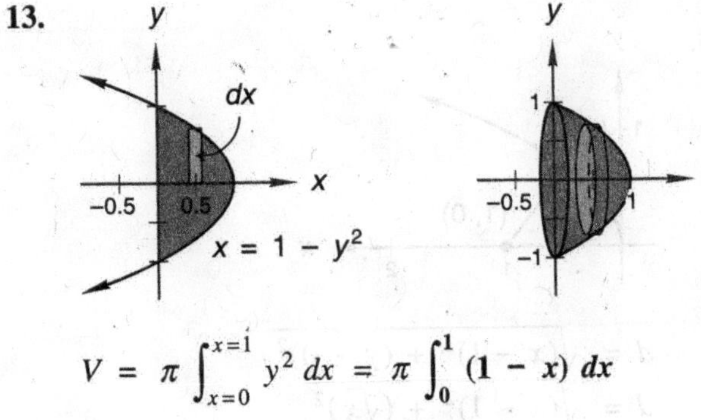

$$V = \pi \int_{x=0}^{x=1} y^2\, dx = \pi \int_0^1 \mathbf{(1 - x)\, dx}$$

14.

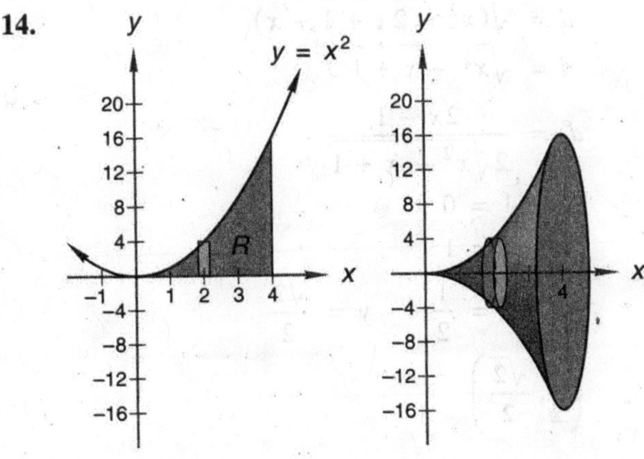

$$V = \pi \int_{x=0}^{x=4} y^2\, dx = \pi \int_0^4 x^4\, dx$$
$$= \pi\left[\frac{1}{5}x^5\right]_0^4 = \mathbf{\frac{1024}{5}\pi\ units^3}$$

15. $y = 5^{x^2+1} + x \arctan \frac{x}{2} + \log_{24} x$

$$y' = 5^{x^2+1}(\ln 5)(2x) + x \cdot \frac{2}{x^2 + 4} + \arctan \frac{x}{2} + \frac{1}{x \ln 24}$$

$$y' = \mathbf{5^{x^2+1} x \ln 25 + \frac{2x}{x^2 + 4} + \arctan \frac{x}{2} + \frac{1}{x \ln 24}}$$

16. $y = x(\ln x)^2$

$$y' = x\left(\frac{2\ln x}{x}\right) + (\ln x)^2$$

$$y' = 2\ln x + (\ln x)^2$$

$$0 = 2\ln x + (\ln x)^2$$

$$0 = \ln x\,(2 + \ln x)$$

$x = 1$ $\qquad \ln x = -2$

$$x = e^{-2}$$

17. $\dfrac{d}{dx}(\arcsin x) + \displaystyle\int \frac{1}{\sqrt{1-x^2}}\,dx$

$$= \mathbf{\frac{1}{\sqrt{1-x^2}} + \arcsin x + C}$$

18. $\displaystyle\int \left(xe^{2x} + xe^{x^2}\right) dx = \int xe^{2x}\,dx + \int xe^{x^2}\,dx$

$u = x \quad du = dx \quad v = \frac{1}{2}e^{2x} \quad dv = e^{2x}\,dx$

$$\int xe^{2x}\,dx + \int xe^{x^2}\,dx$$

$$= \frac{1}{2}xe^{2x} - \int \frac{1}{2}e^{2x}\,dx + \int xe^{x^2}\,dx$$

$$= \mathbf{\frac{1}{2}xe^{2x} - \frac{1}{4}e^{2x} + \frac{1}{2}e^{x^2} + C}$$

19.

$$xy + y^2 = x + 1$$

$$x\frac{dy}{dx} + y + 2y\frac{dy}{dx} = 1$$

$$\frac{dy}{dx} = \frac{1-y}{x+2y}$$

$$\left.\frac{dy}{dx}\right|_{(2,1)} = \frac{1-1}{2+2} = 0$$

$\mathbf{y = 1}$

20.

$$5y - 2x + y^3 - x^2y = 0$$

$$5\frac{dy}{dx} - 2 + 3y^2\frac{dy}{dx} - x^2\frac{dy}{dx} - 2xy = 0$$

$$\frac{2xy + 2}{5 + 3y^2 - x^2} = \frac{dy}{dx}$$

$$\left.\frac{dy}{dx}\right|_{(0,0)} = \frac{2}{5}$$

$$5x + 2y + x^4 - x^3y^2 = 0$$

$$5 + 2\frac{dy}{dx} + 4x^3 - 2x^3y\frac{dy}{dx} - 3x^2y^2 = 0$$

$$\frac{3x^2y^2 - 4x^3 - 5}{2 - 2x^3y} = \frac{dy}{dx}$$

$$\left.\frac{dy}{dx}\right|_{(0,0)} = -\frac{5}{2}$$

The slopes are negative reciprocals of each other. Therefore, the tangents to the two curves are perpendicular at the origin.

21. $\displaystyle\int_0^1 \cos x\, e^{\sin x}\,dx = \int_{x=0}^{x=1} e^u\,du = e^u\Big|_{x=0}^{x=1}$

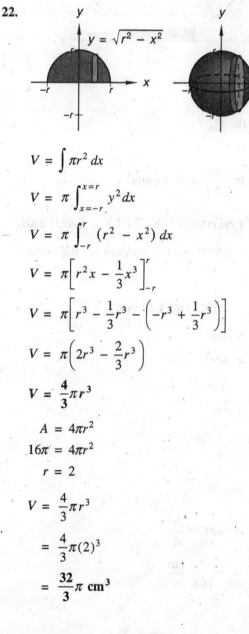

$$= e^{\sin x}\Big|_0^1 = \mathbf{e^{\sin 1} - 1}$$

22.

$$V = \int \pi r^2\,dx$$

$$V = \pi\int_{x=-r}^{x=r} y^2\,dx$$

$$V = \pi\int_{-r}^{r} (r^2 - x^2)\,dx$$

$$V = \pi\left[r^2x - \frac{1}{3}x^3\right]_{-r}^{r}$$

$$V = \pi\left[r^3 - \frac{1}{3}r^3 - \left(-r^3 + \frac{1}{3}r^3\right)\right]$$

$$V = \pi\left(2r^3 - \frac{2}{3}r^3\right)$$

$$\mathbf{V = \frac{4}{3}\pi r^3}$$

$$A = 4\pi r^2$$

$$16\pi = 4\pi r^2$$

$$r = 2$$

$$V = \frac{4}{3}\pi r^3$$

$$= \frac{4}{3}\pi(2)^3$$

$$= \mathbf{\frac{32}{3}\pi\ \text{cm}^3}$$

23. $f(x) = \dfrac{x^5 - 1}{x - 1}$

$f(-a) = \dfrac{(-a)^5 - 1}{-a - 1} = \dfrac{-a^5 - 1}{-a - 1} = \dfrac{a^5 + 1}{a + 1}$

-1	1	0	0	0	0	1
	↓	-1	1	-1	1	-1
	1	-1	1	-1	1	[0]

$f(-a) = \dfrac{a^5 + 1}{a + 1} = a^4 - a^3 + a^2 - a + 1$

The correct choice is **B.**

24.

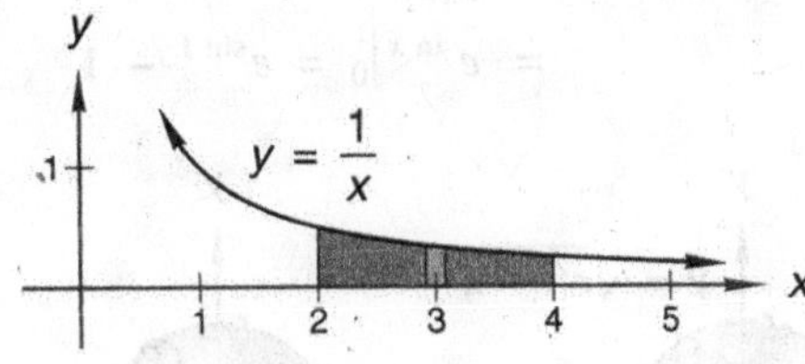

$A = \displaystyle\int_2^4 \frac{1}{x}\,dx$

$= [\ln x]_2^4$

$= \ln 4 - \ln 2$

$= \ln\left(\dfrac{4}{2}\right) = \mathbf{\ln 2\ units^2}$

25. $A =$ `fnInt(X⁻¹,X,2,4)` $\approx$ **0.6931 units²**

$\ln 2 \approx 0.6931$, so **the answers are the same.**

Problem Set 77

1. $A = 4\pi r^2$

$16\pi = 4\pi r^2$

$r^2 = 4$

$r = 2$

$V = \dfrac{4}{3}\pi r^3$

$\dfrac{dV}{dt} = 4\pi r^2 \dfrac{dr}{dt}$

$-3 = 4\pi(2)^2 \dfrac{dr}{dt}$

$\dfrac{dr}{dt} = \mathbf{-\dfrac{3}{16\pi}\ \dfrac{cm}{s}}$

2.

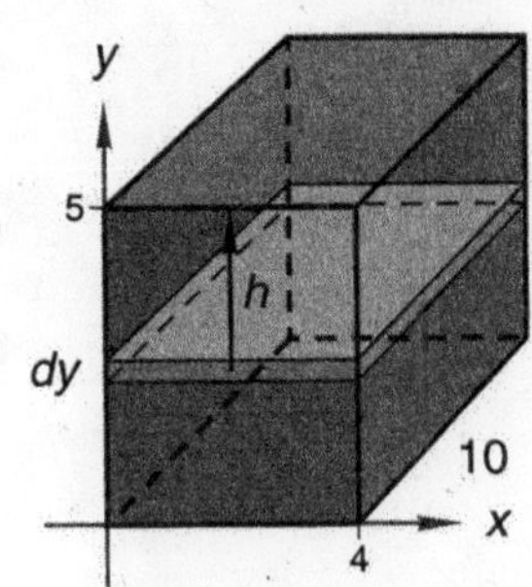

$W = \displaystyle\int$ depth · weight density · volume

$= \displaystyle\int_0^5 (5 - y)(9800)(4)(10)\,dy$

$= 392{,}000 \displaystyle\int_0^5 (5 - y)\,dy$

$= 392{,}000\left[5y - \dfrac{1}{2}y^2\right]_0^5$

$= 392{,}000\left(25 - \dfrac{25}{2}\right)$

$=$ **4,900,000 joules**

3.

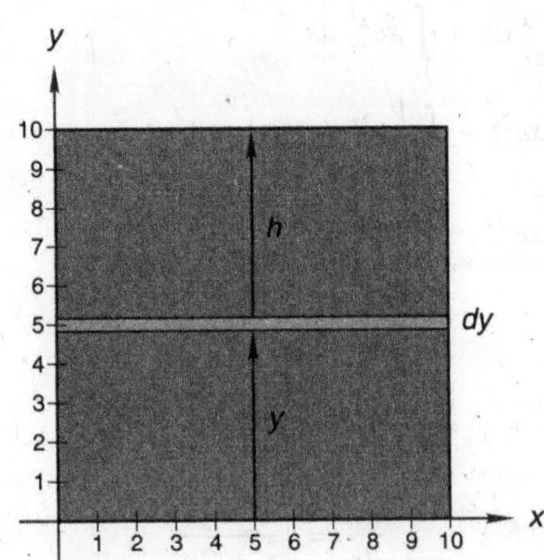

$F = \displaystyle\int$ weight density · depth · area

$= \displaystyle\int_0^{10} 9800(10 - y)(10)\,dy$

$= 98{,}000 \displaystyle\int_0^{10} (10 - y)\,dy$

$= 98{,}000\left[10y - \dfrac{1}{2}y^2\right]_0^{10}$

$= 98{,}000(100 - 50)$

$=$ **4,900,000 newtons**

4.

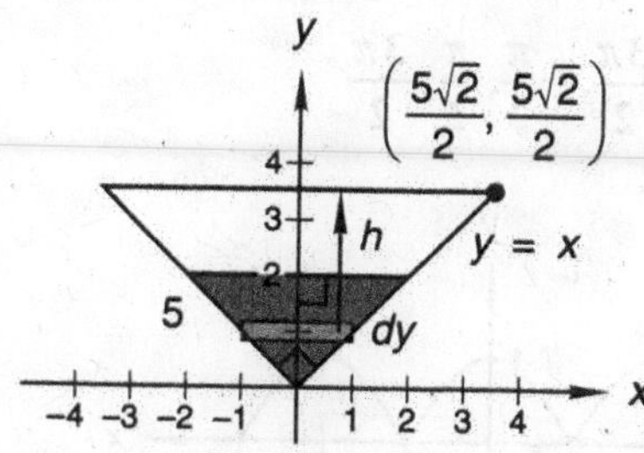

$$W = \int \text{depth} \cdot \text{weight density} \cdot \text{volume}$$

$$= \int_0^2 \left(\frac{5\sqrt{2}}{2} - y\right)(6000)(2x)(15)\,dy$$

$$= \mathbf{180{,}000 \int_0^2 y\left(\frac{5\sqrt{2}}{2} - y\right) dy}$$

5. $\int \sin^2 x \cos^3 x\,dx$

$$= \int \sin^2 x \cos x\,(1 - \sin^2 x)\,dx$$

$$= \int \sin^2 x \cos x\,dx - \int \sin^4 x \cos x\,dx$$

$u = \sin x \qquad du = \cos x\,dx$

$$\int \sin^2 x \cos x\,dx - \int \sin^4 x \cos x\,dx$$

$$= \int u^2\,du - \int u^4\,du$$

$$= \frac{1}{3}u^3 - \frac{1}{5}u^5 + C$$

$$= \mathbf{\frac{1}{3}\sin^3 x - \frac{1}{5}\sin^5 x + C}$$

6. $\int \cos^3 x\,dx = \int \cos x\,(1 - \sin^2 x)\,dx$

$$= \int \cos x\,dx - \int \sin^2 x \cos x\,dx$$

$u = \sin x \qquad du = \cos x\,dx$

$$\int \cos x\,dx - \int \sin^2 x \cos x\,dx$$

$$= \int du - \int u^2\,du$$

$$= u - \frac{1}{3}u^3 + C$$

$$= \mathbf{\sin x - \frac{1}{3}\sin^3 x + C}$$

7. $\int \frac{1}{1 + x^2}\,dx + \int \frac{2 \sin x}{\sqrt{\cos x + 1}}\,dx$

$$= \arctan x + 2\int (\sin x)(\cos x + 1)^{-1/2}\,dx$$

$u = \cos x + 1 \qquad du = -\sin x\,dx$

$$\arctan x + 2\int (\sin x)(\cos x + 1)^{-1/2}\,dx$$

$$= \arctan x - 2\int u^{-1/2}\,du$$

$$= \arctan x - 4u^{1/2} + C$$

$$= \mathbf{\arctan x - 4\sqrt{\cos x + 1} + C}$$

8. $\int \frac{x^2 + 1}{x}\,dx = \int \left(x + \frac{1}{x}\right) dx$

$$= \mathbf{\frac{1}{2}x^2 + \ln|x| + C}$$

9. $\lim_{x\to 1^+} f(x) = f(1)$

$$\lim_{x\to 1^+} (ax + 2) = 1$$

$$a + 2 = 1$$

$$\mathbf{a = -1}$$

10. $a(t) = -9.8$

$$\mathbf{v(t) = -9.8t + 20}$$

$$\mathbf{h(t) = -4.9t^2 + 20t + 100}$$

11. $y = \log_3 x$

$$y' = \frac{1}{x \ln 3}$$

$$y'(3) = \frac{1}{3 \ln 3} = \frac{1}{\ln 27}$$

For the perpendicular line, $m = -\ln 27$.

$$y - 1 = -\ln 27\,(x - 3)$$

$$y = -\ln 27\,(x) + 3 \ln 27 + 1$$

$$\mathbf{y = (-\ln 27)x + \ln(19{,}683e)}$$

12. (a) $\lim_{x\to 0^+} \frac{|x|}{x} = \mathbf{1}$

(b) $\lim_{x\to 0^+} \sin\frac{1}{x}$ **does not exist**

13. (a) $\lim_{x \to 0} \frac{\sin x}{\cos x} = \lim_{x \to 0} \tan x = \mathbf{0}$

(b) $\lim_{x \to 0} \frac{1}{x}$ **does not exist,** because

$$\lim_{x \to 0^+} \frac{1}{x} = \infty \text{ and } \lim_{x \to 0^-} \frac{1}{x} = -\infty$$

14. $$\lim_{x \to \pi} (fg)(x) = \lim_{x \to \pi} (3x^2 \sin x)$$
$$= \lim_{x \to \pi} 3x^2 \cdot \lim_{x \to \pi} \sin x$$
$$= 3\pi^2(0) = \mathbf{0}$$

15. $$h(x) = \frac{3x^2}{\sin x}$$
$$h(-x) = \frac{3(-x)^2}{\sin(-x)}$$
$$h(-x) = \frac{3x^2}{-\sin x}$$
$$h(-x) = -h(x)$$

Therefore h is odd, which implies **origin symmetry.**

16.

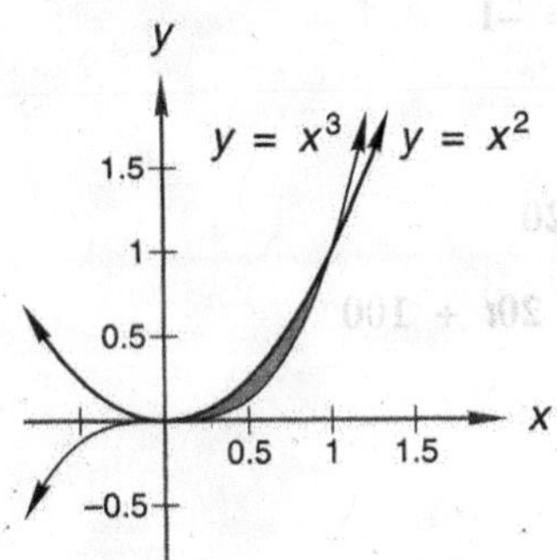

$$A = \int_0^1 (x^2 - x^3)\, dx$$
$$= \left[\frac{1}{3}x^3 - \frac{1}{4}x^4\right]_0^1$$
$$= \frac{1}{3} - \frac{1}{4} - (0) = \mathbf{\frac{1}{12}\ unit^2}$$

17. On the interval [1, 4],

$$-6 \le f(x) \le 4$$
$$(-6)(3) \le \int_1^4 f(x)\, dx \le (4)(3)$$
$$-18 \le \int_1^4 f(x)\, dx \le 12$$

The correct choice is **B.**

18. (a) $x = \mathbf{-\frac{3\pi}{2}, -\frac{\pi}{2}, \frac{\pi}{2}, \frac{3\pi}{2}}$

(b)

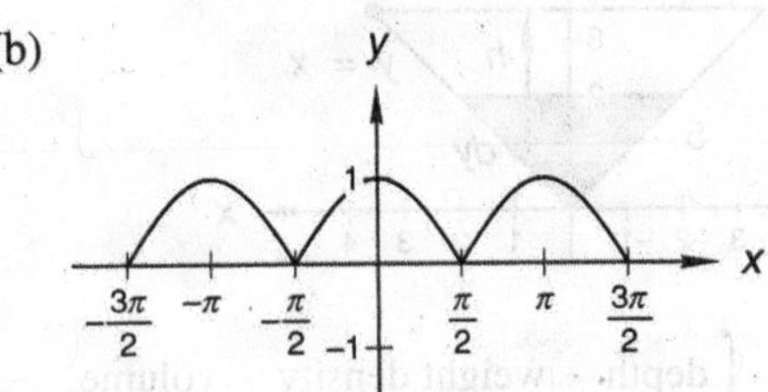

(c) $$f'(x) = \begin{cases} \mathbf{-\sin x \text{ when } -\frac{\pi}{2} < x < \frac{\pi}{2}} \\ \mathbf{\sin x \text{ when } -\frac{3\pi}{2} < x < -\frac{\pi}{2}} \\ \mathbf{\text{or } \frac{\pi}{2} < x < \frac{3\pi}{2}} \end{cases}$$

19. (a) $$h(x) = g(f(x))$$
$$h(x) = g(|\cos x|)$$
$$\mathbf{h(x) = \cos^2 x}$$
$$0 = \cos^2 x$$
$$x = \mathbf{-\frac{3\pi}{2}, -\frac{\pi}{2}, \frac{\pi}{2}, \frac{3\pi}{2}}$$

(b)

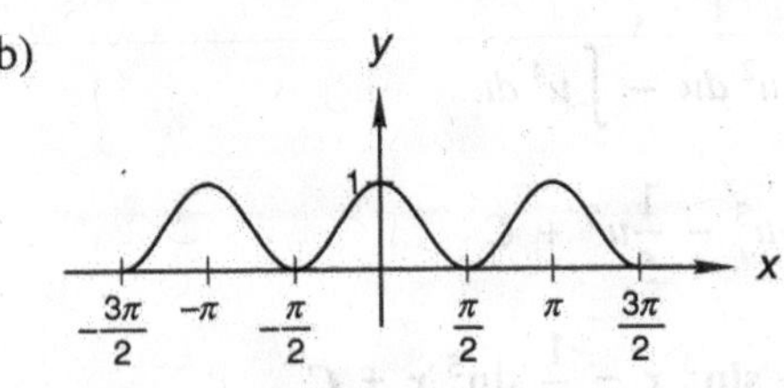

(c) **Domain:** $\{x \in \mathbb{R} \mid 0 \le x \le 2\pi\}$

Range: $\{y \in \mathbb{R} \mid 0 \le y \le 1\}$

(d) $$h\left(\frac{3\pi}{4}\right) = \cos^2 \frac{3\pi}{4} = \frac{1}{2}$$
$$h'(x) = 2\cos x(-\sin x) = -\sin(2x)$$
$$h'\left(\frac{3\pi}{4}\right) = -\sin\left(\frac{3\pi}{2}\right) = 1$$
$$y - \frac{1}{2} = 1\left(x - \frac{3\pi}{4}\right)$$
$$y = x - \frac{3\pi}{4} + \frac{1}{2}$$
$$\mathbf{y = x + \frac{2 - 3\pi}{4}}$$

20. $y = \arctan(2x) + 2\sin x(\cos x + 1)^{-1/2} + \sec x \tan x$

$$y' = \frac{2}{4x^2 + 1} + 2\sin x\left(-\frac{1}{2}(\cos x + 1)^{-3/2}(-\sin x)\right) + (\cos x + 1)^{-1/2}(2\cos x) + \sec x \sec^2 x + \tan x \sec x \tan x$$

$$\boldsymbol{y' = \frac{2}{4x^2 + 1} + \frac{\sin^2 x}{(\cos x + 1)^{3/2}} + \frac{2\cos x}{\sqrt{\cos x + 1}} + \sec^3 x + \sec x \tan^2 x}$$

21. $$\lim_{h\to 0} \frac{\sin\left(\frac{\pi}{2} + h\right) - \sin\frac{\pi}{2}}{h} = \left.\frac{d}{dx}\right|_{\pi/2} \sin x = \cos\frac{\pi}{2} = \mathbf{0}$$

22. $$\lim_{x\to 4} \frac{\ln x - \ln 4}{x - 4} = \left.\frac{d}{dx}\ln x\right|_4 = \mathbf{\frac{1}{4}}$$

23. (a)
$$x^2 - xy + y^2 = 9$$
$$2x - x\frac{dy}{dx} - y + 2y\frac{dy}{dx} = 0$$
$$\boldsymbol{\frac{dy}{dx} = \frac{y - 2x}{2y - x}}$$

(b) Vertical tangents occur when $\frac{dy}{dx}$ is undefined.

$$2y - x = 0$$
$$x = 2y$$
$$x^2 - xy + y^2 = 9$$
$$(2y)^2 - (2y)y + y^2 = 9$$
$$4y^2 - 2y^2 + y^2 = 9$$
$$3y^2 = 9$$
$$y^2 = 3$$
$$y = \pm\sqrt{3}$$

$\mathbf{(2\sqrt{3}, \sqrt{3}), (-2\sqrt{3}, -\sqrt{3})}$

(c) $y^2 - xy + (x^2 - 9) = 0$

$$y = \frac{x \pm \sqrt{x^2 - 4(x^2 - 9)}}{2}$$

```
Y1=(X+√(-3X²+36))/2
Y2=(X-√(-3X²+36))/2
```

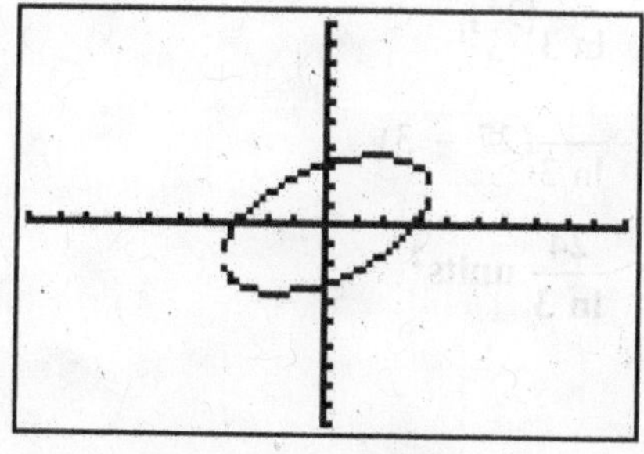

24. The correct choice is **C**.

25. $y = \sin(\arctan x)$

Range of arctan x: $\left\{y \in \mathbb{R} \mid -\frac{\pi}{2} < y < \frac{\pi}{2}\right\}$

Range of sin (arctan x): $\mathbf{\{y \in \mathbb{R} \mid -1 < y < 1\}}$

PROBLEM SET 78

1. (a)
$$\text{Cost} = 2x^2(2.40) + 4xy(1.50)$$
$$\text{Cost} = 4.8x^2 + 6xy$$
$$360 = 4.8x^2 + 6xy$$
$$360 - 4.8x^2 = 6xy$$
$$y = \frac{360 - 4.8x^2}{6x}$$
$$y = 60x^{-1} - 0.8x$$
$$V = x^2y$$
$$V = x^2(60x^{-1} - 0.8x)$$
$$\mathbf{V = 60x - 0.8x^3}$$

(b)
$$V' = 60 - 2.4x^2$$
$$2.4x^2 = 60$$
$$x^2 = 25$$
$$x = 5$$
$$y = \frac{60}{5} - 0.8(5) = 12 - 4 = 8$$
$\mathbf{x = 5\text{ m}, y = 8\text{ m}}$

(c)

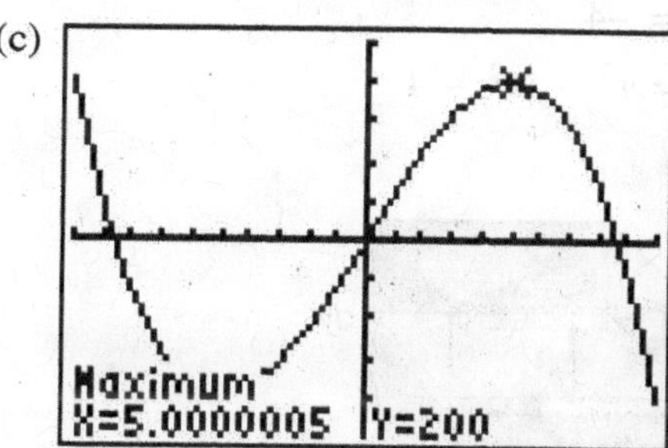

Window: `Xmin=-10, Xmax=10, Ymin=-250, Ymax=250`

2. (a) $a(t) = 2t$

$v(t) = t^2 + C$

$-10 = 0 + C$

$C = -10$

$\mathbf{v(t) = t^2 - 10}$

$x(t) = \frac{1}{3}t^3 - 10t + C$

$4 = 0 - 0 + C$

$C = 4$

$\mathbf{x(t) = \frac{1}{3}t^3 - 10t + 4}$

(b) $\mathbf{v(2) = -6}$ **units/s**

$x(2) = \frac{8}{3} - 20 + 4$

$\mathbf{x(2) = -\frac{40}{3}}$ **units**

3. $a(t) = 6t - 4$

$v(t) = 3t^2 - 4t + C$

$-1 = 3 - 4 + C$

$C = 0$

$\mathbf{v(t) = 3t^2 - 4t}$

$x(t) = t^3 - 2t^2 + C$

$-4 = 0 - 0 + C$

$C = -4$

$\mathbf{x(t) = t^3 - 2t^2 - 4}$

4.

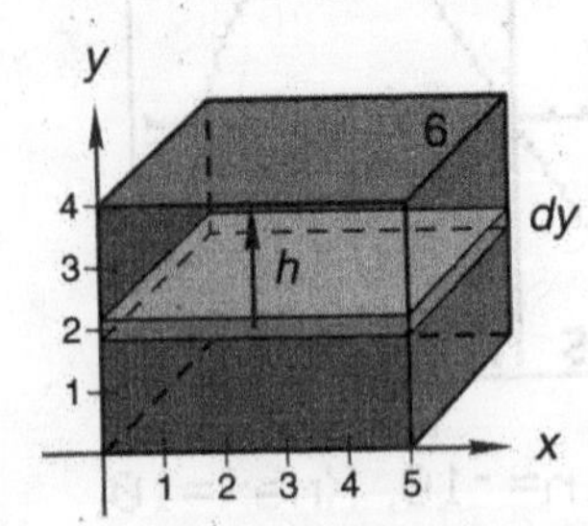

$W = \int \text{depth} \cdot \text{weight density} \cdot \text{volume}$

$= \int_0^4 (4 - y)(5000)(5)(6)\, dy$

$= 150{,}000 \int_0^4 (4 - y)\, dy$

$= 150{,}000 \left[4y - \frac{1}{2}y^2 \right]_0^4$

$=$ **1,200,000 joules**

5. $x^2 + y^2 = 25$

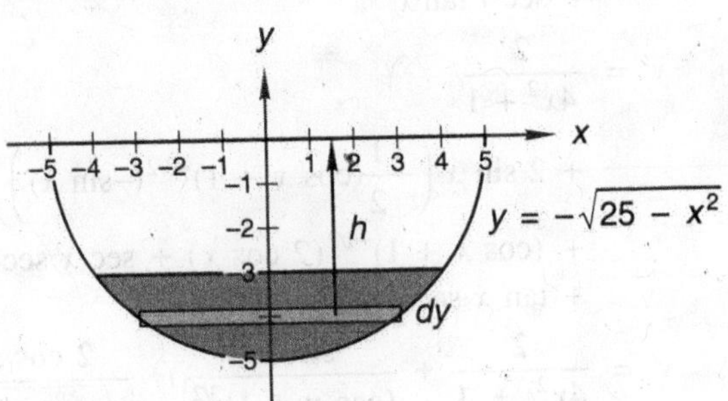

$W = \int \text{depth} \cdot \text{weight density} \cdot \text{volume}$

$= \int_{y=-5}^{y=-3} (-y)(6000)(2x)(20)\, dy$

$= 240{,}000 \int_{-5}^{-3} \sqrt{25 - y^2}\,(-y)\, dy$

$= 120{,}000 \int_{-5}^{-3} (25 - y^2)^{1/2}(-2y)\, dy$

$= 120{,}000\left(\frac{2}{3}\right)\left[(25 - y^2)^{3/2}\right]_{-5}^{-3}$

$= 80{,}000(64 - 0)$

$=$ **5,120,000 joules**

6. This statement would be true if f were a continuous function. Since we do not know whether or not f is continuous, it is possible that f has a discontinuity at $x = 0$. The function could look like:

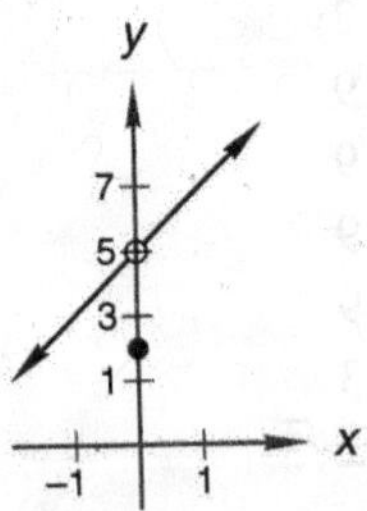

Since this is a possibility, the given statement is **false.**

7. $A = \int_1^3 3^x\, dx$

$= \frac{1}{\ln 3}[3^x]_1^3$

$= \frac{1}{\ln 3}(27 - 3)$

$= \mathbf{\frac{24}{\ln 3}}$ **units²**

8. $u = x \qquad v = \frac{1}{2}e^{2x}$

$du = dx \qquad dv = e^{2x}\,dx$

$$\int x e^{2x}\,dx = \frac{1}{2}xe^{2x} - \int \frac{1}{2}e^{2x}\,dx$$

$$= \frac{1}{2}xe^{2x} - \frac{1}{4}e^{2x} + C$$

$$= \mathbf{\frac{1}{4}e^{2x}(2x - 1) + C}$$

9. $$\int \frac{x+1}{\sqrt{x}}\,dx = \int (x^{1/2} + x^{-1/2})\,dx$$

$$= \frac{2}{3}x^{3/2} + 2x^{1/2} + C$$

$$= \mathbf{\frac{2}{3}\sqrt{x}(x + 3) + C}$$

10. $u = x^2 + 1 \quad du = 2x\,dx$

$$\int \frac{4x}{x^2 + 1}\,dx = 2\int \frac{du}{u}$$

$$= 2\ln|u| + C$$

$$= \mathbf{2\ln(x^2 + 1) + C}$$

11. $$\int \frac{4}{x^2 + 1}\,dx = \mathbf{4\arctan x + C}$$

12. $$\int \sin^6 x \cos^3 x\,dx$$

$$= \int \sin^6 x \cos x\,(1 - \sin^2 x)\,dx$$

$$= \int \sin^6 x \cos x\,dx - \int \sin^8 x \cos x\,dx$$

$u = \sin x \qquad du = \cos x\,dx$

$$\int \sin^6 x \cos x\,dx - \int \sin^8 x \cos x\,dx$$

$$= \int u^6\,du - \int u^8\,du$$

$$= \frac{1}{7}u^7 - \frac{1}{9}u^9 + C$$

$$= \mathbf{\frac{1}{7}\sin^7 x - \frac{1}{9}\sin^9 x + C}$$

13. $u = \sin x + \pi \qquad du = \cos x\,dx$

$$\int (\cos x)(\sin x + \pi)^3\,dx = \int u^3\,du$$

$$= \frac{1}{4}u^4 + C$$

$$= \mathbf{\frac{1}{4}(\sin x + \pi)^4 + C}$$

14.

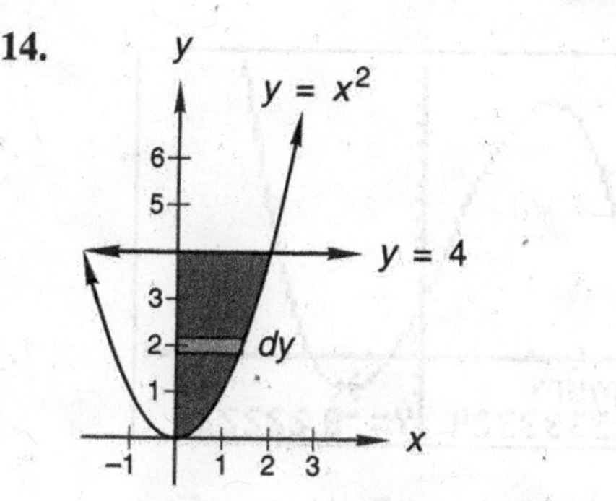

$$A = \int_0^4 x\,dy = \mathbf{\int_0^4 \sqrt{y}\,dy}$$

15. (a) $f(x) = \frac{1}{2}(x - 2)(6x^2 + 21x - 14)$

$$f'(x) = \frac{1}{2}(x - 2)(12x + 21) + \frac{1}{2}(6x^2 + 21x - 14)$$

$$f'(x) = \frac{1}{2}(12x^2 - 3x - 42 + 6x^2 + 21x - 14)$$

$$f'(x) = 9x^2 + 9x - 28$$

$$0 = 9x^2 + 9x - 28$$

$$0 = (3x + 7)(3x - 4)$$

$$x = -\frac{7}{3}, \frac{4}{3}$$

Critical numbers: $x = -4, -\frac{7}{3}, \frac{4}{3}, 2$

$$f(-4) = \frac{1}{2}(-6)(-2) = 6$$

$$f\left(-\frac{7}{3}\right) = \frac{1}{2}\left(-\frac{13}{3}\right)\left(-\frac{91}{3}\right) = 65\frac{13}{18}$$

$$f\left(\frac{4}{3}\right) = \frac{1}{2}\left(-\frac{2}{3}\right)\left(\frac{74}{3}\right) = -8\frac{2}{9}$$

$$f(2) = \frac{1}{2}(0)(52) = 0$$

Maximum: $65\frac{13}{18}$ Minimum: $-8\frac{2}{9}$

(b)

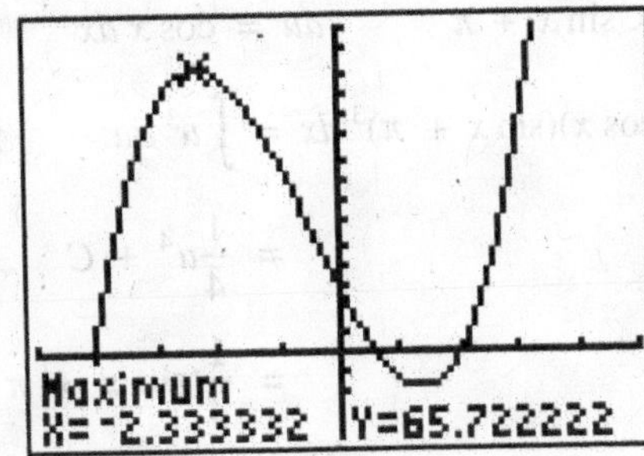

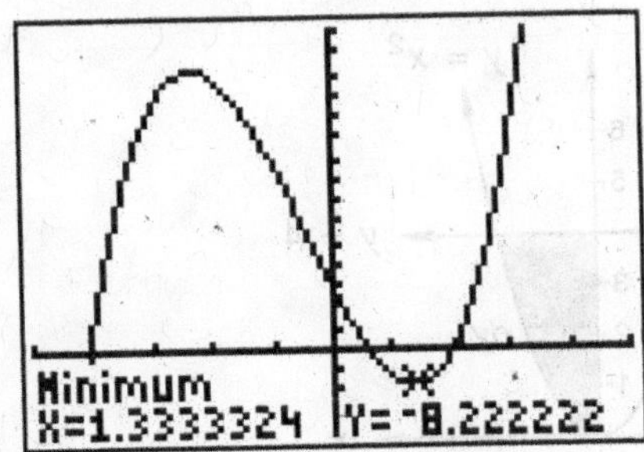

Window: Xmin=-5, Xmax=5, Ymin=-20, Ymax=75, Yscl=5

16.

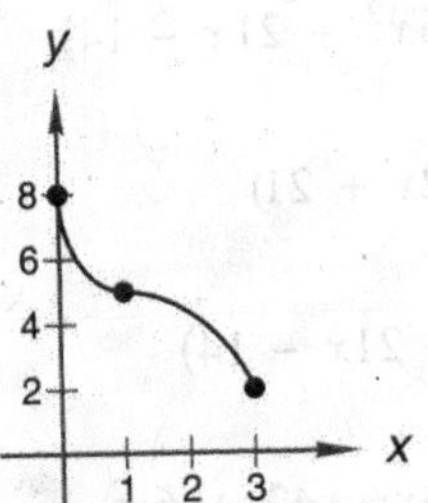

Inflection point: (1, 5)
Absolute maximum: (0, 8)
Absolute minimum: (3, 2)

17. $y = e^x + x$

$\mathbf{x = e^y + y}$

18. $h(x) = f(g(x))$

$h(x) = f(-x)$

$h(x) = (-x)^2 + \cos(-x)$

$h(x) = x^2 + \cos x$

$h(-x) = (-x)^2 + \cos(-x)$

$h(-x) = x^2 + \cos x$

Since $h(x) = h(-x)$, the graph of h is even and therefore **symmetric about the *y*-axis.**

19. $y = x\tan x^2 + \csc(15x) + \dfrac{x}{\sin x + \cos x}$

$$\frac{dy}{dx} = x(\sec^2 x^2)(2x) + \tan x^2 - \csc(15x)\cot(15x)(15) + \frac{(\sin x + \cos x) - x(\cos x - \sin x)}{(\sin x + \cos x)^2}$$

$$\frac{dy}{dx} = \mathbf{2x^2 \sec^2(x^2) + \tan x^2 - 15\csc(15x)\cot(15x) + \frac{1}{\sin x + \cos x} + \frac{x(\sin x - \cos x)}{1 + \sin(2x)}}$$

20. $\dfrac{d}{dx}[\arcsin(2x)] + \displaystyle\int \frac{2}{\sqrt{1 - 4x^2}}\,dx$

$$= \mathbf{\frac{2}{\sqrt{1 - 4x^2}} + \arcsin(2x) + C}$$

21. Maximum value of

$$\int_{-1}^{1} f(x)\,dx = [1 - (-1)](f_{max} \text{ on } [-1, 1])$$
$$= 2(5) = \mathbf{10}$$

The correct choice is **C.**

22. $f''(x) = 12x^2 - 10$

$f'(x) = 4x^3 - 10x + C$

$f'(-1) = 4(-1)^3 - 10(-1) + C$

$-6 = 6 + C$

$C = -12$

$f'(x) = 4x^3 - 10x - 12$

$f(x) = x^4 - 5x^2 - 12x + C$

$f(-1) = (-1)^4 - 5(-1)^2 - 12(-1) + C$

$0 = 1 - 5 + 12 + C$

$C = -8$

$\mathbf{f(x) = x^4 - 5x^2 - 12x - 8}$

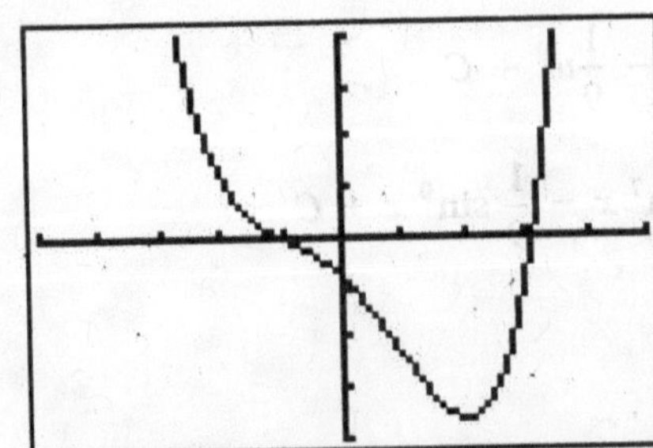

23.

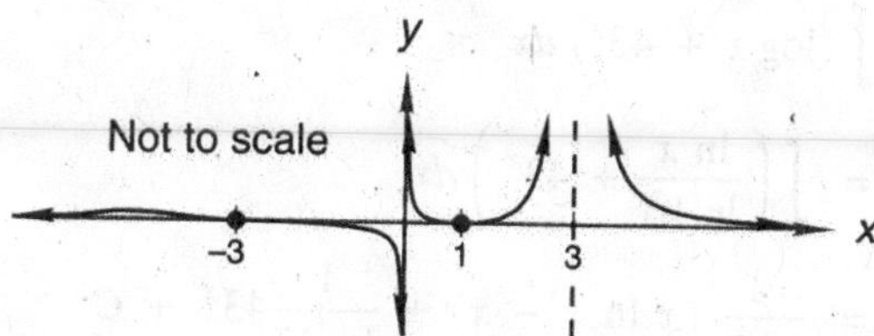

24. $y = \ln(x^3) = 3 \ln x$

The coefficient of 3 "amplifies" the graph of $y = \ln x$.

The correct choice is **A**.

25. Since f is a continuous function, it must cross the x-axis in going from $y = -2$ to $y = 3$.

The correct choice is **B**.

Problem Set 79

1.
$$a(t) = 2\cos t$$
$$v(t) = 2\sin t + C$$
$$v\left(\frac{\pi}{2}\right) = 2\sin\frac{\pi}{2} + C$$
$$-4 = 2 + C$$
$$C = -6$$
$$\mathbf{v(t) = 2\sin t - 6}$$
$$x(t) = -2\cos t - 6t + C$$
$$x(0) = -2\cos 0 - 6(0) + C$$
$$8 = -2 + C$$
$$C = 10$$
$$\mathbf{x(t) = -2\cos t - 6t + 10}$$

2.
$$a(t) = -6t$$
$$v(t) = -3t^2 + C$$
$$v(1) = -3(1^2) + C$$
$$-1 = -3 + C$$
$$C = 2$$
$$v(t) = -3t^2 + 2$$
$$\mathbf{v(3) = -25}$$
$$x(t) = -t^3 + 2t + C$$
$$x(2) = -(2^3) + 2(2) + C$$
$$-3 = -4 + C$$
$$C = 1$$
$$x(t) = -t^3 + 2t + 1$$
$$\mathbf{x(3) = -20}$$

3.

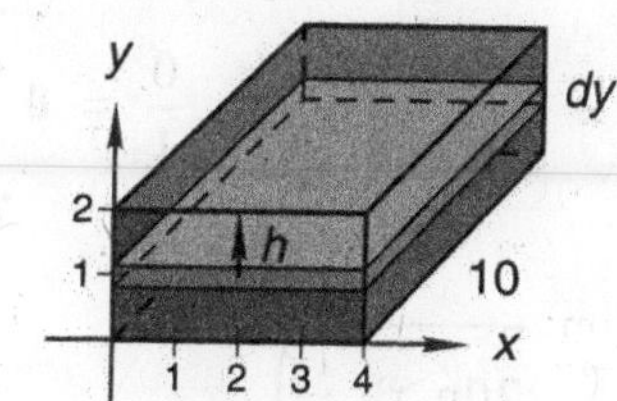

$$W = \int \text{depth} \cdot \text{weight density} \cdot \text{volume}$$
$$= \int_1^2 (2 - y)(9800)(4)(10)\, dy$$
$$= 392{,}000 \int_1^2 (2 - y)\, dy$$
$$= 392{,}000\left[2y - \frac{1}{2}y^2\right]_1^2$$
$$= 392{,}000\left[4 - 2 - \left(2 - \frac{1}{2}\right)\right]$$
$$= 392{,}000\left(\frac{1}{2}\right) = \mathbf{196{,}000 \text{ joules}}$$

4.
$$W = \int \text{depth} \cdot \text{weight density} \cdot \text{volume}$$
$$= \int_0^1 (1 - y)(1000)(2y)(6)\, dy$$
$$= 12{,}000 \int_0^1 (y - y^2)\, dy$$
$$= 12{,}000\left[\frac{1}{2}y^2 - \frac{1}{3}y^3\right]_0^1 = \mathbf{2{,}000 \text{ joules}}$$

5.

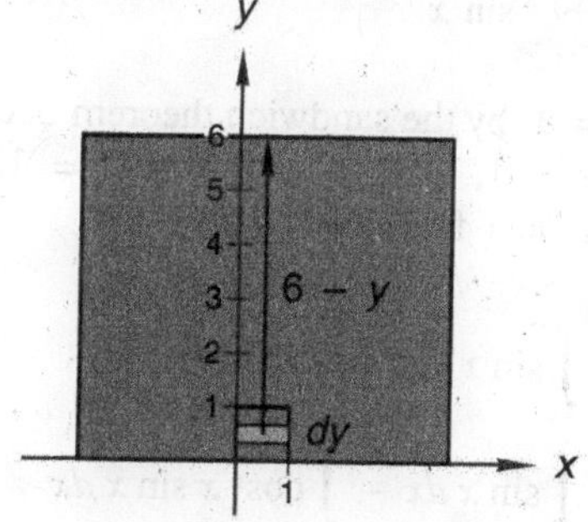

$$F = \int \text{weight density} \cdot \text{depth} \cdot \text{area}$$
$$= \int_0^1 2000(6 - y)(1)\, dy$$
$$= 2000 \int_0^1 (6 - y)\, dy$$
$$= 2000\left[6y - \frac{1}{2}y^2\right]_0^1$$
$$= 2000\left(6 - \frac{1}{2}\right) = \mathbf{11{,}000 \text{ newtons}}$$

6.
$$\lim_{x\to 0} \frac{\sin x}{x} = \lim_{x\to 0} \frac{\cos x}{1} = \mathbf{1}$$

7. $\lim_{x\to 0}\frac{2-2\cos x}{\sin x} = \lim_{x\to 0}\frac{2\sin x}{\cos x} = \frac{0}{1} = \mathbf{0}$

8. $\lim_{x\to\infty}\frac{x}{(\ln x)^2} = \lim_{x\to\infty}\frac{1}{2(\ln x)\left(\frac{1}{x}\right)}$

$= \lim_{x\to\infty}\frac{x}{2\ln x}$

$= \lim_{x\to\infty}\frac{1}{\frac{2}{x}}$

$= \lim_{x\to\infty}\frac{x}{2}$

$= \boldsymbol{\infty}$

9. $\lim_{x\to\infty}\frac{x+\sin x}{x^2} = \lim_{x\to\infty}\frac{1+\cos x}{2x} = \mathbf{0}$

10. $\lim_{x\to 0}\frac{e^x - x}{\sin x} = \frac{1-0}{0} = \frac{1}{0}$

$\lim_{x\to 0^+}\frac{e^x - x}{\sin x} = +\infty$

$\lim_{x\to 0^-}\frac{e^x - x}{\sin x} = -\infty$

Therefore, $\lim_{x\to 0}\frac{e^x - x}{\sin x}$ **does not exist.**

11. $\lim_{x\to\pi} g(x) = \mathbf{1}$ by the sandwich theorem because $\lim_{x\to\pi} -\cos x = 1$, $\lim_{x\to\pi}(2+\cos x) = 1$, and $f(x) \le g(x) \le h(x)$ for values of x near π.

12. $\int \sin^3 x\,dx = \int \sin x(1-\cos^2 x)\,dx$

$= \int \sin x\,dx - \int \cos^2 x \sin x\,dx$

$u = \cos x \qquad du = -\sin x\,dx$

$\int \sin x\,dx - \int \cos^2 x\sin x\,dx$

$= -\int du + \int u^2\,du$

$= -u + \frac{1}{3}u^3 + C$

$= \mathbf{\frac{1}{3}\cos^3 x - \cos x + C}$

13. $\int \cos x \sin^3 x\,dx = \mathbf{\frac{1}{4}\sin^4 x + C}$

14. $\int(\log x + 43^x)\,dx$

$= \int\left(\frac{\ln x}{\ln 10} + 43^x\right)dx$

$= \frac{1}{\ln 10}(x\ln x - x) + \frac{1}{\ln 43}43^x + C$

$= \mathbf{x\log x - \frac{x}{\ln 10} + \frac{43^x}{\ln 43} + C}$

15. (a) $f(x) = |x^2 - 8| = 0$ when $x^2 - 8 = 0$

$x^2 = 8$

$x = \mathbf{\pm 2\sqrt{2}}$

(b)

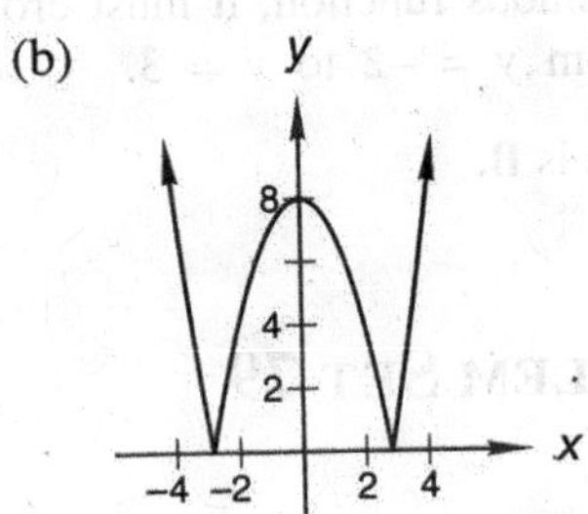

(c) $f'(x) = \begin{cases} \mathbf{2x} & \textbf{when } |x| > 2\sqrt{2} \\ \mathbf{-2x} & \textbf{when } |x| < 2\sqrt{2}\end{cases}$

16. $u = 2x - 1 \qquad x = \frac{1}{2}(u+1)$

$du = 2\,dx \qquad dx = \frac{1}{2}\,du$

$\int_1^2 x\sqrt{2x-1}\,dx = \int_1^3 \frac{1}{2}(u+1)u^{1/2}\frac{1}{2}\,du$

$= \int_1^3 \frac{1}{4}(u^{3/2} + u^{1/2})\,du$

The correct choice is **E**.

17. $h(x) = f(x)g(x) = 3\tan x\sin x$

$h(-x) = 3\tan(-x)\sin(-x)$

$= 3(-\tan x)(-\sin x)$

$= 3\tan x\sin x$

Since $h(-x) = h(x)$, the graph of h is even and therefore **symmetric about the y-axis.**

18. $y = x^3 + 6x^2 + 1$

$y' = 3x^2 + 12x$

$y'' = 6x + 12$

$0 = 6x + 12$

$x = -2$

$y = (-2)^3 + 6(-2)^2 + 1 = 17$

$y'(-2) = 12 - 24 = -12$

$y - 17 = -12(x + 2)$

$y = -12x - 24 + 17$

$\mathbf{y = -12x - 7}$

19. $f(x) = a \sin x + b \cos x$

$f(0) = a \sin 0 + b \cos 0$

$2 = b$

$f(x) = a \sin x + 2 \cos x$

$f'(x) = a \cos x - 2 \sin x$

$f'(0) = a \cos 0 - 2 \sin 0$

$2 = a$

$\mathbf{a + b = 4}$

20. (a)

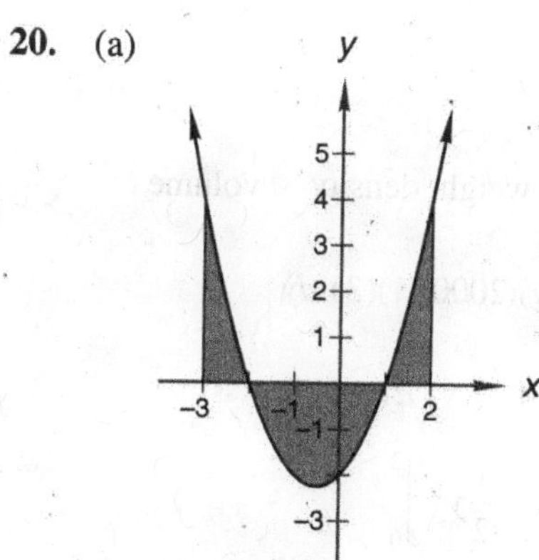

$$A = \int_{-3}^{2} |x^2 + x - 2|\,dx$$

(b) $A =$ `fnInt(abs(X²+X-2),X,-3,2)`

$\approx$ **8.1667 units²**

21. (a)

n	$f^{(n)}(x)$	$f^{(n)}(0)$
0	$\sin x$	0
1	$\cos x$	1
2	$-\sin x$	0
3	$-\cos x$	-1
4	$\sin x$	0
5	$\cos x$	1
6	$-\sin x$	0
⋮	⋮	⋮

$$\sin x = x - \frac{x^3}{3!} + \frac{x^5}{5!} - \frac{x^7}{7!} + \cdots$$

$$\sin x = \sum_{n=1}^{\infty} (-1)^{n-1} \frac{x^{(2n-1)}}{(2n-1)!}$$

(b)

n	$f^{(n)}(x)$	$f^{(n)}(0)$
0	$\sin x^2$	0
1	$2x \cos x^2$	0
2	$-4x^2 \sin x^2 + 2 \cos x^2$	2
3	$-12x \sin x^2 - 8x^3 \cos x^2$	0
4	$(16x^4 - 12) \sin x^2 - 48x^2 \cos x^2$	0
5	$160x^3 \sin x^2 + (32x^5 - 120x) \cos x^2$	0
6	$(-64x^6 + 720x^2) \sin x^2 + (480x^4 - 120) \cos x^2$	-120
⋮	⋮	⋮

$$\sin x^2 = \frac{2x^2}{2!} - \frac{120x^6}{6!} + \cdots$$

$$\sin x^2 = \mathbf{x^2 - \frac{x^6}{3!} + \cdots}$$

(c) $\sin x^2$

$$= x^2 - \frac{(x^2)^3}{3!} + \frac{(x^2)^5}{5!} - \frac{(x^2)^7}{7!} + \cdots$$

$$\sin x^2 = \mathbf{x^2 - \frac{x^6}{3!} + \frac{x^{10}}{5!} - \frac{x^{14}}{7!} + \cdots}$$

They are the same.

22. $y = \dfrac{x + \sin x}{\cos x} + \arctan(x^2) + e^x \csc(2x)$

$$\frac{dy}{dx} = \frac{\cos x(1 + \cos x) - (x + \sin x)(-\sin x)}{\cos^2 x} + \frac{2x}{(x^2)^2 + 1} + e^x[-2\csc(2x)\cot(2x)] + e^x \csc(2x)$$

$$\frac{dy}{dx} = \frac{1 + \cos x}{\cos x} + \frac{\sin x\,(x + \sin x)}{\cos^2 x} + \frac{2x}{x^4 + 1} + e^x \csc(2x)\,[-2\cot(2x) + 1]$$

$$\frac{dy}{dx} = \sec x + 1 + \sec x \tan x\,(x + \sin x) + \frac{2x}{x^4 + 1} + e^x \csc(2x)\,[-2\cot(2x) + 1]$$

$$\frac{dy}{dx} = \sec x + 1 + x \sec x \tan x + \tan^2 x + \frac{2x}{x^4 + 1} + e^x \csc(2x)\,[-2\cot(2x) + 1]$$

$$\frac{dy}{dx} = \sec x + x \sec x \tan x + \sec^2 x + \frac{2x}{x^4 + 1} + e^x \csc(2x)\,[-2\cot(2x) + 1]$$

$$\boldsymbol{\frac{dy}{dx} = \sec x\,(1 + x \tan x + \sec x) + \frac{2x}{x^4 + 1} + e^x \csc(2x)\,[-2\cot(2x) + 1]}$$

23. $h(x) = f(g(x)) = f(\sin x) = \sin^2 x$

$h'(x) = 2 \sin x \cos x$

$h'(x) = \mathbf{\sin(2x)}$

24. $\displaystyle\lim_{h\to 0} \frac{f(a + h) - f(a)}{h} = f'(a) = \lim_{x\to a} \frac{f(x) - f(a)}{x - a}$

The correct choice is **B.**

25. (a)

(b) $f(x) = 2x^3 - 3x^2 - 12x + 20$

$f'(x) = 6x^2 - 6x - 12$

$0 = 6(x^2 - x - 2)$

$0 = (x - 2)(x + 1)$

$x = -1, 2$

$f(-1) = 27,\ f(2) = 0$

(–1, 27), (2, 0)

Problem Set 80

1. $a(t) = 2t$

$v(t) = t^2 + C$

$v(3) = 3^2 + C$

$10 = 9 + C$

$C = 1$

$v(t) = t^2 + 1$

$17 = t^2 + 1$

$t^2 = 16$

$t = \mathbf{-4, 4}$

2.

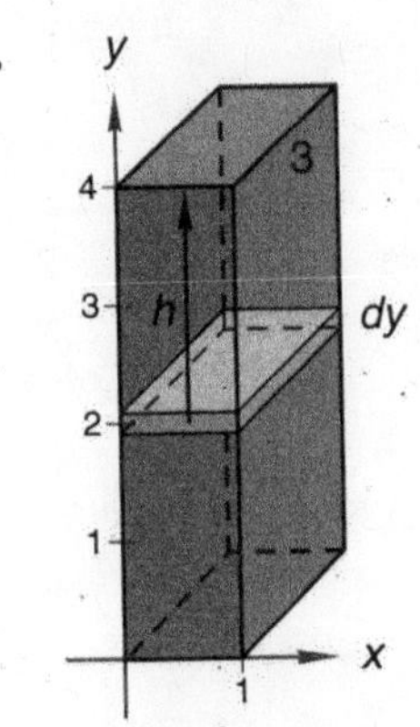

$$W = \int \text{depth} \cdot \text{weight density} \cdot \text{volume}$$

$$= \int_0^2 (4 - y)(2000)(1)(3)\,dy$$

$$= 6000 \int_0^2 (4 - y)\,dy$$

$$= 6000\left[4y - \frac{1}{2}y^2\right]_0^2$$

$$= 6000(8 - 2) = \mathbf{36{,}000\ joules}$$

3. (a) $a(t) = -9.8$

$v(t) = -9.8t + C$

$\mathbf{v(t) = -9.8t + 50}$

$x(t) = -4.9t^2 + 50t + C$

$\mathbf{x(t) = -4.9t^2 + 50t + 160}$

(b) $v(t) = -9.8t + 50$

$0 = -9.8t + 50$

$t \approx \mathbf{5.1020\ s}$

(c) $x(t) = -4.9t^2 + 50t + 160$

$0 = -4.9t^2 + 50t + 160$

$$t = \frac{-50 \pm \sqrt{2500 - 4(-4.9)(160)}}{-9.8}$$

$t \approx \mathbf{12.7626\ s}$ $\quad (t \neq -2.5585\text{ s})$

4. (a)

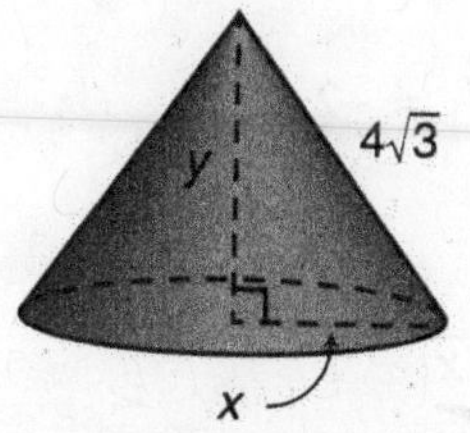

$$x^2 + y^2 = (4\sqrt{3})^2$$
$$y^2 = 48 - x^2$$
$$y = \sqrt{48 - x^2}$$

$$V = \frac{1}{3}\pi r^2 h$$

$$\mathbf{V = \frac{1}{3}\pi x^2\sqrt{48 - x^2}}$$

(b) $$V' = \frac{1}{3}\pi x^2 \cdot \frac{1}{2}(48 - x^2)^{-1/2}(-2x) + \frac{2}{3}\pi x(48 - x^2)^{1/2}$$

$$V' = -\frac{1}{3}\pi x^3(48 - x^2)^{-1/2} + \frac{2}{3}\pi x(48 - x^2)^{1/2}$$

$$V' = \frac{1}{3}\pi x(48 - x^2)^{-1/2}\left[-x^2 + 2(48 - x^2)\right]$$

$$V' = \frac{1}{3}\pi x(48 - x^2)^{-1/2}(-3x^2 + 96)$$

$$0 = \frac{1}{3}\pi x(48 - x^2)^{-1/2}(-3x^2 + 96)$$

$x = 0 \qquad -3x^2 + 96 = 0$

$$x^2 = 32$$

$$\mathbf{x = 4\sqrt{2}\text{ cm}} \qquad \mathbf{y = 4\text{ cm}}$$

(c)

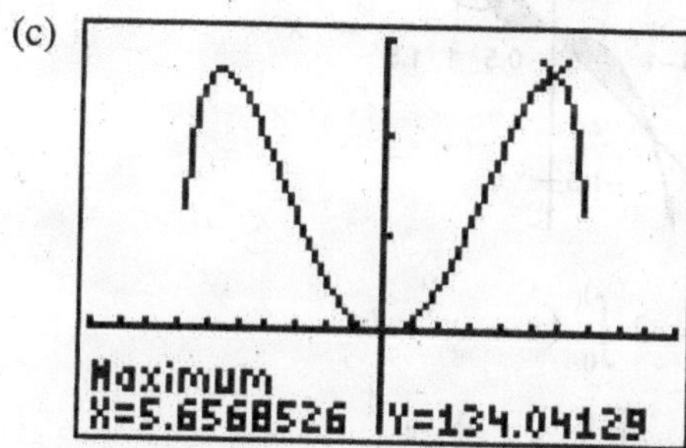

Window: Xmin=-10, Xmax=10,
Ymin=-30, Ymax=150

(d) $$V = \frac{1}{3}\pi(4\sqrt{2})^2\sqrt{48 - (4\sqrt{2})^2}$$

$$= \frac{1}{3}\pi(32)(4) = \mathbf{\frac{128}{3}\pi\text{ cm}^3}$$

5. $$\lim_{x\to\infty} \frac{3x^5 - 2x^3 + 1}{2x^5 - 1} = \frac{3}{2}$$

Horizontal asymptote: $y = \mathbf{\frac{3}{2}}$

6. $$y = \frac{x + 1}{x} = 1 + \frac{1}{x}$$

$$\lim_{x\to\infty} \frac{x + 1}{x} = 1$$

Horizontal asymptote: $y = 1$
Vertical asymptote: $x = 0$
Zero: $x = -1$

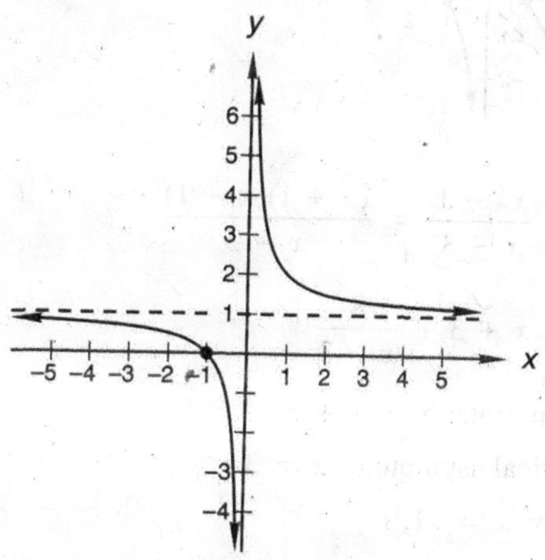

7. $$y = \frac{-24x + 6x^2}{3x^2 - 27} = \frac{6x(x - 4)}{3(x + 3)(x - 3)}$$

$$\lim_{x\to\infty} \frac{-24x + 6x^2}{3x^2 - 27} = 2$$

Horizontal asymptote: $y = 2$
Vertical asymptote: $x = 3,\ x = -3$
Zero: $x = 0, 4$

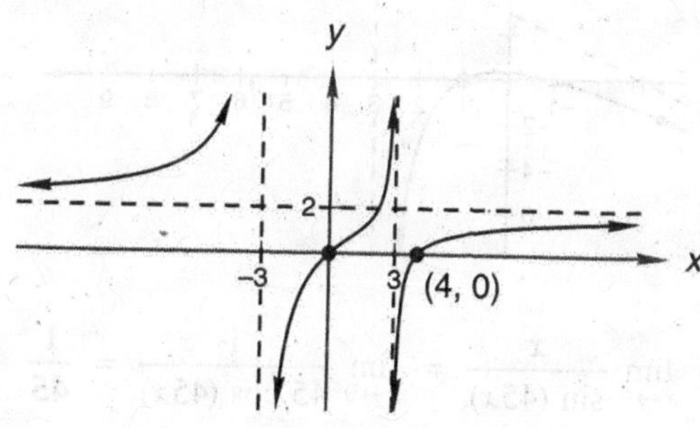

8. $y = \dfrac{x^2 - 1}{x} = \dfrac{(x + 1)(x - 1)}{x}$

$y = x - \dfrac{1}{x}$

Asymptote: $y = x$

Vertical asymptote: $x = 0$

Zero: $x = -1, 1$

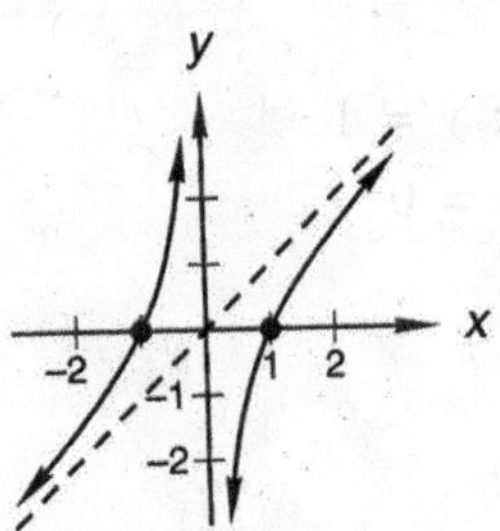

9. $y = \dfrac{x^2 - 1}{x - 3} = \dfrac{(x + 1)(x - 1)}{x - 3}$

$y = x + 3 + \dfrac{8}{x - 3}$

Asymptote: $y = x + 3$

Vertical asymptote: $x = 3$

Zero: $x = -1, 1$

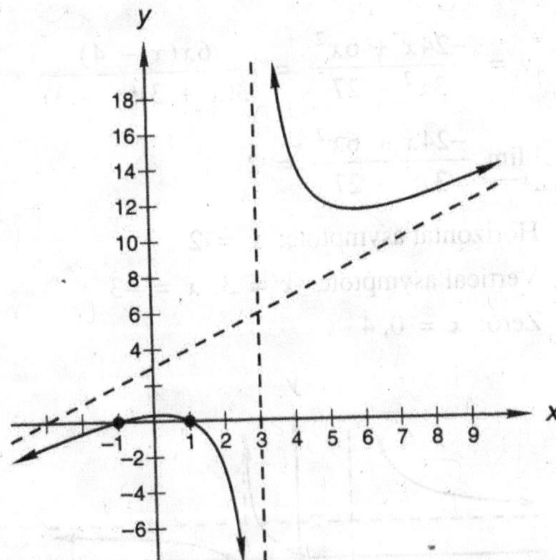

10. $\lim_{x\to 0} \dfrac{x}{\sin (45x)} = \lim_{x\to 0} \dfrac{1}{45 \cos (45x)} = \mathbf{\dfrac{1}{45}}$

11. $\lim_{x\to \infty} \dfrac{x^2}{\ln x} = \lim_{x\to \infty} \dfrac{2x}{\frac{1}{x}} = \lim_{x\to \infty} 2x^2 = \infty$

12. $\lim_{x\to 0} \dfrac{\cos x - 1}{52 \sin x} = \lim_{x\to 0} \dfrac{-\sin x}{52 \cos x} = \dfrac{0}{52} = \mathbf{0}$

13. $\lim_{x\to 1} \dfrac{x^2 - 3}{2x - 1} = \dfrac{-2}{1} = \mathbf{-2}$

14.

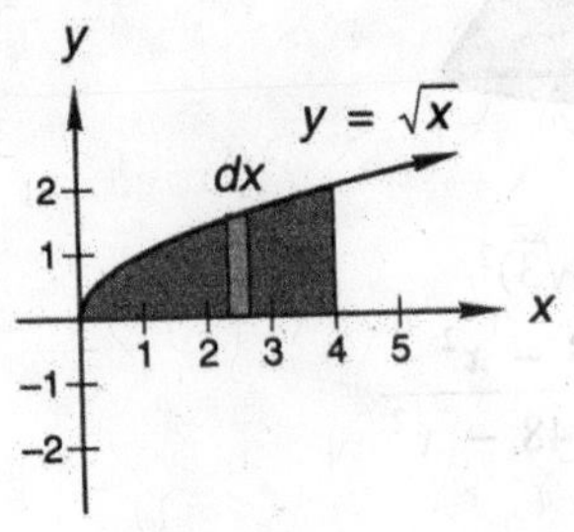

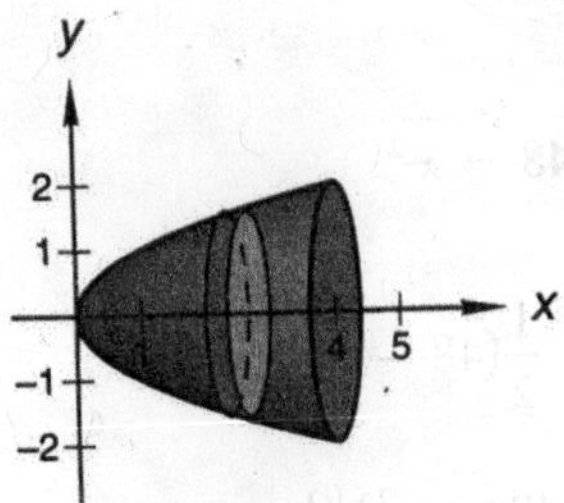

$$V = \int \pi r^2\, dx$$

$$= \pi \int_{x=0}^{x=4} y^2\, dx$$

$$= \pi \int_0^4 x\, dx$$

$$= \pi\left[\frac{1}{2}x^2\right]_0^4$$

$$= \mathbf{8\pi\ units^3}$$

15.

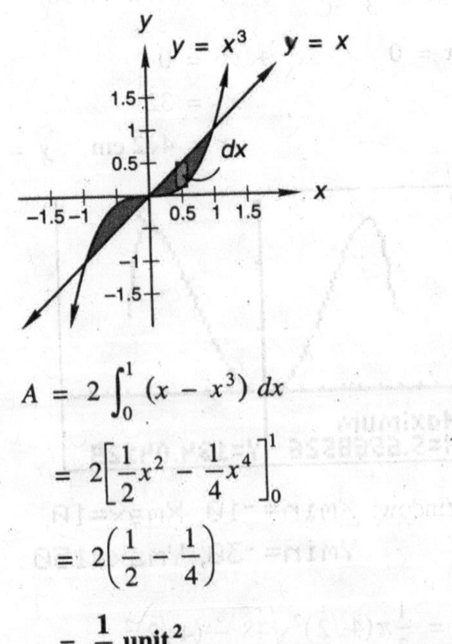

$$A = 2\int_0^1 (x - x^3)\, dx$$

$$= 2\left[\frac{1}{2}x^2 - \frac{1}{4}x^4\right]_0^1$$

$$= 2\left(\frac{1}{2} - \frac{1}{4}\right)$$

$$= \mathbf{\frac{1}{2}\ unit^2}$$

16.
$$x^2 + y^2 = 25$$
$$2x + 2y\frac{dy}{dx} = 0$$
$$\frac{dy}{dx} = -\frac{x}{y}$$
$$2 = -\frac{x}{y}$$
$$2y = -x$$
$$2\sqrt{25 - x^2} = -x$$
$$4(25 - x^2) = x^2$$
$$5x^2 = 100$$
$$x^2 = 20$$
$$x = \pm 2\sqrt{5}$$
$$\mathbf{(2\sqrt{5}, -\sqrt{5}), (-2\sqrt{5}, \sqrt{5})}$$

17.
$$\int_1^c f(x)\,dx + \int_c^b f(x)\,dx = \int_1^b f(x)\,dx$$
$$3 + \int_c^b f(x)\,dx = 5$$
$$\int_c^b f(x)\,dx = \mathbf{2}$$

18.
$$y = \arctan(\sin x) + x^2 \ln|\sin x| + e^{\sec x}$$
$$\frac{dy}{dx} = \frac{\cos x}{\sin^2 x + 1} + x^2\frac{\cos x}{\sin x} + \ln|\sin x|(2x) + \sec x \tan x\, e^{\sec x}$$
$$\frac{dy}{dx} = \mathbf{\frac{\cos x}{\sin^2 x + 1} + x^2 \cot x + 2x \ln|\sin x| + \sec x \tan x\, e^{\sec x}}$$

19.
$$LW = 100$$
$$L\frac{dW}{dt} + W\frac{dL}{dt} = 0$$
$$L(-0.8) + W(5) = 0$$
$$L(-0.8) + \frac{100}{L}(5) = 0$$
$$-0.8L + 500L^{-1} = 0$$
$$\frac{500}{L} = 0.8L$$
$$L^2 = 625$$
$$\mathbf{L = 25 \text{ cm},\ W = 4 \text{ cm}}$$

20. $u = x^3 + e^x \qquad du = (3x^2 + e^x)\,dx$
$$\int \frac{3x^2 + e^x}{x^3 + e^x}\,dx = \int \frac{1}{u}\,du = \ln|u| + C$$
$$= \mathbf{\ln|x^3 + e^x| + C}$$

21.
$$\int (\ln x + 43^x)\,dx = \mathbf{x \ln x - x + \frac{43^x}{\ln 43} + C}$$

22.
$$\int \frac{x}{\sqrt{6 - 4x^4}}\,dx = \frac{1}{4}\int \frac{4x}{\sqrt{(\sqrt{6})^2 - (2x^2)^2}}\,dx$$
$$= \mathbf{\frac{1}{4}\arcsin\frac{2x^2}{\sqrt{6}} + C}$$

23.
$$\int \frac{x}{6 + 4x^4}\,dx = \frac{1}{4\sqrt{6}}\int \frac{\sqrt{6}(4x)}{(\sqrt{6})^2 + (2x^2)^2}\,dx$$
$$= \mathbf{\frac{1}{4\sqrt{6}}\arctan\frac{2x^2}{\sqrt{6}} + C}$$

24. $f(x) = \sin(\arctan x)$

Range of arctan x: $\left\{y \in \mathbb{R} \mid -\frac{\pi}{2} < y < \frac{\pi}{2}\right\}$

Range of sin (arctan x): $\mathbf{\{y \in \mathbb{R} \mid -1 < y < 1\}}$

25.
$$\lim_{x\to 1^-} f(x) = f(1)$$
$$\lim_{x\to 1^-} (2x + 1) = a + 1$$
$$3 = a + 1$$
$$a = \mathbf{2}$$

PROBLEM SET 81

1.

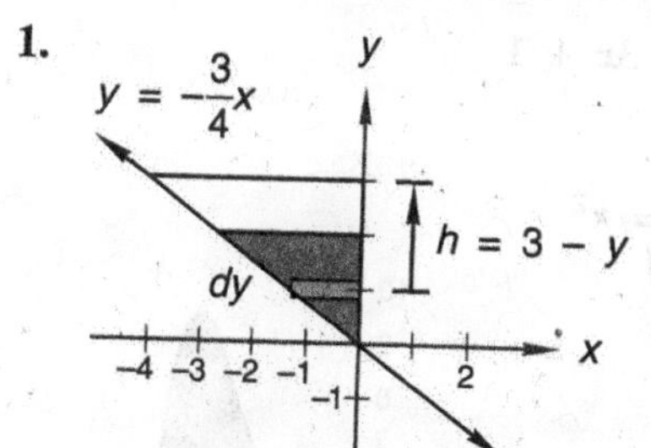

$$W = \int \text{depth} \cdot \text{weight density} \cdot \text{volume}$$
$$= \int_{y=0}^{y=2} (3 - y)(9000)(-x)(10)\,dy$$
$$= 90{,}000 \int_0^2 \frac{4}{3}y(3 - y)\,dy$$
$$= 120{,}000 \int_0^2 (3y - y^2)\,dy$$
$$= 120{,}000\left[\frac{3}{2}y^2 - \frac{1}{3}y^3\right]_0^2$$
$$= 120{,}000\left(6 - \frac{8}{3}\right) = \mathbf{400{,}000 \text{ joules}}$$

2. $$\lim_{x\to 2^+} f(x) = f(2)$$

$$\lim_{x\to 2^+} (3x + b) = 12$$

$$6 + b = 12$$

$$b = \mathbf{6}$$

3. $f(x) = ax^2 + bx + c$

$f'(x) = 2ax + b$

Since the graph of f passes through (0, 1),

$$f(0) = 1$$

$$a(0)^2 + b(0) + c = 1$$

$$c = 1$$

Since the slope of the graph is 1 at $x = 1$,

$$f'(1) = 1$$

$$2a + b = 1$$

$$b = 1 - 2a$$

Since the slope is 5 at $x = 2$,

$$f'(2) = 5$$

$$4a + b = 5$$

$$4a + (1 - 2a) = 5$$

$$2a = 4$$

$$a = 2$$

$$b = 1 - 2a = 1 - 2(2) = -3$$

$$\mathbf{f(x) = 2x^2 - 3x + 1}$$

4. 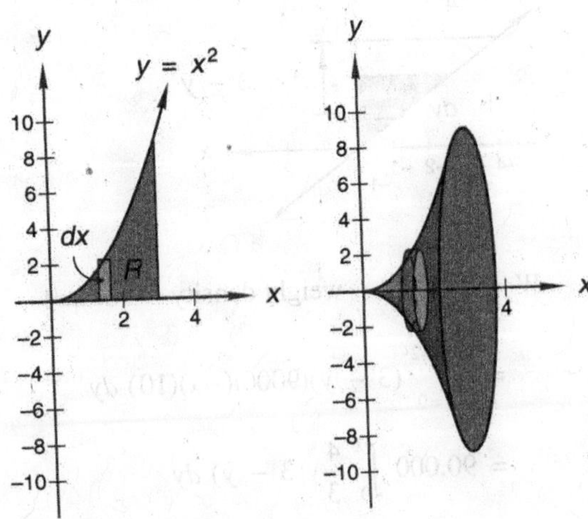

$$V = \pi \int_{x=0}^{x=3} y^2\, dx$$

$$= \pi \int_0^3 x^4\, dx$$

$$= \frac{\pi}{5}\left[x^5\right]_0^3 = \mathbf{\frac{243}{5}\pi\ units^3}$$

5. 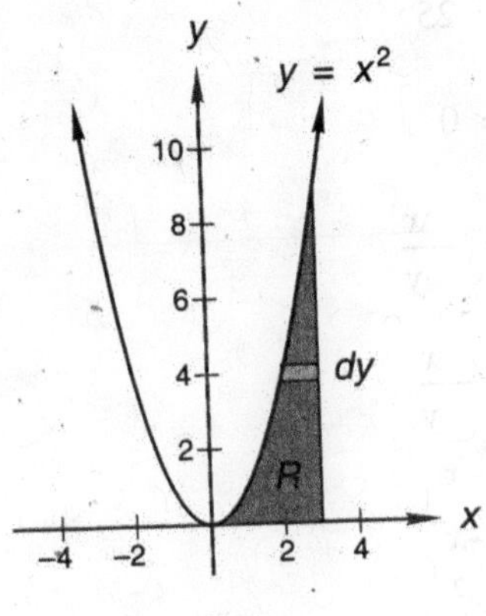

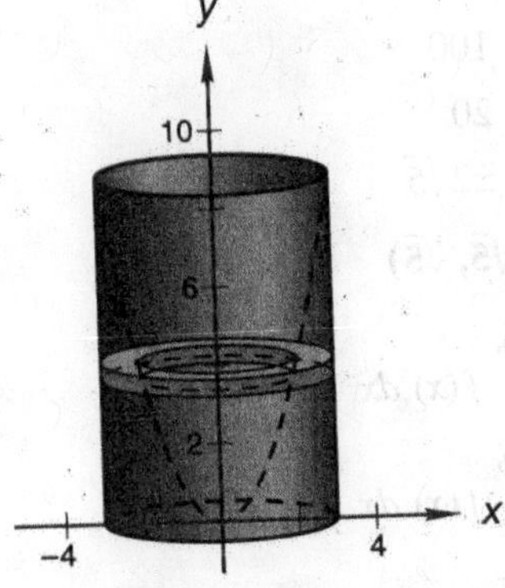

$$V = \pi \int_{y=0}^{y=9} (3^2 - x^2)\, dy$$

$$= \pi \int_0^9 (9 - y)\, dy = \pi\left[9y - \frac{1}{2}y^2\right]_0^9$$

$$= \pi\left(81 - \frac{81}{2}\right) = \mathbf{\frac{81}{2}\pi\ units^3}$$

6. 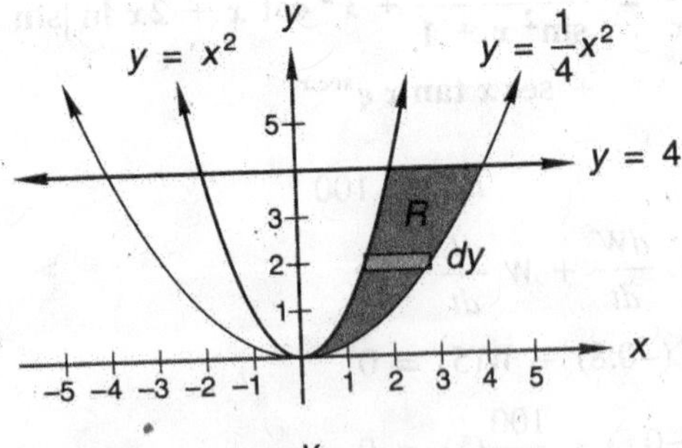

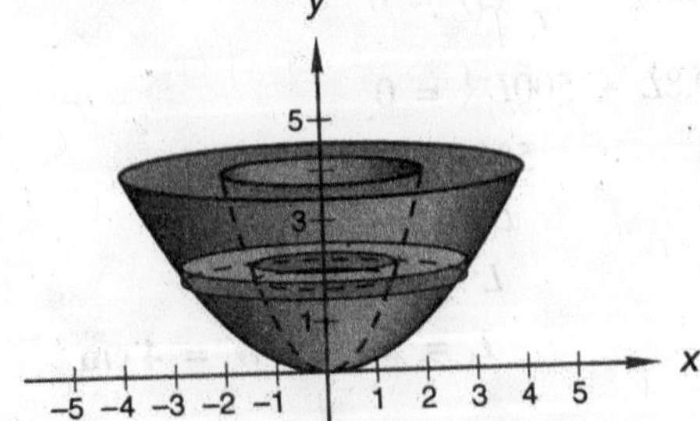

$$V = \pi \int_0^4 (4y - y)\, dy$$

$$= \pi\left[2y^2 - \frac{1}{2}y^2\right]_0^4 = \pi(32 - 8) = \mathbf{24\pi\ units^3}$$

7.

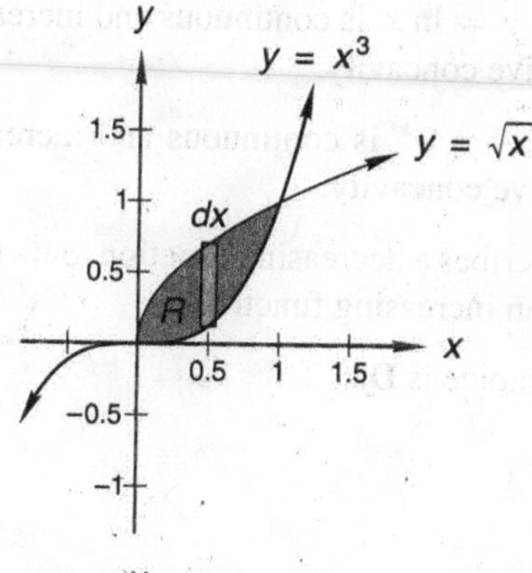

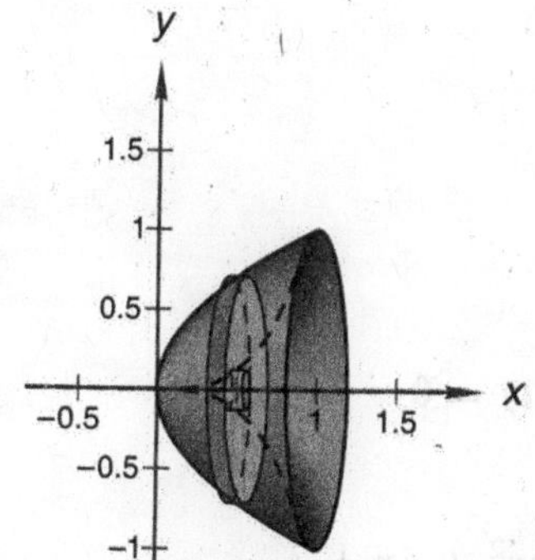

$$V = \pi \int_0^1 \left[(\sqrt{x})^2 - (x^3)^2\right] dx$$

$$= \pi \int_0^1 (x - x^6)\, dx = \pi\left[\frac{1}{2}x^2 - \frac{1}{7}x^7\right]_0^1$$

$$= \pi\left(\frac{1}{2} - \frac{1}{7}\right) = \mathbf{\frac{5}{14}\pi\ units^3}$$

8.

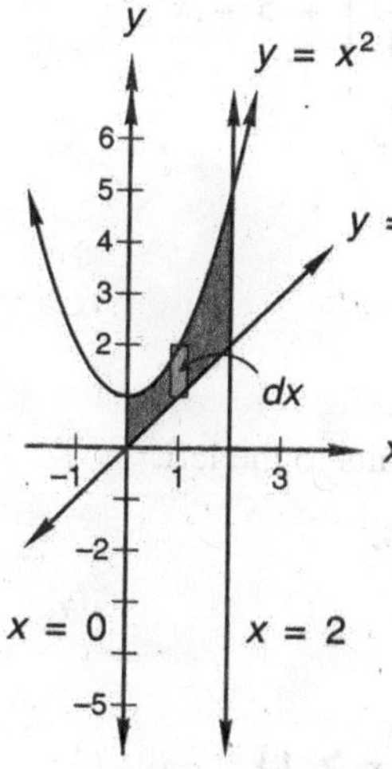

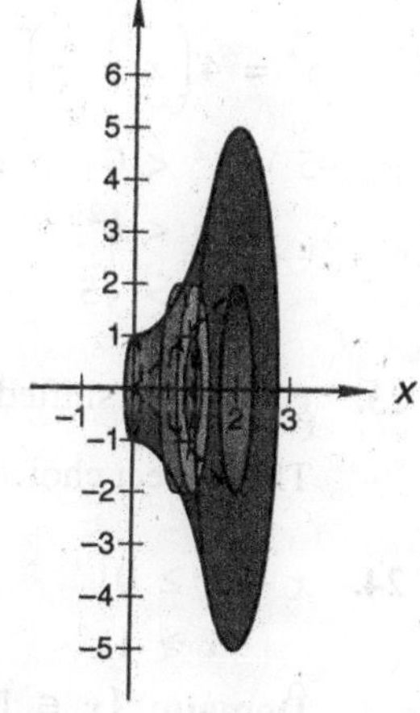

$$V = \pi \int_0^2 \left[(x^2 + 1)^2 - x^2\right] dx$$

$$= \pi \int_0^2 (x^4 + x^2 + 1)\, dx$$

$$= \pi\left[\frac{1}{5}x^5 + \frac{1}{3}x^3 + x\right]_0^2$$

$$= \pi\left(\frac{32}{5} + \frac{8}{3} + 2\right) = \mathbf{\frac{166}{15}\pi\ units^3}$$

9. $y = \dfrac{2x^2 - 2x - 4}{x - 1}$

$$\begin{array}{r|rrr} 1 & 2 & -2 & -4 \\ & \downarrow & 2 & 0 \\ \hline & 2 & 0 & \boxed{-4} \end{array}$$

$$y = 2x - \frac{4}{x - 1}$$

Asymptote: $y = 2x$

Vertical asymptote: $x = 1$

10. $y = \dfrac{x^2 + 1}{2x} = \dfrac{1}{2}x + \dfrac{1}{2x}$

Asymptote: $y = \dfrac{1}{2}x$

Vertical asymptote: $x = 0$

Zeros: none

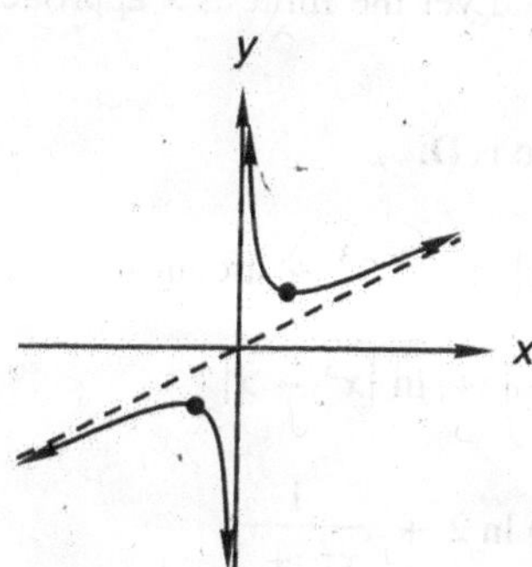

11. $y = \dfrac{x^2 + x - 2}{x + 1} = \dfrac{(x + 2)(x - 1)}{x + 1}$

$$\begin{array}{r|rrr} -1 & 1 & 1 & -2 \\ & \downarrow & -1 & 0 \\ \hline & 1 & 0 & \boxed{-2} \end{array}$$

$$y = x - \frac{2}{x + 1}$$

Asymptote: $y = x$

Vertical asymptote: $x = -1$

Zeros: $-2, 1$

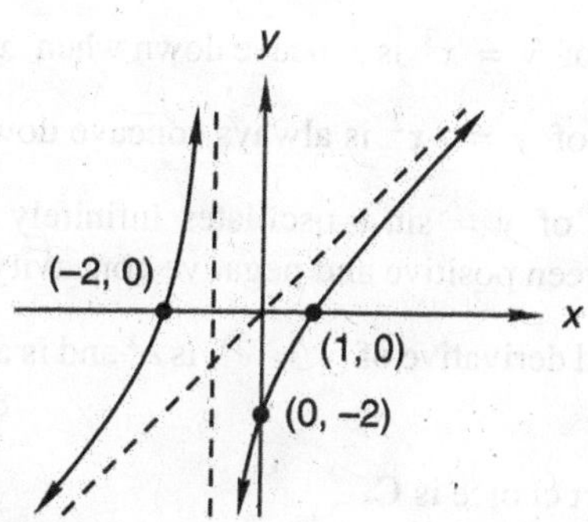

12. $\lim_{x\to 0} \frac{\sin(3x)}{x} = \lim_{x\to 0} \frac{3\cos(3x)}{1} = \mathbf{3}$

13. $\lim_{x\to 2} \frac{x^3 - x^2 - x - 2}{x - 2} = \lim_{x\to 2} \frac{3x^2 - 2x - 1}{1}$

$= \mathbf{7}$

14. $y = 2^x$

$y' = 2^x \ln 2$

$y'(2) = 4\ln 2 = \ln 16$

$y - 4 = \ln 16\,(x - 2)$

$y = (\ln 16)x - 2\ln 16 + 4$

$\mathbf{y = (\ln 16)x + (4 - \ln 256)}$ or

$\mathbf{y \approx 2.7726x - 1.5452}$

15. A, B, and C are false if the graph of f has a hole at the point (2, 7), and yet the limit as x approaches 2 could still be 7.

The correct choice is **D.**

16. $y = x\ln|x^3 - x| + 2^{2x-3} + \arctan x$

$y' = x\left(\frac{3x^2 - 1}{x^3 - x}\right) + \ln|x^3 - x|$

$+ 2^{2x-3}(2)\ln 2 + \frac{1}{x^2 + 1}$

$\mathbf{y' = \frac{3x^2 - 1}{x^2 - 1} + \ln|x^3 - x| + 2^{2x-2}\ln 2}$

$\mathbf{+ \frac{1}{x^2 + 1}}$

17. $\int\left(2^x + \frac{1}{1 + x^2}\right)dx = \mathbf{\frac{2^x}{\ln 2} + \arctan x + C}$

18. $u = \sin x + 1 \qquad du = \cos x\,dx$

$\int_0^\pi \frac{\cos x}{\sqrt{\sin x + 1}}\,dx = \int_1^1 \frac{du}{\sqrt{u}} = \mathbf{0}$

19. The graph of $y = x^3$ is concave down when $x < 0$.

The graph of $y = -x^2$ is always concave down.

The graph of $y = \sin x$ oscillates infinitely many times between positive and negative concavity.

The second derivative of $y = e^x$ is e^x and is always positive.

The correct choice is **C.**

20. The graph of $y = \ln x$ is continuous and increasing but has negative concavity.

The graph of $y = e^x$ is continuous and increasing but has positive concavity.

Choice C describes a decreasing function, but choice D describes an increasing function.

The correct choice is **D.**

21. $y = e^{3x}$

$x = e^{3y}$

$\ln x = 3y$

$y = \frac{1}{3}\ln x$

$f^{-1}(x) = \frac{1}{3}\ln x$

$f^{-1}(1) = \frac{1}{3}\ln(1) = \mathbf{0}$

22. $y = \frac{4}{3}x^3 + 2kx^2 + 5x + 3$

$y' = 4x^2 + 4kx + 5$

For the graph to have 2 tangent lines parallel to the x-axis, $4x^2 + 4kx + 5 = 0$ must have 2 distinct solutions. Thus the vertex of $y' = 4x^2 + 4kx + 5$ must be *below* the x-axis.

$y' = 4(x^2 + kx) + 5$

$y' = 4\left(x^2 + kx + \frac{k^2}{4}\right) + 5 - k^2$

$y' = 4\left(x + \frac{k}{2}\right)^2 + (5 - k^2)$

$5 - k^2 < 0$

$5 < k^2$

$\mathbf{|k| > \sqrt{5}}$

23. $g(x)$ is $f(x)$ shifted 2 units to the left.

The correct choice is **B.**

24. $x - 1 \ge 0$

$x \ge 1$

Domain: $\{x \in \mathbb{R} \mid x \ge 1\}$

Range: $\{y \in \mathbb{R} \mid -1 \le y \le 1\}$

25. $f(x) = -x^2 - 4x + 12$

$f(-3) = -(-3)^2 - 4(-3) + 12 = 15$

$f(1) = -(1)^2 - 4(1) + 12 = 7$

$$\text{slope} = \frac{15 - 7}{-3 - 1} = -2$$

$f'(x) = -2x - 4 = -2$

$x = -1$

$f(-1) = -(-1)^2 - 4(-1) + 12 = 15$

The only point satisfying the conditions is **(–1, 15).**

PROBLEM SET 82

1.

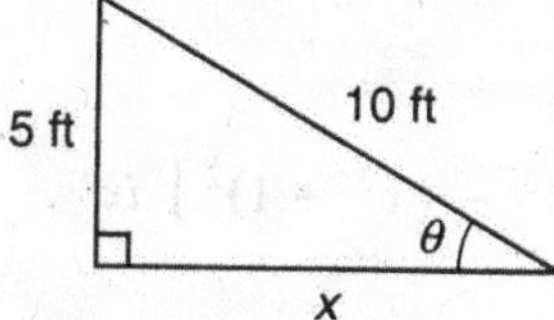

$$\frac{dx}{dt} = 2\,\frac{\text{ft}}{\text{s}}$$

$$\cos\theta = \frac{x}{10}$$

$$x = 10\cos\theta$$

$$\frac{dx}{dt} = -10\sin\theta\,\frac{d\theta}{dt}$$

$$\frac{d\theta}{dt} = -\frac{1}{10}\csc\theta\,\frac{dx}{dt}$$

$$\frac{d\theta}{dt} = -\frac{1}{10}\left(\frac{10}{5}\right)(2) = -\frac{2}{5}\,\frac{\textbf{rad}}{\textbf{s}}$$

2. (a) $y = -x + 4$

$A = bh$

$A = 2xy$

$A = 2x(-x + 4)$

$A = \mathbf{-2x^2 + 8x}$

(b) $A' = -4x + 8 = 0$

$x = 2$

$A = -2(2)^2 + 8(2) = \mathbf{8\ units^2}$

3. $x(t) = t^2 - 6t + 5$

$v(t) = 2t - 6$

$0 = 2t - 6$

$t = 3$

Since $x(t)$ describes a parabola that opens upward, the particle is **at rest when $t = 3$, moving right when $t > 3$, and moving left when $t < 3$.**

4. $a(t) = -9.8$

$\mathbf{v(t) = -9.8t - 25}$

$\mathbf{h(t) = -4.9t^2 - 25t + 100}$

To determine how long it takes for the ball to strike the ground, enter the height function in the TI-83, and have it calculate the zero.

Window: `Xmin=-10, Xmax=10, Ymin=-50, Ymax=150, Yscl=10`

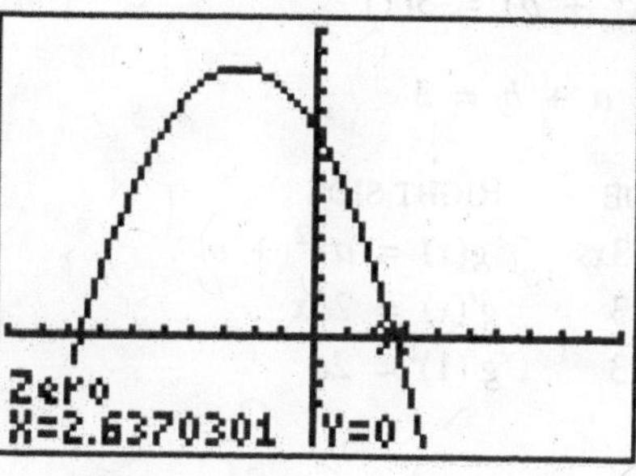

$t \approx \mathbf{2.6370\ s}$

5.

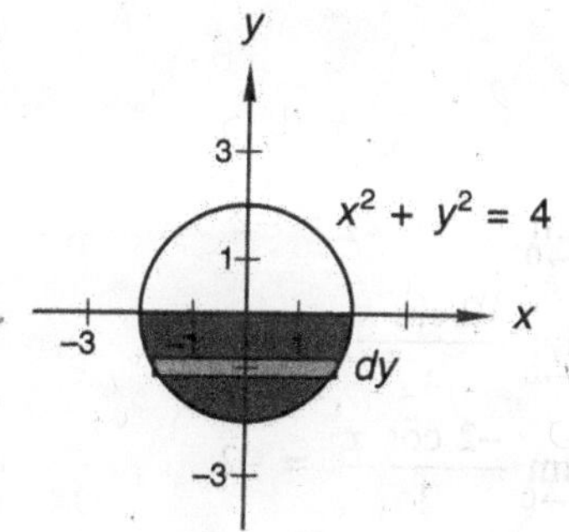

$u = 4 - y^2 \qquad du = -2y\,dy$

$$F = \int \text{weight density} \cdot \text{depth} \cdot \text{area}$$

$$= \int_{-2}^{0} 9000(-y)(2x)\,dy$$

$$= 9000\int_{-2}^{0} (-2y)\sqrt{4 - y^2}\,dy$$

$$= 9000\int_{0}^{4} u^{1/2}\,du$$

$$= 9000\left[\frac{2}{3}u^{3/2}\right]_0^4$$

$$= 9000\,\frac{16}{3} = \textbf{48,000 newtons}$$

6. LEFT SIDE

$f(x) = x^2 + x + 1$

$f'(x) = 2x + 1$

$f'(1) = 3$

RIGHT SIDE

$f(x) = 2x + 1$

$f'(x) = 2$

$\lim_{x\to1^+} f'(x) = 2$

7. The function $f(x)$ is continuous at $x = 1$ because $f(1) = \lim_{x\to 1^+} f(x) = 3$, but because the right-hand derivative does not equal the left-hand derivative at $x = 1$, the function is not differentiable at $x = 1$.

8. The function $g(x) = \begin{cases} 3x & \text{when } x \le 1 \\ ax^2 + b & \text{when } x > 1 \end{cases}$ is already continuous everywhere except at $x = 1$. To establish continuity at $x = 1$, we must have

$$\lim_{x\to 1^+} f(x) = f(1)$$

$$\lim_{x\to 1^+} (ax^2 + b) = 3(1)$$

$$\mathbf{a + b = 3}$$

9.

LEFT SIDE	RIGHT SIDE
$g(x) = 3x$	$g(x) = ax^2 + b$
$g'(x) = 3$	$g'(x) = 2ax$
$g'(1) = 3$	$g'(1) = 2a$

$$2a = 3$$

$$\mathbf{a = \frac{3}{2}}$$

$$a + b = 3$$

$$\mathbf{b = \frac{3}{2}}$$

10. $\lim_{x\to 0} f(x) = \lim_{x\to 0} (x^2 - 2) = -2$

$$\lim_{x\to 0} h(x) = \lim_{x\to 0} \frac{-2\sin x}{x}$$

$$= \lim_{x\to 0} \frac{-2\cos x}{1} = -2$$

$\lim_{x\to 0} g(x) = \mathbf{-2}$ by the sandwich theorem.

11.

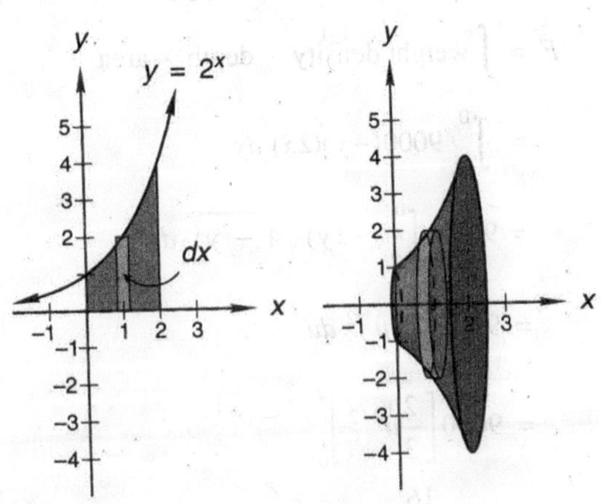

$$u = 2^x \qquad du = (\ln 2)2^x\,dx$$

$$V = \pi \int_0^2 2^x 2^x\,dx = \frac{\pi}{\ln 2}\int_1^4 u\,du$$

$$= \frac{\pi}{2\ln 2}\left[u^2\right]_1^4 = \frac{\pi}{\ln 4}(16 - 1)$$

$$= \mathbf{\frac{15\pi}{\ln 4}\ \text{units}^3}$$

12.

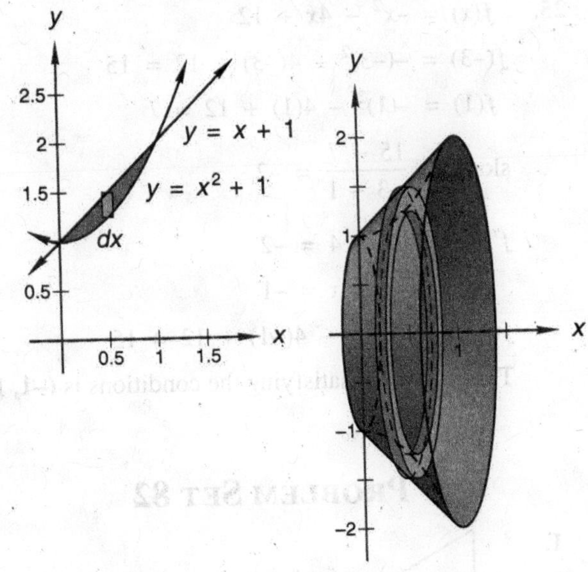

$$V = \pi \int_0^1 \left[(x+1)^2 - (x^2+1)^2\right] dx$$

$$V = \pi \int_0^1 \left[(x^2 + 2x + 1) - (x^4 + 2x^2 + 1)\right] dx$$

$$\mathbf{V = \pi \int_0^1 (-x^4 - x^2 + 2x)\,dx}$$

13.

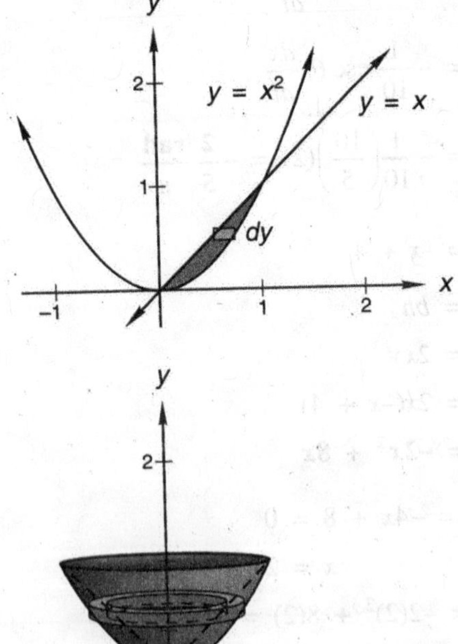

$$V = \pi \int_0^1 \left[(\sqrt{y})^2 - y^2\right] dy = \pi \int_0^1 (y - y^2)\,dy$$

$$= \pi\left[\frac{1}{2}y^2 - \frac{1}{3}y^3\right]_0^1 = \pi\left(\frac{1}{2} - \frac{1}{3}\right) = \mathbf{\frac{\pi}{6}\ \text{units}^3}$$

14. (a) $f(x) = \dfrac{x^2 + x - 6}{x - 1}$

$= \dfrac{(x + 3)(x - 2)}{x - 1}$

$$\begin{array}{r|rrr} 1 & 1 & 1 & -6 \\ & \downarrow & 1 & 2 \\ \hline & 1 & 2 & \boxed{-4} \end{array}$$

$f(x) = x + 2 - \dfrac{4}{x - 1}$

Asymptotes: $\mathbf{y = x + 2}$

$\mathbf{x = 1}$

(b)

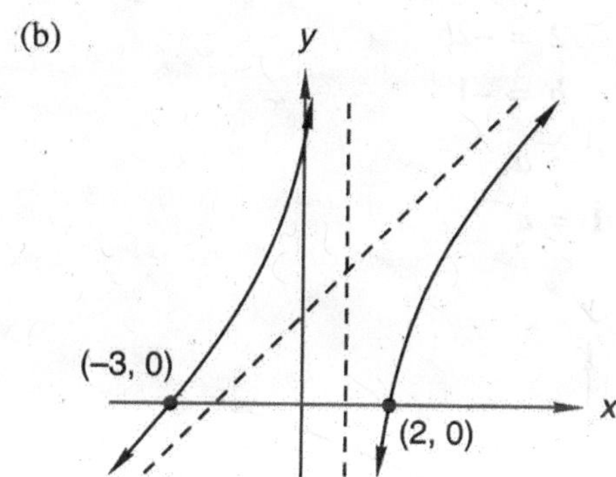

15. $\displaystyle\lim_{x\to\pi} \frac{\sin(x - \pi)}{2x - \frac{\pi}{2}} = \frac{0}{\frac{3\pi}{2}} = \mathbf{0}$

16. $\displaystyle\lim_{x\to\infty} \frac{x \ln x}{e^x} = \lim_{x\to\infty} \frac{x\left(\frac{1}{x}\right) + \ln x}{e^x}$

$\displaystyle= \lim_{x\to\infty} \frac{\frac{1}{x}}{e^x} = \lim_{x\to\infty} \frac{1}{xe^x} = \mathbf{0}$

17. $\displaystyle\lim_{x\to0^+} \left(1 - \frac{|x|}{x}\right) = 1 - 1 = \mathbf{0}$

18. $\displaystyle\int \cos^3 x\,dx = \int \cos x\,(1 - \sin^2 x)\,dx$

$\displaystyle= \int \cos x\,dx - \int \sin^2 x \cos x\,dx$

$\displaystyle= \mathbf{\sin x - \frac{1}{3}\sin^3 x + C}$

19. $\displaystyle\int (\sin x \cos^3 x - \sin x \cos^5 x)\,dx$

$\displaystyle= \mathbf{-\frac{1}{4}\cos^4 x + \frac{1}{6}\cos^6 x + C}$

20. $u = 2^x \qquad du = (\ln 2)2^x\,dx$

$\displaystyle\int 2^x\,dx = \frac{1}{\ln 2}\int (\ln 2)2^x\,dx$

$\displaystyle= \frac{1}{\ln 2}\int du$

$\displaystyle= \frac{1}{\ln 2}u + C$

$\displaystyle= \mathbf{\frac{2^x}{\ln 2} + C}$

21. $u = x \quad du = dx \quad v = e^x \quad dv = e^x\,dx$

$\displaystyle\int xe^x\,dx = xe^x - \int e^x\,dx$

$= xe^x - e^x + C$

$= \mathbf{e^x(x - 1) + C}$

22. $u = e^x + \sin x \qquad du = (e^x + \cos x)\,dx$

$\displaystyle\int \frac{e^x + \cos x}{\sqrt{e^x + \sin x}}\,dx = \int u^{-1/2}\,du$

$= 2u^{1/2} + C$

$= \mathbf{2\sqrt{e^x + \sin x} + C}$

23. $\displaystyle y = \frac{x}{\sin(1 + x^2)} + \arcsin\frac{x}{2} + \log_7 x - 14^x$

$\displaystyle y' = \frac{\sin(1 + x^2) - x(2x)\cos(1 + x^2)}{\sin^2(1 + x^2)}$

$\displaystyle+ \frac{1}{\sqrt{4 - x^2}} + \frac{1}{x \ln 7} - 14^x \ln 14$

$y' = \csc(1 + x^2)$

$- 2x^2 \csc(1 + x^2)\cot(1 + x^2)$

$\displaystyle+ \frac{1}{\sqrt{4 - x^2}} + \frac{1}{x \ln 7} - 14^x \ln 14$

$\mathbf{y' = \csc(1 + x^2)\left[1 - 2x^2 \cot(1 + x^2)\right]}$

$\displaystyle\mathbf{+ \frac{1}{\sqrt{4 - x^2}} + \frac{1}{x \ln 7} - 14^x \ln 14}$

24. The composite function $f(g(x)) = x$ means that f and g are inverses, because the output is the same as the input. Of the given function, this is true only for $f(x) = \ln x$ and $g(x) = e^x$.

The correct choice is **C**.

25. $1 - \sin x \geq 0$

$\sin x \leq 1$

Domain: $\mathbb{R}$

Range: $\{y \in \mathbb{R} \mid 0 \leq y \leq \sqrt{2}\}$

PROBLEM SET 83

1.

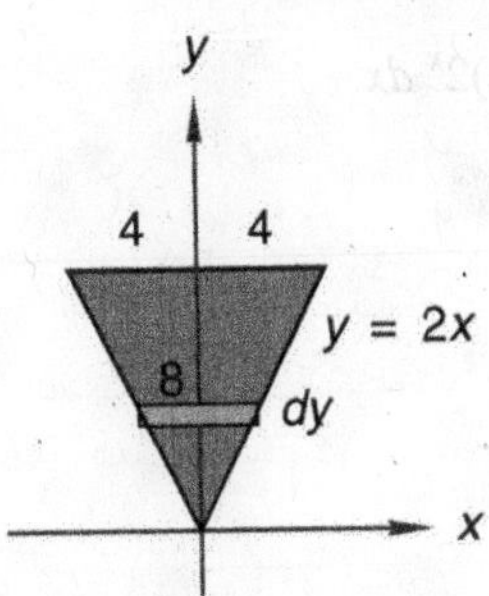

$$W = \int \text{depth} \cdot \text{weight density} \cdot \text{volume}$$

$$= \int_{y=0}^{y=8} (8 - y)(9800)(2x)(3)\,dy$$

$$= 29{,}400 \int_0^8 (8y - y^2)\,dy$$

$$= 29{,}400\left[4y^2 - \frac{1}{3}y^3\right]_0^8$$

$$= 29{,}400\left(256 - \frac{512}{3}\right)$$

$$= \mathbf{2{,}508{,}800 \text{ joules}}$$

2. The function $f(x) = \begin{cases} ax^3 + b & \text{when } x \le 1 \\ x^2 & \text{when } x > 1 \end{cases}$ is already continuous everywhere except at $x = 1$. To be continuous at $x = 1$,

$$\lim_{x\to 1^+} f(x) = f(1)$$

$$\lim_{x\to 1^+} x^2 = a(1)^3 + b$$

$$\mathbf{1 = a + b}$$

3. LEFT SIDE / RIGHT SIDE

LEFT SIDE	RIGHT SIDE
$f(x) = ax^3 + b$	$f(x) = x^2$
$f'(x) = 3ax^2$	$f'(x) = 2x$
$f'(1) = 3a$	$\lim_{x\to 1^+} f'(x) = 2$

$$3a = 2$$

$$\mathbf{a = \frac{2}{3}}$$

$$a + b = 1$$

$$\mathbf{b = \frac{1}{3}}$$

4. Function f is continuous at $x = 1$ if

$$\lim_{x\to 1^+} f(x) = f(1)$$

$$\lim_{x\to 1^+} (2x^2 + bx) = a(1)^3$$

$$2 + b = a$$

LEFT SIDE	RIGHT SIDE
$f(x) = ax^3$	$f(x) = 2x^2 + bx$
$f'(x) = 3ax^2$	$f'(x) = 4x + b$
$f'(1) = 3a$	$\lim_{x\to 1^+} f'(x) = 4 + b$

$$3a = 4 + b$$

$$3(2 + b) = 4 + b$$

$$2 = -2b$$

$$\mathbf{b = -1}$$

$$2 + b = a$$

$$\mathbf{1 = a}$$

5.

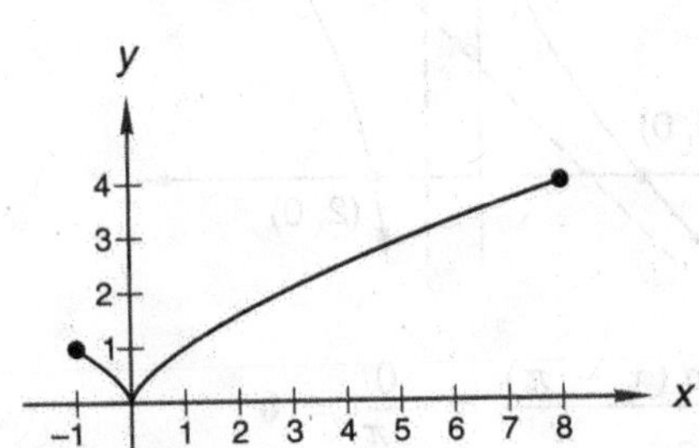

The maximum and minimum can be determined from the graph.

Maximum: 4

Minimum: 0

6.

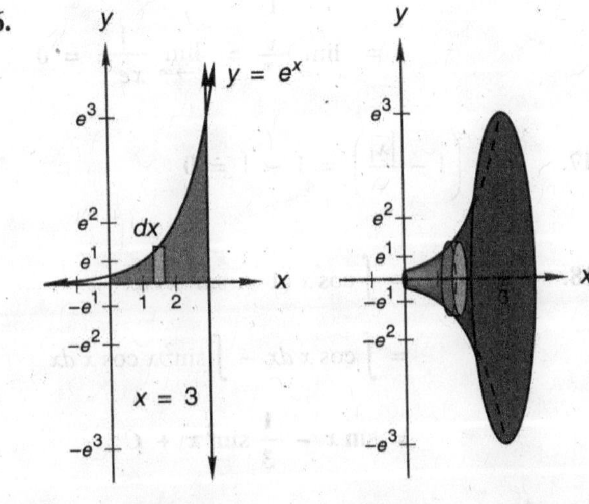

$$V = \pi \int_0^3 (e^x)^2\,dx = \pi \int_0^3 e^{2x}\,dx = \frac{\pi}{2}\left[e^{2x}\right]_0^3$$

$$= \mathbf{\frac{\pi}{2}(e^6 - 1) \text{ units}^3 \approx 632.1337 \text{ units}^3}$$

7.

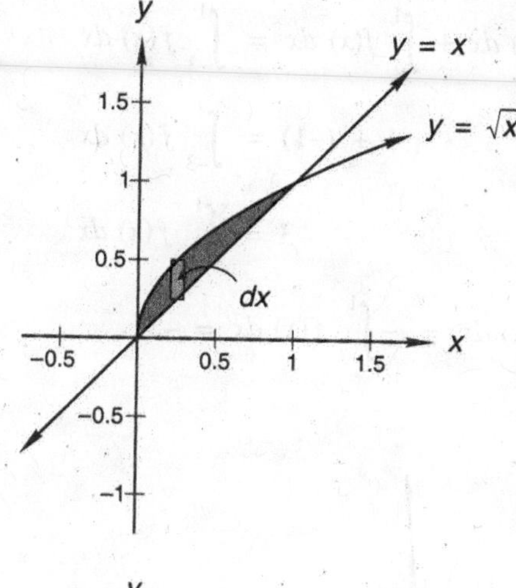

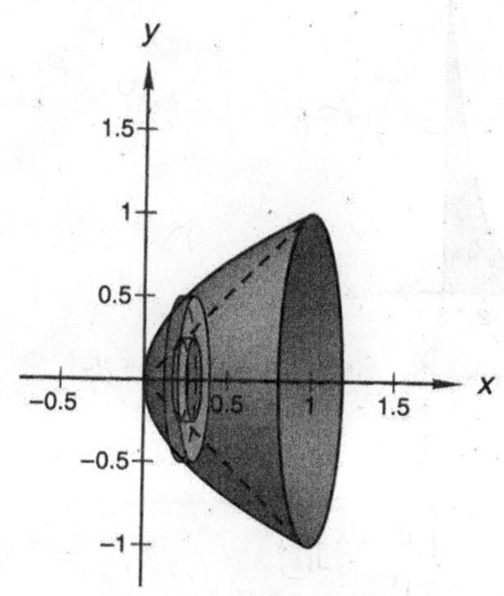

$$V = \pi \int_0^1 \left[(\sqrt{x})^2 - x^2\right] dx$$

$$= \pi \int_0^1 (x - x^2)\, dx$$

$$= \pi \left[\frac{1}{2}x^2 - \frac{1}{3}x^3\right]_0^1$$

$$= \pi\left(\frac{1}{2} - \frac{1}{3}\right) = \boldsymbol{\frac{\pi}{6}} \textbf{ unit}^3$$

8.

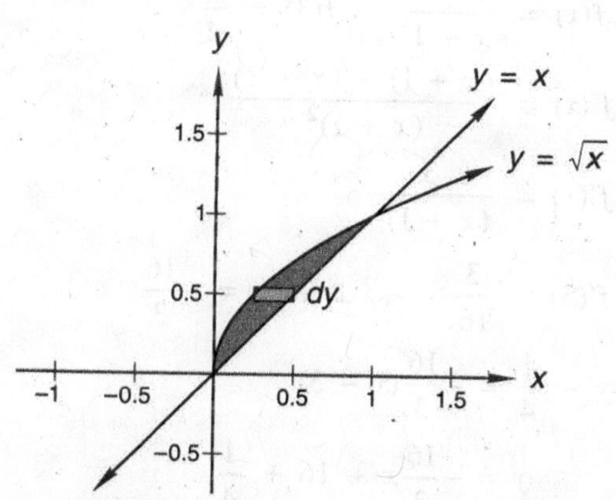

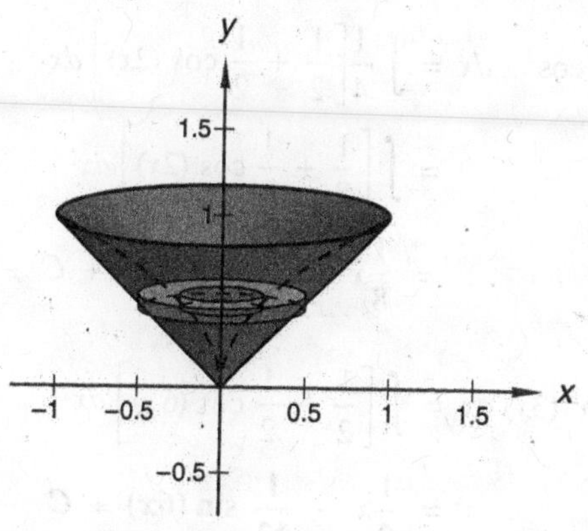

$$V = \pi \int_0^1 \left[y^2 - (y^2)^2\right] dy$$

$$= \pi \int_0^1 (y^2 - y^4)\, dy$$

$$= \pi \left[\frac{1}{3}y^3 - \frac{1}{5}y^5\right]_0^1$$

$$= \pi\left(\frac{1}{3} - \frac{1}{5}\right) = \boldsymbol{\frac{2}{15}\pi} \textbf{ unit}^3$$

9. (a)

n	$f^{(n)}(x)$	$f^{(n)}(0)$
0	$\cos x$	1
1	$-\sin x$	0
2	$-\cos x$	-1
3	$\sin x$	0
4	$\cos x$	1
⋮	⋮	⋮

$$\cos x = 1 - \frac{x^2}{2!} + \frac{x^4}{4!} - \frac{x^6}{6!} + \cdots$$

$$= \boldsymbol{\sum_{n=0}^{\infty} \frac{(-1)^n x^{(2n)}}{(2n)!}}$$

(b) $\cos(x^2)$

$$= 1 - \frac{(x^2)^2}{2!} + \frac{(x^2)^4}{4!} - \frac{(x^2)^6}{6!} + \cdots$$

$$= 1 - \frac{x^4}{2!} + \frac{x^8}{4!} - \frac{x^{12}}{6!} + \cdots$$

$$= \boldsymbol{\sum_{n=0}^{\infty} \frac{(-1)^n x^{(4n)}}{(2n)!}}$$

10. $\int \frac{1}{4}\cos^2 x\,dx = \int \frac{1}{4}\left[\frac{1}{2} + \frac{1}{2}\cos(2x)\right]dx$

$= \int \left[\frac{1}{8} + \frac{1}{8}\cos(2x)\right]dx$

$= \mathbf{\frac{1}{8}x + \frac{1}{16}\sin(2x) + C}$

11. $\int \sin^2(3x)\,dx = \int \left[\frac{1}{2} - \frac{1}{2}\cos(6x)\right]dx$

$= \mathbf{\frac{1}{2}x - \frac{1}{12}\sin(6x) + C}$

12. $\int \sin^3 x\cos^2 x\,dx = \int \sin x(1 - \cos^2 x)\cos^2 x\,dx$

$= \int (\cos^2 x\sin x - \cos^4 x\sin x)\,dx$

$= \mathbf{-\frac{1}{3}\cos^3 x + \frac{1}{5}\cos^5 x + C}$

13. $\int \frac{x - 3}{x^2}\,dx = \int \left(\frac{1}{x} - 3x^{-2}\right)dx$

$= \mathbf{\ln|x| + 3x^{-1} + C}$

14. $u = \sin x \qquad du = \cos x\,dx$

$\int (\pi\cos x)e^{\sin x}\,dx = \pi\int e^u\,du$

$= \pi e^u + C$

$= \mathbf{\pi e^{\sin x} + C}$

15. $\int \frac{x}{x^2 - 1}\,dx = \frac{1}{2}\int \frac{2x}{x^2 - 1}\,dx$

$= \frac{1}{2}\ln|x^2 - 1| + C$

$= \mathbf{\ln\sqrt{x^2 - 1} + C}$

16. $\lim_{x\to 0}\frac{3\sin(2x)}{4x} = \lim_{x\to 0}\frac{6\cos(2x)}{4} = \mathbf{\frac{3}{2}}$

17. $\lim_{x\to 0^+}\frac{x + \sin x}{\ln x} = \frac{0^+}{-\infty} = \mathbf{0}$

18. $\lim_{h\to 0}\frac{e^{x+h} - e^x}{h} = \frac{d}{dx}e^x = \mathbf{e^x}$

19. $\lim_{x\to 2} f(x) = \lim_{x\to 2}\frac{x^2 - x - 2}{x - 2}$

$= \lim_{x\to 2}\frac{2x - 1}{1} = 3$

$\lim_{x\to 2} h(x) = \lim_{x\to 2} 2|x - 2| + 3 = 3$

$\lim_{x\to 2} g(x) = \mathbf{3}$ by the sandwich theorem.

20. $\int_{-3}^{0} f(x)\,dx + \int_{0}^{1} f(x)\,dx = \int_{-3}^{1} f(x)\,dx$

$4 + (-1) = \int_{-3}^{1} f(x)\,dx$

$3 = \int_{-3}^{1} f(x)\,dx$

$\int_{1}^{-3} f(x)\,dx = -\int_{-3}^{1} f(x)\,dx = \mathbf{-3}$

21.

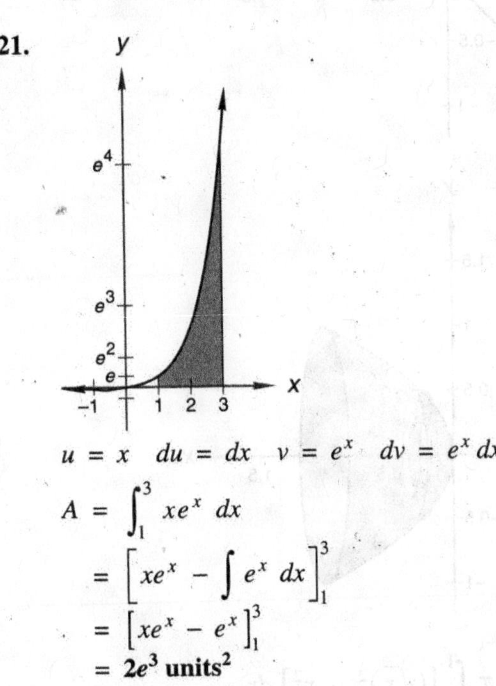

$u = x \quad du = dx \quad v = e^x \quad dv = e^x\,dx$

$A = \int_1^3 xe^x\,dx$

$= \left[xe^x - \int e^x\,dx\right]_1^3$

$= \left[xe^x - e^x\right]_1^3$

$= \mathbf{2e^3\ units^2}$

22. $x = \sqrt{1 - y^2}$

$x^2 = 1 - y^2$

$x^2 + y^2 = 1$

$A = \int_{-1}^{1}\sqrt{1 - y^2}\,dy = \mathbf{\frac{\pi}{2}}$

23. $f(x) = \frac{x - 2}{x + 1} \qquad f(3) = \frac{1}{4}$

$f'(x) = \frac{(x + 1) - (x - 2)}{(x + 1)^2}$

$f'(x) = \frac{3}{(x + 1)^2}$

$f'(3) = \frac{3}{16} \qquad \perp\text{ slope} = -\frac{16}{3}$

$y - \frac{1}{4} = -\frac{16}{3}(x - 3)$

$y = -\frac{16}{3}x + 16 + \frac{1}{4}$

$\mathbf{y = -\frac{16}{3}x + \frac{65}{4}}$

24.

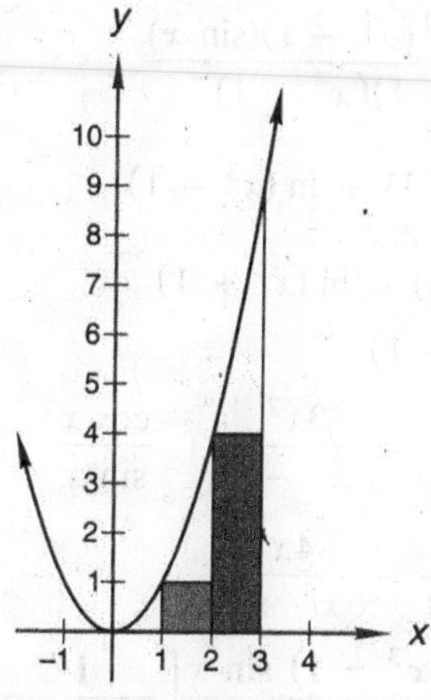

The value of $\int_0^3 x^2\,dx$ equals the exact area under $y = x^2$ on [0, 3], which is 9. Since these rectangles are lower rectangles, the sum of their areas must be less than $\int_0^3 x^2\,dx$.

The correct choice is **A**.

25. $f(x) = x^2 - 3x - 10$

$f(-1) = -6 \qquad f(5) = 0$

$$\text{slope} = \frac{-6 - 0}{-1 - 5} = 1$$

$$f'(x) = 2x - 3 = 1$$

$$x = 2$$

$$f(2) = -12$$

The only point satisfying the given conditions is **(2, –12)**.

PROBLEM SET 84

1.

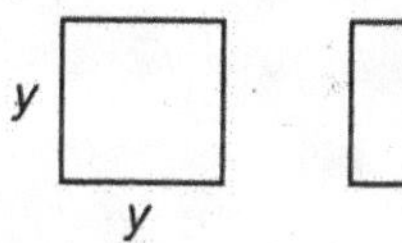

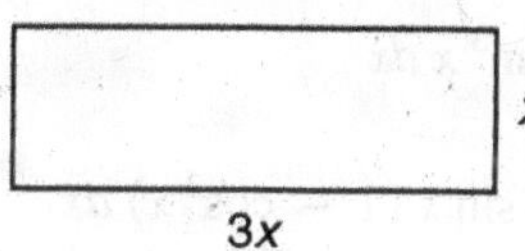

$$4y + 8x = 120$$
$$4y = 120 - 8x$$
$$y = 30 - 2x$$

(a) For the square field,

$$y^2 \ge 100$$
$$y \ge 10$$
$$30 - 2x \ge 10$$
$$-2x \ge -20$$
$$x \le 10$$

For the rectangular field,

$$3x(x) \ge 75$$
$$3x^2 \ge 75$$
$$x^2 \ge 25$$
$$x \ge 5$$

Maximum value of x = 10
Minimum value of x = 5

(b) Total area $= y^2 + 3x^2$

$$= (30 - 2x)^2 + 3x^2$$
$$= \mathbf{7x^2 - 120x + 900}$$

(c) $A' = 14x - 120 = 0$

$$14x = 120$$
$$x = \frac{60}{7}$$

Critical numbers: $x = 5, \frac{60}{7}, 10$

$$A(5) = 475$$
$$A\left(\frac{60}{7}\right) = 385.714$$
$$A(10) = 400$$

Maximum total area when x = **5.**

(d) $A(5) = \mathbf{475\ m^2}$

2. $W = \int_2^4 2x\,dx = [x^2]_2^4 =$ **12 joules**

3. (a) $a(t) = -9.8$

$$v(t) = -9.8t$$
$$\mathbf{h(t) = -4.9t^2 + 100}$$

(b) $-4.9t^2 + 100 = 0$

$$4.9t^2 = 100$$
$$t \approx \mathbf{4.5175\ s}$$

(c) $d = rt \approx 20(4.5175) = \mathbf{90.35\ m}$

4.

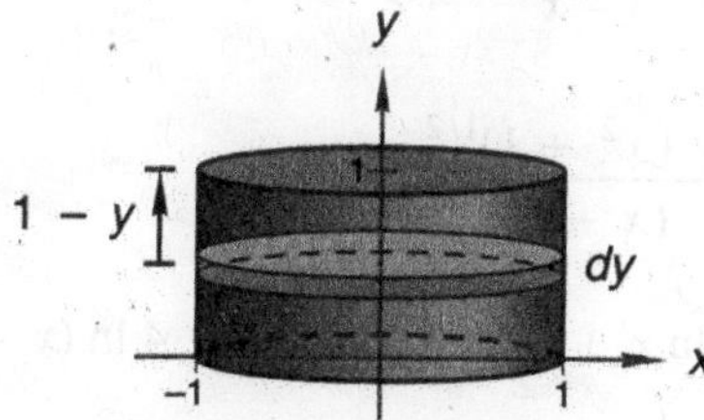

$$W = \int_0^1 100\pi(1 - y)\,dy$$

$$= 100\pi \int_0^1 (1 - y)\,dy = 100\pi\left[y - \frac{1}{2}y^2\right]_0^1$$

$$= 100\pi\left(1 - \frac{1}{2}\right) = \mathbf{50\pi\ joules}$$

5. Function f is continuous at $x = -1$ if

$$\lim_{x\to -1^+} f(x) = f(-1)$$

$$\lim_{x\to -1^+} (ax + b) = (-1)^3$$

$$-a + b = -1$$

LEFT SIDE / RIGHT SIDE

$$f(x) = x^3 \qquad f(x) = ax + b$$

$$f'(x) = 3x^2 \qquad f'(x) = a$$

$$f'(-1) = 3 \qquad \lim_{x\to -1^+} f'(x) = a$$

$$\mathbf{a = 3}$$

$$-a + b = -1$$

$$\mathbf{b = 2}$$

6.
$$y = x^x$$

$$\ln y = x \ln x$$

$$\frac{1}{y}\frac{dy}{dx} = x\left(\frac{1}{x}\right) + \ln x$$

$$\frac{dy}{dx} = y(1 + \ln x)$$

$$\frac{dy}{dx} = \mathbf{x^x(1 + \ln x)}$$

7.
$$y = x^{\sin x}$$

$$\ln y = \sin x \ln x$$

$$\frac{1}{y}\frac{dy}{dx} = \sin x\left(\frac{1}{x}\right) + \ln x(\cos x)$$

$$\frac{dy}{dx} = y\left[\frac{\sin x}{x} + \ln x(\cos x)\right]$$

$$\frac{dy}{dx} = \mathbf{x^{\sin x}\left[\frac{\sin x}{x} + \ln x(\cos x)\right]}$$

8.
$$y = \frac{x^2(x^2 + 1)^{1/2}}{(x - 1)^4}$$

$$\ln y = 2\ln x + \frac{1}{2}\ln(x^2 + 1) - 4\ln(x - 1)$$

$$\frac{1}{y}\frac{dy}{dx} = \frac{2}{x} + \frac{x}{x^2 + 1} - \frac{4}{x - 1}$$

$$\frac{dy}{dx} = y\left(\frac{2}{x} + \frac{x}{x^2 + 1} - \frac{4}{x - 1}\right)$$

$$\frac{dy}{dx} = \mathbf{\frac{x^2\sqrt{x^2 + 1}}{(x - 1)^4}\left(\frac{2}{x} + \frac{x}{x^2 + 1} - \frac{4}{x - 1}\right)}$$

9.
$$y = \frac{(x - 1)^{1/2}(x^3 - 1)(\sin x)}{(x^2 + 1)(x^4 + 1)}$$

$$\ln y = \frac{1}{2}\ln(x - 1) + \ln(x^3 - 1) + \ln(\sin x) - \ln(x^2 + 1) - \ln(x^4 + 1)$$

$$\frac{1}{y}\frac{dy}{dx} = \frac{1}{2(x - 1)} + \frac{3x^2}{x^3 - 1} + \frac{\cos x}{\sin x} - \frac{2x}{x^2 + 1} - \frac{4x^3}{x^4 + 1}$$

$$\frac{dy}{dx} = \mathbf{\frac{\sqrt{x - 1}(x^3 - 1)\sin x}{(x^2 + 1)(x^4 + 1)}\left[\frac{1}{2(x - 1)} + \frac{3x^2}{x^3 - 1} + \cot x - \frac{2x}{x^2 + 1} - \frac{4x^3}{x^4 + 1}\right]}$$

10.
$$\int 2\sin^2 x\,dx = \int 2\left[\frac{1}{2} - \frac{1}{2}\cos(2x)\right]dx$$

$$= \int [1 - \cos(2x)]\,dx$$

$$= \mathbf{x - \frac{1}{2}\sin(2x) + C}$$

11.
$$\int 4\sin^2 x\cos^2 x\,dx = \int \sin^2(2x)\,dx$$

$$= \int\left[\frac{1}{2} - \frac{1}{2}\cos(4x)\right]dx$$

$$= \mathbf{\frac{1}{2}x - \frac{1}{8}\sin(4x) + C}$$

12.
$$\int 2\sin^3 x\,dx$$

$$= 2\int \sin x(1 - \cos^2 x)\,dx$$

$$= 2\int (\sin x - \cos^2 x\sin x)\,dx$$

$$= \mathbf{-2\cos x + \frac{2}{3}\cos^3 x + C}$$

13.
$$\int 2\sin^2 x\cos^3 x\,dx$$

$$= 2\int \sin^2 x\cos x(1 - \sin^2 x)\,dx$$

$$= 2\int (\sin^2 x\cos x - \sin^4 x\cos x)\,dx$$

$$= \mathbf{\frac{2}{3}\sin^3 x - \frac{2}{5}\sin^5 x + C}$$

14. $u = 1 - \sin x \qquad du = -\cos x\,dx$

$$\int \cos x\,(1 - \sin x)^{1/2}\,dx$$

$$= -\int u^{1/2}\,du$$

$$= -\frac{2}{3}u^{3/2} + C$$

$$= \mathbf{-\frac{2}{3}(1 - \sin x)^{3/2} + C}$$

15. (a) $f(x) = \dfrac{x+1}{x^3 - x^2 + x - 1}$

$$= \frac{x+1}{(x-1)(x^2+1)}$$

Asymptote: $y = 0$

Vertical asymptote: $x = 1$

(b)

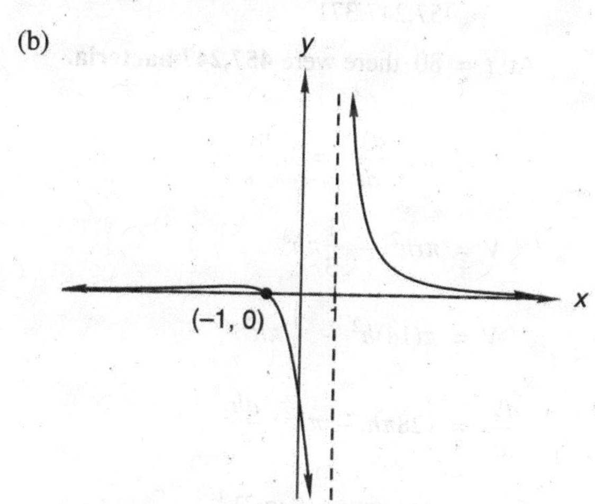

16. $\displaystyle\lim_{x\to 0} \frac{2\sin(3x)}{4x} = \lim_{x\to 0} \frac{6\cos(3x)}{4} = \mathbf{\frac{3}{2}}$

17. $\displaystyle\lim_{x\to\infty} \frac{x^2}{1 - x^2} = \lim_{x\to\infty} \frac{1}{\frac{1}{x^2} - 1} = \mathbf{-1}$

18. $y = \log x = \dfrac{\ln x}{\ln 10}$

$$y' = \frac{1}{x\ln 10}$$

$$y'(2) = \frac{1}{2\ln 10} = \mathbf{\frac{1}{\ln 100}}$$

19. $y = \sin(\cos x)$

$$y\left(\frac{\pi}{2}\right) = 0$$

$$y' = \cos(\cos x)(-\sin x)$$

$$y'\left(\frac{\pi}{2}\right) = 1(-1) = -1$$

$$y - 0 = -\left(x - \frac{\pi}{2}\right)$$

$$\mathbf{y = -x + \frac{\pi}{2}}$$

20. $u = x \quad du = dx \quad v = e^x \quad dv = e^x\,dx$

$$A = \int_1^2 xe^x\,dx$$

$$= \left[xe^x - \int e^x\,dx\right]_1^2$$

$$= \left[xe^x - e^x\right]_1^2$$

$$= 2e^2 - e^2 - (e - e) = \mathbf{e^2 \text{ units}^2}$$

21.

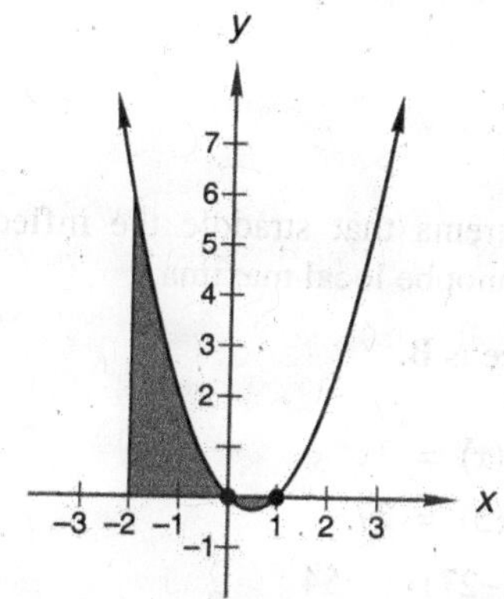

$$A = \int_{-2}^{0} (x^2 - x)\,dx + \int_1^0 (x^2 - x)\,dx$$

$$= \left[\frac{1}{3}x^3 - \frac{1}{2}x^2\right]_{-2}^{0} + \left[\frac{1}{3}x^3 - \frac{1}{2}x^2\right]_1^0$$

$$= -\left(-\frac{8}{3} - 2\right) + 0 - \left(\frac{1}{3} - \frac{1}{2}\right)$$

$$= \mathbf{\frac{29}{6} \text{ units}^2}$$

22. $f(x) = e^x \qquad g(x) = 5$

$h(x) = g(f(x)) = g(e^x) = 5$

$h(x)$ has y-axis symmetry, so $h(x)$ is **even.**

23. $y = \dfrac{\sin(x^2+1)}{e^x - e^{-x}} - \arctan(2x)$

$y' = \dfrac{(e^x - e^{-x})\cos(x^2+1)\,2x}{(e^x - e^{-x})^2} - \dfrac{\sin(x^2+1)(e^x + e^{-x})}{(e^x - e^{-x})^2} - \dfrac{2}{(2x)^2+1}$

$y' = \mathbf{\dfrac{2x\cos(x^2+1)}{e^x - e^{-x}} - \dfrac{(e^x + e^{-x})\sin(x^2+1)}{(e^x - e^{-x})^2} - \dfrac{2}{4x^2+1}}$

24. $y = x^3 - 27x$

$y' = 3x^2 - 27$

$y'' = 6x$

The second derivative is zero only once, when $x = 0$, so the function has exactly one inflection point.

Solving for the local extrema:

$3x^2 - 27 = 0$

$x^2 = 9$

$x = \pm 3$

We find two extrema that straddle the inflection point, so both cannot be local maxima.

The correct choice is **B.**

25. $f(x) = x^3 \quad f'(x) = 3x^2$

$f(-3) = -27 \quad f(3) = 27$

$\text{slope} = \dfrac{27-(-27)}{3-(-3)} = \dfrac{54}{6} = 9$

$3x^2 = 9$

$x^2 = 3$

$x = \pm\sqrt{3}$

$f(\sqrt{3}) = 3\sqrt{3};\ f(-\sqrt{3}) = -3\sqrt{3}$

$\mathbf{(\sqrt{3}, 3\sqrt{3}), (-\sqrt{3}, -3\sqrt{3})}$

PROBLEM SET 85

1. $B_t = B_0 e^{kt}$

$100 = 30e^{10k}$

$\dfrac{10}{3} = e^{10k}$

$\ln\left(\dfrac{10}{3}\right) = 10k$

$k = \dfrac{\ln\left(\frac{10}{3}\right)}{10}$

$B_{80} = 30\,e^{\{[\ln(10/3)]/10\}80}$

$= 30\,e^{8\ln 10/3}$

$= 30\,e^{\ln[(10/3)^8]}$

$= 30\left(\dfrac{10}{3}\right)^8$

$\approx 457{,}247.371$

At $t = 80$ there were **457,247 bacteria.**

2. $r = 14$ in.; $\dfrac{dV}{dt} = 1\,\dfrac{\text{in.}^3}{\text{s}}$; $h = 7$ in.

$V = \pi r h^2 - \dfrac{1}{3}\pi h^3$

$V = \pi(14)h^2 - \dfrac{1}{3}\pi h^3$

$\dfrac{dV}{dt} = (28\pi h - \pi h^2)\dfrac{dh}{dt}$

$(1) = [28\pi(7) - \pi(7)^2]\dfrac{dh}{dt}$

$1 = (196\pi - 49\pi)\dfrac{dh}{dt}$

$\dfrac{dh}{dt} = \mathbf{\dfrac{1}{147\pi}\,\dfrac{in.}{s}}$

3. $f(x) = \sin x + \cos x$

$f'(x) = \cos x - \sin x$

$f''(x) = -\sin x - \cos x$

To determine the critical numbers,

$f'(x) = 0 = \cos x - \sin x$

$\sin x = \cos x$

$\tan x = 1$

$x = \dfrac{\pi}{4}$

Critical numbers: $x = 0, \frac{\pi}{4}, \pi$

$$f(0) = 0 + 1 = 1$$

$$f\left(\frac{\pi}{4}\right) = \frac{\sqrt{2}}{2} + \frac{\sqrt{2}}{2} = \sqrt{2}$$

$$f(\pi) = 0 + (-1) = -1$$

To determine the inflection points,

$$f''(x) = 0 = -\sin x - \cos x$$

$$\sin x = -\cos x$$

$$\tan x = -1$$

$$x = \frac{3\pi}{4}$$

Maximum: $\sqrt{2}$

Minimum: –1

Inflection point: $x = \frac{3\pi}{4}$

4. $v(t) = a \sin t + b \cos t$

$a(t) = a \cos t - b \sin t = 2 \cos t - 4 \sin t$

$\mathbf{a = 2, b = 4}$

5. (a) $f(x) = \begin{cases} 2x^2 - x & \text{when } x \le 1 \\ ax + b & \text{when } x > 1 \end{cases}$

$$\lim_{x \to 1^+} f(x) = f(1)$$

$$\lim_{x \to 1^+} (ax + b) = 2(1^2) - (1)$$

$$\mathbf{a + b = 1}$$

(b) LEFT SIDE | RIGHT SIDE

$f(x) = 2x^2 - x$ | $f(x) = ax + b$

$f'(x) = 4x - 1$ | $f'(x) = a$

$$4(1) - 1 = \lim_{x \to 1^+} a$$

$$\mathbf{3 = a}$$

$$a + b = 1$$

$$\mathbf{b = -2}$$

6. $f(x) = x^2 + 1$

$f'(x) = 2x$

$$f'(c) = \frac{f(3) - f(1)}{3 - 1}$$

$$2c = \frac{10 - 2}{2}$$

$$2c = 4$$

$$\mathbf{c = 2}$$

7. $f(x) = 2x^3 - x$

$f'(x) = 6x^2 - 1$

$$f'(c) = \frac{f(1) - f(-2)}{1 + 2}$$

$$6c^2 - 1 = \frac{1 - (-14)}{3}$$

$$6c^2 - 1 = 5$$

$$6c^2 = 6$$

$$\mathbf{c = -1}$$

Note: $c \neq 1$, because c must not be an endpoint of the interval.

8.

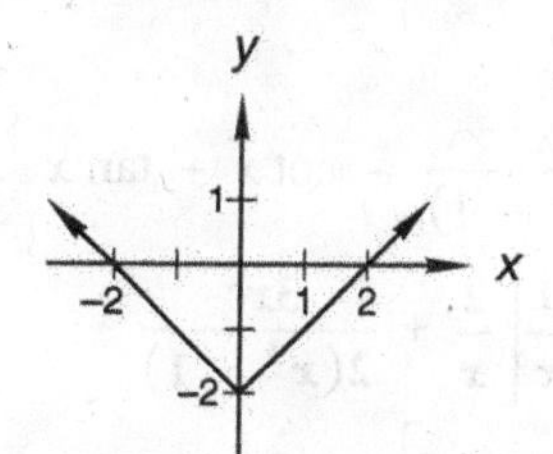

No, the Mean Value Theorem does not apply to $f(x)$. The function is not differentiable at $x = 0$, where there is a cusp point.

9. $f(x) = x^2 - 4x + 3$

$f'(x) = 2x - 4$

$f'(c) = 0$

$2c - 4 = 0$

$\mathbf{c = 2}$

10. $f(x) = x^3 + 3x^2 - 4$

$f'(x) = 3x^2 + 6x$

$f'(c) = 0$

$3c^2 + 6c = 0$

$c(c + 2) = 0$

$\mathbf{c = 0}$

Note: $c \neq -2$, because c must not be an endpoint of the interval.

11.

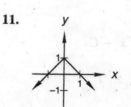

No, Rolle's theorem does not apply to f. The function is not differentiable at $x = 0$, where there is a cusp point.

12. $$y = x^x$$
$$\ln y = x \ln x$$
$$\frac{1}{y}\frac{dy}{dx} = x\left(\frac{1}{x}\right) + \ln x$$
$$\frac{dy}{dx} = y(1 + \ln x)$$
$$\frac{dy}{dx} = \mathbf{x^x(1 + \ln x)}$$

13. $$y = \frac{x^2(x^3 - 1)^{1/2}}{\sin x \cos x}$$
$$\ln y = 2\ln x + \frac{1}{2}\ln(x^3 - 1) - \ln(\sin x) - \ln(\cos x)$$
$$\frac{1}{y}\frac{dy}{dx} = \frac{2}{x} + \frac{3x^2}{2(x^3 - 1)} - \cot x + \tan x$$
$$\frac{dy}{dx} = \frac{x^2\sqrt{x^3 - 1}}{\sin x \cos x}\left[\frac{2}{x} + \frac{3x^2}{2(x^3 - 1)} - \cot x + \tan x\right]$$

14. $$\int 6\cos^2 x\,dx = \int 6\left[\frac{1}{2} + \frac{1}{2}\cos(2x)\right]dx$$
$$= \int [3 + 3\cos(2x)]\,dx$$
$$= \mathbf{3x + \frac{3}{2}\sin(2x) + C}$$

15. $$\int 3\sin^2 x\,dx = \int 3\left[\frac{1}{2} - \frac{1}{2}\cos(2x)\right]dx$$
$$= \int \left[\frac{3}{2} - \frac{3}{2}\cos(2x)\right]dx$$
$$= \mathbf{\frac{3}{2}x - \frac{3}{4}\sin(2x) + C}$$

16. $$\int \sin^3 x\,dx = \int \sin x(1 - \cos^2 x)\,dx$$
$$= \int (\sin x - \cos^2 x \sin x)\,dx$$
$$= \mathbf{-\cos x + \frac{1}{3}\cos^3 x + C}$$

17. $$\int \sin^3 x \cos x\,dx = \mathbf{\frac{1}{4}\sin^4 x + C}$$

18. $u = \tan x \qquad du = \sec^2 x\,dx$
$$\int e^{\tan x}(\sec^2 x)\,dx = \int e^u\,du$$
$$= e^u + C$$
$$= \mathbf{e^{\tan x} + C}$$

19.

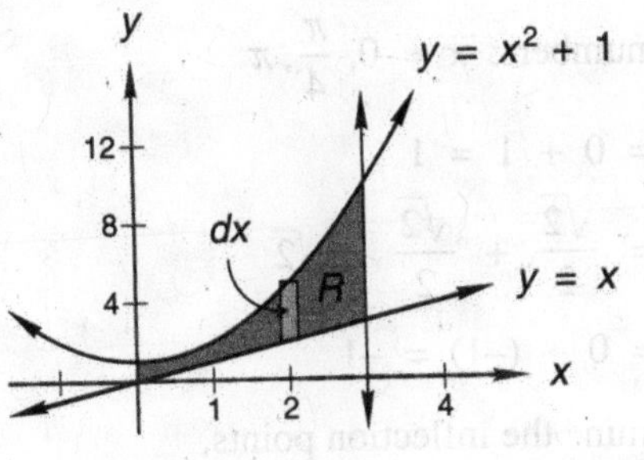

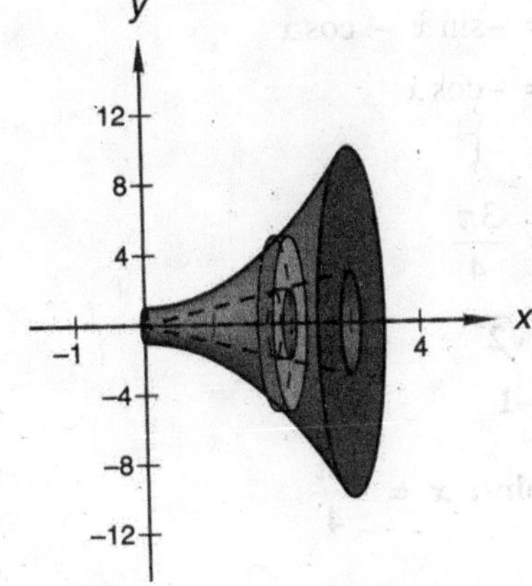

$$V = \pi\int_0^3 [(x^2 + 1)^2 - x^2]\,dx$$
$$= \mathbf{\pi\int_0^3 (x^4 + x^2 + 1)\,dx}$$

20. $$f(x) = \frac{1 - x^2}{x}$$
$$= \frac{(1 + x)(1 - x)}{x}$$
$$= \frac{1}{x} - x$$

Zeros: 1, –1
Vertical asymptote: $x = 0$
Asymptote: $y = -x$

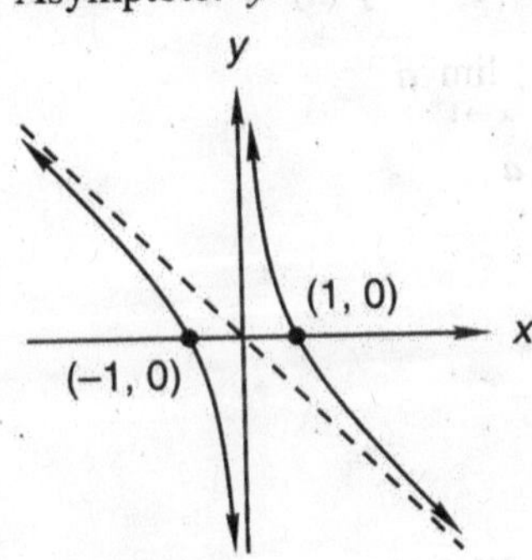

21. $$\lim_{x\to\frac{\pi}{2}} \frac{\sin x - \sin\frac{\pi}{2}}{x - \frac{\pi}{2}} = \frac{d}{dx}\sin x\bigg|_{\frac{\pi}{2}}$$
$$= \cos\left(\frac{\pi}{2}\right) = \mathbf{0}$$

22. $y = x \arcsin \frac{x}{3} + x(1 + x)^{-1/2} + 3^x - \frac{3 \ln x}{\ln 47}$

$$\frac{dy}{dx} = x\left(\frac{1}{\sqrt{9 - x^2}}\right) + \arcsin \frac{x}{3}$$
$$+ x\left[-\frac{1}{2}(1 + x)^{-3/2}\right] + (1 + x)^{-1/2}$$
$$+ 3^x \ln 3 - \frac{3}{x \ln 47}$$

$$\frac{dy}{dx} = \frac{x}{\sqrt{9 - x^2}} + \arcsin \frac{x}{3}$$
$$+ \frac{x + 2}{2(1 + x)^{3/2}} + 3^x \ln 3 - \frac{3}{x \ln 47}$$

23. $y = \arcsin \frac{x}{3}$

$$\frac{dy}{dx} = \frac{1}{\sqrt{9 - x^2}}$$

$$\text{slope} = \left.\frac{dy}{dx}\right|_{x=1} = \frac{1}{\sqrt{8}}$$

slope of normal line $= -\sqrt{8} = \mathbf{-2\sqrt{2}}$

24. Each of the four choices is an attempt to properly state Rolle's theorem. Choice A does not mention differentiability over (1, 3) and is false. Choice B does not require f to be zero at $f(1)$ and $f(3)$, so we do not know if the statement is true or false. Choice C is false, because $f'(c) = 0$ not $f(c) = 0$.

The correct choice is **D**.

25. $(fg)'(1) = f(1)g'(1) + g(1)f'(1)$
$= 2(4) + (-1)(3)$
$= \mathbf{5}$

PROBLEM SET 86

1. (a)

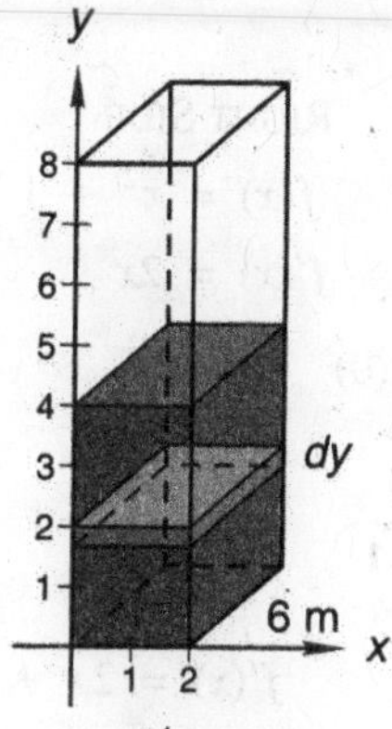

$$F = \int_0^4 3000(4 - y)(2)\,dy$$
$$= 6000 \int_0^4 (4 - y)\,dy$$
$$= 6000\left[4y - \frac{1}{2}y^2\right]_0^4$$
$$= 6000(16 - 8) = \mathbf{48{,}000 \text{ newtons}}$$

(b) $$W = \int_0^4 3000(2)(6)(8 - y)\,dy$$
$$= 36{,}000 \int_0^4 (8 - y)\,dy$$
$$= 36{,}000\left[8y - \frac{1}{2}y^2\right]_0^4$$
$$= 36{,}000(32 - 8)$$
$$= \mathbf{864{,}000 \text{ joules}}$$

2. $a(t) = 6t + 18$
$v(t) = 3t^2 + 18t + C$
$v(0) = 3(0)^2 + 18(0) + C$
$20 = C$
$\mathbf{v(t) = 3t^2 + 18t + 20}$
$x(t) = t^3 + 9t^2 + 20t + C$
$x(1) = (1)^3 + 9(1)^2 + 20(1) + C$
$21 = 30 + C$
$C = -9$
$\mathbf{x(t) = t^3 + 9t^2 + 20t - 9}$

3. $f(x) = ae^x + b \sin x$
$f'(x) = ae^x + b \cos x$
$f'(0) = ae^0 + b \cos 0 = 4$
$a + b = 4$

$f'\left(\frac{\pi}{2}\right) = ae^{\pi/2} + 0 = 1$
$\mathbf{a = e^{-\pi/2}}$
$\mathbf{b = 4 - e^{-\pi/2}}$

4. $\lim_{x \to 0^-} ae^x + bx = f(0)$

$a = \mathbf{1}$

LEFT SIDE	RIGHT SIDE
$f(x) = ae^x + bx$	$f(x) = x^2 + 1$
$f'(x) = ae^x + b$	$f'(x) = 2x$

$$\lim_{x \to 0^-} (ae^x + b) = 2(0)$$
$$a + b = 0$$
$$b = \mathbf{-1}$$

5. $f(x) = x^2 + x + 1 \qquad f'(x) = 2x + 1$

$$f'(c) = \frac{f(3) - f(0)}{3 - 0}$$
$$2c + 1 = \frac{13 - 1}{3}$$
$$c = \mathbf{\frac{3}{2}}$$

6. $f(x) = x^3 + 3x^2 \qquad f'(x) = 3x^2 + 6x$

$$f'(c) = \frac{f(1) - f(-2)}{1 + 2}$$
$$3c^2 + 6c = \frac{4 - 4}{3}$$
$$3c(c + 2) = 0$$
$$c = \mathbf{0}$$

Note: c cannot be an endpoint, so $c \neq -2$.

7. $f(x) = \sin x \qquad f'(x) = \cos x$

$$f'(c) = 0$$
$$\cos c = 0$$
$$c = \mathbf{\frac{\pi}{2}} \text{ on the interval } [0, \pi].$$

8. $f(x) = x^3 - x \qquad f'(x) = 3x^2 - 1$

$$f'(c) = 0$$
$$3c^2 - 1 = 0$$
$$c^2 = \frac{1}{3}$$
$$c = \mathbf{\pm\frac{\sqrt{3}}{3}}$$

9.
$$(fg)(-x) = f(-x)g(-x)$$
$$= -f(x)[-g(x)]$$
$$= f(x)g(x)$$
$$= (fg)(x)$$

10.
$$\int_{-4}^{4} f(x)\,dx = \int_{-4}^{0} f(x)\,dx + \int_{0}^{4} f(x)\,dx$$
$$= -7 + 7 = \mathbf{0}$$

11.
$$\int_{0}^{4} g(x)\,dx = \frac{1}{2}\int_{-4}^{4} g(x)\,dx = \frac{1}{2}(4) = \mathbf{2}$$

12.
$$f(x) = x \sin x \cos x$$
$$\ln[f(x)] = \ln x + \ln(\sin x) + \ln(\cos x)$$
$$\frac{f'(x)}{f(x)} = \mathbf{\frac{1}{x} + \cot x - \tan x}$$

13.
$$\lim_{x \to 0}(x \csc x) = \lim_{x \to 0} \frac{x}{\sin x} = \lim_{x \to 0} \frac{1}{\cos x}$$
$$= \frac{1}{1} = \mathbf{1}$$

14.
$$\lim_{x \to \infty} \frac{x + e^x}{x - e^x} = \lim_{x \to \infty} \frac{1 + e^x}{1 - e^x} = \lim_{x \to \infty} \frac{e^x}{-e^x}$$
$$= \lim_{x \to \infty} -1 = \mathbf{-1}$$

15.

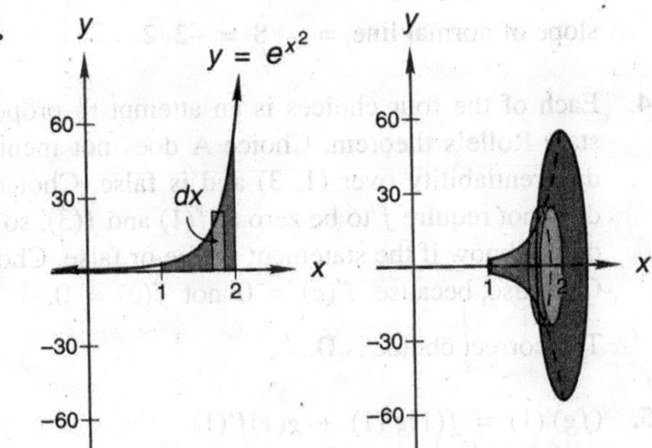

$$V = \pi \int_1^2 \left(e^{x^2}\right)^2 dx = \mathbf{\pi \int_1^2 e^{2x^2}\,dx}$$

16.
$$y = \arcsin \frac{x}{a}$$
$$y' = \mathbf{\frac{1}{\sqrt{a^2 - x^2}}}$$

17. $y = \arcsin(\cos x) + \dfrac{e^x - x}{\sin(2x) + \cos x}$

$- 2\csc^2 x$

$$y' = \frac{-\sin x}{\sqrt{1 - \cos^2 x}}$$

$$+ \frac{[\sin(2x) + \cos x](e^x - 1)}{[\sin(2x) + \cos x]^2}$$

$$- \frac{(e^x - x)[2\cos(2x) - \sin x]}{[\sin(2x) + \cos x]^2}$$

$$- 4\csc x(-\csc x \cot x)$$

$$y' = -1 + \frac{e^x - 1}{\sin(2x) + \cos x}$$

$$- \frac{(e^x - x)[2\cos(2x) - \sin x]}{[\sin(2x) + \cos x]^2}$$

$$+ 4\csc^2 x \cot x$$

18. $\displaystyle\int \frac{dx}{\sqrt{9 - x^2}} = \arcsin\frac{x}{3} + C$

19. $u = 2x \quad du = 2\,dx \quad v = e^x \quad dv = e^x\,dx$

$$\int 2xe^x\,dx = 2xe^x - \int 2e^x\,dx$$

$$= 2xe^x - 2e^x + C$$

$$= 2e^x(x - 1) + C$$

20. $u = -x^2 \qquad du = -2x\,dx$

$$\int 2xe^{-x^2}\,dx = -\int -2xe^{-x^2}\,dx$$

$$= -\int e^u\,du$$

$$= -e^u + C$$

$$= -e^{-x^2} + C$$

21. (a) $\displaystyle\int_1^3 f(x)\,dx + \int_3^5 f(x)\,dx = \int_1^5 f(x)\,dx$

$$\frac{5}{2} + \int_3^5 f(x)\,dx = 10$$

$$\int_3^5 f(x)\,dx = \frac{15}{2}$$

$$\int_3^5 (2f(x) + 6)\,dx = 2\left(\frac{15}{2}\right) + [6x]_3^5$$

$$= 15 + (30 - 18) = 27$$

(b) $\displaystyle\int_1^3 (ax + b)\,dx = \frac{5}{2}$

$$\left[\frac{a}{2}x^2 + bx\right]_1^3 = \frac{5}{2}$$

$$\frac{9}{2}a + 3b - \left(\frac{a}{2} + b\right) = \frac{5}{2}$$

$$8a + 4b = 5$$

$$\int_1^5 (ax + b)\,dx = 10$$

$$\left[\frac{a}{2}x^2 + bx\right]_1^5 = 10$$

$$\frac{25}{2}a + 5b - \left(\frac{a}{2} + b\right) = 10$$

$$12a + 4b = 10$$

$$12a + 4b - (8a + 4b) = 10 - (5)$$

$$4a = 5$$

$$a = \frac{5}{4}$$

$$8a + 4b = 5$$

$$10 + 4b = 5$$

$$b = -\frac{5}{4}$$

22. $\displaystyle\left(\frac{f}{g}\right)'(1) = \frac{g(1)f'(1) - f(1)g'(1)}{[g(1)]^2}$

$$= \frac{1(2) - 4(2)}{1^2} = -6$$

23. $f(x) = x^3 + 1$

$$y = x^3 + 1$$

$$x = y^3 + 1$$

$$y^3 = x - 1$$

$$y = \sqrt[3]{x - 1}$$

$$f^{-1}(x) = \sqrt[3]{x - 1}$$

$$f^{-1}(2) = \sqrt[3]{2 - 1}$$

$$f^{-1}(2) = 1$$

24. The Mean Value Theorem guarantees that there is a number c such that

$$f'(c) = \frac{f(6) - f(1)}{6 - 1} = \frac{2 - 3}{5} = -\frac{1}{5}$$

with $1 < c < 6$. Thus, choice A is true while B and C are not. Choice D is not a statement of the Mean Value Theorem, and we do not know if it is true or false.

The correct choice is **A**.

25. $f(x) = \dfrac{x^3 - 1}{x - 2}$

(a) $x^3 - 1 = 0$
$$x^3 = 1$$
$$x = 1$$

Zero: 1
Vertical asymptote: $x = 2$

(b)

2	1	0	0	−1
	↓	2	4	8
	1	2	4	7

$f(x) = x^2 + 2x + 4 + \dfrac{7}{x - 2}$

End behavior: $y = x^2 + 2x + 4$

(c)

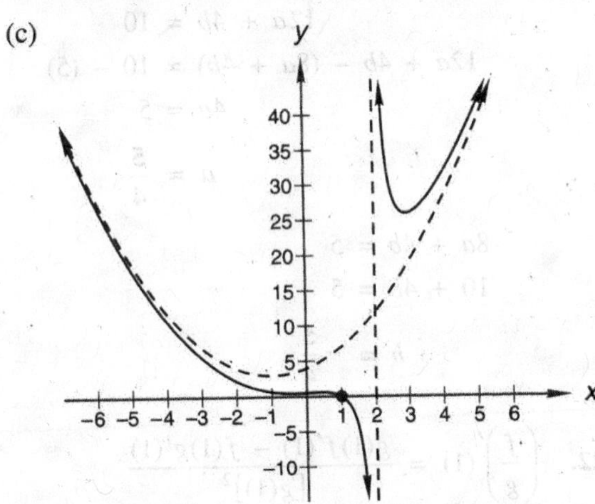

(d) **Domain:** $\{x \in \mathbb{R} \mid x \neq 2\}$
Range: $\mathbb{R}$

PROBLEM SET 87

1.
$$A_t = A_0e^{kt}$$
$$1050 = 1000e^{100k}$$
$$1.05 = e^{100k}$$
$$\ln(1.05) = 100k$$
$$k = \frac{\ln(1.05)}{100}$$
$$A_{200} = 1000e^{[\ln(1.05)/100]200}$$
$$= 1000e^{2\ln(1.05)}$$
$$= 1000(1.05)^2$$
$$= \$1102.50$$

2. (a) $f(x) = xe^{-x}$
$$f'(x) = x(-e^{-x}) + e^{-x}$$
$$f'(x) = e^{-x}(-x + 1)$$
$$0 = e^{-x}(-x + 1)$$

Critical number: $x = 1$

(b) $f''(x) = e^{-x}(-1) + (-x + 1)(-e^{-x})$
$$= e^{-x}(-1 + x - 1)$$
$$= e^{-x}(x - 2)$$

$f''(1) = -e^{-1}$ and $f(1) = \dfrac{1}{e}$

Since f'' is negative at $x = 1$, f attains a maximum at $x = 1$.

Maximum: $\left(1, \dfrac{1}{e}\right)$

(c)
$$f''(x) = 0$$
$$e^{-x}(x - 2) = 0$$
$$x = 2$$

Inflection point: $x = 2$

3. (a) $a(t) = -4t + \sin(\pi t)$
$$v(t) = -2t^2 - \frac{1}{\pi}\cos(\pi t) + C$$
$$v\left(\frac{1}{2}\right) = -2\left(\frac{1}{2}\right)^2 - \frac{1}{\pi}(0) + C = 4$$
$$C = \frac{9}{2}$$
$$v(t) = -2t^2 - \frac{1}{\pi}\cos(\pi t) + \frac{9}{2}$$
$$x(t) = -\frac{2}{3}t^3 - \frac{1}{\pi^2}\sin(\pi t) + \frac{9}{2}t + C$$
$$x(1) = -\frac{2}{3} - 0 + \frac{9}{2} + C$$
$$4 = \frac{23}{6} + C$$
$$C = \frac{1}{6}$$
$$x(t) = -\frac{2}{3}t^3 - \frac{1}{\pi^2}\sin(\pi t) + \frac{9}{2}t + \frac{1}{6}$$

(b) $v(0) = 0 - \dfrac{1}{\pi} + \dfrac{9}{2}$
$$v(0) = \frac{9\pi - 2}{2\pi}\ \frac{\text{linear units}}{\text{time unit}}$$
$$\approx 4.1817 \text{ linear units/time unit}$$
$$x(0) = 0 - 0 + 0 + \frac{1}{6}$$
$$x(0) = \frac{1}{6} \text{ linear unit}$$

4. (a) $a(t) = -9.8$

$v(t) = -9.8t$

$h(t) = -4.9t^2 + 200$

$-4.9t^2 + 200 = 0$

$4.9t^2 = 200$

$t \approx \mathbf{6.3888\ s}$

(b) $d = rt$

$d \approx 40(6.3888) = \mathbf{255.552\ m}$

5. $y = x^3 + kx$

$y' = 3x^2 + k$

$y'(1) = 3 + k = 5$

$k = \mathbf{2}$

6.

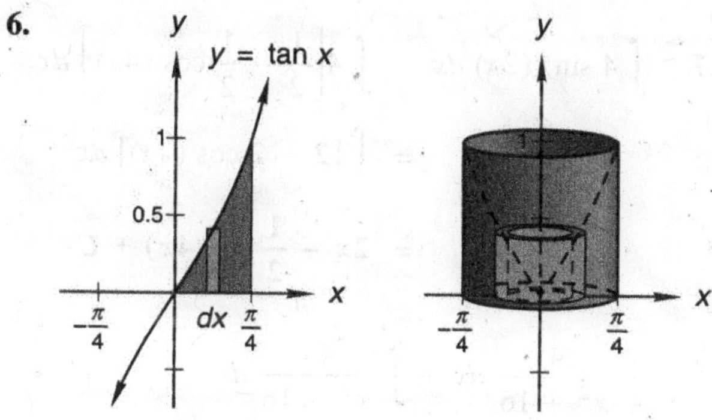

$$V = \int 2\pi rh\,dx = \mathbf{2\pi \int_0^{\pi/4} x \tan x\,dx}$$

7.

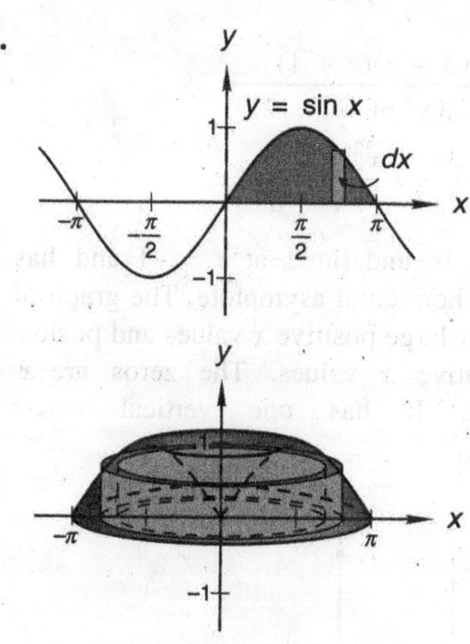

$$V = \int 2\pi rh\,dx = 2\pi \int_0^{\pi} x \sin x\,dx$$

$u = x \quad du = dx \quad v = -\cos x \quad dv = \sin x\,dx$

$$V = 2\pi\left[-x\cos x + \int \cos x\,dx\right]_0^{\pi}$$

$$= 2\pi\left[-x\cos x + \sin x\right]_0^{\pi}$$

$$= \mathbf{2\pi^2\ units^3}$$

8.

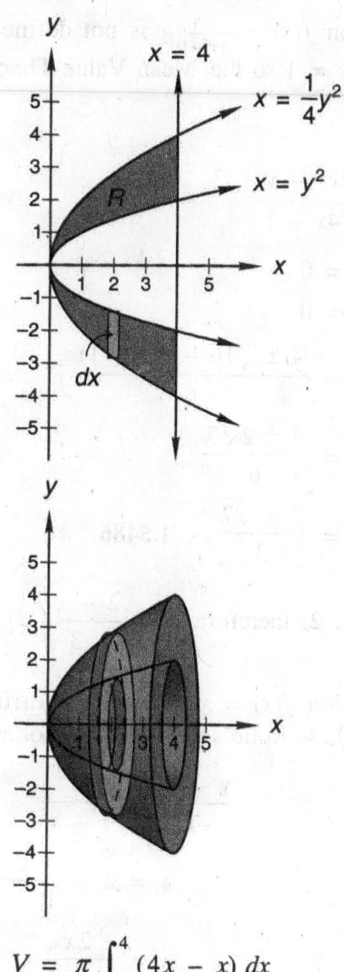

$$V = \pi \int_0^4 (4x - x)\,dx$$

$$= \pi \int_0^4 3x\,dx$$

$$= \pi\left[\frac{3}{2}x^2\right]_0^4 = \mathbf{24\pi\ units^3}$$

9. g is an even function.

$$\int_{-4}^{-1} g(x)\,dx = \int_1^4 g(x)\,dx = \mathbf{k}$$

10. $y = e^{x^2}$ is an even function.

$$\int_{-b}^{b} e^{x^2}\,dx = 2\int_0^b e^{x^2}\,dx = \mathbf{2L}$$

11. $f(x) = x^3 + x \quad f'(x) = 3x^2 + 1$

$$f'(c) = \frac{f(3) - f(1)}{3 - 1}$$

$$3c^2 + 1 = \frac{30 - 2}{2}$$

$3c^2 + 1 = 14$

$3c^2 = 13$

$$c = \mathbf{\frac{\sqrt{39}}{3}} \approx \mathbf{2.0817}$$

12. **No,** the function $f(x) = \frac{1}{(x-1)^2}$ is not defined or continuous at $x = 1$ so the Mean Value Theorem does not apply.

13. $$f(x) = x^3 - 2x^2 - x + 2$$
$$f'(x) = 3x^2 - 4x - 1$$
$$f'(c) = 0$$
$$3c^2 - 4c - 1 = 0$$
$$c = \frac{4 \pm \sqrt{16 - 4(3)(-1)}}{6}$$
$$c = \frac{4 \pm 2\sqrt{7}}{6}$$
$$c = \mathbf{\frac{2 + \sqrt{7}}{3}} \approx \mathbf{1.5486}$$

Note: $1 < c < 2$, therefore $c \neq \frac{2 - \sqrt{7}}{3}$.

14. **No,** the function $f(x) = x^{2/3 - 1}$ is not differentiable at $x = 0$, so Rolle's theorem does not apply.

15. $$\frac{y - 2}{-1} = \frac{2}{1 - x}$$
$$y = 2 - \frac{2}{1 - x}$$
$$y = \frac{2x}{x - 1}$$

$$A = \frac{1}{2}xy \ (x > 1,\ y > 2)$$
$$A = \frac{1}{2}x\left(\frac{2x}{x - 1}\right)$$
$$A = \frac{x^2}{x - 1}$$
$$A' = \frac{(x - 1)(2x) - (x^2)(1)}{(x - 1)^2}$$
$$A' = \frac{x^2 - 2x}{(x - 1)^2}$$
$$A'' = \frac{2}{(x - 1)^3}$$
$$A''(2) > 0$$
$$0 = \frac{x^2 - 2x}{(x - 1)^2}$$
$$0 = x(x - 2)$$
$$x = 2$$

If $x = 2$, then $y = 4$. The slope of the line is $\frac{4 - 0}{0 - 2} = \mathbf{-2}$.

16. $$f(x) = \frac{\sqrt{x - 1}\sin x}{(x^3 + 1)^{100}(x - 1)^5}$$
$$\ln[f(x)] = \ln\sqrt{x - 1} + \ln(\sin x) - \ln(x^3 + 1)^{100} - \ln(x - 1)^5$$
$$\ln[f(x)] = \frac{1}{2}\ln(x - 1) + \ln(\sin x) - 100\ln(x^3 + 1) - 5\ln(x - 1)$$
$$\frac{f'(x)}{f(x)} = \frac{1}{2(x - 1)} + \cot x - \frac{300x^2}{x^3 + 1} - \frac{5}{x - 1}$$
$$\mathbf{\frac{f'(x)}{f(x)} = -\frac{9}{2(x - 1)} + \cot x - \frac{300x^2}{x^3 + 1}}$$

17. $$\int 4\sin^2(2x)\,dx = \int 4\left[\frac{1}{2} - \frac{1}{2}\cos(4x)\right]dx$$
$$= \int [2 - 2\cos(4x)]\,dx$$
$$= \mathbf{2x - \frac{1}{2}\sin(4x) + C}$$

18. $$\int \frac{4}{x^2 + 16}\,dx + \int \frac{4x}{x^2 + 16}\,dx$$
$$= \mathbf{\arctan\frac{x}{4} + 2\ln(x^2 + 16) + C}$$

19. $$y = \frac{x(3 - x)(x + 1)}{(x + 1)(x^2 + 2)(x + 3)}$$
$$y = \frac{3x - x^2}{x^3 + 3x^2 + 2x + 6}$$

The graph is undefined at $x = -1$ and has the x-axis as a horizontal asymptote. The graph of y is negative for large positive x values and positive for large negative x values. The zeros are $x = 0$ and $x = 3$. It has one vertical asymptote at $x = -3$.

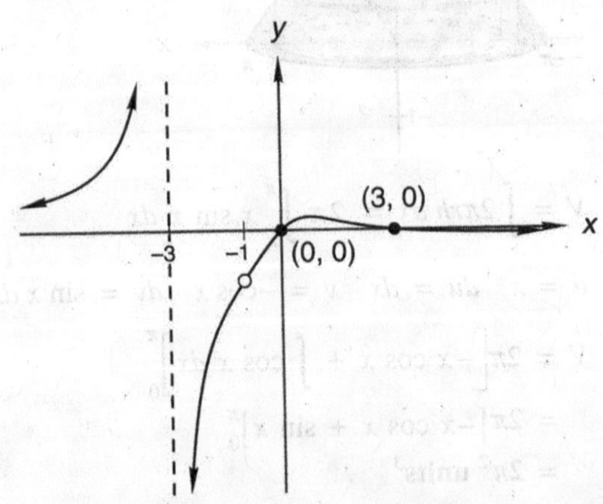

20.

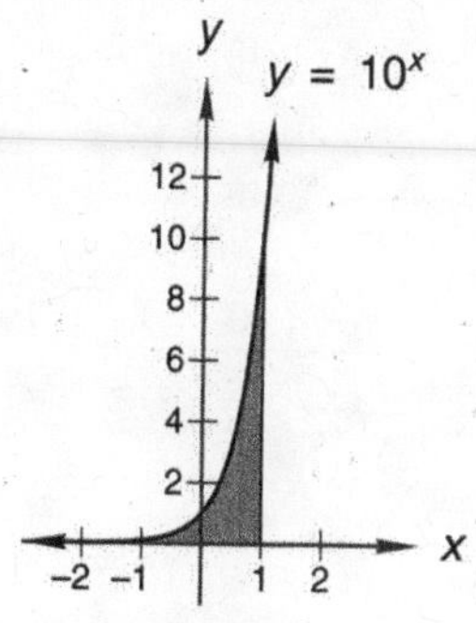

$$A = \int_{-1}^{1} 10^x \, dx$$
$$= \frac{1}{\ln 10}\left[10^x\right]_{-1}^{1}$$
$$= \frac{10}{\ln 10} - \frac{1}{10 \ln 10}$$
$$= \mathbf{\frac{99}{10 \ln 10}} \textbf{ units}^2$$

21.

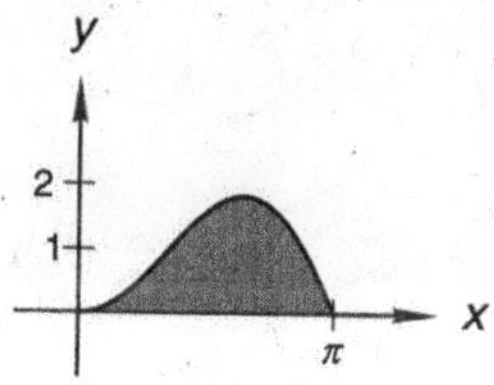

$u = x \quad du = dx \quad v = -\cos x \quad dv = \sin x \, dx$

$$A = \int_0^{\pi} x \sin x \, dx$$
$$= \left[-x \cos x + \int \cos x \, dx\right]_0^{\pi}$$
$$= [-x \cos x + \sin x]_0^{\pi}$$
$$= \pi \textbf{ units}^2$$

22. (a) $y = x^3 + x$

$\mathbf{x = y^3 + y}$

(b) Since $f(1) = (1)^3 + (1) = 2$, we know that $f^{-1}(2) = \mathbf{1}$.

23. $y = \arctan \frac{x}{7} + \frac{1 - e^x}{e^x} + \sin x \cot x$

$y = \arctan \frac{x}{7} + e^{-x} - 1 + \cos x$

$$y' = \mathbf{\frac{7}{x^2 + 49} - e^{-x} - \sin x}$$

24. If a function contains the point (x, y), then its inverse contains the point (y, x). So choice A is false, while choice D is true. Not enough is known about the function to determine the validity of choices B and C.

The correct choice is **D.**

25. (a) The zero of $f(x) = \frac{2x^3 - 4x^2 + 6}{x - 2}$ is the solution to $x^3 - 2x^2 = -3$, which is -1 by inspection.

Zero: −1

Vertical asymptote: $\mathbf{x = 2}$

(b)
$$\begin{array}{r|rrrr} 2 & 2 & -4 & 0 & 6 \\ & \downarrow & 4 & 0 & 0 \\ \hline & 2 & 0 & 0 & \boxed{6} \end{array}$$

End behavior: $\mathbf{y = 2x^2}$

(c)

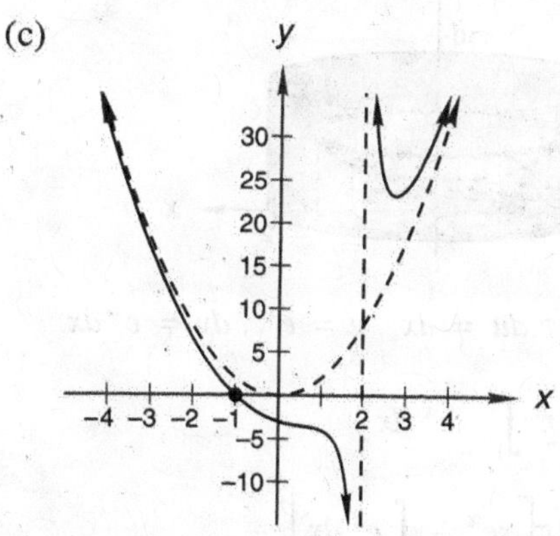

(d) **Domain:** $\{x \in \mathbb{R} \mid x \neq 2\}$

Range: $\mathbb{R}$

Problem Set 88

1. $$W = \int_1^5 (3x^2 + 1) \, dx$$
$$= \left[x^3 + x\right]_1^5$$
$$= 125 + 5 - (1 + 1) = \textbf{128 joules}$$

2.

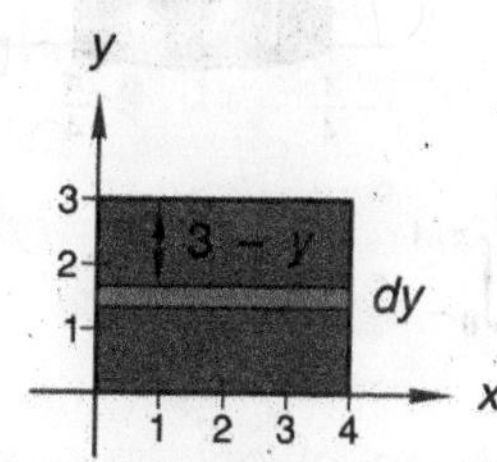

$$F = \int_0^3 2000(3 - y)4 \, dy$$
$$= 8000 \int_0^3 (3 - y) \, dy$$
$$= 8000\left[3y - \frac{1}{2}y^2\right]_0^3$$
$$= 8000\left(9 - \frac{9}{2}\right)$$
$$= \textbf{36,000 newtons}$$

3.

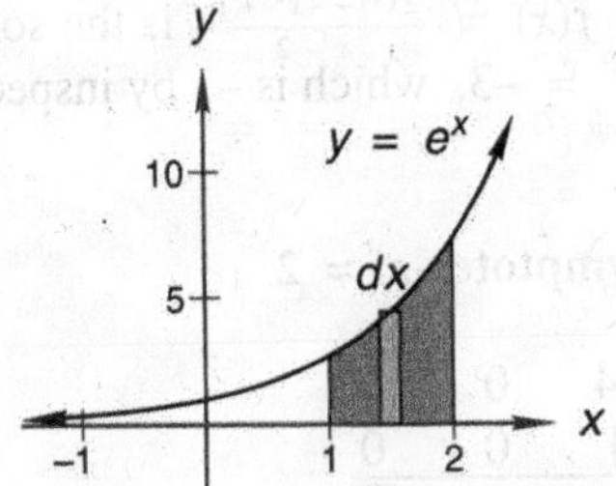

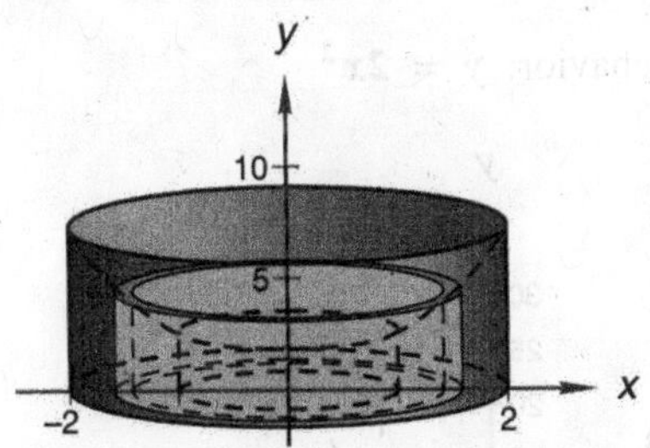

$u = x \quad du = dx \quad v = e^x \quad dv = e^x\,dx$

$$V = 2\pi \int_1^2 xe^x\,dx$$

$$= 2\pi\left[xe^x - \int e^x\,dx\right]_1^2$$

$$= 2\pi\left[xe^x - e^x\right]_1^2$$

$$= 2\pi[2e^2 - e^2 - (e - e)]$$

$$= \mathbf{2\pi e^2\ units^3}$$

4.

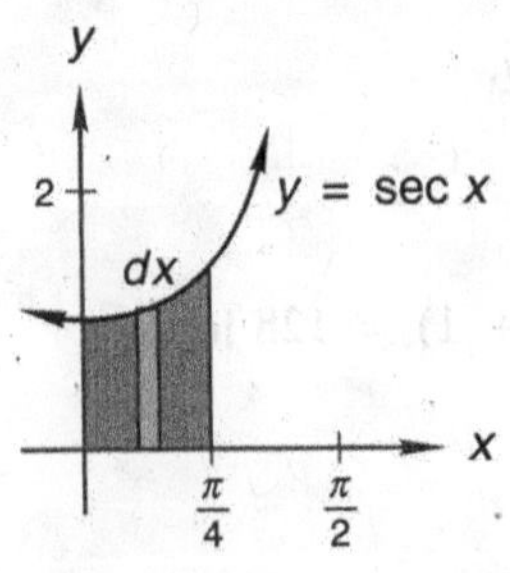

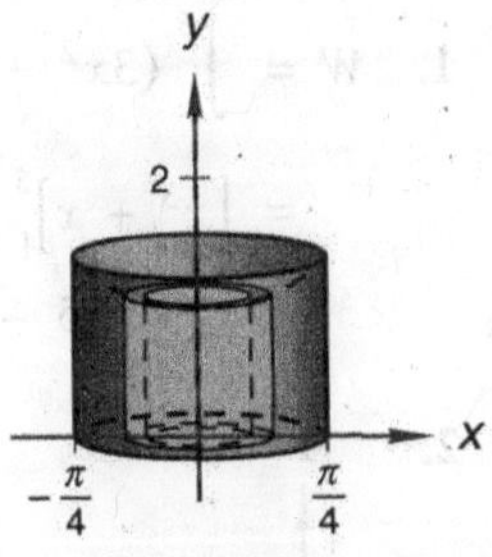

$$V = \int 2\pi rh\,dx = \mathbf{2\pi \int_0^{\pi/4} x \sec x\,dx}$$

5. $f(0) = \lim_{x\to 0^-} f(x)$

$\mathbf{a = 0}$

LEFT SIDE	RIGHT SIDE
$f(x) = bx$	$f(x) = ae^x + \sin x$
$f'(x) = b$	$f'(x) = ae^x + \cos x$

$\lim_{x\to 0^-} f'(x) = f'(0)$

$b = a + 1$

$\mathbf{b = 1}$

6. $x\,dx - y\,dy = 0$

$$x\,dx = y\,dy$$

$$\frac{1}{2}x^2 + C = \frac{1}{2}y^2$$

$$x^2 + C = y^2$$

$$\mathbf{x^2 - y^2 = C}$$

7. $\dfrac{dy}{dx} = 4x^3y^2$

$$y^{-2}\,dy = 4x^3\,dx$$

$$-y^{-1} = x^4 + C$$

$$y^{-1} = -x^4 + C$$

$$\mathbf{y = \frac{1}{-x^4 + C}}$$

8. $\dfrac{dy}{dx} = 3x$

$$dy = 3x\,dx$$

$$y = \frac{3}{2}x^2 + C$$

$$3 = 6 + C$$

$$C = -3$$

$$\mathbf{y = \frac{3}{2}x^2 - 3}$$

9. (a) $(fg)(-x) = f(-x)g(-x)$

$$= \cos(-x)\left[(-x)^5 - (-x)^3 + (-x)\right]$$

$$= \cos x\left[-x^5 + x^3 - x\right]$$

$$= f(x)[-g(x)]$$

$$= -f(x)g(x)$$

$$= -(fg)(x)$$

So $(fg)(x)$ is an **odd function.**

(b) Since fg is odd, $\int_{-3}^{3} (fg)(x)\,dx = \mathbf{0}$.

10. nth term $= \dfrac{9!\,(3x)^{9-(n-1)}\,(y^2)^{n-1}}{[9-(n-1)]!\,(n-1)!}$

6th term $= \dfrac{9!\,(3x)^4\,(y^2)^5}{4!\,5!} = \mathbf{10{,}206x^4y^{10}}$

11. $f(x) = e^{2x} \qquad f'(x) = 2e^{2x}$

$$f'(c) = \frac{f(1) - f(0)}{1 - 0}$$

$$2e^{2c} = e^2 - 1$$

$$e^{2c} = \frac{1}{2}(e^2 - 1)$$

$$2c = \ln\left[\frac{1}{2}(e^2 - 1)\right]$$

$$\mathbf{c = \frac{1}{2}\ln\left[\frac{1}{2}(e^2 - 1)\right]}$$

12. (a) $\dfrac{dV}{dt} = -6\,\dfrac{\text{m}^3}{\text{min}}$ $\quad V = 64\text{ m}^3 \quad s = 4\text{ m}$

$$V = s^{312}$$

$$\frac{dV}{dt} = 3s^2\,\frac{ds}{dt}$$

$$(-6) = 3(4)^2\,\frac{ds}{dt}$$

$$\mathbf{\frac{ds}{dt} = -\frac{1}{8}\,\frac{m}{min}}$$

(b) $A = 6s^2$

$$\frac{dA}{dt} = 12s\,\frac{ds}{dt}$$

$$\frac{dA}{dt} = 12(4)\left(-\frac{1}{8}\right)$$

$$\mathbf{\frac{dA}{dt} = -6\,\frac{m^2}{min}}$$

13.

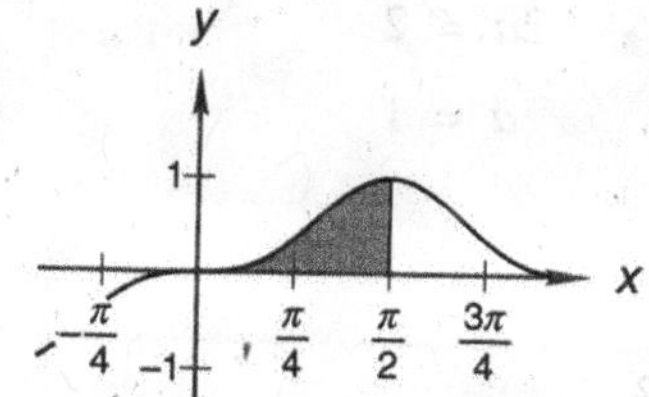

y

1

x

$-\frac{\pi}{4}$ $\quad -1$ $\quad \frac{\pi}{4}$ $\quad \frac{\pi}{2}$ $\quad \frac{3\pi}{4}$

$$A = \int_0^{\pi/2} \sin^3 x\,dx$$

$$= \int_0^{\pi/2} \sin x\,(1 - \cos^2 x)\,dx$$

$$= \int_0^{\pi/2} [\sin x - \sin x \cos^2 x]\,dx$$

$$= \left[-\cos x + \frac{1}{3}\cos^3 x\right]_0^{\pi/2}$$

$$= 0 + 0 - \left(-1 + \frac{1}{3}\right)$$

$$= \mathbf{\frac{2}{3}\ units^2}$$

14. $y = x\sec(2x) - \dfrac{a - \sin x}{b + \cos x} - \arcsin\dfrac{x}{a}$

$$y' = 2x\sec(2x)\tan(2x) + \sec(2x) - \left[\frac{(b + \cos x)(-\cos x)}{(b + \cos x)^2} - \frac{(a - \sin x)(-\sin x)}{(b + \cos x)^2}\right] - \frac{1}{\sqrt{a^2 - x^2}}$$

$$y' = \sec(2x)\,[2x\tan(2x) + 1] - \frac{-b\cos x - \cos^2 x + a\sin x - \sin^2 x}{(b + \cos x)^2} - \frac{1}{\sqrt{a^2 - x^2}}$$

$$\mathbf{y' = \sec(2x)\,[2x\tan(2x) + 1] + \frac{b\cos x - a\sin x + 1}{(b + \cos x)^2} - \frac{1}{\sqrt{a^2 - x^2}}}$$

15. $u = x^3 - 1 \qquad du = 3x^2\,dx$

$$\int x^2(x^3 - 1)^{1/2}\,dx = \frac{1}{3}\int u^{1/2}\,du$$

$$= \frac{2}{9}u^{3/2} + C$$

$$= \mathbf{\frac{2}{9}(x^3 - 1)^{3/2} + C}$$

16. $\displaystyle\int\left(\frac{1}{\sqrt{a^2 - x^2}} + \frac{x}{\sqrt{a^2 - x^2}}\right)dx$

$$= \arcsin\frac{x}{a} + \int\frac{x}{\sqrt{a^2 - x^2}}\,dx$$

$u = a^2 - x^2 \qquad du = -2x\,dx$

$$\arcsin\frac{x}{a} + \int\frac{x}{\sqrt{a^2 - x^2}}\,dx$$

$$= \arcsin\frac{x}{a} - \frac{1}{2}\int u^{-1/2}\,du$$

$$= \arcsin\frac{x}{a} - u^{1/2} + C$$

$$= \mathbf{\arcsin\frac{x}{a} - \sqrt{a^2 - x^2} + C}$$

17. The function must be both continuous and differentiable over $[a, b]$ in order to apply the Mean Value Theorem. Choice A is not differentiable over $[a, b]$, while choice B is not continuous.

Choices C and D are both continuous and differentiable over $[a, b]$, so the correct choices are **C** and **D.**

18. $f(x) = x^2 - 9x + 14 \qquad f'(x) = 2x - 9$

$$f'(c) = 0$$
$$2c - 9 = 0$$
$$2c = 9$$
$$c = \frac{9}{2}$$

The number c is the midpoint of [2, 7].

19. $f(x) = (4x - x^2)^{1/2}$

$$f'(x) = \frac{1}{2}(4x - x^2)^{-1/2}(4 - 2x)$$
$$f'(c) = \frac{1}{2}(4c - c^2)^{-1/2}(4 - 2c)$$
$$0 = \frac{1}{2}(4c - c^2)^{-1/2}(4 - 2c)$$
$$0 = 4 - 2c$$
$$c = \mathbf{2}$$

20. $\lim_{x \to 0} \frac{x^3 - 1}{x - 1} = \frac{-1}{-1} = \mathbf{1}$

21. Since $\lim_{x \to 0^+} \frac{|x|}{x} = 1$ and $\lim_{x \to 0^-} \frac{|x|}{x} = -1$,

$\lim_{x \to 0} \frac{|x|}{x}$ **does not exist.**

22. $\lim_{h \to 0} \frac{\ln(x + h) - \ln x}{h} = \frac{d}{dx}\ln x = \mathbf{\frac{1}{x}}$

23. $\lim_{x \to 0} [x \csc(3x)] = \lim_{x \to 0} \frac{x}{\sin(3x)}$

$$= \lim_{x \to 0} \frac{1}{3\cos(3x)} = \mathbf{\frac{1}{3}}$$

24.
$$y = a\cos x + b\sin x$$
$$\frac{dy}{dx} = -a\sin x + b\cos x$$
$$\frac{d^2y}{dx^2} = -a\cos x - b\sin x$$
$$y + \frac{d^2y}{dx^2} = a\cos x + b\sin x - a\cos x - b\sin x$$
$$y + \frac{d^2y}{dx^2} = \mathbf{0}$$

25. $f(x) = ax^3 + bx^2 + cx + d$

$$f(0) = d$$
$$d = 0$$
$$f(x) = ax^3 + bx^2 + cx$$
$$f(1) = a + b + c$$
$$-2 = a + b + c$$
$$f'(x) = 3ax^2 + 2bx + c$$
$$f'(0) = c$$
$$c = 0$$
$$f''(x) = 6ax + 2b$$
$$f''(1) = 6a + 2b$$
$$0 = 6a + 2b$$
$$0 = 3a + b$$
$$3a + b - (a + b + c) = 0 - (-2)$$
$$2a = 2$$
$$a = 1$$
$$1 + b = -2$$
$$b = -3$$
$$\mathbf{f(x) = x^3 - 3x^2}$$

Problem Set 89

1.

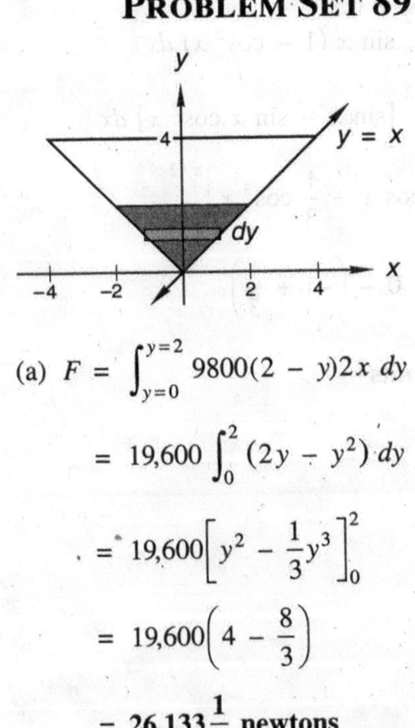

(a) $F = \int_{y=0}^{y=2} 9800(2 - y)2x\,dy$

$$= 19{,}600 \int_0^2 (2y - y^2)\,dy$$
$$= 19{,}600\left[y^2 - \frac{1}{3}y^3\right]_0^2$$
$$= 19{,}600\left(4 - \frac{8}{3}\right)$$
$$= \mathbf{26{,}133\frac{1}{3}}\ \textbf{newtons}$$

(b) $W = \int_0^2 (4 - y)(9800)(2y)(3)\,dy$

$= 58{,}800 \int_0^2 (4y - y^2)\,dy$

$= 58{,}800\left[2y^2 - \frac{1}{3}y^3\right]_0^2$

$= 58{,}800\left(8 - \frac{8}{3}\right)$

$=$ **313,600 joules**

2. $f(x) = 2x^{2/3}$

$f'(x) = \frac{4}{3}x^{-1/3}$

$f'(x) \neq 0$, but $f'(x)$ is undefined when $x = 0$.

Critical numbers: $x = -1, 0, 8$

$f(-1) = 2$ $\quad f(0) = 0$ $\quad f(8) = 8$

Maximum: 8 $\quad$ **Minimum: 0**

3. (a) $\frac{f}{g} = \frac{\text{odd}}{\text{even}} =$ **odd**

(b) $fg = (\text{odd})(\text{even}) =$ **odd**

(c) $f^2g = (\text{odd})(\text{odd})(\text{even})$

$= (\text{even})(\text{even}) =$ **even**

4. $v_{\text{avg}} = \frac{1}{3 - (-1)} \int_{-1}^{3} (x^2 + 6)\,dx$

$= \frac{1}{4}\left[\frac{1}{3}x^3 + 6x\right]_{-1}^{3}$

$= \frac{1}{4}\left[9 + 18 - \left(-\frac{1}{3} - 6\right)\right]$

$= \frac{1}{4}\left(\frac{100}{3}\right) = \mathbf{\frac{25}{3}}$

5. $u = x \quad du = dx \quad v = e^x \quad dv = e^x\,dx$

$v_{\text{avg}} = \frac{1}{2 - 0}\int_0^2 xe^x\,dx$

$= \frac{1}{2}\left[xe^x - \int e^x\,dx\right]_0^2$

$= \frac{1}{2}\left[xe^x - e^x\right]_0^2$

$= \frac{1}{2}[e^2 - (-1)] = \mathbf{\frac{1}{2}(e^2 + 1)} \approx$ **4.1945**

6. $f(x) = x^3 + 4$

$f(c) = \frac{1}{2 - (-2)}\int_{-2}^{2} (x^3 + 4)\,dx$

$c^3 + 4 = \frac{1}{4}\left[\frac{1}{4}x^4 + 4x\right]_{-2}^{2}$

$c^3 + 4 = \frac{1}{4}[4 + 8 - (4 - 8)]$

$c^3 + 4 = 4$

$c =$ **0**

7. $f(x) = 3x^2$

$f(c) = 3$

$3c^2 = 3$

$c^2 = 1$

$c =$ **1**

Note: c must be between -1 and 2, so $c \neq -1$.

8. $x\,dx + 2y\,dy = 0$

$x\,dx = -2y\,dy$

$\frac{1}{2}x^2 + C = -y^2$

$x^2 + C = -2y^2$

$\mathbf{x^2 + 2y^2 = C}$

9. $\frac{dy}{dx} = 6x^2y^2$

$y^{-2}\,dy = 6x^2\,dx$

$-y^{-1} = 2x^3 + C$

$y^{-1} = -2x^3 + C$

$\mathbf{y = \frac{1}{-2x^3 + C}}$

10. $\frac{dy}{dx} = 2x$

$dy = 2x\,dx$

$y = x^2 + C$

$1 = 1 + C$

$C = 0$

$\mathbf{y = x^2}$

11. $B = Pe^{rt}$

$20{,}000 = Pe^{0.08(21)}$

$P = \frac{20{,}000}{e^{1.68}}$

$P =$ **\$3727.48**

12. $f(x) = 4x^2 - 36x + 89 \qquad f'(x) = 8x - 36$

$$f'(c) = \frac{f(6) - f(3)}{6 - 3}$$

$$8c - 36 = \frac{17 - 17}{3}$$

$$8c = 36$$

$$c = 4.5$$

The number c is the midpoint of [3, 6].

13. (a) $\int_0^2 [f(x) + 2g(x)]\,dx$

$$= \int_0^2 f(x)\,dx + 2\int_0^2 g(x)\,dx$$

$$= 2 + 2(4) = \mathbf{10}$$

(b) $\int_1^2 g(x)\,dx + \int_2^0 g(x)\,dx$

$$= -\int_0^1 g(x)\,dx = -(-1) = \mathbf{1}$$

14.

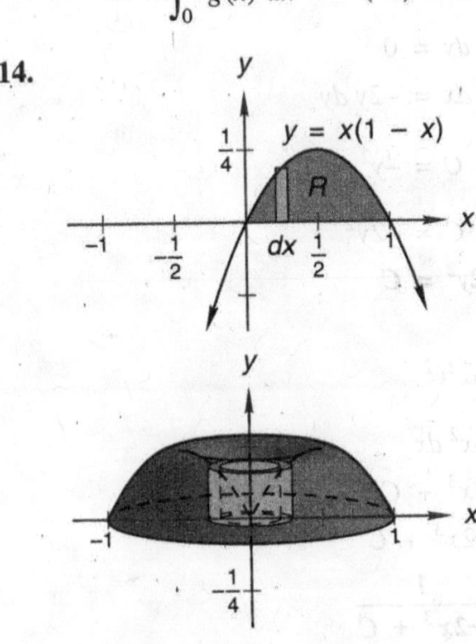

$$V = \int 2\pi rh\,dx$$

$$= 2\pi \int_0^1 x[x(1 - x)]\,dx$$

$$= \mathbf{2\pi \int_0^1 (x^2 - x^3)\,dx}$$

15.

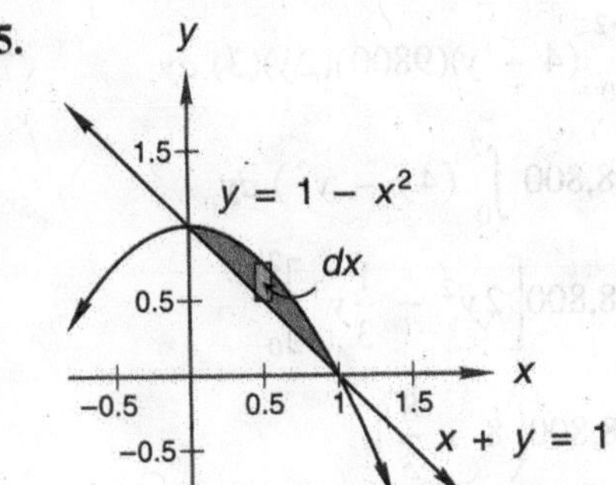

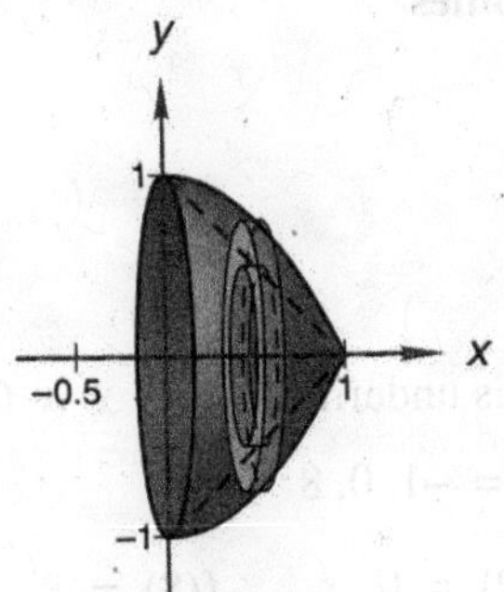

$$V = \pi \int_0^1 [(1 - x^2)^2 - (-x + 1)^2]\,dx$$

$$= \pi \int_0^1 (1 - 2x^2 + x^4 - x^2 + 2x - 1)\,dx$$

$$= \pi \int_0^1 (x^4 - 3x^2 + 2x)\,dx$$

$$= \pi\left[\frac{1}{5}x^5 - x^3 + x^2\right]_0^1 = \mathbf{\frac{\pi}{5}\ units^3}$$

16.

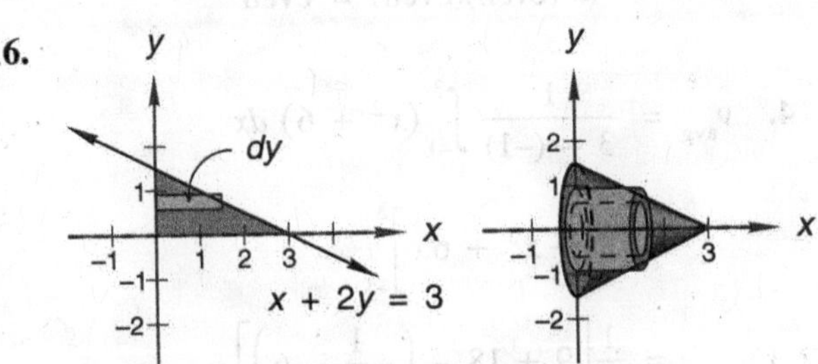

$$V = \int 2\pi rh\,dy$$

$$= 2\pi \int_0^{3/2} y(-2y + 3)\,dy$$

$$= \mathbf{2\pi \int_0^{3/2} (-2y^2 + 3y)\,dy}$$

17.

$$f(x) = 2x^{2x}$$

$$\ln f(x) = \ln (2x^{2x})$$

$$\ln f(x) = \ln 2 + 2x \ln x$$

$$\frac{1}{f(x)} f'(x) = 2x\left(\frac{1}{x}\right) + 2 \ln x$$

$$f'(x) = f(x)[2 + 2 \ln x]$$

$$f'(x) = \mathbf{4x^{2x}(1 + \ln x)}$$

18. $y = \arctan x + \ln|\sin x| + 14^x - \dfrac{\sec x + e^x}{1 + x}$

$$y' = \frac{1}{x^2 + 1} + \frac{\cos x}{\sin x} + 14^x \ln 14 - \frac{(1 + x)(\sec x \tan x + e^x)}{(1 + x)^2} + \frac{\sec x + e^x}{(1 + x)^2}$$

$$\mathbf{y' = \frac{1}{x^2 + 1} + \cot x + 14^x \ln 14 - \frac{\sec x \tan x + e^x}{1 + x} + \frac{\sec x + e^x}{(1 + x)^2}}$$

19.

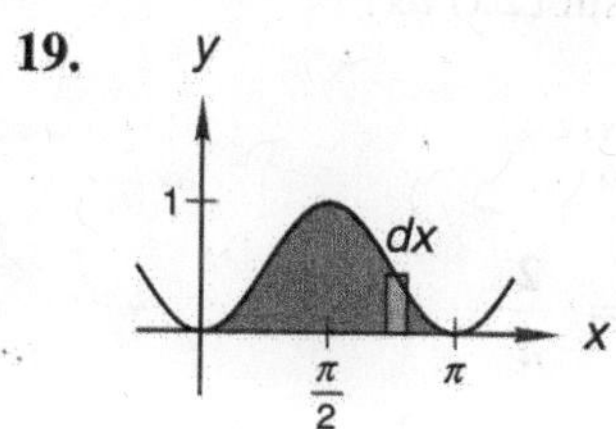

$$A = \int_0^{\pi} \sin^2 x \, dx = \int_0^{\pi} \left[\frac{1}{2} - \frac{1}{2}\cos(2x)\right] dx = \left[\frac{1}{2}x - \frac{1}{4}\sin(2x)\right]_0^{\pi} = \mathbf{\frac{\pi}{2}\ units^2}$$

20. $y = \dfrac{x^2 + 1}{x} = x + \dfrac{1}{x}$

No zeros

Vertical asymptote: $x = 0$

End behavior: $y = x$

21. $u = \sin(2x) \qquad du = 2\cos(2x)\,dx$

$$\int \cos(2x)\, e^{\sin(2x)}\, dx = \frac{1}{2}\int e^u\, du = \frac{1}{2}e^u + C = \mathbf{\frac{1}{2}e^{\sin(2x)} + C}$$

22. $u = x^3 + 1 \qquad du = 3x^2\,dx$

$$\int \frac{x^2}{x^3 + 1}\, dx = \frac{1}{3}\int \frac{du}{u} = \frac{1}{3}\ln|u| + C = \mathbf{\frac{1}{3}\ln\left|x^3 + 1\right| + C}$$

23.
$$x^3 + xy + y^2 = 0$$
$$3x^2 + x\frac{dy}{dx} + y + 2y\frac{dy}{dx} = 0$$
$$\frac{dy}{dx}(x + 2y) = -3x^2 - y$$
$$\mathbf{\frac{dy}{dx} = \frac{-3x^2 - y}{x + 2y}}$$

24. The graph of f' has zeros at both tick marks. The corresponding graph of f must have either a maximum or a minimum at these points. Only one of the four choices possesses this characteristic.

The correct choice is **D**.

25. The phase difference between $\sin x$ and $\cos x$ is $\frac{\pi}{2}$. By reducing the period by a factor of $\frac{1}{2}$ and then shifting it by a multiple of the period $(2x \pm \pi)$, the phase difference reduces to $\frac{\pi}{4}$. With $f(x) = \sin(2x - \pi)$ and $g(x) = \cos(2x + \pi)$, we have the sine and cosine functions with periods shortened to π. They are still odd and even functions, respectively, with equal amplitudes.

The correct choice is **C**.

PROBLEM SET 90

1. 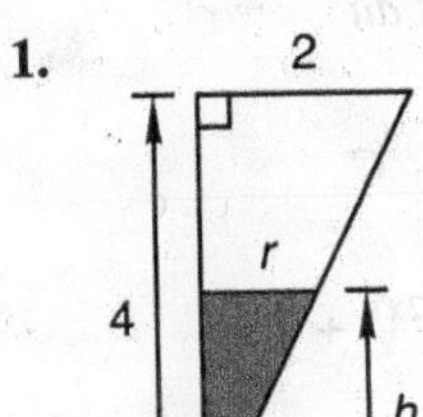

$$V = \frac{1}{3}\pi r^2 h$$
$$V = \frac{1}{3}\pi\left(\frac{1}{2}h\right)^2 h$$
$$V = \frac{1}{12}\pi h^3$$
$$\frac{dV}{dt} = \frac{1}{4}\pi h^2 \frac{dh}{dt}$$
$$\left(-\frac{1}{2}\right) = \frac{1}{4}\pi(2)^2 \frac{dh}{dt}$$
$$-\frac{1}{2} = \pi \frac{dh}{dt}$$
$$\frac{dh}{dt} = \mathbf{-\frac{1}{2\pi}\frac{cm}{s}}$$

2. $x(5) = x(1) + \int_1^2 v(t)\,dt + \int_2^3 v(t)\,dt + \int_3^5 v(t)\,dt$
$= 5 - 5 + 6 - 3 = \mathbf{3}$

3. (a) $x(t) = t^2 - 3t + 2$
$\mathbf{x(0) = 2}$
$x(3) = 3^2 - 3(3) + 2$
$\mathbf{x(3) = 2}$

(b) $v(t) = 2t - 3$
$2t - 3 = 0$
$$t = \frac{3}{2}$$
$$x\left(\frac{3}{2}\right) = \frac{9}{4} - \frac{9}{2} + 2 = -\frac{1}{4}$$
Distance from $t = 0$ to $t = \frac{3}{2}$:
$2 - \left(-\frac{1}{4}\right) = 2\frac{1}{4}$
Distance from $t = \frac{3}{2}$ to $t = 3$:
$2 - \left(-\frac{1}{4}\right) = 2\frac{1}{4}$
Total distance $= 2\frac{1}{4} + 2\frac{1}{4} = \mathbf{4\frac{1}{2}}$ **units**

4. (a) The particle is at rest when
$$v(t) = 2\pi\sin(\pi t) = 0$$
$$\sin(\pi t) = 0$$
$$\pi t = 0, \pi, 2\pi, \ldots$$
On the given interval $t = \mathbf{1.}$

(b) The distance in the negative x-direction is
$$d = \int_{3/2}^{1} 2\pi\sin(\pi t)\,dt$$
$$= 2[-\cos(\pi t)]_{3/2}^{1}$$
$$= \mathbf{2\ units}$$

5. $$v_{avg} = \frac{1}{\frac{\pi}{2} - 0}\int_0^{\pi/2} \sin(2x)\,dx$$
$$= \frac{2}{\pi}\left(\frac{1}{2}\right)\int_0^{\pi/2} 2\sin(2x)\,dx$$
$$= \frac{1}{\pi}[-\cos(2x)]_0^{\pi/2}$$
$$= \frac{1}{\pi}[1 - (-1)] = \mathbf{\frac{2}{\pi}}$$

6. $a(t) = -32$
$v(t) = -32t$
$h(t) = -16t^2 + 576$
$0 = -16t^2 + 576$
$t = 6$
$$\text{Average height} = \frac{1}{6 - 0}\int_0^6 (-16t^2 + 576)\,dt$$
$$= \frac{1}{6}\left[-\frac{16}{3}t^3 + 576t\right]_0^6$$
$$= \frac{1}{6}[-1152 + 3456 - (0)]$$
$$= \frac{1}{6}(2304) = \mathbf{384\ ft}$$

7. $a(t) = 4\pi\sin t$
$v(t) = -4\pi\cos t + C$
$\pi = -4\pi + C$
$C = 5\pi$
$v(t) = -4\pi\cos t + 5\pi$
Average velocity
$$= \frac{1}{\pi - 0}\int_0^{\pi}(-4\pi\cos t + 5\pi)\,dt$$
$$= \frac{1}{\pi}[-4\pi\sin t + 5\pi t]_0^{\pi}$$
$$= \frac{1}{\pi}[0 + 5\pi^2 - (0)]$$
$= \mathbf{5\pi}$ **linear units/time unit**

8. $f(x) = x^2 + 1$

$$f(c) = \frac{1}{4-3}\int_3^4 (x^2+1)\,dx$$

$$c^2 + 1 = \left[\frac{1}{3}x^3 + x\right]_3^4$$

$$c^2 + 1 = \frac{64}{3} + 4 - (9+3)$$

$$c^2 = \frac{37}{3}$$

$$c = \sqrt{\frac{\mathbf{111}}{\mathbf{3}}} \approx \mathbf{3.5119}$$

9. $f(x) = \dfrac{x}{\sqrt{x^2+16}}$

$$f(c) = \frac{c}{\sqrt{c^2+16}}$$

$$\frac{1}{3} = \frac{c}{\sqrt{c^2+16}}$$

$$\sqrt{c^2+16} = 3c$$

$$c^2 + 16 = 9c^2$$

$$16 = 8c^2$$

$$c = \mathbf{\sqrt{2}}$$

10. (a) $B_t = B_0e^{kt}$

$$1100 = 1000e^k$$

$$1.1 = e^k$$

$$k = \ln 1.1 \approx 0.095310$$

Interest rate $\approx$ **9.531%**

(b) $90{,}000 = B_0e^{20\ln 1.1}$

$$90{,}000 = B_0(1.1)^{20}$$

$$B_0 = \frac{90{,}000}{(1.1)^{20}} \approx \mathbf{\$13{,}377.93}$$

11. $4x\,dx - 2y\,dy = 0$

$$2y\,dy = 4x\,dx$$

$$y^2 = 2x^2 + C$$

$$\mathbf{y^2 - 2x^2 = C}$$

12. $\dfrac{dy}{dx} = \dfrac{1}{x}$

$$dy = \frac{1}{x}\,dx$$

$$\mathbf{y = \ln|x| + C}$$

13. $\dfrac{dy}{dx} = \dfrac{1}{x}$

$$dy = \frac{1}{x}\,dx$$

$$y = \ln|x| + C$$

$$3 = \ln e + C$$

$$C = 2$$

$$\mathbf{y = \ln|x| + 2}$$

14. $f(x) = 2\sin x \qquad f'(x) = 2\cos x$

$$f'(c) = 0$$

$$2\cos c = 0$$

$$\cos c = 0$$

$$c = \frac{\mathbf{\pi}}{\mathbf{2}}$$

15. $f(1) = \lim_{x\to1^-} f(x)$

$$a + b = 2$$

LEFT SIDE	RIGHT SIDE
$f(x) = 2x^2$	$f(x) = ax^2 + bx$
$f'(1) = \lim_{x\to1^-} f'(x)$	$f'(x) = 2ax + b$
$f'(1) = 4$	$f'(1) = 2a + b$

$$4 = 2a + b$$

$$4 = 2a + (2 - a)$$

$$4 = a + 2$$

$$\mathbf{2 = a} \qquad \mathbf{b = 0}$$

16. (a)

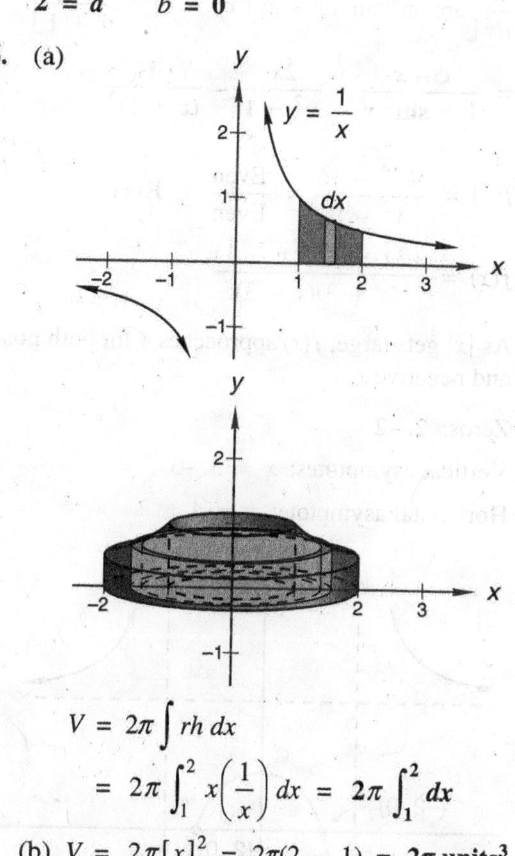

$$V = 2\pi\int rh\,dx$$

$$= 2\pi\int_1^2 x\left(\frac{1}{x}\right)dx = 2\pi\int_1^2 dx$$

(b) $V = 2\pi[x]_1^2 = 2\pi(2-1) = \mathbf{2\pi\ units^3}$

17. $\int 3^x\,dx = \dfrac{\mathbf{3^x}}{\mathbf{\ln 3}} + \mathbf{C}$

18. $u = \ln x \quad du = \dfrac{1}{x}\,dx \quad v = \dfrac{1}{2}x^2 \quad dv = x\,dx$

$$\int x \ln x\,dx = \frac{1}{2}x^2 \ln x - \int \frac{1}{2}x\,dx$$
$$= \frac{1}{2}x^2 \ln x - \frac{1}{4}x^2 + C$$
$$= \mathbf{\frac{1}{4}x^2(2 \ln x - 1) + C}$$

19. $\int 3xe^{x^2}\,dx = \dfrac{3}{2}\int 2xe^{x^2}\,dx = \mathbf{\dfrac{3}{2}e^{x^2} + C}$

20. $\int \cot x \csc^2 x\,dx = \mathbf{-\dfrac{1}{2}\cot^2 x + C}$ or

$$= \mathbf{-\frac{1}{2}\csc^2 x + C}$$

(for a different C)

21. $\int \dfrac{5\,dx}{1 + x^2} = \mathbf{5 \arctan x + C}$

22. $\dfrac{d}{dx}\left[\arctan(\sin x) + \ln(x^2 - 1) + \dfrac{1}{x + 1}\right]$

$$= \mathbf{\frac{\cos x}{1 + \sin^2 x} + \frac{2x}{x^2 - 1} - \frac{1}{(x + 1)^2}}$$

23. $f(x) = \dfrac{4x^2 - 16}{x^2 - 9} = \dfrac{\text{Even}}{\text{Even}} = \mathbf{Even}$

$$f(x) = \frac{(2x + 4)(2x - 4)}{(x + 3)(x - 3)}$$

As $|x|$ gets large, $f(x)$ approaches 4 for both positive and negative x.

Zeros: 2, −2

Vertical asymptotes: $x = 3, -3$

Horizontal asymptote: $y = 4$

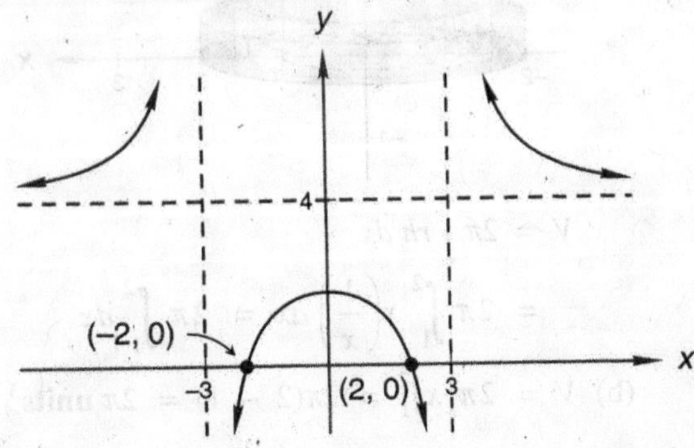

24. If the inverse of a function is also a function, then the functions must be one-to-one. Choice B is not a function. Choices A and D are not one-to-one.

The correct choice is **C**.

25. (a) $f(x) = \dfrac{x^3 - 2x - 1}{x + 2}$

Vertical asymptote: $x = -2$

```
-2| 1   0   -2   -1
    ↓  -2    4   -4
    1  -2    2  [-5]
```

End behavior: $y = x^2 - 2x + 2$

(b) By observation, we see that $x = -1$ is a zero of f. The other two can be found by using synthetic division and the quadratic formula.

```
-1| 1   0   -2   -1
    ↓  -1    1    1
    1  -1   -1   [0]
```

$$x^2 - x - 1 = 0$$
$$x = \frac{1 \pm \sqrt{1 - 4(1)(-1)}}{2}$$
$$x = \frac{1}{2} \pm \frac{\sqrt{5}}{2}$$

Zeros: $-1, \dfrac{1}{2} - \dfrac{\sqrt{5}}{2}, \dfrac{1}{2} + \dfrac{\sqrt{5}}{2}$

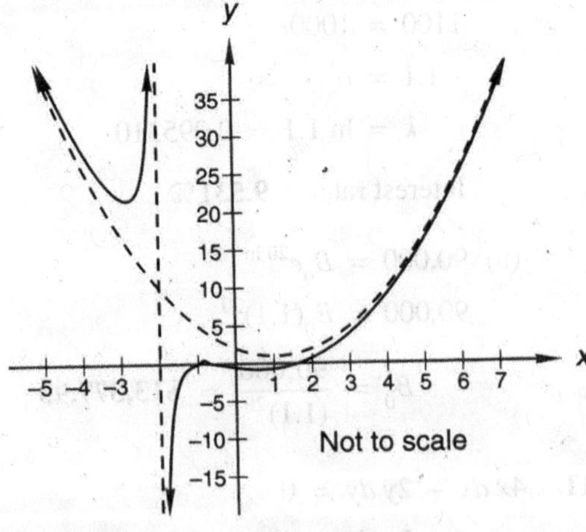

(c) **Domain: $\{x \in \mathbb{R} \mid x \neq -2\}$**

Range: $\mathbb{R}$

PROBLEM SET 91

1. (a) $\dfrac{6-h}{r} = \dfrac{6}{4}$

$$6r = 24 - 4h$$
$$4h = 24 - 6r$$
$$h = 6 - \frac{3}{2}r$$

$$V = \pi r^2 h$$
$$V = \pi r^2\left(6 - \frac{3}{2}r\right)$$
$$\mathbf{V = 6\pi r^2 - \frac{3}{2}\pi r^3}$$

(b) $V' = 12\pi r - \dfrac{9}{2}\pi r^2$

$$0 = 12\pi r - \frac{9}{2}\pi r^2$$
$$0 = \frac{3}{2}\pi r(8 - 3r)$$
$$3r = 8$$
$$\mathbf{r = \frac{8}{3}\ cm}$$
$$h = 6 - \frac{3}{2}\left(\frac{8}{3}\right)$$
$$\mathbf{h = 2\ cm}$$

(c) $V = \pi\left(\dfrac{8}{3}\right)^2(2) = \mathbf{\dfrac{128}{9}\pi\ cm^3}$

2. (a) Displacement $= \displaystyle\int_1^2 v(t)\,dt + \int_2^4 v(t)\,dt + \int_4^6 v(t)\,dt$

$$= 3 - 5 + 10$$
$$= \textbf{8 units to the right}$$

(b) $x(6) = x(2) + \displaystyle\int_2^4 v(t)\,dt + \int_4^6 v(t)\,dt$

$$= 9 - 5 + 10 = \mathbf{14}$$

3. (a) $x(t) = t^3 - 6t^2 + 9t + 2$

$$\mathbf{x(0) = 2}$$
$$x(4) = 64 - 96 + 36 + 2$$
$$\mathbf{x(4) = 6}$$

(b) $v(t) = 3t^2 - 12t + 9$

$$0 = 3(t^2 - 4t + 3)$$
$$0 = (t-3)(t-1)$$
$$t = 1, 3$$

The particle is momentarily at rest when $t = 1, 3$.

$x(0) = 2$; $x(1) = 6$; $x(3) = 2$; $x(4) = 6$

Total distance traveled is the sum of the distances traveled between times $t = 0$ and 1, $t = 1$ and 3, and $t = 3$ and 4. This sum equals $4 + 4 + 4 =$ **12 units.**

4. (a) $4\pi\cos(2\pi t) = 0$

$$2\pi t = \frac{\pi}{2}, \frac{3\pi}{2}, \frac{5\pi}{2}, \ldots$$
$$t = \frac{1}{4}, \frac{3}{4}, \frac{5}{4}, \ldots$$

On the given interval $t = \mathbf{\dfrac{1}{4}}$ and $t = \mathbf{\dfrac{3}{4}}$.

(b) Distance in negative direction

$$= -\int_{1/4}^{3/4} 4\pi\cos(2\pi t)\,dt$$
$$= -2\left[\sin(2\pi t)\right]_{1/4}^{3/4}$$
$$= -2[-1 - (1)] = \textbf{4 units}$$

5. $\displaystyle\lim_{x\to 0}(x\csc x) = \lim_{x\to 0}\frac{x}{\sin x} = \lim_{x\to 0}\frac{1}{\cos x} = \mathbf{1}$

6. $\displaystyle\lim_{x\to 0^+}(x\cdot\ln x) = \lim_{x\to 0^+}\frac{\ln x}{x^{-1}} = \lim_{x\to 0^+}\frac{\frac{1}{x}}{-\frac{1}{x^2}}$

$$= \lim_{x\to 0^+} -x = \mathbf{0}$$

7. $\displaystyle\lim_{x\to(\pi/2)^-}[\sec x\cos(3x)] = \lim_{x\to(\pi/2)^-}\frac{\cos(3x)}{\cos x}$

$$= \lim_{x\to(\pi/2)^-}\frac{-3\sin(3x)}{-\sin x} = -\frac{3}{1} = \mathbf{-3}$$

8. $\displaystyle\lim_{x\to 0}\left(\frac{1}{\sin x} - \frac{1}{x}\right)$

$$= \lim_{x\to 0}\left(\frac{x - \sin x}{x\sin x}\right)$$
$$= \lim_{x\to 0}\left(\frac{1 - \cos x}{x\cos x + \sin x}\right)$$
$$= \lim_{x\to 0}\left(\frac{\sin x}{-x\sin x + \cos x + \cos x}\right)$$
$$= \frac{0}{2} = \mathbf{0}$$

9. $$v_{\text{avg}} = \frac{1}{\frac{\pi}{4} - \left(-\frac{\pi}{4}\right)} \int_{-\pi/4}^{\pi/4} \cos(2x)\,dx$$

$$= \frac{2}{\pi}\left(\frac{1}{2}\right)\int_{-\pi/4}^{\pi/4} 2\cos(2x)\,dx$$

$$= \frac{1}{\pi}\left[\sin(2x)\right]_{-\pi/4}^{\pi/4}$$

$$= \frac{1}{\pi}[1 - (-1)] = \mathbf{\frac{2}{\pi}}$$

10. $a(t) = -32$

$v(t) = -32t$

$h(t) = -16t^2 + 576$

$0 = -16t^2 + 576$

$t = 6$

$$\text{Average velocity} = \frac{1}{6 - 0}\int_0^6 (-32t)\,dt$$

$$= \frac{1}{6}\left[-16t^2\right]_0^6$$

$$= \frac{1}{6}(-576 - 0)$$

$$= \mathbf{-96\ ft/s}$$

11. $a(t) = 2\pi\cos(2t)$

$v(t) = \pi\sin(2t) + C$

$v(0) = \pi\sin 0 + C$

$2 = C$

$v(t) = \pi\sin(2t) + 2$

Average velocity

$$= \frac{1}{2\pi - 0}\int_0^{2\pi} [\pi\sin(2t) + 2]\,dt$$

$$= \frac{1}{2\pi}\left[-\frac{\pi}{2}\cos(2t) + 2t\right]_0^{2\pi}$$

$$= \frac{1}{2\pi}\left[-\frac{\pi}{2} + 4\pi - \left(-\frac{\pi}{2} + 0\right)\right]$$

$$= \frac{1}{2\pi}(4\pi) = \mathbf{2\ \frac{linear\ units}{time\ unit}}$$

12. Average value $= 5$

$$\frac{1}{b - a}\int_a^b f(x)\,dx = 5$$

$$\frac{1}{b - 3}(10) = 5$$

$$\frac{1}{b - 3} = \frac{1}{2}$$

$$b - 3 = 2$$

$$\mathbf{b = 5}$$

13. $$f(c) = \frac{1}{e - 1}\int_1^e \frac{1}{x}\,dx$$

$$\frac{1}{c} = \frac{1}{e - 1}\left[\ln|x|\right]_1^e$$

$$\frac{1}{c} = \frac{1}{e - 1}$$

$$\mathbf{c = e - 1}$$

14. $$f(c) = \frac{1}{b - a}\int_a^b x\,dx$$

$$c = \frac{1}{b - a}\left[\frac{1}{2}x^2\right]_a^b$$

$$c = \frac{1}{b - a}\left[\frac{1}{2}b^2 - \frac{1}{2}a^2\right]$$

$$c = \frac{1}{b - a}\left[\frac{1}{2}(b + a)(b - a)\right]$$

$$c = \frac{b + a}{2}$$

The number c is the midpoint of $[a, b]$.

15.

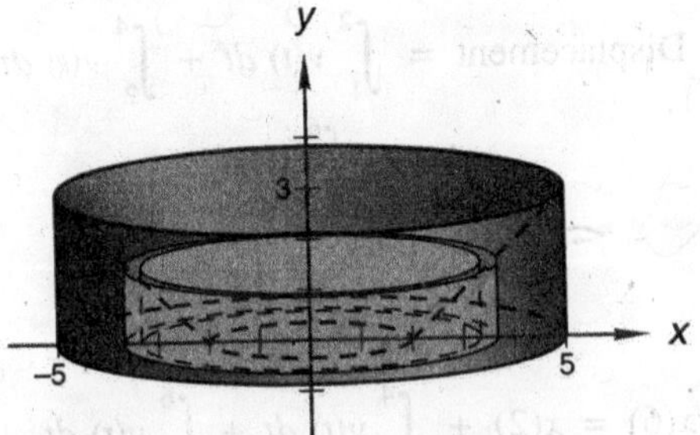

$$V = 2\pi\int rh\,dx$$

$$= 2\pi\int_2^5 x(x - 2)\,dx$$

$$= 2\pi\int_2^5 (x^2 - 2x)\,dx$$

$$= 2\pi\left[\frac{1}{3}x^3 - x^2\right]_2^5$$

$$= 2\pi\left[\frac{125}{3} - 25 - \left(\frac{8}{3} - 4\right)\right]$$

$$= \mathbf{36\pi\ units^3}$$

16.

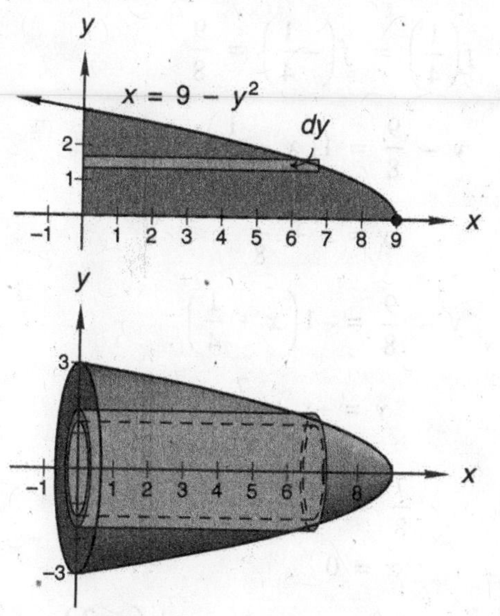

$$V = 2\pi \int rh\, dy$$

$$= 2\pi \int_0^3 y(9 - y^2)\, dy = 2\pi \int_0^3 (9y - y^3)\, dy$$

$$= 2\pi \left[\frac{9}{2}y^2 - \frac{1}{4}y^4\right]_0^3 = 2\pi\left[\frac{81}{2} - \frac{81}{4} - (0)\right]$$

$$= \mathbf{\frac{81}{2}\pi \textbf{ units}^3}$$

17. $\frac{1}{y}\, dx - \frac{1}{x}\, dy = 0$

$$\frac{1}{y}\, dx = \frac{1}{x}\, dy$$

$$y\, dy = x\, dx$$

$$\frac{1}{2}y^2 = \frac{1}{2}x^2 + C$$

$$y^2 = x^2 + C$$

$$\mathbf{y^2 - x^2 = C}$$

18. $\frac{dy}{dx} = 4x^3y^2$

$$y^{-2}\, dy = 4x^3\, dx$$

$$-y^{-1} = x^4 + C$$

$$y^{-1} = -x^4 + C$$

$$\frac{1}{2} = -1 + C$$

$$C = \frac{3}{2}$$

$$\frac{1}{y} = -x^4 + \frac{3}{2}$$

$$\frac{1}{y} = \frac{-2x^4 + 3}{2}$$

$$\mathbf{y = \frac{2}{3 - 2x^4}}$$

19. (a) $\int_0^k f(x)\, dx = 5$

$$\int_{-k}^k f(x)\, dx = 10$$

$$\int_k^{-k} f(x)\, dx = \mathbf{-10}$$

(b) $\int_k^{-k} f(x)\, dx = \mathbf{0}$

20. (a) Average speed $= \frac{\text{distance}}{\text{time}} = \frac{70}{1} =$ **70 mph**

(b) **Yes.** If the driver did not exceed 65 mph, he could not have traveled 70 miles in 1 hour. By the Mean Value Theorem, the driver's speed must have reached 70 mph at some point.

21. $x^3 + y^2 = y$

$$3x^2 + 2y\frac{dy}{dx} = \frac{dy}{dx}$$

$$3x^2 = (1 - 2y)\frac{dy}{dx}$$

$$\frac{dy}{dx} = \frac{3x^2}{1 - 2y}$$

$$\left.\frac{dy}{dx}\right|_{(0,1)} = \frac{0}{-1} = 0$$

$$y - 1 = 0(x - 0)$$

$$\mathbf{y = 1}$$

22. $\int \cos^2(3x)\, dx = \int\left[\frac{1}{2} + \frac{1}{2}\cos(6x)\right] dx$

$$= \mathbf{\frac{1}{2}x + \frac{1}{12}\sin(6x) + C}$$

23. $\int \cos^3(3x)\, dx = \int \cos(3x)\,[1 - \sin^2(3x)]\, dx$

$$= \int [\cos(3x) - \sin^2(3x)\cos(3x)]\, dx$$

$$= \mathbf{\frac{1}{3}\sin(3x) - \frac{1}{9}\sin^3(3x) + C}$$

24. (a) $1 + 6x \geq 0$

$$6x \geq -1$$

$$x \geq -\frac{1}{6}$$

Domain: $\left\{x \in \mathbb{R} \mid x \geq -\frac{1}{6}\right\}$

Range: $\{y \in \mathbb{R} \mid y \geq 0\}$

(b) $f'(x) = \frac{1}{2}(1 + 6x)^{-1/2}(6)$

$$f'(x) = \frac{3}{\sqrt{1 + 6x}}$$

$$1 = \frac{3}{\sqrt{1 + 6x}}$$

$$3 = \sqrt{1 + 6x}$$

$$9 = 1 + 6x$$

$$\frac{4}{3} = x$$

$$f\left(\frac{4}{3}\right) = \sqrt{1 + 6\left(\frac{4}{3}\right)} = 3$$

$$\left(\frac{4}{3}, 3\right)$$

(c) $f\left(\frac{1}{4}\right) = f\left(-\frac{1}{4}\right) = \frac{9}{8}$

$$y - \frac{9}{8} = 1\left(x - \frac{1}{4}\right)$$

$$y = x + \frac{7}{8}$$

$$y - \frac{9}{8} = -1\left(x + \frac{1}{4}\right)$$

$$y = -x + \frac{7}{8}$$

$$x + \frac{7}{8} = -x + \frac{7}{8}$$

$$x = 0$$

The point of intersection is $\left(\mathbf{0}, \frac{\mathbf{7}}{\mathbf{8}}\right)$.

25. (a) $f(x) = 2x^2 + 1$

$$f'(x) = 4x$$

$$f'(x_0) = 4x_0; \quad f'(-x_0) = -4x_0$$

The slopes of $f'(x_0)$ and $f'(-x_0)$ must be negative reciprocals, so their product must equal -1.

$$4x_0(-4x_0) = -1$$

$$-16x_0^2 = -1$$

$$x_0^2 = \frac{1}{16}$$

$$x_0 = \frac{1}{4}, -\frac{1}{4}$$

(b) $f'\left(\frac{1}{4}\right) = 4\left(\frac{1}{4}\right) = \mathbf{1}$

$$f'\left(-\frac{1}{4}\right) = -4\left(\frac{1}{4}\right) = \mathbf{-1}$$

PROBLEM SET 92

1. (a) $v(t) = \frac{4t}{1 + t^2}$

$$a(t) = \frac{(1 + t^2)4 - 4t(2t)}{(1 + t^2)^2}$$

$$a(t) = \frac{4 + 4t^2 - 8t^2}{(1 + t^2)^2}$$

$$\mathbf{a(t) = \frac{4 - 4t^2}{(1 + t^2)^2}}$$

$$x(t) = 2\ln(1 + t^2) + C$$

$$x(0) = 2\ln 1 + C$$

$$C = 4$$

$$\mathbf{x(t) = 2\ln(1 + t^2) + 4}$$

(b) $\lim_{t\to\infty} v(t) = \lim_{t\to\infty} \frac{4t}{1 + t^2} = \mathbf{0}$

2. (a) $x(t) = 2t^3 - 9t^2 + 12t + 9$

$$\mathbf{x(0) = 9}$$

$$x(2) = 16 - 36 + 24 + 9$$

$$\mathbf{x(2) = 13}$$

(b) $v(t) = 6t^2 - 18t + 12$

$$0 = 6t^2 - 18t + 12 = 0$$

$$0 = t^2 - 3t + 2 = 0$$

$$0 = (t - 2)(t - 1) = 0$$

$$t = 2, 1$$

$$x(0) = 9; \; x(1) = 14; \; x(2) = 13$$

Total distance traveled is the sum of the distances traveled between times $t = 0$ and 1 and times $t = 1$ and 2. This sum equals $5 + 1 =$ **6 units.**

3. $f(x) = xe^{-x^2}$

$$f'(x) = x\left(-2xe^{-x^2}\right) + e^{-x^2}$$

$$f'(x) = e^{-x^2}(-2x^2 + 1)$$

$$0 = e^{-x^2}(-2x^2 + 1)$$

$$1 = 2x^2$$

$$\frac{1}{2} = x^2$$

$$x = \pm\frac{\sqrt{2}}{2}$$

$$f'(-1) = e^{-1}(-1) < 0$$

$$f'(0) = 1(1) > 0$$

$$f'(1) = e^{-1}(-1) < 0$$

Since the derivative changes from negative to positive at $x = -\frac{\sqrt{2}}{2}$, the critical number $-\frac{\sqrt{2}}{2}$ **is a local minimum.** Since the derivative changes from positive to negative at $x = \frac{\sqrt{2}}{2}$, the critical number $\frac{\sqrt{2}}{2}$ **is a local maximum.**

4. $f(x) = x^3 - x - 1$ $\qquad f'(x) = 3x^2 - 1$

$$(f^{-1})'(-1) = \frac{1}{f'(0)} = \frac{1}{3(0)^2 - 1} = \mathbf{-1}$$

5. $f(x) = x^3 + 2x$ $\qquad f'(x) = 3x^2 + 2$

The value of $h(3)$ is the solution to

$3 = x^3 + 2x$, which is $x = 1$.

So $\mathbf{h(3) = 1}$

$$h'(3) = \frac{1}{f'(h(3))} = \frac{1}{3(1)^2 + 2}$$

$$\mathbf{h'(3) = \frac{1}{5}}$$

6. $f(x) = x^3 + x$ $\quad f'(x) = 3x^2 + 1$

The value of $h(0)$ is the solution to

$0 = x^3 + x$, which is $x = 0$.

$\mathbf{h(0) = 0}$

$$h'(0) = \frac{1}{f'(h(0))} = \frac{1}{3(0)^2 + 1}$$

$\mathbf{h'(0) = 1}$

7. $$\lim_{x\to 0}\,[4x \csc(2x)] = \lim_{x\to 0}\frac{4x}{\sin(2x)}$$

$$= \lim_{x\to 0}\frac{4}{2\cos(2x)} = \frac{4}{2} = \mathbf{2}$$

8. $$\lim_{x\to\infty}\frac{\ln x}{\sqrt{x}} = \lim_{x\to\infty}\frac{\frac{1}{x}}{\frac{1}{2}x^{-1/2}} = \lim_{x\to\infty}\frac{2}{\sqrt{x}} = \mathbf{0}$$

9. $$\lim_{x\to\infty} e^{-x}\ln x = \lim_{x\to\infty}\frac{\ln x}{e^x} = \lim_{x\to\infty}\frac{\frac{1}{x}}{e^x}$$

$$= \lim_{x\to\infty}\frac{1}{xe^x} = \mathbf{0}$$

10. $$\lim_{x\to\pi/2^-}(\tan x - \sec x)$$

$$= \lim_{x\to\pi/2^-}\left(\frac{\sin x}{\cos x} - \frac{1}{\cos x}\right)$$

$$= \lim_{x\to\pi/2^-}\left(\frac{\sin x - 1}{\cos x}\right)$$

$$= \lim_{x\to\pi/2^-}\frac{\cos x}{-\sin x} = \frac{0}{-1} = \mathbf{0}$$

11. $$B_t = B_0e^{rt}$$

$$50{,}000 = B_0e^{0.09(30)}$$

$$50{,}000 = B_0e^{2.7}$$

$$B_0 = \frac{50{,}000}{e^{2.7}} \approx \mathbf{\$3360.28}$$

12. $y\,dx - dy = 0$

$$y\,dx = dy$$

$$\frac{1}{y}\,dy = dx$$

$$\mathbf{\ln|y| = x + C} \text{ or}$$

$$\mathbf{|y| = Ce^x}$$

13. $a(t) = 3 \sin t$

$v(t) = -3 \cos t + C$

$v(0) = -3 + C$

$3 = -3 + C$

$C = 6$

$v(t) = -3 \cos t + 6$

$$\text{Average velocity} = \frac{1}{\pi}\int_0^{\pi} (-3 \cos t + 6)\, dt$$

$$= \frac{1}{\pi}[-3 \sin t + 6t]_0^{\pi}$$

$$= \mathbf{6 \text{ linear units/time unit}}$$

14. (a) $f(x) = x^3 + ax^2 + bx + c$

$f(0) = 0 + 0 + 0 + c$

$\mathbf{-3 = c}$

$f'(x) = 3x^2 + 2ax + b$

$f''(x) = 6x + 2a$

$f''(0) = 2a$

$0 = 2a$

$\mathbf{a = 0}$

$$-1 = \frac{1}{4}\int_0^4 (x^3 + bx - 3)\, dx$$

$$-1 = \frac{1}{4}\left[\frac{1}{4}x^4 + \frac{b}{2}x^2 - 3x\right]_0^4$$

$$-1 = \frac{1}{4}[64 + 8b - 12 - (0)]$$

$$-1 = \frac{1}{4}[52 + 8b]$$

$-1 = 13 + 2b$

$2b = -14$

$\mathbf{b = -7}$

$\mathbf{f(x) = x^3 - 7x - 3}$

(b) $$f'(c) = \frac{f(3) - f(0)}{3 - 0}$$

$$3c^2 - 7 = \frac{3 - (-3)}{3}$$

$3c^2 - 7 = 2$

$3c^2 = 9$

$c^2 = 3$

$\mathbf{c = \sqrt{3}}$

15. $$f(c) = \frac{1}{2 - (-1)}\int_{-1}^{2} (3x^2 + 2x + 1)\, dx$$

$$3c^2 + 2c + 1 = \frac{1}{3}\left[x^3 + x^2 + x\right]_{-1}^{2}$$

$$3c^2 + 2c + 1 = \frac{1}{3}[8 + 4 + 2 - (-1 + 1 - 1)]$$

$3c^2 + 2c + 1 = 5$

$3c^2 + 2c - 4 = 0$

$$c = \frac{-2 \pm \sqrt{4 - 4(3)(-4)}}{6}$$

$$c = -\frac{1}{3} \pm \frac{\sqrt{13}}{3}$$

On $[-1, 2]$, $\mathbf{c = -\frac{1}{3} + \frac{\sqrt{13}}{3}}$

16. (a) $$\text{Average speed} = \frac{\text{distance}}{\text{time}} = \frac{4 \text{ miles}}{3 \text{ minutes}}$$

$$= \mathbf{80 \text{ mph}}$$

(b) **Yes.** If the driver did not exceed 70 mph, she could not have traveled 4 miles in 3 minutes. By the Mean Value Theorem, she must have been going 80 mph at some point.

17. $$f(x) = \frac{\sin x}{(x^3 + 1)^3 (x^4 + 1)^4}$$

$$\ln [f(x)] = \ln (\sin x) - 3 \ln (x^3 + 1) - 4 \ln (x^4 + 1)$$

$$\mathbf{\frac{f'(x)}{f(x)} = \cot x - \frac{9x^2}{x^3 + 1} - \frac{16x^3}{x^4 + 1}}$$

18.

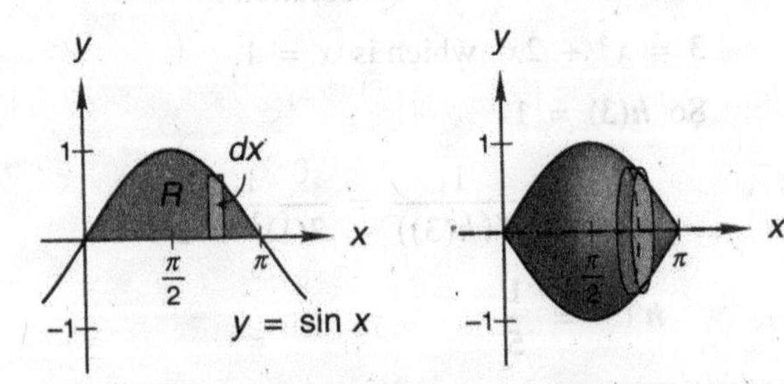

$$V = \pi\int_0^{\pi} (\sin x)^2\, dx$$

$$= \pi\int_0^{\pi}\left[\frac{1}{2} - \frac{1}{2}\cos(2x)\right] dx$$

$$= \pi\left[\frac{1}{2}x - \frac{1}{4}\sin(2x)\right]_0^{\pi}$$

$$= \mathbf{\frac{\pi^2}{2} \text{ units}^3}$$

19. $u = \sin x \qquad du = \cos x\,dx$

$$\int_0^{\pi/2} (\cos x)[\cos(\sin x)]\,dx = \int_0^1 \cos u\,du$$

The correct choice is **D**.

20. (a) $\int_b^a e^{\cos x}\,dx = -\int_a^b e^{\cos x}\,dx = \mathbf{-k}$

(b) $\int_a^b e^{\cos x}\,dx = \int_{-b}^{-a} e^{\cos x}\,dx = \mathbf{k}$

21. $\frac{d}{dx}\arcsin\frac{x}{3} + \int \frac{1}{\sqrt{9 - x^2}}\,dx + \frac{d}{dx}\arctan\frac{x}{3} + \int \frac{3}{x^2 + 9}\,dx$

$$= \mathbf{\frac{1}{\sqrt{9 - x^2}} + \arcsin\frac{x}{3} + \frac{3}{x^2 + 9} + \arctan\frac{x}{3} + C}$$

22. $y = x^{-1/2} + 2\ln|\sin x + \cos x|$

$$\frac{dy}{dx} = \mathbf{-\frac{1}{2}x^{-3/2} + \frac{2(\cos x - \sin x)}{\sin x + \cos x}}$$

23. $\lim_{x\to 0} \frac{x}{\sin x} = \lim_{x\to 0} \frac{1}{\cos x} = 1$

$\lim_{x\to 0} \sin\frac{x}{1} = \lim_{x\to 0} \sin x = 0$

$\lim_{x\to 0} \sin\frac{1}{x} = \lim_{|u|\to\infty} \sin u$

$\lim_{x\to 0} \frac{x^2 - 1}{x - 1} = \lim_{x\to 0} \frac{1 - \frac{1}{x^2}}{\frac{1}{x} - \frac{1}{x^2}} = 1$

The correct choice is **C**.

24. If (x, y) lies on f, then (y, x) lies on f^{-1}.

The correct choice is **D**.

25. 

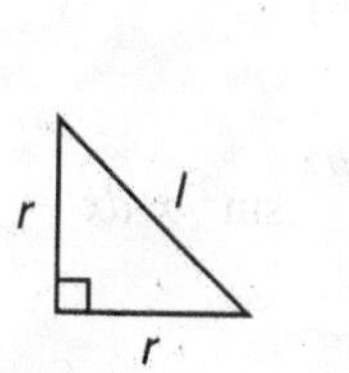

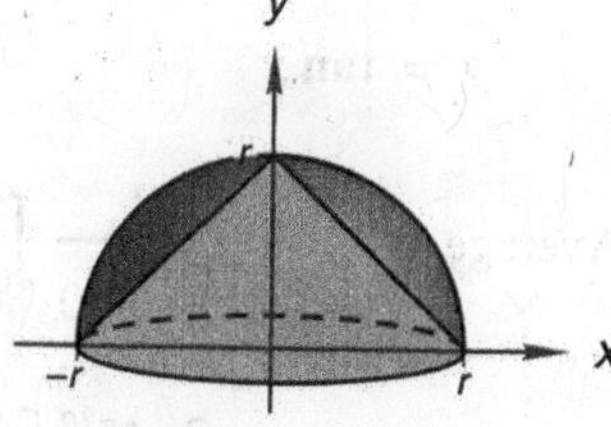

$A = \pi r^2 + \pi r l$

$A = \pi r^2 + \pi r(\sqrt{2}r)$

$A = \pi r^2 + \sqrt{2}\pi r^2$

$A = \mathbf{\pi r^2(1 + \sqrt{2})\ units^2}$

$V = \frac{1}{3}\pi r^2 h = \frac{1}{3}\pi r^2 r = \mathbf{\frac{1}{3}\pi r^3\ units^3}$

Problem Set 93

1. (a) $r^2 + \left(\frac{h}{2}\right)^2 = 3$

$$r^2 + \frac{h^2}{4} = 3$$
$$4r^2 + h^2 = 12$$
$$h^2 = 12 - 4r^2$$
$$h = \sqrt{12 - 4r^2}$$
$$V = \pi r^2 h$$
$$V = \pi r^2\sqrt{12 - 4r^2}$$
$$\mathbf{V = 2\pi r^2\sqrt{3 - r^2}}$$

(b) $V' = \pi r^2(3 - r^2)^{-1/2}(-2r) + 4\pi r(3 - r^2)^{1/2}$

$$V' = -2\pi r^3(3 - r^2)^{-1/2} + 4\pi r(3 - r^2)^{1/2}$$
$$V' = 2\pi r(3 - r^2)^{-1/2}[-r^2 + 2(3 - r^2)]$$
$$V' = 2\pi r(3 - r^2)^{-1/2}(6 - 3r^2)$$
$$0 = 2\pi r(3 - r^2)^{-1/2}(6 - 3r^2)$$

$r = 0$; Local minimum

$$6 - 3r^2 = 0$$
$$3r^2 = 6$$
$$r^2 = 2$$
$$\mathbf{r = \sqrt{2}\ m}$$
$$h = \sqrt{12 - 4(2)}$$
$$h = \sqrt{4} = \mathbf{2\ m}$$

(c) $V = \pi(\sqrt{2})^2(2) = \mathbf{4\pi\ m^3}$

2. (a) Displacement $= \int_1^3 v(t)\,dt + \int_3^4 v(t)\,dt + \int_4^7 v(t)\,dt + \int_7^8 v(t)\,dt$

$$= -4 + 5 - 7 + 3$$
$$= \mathbf{-3\ units}$$

(b) $x(7) = x(3) + \int_3^4 v(t)\,dt + \int_4^7 v(t)\,dt$

$$= 3 + 5 - 7 = \mathbf{1}$$

3. (a) $x(t) = t^3 - 9t^2 + 15t + 3 \qquad \mathbf{x(0) = 3}$

$x(2) = 8 - 36 + 30 + 3 \qquad \mathbf{x(2) = 5}$

(b) $v(t) = 3t^2 - 18t + 15$

$$0 = 3t^2 - 18t + 15$$
$$0 = t^2 - 6t + 5$$
$$0 = (t - 5)(t - 1)$$
$$t = 1, 5$$

$x(0) = 3$; $x(1) = 10$; $x(4) = -17$

The total distance traveled is the sum of the distances traveled between times $t = 0$ and 1 and times $t = 1$ and 4. This sum equals $7 + 27 =$ **34 units.**

4. (a) $6\pi \sin(3\pi t) = 0$

$$3\pi t = 0, \pi, 2\pi, 3\pi, \ldots$$

Over the given interval $t = \mathbf{0, \frac{1}{3}, \frac{2}{3}, 1}$

(b) The velocity is negative between $t = \frac{1}{3}$ and $t = \frac{2}{3}$.

$$\text{Distance} = -\int_{1/3}^{2/3} 6\pi \sin(3\pi t)\, dt$$

$$= [2\cos(3\pi t)]_{1/3}^{2/3}$$

$$= 2[1 - (-1)] = \mathbf{4 \text{ units}}$$

5. Because $f(1) = -1$ and $f(2) = 3$, there is a zero between $x = 1$ and $x = 2$. Let $x_1 = 1.5$, `Y1=X²+X-3`, and `Y2=nDeriv(Y1,X,X)`.

```
1.5→X
                 1.5
X-(Y1/Y2)→X
              1.3125
         1.302801724
         1.302775638
         1.302775638
```

The positive zero is approximately **1.302775638**.

6. Let $x_1 = 0.5$, which is the center of the interval, and assign `Y1=X³+X-1` and `Y2=nDeriv(Y1,X,X)`.

```
                  .5
X-(Y1/Y2)→X
         .7142855918
         .6831797293
         .6823284237
         .6823278038
         .6823278038
```

The zero is approximately **0.6823278038**.

7. $f(x) = x^3 + 2x + 2 \quad f'(x) = 3x^2 + 2$

$$(f^{-1})'(2) = \frac{1}{f'(0)} = \frac{1}{3(0)^2 + 2} = \mathbf{\frac{1}{2}}$$

8. $f(x) = x^3 + 2x \quad f'(x) = 3x^2 + 2$

The value of $f^{-1}(3)$ is a solution to $3 = x^3 + 2x$.

By inspection $\mathbf{f^{-1}(3) = 1}$.

$$(f^{-1})'(3) = \frac{1}{f'(f^{-1}(3))} = \frac{1}{f'(1)}$$

$$= \frac{1}{3(1)^2 + 2} = \mathbf{\frac{1}{5}}$$

9. $$\lim_{x\to 0} [4x \csc(3x)] = \lim_{x\to 0} \frac{4x}{\sin(3x)}$$

$$= \lim_{x\to 0} \frac{4}{3\cos(3x)} = \mathbf{\frac{4}{3}}$$

10. $$\lim_{x\to 1^+} \left(\frac{3}{x^2 - 1} - \frac{2}{x - 1}\right) = \lim_{x\to 1^+} \frac{3 - 2(x + 1)}{x^2 - 1}$$

$$= \lim_{x\to 1^+} \frac{-2x + 1}{x^2 - 1}$$

$$= -\frac{1}{0^+} = \mathbf{-\infty}$$

11. $2\,dx - x\,dy = 0$

$$x\,dy = 2\,dx$$

$$dy = \frac{2}{x}\,dx$$

$$y = 2\ln|x| + C$$

$$2 = 2\ln|e| + C$$

$$2 = 2 + C$$

$$C = 0$$

$$\mathbf{y = 2\ln|x|}$$

12. $$\frac{dy}{dx} = 1 + y^2$$

$$\frac{1}{1 + y^2}\,dy = dx$$

$$\arctan y = x + C$$

$$\arctan(1) = \frac{\pi}{4} + C$$

$$\frac{\pi}{4} = \frac{\pi}{4} + C$$

$$C = 0$$

$$\arctan y = x$$

$$\mathbf{y = \tan x}$$

13. $$\text{Average value} = \frac{1}{\frac{\pi}{2} - 0}\int_0^{\pi/2} \sin^2 x\, dx$$

$$= \frac{2}{\pi}\int_0^{\pi/2} \left[\frac{1}{2} - \frac{1}{2}\cos(2x)\right] dx$$

$$= \frac{2}{\pi}\left[\frac{1}{2}x - \frac{1}{4}\sin(2x)\right]_0^{\pi/2}$$

$$= \mathbf{\frac{1}{2}}$$

14. $$\text{Average value} = \frac{1}{b - a}\int_a^b f(x)\,dx$$

$$3 = \frac{1}{8 - a}(18)$$

$$\frac{1}{6} = \frac{1}{8 - a}$$

$$8 - a = 6$$

$$a = \mathbf{2}$$

15. $$f(c) = \frac{1}{0 - (-2)}\int_{-2}^{0} (x + 1)^{1/3}\,dx$$

$$(c + 1)^{1/3} = \frac{1}{2}\left(\frac{3}{4}\right)\left[(x + 1)^{4/3}\right]_{-2}^{0}$$

$$(c + 1)^{1/3} = \frac{3}{8}(1 - 1)$$

$$(c + 1)^{1/3} = 0$$

$$c + 1 = 0$$

$$c = \mathbf{-1}$$

16. **No.** Rolle's theorem also requires that the function be continuous on the given interval. The function $f(x) = \ln|x|$ has a vertical asymptote at $x = 0$, so it does not meet the requirements of Rolle's theorem.

17. $u = \cos x \qquad du = -\sin x\,dx$

$$\int \cos^2 x \sin x\,dx = -\int u^2\,du$$

$$= -\frac{1}{3}u^3 + C$$

$$= \mathbf{-\frac{1}{3}\cos^3 x + C}$$

18. Method 1:

$u = \cos(2x) \qquad du = -2\sin(2x)\,dx$

$$\int \cos(2x)\sin(2x)\,dx = -\frac{1}{2}\int u\,du$$

$$= -\frac{1}{4}u^2 + C$$

$$= \mathbf{-\frac{1}{4}\cos^2(2x) + C}$$

Method 2:

$v = \sin(2x) \qquad dv = 2\cos(2x)\,dx$

$$\int \cos(2x)\sin(2x)\,dx = \frac{1}{2}\int v\,dv$$

$$= \frac{1}{4}v^2 + C$$

$$= \mathbf{\frac{1}{4}\sin^2(2x) + C}$$

Method 3:

$$\int \cos(2x)\sin(2x)\,dx = \frac{1}{2}\int \sin(4x)\,dx$$

$$= \frac{1}{2}\left(\frac{1}{4}\right)\int 4\sin(4x)\,dx$$

$$= \mathbf{-\frac{1}{8}\cos(4x) + C}$$

All three answers are acceptable. They differ by a constant. Thus C represents a different value for each one.

19. $$\int \frac{\sin(2x)}{\sin^2 x}\,dx = \int \frac{2\sin x\cos x}{\sin^2 x}\,dx$$

$$= 2\int \frac{\cos x}{\sin x}\,dx$$

$$= \mathbf{2\ln|\sin x| + C}$$

20. $y = -x(x^2 - 3x + 2)$

$y = -x(x - 2)(x - 1)$

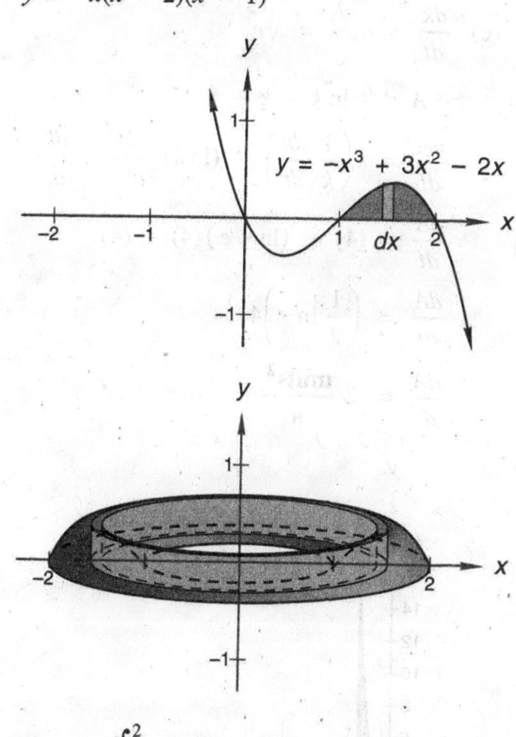

$$V = 2\pi\int_1^2 x(-x^3 + 3x^2 - 2x)\,dx$$

$$= \mathbf{2\pi\int_1^2 (-x^4 + 3x^3 - 2x^2)\,dx}$$

21. $$\int_0^2 [2f(x) - 3g(x)]\,dx$$

$$= 2\int_0^2 f(x)\,dx - 3\int_0^2 g(x)\,dx$$

$$= 2(5) - 3(-6) = \mathbf{28}$$

22.

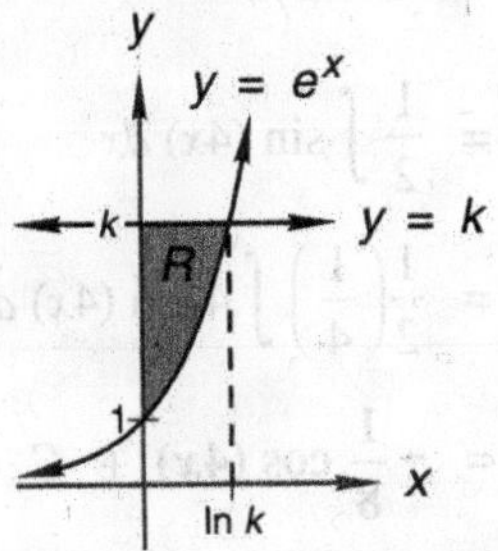

(a) $A = \int_0^{\ln k} (k - e^x)\,dx$

$A = \left[kx - e^x\right]_0^{\ln k}$

$A = k\ln k - k - (0 - 1)$

$\mathbf{A = k\ln k - k + 1}$

(b) $k\ln k - k + 1 = 1$

$k\ln k - k = 0$

$\ln k = 1$

$\mathbf{k = e}$

(c) $\dfrac{dk}{dt} = 4,\ k = \sqrt{e}$

$A = k\ln k - k + 1$

$\dfrac{dA}{dt} = k\left(\dfrac{1}{k}\dfrac{dk}{dt}\right) + (\ln k)\dfrac{dk}{dt} - \dfrac{dk}{dt}$

$\dfrac{dA}{dt} = (4) + (\ln\sqrt{e})(4) - (4)$

$\dfrac{dA}{dt} = \left(\dfrac{1}{2}\ln e\right)4$

$\dfrac{dA}{dt} = \mathbf{2\ \dfrac{units^2}{s}}$

23.

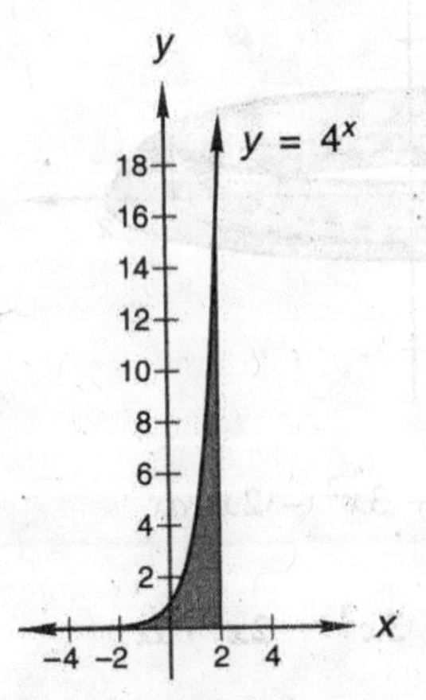

$A = \int_{-2}^{2} 4^x\,dx$

$= \dfrac{1}{\ln 4}\left[4^x\right]_{-2}^{2} = \dfrac{1}{\ln 4}\left(16 - \dfrac{1}{16}\right)$

$= \dfrac{1}{\ln 4}\left(\dfrac{255}{16}\right) = \mathbf{\dfrac{255}{16\ln 4}\ units^2}$

24. $f(x) = ax^2 + bx + c$

$0 = a(0)^2 + b(0) + c$

$\mathbf{c = 0}$

$f'(x) = 2ax + b$

$f'(0) = b$

$\mathbf{2 = b}$

$f(2) = a(2)^2 + 2(2)$

$1 = 4a + 4$

$\mathbf{-\dfrac{3}{4} = a}$

$\mathbf{f(x) = -\dfrac{3}{4}x^2 + 2x}$

25. A. $f + g =$ odd + odd = odd

B. $fg =$ odd · odd = even

C. $(f \circ g)(-x) = f(g(-x)) = f(-g(x)) = -f(g(x))$

So $f \circ g$ is odd.

D. $f - g =$ odd − odd = odd

The correct choice is **C.**

Problem Set 94

1.

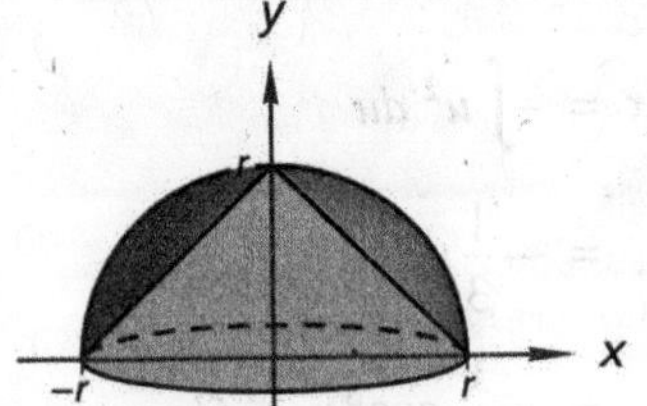

(a) $A = \pi r^2 + 2\pi r^2$

$A = 3\pi r^2$

$\dfrac{dA}{dt} = 6\pi r\dfrac{dr}{dt}$

$(24) = 6\pi(4)\dfrac{dr}{dt}$

$\dfrac{dr}{dt} = \mathbf{\dfrac{1}{\pi}\ \dfrac{cm}{s}}$

(b) $V = \dfrac{1}{3}\pi r^2 h$

$V = \dfrac{1}{3}\pi r^3$

$\dfrac{dV}{dt} = \pi r^2\dfrac{dr}{dt}$

$\dfrac{dV}{dt} = \pi(4)^2\left(\dfrac{1}{\pi}\right) = \mathbf{16\ \dfrac{cm^3}{s}}$

2. (a) Displacement

$$= \int_0^2 v(t)\,dt + \int_2^3 v(t)\,dt + \int_3^6 v(t)\,dt$$

$$= -5 + 7 - 2 = \mathbf{0}$$

(b) $$x(6) = x(0) + \int_0^2 v(t)\,dt + \int_2^3 v(t)\,dt + \int_3^6 v(t)\,dt = 5 + (0) = \mathbf{5}$$

3.

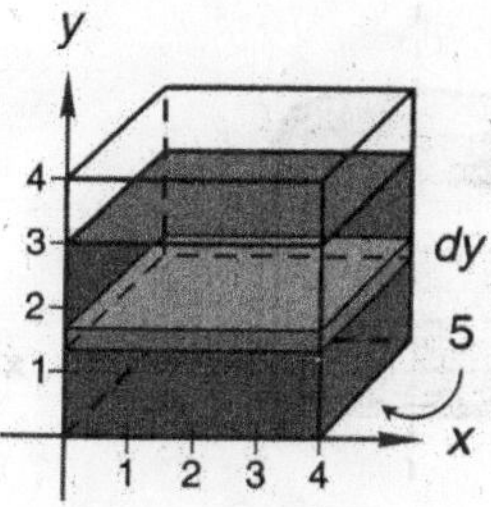

(a) $$F = 5000 \int_0^3 4(3 - y)\,dy$$

$$= 20{,}000\left[3y - \frac{1}{2}y^2\right]_0^3$$

$$= 20{,}000\left(9 - \frac{9}{2}\right) = \textbf{90,000 newtons}$$

(b) $$W = 5000 \int_0^3 4(5)(4 - y)\,dy$$

$$= 100{,}000 \int_0^3 (4 - y)\,dy$$

$$= 100{,}000\left[4y - \frac{1}{2}y^2\right]_0^3$$

$$= 100{,}000\left(12 - \frac{9}{2}\right) = \textbf{750,000 joules}$$

4. (a) $\mathbf{a(t) = -9.8}$

$v(t) = -9.8t + C$

$v(0) = -9.8(0) + C$

$20 = C$

$\mathbf{v(t) = -9.8t + 20}$

$h(t) = -\frac{9.8}{2}t^2 + 20t + C$

$h(0) = 0 + 0 + C$

$20 = C$

$\mathbf{h(t) = -4.9t^2 + 20t + 20}$

(b) $h(2) = -4.9(2)^2 + 20(2) + 20$

$\mathbf{h(2) = 40.4\ m}$

$v(2) = -9.8(2) + 20$

$\mathbf{v(2) = 0.4\ m/s}$

$\mathbf{a(2) = -9.8\ m/s^2}$

(c) $-4.9t^2 + 20t + 20 = 0$

$$t = \frac{-20 \pm \sqrt{400 - 4(20)(-4.9)}}{2(-4.9)}$$

$t \approx$ **4.9125 seconds later**

5.

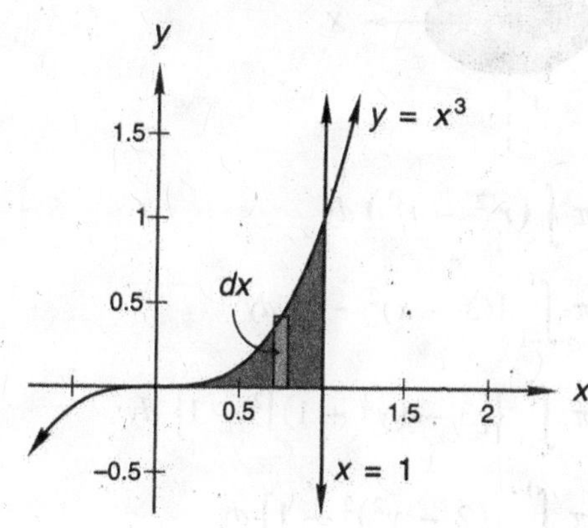

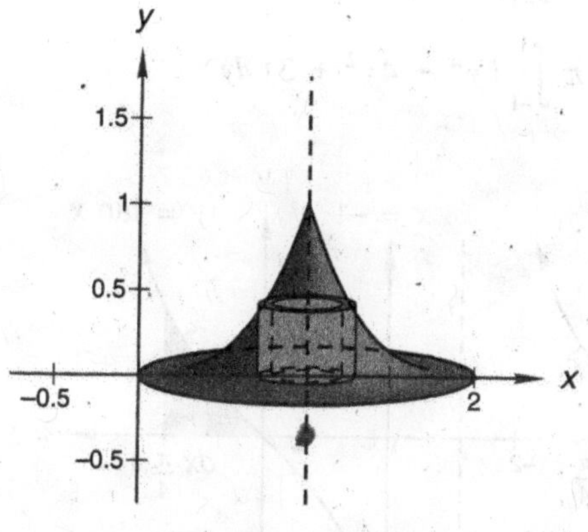

$$V = 2\pi \int rh\,dx$$

$$= 2\pi \int_0^1 (1 - x)x^3\,dx$$

$$= 2\pi \int_0^1 (x^3 - x^4)\,dx$$

$$= 2\pi\left[\frac{1}{4}x^4 - \frac{1}{5}x^5\right]_0^1 = \frac{\mathbf{1}}{\mathbf{10}}\boldsymbol{\pi}\ \textbf{units}^3$$

6.

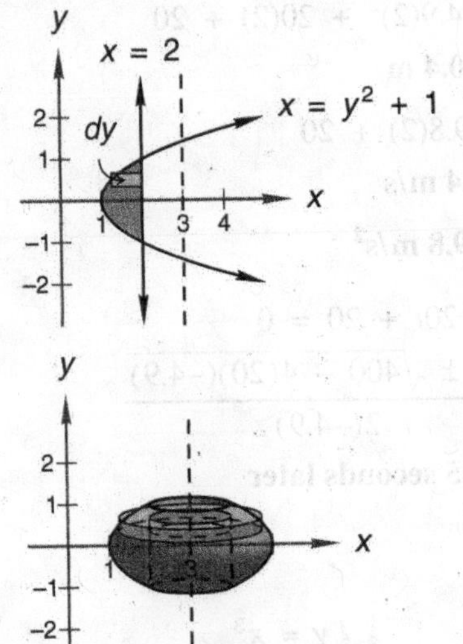

$$V = \pi \int (r_o^2 - r_i^2)\,dy$$

$$= \pi \int_{-1}^{1} [(3 - x)^2 - 1]\,dy$$

$$= \pi \int_{-1}^{1} \{[3 - (y^2 + 1)]^2 - 1\}\,dy$$

$$= \pi \int_{-1}^{1} [(2 - y^2)^2 - 1]\,dy$$

$$= \pi \int_{-1}^{1} (y^4 - 4y^2 + 3)\,dy$$

7.

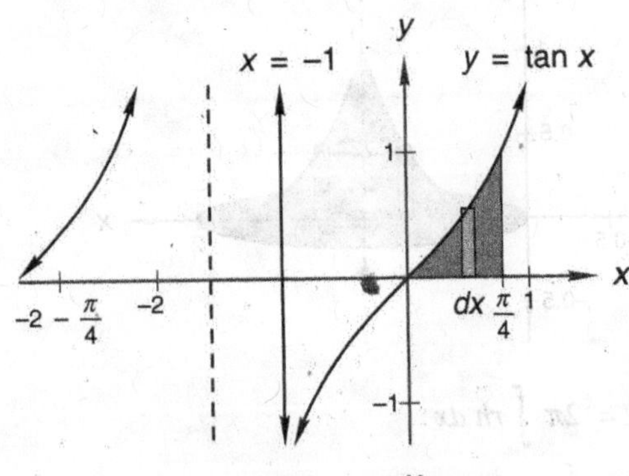

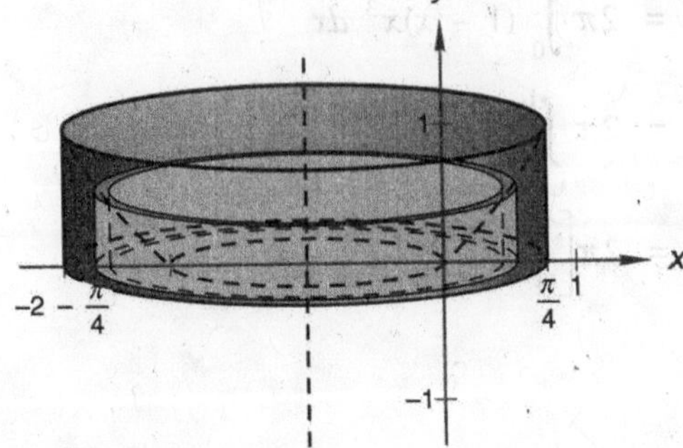

$$V = 2\pi \int rh\,dx$$

$$= 2\pi \int_{0}^{\pi/4} (1 + x)\tan x\,dx$$

8.

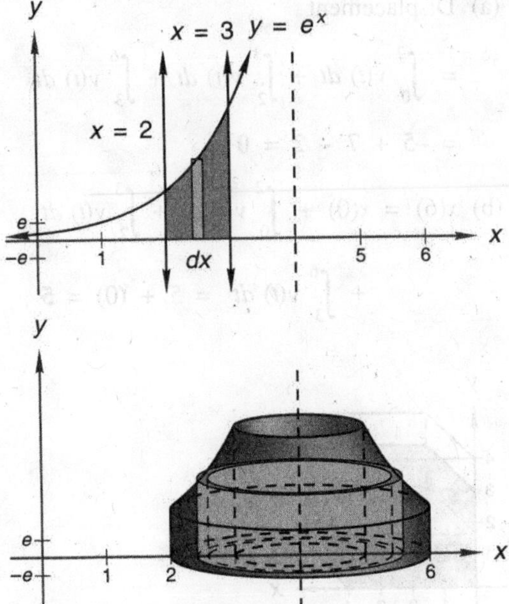

$$V = 2\pi \int rh\,dx$$

$$= 2\pi \int_{2}^{3} (4 - x)e^x\,dx$$

9. Since $f(1) = -1$ and $f(2) = 1$, there is a zero between $x = 1$ and $x = 2$. Let $x_1 = 1.5$, Y1=X²-X-1, and Y2=nDeriv(Y1,X,X).

```
1.5→X
                 1.5
X-(Y1/Y2)→X
               1.625
         1.618055556
         1.618033989
         1.618033989
```

The positive zero is approximately **1.618033989.**

10. Since $f(-3) = -15$ and $f(-2) = 1$, there must be a zero between $x = -3$ and $x = -2$, so we set $x_1 = -2.5$. We assign Y1=X³-3X+3 and Y2=nDeriv(Y1,X,X).

```
-2.5→X
                -2.5
X-(Y1/Y2)→X
        -2.174603195
        -2.106694917
        -2.103808524
        -2.103803403
        -2.103803403
```

The zero is approximately **−2.103803403.**

11. $f(x) = x^3 + x + 1 \qquad f'(x) = 3x^2 + 1$

$$(f^{-1})'(1) = \frac{1}{f'(0)} = \frac{1}{3(0)^2 + 1} = 1$$

$$y - 0 = 1(x - 1)$$

$$\mathbf{y = x - 1}$$

12. $f(x) = \sin x \qquad f'(x) = \cos x$

$$(f^{-1})'\left(\frac{1}{2}\right) = \frac{1}{f'\left(f^{-1}\left(\frac{1}{2}\right)\right)} = \frac{1}{f'\left(\frac{\pi}{6}\right)}$$

$$= \frac{1}{\cos\frac{\pi}{6}} = \frac{1}{\frac{\sqrt{3}}{2}} = \frac{2}{\sqrt{3}} = \mathbf{\frac{2\sqrt{3}}{3}}$$

13. $$\lim_{x\to 0} (\csc x - \cot x) = \lim_{x\to 0}\left(\frac{1 - \cos x}{\sin x}\right)$$

$$= \lim_{x\to 0}\frac{\sin x}{\cos x} = \frac{0}{1} = \mathbf{0}$$

14. $$\lim_{x\to 0}\frac{x - \sin x}{x^3} = \lim_{x\to 0}\frac{1 - \cos x}{3x^2} = \lim_{x\to 0}\frac{\sin x}{6x}$$

$$= \lim_{x\to 0}\frac{\cos x}{6} = \mathbf{\frac{1}{6}}$$

15. $$\frac{dy}{dx} = e^{x-y}$$

$$\frac{dy}{dx} = \frac{e^x}{e^y}$$

$$e^y\,dy = e^x\,dx$$

$$e^y = e^x + C$$

$$e^1 = e^1 + C$$

$$C = 0$$

$$e^y = e^x$$

$$\mathbf{y = x}$$

16.

$$\text{Average value} = \frac{1}{3 - 0}\int_0^3 \sqrt{9 - x^2}\,dx$$

$$= \frac{1}{3}\left(\frac{9\pi}{4}\right) = \mathbf{\frac{3\pi}{4}}$$

17. $$f(c) = \frac{1}{2}\int_0^2 (x^3 + 2)\,dx$$

$$c^3 + 2 = \frac{1}{2}\left[\frac{1}{4}x^4 + 2x\right]_0^2$$

$$c^3 + 2 = \frac{1}{2}(8)$$

$$c^3 = 2$$

$$c = \mathbf{\sqrt[3]{2}}$$

18. $f(x) = x^2 + 1 \quad f'(x) = 2x$

$$f'(c) = \frac{f(1) - f(-1)}{1 - (-1)}$$

$$2c = \frac{2 - 2}{2}$$

$$c = \mathbf{0}$$

19.

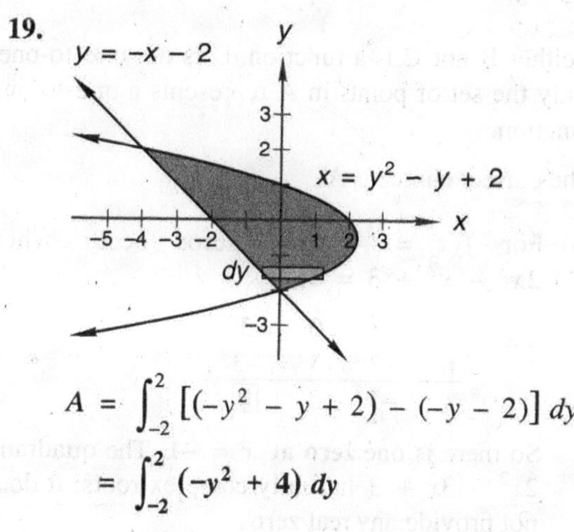

$$A = \int_{-2}^{2}\left[(-y^2 - y + 2) - (-y - 2)\right] dy$$

$$= \mathbf{\int_{-2}^{2}(-y^2 + 4)\,dy}$$

20. $$f\left(\frac{\pi}{2}\right) = \lim_{t\to\pi/2^-} f(t)$$

$$a\sin\frac{\pi}{2} - b\cos\frac{\pi}{2} = \lim_{t\to\pi/2^-}\cos t$$

$$a(1) - b(0) = 0$$

$$\mathbf{a = 0}$$

Since there are no restrictions on b, $\mathbf{b \in \mathbb{R}}$.

21.

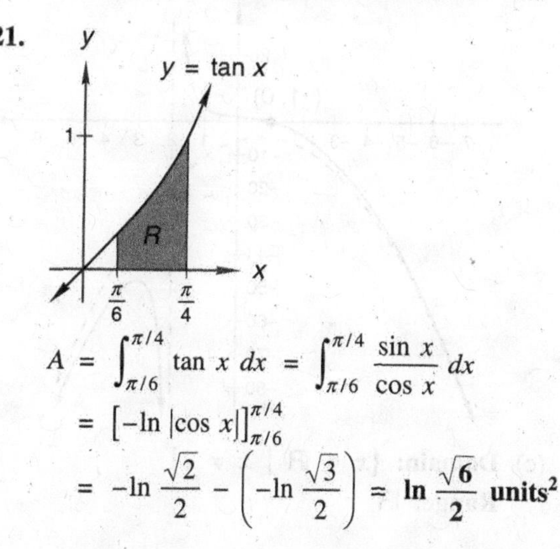

$$A = \int_{\pi/6}^{\pi/4}\tan x\,dx = \int_{\pi/6}^{\pi/4}\frac{\sin x}{\cos x}\,dx$$

$$= \left[-\ln|\cos x|\right]_{\pi/6}^{\pi/4}$$

$$= -\ln\frac{\sqrt{2}}{2} - \left(-\ln\frac{\sqrt{3}}{2}\right) = \mathbf{\ln\frac{\sqrt{6}}{2}\ \text{units}^2}$$

22. $h(x) = f(g(x)) = f(\sin x) = e^{\sin x}$
$h'(x) = \cos x\, e^{\sin x}$
$h'\left(\frac{\pi}{2}\right) = \left(\cos \frac{\pi}{2}\right)e^{\sin \pi/2} = \mathbf{0}$

23. $\frac{d}{dx}\left[\sin(x^2 - 1) + \frac{\sin x + 1}{e^x - 2}\right] + \int \frac{x^2}{x^3 - 1}\,dx$
$= 2x\cos(x^2 - 1) + \frac{(e^x - 2)(\cos x)}{(e^x - 2)^2}$
$- \frac{(\sin x + 1)(e^x)}{(e^x - 2)^2} + \frac{1}{3}\int \frac{3x^2}{x^3 - 1}\,dx$
$= \mathbf{2x\cos(x^2 - 1) + \frac{\cos x}{e^x - 2} - \frac{e^x(\sin x + 1)}{(e^x - 2)^2}}$
$\mathbf{+ \frac{1}{3}\ln|x^3 - 1| + C}$

24. Neither B nor C is a function. D is not one-to-one. Only the set of points in A represents a one-to-one function.

The correct choice is **A.**

25. (a) For $f(x) = \frac{2x^3 - x^2 + 3}{2 - x}$ zeros occur when $2x^3 - x^2 + 3 = 0$.

$\underline{-1|}$	2	−1	0	3
	↓	−2	3	−3
	2	−3	3	$\boxed{0}$

So there is one **zero at $x = -1$.** The quadratic $2x^2 - 3x + 3$ has only complex roots; it does not provide any real zeros.

Vertical asymptote: $x = 2$

$\underline{2|}$	−2	1	0	−3
	↓	−4	−6	−12
	−2	−3	−6	$\boxed{-15}$

End behavior: $y = -2x^2 - 3x - 6$

(b)

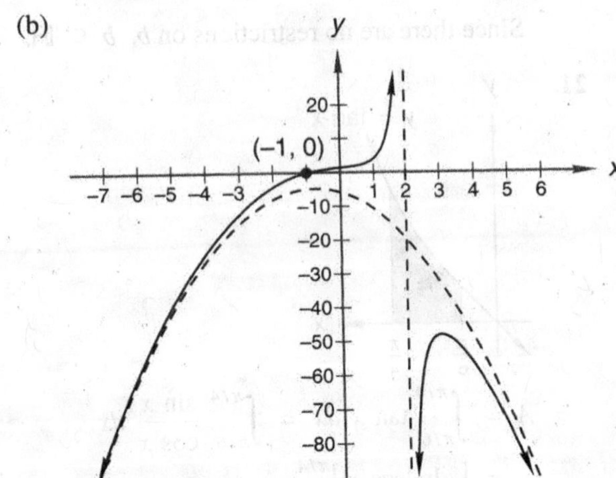

(c) **Domain: $\{x \in \mathbb{R} \mid x \neq 2\}$**
Range: $\mathbb{R}$

PROBLEM SET 95

1. (a) $V = \frac{1}{3}\pi r^2 h$

$100 = \frac{1}{3}\pi r^2 h$

$h = \frac{300}{\pi r^2}$

$r^2 + h^2 = l^2$

$l = \sqrt{r^2 + h^2}$

$A = \pi r l$

$A = \pi r\sqrt{r^2 + h^2}$

$\mathbf{A = \pi r\sqrt{r^2 + \left(\frac{300}{\pi r^2}\right)^2}}$

(b) $A = \pi r\left(r^2 + \frac{90{,}000}{\pi^2 r^4}\right)^{1/2}$

$A' = \pi r\left[\frac{1}{2}\left(r^2 + \frac{90{,}000}{\pi^2}r^{-4}\right)^{-1/2} \cdot \left(2r - \frac{360{,}000}{\pi^2}r^{-5}\right)\right] + \pi\left(r^2 + \frac{90{,}000}{\pi^2}r^{-4}\right)^{1/2}$

$A' = \pi\left(r^2 + \frac{90{,}000}{\pi^2}r^{-4}\right)^{-1/2} \cdot \left(r^2 - \frac{180{,}000}{\pi^2}r^{-4} + r^2 + \frac{90{,}000}{\pi^2}r^{-4}\right)$

$0 = \pi\left(r^2 + \frac{90{,}000}{\pi^2}r^{-4}\right)^{-1/2} \cdot \left(2r^2 - \frac{90{,}000}{\pi^2}r^{-4}\right)$

$2r^2 = \frac{90{,}000}{\pi^2}r^{-4}$

$r^6 = \frac{45{,}000}{\pi^2}$

$r = \sqrt[6]{\frac{45{,}000}{\pi^2}}$ m

$\mathbf{r \approx 4.0721\ m}$

$h \approx \frac{300}{\pi(4.0721)^2}$

$\mathbf{h \approx 5.7588\ m}$

2. 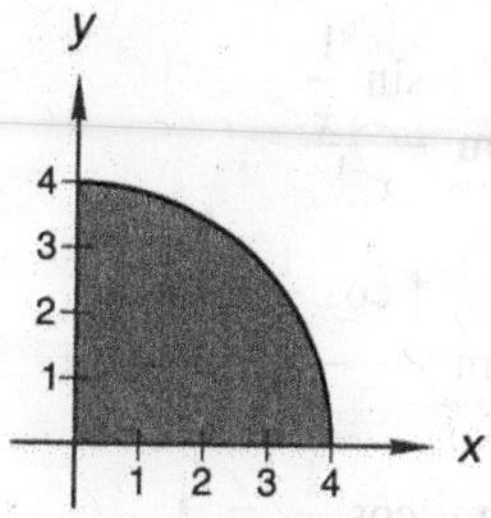

$$\text{Work} = \int_0^4 \sqrt{16 - x^2}\, dx = \frac{16\pi}{4} = \mathbf{4\pi \text{ joules}}$$

3. (a) $\dfrac{dx}{dt} = \dfrac{4}{5}\,\dfrac{\text{units}}{\text{s}}$

$$y = x^2 + 2$$
$$\frac{dy}{dt} = 2x\frac{dx}{dt}$$
$$\frac{dy}{dt} = 2(1)\left(\frac{4}{5}\right) = \mathbf{\frac{8}{5}\,\frac{units}{s}}$$

(b) $s = \sqrt{x^2 + y^2}$

$$\frac{ds}{dt} = \frac{1}{2}(x^2 + y^2)^{-1/2}\left(2x\frac{dx}{dt} + 2y\frac{dy}{dt}\right)$$
$$\frac{ds}{dt} = \frac{1}{2}(1 + 9)^{-1/2}\left[2(1)\left(\frac{4}{5}\right) + 2(3)\left(\frac{8}{5}\right)\right]$$
$$\frac{ds}{dt} = \left(\frac{1}{2\sqrt{10}}\right)\left(\frac{56}{5}\right)$$
$$\frac{ds}{dt} = \frac{56\sqrt{10}}{100}$$
$$\frac{ds}{dt} = \mathbf{\frac{14\sqrt{10}}{25}\,\frac{units}{s}} \approx \mathbf{1.7709\,\frac{units}{s}}$$

4. $x(t) = 2t^3 - 21t^2 + 60t + 2$

$$v(t) = 6t^2 - 42t + 60$$
$$0 = 6t^2 - 42t + 60$$
$$0 = t^2 - 7t + 10$$
$$0 = (t - 5)(t - 2)$$
$$t = 5, 2$$

The particle changes direction **twice**.

5. (a) $8\pi\cos\left(4\pi t + \dfrac{\pi}{2}\right) = 0$

$$\cos\left(4\pi t + \frac{\pi}{2}\right) = 0$$
$$4\pi t + \frac{\pi}{2} = \frac{\pi}{2}, \frac{3\pi}{2}, \frac{5\pi}{2}, \frac{7\pi}{2}, \frac{9\pi}{2}, \ldots$$
$$4\pi t = 0, \pi, 2\pi, 3\pi, 4\pi, \ldots$$

For $0 \le t \le 1$,

$$t = \mathbf{0, \frac{1}{4}, \frac{1}{2}, \frac{3}{4}, 1}$$

(b) $$\text{Distance} = \int_{1/4}^{1/2} v(t)\,dt + \int_{3/4}^{1} v(t)\,dt$$
$$= 2\int_{1/4}^{1/2} 8\pi\cos\left(4\pi t + \frac{\pi}{2}\right)dt$$
$$= 4\int_{1/4}^{1/2} 4\pi\cos\left(4\pi t + \frac{\pi}{2}\right)dt$$
$$= 4\left[\sin\left(4\pi t + \frac{\pi}{2}\right)\right]_{1/4}^{1/2}$$
$$= \mathbf{8 \text{ units}}$$

6. (a) $T = \dfrac{b - a}{2n}(y_0 + 2y_1 + 2y_2 + 2y_3 + y_4)$

$$= \frac{4 - 1}{2(4)}\left[(1)^2 + 2\left(\frac{7}{4}\right)^2 + 2\left(\frac{5}{2}\right)^2 + 2\left(\frac{13}{4}\right)^2 + 4^2\right]$$
$$= \frac{3}{8}\left(1 + \frac{49}{8} + \frac{25}{2} + \frac{169}{8} + 16\right)$$
$$= \frac{681}{32} \approx \mathbf{21.2813}$$

(b) $\displaystyle\int_1^4 x^2\,dx = \left[\frac{1}{3}x^3\right]_1^4 = \frac{64}{3} - \frac{1}{3} = \mathbf{21}$

The trapezoidal approximation is 0.2813 too large.

(c) $\max|f''(x)| = 2$

$$E = \frac{(4 - 1)^3}{12(4)^2}(2) = \frac{27}{12(16)}(2)$$
$$= \mathbf{\frac{9}{32}} \approx \mathbf{0.2813}$$

(d) $$\frac{(4 - 1)^3}{12n^2}(2) < 0.001$$
$$\frac{54}{12n^2} < 0.001$$
$$\frac{1}{n^2} < 0.000\overline{2}$$
$$n^2 > 4500$$
$$n > 67.08$$

The number of subdivisions required is **68**.

7. $T = \dfrac{b - a}{2n}(y_0 + 2y_1 + 2y_2 + 2y_3 + y_4)$

$$= \frac{\frac{\pi}{4}}{8}\left(\sec^3 0 + 2\sec^3\frac{\pi}{16} + 2\sec^3\frac{\pi}{8} + 2\sec^3\frac{3\pi}{16} + \sec^3\frac{\pi}{4}\right) \approx \mathbf{1.1745}$$

8. $x_1 = \dfrac{3}{2}$

$$x_2 = \frac{3}{2} - \frac{\left(\frac{3}{2}\right)^4 - 3}{4\left(\frac{3}{2}\right)^3} = \frac{3}{2} - \frac{81 - 48}{216}$$

$$= \frac{324 - 33}{216} = \mathbf{\frac{97}{72}}$$

9. $f(x) = x^3 - 8 \quad f'(x) = 3x^2$

By inspection $x = 2$ is the solution to $x^3 - 8 = 0$.

$$(f^{-1})'(0) = \frac{1}{f'(f^{-1}(0))} = \frac{1}{f'(2)} = \frac{1}{3(2)^2}$$

$$= \mathbf{\frac{1}{12}}$$

10. $f(x) = \cos x \quad f'(x) = -\sin x$

By inspection $x = \frac{\pi}{3}$ is the solution to $\cos x = \frac{1}{2}$ on the interval $[0, \pi]$.

$$(f^{-1})'\left(\frac{1}{2}\right) = \frac{1}{f'\left(f^{-1}\left(\frac{1}{2}\right)\right)} = \frac{1}{f'\left(\frac{\pi}{3}\right)}$$

$$= \frac{1}{-\sin\frac{\pi}{3}} = \frac{1}{-\frac{\sqrt{3}}{2}} = \mathbf{\frac{-2\sqrt{3}}{3}}$$

11. $$\lim_{x\to\infty}\left(e^{-x^2}\ln x\right) = \lim_{x\to\infty}\frac{\ln x}{e^{x^2}} = \lim_{x\to\infty}\frac{\frac{1}{x}}{2xe^{x^2}}$$

$$= \lim_{x\to\infty}\frac{1}{2x^2e^{x^2}} = \mathbf{0}$$

12.

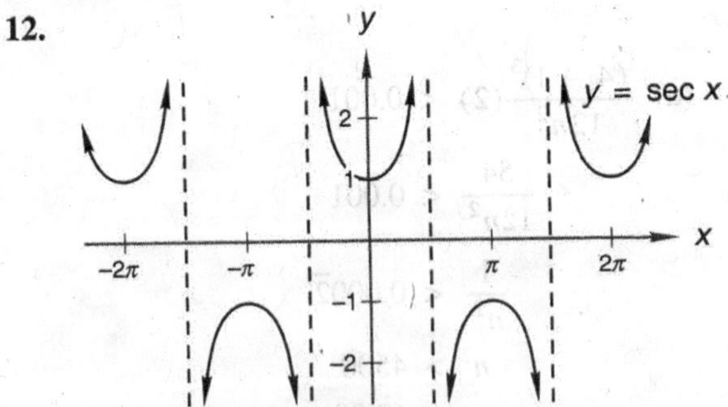

From the graph, $\lim_{x\to\pi/2} \sec x$ **does not exist.**

13. $$\lim_{x\to-3}\left(\frac{2x}{x^2 + 2x - 3} - \frac{3}{x + 3}\right)$$

$$= \lim_{x\to-3}\left[\frac{2x - 3(x - 1)}{x^2 + 2x - 3}\right]$$

$$= \lim_{x\to-3}\left(\frac{-x + 3}{x^2 + 2x - 3}\right)$$

This limit approaches $+\infty$ from the left and $-\infty$ from the right, so the limit **does not exist.**

14. $$\lim_{x\to\infty}\left(x\sin\frac{1}{x}\right) = \lim_{x\to\infty}\frac{\sin\frac{1}{x}}{x^{-1}}$$

$$= \lim_{x\to\infty}\frac{\left(\cos\frac{1}{x}\right)(-x^{-2})}{-x^{-2}}$$

$$= \lim_{x\to\infty}\cos\frac{1}{x} = \mathbf{1}$$

15.

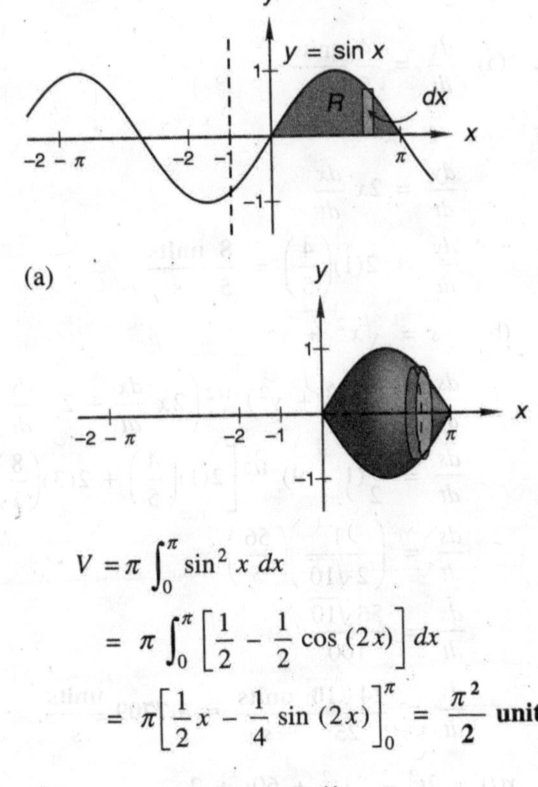

$$V = \pi\int_0^\pi \sin^2 x\,dx$$

$$= \pi\int_0^\pi\left[\frac{1}{2} - \frac{1}{2}\cos(2x)\right]dx$$

$$= \pi\left[\frac{1}{2}x - \frac{1}{4}\sin(2x)\right]_0^\pi = \mathbf{\frac{\pi^2}{2}\ units^3}$$

(b)

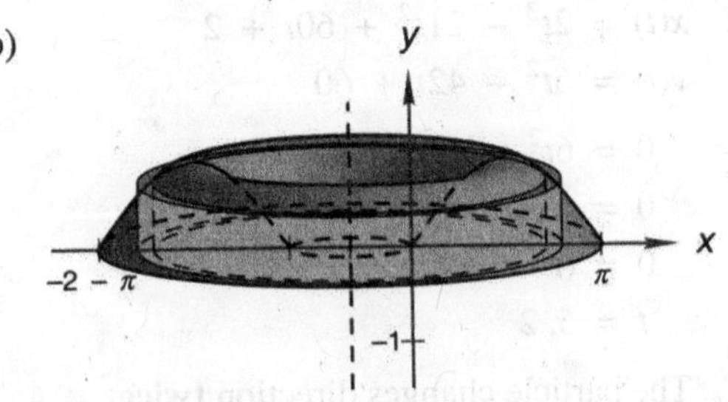

$$V = 2\pi\int_0^\pi (1 + x)\sin x\,dx$$

$$= 2\pi\int_0^\pi (\sin x + x\sin x)\,dx$$

$u = x \quad du = dx \quad v = -\cos x \quad dv = \sin x\,dx$

$$2\pi\int_0^\pi (\sin x + x\sin x)\,dx$$

$$= 2\pi\left[-\cos x - x\cos x + \int\cos x\,dx\right]_0^\pi$$

$$= 2\pi[-\cos x - x\cos x + \sin x]_0^\pi$$

$$= \mathbf{2\pi(2 + \pi)\ units^3}$$

16. $$\frac{dy}{dx} = 2xy^2$$
$$y^{-2}\,dy = 2x\,dx$$
$$-y^{-1} = x^2 + C$$
$$1 = 1 + C$$
$$C = 0$$
$$-y^{-1} = x^2$$
$$y = -\frac{\mathbf{1}}{\mathbf{x^2}}$$

17. $$\frac{dy}{dx} = \frac{1 - 2x}{2y}$$
$$2y\,dy = (1 - 2x)\,dx$$
$$y^2 = x - x^2 + C$$
$$x^2 + y^2 - x = C$$

This describes a family of circles, so the correct choice is **B.**

18.

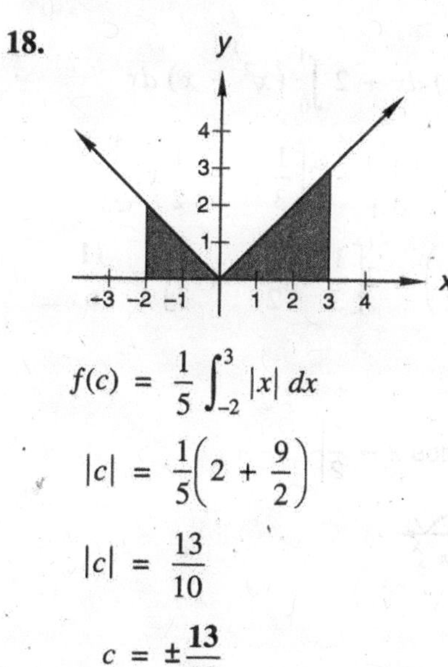

$$f(c) = \frac{1}{5}\int_{-2}^{3} |x|\,dx$$
$$|c| = \frac{1}{5}\left(2 + \frac{9}{2}\right)$$
$$|c| = \frac{13}{10}$$
$$c = \pm\frac{\mathbf{13}}{\mathbf{10}}$$

19. (a) Average speed $= \dfrac{\text{distance}}{\text{time}} = \dfrac{600 \text{ ft}}{12 \text{ s}}$

$= \mathbf{50\ ft/s}$

(b) $\dfrac{50 \text{ ft}}{1 \text{ s}} \cdot \dfrac{60 \text{ s}}{1 \text{ min}} \cdot \dfrac{60 \text{ min}}{1 \text{ hr}} \cdot \dfrac{1 \text{ mile}}{5280 \text{ ft}}$

$= 34.0909$ mph

Yes, the driver was speeding. If the driver did not exceed 30 mph, he could not have traveled 600 feet in 12 seconds. By the Mean Value Theorem, the speed of the car must have been 50 ft/s at some point in the skid, which is just over 34 mph.

20. $$\int \frac{3}{x^2 + 16}\,dx = \frac{3}{4}\int \frac{4}{x^2 + 16}\,dx$$
$$= \frac{\mathbf{3}}{\mathbf{4}}\ \mathbf{arctan}\ \frac{\mathbf{x}}{\mathbf{4}} + \mathbf{C}$$

21. $$\int \frac{e^x + \cos x}{e^x + \sin x}\,dx = \mathbf{\ln|e^x + \sin x| + C}$$

22. $$h(x) = f(g(x)) = f(e^x) = \arctan(e^{2x})$$
$$h'(x) = \frac{2e^{2x}}{1 + e^{4x}}$$
$$h'(0) = \frac{2e^0}{1 + e^0} = \frac{2}{1 + 1} = \mathbf{1}$$

23. $$\lim_{x\to 2^-} f(x) = f(2)$$
$$\lim_{x\to 2^-} (x^2 + 2) = 2a + b$$
$$6 = 2a + b$$
$$\lim_{x\to 2^-} 2x = f'(2)$$
$$\mathbf{4 = a}$$
$$6 = 2(4) + b$$
$$\mathbf{-2 = b}$$

24.

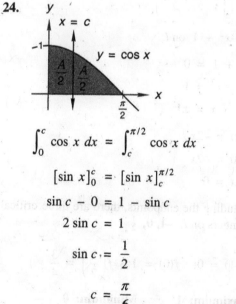

$$\int_0^c \cos x\,dx = \int_c^{\pi/2} \cos x\,dx$$
$$[\sin x]_0^c = [\sin x]_c^{\pi/2}$$
$$\sin c - 0 = 1 - \sin c$$
$$2\sin c = 1$$
$$\sin c = \frac{1}{2}$$
$$c = \frac{\boldsymbol{\pi}}{\mathbf{6}}$$

25. $f(x) = x^2$ is continuous and differentiable everywhere. The graphs of $x^{1/2}$, $x^{5/2}$, and $x^{3/2}$ are not defined for $x < 0$, so these functions are neither continuous nor differentiable at $x = 0$. $f(x) = x^{2/3}$ is continuous at $x = 0$, but it is not differentiable at $x = 0$ because the graph has a cusp at the origin.

The correct choice is **E.**

Problem Set 96

1. (a) $x(t) = 2t^3 - 9t^2 + 12t + 1$

$v(t) = 6t^2 - 18t + 12$

The particle is at rest when

$$6t^2 - 18t + 12 = 0$$
$$t^2 - 3t + 2 = 0$$
$$(t - 2)(t - 1) = 0$$
$$t = 1, 2$$

The particle is moving left when $v(t)$ is negative: **$1 < t < 2$**

(b) $x(0) = 1;\ x(1) = 6;\ x(2) = 5;\ x(4) = 33$

Total distance traveled is the sum of the distances traveled between times $t = 0$ and 1, $t = 1$ and 2, and $t = 2$ and 4.

distance $= 5 + 1 + 28 =$ **34 units**

2.

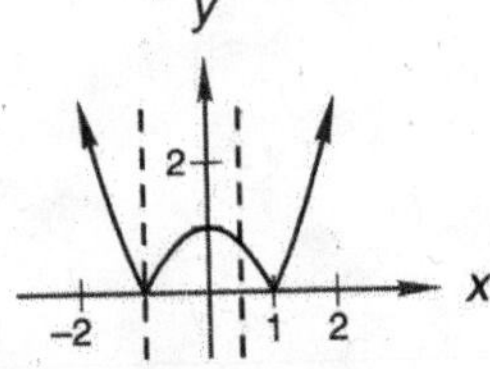

$f(x) = -x^2 + 1$ on I.

(a) $-x^2 + 1 = 0$

$$x^2 = 1$$
$$x = \pm 1$$

$$f'(x) = -2x$$
$$0 = -2x$$
$$x = 0$$

Including the endpoints, there are three critical numbers on I: **$-1, 0, \frac{1}{2}$**

(b) $f(-1) = 0;\quad f(0) = 1;\quad f\left(\frac{1}{2}\right) = \frac{3}{4}$

Maximum: 1 **Minimum: 0**

3.

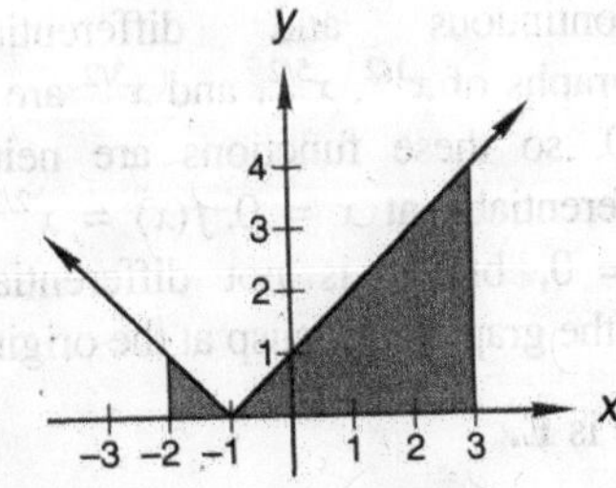

$$\int_{-2}^{3} |x + 1|\, dx$$
$$= \int_{-2}^{-1} (-x - 1)\, dx + \int_{-1}^{3} (x + 1)\, dx$$
$$= \left[-\frac{1}{2}x^2 - x\right]_{-2}^{-1} + \left[\frac{1}{2}x^2 + x\right]_{-1}^{3}$$
$$= -\frac{1}{2} + 1 - (-2 + 2) + \frac{9}{2} + 3 - \left(\frac{1}{2} - 1\right)$$
$$= \mathbf{\frac{17}{2}}$$

4.

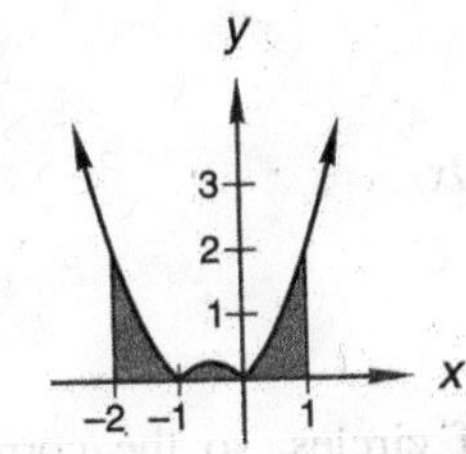

$$\int_{-2}^{1} \left|x^2 + x\right| dx$$
$$= \int_{-1}^{0} (-x^2 - x)\, dx + 2\int_{0}^{1} (x^2 + x)\, dx$$
$$= \left[-\frac{1}{3}x^3 - \frac{1}{2}x^2\right]_{-1}^{0} + 2\left[\frac{1}{3}x^3 + \frac{1}{2}x^2\right]_{0}^{1}$$
$$= 0 - \left(\frac{1}{3} - \frac{1}{2}\right) + 2\left[\frac{1}{3} + \frac{1}{2} - (0)\right] = \mathbf{\frac{11}{6}}$$

5.

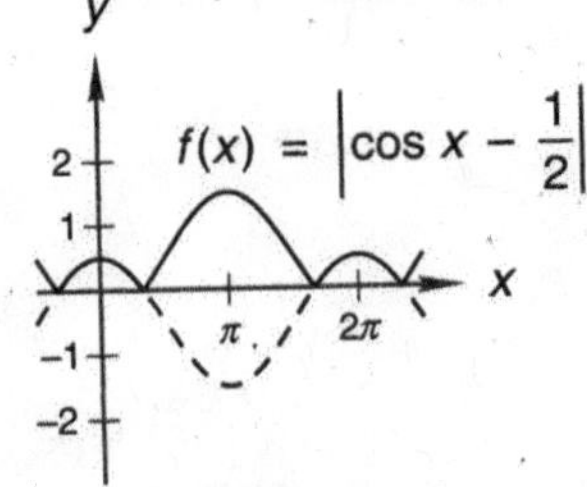

$$f'(x) = -\sin x$$
$$0 = -\sin x$$
$$x = 0, \pi, 2\pi, \ldots$$

$$\cos x = \frac{1}{2}$$
$$x = \frac{\pi}{3}, \frac{5\pi}{3}, \ldots$$

$f(0) = \frac{1}{2};\ f(\pi) = \frac{3}{2};\ f(2\pi) = \frac{1}{2};\ f\left(\frac{\pi}{3}\right) = 0;$

$f\left(\frac{5\pi}{3}\right) = 0$

Maximum: $\mathbf{\frac{3}{2}}$

6. The maximum value of $|f(x)|$ is 10. There is not enough information to determine the minimum value of $f(|x|)$.

The correct choice is **C**.

7. (a) $T = \dfrac{b-a}{2n}(y_0 + 2y_1 + 2y_2 + 2y_3 + 2y_4 + y_5)$

$$= \frac{1}{10}\left[0 + 2\left(\frac{1}{5}\right)^3 + 2\left(\frac{2}{5}\right)^3 + 2\left(\frac{3}{5}\right)^3 + 2\left(\frac{4}{5}\right)^3 + 1\right]$$

$$= \frac{1}{10}\left(\frac{13}{5}\right) = \mathbf{\frac{13}{50}} = \mathbf{0.26}$$

(b) $\displaystyle\int_0^1 x^3\,dx = \left[\frac{1}{4}x^4\right]_0^1 = \mathbf{\frac{1}{4}} = \mathbf{0.25}$

The trapezoidal approximation is $\dfrac{1}{100}$ too large.

(c) $f(x) = x^3 \qquad f''(x) = 6x$

$\max|f''(x)| = 6$

$$E_{\max} = \frac{(1-0)^3}{12(5^2)} \cdot 6 = \frac{6}{12(25)} = \mathbf{\frac{1}{50}} = \mathbf{0.02}$$

(d) $\dfrac{1}{12n^2}(6) < 10^{-4}$

$$\frac{1}{2n^2} < 10^{-4}$$

$$\frac{1}{n^2} < 2 \cdot 10^{-4}$$

$$n^2 > 5000$$

$$n > 70.7107$$

The number of required subdivisions is **71**.

8. $T = \dfrac{b-a}{2n}(y_0 + 2y_1 + 2y_2 + 2y_3 + 2y_4 + y_5)$

$$= \frac{1}{10}\left(1 + 2\sqrt{\frac{126}{125}} + 2\sqrt{\frac{133}{125}} + 2\sqrt{\frac{152}{125}} + 2\sqrt{\frac{189}{125}} + \sqrt{2}\right)$$

$$\approx \mathbf{1.1150}$$

9.

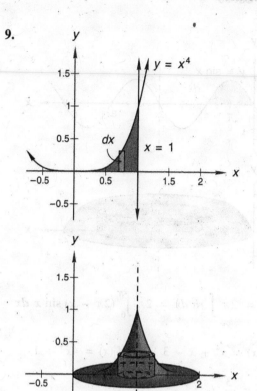

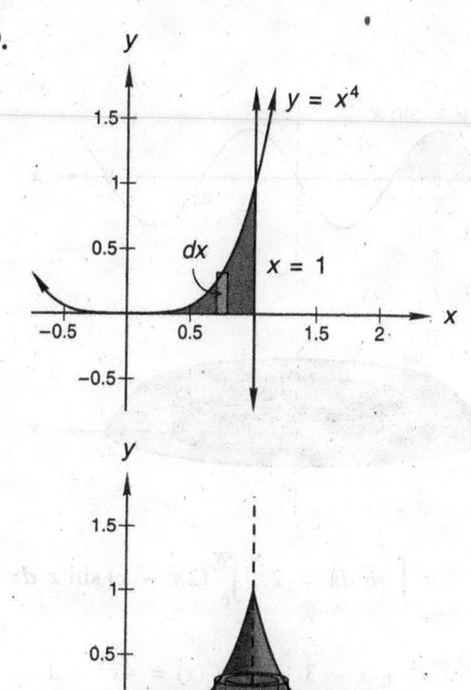

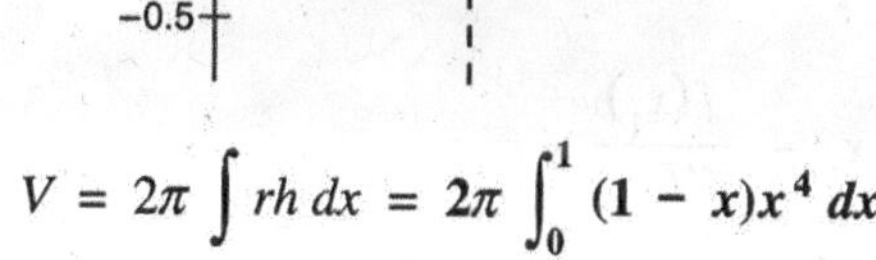

$V = 2\pi \displaystyle\int rh\,dx = \mathbf{2\pi \int_0^1 (1 - x)x^4\,dx}$

10.

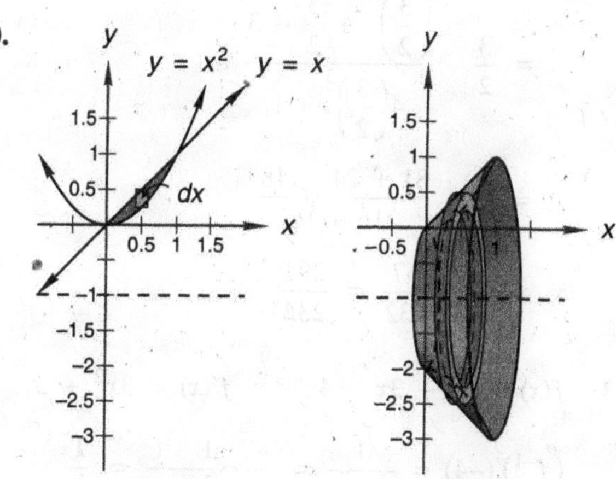

$$V = \pi\int_0^1 \left[(1+x)^2 - (1+x^2)^2\right] dx$$

$$= \pi\int_0^1 [1 + 2x + x^2 - (1 + 2x^2 + x^4)]\,dx$$

$$= \pi\int_0^1 \mathbf{(-x^4 - x^2 + 2x)\,dx}$$

11.

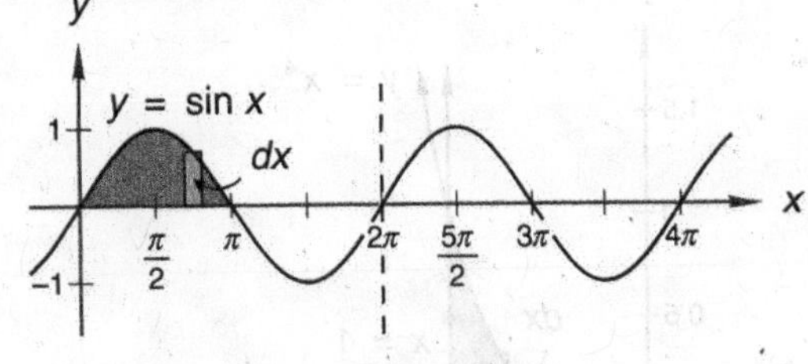

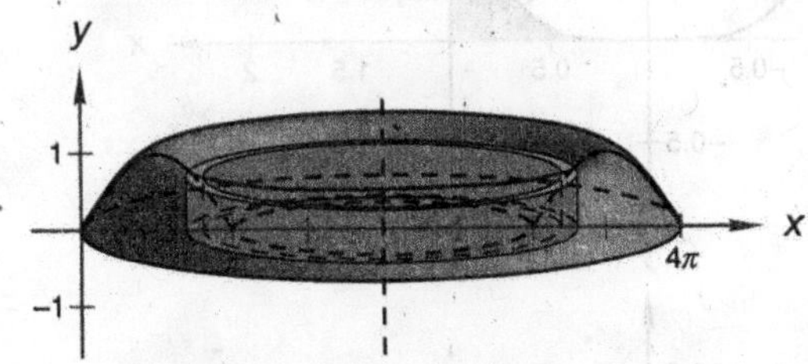

$$V = 2\pi \int rh\,dx = \mathbf{2\pi \int_0^{\pi} (2\pi - x) \sin x\, dx}$$

12. $f(x) = x^4 + x - 3 \qquad f'(x) = 4x^3 + 1$

$$x_1 = \frac{3}{2}$$

$$x_2 = x_1 - \frac{f(x_1)}{f'(x_1)}$$

$$= \frac{3}{2} - \frac{\left(\frac{3}{2}\right)^4 + \frac{3}{2} - 3}{4\left(\frac{3}{2}\right)^3 + 1}$$

$$= \frac{3}{2} - \frac{81 + 24 - 48}{216 + 16}$$

$$= \frac{3}{2} - \frac{57}{232} = \mathbf{\frac{291}{232}}$$

13. $f(x) = x^3 + 3x - 4 \qquad f'(x) = 3x^2 + 3$

$$(f^{-1})'(-4) = \frac{1}{f'(0)} = \frac{1}{3(0)^2 + 3} = \mathbf{\frac{1}{3}}$$

14. $$\lim_{x\to 0^+} (x^2 \ln x) = \lim_{x\to 0^+} \frac{\ln x}{x^{-2}}$$

$$= \lim_{x\to 0^+} \frac{\frac{1}{x}}{\frac{-2}{x^3}}$$

$$= \lim_{x\to 0^+} -\frac{x^2}{2} = \mathbf{0}$$

15. $$\lim_{x\to\pi/2} \frac{1 + \tan x}{\tan x} = \lim_{x\to\pi/2} \frac{\sec^2 x}{\sec^2 x} = \mathbf{1}$$

16. $\lim_{x\to 3} \frac{e^x - e^3}{x - 3}$ is the definition of $f'(3)$ when $f(x) = e^x$, so the limit equals $\mathbf{e^3}$.

17.
$$B_t = B_0 e^{rt}$$
$$911 = 500e^{10r}$$
$$1.822 = e^{10r}$$
$$\ln 1.822 = 10r$$
$$r = \frac{\ln 1.822}{10}$$
$$20{,}000 = B_0 e^{20[(\ln 1.822)/10]}$$
$$20{,}000 = B_0 e^{\ln 1.822^2}$$
$$20{,}000 = B_0 1.822^2$$
$$B_0 = \mathbf{\$6024.67}$$

18. (a) fg = odd · even = **odd**

(b) $\frac{f}{g} = \frac{\text{odd}}{\text{even}}$ = **odd**

(c) f^2 = (odd)(odd) = **even**

(d) f^2g^3 = (odd²)(even³) = (even)(even) = **even**

19.
$$y = x^{\sqrt{x}}$$
$$\ln y = \sqrt{x} \ln x$$
$$\frac{1}{y}\frac{dy}{dx} = \sqrt{x}\frac{1}{x} + \ln x \left(\frac{1}{2}x^{-1/2}\right)$$
$$\frac{dy}{dx} = y\left(x^{-1/2} + \frac{x^{-1/2} \ln x}{2}\right)$$
$$\frac{dy}{dx} = x^{\sqrt{x}} x^{-1/2}\left(1 + \frac{\ln x}{2}\right)$$
$$\frac{dy}{dx} = \mathbf{x^{\sqrt{x} - 1/2}(1 + \ln \sqrt{x})}$$

20.

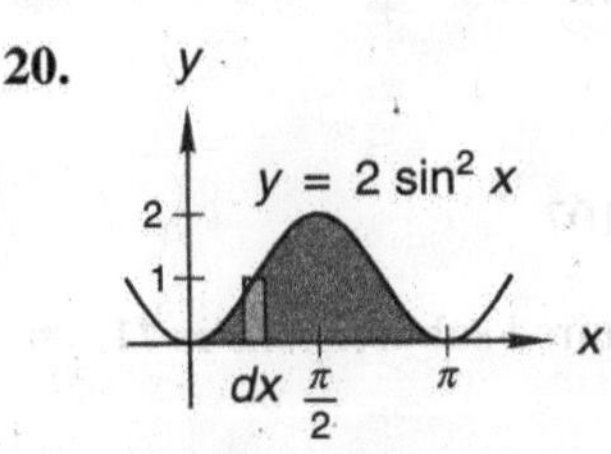

$$A = \int_0^{\pi} 2 \sin^2 x\, dx$$
$$= \int_0^{\pi} 2\left[\frac{1}{2} - \frac{1}{2}\cos(2x)\right] dx$$
$$= \int_0^{\pi} [1 - \cos(2x)]\, dx$$
$$= \left[x - \frac{1}{2}\sin(2x)\right]_0^{\pi} = \mathbf{\pi \text{ units}^2}$$

21. Choice A states the definition of continuity at $x = 2$. Choice B is not necessarily true, because there could be a cusp at $x = 2$. Choice C is true only if f is differentiable at $x = 2$. Choice D could be true, but there is not enough information to determine its validity.

The correct choice is **A.**

22. $$y = x^3 - 6x^2 + 6x + 1$$
$$y' = 3x^2 - 12x + 6$$
$$y'' = 6x - 12$$
$$0 < 6x - 12$$
$$\mathbf{x > 2}$$

23. $$y = (x - 4)^6 + \sin(2x)$$
$$\frac{dy}{dx} = 6(x - 4)^5 + 2\cos(2x)$$
$$\frac{d^2y}{dx^2} = 30(x - 4)^4 - 4\sin(2x)$$
$$\frac{d^3y}{dx^3} = \mathbf{120(x - 4)^3 - 8\cos(2x)}$$

24. $$f(x) = x^3 + kx$$
$$f'(x) = 3x^2 + k$$

The function f has one local maximum and one local minimum if $3x^2 + k$ has two distinct zeros. This can be true only if $k < 0$.

The correct choice is **E.**

25. $y = x$

Switch variables and solve for y.

$$x = y$$
$$y = x$$

The correct choice is **A.**

PROBLEM SET 97

1. $$\frac{r}{h} = \frac{5}{15}$$
$$r = \frac{1}{3}h$$

$$\frac{dv}{dt} = 4\,\frac{\text{m}^3}{\text{min}} \qquad h = 9\text{ m}$$

$$V = \frac{1}{3}\pi r^2 h$$
$$V = \frac{1}{27}\pi h^3$$
$$\frac{dV}{dt} = \frac{1}{9}\pi h^2 \frac{dh}{dt}$$
$$(4) = \frac{1}{9}\pi(9)^2 \frac{dh}{dt}$$
$$\frac{dh}{dt} = \mathbf{\frac{4}{9\pi}\,\frac{m}{min}}$$

2.

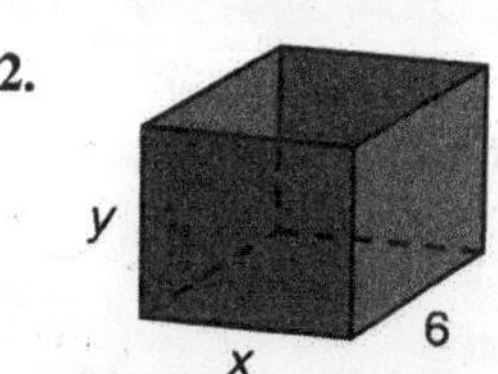

(a) $$V = lwh$$
$$72 = 6xy$$
$$y = \frac{12}{x}$$
$$\text{Cost} = 3(6x) + 2(6y)(2) + 2(xy)(2)$$
$$C = 18x + 24\left(\frac{12}{x}\right) + 4\left[x\left(\frac{12}{x}\right)\right]$$
$$\mathbf{C = 18x + 288x^{-1} + 48}$$

(b) $$C' = 18 - 288x^{-2}$$
$$0 = 18 - 288x^{-2}$$
$$18x^2 = 288$$
$$x^2 = 16$$
$$\mathbf{x = 4\text{ m}}$$
$$y = \frac{12}{4}$$
$$\mathbf{y = 3\text{ m}}$$

(c) $$C = 18(4) + \frac{288}{4} + 48 = \mathbf{\$192}$$

3. (a) Displacement $= \int_0^2 v(t)\,dt + \int_2^3 v(t)\,dt + \int_3^5 v(t)\,dt + \int_5^6 v(t)\,dt$

$= 8 - 3 + 1 - 6 = \mathbf{0}$

(b) $x(6) = x(2) + \int_2^3 v(t)\,dt + \int_3^5 v(t)\,dt + \int_5^6 v(t)\,dt$

$= 4 - 3 + 1 - 6 = \mathbf{-4}$

(c) Distance = 8 + 3 + 1 + 6 = **18 units**

4. (a) $x(t) = (t - 1)^3(t - 5)$

$v(t) = (t - 1)^3 + (t - 5)[3(t - 1)^2]$

$v(t) = (t - 1)^2[(t - 1) + 3(t - 5)]$

$v(t) = (t - 1)^2(4t - 16)$

$v(t) = 4(t - 1)^2(t - 4)$

$0 = 4(t - 1)^2(t - 4)$

$t = \mathbf{1, 4}$

(b)

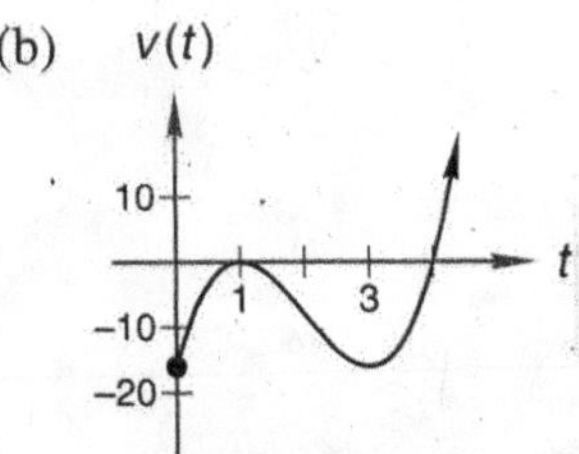

The particle is moving right when $v(t) > 0$. This occurs when $t > \mathbf{4}$.

(c) The particle changes direction when $v(t)$ changes sign. This occurs when $t = \mathbf{4}$.

(d) The particle begins moving left at $t = 0$ and continues moving left until $t = 4$.

$x(4) = (4 - 1)^3(4 - 5) = \mathbf{-27\ units}$

5.

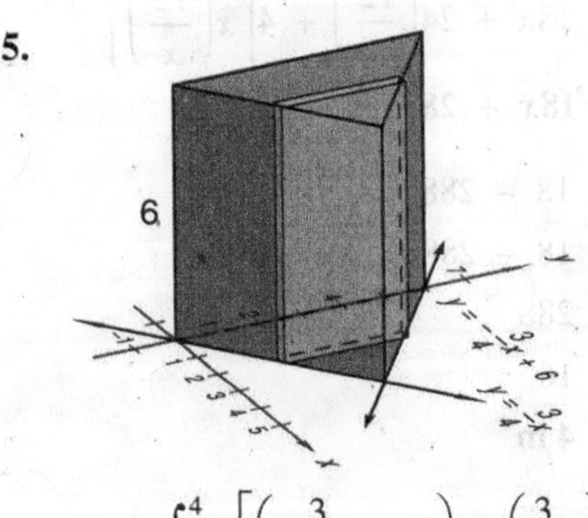

$$V = \int_0^4 6\left[\left(-\frac{3}{4}x + 6\right) - \left(\frac{3}{4}x\right)\right] dx$$

$$= \int_0^4 (-9x + 36)\,dx$$

$$= \left[-\frac{9}{2}x^2 + 36x\right]_0^4 = \mathbf{72\ units^3}$$

6.

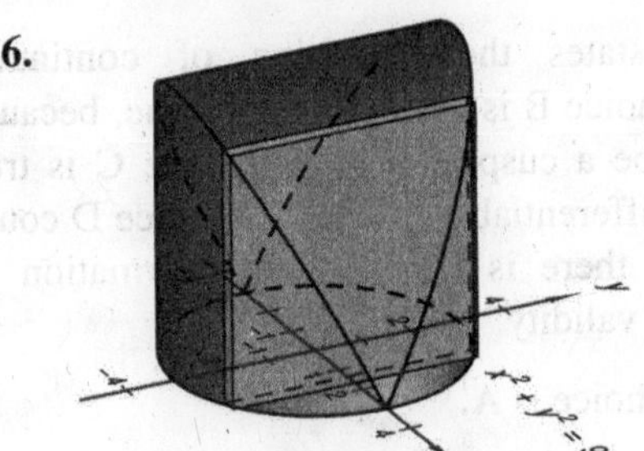

$$V = 2\int_{x=0}^{x=3} (2y)^2\,dx = 2\int_{x=0}^{x=3} 4y^2\,dx$$

$$= 8\int_0^3 (9 - x^2)\,dx = 8\left[9x - \frac{1}{3}x^3\right]_0^3$$

$$= 8(27 - 9) = \mathbf{144\ units^3}$$

7.

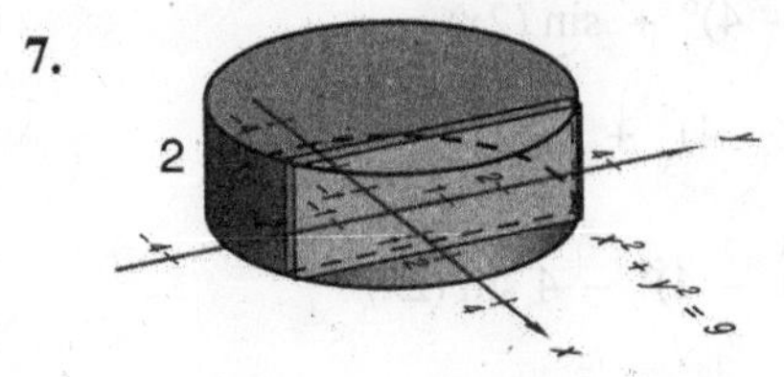

$$V = \pi r^2 h = \pi(3)^2(2) = \mathbf{18\pi\ units^3}$$

8.

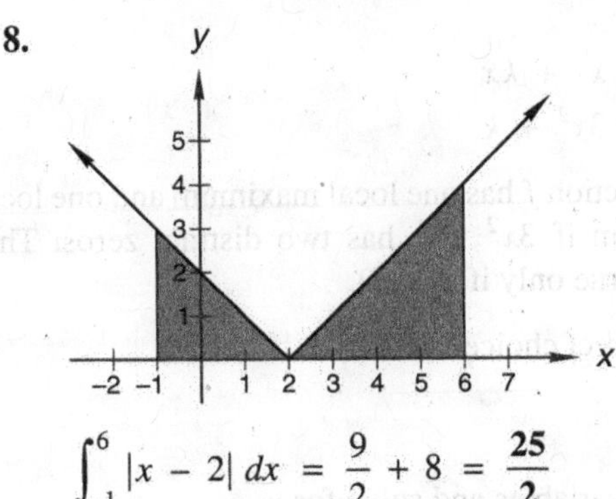

$$\int_{-1}^6 |x - 2|\,dx = \frac{9}{2} + 8 = \mathbf{\frac{25}{2}}$$

9.

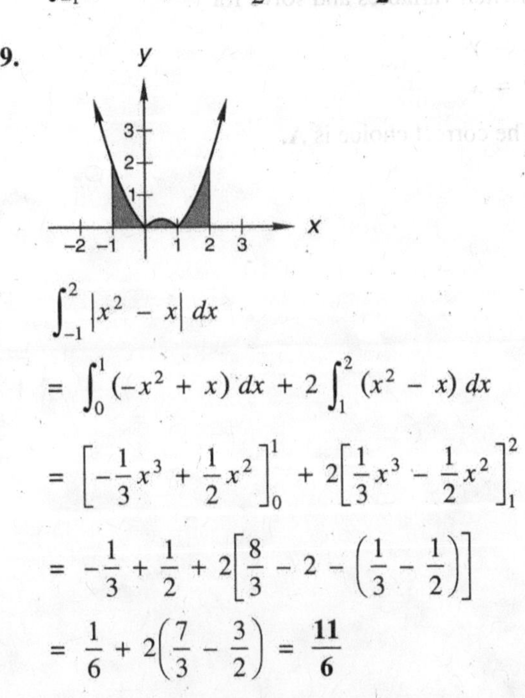

$$\int_{-1}^2 |x^2 - x|\,dx$$

$$= \int_0^1 (-x^2 + x)\,dx + 2\int_1^2 (x^2 - x)\,dx$$

$$= \left[-\frac{1}{3}x^3 + \frac{1}{2}x^2\right]_0^1 + 2\left[\frac{1}{3}x^3 - \frac{1}{2}x^2\right]_1^2$$

$$= -\frac{1}{3} + \frac{1}{2} + 2\left[\frac{8}{3} - 2 - \left(\frac{1}{3} - \frac{1}{2}\right)\right]$$

$$= \frac{1}{6} + 2\left(\frac{7}{3} - \frac{3}{2}\right) = \mathbf{\frac{11}{6}}$$

10.

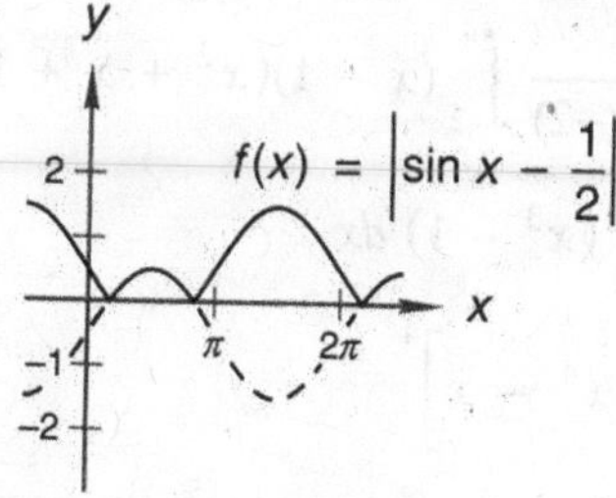

$f'(x) = 0$

$\cos x = 0$

$x = \frac{\pi}{2}, \frac{3\pi}{2}, \frac{5\pi}{2}, \ldots$

$\sin x = \frac{1}{2}$

$x = \frac{\pi}{6}, \frac{5\pi}{6}, \ldots$

$f\left(\frac{\pi}{6}\right) = 0;\; f\left(\frac{5\pi}{6}\right) = 0;\; f\left(\frac{\pi}{2}\right) = \frac{1}{2};$

$f\left(\frac{3\pi}{2}\right) = \frac{3}{2};\; f\left(\frac{5\pi}{2}\right) = \frac{1}{2}$

Maximum: $\mathbf{\frac{3}{2}}$

11. From the given information, the maximum or minimum values of $f(|x|)$ cannot be determined. The max of $|f(x)|$ is 15, and the minimum of $|f(x)|$ is zero.

The correct choice is **D.**

12. (a) $T = \frac{b-a}{2n}(y_0 + 2y_1 + 2y_2 + 2y_3 + y_4)$

$= \frac{2}{8}\left[0 + 2\left(\frac{1}{2}\right)^4 + 2(1)^4 + 2\left(\frac{3}{2}\right)^4 + 2^4\right]$

$= \frac{1}{4}\left(\frac{113}{4}\right) = \mathbf{\frac{113}{16}} = \mathbf{7.0625}$

(b) $\int_0^2 x^4\,dx = \left[\frac{1}{5}x^5\right]_0^2 = \mathbf{\frac{32}{5}} = \mathbf{6.4}$

(c) $f(x) = x^4 \qquad f''(x) = 12x^2$

$\max|f''(x)| = 48$

$E_{\max} = \frac{(2-0)^3}{12(4)^2}(48) = \frac{8}{4} = \mathbf{2}$

(d) $\frac{2^3}{12n^2}(48) < 10^{-3}$

$\frac{32}{n^2} < 10^{-3}$

$\frac{1}{n^2} < 3.125 \times 10^{-5}$

$n^2 > 32{,}000$

$n > 178.8854$

The required number of trapezoids is **179.**

13. $T = \frac{b-a}{2n}(y_0 + 2y_1 + 2y_2 + 2y_3 + 2y_4 + 2y_5 + y_6)$

$= \frac{1}{12}(1 + 2e^{-1/36} + 2e^{-1/9} + 2e^{-1/4} + 2e^{-4/9} + 2e^{-25/36} + e^{-1})$

$\approx \mathbf{0.7451}$

14.

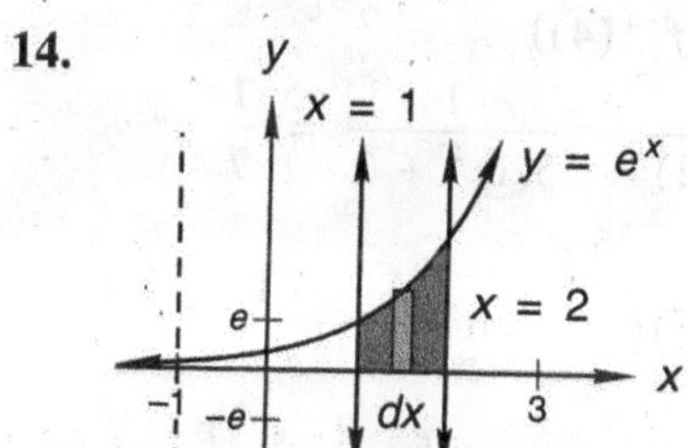

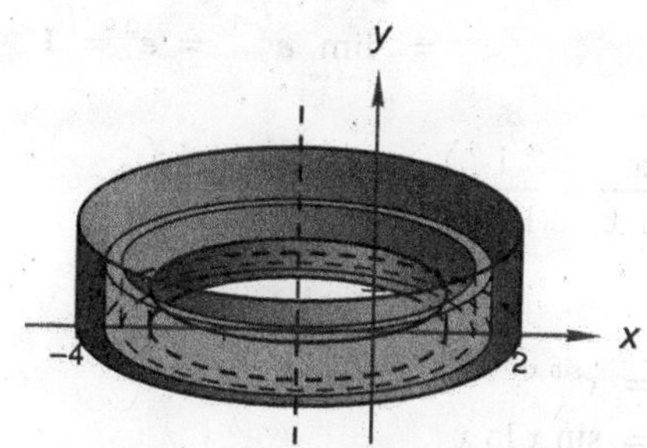

$V = 2\pi\int_1^2 (1 + x)e^x\,dx$

$= 2\pi\int_1^2 (e^x + xe^x)\,dx$

$u = x \quad du = dx \quad v = e^x \quad dv = e^x\,dx$

$V = 2\pi\left[e^x + xe^x - \int e^x\right]_1^2$

$= 2\pi[xe^x]_1^2 = \mathbf{2\pi(2e^2 - e)\ units^3}$

15. Since $f(1) = -1$ and $f(2) = 8$, there must be a zero between $x = 1$ and $x = 2$; so set $x_1 = 1.5$. Assign `Y1=X³+2X-4` and `Y2=nDeriv(Y1,X,X)`.

```
1.5→X
                1.5
X-(Y1/Y2)→X
         1.22857146
         1.180849971
         1.179510055
         1.179509025
         1.179509025
```

The zero is approximately **1.179509025.**

16. $f(x) = x^5 + 2x + 1 \qquad f'(x) = 5x^4 + 2$

By inspection $x = 1$ is a solution to $x^5 + 2x + 1 = 4$.

$$(f^{-1})'(4) = \frac{1}{f'(f^{-1}(4))}$$
$$= \frac{1}{f'(1)} = \frac{1}{5(1)^4 + 2} = \mathbf{\frac{1}{7}}$$

17. $$\lim_{x\to\infty} \left[x(e^{1/x} - 1)\right] = \lim_{x\to\infty} \frac{e^{x^{-1}} - 1}{x^{-1}}$$
$$= \lim_{x\to\infty} \frac{e^{x^{-1}}(-x^{-2})}{-x^{-2}}$$
$$= \lim_{x\to\infty} e^{x^{-1}} = e^0 = \mathbf{1}$$

18. $$\lim_{x\to 1}\left(\frac{x}{\ln x} - \frac{1}{\ln x}\right) = \lim_{x\to 1}\left(\frac{x-1}{\ln x}\right)$$
$$= \lim_{x\to 1} x = \mathbf{1}$$

19. $$y = x^{\sin x}$$
$$\ln y = \sin x \ln x$$
$$\frac{1}{y}\frac{dy}{dx} = \frac{\sin x}{x} + \cos x \ln x$$
$$\frac{dy}{dx} = \mathbf{x^{\sin x}\left(\frac{\sin x}{x} + \cos x \ln x\right)}$$

20. $$\frac{dy}{dx} = y \cos x$$
$$\frac{1}{y}\,dy = \cos x\,dx$$
$$\ln|y| = \sin x + C$$
$$\ln e = \sin\frac{\pi}{2} + C$$
$$1 = 1 + C$$
$$C = 0$$
$$\mathbf{\ln|y| = \sin x} \text{ or}$$
$$\mathbf{|y| = e^{\sin x}}$$

21. $$f(c) = \frac{1}{4 - (-2)}\int_{-2}^{4}(x - 1)(x^2 + x + 1)\,dx$$
$$c^3 - 1 = \frac{1}{6}\int_{-2}^{4}(x^3 - 1)\,dx$$
$$c^3 - 1 = \frac{1}{6}\left[\frac{1}{4}x^4 - x\right]_{-2}^{4}$$
$$c^3 - 1 = \frac{1}{6}[64 - 4 - (4 + 2)]$$
$$c^3 - 1 = 9$$
$$c = \mathbf{\sqrt[3]{10}}$$

22. $$\int \frac{1}{\sqrt{9 - x^2}}\,dx = \mathbf{\arcsin\frac{x}{3} + C}$$

23. $$\lim_{x\to 0}\frac{\sin(2x)}{x} = \lim_{x\to 0} 2\cos(2x) = 2$$
$$\lim_{x\to 1}\frac{x^3 - 1}{x - 1} = \lim_{x\to 1}\frac{3x^2}{1} = 3$$
$$\lim_{x\to 0}\frac{\sqrt{1 + x} - 1}{x} = \lim_{x\to 0}\frac{1}{2}(1 + x)^{-1/2} = \frac{1}{2}$$
$$\lim_{x\to 0}\frac{\sqrt{x^2}}{x} = \lim_{x\to 0}\frac{|x|}{x}$$

From the left this limit is –1, and from the right it is +1. So the limit does not exist.

The correct choice is **D.**

24. $$f(0) = \lim_{x\to 0} f(x)$$
$$= \lim_{x\to 0}\frac{x - \sin(2x)}{\sin x}$$
$$= \lim_{x\to 0}\frac{1 - 2\cos(2x)}{\cos x}$$
$$= -1$$

Define $\mathbf{f(0) = -1}$.

25. $u = f(x) \quad du = f'(x)\,dx \quad v = e^x \quad dv = e^x\,dx$

$$\int f(x)e^x\,dx = f(x)e^x - \int f'(x)e^x\,dx$$
$$= f(x)e^x - \int 2xe^x\,dx$$
$$f'(x) = 2x$$
$$f(x) = \mathbf{x^2 + C}$$

Problem Set 98

1. $\frac{dl}{dt} = 2\ \frac{\text{cm}}{\text{s}}$ $\quad \frac{dw}{dt} = -1\ \frac{\text{cm}}{\text{s}}$

$l = 12$ cm $\quad w = 10$ cm

$$A = lw$$

$$\frac{dA}{dt} = l\frac{dw}{dt} + w\frac{dl}{dt}$$

$$\frac{dA}{dt} = 12(-1) + 10(2) = \mathbf{8\ \frac{cm^2}{s}}$$

2. 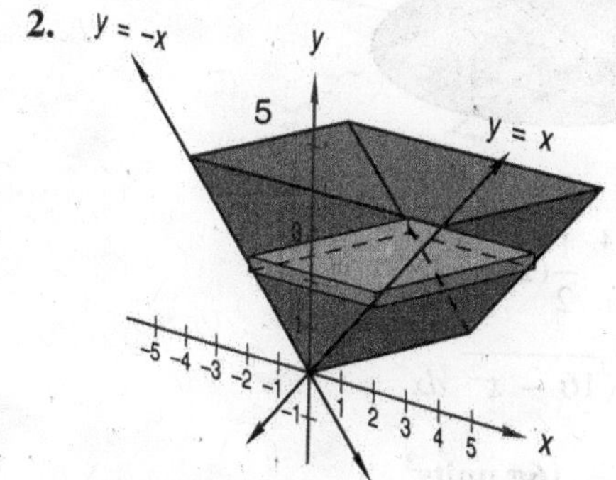

(a) $F = 600\int_{y=0}^{y=4}(4-y)2y\,dy$

$$= 1200\int_0^4 (4y - y^2)\,dy$$

$$= 1200\left[2y^2 - \frac{1}{3}y^3\right]_0^4$$

$$= 1200\left(32 - \frac{64}{3}\right) = \mathbf{12{,}800\ newtons}$$

(b) $W = 600\int_0^4 (4-y)2y(5)\,dy$

$$= 6000\int_0^4 (4y - y^2)\,dy$$

$$= 6000\left[2y^2 - \frac{1}{3}y^3\right]_0^4$$

$$= 6000\left(32 - \frac{64}{3}\right) = \mathbf{64{,}000\ joules}$$

3. (a) $x(t) = (4t-1)(t-1)^2$

$$v(t) = (4t-1)[2(t-1)] + (t-1)^2(4)$$

$$v(t) = 2(t-1)[(4t-1) + 2(t-1)]$$

$$v(t) = 6(t-1)(2t-1)$$

$$0 = 6(t-1)(2t-1)$$

$$t = \mathbf{\frac{1}{2}, 1}$$

(b) 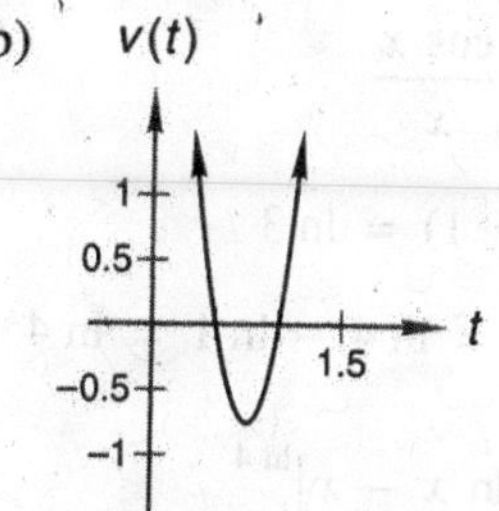

From the graph, the particle is moving left when $\mathbf{\frac{1}{2} < t < 1}$.

(c) The particle reverses direction when $v(t)$ changes sign. This happens **2 times,** at $t = \frac{1}{2}$ and at $t = 1$.

(d) $v'(t) = 6(t-1)(2) + 6(2t-1)$

$$v'(t) = 12t - 12 + 12t - 6$$

$$v'(t) = 24t - 18$$

$$0 = 24t - 18$$

$$t = \mathbf{\frac{3}{4}}$$

4. $a(t) = \pi\sin(\pi t)$

$$v(t) = -\cos(\pi t) + C$$

$$0 = -1 + C$$

$$C = 1$$

$$\text{Average velocity} = \frac{1}{1-0}\int_0^1 [-\cos(\pi t) + 1]\,dt$$

$$= \left[-\frac{1}{\pi}\sin(\pi t) + t\right]_0^1$$

$$= \mathbf{1\ linear\ unit/time\ unit}$$

5. (a) $\frac{d}{dx}\int_1^x t^2\,dt = \frac{d}{dx}\left[\frac{1}{3}t^3\right]_1^x$

$$= \frac{d}{dx}\left[\frac{1}{3}x^3 - \frac{1}{3}\right] = \mathbf{x^2}$$

(b) $\frac{d}{dx}\int_1^x t^2\,dt = \mathbf{x^2}$

6. (a) $\frac{d}{dx}\int_x^3 \sin t\,dt = \frac{d}{dx}[-\cos t]_x^3$

$$= \frac{d}{dx}(-\cos 3 + \cos x)$$

$$= \mathbf{-\sin x}$$

(b) $\frac{d}{dx}\int_x^3 \sin t\,dt = \mathbf{-\sin x}$

7. $\frac{d}{dx}\int_{18}^x e^{-t^2}\,dt = \mathbf{e^{-x^2}}$

8. $\dfrac{d}{dx}\displaystyle\int_x^5 \frac{\cos t}{t}\,dt = -\dfrac{\cos x}{x}$

9. $\ln 3 + \ln 1 = \ln(3 \cdot 1) = \ln 3$

$$\int_1^4 \frac{1}{x}\,dx = [\ln x]_1^4 = \ln 4 - \ln 1 = \ln 4$$

$$\int_1^{\ln 4} \ln x\,dx = [x \ln x - x]_1^{\ln 4}$$

$$= \ln 4 \ln(\ln 4) - \ln 4 - (-1)$$

$$= \ln 4\,[\ln(\ln 4) - 1] + 1$$

$$\int_1^4 \ln x\,dx = [x \ln x - x]_1^4$$

$$= 4 \ln 4 - 4 - (-1) = 4 \ln 4 - 3$$

The correct choice is **B.**

10.

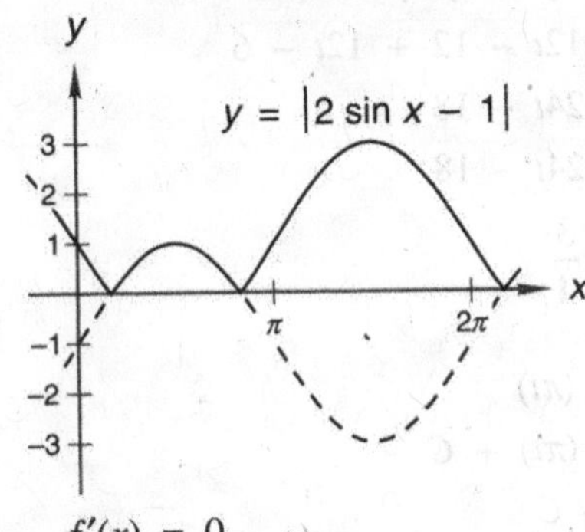

$$f'(x) = 0$$

$$2 \cos x = 0$$

$$x = \frac{\pi}{2}, \frac{3\pi}{2}, \frac{5\pi}{2}, \ldots$$

$$2 \sin x = 1$$

$$\sin x = \frac{1}{2}$$

$$x = \frac{\pi}{6}, \frac{5\pi}{6}, \ldots$$

$$f\left(\frac{\pi}{6}\right) = 0;\; f\left(\frac{5\pi}{6}\right) = 0;\; f\left(\frac{\pi}{2}\right) = 1;$$

$$f\left(\frac{3\pi}{2}\right) = 3;\; f\left(\frac{5\pi}{2}\right) = 1$$

Maximum: **3**

11.

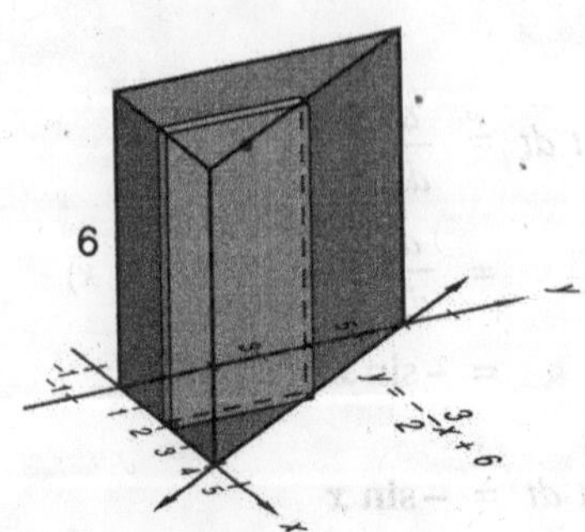

$$V = \int_0^4 6\left(-\frac{3}{2}x + 6\right) dx = 6\left[-\frac{3}{4}x^2 + 6x\right]_0^4$$

$$= 6(-12 + 24) = \mathbf{72\ units^3}$$

12.

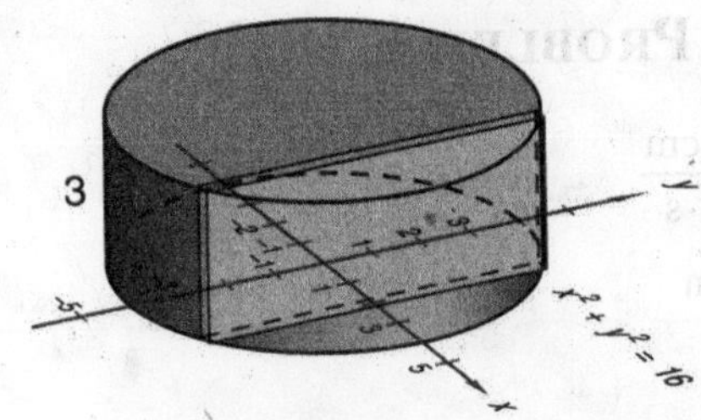

$$V = \pi r^2 h = \pi(4)^2(3) = \mathbf{48\pi\ units^3}$$

13.

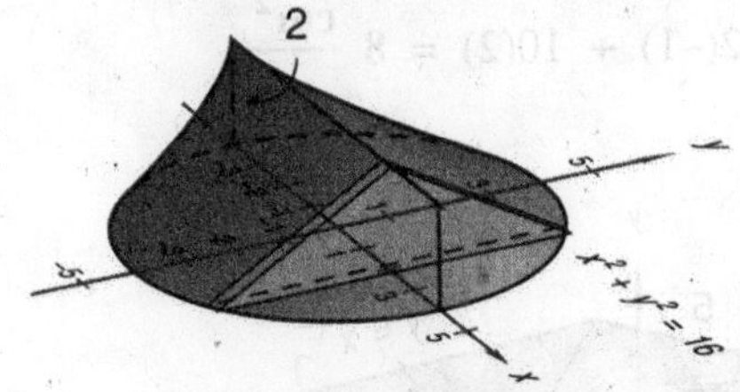

$$V = 2\int_{x=0}^{x=4} \frac{1}{2}(2y)2\,dx$$

$$= 4\int_0^4 \sqrt{16 - x^2}\,dx$$

$$= 4(4\pi) = \mathbf{16\pi\ units^3}$$

14.

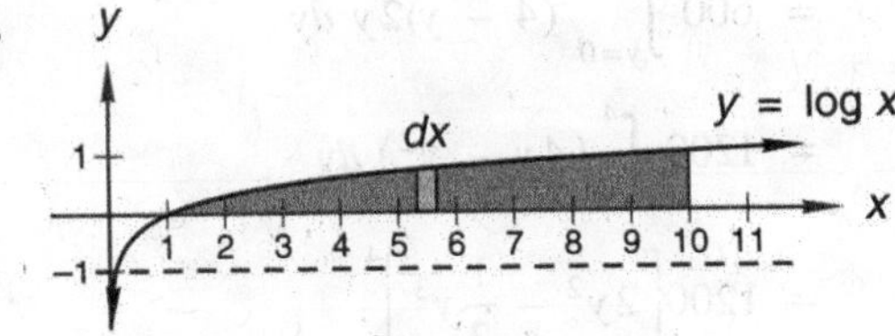

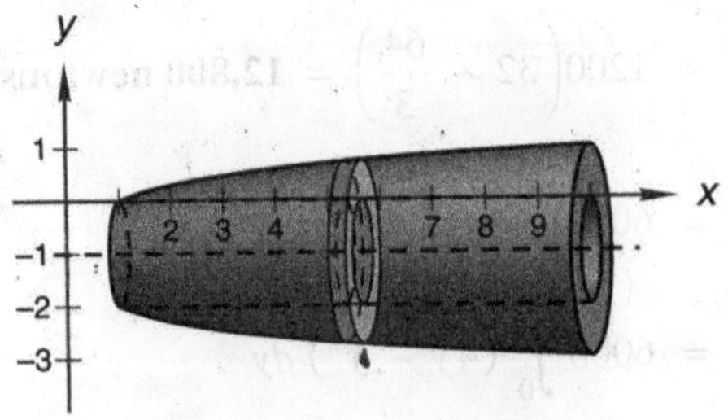

$$V = \pi\int_1^{10} [(1 + \log x)^2 - 1]\,dx$$

$$= \pi\int_1^{10} (2 \log x + \log^2 x)\,dx$$

$$= \pi\int_1^{10} (\log x^2 + \log^2 x)\,dx$$

15. (a) $T = \dfrac{b - a}{2n}(y_0 + 2y_1 + 2y_2 + 2y_3 + y_4)$

$$= \frac{1}{8}\left[1 + 2\left(\frac{4}{5}\right) + 2\left(\frac{2}{3}\right) + 2\left(\frac{4}{7}\right) + \frac{1}{2}\right]$$

$$= \frac{1}{8}\left(\frac{1171}{210}\right) = \mathbf{\frac{1171}{1680}} \approx \mathbf{0.6970}$$

(b) $\int_1^2 \frac{1}{x}\,dx = \mathbf{\ln 2}$

(c) $f(x) = x^{-1} \quad f'(x) = -x^{-2} \quad f''(x) = 2x^{-3}$

$\max|f''(x)| = 2$

$E_{\max} = \frac{(2-1)^3}{12(4)^2}(2) = \frac{2}{12(16)} = \mathbf{\frac{1}{96}}$

(d) $\frac{1}{12n^2}(2) < 10^{-3}$

$\frac{1}{6n^2} < 10^{-3}$

$\frac{1}{n^2} < 6 \times 10^{-3}$

$n^2 > \frac{1}{0.006}$

$n > 12.9099$

The required number of trapezoids is **13.**

16. $T = \frac{b-a}{2n}(y_0 + 2y_1 + 2y_2 + 2y_3 + 2y_4 + 2y_5 + y_6)$

$= \frac{1}{12}(1 + 2e^{1/36} + 2e^{1/9} + 2e^{1/4} + 2e^{4/9} + 2e^{25/36} + e)$

$\approx \mathbf{1.4752}$

17. $\frac{dy}{dx} = \sin(2x)$

$dy = \sin(2x)\,dx$

$\mathbf{y = -\frac{1}{2}\cos(2x) + C}$

18. $f(x) = \sin x$ is odd; $g(x) = e^{x^2}$ is even:

(a) $f + g$ = odd + even = **neither**

(b) f^2 = (odd)(odd) = **even**

(c) $g \circ f$ = even ∘ odd = **even**

(d) fg = (odd)(even) = **odd**

19. $\log|f(x)| = \log|x^2+1| + \log|\sin x|$

$\ln|f(x)| = \ln|x^2+1| + \ln|\sin x|$

$\frac{f'(x)}{f(x)} = \frac{2x}{x^2+1} + \frac{\cos x}{\sin x}$

$\mathbf{\frac{f'(x)}{f(x)} = \frac{2x}{x^2+1} + \cot x}$

20. **(–1, 5)**

21. $\frac{d}{dx}\left[\tan(\sin x) + 3^{x^2}\right] + \int \frac{5}{1+x^2}\,dx$

$= \mathbf{\sec^2(\sin x)\cos x + 2x(\ln 3)3^{x^2}}$

$\mathbf{+\ 5\arctan x + C}$

22. $y = \sin(xy)$

$\frac{dy}{dx} = \cos(xy)\left(x\frac{dy}{dx} + y\right)$

$\frac{dy}{dx} = x\cos(xy)\frac{dy}{dx} + y\cos(xy)$

$-y\cos(xy) = \frac{dy}{dx}[x\cos(xy) - 1]$

$\frac{dy}{dx} = \frac{-y\cos(xy)}{x\cos(xy) - 1}$

$\frac{dy}{dx} = y\left[\frac{\cos(xy)}{1 - x\cos(xy)}\right]$

$\frac{dy}{dx} = y\left[\frac{1}{\frac{1}{\cos(xy)} - x}\right]$

$\mathbf{\frac{dy}{dx} = \frac{y}{\sec(xy) - x}}$

23. $\int_0^{\pi/12} \sin^2(2x)\,dx$

$= \int_0^{\pi/12}\left[\frac{1}{2} - \frac{1}{2}\cos(4x)\right]dx$

$= \left[\frac{1}{2}x - \frac{1}{8}\sin(4x)\right]_0^{\pi/12}$

$= \frac{\pi}{24} - \frac{1}{8}\left(\frac{\sqrt{3}}{2}\right) = \mathbf{\frac{2\pi - 3\sqrt{3}}{48}} \approx \mathbf{0.0226}$

24. $\lim_{x\to1^-} f(x) = f(1)$

$3 = a + b$

$\lim_{x\to1^-} f'(x) = f'(1)$

$1 = 2a + b$

$2a + b - (a + b) = 1 - 3$

$\mathbf{a = -2}$

$3 = -2 + b$

$\mathbf{5 = b}$

25. 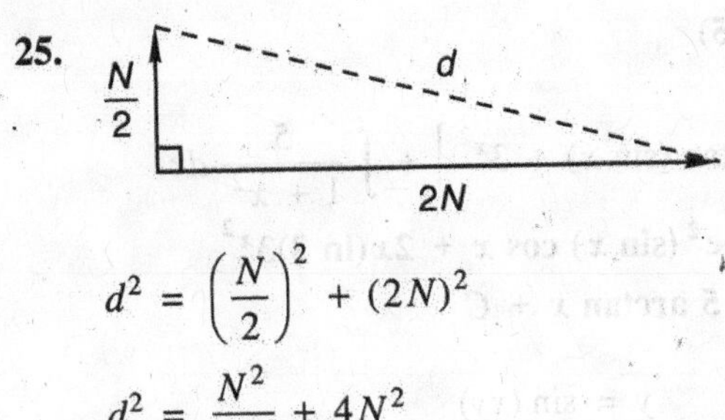

$$d^2 = \left(\frac{N}{2}\right)^2 + (2N)^2$$

$$d^2 = \frac{N^2}{4} + 4N^2$$

$$d^2 = \frac{17}{4}N^2$$

$$d = \mathbf{\frac{\sqrt{17}}{2}N \text{ miles}}$$

PROBLEM SET 99

1. 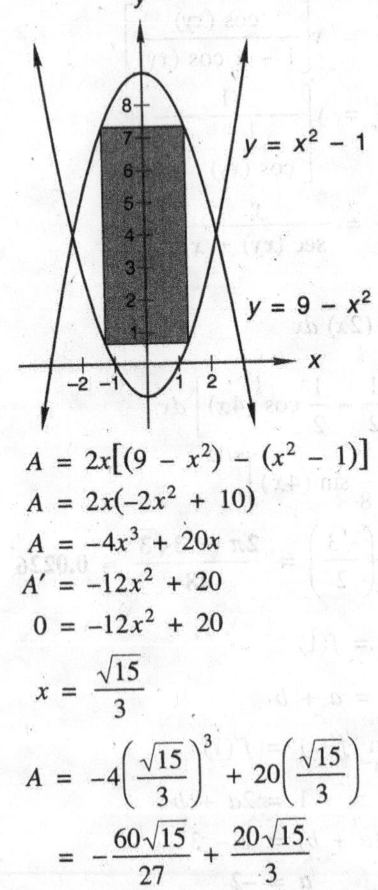

$$A = 2x[(9 - x^2) - (x^2 - 1)]$$
$$A = 2x(-2x^2 + 10)$$
$$A = -4x^3 + 20x$$
$$A' = -12x^2 + 20$$
$$0 = -12x^2 + 20$$
$$x = \frac{\sqrt{15}}{3}$$
$$A = -4\left(\frac{\sqrt{15}}{3}\right)^3 + 20\left(\frac{\sqrt{15}}{3}\right)$$
$$= -\frac{60\sqrt{15}}{27} + \frac{20\sqrt{15}}{3}$$
$$= \mathbf{\frac{40\sqrt{15}}{9} \text{ units}^2}$$

2. $r = 25 \text{ cm} \quad dr = 0.01 \text{ cm}$

$$V = \frac{4}{3}\pi r^3$$
$$dV = 4\pi r^2\, dr$$
$$dV = 4\pi(25)^2(0.01) = \mathbf{25\pi \text{ cm}^3}$$

3. $p(x) = (750x - 2x^2) - (x^2 - 99x + 4000)$

$$dp = [(750 - 4x) - (2x - 99)]\, dx$$
$$\approx \{[750 - 4(125)] - [2(125) - 99]\}(5)$$
$$= \mathbf{\$495}$$

4. 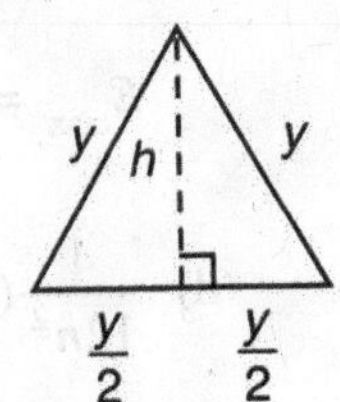

$$h^2 = y^2 - \frac{y^2}{4}$$
$$h = \frac{y\sqrt{3}}{2}$$
$$V = \int_{x=0}^{x=2} \frac{1}{2}y\left(\frac{y\sqrt{3}}{2}\right) dx$$
$$= \frac{\sqrt{3}}{4}\int_0^2 (-2x + 4)^2\, dx$$
$$= -\frac{\sqrt{3}}{8}\left(\frac{1}{3}\right)\left[(-2x + 4)^3\right]_0^2$$
$$= \frac{-\sqrt{3}}{24}(0 - 64)$$
$$= \mathbf{\frac{8\sqrt{3}}{3} \text{ units}^3 \approx 4.6188 \text{ units}^3}$$

5. $v(t) = \frac{t + 1}{t}$

$$v(t) = 1 + \frac{1}{t}$$
$$x(t) = t + \ln t + C$$
$$5 = 3 + \ln 3 + C$$
$$C = 2 - \ln 3$$
$$\mathbf{x(t) = t + \ln t + 2 - \ln 3}$$

6. $W = \int_0^6 \frac{1}{2}x^2\, dx = \left[\frac{1}{6}x^3\right]_0^6 = \mathbf{36 \text{ joules}}$

7. $\frac{d}{dx}\int_2^x e^{t^3}\, dt = \mathbf{e^{x^3}}$

8. $\frac{d}{dx}\int_x^2 e^{1/t}\, dt = \mathbf{-e^{1/x}}$

9.

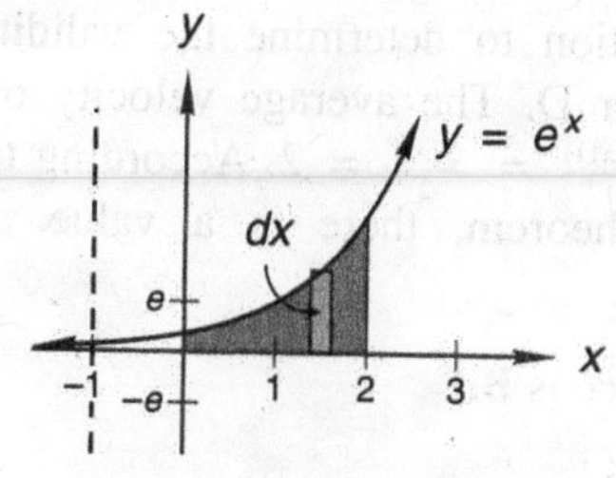

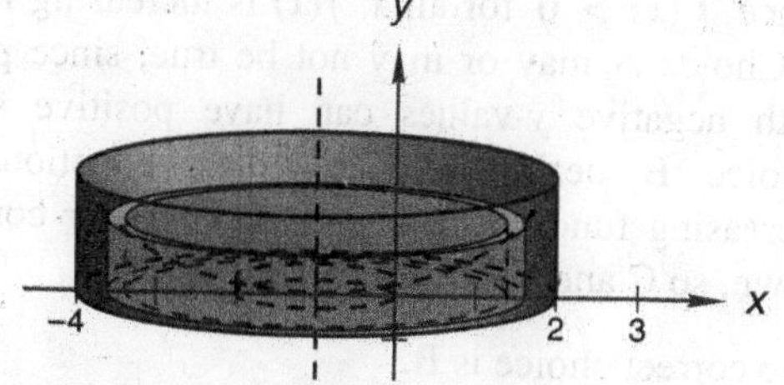

$$V = 2\pi \int_0^2 (1 + x)e^x \, dx$$

$$= 2\pi \int_0^2 (e^x + xe^x) \, dx$$

$u = x \quad du = dx \quad v = e^x \quad dv = e^x \, dx$

$$V = 2\pi\left[e^x + xe^x - e^x\right]_0^2 = \mathbf{4\pi e^2 \text{ units}^3}$$

10. $\int (\sin^2 x + \sin^3 x) \, dx$

$$= \int \left[\frac{1}{2} - \frac{1}{2}\cos(2x) + \sin x\,(1 - \cos^2 x)\right] dx$$

$$= \int \left[\frac{1}{2} - \frac{1}{2}\cos(2x) + \sin x - \cos^2 x \sin x\right] dx$$

$$= \mathbf{\frac{1}{2}x - \frac{1}{4}\sin(2x) - \cos x + \frac{1}{3}\cos^3 x + C}$$

11. $T = \dfrac{b - a}{2n}(y_0 + 2y_1 + 2y_2 + 2y_3 + 2y_4 + 2y_5 + y_6)$

$$= \frac{3}{12}\left(1 + \frac{4}{3} + 1 + \frac{4}{5} + \frac{2}{3} + \frac{4}{7} + \frac{1}{4}\right)$$

$$= \frac{1}{4}\left(\frac{787}{140}\right) = \mathbf{\frac{787}{560} \text{ units}^2} \approx \mathbf{1.4054 \text{ units}^2}$$

12. $\lim_{h \to 0} \dfrac{f(x + h) - f(x - h)}{2h} = \dfrac{d}{dx}f(x)$

$$= \frac{d}{dx}\sqrt{x} = \mathbf{\frac{1}{2\sqrt{x}}}$$

13. $f(x) = x^5 + x \qquad f'(x) = 5x^4 + 1$

By inspection $x = 1$ is a solution to $x^5 + x = 2$.

$$(f^{-1})'(2) = \frac{1}{f'(f^{-1}(2))}$$

$$= \frac{1}{f'(1)} = \frac{1}{5(1)^4 + 1} = \mathbf{\frac{1}{6}}$$

14. The absolute maximum value of $|f(x)|$ is $|-6|$, or **6**.

15. $\int_2^4 |x + 2| \, dx = \int_2^4 (x + 2) \, dx$

$$= \left[\frac{1}{2}x^2 + 2x\right]_2^4$$

$$= 8 + 8 - (2 + 4) = \mathbf{10}$$

16. $\int_{-1}^4 |x^2 + 4| \, dx = \int_{-1}^4 (x^2 + 4) \, dx$

$$= \left[\frac{1}{3}x^3 + 4x\right]_{-1}^4$$

$$= \frac{64}{3} + 16 - \left(-\frac{1}{3} - 4\right)$$

$$= \mathbf{\frac{125}{3}}$$

17.

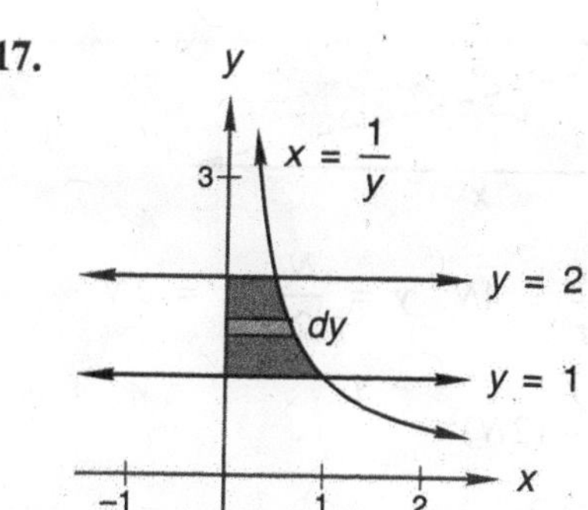

$$A = \int_{y=1}^{y=2} x \, dy = \mathbf{\int_1^2 \frac{1}{y} \, dy}$$

18. $\dfrac{dy}{dx} = e^{2x - 3y}$

$$\frac{dy}{dx} = \frac{e^{2x}}{e^{3y}}$$

$$e^{3y} \, dy = e^{2x} \, dx$$

$$\frac{1}{3}e^{3y} = \frac{1}{2}e^{2x} + C$$

$$e^{3y} = \frac{3}{2}e^{2x} + C$$

$$3y = \ln\left(\frac{3}{2}e^{2x} + C\right)$$

$$\mathbf{y = \frac{1}{3}\ln\left(\frac{3}{2}e^{2x} + C\right)}$$

19. $\lim_{x \to 2} [f(x)]^2 g(x) = \left[\lim_{x \to 2} f(x)\right]^2 \cdot \left[\lim_{x \to 2} g(x)\right]$

$= 4^2(-1) = \mathbf{-16}$

20. **(–4, –2)**

21.

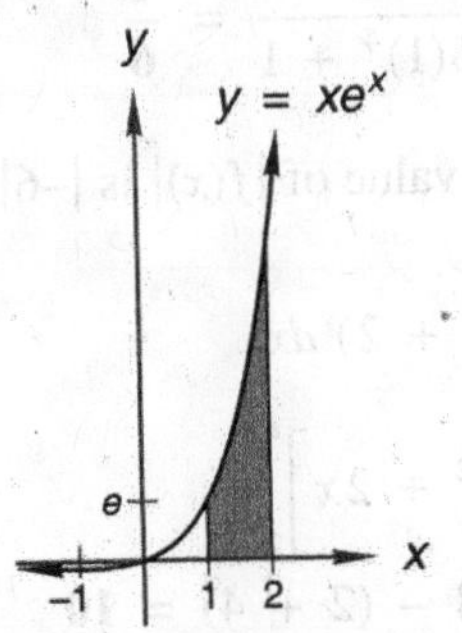

$u = x \quad du = dx \quad v = e^x \quad dv = e^x\, dx$

$$A = \int_1^2 xe^x\, dx$$

$$= \left[xe^x - \int e^x\, dx\right]_1^2$$

$$= \left[xe^x - e^x\right]_1^2$$

$$= 2e^2 - e^2 - (e - e) = \mathbf{e^2\ units^2}$$

22.

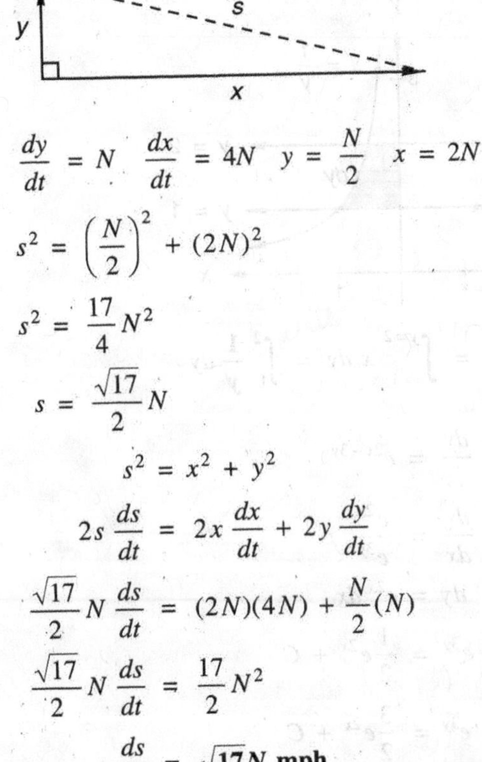

$\frac{dy}{dt} = N \quad \frac{dx}{dt} = 4N \quad y = \frac{N}{2} \quad x = 2N$

$$s^2 = \left(\frac{N}{2}\right)^2 + (2N)^2$$

$$s^2 = \frac{17}{4}N^2$$

$$s = \frac{\sqrt{17}}{2}N$$

$$s^2 = x^2 + y^2$$

$$2s\frac{ds}{dt} = 2x\frac{dx}{dt} + 2y\frac{dy}{dt}$$

$$\frac{\sqrt{17}}{2}N\frac{ds}{dt} = (2N)(4N) + \frac{N}{2}(N)$$

$$\frac{\sqrt{17}}{2}N\frac{ds}{dt} = \frac{17}{2}N^2$$

$$\frac{ds}{dt} = \mathbf{\sqrt{17}N\ mph}$$

23. Not all characteristics of the velocity on the interval [1, 3] are known. It could change direction on the interval or always be positive. There is not enough information to determine the validity of choices A, C, or D. The average velocity of the particle is $\frac{x(3) - x(1)}{3 - 1} = \frac{5 - 1}{2} = 2$. According to the Mean Value Theorem, there is a value c for which $v(c) = 2$.

The correct choice is **B.**

24. Since $f'(x) > 0$ for all x, $f(x)$ is increasing for all x. Choice A may or may not be true, since points with negative y-values can have positive slope. Choice B defines an increasing function. An increasing function can be concave up or concave down, so C and D are not necessarily true.

The correct choice is **B.**

25. The statement expresses the definition of continuity. Choices A and B may or may not be true for $f(x)$. Continuity does not guarantee differentiability, so choice C is not necessarily true.

The correct choice is **D.**

PROBLEM SET 100

1.

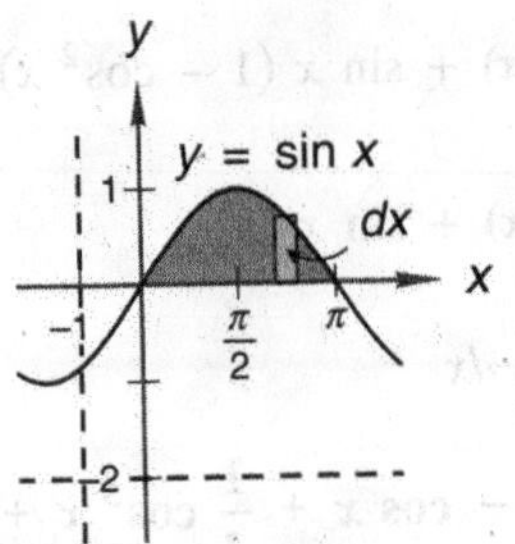

(a)

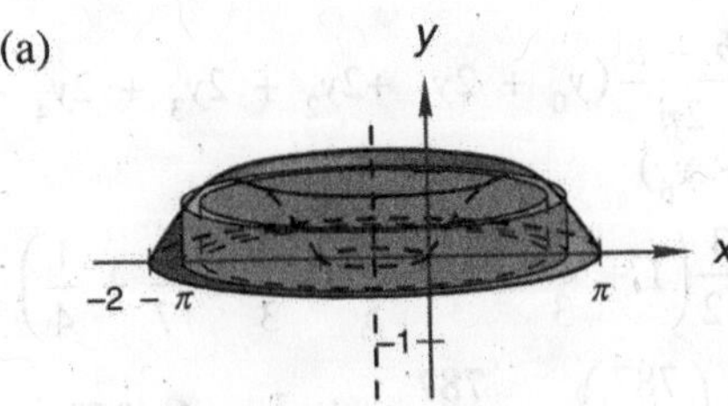

$$V = 2\pi \int_0^\pi (1 + x) \sin x\, dx$$

$$= 2\pi \int_0^\pi (\sin x + x \sin x)\, dx$$

$u = x \quad du = dx \quad v = -\cos x \quad dv = \sin x\, dx$

$$V = 2\pi\left[-\cos x - x \cos x - \int -\cos x\, dx\right]_0^\pi$$

$$= 2\pi[-\cos x - x\cos x + \sin x]_0^\pi$$

$$= 2\pi[1 + \pi + 0 - (-1 - 0 + 0)]$$

$$= \mathbf{2\pi(2 + \pi)\ units^3}$$

(b)

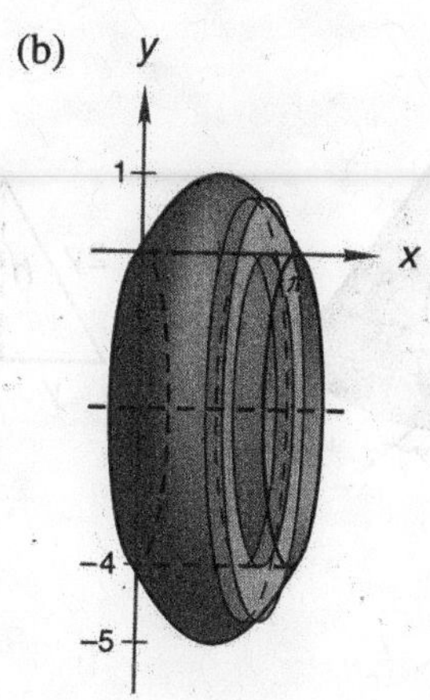

$$V = \pi \int_0^{\pi} [(2 + \sin x)^2 - (2)^2]\, dx$$

$$= \pi \int_0^{\pi} (4 \sin x + \sin^2 x)\, dx$$

$$= \pi \int_0^{\pi} \left[4 \sin x + \frac{1}{2} - \frac{1}{2} \cos (2x)\right] dx$$

$$= \pi\left[-4 \cos x + \frac{1}{2}x - \frac{1}{4} \sin (2x)\right]_0^{\pi}$$

$$= \pi\left[4 + \frac{\pi}{2} - 0 - (-4 + 0 - 0)\right]$$

$$= \pi\left(\mathbf{8} + \frac{\boldsymbol{\pi}}{\mathbf{2}}\right) \textbf{ units}^3$$

2. $f(c) = \dfrac{1}{\frac{\pi}{2}} \displaystyle\int_{-\pi/4}^{\pi/4} \tan x\, dx$

$$\tan c = \frac{2}{\pi}\left[-\ln |\cos x|\right]_{-\pi/4}^{\pi/4}$$

$$\tan c = \frac{2}{\pi}\left(-\ln \frac{\sqrt{2}}{2} + \ln \frac{\sqrt{2}}{2}\right)$$

$$\tan c = 0$$

$$c = \mathbf{0}$$

3. $f(x) = x^3 + 2x + 1 \qquad f'(x) = 3x^2 + 2$

$$\text{slope} = \frac{f(3) - f(1)}{3 - 1} = \frac{34 - 4}{2} = \mathbf{15}$$

$$f'(c) = 15$$

$$3c^2 + 2 = 15$$

$$3c^2 = 13$$

$$c^2 = \frac{13}{3}$$

$$c = \frac{\sqrt{39}}{3} \approx \mathbf{2.0817}$$

4. $T = \dfrac{b - a}{2n}(y_0 + 2y_1 + 2y_2 + 2y_3 + 2y_4 + 2y_5 + y_6)$

$$= \frac{2}{12}\left[1 + 2\left(\frac{1}{\sqrt{\frac{10}{9}}}\right) + 2\left(\frac{1}{\sqrt{\frac{13}{9}}}\right) + 2\left(\frac{1}{\sqrt{2}}\right) + 2\left(\frac{1}{\sqrt{\frac{25}{9}}}\right) + 2\left(\frac{1}{\sqrt{\frac{34}{9}}}\right) + \frac{1}{\sqrt{5}}\right]$$

$$\approx \mathbf{1.4420}$$

5. (a) Maximum of $|f(x)| = |-10| = \mathbf{10.}$

(b) Maximum of $f(|x|)$ **cannot be determined** from the given information.

(c) Minimum of $|f(x)|$ will be **zero.**

(d) Minimum of $f(|x|)$ **cannot be determined** from the given information.

6. $\displaystyle\lim_{x\to 0^+} (\ln x \tan x) = \lim_{x\to 0^+} \left(\frac{\ln x}{\cot x}\right)$

$$= \lim_{x\to 0^+} \frac{\frac{1}{x}}{-\csc^2 x}$$

$$= \lim_{x\to 0^+} -\frac{\sin^2 x}{x}$$

$$= \lim_{x\to 0^+} -\frac{2 \sin x \cos x}{1}$$

$$= \mathbf{0}$$

7. $\displaystyle\lim_{h\to 0} \frac{f(x + h) - f(x - h)}{2h} = f'(x)$

$$= \frac{d}{dx}(x^2)$$

$$= \mathbf{2x}$$

8.
$$y' = \sqrt{x}y^2$$
$$\frac{dy}{dx} = \sqrt{x}y^2$$
$$y^{-2}\,dy = \sqrt{x}\,dx$$
$$-y^{-1} = \frac{2}{3}x^{3/2} + C$$
$$\frac{1}{y} = C - \frac{2}{3}x^{3/2}$$
$$y = \frac{1}{C - \frac{2}{3}x^{3/2}}$$
$$\mathbf{y = \frac{3}{C - 2x^{3/2}}}$$

9. $\int \tan x\,dx = \int \frac{\sin x}{\cos x}\,dx$
$$= \mathbf{-\ln|\cos x| + C}$$
$$= \mathbf{\ln|\sec x| + C}$$

10. $\int \cot x\,dx = \int \frac{\cos x}{\sin x}\,dx$
$$= \mathbf{\ln|\sin x| + C}$$

11. $\int \sec x\,dx = \int \frac{\sec x\,(\sec x + \tan x)}{\sec x + \tan x}\,dx$
$$= \mathbf{\ln|\sec x + \tan x| + C}$$

12. $\int \tan^2 x\,dx = \int (\sec^2 x - 1)\,dx$
$$= \mathbf{\tan x - x + C}$$

13. $\int \tan^3 x\,dx = \int \tan x\,(\sec^2 x - 1)\,dx$
$$= \int (\tan x \sec^2 x - \tan x)\,dx$$

$u = \tan x \qquad du = \sec^2 x\,dx$

$$\int (\tan x \sec^2 x - \tan x)\,dx$$
$$= \int u\,du - \int \tan x\,dx$$
$$= \frac{1}{2}u^2 - \ln|\sec x| + C$$
$$= \mathbf{\frac{1}{2}\tan^2 x - \ln|\sec x| + C}$$
$$= \mathbf{\frac{1}{2}\sec^2 x + \ln|\cos x| + C}$$

14. $\int \sec^2 x\,dx = \mathbf{\tan x + C}$

15.

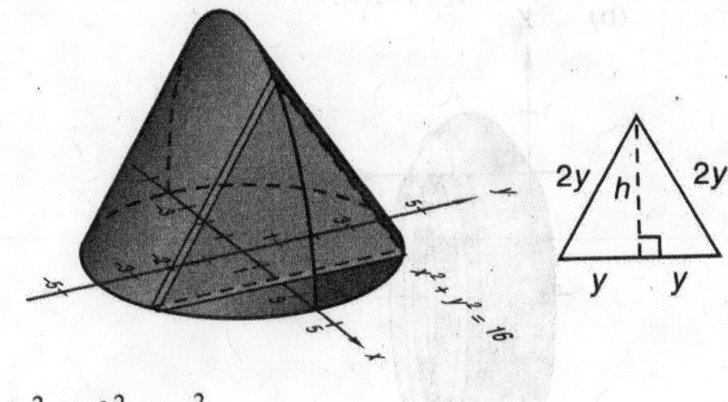

$$4y^2 = h^2 + y^2$$
$$h^2 = 3y^2$$
$$h = \sqrt{3}y$$

$$V = 2\int_{x=0}^{x=4} y(\sqrt{3}y)\,dx$$
$$= 2\sqrt{3}\int_{x=0}^{x=4} y^2\,dx$$
$$= 2\sqrt{3}\int_0^4 (16 - x^2)\,dx = 2\sqrt{3}\left[16x - \frac{1}{3}x^3\right]_0^4$$
$$= 2\sqrt{3}\left(64 - \frac{64}{3}\right) = \mathbf{\frac{256\sqrt{3}}{3}\ units^3}$$

16.

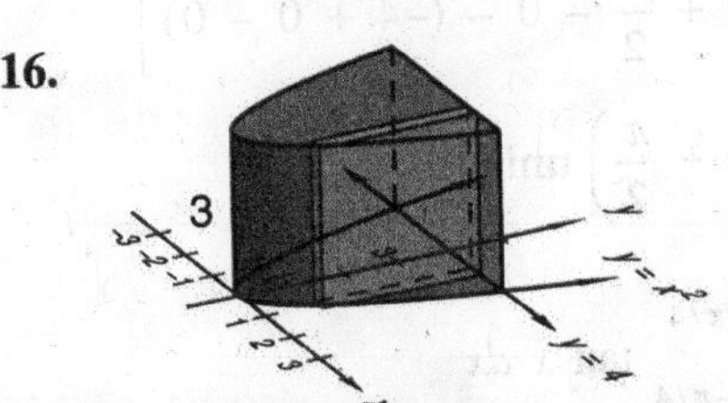

$$V = 2\int_{x=0}^{x=2} 3(4 - y)\,dx$$
$$= 6\int_0^2 (4 - x^2)\,dx = 6\left[4x - \frac{1}{3}x^3\right]_0^2$$
$$= 6\left(8 - \frac{8}{3}\right) = \mathbf{32\ units^3}$$

17. Since $y(2) = -1$ and $y(3) = 17$, there is a root between $x = 2$ and $x = 3$. Set $x_1 = 2.5$ and let `Y1=X³-X-7` and `Y2=nDeriv(Y1,X,X)`.

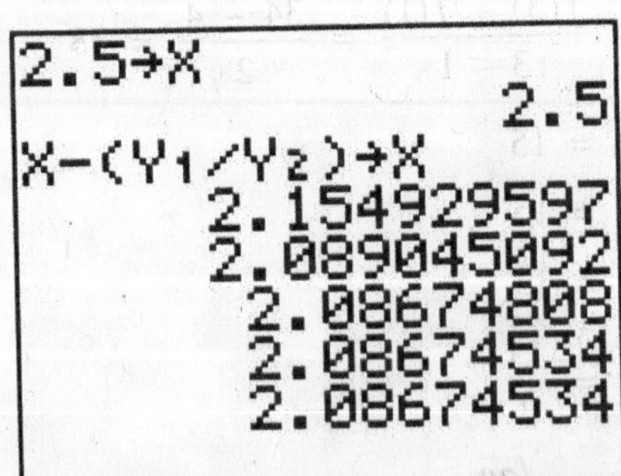

```
2.5→X
                2.5
X-(Y1/Y2)→X
        2.154929597
        2.089045092
         2.08674808
         2.08674534
         2.08674534
```

The root is approximately **2.086745340.**

18.

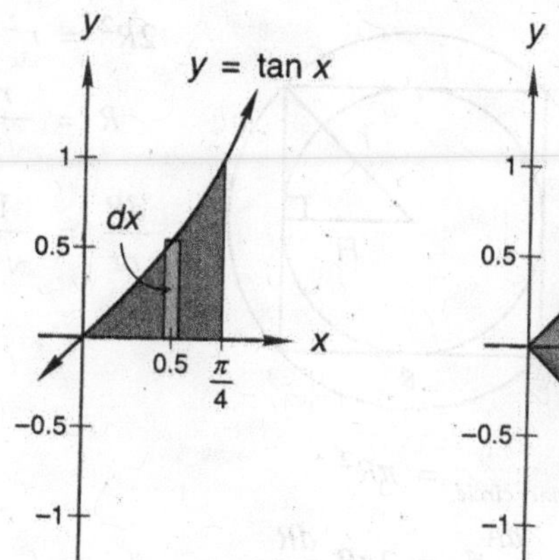

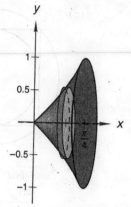

$$V = \pi \int_0^{\pi/4} \tan^2 x \, dx$$
$$= \pi \int_0^{\pi/4} (\sec^2 x - 1) \, dx$$
$$= \pi[\tan x - x]_0^{\pi/4}$$
$$= \pi\left(\mathbf{1} - \frac{\pi}{4}\right) \textbf{ units}^3$$

19.

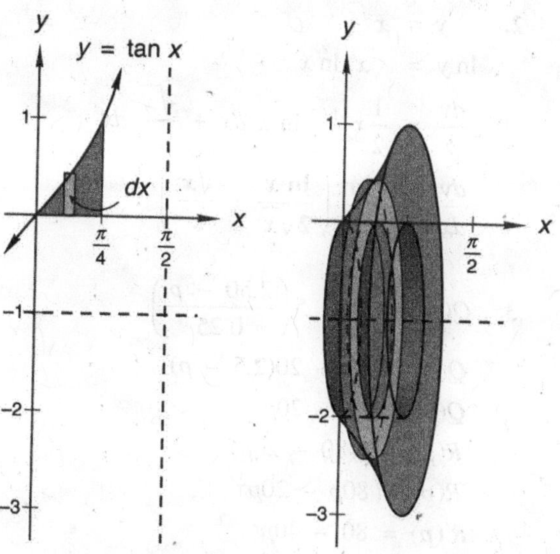

$$V = \pi \int_0^{\pi/4} [(1 + \tan x)^2 - 1] \, dx$$
$$= \pi \int_0^{\pi/4} (\mathbf{2 \tan x + \tan^2 x}) \, dx$$

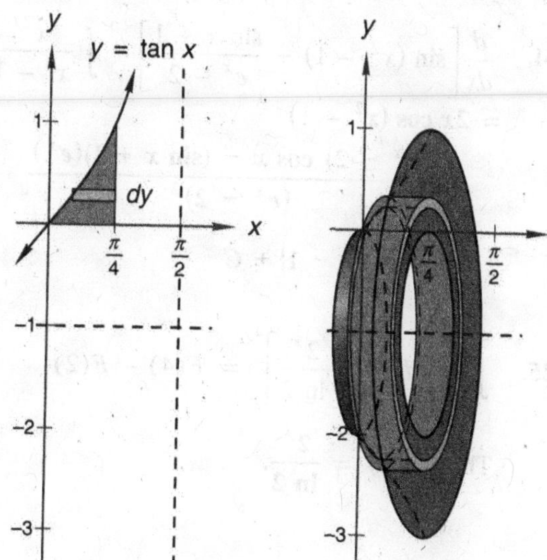

An alternative solution uses shells.

$$V = 2\pi \int rh \, dy$$
$$= \mathbf{2\pi \int_0^1 (1 + y)\left(\frac{\pi}{4} - \arctan y\right) dy}$$

20. $f(x) = x^4 \quad f'(x) = 4x^3$

$$f(4.1) - f(4) \approx f'(4)(4.1 - 4)$$
$$f(4.1) \approx f(4) + f'(4)(0.1)$$
$$4.1^4 \approx 4^4 + 4(4)^3(0.1)$$
$$4.1^4 \approx \mathbf{281.6}$$

21. $y = 2^x$

$$y' = 2^x \ln 2$$
$$y'(2) = 4 \ln 2 = \ln 16$$
At $x = 2$, $y = 4$
$$y - 4 = \ln 16 \,(x - 2)$$
$$y = (\ln 16)x - 2 \ln 16 + 4$$
$$\mathbf{y = (\ln 16)x - \ln 256 + 4}$$
or $\mathbf{y \approx 2.7726x - 1.5452}$

22. $y = (\ln 16)x - \ln 256 + 4$

$$= (\ln 16)(1.9) - \ln 256 + 4$$
$$\approx \mathbf{3.7227}$$

23. **(1.25, 1.75)**

24. $\frac{d}{dx}\left[\sin(x^2 - 1) + \frac{\sin x + 1}{e^x - 2}\right] + \int \frac{x^2}{x^3 - 1}\,dx$

$= \mathbf{2x\cos(x^2 - 1)}$

$+ \mathbf{\frac{(e^x - 2)\cos x - (\sin x + 1)(e^x)}{(e^x - 2)^2}}$

$+ \mathbf{\frac{1}{3}\ln|x^3 - 1| + C}$

25. $\int_2^4 2^x\,dx = \left[\frac{2^x}{\ln 2}\right]_2^4 = F(4) - F(2)$

Thus, $F(x) = \mathbf{\frac{2^x}{\ln 2}}$.

PROBLEM SET 101

1.

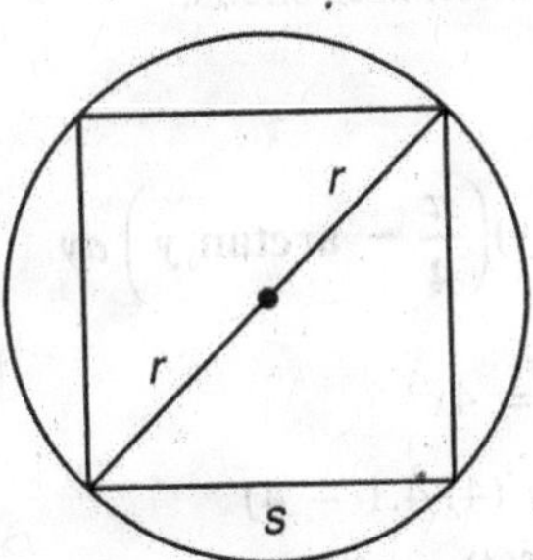

$$2s^2 = (2r)^2$$
$$s = \sqrt{2}r$$
$$\frac{ds}{dt} = \sqrt{2}\frac{dr}{dt}$$
$$\frac{dr}{dt} = 5\,\frac{\text{cm}}{\text{min}} \qquad r = 10\text{ cm}$$

(a) $A_{circle} = \pi r^2$

$$\frac{dA_c}{dt} = 2\pi r\frac{dr}{dt}$$
$$\frac{dA_c}{dt} = 2\pi(10)(5)$$
$$\frac{dA_c}{dt} = \mathbf{100\pi\,\frac{cm^2}{min}}$$

(b) $A_{square} = s^2$

$$\frac{dA_s}{dt} = 2s\frac{ds}{dt}$$
$$\frac{dA_s}{dt} = 2(\sqrt{2}r)(\sqrt{2})\frac{dr}{dt}$$
$$\frac{dA_s}{dt} = 4(10)(5)$$
$$\frac{dA_s}{dt} = \mathbf{200\,\frac{cm^2}{min}}$$

(c)

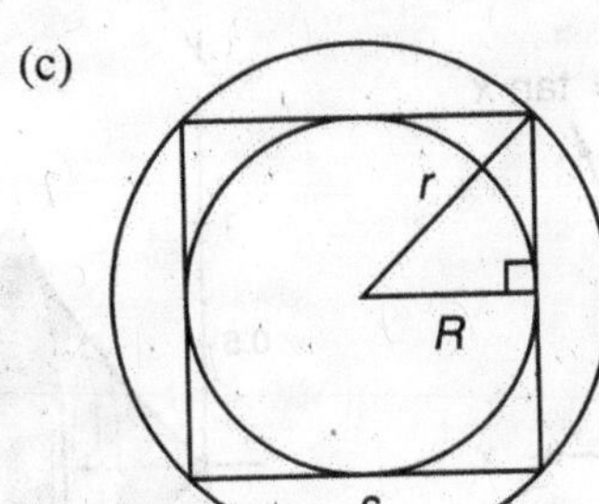

$$2R^2 = r^2$$
$$R = \frac{r}{\sqrt{2}}$$
$$\frac{dR}{dt} = \frac{1}{\sqrt{2}}\frac{dr}{dt}$$

$$A_{inner\,circle} = \pi R^2$$
$$\frac{dA_{ic}}{dt} = 2\pi R\frac{dR}{dt}$$
$$\frac{dA_{ic}}{dt} = 2\pi\left(\frac{r}{\sqrt{2}}\right)\left(\frac{1}{\sqrt{2}}\right)\frac{dr}{dt}$$
$$\frac{dA_{ic}}{dt} = 2\pi\left(\frac{10}{\sqrt{2}}\right)\left(\frac{1}{\sqrt{2}}\right)(5)$$
$$\frac{dA_{ic}}{dt} = \mathbf{50\pi\,\frac{cm^2}{min}}$$

2.

$$y = x^{\sqrt{x}}$$
$$\ln y = \sqrt{x}\,\ln x$$
$$\frac{dy}{y} = \frac{1}{2}x^{-1/2}\ln x\,dx + \frac{\sqrt{x}}{x}\,dx$$
$$\frac{dy}{dx} = \mathbf{x^{\sqrt{x}}\left(\frac{\ln x}{2\sqrt{x}} + \frac{\sqrt{x}}{x}\right)}$$

3.

$$Q(p) = 30 + 5\left(\frac{2.50 - p}{0.25}\right)$$
$$Q(p) = 30 + 20(2.5 - p)$$
$$Q(p) = 80 - 20p$$
$$R(p) = p(80 - 20p)$$
$$R(p) = 80p - 20p^2$$
$$R'(p) = 80 - 40p$$
$$0 = 80 - 40p$$
$$p = \mathbf{\$2}$$

4.

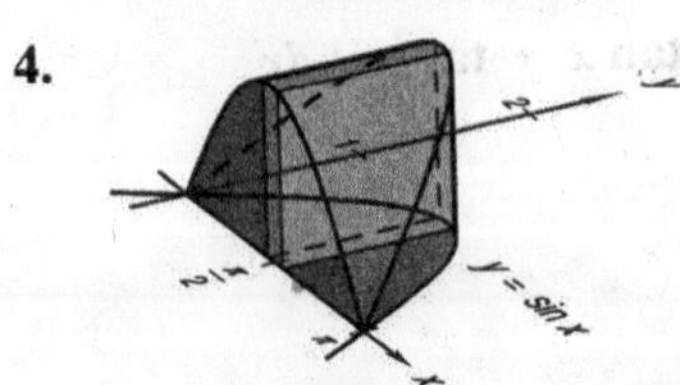

(a) $V = \mathbf{\int_0^\pi \sin^2 x\,dx}$

(b) $V = \int_0^\pi \left[\frac{1}{2} - \frac{1}{2}\cos(2x)\right]dx$

$$= \left[\frac{1}{2}x - \frac{1}{4}\sin(2x)\right]_0^\pi = \mathbf{\frac{\pi}{2}\text{ units}^3}$$

5. (a)

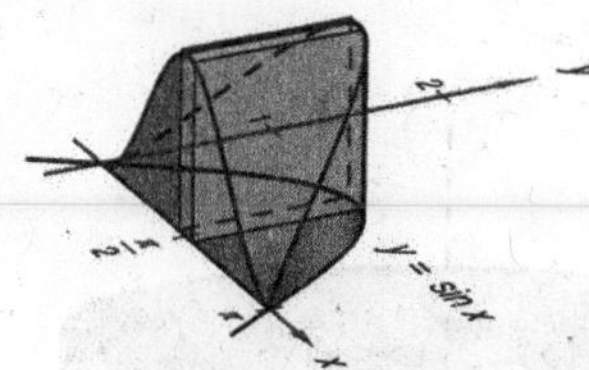

$$V = \int_0^{\pi} \sin x\,(\sin^2 x)\,dx = \int_0^{\pi} \mathbf{\sin^3 x\,dx}$$

(b) $$V = \int_0^{\pi} \sin x\,(1 - \cos^2 x)\,dx$$

$$= \int_0^{\pi} (\sin x - \cos^2 x \sin x)\,dx$$

$$= \left[-\cos x + \frac{1}{3}\cos^3 x\right]_0^{\pi} = \mathbf{\frac{4}{3}\ units^3}$$

6. $$T = \frac{b - a}{2n}(y_0 + 2y_1 + 2y_2 + 2y_3 + y_4)$$

$$= \frac{3}{8}\left(e + \frac{2e^{7/4}}{\frac{49}{16}} + \frac{2e^{5/2}}{\frac{25}{4}} + \frac{2e^{13/4}}{\frac{169}{16}} + \frac{e^4}{16}\right)$$

$$\approx \mathbf{7.0015}$$

7. $$f(x) = e^{|x|} = \begin{cases} e^x & \text{when } x \geq 0 \\ e^{-x} & \text{when } x < 0 \end{cases}$$

$$\mathbf{f'(x) = \begin{cases} e^x & \text{when } x > 0 \\ -e^{-x} & \text{when } x < 0 \end{cases}}$$

8. $$\int_{-1}^{2} e^{|x|}\,dx = \int_{-1}^{0} e^{-x}\,dx + \int_0^2 e^x\,dx$$

$$= [-e^{-x}]_{-1}^{0} + [e^x]_0^2$$

$$= -1 - (-e) + e^2 - 1 = \mathbf{e^2 + e - 2}$$

9. $$\lim_{x\to 0} \frac{\sin x}{x} = \mathbf{1}$$

10. $$\lim_{x\to 0} \frac{8x}{\sin(3x)} = \mathbf{\frac{8}{3}}$$

11. $$\lim_{x\to 0}\left(\frac{1}{x} - \frac{1}{x^2}\right) = \lim_{x\to 0} \frac{x - 1}{x^2} = \frac{-1}{0^+} = \mathbf{-\infty}$$

12. $$\lim_{x\to\infty} xe^{-3x} = \lim_{x\to\infty} \frac{x}{e^{3x}} = \lim_{x\to\infty} \frac{1}{3e^{3x}} = \mathbf{0}$$

13. $$\lim_{h\to 0} \frac{\sin(x + h) - \sin x}{h}$$

$$= \lim_{h\to 0} \frac{\sin x \cos h + \cos x \sin h - \sin x}{h}$$

$$= \lim_{h\to 0} \frac{\sin x(\cos h - 1) + \cos x \sin h}{h}$$

$$= \sin x \lim_{h\to 0} \frac{\cos h - 1}{h} + \cos x \lim_{h\to 0} \frac{\sin h}{h}$$

$$= (\sin x)(0) + (\cos x)(1)$$

$$= \cos x$$

14. $$\int \tan x\,dx = \int \frac{\sin x}{\cos x}\,dx$$

$$= -\ln|\cos x| + C$$

$$= \mathbf{\ln|\sec x| + C}$$

15. $$\int \sec x\,dx = \int \frac{\sec x(\sec x + \tan x)}{\sec x + \tan x}\,dx$$

$$= \mathbf{\ln|\sec x + \tan x| + C}$$

16. $$\int \sec^2 x\,dx = \mathbf{\tan x + C}$$

17. $$\int \tan^4 x\,dx = \int \tan^2 x(\sec^2 x - 1)\,dx$$

$$= \int (\tan^2 x \sec^2 x - \tan^2 x)\,dx$$

$$= \int (\tan^2 x \sec^2 x - \sec^2 x + 1)\,dx$$

$$= \mathbf{\frac{1}{3}\tan^3 x - \tan x + x + C}$$

18. $$y = \sqrt[3]{x}$$

$$dy = \frac{1}{3}x^{-2/3}\,dx$$

$$dy = \frac{1}{3}(64)^{-2/3}(-4)$$

$$dy = -\frac{1}{12}$$

$$\sqrt[3]{60} \approx \sqrt[3]{64} + dy = 4 - \frac{1}{12} = \mathbf{3\frac{11}{12} = 3.91\overline{6}}$$

19. $y = x^3 - 60$; $y(3) = -33$; $y(4) = 4$

There must be a root between $x = 3$ and $x = 4$.

Set $x_1 = 3.5$ and define `Y1=X³-60` and `Y2=nDeriv(Y1,X,X)`.

```
3.5→X
                3.5
X-(Y1/Y2)→X
        3.965986382
        3.915523696
        3.91486751
        3.914867641
        3.914867641
```

3.914867641

20. (a) $x(t) = \sin t$

$v(t) = \cos t$

$$\text{Distance} = \int_0^5 |\cos t|\, dt \approx \mathbf{3.0411\ units}$$

(b) Average velocity

$$= \frac{1}{5-0}\int_0^5 \cos t\, dt = \frac{1}{5}[\sin t]_0^5$$

$$= \frac{\sin 5}{5} \textbf{ linear units/time unit}$$

$$\approx \mathbf{-0.1918\ linear\ units/time\ unit}$$

21. $f(x) = 3e^{4x}$

$x = 3e^{4y}$ Implicit inverse

$$\frac{x}{3} = e^{4y}$$

$$\ln\frac{x}{3} = 4y$$

$$y = \frac{1}{4}(\ln x - \ln 3) \quad \text{Explicit inverse}$$

$$f^{-1}(x) = \frac{1}{4}(\ln x - \ln 3)$$

$$f^{-1}(e) = \mathbf{\frac{1}{4}(1 - \ln 3)}$$

22.

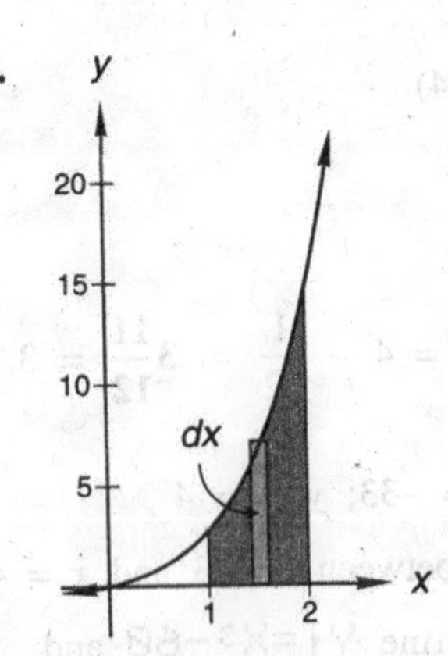

$u = x \quad du = dx \quad v = e^x \quad dv = e^x\, dx$

$$A = \int_1^2 xe^x\, dx = [xe^x - e^x]_1^2 = \mathbf{e^2\ units^2}$$

23.

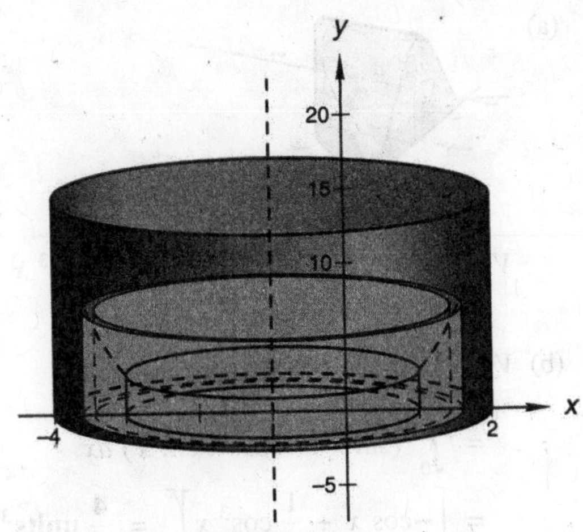

$$V = 2\pi\int_1^2 (1 + x)xe^x\, dx$$

$$= 2\pi\int_1^2 (xe^x + x^2e^x)\, dx$$

$u = x \quad du = dx \quad v = e^x \quad dv = e^x\, dx$

$$V = 2\pi\left[xe^x - e^x\right]_1^2 + 2\pi\int_1^2 x^2e^x\, dx$$

$$= 2\pi e^2 + 2\pi\int_1^2 x^2e^x\, dx$$

$u = x^2 \quad du = 2x\, dx \quad v = e^x \quad dv = e^x\, dx$

$$V = 2\pi e^2 + 2\pi\left(x^2e^x\Big|_1^2 - \int_1^2 2xe^x\, dx\right)$$

$$= 2\pi(5e^2 - e) - 2\pi\int_1^2 2xe^x\, dx$$

$$V = 2\pi(5e^2 - e) - 4\pi\left[xe^x - e^x\right]_1^2$$

$$= 2\pi(5e^2 - e) - 4\pi(e^2)$$

$$= \mathbf{2\pi(3e^2 - e)\ units^3}$$

24. For the sequence 0, 3, 8, 15, 24, ...

$a_n = n^2 - 1$ with $n = 1, 2, 3, \ldots$

$a_6 = 6^2 - 1 = \mathbf{35}$

25. $y = ax^2 + bx + c$

$$\begin{cases} -1 = a - b + c \\ 0 = a + b + c \\ 6 = 9a + 3b + c \end{cases}$$

$$-1 - (0) = a - b + c - (a + b + c)$$

$$-1 = -2b$$

$$b = \frac{1}{2}$$

$$6 - (0) = 9a + 3b + c - (a + b + c)$$
$$6 = 8a + 2b$$
$$6 = 8a + 1$$
$$a = \frac{5}{8}$$
$$0 = \frac{5}{8} + \frac{1}{2} + c$$
$$c = -\frac{9}{8}$$
$$\mathbf{y = \frac{5}{8}x^2 + \frac{1}{2}x - \frac{9}{8}}$$

Problem Set 102

1.

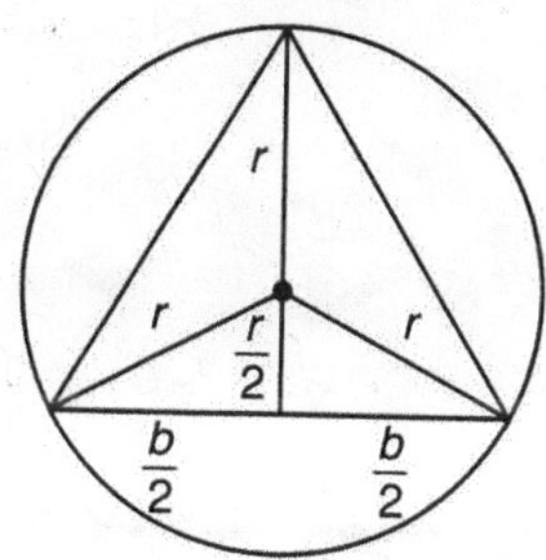

(a) $A_c = \pi r^2$

$$\frac{dA_c}{dt} = 2\pi r \frac{dr}{dt}$$
$$\frac{dA_c}{dt} = 2\pi(8)(5) = \mathbf{80\pi \frac{cm^2}{s}}$$

(b) $\left(\frac{b}{2}\right)^2 = r^2 - \left(\frac{r}{2}\right)^2$

$$\frac{b^2}{4} = \frac{3}{4}r^2$$
$$b = \sqrt{3}r$$
$$A_t = \frac{1}{2}(\sqrt{3}r)\left(\frac{3}{2}r\right)$$
$$A_t = \frac{3\sqrt{3}}{4}r^2$$
$$\frac{dA_t}{dt} = \frac{3\sqrt{3}}{2}r\frac{dr}{dt}$$
$$\frac{dA}{dt} = \frac{3\sqrt{3}}{2}(8)(5)$$
$$\frac{dA}{dt} = \mathbf{60\sqrt{3} \frac{cm^2}{s}}$$

2.

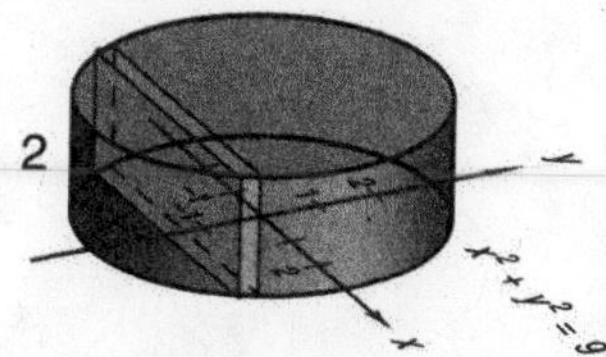

$$V = 2\int_{y=0}^{y=3} 2x(2)\, dy$$
$$= 8\int_0^3 \sqrt{9 - y^2}\, dy$$
$$= 8\left(\frac{9}{4}\pi\right) = \mathbf{18\pi \text{ units}^3}$$

3. (a) $x(t) = t^3 - 9t^2 + 24t - 8$

$$v(t) = 3t^2 - 18t + 24$$
$$0 = 3t^2 - 18t + 24$$
$$0 = t^2 - 6t + 8$$
$$0 = (t - 2)(t - 4)$$
$$t = 2, 4$$

$x(0) = -8$; $x(2) = 12$; $x(4) = 8$; $x(5) = 12$

The total distance traveled is the sum of the change in position from $t = 0$ to 2, $t = 2$ to 4, and $t = 4$ to 5.

$$D = 20 + 4 + 4 = \mathbf{28 \text{ units}}$$

(b) Average velocity $= \frac{1}{5}\int_0^5 (3t^2 - 18t + 24)\, dt$

$$= \frac{1}{5}[t^3 - 9t^2 + 24t]_0^5$$
$$= \frac{1}{5}(125 - 225 + 120)$$
$$= \mathbf{4 \text{ linear units/time unit}}$$

(c) $v(t) = 3t^2 - 18t + 24$

$$v'(t) = a(t) = 6t - 18$$
$$0 = 6t - 18$$
$$t = 3$$

Critical numbers: $t = 0, 3, 5$

$v(0) = 24$; $v(3) = -3$; $v(5) = 9$

Maximum velocity: **24 linear units/time unit**

4.

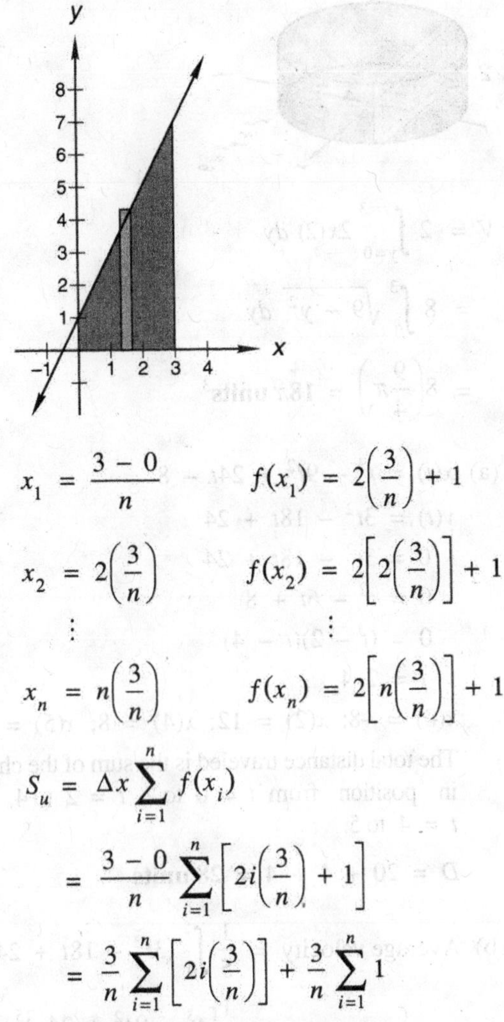

$$x_1 = \frac{3 - 0}{n} \qquad f(x_1) = 2\left(\frac{3}{n}\right) + 1$$

$$x_2 = 2\left(\frac{3}{n}\right) \qquad f(x_2) = 2\left[2\left(\frac{3}{n}\right)\right] + 1$$

$$\vdots \qquad\qquad \vdots$$

$$x_n = n\left(\frac{3}{n}\right) \qquad f(x_n) = 2\left[n\left(\frac{3}{n}\right)\right] + 1$$

$$S_u = \Delta x \sum_{i=1}^{n} f(x_i)$$

$$= \frac{3 - 0}{n} \sum_{i=1}^{n} \left[2i\left(\frac{3}{n}\right) + 1\right]$$

$$= \frac{3}{n} \sum_{i=1}^{n} \left[2i\left(\frac{3}{n}\right)\right] + \frac{3}{n} \sum_{i=1}^{n} 1$$

$$= \left(\frac{3}{n}\right)(2)\left(\frac{3}{n}\right)\frac{(n + 1)(n)}{2} + \left(\frac{3}{n}\right)(n)$$

$$= \frac{9n^2 + 9n}{n^2} + 3$$

$$A = \lim_{n\to\infty} S_u$$

$$= \lim_{n\to\infty} \left(\frac{9n^2 + 9n}{n^2} + 3\right)$$

$$= \lim_{n\to\infty} \left(9 + \frac{9}{n} + 3\right)$$

$$= \mathbf{12\ units^2}$$

5. Both x^2 and y^2 are positive terms and their coefficients are unequal, so this is an **ellipse.**

$$9x^2 - 18x + y^2 = 18$$

$$9(x^2 - 2x) + y^2 = 18$$

$$9(x^2 - 2x + 1) + y^2 = 18 + 9$$

$$9(x - 1)^2 + y^2 = 27$$

$$\mathbf{\frac{(x - 1)^2}{3} + \frac{y^2}{27} = 1}$$

6. $$\lim_{h\to 0} \frac{\ln(x + h) - \ln x}{h}$$

$$= \lim_{h\to 0} \frac{1}{h}[\ln(x + h) - \ln x]$$

$$= \lim_{h\to 0} \frac{1}{h} \cdot \frac{x}{x}\left[\ln\left(\frac{x + h}{x}\right)\right]$$

$$= \lim_{h\to 0} \frac{1}{x} \cdot \frac{x}{h}\left[\ln\left(\frac{x + h}{x}\right)\right]$$

$$= \frac{1}{x} \lim_{h\to 0} \ln\left(\frac{x + h}{x}\right)^{x/h} = \frac{1}{x} \ln e = \frac{1}{x}$$

7. $$y = e^x$$

$$\ln y = x$$

$$\frac{1}{y}\frac{dy}{dx} = 1$$

$$\frac{dy}{dx} = y$$

$$\frac{dy}{dx} = e^x$$

8. $$R = k\frac{T}{H}$$

$$1.5 = k\frac{3}{0.6}$$

$$k = 0.3$$

$$R = 0.3\frac{T}{H}$$

$$= 0.3\left(\frac{2}{0.75}\right)$$

$$= \mathbf{0.8\ mm}$$

9. (a) $$\frac{d}{ds}\int_{\pi}^{s} \cos t\, dt = \frac{d}{ds}[\sin t]_{\pi}^{s}$$

$$= \frac{d}{ds}(\sin s - \sin \pi)$$

$$= \mathbf{\cos s}$$

(b) $$\frac{d}{ds}\int_{\pi}^{s} \cos t\, dt = \mathbf{\cos s}$$

10. $$\frac{d}{ds}\int_{\pi}^{s} \cos t^2\, dt = \mathbf{\cos s^2}$$

11. $T = \frac{b-a}{2n}(y_0 + 2y_1 + 2y_2 + 2y_3 + 2y_4 + y_5)$

$= \frac{1}{10}\left(1 + 2\sqrt{\frac{126}{125}} + 2\sqrt{\frac{133}{125}} + 2\sqrt{\frac{152}{125}}\right.$

$\left. + 2\sqrt{\frac{189}{125}} + \sqrt{2}\right)$

$\approx \mathbf{1.1150}$

12. $\lim_{x\to 0} \frac{\sin(7x)}{13x} = \frac{7}{13} \lim_{7x\to 0} \frac{\sin(7x)}{7x} = \mathbf{\frac{7}{13}}$

13. $\lim_{x\to 0}\left(\frac{1}{x^2} - \frac{1}{x^4}\right) = \lim_{x\to 0}\left(\frac{x^2-1}{x^4}\right)$

$\lim_{x\to 0} \frac{x^2 - 1}{x^4} = \frac{-1}{0^+} = -\infty$

14. $\lim_{x\to\infty} xe^{-7x} = \lim_{x\to\infty} \frac{x}{e^{7x}} = \lim_{x\to\infty} \frac{1}{7e^{7x}} = \mathbf{0}$

15. $\int \csc x\, dx = \int \frac{\csc x(\csc x - \cot x)}{\csc x - \cot x}\, dx$

$= \mathbf{\ln|\csc x - \cot x| + C}$

16. $\int \cot x\, dx = \int \frac{\cos x}{\sin x}\, dx = \mathbf{\ln|\sin x| + C}$

17. $\int \tan^3 x\, dx = \int \tan x(\sec^2 x - 1)\, dx$

$= \int (\tan x \sec^2 x - \tan x)\, dx$

$u = \tan x \qquad du = \sec^2 x\, dx$

$\int (\tan x \sec^2 x - \tan x)\, dx$

$= \int u\, du - \int \tan x\, dx$

$= \frac{1}{2}u^2 - \ln|\sec x| + C$

$= \mathbf{\frac{1}{2}\tan^2 x - \ln|\sec x| + C}$

$= \mathbf{\frac{1}{2}\sec^2 x + \ln|\cos x| + C}$

18. $\int \cot^2 x\, dx = \int (\csc^2 x - 1)\, dx$

$= \mathbf{-\cot x - x + C}$

19. $\frac{dy}{dx} = \sin(2x)$

$dy = \sin(2x)\, dx$

$y = \mathbf{-\frac{1}{2}\cos(2x) + C}$

20. $\int_0^{\pi/4} \tan x\, dx = \left[-\ln|\cos x|\right]_0^{\pi/4}$

$= -\ln\frac{\sqrt{2}}{2} - 0$

$= \mathbf{\ln\sqrt{2}}$

21. $f(x) = x^3 - 6x^2 + 12x - 4;$
$f'(x) = 3x^2 - 12x + 12$

$(3, f(3)) = (3, 5)$

By reflecting $f(x)$ about the line $y = x$, we obtain its inverse. The slope of the inverse is given by

$(f^{-1})'(5) = \frac{1}{f'(3)}$

$= \frac{1}{3(3)^2 - 12(3) + 12}$

$= \mathbf{\frac{1}{3}}$

22. **(–3.004, –2.996)**

23.

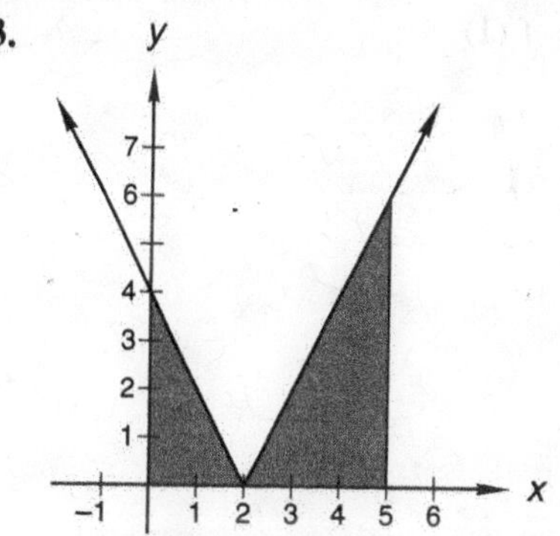

$\int_0^5 |2x - 4|\, dx$ = the area of the 2 triangles

$= \frac{1}{2}(2)(4) + \frac{1}{2}(3)(6)$

$= 4 + 9 = \mathbf{13}$

24. $$x^2y + 6 = xy^3$$

$$x^2\frac{dy}{dx} + y(2x) = x(3y^2)\frac{dy}{dx} + y^3$$

$$(3xy^2 - x^2)\frac{dy}{dx} = 2xy - y^3$$

$$\frac{dy}{dx} = \frac{2xy - y^3}{3xy^2 - x^2}$$

At (1,2) slope $= \dfrac{2(1)(2) - 8}{3(1)(4) - 1} = -\dfrac{4}{11}$

$$y - 2 = -\frac{4}{11}(x - 1)$$

$$y = -\frac{4}{11}x + \frac{26}{11}$$

$$x = 1.2 = \frac{6}{5}$$

$$y = -\frac{4}{11}\left(\frac{6}{5}\right) + \frac{26}{11}$$

$$= -\frac{24}{55} + \frac{26}{11} = \frac{106}{55}$$

The approximate coordinates based on the prescribed method are exactly $\left(\mathbf{1.2}, \frac{\mathbf{106}}{\mathbf{55}}\right)$.

25. $$\lim_{x\to 1^-} f(x) = f(1)$$

$$3 = a + b$$

$$\lim_{x\to 1^-} f'(x) = f'(1)$$

$$1 = 2a$$

$$\mathbf{a = \frac{1}{2}}$$

$$\frac{1}{2} + b = 3$$

$$\mathbf{b = \frac{5}{2}}$$

Problem Set 103

1. $$Q(p) = 25 + 7\left(\frac{20 - p}{1.5}\right)$$

$$R(p) = \left[25 + 7\left(\frac{20 - p}{1.5}\right)\right]p$$

$$R(p) = \frac{355}{3}p - \frac{14}{3}p^2$$

$$R'(p) = \frac{355}{3} - \frac{28}{3}p$$

$$0 = \frac{355}{3} - \frac{28}{3}p$$

$$p = \$12.68$$

$$Q(\$12.68) = 59.16 \text{ trees}$$

Forrest cannot sell partial trees, so we need to check profit for 59 trees and for 60 trees.

$$Q(p) = 59 = 25 + 7\left(\frac{20 - p}{1.5}\right)$$

$p = \$12.71$ and profit $= (12.71)(59) = \$749.89$

$$Q(p) = 60 = 25 + 7\left(\frac{20 - p}{1.5}\right)$$

$p = \$12.50$ and profit $= (12.50)(60) = \$750$

The trees should be sold at **\$12.50.** Forrest should expect to sell **60 trees.**

2.

W, S, D

$$W = 60 \text{ mi} \qquad S = 50 \text{ mi}$$

$$\frac{dW}{dt} = 40 \text{ mph} \qquad \frac{dS}{dt} = 50 \text{ mph}$$

$$D = \sqrt{60^2 + 50^2} = \sqrt{6100} = 10\sqrt{61}$$

$$D^2 = W^2 + S^2$$

$$2D\frac{dD}{dt} = 2W\frac{dW}{dt} + 2S\frac{dS}{dt}$$

$$D\frac{dD}{dt} = W\frac{dW}{dt} + S\frac{dS}{dt}$$

$$10\sqrt{61}\frac{dD}{dt} = 60(40) + 50(50)$$

$$10\sqrt{61}\frac{dD}{dt} = 4900$$

$$\frac{dD}{dt} = \mathbf{\frac{490\sqrt{61}}{61}\ mph \approx 62.7381\ mph}$$

3. $f(x) = 2^x \qquad f'(x) = 2^x \ln 2$

$$f'(c) = \frac{f(3) - f(0)}{3 - 0}$$

$$2^c \ln 2 = \frac{7}{3}$$

$$2^c = \frac{7}{\ln 8}$$

$$c = \log_2\left(\frac{7}{\ln 8}\right) = \frac{\ln\left(\frac{7}{\ln 8}\right)}{\ln 2} \approx 1.7512$$

$$f(c) \approx 2^{1.7512} \approx 3.3664$$

$$y - 3.3664 \approx \frac{7}{3}(x - 1.7512)$$

$$\mathbf{y \approx \frac{7}{3}x - 0.7197}$$

4. (a) Average value $= \dfrac{1}{3}\displaystyle\int_0^3 2^x\,dx$

$= \dfrac{1}{3\ln 2}\left[2^x\right]_0^3$

$= \mathbf{\dfrac{7}{\ln 8}} \approx \mathbf{3.3663}$

(b) $f(c) = \dfrac{7}{\ln 8}$

$2^c = \dfrac{7}{\ln 8}$

$c = \log_2 \dfrac{7}{\ln 8}$

$c = \dfrac{\ln\left(\dfrac{7}{\ln 8}\right)}{\ln 2}$

$c \approx \mathbf{1.7512}$

5.

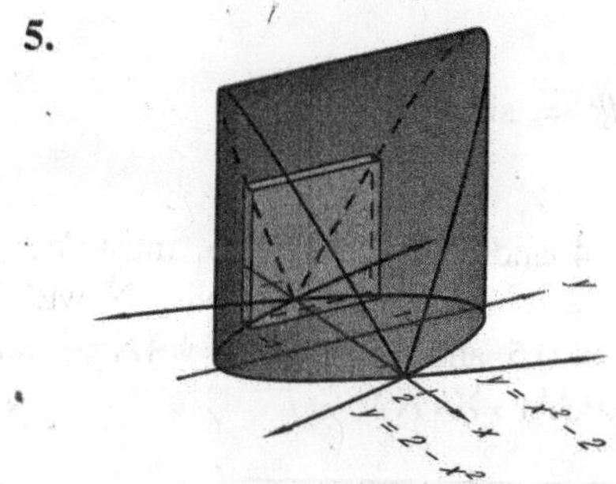

$x^2 - 2 = 2 - x^2$

$2x^2 = 4$

$x = \pm\sqrt{2}$

$V = 2\displaystyle\int_0^{\sqrt{2}} [(2 - x^2) - (x^2 - 2)]^2\,dx$

$= 2\displaystyle\int_0^{\sqrt{2}} (-2x^2 + 4)^2\,dx$

$= 2\displaystyle\int_0^{\sqrt{2}} (4x^4 - 16x^2 + 16)\,dx$

$= 2\left[\dfrac{4}{5}x^5 - \dfrac{16}{3}x^3 + 16x\right]_0^{\sqrt{2}}$

$= 2\left(\dfrac{16\sqrt{2}}{5} - \dfrac{32\sqrt{2}}{3} + 16\sqrt{2}\right)$

$= \mathbf{\dfrac{256\sqrt{2}}{15}}$ **units³** $\approx$ **24.1359 units³**

6.

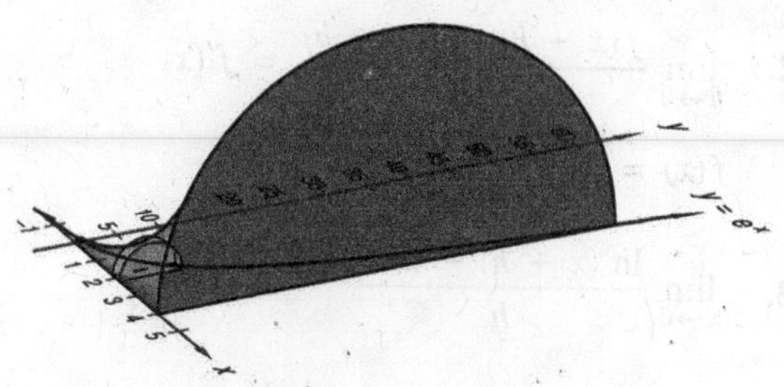

(a) $V = \displaystyle\int_0^4 \frac{1}{2}\pi r^2\,dx$

$= \dfrac{\pi}{2}\displaystyle\int_0^4 \left(\frac{e^x}{2}\right)^2 dx$

$= \mathbf{\dfrac{\pi}{8}\displaystyle\int_0^4 e^{2x}\,dx}$

(b) $\dfrac{\pi}{8}\displaystyle\int_0^4 e^{2x}\,dx = \dfrac{\pi}{16}\left[e^{2x}\right]_0^4$

$= \mathbf{\dfrac{\pi}{16}(e^8 - 1)}$ **units³**

$\approx$ **585.1134 units³**

7. Find a rule for $\delta(\varepsilon)$ for $y = x - 3$.

$|y - 1| < \varepsilon$

$|x - 3 - 1| < \varepsilon$

$|x - 4| < \varepsilon$

Thus, $\delta = \varepsilon$.

8. $|y - 5| < \varepsilon$

$|3x - 1 - 5| < \varepsilon$

$|3x - 6| < \varepsilon$

$|x - 2| < \dfrac{\varepsilon}{3}$

$\delta = \dfrac{\varepsilon}{3}$

9. $\displaystyle\lim_{x\to 0} \frac{\cos x - 1}{x} = \lim_{x\to 0} \frac{-\sin x}{1} = \mathbf{0}$

10. $\displaystyle\lim_{n\to\infty} \left(1 + \frac{1}{n}\right)^n = \mathbf{e}$

11. $\displaystyle\lim_{x\to\infty} x^2 e^{-2x} = \lim_{x\to\infty} \frac{x^2}{e^{2x}}$

$= \displaystyle\lim_{x\to\infty} \frac{2x}{2e^{2x}}$

$= \displaystyle\lim_{x\to\infty} \frac{2}{4e^{2x}} = \frac{2}{\infty} = \mathbf{0}$

12. $\lim_{h\to 0} \frac{f(x+h) - f(x-h)}{2h} = f'(x)$

$f(x) = 3x^2, \ f'(x) = \mathbf{6x}$

13. $\lim_{h\to 0} \frac{\ln(x+h) - \ln x}{h}$

$= \lim_{h\to 0} \frac{1}{h}[\ln(x+h) - \ln x]$

$= \lim_{h\to 0} \frac{1}{h} \cdot \frac{x}{x}\left[\ln\left(\frac{x+h}{x}\right)\right]$

$= \lim_{h\to 0} \frac{1}{x} \cdot \frac{x}{h}\left[\ln\left(\frac{x+h}{x}\right)\right]$

$= \frac{1}{x} \lim_{h\to 0} \ln\left(\frac{x+h}{x}\right)^{x/h} = \frac{1}{x}\ln e = \frac{1}{x}$

14.

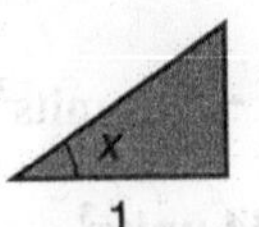

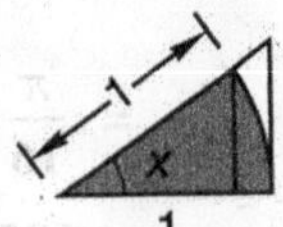

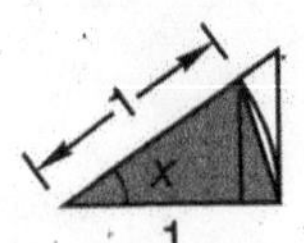

$A_1 = \frac{1}{2}(1)\tan x \quad A = \pi(1)^2\frac{x}{2\pi} \quad A = \frac{1}{2}(1)\sin x$

$A = \frac{\tan x}{2} \quad A = \frac{x}{2} \quad A = \frac{\sin x}{2}$

$\frac{\tan x}{2} > \frac{x}{2} > \frac{\sin x}{2}$

$\tan x > x > \sin x$

$\frac{1}{\cos x} > \frac{x}{\sin x} > 1$

$\cos x < \frac{\sin x}{x} < 1$

$\lim_{x\to 0} \cos x \le \lim_{x\to 0} \frac{\sin x}{x} \le \lim_{x\to 0} 1$

$1 \le \lim_{x\to 0} \frac{\sin x}{x} \le 1$

By the squeeze theorem, $\lim_{x\to 0} \frac{\sin x}{x} = 1$.

15. $\lim_{h\to 0} \frac{\sin(x+h) - \sin x}{h}$

$= \lim_{h\to 0} \frac{\sin x\cos h + \cos x\sin h - \sin x}{h}$

$= \lim_{h\to 0} \frac{\sin x(\cos h - 1) + \cos x\sin h}{h}$

$= \sin x \lim_{h\to 0} \frac{\cos h - 1}{h} + \cos x \lim_{h\to 0} \frac{\sin h}{h}$

$= (\sin x)(0) + (\cos x)(1)$

$= \cos x$

16.

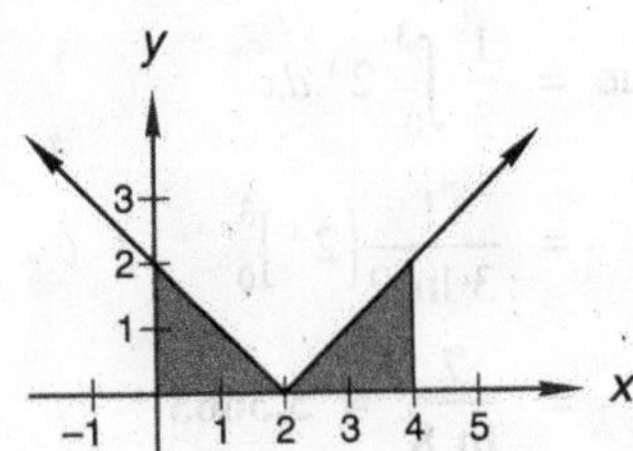

$\int_0^4 |-x + 2|\,dx = \frac{1}{2}(2)(2) + \frac{1}{2}(2)(2)$

$= \mathbf{4}$

17. $T = \frac{b-a}{2n}(y_0 + 2y_1 + 2y_2 + 2y_3 + y_4)$

$= \frac{1.4}{8}[0 + 2\sin(0.35^3) + 2\sin(0.7^3)$

$+ 2\sin(1.05^3) + \sin(1.4^3)]$

$\approx \mathbf{0.5210}$

18. $\frac{d}{dx}\int_0^x \sin k^3\,dk = \mathbf{\sin x^3}$

19. Since $f(0) = -4$ and $f(1) = 1$, there must be a root between $x = 0$ and $x = 1$. Applying Newton's method, let $x_1 = 0.5$ and set Y1=X³+4X−4 and Y2=nDeriv(Y1,X,X).

```
.5→X
                .5
X-(Y1/Y2)→X
       .894736759
       .8486187382
       .8477079412
       .8477075981
       .8477075981
```

The root is approximately **0.8477075981.**

20. $y = \frac{x^2 - 2x}{1 - x^2}$

Zeros: $x^2 - 2x = 0$

$x(x - 2) = 0$

$x = 0, 2$

Vertical asymptotes:

$1 - x^2 = 0$

$(1 + x)(1 - x) = 0$

$x = -1, 1$

Horizontal asymptote:

$$\lim_{x\to\infty}\frac{x^2-2x}{1-x^2}=\lim_{x\to\infty}\frac{1-\dfrac{2}{x}}{\dfrac{1}{x^2}-1}=-1$$

$y = -1$

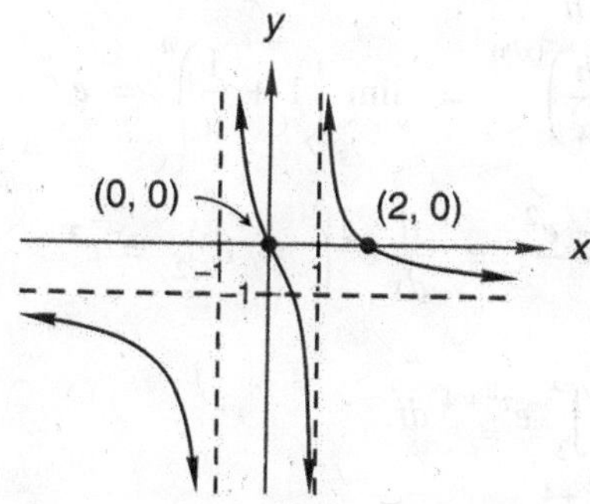

21. $\int \tan^4 x\,dx = \int \tan^2 x(\sec^2 x - 1)\,dx$

$= \int (\tan^2 x \sec^2 x - \tan^2 x)\,dx$

$= \int (\tan^2 x \sec^2 x - \sec^2 x + 1)\,dx$

$= \mathbf{\frac{1}{3}\tan^3 x - \tan x + x + C}$

22. $y = x^3y^3 - 4x^3y^2 + 25$

$\frac{dy}{dx} = x^3(3y^2)\frac{dy}{dx} + y^3(3x^2)$

$- 4x^3(2y)\frac{dy}{dx} - y^2(12x^2)$

$12x^2y^2 - 3x^2y^3 = \frac{dy}{dx}(3x^3y^2 - 8x^3y - 1)$

$\frac{dy}{dx} = \frac{12x^2y^2 - 3x^2y^3}{3x^3y^2 - 8x^3y - 1}$

$\frac{dy}{dx} = \frac{12(4) - 3(4)}{3(8) - 8(8) - 1} = -\frac{36}{41}$

$y - 1 = -\frac{36}{41}(x - 2)$

$y = -\frac{36}{41}x + \frac{113}{41}$

$y = -\frac{36}{41}\left(\frac{9}{5}\right) + \frac{113}{41}$

$y = \frac{241}{205}$

The approximate coordinates based on the prescribed method are exactly $\mathbf{(1.8, \frac{241}{205})}$.

23. $f(x) = ax^2 + bx + c$

$f(2) = 0 = 4a + 2b + c$

$f(-1) = 13 = a - b + c$

$f(4) = 38 = 16a + 4b + c$

$4a + 2b + c - (a - b + c) = 0 - 13$

$3a + 3b = -13$

$16a + 4b + c - (a - b + c) = 38 - 13$

$15a + 5b = 25$

$3a + b = 5$

$3a + 3b - (3a + b) = -13 - 5$

$2b = -18$

$b = -9$

$3a - 9 = 5$

$a = \frac{14}{3}$

$\frac{14}{3} + 9 + c = 13$

$c = -\frac{2}{3}$

$\mathbf{f(x) = \frac{14}{3}x^2 - 9x - \frac{2}{3}}$

24. −5, −2, 1, 4, ...

$a_1 = -5$

$a_2 = -5 + (1)3 = -2$

$a_3 = -5 + 2(3) = 1$

$a_4 = -5 + 3(3) = 4$

$a_{40} = -5 + 39(3) = \mathbf{112}$

25. **If a building is not a skyscraper, then it is not tall.**

Problem Set 104

1. $v(t) = 2t^{1/2} + 4t^3$

$0 = 2t^{1/2}(1 + 2t^{5/2})$

$2t^{1/2} = 0 \qquad 2t^{5/2} = -1$

$t = 0$

$\text{Distance} = \int_0^9 (2t^{1/2} + 4t^3)\,dt$

$= \left[\frac{4}{3}t^{3/2} + t^4\right]_0^9$

$= \mathbf{6597\ m}$

2. $V = s^3$
$dV = 3s^2\,ds$
$dV = 3(5)^2(0.02)$
$dV = \mathbf{1.5\ cm^3}$

3. $x = 151 \qquad dx = 1$
$c(x) = x(x - 150)^2 + 140$
$d[c(x)] = [2x(x - 150) + (x - 150)^2]\,dx$
$d[c(151)] = [2(151)(1) + 1](1)$
$d[c(151)] = 302 + 1 = \mathbf{\$303}$

4.

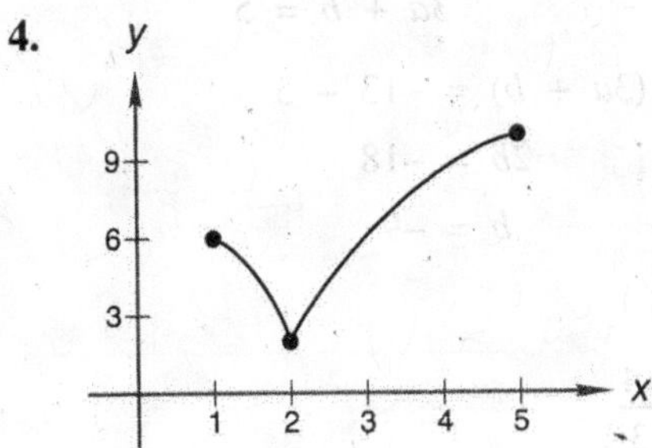

5.

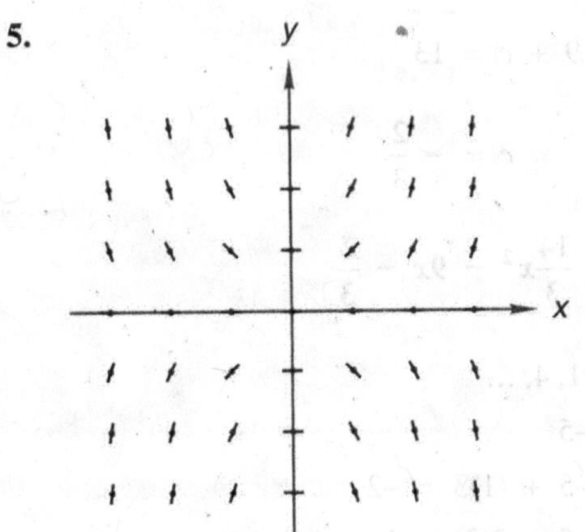

6. $T = \frac{b - a}{2n}(y_0 + 2y_1 + 2y_2 + 2y_3 + 2y_4 + 2y_5 + y_6)$

$= \frac{\pi}{12}\left[0 + 2\sin\left(\frac{\pi}{6}\right)^2 + 2\sin\left(\frac{\pi}{3}\right)^2 + 2\sin\left(\frac{\pi}{2}\right)^2 + 2\sin\left(\frac{2\pi}{3}\right)^2 + 2\sin\left(\frac{5\pi}{6}\right)^2 + \sin\pi^2\right]$

$\approx \mathbf{0.6086}$

7. The given slope field does not have uniform slope in any row or column, so the slope is dependent upon both x and y. This eliminates choices A and B. The differential equation in choice C has a slope of zero along both axes, so it cannot describe the given slope field.

The correct choice is **D.**

8. $\lim_{x\to 0}\frac{\sin(2x)}{x} = 2\lim_{2x\to 0}\frac{\sin(2x)}{2x} = 2(1) = \mathbf{2}$

9. $\lim_{x\to 0}\frac{4x}{\sin(7x)} = \frac{4}{7}\lim_{7x\to 0}\frac{7x}{\sin(7x)} = \frac{4}{7}(1) = \mathbf{\frac{4}{7}}$

10. With $u = \frac{x}{h}$, u goes to infinity as h goes to zero.

$\lim_{h\to 0}\left(1 + \frac{h}{x}\right)^{(x/h)} = \lim_{u\to\infty}\left(1 + \frac{1}{u}\right)^u = \mathbf{e}$

11. $\lim_{h\to 0}\frac{e^{2+h} - e^2}{h} = \frac{d}{dx}e^x\Big|_2 = e^x\big|_2 = \mathbf{e^2}$

12. $f(x) = \frac{d}{dx}\int_3^x e^{t^2+4}\,dt$
$f(x) = e^{x^2+4}$
$f(0) = e^{0+4} = \mathbf{e^4}$

13. $\frac{d}{dx}\int_3^x (\sin t)e^{t^2+1}\,dt = \mathbf{(\sin x)e^{x^2+1}}$

14.

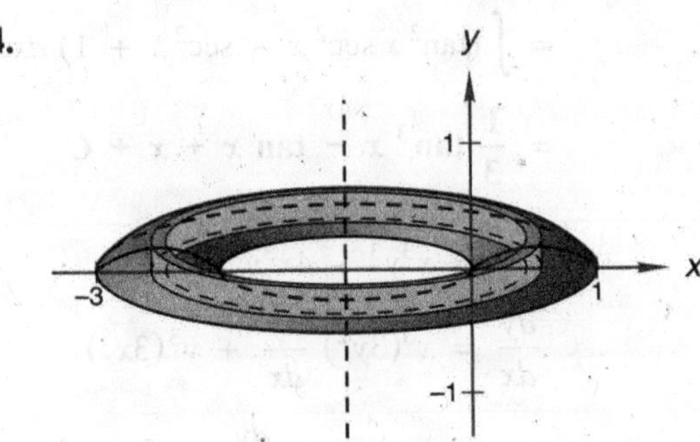

$V = \mathbf{2\pi\int_0^1 (1 + x)(x - x^2)\,dx}$

15. $\int \cot^3 x\,dx = \int \cot x(\csc^2 x - 1)\,dx$
$= \int \cot x\csc^2 x\,dx - \int \cot x\,dx$
$= \mathbf{-\frac{1}{2}\cot^2 x - \ln|\sin x| + C}$
$= \mathbf{-\frac{1}{2}\csc^2 x + \ln|\csc x| + C}$

16. $\int (\pi\sec^2 x)(e^{\tan x})\,dx = \pi\int \sec^2 x\, e^{\tan x}\,dx$
$= \mathbf{\pi e^{\tan x} + C}$

17.

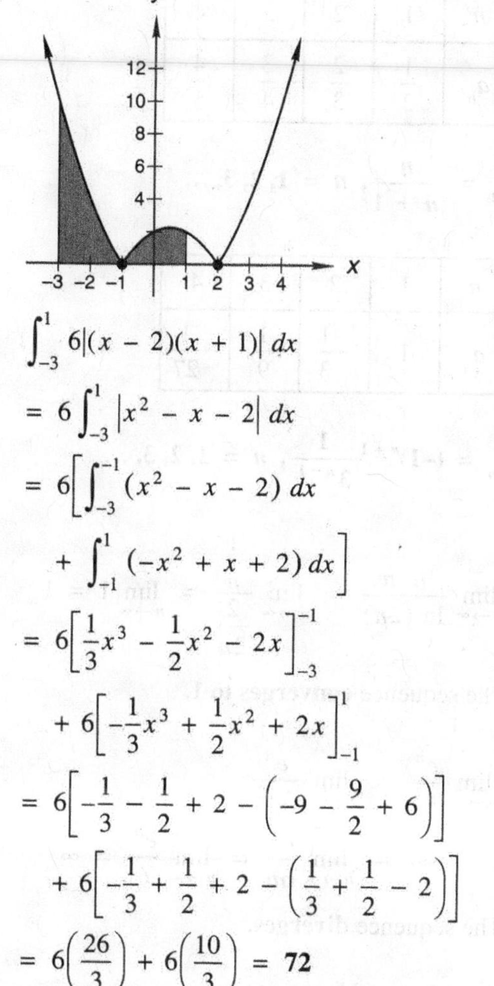

$$\int_{-3}^{1} 6|(x-2)(x+1)|\,dx$$

$$= 6\int_{-3}^{1} |x^2 - x - 2|\,dx$$

$$= 6\left[\int_{-3}^{-1} (x^2 - x - 2)\,dx + \int_{-1}^{1} (-x^2 + x + 2)\,dx\right]$$

$$= 6\left[\frac{1}{3}x^3 - \frac{1}{2}x^2 - 2x\right]_{-3}^{-1} + 6\left[-\frac{1}{3}x^3 + \frac{1}{2}x^2 + 2x\right]_{-1}^{1}$$

$$= 6\left[-\frac{1}{3} - \frac{1}{2} + 2 - \left(-9 - \frac{9}{2} + 6\right)\right] + 6\left[-\frac{1}{3} + \frac{1}{2} + 2 - \left(\frac{1}{3} + \frac{1}{2} - 2\right)\right]$$

$$= 6\left(\frac{26}{3}\right) + 6\left(\frac{10}{3}\right) = \mathbf{72}$$

18. $f(x) = x^3 + 3x - 1$ $\qquad f'(x) = 3x^2 + 3$

By inspection $x = 3$ is a solution of $x^3 + 3x - 1 = 35$.

$$g'(35) = \frac{1}{f'(g(35))} = \frac{1}{f'(3)} = \frac{1}{3(3)^2 + 3} = \mathbf{\frac{1}{30}}$$

19.

$$\frac{dy}{dx} = x^2\sqrt{1 - y^2}$$

$$\frac{1}{\sqrt{1 - y^2}}\,dy = x^2\,dx$$

$$\arcsin y = \frac{1}{3}x^3 + C$$

$$\arcsin 0 = 9 + C$$

$$C = -9$$

$$\arcsin y = \frac{1}{3}x^3 - 9$$

$$\mathbf{y = \sin\left(\frac{1}{3}x^3 - 9\right)}$$

20.

$$y = \frac{2\sqrt{x^3 - 1}}{\sin x + \cos(2x)} + e^{\sin x}$$

$$y' = \frac{[\sin x + \cos(2x)](x^3 - 1)^{-1/2}(3x^2)}{[\sin x + \cos(2x)]^2} - \frac{2(x^3 - 1)^{1/2}[\cos x - 2\sin(2x)]}{[\sin x + \cos(2x)]^2} + \cos x\, e^{\sin x}$$

$$\mathbf{y' = \frac{3x^2}{\sqrt{x^3 - 1}[\sin x + \cos(2x)]} - \frac{2\sqrt{x^3 - 1}\,[\cos x - 2\sin(2x)]}{[\sin x + \cos(2x)]^2} + \cos x\, e^{\sin x}}$$

21.

$$|y - 1| < \varepsilon$$

$$|2x - 5 - 1| < \varepsilon$$

$$|2x - 6| < \varepsilon$$

$$|x - 3| < \frac{\varepsilon}{2}$$

$$\mathbf{\delta = \frac{\varepsilon}{2}}$$

22.

$$|y - 2| < \varepsilon$$

$$\left|\frac{3}{2}x - 4 - 2\right| < \varepsilon$$

$$\left|\frac{3}{2}x - 6\right| < \varepsilon$$

$$|x - 4| < \frac{2}{3}\varepsilon$$

$$\mathbf{\delta = \frac{2}{3}\varepsilon}$$

23.

$$y = e^x,$$

$$\ln y = x$$

$$\frac{1}{y}\frac{dy}{dx} = 1$$

$$\frac{dy}{dx} = y$$

$$\frac{dy}{dx} = e^x$$

24.

$$f(x) = \sin|x| = \begin{cases} \sin x & \text{when } x \geq 0 \\ \sin(-x) & \text{when } x < 0 \end{cases}$$

$$f'(x) = \begin{cases} \cos x & \text{when } x > 0 \\ -\cos x & \text{when } x < 0 \end{cases}$$

$$f'\left(-\frac{5\pi}{6}\right) = -\cos\left(-\frac{5\pi}{6}\right) = \mathbf{\frac{\sqrt{3}}{2}}$$

25.

$$\lim_{n\to\infty} \frac{1}{n}\sum_{i=1}^{n} f(x_i) = \mathbf{\int_0^1 (x^3 + 2x)\,dx}$$

Problem Set 105

1.

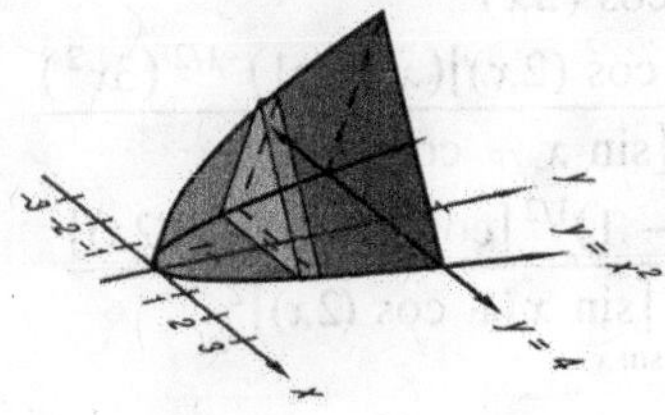

$$h^2 = 4x^2 - x^2$$
$$h = \sqrt{3}x$$

$$V = \int_{y=0}^{y=4} \frac{1}{2}(2x)(\sqrt{3}x)\,dy$$
$$= \sqrt{3}\int_{y=0}^{y=4} x^2\,dy$$
$$= \sqrt{3}\int_0^4 y\,dy$$
$$= \sqrt{3}\left[\frac{1}{2}y^2\right]_0^4$$
$$= \mathbf{8\sqrt{3}\ units^3}$$

2. $B(t) = B_0e^{kt}$
$$3000 = 1000e^{10k}$$
$$3 = e^{10k}$$
$$\ln 3 = 10k$$
$$k = \frac{\ln 3}{10}$$
$$B(t) = 1000e^{[(\ln 3)/10]t}$$
$$B(t) = 1000e^{(t/10)\ln 3}$$
$$\mathbf{B(t) = (1000)\,3^{t/10}}$$

3. $a_n = \dfrac{n+1}{n}$, $n = 1, 2, 3, \ldots$

$a_1 = \mathbf{2}$, $a_2 = \mathbf{\frac{3}{2}}$, $a_3 = \mathbf{\frac{4}{3}}$, $a_4 = \mathbf{\frac{5}{4}}$

4. $a_n = \dfrac{2-n}{n^2}$, $n = 1, 2, 3, \ldots$

$a_1 = \mathbf{1}$, $a_2 = \mathbf{0}$, $a_3 = \mathbf{-\frac{1}{9}}$, $a_4 = \mathbf{-\frac{1}{8}}$

5. $a_n = \dfrac{\ln n}{n}$, $n = 1, 2, 3, \ldots$

$a_1 = \mathbf{0}$, $a_2 = \mathbf{\frac{\ln 2}{2}}$, $a_3 = \mathbf{\frac{\ln 3}{3}}$, $a_4 = \mathbf{\frac{\ln 4}{4}}$

6.

n	1	2	3	4
a_n	$\frac{1}{2}$	$\frac{2}{3}$	$\frac{3}{4}$	$\frac{4}{5}$

$$\mathbf{a_n = \frac{n}{n+1},\ n = 1, 2, 3, \ldots}$$

7.

n	1	2	3	4
a_n	1	$-\frac{1}{3}$	$\frac{1}{9}$	$-\frac{1}{27}$

$$\mathbf{a_n = (-1)^{n+1}\frac{1}{3^{n-1}},\ n = 1, 2, 3, \ldots}$$

8. $$\lim_{n\to\infty}\frac{\ln n}{\ln(2n)} = \lim_{n\to\infty}\frac{\frac{1}{n}}{\frac{2}{2n}} = \lim_{n\to\infty} 1 = 1$$

The sequence **converges to 1.**

9. $$\lim_{n\to\infty}\frac{e^n}{n^3} = \lim_{n\to\infty}\frac{e^n}{3n^2}$$
$$= \lim_{n\to\infty}\frac{e^n}{6n} = \lim_{n\to\infty}\frac{e^n}{6} = \infty$$

The sequence **diverges.**

10. $$\lim_{n\to\infty}\left(1 + \frac{1}{n}\right)^n = e \text{ by definition}$$

The sequence **converges to *e*.**

11. $$\lim_{x\to 0}\frac{7x}{\sin(13x)} = \frac{7}{13}\lim_{13x\to 0}\frac{13x}{\sin(13x)}$$
$$= \frac{7}{13}(1) = \mathbf{\frac{7}{13}}$$

12. $$\lim_{x\to 0}\frac{1-\cos x}{x} = \lim_{x\to 0}\frac{\sin x}{1} = \mathbf{0}$$

13. $$\lim_{x\to 0^+}\frac{2x^2 + x}{(\ln x)^2} = \frac{0}{\infty} = \mathbf{0}$$

14. $$\lim_{x\to 0}\left[(1 - \cos x)(\csc x)\right] = \lim_{x\to 0}\frac{1-\cos x}{\sin x}$$
$$= \lim_{x\to 0}\frac{\sin x}{\cos x} = \frac{0}{1} = \mathbf{0}$$

15. $y = x^2 - \sqrt{x}$

$$dy = \left(2x - \frac{1}{2\sqrt{x}}\right)dx$$

$$dy = \left[2(9) - \frac{1}{2\sqrt{9}}\right](0.3)$$

$$dy = \left(18 - \frac{1}{6}\right)(0.3)$$

$$dy = \frac{107}{6}\left(\frac{3}{10}\right)$$

$$dy = \frac{107}{20}$$

$$(9.3)^2 - \sqrt{9.3} \approx 9^2 - \sqrt{9} + dy$$

$$= 78 + \frac{107}{20} = \mathbf{83\frac{7}{20}} = \mathbf{83.35}$$

16. $\frac{d}{dx}\int_7^x (t^3 - 4t^2 + 3t - 7)\,dt$

$= \mathbf{x^3 - 4x^2 + 3x - 7}$

17. $\int_3^x \left[\frac{d}{dx}\left(\int_3^x (t^3 - 4t^2 + 3t - 7)\,dt\right)\right] dx$

$$= \int_3^x (x^3 - 4x^2 + 3x - 7)\,dx$$

$$= \left[\frac{x^4}{4} - \frac{4x^3}{3} + \frac{3x^2}{2} - 7x\right]_3^x$$

$$= \left(\frac{x^4}{4} - \frac{4x^3}{3} + \frac{3x^2}{2} - 7x\right) - \left(\frac{3^4}{4} - \frac{4(3)^3}{3} + \frac{3(3)^2}{2} - 7(3)\right)$$

$$= \mathbf{\frac{x^4}{4} - \frac{4x^3}{3} + \frac{3x^2}{2} - 7x + \frac{93}{4}}$$

18. Since $y(-1) = 1$ and $y(-2) = -18$, there must be a root between $x = -1$ and $x = -2$. Apply Newton's method by setting $x_1 = -1.5$, `Y1=X³-4X²+6`, and `Y2=nDeriv(Y1,X,X)`.

```
-1.5→X
                 -1.5
X-(Y1/Y2)→X
          -1.160000018
          -1.089164971
           -1.08613565
          -1.086130198
          -1.086130198
```

The root is approximately **−1.086130198.**

19. (a)

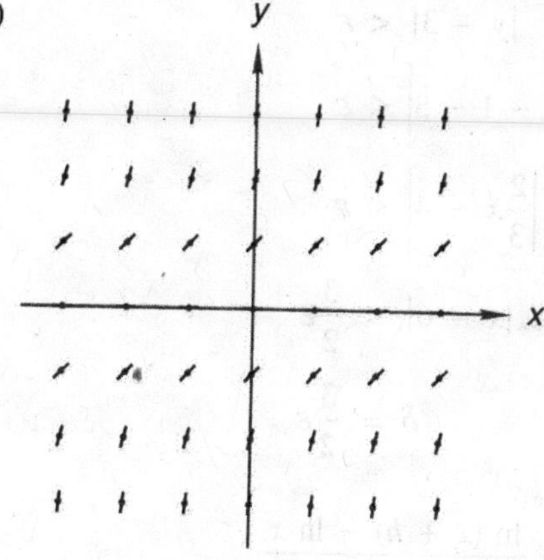

(b)

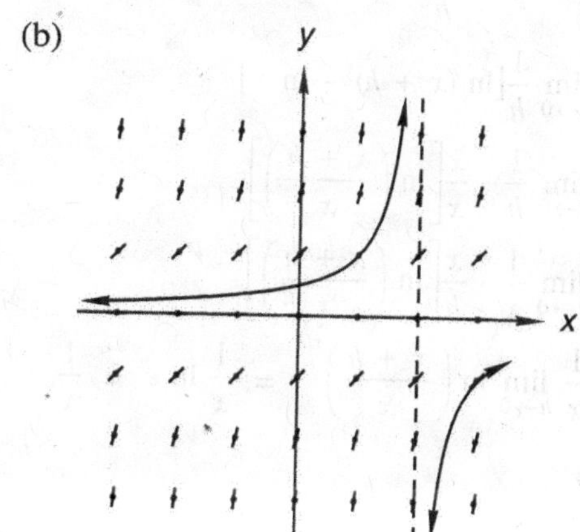

20. $T = \frac{b-a}{2n}(y_0 + 2y_1 + 2y_2 + 2y_3 + y_4)$

$$= \frac{\frac{\pi}{2}}{8}\left[\frac{\sin\frac{\pi}{2}}{\frac{\pi}{2}} + \frac{2\sin\left(\frac{5\pi}{8}\right)}{\frac{5\pi}{8}} + \frac{2\sin\left(\frac{3\pi}{4}\right)}{\frac{3\pi}{4}} + \frac{2\sin\left(\frac{7\pi}{8}\right)}{\frac{7\pi}{8}} + \frac{\sin\pi}{\pi}\right]$$

$\approx$ **0.4823**

21. $u = x^2 \qquad du = 2x\,dx$

$$\int \ln(x^x x^x x^x x^x)\,dx = \int \ln(x^{4x})\,dx$$

$$= \int 2x\ln(x^2)\,dx$$

$$= \int \ln u\,du$$

$$= u\ln u - u + C$$

$$= \mathbf{x^2\ln(x^2) - x^2 + C}$$

22.
$$|y - 3| < \varepsilon$$
$$\left|\frac{2}{3}x - 1 - 3\right| < \varepsilon$$
$$\left|\frac{2}{3}x - 4\right| < \varepsilon$$
$$|x - 6| < \frac{3}{2}\varepsilon$$
$$\boldsymbol{\delta = \frac{3}{2}\varepsilon}$$

23.
$$\lim_{h\to 0} \frac{\ln(x + h) - \ln x}{h}$$
$$= \lim_{h\to 0} \frac{1}{h}[\ln(x + h) - \ln x]$$
$$= \lim_{h\to 0} \frac{1}{h} \cdot \frac{x}{x}\left[\ln\left(\frac{x + h}{x}\right)\right]$$
$$= \lim_{h\to 0} \frac{1}{x} \cdot \frac{x}{h}\left[\ln\left(\frac{x + h}{x}\right)\right]$$
$$= \frac{1}{x} \lim_{h\to 0} \ln\left(\frac{x + h}{x}\right)^{x/h} = \frac{1}{x}\ln e = \boldsymbol{\frac{1}{x}}$$

24.

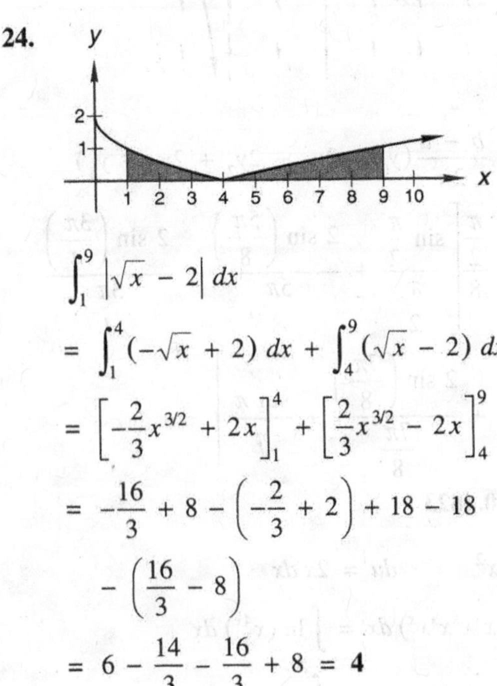

$$\int_1^9 \left|\sqrt{x} - 2\right| dx$$
$$= \int_1^4 (-\sqrt{x} + 2)\, dx + \int_4^9 (\sqrt{x} - 2)\, dx$$
$$= \left[-\frac{2}{3}x^{3/2} + 2x\right]_1^4 + \left[\frac{2}{3}x^{3/2} - 2x\right]_4^9$$
$$= -\frac{16}{3} + 8 - \left(-\frac{2}{3} + 2\right) + 18 - 18$$
$$- \left(\frac{16}{3} - 8\right)$$
$$= 6 - \frac{14}{3} - \frac{16}{3} + 8 = \mathbf{4}$$

25.

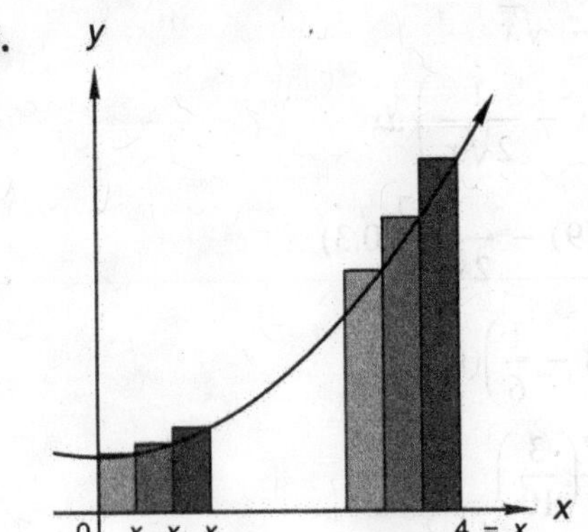

$$S_u = \frac{4}{n}\left[(x_1^2 + 3) + (x_2^2 + 3) + (x_3^2 + 3) + \cdots + (x_n^2 + 3)\right]$$
$$= \frac{4}{n}\left[(\Delta x)^2 + 3 + (2\Delta x)^2 + 3 + (3\Delta x)^2 + 3 + \cdots + (n\Delta x)^2 + 3\right]$$
$$= \frac{4}{n}\left[3n + (\Delta x)^2 + 2^2(\Delta x)^2 + 3^2(\Delta x)^2 + \cdots + n^2(\Delta x)^2\right]$$
$$= \frac{4}{n}\left[3n + (\Delta x)^2(1^2 + 2^2 + 3^2 + \cdots + n^2)\right]$$
$$= \frac{4}{n}\left[3n + \left(\frac{4}{n}\right)^2\left(\frac{n(n + 1)(2n + 1)}{6}\right)\right]$$
$$= 12 + \frac{64}{n^3}\left(\frac{n(n + 1)(2n + 1)}{6}\right)$$
$$= 12 + \frac{32(n + 1)(2n + 1)}{3n^2}$$
$$A = \lim_{n\to\infty}\left(12 + \frac{32(n + 1)(2n + 1)}{3n^2}\right)$$
$$= 12 + \frac{64}{3} = \boldsymbol{\frac{100}{3}}\ \textbf{units}^2$$

PROBLEM SET 106

1. (a)

t	−3	−2	−1	0	1	2	3
x	−7	−4	−1	2	5	8	11
y	9	4	1	0	1	4	9

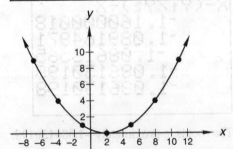

(b) $x = 3t + 2 \qquad y = t^2$

$$\frac{dy}{dx} = \frac{\frac{dy}{dt}}{\frac{dx}{dt}} = \frac{2t}{3} = \frac{2}{3}\left(\frac{x-2}{3}\right) = \mathbf{\frac{2}{9}x - \frac{4}{9}}$$

(c) $t = \dfrac{x-2}{3}$

$$y = \left(\frac{1}{3}x - \frac{2}{3}\right)^2$$

$$\mathbf{y = \frac{1}{9}x^2 - \frac{4}{9}x + \frac{4}{9}}$$

2. (a)

t	−2	−1	0	1	2
x	−8	−1	0	1	8
y	4	1	0	1	4

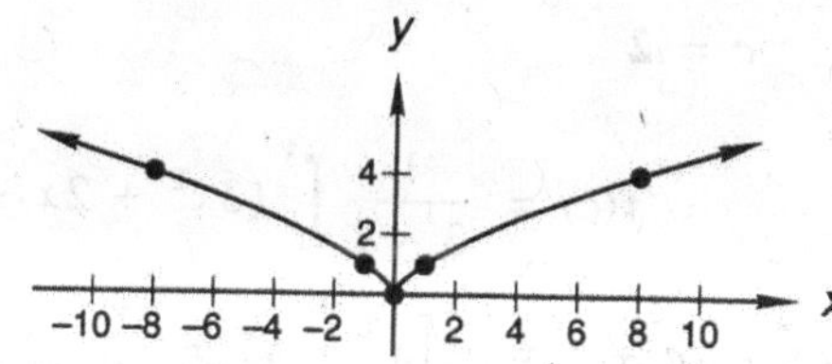

(b) $x = t^3 \qquad y = t^2$

$$\frac{dy}{dx} = \frac{\frac{dy}{dt}}{\frac{dx}{dt}} = \frac{2t}{3t^2} = \frac{2}{3}t^{-1} = \mathbf{\frac{2}{3}x^{-1/3}}$$

(c) $t = x^{1/3}$

$$y = (x^{1/3})^2$$

$$\mathbf{y = x^{2/3}}$$

3. $x = 100 \qquad dx = 1$

$$p(x) = -(x - 100)^2 + 200x$$

$$d(p(x)) = [-2(x - 100) + 200]\,dx$$

$$d(p(100)) = [-2(0) + 200](1)$$

$$d(p(100)) = \mathbf{\$200}$$

4. $y = \sqrt[3]{x}$

$$dy = \frac{1}{3}x^{-2/3}\,dx$$

$$dy = \frac{1}{3}(64)^{-2/3}(4) = \frac{1}{12}$$

$$\sqrt[3]{68} \approx \sqrt[3]{64} + dy = \mathbf{4\frac{1}{12}}$$

5. $y = x^3 - 68$ has a root between $x = 4$ and $x = 5$. Let $x_1 = 4.5$, `Y1=X³-68`, and `Y2=nDeriv(Y1,X,X)`.

```
4.5→X
                4.5
X-(Y1/Y2)→X
         4.11934157
        4.081998832
        4.081655131
        4.081655102
        4.081655102
```

$\sqrt[3]{68} \approx \mathbf{4.081655102}$

6. $$T = \frac{1}{12}\left(0 + 2\sin\frac{1}{36} + 2\sin\frac{1}{9} + 2\sin\frac{1}{4} + 2\sin\frac{4}{9} + 2\sin\frac{25}{36} + \sin 1\right)$$

$$\approx \mathbf{0.3128}$$

7. $A = \displaystyle\int_1^4 \frac{1}{x}\,dx = [\ln x]_1^4 = \mathbf{\ln 4 \text{ units}^2}$

8.

$$y = x^{-1}$$

$$y' = -x^{-2}$$

$$y'' = 2x^{-3}$$

$$|y'' \max| = 2 \text{ when } x = 1$$

$$\frac{(3)^3}{12N^2}(2) < 0.01$$

$$\frac{9}{2N^2} < 0.01$$

$$\frac{1}{N^2} < \frac{1}{450}$$

$$N^2 > 450$$

$$N > 21.2$$

Therefore, **22 intervals** are needed.

9.

6

6

$\frac{b}{2}$ $\frac{b}{2}$

$$V = 2\int_{x=0}^{x=2} \frac{1}{2}(4 - y)6\,dx = 6\int_0^2 (4 - x^2)\,dx$$

$$= 6\left[4x - \frac{1}{3}x^3\right]_0^2 = \mathbf{32 \text{ units}^3}$$

10. $\lim_{x\to 0} \frac{1 - \cos x}{x} = \lim_{x\to 0} \frac{\sin x}{1} = \mathbf{0}$

11. With $u = \frac{3}{x}$, u goes to infinity as x goes to zero.

$$\lim_{x\to 0}\left(1 + \frac{x}{3}\right)^{3/x} = \lim_{u\to\infty}\left(1 + \frac{1}{u}\right)^{u} = e$$

12. $\lim_{x\to 0}\left(\frac{1}{x} - \frac{1}{2e^x - 2}\right) = \lim_{x\to 0}\left[\frac{2e^x - 2 - x}{x(2e^x - 2)}\right]$

$$= \lim_{x\to 0}\frac{2e^x - 1}{x2e^x + 2e^x - 2}$$

$$\lim_{x\to 0^+}\frac{2e^x - 1}{x2e^x + 2e^x - 2} = \frac{1}{0^+} = \infty$$

$$\lim_{x\to 0^-}\frac{2e^x - 1}{x2e^x + 2e^x - 2} = \frac{1}{0^-} = -\infty$$

$\lim_{x\to 0}\left(\frac{1}{x} - \frac{1}{2e^x - 2}\right)$ **does not exist.**

13. $\frac{d}{dx}\int_{12}^{x}\frac{\sin k}{k}\,dk = \frac{\sin x}{x}$

14. $\int 2\cot^2 x\,dx + \int \frac{1}{2}\tan^2 x\,dx$

$$= 2\int(\csc^2 x - 1)\,dx + \frac{1}{2}\int(\sec^2 x - 1)\,dx$$

$$= -2\cot x - 2x + \frac{1}{2}\tan x - \frac{1}{2}x + C$$

$$= \mathbf{-2\cot x + \frac{1}{2}\tan x - \frac{5}{2}x + C}$$

15. $\int 2\sin^2 x\,dx + \int \sin^3 x\,dx$

$$= \int 2\left[\frac{1}{2} - \frac{1}{2}\cos(2x)\right]dx + \int \sin x\,(1 - \cos^2 x)\,dx$$

$$= x - \frac{1}{2}\sin(2x) + \int(\sin x - \cos^2 x\sin x)\,dx$$

$$= \mathbf{x - \frac{1}{2}\sin(2x) - \cos x + \frac{1}{3}\cos^3 x + C}$$

16.

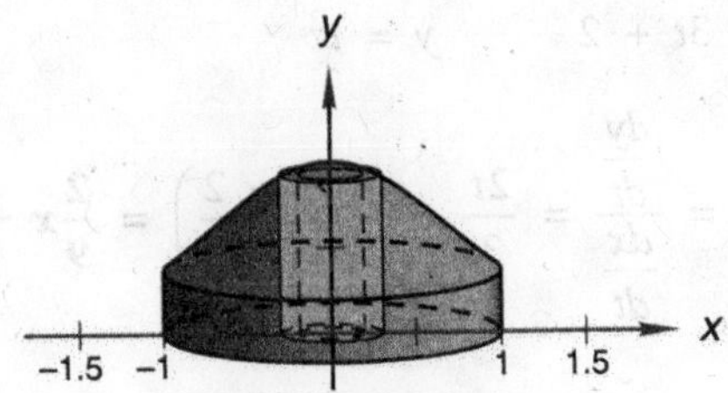

$$V = 2\pi\int_0^1 x(e^{-x^2})\,dx$$

$$= 2\pi\left(-\frac{1}{2}\right)\int_0^1 -2xe^{-x^2}\,dx$$

$$= -\pi\left[e^{-x^2}\right]_0^1 = \mathbf{-\pi(e^{-1} - 1)\ units^3}$$

17. $f(x) = x^2 + x + 1 \qquad f'(x) = 2x + 1$

$$f'(c) = \frac{f(3) - f(1)}{3 - 1}$$

$$2c + 1 = \frac{13 - 3}{2}$$

$$2c + 1 = 5$$

$$\mathbf{c = 2}$$

18. $f(c) = \frac{1}{3 - 1}\int_1^3(3x^2 + 2x + 1)\,dx$

$$3c^2 + 2c + 1 = \frac{1}{2}\left[x^3 + x^2 + x\right]_1^3$$

$$3c^2 + 2c + 1 = \frac{1}{2}[27 + 9 + 3 - (1 + 1 + 1)]$$

$$3c^2 + 2c + 1 = 18$$

$$3c^2 + 2c - 17 = 0$$

$$\mathbf{c = -\frac{1}{3} + \frac{2\sqrt{13}}{3}}$$

19. $f(x) = a\sin x + b\cos x$

$f'(x) = a\cos x - b\sin x$

$2 = a\cos\pi - b\sin\pi \qquad 4 = a\cos\frac{\pi}{2} - b\sin\frac{\pi}{2}$

$\mathbf{a = -2} \qquad \mathbf{b = -4}$

20. (a) $\mathbf{a_1 = \frac{1}{3},\ a_2 = -\frac{2}{9},\ a_3 = -\frac{15}{43},\ a_4 = -\frac{16}{39}}$

(b) $\lim_{n\to\infty}\frac{3n^2 - 4n}{2 - 5n^2} = -\frac{3}{5}$

The sequence **converges to $-\frac{3}{5}$.**

21.

n	1	2	3	4
a_n	$\frac{1}{2}$	$\frac{4}{3}$	$\frac{9}{4}$	$\frac{16}{5}$

$$a_n = \frac{n^2}{n+1},\ n = 1, 2, 3, \ldots$$

22. The terms in this sequence are the same ones as in the previous problem, but the index for this one begins with 3. Therefore, replace n in the previous problem with $n - 2$.

$$a_n = \frac{(n-2)^2}{(n-2)+1} = \frac{(n-2)^2}{n-1},\ n = 3, 4, 5, \ldots$$

23. $$\lim_{n\to\infty} \frac{n^2 - 3n + 98}{4^n} = \lim_{n\to\infty} \frac{2n-3}{4^n \ln 4}$$

$$= \lim_{n\to\infty} \frac{2}{4^n(\ln 4)^2} = 0$$

The sequence **converges to 0.**

24. $$\lim_{n\to\infty} \frac{e^n}{n^2} = \lim_{n\to\infty} \frac{e^n}{2n} = \lim_{n\to\infty} \frac{e^n}{2} = \infty$$

The sequence **diverges.**

25. (a) $x(t)$

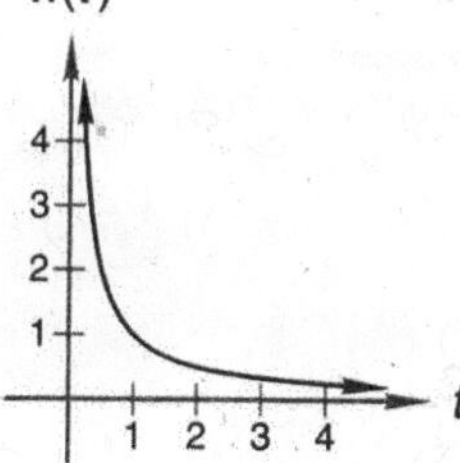

(b) $y(t)$

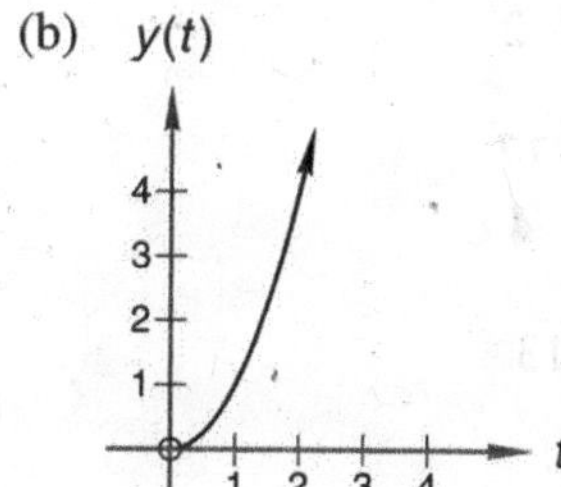

(c) $x(t) = \frac{1}{t} \qquad y = t^2$

$$y = \frac{1}{x^2} \text{ for } x > 0$$

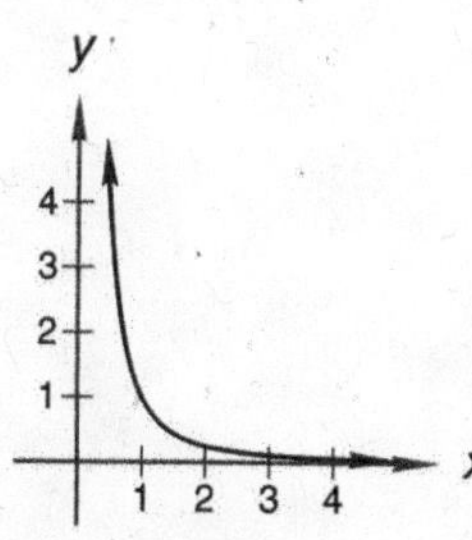

PROBLEM SET 107

1.

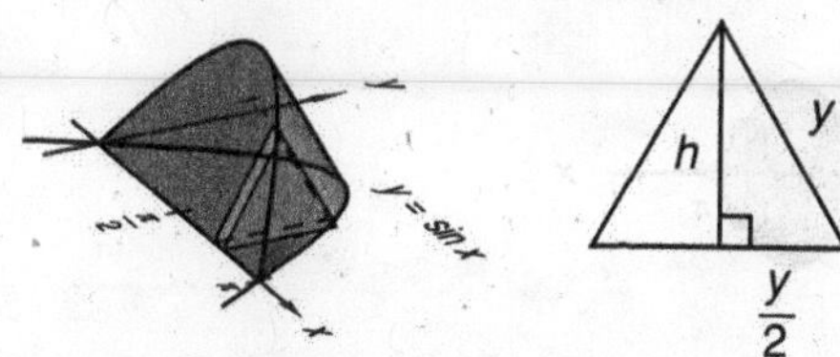

$$h^2 = y^2 - \frac{y^2}{4}$$

$$h = \frac{\sqrt{3}}{2}y = \frac{\sqrt{3}\sin x}{2}$$

$$V = 2\int_0^{\pi/2} \frac{1}{2}bh\,dx$$

$$= \int_0^{\pi/2} \sin x\left(\frac{\sqrt{3}\sin x}{2}\right) dx$$

$$= \frac{\sqrt{3}}{2}\int_0^{\pi/2} \sin^2 x\,dx$$

$$= \frac{\sqrt{3}}{2}\int_0^{\pi/2} \left[\frac{1}{2} - \frac{1}{2}\cos(2x)\right] dx$$

$$= \frac{\sqrt{3}}{2}\left[\frac{1}{2}x - \frac{1}{4}\sin(2x)\right]_0^{\pi/2}$$

$$= \frac{\sqrt{3}}{2}\left(\frac{\pi}{4}\right) = \frac{\sqrt{3}\pi}{8} \textbf{ units}^3$$

2. (a) $x(t) = t^3 - 6t^2 + 9t + 1$
$\mathbf{v(t) = 3t^2 - 12t + 9}$
$\mathbf{a(t) = 6t - 12}$

(b) $v(4) = 3(4)^2 - 12(4) + 9 = \mathbf{9}$
$a(3) = 6(3) - 12 = \mathbf{6}$

3. (a) $x(t) = t^3 - 6t^2 + 9t + 1$
$v(t) = 3t^2 - 12t + 9$
The particle is moving left when $v(t) < 0$
$3t^2 - 12t + 9 = 0$
$t^2 - 4t + 3 = 0$
$(t-3)(t-1) = 0$
sign of $v(t)$:

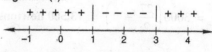

+ + + + + | − − − − | + + +
(number line: −1, 0, 1, 2, 3, 4)

$\mathbf{1 < t < 3}$

(b) The particle is moving right when $v(t) > 0$.
$\mathbf{t < 1,\ t > 3}$

(c) $x(0) = 1,\ x(1) = 5,\ x(3) = 1,\ x(4) = 5$
The total distance traveled is the sum of the distances traveled from $t = 0$ to 1, $t = 1$ to 3, and $t = 3$ to 4.

$D = 4 + 4 + 4 = \mathbf{12\ units}$

4. 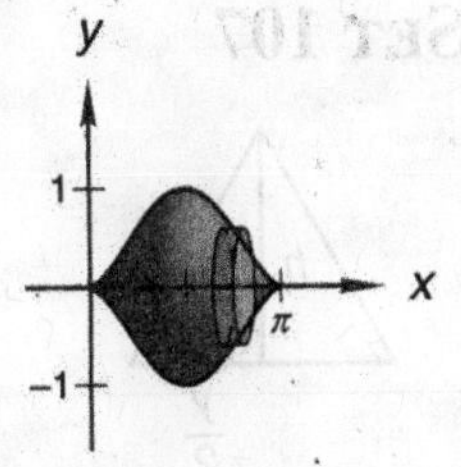

$$V = \pi \int_0^{\pi} (\sin^{3/2} x)^2\, dx$$
$$= \pi \int_0^{\pi} \sin^3 x\, dx$$
$$= \pi \int_0^{\pi} [\sin x\,(1 - \cos^2 x)]\, dx$$
$$= \pi \int_0^{\pi} (\sin x - \cos^2 x \sin x)\, dx$$
$$= \pi\left[-\cos x + \frac{1}{3}\cos^3 x\right]_0^{\pi}$$
$$= \pi\left[1 - \frac{1}{3} - \left(-1 + \frac{1}{3}\right)\right]$$
$$= \pi\left(2 - \frac{2}{3}\right) = \mathbf{\frac{4}{3}\pi\ units^3}$$

5. 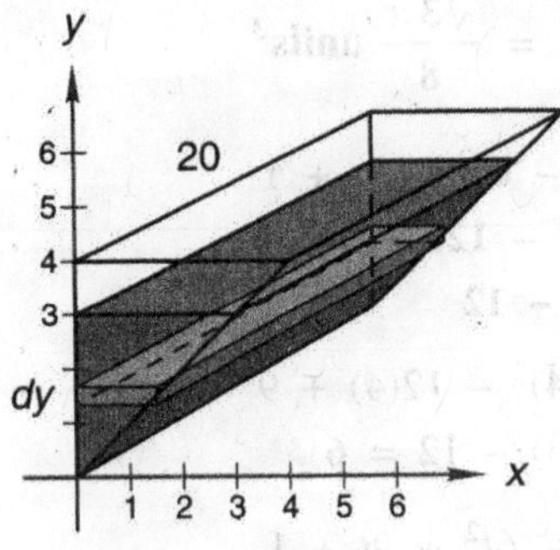

$$F = 3000 \int_0^3 (3 - y)\, y\, dy$$
$$= 3000 \int_0^3 (3y - y^2)\, dy$$
$$= 3000\left[\frac{3}{2}y^2 - \frac{1}{3}y^3\right]_0^3$$
$$= 3000\left(\frac{27}{2} - 9\right) = \mathbf{13{,}500\ newtons}$$

6.

t	−3	−2	−1	0	1	2	3
x	−9	−7	−5	−3	−1	1	3
y	11	6	3	2	3	6	11

$x = 2t - 3 \qquad y = t^2 + 2$

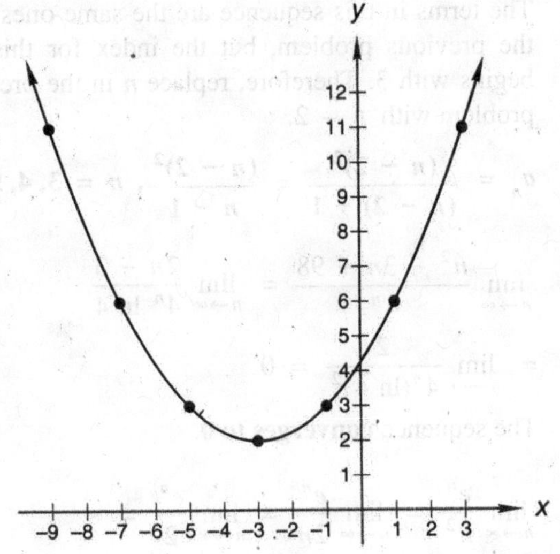

$$\frac{dy}{dx} = \frac{\frac{dy}{dt}}{\frac{dx}{dt}} = \frac{2t}{2} = t$$
$$\mathbf{\frac{dy}{dx} = \frac{x + 3}{2}}$$
$$y = \left(\frac{x+3}{2}\right)^2 + 2$$
$$y = \left(\frac{1}{2}x + \frac{3}{2}\right)^2 + 2$$
$$\mathbf{y = \frac{1}{4}x^2 + \frac{3}{2}x + \frac{17}{4}}$$

7. $r = \sqrt{4 + 9} = \sqrt{13}$

$\tan\theta = -\frac{3}{2}$

$\theta \approx 123.6901°$

$\mathbf{\sqrt{13}\ \underline{/123.6901°}}$

8. $r = \sqrt{1 + \frac{1}{4}} = \frac{\sqrt{5}}{2}$

$\theta = \tan^{-1}\left(\frac{1}{2}\right) \approx 26.5651°$

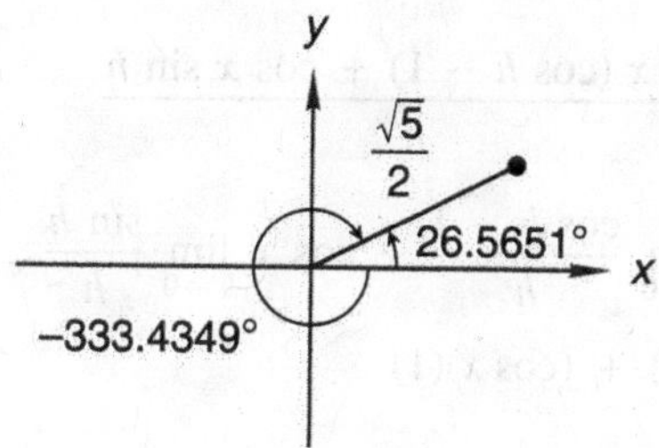

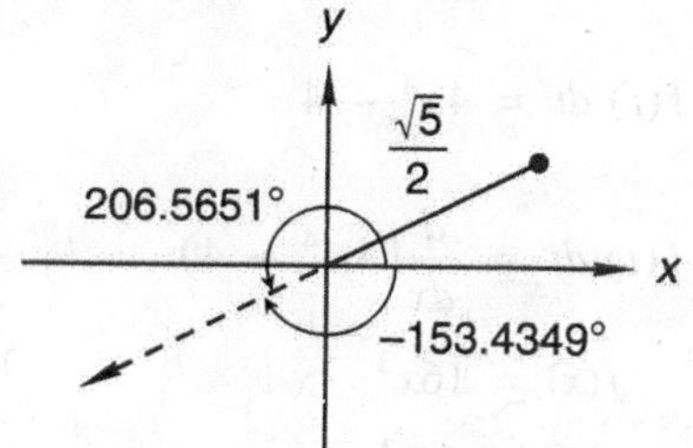

$\frac{\sqrt{5}}{2}\angle 26.5651°$, $\frac{\sqrt{5}}{2}\angle -333.4349°$, $-\frac{\sqrt{5}}{2}\angle -153.4349°$, or $-\frac{\sqrt{5}}{2}\angle 206.5651°$

9.
$$y = 2x^2$$
$$r\sin\theta = 2(r\cos\theta)^2$$
$$r\sin\theta = 2r^2\cos^2\theta$$
$$r = \frac{\sin\theta}{2\cos^2\theta}$$
$$r = \frac{1}{2}\tan\theta\sec\theta$$

10.
$$r = \sin\theta$$
$$\sqrt{x^2 + y^2} = \frac{y}{\sqrt{x^2 + y^2}}$$
$$x^2 + y^2 = y$$
$$x^2 + y^2 - y = 0$$

11. $\lim_{n\to\infty} \frac{2n^2}{(2n+1)^2} = \lim_{n\to\infty} \frac{2n^2}{4n^2 + 4n + 1} = \frac{1}{2}$

The sequence **converges to $\frac{1}{2}$.**

12. $\lim_{n\to\infty} \frac{7}{n!} = \frac{7}{\infty} = 0$

The sequence **converges to 0.**

13.

n	2	3	4	5	6	7
a_n	1	$-\frac{8}{9}$	1	$-\frac{32}{25}$	$\frac{64}{36}$	$-\frac{128}{49}$

$$a_n = (-1)^n\frac{2^n}{n^2},\ n = 2, 3, 4, 5, \ldots$$

14.
$$T = \frac{2}{12}\left[\frac{1}{9} + 2\left(\frac{9}{82}\right) + 2\left(\frac{9}{85}\right) + 2\left(\frac{1}{10}\right) + 2\left(\frac{9}{97}\right) + 2\left(\frac{9}{106}\right) + \frac{1}{13}\right]$$
$$\approx \mathbf{0.1958}$$

15.
$$\int_0^2 \frac{1}{x^2+9}\,dx = \frac{1}{3}\int_0^2 \frac{3}{x^2+9}\,dx = \frac{1}{3}\left[\arctan\frac{x}{3}\right]_0^2 \approx \mathbf{0.1960}$$

16.
$$\left|y - \frac{11}{4}\right| < \varepsilon$$
$$\left|\frac{3}{4}x + 2 - \frac{11}{4}\right| < \varepsilon$$
$$\left|\frac{3}{4}x - \frac{3}{4}\right| < \varepsilon$$
$$|x - 1| < \frac{4}{3}\varepsilon$$
$$\delta = \frac{4}{3}\varepsilon$$

17.
$$\lim_{x\to 0}\frac{x - \sin x}{x} = \lim_{x\to 0}\frac{1-\cos x}{1} = \frac{0}{1} = \mathbf{0}$$

18.
$$\lim_{x\to\infty}\frac{(\ln x)^2}{x} = \lim_{x\to\infty}\frac{2\ln x}{x} = \lim_{x\to\infty}\frac{2}{x} = \frac{2}{\infty} = \mathbf{0}$$

19.
$$\lim_{x\to\infty}\left(1+\frac{1}{x}\right)^{4x} = \lim_{x\to\infty}\left[\left(1+\frac{1}{x}\right)^x\right]^4 = \mathbf{e^4}$$

20. $f(x) = \tan x \qquad f'(x) = \sec^2 x$

$$f'(c) = \frac{f\left(\frac{\pi}{4}\right) - f(0)}{\frac{\pi}{4} - 0}$$

$$\sec^2 c = \frac{1}{\frac{\pi}{4}}$$

$$\sec^2 c = \frac{4}{\pi}$$

$$\sec c = \frac{2}{\sqrt{\pi}}$$

$$\cos c = \frac{\sqrt{\pi}}{2}$$

$$c = \mathbf{\cos^{-1}\frac{\sqrt{\pi}}{2}} \approx \mathbf{0.4817}$$

21.
$$f(x) = ae^x + b\sin x$$
$$f'(x) = ae^x + b\cos x$$
$$4 = ae^0 + b(1)$$
$$4 = a + b$$
$$f''(x) = ae^x - b\sin x$$
$$7 = ae^0 + b(0)$$
$$\mathbf{a = 7}$$
$$7 + b = 4$$
$$\mathbf{b = -3}$$

22.

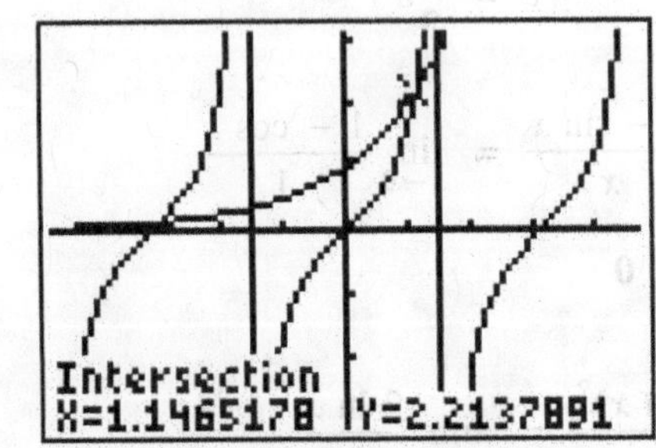

The smallest positive solution is approximately **1.1465.**

23.
$$f(x) = (x-3)^2 + 1$$
$$f(x) = (x^2 - 6x + 9) + 1$$
$$f(-x) = (x^2 + 6x + 9) + 1$$
$$f(-x) = (x+3)^2 + 1$$
$$f(|x|) = \begin{cases}(x-3)^2 + 1 \text{ when } x \geq 0 \\ (x+3)^2 + 1 \text{ when } x < 0\end{cases}$$
$$\frac{d}{dx}f(|x|) = \begin{cases}\mathbf{2x - 6 \text{ when } x > 0} \\ \mathbf{2x + 6 \text{ when } x < 0}\end{cases}$$

24.
$$\lim_{h\to0}\frac{\sin(x+h) - \sin x}{h}$$
$$= \lim_{h\to0}\frac{\sin x\cos h + \cos x\sin h - \sin x}{h}$$
$$= \lim_{h\to0}\frac{\sin x(\cos h - 1) + \cos x\sin h}{h}$$
$$= \sin x\lim_{h\to0}\frac{\cos h - 1}{h} + \cos x\lim_{h\to0}\frac{\sin h}{h}$$
$$= (\sin x)(0) + (\cos x)(1)$$
$$= \cos x$$

25. (a)
$$\int_c^x f(t)\,dt = 4x^4 - 4$$
$$\frac{d}{dx}\int_c^x f(t)\,dt = \frac{d}{dx}(4x^4 - 4)$$
$$f(x) = 16x^3$$
$$\mathbf{f(t) = 16t^3}$$

(b)
$$\int_c^x 16t^3\,dt = 4x^4 - 4$$
$$\left[4t^4\right]_c^x = 4x^4 - 4$$
$$4x^4 - 4c^4 = 4x^4 - 4$$
$$-4c^4 = -4$$
$$c^4 = 1$$
$$\mathbf{c = \pm 1}$$

Problem Set 108

1. $\vec{V} = (3-1)\hat{i} + (-2-2)\hat{j} = \mathbf{2\hat{i} - 4\hat{j}}$

2. $\vec{V} = (0+3)\hat{i} + (0-4)\hat{j} = \mathbf{3\hat{i} - 4\hat{j}}$

3.

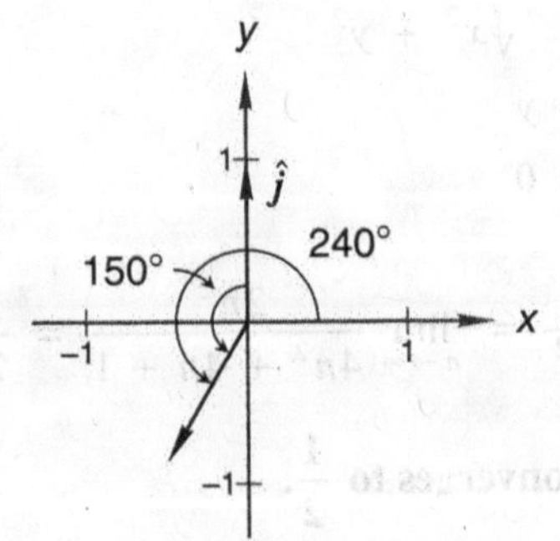

$$b = \sin\theta = \sin 240° \approx -0.8660$$
$$a = \cos\theta = \cos 240° = -0.5$$
$$1\angle 240° \approx \mathbf{\langle -0.5, -0.8660\rangle}$$

4. $r = 1$

$\theta = \tan^{-1} -\frac{6}{8} \approx -36.8699°$

$\underline{1\angle -36.8699°}$

5. $y = 3x^2 - 4$

$\frac{dy}{dx} = 6x = 6(2) = 12$

One vector with this slope is $\langle 1, 12 \rangle$.

$|\langle 1, 12 \rangle| = \sqrt{1^2 + 12^2} = \sqrt{145}$

A unit vector parallel to y at $(2, 8)$ is $\left\langle \frac{1}{\sqrt{145}}, \frac{12}{\sqrt{145}} \right\rangle$, and a unit normal vector is $\left\langle -\frac{12}{\sqrt{145}}, \frac{1}{\sqrt{145}} \right\rangle$.

6. (a) **True**

(b) **False.** A counterexample is $y = \sqrt[3]{x}$, which is continuous everywhere but not differentiable at $x = 0$.

(c) **False.** A counterexample is $y = |x|$, which is integrable on any interval but not differentiable at $x = 0$.

(d) **True**

7.

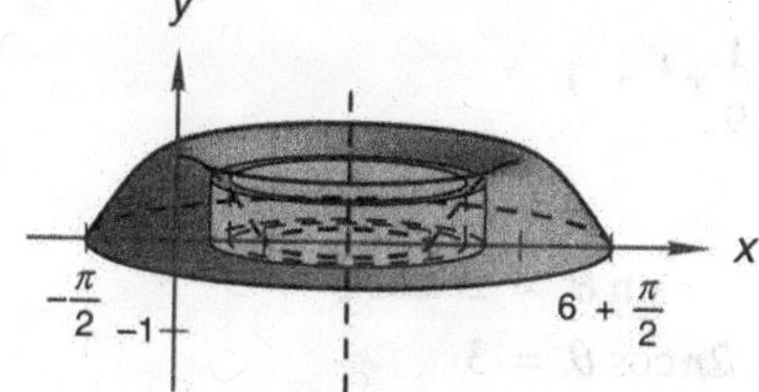

$$V = 2\pi \int_{-\pi/2}^{\pi/2} (3 - x) \cos x \, dx$$

$$= 2\pi \int_{-\pi/2}^{\pi/2} (3 \cos x - x \cos x) \, dx$$

$u = x \quad du = dx \quad v = \sin x \quad dv = \cos x \, dx$

$$2\pi \int_{-\pi/2}^{\pi/2} (3 \cos x - x \cos x) \, dx$$

$$= 2\pi \left[3 \sin x - x \sin x + \int \sin x \, dx \right]_{-\pi/2}^{\pi/2}$$

$$= 2\pi [3 \sin x - x \sin x - \cos x]_{-\pi/2}^{\pi/2}$$

$$= 2\pi \left[3 - \frac{\pi}{2} - 0 - \left(-3 - \frac{\pi}{2} - 0 \right) \right]$$

$$= 2\pi(6) = \mathbf{12\pi \text{ units}^3}$$

8.

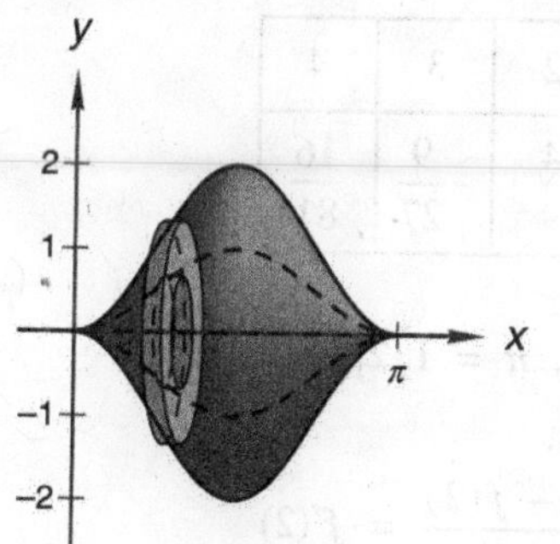

$$V = \pi \int_0^{\pi} [(2 \sin^2 x)^2 - (\sin^2 x)^2] \, dx$$

$$= \mathbf{3\pi \int_0^{\pi} \sin^4 x \, dx}$$

9.

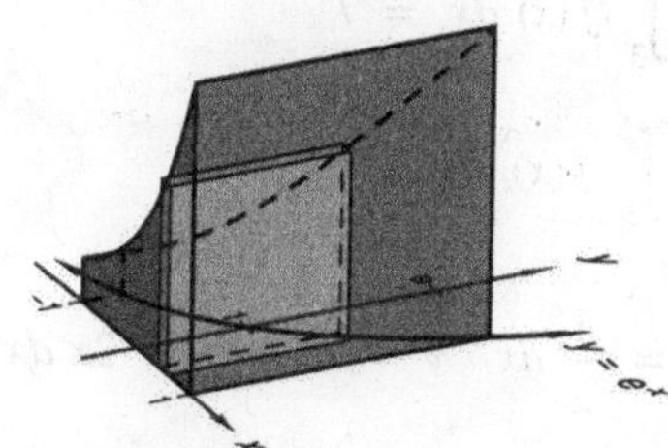

$$V = \int_{-1}^{1} (e^x)^2 \, dx = \int_{-1}^{1} e^{2x} \, dx$$

$$= \left[\frac{1}{2} e^{2x} \right]_{-1}^{1} = \mathbf{\frac{1}{2}(e^2 - e^{-2}) \text{ units}^3}$$

10. $y = 4^x$

$\frac{dy}{dx} = 4^x \ln 4$

$\left. \frac{dy}{dx} \right|_1 = 4 \ln 4$

$y - 4 = 4 \ln 4 (x - 1)$

$y = \ln 4^4 (x - 1) + 4$

$\mathbf{y = (\ln 256)x - \ln 256 + 4}$

11. Because e^{x^2} is an even function

$$\int_{-k}^{k} e^{x^2} \, dx = 2 \int_0^k e^{x^2} \, dx = \mathbf{2c}$$

12. $\lim_{n \to \infty} \frac{3^n}{n^3} = \lim_{n \to \infty} \frac{3^n \ln 3}{3n^2} = \lim_{n \to \infty} \frac{3^n (\ln 3)^2}{6n}$

$= \lim_{n \to \infty} \frac{3^n (\ln 3)^3}{6} = \frac{\infty}{6} = \infty$

The sequence **diverges.**

13. $\lim_{n \to \infty} \left(\frac{1}{3} \right)^n = \frac{1}{\infty} = 0$

The sequence **converges to 0.**

14.

n	1	2	3	4
a_n	$-\frac{1}{3}$	$\frac{4}{9}$	$-\frac{9}{27}$	$\frac{16}{81}$

$$\mathbf{a_n = (-1)^n \frac{n^2}{3^n},\ n = 1, 2, 3, \ldots}$$

15. $$\lim_{h \to 0} \frac{f(2+h) - f(2)}{h} = f'(2)$$
$$= \mathbf{\cos 2}$$

16. $$\int_{-1}^{3} f(x)\,dx + \int_{3}^{5} f(x)\,dx = \int_{-1}^{5} f(x)\,dx$$
$$-3 + \int_{3}^{5} f(x)\,dx = 7$$
$$\mathbf{\int_{3}^{5} f(x)\,dx = 10}$$

17. $u = \ln x \quad du = \frac{1}{x}\,dx \quad v = x^2 \quad dv = 2x\,dx$

$$\int 2x \ln x\,dx = x^2 \ln x - \int x\,dx$$
$$= x^2 \ln x - \frac{1}{2}x^2 + C$$
$$= \mathbf{x^2\left(\ln x - \frac{1}{2}\right) + C}$$

18. $$\int \tan^3(2x)\,dx = \int \tan(2x)\,[\sec^2(2x) - 1]\,dx$$
$$= \int [\tan(2x)\sec^2(2x) - \tan(2x)]\,dx$$

$u = \tan(2x) \qquad du = 2\sec^2(2x)\,dx$

$$\int [\tan(2x)\sec^2(2x) - \tan(2x)]\,dx$$
$$= \frac{1}{2}\int u\,du - \frac{1}{2}\int 2\tan(2x)\,dx$$
$$= \frac{1}{4}u^2 - \frac{1}{2}\ln|\sec(2x)| + C$$
$$= \mathbf{\frac{1}{4}\tan^2(2x) - \ln\sqrt{\sec(2x)} + C}$$
$$= \mathbf{\frac{1}{4}\sec^2(2x) + \ln\sqrt{\cos(2x)} + C}$$

19. $$\int \frac{x^3 + 4x^2 - 3x + 7}{x^2}\,dx$$
$$= \int \left(x + 4 - \frac{3}{x} + 7x^{-2}\right) dx$$
$$= \mathbf{\frac{1}{2}x^2 + 4x - 3\ln|x| - 7x^{-1} + C}$$

20. $$\frac{d}{dx}[\arcsin(2x)] + \int \frac{2}{\sqrt{1 - 4x^2}}\,dx$$
$$= \mathbf{\frac{2}{\sqrt{1 - 4x^2}} + \arcsin(2x) + C}$$

21. $x = 3t$
$9 = 3t$
$t = 3$

$y = t^2 + 1$
$y = 3^2 + 1$
$\mathbf{y = 10}$

22. (a)

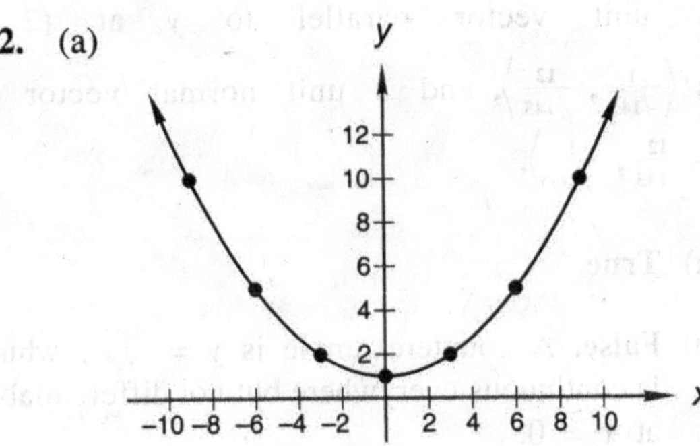

(b) $$\frac{dy}{dx} = \frac{\frac{dy}{dt}}{\frac{dx}{dt}} = \frac{2t}{3} = \frac{2}{3}\left(\frac{x}{3}\right) = \mathbf{\frac{2}{9}x}$$

(c) $$y = \left(\frac{x}{3}\right)^2 + 1$$
$$\mathbf{y = \frac{1}{9}x^2 + 1}$$

23. $$y = 2x + 3$$
$$r\sin\theta = 2r\cos\theta + 3$$
$$r\sin\theta - 2r\cos\theta = 3$$
$$r(\sin\theta - 2\cos\theta) = 3$$
$$\mathbf{r = \frac{3}{\sin\theta - 2\cos\theta}}$$

24. $y = 3x^4 - 12x^3 - 24x^2$
$y' = 12x^3 - 36x^2 - 48x$
$y' = 12x(x^2 - 3x - 4)$
$0 = 12x(x - 4)(x + 1)$
$x = 0, 4, -1$

$y'' = 36x^2 - 72x - 48$
$y'' = 12(3x^2 - 6x - 4)$
$0 = 12(3x^2 - 6x - 4)$
$$x = \frac{6 \pm \sqrt{36 - 4(3)(-4)}}{6}$$
$$x = 1 \pm \frac{\sqrt{21}}{3}$$

$y''(0) = -48$ implies concave down
$y''(4) = 240$ implies concave up
$y''(-1) = 60$ implies concave up

Local maximum: $x = 0$
Local minima: $x = -1, 4$

Inflection points: $x = 1 \pm \frac{\sqrt{21}}{3}$

25.

n	$f^{(n)}(x)$	$f^{(n)}(0)$
0	$\ln(1 - x)$	0
1	$-\frac{1}{1-x} = -(1-x)^{-1}$	-1
2	$-(1-x)^{-2}$	-1
3	$-2(1-x)^{-3}$	-2
4	$-6(1-x)^{-4}$	-6
$\vdots$	$\vdots$	$\vdots$

$$\ln(1 - x) = -x - \frac{x^2}{2!} - \frac{2x^3}{3!} - \frac{6x^4}{4!} - \cdots$$

$$\ln(1 - x) = \mathbf{-x - \frac{x^2}{2} - \frac{x^3}{3} - \frac{x^4}{4} - \cdots}$$

$$1 - x = 1.1$$
$$x = -0.1$$

$$\ln(1.1) \approx 0.1 - \frac{1}{2}(-0.1)^2 - \frac{1}{3}(-0.1)^3$$
$$\approx \mathbf{0.0953}$$

PROBLEM SET 109

1. $r = 10 \qquad dr = 0.5$

$$w(r) = r(r - 9)^2 + 40$$
$$d(w(r)) = [2r(r - 9) + (r - 9)^2]\,dr$$
$$d(w(10)) = [2(10)(1) + 1]0.5$$
$$d(w(10)) = \mathbf{10.5\ gallons}$$

2. $f(x) = x^{3/2} \qquad f'(x) = \frac{3}{2}x^{1/2}$

$$L_0^4 = \int_0^4 \sqrt{1 + \left(\frac{3}{2}x^{1/2}\right)^2}\,dx$$
$$= \int_0^4 \sqrt{1 + \frac{9}{4}x}\,dx$$
$$= \frac{4}{9}\int_0^4 \frac{9}{4}\left(1 + \frac{9}{4}x\right)^{1/2} dx$$
$$= \frac{8}{27}\left[\left(1 + \frac{9}{4}x\right)^{3/2}\right]_0^4$$
$$= \mathbf{\frac{8}{27}(10\sqrt{10} - 1)\ units}$$

3.
$$y = x^{2/3}$$
$$x = y^{3/2}$$
$$\frac{dx}{dy} = \frac{3}{2}y^{1/2}$$

$$L_0^4 = \int_0^4 \sqrt{1 + \left(\frac{3}{2}y^{1/2}\right)^2}\,dy$$
$$= \int_0^4 \sqrt{1 + \frac{9}{4}y}\,dy$$
$$= \frac{4}{9}\int_0^4 \frac{9}{4}\left(1 + \frac{9}{4}y\right)^{1/2} dy$$
$$= \frac{8}{27}\left[\left(1 + \frac{9}{4}y\right)^{3/2}\right]_0^4$$
$$= \mathbf{\frac{8}{27}(10\sqrt{10} - 1)\ units}$$

4. $f(x) = \sin x + x^2 \qquad f'(x) = \cos x + 2x$

$$L_0^3 = \mathbf{\int_0^3 \sqrt{1 + (\cos x + 2x)^2}\,dx}$$

5.
$$v(t) = te^{-t}$$
$$a(t) = -te^{-t} + e^{-t}$$
$$a(t) = e^{-t}(-t + 1)$$
$$\mathbf{a(4) = -3e^{-4}}$$

$u = t \quad du = dt \quad v = -e^{-t} \quad dv = e^{-t}\,dt$

$$x(t) = \int v(t)\,dt$$
$$x(t) = -te^{-t} + \int e^{-t}\,dt$$
$$x(t) = -te^{-t} - e^{-t} + C$$
$$x(t) = -e^{-t}(t + 1) + C$$
$$x(0) = -(1) + C$$
$$0 = -1 + C$$
$$C = 1$$
$$x(t) = -e^{-t}(t + 1) + 1$$
$$\mathbf{x(3) = -4e^{-3} + 1}$$

6. $x = 3\sin^2 t \qquad y = 4\cos^2 t$

$$\frac{dy}{dx} = \frac{\frac{dy}{dt}}{\frac{dx}{dt}} = \frac{-8\cos t \sin t}{6 \sin t \cos t} = -\frac{4}{3}$$

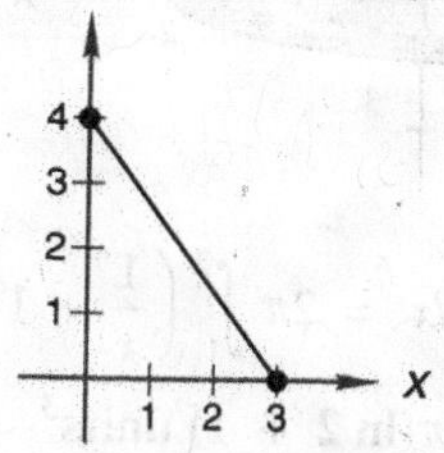

y
4
3
2
1
x
1
2
3

7. $\theta = \frac{\pi}{4}$

$\tan^{-1}\frac{y}{x} = \frac{\pi}{4}$

$\frac{y}{x} = \tan\frac{\pi}{4}$

$\frac{y}{x} = 1$

$y = x$

8. $x^2 + y^2 = 9$

$r^2 = 9$

$\mathbf{r = 3}$

9. $\lim_{x\to\infty}\frac{x\ln x}{x^2+1} = \lim_{x\to\infty}\frac{1+\ln x}{2x} = \lim_{x\to\infty}\frac{1}{2x}$

$= \mathbf{0}$

10. $\lim_{x\to 0}\frac{\sin(17x)}{12x} = \frac{17}{12}\lim_{17x\to 0}\frac{\sin(17x)}{17x}$

$= \mathbf{\frac{17}{12}}$

11. $\lim_{h\to 0}\frac{\sin\left(\frac{\pi}{2}+h\right) - \sin\frac{\pi}{2}}{h} = \frac{d}{dx}\sin x\Big|_{\pi/2}$

$= \cos\frac{\pi}{2} = \mathbf{0}$

12. $\frac{d}{dx}\int_x^2 \frac{\ln t}{t}\,dt = \frac{d}{dx} - \int_2^x \frac{\ln t}{t}\,dt = \mathbf{-\frac{\ln x}{x}}$

13. Any graph of the form $y = f(|x|)$ has y-axis symmetry, so its graph is the same as $y = f(x)$ provided f is an even function.

The correct choice is **C**.

14.

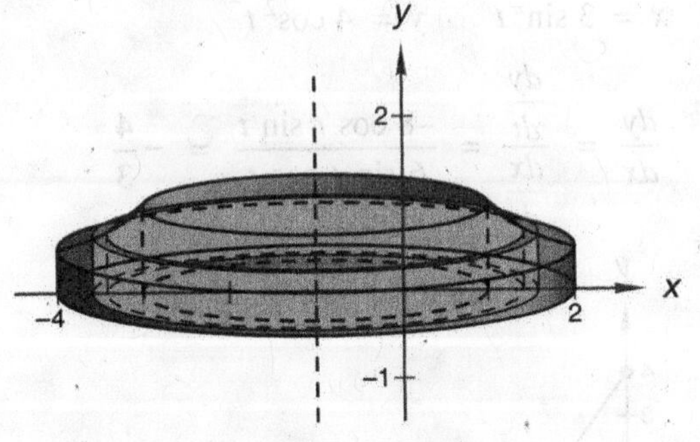

$V = 2\pi\int_1^2 (1+x)\left(\frac{1}{x}\right)dx = 2\pi\int_1^2\left(\frac{1}{x}+1\right)dx$

$= 2\pi[\ln x + x]_1^2 = \mathbf{2\pi(\ln 2 + 1)\ units^3}$

15. $u = 25 - x^2 \qquad du = -2x\,dx$

$\int\frac{2x}{\sqrt{25-x^2}}\,dx = -\int u^{-1/2}\,du$

$= -2u^{1/2} + C$

$= \mathbf{-2\sqrt{25 - x^2} + C}$

16. $\int \cot^2(2x)\,dx = \int[\csc^2(2x) - 1]\,dx$

$= \mathbf{-\frac{1}{2}\cot(2x) - x + C}$

17. $e^{2x} - 2 = 0$

$e^{2x} = 2$

$2x = \ln 2$

$x = \frac{1}{2}\ln 2$

$x = \ln\sqrt{2}$

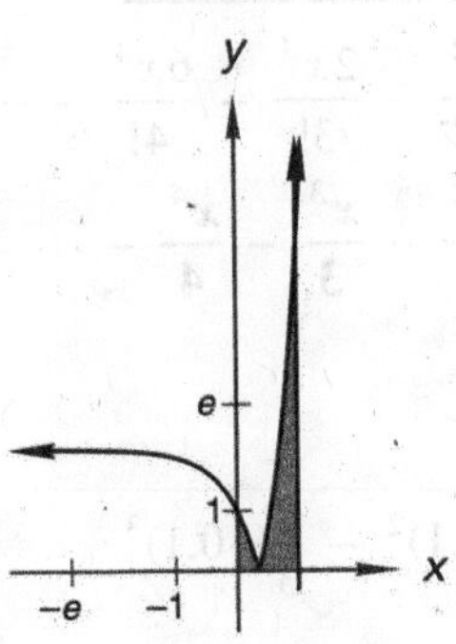

$\int_0^1 |e^{2x} - 2|\,dx$

$= \mathbf{\int_0^{\ln\sqrt{2}}(-e^{2x}+2)\,dx + \int_{\ln\sqrt{2}}^1 (e^{2x}-2)\,dx}$

18. $(f^{-1})'\left(\frac{1}{2}\right) = \frac{1}{f'\left(f^{-1}\left(\frac{1}{2}\right)\right)} = \frac{1}{f'\left(\frac{\pi}{6}\right)}$

$= \frac{1}{\cos\frac{\pi}{6}} = \frac{1}{\frac{\sqrt{3}}{2}} = \mathbf{\frac{2\sqrt{3}}{3}}$

19. $f(c) = \frac{1}{1}\int_0^1\sqrt{x}\,dx$

$\sqrt{c} = \left[\frac{2}{3}x^{3/2}\right]_0^1$

$\sqrt{c} = \frac{2}{3}$

$c = \mathbf{\frac{4}{9}}$

20. 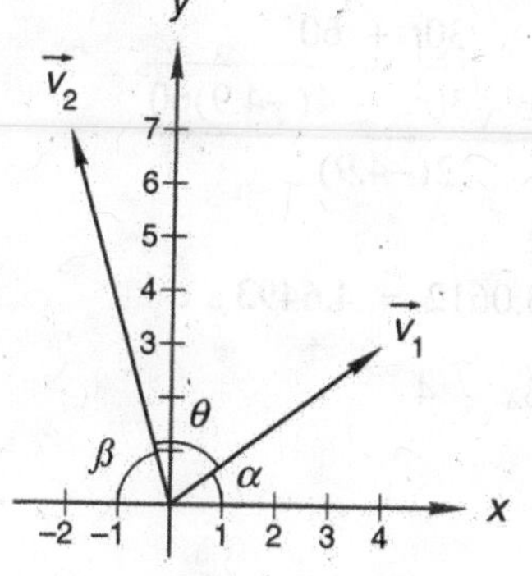

$\alpha = \tan^{-1}\frac{3}{4} \approx 36.8699°$

$\beta = \tan^{-1}\frac{7}{2} \approx 74.0546°$

$\alpha + \beta + \theta = 180°$ implies $\theta \approx$ **69.0755°**

21. $y = x^2 - 4$

$\frac{dy}{dx} = 2x$

$\left.\frac{dy}{dx}\right|_3 = 6$

One vector with a slope of 6 is $\langle 1, 6\rangle$.

$|\langle 1, 6\rangle| = \sqrt{1^2 + 6^3} = \sqrt{37}$

A vector with magnitude 1 is $\left\langle \frac{1}{\sqrt{37}}, \frac{6}{\sqrt{37}} \right\rangle$.

A vector with magnitude 6 is $\left\langle \mathbf{\frac{6}{\sqrt{37}}}, \mathbf{\frac{36}{\sqrt{37}}} \right\rangle$.

22. $y = \arctan\frac{x}{2} + e^{\sin x + \cos x} - \frac{1 + x}{e^x - \sin x}$

$$\frac{dy}{dx} = \frac{2}{x^2 + 4} + (\cos x - \sin x)e^{\sin x + \cos x} - \frac{(e^x - \sin x) - (1 + x)(e^x - \cos x)}{(e^x - \sin x)^2}$$

$$\frac{dy}{dx} = \mathbf{\frac{2}{x^2 + 4} + (\cos x - \sin x)e^{\sin x + \cos x} - \frac{1}{e^x - \sin x} + \frac{(1 + x)(e^x - \cos x)}{(e^x - \sin x)^2}}$$

23. (a) $a_n = \frac{(-1)^{n+1}n}{2^n}$, $n = 1, 2, 3, \ldots$

$a_1 = \mathbf{\frac{1}{2}}$, $a_2 = \mathbf{-\frac{1}{2}}$, $a_3 = \mathbf{\frac{3}{8}}$, $a_4 = \mathbf{-\frac{1}{4}}$

(b) $\lim_{n\to\infty} \frac{(-1)^{n+1}n}{2^n}$

$= \lim_{n\to\infty} (-1)^{n+1} \cdot \lim_{n\to\infty} \frac{n}{2^n}$

$= \lim_{n\to\infty} (-1)^{n+1} \cdot \lim_{n\to\infty} \frac{1}{2^n \ln 2}$

$= \lim_{n\to\infty} (-1)^{n+1} \cdot 0 = 0$

The sequence **converges to zero.**

24.

n	1	2	3	4
a_n	$\frac{1}{2}$	$\frac{3}{4}$	$\frac{7}{8}$	$\frac{15}{16}$

$\mathbf{a_n = \frac{2^n - 1}{2^n}, n = 1, 2, 3, \ldots}$

25. (a) $f(x) = \frac{x^2 + x - 2}{x} = x + 1 - \frac{2}{x}$

Vertical asymptote: $x = 0$

End behavior: $y = x + 1$

(b) $\frac{f(x)}{x} = \frac{x^2 + x - 2}{x^2} = 1 + \frac{1}{x} - \frac{2}{x^2} \approx \mathbf{1}$ when x is large

(c) $xf(x) = x^2 + x - 2 \approx \mathbf{x^2}$ when x is large

PROBLEM SET 110

1. $y = \sqrt{x}$

$dy = \frac{1}{2\sqrt{x}}\,dx$

$dy = \frac{1}{2\sqrt{16}}(1)$

$dy = \frac{1}{8}$

$\sqrt{17} \approx \sqrt{16} + dy = 4 + \frac{1}{8} = \mathbf{4\frac{1}{8}}$

2. 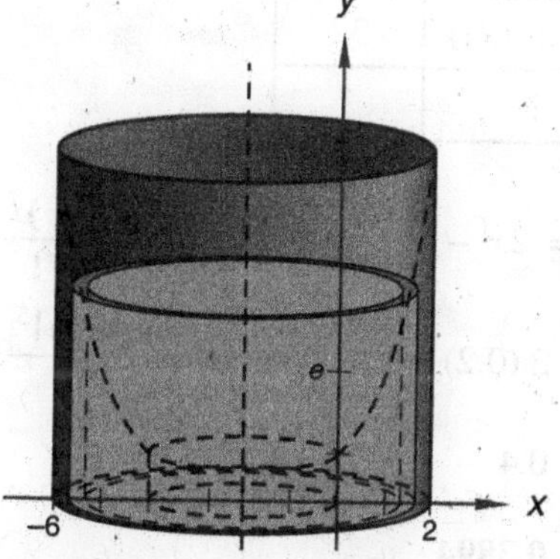

$V = 2\pi \int_0^2 (2 + x)e^x\,dx$

$= 2\pi \int_0^2 (2e^x + xe^x)\,dx$

$u = x \quad du = dx \quad v = e^x \quad dv = e^x\,dx$

$2\pi \int_0^2 (2e^x + xe^x)\,dx = 2\pi\left[2e^x + xe^x - e^x\right]_0^2$

$= \mathbf{2\pi(3e^2 - 1)}$ **units³**

3. $|\langle 2, -3\rangle| = \sqrt{2^2 + (-3)^2} = \sqrt{13}$

The unit vector with identical slope is $\left\langle \frac{2}{\sqrt{13}}, -\frac{3}{\sqrt{13}} \right\rangle$.

The normal unit vector is then $\left\langle \frac{3}{\sqrt{13}}, \frac{2}{\sqrt{13}} \right\rangle$.

A normal vector with length 4 is $4\left\langle \frac{3}{\sqrt{13}}, \frac{2}{\sqrt{13}} \right\rangle = \left\langle \frac{12}{\sqrt{13}}, \frac{8}{\sqrt{13}} \right\rangle$.

4. $\frac{dy}{dx} = \frac{1}{x}$

$dy = \frac{1}{x}\,dx$

$y = \ln|x| + C$

$1 = \ln 1 + C$

$C = 1$

$\mathbf{f(x) = \ln|x| + 1}$

5. $\sin 0.4 = \sin(2x)$

$0.4 = 2x$

$0.2 = x$

n	$f^{(n)}(x)$	$f^{(n)}(0)$
0	$\sin(2x)$	0
1	$2\cos(2x)$	2
2	$-4\sin(2x)$	0
3	$-8\cos(2x)$	-8
4	$16\sin(2x)$	0
5	$32\cos(2x)$	32
⋮	⋮	⋮

$$\sin(2x) = 2x - \frac{(2x)^3}{3!} + \frac{(2x)^5}{5!} - \frac{(2x)^7}{7!} + \cdots$$

$$\sin 0.4 \approx 2(0.2) - \frac{[2(0.2)]^3}{3!} + \frac{[2(0.2)]^5}{5!}$$

$$\approx 0.4 - \frac{0.4^3}{6} + \frac{0.4^5}{120}$$

$$\approx \mathbf{0.3894}$$

6. (a) $a(t) = -9.8 \text{ m/s}^2$

$\mathbf{v(t) = -9.8t + 30}$

$\mathbf{h(t) = -4.9t^2 + 30t + 60}$

(b) $v(t) = 0$

$-9.8t + 30 = 0$

$9.8t = 30$

$t \approx \mathbf{3.0612\ s}$

(c) $0 = -4.9t^2 + 30t + 60$

$$t = \frac{-30 \pm \sqrt{30^2 - 4(-4.9)60}}{2(-4.9)}$$

$t \approx 7.7105$

$7.7105 - 3.0612 = \mathbf{4.6493\ s}$

7. $y = 2x^2 + 3x - 4$

$\frac{dy}{dx} = 4x + 3$

$$L_2^6 = \int_2^6 \sqrt{1 + (4x + 3)^2}\,dx$$

$$= \int_2^6 \sqrt{\mathbf{16x^2 + 24x + 10}}\,\mathbf{dx}$$

8. $y = x^{3/2}$

$\frac{dy}{dx} = \frac{3}{2}x^{1/2}$

$$L_1^4 = \int_1^4 \sqrt{1 + \left(\frac{3}{2}x^{1/2}\right)^2}\,dx$$

$$= \frac{4}{9}\int_1^4 \frac{9}{4}\left(1 + \frac{9}{4}x\right)^{1/2} dx$$

$$= \left(\frac{4}{9}\right)\left(\frac{2}{3}\right)\left[\left(1 + \frac{9}{4}x\right)^{3/2}\right]_1^4$$

$$= \mathbf{\frac{8}{27}\left(10\sqrt{10} - \frac{13\sqrt{13}}{8}\right)\ units}$$

$$\approx \mathbf{7.6337\ units}$$

9. $(y + 1)^2 = (x - 4)^3$

$y + 1 = (x - 4)^{3/2}$

$y = (x - 4)^{3/2} - 1$

$\frac{dy}{dx} = \frac{3}{2}\sqrt{x - 4}$

$$L_5^8 = \int_5^8 \sqrt{1 + \left[\frac{3}{2}(x - 4)^{1/2}\right]^2}\,dx$$

$$= \frac{4}{9}\int_5^8 \frac{9}{4}\left[1 + \frac{9}{4}(x - 4)\right]^{1/2} dx$$

$$= \left(\frac{4}{9}\right)\left(\frac{2}{3}\right)\left[\left(1 + \frac{9}{4}(x - 4)\right)^{3/2}\right]_5^8$$

$$= \mathbf{\frac{8}{27}\left(10\sqrt{10} - \frac{13\sqrt{13}}{8}\right)\ units}$$

$$\approx \mathbf{7.6337\ units}$$

10. $f(x) = \int_4^x t^2\sqrt{1 + t^2}\,dt$

$f'(x) = \frac{d}{dx}\int_4^x t^2\sqrt{1 + t^2}\,dt$

$f'(x) = x^2\sqrt{1 + x^2}$

$f'(1.4) = (1.4)^2\sqrt{1 + (1.4)^2} \approx \mathbf{3.3721}$

11.
$$r = 2 + \sin\theta$$
$$\sqrt{x^2 + y^2} = 2 + \frac{y}{\sqrt{x^2 + y^2}}$$
$$\sqrt{x^2 + y^2} = \frac{2\sqrt{x^2 + y^2} + y}{\sqrt{x^2 + y^2}}$$
$$\mathbf{x^2 + y^2 = 2\sqrt{x^2 + y^2} + y}$$

12.
$$y = 2x + 3$$
$$r\sin\theta = 2r\cos\theta + 3$$
$$r(\sin\theta - 2\cos\theta) = 3$$
$$\mathbf{r = \frac{3}{\sin\theta - 2\cos\theta}}$$

13.

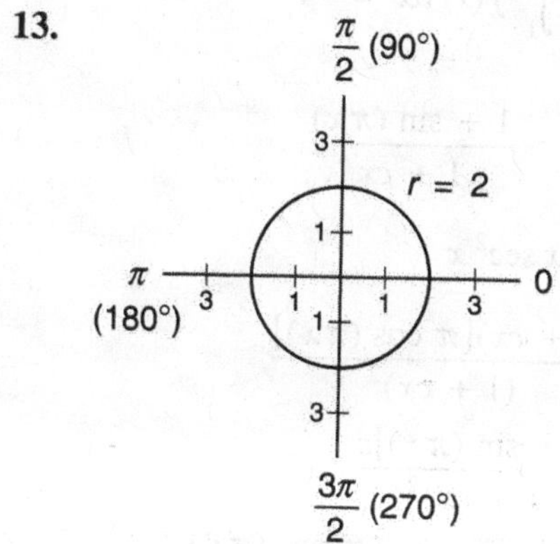

14.

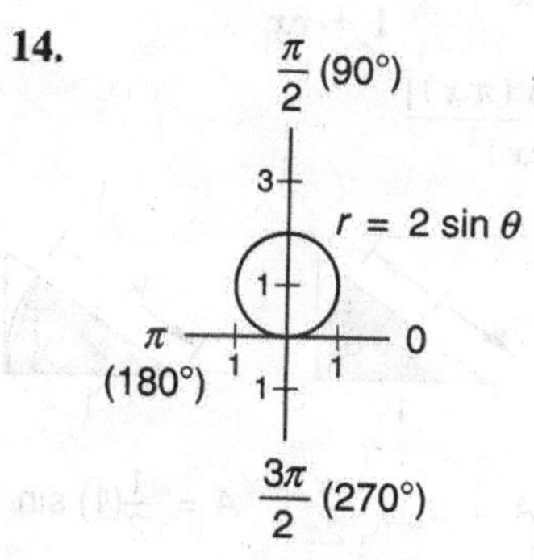

15.

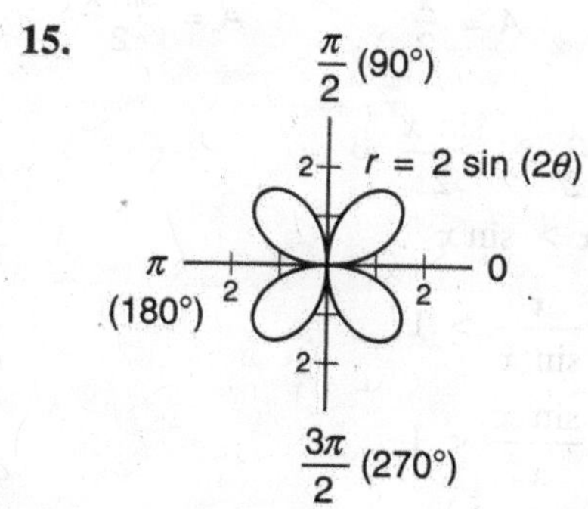

16.

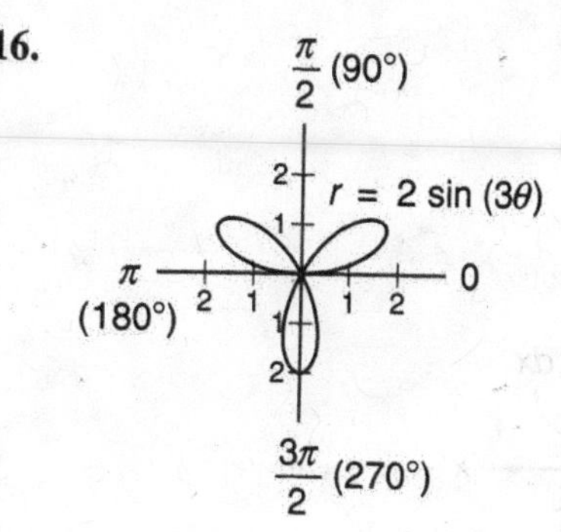

17. $x = e^t \qquad y = e^{-3t}$

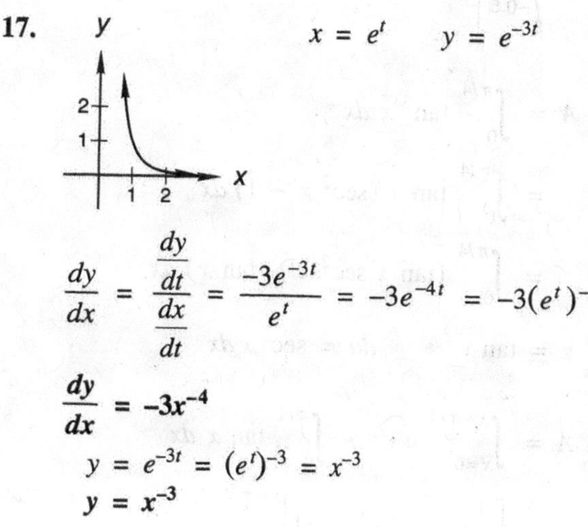

$$\frac{dy}{dx} = \frac{\frac{dy}{dt}}{\frac{dx}{dt}} = \frac{-3e^{-3t}}{e^t} = -3e^{-4t} = -3(e^t)^{-4}$$
$$\mathbf{\frac{dy}{dx} = -3x^{-4}}$$
$$y = e^{-3t} = (e^t)^{-3} = x^{-3}$$
$$\mathbf{y = x^{-3}}$$

18.

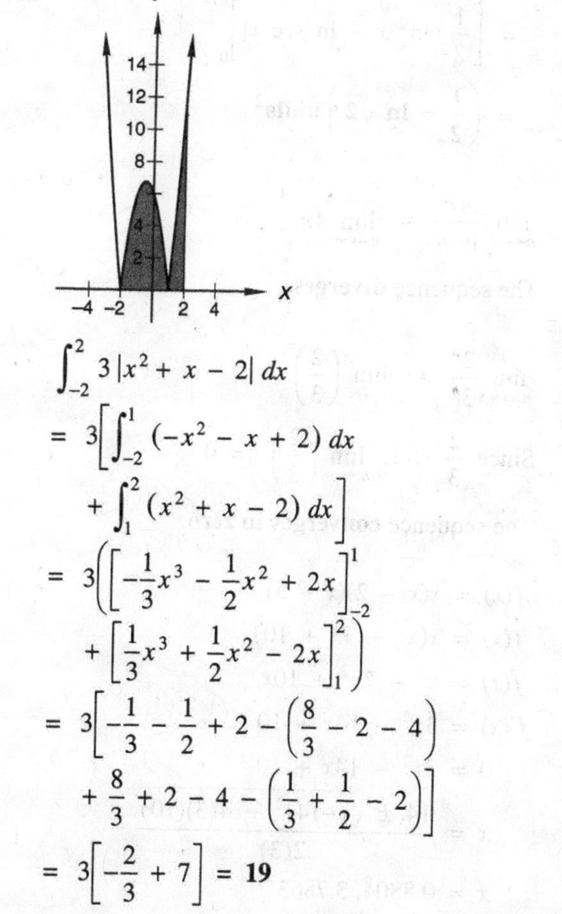

$$\int_{-2}^{2} 3|x^2 + x - 2|\,dx$$
$$= 3\left[\int_{-2}^{1} (-x^2 - x + 2)\,dx + \int_{1}^{2} (x^2 + x - 2)\,dx\right]$$
$$= 3\left(\left[-\frac{1}{3}x^3 - \frac{1}{2}x^2 + 2x\right]_{-2}^{1} + \left[\frac{1}{3}x^3 + \frac{1}{2}x^2 - 2x\right]_{1}^{2}\right)$$
$$= 3\left[-\frac{1}{3} - \frac{1}{2} + 2 - \left(\frac{8}{3} - 2 - 4\right) + \frac{8}{3} + 2 - 4 - \left(\frac{1}{3} + \frac{1}{2} - 2\right)\right]$$
$$= 3\left[-\frac{2}{3} + 7\right] = \mathbf{19}$$

19.

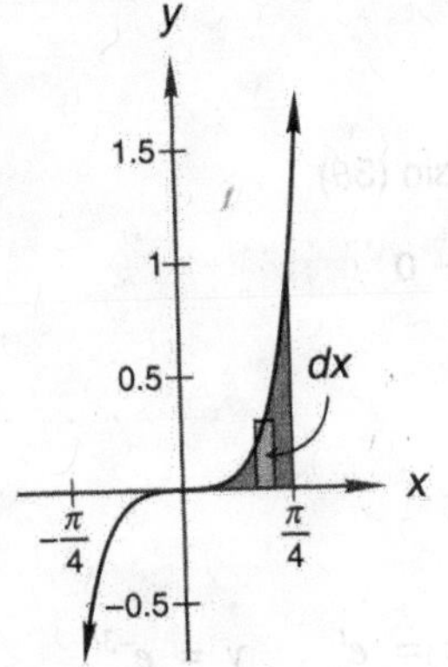

$$A = \int_0^{\pi/4} \tan^3 x\, dx$$
$$= \int_0^{\pi/4} \tan x\,(\sec^2 x - 1)\, dx$$
$$= \int_0^{\pi/4} (\tan x \sec^2 x - \tan x)\, dx$$

$u = \tan x \qquad du = \sec^2 x\, dx$

$$A = \int_{x=0}^{x=\pi/4} u\, du - \int_0^{\pi/4} \tan x\, dx$$
$$= \left[\frac{1}{2}u^2 - \ln|\sec x|\right]_{x=0}^{x=\pi/4}$$
$$= \left[\frac{1}{2}\tan^2 x - \ln|\sec x|\right]_0^{\pi/4}$$
$$= \left(\frac{1}{2} - \ln\sqrt{2}\right) \textbf{ units}^2$$

20. $\displaystyle\lim_{n\to\infty} \frac{4n}{\ln n} = \lim_{n\to\infty} 4n = \infty$

The sequence **diverges.**

21. $\displaystyle\lim_{n\to\infty} \frac{2^n}{3^n} = \lim_{n\to\infty} \left(\frac{2}{3}\right)^n$

Since $\frac{2}{3} < 1$, $\displaystyle\lim_{n\to\infty} \left(\frac{2}{3}\right)^n = 0$

The sequence **converges to zero.**

22.
$$f(x) = x(x-2)(x-5)$$
$$f(x) = x(x^2 - 7x + 10)$$
$$f(x) = x^3 - 7x^2 + 10x$$
$$f'(x) = 3x^2 - 14x + 10$$
$$0 = 3x^2 - 14x + 10$$
$$x = \frac{14 \pm \sqrt{(-14)^2 - 4(3)(10)}}{2(3)}$$
$$x \approx 0.8804,\ 3.7863$$

Critical numbers: $x = -1, 0.8804, 3.7863, 5$
$$f(-1) = -18$$
$$f(0.8804) \approx 4.0607$$
$$f(3.7863) \approx -8.2088$$
$$f(5) = 0$$

Maximum: (0.8804, 4.0607)
Minimum: (−1, −18)

23.
$$\int_1^3 f(x)\,dx + \int_3^7 f(x)\,dx = \int_1^7 f(x)\,dx$$
$$\int_1^3 f(x)\,dx + 5 = 4$$
$$\int_1^3 f(x)\,dx = \mathbf{-1}$$

24.
$$y = \tan^3 x - \frac{1 + \sin(\pi x)}{1 + cx}$$
$$\frac{dy}{dx} = 3\tan^2 x \sec^2 x - \frac{(1+cx)[\pi\cos(\pi x)]}{(1+cx)^2} + \frac{[1+\sin(\pi x)]c}{(1+cx)^2}$$
$$\frac{dy}{dx} = \mathbf{3\tan^2 x \sec^2 x - \frac{\pi\cos(\pi x)}{1+cx} + \frac{c[1+\sin(\pi x)]}{(1+cx)^2}}$$

25.

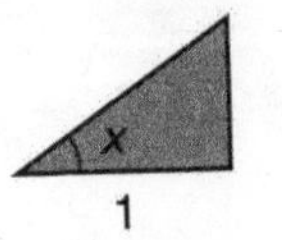

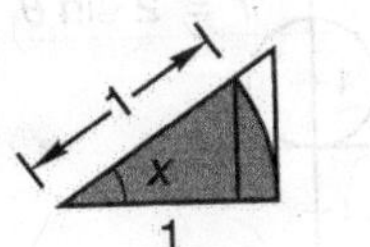

$A_1 = \frac{1}{2}(1)\tan x \qquad A = \pi(1)^2\frac{x}{2\pi} \qquad A = \frac{1}{2}(1)\sin x$

$A = \frac{\tan x}{2} \qquad A = \frac{x}{2} \qquad A = \frac{\sin x}{2}$

$$\frac{\tan x}{2} > \frac{x}{2} > \frac{\sin x}{2}$$
$$\tan x > x > \sin x$$
$$\frac{1}{\cos x} > \frac{x}{\sin x} > 1$$
$$\cos x < \frac{\sin x}{x} < 1$$
$$\lim_{x\to 0} \cos x \le \lim_{x\to 0} \frac{\sin x}{x} < \lim_{x\to 0} 1$$
$$1 < \lim_{x\to 0} \frac{\sin x}{x} < 1$$

By the squeeze theorem, $\displaystyle\lim_{x\to 0} \frac{\sin x}{x} = 1.$

Problem Set 111

1.

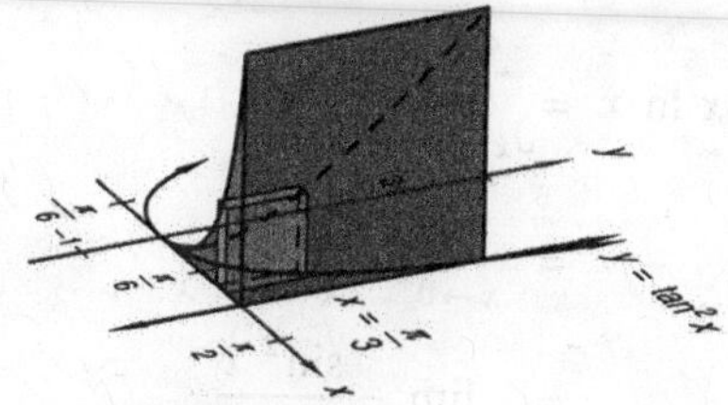

$$V = \int_0^{\pi/3} (\tan^2 x)^2\,dx$$
$$= \int_0^{\pi/3} \left[\tan^2 x\,(\sec^2 x - 1)\right] dx$$
$$= \int_0^{\pi/3} (\tan^2 x \sec^2 x - \tan^2 x)\,dx$$
$$= \int_0^{\pi/3} (\tan^2 x \sec^2 x - \sec^2 x + 1)\,dx$$
$$= \left[\frac{1}{3}\tan^3 x - \tan x + x\right]_0^{\pi/3}$$
$$= \frac{1}{3}(\sqrt{3})^3 - \sqrt{3} + \frac{\pi}{3} = \mathbf{\frac{\pi}{3}\ units^3}$$

2. $x(t) = \frac{1}{4}t^4 - \frac{7}{3}t^3 + 5t^2 + 7$

$v(t) = t^3 - 7t^2 + 10t$
$0 = t(t^2 - 7t + 10)$
$0 = t(t-5)(t-2)$
$t = 0, 5, 2$

$x(0) = 7;\ x(2) = 12\frac{1}{3};\ x(5) = -3\frac{5}{12};\ x(6) = 7$

The total distance traveled is the sum of the distances traveled from time $t = 0$ to 2, $t = 2$ to 5, and $t = 5$ to 6.

$$5\frac{1}{3} + 15\frac{3}{4} + 10\frac{5}{12} = \mathbf{31\frac{1}{2}\ units}$$

3.
$$xy^2 - 4x^2y + 14 = 0$$
$$2xy\frac{dy}{dx} + y^2 - 4x^2\frac{dy}{dx} - 8xy = 0$$
$$\frac{dy}{dx}(2xy - 4x^2) = 8xy - y^2$$
$$\frac{dy}{dx} = \frac{8xy - y^2}{2xy - 4x^2}$$

At (2, 1), slope $= \frac{8(2) - 1}{2(2) - 4(4)} = -\frac{15}{12} = -\frac{5}{4}$

$$y - 1 = -\frac{5}{4}(x - 2)$$
$$y = -\frac{5}{4}x + \frac{7}{2} \approx -\frac{5}{4}\left(\frac{21}{10}\right) + \frac{7}{2}$$
$$\approx -\frac{105}{40} + \frac{7}{2} = \mathbf{\frac{7}{8}}$$

4.

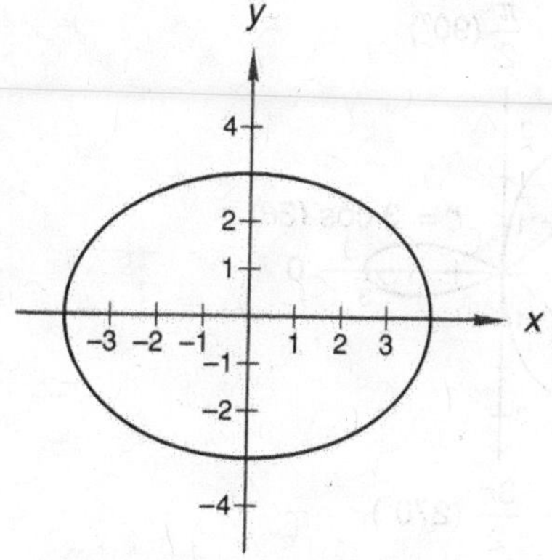

$x = 4\sin t \qquad y = 3\cos t$

$$\frac{dy}{dx} = \frac{\frac{dy}{dt}}{\frac{dx}{dt}} = \frac{-3\sin t}{4\cos t} = \frac{-3\left(\frac{x}{4}\right)}{4\left(\frac{y}{3}\right)} = \frac{\frac{-3x}{4}}{\frac{4y}{3}}$$
$$= \mathbf{-\frac{9x}{16y}}$$

5.

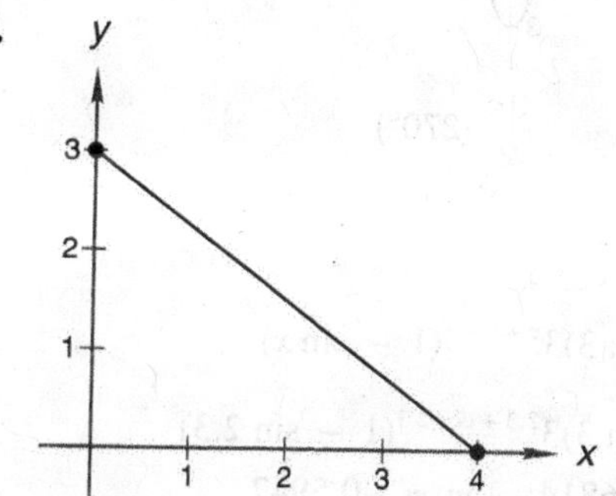

$x = 4\sin^2 t \qquad y = 3\cos^2 t$

$$\frac{dy}{dx} = \frac{\frac{dy}{dt}}{\frac{dx}{dt}} = \frac{-6\cos t\sin t}{8\sin t\cos t} = \mathbf{-\frac{3}{4}}$$

6. $0 = x^2 + y^2 - 6x$
$0 = r^2 - 6r\cos\theta$
$\mathbf{r = 6\cos\theta}$

7.

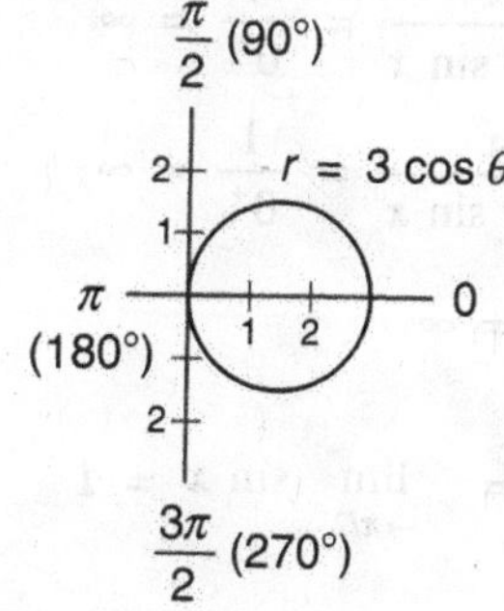

8.

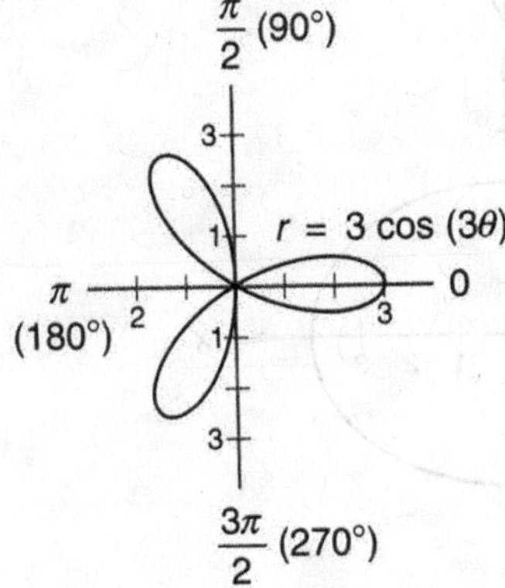

9.

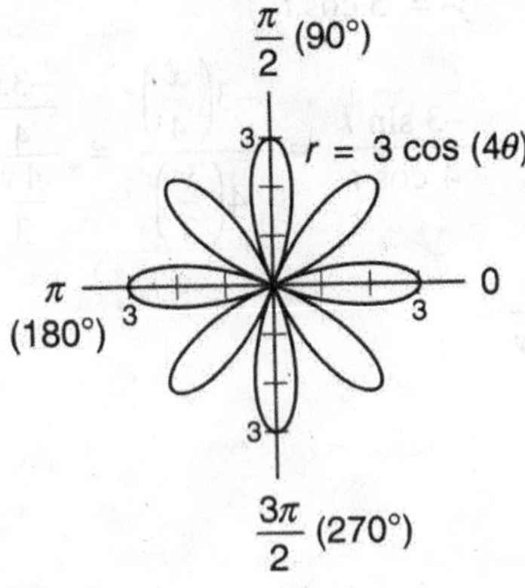

10. $y = 3^{x + \cos x}$

$$\frac{dy}{dx} = (\ln 3)3^{x + \cos x}(1 - \sin x)$$

$$m = (\ln 3)3^{2.3 + \cos 2.3}(1 - \sin 2.3)$$

$m \approx 1.6814$; $\perp m \approx -0.5947$

$|\langle 1, -0.5947\rangle| \approx 1.1635$

Normal unit vector: $\langle 0.8595, -0.5111\rangle$

Magnitude 7 vector: $\mathbf{\langle 6.0163, -3.5779\rangle}$

11. $$\lim_{x\to 0}\left(\frac{1}{x^2} - \frac{1}{\sin x}\right) = \lim_{x\to 0}\left(\frac{\sin x - x^2}{x^2 \sin x}\right)$$

$$= \lim_{x\to 0}\frac{\cos x - 2x}{x^2\cos x + 2x\sin x}$$

Examine the left- and right-hand limits.

$$\lim_{x\to 0^+}\frac{\cos x - 2x}{x^2\cos x + 2x\sin x} = \frac{1}{0^+} = \infty$$

$$\lim_{x\to 0^-}\frac{\cos x - 2x}{x^2\cos x + 2x\sin x} = \frac{1}{0^+} = \infty$$

$$\lim_{x\to 0}\left(\frac{1}{x^2} - \frac{1}{\sin x}\right) = \infty$$

12. $$\lim_{x\to\pi/2^-}\cos x\tan x = \lim_{x\to\pi/2^-}\sin x = \mathbf{1}$$

13. $$\lim_{x\to 0^+} x^{\tan x} = 0^0$$

$$\lim_{x\to 0^+}\tan x\ln x = \lim_{x\to 0^+}\frac{\ln x}{\cot x}$$

$$= \lim_{x\to 0^+} -\frac{1}{x\csc^2 x}$$

$$= \lim_{x\to 0^+} -\frac{\sin^2 x}{x}$$

$$= \lim_{x\to 0^+} -\frac{2\sin x\cos x}{1} = 0$$

$$\lim_{x\to 0^+} x^{\tan x} = e^0 = \mathbf{1}$$

14. $$\lim_{x\to\infty} x^{1/x} = \infty^0$$

$$\lim_{x\to\infty}\frac{1}{x}\ln x = \lim_{x\to\infty}\frac{\ln x}{x}$$

$$= \lim_{x\to\infty}\frac{1}{x} = 0$$

$$\lim_{x\to\infty} x^{1/x} = e^0 = \mathbf{1}$$

15. $$\lim_{x\to\pi/2^-}(\sin x)^{\tan x} = 1^\infty$$

$$\lim_{x\to\pi/2^-}\tan x\ln(\sin x)$$

$$= \lim_{x\to\pi/2^-}\frac{\ln(\sin x)}{\cot x}$$

$$= \lim_{x\to\pi/2^-}\frac{\frac{\cos x}{\sin x}}{-\csc^2 x}$$

$$= \lim_{x\to\pi/2^-} -\sin x\cos x = 0$$

$$\lim_{x\to\pi/2^-}(\sin x)^{\tan x} = e^0 = \mathbf{1}$$

16. $$\lim_{x\to\infty}\left[\left(1 + \frac{1}{x}\right)^x\right]^3 = \mathbf{e^3}$$

17. $$\lim_{x\to 0}\frac{\tan\left(\frac{\pi}{4} + x\right) - \tan\frac{\pi}{4}}{x} = \left.\frac{d}{dx}\tan x\right|_{\pi/4}$$

$$= \sec^2\left(\frac{\pi}{4}\right) = \mathbf{2}$$

18. $$\lim_{x\to\pi/4}\frac{\sin x - \sin\left(\frac{\pi}{4}\right)}{x - \frac{\pi}{4}} = \left.\frac{d}{dx}\sin x\right|_{\pi/4}$$

$$= \cos\left(\frac{\pi}{4}\right) = \mathbf{\frac{\sqrt{2}}{2}}$$

19. $\lim_{x\to 0} \frac{\sin(31x)}{13x} = \frac{31}{13} \lim_{31x\to 0} \frac{\sin(31x)}{31x}$

$= \frac{31}{13}(1) = \mathbf{\frac{31}{13}}$

20. $y = \sin x$

$\frac{dy}{dx} = \cos x$

$\mathbf{L_0^\pi = \int_0^\pi \sqrt{1 + \cos^2 x}\, dx}$

21. $T = \frac{\pi}{12}\left[\sqrt{2} + 2\sqrt{\frac{7}{4}} + 2\sqrt{\frac{5}{4}} + 2 + 2\sqrt{\frac{5}{4}} + 2\sqrt{\frac{7}{4}} + \sqrt{2}\right]$

$\approx \mathbf{3.8202}$

22. $\lim_{n\to\infty} \frac{e^{2n}}{e^{3n}} = \lim_{n\to\infty} e^{-n} = 0$

The sequence **converges to 0.**

23. (a)

n	1	2	3	4
a_n	$\frac{3}{2}$	$\frac{9}{5}$	$\frac{27}{10}$	$\frac{81}{17}$

$\mathbf{a_n = \frac{3^n}{n^2 + 1},\ n = 1, 2, 3, \ldots}$

(b) $\lim_{n\to\infty} \frac{3^n}{n^2 + 1} = \lim_{n\to\infty} \frac{3^n \ln 3}{2n}$

$= \lim_{n\to\infty} \frac{3^n(\ln 3)^2}{2} = \infty$

The sequence **diverges.**

24. $u = \sin x \qquad du = \cos x\, dx$

$\int_0^{\pi/2} \sin^2 x \cos x\, dx = \int_0^1 u^2\, du$

The correct choice is **B.**

25. $u = x + 4 \quad du = dx \quad x = u - 4$

$\int x\sqrt{x + 4}\, dx$

$= \int (u - 4)u^{1/2}\, du$

$= \int (u^{3/2} - 4u^{1/2})\, du$

$= \frac{2}{5}u^{5/2} - \frac{8}{3}u^{3/2} + C$

$= \frac{2}{15}u^{3/2}(3u - 20) + C$

$= \frac{2}{15}(x + 4)^{3/2}[3(x + 4) - 20] + C$

$= \mathbf{\frac{2}{15}(x + 4)^{3/2}(3x - 8) + C}$

Problem Set 112

1. (a) $A = \int_1^k \frac{1}{x}\, dx = [\ln x]_1^k$

$= \mathbf{\ln k \text{ units}^2}$

(b) $\frac{dk}{dt} = 1 \frac{\text{unit}}{\text{s}} \qquad k = 10$

$\frac{dA}{dt} = \frac{1}{k}\frac{dk}{dt}$

$= \frac{1}{10}(1) = \mathbf{\frac{1}{10} \frac{\text{unit}^2}{\text{s}}}$

2. $y = \sqrt{x}$

$dy = \frac{1}{2\sqrt{x}}\, dx$

$dy = \frac{1}{2(3)}(1) = \frac{1}{6}$

$\sqrt{10} \approx \sqrt{9} + dy = 3 + \frac{1}{6} = \mathbf{3\frac{1}{6}}$

3.

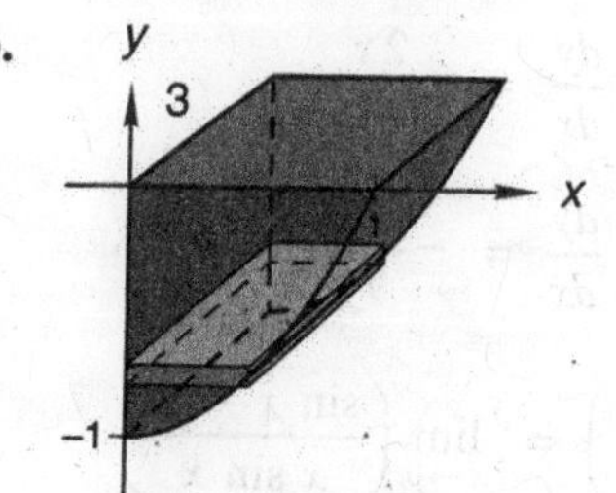

$W = 3000 \int_{y=-1}^{y=0} x(3)(-y)\, dy$

$= 9000 \int_{-1}^{0} \sqrt{y + 1}(-y)\, dy$

$= \mathbf{-9000 \int_{-1}^{0} y\sqrt{y + 1}\, dy}$

4. (a)

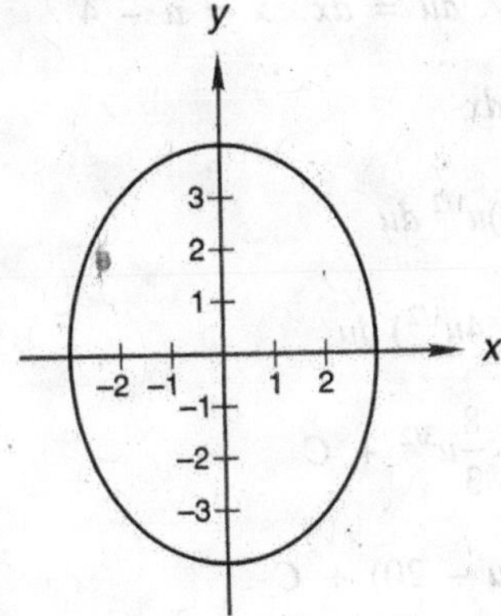

(b) $x = 3\cos\theta$

$$\cos\theta = \frac{x}{3}$$

$$y = 4\sin\theta$$

$$\sin\theta = \frac{y}{4}$$

$$\sin^2\theta + \cos^2\theta = 1$$

$$\left(\frac{y}{4}\right)^2 + \left(\frac{x}{3}\right)^2 = 1$$

$$\mathbf{\frac{x^2}{9} + \frac{y^2}{16} = 1}$$

(c) $$\frac{dy}{dx} = \frac{\frac{dy}{dt}}{\frac{dx}{dt}} = \frac{4\cos\theta}{-3\sin\theta}$$

$$= \frac{4\left(\frac{x}{3}\right)}{-3\left(\frac{y}{4}\right)} = \mathbf{-\frac{16x}{9y}}$$

$$\frac{x^2}{9} + \frac{y^2}{16} = 1$$

$$\frac{2x}{9} + \left(\frac{2y}{16}\right)\frac{dy}{dx} = 0$$

$$\left(\frac{y}{8}\right)\frac{dy}{dx} = -\frac{2x}{9}$$

$$\mathbf{\frac{dy}{dx} = -\frac{16x}{9y}}$$

5. $$\lim_{x\to 0}\left(\frac{1}{x} - \frac{1}{\sin x}\right) = \lim_{x\to 0}\left(\frac{\sin x - x}{x\sin x}\right)$$

$$= \lim_{x\to 0}\left(\frac{\cos x - 1}{x\cos x + \sin x}\right)$$

$$= \lim_{x\to 0}\left(\frac{-\sin x}{-x\sin x + \cos x + \cos x}\right)$$

$$= \frac{0}{2} = \mathbf{0}$$

6. $$\lim_{x\to 0}\frac{\sin(2x)}{4x} = \frac{2}{4}\lim_{2x\to 0}\frac{\sin(2x)}{2x}$$

$$= \frac{1}{2}(1) = \mathbf{\frac{1}{2}}$$

7. $$\lim_{x\to 0^+}(\sin x)^x = 0^0$$

$$\lim_{x\to 0^+} x\ln(\sin x)$$

$$= \lim_{x\to 0^+}\frac{\ln(\sin x)}{x^{-1}}$$

$$= \lim_{x\to 0^+}\frac{\cot x}{-x^{-2}}$$

$$= \lim_{x\to 0^+} -\frac{x^2\cos x}{\sin x}$$

$$= \lim_{x\to 0^+} -\frac{x^2(-\sin x) + (\cos x)(2x)}{\cos x}$$

$$= \frac{0}{1} = 0$$

$$\lim_{x\to 0^+}(\sin x)^x = e^0 = \mathbf{1}$$

8. $$r = \frac{1}{2\sin\theta - 3\cos\theta}$$

$$r(2\sin\theta - 3\cos\theta) = 1$$

$$2r\sin\theta - 3r\cos\theta = 1$$

$$2y - 3x = 1$$

$$\mathbf{y = \frac{3}{2}x + \frac{1}{2}}$$

9.

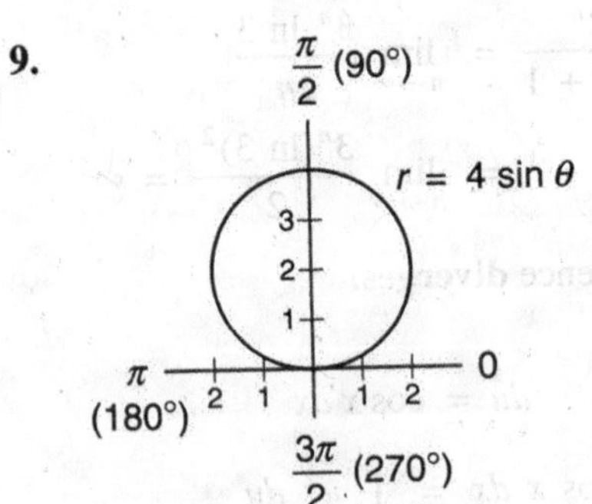

10.

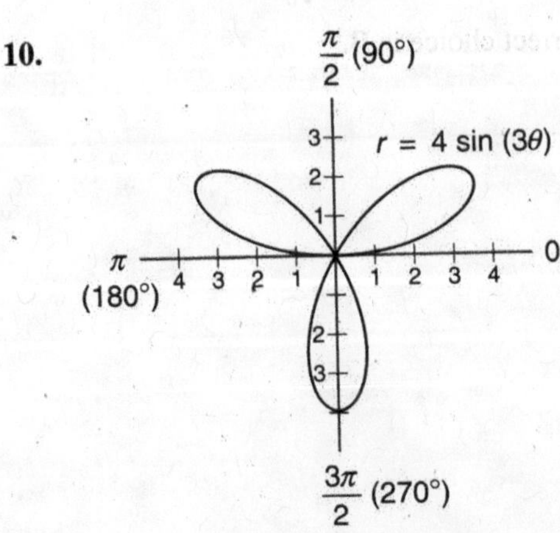

11. $y = e^{x^2}$

$$\frac{dy}{dx} = 2xe^{x^2}$$

$$\left(\frac{dy}{dx}\right)^2 = 4x^2e^{2x^2}$$

$$L_{-2}^{2} = \int_{-2}^{2} \sqrt{1 + 4x^2e^{2x^2}}\, dx$$

12.

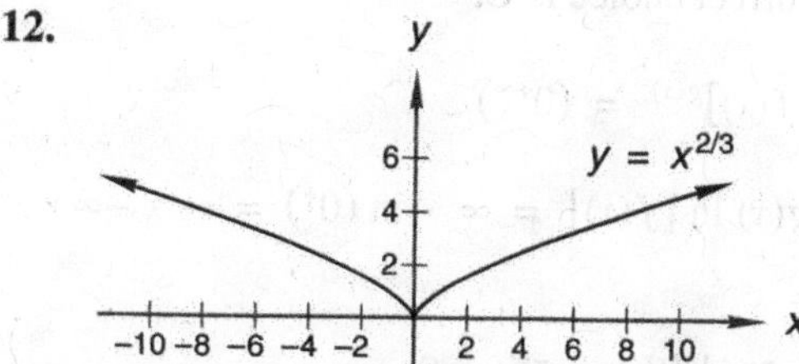

$y = x^{2/3}$ is not differentiable at (0, 0). We must split the arc length integral at $x = 0$. Since $y = x^{2/3}$ is an even function, double the integral from (0, 0) to (8, 4). For simplicity, integrate with respect to y from 0 to 4.

$$y = x^{2/3}$$

$$x = y^{3/2}$$

$$\frac{dx}{dy} = \frac{3}{2}y^{1/2}$$

$$\left(\frac{dx}{dy}\right)^2 = \frac{9}{4}y$$

$$L_{x=-8}^{x=8} = 2\int_0^4 \sqrt{1 + \frac{9}{4}y}\, dy$$

$$= \frac{8}{9}\int_0^4 \frac{9}{4}\left(1 + \frac{9}{4}y\right)^{1/2} dy$$

$$= \left(\frac{8}{9}\right)\left(\frac{2}{3}\right)\left[\left(1 + \frac{9}{4}y\right)^{3/2}\right]_0^4$$

$$= \mathbf{\frac{16}{27}(10\sqrt{10} - 1)\ units}$$

13. $|3\hat{i} - 2\hat{j}| = \sqrt{9 + 4} = \mathbf{\sqrt{13}}$

14. $y = x^2 + 2x - 1$

$y' = 2x + 2$

$y' = 2(2) + 2 = 6$

One possible vector with a slope of 6 is $\langle 1, 6\rangle$.

$|\langle 1, 6\rangle| = \sqrt{37}$

Unit tangent vector: $\left\langle \frac{1}{\sqrt{37}}, \frac{6}{\sqrt{37}}\right\rangle$

Unit normal vector: $\left\langle -\frac{6}{\sqrt{37}}, \frac{1}{\sqrt{37}}\right\rangle$

15. $f(t) = e^{\sin t + \cos t} - \dfrac{1 + t}{e^t - \sin t}$

$$f'(t) = (\cos t - \sin t)e^{\sin t + \cos t} - \frac{e^t - \sin t - (1 + t)(e^t - \cos t)}{(e^t - \sin t)^2}$$

$$f'(0) = (1 - 0)e^{0+1} - \frac{e^0 - 0 - (1 + 0)(e^0 - 1)}{(e^0 - 0)^2}$$

$$f'(0) = \mathbf{e - 1}$$

16. $$\lim_{n\to\infty} (-1)^{n+1}\frac{\sqrt{n}}{n} = \lim_{n\to\infty} (-1)^{n+1}\frac{1}{\sqrt{n}}$$

$$= \lim_{n\to\infty} (-1)^{n+1} \cdot \lim_{n\to\infty} \frac{1}{\sqrt{n}} = \lim_{n\to\infty} (-1)^{n+1} \cdot 0$$

The sequence **converges to 0.**

17. $$\lim_{n\to\infty} \frac{\ln n}{e^n} = \lim_{n\to\infty} \frac{1}{ne^n} = 0$$

The sequence **converges to 0.**

18.

n	1	2	3	4
a_n	$\frac{3}{2}$	$-\frac{9}{4}$	$\frac{27}{8}$	$-\frac{81}{16}$

$$\mathbf{a_n = (-1)^{n+1}\frac{3^n}{2^n},\ n = 1, 2, 3, \ldots}$$

19. $$T = \frac{3 - 1}{8}\left[\frac{1}{\sqrt{2}} + \frac{\frac{9}{2}}{\sqrt{\frac{13}{4}}} + \frac{8}{\sqrt{5}} + \frac{\frac{25}{2}}{\sqrt{\frac{29}{4}}} + \frac{9}{\sqrt{10}}\right]$$

$$\approx \mathbf{3.5673}$$

20. $$\frac{1}{4}x = \sin x$$

$$\frac{1}{4}x - \sin x = 0$$

The values of $\sin x$ in the first quadrant lie between 0 and 1. The values of $\frac{1}{4}x$ less than 1 in this quadrant are between 0 and 4. Let $x_1 = 2$ and assign `Y1=0.25X-sin(X)` and `Y2=nDeriv(Y1,X,X)`.

```
2→X
                 2
X-(Y1/Y2)→X
       2.614425299
       2.479338021
       2.474583511
       2.474576787
       2.474576787
```

(2.474576787, 0.6186441968)

21. $x = \tan\theta \qquad dx = \sec^2\theta\, d\theta$

$$\frac{2\,dx}{(1 + x^2)^3} = \frac{2\sec^2\theta\, d\theta}{(1 + \tan^2\theta)^3} = \frac{2\sec^2\theta\, d\theta}{(\sec^2\theta)^3}$$

$$= \mathbf{2\cos^4\theta\, d\theta}$$

22. $r = x^2 \qquad dr = 2x\,dx$

$$\int 2x\ln(x^2)\,dx = \int \ln r\,dr$$

$$= r\ln r - r + C$$

$$= x^2\ln x^2 - x^2 + C$$

$$\int_{\sqrt{e}}^{e} 2x\ln(x^2)\,dx$$

$$= \left[e^2\ln(e^2) - e^2\right] - (e\ln e - e)$$

$$= (2e^2 - e^2) - (e - e) = \mathbf{e^2}$$

23. $$u = \sin\left(\frac{\pi}{2}x\right)$$

$$du = \frac{\pi}{2}\cos\left(\frac{\pi}{2}x\right)dx$$

$$\cos\left(\frac{\pi}{2}x\right)dx = \frac{2}{\pi}\,du$$

$$\int_0^1 \sin\left(\frac{\pi}{2}x\right)\cos\left(\frac{\pi}{2}x\right)dx = \int_0^1 \frac{2}{\pi}u\,du$$

The correct choice is **C.**

24. The function $|x - 3| - 3$ is not differentiable on (0, 6), so choice A is not true.

The function $f(x) = 2 - \frac{1}{x^2 - 1} \neq 0$ at the stated endpoints, because it is not defined.

Choice C meets all the requirements for Rolle's theorem.

Choice D states the inverse of Rolle's theorem, but it is not necessarily true.

The correct choice is **C.**

25. $$\lim_{x\to a}\,[f(x)]^{g(x)} = (0^{+\infty})$$

$$\lim_{x\to a} g(x)\ln[f(x)] = \infty \cdot \ln(0^+) = \infty \cdot -\infty$$

$$= -\infty$$

$$\lim_{x\to a}\,[f(x)]^{g(x)} = e^{-\infty} = 0$$

Problem Set 113

1.

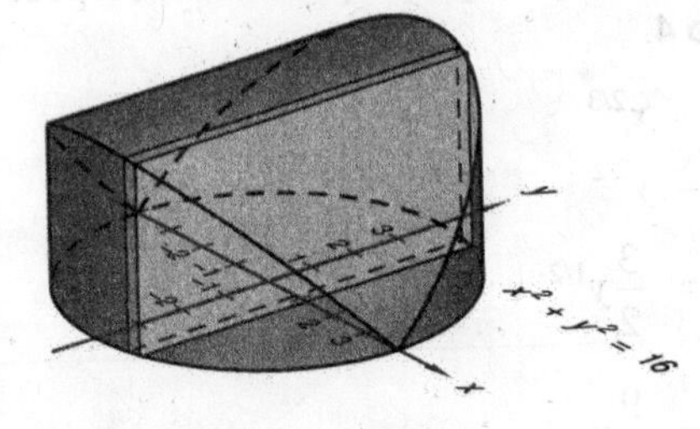

$$V = 2\int_0^4 2y(y)\,dx$$

$$= 4\int_0^4 (16 - x^2)\,dx$$

$$= 4\left[16x - \frac{1}{3}x^3\right]_0^4$$

$$= 4\left(64 - \frac{64}{3}\right) = \mathbf{\frac{512}{3}\ units^3}$$

2. $u = a\sin\theta \qquad du = a\cos\theta\, d\theta$

$$\sqrt{a^2 - u^2} = \sqrt{a^2 - a^2\sin^2\theta} = \sqrt{a^2(\cos^2\theta)}$$

$$= a\cos\theta$$

$a\cos\theta$ is a much easier expression to integrate.

3. $$y = \frac{x^{3/4}\,4\sqrt{x}}{(4 + x^3)^6} = \frac{4x^{5/4}}{(4 + x^3)^6}$$

$$\frac{dy}{dx} = \frac{5x^{1/4}(4 + x^3)^6}{[(4 + x^3)^6]^2} - \frac{4x^{5/4}[6(4 + x^3)^5(3x^2)]}{[(4 + x^3)^6]^2}$$

$$\frac{dy}{dx} = \mathbf{\frac{5x^{1/4}(4 + x^3) - 72x^{13/4}}{(4 + x^3)^7}}$$

4. $f'(x) = \lim_{h\to 0} \dfrac{f(x+h) - f(x-h)}{2h}$

$$= \lim_{h\to 0} \frac{-5(x^2 + 2xh + h^2) + \frac{1}{2}}{2h} - \frac{-5(x^2 - 2xh + h^2) + \frac{1}{2}}{2h}$$

$$= \lim_{h\to 0} \frac{-10xh - 10xh}{2h} = \mathbf{-10x}$$

5. $\displaystyle\int \frac{dx}{\sqrt{1-x^2}} = \mathbf{\arcsin x + C}$

6. $x = \sin\theta \qquad dx = \cos\theta\, d\theta$

$\sqrt{1-x^2} = \sqrt{1-\sin^2\theta} = \cos\theta$

$$\int \frac{dx}{\sqrt{1-x^2}} = \int \frac{\cos\theta\, d\theta}{\cos\theta}$$

$$= \int d\theta$$

$$= \theta + C$$

$$= \mathbf{\arcsin x + C}$$

7. $\displaystyle\int \frac{dx}{1+x^2} = \mathbf{\arctan x + C}$

8. $x = \tan\theta \qquad dx = \sec^2\theta\, d\theta$

$1 + x^2 = 1 + \tan^2\theta = \sec^2\theta$

$$\int \frac{dx}{1+x^2} = \int \frac{\sec^2\theta\, d\theta}{\sec^2\theta}$$

$$= \int d\theta$$

$$= \theta + C$$

$$= \mathbf{\arctan x + C}$$

9.

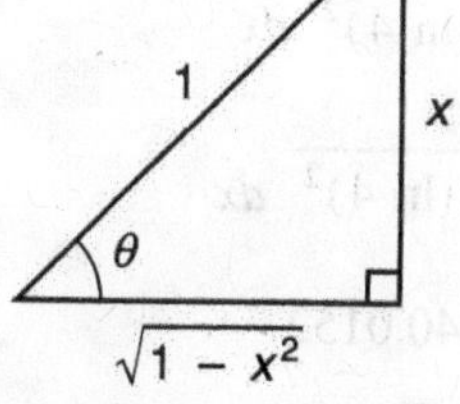

$x = \sin\theta$

$dx = \cos\theta\, d\theta$

$$\int \frac{x^3\, dx}{\sqrt{1-x^2}}$$

$$= \int \frac{\sin^3\theta \cos\theta\, d\theta}{\sqrt{1-\sin^2\theta}} = \int \frac{\sin^3\theta\cos\theta\, d\theta}{\cos\theta}$$

$$= \int \sin^3\theta\, d\theta = \int \sin\theta(1-\cos^2\theta)\, d\theta$$

$$= \int \sin\theta\, d\theta - \int \sin\theta\cos^2\theta\, d\theta$$

$$= -\cos\theta + \frac{\cos^3\theta}{3} + C$$

$$= -\sqrt{1-x^2} + \frac{(1-x^2)\sqrt{1-x^2}}{3} + C$$

$$= \left(-1 + \frac{1}{3} - \frac{1}{3}x^2\right)\sqrt{1-x^2} + C$$

$$= \mathbf{\frac{(-2-x^2)\sqrt{1-x^2}}{3} + C}$$

10.

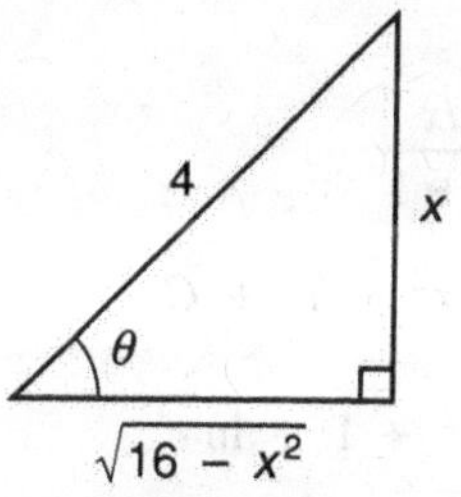

$x = 4\sin\theta$

$dx = 4\cos\theta\, d\theta$

$$\int \frac{\sqrt{16-x^2}}{x^2}\, dx$$

$$= \int \frac{\sqrt{16 - 16\sin^2\theta}(4\cos\theta\, d\theta)}{16\sin^2\theta}$$

$$= \int \frac{4\sqrt{1-\sin^2\theta}(4\cos\theta)\, d\theta}{16\sin^2\theta}$$

$$= \int \frac{\cos^2\theta}{\sin^2\theta}\, d\theta$$

$$= \int \cot^2\theta\, d\theta$$

$$= \int (\csc^2\theta - 1)\, d\theta$$

$$= -\cot\theta - \theta + C$$

$$= \mathbf{\frac{-\sqrt{16-x^2}}{x} - \sin^{-1}\frac{x}{4} + C}$$

11. $2\int \sec^3 x\,dx$

$= 2\int \sec x\,(1 + \tan^2 x)\,dx$

$= 2\int \sec x\,dx + 2\int \sec x \tan^2 x\,dx$

$u = \tan x \qquad v = \sec x$

$du = \sec^2 x\,dx \qquad dv = \sec x \tan x\,dx$

$2\int \sec^3 x\,dx$

$= 2\ln|\sec x + \tan x| + 2\sec x \tan x - 2\int \sec^3 x\,dx$

$4\int \sec^3 x\,dx$

$= 2\ln|\sec x + \tan x| + 2\sec x \tan x + C$

$2\int \sec^3 x$

$= \mathbf{\ln|\sec x + \tan x| + \sec x \tan x + C}$

12. $y(x^2 + 1)\dfrac{dy}{dx} = xy^2$

$\int \dfrac{dy}{y} = \int \dfrac{x\,dx}{x^2 + 1}$

$\ln|y| = \dfrac{1}{2}\ln|x^2 + 1| + C$

$\ln|y| = \ln\sqrt{x^2 + 1} + \ln e^C$

$|y| = e^{\ln\sqrt{x^2+1} + \ln e^C}$

$|y| = k\sqrt{x^2 + 1}$

$\mathbf{y = \pm k\sqrt{x^2 + 1}}$

13. $\vec{v}_1 + \vec{v}_2 = \langle 6, 5\rangle + \langle -2, 11\rangle = \mathbf{\langle 4, 16\rangle}$

14. $4\vec{v}_1 - 7\vec{v}_2$

$= 4\langle 2, 2\rangle - 7\langle -1, 3\rangle$

$= \langle 8, 8\rangle - \langle -7, 21\rangle$

$= \mathbf{\langle 15, -13\rangle}$

15. $-4\angle 150^\circ + 6\angle -200^\circ$

$= 4\angle -30^\circ + 6\angle 160^\circ$

$= 4\cos(-30^\circ)\,\hat{i} + 4\sin(-30^\circ)\,\hat{j} + 6\cos 160^\circ\,\hat{i}$

$+ 6\sin 160^\circ\,\hat{j}$

$\approx -2.1741\hat{i} + 0.0521\hat{j}$

$\approx \mathbf{2.1747\angle 178.6272^\circ}$

16. $y = \dfrac{1}{x}$

$r\sin\theta = \dfrac{1}{r\cos\theta}$

$\mathbf{r^2 = \dfrac{1}{\sin\theta\cos\theta}}$

17. $y = \sqrt{16 - (x + 2)^2} + 4$

$\dfrac{dy}{dx} = \dfrac{-(x + 2)}{\sqrt{16 - (x + 2)^2}}$

$\left(\dfrac{dy}{dx}\right)^2 = \dfrac{x^2 + 4x + 4}{16 - (x + 2)^2}$

$L_0^2 = \int_0^2 \sqrt{1 + \dfrac{x^2 + 4x + 4}{16 - (x + 2)^2}}\,dx$

$= \int_0^2 \sqrt{\dfrac{-x^2 - 4x + 12 + x^2 + 4x + 4}{16 - (x + 2)^2}}\,dx$

$= \int_0^2 \dfrac{4\,dx}{\sqrt{16 - (x + 2)^2}}$

$x + 2 = 4\sin\theta \qquad dx = 4\cos\theta\,d\theta$

At $x = 0$, $\sin\theta = \dfrac{1}{2}$ so $\theta = \dfrac{\pi}{6}$.

At $x = 2$, $\sin\theta = 1$ so $\theta = \dfrac{\pi}{2}$.

$4^2 - (x + 2)^2 = 4^2(1 - \sin^2\theta) = 4^2\cos^2\theta$

$\int_0^2 \dfrac{4\,dx}{\sqrt{16 - (x + 2)^2}} = 4\int_{\pi/6}^{\pi/2} \dfrac{4\cos\theta\,d\theta}{\sqrt{4^2\cos^2\theta}}$

$= 4\int_{\pi/6}^{\pi/2} d\theta = 4\theta\Big|_{\pi/6}^{\pi/2}$

$= 4\left(\dfrac{\pi}{2} - \dfrac{\pi}{6}\right)$

$= \mathbf{\dfrac{4\pi}{3}}$ **units**

18. $y = 4^{|x|}$ has a cusp at (0, 1), so a single integral cannot be used. This is an even function.

If $x \ge 0$

$y = 4^x$

$\dfrac{dy}{dx} = 4^x \ln 4$

$\left(\dfrac{dy}{dx}\right)^2 = 4^{2x}(\ln 4)^2$

$L_{-2}^4 = 2\int_0^2 \sqrt{1 + 4^{2x}(\ln 4)^2}\,dx$

$+ \int_2^4 \sqrt{1 + 4^{2x}(\ln 4)^2}\,dx$

$\approx 2(15.2341) + 240.0152$

$\approx$ **270.4834 units**

19. $\lim_{x\to\infty}\left(1+\frac{1}{x}\right)^x = e$

20. $\lim_{x\to 0^+}(e^x-1)^x = 0^0$

$$\lim_{x\to 0^+} x\ln(e^x-1)$$

$$= \lim_{x\to 0^+}\frac{\ln(e^x-1)}{x^{-1}}$$

$$= \lim_{x\to 0^+}\frac{-x^2e^x}{e^x-1}$$

$$= \lim_{x\to 0^+}\frac{-x^2e^x-2xe^x}{e^x}$$

$$= \lim_{x\to 0^+}(-x^2-2x) = 0$$

$$\lim_{x\to 0^+}(e^x-1)^x = e^0 = \mathbf{1}$$

21. $\lim_{x\to 1} x^{1/(1-x)} = 1^{\pm\infty}$

$$\lim_{x\to 1}\frac{\ln x}{1-x} = \lim_{x\to 1} -\frac{1}{x} = -1$$

$$\lim_{x\to 1} x^{1/1-x} = e^{-1} = \mathbf{\frac{1}{e}}$$

22.

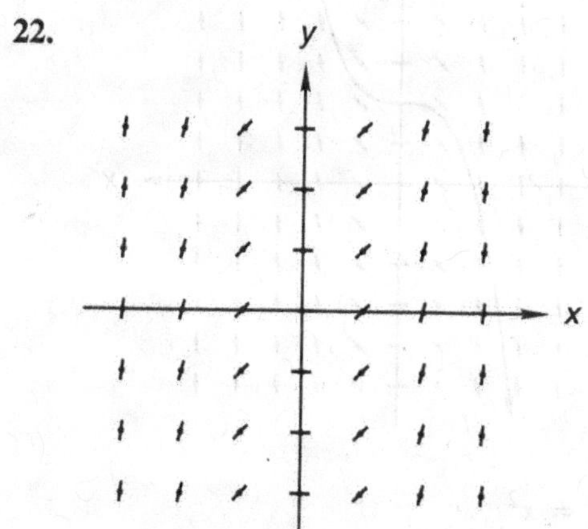

23.

$\frac{\pi}{2}$ (90°)

$r = 4\cos\theta$

π (180°) — 0

$\frac{3\pi}{2}$ (270°)

24.

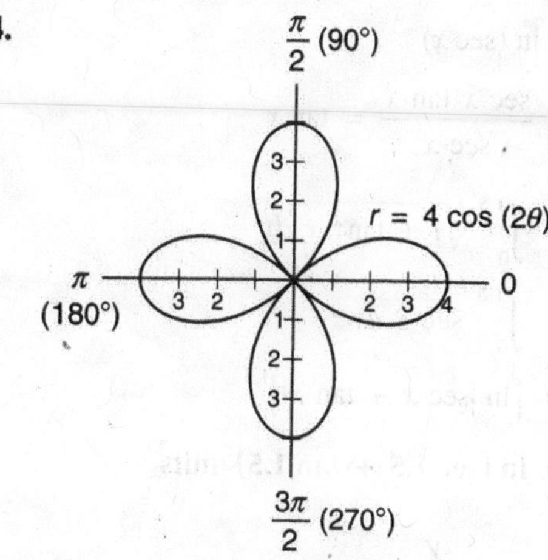

25. $\lim_{x\to a}[f(x)]^{g(x)} = 0^{-\infty}$

$$\lim_{x\to a} g(x)\ln[f(x)] = -\infty\cdot\ln(0^+)$$

$$= -\infty\cdot-\infty = \infty$$

$$\lim_{x\to a}[f(x)]^{g(x)} = e^{\infty} = \infty$$

PROBLEM SET 114

1.

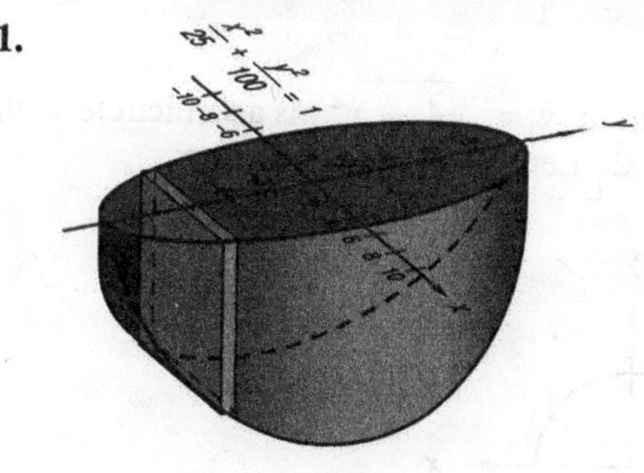

$$V = 2\int_{y=0}^{y=10}(2x)^2\,dy$$

$$= 8\int_0^{10}\left(25-\frac{1}{4}y^2\right)dy$$

$$= 8\left[25y-\frac{1}{12}y^3\right]_0^{10}$$

$$= 8\left(250-\frac{250}{3}\right) = \mathbf{1333\frac{1}{3}\ ft^3}$$

2. $y = \tan x - 3^x$

$$\frac{dy}{dx} = \sec^2 x - 3^x\ln 3$$

$$L_0^{1.5} = \mathbf{\int_0^{1.5}\sqrt{1+(\sec^2 x - 3^x\ln 3)^2}\,dx}$$

3. $y = \ln(\sec x)$

$$\frac{dy}{dx} = \frac{\sec x \tan x}{\sec x} = \tan x$$

$$L_0^{1.5} = \int_0^{1.5} \sqrt{1 + \tan^2 x}\, dx$$

$$= \int_0^{1.5} \sec x\, dx$$

$$= \left[\ln|\sec x + \tan x|\right]_0^{1.5}$$

$$= \mathbf{\ln(\sec 1.5 + \tan 1.5)\ units}$$

4.

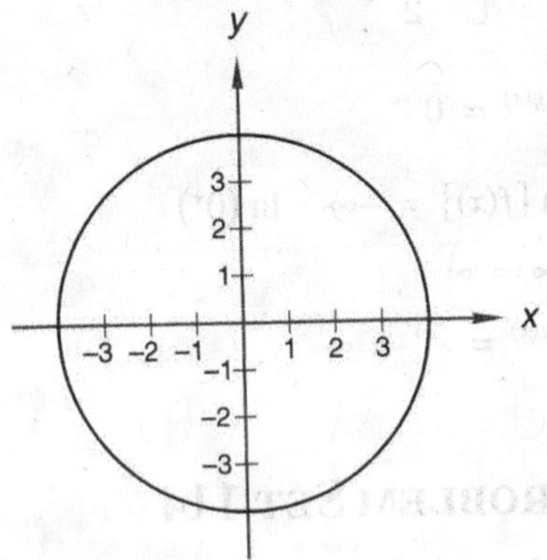

5. The graph of $y = \sqrt{4 - x^2}$ is a semicircle with a radius of 2. Length $= \pi r =$ **2π units**

6.

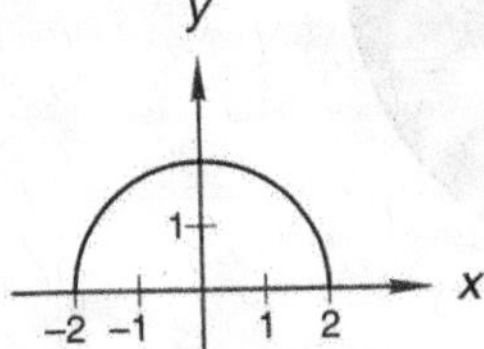

The parametric equations trace the semicircle in problem 5.

$L_0^{\pi} = \pi r =$ **2π units**

7. The parametric equations trace a circle of radius 4. Length $= 2\pi(4) =$ **8π units**

8.

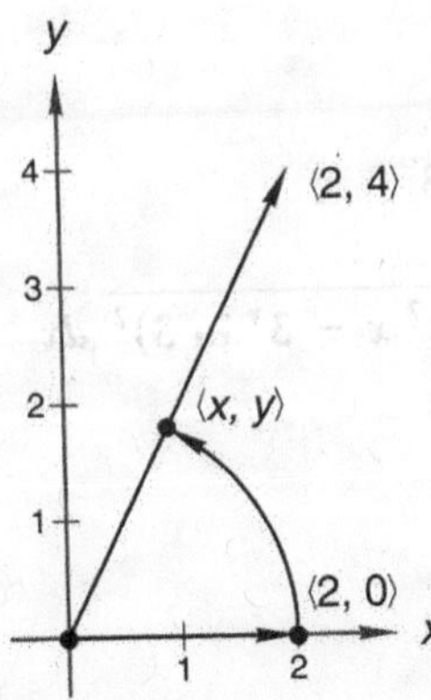

$$|\langle 2, 4\rangle| = \sqrt{20} = 2\sqrt{5}$$

$$2\left(\frac{2}{2\sqrt{5}}, \frac{4}{2\sqrt{5}}\right) = \mathbf{\left(\frac{2}{\sqrt{5}}, \frac{4}{\sqrt{5}}\right)}$$

9. Newton's method can provide the desired accuracy.

$$x^2 = \sin x$$

$$x^2 - \sin x = 0$$

Since the sine function varies between 0 and 1 in the first quadrant, let $x_1 = 0.5$ and assign `Y1=X²-sin(X)` and `Y2=nDeriv(Y1,X,X)`.

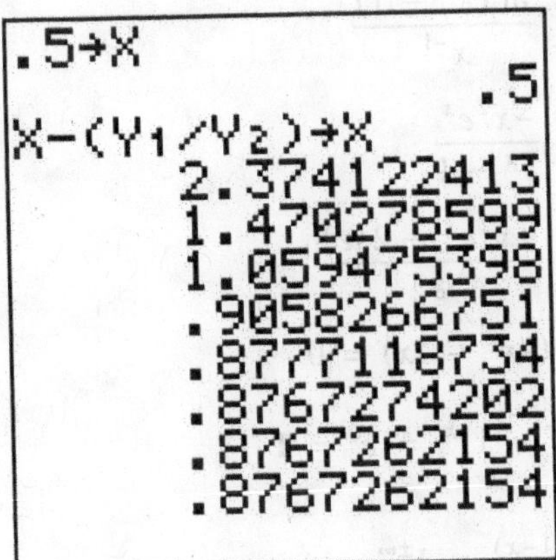

```
.5→X
                .5
X-(Y1/Y2)→X
       2.374122413
       1.470278599
       1.059475398
       .9058266751
       .877118734
       .8767274202
       .8767262154
       .8767262154
```

0.8767262154

10. (a)

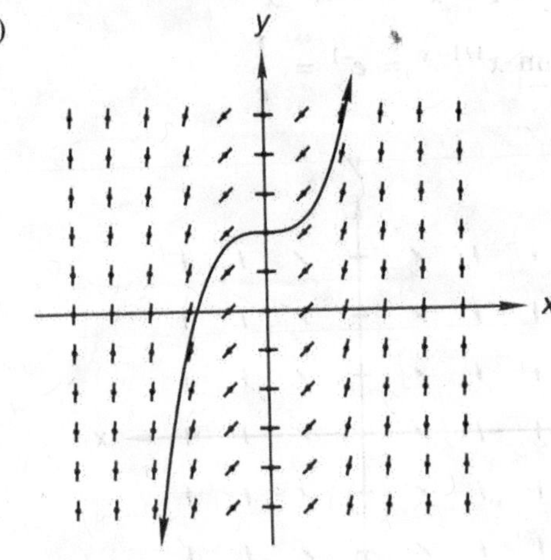

(b) $\frac{dy}{dx} = x^2$

$$\int dy = \int x^2\, dx$$

$$\mathbf{y = \frac{1}{3}x^3 + C}$$

11. $T = \frac{\pi}{12}\left[1 + \frac{2\cos\left(\frac{\pi}{6}\right)}{\sqrt{\sin\left(\frac{\pi}{6}\right) + 1}} + \frac{2\cos\left(\frac{\pi}{3}\right)}{\sqrt{\sin\left(\frac{\pi}{3}\right) + 1}}\right.$

$+ 0 + \frac{2\cos\left(\frac{2\pi}{3}\right)}{\sqrt{\sin\left(\frac{2\pi}{3}\right) + 1}}$

$\left. + \frac{2\cos\left(\frac{5\pi}{6}\right)}{\sqrt{\sin\left(\frac{5\pi}{6}\right) + 1}} + -1\right]$

$= \frac{\pi}{12}[0] = \mathbf{0}$

$\int_0^\pi \cos x\,(\sin x + 1)^{-1/2}\,dx = \left[2\sqrt{\sin x + 1}\right]_0^\pi$

$= 2 - 2 = 0$

Both methods yield the same answer.

12. $4 = x^2 + (y - 2)^2$

$4 = (r\cos\theta)^2 + (r\sin\theta - 2)^2$

$4 = r^2\cos^2\theta + r^2\sin^2\theta - 4r\sin\theta + 4$

$0 = r^2 - 4r\sin\theta$

$\mathbf{r = 4\sin\theta}$

13. $r = 3\csc\theta$

$r\sin\theta = 3$

$\mathbf{y = 3}$

14. $\frac{\pi}{2}$ (90°)

$r = \cos(3\theta)$

π (180°) 1 1 0

$\frac{3\pi}{2}$ (270°)

15. $\frac{\pi}{2}$ (90°)

$r = 3\cos\theta$

2 1 π (180°) 1 2 0 2

$\frac{3\pi}{2}$ (270°)

16. $\lim_{x\to\pi/2^-}(\tan x)^{\cos x} = \infty^0$

$\lim_{x\to\pi/2^-}\cos x \ln(\tan x)$

$= \lim_{x\to\pi/2^-}\frac{\ln(\tan x)}{\sec x}$

$= \lim_{x\to\pi/2^-}\frac{\cos x}{\sin^2 x} = \frac{0}{1} = 0$

$\lim_{x\to\pi/2^-}(\tan x)^{\cos x} = e^0 = \mathbf{1}$

17. $\lim_{x\to 0^+} x^{x^2} = 0^0$

$\lim_{x\to 0^+} x^2\ln x = \lim_{x\to 0^+}\frac{\ln x}{x^{-2}}$

$= \lim_{x\to 0^+} -\frac{x^2}{2} = 0$

$\lim_{x\to 0^+} x^{x^2} = e^0 = \mathbf{1}$

18. $\lim_{n\to\infty}(1 + 4n^{-1})^n = 1^\infty$

$\lim_{n\to\infty} n\ln(1 + 4n^{-1})$

$= \lim_{n\to\infty}\frac{\ln(1 + 4n^{-1})}{n^{-1}}$

$= \lim_{n\to\infty}\frac{4}{1 + 4n^{-1}} = 4$

The sequence **converges to e^4.**

19. $u = \cos x + 1 \qquad du = \sin x\,dx$

$\int_0^\pi \frac{-\sin x}{\sqrt{\cos x + 1}}\,dx = \int_2^0 u^{-1/2}\,du$

$= \left[2u^{1/2}\right]_2^0 = \mathbf{-2\sqrt{2}}$

20. $x = 2\sec\theta \qquad dx = 2\sec\theta\tan\theta\,d\theta$

$\sqrt{x^2 - 4} = 2\tan\theta$

$\int \frac{dx}{\sqrt{x^2 - 4}} = \int \frac{2\sec\theta\tan\theta\,d\theta}{2\tan\theta}$

$= \int \sec\theta\,d\theta$

$= \ln|\sec\theta + \tan\theta|$

$= \ln\left|\frac{x}{2} + \frac{\sqrt{x^2 - 4}}{2}\right| + C$

$= \ln\left|\frac{x + \sqrt{x^2 - 4}}{2}\right| + C$

$= \mathbf{\ln\left|x + \sqrt{x^2 - 4}\right| + C}$

21. $x = 2\sin\theta \qquad dx = 2\cos\theta\, d\theta$

$\sqrt{4 - x^2} = 2\cos\theta$

$$\int \frac{dx}{\sqrt{4-x^2}} = \int \frac{2\cos\theta\, d\theta}{2\cos\theta}$$
$$= \int d\theta$$
$$= \theta + C$$
$$= \mathbf{arcsin}\,\frac{\mathbf{x}}{\mathbf{2}} + \mathbf{C}$$

22. $x = \sqrt{6}\tan\theta \quad dx = \sqrt{6}\sec^2\theta\, d\theta$

$\sqrt{x^2 + 6} = \sqrt{6}\sec\theta$

$$\int_0^1 \frac{1}{\sqrt{x^2+6}}\, dx$$
$$= \int \frac{\sqrt{6}\sec^2\theta\, d\theta}{\sqrt{6}\sec\theta}$$
$$= \int \sec\theta\, d\theta$$
$$= \ln|\sec\theta + \tan\theta|$$
$$= \left[\ln\left|\frac{\sqrt{x^2+6}}{\sqrt{6}} + \frac{x}{\sqrt{6}}\right|\right]_0^1$$
$$= \ln\left(\frac{\sqrt{7}+1}{\sqrt{6}}\right) - \ln(1)$$
$$= \mathbf{ln}\,\frac{\sqrt{\mathbf{7}} + \mathbf{1}}{\sqrt{\mathbf{6}}}$$

23.

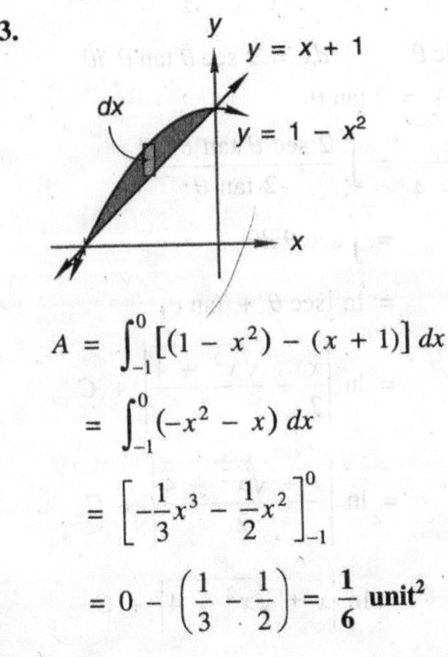

$$A = \int_{-1}^{0} [(1 - x^2) - (x + 1)]\, dx$$
$$= \int_{-1}^{0} (-x^2 - x)\, dx$$
$$= \left[-\frac{1}{3}x^3 - \frac{1}{2}x^2\right]_{-1}^{0}$$
$$= 0 - \left(\frac{1}{3} - \frac{1}{2}\right) = \frac{\mathbf{1}}{\mathbf{6}}\ \mathbf{unit^2}$$

24. Let `Y1=2X²-2X-3`, `Xmin=1.985`, `Xmax=2.015`, `Ymin=0.985`, and `Ymax=1.015`. Performing a `TRACE` results in the following:

x	y
1.9996809	0.99808531
2	1
2.0003191	1.0019151

If $|x - 2| < 0.0003191$, then $|y - 1| < 0.01$. Thus $\delta = \mathbf{0.0003191}$. Answers may vary.

25. Each graph passes through the point (1, 0).

$0 = c - 1 \qquad 0 = 1 + a + b$

$\mathbf{c = 1} \qquad -1 = a + b$

Since the graphs are tangent to each other, they must have the same slope at the point (1, 0).

$y_1 = x - x^2$

$y_1' = 1 - 2x$

$y_1' = 1 - 2 = -1$

$y_2 = x^2 + ax + b$

$y_2' = 2x + a$

$y_2' = 2 + a$

$-1 = 2 + a$

$\mathbf{a = -3}$

$a + b = -1$

$-3 + b = -1$

$\mathbf{b = 2}$

Problem Set 115

1.

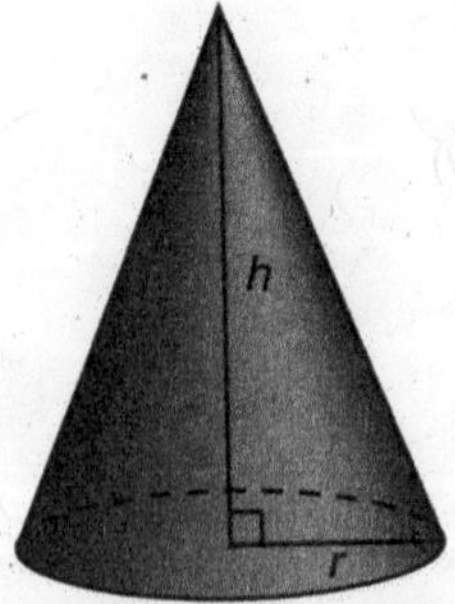

$$V = \frac{1}{3}\pi r^2 h$$
$$\frac{dV}{dt} = \frac{1}{3}\pi r^2 \frac{dh}{dt} + \frac{2}{3}\pi r h \frac{dr}{dt}$$
$$\frac{dV}{dt} = \frac{1}{3}\pi(16)(3) + \frac{2}{3}\pi(4)(10)(-1)$$
$$\frac{dV}{dt} = -\frac{\mathbf{32}}{\mathbf{3}}\pi\ \frac{\mathbf{cm^3}}{\mathbf{s}}$$

2. $y = \sqrt[3]{x}$

$$dy = \frac{1}{3}x^{-2/3}\,dx$$

$$dy = \frac{1}{3}\left(\frac{1}{4}\right)(1)$$

$$dy = \frac{1}{12}$$

$$\sqrt[3]{9} \approx \sqrt[3]{8} + dy = \mathbf{2\frac{1}{12}}$$

3.

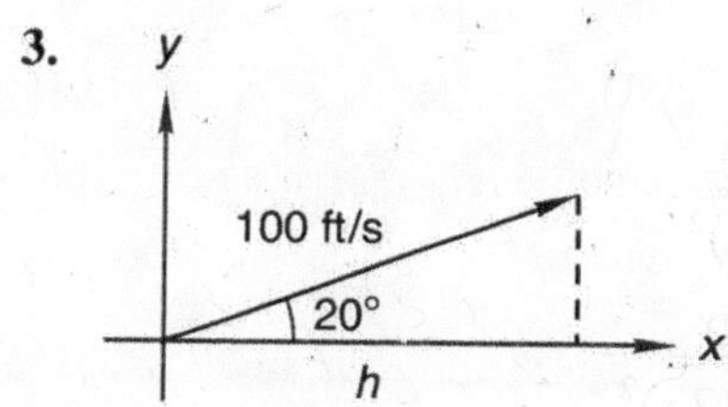

$$\cos 20° = \frac{h}{100}$$

$$h \approx \mathbf{93.9693\ ft/s}$$

distance = rate × time

$$d \approx (93.9693)(3)$$

$$d \approx \mathbf{281.9079\ ft}$$

4.

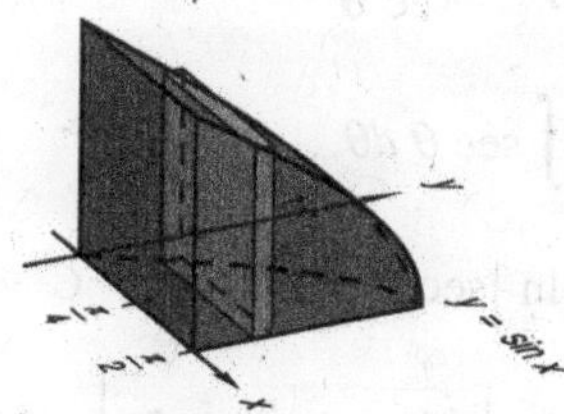

$y = \sin x \qquad dy = \cos x\,dx$

$$V = \int_{y=0}^{y=1}\left(\frac{\pi}{2} - x\right)^2 dy$$

$$= \int_0^{\pi/2}\left(\frac{\pi^2}{4} - \pi x + x^2\right)\cos x\,dx$$

$$= \frac{\pi^2}{4}\int_0^{\pi/2}\cos x\,dx - \pi\int_0^{\pi/2} x\cos x\,dx + \int_0^{\pi/2} x^2\cos x\,dx$$

$u = x \quad du = dx \quad v = \sin x \quad dv = \cos x\,dx$

$$V = \frac{\pi^2}{4}[\sin x]_0^{\pi/2} - \pi[x\sin x + \cos x]_0^{\pi/2} + \int_0^{\pi/2} x^2\cos x\,dx$$

$$= \frac{\pi^2}{4} - \frac{\pi^2}{2} + \pi + \int_0^{\pi/2} x^2\cos x\,dx$$

$u = x^2 \quad du = 2x\,dx \quad v = \sin x \quad dv = \cos x\,dx$

$$\frac{\pi^2}{4} - \frac{\pi^2}{2} + \pi + \int_0^{\pi/2} x^2\cos x\,dx$$

$$= -\frac{\pi^2}{4} + \pi + \left[x^2\sin x\right]_0^{\pi/2} - \int_0^{\pi/2} 2x\sin x\,dx$$

$$= -\frac{\pi^2}{4} + \pi + \frac{\pi^2}{4} - \int_0^{\pi/2} 2x\sin x\,dx$$

$$= \pi - 2\int_0^{\pi/2} x\sin x\,dx$$

$u = x \quad du = dx \quad v = -\cos x \quad dv = \sin x\,dx$

$$V = \pi - 2[-x\cos x + \sin x]_0^{\pi/2}$$

$$= \mathbf{(\pi - 2)\ units^3}$$

5. $y = \frac{1}{12}x^3 + x^{-1}$

$$\frac{dy}{dx} = \frac{1}{4}x^2 - \frac{1}{x^2}$$

$$L_1^2 = \int_1^2\sqrt{1 + \left(\frac{1}{4}x^2 - \frac{1}{x^2}\right)^2}\,dx$$

$$= \int_1^2\sqrt{\frac{1}{16}x^4 + \frac{1}{2} + \frac{1}{x^4}}\,dx$$

$$= \int_1^2\sqrt{\left(\frac{1}{4}x^2 + \frac{1}{x^2}\right)^2}\,dx$$

$$= \int_1^2\left(\frac{1}{4}x^2 + x^{-2}\right)dx$$

$$= \left[\frac{1}{12}x^3 - x^{-1}\right]_1^2$$

$$= \frac{2}{3} - \frac{1}{2} - \left(\frac{1}{12} - 1\right) = \mathbf{\frac{13}{12}\ units}$$

6. $\displaystyle\int\frac{3x}{(x-1)(x+2)}\,dx = \int\left(\frac{A}{x-1} + \frac{B}{x+2}\right)dx$

$$A(x+2) + B(x-1) = 3x$$

$x = 1: \quad 3A = 3$

$\qquad A = 1$

$x = -2: \quad -3B = -6$

$\qquad B = 2$

$$\int\left(\frac{A}{x-1} + \frac{B}{x+2}\right)dx$$

$$= \int\left(\frac{1}{x-1} + \frac{2}{x+2}\right)dx$$

$$= \mathbf{\ln|x-1| + 2\ln|x+2| + C}$$

7. $\int \frac{x^2 - 2}{x(x-2)(x-1)}\,dx$

$= \int \left(\frac{A}{x} + \frac{B}{x-2} + \frac{C}{x-1} \right) dx$

$A(x-2)(x-1) + B(x-1)x + C(x-2)x$
$= x^2 - 2$

$x = 0$: $\quad 2A = -2$
$\quad A = -1$

$x = 1$: $\quad -C = -1$
$\quad C = 1$

$x = 2$: $\quad 2B = 2$
$\quad B = 1$

$\int \left(\frac{A}{x} + \frac{B}{x-2} + \frac{C}{x-1} \right) dx$

$= \int \left(\frac{-1}{x} + \frac{1}{x-2} + \frac{1}{x-1} \right) dx$

$= \mathbf{-\ln|x| + \ln|x-2| + \ln|x-1| + C}$

8. $x = \sin t + 3 \qquad y = 3^t + \cos t$

$\frac{dx}{dt} = \cos t \qquad \frac{dy}{dt} = 3^t \ln 3 - \sin t$

$L_2^6 = \int_2^6 \sqrt{\cos^2 t + (3^t \ln 3 - \sin t)^2}\, dt$

$= \mathbf{\int_2^6 \sqrt{1 + 3^{2t}(\ln 3)^2 - (\ln 9)3^t \sin t}\, dt}$

9. The graph of the parametric equations is a circle of radius 6. The given interval accounts for the $\frac{3}{4}$ of the circle in quadrants II, III, and IV. Thus the length of the graph is

$\frac{3}{4}(12\pi) = \mathbf{9\pi}$ **units**

10. $r = 2$

$\sqrt{x^2 + y^2} = 2$

$\mathbf{x^2 + y^2 = 4}$

11.

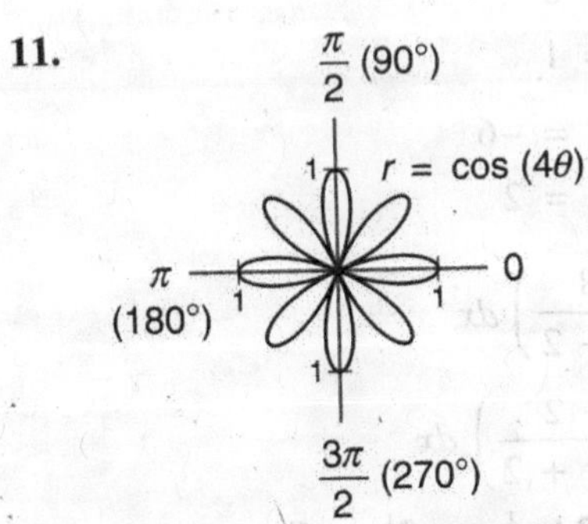

12.

$\frac{\pi}{2}$ (90°)
$r = 2\cos(2\theta)$
2
π (180°)
2
2
0
$\frac{3\pi}{2}$ (270°)

13. $\int \frac{dx}{\sqrt{1 - 4x^2}}$

$= \int \frac{dx}{\sqrt{1 - (2x)^2}}$

$= \frac{1}{2} \int \frac{2\,dx}{\sqrt{1 - (2x)^2}}$

$= \mathbf{\frac{1}{2} \arcsin(2x) + C}$

14. $x = \frac{1}{2}\tan\theta \qquad dx = \frac{1}{2}\sec^2\theta\, d\theta$

$\sqrt{1 + 4x^2} = \sec\theta$

$\int \frac{dx}{\sqrt{1+4x^2}} = \frac{1}{2}\int \frac{\sec^2\theta\, d\theta}{\sec\theta}$

$= \frac{1}{2}\int \sec\theta\, d\theta$

$= \frac{1}{2}\ln|\sec\theta + \tan\theta| + C$

$= \mathbf{\frac{1}{2}\ln\left|\sqrt{1+4x^2} + 2x\right| + C}$

15. $\int \frac{dx}{1 + 4x^2} = \int \frac{dx}{1 + (2x)^2}$

$= \frac{1}{2}\int \frac{2\,dx}{1 + (2x)^2}$

$= \mathbf{\frac{1}{2}\arctan(2x) + C}$

16. $x = \frac{1}{2}\sec\theta \qquad dx = \frac{1}{2}\sec\theta\tan\theta\, d\theta$

$\sqrt{4x^2 - 1} = \tan\theta$

$\int \frac{dx}{\sqrt{4x^2 - 1}} = \frac{1}{2}\int \frac{\sec\theta\tan\theta\, d\theta}{\tan\theta}$

$= \frac{1}{2}\int \sec\theta\, d\theta$

$= \frac{1}{2}\ln|\sec\theta + \tan\theta| + C$

$= \mathbf{\frac{1}{2}\ln\left|2x + \sqrt{4x^2 - 1}\right| + C}$

17. $\int \frac{x}{1 + 4x^2}\,dx = \frac{1}{8}\int \frac{8x}{1 + 4x^2}\,dx$

$= \mathbf{\frac{1}{8} \ln (1 + 4x^2) + C}$

18. $\int \frac{1 + 4x^2}{x}\,dx = \int \left(\frac{1}{x} + 4x\right) dx$

$= \mathbf{\ln |x| + 2x^2 + C}$

19. $\lim_{x\to 0} \frac{27x}{\sin (4x)} = \frac{27}{4} \lim_{4x\to 0} \frac{4x}{\sin (4x)}$

$= \frac{27}{4}(1) = \mathbf{\frac{27}{4}}$

20. $\lim_{x\to \pi/2^-} (\tan x)^{\pi - 2x} = \infty^0$

$\lim_{x\to \pi/2^-} (\pi - 2x) \ln (\tan x)$

$= \lim_{x\to \pi/2^-} \frac{\ln (\tan x)}{(\pi - 2x)^{-1}}$

$= \lim_{x\to \pi/2^-} \frac{(\pi - 2x)^2}{2 \sin x \cos x}$

$= \lim_{x\to \pi/2^-} \frac{-4(\pi - 2x)}{2 \cos (2x)} = \frac{0}{-2} = 0$

$\lim_{x\to \pi/2^-} (\tan x)^{\pi - 2x} = e^0 = \mathbf{1}$

21. $g(x) = \frac{d}{dx}\int_2^x \sqrt{1 + t^3}\,dt$

$g(x) = \sqrt{1 + x^3}$

$g'(x) = \frac{1}{2}(1 + x^3)^{-1/2}\, 3x^2$

$g'(x) = \mathbf{\frac{3x^2}{2\sqrt{1 + x^3}}}$

22. The graphs of $y = |f(x)|$ and $y = f(x)$ are identical only if the graph of $y = f(x)$ always stays on or above the x-axis.

The correct choice is **C.**

23. If f is everywhere increasing, then it is a one-to-one function. The inverse of a one-to-one function is also a function, so choice A is true. Choices B, C, D, and E can be shown to be false by counterexample. For B, D, and E let $f(x) = e^x$, which is a continuous increasing function. The inverse of e^x is $f^{-1}(x) = \ln x$, which is also a continuous increasing function. So $f^{-1} \neq f$ and $\frac{1}{f} = e^{-x} \neq \ln x$. For C let $f(x) = \sqrt[3]{x}$. This function is everywhere continuous and increasing, but it is not differentiable at $x = 0$.

The correct choice is **A.**

24.

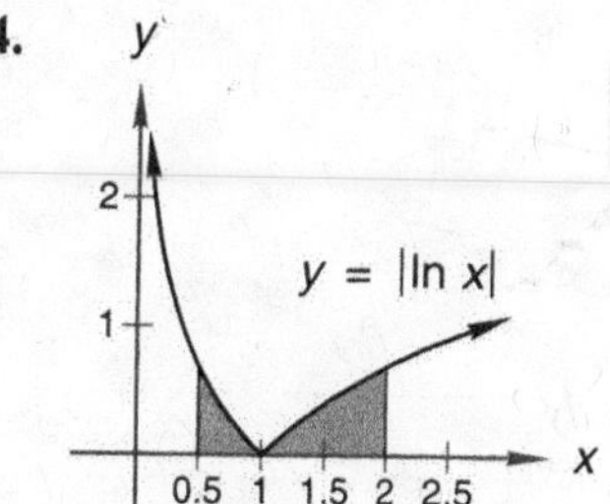

$\int_{0.5}^{2} |\ln x|\,dx = \int_{0.5}^{1} (-\ln x)\,dx + \int_1^2 \ln x\,dx$

$= \int_1^{0.5} \ln x\,dx + \int_1^2 \ln x\,dx$

$= [x \ln x - x]_1^{0.5} + [x \ln x - x]_1^2$

$= 0.5 \ln (0.5) - 0.5 - (0 - 1) + 2 \ln 2 - 2 - (0 - 1)$

$= \ln \sqrt{0.5} + \ln 4 - 0.5$

$= \mathbf{\ln 2\sqrt{2} - \frac{1}{2}}$

25. $f(x + b)$ is the graph of $f(x)$ shifted left b units, so I and II are equivalent.

$f(x + a)$ is the graph of $f(x)$ shifted left a units, so I and III are equivalent. This implies that all three integrals are equivalent.

The correct choice is **D.**

PROBLEM SET 116

1. Newton's method can provide the desired accuracy by restating the problem as

$x = \cos x$

$x - \cos x = 0$

The zero must lie between $x = 0$ and $x = 1$, since the graph of $y = x$ exceeds the limits of $y = \cos x$ outside this interval. So set $x_1 = 0.5$, `Y1=X-cos(X)`, and `Y2=nDeriv(Y1,X,X)`.

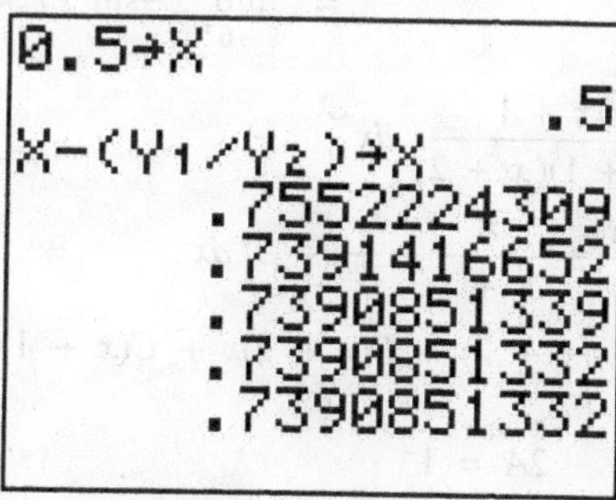

0.7390851332

2. 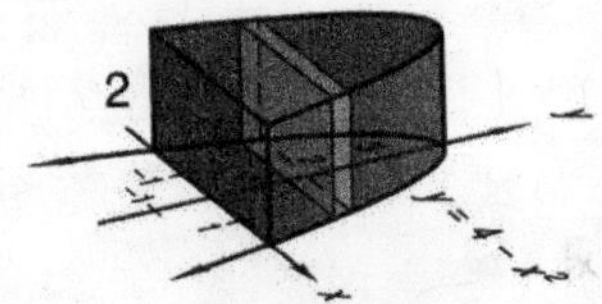

$$V = \int_{y=0}^{y=4} (2x)(2)\,dy$$
$$= 4\int_0^4 (4 - y)^{1/2}\,dy$$
$$= -\frac{8}{3}[(4 - y)^{3/2}]_0^4$$
$$= \mathbf{\frac{64}{3}\ units^3}$$

3. $\text{Average} = \frac{1}{\pi - 0}\int_0^{\pi} \sin x\,dx$
$$= \frac{1}{\pi}[-\cos x]_0^{\pi}$$
$$= \frac{1}{\pi}[1 - (-1)] = \frac{2}{\pi}$$

$$f(c) = \frac{2}{\pi}$$
$$\sin c = \frac{2}{\pi}$$
$$\mathbf{c = \arcsin\left(\frac{2}{\pi}\right)\ \text{or}\ \pi - \arcsin\left(\frac{2}{\pi}\right)}$$

4. **A *series* is the sum of the terms of an infinite sequence.**

5. $W = \int_0^3 xe^{x^2}\,dx$
$$= \frac{1}{2}[e^{x^2}]_0^3$$
$$= \mathbf{\frac{1}{2}(e^9 - 1)\ joules}$$

6. $\lim_{x\to 0^+} [\sin x \ln(\sin x)] = \lim_{x\to 0^+} \frac{\ln(\sin x)}{\csc x}$
$$= \lim_{x\to 0^+} \frac{\cot x}{-\csc x \cot x}$$
$$= \lim_{x\to 0^+} (-\sin x) = \mathbf{0}$$

7. $\int \frac{6x + 1}{x(x + 1)(x + 2)}\,dx$
$$= \int \left(\frac{A}{x} + \frac{B}{x + 1} + \frac{C}{x + 2}\right) dx$$

$A(x + 1)(x + 2) + B(x + 2)x + C(x + 1)x$
$= 6x + 1$

$x = 0$: $2A = 1$, $A = \frac{1}{2}$

$x = -1$: $-B = -5$, $B = 5$

$x = -2$: $2C = -11$, $C = -\frac{11}{2}$

$$\int \left(\frac{A}{x} + \frac{B}{x + 1} + \frac{C}{x + 2}\right) dx$$
$$= \int \left(\frac{\frac{1}{2}}{x} + \frac{5}{x + 1} - \frac{\frac{11}{2}}{x + 2}\right) dx$$
$$= \mathbf{\frac{1}{2}\ln|x| + 5\ln|x + 1| - \frac{11}{2}\ln|x + 2| + C}$$

8. $\int \frac{-x - 7}{(x + 1)(x - 2)}\,dx$
$$= \int \left(\frac{A}{x + 1} + \frac{B}{x - 2}\right) dx$$

$A(x - 2) + B(x + 1) = -x - 7$

$x = -1$: $-3A = -6$, $A = 2$

$x = 2$: $3B = -9$, $B = -3$

$$\int \left(\frac{A}{x + 1} + \frac{B}{x - 2}\right) dx$$
$$= \int \left(\frac{2}{x + 1} - \frac{3}{x - 2}\right) dx$$
$$= \mathbf{2\ln|x + 1| - 3\ln|x - 2| + C}$$

9. **$x^2 + y^2 = 4$ is the equation of an origin-centered circle of radius 2, so its polar equation is $r = 2$.**

10. $x = e^t \sin t$
$$\frac{dx}{dt} = e^t \cos t + (\sin t)e^t$$
$$\frac{dx}{dt} = e^t(\cos t + \sin t)$$
$$\left(\frac{dx}{dt}\right)^2 = e^{2t}(\cos t + \sin t)^2$$
$$\left(\frac{dx}{dt}\right)^2 = e^{2t}(\cos^2 t + 2\sin t\cos t + \sin^2 t)$$
$$\left(\frac{dx}{dt}\right)^2 = e^{2t}[1 + \sin(2t)]$$

$$y = e^t \cos t$$

$$\frac{dy}{dt} = -e^t \sin t + (\cos t)e^t$$

$$\frac{dy}{dt} = e^t(\cos t - \sin t)$$

$$\left(\frac{dy}{dt}\right)^2 = e^{2t}(\cos t - \sin t)^2$$

$$\left(\frac{dy}{dt}\right)^2 = e^{2t}(\cos^2 t - 2 \sin t \cos t + \sin^2 t)$$

$$\left(\frac{dy}{dt}\right)^2 = e^{2t}[1 - \sin (2t)]$$

$$L_0^2 = \int_0^2 \sqrt{\left(\frac{dx}{dt}\right)^2 + \left(\frac{dy}{dt}\right)^2}\, dt$$

$$= \int_0^2 \sqrt{e^{2t}[1 + \sin (2t)] + e^{2t}[1 - \sin (2t)]}\, dt$$

$$= \int_0^2 \sqrt{2e^{2t}}\, dt$$

$$= \sqrt{2} \int_0^2 e^t\, dt$$

$$= \sqrt{2}[e^t]_0^2 = \boldsymbol{\sqrt{2}(e^2 - 1)} \textbf{ units}$$

11. $$x = \frac{t^2}{2}$$

$$\frac{dx}{dt} = t$$

$$\left(\frac{dx}{dt}\right)^2 = t^2$$

$$y = \frac{1}{3}(2t + 1)^{3/2}$$

$$\frac{dy}{dt} = (2t + 1)^{1/2}$$

$$\left(\frac{dy}{dt}\right)^2 = 2t + 1$$

$$L_0^4 = \int_0^4 \sqrt{t^2 + 2t + 1}\, dt$$

$$= \int_0^4 \sqrt{(t + 1)^2}\, dt$$

$$= \int_0^4 (t + 1)\, dt$$

$$= \left[\frac{1}{2}t^2 + t\right]_0^4$$

$$= \textbf{12 units}$$

12.

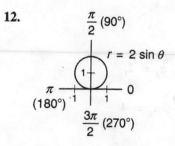

$\frac{\pi}{2}$ (90°)

$r = 2 \sin \theta$

1

π (180°)   1   1   0

$\frac{3\pi}{2}$ (270°)

13.

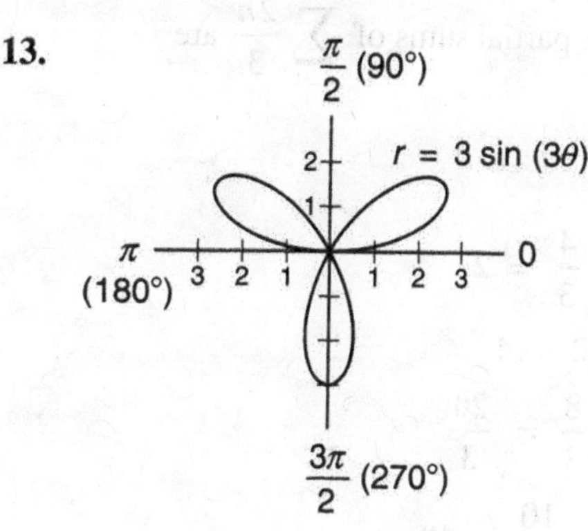

14. $$\int \frac{2x}{4 + 9x^2}\, dx = \frac{1}{9} \int \frac{18x}{4 + 9x^2}\, dx$$

$$= \boldsymbol{\frac{1}{9} \ln (4 + 9x^2) + C}$$

15. $$\int \frac{4 + 9x^2}{2x}\, dx = \int \left(\frac{2}{x} + \frac{9}{2}x\right) dx$$

$$= \boldsymbol{2 \ln |x| + \frac{9}{4}x^2 + C}$$

16. $$\int \frac{2x}{\sqrt{4 + 9x^2}}\, dx = \frac{1}{9} \int 18x(4 + 9x^2)^{-1/2}\, dx$$

$$= \boldsymbol{\frac{2}{9}\sqrt{4 + 9x^2} + C}$$

17. $x = \frac{2}{3} \tan \theta \qquad dx = \frac{2}{3} \sec^2 \theta\, d\theta$

$$\sqrt{4 + 9x^2} = 2 \sec \theta$$

$$\int \frac{2}{\sqrt{4 + 9x^2}}\, dx = \int \frac{\frac{4}{3} \sec^2 \theta\, d\theta}{2 \sec \theta}$$

$$= \frac{2}{3} \int \sec \theta\, d\theta$$

$$= \frac{2}{3} \ln |\sec \theta + \tan \theta| + C$$

$$= \frac{2}{3} \ln \left|\frac{\sqrt{4 + 9x^2}}{2} + \frac{3x}{2}\right| + C$$

$$= \boldsymbol{\frac{2}{3} \ln \left|\sqrt{4 + 9x^2} + 3x\right| + C}$$

18. $a_n = \dfrac{2n}{3}$

$a_1 = \mathbf{\dfrac{2}{3}},\ a_2 = \mathbf{\dfrac{4}{3}},\ a_3 = \mathbf{2},$

$a_4 = \mathbf{\dfrac{8}{3}},\ a_5 = \mathbf{\dfrac{10}{3}},\ a_6 = \mathbf{4}$

19. The first six partial sums of $\sum_{n=1}^{\infty} \dfrac{2n}{3}$ are

$S_1 = \mathbf{\dfrac{2}{3}}$

$S_2 = \dfrac{2}{3} + \dfrac{4}{3} = \mathbf{2}$

$S_3 = 2 + 2 = \mathbf{4}$

$S_4 = 4 + \dfrac{8}{3} = \mathbf{\dfrac{20}{3}}$

$S_5 = \dfrac{20}{3} + \dfrac{10}{3} = \mathbf{10}$

$S_6 = 10 + 4 = \mathbf{14}$

20. In problem 19 the partial sums were found to increase from $S_1 = \frac{2}{3}$ to $S_6 = 14$. Because of this rate of increase, the series most likely **diverges.**

21. $a_n = \dfrac{3}{2^n}$

$a_1 = \mathbf{\dfrac{3}{2}},\ a_2 = \mathbf{\dfrac{3}{4}},\ a_3 = \mathbf{\dfrac{3}{8}},$

$a_4 = \mathbf{\dfrac{3}{16}},\ a_5 = \mathbf{\dfrac{3}{32}},\ a_6 = \mathbf{\dfrac{3}{64}}$

22. The first six partial sums of $\sum_{n=1}^{\infty} \dfrac{3}{2^n}$ are

$S_1 = \mathbf{\dfrac{3}{2}} = \mathbf{1.5}$

$S_2 = \dfrac{3}{2} + \dfrac{3}{4} = \mathbf{\dfrac{9}{4}} = \mathbf{2.25}$

$S_3 = \dfrac{9}{4} + \dfrac{3}{8} = \mathbf{\dfrac{21}{8}} = \mathbf{2.625}$

$S_4 = \dfrac{21}{8} + \dfrac{3}{16} = \mathbf{\dfrac{45}{16}} = \mathbf{2.8125}$

$S_5 = \dfrac{45}{16} + \dfrac{3}{32} = \mathbf{\dfrac{93}{32}} \approx \mathbf{2.9063}$

$S_6 = \dfrac{93}{32} + \dfrac{3}{64} = \mathbf{\dfrac{189}{64}} \approx \mathbf{2.9531}$

23. From the partial sums computed in problem 22, the series appears to **converge to 3.**

24. $y = x^{-1/2} - x \ln|\sin x| + \arcsin\dfrac{x}{2}$

$\dfrac{dy}{dx} = -\dfrac{1}{2}x^{-3/2} - x\cot x - \ln|\sin x| + \dfrac{1}{\sqrt{4 - x^2}}$

$\mathbf{\dfrac{dy}{dx} = -\dfrac{1}{2x\sqrt{x}} - x\cot x - \ln|\sin x| + \dfrac{1}{\sqrt{4 - x^2}}}$

25. $\int_2^5 f(x)\,dx \approx$

$T = \dfrac{3}{12}(2.7 + 7 + 8.2 + 8 + 7.6 + 6.4 + 2.4)$

$= \mathbf{10.575}$

PROBLEM SET 117

1.
$$\begin{array}{rl} 1000N = & 1476.\overline{476} \\ - \quad N = & 1.476 \\ \hline 999N = & 1475 \end{array}$$

$N = \mathbf{\dfrac{1475}{999}}$

2. The ball falls distances of 15, $15(\frac{3}{5})$, $15(\frac{3}{5})^2$, ... with each consecutive bounce. The sum of these terms forms a geometric series with $a = 15$ and $r = \frac{3}{5}$. This series converges to

$S = \dfrac{a}{1 - r} = \dfrac{15}{1 - \frac{3}{5}} = \dfrac{15}{\frac{2}{5}} = \dfrac{75}{2} = \mathbf{37.5\ ft}$

3. The ball falls 37.5 ft.
It rebounds $37.5 - 15 = 22.5$ ft.
Therefore, it travels $37.5 + 22.5 = \mathbf{60\ ft.}$

4. $\lim_{n\to\infty} \dfrac{3}{4^n} = \dfrac{3}{\infty} \doteq 0$

The sequence **converges to 0.**

5. $\lim_{n\to\infty} \dfrac{3^n}{5^n} = \lim_{n\to\infty}\left(\dfrac{3}{5}\right)^n = 0$

The sequence **converges to 0.**

6. $\lim_{n\to\infty} \dfrac{5^n}{3^n} = \lim_{n\to\infty}\left(\dfrac{5}{3}\right)^n = \infty$

The sequence **diverges.**

7. $\sum_{n=1}^{\infty} \frac{3}{4^n}$ is geometric with $a = \frac{3}{4}$ and $r = \frac{1}{4}$.

$$S = \frac{\frac{3}{4}}{1 - \frac{1}{4}} = 1$$

The series **converges to 1.**

8. $\sum_{n=1}^{\infty} \frac{3^n}{5^n}$ is geometric with $a = \frac{3}{5}$ and $r = \frac{3}{5}$.

$$S = \frac{\frac{3}{5}}{1 - \frac{3}{5}} = \frac{\frac{3}{5}}{\frac{2}{5}} = \frac{3}{2}$$

The series **converges to $\frac{3}{2}$.**

9. $\sum_{n=1}^{\infty} \frac{5^n}{3^n}$ is a geometric series with $a = \frac{5}{3}$ and $r = \frac{5}{3}$. Because $r = \frac{5}{3} > 1$, the series **diverges.**

10. If $\sec \theta = \frac{x}{a}$, then $dx = a \sec \theta \tan \theta \, d\theta$.

$$\int \frac{dx}{\sqrt{x^2 - a^2}} = \int \frac{a \sec \theta \tan \theta \, d\theta}{\sqrt{a^2 \sec^2 \theta - a^2}} = \int \sec \theta \, d\theta$$

$\sec \theta \, d\theta$ is easy to integrate.

11. $\lim_{n\to\infty} \left(1 + \frac{3}{n}\right)^n = 1^\infty$

$$\lim_{n\to\infty} n \ln\left(1 + \frac{3}{n}\right) = \lim_{n\to\infty} \frac{\ln\left(1 + \frac{3}{n}\right)}{n^{-1}} = \lim_{n\to\infty} \frac{3}{1 + \frac{3}{n}} = 3$$

The original limit **converges to e^3.**

12. $\sum_{n=1}^{\infty} \frac{1}{2^n}$ is a geometric series with $a = \frac{1}{2}$ and $r = \frac{1}{2}$.

$$S = \frac{\frac{1}{2}}{1 - \frac{1}{2}} = \frac{\frac{1}{2}}{\frac{1}{2}} = 1$$

The series **converges to 1.**

13. $\sum_{n=1}^{\infty} 2^n$ is a geometric series with $a = 2$ and $r = 2$. Because $r > 1$, the series **diverges.**

14. $\sum_{n=1}^{\infty} (-1)^{n-1} 2^{n-1} = \sum_{n=1}^{\infty} (-2)^{n-1}$

This is a geometric series with $a = 1$ and $r = -2$. Because $|r| > 1$, the series **diverges.**

15. $\sum_{n=1}^{\infty} \frac{1}{(n + 1)(n + 2)} = \sum_{n=1}^{\infty} \left(\frac{1}{n + 1} - \frac{1}{n + 2}\right)$

First 4 terms: $\frac{1}{2} - \frac{1}{3}, \frac{1}{3} - \frac{1}{4}, \frac{1}{4} - \frac{1}{5}, \frac{1}{5} - \frac{1}{6}$

$$S_n = \frac{1}{2} - \frac{1}{n + 2}$$

$$\lim_{n\to\infty} S_n = \frac{1}{2} - 0 = \frac{1}{2}$$

The series **converges to $\frac{1}{2}$.**

16. $\sum_{n=1}^{\infty} \ln \frac{n}{n + 1} = \sum_{n=1}^{\infty} [\ln n - \ln (n + 1)]$

First 4 terms: $\ln 1 - \ln 2$, $\ln 2 - \ln 3$, $\ln 3 - \ln 4$, $\ln 4 - \ln 5$

$$S_n = \ln 1 - \ln (n + 1)$$

$$\lim_{n\to\infty} S_n = 0 - \infty = -\infty$$

The series **diverges.**

17. $\sum_{n=1}^{\infty} \frac{1}{n(n + 1)} = \sum_{n=1}^{\infty} \left(\frac{1}{n} - \frac{1}{n + 1}\right)$

First 4 terms: $1 - \frac{1}{2}, \frac{1}{2} - \frac{1}{3}, \frac{1}{3} - \frac{1}{4}, \frac{1}{4} - \frac{1}{5}$

$$S_n = 1 - \frac{1}{n + 1}$$

$$\lim_{n\to\infty} S_n = 1 - 0 = 1$$

The series **converges to 1.**

18. $\int \frac{x+2}{x^2+2x-8}\,dx = \int \frac{x+2}{(x+4)(x-2)}\,dx$

$= \int \left(\frac{A}{x+4} + \frac{B}{x-2} \right) dx$

$A(x-2) + B(x+4) = x+2$

$x = -4$: $\quad -6A = -2$

$A = \frac{1}{3}$

$x = 2$: $\quad 6B = 4$

$B = \frac{2}{3}$

$\int \left(\frac{A}{x+4} + \frac{B}{x-2} \right) dx$

$= \int \left(\frac{\frac{1}{3}}{x+4} + \frac{\frac{2}{3}}{x-2} \right) dx$

$= \mathbf{\frac{1}{3} \ln|x+4| + \frac{2}{3} \ln|x-2| + C}$

19. $x = 3\sin\theta \quad dx = 3\cos\theta\, d\theta$

$\sqrt{9-x^2} = 3\cos\theta$

$\int \sqrt{9-x^2}\,dx$

$= \int (3\cos\theta)(3\cos\theta)\,d\theta$

$= 9\int \cos^2\theta\,d\theta$

$= 9\int \left[\frac{1}{2} + \frac{1}{2}\cos(2\theta)\right] d\theta$

$= 9\left[\frac{1}{2}\theta + \frac{1}{4}\sin(2\theta)\right] + C$

$= 9\left[\frac{1}{2}\theta + \frac{1}{4}(2\sin\theta\cos\theta)\right] + C$

$= 9\left[\frac{1}{2}\arcsin\frac{x}{3} + \frac{1}{2}\left(\frac{x}{3}\right)\frac{\sqrt{9-x^2}}{3}\right] + C$

$= \mathbf{\frac{9}{2}\arcsin\frac{x}{3} + \frac{x\sqrt{9-x^2}}{2} + C}$

20. (a) The expression represents the area in one quadrant of a circle of radius 3.

$\int_0^3 \sqrt{9-x^2}\,dx = \mathbf{\frac{9\pi}{4}}$

(b) From problem 19,

$\int_0^3 \sqrt{9-x^2}\,dx$

$= \left[\frac{9}{2}\arcsin\frac{x}{3} + \frac{x\sqrt{9-x^2}}{2}\right]_0^3$

$= \frac{9}{2}\left(\frac{\pi}{2}\right) + 0 - (0+0) = \mathbf{\frac{9\pi}{4}}$

21. $x = e^{2t} \qquad y = 2e^t$

$\frac{dx}{dt} = 2e^{2t} \qquad \frac{dy}{dt} = 2e^t$

$\left(\frac{dx}{dt}\right)^2 = 4e^{4t} \qquad \left(\frac{dy}{dt}\right)^2 = 4e^{2t}$

$L_0^5 = \int_0^5 \sqrt{4e^{4t} + 4e^{2t}}\,dt$

$= \int_0^5 2e^t\sqrt{e^{2t}+1}\,dt$

$\approx$ **22,030.3634 units**

22.

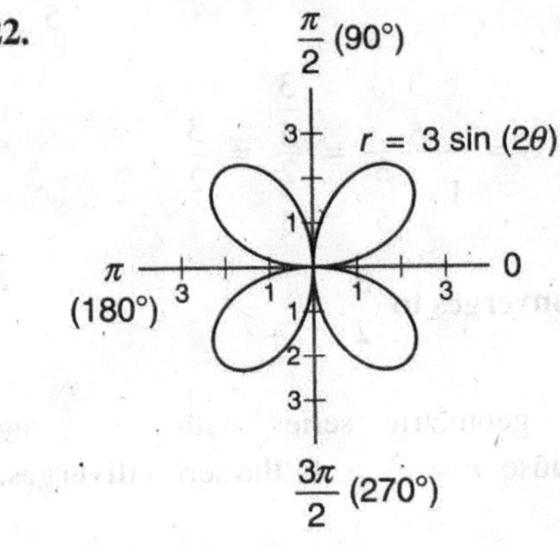

23.

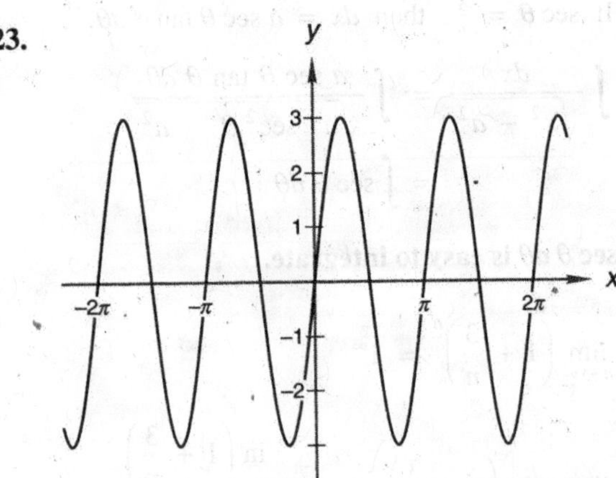

24. $(x-2)^2 + y^2 = 4$ is a circle centered at (2, 0) with a radius of 2. So the polar equation is $\mathbf{r = 4\cos\theta}$.

25. $S_1 = \mathbf{1}$

$S_2 = 1 + \frac{1}{2} = \mathbf{\frac{3}{2}} = 1.5$

$S_3 = \frac{3}{2} + \frac{1}{3} = \mathbf{\frac{11}{6}} = 1.8\overline{3}$

$S_4 = \frac{11}{6} + \frac{1}{4} = \mathbf{\frac{25}{12}} = 2.08\overline{3}$

$S_5 = \frac{25}{12} + \frac{1}{5} = \mathbf{\frac{137}{60}} = 2.28\overline{3}$

$S_6 = \frac{137}{60} + \frac{1}{6} = \mathbf{\frac{49}{20}} = 2.45$

$S_7 = \frac{49}{20} + \frac{1}{7} = \mathbf{\frac{363}{140}} \approx 2.5929$

$$S_8 = \frac{363}{140} + \frac{1}{8} = \mathbf{\frac{761}{280}} \approx 2.7179$$

$$S_9 = \frac{761}{280} + \frac{1}{9} = \mathbf{\frac{7129}{2520}} \approx 2.8290$$

$$S_{10} = \frac{7129}{2520} + \frac{1}{10} = \mathbf{\frac{7381}{2520}} \approx 2.9290$$

$$S_{11} = \frac{7381}{2520} + \frac{1}{11} = \mathbf{\frac{83{,}711}{27{,}720}} \approx 3.0199$$

The partial sums continue to increase without any apparent bound, so the series appears to **diverge.** *Note:* This is an opinion question. Students should not lose credit for incorrectly presuming that the series converges.

PROBLEM SET 118

1. $V = 2Lh$

$16 = 2Lh$

$h = 8L^{-1}$

$C = 2(2L)8 + 4[2(2h) + 2(Lh)]$

$C = 32L + 16h + 8Lh$

$C = 32L + 16(8L^{-1}) + 8L(8L^{-1})$

$C = 32L + 128L^{-1} + 64$

$C' = 32 - 128L^{-2}$

$\frac{128}{L^2} = 32$

$L^2 = 4$

$\mathbf{L = 2\text{ m}, h = 4\text{ m}, C = \$192}$

2. $x = \cos^3\theta$

$\frac{dx}{d\theta} = -3\cos^2\theta\sin\theta$

$\left(\frac{dx}{d\theta}\right)^2 = 9\cos^4\theta\sin^2\theta$

$y = \sin^3\theta$

$\frac{dy}{d\theta} = 3\sin^2\theta\cos\theta$

$\left(\frac{dy}{d\theta}\right)^2 = 9\sin^4\theta\cos^2\theta$

$L_0^{\pi/2}$

$$= \int_0^{\pi/2}\sqrt{9\cos^4\theta\sin^2\theta + 9\sin^4\theta\cos^2\theta}\,d\theta$$

$$= \int_0^{\pi/2}\sqrt{9\sin^2\theta\cos^2\theta(\cos^2\theta + \sin^2\theta)}\,d\theta$$

$$= \int_0^{\pi/2} 3\sin\theta\cos\theta\,d\theta$$

$$= \frac{3}{2}[\sin^2\theta]_0^{\pi/2} = \mathbf{\frac{3}{2}\text{ units}}$$

3. $r = 50\text{ cm} \qquad dr = \frac{1}{100}\text{ cm}$

$A = 4\pi r^2$

$dA = 8\pi r\,dr$

$dA = 8\pi(50)\left(\frac{1}{100}\right) = \mathbf{4\pi\text{ cm}^2}$

4. $y = \frac{1}{4}x^4 + \frac{1}{8}x^{-2}$

$\frac{dy}{dx} = x^3 - \frac{1}{4}x^{-3}$

$$L_2^4 = \int_2^4\sqrt{1 + \left(x^3 - \frac{1}{4}x^{-3}\right)^2}\,dx$$

$$= \int_2^4\sqrt{1 + x^6 - \frac{1}{2} + \frac{1}{16}x^{-6}}\,dx$$

$$= \int_2^4\sqrt{x^6 + \frac{1}{2} + \frac{1}{16}x^{-6}}\,dx$$

$$= \int_2^4\sqrt{\left(x^3 + \frac{1}{4}x^{-3}\right)^2}\,dx$$

$$= \int_2^4\left(x^3 + \frac{1}{4}x^{-3}\right)dx$$

$$= \left[\frac{1}{4}x^4 - \frac{1}{8}x^{-2}\right]_2^4$$

$$= 64 - \frac{1}{128} - \left(4 - \frac{1}{32}\right)$$

$$= \mathbf{60\frac{3}{128}\text{ units}}$$

5. $x = y^2$

$r\cos\theta = (r\sin\theta)^2$

$r\cos\theta = r^2\sin^2\theta$

$\cos\theta = r\sin^2\theta$

$\mathbf{r = \cot\theta\csc\theta}$

6.

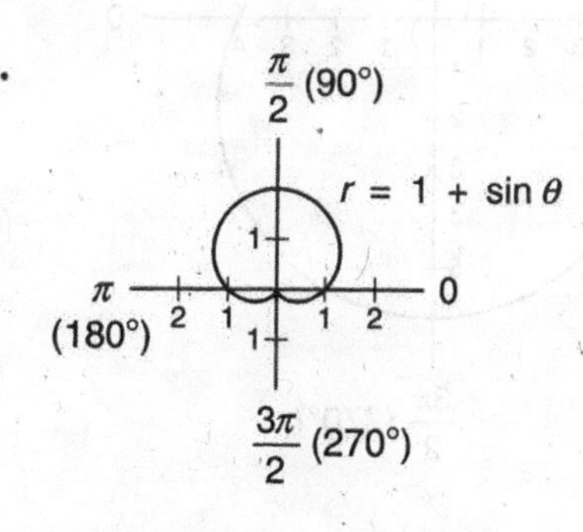

7.

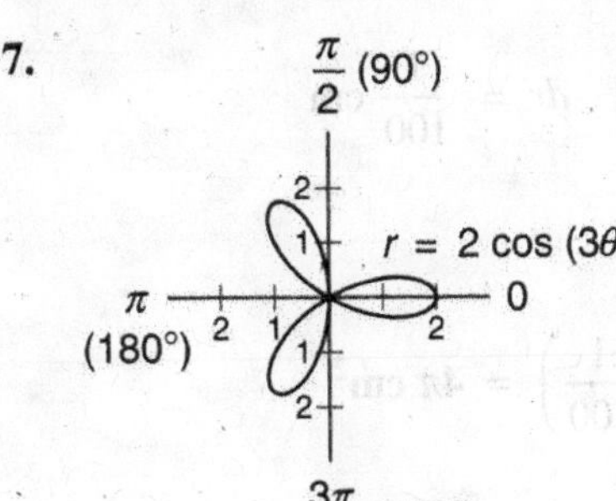

8.

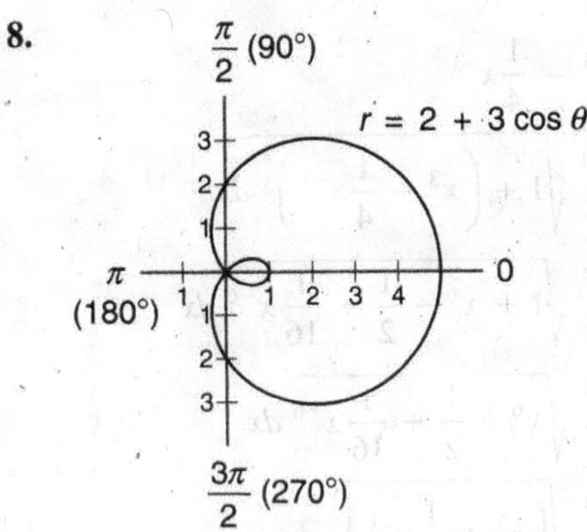

9.

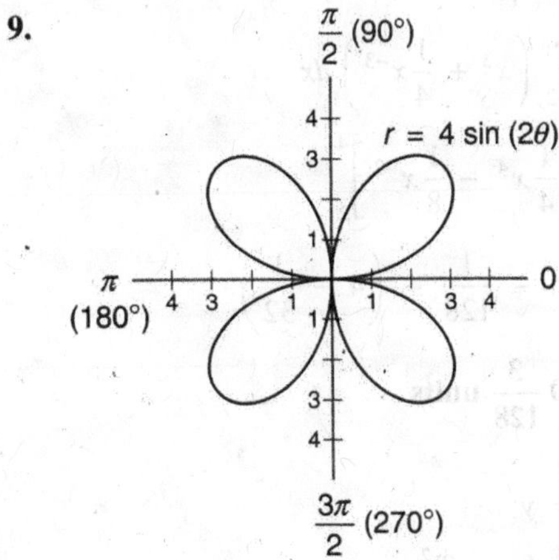

10.

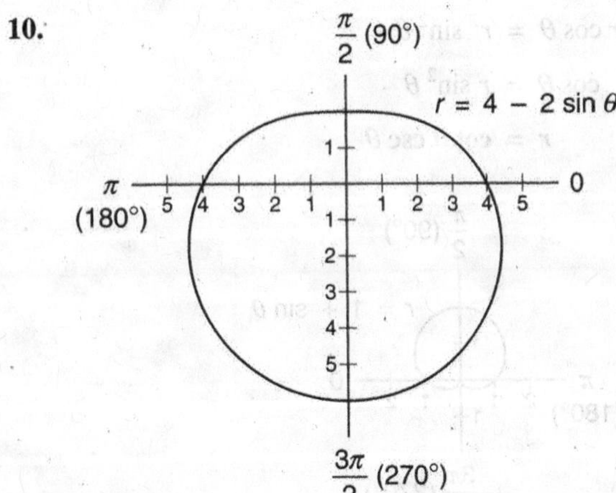

11. $y = x^3 - 3x + 4$

$$\frac{dy}{dx} = 3x^2 - 3$$

$$\frac{dy}{dx} = 3(2)^2 - 3 = 9$$

One possible vector with a slope of 9 is $\langle 1, 9\rangle$.

$|\langle 1, 9\rangle| = \sqrt{82}$

Unit tangent vector: $\left\langle \frac{1}{\sqrt{82}}, \frac{9}{\sqrt{82}} \right\rangle$

Unit normal vector: $\left\langle -\frac{9}{\sqrt{82}}, \frac{1}{\sqrt{82}} \right\rangle$

12. $$\int \frac{dx}{x^2 - x} = \int \frac{dx}{x(x-1)}$$

$$= \int \left(\frac{A}{x} + \frac{B}{x-1} \right) dx$$

$A(x - 1) + Bx = 1$

$x = 0$: $A = -1$

$x = 1$: $B = 1$

$$\int \left(\frac{A}{x} + \frac{B}{x-1} \right) dx = \int \left(-\frac{1}{x} + \frac{1}{x-1} \right) dx$$

$$= \mathbf{-\ln|x| + \ln|x - 1| + C}$$

13. $$\int \frac{3x^2 + 9x + 7}{x(x+1)(x+2)}\, dx$$

$$= \int \left(\frac{A}{x} + \frac{B}{x+1} + \frac{C}{x+2} \right) dx$$

$A(x + 1)(x + 2) + B(x + 2)x + C(x + 1)x$
$= 3x^2 + 9x + 7$

$x = 0$: $2A = 7$

$$A = \frac{7}{2}$$

$x = -1$: $B = -1$

$x = -2$: $2C = 1$

$$C = \frac{1}{2}$$

$$\int \left(\frac{A}{x} + \frac{B}{x+1} + \frac{C}{x+2} \right) dx$$

$$= \int \left(\frac{\frac{7}{2}}{x} - \frac{1}{x+1} + \frac{\frac{1}{2}}{x+2} \right) dx$$

$$= \mathbf{\frac{7}{2}\ln|x| - \ln|x + 1| + \frac{1}{2}\ln|x + 2| + C}$$

14. $x = 4 \sec \theta \qquad dx = 4 \sec \theta \tan \theta \, d\theta$

$\sqrt{x^2 - 16} = 4 \tan \theta$

$$\int \frac{dx}{\sqrt{x^2 - 16}} = \int \frac{4 \sec \theta \tan \theta \, d\theta}{4 \tan \theta}$$
$$= \int \sec \theta \, d\theta$$
$$= \ln |\sec \theta + \tan \theta| + C$$
$$= \ln \left| \frac{x}{4} + \frac{\sqrt{x^2 - 16}}{4} \right| + C$$
$$= \mathbf{\ln \left| x + \sqrt{x^2 - 16} \right| + C}$$

15. $x = 4 \sin \theta \qquad dx = 4 \cos \theta \, d\theta$

$\sqrt{16 - x^2} = 4 \cos \theta$

$$\int \sqrt{16 - x^2} \, dx$$
$$= \int (4 \cos \theta)(4 \cos \theta) \, d\theta$$
$$= \int 16 \cos^2 \theta \, d\theta$$
$$= \int [8 + 8 \cos (2\theta)] \, d\theta$$
$$= 8\theta + 4 \sin (2\theta) + C$$
$$= 8\theta + 8 \sin \theta \cos \theta + C$$
$$= 8 \arcsin \frac{x}{4} + 8\left(\frac{x}{4}\right)\left(\frac{\sqrt{16 - x^2}}{4}\right) + C$$
$$= \mathbf{8 \arcsin \frac{x}{4} + \frac{x\sqrt{16 - x^2}}{2} + C}$$

16. $\int \tan^2 x \, dx = \int (\sec^2 x - 1) \, dx = \mathbf{\tan x - x + C}$

17. $\sum_{n=3}^{\infty} \frac{1}{2^n}$ is a geometric series with $a = \frac{1}{8}$ and $r = \frac{1}{2}$.

$$S = \frac{\frac{1}{8}}{1 - \frac{1}{2}} = \frac{1}{4}$$

The series **converges to $\frac{1}{4}$.**

18. $$\sum_{n=3}^{\infty} (-1)^{n-1} \frac{1}{2^{n-1}} = \sum_{n=3}^{\infty} \left(-\frac{1}{2}\right)^{n-1}$$

This is a geometric series with $a = \frac{1}{4}$ and $r = -\frac{1}{2}$.

$$S = \frac{\frac{1}{4}}{1 + \frac{1}{2}} = \frac{1}{6}$$

The series **converges to $\frac{1}{6}$.**

19. $\sum_{n=3}^{\infty} \frac{4^n}{3}$ is a geometric series with $a = \frac{64}{3}$ and $r = 4$.

Because $|r| > 1$, the series **diverges.**

20. $$\sum_{n=1}^{\infty} \frac{1}{n^2 + 3n + 2} = \sum_{n=1}^{\infty} \frac{1}{(n + 1)(n + 2)}$$
$$= \sum_{n=1}^{\infty} \left(\frac{1}{n + 1} - \frac{1}{n + 2} \right)$$

This is a telescoping series that will collapse to

$$\frac{1}{2} - \lim_{n \to \infty} \frac{1}{n + 2} = \frac{1}{2} - 0 = \frac{1}{2}$$

The series **converges to $\frac{1}{2}$.**

21. $$\lim_{2x \to 0} \frac{\sin (137x)}{217x} = \frac{137}{217} \lim_{137x \to 0} \frac{\sin (137x)}{137x}$$
$$= \frac{137}{217}(1) = \mathbf{\frac{137}{217}}$$

22. $$\lim_{x \to (\pi/2)^-} (1 + \cos x)^{\tan x} = 1^\infty$$
$$\lim_{x \to (\pi/2)^-} \tan x \ln (1 + \cos x)$$
$$= \lim_{x \to (\pi/2)^-} \frac{\ln (1 + \cos x)}{\cot x}$$
$$= \lim_{x \to (\pi/2)^-} \frac{\sin^3 x}{1 + \cos x} = \frac{1}{1} = 1$$

The original limit is $e^1 = \mathbf{e}$.

23. $$\int_c^x f(t) \, dt = \sin x + 1$$
$$\frac{d}{dx} \int_c^x f(t) \, dt = \frac{d}{dx}(\sin x + 1)$$
$$f(x) = \cos x$$
$$\int_c^x \cos t \, dt = \sin x + 1$$
$$[\sin t]_c^x = \sin x + 1$$
$$\sin x - \sin c = \sin x + 1$$
$$-\sin c = 1$$
$$\sin c = -1$$
$$c = \mathbf{\frac{3\pi}{2}}$$

24. $$(f \circ f)'(2) = f'(f(2)) \cdot f'(2)$$
$$= f'(3) \cdot (-4)$$
$$= 2(-4)$$
$$= -8$$

The correct choice is **B.**

25. $\lim_{x\to 2^+} f(x) = f(2)$

$$8 = a + 4b$$

$$\lim_{x\to 2^+} f'(x) = f'(2)$$

$$\lim_{x\to 2^+} (3x^2) = 4b$$

$$12 = 4b$$

$$\mathbf{b = 3}$$

$$8 = a + 4(3)$$

$$\mathbf{-4 = a}$$

PROBLEM SET 119

1. $x = 2 + \sin t \qquad y = -1 + \cos t$

$$\frac{dy}{dx} = \frac{\frac{dy}{dt}}{\frac{dx}{dt}} = \frac{-\sin t}{\cos t} = \mathbf{-\tan t}$$

$$\frac{d^2y}{dx^2} = \frac{\frac{d}{dt}\left(\frac{dy}{dx}\right)}{\frac{dx}{dt}} = \frac{-\sec^2 t}{\cos t} = \mathbf{-\sec^3 t}$$

2. $a(t) = 2\pi \sin t \cos t$

$$v(t) = \pi \sin^2 t + C$$

$$v(0) = \pi(0) + C$$

$$0 = C$$

$$v(t) = \pi \sin^2 t$$

$$\text{Average velocity} = \frac{1}{\pi - 0}\int_0^{\pi} \pi \sin^2 t\, dt$$

$$= \int_0^{\pi}\left[\frac{1}{2} - \frac{1}{2}\cos(2t)\right] dt$$

$$= \left[\frac{1}{2}t - \frac{1}{4}\sin(2t)\right]_0^{\pi}$$

$$= \mathbf{\frac{\pi}{2}\ \frac{\text{linear units}}{\text{time unit}}}$$

3. $x = t^2 + t \qquad y = t + 3$

$$\frac{dy}{dx} = \frac{1}{2t + 1} = (2t + 1)^{-1}$$

$$\frac{d^2y}{dx^2} = \frac{\frac{d}{dt}\left(\frac{dy}{dx}\right)}{\frac{dx}{dt}}$$

$$\frac{d^2y}{dx^2} = \frac{-2(2t + 1)^{-2}}{2t + 1} = -2(2t + 1)^{-3}$$

$$\left.\frac{dy}{dx}\right|_{t=1} = \frac{1}{3} \text{ and } \left.\frac{d^2y}{dx^2}\right|_{t=1} = -\frac{2}{27}$$

This implies **negative concavity.**

$$y - 4 = \frac{1}{3}(x - 2)$$

$$\mathbf{y = \frac{1}{3}x + \frac{10}{3}}$$

4. $f(x) = \sin^2 x - 2\sin x$

$$f'(x) = 2\sin x \cos x - 2\cos x$$

$$f'(x) = 2\cos x(\sin x - 1)$$

Critical numbers on I:

$$x = \mathbf{0, \frac{\pi}{2}, \frac{3\pi}{2}, 2\pi}$$

$$f(0) = 0;\quad f\left(\frac{\pi}{2}\right) = -1;\quad f\left(\frac{3\pi}{2}\right) = 3;$$

$$f(2\pi) = 0$$

Maximum: 3 Minimum: −1

5. $x = t + 3 \qquad y = t^3 - 3t^2$

$$\frac{dx}{dt} = 1 \qquad \frac{dy}{dt} = 3t^2 - 6t$$

$$\left(\frac{dx}{dt}\right)^2 = 1 \qquad \left(\frac{dy}{dt}\right)^2 = 9t^4 - 36t^3 + 36t^2$$

$$L_2^5 = \mathbf{\int_2^5 \sqrt{9t^4 - 36t^3 + 36t^2 + 1}\, dt}$$

6. $r = \sin\theta\cos\theta$

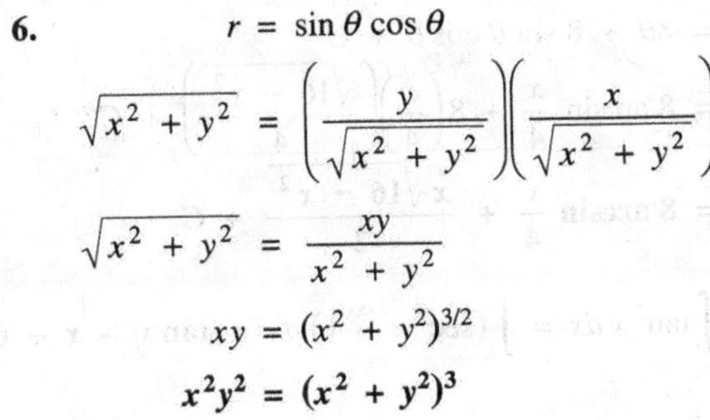

$$\sqrt{x^2 + y^2} = \left(\frac{y}{\sqrt{x^2 + y^2}}\right)\left(\frac{x}{\sqrt{x^2 + y^2}}\right)$$

$$\sqrt{x^2 + y^2} = \frac{xy}{x^2 + y^2}$$

$$xy = (x^2 + y^2)^{3/2}$$

$$\mathbf{x^2y^2 = (x^2 + y^2)^3}$$

7.

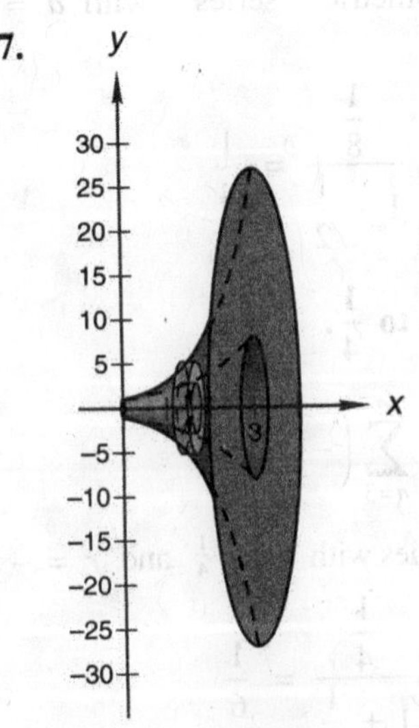

$$\mathbf{V = \pi\int_0^3 (3^{2x} - 2^{2x})\, dx}$$

8.

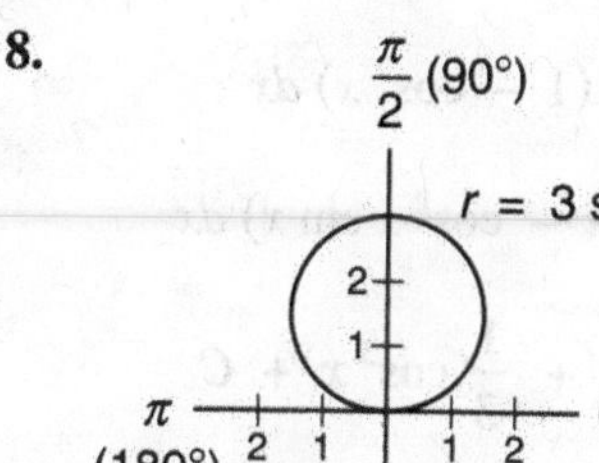

9.

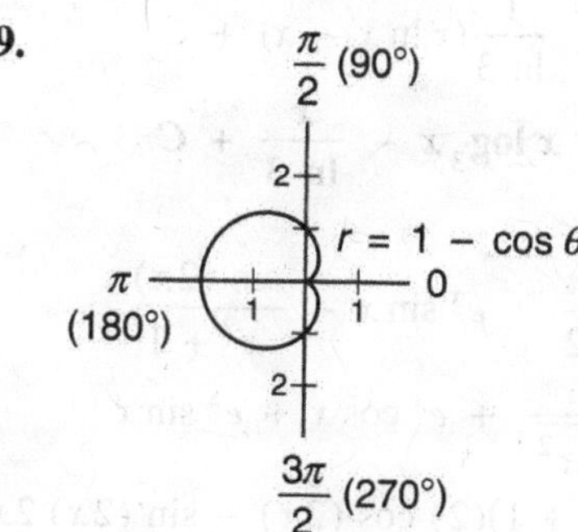

10.

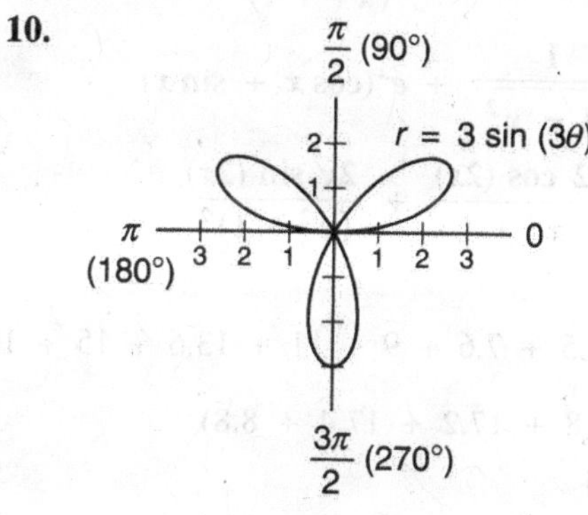

11.

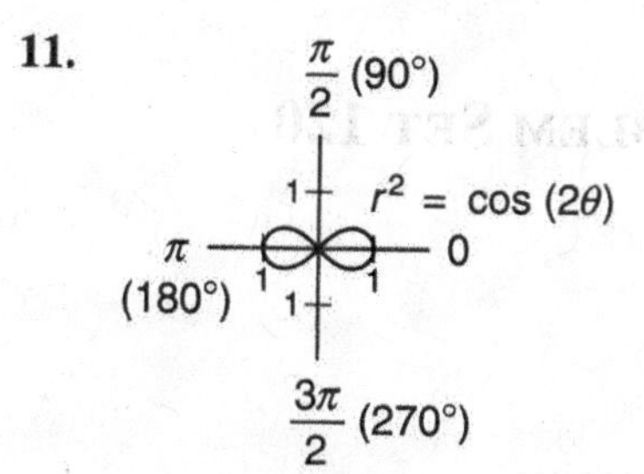

12. This series is geometric with $a = \frac{23}{100}$ and $r = \frac{1}{100}$.

$$S = \frac{\frac{23}{100}}{1 - \frac{1}{100}} = \frac{23}{99}$$

This series **converges to $\frac{23}{99}$.**

13. $$\sum_{n=1}^{\infty} (-1)^n \left(\frac{4}{3}\right)^n = \sum_{n=1}^{\infty} \left(-\frac{4}{3}\right)^n$$

This is a geometric series with $a = -\frac{4}{3}$ and $r = -\frac{4}{3}$. Because $|r| > 1$, the series **diverges.**

14. $$\sum_{n=1}^{\infty} \frac{n+1}{n} = \sum_{n=1}^{\infty} \left(1 + \frac{1}{n}\right)$$

Each term is greater than one, so the sum of infinitely many such terms would be ∞. This series **diverges.**

15. $$y = \frac{(x-1)(x^2+1)}{(x-2)^2}$$

Zero: 1

Vertical asymptote: $x = 2$

$$\frac{x^3 - x^2 + x - 1}{x^2 - 4x + 4} = x + 3 + \frac{9x - 13}{x^2 - 4x + 4}$$

End behavior: $y = x + 3$

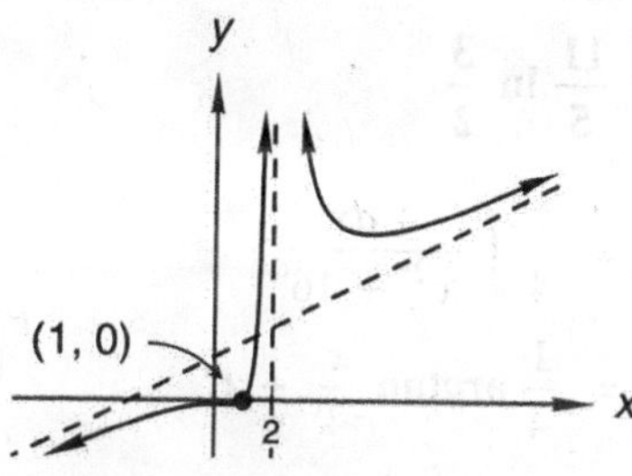

16. $$\lim_{x \to 0} (1 - e^x)^{\tan x} = 0^0$$

$$\lim_{x \to 0} \tan x \ln (1 - e^x)$$

$$= \lim_{x \to 0} \frac{\ln (1 - e^x)}{\cot x}$$

$$= \lim_{x \to 0} \frac{e^x \sin^2 x}{1 - e^x}$$

$$= \lim_{x \to 0} \frac{e^x 2 \sin x \cos x + (\sin^2 x)e^x}{-e^x}$$

$$= \lim_{x \to 0} (-2 \sin x \cos x - \sin^2 x) = 0$$

$$= \lim_{x \to 0} (1 - e^x) \tan x = e^0 = \mathbf{1}$$

17. $u = \frac{x}{3} \qquad x = 3u$

$$\lim_{x \to \infty} \left(1 + \frac{3}{x}\right)^x = \lim_{3u \to \infty} \left(1 + \frac{1}{u}\right)^{3u} = e^3$$

18. $$\lim_{x \to \infty} \left(1 + \frac{1}{x}\right)^{3x} = \lim_{x \to \infty} \left[\left(1 + \frac{1}{x}\right)^x\right]^3 = e^3$$

19. $\displaystyle\int_4^7 \frac{3x - 5}{(x - 3)(x + 2)}\,dx$

$$= \int_4^7 \left(\frac{A}{x - 3} + \frac{B}{x + 2}\right)dx$$

$A(x + 2) + B(x - 3) = 3x - 5$

$x = 3$: $\quad 5A = 4$

$$A = \frac{4}{5}$$

$x = -2$: $\quad -5B = -11$

$$B = \frac{11}{5}$$

$$\int_4^7 \left(\frac{A}{x - 3} + \frac{B}{x + 2}\right) dx$$

$$= \int_4^7 \left(\frac{\frac{4}{5}}{x - 3} + \frac{\frac{11}{5}}{x + 2}\right) dx$$

$$= \left[\frac{4}{5} \ln|x - 3| + \frac{11}{5} \ln|x + 2|\right]_4^7$$

$$= \frac{4}{5} \ln 4 + \frac{11}{5} \ln 9 - \frac{4}{5} \ln 1 - \frac{11}{5} \ln 6$$

$$= \mathbf{\frac{4}{5} \ln 4 + \frac{11}{5} \ln \frac{3}{2}}$$

20. $\displaystyle\int \frac{dx}{x^2 + 16} = \frac{1}{4}\int \frac{4\,dx}{x^2 + 16}$

$$= \mathbf{\frac{1}{4} \arctan \frac{x}{4} + C}$$

21. $x = 4 \sec\theta \qquad dx = 4 \sec\theta \tan\theta \, d\theta$

$\sqrt{x^2 - 16} = 4 \tan\theta$

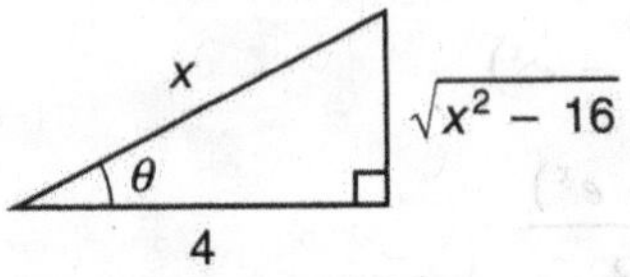

$$\int \frac{dx}{x^2 - 16} = \int \frac{4 \sec\theta \tan\theta \, d\theta}{16 \tan^2\theta}$$

$$= \frac{1}{4} \int \csc\theta \, d\theta$$

$$= \frac{1}{4} \ln|\csc\theta - \cot\theta| + C$$

$$= \frac{1}{4} \ln\left|\frac{x}{\sqrt{x^2 - 16}} - \frac{4}{\sqrt{x^2 - 16}}\right| + C$$

$$= \frac{1}{4} \ln\left|\frac{x - 4}{\sqrt{x^2 - 16}}\right| + C$$

$$= \frac{1}{4} \ln\left|\frac{x - 4}{\sqrt{x - 4}\sqrt{x + 4}}\right| + C$$

$$= \frac{1}{4} \ln\left|\frac{\sqrt{x - 4}}{\sqrt{x + 4}}\right| + C = \mathbf{\frac{1}{8} \ln\left|\frac{x - 4}{x + 4}\right| + C}$$

22. $\displaystyle\int \sin^3 x \, dx = \int \sin x\,(1 - \cos^2 x)\,dx$

$$= \int (\sin x - \cos^2 x \sin x)\,dx$$

$$= \mathbf{-\cos x + \frac{1}{3} \cos^3 x + C}$$

23. $\displaystyle\int \log_3 x \, dx = \int \frac{\ln x}{\ln 3}\,dx$

$$= \frac{1}{\ln 3}(x \ln x - x) + C$$

$$= \mathbf{x \log_3 x - \frac{x}{\ln 3} + C}$$

24. $\displaystyle y = \arcsin \frac{x}{2} + e^x \sin x - \frac{\sin(2x)}{x^2 + 1}$

$$\frac{dy}{dx} = \frac{1}{\sqrt{4 - x^2}} + e^x \cos x + e^x \sin x - \frac{(x^2 + 1)(2)\cos(2x) - \sin(2x)\,2x}{(x^2 + 1)^2}$$

$$\mathbf{\frac{dy}{dx} = \frac{1}{\sqrt{4 - x^2}} + e^x(\cos x + \sin x) - \frac{2\cos(2x)}{x^2 + 1} + \frac{2x \sin(2x)}{(x^2 + 1)^2}}$$

25. $T = \dfrac{4}{20}(3.5 + 7.6 + 9 + 11 + 13.6 + 15 + 16 + 16.8 + 17.2 + 17.4 + 8.8)$

$= \mathbf{27.18}$

Problem Set 120

1. $R(t) = R_0 e^{kt}$

$3000 = 2000e^k$

$1.5 = e^k$

$k = \ln 1.5$

$R(t) = 2000e^{t(\ln 1.5)}$

$\mathbf{R(t) = 2000(1.5)^t}$

2.

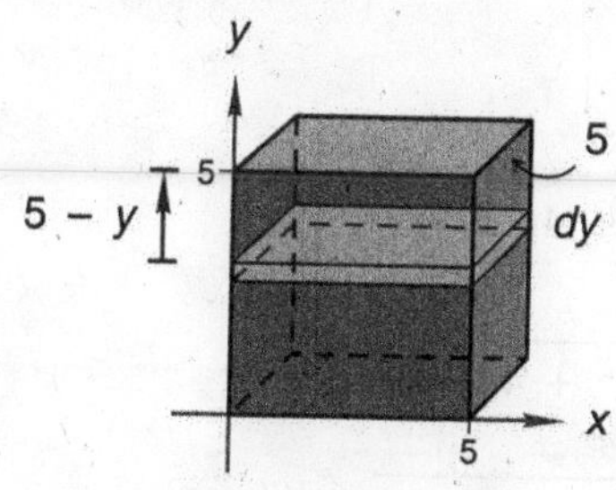

$$W = 5000\int_0^5 (5-y)25\,dy$$
$$= 125{,}000\int_0^5 (5-y)\,dy$$
$$= 125{,}000\left[5y - \frac{1}{2}y^2\right]_0^5$$
$$= 125{,}000\left(25 - \frac{25}{2}\right) = \mathbf{1{,}562{,}500\ joules}$$

3. $y = \sqrt[3]{x}$

$$dy = \frac{1}{3}x^{-2/3}\,dx$$
$$dy = \frac{1}{3}\left(\frac{1}{9}\right)(1) = \frac{1}{27}$$
$$\sqrt[3]{28} \approx \sqrt[3]{27} + dy = \mathbf{3\frac{1}{27}}$$

4. $\displaystyle\int \frac{5x-9}{(x-3)(x-3)}\,dx$

$$= \int\left(\frac{A}{x-3} + \frac{B}{(x-3)^2}\right)dx$$

$A(x-3) + B = 5x - 9$

$x = 3$: $\quad B = 6$

$x = 0$: $\quad -3A + B = -9$

$\quad A = 5$

$$\int\left(\frac{A}{x-3} + \frac{B}{(x-3)^2}\right)dx$$
$$= \int\left(\frac{5}{x-3} + \frac{6}{(x-3)^2}\right)dx$$
$$= \mathbf{5\ln|x-3| - \frac{6}{x-3} + C}$$

5. $\displaystyle\int \frac{8}{x(x+2)^2}\,dx$

$$= \int\left(\frac{A}{x} + \frac{B}{x+2} + \frac{C}{(x+2)^2}\right)dx$$

$A(x+2)^2 + B(x+2)x + Cx = 8$

$x = 0$: $\quad 4A = 8$

$\quad A = 2$

$x = -2$: $\quad -2C = 8$

$\quad C = -4$

$x = 1$: $\quad 9A + 3B + C = 8$

$\quad 3B = 8 + 4 - 18$

$\quad B = -2$

$$\int\left(\frac{A}{x} + \frac{B}{x+2} + \frac{C}{(x+2)^2}\right)dx$$
$$= \int\left(\frac{2}{x} - \frac{2}{x+2} - \frac{4}{(x+2)^2}\right)dx$$
$$= \mathbf{2\ln|x| - 2\ln|x+2| + \frac{4}{x+2} + C}$$

6. $\displaystyle\int \frac{dx}{x^2(x-1)} = \int\left(\frac{A}{x} + \frac{B}{x^2} + \frac{C}{x-1}\right)dx$

$A(x-1)x + B(x-1) + Cx^2 = 1$

$x = 0$: $\quad -B = 1$

$\quad B = -1$

$x = 1$: $\quad C = 1$

$x = 2$: $\quad 2A + B + 4C = 1$

$\quad 2A = 1 + 1 - 4$

$\quad A = -1$

$$\int\left(\frac{A}{x} + \frac{B}{x^2} + \frac{C}{x-1}\right)dx$$
$$= \int\left(\frac{-1}{x} - \frac{1}{x^2} + \frac{1}{x-1}\right)dx$$
$$= \mathbf{-\ln|x| + \frac{1}{x} + \ln|x-1| + C}$$

7. $y = 3x^2 - 4x + 1$

$$\frac{dy}{dx} = 6x - 4$$
$$\left.\frac{dy}{dx}\right|_{x=1} = 2$$

One possible vector with a slope of 2 is $\langle 1, 2\rangle$.

$|\langle 1, 2\rangle| = \sqrt{5}$

Unit tangent vector: $\left\langle \frac{1}{\sqrt{5}}, \frac{2}{\sqrt{5}}\right\rangle$

Unit normal vector: $\left\langle -\frac{2}{\sqrt{5}}, \frac{1}{\sqrt{5}}\right\rangle$

8.

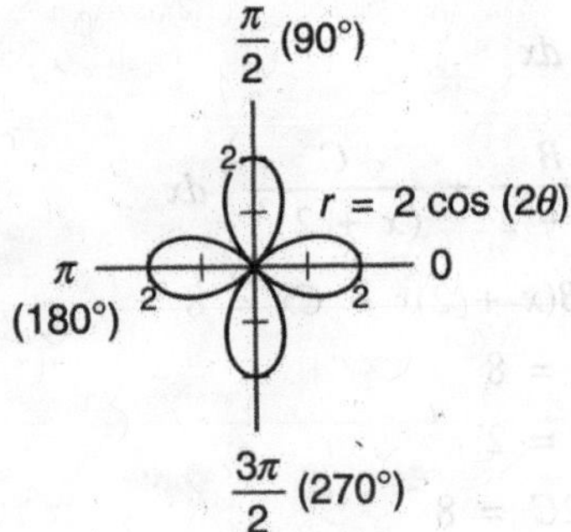

9.

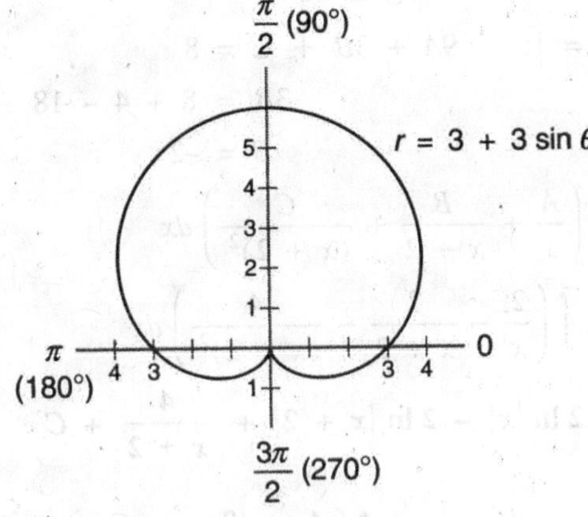

10.

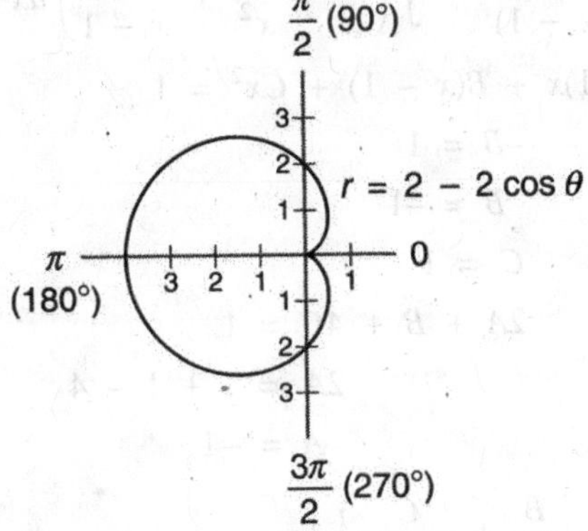

11. $x = 4t \qquad y = t^2 + t$

$$\frac{dx}{dt} = 4 \qquad \frac{dy}{dt} = 2t + 1$$

$$\frac{dy}{dx} = \frac{2t+1}{4} = \mathbf{\frac{1}{2}t + \frac{1}{4}}$$

$$\frac{d^2y}{dx^2} = \frac{\frac{1}{2}}{4} = \mathbf{\frac{1}{8}}$$

12. At $t = 2$, $x = 8$, $y = 6$, and slope $= \frac{5}{4}$.

$$y - 6 = \frac{5}{4}(x - 8)$$

$$\mathbf{y = \frac{5}{4}x - 4}$$

The positive second derivative in problem 11 indicates **positive concavity.**

13. $$\left(\frac{dx}{dt}\right)^2 = 16$$

$$\left(\frac{dy}{dt}\right)^2 = 4t^2 + 4t + 1$$

$$L_0^5 = \int_0^5 \sqrt{4t^2 + 4t + 1 + 16}\,dt$$

$$= \mathbf{\int_0^5 \sqrt{4t^2 + 4t + 17}\,dt}$$

14. The sum of infinitely many terms that get infinitely large must be infinite. The series **diverges.**

15. $$\sum_{n=1}^{\infty} \frac{1}{(n+3)(n+4)} = \sum_{n=1}^{\infty} \frac{1}{n+3} - \frac{1}{n+4}$$

This telescoping series collapses to

$$\frac{1}{4} - \lim_{n\to\infty} \frac{1}{n+4} = \frac{1}{4} - 0$$

The series **converges to $\frac{1}{4}$.**

16. $\sum_{n=1}^{\infty} \frac{2}{3^n}$ is a geometric series with $a = \frac{2}{3}$, and $r = \frac{1}{3}$.

$$S = \frac{\frac{2}{3}}{1 - \frac{1}{3}} = 1$$

The series **converges to 1.**

17. $$y = \frac{1}{3}(x^2 + 2)^{3/2}$$

$$\frac{dy}{dx} = \frac{1}{2}(x^2 + 2)^{1/2}(2x)$$

$$\frac{dy}{dx} = x\sqrt{x^2 + 2}$$

$$\left(\frac{dy}{dx}\right)^2 = x^2(x^2 + 2) = x^4 + 2x^2$$

$$L_0^4 = \int_0^4 \sqrt{x^4 + 2x^2 + 1}\,dx$$

$$= \int_0^4 \sqrt{(x^2 + 1)^2}\,dx$$

$$= \int_0^4 (x^2 + 1)\,dx$$

$$= \left[\frac{1}{3}x^3 + x\right]_0^4$$

$$= \frac{64}{3} + 4 - (0) = \mathbf{\frac{76}{3}\ units}$$

18. $x = 5\sin\theta \qquad dx = 5\cos\theta\, d\theta$

$\sqrt{25 - x^2} = 5\cos\theta$

$$\int \sqrt{25 - x^2}\, dx = \int (5\cos\theta)(5\cos\theta)\, d\theta$$

$$= 25\int \cos^2\theta\, d\theta$$

$$= 25\int\left[\frac{1}{2} + \frac{1}{2}\cos(2\theta)\right] d\theta$$

$$= 25\left[\frac{1}{2}\theta + \frac{1}{4}\sin(2\theta)\right] + C$$

$$= 25\left[\frac{1}{2}\theta + \frac{1}{4}(2\sin\theta\cos\theta)\right] + C$$

$$= 25\left[\frac{1}{2}\arcsin\frac{x}{5} + \frac{1}{2}\left(\frac{x}{5}\right)\left(\frac{\sqrt{25 - x^2}}{5}\right)\right] + C$$

$$= \mathbf{\frac{25}{2}\arcsin\frac{x}{5} + \frac{x\sqrt{25 - x^2}}{2} + C}$$

19. The result of problem 18 can be used to write

$$\int_{-4}^{4}\sqrt{25 - x^2}$$

$$= 2\left[\frac{25}{2}\arcsin\frac{x}{5} + \frac{x\sqrt{25 - x^2}}{2}\right]_0^4$$

$$= \mathbf{25\arcsin\frac{4}{5} + 12}$$

20. $x = 5\sec\theta \qquad dx = 5\sec\theta\tan\theta\, d\theta$

$\sqrt{x^2 - 25} = 5\tan\theta$

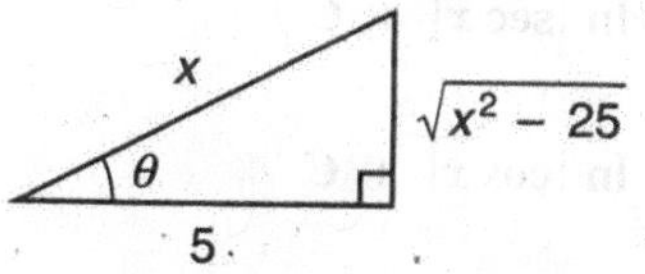

$$\int\frac{dx}{x^2 - 25} = \int\frac{5\sec\theta\tan\theta\, d\theta}{25\tan^2\theta}$$

$$= \frac{1}{5}\int\csc\theta\, d\theta$$

$$= \frac{1}{5}\ln|\csc\theta - \cot\theta| + C$$

$$= \frac{1}{5}\ln\left|\frac{x}{\sqrt{x^2 - 25}} - \frac{5}{\sqrt{x^2 - 25}}\right| + C$$

$$= \frac{1}{5}\ln\left|\frac{x - 5}{\sqrt{x^2 - 25}}\right| + C$$

$$= \frac{1}{5}\ln\left|\frac{x - 5}{\sqrt{x - 5}\sqrt{x + 5}}\right| + C$$

$$= \frac{1}{5}\ln\left|\frac{\sqrt{x - 5}}{\sqrt{x + 5}}\right| + C = \mathbf{\frac{1}{10}\ln\left|\frac{x - 5}{x + 5}\right| + C}$$

21. $\dfrac{d}{dx}\displaystyle\int_1^x \sin(t^2)\, dt = \mathbf{\sin(x^2)}$

22. Choices A, C, and D can be shown to be false by counterexample. For example, let $f(x) = \cos x$. Then $f(|x|) = \cos x$ as well. Its graph is not strictly above the x-axis. It is not an odd function. And $\int_{-\pi/2}^{\pi/2} f(|x|)\, dx = 2 \neq 0$.

The correct choice is **B.**

23. $f(x) = x^3 + x - 1$

$f'(x) = 3x^2 + 1$

$$(f^{-1})'(1) = \frac{1}{f'(f^{-1}(1))} = \frac{1}{f'(1)} = \frac{1}{3(1)^2 + 1}$$

$$= \mathbf{\frac{1}{4}}$$

24. $y = 3^{x^2} + \dfrac{2x - 1}{(x - 2)^{1/2}} + \ln|1 + \sin x|$

$$\frac{dy}{dx} = 2x(\ln 3)3^{x^2}$$

$$+ \frac{2(x - 2)^{1/2} - (2x - 1)\frac{1}{2}(x - 2)^{-1/2}}{x - 2}$$

$$+ \frac{\cos x}{1 + \sin x}$$

$$\frac{dy}{dx} = \mathbf{x(\ln 9)3^{x^2} + \frac{2}{\sqrt{x - 2}} - \frac{2x - 1}{2(x - 2)^{3/2}}}$$

$$\mathbf{+ \frac{\cos x}{1 + \sin x}}$$

25. Choice A is a statement of the mean value theorem for derivatives and is true for f. Choice B is a property of integrals and is true for the given f as well. Choice D is a statement of the mean value theorem for integrals, which is also true for f.

If $f(x) < 0$ on the interval $[a, b]$, then $\int_a^b f(x)\, dx < 0$.

The correct choice is **C.**

Problem Set 121

1. $\dfrac{dy}{dx} = \dfrac{3t^2}{2t} = \dfrac{3}{2}t$

At $t = 4$, $x = 17$, $y = 65$

$\left.\dfrac{dy}{dx}\right|_{t=4} = 6$

$y - 65 = 6(x - 17)$

$\mathbf{y = 6x - 37}$

2. $\dfrac{d^2y}{dx^2} = \dfrac{\frac{3}{2}}{2t} = \dfrac{3}{4t}$

$\left.\dfrac{d^2y}{dx^2}\right|_{t=4} = \dfrac{3}{16}$

The curve has **positive concavity** at the point of tangency.

3. $\dfrac{dy}{dx} = \dfrac{3t^2 - 6t}{1} = 3t^2 - 6t$

There are horizontal tangents when $\dfrac{dy}{dx} = 0$.

$3t^2 - 6t = 0$

$3t(t - 2) = 0$

$t = 0, 2$

A horizontal tangent exists when $t = 0$ at **(3, 0)** and when $t = 2$ at **(5, –4).**

The derivative $\frac{dy}{dx}$ is never undefined, so **the curve has no vertical tangents.**

4. $r = \sin\theta + \cos\theta$

$r^2 = r\sin\theta + r\cos\theta$

$x^2 + y^2 = y + x$

$\mathbf{x^2 - x + y^2 - y = 0}$

5.

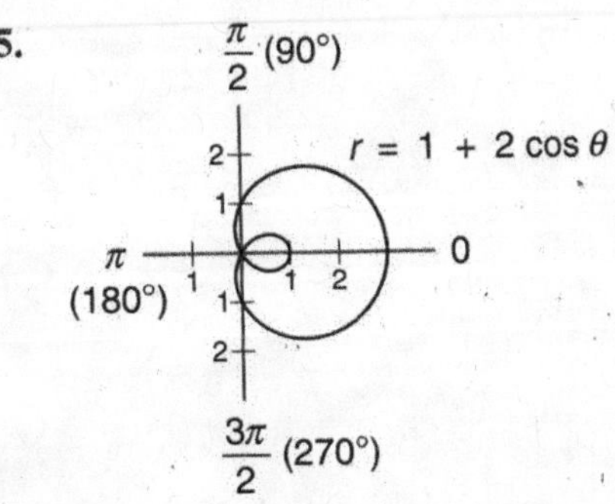

6.

$A = \displaystyle\int_0^{\pi/4} \cos^2 x\, dx$

$= \displaystyle\int_0^{\pi/4} \left[\frac{1}{2} + \frac{1}{2}\cos(2x)\right] dx$

$= \left[\dfrac{1}{2}x + \dfrac{1}{4}\sin(2x)\right]_0^{\pi/4}$

$= \dfrac{\pi}{8} + \dfrac{1}{4} - (0 + 0)$

$= \mathbf{\dfrac{2 + \pi}{8}\ units^2}$

7. $\displaystyle\int \tan^3 x\, dx = \int \tan x(\sec^2 x - 1)\, dx$

$= \displaystyle\int (\tan x \sec^2 x - \tan x)\, dx$

$u = \tan x \qquad du = \sec^2 x\, dx$

$\displaystyle\int (\tan x \sec^2 x - \tan x)\, dx$

$= \displaystyle\int u\, du - \int \tan x\, dx$

$= \dfrac{1}{2}u^2 - \ln|\sec x| + C$

$= \mathbf{\dfrac{1}{2}\tan^2 x - \ln|\sec x| + C}$

$= \mathbf{\dfrac{1}{2}\sec^2 x + \ln|\cos x| + C}$

8. $\displaystyle\int \frac{-x + 26}{x^2 + 2x - 8}\, dx = \int \frac{-x + 26}{(x + 4)(x - 2)}\, dx$

$= \displaystyle\int \left(\frac{A}{x + 4} + \frac{B}{x - 2}\right) dx$

$A(x - 2) + B(x + 4) = -x + 26$

$x = -4$: $\quad -6A = 30$

$A = -5$

$x = 2$: $\quad 6B = 24$

$B = 4$

$\displaystyle\int \left(\frac{A}{x + 4} + \frac{B}{x - 2}\right) dx$

$= \displaystyle\int \left(\frac{-5}{x + 4} + \frac{4}{x - 2}\right) dx$

$= \mathbf{-5\ln|x + 4| + 4\ln|x - 2| + C}$

9. $\int \frac{x^2 - x - 1}{x^3 - x^2}\,dx = \int \frac{x^2 - x - 1}{x^2(x-1)}\,dx$

$= \int \left(\frac{A}{x} + \frac{B}{x^2} + \frac{C}{x-1}\right) dx$

$A(x-1)x + B(x-1) + Cx^2 = x^2 - x - 1$

$x = 0$: $-B = -1$

$B = 1$

$x = 1$: $C = -1$

$x = 2$: $2A + B + 4C = 1$

$2A + 1 - 4 = 1$

$A = 2$

$\int \left(\frac{A}{x} + \frac{B}{x^2} + \frac{C}{x-1}\right) dx$

$= \int \left(\frac{2}{x} + \frac{1}{x^2} - \frac{1}{x-1}\right) dx$

$= \mathbf{2 \ln|x| - \frac{1}{x} - \ln|x-1| + C}$

10. $\int \frac{-x^3 + 2x^2 + 4x + 2}{x^2(x+1)^2}\,dx$

$= \int \left(\frac{A}{x} + \frac{B}{x^2} + \frac{C}{x+1} + \frac{D}{(x+1)^2}\right) dx$

$Ax(x+1)^2 + B(x+1)^2 + C(x+1)x^2 + Dx^2$

$= -x^3 + 2x^2 + 4x + 2$

$x = 0$: $B = 2$

$x = -1$: $D = 1$

$x = 1$: $4A + 4B + 2C + D = 7$

$4A + 2C = -2$

$A = -\frac{1}{2}(1 + C)$

$x = -2$: $-2A + B - 4C + 4D = 10$

$-2\left[-\frac{1}{2}(1 + C)\right] - 4C = 4$

$C = -1$

$A = -\frac{1}{2}[1 + (-1)] = 0$

$\int \left(\frac{A}{x} + \frac{B}{x^2} + \frac{C}{x+1} + \frac{D}{(x+1)^2}\right) dx$

$= \int \left(\frac{2}{x^2} - \frac{1}{x+1} + \frac{1}{(x+1)^2}\right) dx$

$= \mathbf{-\frac{2}{x} - \ln|x+1| - \frac{1}{x+1} + C}$

11. $x = 2\tan\theta$ $\qquad dx = 2\sec^2\theta\,d\theta$

$\sqrt{4 + x^2} = 2\sec\theta$

$\int \frac{dx}{\sqrt{4 + x^2}} = \int \frac{2\sec^2\theta\,d\theta}{2\sec\theta}$

$= \int \sec\theta\,d\theta$

$= \ln|\sec\theta + \tan\theta| + C$

$= \ln\left|\frac{\sqrt{4 + x^2}}{2} + \frac{x}{2}\right| + C$

$= \mathbf{\ln\left|\sqrt{4 + x^2} + x\right| + C}$

12. $x = 2\sec\theta$ $\qquad dx = 2\sec\theta\tan\theta\,d\theta$

$\sqrt{x^2 - 4} = 2\tan\theta$

$\int \frac{dx}{\sqrt{x^2 - 4}} = \int \frac{2\sec\theta\tan\theta\,d\theta}{2\tan\theta}$

$= \int \sec\theta\,d\theta$

$= \ln|\sec\theta + \tan\theta| + C$

$= \ln\left|\frac{x}{2} + \frac{\sqrt{x^2 - 4}}{2}\right| + C$

$= \mathbf{\ln\left|x + \sqrt{x^2 - 4}\right| + C}$

13. $\int \frac{2\,dx}{\sqrt{4 - x^2}} = 2\int \frac{dx}{\sqrt{4 - x^2}}$

$= \mathbf{2 \arcsin \frac{x}{2} + C}$

14. $\int \frac{3\,dx}{9 + x^2} = \mathbf{\arctan \frac{x}{3} + C}$

15. $\int \frac{\cos^3 x \sin x}{\cos^4 x + 1}\,dx = -\frac{1}{4}\int \frac{-4\cos^3 x \sin x}{\cos^4 x + 1}\,dx$

$= \mathbf{-\frac{1}{4} \ln(\cos^4 x + 1) + C}$

16. $u = 2x \quad du = 2\,dx \quad v = \sin x \quad dv = \cos x\,dx$

$\int 2x\cos x\,dx = 2x\sin x - \int 2\sin x\,dx$

$= \mathbf{2x\sin x + 2\cos x + C}$

17. $\lim_{x\to 0} \frac{\cos x - 1}{3x} = \lim_{x\to 0} \frac{-\sin x}{3} = \frac{0}{3} = \mathbf{0}$

18. $u = \frac{x}{3} \qquad x = 3u$

$\lim_{x\to\infty} \left(1 + \frac{3}{x}\right)^x = \lim_{3u\to\infty} \left(1 + \frac{1}{u}\right)^{3u}$

$= \lim_{u\to\infty} \left[\left(1 + \frac{1}{u}\right)^u\right]^3 = \mathbf{e^3}$

19. $u = \frac{3}{x}$

$$\lim_{x\to 0}\left(1 + \frac{x}{3}\right)^{3/x} = \lim_{u\to\infty}\left(1 + \frac{1}{u}\right)^{u} = e$$

20. $\lim_{n\to\infty} \frac{n}{n+1} = 1$

The series **diverges** by the divergence theorem.

21. $$\sum_{n=1}^{\infty} \frac{4}{(4n-3)(4n+1)}$$

$$= \sum_{n=1}^{\infty}\left(\frac{1}{4n-3} - \frac{1}{4n+1}\right)$$

$$= \left(1 - \frac{1}{5}\right) + \left(\frac{1}{5} - \frac{1}{9}\right) + \left(\frac{1}{9} - \frac{1}{13}\right) + \cdots$$

$$= 1 - \lim_{n\to\infty}\frac{1}{4n+1} = 1$$

The series **converges to 1.**

22. $$\sum_{n=1}^{\infty} (-1)^n \frac{4}{2^n} = \sum_{n=1}^{\infty} 4\left(-\frac{1}{2}\right)^n$$

This is a geometric series with $a = -2$ and $r = -\frac{1}{2}$.

$$S = \frac{-2}{1 + \frac{1}{2}} = -\frac{4}{3}$$

The series **converges to $-\frac{4}{3}$.**

23. $\lim_{n\to\infty} \frac{5n}{4n+7} = \frac{5}{4}$

The series **diverges** by the divergence theorem.

24. $$a^3 + b^3 = (a+b)(a^2 - ab + b^2)$$
$$10 = 5(a^2 - ab + b^2)$$
$$\mathbf{a^2 - ab + b^2 = 2}$$

25. $$T = \frac{3}{20}(3.5 + 7.6 + 9 + 11 + 13.6 + 13.4 + 11.2 + 10.2 + 9.6 + 9 + 4.3)$$
$$= \mathbf{15.36}$$

PROBLEM SET 122

1. $$\frac{1}{4}x^2 - \frac{1}{9}y^2 = 1$$

$$\frac{1}{2}x\frac{dx}{dt} - \frac{2}{9}y\frac{dy}{dt} = 0$$

$$\frac{1}{2}\left(\frac{2\sqrt{10}}{3}\right)(2) - \frac{2}{9}(1)\frac{dy}{dt} = 0$$

$$\frac{2\sqrt{10}}{3} - \frac{2}{9}\frac{dy}{dt} = 0$$

$$\frac{dy}{dt} = \mathbf{3\sqrt{10}\ \frac{units}{s}}$$

2. (a) $a(t) = \frac{1}{t}$

$$v(t) = \ln t + C$$
$$v(1) = \ln 1 + C$$
$$4 = 0 + C$$
$$C = 4$$
$$\mathbf{v(t) = \ln t + 4}$$

$$x(t) = t\ln t - t + 4t + C$$
$$x(t) = t(\ln t + 3) + C$$
$$x(1) = \ln 1 + 3 + C$$
$$5 = 3 + C$$
$$C = 2$$
$$\mathbf{x(t) = t(\ln t + 3) + 2}$$

(b) $v(3) =$ **($\ln 3 + 4$) length units/time unit**

$$x(3) = 3(\ln 3 + 3) + 2$$
$$x(3) = \ln 3^3 + 9 + 2$$

$x(3) =$ **($\ln 27 + 11$) length units**

3. $y = 3x^3 - 6x + 2$

$$\frac{dy}{dx} = 9x^2 - 6$$

$$\left.\frac{dy}{dx}\right|_{x=2} = 30$$

One possible vector with a slope of 30 is $\langle 1, 30\rangle$.

$|\langle 1, 30\rangle| = \sqrt{901}$

A unit normal vector to $\langle 1, 30\rangle$ is $\mathbf{\left\langle -\frac{30}{\sqrt{901}}, \frac{1}{\sqrt{901}}\right\rangle}$.

A normal vector with length 5 is $\mathbf{\left\langle -\frac{150}{\sqrt{901}}, \frac{5}{\sqrt{901}}\right\rangle}$.

4. The distance the ball falls can be represented by a geometric series with $a = 8$ and $r = \frac{3}{5}$.

$$\text{Fall distance} = \frac{8}{1 - \frac{3}{5}} = 20 \text{ m}$$

Rebound distance = 20 − 8 = 12 m

Total distance traveled = 20 m + 12 m = **32 m**

5. $u = x^2 \qquad v = \frac{1}{2}\sin(2x)$

$du = 2x\,dx \qquad dv = \cos(2x)\,dx$

$$\int x^2 \cos(2x)\,dx = \frac{1}{2}x^2 \sin(2x) - \int x \sin(2x)\,dx$$

$u = x \qquad v = -\frac{1}{2}\cos(2x)$

$du = dx \qquad dv = \sin(2x)\,dx$

$$\frac{1}{2}x^2 \sin(2x) - \int x\sin(2x)\,dx$$

$$= \frac{1}{2}x^2\sin(2x) - \left[-\frac{1}{2}x\cos(2x) + \int \frac{1}{2}\cos(2x)\,dx\right]$$

$$= \mathbf{\frac{1}{2}x^2\sin(2x) + \frac{1}{2}x\cos(2x) - \frac{1}{4}\sin(2x) + C}$$

6. $u = \sin x \quad du = \cos x\,dx \quad v = e^x \quad dv = e^x\,dx$

$$\int e^x \sin x\,dx = e^x \sin x - \int e^x \cos x\,dx$$

$u = \cos x \quad du = -\sin x\,dx \quad v = e^x \quad dv = e^x\,dx$

$$\int e^x \sin x\,dx$$

$$= e^x \sin x - \left(e^x\cos x + \int e^x \sin x\,dx\right)$$

$$2\int e^x \sin^x dx = e^x\sin x - e^x\cos x + C$$

$$\int e^x \sin x\,dx = \mathbf{\frac{1}{2}e^x(\sin x - \cos x) + C}$$

7. $$\int \frac{2x}{(x-1)(x+1)^2}\,dx$$

$$= \int\left(\frac{A}{x-1} + \frac{B}{x+1} + \frac{C}{(x+1)^2}\right)dx$$

$A(x+1)^2 + B(x-1)(x+1) + C(x-1) = 2x$

$x = 1: \quad 4A = 2$

$A = \frac{1}{2}$

$x = -1: \quad -2C = -2$

$C = 1$

$x = 0: \quad A - B - C = 0$

$B = -\frac{1}{2}$

$$\int\left(\frac{A}{x-1} + \frac{B}{x+1} + \frac{C}{(x+1)^2}\right)dx$$

$$= \int\left(\frac{\frac{1}{2}}{x-1} - \frac{\frac{1}{2}}{x+1} + \frac{1}{(x+1)^2}\right)dx$$

$$= \mathbf{\frac{1}{2}\ln|x-1| - \frac{1}{2}\ln|x+1| - \frac{1}{x+1} + C}$$

8. $$\int \frac{2x+4}{x^3(x-1)}\,dx$$

$$= \int\left(\frac{A}{x} + \frac{B}{x^2} + \frac{C}{x^3} + \frac{D}{x-1}\right)dx$$

$A(x-1)x^2 + B(x-1)x + C(x-1) + Dx^3 = 2x + 4$

$x = 0: \quad C = -4$

$x = 1: \quad D = 6$

$x = -1: \quad -2A + 2B - 2C - D = 2$

$-2A + 2B = 0$

$A = B$

$x = 2: \quad 4A + 2B + C + 8D = 8$

$4A + 2A = -36$

$A = -6$

So, $B = -6$

$$\int\left(\frac{A}{x} + \frac{B}{x^2} + \frac{C}{x^3} + \frac{D}{x-1}\right)dx$$

$$= \int\left(\frac{-6}{x} - \frac{6}{x^2} - \frac{4}{x^3} + \frac{6}{x-1}\right)dx$$

$$= \mathbf{-6\ln|x| + \frac{6}{x} + \frac{2}{x^2} + 6\ln|x-1| + C}$$

9. $$\int \frac{dx}{\sqrt{9-x^2}} = \mathbf{\arcsin\frac{x}{3} + C}$$

10. $x = 3\sec\theta \qquad dx = 3\sec\theta\tan\theta\, d\theta$

$\sqrt{x^2 - 9} = 3\tan\theta$

$$\int \frac{dx}{\sqrt{x^2-9}} = \int \frac{3\sec\theta\tan\theta\, d\theta}{3\tan\theta}$$

$$= \int \sec\theta\, d\theta$$

$$= \ln|\sec\theta + \tan\theta| + C$$

$$= \ln\left|\frac{x}{3} + \frac{\sqrt{x^2-9}}{3}\right| + C$$

$$= \mathbf{\ln\left|x + \sqrt{x^2-9}\right| + C}$$

11. $$\lim_{n\to\infty} \frac{2^n}{n^3} = \lim_{n\to\infty} \frac{2^n \ln 2}{3n^2}$$

$$= \lim_{n\to\infty} \frac{2^n (\ln 2)^2}{6n}$$

$$= \lim_{n\to\infty} \frac{2^n (\ln 2)^3}{6} = \infty$$

The series **diverges** by the divergence theorem.

12. $$S = \sum_{n=3}^{\infty} \frac{6 - 2^n}{3^n} = \sum_{n=3}^{\infty} \frac{6}{3^n} - \sum_{n=3}^{\infty} \left(\frac{2}{3}\right)^n$$

Both of these series are geometric. The first has $a = \frac{2}{9}$ and $r = \frac{1}{3}$. The second has $a = \frac{8}{27}$ and $r = \frac{2}{3}$.

$$S = \frac{\frac{2}{9}}{1 - \frac{1}{3}} - \frac{\frac{8}{27}}{1 - \frac{2}{3}} = \frac{1}{3} - \frac{8}{9} = -\frac{5}{9}$$

The series **converges to $-\frac{5}{9}$.**

13.

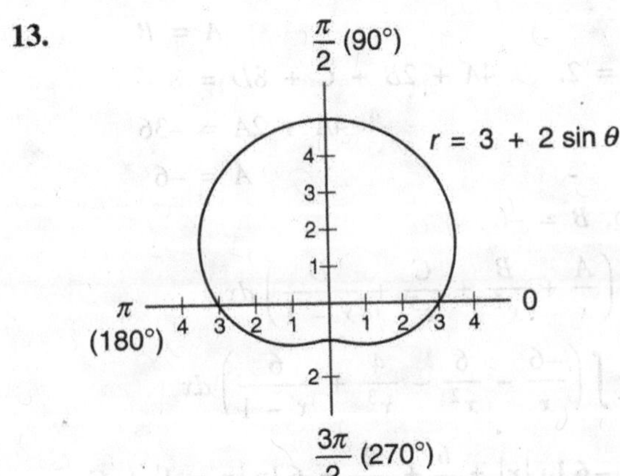

14. The equation $(x - 3)^2 + y^2 = 9$ is a circle of radius 3 whose center is the point (3, 0). In polar form this is $\boldsymbol{r = 6\cos\theta}$.

15. $x = 4\sin^2\theta \ge 0$

$y = 5\cos^2\theta \ge 0$

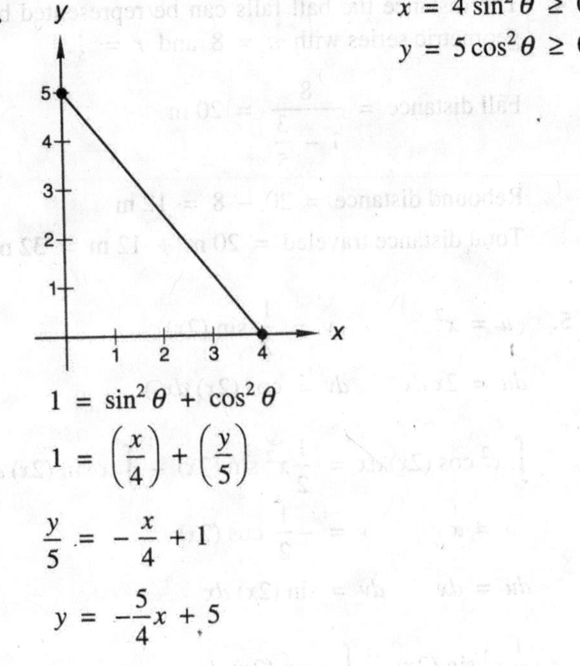

$1 = \sin^2\theta + \cos^2\theta$

$$1 = \left(\frac{x}{4}\right) + \left(\frac{y}{5}\right)$$

$$\frac{y}{5} = -\frac{x}{4} + 1$$

$$y = -\frac{5}{4}x + 5$$

16. $x = \sin^2 t$

$y = \cos^2 t$

$0 \le t \le \frac{\pi}{2}$

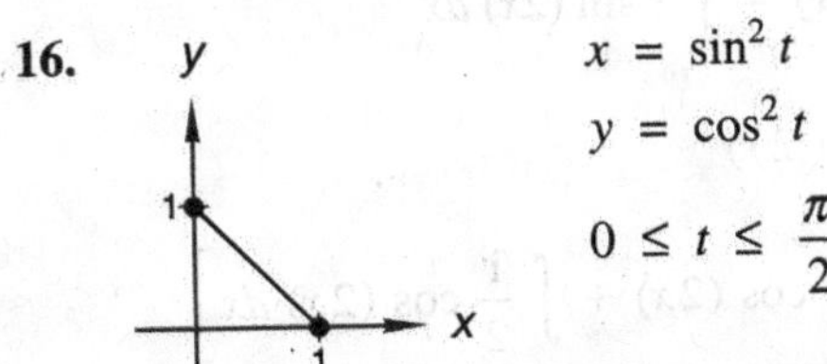

This length is the hypotenuse of a 45°–45°–90° triangle that has legs of length 1, so the length of the curve is $\sqrt{2}$ **units.**

17. $u = \cos x \qquad du = -\sin x\, dx$

$$\int_{\pi}^{2\pi} (\sin x)(e^{2\cos x})\, dx = -\int_{-1}^{1} e^{2u}\, du$$

The correct choice is **B.**

18. $$\frac{dy}{dx} = \frac{t\cos t + \sin t}{te^t + e^t}$$

$$\frac{d}{dt}\left(\frac{dy}{dx}\right) = \frac{(te^t + e^t)(-t\sin t + 2\cos t)}{(te^t + e^t)^2} - \frac{(t\cos t + \sin t)(te^t + 2e^t)}{(te^t + e^t)^2}$$

$$\frac{d^2y}{dx^2} = \frac{d}{dt}\left(\frac{dy}{dx}\right) \div \frac{dx}{dt}$$

$$= \frac{(te^t + e^t)(-t\sin t + 2\cos t)}{(te^t + e^t)^3} - \frac{(t\cos t + \sin t)(te^t + 2e^t)}{(te^t + e^t)^3}$$

$$\left.\frac{d^2y}{dx^2}\right|_{t=2} \approx -0.0056$$

The curve has **negative concavity** at $t = 2$.

19. $f(x) = \dfrac{\sin x}{x}$ is an even function.

$$\int_{-k}^{-1} \frac{\sin x}{x}\,dx = \int_{1}^{k} \frac{\sin x}{x}\,dx = \mathbf{1}$$

20. If $h(x) = f(x)g(x)$, then $g(x) = \dfrac{h(x)}{f(x)}$.

$$\lim_{x\to\pi} g(x) = \lim_{x\to\pi} \frac{h(x)}{f(x)} = \frac{\frac{1}{\pi}}{3} = \mathbf{\frac{1}{3\pi}}$$

21. $f(x) = \dfrac{x-1}{x+1}$

$$f'(x) = \frac{x + 1 - (x - 1)}{(x+1)^2}$$

$$f'(x) = \frac{2}{(x+1)^2}$$

$$f'(1) = \frac{1}{2}$$

$$\mathbf{y = \frac{1}{2}(x - 1)}$$

22.

$$y = x^2$$

$$\frac{dy}{dx} = 2x$$

$$\left(\frac{dy}{dx}\right)^2 = 4x^2$$

$$L_{-3}^{3} = 2\int_0^3 \sqrt{1 + 4x^2}\,dx$$

$$x = \frac{1}{2}\tan\theta \qquad dx = \frac{1}{2}\sec^2\theta\,d\theta$$

$$\sqrt{1 + 4x^2} = \sec\theta$$

$$2\int \sqrt{1 + 4x^2}\,dx$$

$$= 2\int (\sec\theta)\left(\frac{1}{2}\right)(\sec^2\theta)\,d\theta$$

$$= \int (\sec\theta)(\sec^2\theta)\,d\theta$$

$$u = \sec\theta \qquad v = \tan\theta$$

$$du = \sec\theta\tan\theta\,d\theta \qquad dv = \sec^2\theta\,d\theta$$

$$\int \sec^3\theta\,d\theta$$

$$= \sec\theta\tan\theta - \int \sec\theta\tan^2\theta\,d\theta$$

$$= \sec\theta\tan\theta - \int \sec\theta(\sec^2\theta - 1)\,d\theta$$

$$= \sec\theta\tan\theta - \int (\sec^3\theta - \sec\theta)\,d\theta$$

$$= \sec\theta\tan\theta - \int \sec^3\theta\,d\theta + \ln|\sec\theta + \tan\theta|$$

$$2\int \sec^3\theta\,d\theta$$

$$= \sec\theta\tan\theta + \ln|\sec\theta + \tan\theta| + C$$

$$\int \sec^3\theta\,d\theta$$

$$= \frac{1}{2}\sec\theta\tan\theta + \frac{1}{2}\ln|\sec\theta + \tan\theta| + C$$

$$L_{-3}^{3} = \left[\frac{1}{2}\sqrt{1 + 4x^2}\,(2x) + \frac{1}{2}\ln\left|\sqrt{1 + 4x^2} + 2x\right|\right]_0^3$$

$$= \left[\mathbf{3\sqrt{37} + \frac{1}{2}\ln\left(\sqrt{37} + 6\right)}\right] \textbf{ units}$$

23.

$$4 = xy^3 - x^2y + 3x$$

$$0 = 3xy^2\frac{dy}{dx} + y^3 - x^2\frac{dy}{dx} - 2xy + 3$$

$$\frac{dy}{dx} = \frac{2xy - y^3 - 3}{3xy^2 - x^2}$$

At (2, 1) slope $= \dfrac{2(2) - 1 - 3}{3(2) - 4} = \dfrac{0}{2} = 0$

The tangent line is $y = 1$.

At $x = 1.95$, $y \approx \mathbf{1}$.

24. $y = (e^x)^{\sin x} = e^{x\sin x}$

$$\mathbf{y' = e^{x\sin x}(x\cos x + \sin x)}$$

25. $f(x) = \sin^3 x$ is the only one of the four choices that is an odd function, and the integral from $-a$ to a of any odd function is zero.

$$\int_{-\pi}^{\pi} \sin^3 x\,dx = 0$$

The correct choice is **C.**

PROBLEM SET 123

1. $y = x^2$

$$\frac{dy}{dx} = 2x$$

$$\left(\frac{dy}{dx}\right)^2 = 4x^2$$

$$L_0^6 = \int_0^6 \sqrt{4x^2 + 1}\, dx$$

$$x = \frac{1}{2}\tan\theta \qquad dx = \frac{1}{2}\sec^2\theta\, d\theta$$

$$\sqrt{4x^2 + 1} = \sec\theta$$

$$\int \sqrt{4x^2 + 1}\, dx = \int (\sec\theta)\left(\frac{1}{2}\right)(\sec^2\theta)\, d\theta$$

$$= \frac{1}{2}\int \sec\theta \sec^2\theta\, d\theta$$

$$u = \sec\theta \qquad v = \tan\theta$$

$$du = \sec\theta\tan\theta\, d\theta \qquad dv = \sec^2\theta\, d\theta$$

$$\int \sec^3\theta\, d\theta$$

$$= \sec\theta\tan\theta - \int \sec\theta\tan^2\theta\, d\theta$$

$$= \sec\theta\tan\theta - \int \sec\theta(\sec^2\theta - 1)\, d\theta$$

$$= \sec\theta\tan\theta - \int (\sec^3\theta - \sec\theta)\, d\theta$$

$$= \sec\theta\tan\theta - \int \sec^3\theta\, d\theta + \ln|\sec\theta + \tan\theta|$$

$$2\int \sec^3\theta\, d\theta$$

$$= \sec\theta\tan\theta + \ln|\sec\theta + \tan\theta| + C$$

$$\frac{1}{2}\int \sec^3\theta\, d\theta$$

$$= \frac{1}{4}[\sec\theta\tan\theta + \ln|\sec\theta + \tan\theta|] + C$$

$$L_0^6 = \frac{1}{4}\Big[\sqrt{4x^2+1}(2x)$$

$$+ \ln\left|\sqrt{4x^2+1} + 2x\right|\Big]_0^6$$

$$= \frac{1}{4}[\sqrt{145}(12) + \ln(\sqrt{145} + 12) - (0 + 0)]$$

$$= \boxed{\mathbf{3\sqrt{145} + \frac{1}{4}\ln(\sqrt{145} + 12)}} \textbf{ units}$$

2. $$\frac{dy}{dx} = \frac{\frac{2}{t}}{6e^{3t}} = \frac{1}{3te^{3t}} = (3te^{3t})^{-1}$$

$$\frac{d^2y}{dx^2} = \frac{-(3te^{3t})^{-2}(3t3e^{3t} + 3e^{3t})}{6e^{3t}}$$

$$\frac{d^2y}{dx^2} = \frac{-3e^{3t}(3t + 1)}{6e^{3t}(3te^{3t})^2}$$

$$\frac{d^2y}{dx^2} = -\frac{3t + 1}{18t^2e^{6t}}$$

$$\left.\frac{d^2y}{dx^2}\right|_{t=4} = -\frac{13}{288e^{24}}$$

The curve has **negative concavity** when $t = 4$.

3.

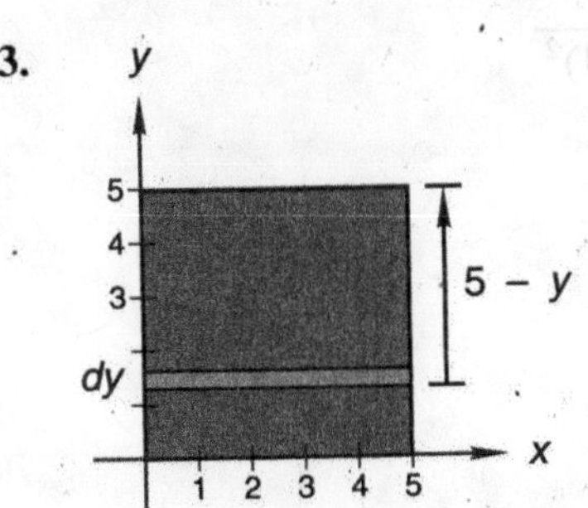

$$F = 5000\int_0^5 (5 - y)(5)\, dy$$

$$= 25{,}000\int_0^5 (5 - y)\, dy$$

$$= 25{,}000\left[5y - \frac{1}{2}y^2\right]_0^5$$

$$= 25{,}000\left[25 - \frac{25}{2}\right]$$

$$= \textbf{312,500 newtons}$$

4. (a) $a(t) = -15\text{ m/s}^2$

$$\mathbf{v(t) = -15t + 40}$$

$$\mathbf{h(t) = -\frac{15}{2}t^2 + 40t}$$

(b) $h(t) = 0$

$$0 = -\frac{15}{2}t^2 + 40t$$

$$0 = \frac{5}{2}t(-3t + 16)$$

$$t = \mathbf{\frac{16}{3}\ s}$$

5. $\displaystyle\int \frac{2x+5}{x^2+2x+1}\,dx = \int \frac{2x+5}{(x+1)^2}\,dx$

$\displaystyle = \int \left(\frac{A}{x+1} + \frac{B}{(x+1)^2}\right) dx$

$A(x+1) + B = 2x + 5$

$x = -1$: $\quad B = 3$

$x = 0$: $\quad A + B = 5$

$A = 2$

$\displaystyle\int \left(\frac{A}{x+1} + \frac{B}{(x+1)^2}\right) dx$

$\displaystyle = \int \left(\frac{2}{x+1} + \frac{3}{(x+1)^2}\right) dx$

$\displaystyle = \mathbf{2 \ln|x+1| - \frac{3}{x+1} + C}$

6. $u = \sin(2x) \qquad v = e^x$

$du = 2\cos(2x)\,dx \qquad dv = e^x\,dx$

$\displaystyle\int e^x \sin(2x)\,dx$

$\displaystyle = e^x \sin(2x) - \int 2e^x \cos(2x)\,dx$

$u = 2\cos(2x) \qquad v = e^x$

$du = -4\sin(2x)\,dx \qquad dv = e^x\,dx$

$\displaystyle\int e^x \sin(2x)\,dx = e^x \sin(2x) - \left[2e^x\cos(2x) + \int 4e^x \sin(2x)\,dx\right]$

$\displaystyle 5\int e^x \sin(2x)\,dx = e^x \sin(2x) - 2e^x\cos(2x) + C$

$\displaystyle\int e^x \sin(2x)\,dx$

$\displaystyle = \mathbf{\frac{1}{5}e^x \sin(2x) - \frac{2}{5}e^x\cos(2x) + C}$

7. $u = x^2 \quad du = 2x\,dx \quad v = e^x \quad dv = e^x\,dx$

$\displaystyle\int x^2e^x\,dx = x^2e^x - \int 2xe^x\,dx$

$u = 2x \quad du = 2\,dx \quad v = e^x \quad dv = e^x\,dx$

$\displaystyle\int x^2e^x\,dx = x^2e^x - \left(2xe^x - \int 2e^x\,dx\right)$

$= x^2e^x - 2xe^x + 2e^x + C$

$= \mathbf{e^x(x^2 - 2x + 2) + C}$

8. $\displaystyle\int \frac{2x+1}{(x-3)(x+2)}\,dx$

$\displaystyle = \int \left(\frac{A}{x-3} + \frac{B}{x+2}\right) dx$

$A(x+2) + B(x-3) = 2x + 1$

$x = 3$: $\quad 5A = 7$

$A = \frac{7}{5}$

$x = -2$: $\quad -5B = -3$

$B = \frac{3}{5}$

$\displaystyle\int \left(\frac{A}{x-3} + \frac{B}{x+2}\right) dx$

$\displaystyle = \int \left(\frac{\frac{7}{5}}{x-3} + \frac{\frac{3}{5}}{x+2}\right) dx$

$\displaystyle = \mathbf{\frac{7}{5}\ln|x-3| + \frac{3}{5}\ln|x+2| + C}$

9. $\vec{f}(t) = 2\cos(t)\,\hat{i} + \ln(t)\,\hat{j}$

$\mathbf{\vec{f}'(t) = -2\sin(t)\,\hat{i} + \frac{1}{t}\hat{j}}$

Domain: $\{t \in \mathbb{R} \mid t > 0\}$

10. $\displaystyle\vec{f}(t) = 3^{2t^2}\hat{i} + \frac{2t-3}{2t+4}\hat{j}$

$\vec{f}'(t) = 4t(\ln 3)3^{2t^2}\hat{i}$

$\displaystyle + \frac{(2t+4)(2) - (2t-3)(2)}{(2t+4)^2}\hat{j}$

$\displaystyle\mathbf{\vec{f}'(t) = t(\ln 81)3^{2t^2}\hat{i} + \frac{14}{(2t+4)^2}\hat{j}}$

Domain: $\{t \in \mathbb{R} \mid t \neq -2\}$

11.

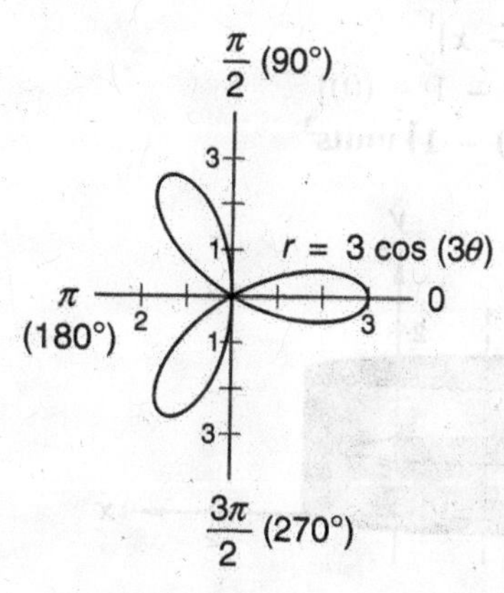

12.

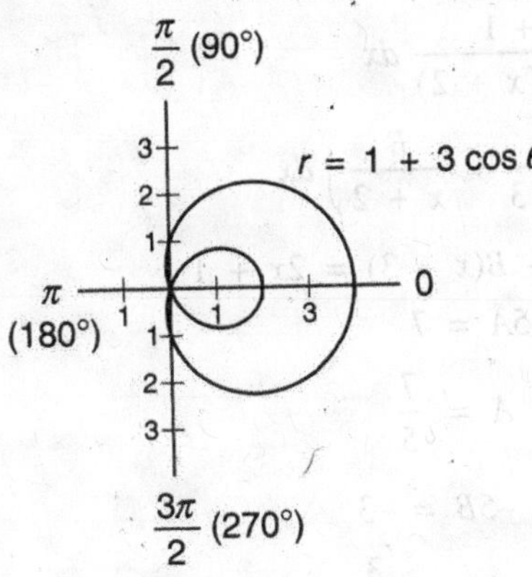

13. Average value $= \dfrac{1}{2\pi - \pi}\displaystyle\int_{\pi}^{2\pi} \sin x\, e^{2\cos x}\, dx$

$$= \frac{1}{\pi}\left(-\frac{1}{2}\right)\int_{\pi}^{2\pi} -2\sin x\, e^{2\cos x}\, dx$$

$$= -\frac{1}{2\pi}\left[e^{2\cos x}\right]_{\pi}^{2\pi}$$

$$= -\frac{1}{2\pi}\left(e^{2} - e^{-2}\right)$$

14.

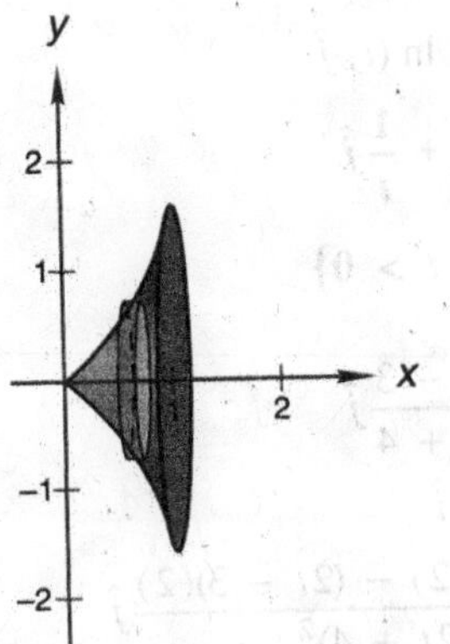

$$V = \pi\int_0^1 \tan^2 x\, dx$$

$$= \pi\int_0^1 (\sec^2 x - 1)\, dx$$

$$= \pi[\tan x - x]_0^1$$

$$= \pi[\tan(1) - 1 - (0)]$$

$$= \boldsymbol{\pi[\tan(1) - 1]\ \text{units}^3}$$

15.

$$V = 2\pi\int_0^1 (1 + x)\tan x\, dx$$

$$= 2\pi\int_0^1 (\tan x + x\tan x)\, dx$$

16. $\displaystyle\sum_{n=3}^{\infty} e^{-n} = \sum_{n=3}^{\infty} \frac{1}{e^n}$

This is a geometric series with $a = \frac{1}{e^3}$ and $r = \frac{1}{e}$.

$$S = \frac{\frac{1}{e^3}}{1 - \frac{1}{e}} = \frac{\frac{1}{e^3}}{\frac{e-1}{e}} = \frac{1}{e^2(e-1)}$$

The series **converges to** $\boldsymbol{\dfrac{1}{e^2(e-1)}}$.

17. $\displaystyle S = \sum_{n=1}^{\infty} \frac{2^n - 5}{3^{n+1}} = \sum_{n=1}^{\infty} \frac{2^n}{3^{n+1}} - \sum_{n=1}^{\infty} \frac{5}{3^{n+1}}$

The first series is geometric with $a = \frac{2}{9}$ and $r = \frac{2}{3}$. The second series is also geometric, with $a = \frac{5}{9}$ and $r = \frac{1}{3}$.

$$S = \frac{\frac{2}{9}}{1 - \frac{2}{3}} - \frac{\frac{5}{9}}{1 - \frac{1}{3}} = \frac{2}{3} - \frac{5}{6} = -\frac{1}{6}$$

The series **converges to** $\boldsymbol{-\dfrac{1}{6}}$.

18. $\displaystyle\lim_{n\to\infty} \frac{2^n + 4}{n^3} = \infty$

The series **diverges** by the divergence theorem.

19. $\displaystyle A = \int_1^5 \sqrt{x^2 - 1}\, dx$

$x = \sec\theta \quad dx = \sec\theta\tan\theta\, d\theta$

$\sqrt{x^2 - 1} = \tan\theta$

$$\int \sqrt{x^2 - 1}\, dx = \int \tan\theta\sec\theta\tan\theta\, d\theta$$

$$= \int \tan^2\theta\sec\theta\, d\theta$$

$$= \int (\sec^2\theta - 1)\sec\theta\, d\theta$$

$$= \int (\sec^3\theta - \sec\theta)\, d\theta$$

In problem 1 the solution to $\int \sec^3\theta\, d\theta$ was determined, so

$$\int (\sec^3\theta - \sec\theta)\, d\theta$$

$$= \frac{1}{2}\sec\theta\tan\theta + \frac{1}{2}\ln|\sec\theta + \tan\theta|$$

$$- \ln|\sec\theta + \tan\theta| + C$$

$$= \frac{1}{2}\sec\theta\tan\theta - \frac{1}{2}\ln|\sec\theta + \tan\theta| + C$$

$$\int_1^5 \sqrt{x^2 - 1}\, dx$$

$$= \left[\frac{1}{2}x\sqrt{x^2 - 1} - \frac{1}{2}\ln\left|x + \sqrt{x^2 - 1}\right|\right]_1^5$$

$$= \left[\mathbf{5\sqrt{6} - \frac{1}{2}\ln(5 + 2\sqrt{6})}\right] \textbf{units}^2$$

20. $$y = \arcsin(\tan x) + \frac{3 - x}{\sin x + \cos x}$$

$$\frac{dy}{dx} = \frac{\sec^2 x}{\sqrt{1 - \tan^2 x}} + \frac{(\sin x + \cos x)(-1)}{(\sin x + \cos x)^2}$$

$$- \frac{(3 - x)(\cos x - \sin x)}{(\sin x + \cos x)^2}$$

$$\frac{dy}{dx} = \frac{\mathbf{\sec^2 x}}{\mathbf{\sqrt{1 - \tan^2 x}}} - \frac{\mathbf{1}}{\mathbf{\sin x + \cos x}}$$

$$+ \frac{\mathbf{(x - 3)(\cos x - \sin x)}}{\mathbf{(\sin x + \cos x)^2}}$$

21. $$x^2y^3 - 4y^2 + 3x = 6xy^4$$

$$3x^2y^2\frac{dy}{dx} + 2xy^3 - 8y\frac{dy}{dx} + 3$$

$$= (6x)4y^3\frac{dy}{dx} + 6y^4$$

$$2xy^3 + 3 - 6y^4 = (24xy^3 + 8y - 3x^2y^2)\frac{dy}{dx}$$

$$\frac{dy}{dx} = \frac{\mathbf{2xy^3 + 3 - 6y^4}}{\mathbf{24xy^3 + 8y - 3x^2y^2}}$$

22. $$\lim_{x\to\infty}\left(1 + \frac{c}{x}\right)^x = 1^\infty$$

$$\lim_{x\to\infty} x\ln\left(1 + \frac{c}{x}\right) = \lim_{x\to\infty}\frac{\ln\left(1 + \frac{c}{x}\right)}{x^{-1}}$$

$$= \lim_{x\to\infty}\frac{\frac{-c}{x(x + c)}}{-\frac{1}{x^2}} = \lim_{x\to\infty}\frac{cx}{x + c} = \lim_{x\to\infty}\frac{c}{1} = c$$

So the original limit, $\lim_{x\to\infty}\left(1 + \frac{c}{x}\right)^x = e^c$.

23. $$u = \frac{x}{5} \qquad x = 5u$$

$$\lim_{x\to\infty}\left(1 + \frac{5}{x}\right)^x = \lim_{5u\to\infty}\left(1 + \frac{1}{u}\right)^{5u}$$

$$= \lim_{u\to\infty}\left[\left(1 + \frac{1}{u}\right)^u\right]^5 = \mathbf{e^5}$$

24. $$\lim_{x\to\infty}\left(1 + \frac{1}{x}\right)^{5x} = \lim_{x\to\infty}\left[\left(1 + \frac{1}{x}\right)^x\right]^5 = \mathbf{e^5}$$

25. $$u = \frac{5}{x}$$

$$\lim_{x\to 0}\left(1 + \frac{x}{5}\right)^{5/x} = \lim_{u\to\infty}\left(1 + \frac{1}{u}\right)^u = \mathbf{e}$$

PROBLEM SET 124

1.

$$V = \pi\int_2^5\left(\frac{1}{\sqrt{x^2 + 10}}\right)^2 dx$$

$$= \pi\int_2^5\frac{1}{x^2 + 10}\, dx$$

$$= \frac{\pi}{\sqrt{10}}\int_2^5\frac{\sqrt{10}}{x^2 + 10}\, dx$$

$$= \frac{\pi}{\sqrt{10}}\left[\arctan\frac{x}{\sqrt{10}}\right]_2^5$$

$$= \frac{\pi}{\sqrt{10}}\left[\arctan\frac{\sqrt{10}}{2} - \arctan\frac{\sqrt{10}}{5}\right] \textbf{units}^3$$

2. (a) $$f(x) = \frac{3}{4}x^{4/3} + 3x^{1/3}$$

$$f'(x) = x^{1/3} + x^{-2/3}$$

$$f'(x) = x^{1/3} + \frac{1}{x^{2/3}}$$

$$f'(x) = \frac{\mathbf{x + 1}}{\mathbf{x^{2/3}}}$$

(b) Critical numbers: $\mathbf{x = -8, -1, 0, 8}$

(c) **Horizontal tangent: $x = -1$**

Vertical tangent: $x = 0$

3. (a) $f(-8) = 6 \quad f(-1) = -2\frac{1}{4}$

$f(0) = 0 \quad f(8) = 18$

Relative maxima: (–8, 6), (8, 18)

Relative minimum: $\left(-1, -2\frac{1}{4}\right)$

(b) $$f''(x) = \frac{x^{2/3} - (x+1)\frac{2}{3}x^{-1/3}}{(x^{2/3})^2}$$

$$= \frac{1}{x^{2/3}} - \frac{2(x+1)}{3x^{5/3}}$$

$$= \frac{3x - (2x+2)}{3x^{5/3}}$$

$$= \frac{x-2}{3x^{5/3}}$$

$f''(x) = 0$ at $x = 2$ and is undefined at $x = 0$.

Sign of f'':

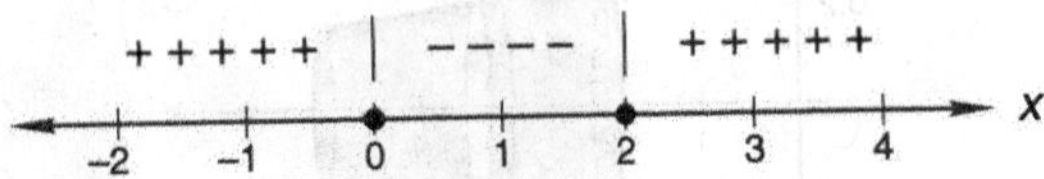

Concave up: (–8, 0), (2, 8)

Concave down: (0, 2)

(c) Inflection points: $\boldsymbol{x = 0, 2}$

(d)

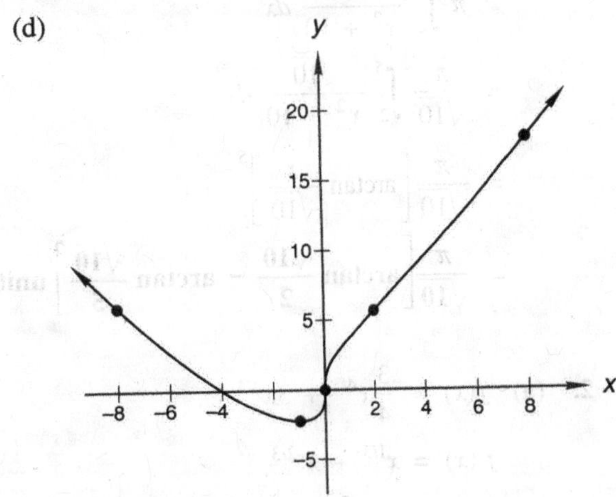

4. $$x^3 + y^3 = 100$$

$$3x^2 + 3y^2\frac{dy}{dx} = 0$$

$$\frac{dy}{dx} = \frac{-3x^2}{3y^2}$$

$$\boldsymbol{\frac{dy}{dx} = -\frac{x^2}{y^2}}$$

$$\frac{d^2y}{dx^2} = \frac{y^2(-2x) - (-x^2)\left(2y\frac{dy}{dx}\right)}{y^4}$$

$$\frac{d^2y}{dx^2} = \frac{-2xy^2 + 2x^2y\frac{dy}{dx}}{y^4}$$

$$\frac{d^2y}{dx^2} = \frac{-2xy^2 + 2x^2y\left(-\frac{x^2}{y^2}\right)}{y^4}$$

$$\frac{d^2y}{dx^2} = \frac{-2xy^2 - 2x^4y^{-1}}{y^4}$$

$$\boldsymbol{\frac{d^2y}{dx^2} = \frac{-2xy^3 - 2x^4}{y^5}}$$

5. $$x^2 = y^3 + y$$

$$2x = (3y^2 + 1)\frac{dy}{dx}$$

$$\boldsymbol{\frac{dy}{dx} = \frac{2x}{3y^2 + 1}}$$

$$\frac{d^2y}{dx^2} = \frac{(3y^2+1)2 - 2x6y\frac{dy}{dx}}{(3y^2+1)^2}$$

$$\frac{d^2y}{dx^2} = \frac{6y^2 + 2 - 12xy\left(\frac{2x}{3y^2+1}\right)}{(3y^2+1)^2}$$

$$\frac{d^2y}{dx^2} = \frac{6y^2+2}{(3y^2+1)^2} - \frac{24x^2y}{(3y^2+1)^3}$$

$$\frac{d^2y}{dx^2} = \frac{18y^4 + 6y^2 + 6y^2 + 2 - 24x^2y}{(3y^2+1)^3}$$

$$\boldsymbol{\frac{d^2y}{dx^2} = \frac{18y^4 + 12y^2 + 2 - 24x^2y}{(3y^2+1)^3}}$$

6. $$S_4 = \sin(1) + \frac{\sin(2)}{2} + \frac{\sin(3)}{3} + \frac{\sin(4)}{4}$$

$$\approx \mathbf{1.1540}$$

7. $u = x^2 \quad du = 2x\,dx \quad v = -\cos x \quad dv = \sin x\,dx$

$$\int x^2 \sin x\,dx = -x^2\cos x + \int 2x\cos x\,dx$$

$u = 2x \quad du = 2\,dx \quad v = \sin x \quad dv = \cos x\,dx$

$$\int x^2\sin x\,dx$$

$$= -x^2\cos x + \left(2x\sin x - \int 2\sin x\,dx\right)$$

$$\boldsymbol{= -x^2\cos x + 2x\sin x + 2\cos x + C}$$

8.
$u = \sin x \qquad v = \frac{1}{2}e^{2x}$

$du = \cos x\,dx \qquad dv = e^{2x}\,dx$

$$\int e^{2x}\sin x\,dx = \frac{1}{2}e^{2x}\sin x - \int \frac{1}{2}e^{2x}\cos x\,dx$$

$u = \cos x \qquad v = \frac{1}{4}e^{2x}$

$du = -\sin x\,dx \qquad dv = \frac{1}{2}e^{2x}\,dx$

$$\int e^{2x}\sin x\,dx$$
$$= \frac{1}{2}e^{2x}\sin x - \left(\frac{1}{4}e^{2x}\cos x + \int \frac{1}{4}e^{2x}\sin x\,dx\right)$$
$$\frac{5}{4}\int e^{2x}\sin x\,dx$$
$$= \frac{1}{2}e^{2x}\sin x - \frac{1}{4}e^{2x}\cos x + C$$
$$\int e^{2x}\sin x\,dx = \frac{2}{5}e^{2x}\sin x - \frac{1}{5}e^{2x}\cos x + C$$
$$= \boldsymbol{\frac{1}{5}e^{2x}(2\sin x - \cos x) + C}$$

9.
$$\int \frac{8x - 4}{(x-1)^2 x}\,dx$$
$$= \int\left(\frac{A}{x-1} + \frac{B}{(x-1)^2} + \frac{C}{x}\right)dx$$

$A(x-1)x + Bx + C(x-1)^2 = 8x - 4$

$x = 0$: $\quad C = -4$

$x = 1$: $\quad B = 4$

$x = 2$: $\quad 2A + 2B + C = 12$

$A = 4$

$$\int\left(\frac{A}{x-1} + \frac{B}{(x-1)^2} + \frac{C}{x}\right)dx$$
$$= \int\left(\frac{4}{x-1} + \frac{4}{(x-1)^2} - \frac{4}{x}\right)dx$$
$$= 4\ln|x-1| - \frac{4}{x-1} - 4\ln|x| + C$$
$$= \boldsymbol{4\left(\ln|x-1| - \ln|x| - \frac{1}{x-1}\right) + C}$$

10.
$x = \tan\theta \qquad dx = \sec^2\theta\,d\theta$

$1 + x^2 = \sec^2\theta$

$$\int \frac{dx}{(1+x^2)^2} = \int \frac{\sec^2\theta}{\sec^4\theta}\,d\theta = \int \cos^2\theta\,d\theta$$
$$= \int\left[\frac{1}{2} + \frac{1}{2}\cos(2\theta)\right]d\theta$$
$$= \frac{1}{2}\theta + \frac{1}{4}\sin(2\theta) + C$$
$$= \frac{1}{2}\theta + \frac{1}{2}\sin\theta\cos\theta + C$$

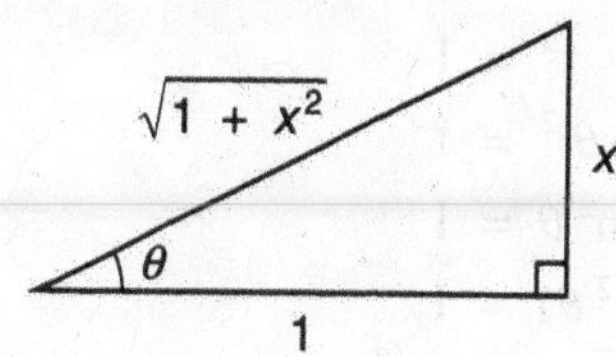

$$\int \frac{dx}{(1+x^2)^2}$$
$$= \frac{1}{2}\arctan x + \frac{1}{2}\left(\frac{x}{\sqrt{1+x^2}}\right)\left(\frac{1}{\sqrt{1+x^2}}\right) + C$$
$$= \boldsymbol{\frac{1}{2}\left(\arctan x + \frac{x}{1+x^2}\right) + C}$$

11.
$$x = e^t \sin t$$
$$\frac{dx}{dt} = e^t\cos t + (\sin t)e^t$$
$$\frac{dx}{dt} = e^t(\cos t + \sin t)$$
$$\left(\frac{dx}{dt}\right)^2 = e^{2t}(\cos t + \sin t)^2$$
$$\left(\frac{dx}{dt}\right)^2 = e^{2t}(\cos^2 t + 2\cos t\sin t + \sin^2 t)$$
$$\left(\frac{dx}{dt}\right)^2 = e^{2t}[1 + \sin(2t)]$$
$$y = e^t\cos t$$
$$\frac{dy}{dt} = e^t(-\sin t) + (\cos t)e^t$$
$$\frac{dy}{dt} = e^t(\cos t - \sin t)$$
$$\left(\frac{dy}{dt}\right)^2 = e^{2t}(\cos t - \sin t)^2$$
$$\left(\frac{dy}{dt}\right)^2 = e^{2t}(\cos^2 t - 2\sin t\cos t + \sin^2 t)$$
$$\left(\frac{dy}{dt}\right)^2 = e^{2t}[1 - \sin(2t)]$$
$$L_0^\pi = \int_0^\pi \sqrt{\left(\frac{dx}{dt}\right)^2 + \left(\frac{dy}{dt}\right)^2}\,dt$$
$$= \int_0^\pi \sqrt{e^{2t}[1 + \sin(2t)] + e^{2t}[1 - \sin(2t)]}\,dt$$
$$= \int_0^\pi \sqrt{e^{2t}(2)}\,dt$$
$$= \int_0^\pi \sqrt{2}e^t\,dt = \sqrt{2}[e^t]_0^\pi = \boldsymbol{\sqrt{2}(e^\pi - 1)\text{ units}}$$

12.
$$x^2 - y^2 = 1$$
$$(r\cos\theta)^2 - (r\sin\theta)^2 = 1$$
$$r^2\cos^2\theta - r^2\sin^2\theta = 1$$
$$r^2(\cos^2\theta - \sin^2\theta) = 1$$
$$r^2\cos(2\theta) = 1$$
$$r^2 = \sec(2\theta)$$
$$r = \sqrt{\sec(2\theta)}$$

13.

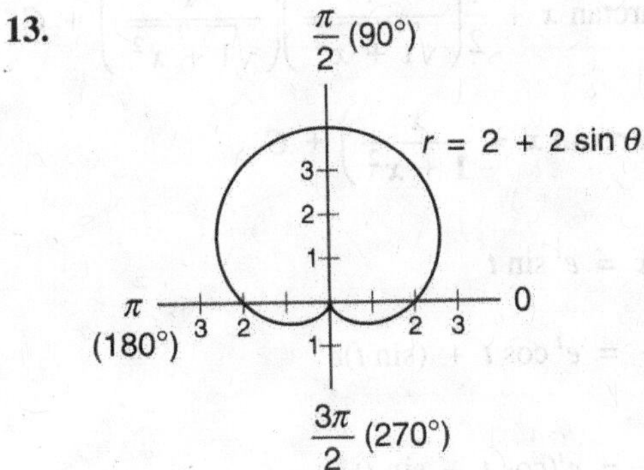

14. $\lim_{n\to\infty}\left(1 + \frac{1}{n}\right)^n = e$

This series **diverges** by the divergence theorem.

15. $S = \sum_{n=4}^{\infty}\frac{3 - \pi^n}{5^n} = \sum_{n=4}^{\infty}\frac{3}{5^n} - \sum_{n=4}^{\infty}\frac{\pi^n}{5^n}$

The first series is geometric with $a = \frac{3}{625}$ and $r = \frac{1}{5}$. The second series is also geometric, with $a = \frac{\pi^4}{625}$ and $r = \frac{\pi}{5}$.

$$S = \frac{\frac{3}{625}}{1 - \frac{1}{5}} - \frac{\frac{\pi^4}{625}}{1 - \frac{\pi}{5}}$$
$$= \frac{3}{500} - \frac{\pi^4}{125(5 - \pi)}$$

The series **converges to** $\mathbf{\frac{3}{500} - \frac{\pi^4}{125(5 - \pi)}}$.

16. $\vec{f}(t) = (\ln t)\hat{i} - 2e^{-t}\hat{j}$

$\vec{f}'(t) = \mathbf{\frac{1}{t}\hat{i} + 2e^{-t}\hat{j}}$

Domain: $\{t \in \mathbb{R} \mid t > 0\}$

17. $\vec{f}(t) = 3\tan(2t)\,\hat{i} + \sqrt{t^2 - 4}\,\hat{j}$

$$\vec{f}'(t) = 6\sec^2(2t)\,\hat{i} + \frac{1}{2}(t^2 - 4)^{-1/2}(2t)\,\hat{j}$$
$$\vec{f}'(t) = \mathbf{6\sec^2(2t)\,\hat{i} + \frac{t}{\sqrt{t^2 - 4}}\hat{j}}$$

Domain: $\{t \in \mathbb{R} \mid t \neq \frac{(2n+1)\pi}{4}, n \in \mathbb{Z}, |t| > 2\}$

18.
$$\frac{dy}{dx} = \frac{2t}{3t^2}$$
$$\frac{dy}{dx} = \frac{2}{3t}$$
$$\left.\frac{dy}{dx}\right|_{t=-3} = \mathbf{-\frac{2}{9}}$$
$$\frac{d^2y}{dx^2} = \frac{\frac{-2}{3t^2}}{3t^2}$$
$$\frac{d^2y}{dx^2} = \frac{-2}{9t^4}$$
$$\left.\frac{d^2y}{dx^2}\right|_{t=-3} = \mathbf{-\frac{2}{729}}$$
$$y - 9 = -\frac{2}{9}(x + 27)$$
$$\mathbf{y = -\frac{2}{9}x + 3}$$

19.

n	$f^{(n)}(x)$	$f^{(n)}(0)$
0	$\ln(1 - x)$	0
1	$-(1 - x)^{-1}$	-1
2	$-(1 - x)^{-2}$	-1
3	$-2(1 - x)^{-3}$	-2
4	$-6(1 - x)^{-4}$	-6
⋮	⋮	⋮

$$\ln(1 - x) = -x - \frac{x^2}{2!} - \frac{2x^3}{3!} - \frac{6x^4}{4!} - \cdots$$
$$\ln(1 - x) = -x - \frac{x^2}{2} - \frac{x^3}{3} - \frac{x^4}{4} - \cdots$$
$$\ln(1 - x) = \mathbf{\sum_{n=1}^{\infty} -\frac{x^n}{n}}$$

20.

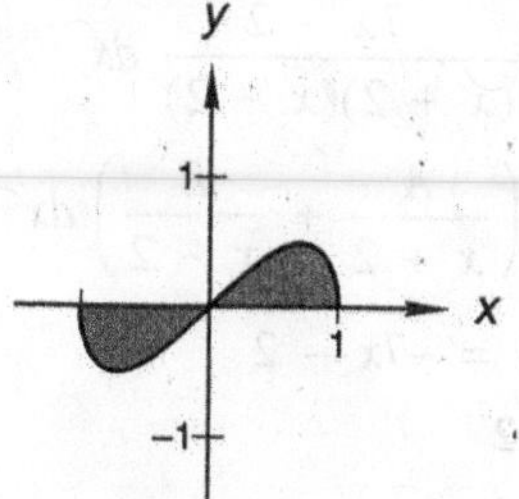

$$A = 2\int_0^1 x(1 - x^2)^{1/2}\,dx$$
$$= -\int_0^1 -2x(1 - x^2)^{1/2}\,dx$$
$$= -\frac{2}{3}\left[(1 - x^2)^{3/2}\right]_0^1$$
$$= \frac{2}{3}\text{ units}^2$$

21. $u = \dfrac{x}{4}$

$$\lim_{x\to\infty}\left(1 + \frac{4}{x}\right)^x = \lim_{4u\to\infty}\left(1 + \frac{1}{u}\right)^{4u}$$
$$= \lim_{u\to\infty}\left[\left(1 + \frac{1}{u}\right)^u\right]^4 = e^4$$

22. $\displaystyle\lim_{x\to\infty}\left(1 + \frac{1}{x}\right)^{4x} = \lim_{x\to\infty}\left[\left(1 + \frac{1}{x}\right)^x\right]^4$

$= e^4$

23. $u = \dfrac{4}{x}$

$$\lim_{x\to 0}\left(1 + \frac{x}{4}\right)^{4/x} = \lim_{u\to\infty}\left(1 + \frac{1}{u}\right)^u = e$$

24. $\displaystyle\lim_{x\to 0^-} f(x) = f(0)$

$$0 = a + b$$
$$b = -a$$
$$\lim_{x\to 0^-} f'(x) = f'(0)$$
$$\pi = a$$

So $b = -\pi$.

25.
$$f(x + h) - f(x) = x^2h + xh^2 + \frac{h^3}{3}$$
$$\frac{f(x + h) - f(x)}{h} = x^2 + xh + \frac{h^2}{3}$$
$$\lim_{h\to 0}\frac{f(x + h) - f(x)}{h} = \lim_{h\to 0}\left(x^2 + xh + \frac{h^2}{3}\right)$$
$$f'(x) = x^2$$
$$f'(3) = 9$$

PROBLEM SET 125

1.
$$a(t) = 20e^{4t}$$
$$v(t) = 5e^{4t} + C$$
$$v(0) = 5e^{4(0)} + C$$
$$10 = 5 + C$$
$$C = 5$$
$$v(t) = 5e^{4t} + 5$$
$$x(t) = \frac{5}{4}e^{4t} + 5t + C$$
$$x(0) = \frac{5}{4}e^{4(0)} + 5(0) + C$$
$$4 = \frac{5}{4} + 0 + C$$
$$C = \frac{11}{4}$$
$$x(t) = \frac{5}{4}e^{4t} + 5t + \frac{11}{4}$$

The particle is at rest when $5e^{4t} + 5 = 0$
$$5e^{4t} = -5$$
$$e^{4t} = -1$$

The value of e^{4t} is never negative, so the particle is never at rest. The distance traveled equals the difference in position at the endpoints.

$$x(5) = \frac{5}{4}e^{20} + 25 + \frac{11}{4}$$
$$x(20) = \frac{5}{4}e^{80} + 100 + \frac{11}{4}$$

Total distance traveled

$$= \left[\frac{5}{4}(e^{80} - e^{20}) + 75\right]\text{ units}$$

2.
$$y = x^{3/2}$$
$$\frac{dy}{dx} = \frac{3}{2}x^{1/2}$$
$$\left(\frac{dy}{dx}\right)^2 = \frac{9}{4}x$$
$$L_0^{4/3} = \int_0^{4/3}\sqrt{1 + \frac{9}{4}x}\,dx$$
$$= \frac{4}{9}\int_0^{4/3}\frac{9}{4}\left(1 + \frac{9}{4}x\right)^{1/2}dx$$
$$= \left(\frac{4}{9}\right)\left(\frac{2}{3}\right)\left[\left(1 + \frac{9}{4}x\right)^{3/2}\right]_0^{4/3}$$
$$= \frac{8}{27}[8 - 1]$$
$$= \frac{56}{27}\text{ units}$$

3. $\vec{f}(t) = 2^t\,\hat{i} - \log_2 t\,\hat{j}$

$$\vec{f}'(t) = 2^t \ln 2\,\hat{i} - \frac{1}{t \ln 2}\hat{j}$$

Domain: $\{t \in \mathbb{R} \mid t > 0\}$

4. $T = \frac{36}{12}[10 + 30 + 24 + 18 + 14 + 10 + 3]$

$= 327 \text{ ft}^2$

$V \approx 20(327) = \mathbf{6540\ ft^3}$

5. $x^2 - y^2 = 4$

$$2x - 2y\frac{dy}{dx} = 0$$

$$\frac{dy}{dx} = \frac{x}{y}$$

$$\frac{d^2y}{dx^2} = \frac{y - x\frac{dy}{dx}}{y^2}$$

$$\frac{d^2y}{dx^2} = \frac{y - x\left(\frac{x}{y}\right)}{y^2}$$

$$\frac{d^2y}{dx^2} = \frac{y - \frac{x^2}{y}}{y^2}$$

$$\frac{d^2y}{dx^2} = \frac{y^2 - x^2}{y^3}$$

$$\frac{d^2y}{dx^2} = -\frac{4}{y^3}$$

6. $x = x^3 + y^2 + y$

$$1 = 3x^2 + (2y + 1)\frac{dy}{dx}$$

$$\frac{dy}{dx} = \frac{1 - 3x^2}{2y + 1}$$

$$\frac{d^2y}{dx^2} = \frac{(2y + 1)(-6x) - (1 - 3x^2)2\frac{dy}{dx}}{(2y + 1)^2}$$

$$\frac{d^2y}{dx^2} = \frac{(2y + 1)(-6x)}{(2y + 1)^2} - \frac{2(1 - 3x^2)\left(\frac{1 - 3x^2}{2y + 1}\right)}{(2y + 1)^2}$$

$$\frac{d^2y}{dx^2} = \frac{-6x}{2y + 1} - \frac{2(1 - 3x^2)^2}{(2y + 1)^3}$$

7. $\int \frac{-7x - 2}{x^2 - 4}\,dx = \int \frac{-7x - 2}{(x + 2)(x - 2)}\,dx$

$$= \int \left(\frac{A}{x + 2} + \frac{B}{x - 2}\right) dx$$

$A(x - 2) + B(x + 2) = -7x - 2$

$x = -2$: $\quad -4A = 12$

$A = -3$

$x = 2$: $\quad 4B = -16$

$B = -4$

$$\int \left(\frac{A}{x + 2} + \frac{B}{x - 2}\right) dx$$

$$= \int \left(\frac{-3}{x + 2} - \frac{4}{x - 2}\right) dx$$

$$= \mathbf{-3 \ln |x + 2| - 4 \ln |x - 2| + C}$$

8. $\int \frac{x^2 + 4x + 1}{x^2(x + 2)}dx = \int \left(\frac{A}{x} + \frac{B}{x^2} + \frac{C}{x + 2}\right) dx$

$A(x + 2)x + B(x + 2) + Cx^2 = x^2 + 4x + 1$

$x = 0$: $\quad 2B = 1$

$B = \frac{1}{2}$

$x = -2$: $\quad 4C = -3$

$C = -\frac{3}{4}$

$x = 1$: $\quad 3A + 3B + C = 6$

$3A = 6 + \frac{3}{4} - \frac{3}{2}$

$A = \frac{7}{4}$

$$\int \left(\frac{A}{x} + \frac{B}{x^2} + \frac{C}{x + 2}\right) dx$$

$$= \int \left(\frac{\frac{7}{4}}{x} + \frac{\frac{1}{2}}{x^2} - \frac{\frac{3}{4}}{x + 2}\right) dx$$

$$= \mathbf{\frac{7}{4} \ln |x| - \frac{1}{2x} - \frac{3}{4} \ln |x + 2| + C}$$

9. $u = \sec x \qquad v = \tan x$

$du = \sec x \tan x \, dx \qquad dv = \sec^2 x \, dx$

$$\int \sec^3 x \, dx$$

$$= \sec x \tan x - \int \tan^2 x \sec x \, dx$$

$$= \sec x \tan x - \int (\sec^2 x - 1) \sec x \, dx$$

$$= \sec x \tan x - \int \sec^3 x \, dx + \int \sec x \, dx$$

$$2\int \sec^3 x \, dx =$$

$$\sec x \tan x + \ln|\sec x + \tan x| + C$$

$$\int \sec^3 x \, dx =$$

$$\mathbf{\frac{1}{2}(\sec x \tan x + \ln|\sec x + \tan x|) + C}$$

10. $$\int_0^\infty \frac{1}{x^2+1} dx = \lim_{b\to\infty} \int_0^b \frac{1}{x^2+1} dx$$

$$= \lim_{b\to\infty} [\arctan x]_0^b$$

$$= \lim_{b\to\infty} [\arctan b - \arctan 0] = \mathbf{\frac{\pi}{2}}$$

11. $$\int_1^\infty \frac{1}{x^3} dx = \lim_{b\to\infty} \int_1^b \frac{1}{x^3} dx$$

$$= \lim_{b\to\infty} \left[\frac{-1}{2x^2}\right]_1^b$$

$$= \lim_{b\to\infty} \left[\frac{-1}{2b^2} + \frac{1}{2}\right] = 0 + \frac{1}{2} = \mathbf{\frac{1}{2}}$$

12. $$\int_1^\infty x^{-1/2} dx = \lim_{b\to\infty} \int_1^b x^{-1/2} dx$$

$$= \lim_{b\to\infty} [2\sqrt{x}]_1^b$$

$$= \lim_{b\to\infty} [2\sqrt{b} - 2]$$

$$= \infty - 2$$

This integral **diverges.**

13. $$I = \int_0^\infty (e^{-x} \cos x) \, dx$$

$$= \lim_{b\to\infty} \int_0^b (e^{-x} \cos x) \, dx$$

$u = \cos x \qquad v = -e^{-x}$

$du = -\sin x \, dx \qquad dv = e^{-x} \, dx$

$$I = \lim_{b\to\infty} \left[-e^{-x} \cos x - \int (e^{-x} \sin x) \, dx\right]_0^b$$

$u = \sin x \qquad v = -e^{-x}$

$du = \cos x \, dx \qquad dv = e^{-x} \, dx$

$$I = \lim_{b\to\infty} \left[-e^{-x} \cos x - \left(-e^{-x} \sin x + \int e^{-x} \cos x \, dx\right)\right]_0^b$$

$$I = \lim_{b\to\infty} \left[-e^{-x} \cos x + e^{-x} \sin x\right]_0^b - \lim_{b\to\infty} \int_0^b (e^{-x} \cos x) \, dx$$

$$2I = \lim_{b\to\infty} \left[e^{-x}(-\cos x + \sin x)\right]_0^b$$

$$I = \frac{1}{2} \lim_{b\to\infty} [e^{-b}(-\cos b + \sin b) - e^0(-\cos 0 + \sin 0)]$$

$$I = \frac{1}{2}[0 - (-1)] = \mathbf{\frac{1}{2}}$$

14. $$\lim_{x\to 0} \frac{2\cos x - 2}{3x}$$

$$= \lim_{x\to 0} \frac{-2\sin x}{3} = \frac{0}{3} = \mathbf{0}$$

15. $$f(x) = \frac{d}{dx} \int_x^3 \frac{\cos t - 1}{t} dt$$

$$f(x) = \frac{1 - \cos x}{x}$$

$$f(\pi) = \frac{1 - \cos \pi}{\pi} = \mathbf{\frac{2}{\pi}}$$

16.

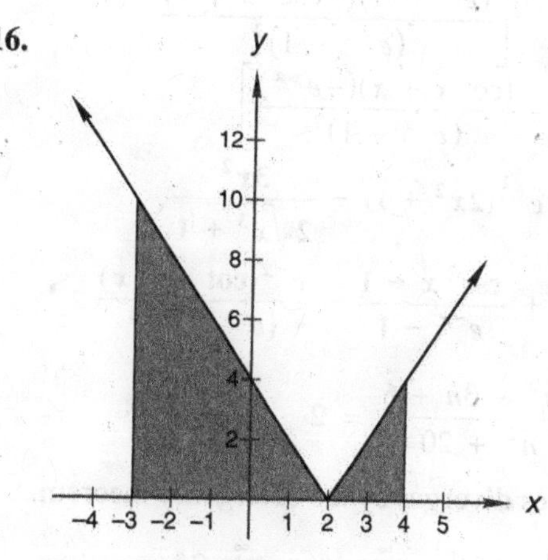

$$\int_{-3}^4 |2x - 4| \, dx$$

= area of large triangle + area of small triangle

$$= \frac{1}{2}(5)(10) + \frac{1}{2}(2)(4) = \mathbf{29}$$

17. 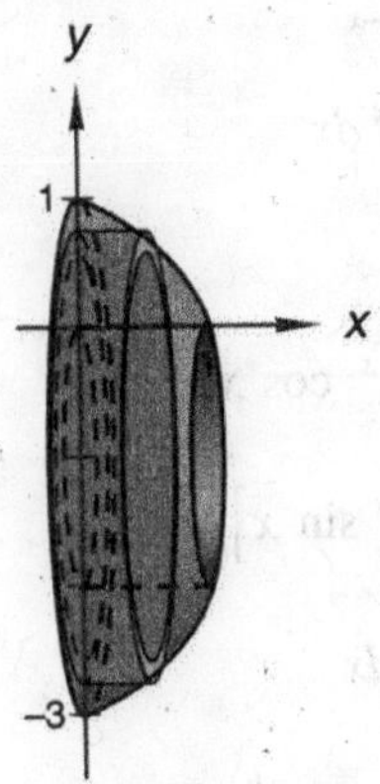

$$V = 2\pi \int rh\,dy$$

$$= 2\pi \int_0^1 (1 + y)(1 - y^2)\,dy$$

18. $$f(x) = (x)^{x^2}$$
$$\ln(f(x)) = x^2 \ln x$$
$$\frac{f'(x)}{f(x)} = x + (\ln x)(2x)$$
$$\mathbf{\frac{f'(x)}{f(x)} = x + x\ln x^2}$$

19. If $\int_a^b f(x)\,dx$ is positive, then $\int_b^a f(x)$ must be negative. Choices A, C, and D cannot be confirmed with the given information.

The correct choice is **B.**

20. $$f(x) = xe^{x^2} - (x^3 + 1)^{1/2} - \frac{\cot x + x}{e^{-x} - 1}$$

$$f'(x) = xe^{x^2}2x + e^{x^2} - \frac{1}{2}(x^3 + 1)^{-1/2}3x^2 - \left[\frac{(e^{-x} - 1)(-\csc^2 x + 1)}{(e^{-x} - 1)^2} - \frac{(\cot x + x)(-e^{-x})}{(e^{-x} - 1)^2}\right]$$

$$\mathbf{f'(x) = e^{x^2}(2x^2 + 1) - \frac{3x^2}{2\sqrt{x^3 + 1}} + \frac{\csc^2 x - 1}{e^{-x} - 1} - \frac{e^{-x}(\cot x + x)}{(e^{-x} - 1)^2}}$$

21. $$\lim_{n\to\infty} \frac{2n^2 - 3n + 6}{n^2 + 20} = 2$$

The series **diverges** by the divergence theorem.

22. $$\sum_{n=1}^{\infty} \frac{4^n - 2^n}{3^n} = \sum_{n=1}^{\infty} \frac{4^n}{3^n} - \sum_{n=1}^{\infty} \frac{2^n}{3^n}$$

The series **diverges** because it is the sum of a divergent series and a convergent series. The first series is a geometric series with $r = \frac{4}{3} > 1$, and the second is a geometric series with $r = \frac{2}{3} < 1$.

23. 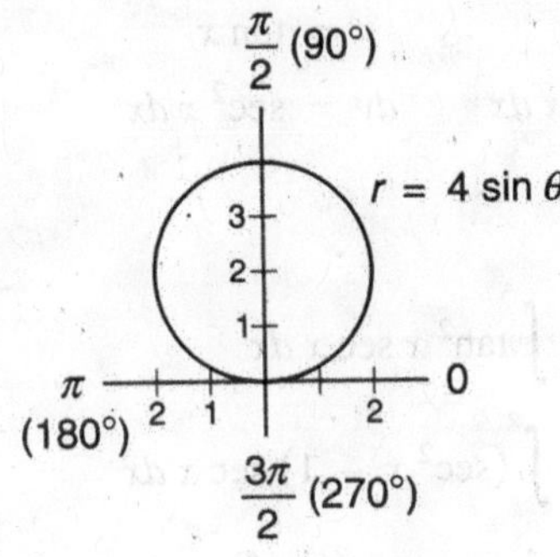

24. 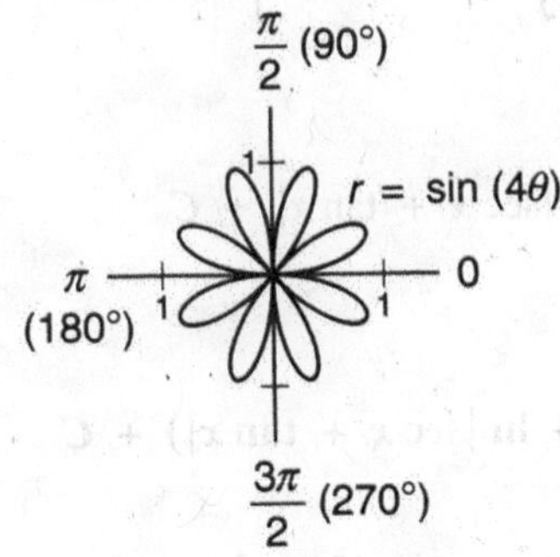

25. Let `Y1=2^X`, `Xmin=2.99`, `Xmax=3.01`, `Ymin=7.99`, and `Ymax=8.01`. Performing a `TRACE` results in the following:

x	y
2.9997872	7.9988203
3	8
3.0002128	8.0011799

If $|x - 3| < 0.0002128$, then

$|y - 8| < 0.01$, thus $\delta =$ **0.0002128.**

Answers may vary.

Problem Set 126

1. $$\frac{1}{9}x^2 + \frac{1}{8}y^2 = 1$$

$$\frac{2}{9}x\frac{dx}{dt} + \frac{1}{4}y\frac{dy}{dt} = 0$$

$$\frac{2}{9}(1)(1) + \frac{1}{4}\left(\frac{8}{3}\right)\frac{dy}{dt} = 0$$

$$\frac{2}{3}\frac{dy}{dt} = -\frac{2}{9}$$

$$\frac{dy}{dt} = -\mathbf{\frac{1}{3}\frac{unit}{s}}$$

2. $y = \sqrt[3]{x}$

$$dy = \frac{1}{3}x^{-2/3}\,dx$$

$$dy = \frac{1}{3}\left(\frac{1}{25}\right)(-1)$$

$$dy = -\frac{1}{75}$$

$$\sqrt[3]{124} \approx \sqrt[3]{125} + dy = 5 - \frac{1}{75} = \mathbf{4\frac{74}{75}}$$

3. $$\int_1^\infty \frac{dx}{x+1} = \lim_{b\to\infty}\int_1^b \frac{dx}{x+1}$$

$$= \lim_{b\to\infty}\left[\ln|x+1|\right]_1^b$$

$$= \lim_{b\to\infty}\left[\ln|b+1| - \ln|2|\right]$$

$$= \infty - \ln 2$$

The integral **diverges.**

4. $$\int_1^\infty \frac{dx}{x^2+1} = \lim_{b\to\infty}\int_1^b \frac{dx}{x^2+1}$$

$$= \lim_{b\to\infty}[\arctan x]_1^b$$

$$= \lim_{b\to\infty}[\arctan b - \arctan 1]$$

$$= \frac{\pi}{2} - \frac{\pi}{4} = \mathbf{\frac{\pi}{4}}$$

5. $\vec{f}(t) = 2^t\hat{i} - t^2\hat{j}$

$\vec{f}'(t) = 2^t \ln 2\,\hat{i} - 2t\hat{j}$

$\vec{f}'(2) = \ln 16\,\hat{i} - 4\hat{j}$

$\vec{f}'(2) \approx 2.7726\hat{i} - 4\hat{j}$

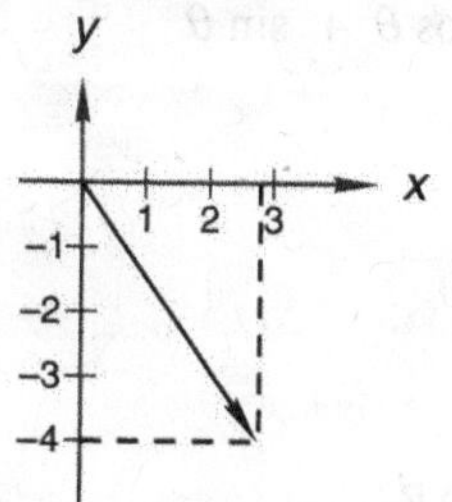

6. $$\int \frac{3x^2 - x}{(x^2+1)(x-1)}\,dx$$

$$= \int\left(\frac{Ax+B}{x^2+1} + \frac{C}{x-1}\right)dx$$

$$(Ax+B)(x-1) + C(x^2+1) = 3x^2 - x$$

$x = 1$: $\quad 2C = 2$

$\qquad C = 1$

$x = 0$: $\quad -B + C = 0$

$\qquad B = 1$

$x = 2$: $\quad 2A + B + 5C = 10$

$\qquad 2A = 4$

$\qquad A = 2$

$$\int\left(\frac{Ax+B}{x^2+1} + \frac{C}{x-1}\right)dx$$

$$= \int\left(\frac{2x+1}{x^2+1} + \frac{1}{x-1}\right)dx$$

$$= \int\left(\frac{2x}{x^2+1} + \frac{1}{x^2+1} + \frac{1}{x-1}\right)dx$$

$$= \mathbf{\ln(x^2+1) + \arctan x + \ln|x-1| + C}$$

7. $$\int \frac{-x^2 + 2x - 3}{(x^2+2)(x+1)}\,dx$$

$$= \int\left(\frac{Ax+B}{x^2+2} + \frac{C}{x+1}\right)dx$$

$$(Ax+B)(x+1) + C(x^2+2) = -x^2 + 2x - 3$$

$x = -1$: $\quad 3C = -6$

$\qquad C = -2$

$x = 0$: $\quad B + 2C = -3$

$\qquad B = 1$

$x = -2$: $\quad 2A - B + 6C = -11$

$\qquad 2A = 2$

$\qquad A = 1$

$$\int\left(\frac{Ax+B}{x^2+2} + \frac{C}{x+1}\right)dx$$

$$= \int\left(\frac{x+1}{x^2+2} - \frac{2}{x+1}\right)dx$$

$$= \int\left(\frac{x}{x^2+2} + \frac{1}{x^2+2} - \frac{2}{x+1}\right)dx$$

$$= \mathbf{\frac{1}{2}\ln(x^2+2) + \frac{1}{\sqrt{2}}\arctan\frac{x}{\sqrt{2}}}$$

$$\mathbf{- 2\ln|x+1| + C}$$

8. $$\int \frac{-x^2 + 2}{(x + 1)^2(x + 2)}\,dx$$

$$= \int \left(\frac{A}{x + 1} + \frac{B}{(x + 1)^2} + \frac{C}{x + 2}\right) dx$$

$$A(x + 1)(x + 2) + B(x + 2) + C(x + 1)^2 = -x^2 + 2$$

$x = -2$: $\quad C = -2$

$x = -1$: $\quad B = 1$

$x = 0$: $\quad 2A + 2B + C = 2$

$\quad A = 1$

$$\int \left(\frac{A}{x + 1} + \frac{B}{(x + 1)^2} + \frac{C}{x + 2}\right) dx$$

$$= \int \left(\frac{1}{x + 1} + \frac{1}{(x + 1)^2} - \frac{2}{x + 2}\right) dx$$

$$= \mathbf{\ln|x + 1| - \frac{1}{x + 1} - 2\ln|x + 2| + C}$$

9.
$$r = 2\sin\theta + \cos\theta$$
$$r^2 = 2r\sin\theta + r\cos\theta$$
$$x^2 + y^2 = 2y + x$$
$$\mathbf{x^2 - x + y^2 - 2y = 0}$$

10.
$$y^3 - x^2 = y$$
$$3y^2\frac{dy}{dx} - 2x = \frac{dy}{dx}$$
$$\frac{dy}{dx} = \frac{2x}{3y^2 - 1}$$
$$\frac{d^2y}{dx^2} = \frac{2(3y^2 - 1) - 2x(6y)\frac{dy}{dx}}{(3y^2 - 1)^2}$$
$$\frac{d^2y}{dx^2} = \frac{2}{3y^2 - 1} - \frac{12xy\left(\frac{2x}{3y^2 - 1}\right)}{(3y^2 - 1)^2}$$
$$\frac{d^2y}{dx^2} = \mathbf{\frac{2}{3y^2 - 1} - \frac{24x^2y}{(3y^2 - 1)^3}}$$

11.

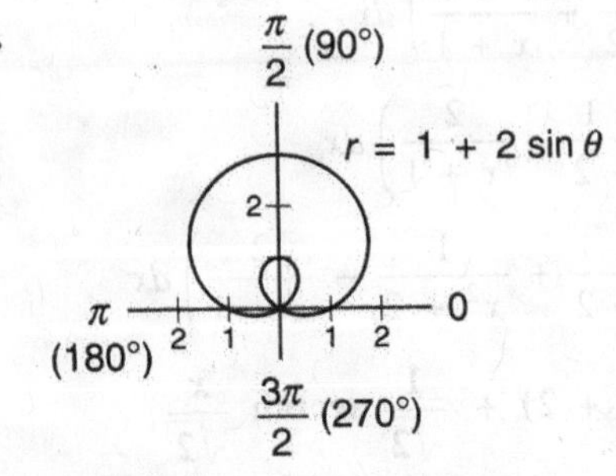

12.

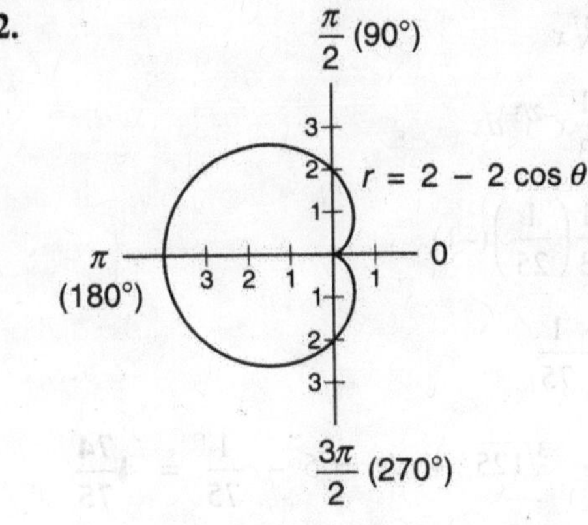

13. $f(x) = x^3 + 1 \quad f'(x) = 3x^2$
$$f'(c) = \frac{f(3) - f(-1)}{3 - (-1)}$$
$$3c^2 = \frac{28 - 0}{4}$$
$$3c^2 = 7$$
$$c^2 = \frac{7}{3}$$
$$c = \mathbf{\frac{\sqrt{21}}{3}}$$

14. $$S_4 = \frac{4}{4} + \frac{9}{8} + \frac{16}{16} + \frac{25}{32} = \mathbf{\frac{125}{32}}$$

15. $$\sum_{n=1}^{\infty}\left(\frac{1}{n(n + 1)} - \frac{3^n}{10}\right) = \sum_{n=1}^{\infty}\frac{1}{n(n + 1)} - \sum_{n=1}^{\infty}\frac{3^n}{10}$$

The first series in the sum is a convergent telescoping series, but the second series in the sum is a divergent geometric series because $r = 3 > 0$. Therefore, the original series **diverges.**

16.
$$x = \cos\theta + \theta\sin\theta$$
$$\frac{dx}{d\theta} = -\sin\theta + \theta\cos\theta + \sin\theta$$
$$\frac{dx}{d\theta} = \theta\cos\theta$$
$$\left(\frac{dx}{d\theta}\right)^2 = \theta^2\cos^2\theta$$
$$y = \sin\theta - \theta\cos\theta$$
$$\frac{dy}{d\theta} = \cos\theta + \theta\sin\theta - \cos\theta$$
$$\frac{dy}{d\theta} = \theta\sin\theta$$
$$\left(\frac{dy}{d\theta}\right)^2 = \theta^2\sin^2\theta$$

$$L_0^{\pi} = \int_0^{\pi} \sqrt{\theta^2 \cos^2 \theta + \theta^2 \sin^2 \theta}\, d\theta$$
$$= \int_0^{\pi} \sqrt{\theta^2}\, d\theta$$
$$= \int_0^{\pi} \theta\, d\theta = \left[\frac{1}{2}\theta^2\right]_0^{\pi} = \frac{\pi^2}{2} \textbf{ units}$$

17. $\int (2x + 1)(x^2 + x + 1)^{-1/2}\, dx$

$= \mathbf{2\sqrt{x^2 + x + 1} + C}$

18. $u = x^2 \quad du = 2x\, dx \quad v = e^x \quad dv = e^x\, dx$

$\int x^2 e^x\, dx = x^2 e^x - \int 2x\, e^x\, dx$

$u = 2x \quad du = 2\, dx \quad v = e^x \quad dv = e^x\, dx$

$x^2 e^x - \int 2x\, e^x\, dx$

$= x^2 e^x - \left(2xe^x - \int 2e^x\, dx\right)$

$= x^2 e^x - 2xe^x + 2e^x + C$

$= \mathbf{e^x(x^2 - 2x + 2) + C}$

19. $\int \frac{4}{\sqrt{4 - x^2}}\, dx = \mathbf{4 \arcsin \frac{x}{2} + C}$

20. $x = 2 \sec \theta \qquad dx = 2 \sec \theta \tan \theta\, d\theta$

$\sqrt{x^2 - 4} = 2 \tan \theta$

$\int \frac{4}{\sqrt{x^2 - 4}}\, dx = \int \frac{8 \sec \theta \tan \theta\, d\theta}{2 \tan \theta}$

$= 4 \int \sec \theta\, d\theta$

$= 4 \ln |\sec \theta + \tan \theta| + C$

$= 4 \ln \left|\frac{x}{2} + \frac{\sqrt{x^2 - 4}}{2}\right| + C$

$= \mathbf{4 \ln \left|x + \sqrt{x^2 - 4}\right| + C}$

21. $\int \frac{4}{x\sqrt{x^2 - 4}}\, dx = \mathbf{2\, \mathrm{arcsec}\, \frac{x}{2} + C}$

22. $x = 2 \sec \theta \qquad dx = 2 \sec \theta \tan \theta\, d\theta$

$\sqrt{x^2 - 4} = 2 \tan \theta$

$\int \sqrt{x^2 - 4}\, dx$

$= \int 2 \tan \theta\, 2 \sec \theta \tan \theta\, d\theta$

$= 4 \int \tan^2 \theta \sec \theta\, d\theta$

$= 4 \int (\sec^2 \theta - 1) \sec \theta\, d\theta$

$= 4 \int (\sec^3 \theta - \sec \theta)\, d\theta$

$= 4\left(\frac{1}{2} \sec \theta \tan \theta + \frac{1}{2} \ln |\sec \theta + \tan \theta| - \ln |\sec \theta + \tan \theta|\right) + C$

$= 2(\sec \theta \tan \theta - \ln |\sec \theta + \tan \theta|) + C$

$= 2\left(\frac{x}{2} \frac{\sqrt{x^2 - 4}}{2} - \ln \left|\frac{x}{2} + \frac{\sqrt{x^2 - 4}}{2}\right|\right) + C$

$= \mathbf{\frac{x\sqrt{x^2 - 4}}{2} - 2 \ln \left|x + \sqrt{x^2 - 4}\right| + C}$

23. $x(t) = t^2 - 3t - 4$

$v(t) = 2t - 3$

The particle is at rest when

$2t - 3 = 0$

$t = \frac{3}{2}$

$x(-2) = 6 \qquad x\left(\frac{3}{2}\right) = -\frac{25}{4} \qquad x(5) = 6$

The total distance traveled from $t = -2$ to $t = 5$ is the sum of distances traveled from $t = -2$ to $\frac{3}{2}$ and $t = \frac{3}{2}$ to 5.

Distance $= 12\frac{1}{4} + 12\frac{1}{4} = \mathbf{24\frac{1}{2}}$ **units**

24. $y = x^2 - 3x - 4$

$\frac{dy}{dx} = 2x - 3$

$\left(\frac{dy}{dx}\right)^2 = 4x^2 - 12x + 9$

$L_{-2}^{5} = \int_{-2}^{5} \sqrt{4x^2 - 12x + 9 + 1}\, dx$

$= \int_{-2}^{5} \sqrt{4x^2 - 12x + 10}\, dx$

$\approx$ **26.0708 units**

25. Since $p(x)$ is an odd function, b and d must equal 0.

$$p(x) = x^3 + cx$$
$$p'(x) = 3x^2 + c$$

Critical numbers: $3x^2 + c = 0$

$$x^2 = -\frac{c}{3}$$
$$x = \pm\sqrt{-\frac{c}{3}}$$

Since the critical numbers are $x = q$ and $x = -q$,

$$\sqrt{-\frac{c}{3}} = q$$
$$-\frac{c}{3} = q^2$$
$$\mathbf{c = -3q^2,\ b = 0,\ d = 0}$$

PROBLEM SET 127

1.

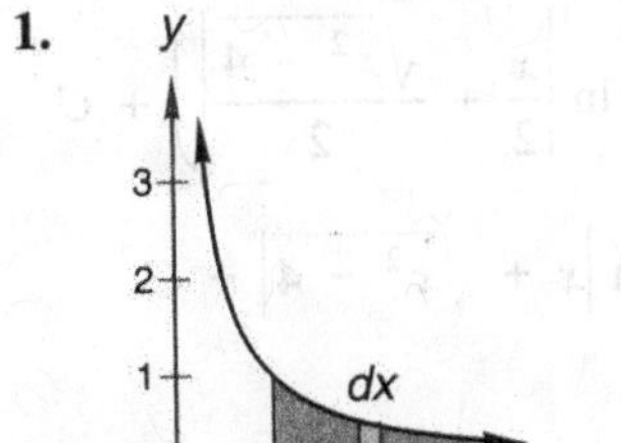

$$A = \int_1^{\infty} \frac{1}{x}\,dx = \lim_{b\to\infty} \int_1^b \frac{1}{x}\,dx$$
$$= \lim_{b\to\infty} [\ln |x|]_1^b$$
$$= \lim_{b\to\infty} (\ln b - \ln 1)$$
$$= \infty - 0$$

The integral diverges, so the area is **infinite.**

2. (a)

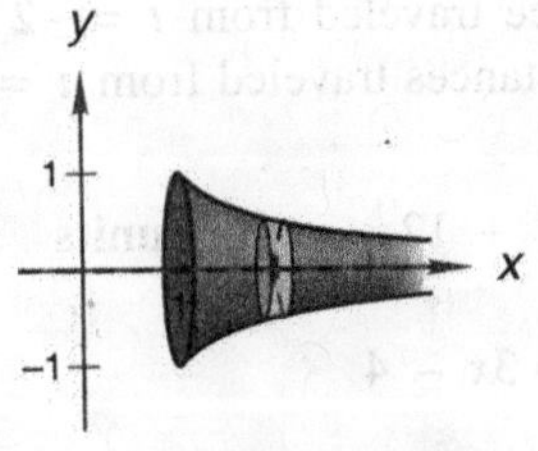

$$V = \pi \int_1^{\infty} \left(\frac{1}{x}\right)^2 dx$$
$$= \pi \lim_{b\to\infty} \int_1^b \frac{1}{x^2}\,dx$$
$$= \pi \lim_{b\to\infty} \left[-\frac{1}{x}\right]_1^b$$
$$= \pi \lim_{b\to\infty} \left[-\frac{1}{b} + 1\right]$$
$$= \pi(0 + 1) = \boldsymbol{\pi}\ \textbf{units}^3$$

(b) **Infinite**

(c) **Finite**

3.

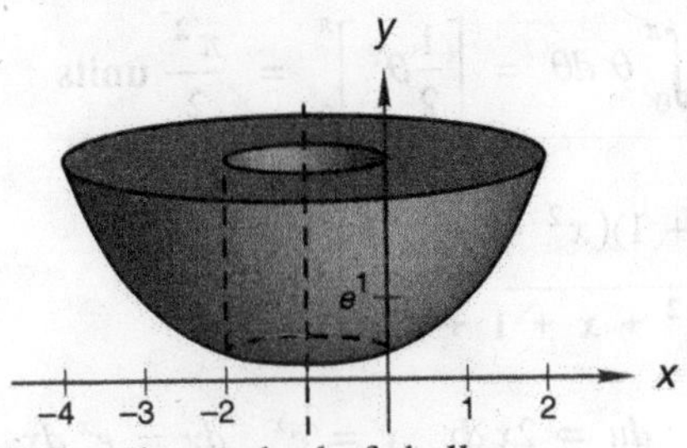

Using the method of shells,

$$V = 2\pi \int_0^2 (1 + x)(e^2 - e^x)\,dx$$

Using the washer method with $x = \ln y$,

$$V = \pi \int_0^{e^2} \left[(1 + \ln y)^2 - 1^2\right] dy$$
$$= \pi \int_0^{e^2} \left[2 \ln y + (\ln y)^2\right] dy$$

4.

$$\frac{dy}{dx} = \frac{x}{y}$$
$$y\,dy = x\,dx$$
$$\frac{1}{2}y^2 = \frac{1}{2}x^2 + C$$
$$y^2 = x^2 + C$$
$$y^2 - x^2 = C$$
$$(9) - (1) = C$$
$$C = 8$$
$$\mathbf{y^2 - x^2 = 8}$$

5.

$$W = \int_1^5 x(x^2 - 1)^{1/2}\,dx$$
$$= \frac{1}{3}\left[(x^2 - 1)^{3/2}\right]_1^5$$
$$= \mathbf{16\sqrt{6}}\ \textbf{joules}$$

6.

$$x^2 = \frac{4}{9}y^3$$
$$x = \frac{2}{3}y^{3/2}$$
$$\frac{dx}{dy} = y^{1/2}$$
$$\left(\frac{dx}{dy}\right)^2 = y$$
$$L_0^3 = \int_0^3 \sqrt{1 + y}\,dy = \frac{2}{3}\left[(1 + y)^{3/2}\right]_0^3$$
$$= \frac{2}{3}(8 - 1) = \frac{\mathbf{14}}{\mathbf{3}}\ \textbf{units}$$

7. $y = \sin(2t) \qquad x = \cos t$

$$\frac{dy}{dx} = \frac{2\cos(2t)}{-\sin t}$$

$$\frac{dy}{dx} = \frac{2 - 4\sin^2 t}{-\sin t}$$

$$\frac{dy}{dx} = -2\csc t + 4\sin t$$

$$\frac{d^2y}{dx^2} = \frac{-2(-\csc t \cot t) + 4\cos t}{-\sin t}$$

$$\frac{d^2y}{dx^2} = -2\csc^2 t \cot t - 4\cot t$$

$$\mathbf{\frac{d^2y}{dx^2} = -2\cot t\,(\csc^2 t + 2)}$$

8. $\displaystyle\int \frac{2x^2 + x + 3}{(x^2+1)(x+1)}\,dx$

$$= \int\left(\frac{Ax + B}{x^2+1} + \frac{C}{x+1}\right)dx$$

$(Ax + B)(x + 1) + C(x^2 + 1) = 2x^2 + x + 3$

$x = -1$: $\quad 2C = 4$
$\qquad C = 2$

$x = 0$: $\quad B + C = 3$
$\qquad B = 1$

$x = 1$: $\quad 2A + 2B + 2C = 6$
$\qquad A = 0$

$$\int\left(\frac{Ax + B}{x^2+1} + \frac{C}{x+1}\right)dx$$

$$= \int\left(\frac{1}{x^2+1} + \frac{2}{x+1}\right)dx$$

$$= \mathbf{\arctan x + 2\ln|x+1| + C}$$

9. $\displaystyle\int \frac{3x^2 + 7x + 6}{x^2(x+2)}\,dx$

$$= \int\left(\frac{A}{x} + \frac{B}{x^2} + \frac{C}{x+2}\right)dx$$

$A(x + 2)x + B(x + 2) + Cx^2 = 3x^2 + 7x + 6$

$x = -2$: $\quad 4C = 4$
$\qquad C = 1$

$x = 0$: $\quad 2B = 6$
$\qquad B = 3$

$x = 1$: $\quad 3A + 3B + C = 16$
$\qquad A = 2$

$$\int\left(\frac{A}{x} + \frac{B}{x^2} + \frac{C}{x+2}\right)dx$$

$$= \int\left(\frac{2}{x} + \frac{3}{x^2} + \frac{1}{x+2}\right)dx$$

$$= \mathbf{2\ln|x| - \frac{3}{x} + \ln|x+2| + C}$$

10. $u = \sin(2x) \qquad v = \frac{1}{3}e^{3x}$

$du = 2\cos(2x)\,dx \quad dv = e^{3x}\,dx$

$$\int e^{3x}\sin(2x)\,dx$$

$$= \frac{1}{3}e^{3x}\sin(2x) - \int \frac{2}{3}e^{3x}\cos(2x)\,dx$$

$u = \cos(2x) \qquad v = \frac{2}{9}e^{3x}$

$du = -2\sin(2x)\,dx \quad dv = \frac{2}{3}e^{3x}\,dx$

$$\int e^{3x}\sin(2x)\,dx$$

$$= \frac{1}{3}e^{3x}\sin(2x) - \frac{2}{9}e^{3x}\cos(2x) - \frac{4}{9}\int e^{3x}\sin(2x)\,dx$$

$$\frac{13}{9}\int e^{3x}\sin(2x)\,dx$$

$$= \frac{1}{3}e^{3x}\sin(2x) - \frac{2}{9}e^{3x}\cos(2x) + C$$

$$\int e^{3x}\sin(2x)\,dx$$

$$= \frac{3}{13}e^{3x}\sin(2x) - \frac{2}{13}e^{3x}\cos(2x) + C$$

$$= \mathbf{\frac{1}{13}e^{3x}[3\sin(2x) - 2\cos(2x)] + C}$$

11.

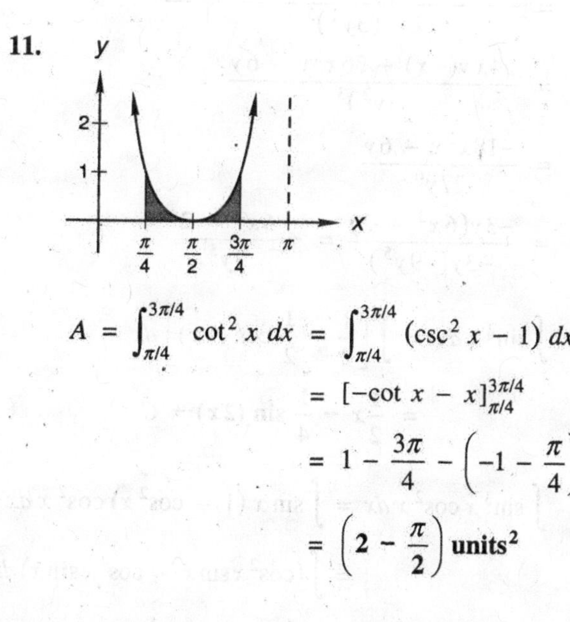

$$A = \int_{\pi/4}^{3\pi/4} \cot^2 x\,dx = \int_{\pi/4}^{3\pi/4}(\csc^2 x - 1)\,dx$$

$$= [-\cot x - x]_{\pi/4}^{3\pi/4}$$

$$= 1 - \frac{3\pi}{4} - \left(-1 - \frac{\pi}{4}\right)$$

$$= \mathbf{\left(2 - \frac{\pi}{2}\right)\text{ units}^2}$$

12.
$$y = \frac{x+1}{x}$$
$$x = \frac{y+1}{y} \quad \text{Implicit inverse}$$
$$x = 1 + \frac{1}{y}$$
$$x - 1 = \frac{1}{y}$$
$$y = \frac{1}{x-1}$$
$$f^{-1}(x) = \mathbf{\frac{1}{x-1}}$$
$$(f^{-1})'(2) = \frac{1}{f'(f^{-1}(2))} = \frac{1}{f'(1)} = \frac{1}{-1} = \mathbf{-1}$$

13.
$$x^3 - y^3 = x$$
$$3x^2 - 3y^2\frac{dy}{dx} = 1$$
$$\frac{dy}{dx} = \frac{3x^2 - 1}{3y^2}$$
$$\frac{d^2y}{dx^2} = \frac{3y^2(6x) - (3x^2 - 1)6y\frac{dy}{dx}}{(3y^2)^2}$$
$$= \frac{18xy^2 - (18x^2y - 6y)\left(\frac{3x^2 - 1}{3y^2}\right)}{(3y^2)^2}$$
$$= \frac{54xy^4 - 54x^4y + 18x^2y + 18x^2y - 6y}{(3y^2)^3}$$
$$= \frac{54xy(y^3 - x^3) + 36x^2y - 6y}{(3y^2)^3}$$
$$= \frac{54xy(-x) + 36x^2y - 6y}{(3y^2)^3}$$
$$= \frac{-18x^2y - 6y}{27y^6}$$
$$= \frac{-3y(6x^2 + 2)}{-3y(-9y^5)} = \mathbf{-\frac{6x^2 + 2}{9y^5}}$$

14.
$$\int \sin^2 x\,dx = \int\left[\frac{1}{2} - \frac{1}{2}\cos(2x)\right]dx$$
$$= \mathbf{\frac{1}{2}x - \frac{1}{4}\sin(2x) + C}$$

15.
$$\int \sin^3 x\cos^2 x\,dx = \int \sin x(1 - \cos^2 x)\cos^2 x\,dx$$
$$= \int(\cos^2 x\sin x - \cos^4 x\sin x)\,dx$$
$$= \mathbf{-\frac{1}{3}\cos^3 x + \frac{1}{5}\cos^5 x + C}$$

16. $\int 10^x\,dx = \mathbf{\frac{10^x}{\ln 10} + C}$

17. $\sum_{n=1}^{\infty}\frac{5}{n} = 5\sum_{n=1}^{\infty}\frac{1}{n}$, which **diverges** because it is a **multiple of the harmonic series.**

18. $\sum_{n=1}^{\infty}\frac{1}{5n} = \frac{1}{5}\sum_{n=1}^{\infty}\frac{1}{n}$, which **diverges** because it is a **multiple of the harmonic series.**

19. $\sum_{n=1}^{\infty}\frac{1}{n^5}$ **converges** because it is a ***p*-series with $p = 5$.**

20. $\sum_{n=1}^{\infty}\frac{1}{5^n}$ is a geometric series with $a = \frac{1}{5}$ and $r = \frac{1}{5}$. $S = \frac{\frac{1}{5}}{1 - \frac{1}{5}} = \frac{1}{4}$ and the series **converges to $\frac{1}{4}$,** because it is a **geometric series with $|r| < 1$.**

21. $\sum_{n=1}^{\infty}\frac{1 + 2^n}{3}$ **diverges** by the **divergence theorem** because $\lim_{n\to\infty}\frac{1 + 2^n}{3} = \infty$.

22.
$$\sum_{n=1}^{\infty}\frac{1}{(4n-3)(4n+1)}$$
$$= \sum_{n=1}^{\infty}\left(\frac{\frac{1}{4}}{4n-3} - \frac{\frac{1}{4}}{4n+1}\right)$$
$$= \left(\frac{1}{4} - \frac{1}{20}\right) + \left(\frac{1}{20} - \frac{1}{36}\right) + \left(\frac{1}{36} - \frac{1}{52}\right) + \cdots$$
$$= \frac{1}{4} + \lim_{n\to\infty}\left(-\frac{\frac{1}{4}}{4n+1}\right) = \frac{1}{4} + 0$$

The series **converges to $\frac{1}{4}$,** because it is a **telescoping series.**

23.

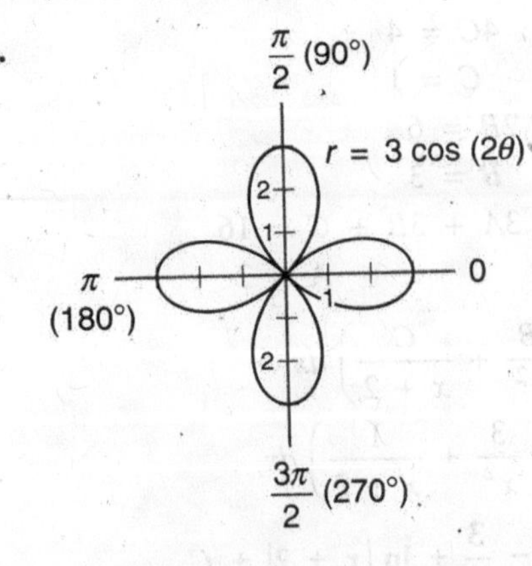

24. $f(x) = \dfrac{x}{1 - x^2} = \dfrac{x}{(1 - x)(1 + x)}$

Vertical asymptotes: $x = 1, x = -1$

Horizontal asymptote: $y = 0$

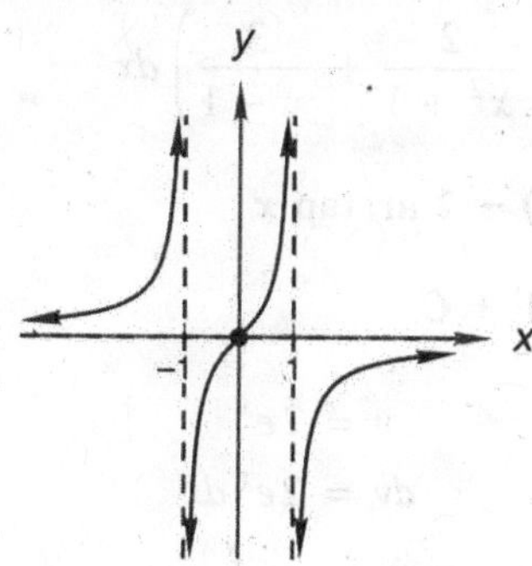

25. $y = x^2 + 2 \qquad \Delta x = \dfrac{4}{n}$

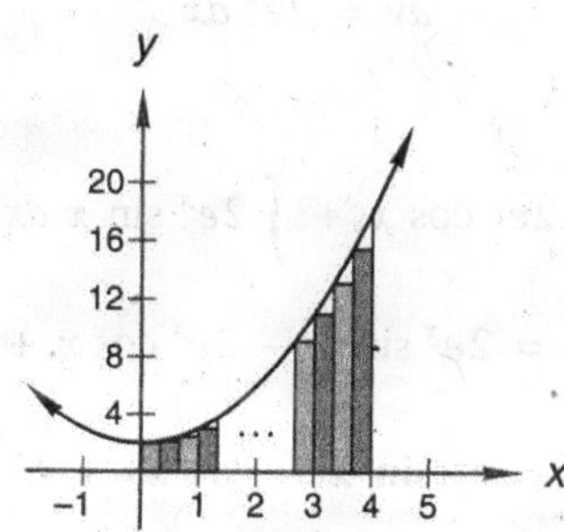

$$\begin{aligned} S_L &= \Delta x\{2 + [(\Delta x)^2 + 2] + [(2\Delta x)^2 + 2] \\ &\quad + [(3\Delta x)^2 + 2] + \cdots \\ &\quad + ([(n - 1)\Delta x]^2 + 2)\} \\ &= \Delta x[2n + (\Delta x)^2 + 2^2(\Delta x)^2 + 3^2(\Delta x)^2 + \cdots \\ &\quad + (n - 1)^2(\Delta x)^2] \\ &= \Delta x\{2n + (\Delta x)^2[1^2 + 2^2 + 3^2 + \cdots \\ &\quad + (n - 1)^2]\} \\ &= \frac{4}{n}\left[2n + \left(\frac{4}{n}\right)^2 \frac{(n - 1)n(2n - 1)}{6}\right] \\ &= 8 + \frac{64(n - 1)(n)(2n - 1)}{6n^3} \\ &= 8 + \frac{32(n - 1)(2n - 1)}{3n^2} \end{aligned}$$

$$A = \lim_{n\to\infty} S_L = 8 + \frac{64}{3} = \mathbf{\frac{88}{3}}\ \textbf{units}^2$$

PROBLEM SET 128

1.

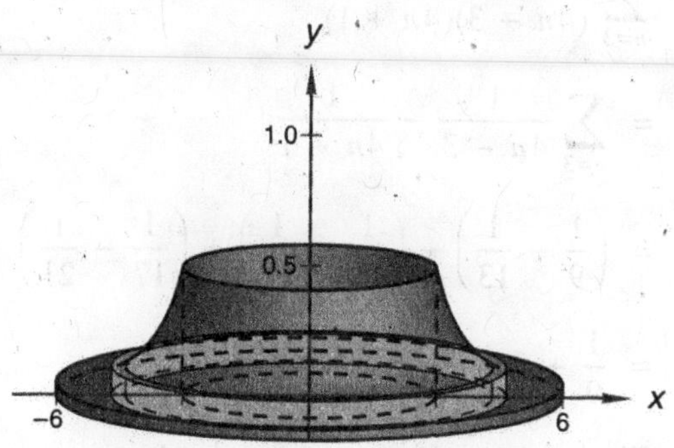

$$\begin{aligned} V &= 2\pi \int_3^6 \frac{x}{x^2 - 3x + 2}\,dx \\ &= 2\pi \int_3^6 \left(\frac{2}{x - 2} - \frac{1}{x - 1}\right) dx \\ &= 2\pi\big[2 \ln |x - 2| - \ln |x - 1|\big]_3^6 \\ &= 2\pi[\ln 16 - \ln 5 - (0 - \ln 2)] \\ &= \mathbf{2\pi\left(\ln \frac{32}{5}\right)}\ \textbf{units}^3 \end{aligned}$$

2.
$$\begin{aligned} A &= \int_3^\infty \frac{1}{x^2 - 3x + 2}\,dx \\ &= \int_3^\infty \left(\frac{1}{x - 2} - \frac{1}{x - 1}\right) dx \\ &= \lim_{b\to\infty} \int_3^b \left(\frac{1}{x - 2} - \frac{1}{x - 1}\right) dx \\ &= \lim_{b\to\infty} [\ln |x - 2| - \ln |x - 1|]_3^b \\ &= \lim_{b\to\infty} \left[\ln \frac{|x - 2|}{|x - 1|}\right]_3^b \\ &= \lim_{b\to\infty} \left[\ln \frac{b - 2}{b - 1} - \ln \frac{1}{2}\right] = \ln 2 \end{aligned}$$

The area is **finite** and equal to **ln 2 units²**.

3. $\sum_{n=1}^{\infty} \frac{2^n}{3}$ **diverges** by the **divergence theorem** because $\lim_{n\to\infty} \frac{2^n}{3} = \infty$.

4. $\sum_{n=1}^{\infty} \frac{3}{2^n}$ is a geometric series with $a = \frac{3}{2}$ and $r = \frac{1}{2}$.

$$S = \frac{\frac{3}{2}}{1 - \frac{1}{2}} = 3$$

The series **converges to 3,** because it is a **geometric series with $|r| < 1$.**

5. $\sum_{n=3}^{\infty} \frac{4}{(4n-3)(4n+1)}$

$= \sum_{n=3}^{\infty} \frac{1}{4n-3} - \frac{1}{4n+1}$

$= \left(\frac{1}{9} - \frac{1}{13}\right) + \left(\frac{1}{13} - \frac{1}{17}\right) + \left(\frac{1}{17} - \frac{1}{21}\right) + \cdots$

$= \frac{1}{9} + \lim_{n\to\infty} \frac{-1}{4n+1} = \frac{1}{9} + 0$

The series **converges** to $\frac{1}{9}$, because it is a **telescoping series.**

6. $\sum_{n=1}^{\infty} \frac{4}{n}$ **diverges** because it is a **multiple of the harmonic series.**

7. $\sum_{n=2}^{\infty} \frac{3}{\sqrt{n}}$ **diverges** because it is a **multiple of the *p*-series with $p = \frac{1}{2} \le 1$.**

8. $\sum_{n=1}^{\infty} \frac{3}{n^2}$ **converges** because the series is a **multiple of the *p*-series with $p = 2 > 1$.**

9. Note that $\frac{3}{\sqrt{n}} < \frac{3}{\sqrt{n}-2}$ for $n > 4$ and $\sum_{n=5}^{\infty} \frac{3}{\sqrt{n}}$ diverges because it is a multiple of the *p*-series with $p = \frac{1}{2} < 1$. So by the **comparison test,** $\sum_{n=5}^{\infty} \frac{3}{\sqrt{n}-2}$ also **diverges.**

10. Note that $\frac{3}{n^2} > \frac{3}{n^2+2}$. $\sum_{n=1}^{\infty} \frac{3}{n^2+2}$ **converges** by using the **comparison test** with $\sum_{n=1}^{\infty} \frac{3}{n^2}$, a known convergent series (problem 8).

11. $\sum_{n=1}^{\infty} \frac{5}{n^{5/3}}$ **converges** because the series is a **multiple of the *p*-series with $p = \frac{5}{3} > 1$.**

12. $\int \frac{4x^2 - 3x + 5}{(x^2+1)(x-1)}\,dx$

$= \int \left(\frac{Ax+B}{x^2+1} + \frac{C}{x-1}\right) dx$

$(Ax + B)(x - 1) + C(x^2 + 1) = 4x^2 - 3x + 5$

$x = 1$: $\quad 2C = 6$

$C = 3$

$x = 0$: $\quad -B + C = 5$

$B = -2$

$x = 2$: $\quad 2A + B + 5C = 15$

$2A = 2$

$A = 1$

$\int \left(\frac{Ax+B}{x^2+1} + \frac{C}{x-1}\right) dx$

$= \int \left(\frac{x-2}{x^2+1} + \frac{3}{x-1}\right) dx$

$= \int \left(\frac{x}{x^2+1} - \frac{2}{x^2+1} + \frac{3}{x-1}\right) dx$

$= \mathbf{\frac{1}{2} \ln (x^2 + 1) - 2 \arctan x}$

$\mathbf{+\ 3 \ln |x - 1| + C}$

13. $u = \sin x \qquad v = 2e^x$

$du = \cos x\,dx \qquad dv = 2e^x\,dx$

$\int 2e^x \sin x\,dx = 2e^x \sin x - \int 2e^x \cos x\,dx$

$u = \cos x \qquad v = 2e^x$

$du = -\sin x\,dx \qquad dv = 2e^x\,dx$

$\int 2e^x \sin x\,dx$

$= 2e^x \sin x - \left(2e^x \cos x + \int 2e^x \sin x\,dx\right)$

$2\int 2e^x \sin x\,dx = 2e^x \sin x - 2e^x \cos x + C$

$\int 2e^x \sin x\,dx = \mathbf{e^x(\sin x - \cos x) + C}$

14. $\lim_{x\to 0} \frac{\tan(2x)}{3x} = \lim_{x\to 0} \frac{2\sec^2(2x)}{3} = \mathbf{\frac{2}{3}}$

15. $\lim_{x\to\infty} \frac{x - x\ln x}{1 + x^2} = \lim_{x\to\infty} \frac{1 - 1 - \ln x}{2x}$

$= \lim_{x\to\infty} -\frac{\frac{1}{x}}{2x} = \mathbf{0}$

16. $u = \frac{x}{7}$

$\lim_{x\to\infty} \left(1 + \frac{7}{x}\right)^x = \lim_{7u\to\infty} \left(1 + \frac{1}{u}\right)^{7u}$

$= \lim_{u\to\infty} \left[\left(1 + \frac{1}{u}\right)^u\right]^7 = \mathbf{e^7}$

17. $u = \frac{x}{\Delta x}$; as Δx goes to 0, u goes to ∞.

$\lim_{\Delta x\to 0} \frac{1}{x} \log_e \left(1 + \frac{\Delta x}{x}\right)^{x/\Delta x}$

$= \lim_{u\to\infty} \frac{1}{x} \log_e \left(1 + \frac{1}{u}\right)^u$

$= \frac{1}{x} \log_e e = \frac{1}{x}(1) = \mathbf{\frac{1}{x}}$

18. $$\frac{dy}{dx} = \frac{-2}{4t} = -\frac{1}{2t} = -\frac{1}{2}t^{-1}$$

$$\frac{d^2y}{dx^2} = \frac{\frac{1}{2}t^{-2}}{4t} = \frac{1}{8}t^{-3}$$

$$\left.\frac{d^2y}{dx^2}\right|_{t=2} = \frac{1}{8}\left(\frac{1}{8}\right) = \frac{1}{64}$$

The curve has **positive concavity** at $t = 2$.

19.

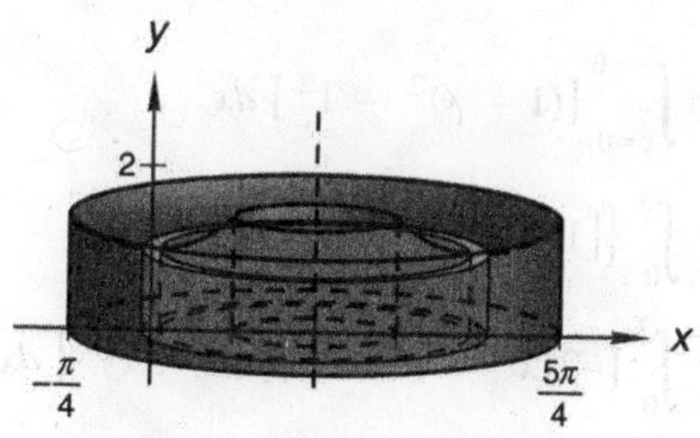

$$V = 2\pi \int_{-\pi/4}^{\pi/4} \left(\frac{\pi}{2} - x\right) \sec x \, dx$$

20. $v(t) = t^2 - 4t + 3$

Average velocity

$$= \frac{1}{5 - 0}\int_0^5 (t^2 - 4t + 3)\, dt$$

$$= \frac{1}{5}\left[\frac{1}{3}t^3 - 2t^2 + 3t\right]_0^5$$

$$= \frac{1}{5}\left[\frac{125}{3} - 50 + 15 - (0)\right]$$

$$= \frac{1}{5}\left[\frac{20}{3}\right] = \frac{4}{3}\,\frac{\textbf{linear units}}{\textbf{time unit}}$$

Average velocity is attained when

$$t^2 - 4t + 3 = \frac{4}{3}$$

$$t^2 - 4t + \frac{5}{3} = 0$$

$$t = 2 \pm \frac{\sqrt{21}}{3}$$

21.

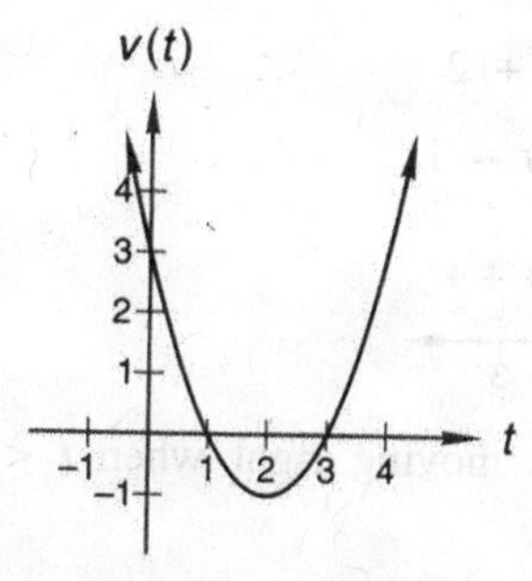

$$\text{Total distance} = \int_0^5 |t^2 - 4t + 3|\, dt$$

$$= \int_0^1 (t^2 - 4t + 3)\, dt + \int_1^3 (-t^2 + 4t - 3)\, dt + \int_3^5 (t^2 - 4t + 3)\, dt$$

$$= \left[\frac{1}{3}t^3 - 2t^2 + 3t\right]_0^1 + \left[-\frac{1}{3}t^3 + 2t^2 - 3t\right]_1^3 + \left[\frac{1}{3}t^3 - 2t^2 + 3t\right]_3^5$$

$$= \left(\frac{1}{3} - 2 + 3 - 0\right) + \left(-9 + 18 - 9 + \frac{1}{3} - 2 + 3\right) + \left(\frac{125}{3} - 50 + 15 - 9 + 18 - 9\right)$$

$$= \frac{28}{3} \text{ linear units}$$

$$\text{Average speed} = \frac{\text{total distance}}{\text{time}} = \frac{\frac{28}{3}}{5} = \frac{\textbf{28}}{\textbf{15}}\,\frac{\textbf{linear units}}{\textbf{time unit}}$$

22. $$y = \arctan(\sin x) - \frac{2^x}{e^{2x} - \sin x}$$

$$\frac{dy}{dx} = \frac{\cos x}{1 + \sin^2 x} - \left[\frac{(e^{2x} - \sin x)2^x \ln 2}{(e^{2x} - \sin x)^2} - \frac{2^x(2e^{2x} - \cos x)}{(e^{2x} - \sin x)^2}\right]$$

$$\frac{dy}{dx} = \frac{\cos x}{1 + \sin^2 x} - \frac{2^x \ln 2}{e^{2x} - \sin x} + \frac{2^x(2e^{2x} - \cos x)}{(e^{2x} - \sin x)^2}$$

23.

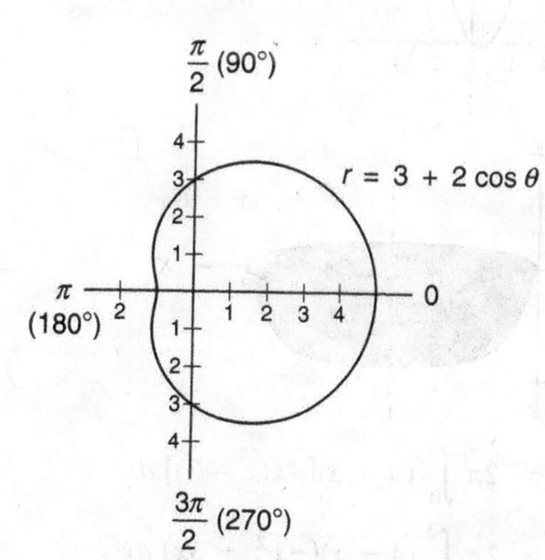

24. Let `Y1=ln(X)/ln(2)` and adjust the window settings to $x[7.5, 8.5]$ and $y[2.5, 3.5]$. Performing a `TRACE` results in the following.

x	y
7.9893617	2.998082
8	3
8.0106383	3.0019172

If $|x - 8| < 0.0106383$, then $|y - 3| < 0.01$, thus $\delta = \mathbf{0.0106383}$. **Answers may vary.**

25. $y = x^3 - 12x$

$y' = 3x^2 - 12$

Relative maximums and minimums occur when

$3x^2 = 12$

$x = \pm 2$

$y(-3) = 9 \quad y(-2) = 16 \quad y(2) = -16 \quad y(5) = 65$

Absolute maximum = 65

Absolute minimum = −16

PROBLEM SET 129

1. $$\frac{dy}{dx} = \frac{8t - 2}{2} = \mathbf{4t - 1}$$

$$\frac{d^2y}{dx^2} = \frac{4}{2} = \mathbf{2}$$

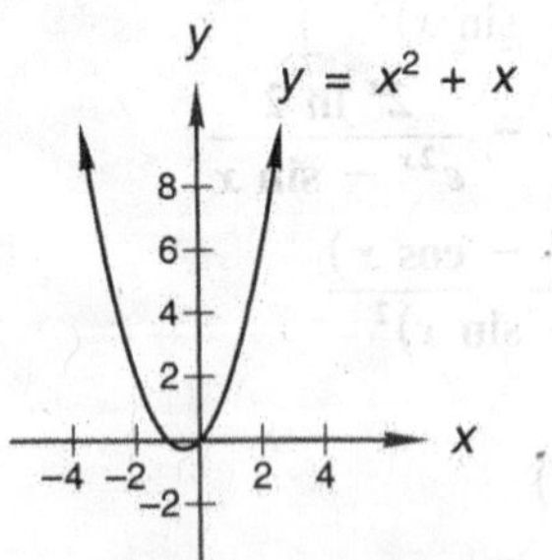

2.

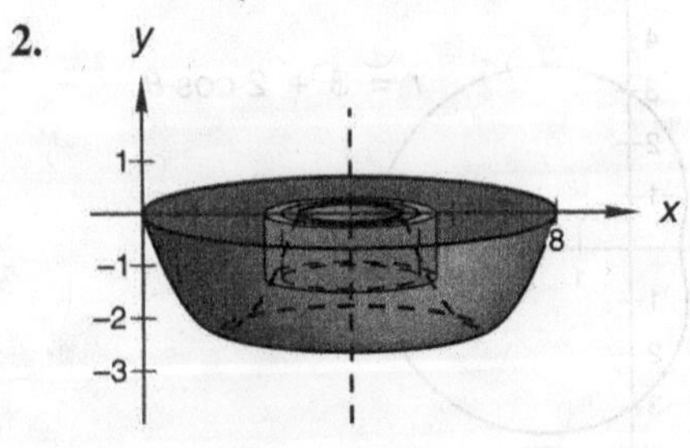

$$V = 2\pi \int_0^3 (4 - x)[-x(x - 3)]\,dx$$

$$= \mathbf{2\pi \int_0^3 (4 - x)(-x^2 + 3x)\,dx}$$

3.

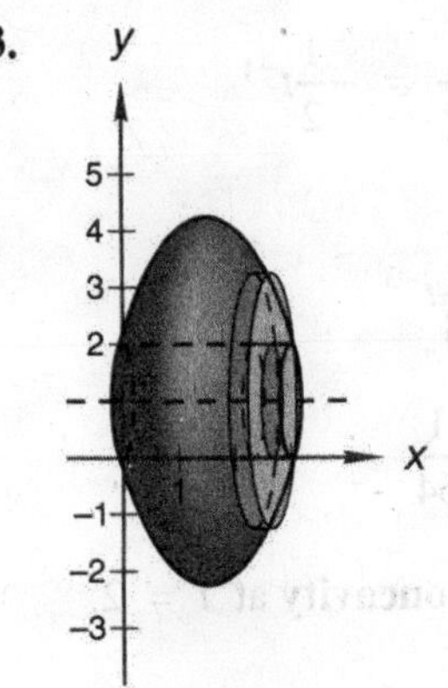

$$V = \pi \int_{x=0}^{x=3} [(1 - y)^2 - 1^2]\,dx$$

$$= \pi \int_0^3 \{[1 - (x^2 - 3x)]^2 - 1\}\,dx$$

$$= \pi \int_0^3 [-2(x^2 - 3x) + (x^2 - 3x)^2]\,dx$$

$$= \pi \int_0^3 [(-2x^2 + 6x) + (x^4 - 6x^3 + 9x^2)]\,dx$$

$$= \mathbf{\pi \int_0^3 (x^4 - 6x^3 + 7x^2 + 6x)\,dx}$$

4.

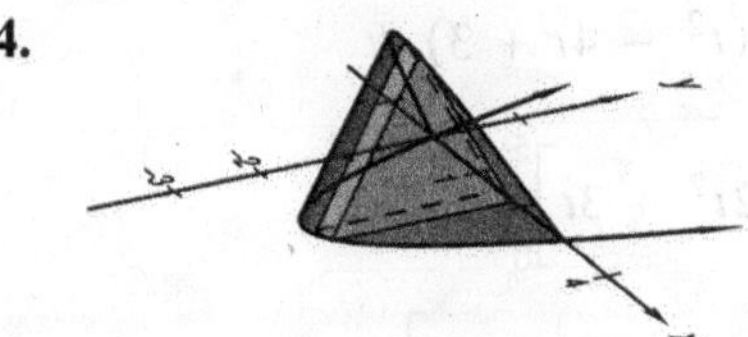

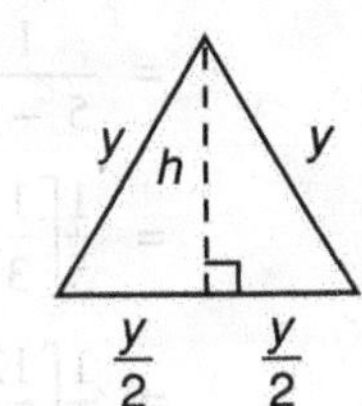

$$V = \int \frac{1}{2} bh\,dx$$

$$= \int_{x=0}^{x=3} \frac{1}{2}(-y)\left(-\frac{\sqrt{3}}{2}y\right)dx$$

$$= \frac{\sqrt{3}}{4} \int_{x=0}^{x=3} y^2\,dx$$

$$= \mathbf{\frac{\sqrt{3}}{4} \int_0^3 (x^2 - 3x)^2\,dx}$$

5. (a) $x(t) = \frac{1}{3}t^3 - \frac{3}{2}t^2 + 2t + 1$

$v(t) = t^2 - 3t + 2$

$= (t - 2)(t - 1)$

+ + + + | − | + + +

−1 0 1 2 3

The particle is moving right when $t < 1$ or when $t > 2$.

(b) $x(0) = 1$; $x(1) = \frac{11}{6}$; $x(2) = \frac{5}{3}$; $x(3) = \frac{5}{2}$

The total distance traveled is the sum of distances traveled between $t = 0$ and 1, $t = 1$ and 2, and $t = 2$ and 3.

$$\text{Total distance} = \frac{5}{6} + \frac{1}{6} + \frac{5}{6} = \mathbf{\frac{11}{6}\ units}$$

6. The graph of $r = 4 \sin \theta$ is a circle of radius 2 traced out once from $\theta = 0$ to $\theta = \pi$.

$$\begin{aligned} A &= \int_0^{\pi} \frac{1}{2}(4 \sin \theta)^2 \, d\theta \\ &= \int_0^{\pi} 8\left[\frac{1}{2} - \frac{1}{2}\cos(2\theta)\right] d\theta \\ &= [4\theta - 2\sin(2\theta)]_0^{\pi} \\ &= \mathbf{4\pi\ units^2} \end{aligned}$$

This area can be confirmed using geometry.

$A = \pi r^2 = \pi 2^2 = 4\pi$ units^2

7.

$\frac{\pi}{2}$ (90°)

$r = 1 + \sin\theta$

π (180°) 2 1 1 2 0

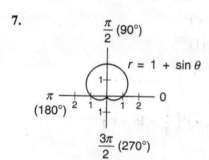

$\frac{3\pi}{2}$ (270°)

$$\begin{aligned} A &= \frac{1}{2}\int_0^{2\pi} (1 + \sin\theta)^2 \, d\theta \\ &= \frac{1}{2}\int_0^{2\pi} (1 + 2\sin\theta + \sin^2\theta) \, d\theta \\ &= \frac{1}{2}\int_0^{2\pi} \left[1 + 2\sin\theta + \frac{1}{2} - \frac{1}{2}\cos(2\theta)\right] d\theta \\ &= \frac{1}{2}\int_0^{2\pi} \left[\frac{3}{2} + 2\sin\theta - \frac{1}{2}\cos(2\theta)\right] d\theta \\ &= \frac{1}{2}\left[\frac{3}{2}\theta - 2\cos\theta - \frac{1}{4}\sin(2\theta)\right]_0^{2\pi} \\ &= \frac{1}{2}[3\pi - 2 - 0 - (0 - 2 - 0)] \\ &= \mathbf{\frac{3\pi}{2}\ units^2} \end{aligned}$$

8.

$\frac{\pi}{2}$ (90°)

π (180°) 2 1 1 2 0

$r = 1 - 2\sin\theta$

$\frac{3\pi}{2}$ (270°)

$$1 - 2\sin\theta = 0$$

$$\sin\theta = \frac{1}{2}$$

$$\theta = \frac{\pi}{6}, \frac{5\pi}{6}$$

$$\begin{aligned} A &= 2\left(\frac{1}{2}\right)\int_{\pi/6}^{\pi/2} (1 - 2\sin\theta)^2 \, d\theta \\ &= \int_{\pi/6}^{\pi/2} (1 - 4\sin\theta + 4\sin^2\theta) \, d\theta \\ &= \int_{\pi/6}^{\pi/2} \left\{1 - 4\sin\theta + 4\left[\frac{1}{2} - \frac{1}{2}\cos(2\theta)\right]\right\} d\theta \\ &= \int_{\pi/6}^{\pi/2} [3 - 4\sin\theta - 2\cos(2\theta)] \, d\theta \\ &= [3\theta + 4\cos\theta - \sin(2\theta)]_{\pi/6}^{\pi/2} \\ &= \left[\frac{3\pi}{2} + 0 - 0 - \left(\frac{\pi}{2} + 2\sqrt{3} - \frac{\sqrt{3}}{2}\right)\right] \\ &= \mathbf{\left(\pi - \frac{3\sqrt{3}}{2}\right)\ units^2} \end{aligned}$$

9. $\lim_{x \to 0^+} \frac{|x|}{x} = \lim_{x \to 0^+} \frac{x}{x} = \mathbf{1}$

10. $\lim_{x \to 0^+} \sin\frac{1}{x}$ **does not exist.**

11. $\sum_{n=2}^{\infty} \frac{3 - 3^n}{4^n} = \sum_{n=2}^{\infty} \frac{3}{4^n} - \sum_{n=2}^{\infty} \frac{3^n}{4^n}$

Both series are geometric. The first has $a = \frac{3}{16}$ and $r = \frac{1}{4}$. The second has $a = \frac{9}{16}$ and $r = \frac{3}{4}$.

$$S = \frac{\frac{3}{16}}{1 - \frac{1}{4}} - \frac{\frac{9}{16}}{1 - \frac{3}{4}} = \frac{1}{4} - \frac{9}{4} = -2$$

The series **converges to −2,** because it is the **sum of two convergent geometric series.**

12. $\sum_{n=1}^{\infty} \frac{3}{n^{2/3}}$ **diverges** because it is **multiple of a p-series with $p = \frac{2}{3} \leq 1$.**

13. $\sum_{n=2}^{\infty} \frac{n^3}{\ln n}$ **diverges** by the **divergence theorem** since

$$\lim_{n\to\infty} \frac{n^3}{\ln n} = \lim_{n\to\infty} \frac{3n^2}{\frac{1}{n}} = \lim_{n\to\infty} 3n^3 = \infty$$

14. $$\frac{d}{dx}(x \ln x)^{-1} = -(x \ln x)^{-2}(1 + \ln x)$$

$$= -\frac{1 + \ln x}{(x \ln x)^2}$$

is negative for all $x > 2$ so the function decreases.

$$\int_2^{\infty} \frac{1}{x \ln x}\, dx = \lim_{b\to\infty} \int_2^b \frac{1}{x}(\ln x)^{-1}\, dx$$

$$= \lim_{b\to\infty} \left[\ln (\ln x)\right]_2^b$$

$$= \infty$$

The series **diverges** by the **integral test.**

15. Term for term, $\frac{1}{n-1} > \frac{1}{n}$.

Since $\sum_{n=2}^{\infty} \frac{1}{n}$ diverges, $\sum_{n=2}^{\infty} \frac{1}{n-1}$ also **diverges** by the **comparison test.**

16. $\sum_{n=1}^{\infty} \frac{4}{3n}$ **diverges** because it is a **multiple of the harmonic series.**

17. $$\int \frac{8}{\sqrt{9 - 4x^2}}\, dx = \mathbf{4 \arcsin \frac{2x}{3} + C}$$

18. $$\int \frac{8}{9 + 4x^2}\, dx = \frac{8}{6} \int \frac{2(3)}{9 + 4x^2}\, dx$$

$$= \mathbf{\frac{4}{3} \arctan \frac{2x}{3} + C}$$

19. $$\int \frac{9 + 4x^2}{8}\, dx = \int \left(\frac{9}{8} + \frac{1}{2}x^2\right) dx$$

$$= \mathbf{\frac{9}{8}x + \frac{1}{6}x^3 + C}$$

20. $$\int_1^{\infty} \frac{4}{x^{4/5}}\, dx = \lim_{b\to\infty} \int_1^b 4x^{-4/5}\, dx$$

$$= \lim_{b\to\infty} \left[20x^{1/5}\right]_1^b$$

$$= \lim_{b\to\infty} \left[20b^{1/5} - 20\right]$$

$$= \infty - 20$$

The integral **diverges.**

21. $$y = \arcsin (\tan x) - xe^{-x}$$

$$\frac{dy}{dx} = \frac{\sec^2 x}{\sqrt{1 - \tan^2 x}} - \left[x(-e^{-x}) + e^{-x}\right]$$

$$\frac{dy}{dx} = \mathbf{\frac{\sec^2 x}{\sqrt{1 - \tan^2 x}} + e^{-x}(x - 1)}$$

22. $$y = \ln |x|$$

$$y' = \frac{1}{x}$$

When $x = -\frac{1}{2}$, $y = -\ln 2$ and the slope $= -2$.

So the slope of the normal line will be $\frac{1}{2}$.

$$y + \ln 2 = \frac{1}{2}\left(x + \frac{1}{2}\right)$$

$$\mathbf{y = \frac{1}{2}x + \frac{1}{4} - \ln 2}$$

23. $$y = (\sqrt{x})^x$$

$$\ln y = x \ln (x^{1/2})$$

$$\frac{1}{y}\frac{dy}{dx} = x\left(\frac{1}{2x}\right) + \ln \sqrt{x}$$

$$\frac{dy}{dx} = \mathbf{(\sqrt{x})^x\left(\frac{1}{2} + \ln \sqrt{x}\right)}$$

24. 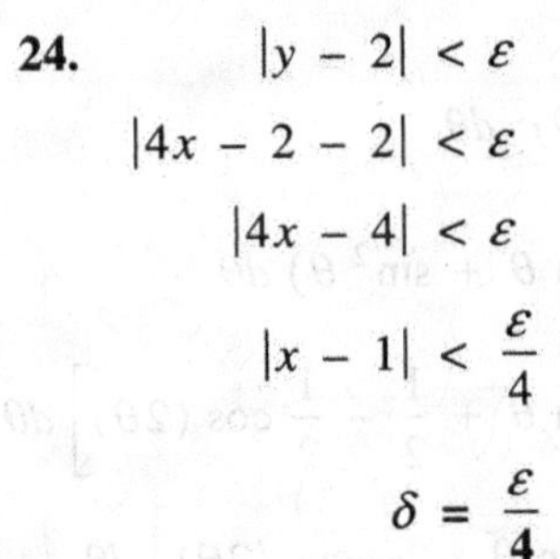

$$|y - 2| < \varepsilon$$

$$|4x - 2 - 2| < \varepsilon$$

$$|4x - 4| < \varepsilon$$

$$|x - 1| < \frac{\varepsilon}{4}$$

$$\mathbf{\delta = \frac{\varepsilon}{4}}$$

25. (a)

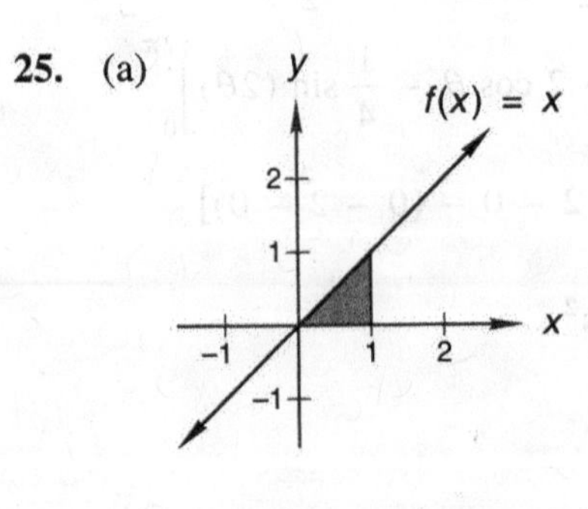

$$A = \frac{1}{2}bh = \frac{1}{2}(1)(1) = \mathbf{\frac{1}{2}\ \text{unit}^2}$$

(b) $\lim_{n\to\infty} \sum_{i=1}^{\infty} \frac{1}{n} f(x_i)$

$$= \lim_{n\to\infty} \left[\frac{1}{n}\left(\frac{1}{n} + \frac{2}{n} + \frac{3}{n} + \cdots \frac{n}{n}\right)\right]$$

$$= \lim_{n\to\infty} \left\{\frac{1}{n}\left[\frac{1}{n}(1 + 2 + 3 + \cdots + n)\right]\right\}$$

$$= \lim_{n\to\infty} \left\{\frac{1}{n}\left[\frac{1}{n}\left(\frac{n(n+1)}{2}\right)\right]\right\}$$

$$= \lim_{n\to\infty} \left[\frac{n+1}{2n}\right] = \mathbf{\frac{1}{2}}$$

(c) $\lim_{n\to\infty} \sum_{i=1}^{n} \frac{1}{n} f(x_i) = \int_0^1 x\,dx = \left[\frac{1}{2}x^2\right]_0^1$

$$= \mathbf{\frac{1}{2}}$$

PROBLEM SET 130

1.

$$4x^2 - 3y^2 = 36$$

$$8x\frac{dx}{dt} - 6y\frac{dy}{dt} = 0$$

$$8(6)\frac{dx}{dt} - 6y(12) = 0$$

$$\frac{dx}{dt} = \frac{72y}{48}$$

$$\frac{dx}{dt} = \frac{3y}{2}$$

If $y = 6$ m, $\frac{dx}{dt} = 9\ \frac{\text{m}}{\text{s}}$;

if $y = -6$ m, $\frac{dx}{dt} = -9\ \frac{\text{m}}{\text{s}}$.

2. Let Y1=X² and Y2=sin(X).

Window: $x[-2, 2]$, $y[-1.5, 1.5]$

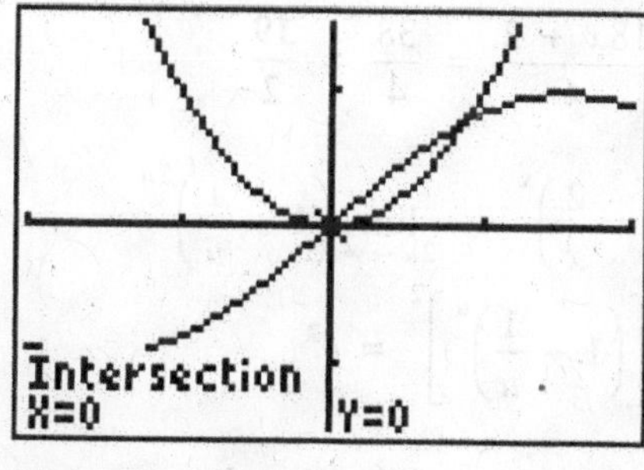

(0, 0)

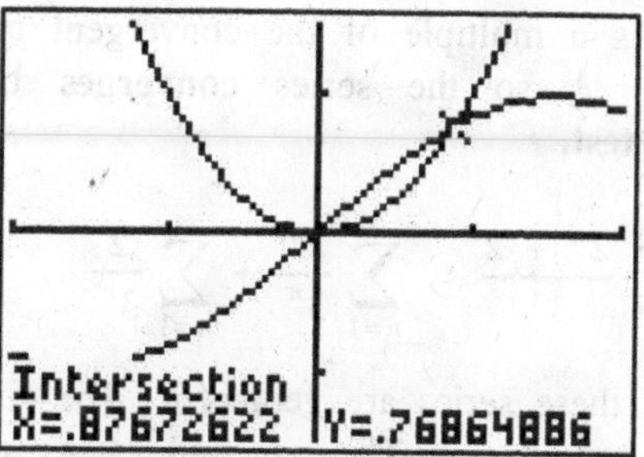

(0.87672622, 0.76864886)

$$A \approx \int_0^{0.8767} (\sin x - x^2)\,dx$$

$$\approx \left[-\cos x - \frac{1}{3}x^3\right]_0^{0.8767}$$

$$\approx -0.6397 - 0.2246 - (-1 - 0)$$

$$\approx \mathbf{0.1357\ units^2}$$

3. $L = \lim_{n\to\infty} \dfrac{\frac{n+2}{(n+1)!}}{\frac{n+1}{n!}} = \lim_{n\to\infty} \dfrac{n+2}{(n+1)(n+1)} = 0$

Since $L < 1$, the series **converges** by the **ratio test.**

4. $L = \lim_{n\to\infty} \dfrac{\frac{3^{n+1}}{(n+1)!}}{\frac{3^n}{n!}} = \lim_{n\to\infty} \dfrac{3}{(n+1)} = 0$

Since $L < 1$, the series **converges** by the **ratio test.**

5. $\frac{d}{dx}\frac{1}{x(\ln x)^3} = \frac{d}{dx}x^{-1}(\ln x)^{-3}$

$$= x^{-1}\left(-3(\ln x)^{-4}\frac{1}{x}\right) + (\ln x)^{-3}\left(-\frac{1}{x^2}\right)$$

$$= \frac{-3}{x^2(\ln x)^4} - \frac{1}{x^2(\ln x)^3}$$

which is negative for all $x > 2$, so the function is decreasing.

$$\int_2^\infty \frac{1}{x}(\ln x)^{-3}\,dx = \lim_{b\to\infty}\left[-\frac{1}{2}(\ln x)^{-2}\right]_2^b$$

$$= \lim_{b\to\infty}\left[\frac{-1}{2b} + \frac{1}{2(\ln 2)^2}\right]$$

$$= \frac{1}{2(\ln 2)^2}$$

Since the integral converges, the series also **converges** by the **integral test.**

6. Every term of $\sum_{n=2}^{\infty} \frac{2}{\sqrt{n}-1}$ is larger than the corresponding term of $\sum_{n=2}^{\infty} \frac{2}{n^{1/2}}$, a divergent p-series. So the original series **diverges** by the **comparison test.**

7. $\sum_{n=1}^{\infty} \frac{4}{n^{3/2}}$ is a multiple of the convergent p-series with $p = \frac{3}{2}$, so the series **converges** by the ***p*-series test.**

8. $$S = \sum_{n=1}^{\infty} \frac{2^n + 2}{3^n} = \sum_{n=1}^{\infty} \frac{2^n}{3^n} + \sum_{n=1}^{\infty} \frac{2}{3^n}$$

Both of these series are geometric. The first has $a = \frac{2}{3}$ and $r = \frac{2}{3}$. The second has $a = \frac{2}{3}$ and $r = \frac{1}{3}$.

$$S = \frac{\frac{2}{3}}{1 - \frac{2}{3}} + \frac{\frac{2}{3}}{1 - \frac{1}{3}} = 2 + 1 = 3$$

The series **converges to 3,** because it is the **sum of two convergent geometric series.**

9. $$|y - 8| < \varepsilon$$
$$|3x + 2 - 8| < \varepsilon$$
$$|3x - 6| < \varepsilon$$
$$|x - 2| < \frac{\varepsilon}{3}$$
$$\delta = \boldsymbol{\frac{\varepsilon}{3}}$$

10. $$f(x) = \frac{d}{dx}\int_x^3 e^{\sin t}\,dt$$
$$f(x) = -e^{\sin x}$$
$$f(1) = -e^{\sin(1)} \approx \mathbf{-2.3198}$$

11.

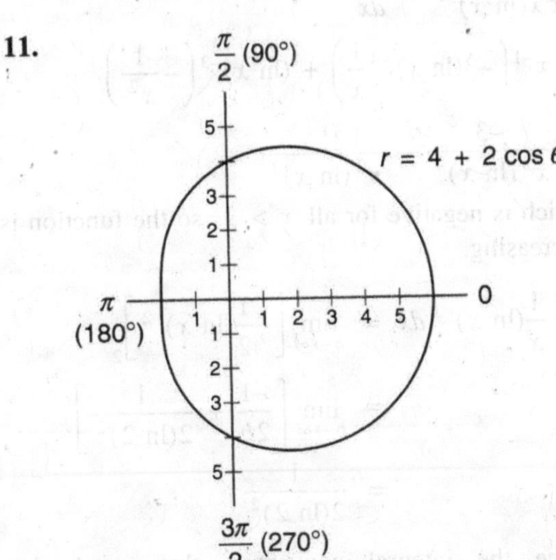

12. $$A = \int_0^{\pi} \frac{1}{2}(4\cos\theta)^2\,d\theta$$
$$= \int_0^{\pi} \frac{1}{2}(16\cos^2\theta)\,d\theta$$
$$= \int_0^{\pi} 8\left[\frac{1}{2} + \frac{1}{2}\cos(2\theta)\right] d\theta$$
$$= \int_0^{\pi} [4 + 4\cos(2\theta)]\,d\theta$$
$$= [4\theta + 2\sin(2\theta)]_0^{\pi} = \mathbf{4\pi\ units^2}$$

13.

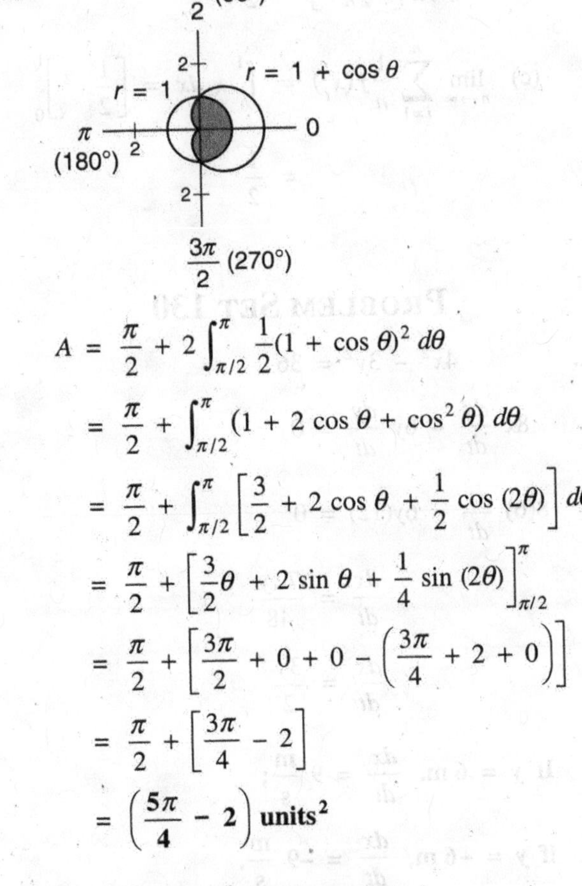

$$A = \frac{\pi}{2} + 2\int_{\pi/2}^{\pi} \frac{1}{2}(1 + \cos\theta)^2\,d\theta$$
$$= \frac{\pi}{2} + \int_{\pi/2}^{\pi} (1 + 2\cos\theta + \cos^2\theta)\,d\theta$$
$$= \frac{\pi}{2} + \int_{\pi/2}^{\pi} \left[\frac{3}{2} + 2\cos\theta + \frac{1}{2}\cos(2\theta)\right] d\theta$$
$$= \frac{\pi}{2} + \left[\frac{3}{2}\theta + 2\sin\theta + \frac{1}{4}\sin(2\theta)\right]_{\pi/2}^{\pi}$$
$$= \frac{\pi}{2} + \left[\frac{3\pi}{2} + 0 + 0 - \left(\frac{3\pi}{4} + 2 + 0\right)\right]$$
$$= \frac{\pi}{2} + \left[\frac{3\pi}{4} - 2\right]$$
$$= \left(\frac{5\pi}{4} - 2\right)\ \mathbf{units^2}$$

14. $$\lim_{x\to 2} \frac{3x^3 + x^2 - 40x + 52}{2x^2 - 8x + 8}$$
$$= \lim_{x\to 2} \frac{9x^2 + 2x - 40}{4x - 8}$$
$$= \lim_{x\to 2} \frac{18x + 2}{4} = \frac{38}{4} = \mathbf{\frac{19}{2}}$$

15. $$\lim_{x\to\infty}\left(1 + \frac{2}{x}\right)^x = \lim_{2u\to\infty}\left(1 + \frac{1}{u}\right)^{2u}$$
$$= \lim_{u\to\infty}\left[\left(1 + \frac{1}{u}\right)^u\right]^2 = \mathbf{e^2}$$

16. $$\lim_{h\to 0} \frac{\sin(x + h) - \sin x}{h} = \frac{d}{dx}\sin x = \mathbf{\cos x}$$

17. $\lim_{h\to 0} \frac{\sin(3+h) - \sin 3}{h} = \left.\frac{d}{dx}\right|_3 \sin x = \mathbf{\cos 3}$

18.
$$9 = x^2 + y^2$$
$$0 = 2x + 2y\frac{dy}{dx}$$
$$\frac{dy}{dx} = -\frac{x}{y}$$
$$\frac{d^2y}{dx^2} = \frac{y(-1) - (-x)\frac{dy}{dx}}{y^2}$$
$$\frac{d^2y}{dx^2} = \frac{-y + x\left(-\frac{x}{y}\right)}{y^2}$$
$$\frac{d^2y}{dx^2} = \frac{-y^2 - x^2}{y^3}$$
$$\frac{d^2y}{dx^2} = \mathbf{-\frac{9}{y^3}}$$

19. $u = 2x^2 \qquad v = \frac{1}{2}\sin(2x)$

$du = 4x\,dx \qquad dv = \cos(2x)\,dx$

$$\int 2x^2 \cos(2x)\,dx$$
$$= x^2\sin(2x) - \int 2x\sin(2x)\,dx$$

$u = 2x \qquad v = -\frac{1}{2}\cos(2x)$

$du = 2\,dx \qquad dv = \sin(2x)\,dx$

$$\int 2x^2\cos(2x)\,dx$$
$$= x^2\sin(2x) - \left[-x\cos(2x) + \int \cos(2x)\,dx\right]$$
$$= \mathbf{x^2\sin(2x) + x\cos(2x) - \frac{1}{2}\sin(2x) + C}$$

20. $\int_1^2 \frac{-x^2 - x + 2}{(x+1)^2x^2}\,dx$

$$= \int_1^2 \left(\frac{A}{x+1} + \frac{B}{(x+1)^2} + \frac{C}{x} + \frac{D}{x^2}\right)dx$$

$A(x+1)x^2 + Bx^2 + C(x+1)^2x + D(x+1)^2$
$= -x^2 - x + 2$

$x = 0$: $\quad D = 2$

$x = -1$: $\quad B = 2$

$x = 1$: $\quad 2A + B + 4C + 4D = 0$
$$A + 2C = -5$$
$$A = -5 - 2C$$

$x = -2$: $\quad -4A + 4B - 2C + D = 0$
$$2A + C = 5$$
$$2(-5 - 2C) + C = 5$$
$$-3C = 15$$
$$C = -5$$

$A = -5 - 2(-5) = 5$

$$\int_1^2 \left(\frac{A}{x+1} + \frac{B}{(x+1)^2} + \frac{C}{x} + \frac{D}{x^2}\right)dx$$
$$= \int_1^2 \left(\frac{5}{x+1} + \frac{2}{(x+1)^2} - \frac{5}{x} + \frac{2}{x^2}\right)dx$$
$$= \left[5\ln|x+1| - \frac{2}{x+1} - 5\ln|x| - \frac{2}{x}\right]_1^2$$
$$= 5\ln 3 - \frac{2}{3} - 5\ln 2 - 1$$
$$- (5\ln 2 - 1 - 0 - 2)$$
$$= 5\ln 3 - 10\ln 2 + \frac{4}{3}$$
$$= 5(\ln 3 - \ln 4) + \frac{4}{3} = \mathbf{5\ln\left(\frac{3}{4}\right) + \frac{4}{3}}$$

21. $\int_1^\infty \frac{1}{x^2+1}\,dx = \lim_{b\to\infty}\int_1^b \frac{1}{x^2+1}\,dx$
$$= \lim_{b\to\infty}[\arctan x]_1^b$$
$$= \lim_{b\to\infty}[\arctan b - \arctan(1)]$$
$$= \frac{\pi}{2} - \frac{\pi}{4} = \mathbf{\frac{\pi}{4}}$$

22. $u = \sqrt{x} \quad du = \frac{1}{2}x^{-1/2}\,dx \quad \frac{1}{\sqrt{x}}dx = 2\,du$

$$\int_1^2 \frac{e^{\sqrt{x}}}{\sqrt{x}}\,dx = \int_1^{\sqrt{2}} 2e^u\,du$$

The correct choice is **D**.

23. $S_3 = \frac{2+4}{4} + \frac{2+9}{8} + \frac{2+16}{16}$
$$= \frac{3}{2} + \frac{11}{8} + \frac{9}{8} = \mathbf{4}$$

24. $x = 4t^3 \qquad y = 3t^2$

$$\frac{dx}{dt} = 12t^2 \qquad \frac{dy}{dt} = 6t$$

$$\left(\frac{dx}{dt}\right)^2 = 144t^4 \qquad \left(\frac{dy}{dt}\right)^2 = 36t^2$$

$$L_0^1 = \int_0^1 \sqrt{144t^4 + 36t^2}\,dt$$
$$= \int_0^1 \sqrt{36t^2(4t^2+1)}\,dt$$
$$= \int_0^1 6t(4t^2+1)^{1/2}\,dt$$
$$= \frac{6}{8}\int_0^1 8t(4t^2+1)^{1/2}\,dt$$
$$= \left(\frac{6}{8}\right)\left(\frac{2}{3}\right)\left[(4t^2+1)^{3/2}\right]_0^1$$
$$= \mathbf{\frac{1}{2}(5\sqrt{5} - 1)\ units}$$

25. (a)

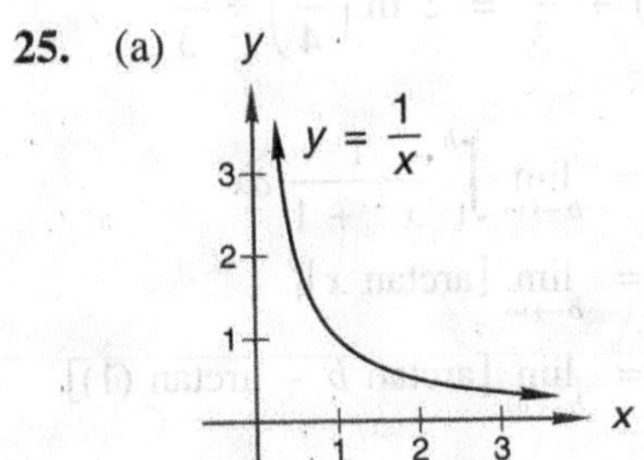

(b) $A = \int_1^\infty \frac{1}{x}\,dx$
$$= \lim_{b\to\infty} \int_1^b \frac{1}{x}\,dx$$
$$= \lim_{b\to\infty} [\ln x]_1^b$$
$$= \lim_{b\to\infty} [\ln b - 0] = \infty$$

The integral **diverges.**

(c) $A = \int_1^\infty \frac{1}{y}\,dy$
$$= \lim_{b\to\infty} \int_1^b \frac{1}{y}\,dy$$
$$= \lim_{b\to\infty} [\ln y]_1^b$$
$$= \lim_{b\to\infty} [\ln b - 0] = \infty$$

The integral **diverges.**

(d) $\int_0^1 \left(\frac{1}{x} - 1\right) dx = \lim_{b\to 0^+} \int_b^1 \left(\frac{1}{x} - 1\right) dx$

PROBLEM SET 131

1. $V = lwh$
$$36 = l(4)h$$
$$h = \frac{9}{l}$$
$$C = 4l(15) + 2(4h)(12) + 2(hl)(12)$$
$$C = 60l + 96h + 24hl$$
$$C = 60l + 96\left(\frac{9}{l}\right) + 24\left(\frac{9}{l}\right)l$$
$$C = 60l + 864l^{-1} + 216$$
$$C' = 60 - \frac{864}{l^2}$$
$$0 = 60 - \frac{864}{l^2}$$
$$60l^2 = 864$$
$$l^2 = 14.4$$
$$l = \sqrt{14.4}$$
$$C(\sqrt{14.4}) = \mathbf{\$671.37}$$

2. $x = 2\cos\theta \qquad y = 3\sin\theta$

$$\frac{dy}{dx} = \frac{3\cos\theta}{-2\sin\theta} = -\frac{3}{2}\cot\theta$$

When $\theta = \frac{\pi}{4}$, $x = \sqrt{2}$, $y = \frac{3\sqrt{2}}{2}$, and slope $= -\frac{3}{2}$.

$$y - \frac{3\sqrt{2}}{2} = -\frac{3}{2}(x - \sqrt{2})$$
$$\mathbf{y = -\frac{3}{2}x + 3\sqrt{2}}$$

$$\frac{d^2y}{dx^2} = \frac{\frac{3}{2}\csc^2\theta}{-2\sin\theta}$$

At $\theta = \frac{\pi}{4}$, $\frac{d^2y}{dx^2}$ is negative, so the curve has **negative concavity.**

3. $x = 3(t-1)^2 \qquad y = 8t^{3/2}$

$$\frac{dx}{dt} = 6(t-1) \qquad \frac{dy}{dt} = 12t^{1/2}$$

$$\left(\frac{dx}{dt}\right)^2 = 36(t-1)^2 \qquad \left(\frac{dy}{dt}\right)^2 = 144t$$

$$L_0^1 = \int_0^1 \sqrt{36(t-1)^2 + 144t}\,dt$$
$$= \int_0^1 \sqrt{36[(t-1)^2 + 4t]}\,dt$$
$$= \int_0^1 6\sqrt{t^2 - 2t + 1 + 4t}\,dt$$
$$= \int_0^1 6\sqrt{t^2 + 2t + 1}\,dt$$
$$= \int_0^1 6\sqrt{(t+1)^2}\,dt = \int_0^1 6(t+1)\,dt$$
$$= \left[3t^2 + 6t\right]_0^1 = \mathbf{9\ units}$$

4.

$$y = \frac{1}{8}x^2 - \ln x$$

$$\frac{dy}{dx} = \frac{1}{4}x - \frac{1}{x}$$

$$\left(\frac{dy}{dx}\right)^2 = \frac{1}{16}x^2 - \frac{1}{2} + \frac{1}{x^2}$$

$$L_1^2 = \int_1^2 \sqrt{1 + \frac{1}{16}x^2 - \frac{1}{2} + \frac{1}{x^2}}\,dx$$

$$= \int_1^2 \sqrt{\left(\frac{1}{4}x + \frac{1}{x}\right)^2}\,dx$$

$$= \int_1^2 \left(\frac{1}{4}x + \frac{1}{x}\right) dx$$

$$= \left[\frac{1}{8}x^2 + \ln x\right]_1^2$$

$$= \frac{1}{2} + \ln 2 - \left(\frac{1}{8} + 0\right)$$

$$= \left(\mathbf{\frac{3}{8} + \ln 2}\right) \textbf{ units}$$

5.

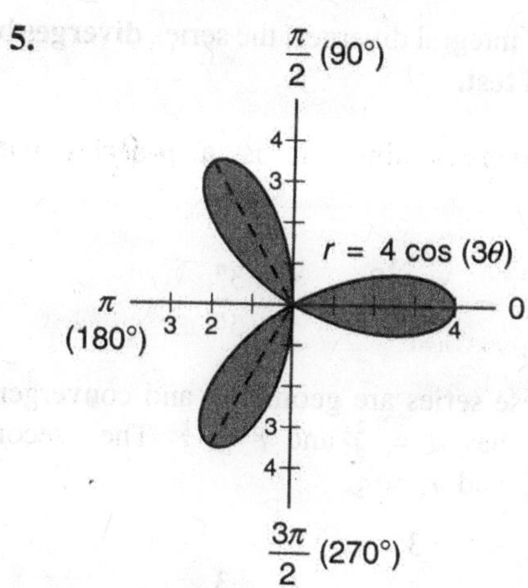

$$A = 6\int_0^{\pi/6} \frac{1}{2}[4\cos(3\theta)]^2\,d\theta$$

$$= 48\int_0^{\pi/6} \cos^2(3\theta)\,d\theta$$

$$= 48\int_0^{\pi/6} \left[\frac{1}{2} + \frac{1}{2}\cos(6\theta)\right] d\theta$$

$$= 48\left[\frac{1}{2}\theta + \frac{1}{12}\sin(6\theta)\right]_0^{\pi/6}$$

$$= \mathbf{4\pi} \textbf{ units}^2$$

6.

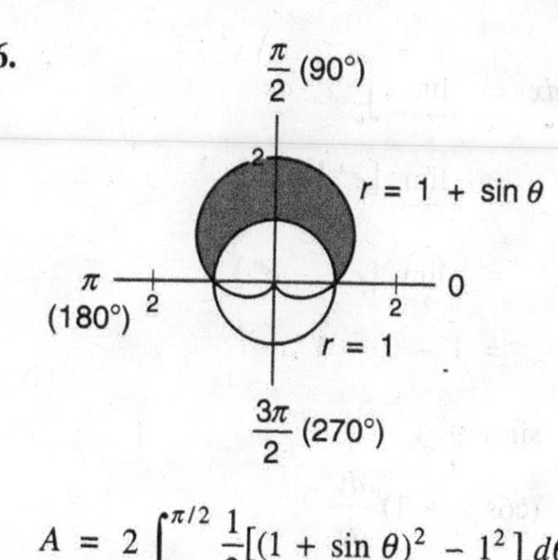

$$A = 2\int_0^{\pi/2} \frac{1}{2}[(1 + \sin\theta)^2 - 1^2]\,d\theta$$

$$= \int_0^{\pi/2} (2\sin\theta + \sin^2\theta)\,d\theta$$

$$= \int_0^{\pi/2} \left[2\sin\theta + \frac{1}{2} - \frac{1}{2}\cos(2\theta)\right] d\theta$$

$$= \left[-2\cos\theta + \frac{1}{2}\theta - \frac{1}{4}\sin(2\theta)\right]_0^{\pi/2}$$

$$= 0 + \frac{\pi}{4} - 0 - (-2 + 0 - 0)$$

$$= \left(\mathbf{\frac{\pi}{4} + 2}\right) \textbf{ units}^2$$

7. $\lim_{x \to 0} e^{-x} \sin x = 1(0) = \mathbf{0}$

8.

$$\int_0^8 \frac{1}{\sqrt[3]{x}}\,dx = \lim_{a \to 0^+} \int_a^8 x^{-1/3}\,dx$$

$$= \lim_{a \to 0^+} \left[\frac{3}{2}x^{2/3}\right]_a^8$$

$$= \lim_{a \to 0^+} \left[6 - \frac{3}{2}a^{2/3}\right]$$

$$= 6 - 0 = \mathbf{6}$$

9.

$$\int_{-1}^1 \frac{1}{x}\,dx = \int_{-1}^0 \frac{1}{x}\,dx + \int_0^1 \frac{1}{x}\,dx$$

$$= \lim_{a \to 0^-} \int_{-1}^a \frac{1}{x}\,dx + \lim_{b \to 0^+} \int_b^1 \frac{1}{x}\,dx$$

$$= \lim_{a \to 0^-} [\ln|x|]_{-1}^a + \lim_{b \to 0^+} [\ln|x|]_b^1$$

$$= \lim_{a \to 0^-} [\ln|a| - 0] + \lim_{b \to 0^+} [0 - \ln|b|]$$

$$= -\infty - 0 + 0 + \infty$$

The integral is **undefined.**

10. $$\int_{-\infty}^{0} e^x\,dx = \lim_{a\to-\infty}\int_a^0 e^x\,dx$$
$$= \lim_{a\to-\infty}[e^x]_a^0$$
$$= \lim_{a\to-\infty}[e^0 - e^a]$$
$$= 1 - 0 = \mathbf{1}$$

11. $$x = \sin y + y$$
$$1 = (\cos y + 1)\frac{dy}{dx}$$
$$\frac{dy}{dx} = \frac{1}{\cos y + 1} = (\cos y + 1)^{-1}$$
$$\frac{d^2y}{dx^2} = -(\cos y + 1)^{-2}(-\sin y)\frac{dy}{dx}$$
$$= \frac{\sin y}{(\cos y + 1)^2}\,\frac{1}{\cos y + 1} = \mathbf{\frac{\sin y}{(\cos y + 1)^3}}$$

12. Let Y1=2^X and adjust the window settings to $x[1.88,\ 2.12]$ and $y[3.88,\ 4.12]$. Performing a TRACE results in the following.

x	y
1.9974468	3.9929273
2	4
2.0025532	4.0070852

If $|x - 2| < 0.003602$, then $|y - 4| < 0.01$, thus δ = **0.0070852.** Answers may vary.

13. $$\sum_{n=1}^{\infty}\frac{n+1}{n\cdot 2^n}$$
$$L = \lim_{n\to\infty}\frac{n+2}{(n+1)2^{n+1}}\cdot\frac{n\cdot 2^n}{n+1}$$
$$= \lim_{n\to\infty}\frac{n(n+2)}{2(n+1)^2} = \frac{1}{2}$$

Since $L < 1$, the series **converges** by the **ratio test.**

14. $$\sum_{n=2}^{\infty}\frac{1}{n\sqrt{\ln n}}$$
$$f(x) = \frac{1}{x\sqrt{\ln x}}$$
$$f'(x) = \frac{x\sqrt{\ln x}\,(0)}{x^2\ln x} - \frac{\left[x\frac{1}{2}(\ln x)^{-1/2}\frac{1}{x} + \sqrt{\ln x}\right]}{x^2\ln x}$$
$$= \frac{-1}{2x^2(\ln x)^{3/2}} - \frac{1}{x^2\sqrt{\ln x}}$$

$f'(x)$ is negative, therefore $f(x)$ is a decreasing function.

$$\int_2^{\infty}\frac{1}{x}(\ln x)^{-1/2}\,dx$$
$$= \lim_{b\to\infty}2\left[(\ln x)^{1/2}\right]_2^b = 2(\infty - \sqrt{\ln 2}) = \infty$$

Because the integral diverges, the series **diverges** by the **integral test.**

15. $\sum_{n=1}^{\infty}\frac{1}{n^{5/3}}$ **converges** since it is a ***p*-series with** $\mathbf{p = \frac{5}{3} > 1}$**.**

16. $$\sum_{n=1}^{\infty}\frac{2+3^n}{5^n} = \sum_{n=1}^{\infty}\frac{2}{5^n} + \sum_{n=1}^{\infty}\frac{3^n}{5^n}$$

Both of these series are geometric and convergent. The first has $a = \frac{2}{5}$ and $r = \frac{1}{5}$. The second has $a = \frac{3}{5}$ and $r = \frac{3}{5}$.

$$S = \frac{\frac{2}{5}}{1-\frac{1}{5}} + \frac{\frac{3}{5}}{1-\frac{3}{5}} = \frac{1}{2} + \frac{3}{2} = 2$$

The series **converges to 2,** because it is the **sum of two convergent geometric series.**

17. $$\lim_{n\to\infty}\frac{n^2}{\ln n} = \lim_{n\to\infty}\frac{2n}{\frac{1}{n}}$$
$$= \lim_{n\to\infty}2n^2 = \infty$$

$\sum_{n=2}^{\infty}\frac{n^2}{\ln n}$ **diverges** by the **divergence theorem.**

18. $$\lim_{n\to\infty}\frac{3+4n}{5n+2} = \frac{4}{5} \neq 0$$

$\sum_{n=1}^{\infty}\frac{3+4n}{5n+2}$ **diverges** by the **divergence theorem.**

19. For $\sum_{n=2}^{\infty} \frac{2+n}{n^3}$,

$$S_3 = \frac{4}{8} + \frac{5}{27} + \frac{6}{64} = \mathbf{\frac{673}{864}}$$

20. $\lim_{h \to 0} \frac{\sin(x+h) - \sin x}{h}$

$$= \lim_{h \to 0} \frac{\sin x \cos h + \cos x \sin h - \sin x}{h}$$

$$= \lim_{h \to 0} \frac{\sin x (\cos h - 1) + \cos x \sin h}{h}$$

$$= \sin x \lim_{h \to 0} \frac{\cos h - 1}{h} + \cos x \lim_{h \to 0} \frac{\sin h}{h}$$

$$= (\sin x)(0) + (\cos x)(1) = \cos x$$

21. $x = 2 \sin \theta \qquad dx = 2 \cos \theta \, d\theta$

$\sqrt{4 - x^2} = 2 \cos \theta$

$$\int \frac{x^2}{\sqrt{4 - x^2}} \, dx$$

$$= \int \frac{(4 \sin^2 \theta)(2 \cos \theta) \, d\theta}{2 \cos \theta}$$

$$= \int 4 \sin^2 \theta \, d\theta$$

$$= \int 4 \left[\frac{1}{2} - \frac{1}{2} \cos(2\theta) \right] d\theta$$

$$= 2\theta - \sin(2\theta) + C$$

$$= 2\theta - 2 \sin \theta \cos \theta + C$$

$$= 2 \arcsin \frac{x}{2} - 2 \left(\frac{x}{2} \right) \left(\frac{\sqrt{4 - x^2}}{2} \right) + C$$

$$= \mathbf{2 \arcsin \frac{x}{2} - \frac{x\sqrt{4 - x^2}}{2} + C}$$

22. $\int \frac{3x^2 - x + 4}{x(x^2 + 4)} \, dx = \int \left(\frac{A}{x} + \frac{Bx + C}{x^2 + 4} \right) dx$

$A(x^2 + 4) + (Bx + C)x = 3x^2 - x + 4$

$x = 0$: $\quad A = 1$

$x = 1$: $\quad 5A + B + C = 6$

$B + C = 1$

$B = 1 - C$

$x = -1$: $\quad 5A + B - C = 8$

$(1 - C) - C = 3$

$C = -1$

$B = 1 - C = 1 - (-1) = 2$

$$\int \left(\frac{A}{x} + \frac{Bx + C}{x^2 + 4} \right) dx1 = \int \left(\frac{1}{x} + \frac{2x - 1}{x^2 + 4} \right) dx$$

$$= \int \left(\frac{1}{x} + \frac{2x}{x^2 + 4} - \frac{1}{x^2 + 4} \right) dx$$

$$= \mathbf{\ln|x| + \ln(x^2 + 4) - \frac{1}{2} \arctan \frac{x}{2} + C}$$

23. $u = \ln x \quad du = \frac{1}{x} \, dx \quad v = \frac{1}{3}x^3 \quad dv = x^2 \, dx$

$$\int x^2 \ln x \, dx = \frac{1}{3}x^3 \ln x - \int \frac{1}{3}x^2 \, dx$$

$$= \frac{1}{3}x^3 \ln x - \frac{1}{9}x^3 + C$$

$$= \mathbf{\frac{1}{9}x^3(3 \ln x - 1) + C}$$

24. $T = \frac{1.2}{8} \left[\frac{(0.2)^2}{\sin(0.2)} + \frac{2(0.5)^2}{\sin(0.5)} + \frac{2(0.8)^2}{\sin(0.8)} + \frac{2(1.1)^2}{\sin(1.1)} + \frac{(1.4)^2}{\sin(1.4)} \right]$

$\approx$ **1.1599 units²**

25. (a) Zeros when $x^2 + 2x - 8 = 0$

$(x + 4)(x - 2) = 0$

$x = -4, 2$

Vertical asymptote: $x = -1$

-1	1	2	-8
	↓	-1	-1
	1	1	$\boxed{-9}$

End behavior: $y = x + 1$

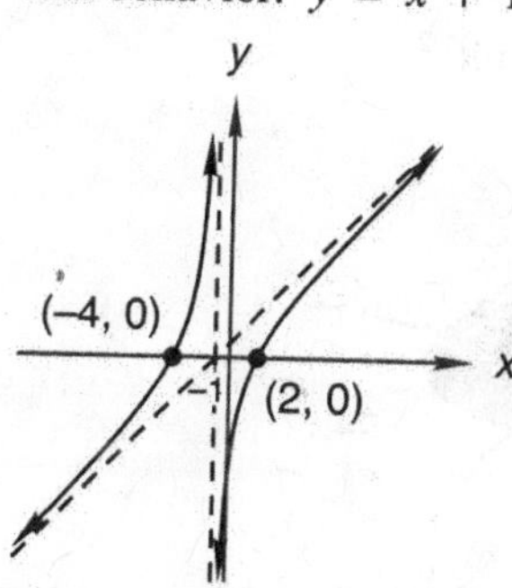

(b) $A = \int_2^4 \frac{x^2 + 2x - 8}{x + 1} \, dx$

$$= \int_2^4 \left(x + 1 - \frac{9}{x + 1} \right) dx$$

$$= \left[\frac{1}{2}x^2 + x - 9 \ln|x + 1| \right]_2^4$$

$$= 8 + 4 - 9 \ln 5 - (2 + 2 - 9 \ln 3)$$

$$= 8 - 9(\ln 5 - \ln 3)$$

$$= \mathbf{\left(8 - 9 \ln \frac{5}{3} \right) units^2}$$

PROBLEM SET 132

1.

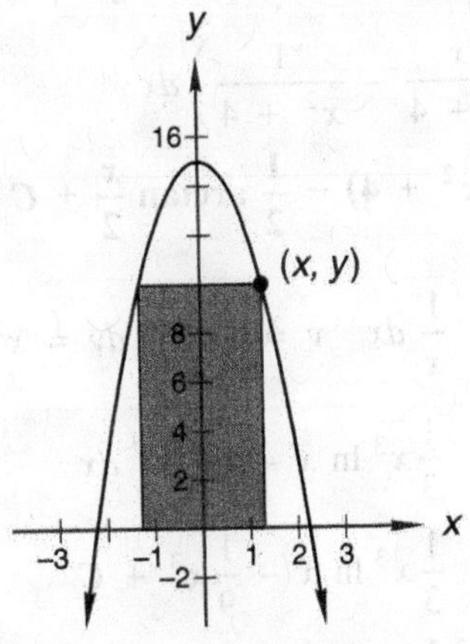

$$A = 2xy$$
$$A = 2x(15 - 3x^2)$$
$$A = 30x - 6x^3$$
$$A' = 30 - 18x^2$$
$$0 = 30 - 18x^2$$
$$18x^2 = 30$$
$$x^2 = \frac{5}{3}$$
$$x = \sqrt{\frac{5}{3}}$$
$$A = 30\sqrt{\frac{5}{3}} - 6\left(\sqrt{\frac{5}{3}}\right)^3$$
$$= \frac{20\sqrt{15}}{3} \textbf{ units}^2$$

2.

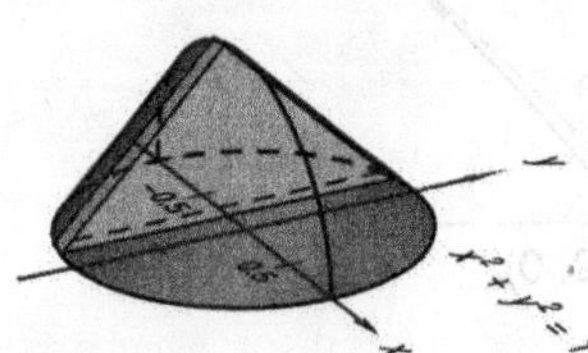

$$V = 2\int_0^1 \frac{1}{2}bh\,dx$$
$$= \int_{x=0}^{x=1} 2y(y)\,dx$$
$$= 2\int_0^1 (1 - x^2)\,dx$$
$$= 2\left[x - \frac{1}{3}x^3\right]_0^1$$
$$= 2\left(1 - \frac{1}{3}\right) = \frac{4}{3} \textbf{ units}^3$$

3.

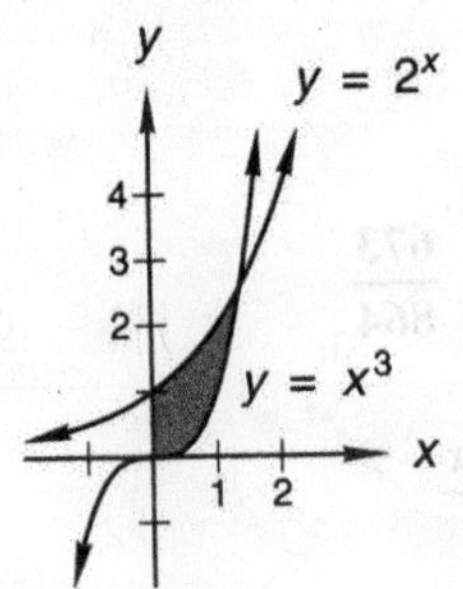

$$A \approx \int_0^{1.3735} (2^x - x^3)\,dx$$
$$= \left[\frac{2^x}{\ln 2} - \frac{1}{4}x^4\right]_0^{1.3735}$$
$$\approx \textbf{1.4056 units}^2$$

4.

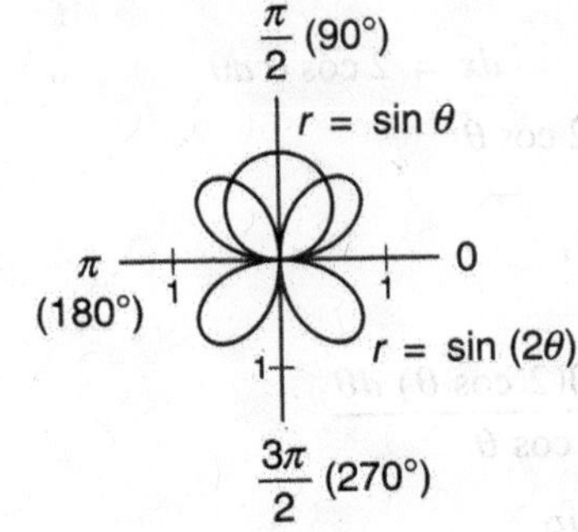

5.
$$\sin\theta = \sin(2\theta)$$
$$\sin\theta = 2\sin\theta\cos\theta$$
$$\cos\theta = \frac{1}{2}$$
$$\theta = \frac{\pi}{3}, \frac{5\pi}{3}$$

Area

$$= 2\left[\int_0^{\pi/3} \frac{1}{2}\sin^2\theta\,d\theta + \int_{\pi/3}^{\pi/2} \frac{1}{2}\sin^2(2\theta)\,d\theta\right]$$
$$= \int_0^{\pi/3}\left[\frac{1}{2} - \frac{1}{2}\cos(2\theta)\right]d\theta$$
$$+ \int_{\pi/3}^{\pi/2}\left[\frac{1}{2} - \frac{1}{2}\cos(4\theta)\right]d\theta$$
$$= \left[\frac{1}{2}\theta - \frac{1}{4}\sin(2\theta)\right]_0^{\pi/3}$$
$$+ \left[\frac{1}{2}\theta - \frac{1}{8}\sin(4\theta)\right]_{\pi/3}^{\pi/2}$$
$$= \frac{\pi}{6} - \frac{\sqrt{3}}{8} - (0) + \frac{\pi}{4} - 0 - \left(\frac{\pi}{6} + \frac{\sqrt{3}}{16}\right)$$
$$= \left(\frac{\pi}{4} - \frac{3\sqrt{3}}{16}\right) \textbf{ unit}^2$$

6. $\lim_{h\to 0} \frac{\ln(x+h) - \ln x}{h}$

$= \lim_{h\to 0} \frac{1}{h}\frac{x}{x}\left[\ln\left(\frac{x+h}{x}\right)\right]$

$= \frac{1}{x}\lim_{h\to 0}\frac{x}{h}\left[\ln\left(1+\frac{h}{x}\right)\right]$

$= \frac{1}{x}\lim_{h\to 0}\ln\left(1+\frac{h}{x}\right)^{x/h}$

$= \frac{1}{x}\ln e = \frac{1}{x}$

7. $\lim_{n\to\infty}\frac{n}{n+1} = \lim_{n\to\infty}\frac{1}{1} = 1 \neq 0$

$\sum_{n=1}^{\infty}\frac{n}{n+1}$ **diverges** by the **divergence theorem.**

8. $\lim_{n\to\infty}\frac{\frac{1}{n+1}}{\frac{1}{n}} = \lim_{n\to\infty}\frac{n}{n+1} = 1$

$\sum_{n=1}^{\infty}\frac{1}{n+1}$ **diverges** by the **limit comparison test** with the harmonic series.

9. $\sum_{n=1}^{\infty} n^{-4/3} = \sum_{n=1}^{\infty}\frac{1}{n^{4/3}}$

The series **converges** because it is a **p-series with $p = \frac{4}{3} > 1$.**

10. $\lim_{n\to\infty}\frac{\frac{2n+1}{(n+1)^2}}{\frac{1}{n}} = \lim_{n\to\infty}\frac{2n^2+n}{(n+1)^2} = 2$

$\sum_{n=1}^{\infty}\frac{2n+1}{(n+1)^2}$ **diverges** by the **limit comparison test** with the harmonic series.

11. $\sum_{n=1}^{\infty}\frac{2^{n+1}}{3^n}$ is a geometric series with $a = \frac{4}{3}$, $r = \frac{2}{3}$, and

$$S = \frac{\frac{4}{3}}{1-\frac{2}{3}} = 4$$

The series **converges to 4,** because it is a **geometric series with $|r| < 1$.**

12. $\lim_{n\to\infty}\frac{\frac{1}{(2+3n)^3}}{\frac{1}{n^3}} = \lim_{n\to\infty}\frac{n^3}{(2+3n)^3} = \frac{1}{27}$

$\sum_{n=1}^{\infty}\frac{1}{(2+3n)^3}$ **converges** by the **limit comparison test** with a convergent p-series.

13. $L = \lim_{n\to\infty}\frac{\frac{2^{n+1}}{(n+1)!}}{\frac{2^n}{n!}} = \lim_{n\to\infty}\frac{2}{n+1} = 0$

By the **ratio test** with $L = 0$, $\sum_{n=1}^{\infty}\frac{2^n}{n!}$ **converges.**

14. $\sum_{n=1}^{\infty}\frac{7}{4n}$ **diverges** because it is a **multiple of the harmonic series.**

15. $\int_3^{\infty}\frac{1}{(x-1)^3}\,dx = \lim_{b\to\infty}\int_3^b\frac{1}{(x-1)^3}\,dx$

$= \lim_{b\to\infty}\left[\frac{-1}{2(x-1)^2}\right]_3^b$

$= \lim_{b\to\infty}\left[\frac{-1}{2(b-1)^2} + \frac{1}{2(2)^2}\right]$

$= 0 + \frac{1}{8} = \mathbf{\frac{1}{8}}$

16. $\int_0^1\frac{1}{(x-1)^{2/3}}\,dx$

$= \lim_{b\to 1^-}\int_0^b (x-1)^{-2/3}\,dx$

$= \lim_{b\to 1^-}\left[3(x-1)^{1/3}\right]_0^b$

$= \lim_{b\to 1^-}\left[3(b-1)^{1/3} - 3(-1)^{1/3}\right]$

$= 0 + 3 = \mathbf{3}$

17. $u = 2x^2 \qquad v = \frac{1}{2}\sin(2x)$

$du = 4x\,dx \qquad dv = \cos(2x)\,dx$

$$\int_0^1 2x^2 \cos(2x)\,dx$$

$$= \left[x^2 \sin(2x) - \int 2x \sin(2x)\,dx\right]_0^1$$

$u = x \qquad v = -\cos(2x)$

$du = dx \qquad dv = 2\sin(2x)\,dx$

$$\int_0^1 2x^2 \cos(2x)\,dx$$

$$= \left[x^2 \sin(2x) - \left(-x\cos(2x) + \int \cos(2x)\,dx\right)\right]_0^1$$

$$= \left[x^2 \sin(2x) + x\cos(2x) - \frac{1}{2}\sin(2x)\right]_0^1$$

$$= \sin 2 + \cos 2 - \frac{1}{2}\sin 2 - (0)$$

$$= \mathbf{\cos 2 + \frac{1}{2}\sin 2}$$

18. $\displaystyle\int \frac{x^2 + 5x + 2}{(x-1)(x+1)^2}\,dx$

$$= \int\left(\frac{A}{x-1} + \frac{B}{x+1} + \frac{C}{(x+1)^2}\right)dx$$

$A(x+1)^2 + B(x-1)(x+1) + C(x-1)$

$= x^2 + 5x + 2$

$x = 1: \quad A = 2$

$x = -1: \quad C = 1$

$x = 0: \quad A - B - C = 2$

$\qquad B = -1$

$$\int\left(\frac{A}{x-1} + \frac{B}{x+1} + \frac{C}{(x+1)^2}\right)dx$$

$$= \int\left(\frac{2}{x-1} - \frac{1}{x+1} + \frac{1}{(x+1)^2}\right)dx$$

$$= \mathbf{2\ln|x-1| - \ln|x+1| - \frac{1}{x+1} + C}$$

19.

$$\begin{array}{r} x + 1 \\ x^2 + 1\overline{)\,x^3 + x^2 + x + 3} \\ \underline{x^3 \quad\;\; + x\quad\;} \\ x^2 \quad\;\; + 3 \\ \underline{x^2 \quad\;\; + 1} \\ 2 \end{array}$$

$$\int \frac{x^3 + x^2 + x + 3}{x^2 + 1}\,dx$$

$$= \int\left(x + 1 + \frac{2}{x^2+1}\right)dx$$

$$= \mathbf{\frac{1}{2}x^2 + x + 2\arctan x + C}$$

20. $\displaystyle\int \frac{-x^2 + x - 10}{(x^2+9)(x-1)}\,dx$

$$= \int\left(\frac{Ax + B}{x^2 + 9} + \frac{C}{x-1}\right)dx$$

$(Ax + B)(x - 1) + C(x^2 + 9) = -x^2 + x - 10$

$x = 1: \quad C = -1$

$x = 0: \quad -B + 9C = -10$

$\qquad B = 1$

$x = 2: \quad 2A + B + 13C = -12$

$\qquad A = 0$

$$\int\left(\frac{Ax + B}{x^2 + 9} + \frac{C}{x-1}\right)dx$$

$$= \int\left(\frac{1}{x^2+9} - \frac{1}{x-1}\right)dx$$

$$= \mathbf{\frac{1}{3}\arctan\frac{x}{3} - \ln|x-1| + C}$$

21. $\displaystyle\lim_{x\to 0}\,[x + \cos(2x)]^{\csc(3x)} = 1^\infty$

$$\lim_{x\to 0}\frac{\ln[x + \cos(2x)]}{\sin(3x)}$$

$$= \lim_{x\to 0}\frac{1 - 2\sin(2x)}{3\cos(3x)\,(x + \cos(2x))} = \frac{1}{3(1)} = \frac{1}{3}$$

So the original limit is $\mathbf{e^{1/3}}$.

22. $\displaystyle\lim_{x\to\infty}\left(1 + \frac{1}{x}\right)^x = e$

23. $\displaystyle\lim_{x\to\infty}\left(\frac{x+4}{x}\right)^x = \lim_{x\to\infty}\left(1 + \frac{4}{x}\right)^x$

With $u = \frac{x}{4}$,

$$\lim_{x\to\infty}\left(1 + \frac{4}{x}\right)^x = \lim_{4u\to\infty}\left(1 + \frac{1}{u}\right)^{4u}$$

$$= \lim_{u\to\infty}\left[\left(1 + \frac{1}{u}\right)^u\right]^4 = \mathbf{e^4}$$

24. $x = 32 \quad dx = -2 \quad y = 2$

$$y = \sqrt[5]{x}$$

$$dy = \frac{1}{5}x^{-4/5}\,dx = \frac{1}{5}\left(\frac{1}{16}\right)(-2) = -\frac{1}{40}$$

$$\sqrt[5]{30} \approx y + dy = 2 - \frac{1}{40} = \mathbf{1\frac{39}{40}}$$

25. $f(x) = x^3 + x \qquad f'(x) = 3x^2 + 1$

Note that $f(x) = 10$ when $x = 2$, so

$$g'(10) = \frac{1}{f'(g(10))} = \frac{1}{f'(2)} = \frac{1}{3(2)^2 + 1}$$

$$= \mathbf{\frac{1}{13}}$$

PROBLEM SET 133

1.

$$a(t) = 16t - 10$$
$$v(t) = 8t^2 - 10t + C$$
$$v(1) = 8(1)^2 - 10(1) + C$$
$$1 = 8 - 10 + C$$
$$C = 3$$
$$v(t) = 8t^2 - 10t + 3$$
$$0 = 8t^2 - 10t + 3$$
$$0 = (4t - 3)(2t - 1)$$
$$t = \frac{3}{4}, \frac{1}{2}$$

+ + + + | − | + + +

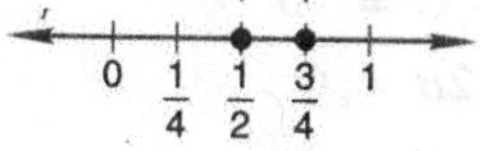

Total distance

$$= \int_0^{1/2} (8t^2 - 10t + 3)\,dt$$
$$+ \int_{3/4}^{1/2} (8t^2 - 10t + 3)\,dt$$
$$+ \int_{3/4}^{2} (8t^2 - 10t + 3)\,dt$$
$$= \left[\frac{8}{3}t^3 - 5t^2 + 3t\right]_0^{1/2} + \left[\frac{8}{3}t^3 - 5t^2 + 3t\right]_{3/4}^{1/2}$$
$$+ \left[\frac{8}{3}t^3 - 5t^2 + 3t\right]_{3/4}^{2}$$
$$= \frac{1}{3} - \frac{5}{4} + \frac{3}{2} - (0) + \frac{1}{3} - \frac{5}{4} + \frac{3}{2}$$
$$- \left(\frac{9}{8} - \frac{45}{16} + \frac{9}{4}\right) + \frac{64}{3} - 20 + 6$$
$$- \left(\frac{9}{8} - \frac{45}{16} + \frac{9}{4}\right) = \mathbf{\frac{59}{8}\ units}$$

2. The total distance the ball falls can be represented as a geometric series with $a = 10$ and $r = \frac{2}{5}$.

$$\text{Fall distance: } S = \frac{10}{1 - \frac{2}{5}} = \frac{50}{3}$$

$$\text{Rebound distance: } \frac{50}{3} - 10 = \frac{20}{3}$$

$$\text{Total distance: } \frac{50}{3} + \frac{20}{3} = \mathbf{\frac{70}{3}\ m}$$

3. $f(x, y) = y$

$$\Delta x = \frac{1 - 0}{4} = 0.25$$

$$y_n = y_{n-1} + f(x_{n-1}, y_{n-1})\Delta x$$

i	x_i	y_i
0	0	4
1	0.25	5
2	0.50	6.25
3	0.75	7.8125
4	1	9.765625

$y(1) \approx$ **9.765625**

4. $\frac{dy}{dx} = y$

$$\int \frac{1}{y}\,dy = \int dx$$
$$\ln|y| = x + C$$
$$|y| = Ce^x$$
$$|4| = Ce^0$$
$$C = 4$$
$$|y| = 4e^x$$
$$y = 4e^1 \approx \mathbf{10.873127}$$

The answers to problems 3 and 4 are not very close.

5. $$y = \frac{1}{4}x^2 - \frac{1}{2}\ln x$$

$$\frac{dy}{dx} = \frac{1}{2}x - \frac{1}{2x}$$

$$\left(\frac{dy}{dx}\right)^2 = \frac{1}{4}x^2 - \frac{1}{2} + \frac{1}{4x^2}$$

$$L_1^4 = \int_1^4 \sqrt{\frac{1}{4}x^2 - \frac{1}{2} + \frac{1}{4x^2} + 1}\, dx$$

$$= \int_1^4 \sqrt{\frac{1}{4}x^2 + \frac{1}{2} + \frac{1}{4x^2}}\, dx$$

$$= \int_1^4 \sqrt{\left(\frac{1}{2}x + \frac{1}{2x}\right)^2}\, dx$$

$$= \int_1^4 \left(\frac{1}{2}x + \frac{1}{2x}\right) dx$$

$$= \left[\frac{1}{4}x^2 + \frac{1}{2}\ln|x|\right]_1^4$$

$$= 4 + \frac{1}{2}\ln 4 - \left(\frac{1}{4} + 0\right)$$

$$= \left(\mathbf{\frac{15}{4} + \ln 2}\right) \textbf{ units}$$

6. $$\sum_{n=2}^{\infty} \frac{2 + 2^n}{4^n} = \sum_{n=2}^{\infty} \frac{2}{4^n} + \sum_{n=2}^{\infty} \frac{2^n}{4^n}$$

Both series are geometric. The first has $a = \frac{1}{8}$ and $r = \frac{1}{4}$. The second has $a = \frac{1}{4}$ and $r = \frac{1}{2}$.

$$S = \frac{\frac{1}{8}}{1 - \frac{1}{4}} + \frac{\frac{1}{4}}{1 - \frac{1}{2}} = \frac{1}{6} + \frac{1}{2} = \frac{2}{3}$$

The series **converges to $\frac{2}{3}$**, because it is the **sum of two convergent geometric series.**

7. $$\lim_{n\to\infty} \frac{n^2 + 10}{n} = \lim_{n\to\infty} \frac{2n}{1} = \infty \neq 0$$

$\sum_{n=1}^{\infty} \frac{n^2 + 10}{n}$ **diverges** by the **divergence theorem.**

8. $$\lim_{n\to\infty} \frac{\frac{n}{n^2 + 10}}{\frac{1}{n}} = \lim_{n\to\infty} \frac{n^2}{n^2 + 10} = 1$$

$\sum_{n=1}^{\infty} \frac{n}{n^2 + 10}$ **diverges** by the **limit comparison test** with the harmonic series.

9. $$\lim_{n\to\infty} \frac{\frac{1}{n^2 + 10}}{\frac{1}{n^2}} = \lim_{n\to\infty} \frac{n^2}{n^2 + 10} = 1$$

$\sum_{n=1}^{\infty} \frac{1}{n^2 + 10}$ **converges** by the **limit comparison test** with a convergent p-series.

10. $$\lim_{n\to\infty} \frac{\frac{100 + n}{n^3 + 2}}{\frac{1}{n^2}} = \lim_{n\to\infty} \frac{100n^2 + n^3}{n^3 + 2} = 1$$

$\sum_{n=1}^{\infty} \frac{100 + n}{n^3 + 2}$ **converges** by the **limit comparsion test** with a convergent p-series.

11. $$\lim_{n\to\infty} \frac{\frac{27}{n - 21}}{\frac{1}{n}} = \lim_{n\to\infty} \frac{27n}{n - 21} = 27$$

$\sum_{n=1}^{\infty} \frac{27}{n - 21}$ **diverges** by the **limit comparison test** with the harmonic series.

12. $$\int \frac{5x^2 + 3x + 2}{x(x + 1)^2}\, dx$$

$$= \int \left[\frac{A}{x} + \frac{B}{x + 1} + \frac{C}{(x + 1)^2}\right] dx$$

$$A(x + 1)^2 + B(x + 1)x + Cx = 5x^2 + 3x + 2$$

$x = -1$: $\quad C = -4$

$x = 0$: $\quad A = 2$

$x = 1$: $\quad 4A + 2B + C = 10$

$\quad 2B = 6$

$\quad B = 3$

$$\int \left[\frac{A}{x} + \frac{B}{x + 1} + \frac{C}{(x + 1)^2}\right] dx$$

$$= \int \left[\frac{2}{x} + \frac{3}{x + 1} - \frac{4}{(x + 1)^2}\right] dx$$

$$= \mathbf{2\ln|x| + 3\ln|x + 1| + \frac{4}{x + 1} + C}$$

13. $u = x^2 \quad du = 2x\, dx \quad v = \sin x \quad dv = \cos x\, dx$

$$\int x^2 \cos x\, dx = x^2 \sin x - \int 2x \sin x\, dx$$

$u = 2x \quad du = 2\, dx \quad v = -\cos x \quad dv = \sin x\, dx$

$$x^2 \sin x - \int 2x \sin x\, dx$$

$$= x^2 \sin x - \left(-2x \cos x + \int 2 \cos x\, dx\right)$$

$$= \mathbf{x^2 \sin x + 2x \cos x - 2 \sin x + C}$$

14. $\int_0^4 \frac{1}{(x-2)^3}\,dx$

$$= \lim_{b\to 2^-} \int_0^b \frac{1}{(x-2)^3}\,dx + \lim_{a\to 2^+} \int_a^4 \frac{1}{(x-2)^3}\,dx$$

$$= \lim_{b\to 2^-} \left[\frac{-1}{2(x-2)^2}\right]_0^b + \lim_{a\to 2^+} \left[\frac{-1}{2(x-2)^2}\right]_a^4$$

$$= \lim_{b\to 2^-} \left[\frac{-1}{2(b-2)^2} + \frac{1}{2(-2)^2}\right] + \lim_{a\to 2^+} \left[\frac{-1}{2(2)^2} + \frac{1}{2(a-2)^2}\right]$$

$$= \infty + \frac{1}{8} - \frac{1}{8} + \infty = \infty$$

The integral **diverges.**

15. $\int_1^\infty \frac{1}{x^3}\,dx = \lim_{b\to\infty} \int_1^b \frac{1}{x^3}\,dx$

$$= \lim_{b\to\infty} \left[\frac{-1}{2x^2}\right]_1^b = \mathbf{\frac{1}{2}}$$

16.

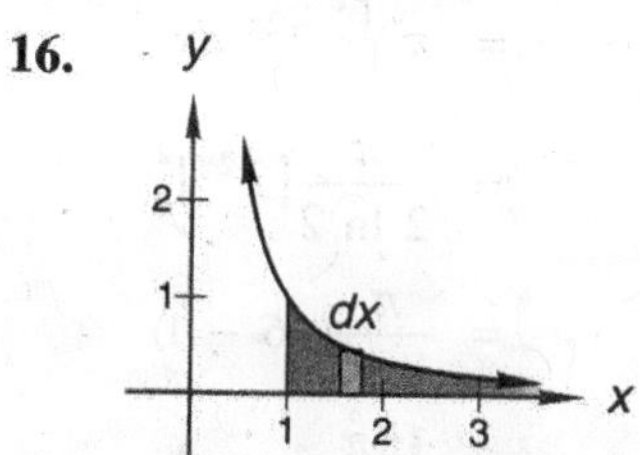

$$A = \int_1^\infty \frac{1}{x^{3/2}}\,dx = \lim_{b\to\infty} \int_1^b x^{-3/2}\,dx$$

$$= \lim_{b\to\infty} \left[-2x^{-1/2}\right]_1^b$$

$$= \lim_{b\to\infty} \left[\frac{-2}{\sqrt{b}} + \frac{2}{\sqrt{1}}\right]$$

$$= \mathbf{2\ units^2}$$

17. $V = \lim_{b\to\infty} 2\pi \int_1^b x\left(\frac{1}{x^{3/2}}\right) dx$

$$= \lim_{b\to\infty} 2\pi \int_1^b x^{-1/2}\,dx$$

$$= \lim_{b\to\infty} 2\pi\left[2\sqrt{x}\right]_1^b = \infty$$

18. $3\sin\theta = 2 - \sin\theta$

$4\sin\theta = 2$

$\sin\theta = \frac{1}{2}$

$\theta = \frac{\pi}{6}, \frac{5\pi}{6}$

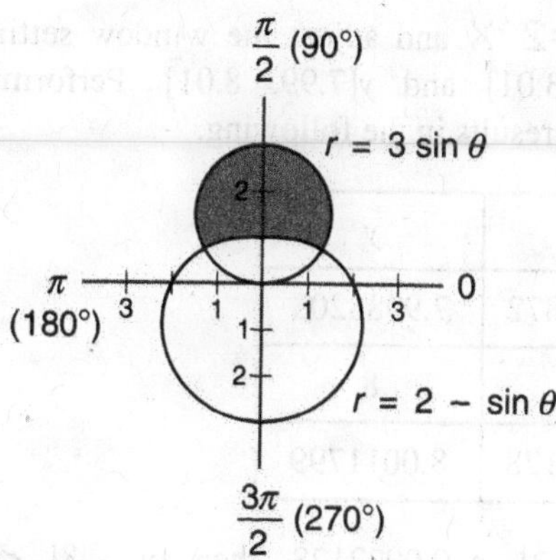

Area

$$= 2\int_{\pi/6}^{\pi/2} \frac{1}{2}\left[(3\sin\theta)^2 - (2-\sin\theta)^2\right] d\theta$$

$$= \int_{\pi/6}^{\pi/2} \left[9\sin^2\theta - (4 - 4\sin\theta + \sin^2\theta)\right] d\theta$$

$$= \int_{\pi/6}^{\pi/2} (8\sin^2\theta + 4\sin\theta - 4)\,d\theta$$

$$= \int_{\pi/6}^{\pi/2} \left[4 - 4\cos(2\theta) + 4\sin\theta - 4\right] d\theta$$

$$= \int_{\pi/6}^{\pi/2} \left[-4\cos(2\theta) + 4\sin\theta\right] d\theta$$

$$= \left[-2\sin(2\theta) - 4\cos\theta\right]_{\pi/6}^{\pi/2}$$

$$= 0 - 0 - \left[-2\left(\frac{\sqrt{3}}{2}\right) - 4\left(\frac{\sqrt{3}}{2}\right)\right]$$

$$= \mathbf{3\sqrt{3}\ units^2}$$

19. $\vec{f}(t) = \arcsin(e^{2t})\,\hat{i} + 4e^{3t}\,\hat{j}$

$$\vec{f}'(t) = \frac{2e^{2t}}{\sqrt{1-e^{4t}}}\hat{i} + 12e^{3t}\,\hat{j}$$

20. To prove the limit, a value for δ must be determined.

$$|y + 5| < \varepsilon$$
$$|-2x + 3 + 5| < \varepsilon$$
$$|-2x + 8| < \varepsilon$$
$$|x - 4| < \frac{\varepsilon}{2}$$
$$\delta = \frac{\varepsilon}{2}$$

21. Let Y1=2^X and adjust the window settings to $x[2.99, 3.01]$ and $y[7.99, 8.01]$. Performing a TRACE results in the following.

x	y
2.9997872	7.9988203
3	8
3.0002128	8.0011799

If $|x - 3| < 0.0002128$, then $|y - 8| < 0.01$, thus $\delta = \mathbf{0.0002128}$. Answers may vary.

22. $x = \dfrac{\ln(t^2)}{\ln 4} \qquad y = \arctan \dfrac{t}{4}$

$$\frac{dy}{dx} = \frac{\dfrac{4}{16 + t^2}}{\dfrac{2t}{(\ln 4)t^2}} = \frac{4(\ln 4)t}{2(16 + t^2)} = \frac{(\ln 16)t}{16 + t^2}$$

When $t = 5$, $x = \log_4 25$, $y = \arctan \frac{5}{4}$, and the slope $= \frac{5 \ln 16}{41}$.

$$y - \arctan \frac{5}{4} = \frac{5 \ln 16}{41}(x - \log_4 25)$$

$$\mathbf{y \approx 0.3381x + 0.1110}$$

23.
$$y = x(\ln x)^2$$
$$\frac{dy}{dx} = x(2)(\ln x)\frac{1}{x} + (\ln x)^2$$
$$\frac{dy}{dx} = 2 \ln x + (\ln x)^2$$
$$0 = \ln x\,(2 + \ln x)$$

Critical numbers: $x = \mathbf{1, e^{-2}}$

24. $\lim\limits_{x \to 0} -x^4 = 0 \qquad \lim\limits_{x \to 0} x^4 = 0$

By the sandwich theorem, $\lim\limits_{x \to 0} f(x) = \mathbf{0}$.

25. Using the trapezoidal rule,

$$T = \frac{1000}{20}[600 + 1180 + 1100 + 940 + 860 + 840 + 500 + 460 + 440 + 400 + 0]$$
$$= \mathbf{366{,}000\ ft^2}$$

PROBLEM SET 134

1.

$y = \sqrt{1 - x^2}$

$$F = 9800 \int_{y=-1}^{y=0} -y(2x)\,dy$$
$$= 9800 \int_{-1}^{0} -2y\sqrt{1 - y^2}\,dy$$
$$= \frac{19{,}600}{3}\left[(1 - y^2)^{3/2}\right]_{-1}^{0} = \mathbf{\frac{19{,}600}{3}\ newtons}$$

2.
$$W = 9800 \int_{y=-1}^{y=0} 2x(3)(-y)\,dy$$
$$= 29{,}400 \int_{-1}^{0} -2y\sqrt{1 - y^2}\,dy$$
$$= 19{,}600\left[(1 - y^2)^{3/2}\right]_{-1}^{0} = \mathbf{19{,}600\ joules}$$

3.

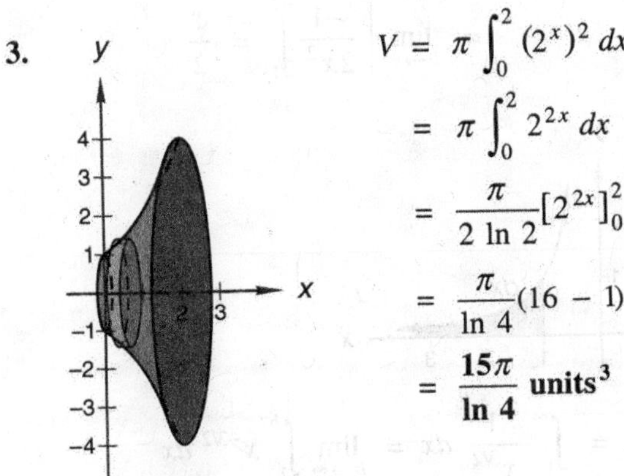

$$V = \pi \int_0^2 (2^x)^2\,dx$$
$$= \pi \int_0^2 2^{2x}\,dx$$
$$= \frac{\pi}{2 \ln 2}\left[2^{2x}\right]_0^2$$
$$= \frac{\pi}{\ln 4}(16 - 1)$$
$$= \mathbf{\frac{15\pi}{\ln 4}\ units^3}$$

4.

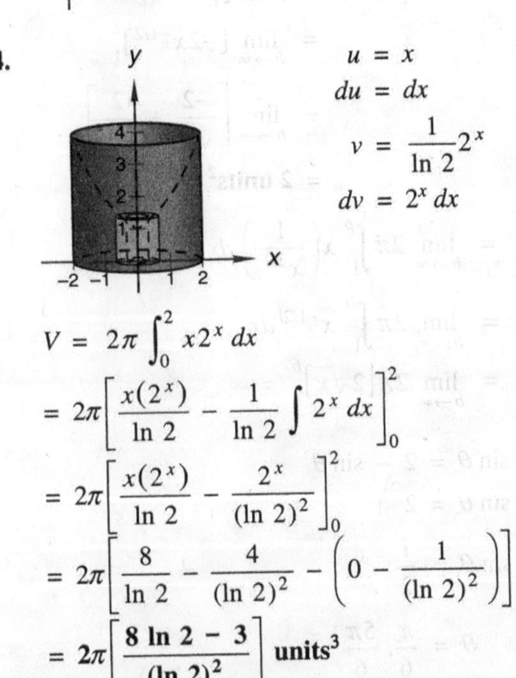

$$u = x \qquad du = dx \qquad v = \frac{1}{\ln 2}2^x \qquad dv = 2^x\,dx$$

$$V = 2\pi \int_0^2 x2^x\,dx$$
$$= 2\pi\left[\frac{x(2^x)}{\ln 2} - \frac{1}{\ln 2}\int 2^x\,dx\right]_0^2$$
$$= 2\pi\left[\frac{x(2^x)}{\ln 2} - \frac{2^x}{(\ln 2)^2}\right]_0^2$$
$$= 2\pi\left[\frac{8}{\ln 2} - \frac{4}{(\ln 2)^2} - \left(0 - \frac{1}{(\ln 2)^2}\right)\right]$$
$$= \mathbf{2\pi\left[\frac{8 \ln 2 - 3}{(\ln 2)^2}\right]\ units^3}$$

5.

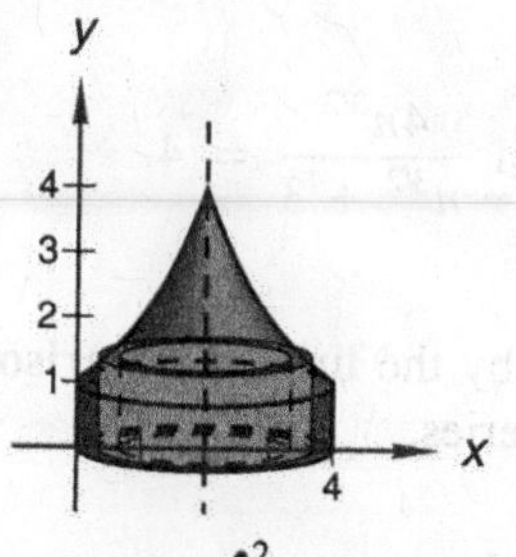

$$V = 2\pi \int_0^2 (2 - x)2^x\, dx$$

$$= 2\pi \int_0^2 [2(2^x) - x(2^x)]\, dx$$

$$= 2\pi\left[\frac{2(2^x)}{\ln 2} - \frac{x(2^x)}{\ln 2} + \frac{2^x}{(\ln 2)^2}\right]_0^2$$

$$= 2\pi\left[\frac{8}{\ln 2} - \frac{8}{\ln 2} + \frac{4}{(\ln 2)^2} - \left(\frac{2}{\ln 2} - 0 + \frac{1}{(\ln 2)^2}\right)\right]$$

$$= \mathbf{2\pi\left[\frac{3 - \ln 4}{(\ln 2)^2}\right]\ units^3}$$

6.

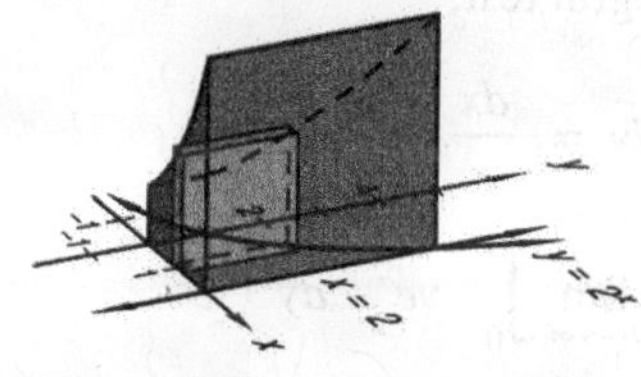

$$V = \int_0^2 (2^x)^2\, dx$$

$$= \int_0^2 2^{2x}\, dx$$

$$= \frac{1}{2 \ln 2}[2^{2x}]_0^2$$

$$= \frac{1}{\ln 4}(16 - 1) = \mathbf{\frac{15}{\ln 4}\ units^3}$$

7.

$$y = 2x + 1$$

$$r \sin\theta = 2(r\cos\theta) + 1$$

$$r\sin\theta - 2r\cos\theta = 1$$

$$r(\sin\theta - 2\cos\theta) = 1$$

$$\mathbf{r = \frac{1}{\sin\theta - 2\cos\theta}}$$

8.

$$r = 2 + 2\cos\theta$$

$$r^2 = 2r + 2r\cos\theta$$

$$x^2 + y^2 = 2\sqrt{x^2 + y^2} + 2x$$

$$x^2 + y^2 - 2x = 2\sqrt{x^2 + y^2}$$

$$x^4 + y^4 - 4x^3 + 2x^2y^2 - 4xy^2 + 4x^2 = 4x^2 + 4y^2$$

$$\mathbf{x^4 + y^4 - 4x^3 + 2x^2y^2 - 4xy^2 - 4y^2 = 0}$$

9.

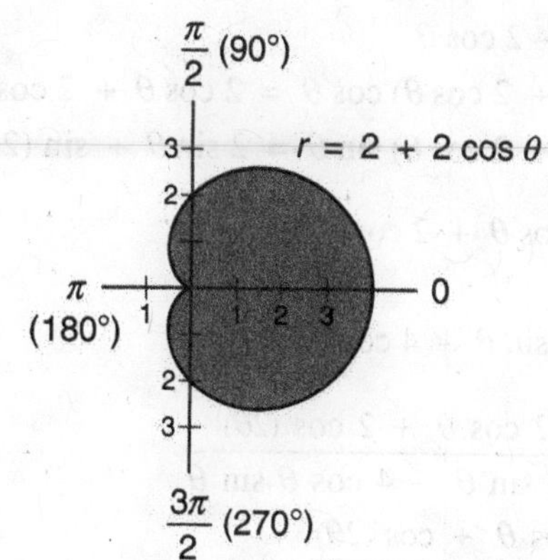

$$A = 2\int_0^\pi \frac{1}{2}(2 + 2\cos\theta)^2\, d\theta$$

$$= \int_0^\pi (4 + 2\cos\theta + 4\cos^2\theta)\, d\theta$$

$$= 4\int_0^\pi \left[\frac{3}{2} + 2\cos\theta + \frac{1}{2}\cos(2\theta)\right] d\theta$$

$$= 4\left[\frac{3}{2}\theta + 2\sin\theta + \frac{1}{4}\sin(2\theta)\right]_0^\pi$$

$$= 4\left[\frac{3\pi}{2} - (0)\right] = \mathbf{6\pi\ units^2}$$

10. $f(x, y) = 7x$

$$\Delta x = \frac{1.1 - 1}{5} = 0.02$$

$$y_n = y_{n-1} + f(x_{n-1}, y_{n-1})\Delta x$$

i	x_i	y_i
0	1	2
1	1.02	2.14
2	1.04	2.2828
3	1.06	2.4284
4	1.08	2.5768
5	1.10	2.728

$y(1.1) \approx$ **2.728**

11. $r = 2 + 2\cos\theta$

$x = (2 + 2\cos\theta)\cos\theta = 2\cos\theta + 2\cos^2\theta$

$y = (2 + 2\cos\theta)\sin\theta = 2\sin\theta + \sin(2\theta)$

$\frac{dy}{d\theta} = 2\cos\theta + 2\cos(2\theta)$

$\frac{dx}{d\theta} = -2\sin\theta - 4\cos\theta\sin\theta$

$\frac{dy}{dx} = \frac{2\cos\theta + 2\cos(2\theta)}{-2\sin\theta - 4\cos\theta\sin\theta}$

$\frac{dy}{dx} = \frac{\cos\theta + \cos(2\theta)}{-\sin\theta - \sin(2\theta)}$

When $\theta = \frac{4\pi}{3}$,

$$\frac{dy}{dx} = \frac{-\frac{1}{2} - \frac{1}{2}}{-\left(-\frac{\sqrt{3}}{2}\right) - \frac{\sqrt{3}}{2}} = \frac{-1}{0}$$

The slope is **undefined.**

12. Problem 11 revealed a vertical tangent line for $r = 2 + 2\cos\frac{4\pi}{3}$, which can be expressed as

$x(\theta) = 2\cos\theta + 2\cos^2\theta$

$x\left(\frac{4\pi}{3}\right) = 2\left(-\frac{1}{2}\right) + 2\left(-\frac{1}{2}\right)^2$

$x = -1 + \frac{1}{2}$

$x = -\frac{1}{2}$

13. With θstep=.1 in the WINDOW screen, the following is obtained.

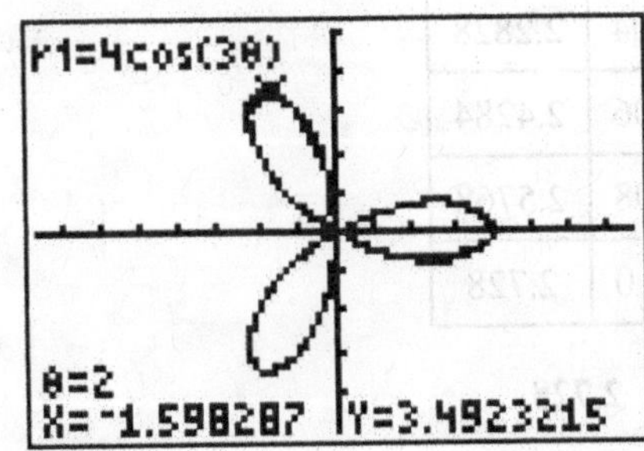

Using option 2:dy/dx from the CALCULATE menu, the calculator gives approximately **−0.2968** as the slope.

14. From problem 13 the following is known for $r = 4\cos(3\theta)$ at $\theta = 2$:

$x \approx -1.5983;\ y \approx 3.4923;\ \text{slope} \approx -0.2968$

$y - 3.4923 \approx -0.2968(x + 1.5983)$

$y \approx \mathbf{-0.2968x + 3.0179}$

15. $$\lim_{n\to\infty} \frac{\frac{4}{n^{3/2} + 3}}{\frac{1}{n^{3/2}}} = \lim_{n\to\infty} \frac{4n^{3/2}}{n^{3/2} + 3} = 4$$

$\sum_{n=1}^{\infty} \frac{4}{n^{3/2} + 3}$ **converges** by the **limit comparison test** with a convergent p-series.

16. $$L = \lim_{n\to\infty} \sqrt[n]{\frac{n^{3/2}}{3^n}} = \frac{1}{3}$$

$\sum_{n=1}^{\infty} \frac{n^{3/2}}{3^n}$ **converges** by the **root test.**

17. $$r = \lim_{n\to\infty} \frac{\frac{3^{n+1}}{(n+1)!}}{\frac{3^n}{n!}} = \lim_{n\to\infty} \frac{3}{n+1} = 0$$

Since $r < 1$, the series **converges** by the **ratio test.**

18. $\frac{d}{dx}\left(\frac{\ln x}{x^2}\right) = \frac{1 - 2\ln x}{x^3}$ is negative for all $x > e^{1/2}$, so the function decreases.

Applying the integral test,

$y = \ln x \qquad dy = \frac{dx}{x} \qquad x = e^y$

$$\int_1^{\infty} \frac{\ln x}{x^2}\,dx = \lim_{b\to\infty} \int_0^b ye^{-y}\,dy$$

$u = y \quad du = dy \quad v = -e^{-y} \quad dv = e^{-y}\,dy$

$$\lim_{b\to\infty} \int_0^b ye^{-y}\,dy$$

$$= \lim_{b\to\infty}\left[-ye^{-y} - \int(-e^{-y})\,dy\right]_0^b$$

$$= \lim_{b\to\infty}\left[-ye^{-y} - e^{-y}\right]_0^b$$

$$= 0 - (-1) = 1$$

So $\sum_{n=1}^{\infty} \frac{\ln n}{n^2}$ **converges** by the **integral test.**

19. $$\sum_{n=1}^{\infty} \frac{7 + 3^n}{4^n} = \sum_{n=1}^{\infty} \frac{7}{4^n} + \sum_{n=1}^{\infty} \frac{3^n}{4^n}$$

This series is the sum of two convergent geometric series with

$$S = \frac{\frac{7}{4}}{1 - \frac{1}{4}} + \frac{\frac{3}{4}}{1 - \frac{3}{4}} = \frac{7}{3} + 3$$

This series **converges to** $\frac{16}{3}$, because it is the **sum of two convergent geometric series.**

20. $\displaystyle\lim_{n\to\infty} \frac{\frac{2}{n^{3/2} - 3}}{\frac{1}{n^{3/2}}} = \lim_{n\to\infty} \frac{2n^{3/2}}{n^{3/2} - 3} = 2$

$\sum_{n=1}^{\infty} \frac{2}{n^{3/2} - 3}$ **converges** by the **limit comparison test** with a convergent p-series.

21. $\displaystyle\int \frac{(x + 1)^3}{x^2 + x - 2}\,dx$

$$= \int \left[x + 2 + \frac{3x + 5}{(x + 2)(x - 1)}\right] dx$$

$$\frac{3x + 5}{(x + 2)(x - 1)} = \frac{A}{x + 2} + \frac{B}{x - 1}$$

$A(x - 1) + B(x + 2) = 3x + 5$

$x = -2$: $\quad -3A = -1$

$A = \frac{1}{3}$

$x = 1$: $\quad 3B = 8$

$B = \frac{8}{3}$

$$\int \left[x + 2 + \frac{3x + 5}{(x + 2)(x - 1)}\right] dx$$

$$= \int \left(x + 2 + \frac{\frac{1}{3}}{x + 2} + \frac{\frac{8}{3}}{x - 1}\right) dx$$

$$= \boldsymbol{\frac{1}{2}x^2 + 2x + \frac{1}{3}\ln|x + 2| + \frac{8}{3}\ln|x - 1| + C}$$

22. $\displaystyle\int_0^{\pi} \sec x\,dx$

$$= \lim_{b\to\pi/2^-} \int_0^b \sec x\,dx + \lim_{a\to\pi/2^+} \int_a^{\pi} \sec x\,dx$$

$$= \lim_{b\to\pi/2^-} [\ln|\sec x + \tan x|]_0^b$$

$$+ \lim_{a\to\pi/2^+} [\ln|\sec x + \tan x|]_a^{\pi}$$

$$= (\ln|\infty + \infty| - \ln|1 + 0|) + (\ln|-1 + 0| - \ln|\infty + \infty|)$$

$$= \infty - 0 + 0 - \infty$$

The integral is **undefined**.

23. $f(x) \geq g(x)$ on $[1, 3]$; $f(x)$ and $g(x)$ intersect at $x = 3$; $f(x) \leq g(x)$ on $[3, 6]$.

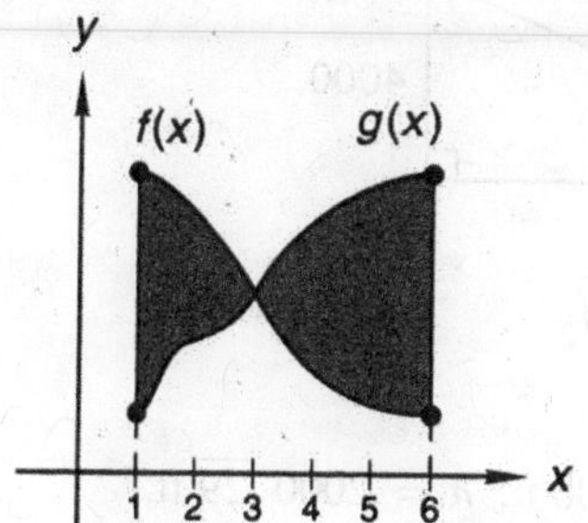

$$A = \int_1^3 [f(x) - g(x)]\,dx + \int_3^6 [g(x) - f(x)]\,dx$$

The correct choice is **B**.

24. $\displaystyle\lim_{x\to 0} (e^x + x)^{1/x} = 1^{\infty}$

$$\lim_{x\to 0} \frac{\ln(e^x + x)}{x} = \lim_{x\to 0} \frac{e^x + 1}{e^x + x} = \frac{2}{1}$$

So the original limit is $\boldsymbol{e^2}$.

25. Darius walks distances of 100, 25, $\frac{25}{4}$, $\frac{25}{16}$, ... in the direction of the 100-meter line. The total of these distances can be represented by a geometric series with $a = 100$, $r = \frac{1}{4}$, and $S = \frac{a}{1 - r} = \frac{400}{3}$ m.

Darius walks distances of 50, $\frac{50}{4}$, $\frac{50}{16}$, ... in the direction of the 0-meter line. The total of these distances can be represented by a geometric series with $a = 50$, $r = \frac{1}{4}$, and $S = \frac{a}{1 - r} = \frac{200}{3}$ m.

Darius's location:

$$\frac{400}{3} - \frac{200}{3} = \frac{200}{3} = \mathbf{66\tfrac{2}{3}\ \textbf{m line}}$$

Total distance: $\frac{400}{3} + \frac{200}{3} = \frac{600}{3} = \mathbf{200\ m}$

PROBLEM SET 135

1.

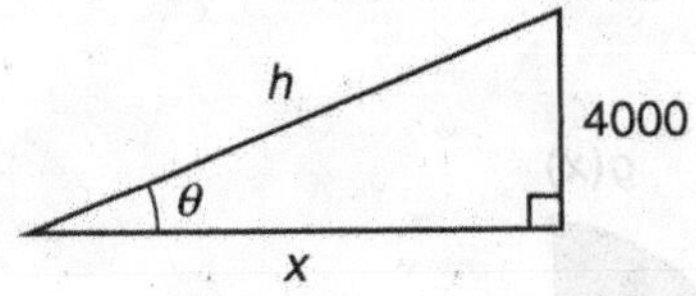

$$\frac{d\theta}{dt} = 0.1\ \frac{\text{rad}}{\text{s}}$$

When $x = 10{,}000$ ft, $h = 2000\sqrt{29}$ ft.

$$\cot\theta = \frac{x}{4000}$$

$$x = 4000\cot\theta$$

$$\frac{dx}{dt} = -4000\csc^2\theta\,\frac{d\theta}{dt}$$

$$= -4000\left(\frac{2000\sqrt{29}}{4000}\right)^2(0.1) = \mathbf{-2900\ \frac{ft}{s}}$$

2. $v(t) = 24\sin t + 7\cos t$

$$v'(t) = 24\cos t - 7\sin t$$

$$0 = 24\cos t - 7\sin t$$

$$7\sin t = 24\cos t$$

$$\tan t = \frac{24}{7}$$

$$t \approx 1.2870$$

$v(1.2870) =$ **25 linear units/time unit**

3.

$$r^2 = \sin^2\theta - 2\cos^2\theta$$

$$r^4 = r^2\sin^2\theta - 2r^2\cos^2\theta$$

$$(x^2 + y^2)^2 = y^2 - 2x^2$$

$$y^2 - 2x^2 = x^4 + 2x^2y^2 + y^4$$

$$\mathbf{0 = x^4 + 2x^2y^2 + y^4 + 2x^2 - y^2}$$

4. $f(x, y) = x^2 \qquad \Delta x = \dfrac{2.3 - 2}{3} = 0.1$

i	x_i	y_i
0	2	4
1	2.1	4.4
2	2.2	4.841
3	2.3	5.325

$y(2.3) \approx$ **5.3250**

5.

$$3 = 3 - 3\cos\theta$$

$$3\cos\theta = 0$$

$$\cos\theta = 0$$

$$\theta = \frac{\pi}{2}, \frac{3\pi}{2}$$

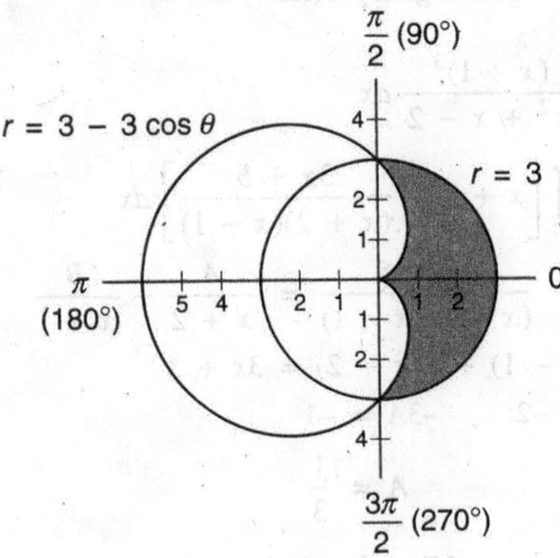

$$A = 2\int_0^{\pi/2}\frac{1}{2}[3^2 - (3 - 3\cos\theta)^2]\,d\theta$$

$$= \int_0^{\pi/2}(18\cos\theta - 9\cos^2\theta)\,d\theta$$

$$= 9\int_0^{\pi/2}\left\{2\cos\theta - \left[\frac{1}{2} + \frac{1}{2}\cos(2\theta)\right]\right\}d\theta$$

$$= 9\left[2\sin\theta - \frac{\theta}{2} - \frac{1}{4}\sin(2\theta)\right]_0^{\pi/2}$$

$$= 9\left[2 - \frac{\pi}{4} - 0 - (0)\right] = \mathbf{\left(18 - \frac{9\pi}{4}\right)\ units^2}$$

6.

$$\vec{f}(t) = \frac{\sin(2t)}{\cos t}\hat{i} + t\sin t\,\hat{j}$$

$$= \frac{2\sin t\cos t}{\cos t}\hat{i} + t\sin t\,\hat{j}$$

$$= 2\sin t\,\hat{i} + t\sin t\,\hat{j}$$

$$\mathbf{\vec{f}'(t) = 2\cos t\,\hat{i} + (t\cos t + \sin t)\hat{j}}$$

Domain: $\left\{t \in \mathbb{R} \mid t \neq \frac{\pi(2n+1)}{2},\ n \in \mathbb{Z}\right\}$

7.

$$L = \lim_{n\to\infty}\frac{\frac{3^{n+1}}{(n+1)!}}{\frac{3^n}{n!}} = \lim_{n\to\infty}\frac{3}{n+1} = 0$$

Since $L < 1$, the series **converges** by the **ratio test.**

8.

$$L = \lim_{n\to\infty}\sqrt[n]{\frac{2^n}{n^n}} = \lim_{n\to\infty}\frac{2}{n} = 0$$

$\sum_{n=1}^{\infty}\frac{2^n}{n^n}$ **converges** by the **root test.**

9. $\sum_{n=1}^{\infty}\left|\frac{(-1)^{n+1}}{n^2}\right| = \sum_{n=1}^{\infty}\frac{1}{n^2}$

which converges (p-series with $p = 2$). This series **converges absolutely,** because $\sum_{n=1}^{\infty}|a_n|$ **converges.**

10. $\lim_{n\to\infty}\frac{\frac{1}{2^n-1}}{\frac{1}{2^n}} = \lim_{n\to\infty}\frac{2^n}{2^n-1} = 1$

$\sum_{n=1}^{\infty}\frac{1}{2^n-1}$ **converges** by the **limit comparison test** with a convergent geometric series.

11. $\sum_{n=1}^{\infty}\left|\frac{(-1)^{n+1}}{2n}\right| = \sum_{n=1}^{\infty}\frac{1}{2n}$

which is a multiple of the harmonic series. This series does not converge absolutely, so **no conclusion can be drawn** about its convergence or divergence at this point.

12. $\sum_{n=1}^{\infty}\frac{3}{\left(\frac{1}{4}\right)^n}$ is geometric with $a = 12$ and $r = 4$.

This series **diverges,** because it is a **geometric series with $r > 1$.**

13. $\lim_{x\to\infty}(x^2-1)e^{-x^2} = \lim_{x\to\infty}\frac{x^2-1}{e^{x^2}}$

$= \lim_{x\to\infty}\frac{2x}{2xe^{x^2}} = \lim_{x\to\infty}\frac{1}{e^{x^2}} = \mathbf{0}$

14. $\lim_{x\to\infty}\left(\frac{x+1}{x}\right)^{7x} = \left[\lim_{x\to\infty}\left(1+\frac{1}{x}\right)^x\right]^7$

$= \boldsymbol{e^7}$

15. $u = \frac{7}{h}$

$\lim_{h\to 0}\left(1+\frac{h}{7}\right)^{7/h} = \lim_{u\to\infty}\left(1+\frac{1}{u}\right)^u = \boldsymbol{e}$

16. $y^2 = x^2 + 4$

$2y\frac{dy}{dx} = 2x$

$\frac{dy}{dx} = \frac{x}{y}$

$\frac{d^2y}{dx^2} = \frac{y - x\frac{dy}{dx}}{y^2}$

$= \frac{y - x\left(\frac{x}{y}\right)}{y^2} = \frac{y^2-x^2}{y^3} = \boldsymbol{\frac{4}{y^3}}$

17. $r = 3 + 2\sin\theta$

$x = (3 + 2\sin\theta)\cos\theta$

$= 3\cos\theta + 2\sin\theta\cos\theta$

$y = (3 + 2\sin\theta)\sin\theta$

$= 3\sin\theta + 2\sin^2\theta$

$\frac{dy}{d\theta} = 3\cos\theta + 4\sin\theta\cos\theta$

$\frac{dx}{d\theta} = -3\sin\theta + 2\sin\theta(-\sin\theta) + 2\cos\theta\cos\theta$

$\frac{dy}{dx} = \frac{3\cos\theta + 4\sin\theta\cos\theta}{-3\sin\theta - 2\sin^2\theta + 2\cos^2\theta}$

When $\theta = 0$, $x = 3$, $y = 0$, and $\frac{dy}{dx} = \frac{3}{2}$

$y - 0 = \frac{3}{2}(x - 3)$

$\boldsymbol{y = \frac{3}{2}x - \frac{9}{2}}$

18. $\int_2^4 \frac{x^2+6x-4}{x^3+x^2-2x}\,dx$

$= \int_2^4 \frac{x^2+6x-4}{x(x+2)(x-1)}\,dx$

$= \int_2^4\left(\frac{A}{x} + \frac{B}{x+2} + \frac{C}{x-1}\right)dx$

$A(x+2)(x-1) + B(x-1)x + C(x+2)x$

$= x^2 + 6x - 4$

$x = 0$: $\quad -2A = -4$

$A = 2$

$x = -2$: $\quad 6B = -12$

$B = -2$

$x = 1$: $\quad 3C = 3$

$C = 1$

$\int_2^4\left(\frac{A}{x} + \frac{B}{x+2} + \frac{C}{x-1}\right)dx$

$= \int_2^4\left(\frac{2}{x} - \frac{2}{x+2} + \frac{1}{x-1}\right)dx$

$= [2\ln x - 2\ln(x+2) + \ln(x-1)]_2^4$

$= 2\ln 4 - 2\ln 6 + \ln 3 - (2\ln 2 - 2\ln 4$

$+ \ln 1)$

$= 2\ln 4 - \ln 4 + 2\ln 4 - \ln 36 + \ln 3$

$= 3\ln 4 - \ln 36 + \ln 3$

$= \ln\left(\frac{64\cdot 3}{36}\right) = \mathbf{\ln\frac{16}{3}}$

19. $\int_2^4 \frac{-4}{(x+1)^2(x-1)}\,dx$

$= \int_2^4 \left(\frac{A}{x+1} + \frac{B}{(x+1)^2} + \frac{C}{x-1}\right) dx$

$A(x+1)(x-1) + B(x-1) + C(x+1)^2 = -4$

$x = 1$: $\quad C = -1$

$x = -1$: $\quad B = 2$

$x = 0$: $\quad -A - B + C = -4$

$\qquad A = 1$

$\int_2^4 \left(\frac{A}{x+1} + \frac{B}{(x+1)^2} + \frac{C}{x-1}\right) dx$

$= \int_2^4 \left(\frac{1}{x+1} + \frac{2}{(x+1)^2} - \frac{1}{x-1}\right) dx$

$= \left[\ln(x+1) - \frac{2}{x+1} - \ln(x-1)\right]_2^4$

$= \ln 5 - \frac{2}{5} - \ln 3 - \left(\ln 3 - \frac{2}{3} - \ln 1\right)$

$= \ln 5 - 2\ln 3 - \frac{2}{5} + \frac{2}{3} = \mathbf{\ln\frac{5}{9} + \frac{4}{15}}$

20. $\int_0^4 \frac{-7}{(x^2+3)(x+2)}\,dx$

$= \int_0^4 \left(\frac{Ax+B}{x^2+3} + \frac{C}{x+2}\right) dx$

$(Ax+B)(x+2) + C(x^2+3) = -7$

$x = -2$: $\quad C = -1$

$x = 0$: $\quad 2B + 3C = -7$

$\qquad B = -2$

$x = 1$: $\quad 3A + 3B + 4C = -7$

$\qquad A = 1$

$\int_0^4 \left(\frac{Ax+B}{x^2+3} + \frac{C}{x+2}\right) dx$

$= \int_0^4 \left(\frac{x-2}{x^2+3} - \frac{1}{x+2}\right) dx$

$= \int_0^4 \left(\frac{x}{x^2+3} - \frac{2}{x^2+3} - \frac{1}{x+2}\right) dx$

$= \left[\frac{1}{2}\ln(x^2+3) - \frac{2}{\sqrt{3}}\arctan\frac{x}{\sqrt{3}}\right.$

$\left. - \ln(x+2)\right]_0^4$

$= \frac{1}{2}\ln 19 - \frac{2}{\sqrt{3}}\arctan\frac{4}{\sqrt{3}} - \ln 6$

$- \left(\frac{1}{2}\ln 3 - 0 - \ln 2\right)$

$= \ln\sqrt{19} - \ln 6 - \ln\sqrt{3} + \ln 2$

$- \frac{2}{\sqrt{3}}\arctan\frac{4}{\sqrt{3}}$

$= \mathbf{\ln\left(\frac{\sqrt{57}}{9}\right) - \frac{2}{\sqrt{3}}\arctan\frac{4}{\sqrt{3}}}$

21. $x = 2\tan\theta \qquad dx = 2\sec^2\theta\,d\theta$

$\sqrt{x^2+4} = 2\sec\theta$

$\int_0^1 \frac{x+2}{\sqrt{x^2+4}}\,dx$

$= \int \frac{(2\tan\theta + 2)2\sec^2\theta\,d\theta}{2\sec\theta}$

$= \int (2\sec\theta\tan\theta + 2\sec\theta)\,d\theta$

$= 2\sec\theta + 2\ln|\sec\theta + \tan\theta|$

$= \left[\sqrt{x^2+4} + 2\ln\left|\frac{\sqrt{x^2+4}}{2} + \frac{x}{2}\right|\right]_0^1$

$= \sqrt{5} + 2\ln\left|\frac{\sqrt{5}}{2} + \frac{1}{2}\right| - (2 + 2\ln|1|)$

$= \mathbf{\sqrt{5} + 2\ln\left(\frac{\sqrt{5}+1}{2}\right) - 2}$

22. $u = \sin(2x) \qquad v = \frac{1}{2}e^{2x}$

$du = 2\cos(2x) \qquad dv = e^{2x}\,dx$

$\int_0^\pi e^{2x}\sin(2x)\,dx$

$= \left[\frac{1}{2}e^{2x}\sin(2x) - \int e^{2x}\cos(2x)\,dx\right]_0^\pi$

$u = \cos(2x) \qquad v = \frac{1}{2}e^{2x}$

$du = -2\sin(2x)\,dx \qquad dv = e^{2x}\,dx$

$\int_0^\pi e^{2x}\sin(2x)\,dx$

$= \left[\frac{1}{2}e^{2x}\sin(2x)\right.$

$\left. - \left(\frac{1}{2}e^{2x}\cos(2x) + \int e^{2x}\sin(2x)\,dx\right)\right]_0^\pi$

$2\int_0^\pi e^{2x}\sin(2x)\,dx$

$= \left[\frac{1}{2}e^{2x}\sin(2x) - \frac{1}{2}e^{2x}\cos(2x)\right]_0^\pi$

$\int_0^\pi e^{2x}\sin(2x)\,dx$

$= \left\{\frac{1}{4}e^{2x}[\sin(2x) - \cos(2x)]\right\}_0^\pi$

$= \frac{1}{4}e^{2\pi}(0-1) - \frac{1}{4}(0-1) = \mathbf{\frac{1}{4}(-e^{2\pi} + 1)}$

23. $\int_0^4 \frac{1}{(x-2)^2}\,dx$

$$= \lim_{b\to 2^-} \int_0^b \frac{1}{(x-2)^2}\,dx + \lim_{a\to 2^+} \int_a^4 \frac{1}{(x-2)^2}\,dx$$

$$= \lim_{b\to 2^-} \left[\frac{-1}{x-2}\right]_0^b + \lim_{a\to 2^+} \left[\frac{-1}{x-2}\right]_a^4$$

$$= \lim_{b\to 2^-} \left[\frac{-1}{b-2} + \frac{1}{-2}\right] + \lim_{a\to 2^+} \left[\frac{-1}{2} + \frac{1}{a-2}\right]$$

$$= \infty - \frac{1}{2} - \frac{1}{2} + \infty = \infty$$

The integral **diverges.**

24. $x = 2 \quad dx = 0.02 \qquad y = 12$

$$y = x^3 + x^2$$
$$dy = (3x^2 + 2x)\,dx$$
$$dy = (16)(0.02) = 0.32$$
$$2.02^3 + 2.02^2 \approx y + dy = \mathbf{12.32}$$

25. $a(t) = -32$

$$v(t) = -32t$$
$$h(t) = -16t^2 + 6$$

The ball hits the ground when $-16t^2 + 6 = 0$

$$t^2 = \frac{3}{8}$$
$$t = \frac{\sqrt{6}}{4}$$

$$d = r \cdot t = (150)\left(\frac{\sqrt{6}}{4}\right) = \mathbf{\frac{75\sqrt{6}}{2}\ ft} \approx \mathbf{91.8559\ ft}$$

PROBLEM SET 136

1. $y = \frac{1}{6}x^3 + \frac{1}{2x}$

$$\frac{dy}{dx} = \frac{1}{2}x^2 - \frac{1}{2x^2}$$

$$\left(\frac{dy}{dx}\right)^2 = \frac{1}{4}x^4 - \frac{1}{2} + \frac{1}{4x^4}$$

$$L_1^3 = \int_1^3 \sqrt{\frac{1}{4}x^4 - \frac{1}{2} + \frac{1}{4x^4} + 1}\;dx$$

$$= \int_1^3 \sqrt{\frac{1}{4}x^4 + \frac{1}{2} + \frac{1}{4x^4}}\;dx$$

$$= \int_1^3 \sqrt{\left(\frac{1}{2}x^2 + \frac{1}{2x^2}\right)^2}\;dx$$

$$= \int_1^3 \left(\frac{1}{2}x^2 + \frac{1}{2x^2}\right) dx$$

$$= \left[\frac{1}{6}x^3 - \frac{1}{2x}\right]_1^3$$

$$= \frac{9}{2} - \frac{1}{6} - \left(\frac{1}{6} - \frac{1}{2}\right) = \mathbf{\frac{14}{3}\ units}$$

2. $f(x) = xe^{-2x}$

$$f'(x) = -2xe^{-2x} + e^{-2x} = e^{-2x}(-2x + 1)$$
$$-2x + 1 = 0$$
$$x = \frac{1}{2}$$

Critical numbers: $x = 0, \frac{1}{2}, 10$

$f(0) = 0$; $f\left(\frac{1}{2}\right) = \frac{1}{2e}$; $f(10) = \frac{10}{e^{20}}$

Maximum: $\mathbf{\frac{1}{2e}}$ **Minimum: 0**

3.

$$F = 400\int_{y=-1}^{y=0} -y(2x)\,dy$$

$$= 400\int_{-1}^{0} -2y\sqrt{1-y^2}\,dy$$

$$= \frac{800}{3}\left[(1-y^2)^{3/2}\right]_{-1}^{0} = \mathbf{\frac{800}{3}\ newtons}$$

4. $x = e^t + 1 \quad y = e^t + e^{-t}$

$$\frac{dy}{dx} = \frac{e^t - e^{-t}}{e^t} = 1 - e^{-2t}$$

When $t = 0$, $x = 2$, $y = 2$, and the slope $= 0$.

$$y - 2 = 0(x - 2)$$
$$\mathbf{y = 2}$$

5. $$\frac{d^2y}{dx^2} = \frac{2e^{-2t}}{e^t} = 2e^{-3t}$$

$$\left.\frac{d^2y}{dx^2}\right|_{t=0} = 2$$

The curve has **positive concavity.**

6. $r = 2 + 3\sin\theta$

$$x = r\cos\theta = 2\cos\theta + 3\sin\theta\cos\theta$$
$$y = r\sin\theta = 2\sin\theta + 3\sin^2\theta$$
$$\frac{dy}{dx} = \frac{2\cos\theta + 6\sin\theta\cos\theta}{-2\sin\theta - 3\sin^2\theta + 3\cos^2\theta}$$

At $\theta = \pi$, $x = -2$, $y = 0$, and the slope $= -\frac{2}{3}$.

$$y - 0 = -\frac{2}{3}(x + 2)$$
$$\mathbf{y = -\frac{2}{3}x - \frac{4}{3}}$$

7. $$f'(x) = \frac{d}{dx}\int_2^x \frac{\sin t}{t}\,dt = \mathbf{\frac{\sin x}{x}}$$

8. $$f'(x) = \frac{d}{dx}\int_3^{\cos x} \sin t^2\,dt$$
$$= \sin(\cos^2 x)\left[\frac{d}{dx}(\cos x)\right]$$
$$= \mathbf{-\sin x \sin(\cos^2 x)}$$

9. $$\sum_{n=1}^{\infty}\left|\frac{(-1)^{n+1}}{n^2+1}\right| = \sum_{n=1}^{\infty}\frac{1}{n^2+1}$$

which converges by comparison ($\frac{1}{n^2+1} < \frac{1}{n^2}$) with a convergent p-series.

The given series **converges absolutely,** because $\sum_{n=1}^{\infty}|a_n|$ **converges.**

10. $$\sum_{n=1}^{\infty}\left|\frac{(-1)^{n+1}}{n!}\right| = \sum_{n=1}^{\infty}\frac{1}{n!}$$

which converges by the ratio test.

$$\lim_{n\to\infty}\frac{\frac{1}{(n+1)!}}{\frac{1}{n!}} = \lim_{n\to\infty}\frac{1}{n+1} = 0$$

The given series **converges absolutely,** because $\sum_{n=1}^{\infty}|a_n|$ **converges.**

11. $$\lim_{n\to\infty}\frac{\frac{4}{3n+1}}{\frac{1}{n}} = \lim_{n\to\infty}\frac{4n}{3n+1} = \frac{4}{3}$$

$\sum_{n=1}^{\infty}\frac{4}{3n+1}$ **diverges** by the **limit comparison test** with the harmonic series.

12. $$\lim_{n\to\infty}\sqrt[n]{\frac{3^n}{n\cdot 2^n}} = \frac{3}{2}$$

$\sum_{n=1}^{\infty}\frac{3^n}{n\cdot 2^n}$ **diverges** by the **root test.**

13. $$\lim_{n\to\infty}\frac{\frac{1}{3^n+3}}{\frac{1}{3^n}} = \lim_{n\to\infty}\frac{3^n}{3^n+3} = 1$$

$\sum_{n=1}^{\infty}\frac{1}{3^n+3}$ **converges** by the **limit comparison test** with a convergent geometric series.

14. $$\lim_{n\to\infty}\frac{3^n}{2^n+3} = \lim_{n\to\infty}\frac{3^n\ln 3}{2^n\ln 2}$$
$$= \frac{\ln 3}{\ln 2}\lim_{n\to\infty}\left(\frac{3}{2}\right)^n = \infty$$

$\sum_{n=1}^{\infty}\frac{3^n}{2^n+3}$ **diverges** by the **divergence theorem.**

15. $x = 2t^2 + 3 \qquad y = -2t + 3$

$$\frac{dx}{dt} = 4t \qquad \frac{dy}{dt} = -2$$

$$L_2^6 = \int_2^6 \sqrt{16t^2 + 4}\,dt = \mathbf{2\int_2^6 \sqrt{4t^2 + 1}\,dt}$$

16. (a) $f(x, y) = \frac{x}{y} \qquad \Delta x = \frac{1.4 - 1}{4} = 0.1$

i	x_i	y_i
0	1	3
1	1.1	$3.0\overline{3}$
2	1.2	$3.\overline{069597}$
3	1.3	3.108690148
4	1.4	3.150508404

$y(1.4) \approx$ **3.1505**

(b) $$\frac{dy}{dx} = \frac{x}{y}$$

$$y\,dy = x\,dx$$

$$\frac{1}{2}y^2 = \frac{1}{2}x^2 + C$$

$$y^2 = x^2 + C$$

$$(9) = (1) + C$$

$$C = 8$$

$$y^2 = x^2 + 8$$

When $x = 1.4$, $y \approx$ **3.1559.**

The solutions differ by only 0.0054.

17.

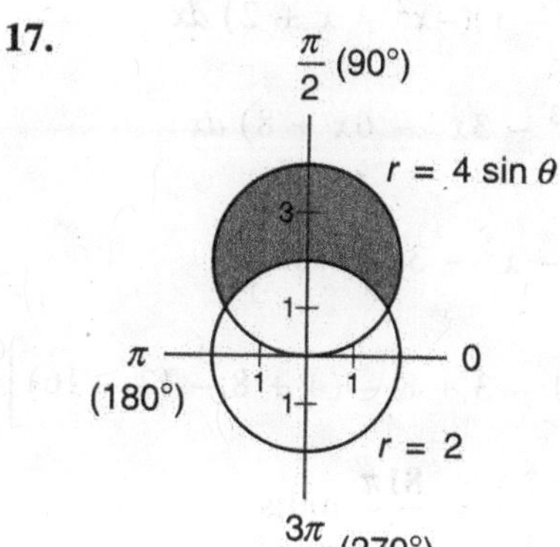

$$4 \sin \theta = 2$$

$$\sin \theta = \frac{1}{2}$$

$$\theta = \frac{\pi}{6}, \frac{5\pi}{6}$$

$$A = 2\int_{\pi/6}^{\pi/2} \frac{1}{2}[(4 \sin \theta)^2 - 2^2]\, d\theta$$

$$= \int_{\pi/6}^{\pi/2} (16 \sin^2 \theta - 4)\, d\theta$$

$$= \int_{\pi/6}^{\pi/2} \left\{16\left[\frac{1}{2} - \frac{1}{2}\cos(2\theta)\right] - 4\right\} d\theta$$

$$= \int_{\pi/6}^{\pi/2} [4 - 8\cos(2\theta)]\, d\theta$$

$$= [4\theta - 4\sin(2\theta)]_{\pi/6}^{\pi/2}$$

$$= 2\pi - 0 - \left(\frac{2\pi}{3} - 2\sqrt{3}\right)$$

$$= \boldsymbol{\left(\frac{4\pi}{3} + 2\sqrt{3}\right)} \textbf{ units}^2$$

18. $$\int_2^{\infty} \frac{1}{(x+2)^2}\, dx = \lim_{b\to\infty} \int_2^b \frac{1}{(x+2)^2}\, dx$$

$$= \lim_{b\to\infty} \left[\frac{-1}{x+2}\right]_2^b$$

$$= \lim_{b\to\infty} \left[\frac{-1}{b+2} + \frac{1}{4}\right]$$

$$= 0 + \frac{1}{4} = \boldsymbol{\frac{1}{4}}$$

19. $$\int_0^{\infty} \frac{1}{(x-1)^3}\, dx$$

$$= \int_0^1 \frac{1}{(x-1)^3}\, dx + \int_1^2 \frac{1}{(x-1)^3}\, dx + \int_2^{\infty} \frac{1}{(x-1)^3}\, dx$$

$$\int_1^2 \frac{1}{(x-1)^3}\, dx = \lim_{b\to 1^+} \int_b^2 \frac{1}{(x-1)^3}\, dx$$

$$= \lim_{b\to 1^+} \left[\frac{-1}{2(x-1)^2}\right]_b^2$$

$$= \lim_{b\to 1^+} \left[\frac{-1}{2} - \left(\frac{-1}{2(b-1)^2}\right)\right]$$

$$= -\frac{1}{2} + \lim_{b\to 1^+} \frac{1}{2(b-1)^2}$$

This limit is undefined. Therefore, the given integral **diverges.**

20. $$\int_4^6 \frac{x^2 - 3x - 1}{x^3 - 2x^2 + x}\, dx = \int_4^6 \frac{x^2 - 3x - 1}{x(x-1)^2}\, dx$$

$$= \int_4^6 \left(\frac{A}{x} + \frac{B}{x-1} + \frac{C}{(x-1)^2}\right) dx$$

$$A(x-1)^2 + B(x-1)x + Cx = x^2 - 3x - 1$$

$x = 1$: $C = -3$

$x = 0$: $A = -1$

$x = 2$: $A + 2B + 2C = -3$

$B = 2$

$$\int_4^6 \left(\frac{A}{x} + \frac{B}{x-1} + \frac{C}{(x-1)^2}\right) dx$$

$$= \int_4^6 \left(-\frac{1}{x} + \frac{2}{x-1} - \frac{3}{(x-1)^2}\right) dx$$

$$= \left[-\ln x + 2\ln(x-1) + \frac{3}{x-1}\right]_4^6$$

$$= -\ln 6 + 2\ln 5 + \frac{3}{5} - (-\ln 4 + 2\ln 3 + 1)$$

$$= -\ln 6 + \ln 25 + \frac{3}{5} + \ln 4 - \ln 9 - 1$$

$$= \boldsymbol{\ln\left(\frac{50}{27}\right) - \frac{2}{5}}$$

21. $$T = \frac{1}{12}\left[27\sqrt{5} + 2\left(\frac{19}{6}\right)^3\sqrt{\left(\frac{19}{6}\right)^2 - 4} + 2\left(\frac{10}{3}\right)^3\sqrt{\left(\frac{10}{3}\right)^2 - 4} + 2\left(\frac{7}{2}\right)^3\sqrt{\left(\frac{7}{2}\right)^2 - 4} + 2\left(\frac{11}{3}\right)^3\sqrt{\left(\frac{11}{3}\right)^2 - 4} + 2\left(\frac{23}{6}\right)^3\sqrt{\left(\frac{23}{6}\right)^2 - 4} + 64\sqrt{12}\right]$$

$$\approx \mathbf{129.4366}$$

22. $x = 2\sec\theta \qquad dx = 2\sec\theta\tan\theta\, d\theta$

$$\theta|_{x=4} = \sec^{-1} 2 = \cos^{-1}\frac{1}{2} = \frac{\pi}{3}$$

$$\theta|_{x=3} = \sec^{-1} 1.5 = \cos^{-1}\frac{2}{3}$$

$$\int_3^4 x^3\sqrt{x^2 - 4}\, dx = \int_{\cos^{-1} 2/3}^{\pi/3} 8\sec^3\theta\sqrt{4(\sec^2\theta - 1)} \cdot (2\sec\theta\tan\theta\, d\theta) = \int_{\cos^{-1} 2/3}^{\pi/3} \mathbf{32\sec^4\theta\tan^2\theta\, d\theta}$$

23.

```
fnInt(X³√(X²-4),
X,3,4)
           129.1042926
fnInt(32tan(X)²*
(1/cos(X))^4,X,c
os⁻¹(2/3),π/3)
           129.1042926
```

The numerical values for the two integrals both equal **129.1043**.

24. (a)

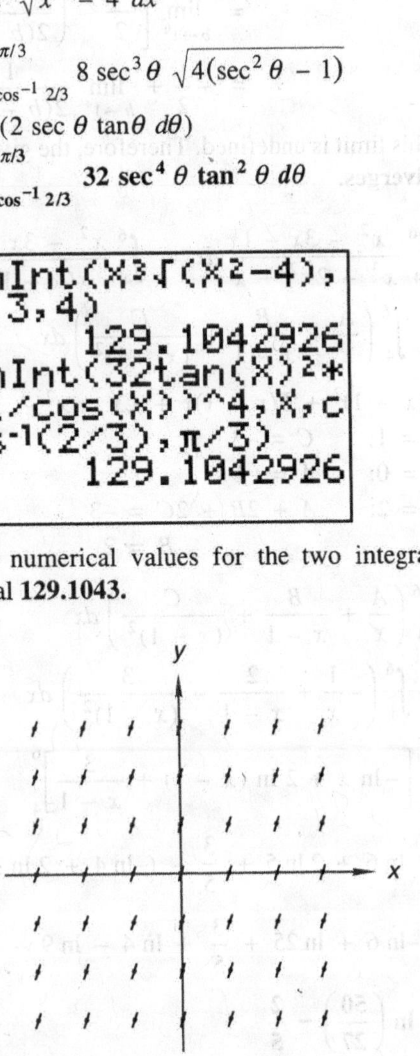

(b) $$\frac{dy}{dx} = 3$$

$$dy = 3\, dx$$

$$\mathbf{y = 3x + C}$$

25.

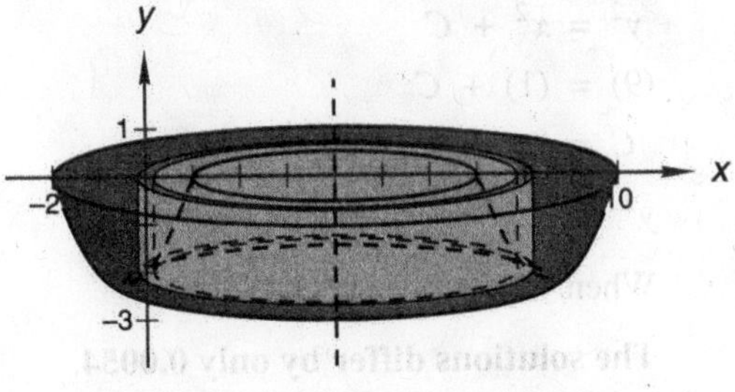

$$V = 2\pi\int_{-2}^{1}(4 - x)(-x^2 - x + 2)\, dx$$

$$= 2\pi\int_{-2}^{1}(x^3 - 3x^2 - 6x + 8)\, dx$$

$$= 2\pi\left[\frac{1}{4}x^4 - x^3 - 3x^2 + 8x\right]_{-2}^{1}$$

$$= 2\pi\left[\frac{1}{4} - 1 - 3 + 8 - (4 + 8 - 12 - 16)\right]$$

$$= 2\pi\left(20 + \frac{1}{4}\right) = \mathbf{\frac{81\pi}{2}\ units^3}$$

PROBLEM SET 137

1. $$R_t = R_0e^{kt}$$

$$4800 = 1200e^{k(1)}$$

$$4 = e^k$$

$$k = \ln 4$$

$$R_{14} = 1200e^{14\ln 4}$$

$$= 1200e^{\ln 4^{14}}$$

$$= 1200(4^{14}) = \mathbf{322{,}122{,}547{,}200\ rabbits}$$

2. **Not necessarily.** For $\lim_{x\to 2} f(x) = 7$, the left- and right-hand limits at $x = 7$ must be equal. This is not guaranteed by the statement $f(2) = 7$, which could be part of a piecewise description of f.

3. After proving that $\frac{d}{dx}\sin x = \cos x$, the proof of $\frac{d}{dx}\cos x = -\sin x$ can be done as follows:

$$\frac{d}{dx}\cos x = \frac{d}{dx}\sin\left(\frac{\pi}{2} - x\right)$$

$$= \cos\left(\frac{\pi}{2} - x\right)(-1)$$

$$= \sin x\,(-1)$$

$$= -\sin x$$

4. Let Y1=3^X and adjust the window settings to $x[1.98, 2.02]$ and $y[8.98, 9.02]$. Performing a TRACE results in the following.

x	y
1.9995745	8.9957935
2	9
2.0004255	9.0042084

If $|x - 2| < 0.0004255$, then $|y - 9| < 0.01$, thus δ = **0.0004255.** Answers may vary.

5. $$\int_{-4}^{4} f(x)\,dx = \lim_{a\to -2^-} \int_{-4}^{a} (x + 4)\,dx + \int_{-2}^{1} x^2\,dx + \lim_{b\to 1^+} \int_{b}^{4} 3\,dx$$
$$= \lim_{a\to -2^-} \left[\frac{1}{2}x^2 + 4x\right]_{-4}^{a} + \left[\frac{1}{3}x^3\right]_{-2}^{1} + \lim_{b\to 1^+} [3x]_b^4$$
$$= (2 - 8 - 8 + 16) + \left(\frac{1}{3} + \frac{8}{3}\right) + (12 - 3)$$
$$= \mathbf{14}$$

6. $$f'(x) = \frac{d}{dx}\int_{3x^2}^{\ln x} \sin(t^2)\,dt$$
$$= \frac{\sin(\ln x)^2}{x} - 6x \sin(3x^2)^2$$
$$= \frac{\sin(\ln x)^2}{x} - 6x \sin(9x^4)$$

7. $$f'(x) = \frac{d}{dx}\int_{x}^{\cos x} \sqrt[3]{t^4 - 4}\,dt$$
$$= -\sin x \sqrt[3]{\cos^4 x - 4} - \sqrt[3]{x^4 - 4}$$
$$f'(2) = -\sin(2)\sqrt[3]{\cos^4(2) - 4} - \sqrt[3]{12}$$
$$\approx \mathbf{-0.8496}$$

8. $$\sum_{n=1}^{\infty}\left|\frac{\sin n}{n}\right| \le \sum_{n=1}^{\infty}\frac{1}{n}$$
At this point **no conclusion can be drawn** by comparison with the harmonic series.

9. $$\sum_{n=1}^{\infty}\left|(-1)^n\frac{n^3}{2^n}\right| = \sum_{n=1}^{\infty}\frac{n^3}{2^n}$$
$$L = \lim_{n\to\infty}\frac{\frac{(n+1)^3}{2^{n+1}}}{\frac{n^3}{2^n}} = \lim_{n\to\infty}\frac{(n+1)^3}{2n^3} = \frac{1}{2}$$
Since $\sum_{n=1}^{\infty}\frac{n^3}{2^n}$ **converges** (by the ratio test), the original series **converges absolutely.**

10. $$\lim_{n\to\infty}\frac{\frac{2n+7}{4n^3 - 4n^2 + 2n - 1}}{\frac{1}{n^2}}$$
$$= \lim_{n\to\infty}\frac{(2n+7)n^2}{4n^3 - 4n^2 + 2n - 1} = \frac{1}{2}$$
$\sum_{n=1}^{\infty}\frac{2n+7}{4n^3 - 4n^2 + 2n - 1}$ **converges** by the **limit comparison test** with a convergent p-series.

11. $$L = \lim_{n\to\infty}\frac{\frac{3^{n+1}}{(n+1)!}}{\frac{3^n}{n!}} = \lim_{n\to\infty}\frac{3}{n+1} = 0$$
$\sum_{n=1}^{\infty}\frac{3^n}{n!}$ **converges by the ratio test.**

12. $$L = \lim_{n\to\infty}\sqrt[n]{\frac{2^n + 3}{n^n}} = \lim_{n\to\infty}\frac{2}{n} = 0$$
$\sum_{n\to 1}^{\infty}\frac{2^n + 3}{n^n}$ **converges** by the **root test.**

13. $$\sum_{n=1}^{\infty}\frac{2^n + 3}{3^n} = \sum_{n=1}^{\infty}\left(\frac{2}{3}\right)^n + \sum_{n=1}^{\infty}\frac{3}{3^n}$$
Both of these series are geometric. The first has $a = \frac{2}{3}$ and $r = \frac{2}{3}$. The second has $a = 1$ and $r = \frac{1}{3}$.
$$S = \frac{\frac{2}{3}}{1 - \frac{2}{3}} + \frac{1}{1 - \frac{1}{3}} = 2 + \frac{3}{2}$$
The original series **converges to** $\frac{7}{2}$**,** because it is the **sum of two convergent geometric series.**

14. For $\sum_{n=3}^{\infty}\frac{4}{n^2}$,
$$S_6 = \frac{4}{9} + \frac{4}{16} + \frac{4}{25} + \frac{4}{36} + \frac{4}{49} + \frac{4}{64}$$
$$= \frac{782{,}996}{705{,}600} = \mathbf{\frac{195{,}749}{176{,}400}}$$

15.

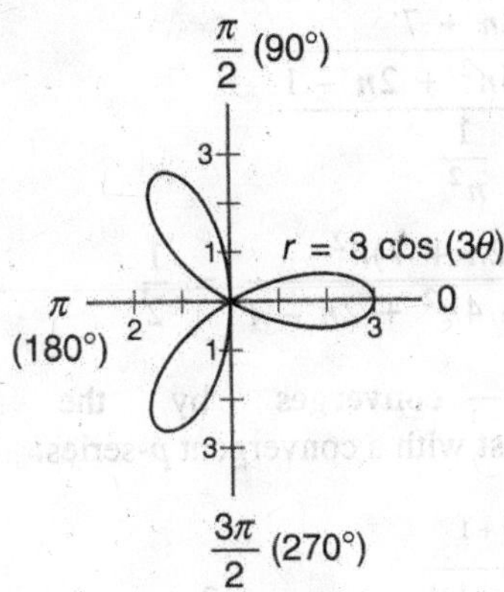

16.

$$r = 3\cos(3\theta)$$
$$x = r\cos\theta = 3\cos(3\theta)\cos\theta$$
$$y = r\sin\theta = 3\cos(3\theta)\sin\theta$$
$$\frac{dy}{dx} = \frac{-3\sin(3\theta)\sin\theta + \cos(3\theta)\cos\theta}{-3\sin(3\theta)\cos\theta - \cos(3\theta)\sin\theta}$$

At $\theta = \frac{\pi}{6}$, $x = 0$, $y = 0$, and the slope $= \frac{\sqrt{3}}{3}$.

$$y = \frac{\sqrt{3}}{3}x$$

17. The slope is not defined at the origin, which eliminates $y = (\frac{1}{2})^x$. With the exception of the origin, all points along the x-axis have identical slope, which eliminates $y = \frac{1}{x^2}$. The graph of $x^2 + 3y^2 = 1$ is an ellipse, while the graph of $x^2 - 2y^2 = 1$ is a hyperbola. By inspection one can see that the slope field represents a family of ellipses.

The correct choice is **A.**

18.

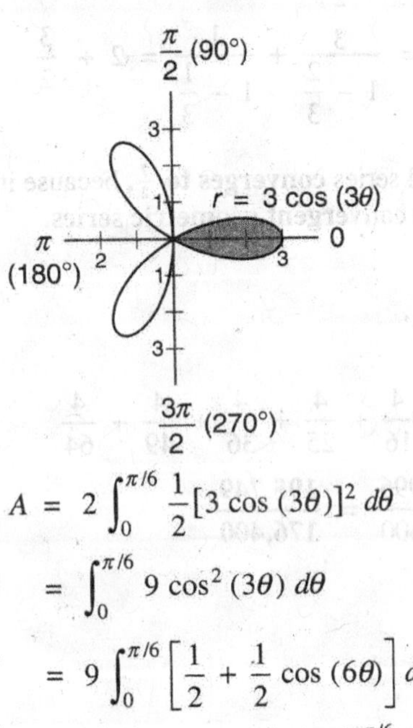

$$A = 2\int_0^{\pi/6} \frac{1}{2}[3\cos(3\theta)]^2\, d\theta$$
$$= \int_0^{\pi/6} 9\cos^2(3\theta)\, d\theta$$
$$= 9\int_0^{\pi/6}\left[\frac{1}{2} + \frac{1}{2}\cos(6\theta)\right] d\theta$$
$$= 9\left[\frac{1}{2}\theta + \frac{1}{12}\sin(6\theta)\right]_0^{\pi/6}$$
$$= 9\left[\frac{\pi}{12} + 0 - (0 + 0)\right] = \mathbf{\frac{3\pi}{4}\ units^2}$$

19.

$\frac{\pi}{2}$ (90°)

$r = 2 - 2\sin\theta$

π (180°) 0

$\frac{3\pi}{2}$ (270°)

20. $f(x, y) = xy^2$ $\qquad \Delta x = \frac{2.2 - 2}{4} = 0.05$

i	x_i	y_i
0	2	−2
1	2.05	−1.6
2	2.1	−1.3376
3	2.15	−1.149736755
4	2.2	−1.007633085

$y(2.2) \approx$ **−1.0076**

21.

$$\int_1^{\infty} \frac{2}{(x+2)^2}\, dx = \lim_{a\to\infty}\int_1^a \frac{2}{(x+2)^2}\, dx$$
$$= \lim_{a\to\infty}\left[-\frac{2}{x+2}\right]_1^a$$
$$= \lim_{a\to\infty}\left(-\frac{2}{a+2} + \frac{2}{3}\right)$$
$$= \mathbf{\frac{2}{3}}$$

22.

$$\int_{-4}^{2} \frac{2}{(x+2)^2}\, dx$$
$$= \int_{-4}^{-2} \frac{2}{(x+2)^2}\, dx + \int_{-2}^{2} \frac{2}{(x+2)^2}\, dx$$
$$\int_{-4}^{-2} \frac{2}{(x+2)^2}\, dx$$
$$= \lim_{b\to -2^-}\int_{-4}^{b} \frac{2}{(x+2)^2}\, dx$$
$$= \lim_{b\to -2^-}\left[\frac{-2}{(x+2)}\right]_{-4}^{b}$$
$$= \lim_{b\to -2^-}\left[\frac{-2}{(b+2)} - (1)\right]$$

This limit is undefined. Therefore, the original integral **diverges.**

23.
$$y = x^{e^{2x^2}}$$
$$\ln y = e^{2x^2} \ln x$$
$$\frac{1}{y}\frac{dy}{dx} = e^{2x^2}\left(\frac{1}{x}\right) + (\ln x)e^{2x^2}(4x)$$
$$\frac{dy}{dx} = x^{e^{2x^2}}\left[\frac{e^{2x^2}}{x} + 4x(\ln x)e^{2x^2}\right]$$
$$\boldsymbol{\frac{dy}{dx} = e^{2x^2}x^{e^{2x^2}}\left(\frac{1}{x} + 4x \ln x\right)}$$

24.
$$\lim_{x\to 1^-} f(x) = f(1)$$
$$\lim_{x\to 1^-} (e^{2x} + 4) = a(1)^2 + b$$
$$e^2 + 4 = a + b$$
$$b = e^2 + 4 - a$$
$$\lim_{x\to 1^-} f'(x) = f'(1)$$
$$\lim_{x\to 1^-} (2e^{2x}) = 2a(1)$$
$$2e^2 = 2a$$
$$\boldsymbol{e^2 = a}$$
$$b = e^2 + 4 - e^2$$
$$\boldsymbol{b = 4}$$

25.
$$y = 18x^3 + 15x^2 - 16x - 5$$
$$y' = 54x^2 + 30x - 16$$
$$0 = 27x^2 + 15x - 8$$
$$0 = (9x + 8)(3x - 1)$$
$$x = -\frac{8}{9}, \frac{1}{3}$$
$$y'' = 108x + 30$$
$$0 = 108x + 30$$
$$x = -\frac{5}{18}$$
$$f\left(-\frac{8}{9}\right) = \frac{683}{81} \qquad f\left(\frac{1}{3}\right) = -8$$
$$f\left(-\frac{5}{18}\right) = \frac{70}{324} = \frac{35}{162}$$

Maximum: $\boldsymbol{\left(-\frac{8}{9}, \frac{683}{81}\right)}$

Minimum: $\boldsymbol{\left(\frac{1}{3}, -8\right)}$

Inflection point: $\boldsymbol{\left(-\frac{5}{18}, \frac{35}{162}\right)}$

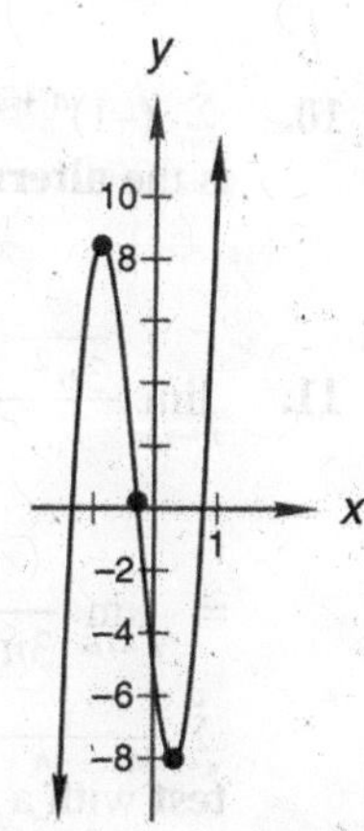

PROBLEM SET 138

1. (a) $\sum_{n=1}^{\infty} (-1)^{n+1} \frac{1}{2^n} = \sum_{n=1}^{\infty} (-1)\left(-\frac{1}{2}\right)^n$

This series is geometric with $a = \frac{1}{2}$ and $r = -\frac{1}{2}$. Since $|r| < 1$, the series converges.

(b) $S = \dfrac{\frac{1}{2}}{1 + \frac{1}{2}} = \boldsymbol{\frac{1}{3}}$

(c) $S_4 = \frac{1}{2} - \frac{1}{4} + \frac{1}{8} - \frac{1}{16} = \frac{5}{16}$

$$\text{error} = \frac{1}{3} - \frac{5}{16} = \boldsymbol{\frac{1}{48}}$$

(d) $a_5 = \left(\frac{1}{2}\right)^5 = \frac{1}{32}$

The error in S_4 is smaller than a_5.

2. $\frac{dV}{dt} = 110 \text{ ft}^3/\text{min} \qquad r = 4$
$$V = \frac{4}{3}\pi r^3$$
$$\frac{dV}{dt} = 4\pi r^2 \frac{dr}{dt}$$
$$(110) = 4\pi(4)^2 \frac{dr}{dt}$$
$$\frac{dr}{dt} = \frac{110}{64\pi} = \boldsymbol{\frac{55}{32\pi}\frac{\text{ft}}{\text{min}}}$$

3. The trapezoidal rule can be used to approximate the area.
$$\text{Area} \approx T = \frac{80}{16}(50 + 104 + 136 + 140 + 130 + 106 + 68 + 60 + 28)$$
$$= \boldsymbol{4110 \text{ ft}^2}$$

4.

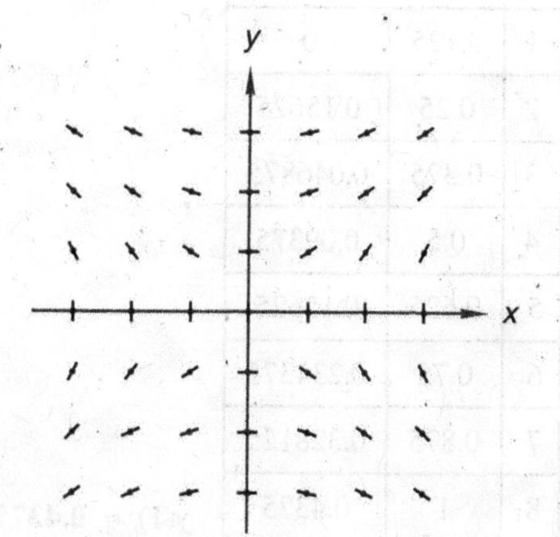

5.

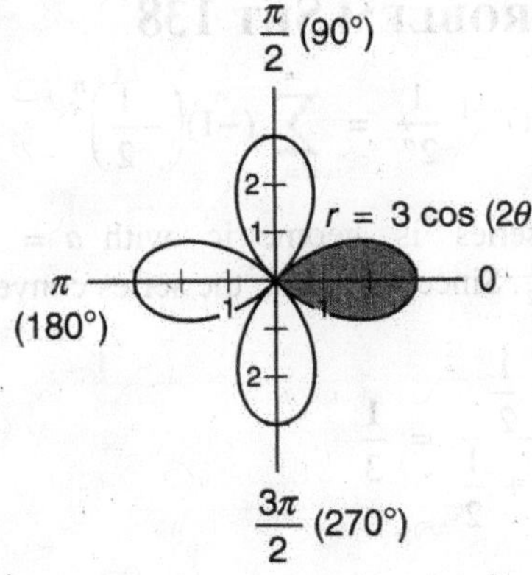

$$A = 2\int_0^{\pi/4} \frac{1}{2}[3\cos(2\theta)]^2\, d\theta$$

$$= \int_0^{\pi/4} 9\cos^2(2\theta)\, d\theta$$

$$= 9\int_0^{\pi/4}\left[\frac{1}{2} + \frac{1}{2}\cos(4\theta)\right] d\theta$$

$$= 9\left[\frac{1}{2}\theta + \frac{1}{8}\sin(4\theta)\right]_0^{\pi/4} = \mathbf{\frac{9\pi}{8}\ units^2}$$

6. (a) $f(x, y) = x$ $\qquad \Delta x = \frac{1-0}{4} = 0.25$

i	x_i	y_i
0	0	0
1	0.25	0
2	0.5	0.0625
3	0.75	0.1875
4	1	0.375

$y(1) \approx \mathbf{0.375}$

(b) $f(x, y) = x$ $\qquad \Delta x = \frac{1-0}{8} = 0.125$

i	x_i	y_i
0	0	0
1	0.125	0
2	0.25	0.15625
3	0.375	0.046875
4	0.5	0.09375
5	0.625	0.15625
6	0.75	0.234375
7	0.875	0.328125
8	1	0.4375

$y(1) \approx \mathbf{0.4375}$

(c) $\frac{dy}{dx} = x$

$dy = x\, dx$

$y = \frac{1}{2}x^2 + C$

At (0, 0), $C = 0$

$\mathbf{y = \frac{1}{2}x^2}$

At $x = 1$, $y = \frac{1}{2} = \mathbf{0.5}$, which means that the part (a) solution is in error by **0.125** and the part (b) solution is in error by **0.0625.**

7. $r = 3\cos(2\theta)$

$x = r\cos\theta = 3\cos(2\theta)\cos\theta$

$y = r\sin\theta = 3\cos(2\theta)\sin\theta$

$$\frac{dy}{dx} = \frac{-6\sin(2\theta)\sin\theta + 3\cos(2\theta)\cos\theta}{-6\sin(2\theta)\cos\theta - 3\cos(2\theta)\sin\theta}$$

When $\theta = 2.5$, $x \approx -0.6818$, $y \approx 0.5093$, and the slope ≈ -0.5395.

$y - 0.5093 \approx -0.5395(x + 0.6818)$

$\mathbf{y \approx -0.5395x + 0.1415}$

8. $$f'(x) = \frac{d}{dx}\int_2^{3x^4} e^{t^2}\, dt$$

$$= 12x^3 e^{(3x^4)^2} = \mathbf{12x^3 e^{9x^8}}$$

9. $$\int_{-1}^{1} f(x)\, dx = \int_{-1}^{0} x\, dx + \lim_{b\to 0+}\int_b^1 \sin x\, dx$$

$$= \left[\frac{1}{2}x^2\right]_{-1}^{0} + \lim_{b\to 0+}[-\cos x]_b^1$$

$$= -\frac{1}{2} + \lim_{b\to 0+}[-\cos 1 + \cos b]$$

$$= -\frac{1}{2} - \cos 1 + 1$$

$$= \mathbf{\frac{1}{2} - \cos 1}$$

10. $\sum_{n=1}^{\infty} (-1)^{n+1}\frac{1}{n}$ **converges conditionally,** because it is the **alternating harmonic series.**

11. $$\lim_{n\to\infty} \frac{\frac{1}{3n^2 - 4n + 5}}{\frac{1}{n^2}}$$

$$= \lim_{n\to\infty} \frac{n^2}{3n^2 - 4n + 5} = \frac{1}{3}$$

$\sum_{n=1}^{\infty} \frac{1}{3n^2 - 4n + 5}$ **converges** by the **limit comparison test** with a convergent p-series.

12. $\displaystyle\sum_{n=1}^{\infty}\left|(-1)^{n+1}\frac{2^n}{n^3+2}\right| = \sum_{n=1}^{\infty}\frac{2^n}{n^3+2}$

$$\lim_{n\to\infty}\frac{2^n}{n^3+2} = \infty$$

This series **diverges** by the **divergence theorem** because its nth term does not approach 0.

13. $\displaystyle L = \lim_{n\to\infty}\sqrt[n]{\frac{3^n}{n^2 2^n}} = \frac{3}{2}$

$\sum_{n=1}^{\infty}\frac{3^n}{n^2 2^n}$ **diverges** because its **root test L-value is $\frac{3}{2}$.**

14. $$\lim_{n\to\infty}\frac{\dfrac{1}{(3n+2)^{1/3}}}{\dfrac{1}{n^{1/3}}} = \lim_{n\to\infty}\frac{n^{1/3}}{(3n+2)^{1/3}} = \frac{1}{\sqrt[3]{3}}$$

$\sum_{n=1}^{\infty}\frac{1}{\sqrt[3]{3n+2}}$ **diverges** by the **limit comparison test** with a divergent p-series.

15. $\sum_{n=2}^{\infty}(-1)^n\frac{2}{5^n}$ is a geometric series with $a = \frac{2}{25}$ and $r = -\frac{1}{5}$.

$$S = \frac{\frac{2}{25}}{1+\frac{1}{5}} = \frac{2}{25}\left(\frac{5}{6}\right) = \frac{1}{15}$$

This series **converges to $\frac{1}{15}$**, because it is a **geometric series with $|r| < 1$.**

16. $u = \sec x \qquad v = \tan x$

$du = \sec x\tan x\,dx \qquad dv = \sec^2 x\,dx$

$$\int \sec^3 x\,dx$$
$$= \sec x\tan x - \int \tan^2 x\sec x\,dx$$
$$= \sec x\tan x - \int(\sec^2 x - 1)\sec x\,dx$$
$$= \sec x\tan x - \int\sec^3 x\,dx + \int\sec x\,dx$$
$$2\int\sec^3 x\,dx$$
$$= \sec x\tan x + \ln|\sec x + \tan x| + C$$
$$\int\sec^3 x\,dx$$
$$= \mathbf{\frac{1}{2}\sec x\tan x + \frac{1}{2}\ln|\sec x + \tan x| + C}$$

17. $$\int\frac{x^2}{x^2+1}\,dx = \int\left(1 - \frac{1}{x^2+1}\right)dx$$
$$= \mathbf{x - \arctan x + C}$$

18. $$\int_0^4\frac{1}{x^2-4}\,dx$$
$$= \int_0^2\frac{1}{x^2-4}\,dx + \int_2^4\frac{1}{x^2-4}\,dx$$
$$\int_0^2\frac{1}{x^2-4}\,dx = \lim_{b\to 2^-}\int_0^b\frac{1}{x^2-4}\,dx$$
$$= \lim_{b\to 2^-}\int_0^b\left(\frac{-\frac{1}{4}}{x+2} + \frac{\frac{1}{4}}{x-2}\right)dx$$
$$= \lim_{b\to 2^-}\left[\frac{-1}{4}\ln|x+2| + \frac{1}{4}\ln|x-2|\right]_0^b$$
$$= \lim_{b\to 2^-}\left(\frac{-1}{4}\ln|b+2| + \frac{1}{4}\ln|b-2|\right)$$
$$- \left(-\frac{1}{4}\ln 2 + \frac{1}{4}\ln|-2|\right)$$

This limit is undefined. Therefore the original integral **diverges.**

19. $$\int_0^1\frac{x+1}{x^2+1}\,dx = \int_0^1\left(\frac{x}{x^2+1} + \frac{1}{x^2+1}\right)dx$$
$$= \left[\frac{1}{2}\ln(x^2+1) + \arctan x\right]_0^1$$
$$= \frac{1}{2}\ln 2 + \frac{\pi}{4} - (0+0)$$
$$= \mathbf{\ln\sqrt{2} + \frac{\pi}{4} \approx 1.1320}$$

20. $$\lim_{h\to 0}\frac{\ln(x+h) - \ln x}{h}$$
$$= \lim_{h\to 0}\frac{x}{x}\frac{1}{h}\left[\ln\left(\frac{x+h}{x}\right)\right]$$
$$= \frac{1}{x}\lim_{h\to 0}\frac{x}{h}\left[\ln\left(1+\frac{h}{x}\right)\right]$$
$$= \frac{1}{x}\lim_{h\to 0}\ln\left(1+\frac{h}{x}\right)^{x/h}$$
$$= \frac{1}{x}\ln e = \frac{1}{x}$$

21. $$|y - 13| < \varepsilon$$
$$|5x + 3 - 13| < \varepsilon$$
$$|5x - 10| < \varepsilon$$
$$|x - 2| < \frac{\varepsilon}{5}$$
$$\delta = \frac{\varepsilon}{5}$$

Any choice for δ that is less than $\frac{\varepsilon}{5}$ would also be acceptable. The largest choice that is less than $\frac{\varepsilon}{5}$ is $\frac{\varepsilon}{6}$.

The correct choice is **D.**

22.

$$x^2 - y^2 = 10$$

$$2x - 2y\frac{dy}{dx} = 0$$

$$\frac{dy}{dx} = \frac{x}{y}$$

$$\frac{d^2y}{dx^2} = \frac{y - x\frac{dy}{dx}}{y^2} = \frac{y - x\left(\frac{x}{y}\right)}{y^2} = \frac{y^2 - x^2}{y^3} = -\frac{\mathbf{10}}{\mathbf{y^3}}$$

23. Since $F(x)$ is an antiderivative of $f(x)$,

$$\frac{d}{dx}F(x) = F'(x) = f(x)$$

Also, $\frac{d}{dx}\int_a^x f(t)\,dt = f(x)$ and $\int_a^x f(t)\,dt = F(x) - F(a)$.

Thus, the correct choice is **D.**

24.

n	$f^{(n)}(x)$	$f^{(n)}(0)$
0	$\sin x$	0
1	$\cos x$	1
2	$-\sin x$	0
3	$-\cos x$	-1
4	$\sin x$	0
5	$\cos x$	1
6	$-\sin x$	0
⋮	⋮	⋮

$$\sin x = x - \frac{x^3}{3!} + \frac{x^5}{5!} - \frac{x^7}{7!} + \cdots = \boldsymbol{\sum_{n=1}^{\infty}(-1)^{n+1}\frac{x^{(2n-1)}}{(2n-1)!}}$$

25.

n	$f^{(n)}(x)$	$f^{(n)}(0)$
0	$(1 + x)^{-1}$	1
1	$-(1 + x)^{-2}$	-1
2	$2(1 + x)^{-3}$	2
3	$-6(1 + x)^{-4}$	-6
4	$24(1 + x)^{-5}$	24
⋮	⋮	⋮

$$\frac{1}{1+x} = 1 - x + \frac{2x^2}{2!} - \frac{6x^3}{3!} + \frac{24x^4}{4!} + \cdots = 1 - x + x^2 - x^3 + x^4 + \cdots = \boldsymbol{\sum_{n=0}^{\infty}(-1)^n x^n}$$

PROBLEM SET 139

1. (a) $\frac{1}{n^2} \geq \frac{1}{(n+1)^2}$ and $\lim_{n\to\infty}\frac{1}{n^2} = 0$, so $\sum_{n=1}^{\infty}(-1)^{n+1}\frac{1}{n^2}$ **meets the conditions of Leibniz's theorem and converges.**

(b) $S_4 = 1 - \frac{1}{4} + \frac{1}{9} - \frac{1}{16} = \mathbf{\frac{115}{144}}$

(c) This approximation is too small, but by no more than $a_5 = \frac{1}{25}$. Therefore, the actual sum of the series is **within 0.04** of S_4.

2. (a)

n	$f^{(n)}(x)$	$f^{(n)}(0)$
0	$\cos x$	1
1	$-\sin x$	0
2	$-\cos x$	-1
3	$\sin x$	0
4	$\cos x$	1
5	$-\sin x$	0
6	$-\cos x$	-1
⋮	⋮	⋮

$$\cos x = 1 - \frac{x^2}{2!} + \frac{x^4}{4!} - \frac{x^6}{6!} + \cdots = \boldsymbol{\sum_{n=0}^{\infty}(-1)^n\frac{x^{2n}}{(2n)!}}$$

(b) To approximate cos (1), the value of x must equal 1. For accuracy to 6 decimal places, the error must be less than 5×10^{-7}.

Since $a_5 = -\frac{1}{10!} = -2.756 \times 10^{-7}$, S_5 will produce the desired approximation. (Note that the index begins at zero.)

$$S_5 = 1 - \frac{1}{2} + \frac{1}{4!} - \frac{1}{6!} + \frac{1}{8!}$$
$$= \mathbf{0.5403025794}$$

3. $a(t) = 2t - 1$

$v(t) = t^2 - t + C$

$v(2) = 4 - 2 + C = -4$

$C = -6$

$v(t) = t^2 - t - 6$

Average velocity

$$= \frac{1}{4}\int_0^4 (t^2 - t - 6)\,dt$$
$$= \frac{1}{4}\left[\frac{1}{3}t^3 - \frac{1}{2}t^2 - 6t\right]_0^4$$
$$= -\frac{8}{3}\,\frac{\textbf{linear units}}{\textbf{time unit}}$$

Average speed

$$= \frac{1}{4}\int_0^4 |t^2 - t - 6|\,dt$$
$$= -\frac{1}{4}\int_0^3 (t^2 - t - 6)\,dt + \frac{1}{4}\int_3^4 (t^2 - t - 6)\,dt$$
$$= -\frac{1}{4}\left[\frac{1}{3}t^3 - \frac{1}{2}t^2 - 6t\right]_0^3 + \frac{1}{4}\left[\frac{1}{3}t^3 - \frac{1}{2}t^2 - 6t\right]_3^4$$
$$= -\frac{1}{4}\left(9 - \frac{9}{2} - 18\right) + \frac{1}{4}\left(\frac{64}{3} - 8 - 24 - 9 + \frac{9}{2} + 18\right)$$
$$= \frac{49}{12}\,\frac{\textbf{linear units}}{\textbf{time unit}}$$

4.

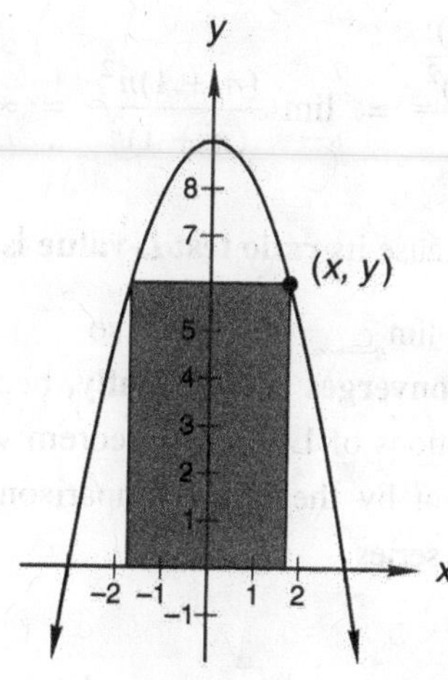

$$A = 2xy$$
$$= 2x(-x^2 + 9)$$
$$= -2x^3 + 18x$$
$$A' = -6x^2 + 18$$
$$0 = -6x^2 + 18$$
$$x^2 = 3$$
$$x = \sqrt{3}$$
$$A = -2(3\sqrt{3}) + 18\sqrt{3} = \mathbf{12\sqrt{3}\ units^2}$$

5. $$f'(x) = \frac{d}{dx}\int_{-\tan x}^{4} t^2\sqrt{1 + t^2}\,dt$$
$$= -\tan^2 x\sqrt{1 + \tan^2 x}\,(-\sec^2 x)$$
$$= \mathbf{\tan^2 x \sec^3 x}$$

6. $$\int_{-2}^{2} f(x)\,dx$$
$$= \lim_{a\to 0^-}\int_{-2}^{a} (x + 1)\,dx + \int_0^2 \cos(\pi x)\,dx$$
$$= \lim_{a\to 0^-}\left[\frac{1}{2}x^2 + x\right]_{-2}^{a} + \frac{1}{\pi}[\sin(\pi x)]_0^2$$
$$= \lim_{a\to 0^-}\left(\frac{1}{2}a^2 + a\right) - (0) + \frac{1}{\pi}(0 - 0)$$
$$= \mathbf{0}$$

7. $\frac{1}{n^{3/2}} \ge \frac{1}{(n+1)^{3/2}}$ and $\lim_{n\to\infty} \frac{1}{n^{3/2}} = 0$, so $\sum_{n=1}^{\infty} (-1)^{n+1}\frac{1}{n^{3/2}}$ **converges absolutely,** because it meets the conditions of Leibniz's theorem and $\sum_{n=1}^{\infty} |a_n|$ is a convergent p-series.

8. $\frac{2}{\sqrt{n}} \ge \frac{2}{\sqrt{n+1}}$ and $\lim_{n\to\infty} \frac{2}{\sqrt{n}} = 0$, so $\sum_{n=1}^{\infty} (-1)^{n+1}\frac{2}{\sqrt{n}}$ **converges conditionally,** because it meets the condition of Leibniz's theorem while $\sum_{n=1}^{\infty} \left|(-1)^{n+1}\frac{2}{\sqrt{n}}\right|$ is a divergent p-series.

9. $L = \lim_{n\to\infty} \dfrac{\dfrac{(n+1)!}{(n+1)^2}}{\dfrac{n!}{n^2}} = \lim_{n\to\infty} \dfrac{(n+1)n^2}{(n+1)^2} = \infty$

$\sum_{n=1}^{\infty} \frac{n!}{n^2}$ **diverges** because its **ratio test** ***L*-value is ∞.**

10. $\frac{2}{n+2} \geq \frac{2}{n+3}$ and $\lim_{n\to\infty} \frac{2}{n+2} = 0$, so $\sum_{n=1}^{\infty} (-1)^{n+1} \frac{2}{n+2}$ **converges conditionally,** because it meets the conditions of Leibniz's theorem while $\sum_{n=1}^{\infty} |a_n|$ is divergent by the limit comparison test with the harmonic series.

11. $\lim_{n\to\infty} \dfrac{\dfrac{1}{\sqrt{3n-2}}}{\dfrac{1}{\sqrt{n}}} = \lim_{n\to\infty} \dfrac{\sqrt{n}}{\sqrt{3n-2}} = \dfrac{1}{\sqrt{3}}$

$\sum_{n=1}^{\infty} \frac{1}{\sqrt{3n-2}}$ **diverges** by the **limit comparison test** with a divergent *p*-series.

12. $\dfrac{d}{dx}\dfrac{x}{e^{x^2}} = \dfrac{e^{x^2} - x(2x)e^{x^2}}{e^{2x^2}}$

$= \dfrac{e^{x^2}(1-2x^2)}{e^{2x^2}} = e^{-x^2}(1-2x^2)$

This is negative for all $x > 1$, so the series is decreasing.

Applying the integral test:

$\int_1^{\infty} \dfrac{x}{e^{x^2}}\,dx = \lim_{b\to\infty} -\dfrac{1}{2}\int_1^b e^{-x^2}(-2x)\,dx$

$= \lim_{b\to\infty} -\dfrac{1}{2}\left[e^{-x^2}\right]_1^b$

$= \lim_{b\to\infty} -\dfrac{1}{2}\left(e^{-b^2} - e^{-1}\right)$

$= -\dfrac{1}{2}(0 - e^{-1}) = \dfrac{1}{2e}$

Since the integral converges, the series also **converges** by the **integral test.**

13.

14. $A = 2\int_0^{\pi} \frac{1}{2}(2 + 2\cos\theta)^2\,d\theta - \pi(2)^2$

$= \int_0^{\pi} (4 + 8\cos\theta + 4\cos^2\theta)\,d\theta - 4\pi$

$= \int_0^{\pi} \left\{4 + 8\cos\theta + 4\left[\frac{1}{2} + \frac{1}{2}\cos(2\theta)\right]\right\} d\theta - 4\pi$

$= \int_0^{\pi} [6 + 8\cos\theta + 2\cos(2\theta)]\,d\theta - 4\pi$

$= [6\theta + 8\sin\theta + \sin(2\theta)]_0^{\pi} - 4\pi$

$= 6\pi + 0 + 0 - (0) - 4\pi =$ $\mathbf{2\pi}$ **units²**

15. $\lim_{x\to\infty} (1+x)^{1/x} = \infty^0$

$\lim_{x\to\infty} \dfrac{\ln(1+x)}{x} = \lim_{x\to\infty} \dfrac{1}{1+x} = 0$

So the original limit is $e^0 =$ **1.**

16. $\lim_{h\to\infty}\left(1 + \dfrac{1}{h}\right)^h = \boldsymbol{e}$

17. $\int_{\pi/4}^{\pi/2} \cot x\,dx = \int_{\pi/4}^{\pi/2} \dfrac{\cos x}{\sin x}\,dx$

$= [\ln|\sin x|]_{\pi/4}^{\pi/2}$

$= \ln(1) - \ln\left(\dfrac{\sqrt{2}}{2}\right)$

$= -\ln\left(\dfrac{\sqrt{2}}{2}\right) = \mathbf{\ln\sqrt{2}}$

18. $\int_2^{\infty} \dfrac{1}{(x-1)^3}\,dx = \lim_{b\to\infty}\left[\dfrac{-1}{2(x-1)^2}\right]_2^b$

$= \lim_{b\to\infty}\left[\dfrac{-1}{2(b-1)^2}\right] + \dfrac{1}{2}$

$= \mathbf{\dfrac{1}{2}}$

19. $\int \dfrac{2x^2 - 5x + 2}{x(x-1)^2}\,dx$

$= \int \left(\dfrac{A}{x} + \dfrac{B}{x-1} + \dfrac{C}{(x-1)^2}\right) dx$

$A(x-1)^2 + B(x-1)x + Cx = 2x^2 - 5x + 2$

$x = 0$: $A = 2$

$x = 1$: $C = -1$

$x = 2$: $A + 2B + 2C = 0$

$B = 0$

$\int \left(\dfrac{A}{x} + \dfrac{B}{x-1} + \dfrac{C}{(x-1)^2}\right) dx$

$= \int \left(\dfrac{2}{x} - \dfrac{1}{(x-1)^2}\right) dx$

$= \mathbf{2\ln|x| + \dfrac{1}{x-1} + C}$

20. $\int (e^x + \cos x)(e^x + \sin x)^{-1/2}\, dx$

$= \mathbf{2\sqrt{e^x + \sin x} + C}$

21.
$$y = \sin(xy)$$
$$\frac{dy}{dx} = \cos(xy)\left(x\frac{dy}{dx} + y\right)$$
$$\frac{dy}{dx} = x\cos(xy)\frac{dy}{dx} + y\cos(xy)$$
$$y\cos(xy) = \frac{dy}{dx}[1 - x\cos(xy)]$$
$$\frac{dy}{dx} = \frac{y\cos(xy)}{1 - x\cos(xy)}$$
$$\frac{dy}{dx} = \mathbf{\frac{y}{\sec(xy) - x}}$$

PROBLEM SET 140

1.
$$x = v_0 t\cos\theta$$
$$10{,}000 = 800t\cos\theta$$
$$t = \frac{12.5}{\cos\theta}$$
$$y = -16t^2 + v_0 t\sin\theta$$
$$0 = -16\left(\frac{12.5}{\cos\theta}\right)^2 + 800\left(\frac{12.5}{\cos\theta}\right)\sin\theta$$
$$16\left(\frac{12.5}{\cos\theta}\right)^2 = 800\left(\frac{12.5}{\cos\theta}\right)\sin\theta$$
$$\frac{200}{\cos\theta} = 800\sin\theta$$
$$0.25 = \sin\theta\cos\theta$$
$$0.5 = 2\sin\theta\cos\theta$$
$$\sin(2\theta) = 0.5$$
$$2\theta = 30°, 150°$$
$$\theta = \mathbf{15°, 75°}$$

2. (a) $\sin x = x - \frac{x^3}{3!} + \frac{x^5}{5!} - \frac{x^7}{7!} + \cdots$

(b) $\sin x = \sum_{n=1}^{\infty} (-1)^{n+1}\frac{x^{(2n-1)}}{(2n-1)!}$

(c) $\sin(0.5) \approx S_3(0.5) = 0.5 - \frac{(0.5)^3}{3!} + \frac{(0.5)^5}{5!}$

$\approx \mathbf{0.4794270833}$

(d) This approximation is too large because the next term in this alternating series is negative, but by no more than $|a_4| = \frac{(0.5)^7}{7!} \doteq 0.0000015501$. Thus the actual value of sin (0.5) is in the interval **(0.4794255332, 0.4794270833).**

3. For accuracy to eight decimal places, the error must be less than 5×10^{-9}.

$$|a_5| = \frac{(0.5)^9}{9!} \approx 5.382 \times 10^{-9}$$
$$|a_6| = \frac{(0.5)^{11}}{11!} \approx 1.223 \times 10^{-11}$$

The sum of the first **5 terms** produces the desired accuracy.

4. $x = t^2 + 7 \qquad y = t^2 + 1$

$$\frac{dy}{dx} = \frac{2t}{2t}$$

When $t = 2$, $x = 11$, $y = 5$ and slope $= 1$.

$$y - 5 = 1(x - 11)$$
$$\mathbf{y = x - 6}$$
$$\frac{d^2y}{dx^2} = \frac{0}{2(1)} = 0$$

The concavity is 0.

5. $\lim_{x\to\infty}\left(\frac{x+1}{x}\right)^{6x} = \lim_{x\to\infty}\left[\left(1 + \frac{1}{x}\right)^x\right]^6$

$= \mathbf{e^6}$

6. $\sum_{n=1}^{\infty}\left|(-1)^{n+1}\frac{n+2}{n^2}\right| = \sum_{n=1}^{\infty}\frac{1 + \frac{2}{n}}{n}$

$$\frac{1 + \frac{2}{n}}{n} > \frac{1}{n}$$

This series does not converge absolutely by comparison with the divergent harmonic series.

$\frac{n+2}{n^2} \geq \frac{n+3}{(n+1)^2}$ for every n, and $\lim_{n\to\infty}\frac{n+2}{n^2} = 0$, so this series meets the conditions of Leibniz's theorem and **converges conditionally.**

7. $\sum_{n=1}^{\infty}(-1)^{n+1}\frac{n+2}{n}$ This series **diverges** by the **divergence theorem,** because its nth term does not approach zero.

8. $$L = \lim_{n\to\infty} \frac{\dfrac{(n+1)!}{(n+1)^{n+1}}}{\dfrac{n!}{n^n}} = \lim_{n\to\infty} \frac{n^n(n+1)}{(n+1)^{n+1}}$$
$$= \lim_{n\to\infty} \frac{n^n}{(n+1)^n}$$
$$= \lim_{n\to\infty} \left(\frac{n}{n+1}\right)^n$$
$$= \lim_{n\to\infty} \left(\frac{n+1}{n}\right)^{-n}$$
$$= e^{-1}$$

$\sum_{n=1}^{\infty} \frac{n!}{n^n}$ **converges by the ratio test.**

9. $\sum_{n=1}^{\infty} \frac{\sin n}{2^n}$ **converges absolutely,** because every term of $\sum_{n=1}^{\infty} \frac{|\sin n|}{2^n}$ is less than, or equal to, the corresponding term of $\sum_{n=1}^{\infty} \frac{1}{2^n}$, which is a convergent geometric series.

10. $$\lim_{n\to\infty} \frac{\dfrac{2n^2 + 4n}{4n + 3n^4}}{\dfrac{1}{n^2}} = \lim_{n\to\infty} \frac{2n^4 + 4n^3}{4n + 3n^4} = \frac{2}{3}$$

$\sum_{n=1}^{\infty} \frac{2n^2 + 4n}{4n + 3n^4}$ **converges by the limit comparison test** with a convergent p-series.

11.

$\frac{\pi}{2}$ (90°)

$r = 2 + 2\cos\theta$

$r = 2$

π (180°)

0

$\frac{3\pi}{2}$ (270°)

$$A = \frac{1}{2}(\pi 2^2) + 2\int_{\pi/2}^{\pi} \frac{1}{2}(2 + 2\cos\theta)^2\, d\theta$$
$$= 2\pi + \int_{\pi/2}^{\pi} (4 + 8\cos\theta + 4\cos^2\theta)\, d\theta$$
$$= 2\pi + \int_{\pi/2}^{\pi} \left\{4 + 8\cos\theta + 4\left[\frac{1}{2} + \frac{1}{2}\cos(2\theta)\right]\right\} d\theta$$
$$= 2\pi + \int_{\pi/2}^{\pi} [6 + 8\cos\theta + 2\cos(2\theta)]\, d\theta$$
$$= 2\pi + [6\theta + 8\sin\theta + \sin(2\theta)]_{\pi/2}^{\pi}$$
$$= 2\pi + [6\pi + 0 + 0 - (3\pi + 8 + 0)]$$
$$= \mathbf{(5\pi - 8)\ units^2}$$

12. $$y = \frac{1}{3}x^3 + \frac{1}{4}x^{-1}$$
$$\frac{dy}{dx} = x^2 - \frac{1}{4x^2}$$
$$\left(\frac{dy}{dx}\right)^2 = x^4 - \frac{1}{2} + \frac{1}{16x^4}$$
$$L_1^4 = \int_1^4 \sqrt{1 + \left(x^4 - \frac{1}{2} + \frac{1}{16x^4}\right)}\, dx$$
$$= \int_1^4 \sqrt{x^4 + \frac{1}{2} + \frac{1}{16x^4}}\, dx$$
$$= \int_1^4 \sqrt{\left(x^2 + \frac{1}{4x^2}\right)^2}\, dx$$
$$= \int_1^4 \left(x^2 + \frac{1}{4}x^{-2}\right) dx$$
$$= \left[\frac{1}{3}x^3 - \frac{1}{4}x^{-1}\right]_1^4$$
$$= \frac{64}{3} - \frac{1}{16} - \left(\frac{1}{3} - \frac{1}{4}\right)$$
$$= \mathbf{21\frac{3}{16}\ units}$$

13. $$\int \frac{x^4 + 4x^2 + 2}{x^2 + 2}\, dx$$
$$= \int \left(x^2 + 2 - \frac{2}{x^2 + 2}\right) dx$$
$$= \int \left(x^2 + 2 - \frac{\sqrt{2}(\sqrt{2})}{x^2 + (\sqrt{2})^2}\right) dx$$
$$= \mathbf{\frac{1}{3}x^3 + 2x - \sqrt{2}\arctan\frac{x}{\sqrt{2}} + C}$$

14. $$\int \frac{6}{4x^2 + 9}\, dx = \int \frac{2(3)}{(2x)^2 + 3^2}\, dx$$
$$= \mathbf{\arctan\frac{2x}{3} + C}$$

15. $\int \frac{3x^2 - x + 8}{(x + 1)(x^2 + 3)}\,dx$

$= \int \left(\frac{A}{x + 1} + \frac{Bx + C}{x^2 + 3} \right) dx$

$A(x^2 + 3) + (Bx + C)(x + 1) = 3x^2 - x + 8$

$x = -1$: $\quad 4A = 12$

$A = 3$

$x = 0$: $\quad 3A + C = 8$

$C = -1$

$x = 1$: $\quad 4A + 2B + 2C = 10$

$B = 0$

$\int \left(\frac{A}{x + 1} + \frac{Bx + C}{x^2 + 3} \right) dx$

$= \int \left(\frac{3}{x + 1} - \frac{1}{x^2 + 3} \right) dx$

$= \mathbf{3 \ln |x + 1| - \frac{1}{\sqrt{3}} \arctan \frac{x}{\sqrt{3}} + C}$

16. $|f(x) - 9| < \varepsilon$

$|4x - 3 - 9| < \varepsilon$

$|4x - 12| < \varepsilon$

$|x - 3| < \frac{\varepsilon}{4}$

$\delta = \frac{\varepsilon}{4}$

The correct choice is **D.**

17. $f(x) = x^3 + 2x - 1 \qquad f'(x) = 3x^2 + 2$

The solution to $f(x) = 11$, is $x = 2$.

$h'(11) = \frac{1}{f'(h(11))} = \frac{1}{f'(2)} = \frac{1}{3(2)^2 + 2}$

$= \mathbf{\frac{1}{14}}$

18. $\lim_{n\to\infty} \frac{9}{n} \sum_{i=1}^{\infty} \frac{1}{x_i} = \int_1^{10} \frac{1}{x}\,dx = \mathbf{\ln 10}$

19. $f'(x) = \frac{d}{dx} \int_{-2}^{e^{x^2}} \cos t^2\,dt$

$= \mathbf{\cos\left(e^{2x^2}\right) e^{x^2} (2x)}$

20.

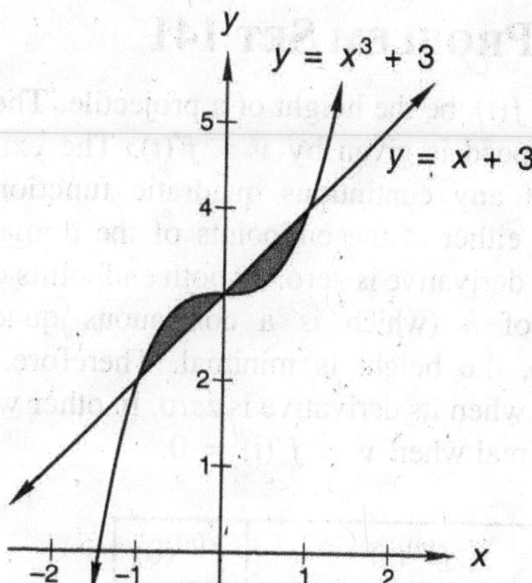

$A = 2\int_0^1 [(x + 3) - (x^3 + 3)]\,dx$

$= 2\int_0^1 (-x^3 + x)\,dx$

$= 2\left[-\frac{1}{4}x^4 + \frac{1}{2}x^2 \right]_0^1$

$= 2\left[-\frac{1}{4} + \frac{1}{2} - (0) \right] = \mathbf{\frac{1}{2}\ \text{unit}^2}$

21.

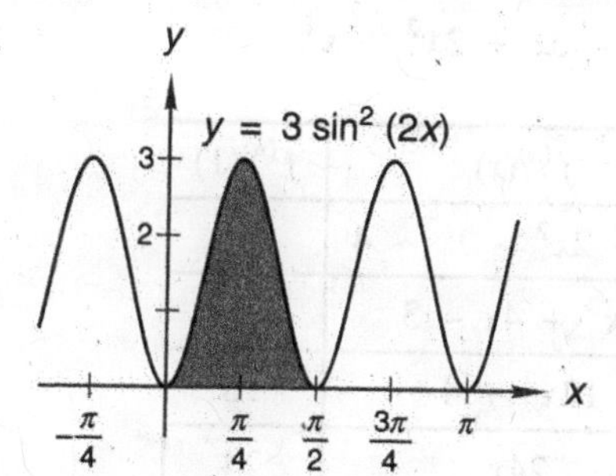

$A = \int_0^{\pi/2} 3 \sin^2 (2x)\,dx$

$= 3\int_0^{\pi/2} \left[\frac{1}{2} - \frac{1}{2}\cos (4x) \right] dx$

$= 3\left[\frac{1}{2}x - \frac{1}{8}\sin (4x) \right]_0^{\pi/2}$

$= 3\left[\frac{\pi}{4} - 0 - (0 - 0) \right] = \mathbf{\frac{3\pi}{4}\ \text{units}^2}$

PROBLEM SET 141

1. Let $h = f(t)$ be the height of a projectile. Then its vertical speed is given by $v = f'(t)$. The extreme values of any continuous quadratic function are achieved either at the endpoints of the domain or when the derivative is zero. At both endpoints of the domain of h (which is a continuous quadratic function), the height is minimal. Therefore, h is maximal when its derivative is zero. In other words, h is maximal when $v = f'(t) = 0$.

2.

n	$f^{(n)}(x)$	$f^{(n)}(0)$
0	$x^4 + 2x^2 - 3x - 4$	-4
1	$4x^3 + 4x - 3$	-3
2	$12x^2 + 4$	4
3	$24x$	0
4	24	24
5	0	0

$$f(x) = -4 - 3x + \frac{4x^2}{2!} + \frac{24x^4}{4!}$$
$$= \mathbf{-4 - 3x + 2x^2 + x^4}$$

3.

n	$f^{(n)}(x)$	$f^{(n)}(1)$
0	$x^4 + 2x^2 - 3x - 4$	-4
1	$4x^3 + 4x - 3$	5
2	$12x^2 + 4$	16
3	$24x$	24
4	24	24
5	0	0

$$f(x) = -4 + 5(x-1) + \frac{16(x-1)^2}{2!} + \frac{24(x-1)^3}{3!} + \frac{24(x-1)^4}{4!}$$
$$= \mathbf{-4 + 5(x-1) + 8(x-1)^2 + 4(x-1)^3 + (x-1)^4}$$

4.

n	$f^{(n)}(x)$	$f^{(n)}(0)$
0	$\sin x$	0
1	$\cos x$	1
2	$-\sin x$	0
3	$-\cos x$	-1
4	$\sin x$	0
⋮	⋮	⋮

$$\sin x = x - \frac{x^3}{3!} + \frac{x^5}{5!} - \frac{x^7}{7!} + \cdots$$
$$= \boldsymbol{\sum_{n=1}^{\infty} (-1)^{n+1} \frac{x^{2n-1}}{(2n-1)!}}$$

5.

n	$f^{(n)}(x)$	$f^{(n)}(\pi)$
0	$\sin x$	0
1	$\cos x$	-1
2	$-\sin x$	0
3	$-\cos x$	1
4	$\sin x$	0
⋮	⋮	⋮

$$\sin x = -(x-\pi) + \frac{(x-\pi)^3}{3!} - \frac{(x-\pi)^5}{5!} + \frac{(x-\pi)^7}{7!} + \cdots$$
$$= \boldsymbol{\sum_{n=1}^{\infty} (-1)^{n} \frac{(x-\pi)^{2n-1}}{(2n-1)!}}$$

6. $\sin 3 \approx S_4 = 3 - \frac{3^3}{3!} + \frac{3^5}{5!} - \frac{3^7}{7!}$
$\approx \mathbf{0.0910714286}$

Because the next term in this alternating series is positive, this approximation is too small, but by no more than $a_5 = \frac{3^9}{9!} \approx 0.0542410714$. Thus the actual value of sin 3 is in the interval **(0.0910714286, 0.1453125)**.

7. $\sin 3 \approx S_4$
$$\approx -(3-\pi) + \frac{(3-\pi)^3}{3!} - \frac{(3-\pi)^5}{5!} + \frac{(3-\pi)^7}{7!}$$
$\approx \mathbf{0.1411200081}$

Because the next term of this alternating series is positive (the opposite of a negative number), this approximation is too small, but by no more than $|a_5| = \left|\frac{(3-\pi)^9}{9!}\right| = 6.3038 \times 10^{-14}$. In other words this approximation is accurate to the 10 decimal places given. This approximation is more accurate than the one in problem 6, because the series was expanded around $x = \pi$ which is much closer to 3 than 0.

8. $y = e^x$

$dy = e^x\,dx$

$dy = e^0(0.1)$

$dy = 0.1$

$y + dy = 1 + 0.1 = 1.1$

location $\approx$ **(0.1, 1.1)**

9. $$\sum_{n=1}^{\infty}\left|(-1)^{n-1}\frac{n^2}{2^n}\right| = \sum_{n=1}^{\infty}\frac{n^2}{2^n}$$

$$\lim_{n\to\infty}\frac{\dfrac{(n+1)^2}{2^{n+1}}}{\dfrac{n^2}{2^n}} = \lim_{n\to\infty}\frac{(n+1)^2}{2n^2} = \frac{1}{2}$$

This series **converges absolutely** by the ratio test.

10. $$f(x) = \int_{x^2}^{\cos x}\frac{\sin t}{t}\,dt$$

$$f'(x) = \frac{d}{dx}\int_{x^2}^{\cos x}\frac{\sin t}{t}\,dt$$

$$= \frac{\sin(\cos x)}{\cos x}(-\sin x) - \frac{2x\sin(x^2)}{x^2}$$

$$f'(2) = -(\tan 2)\sin(\cos 2) - \frac{4\sin 4}{4}$$

$$= \mathbf{-(\tan 2)\sin(\cos 2) - \sin 4} \approx \mathbf{-0.1265}$$

11.

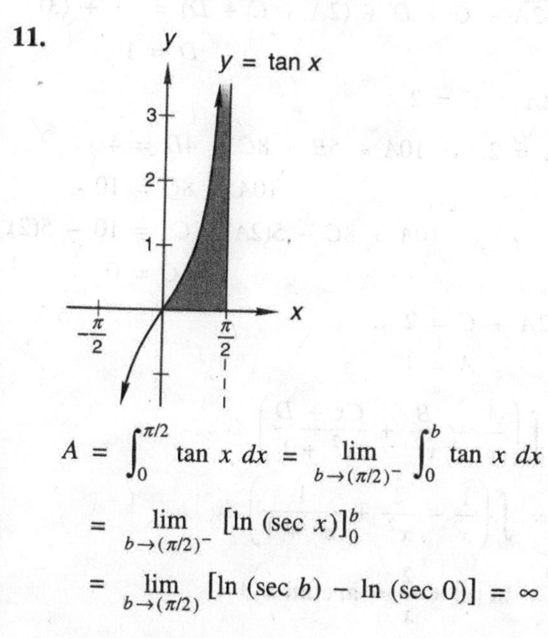

$$A = \int_0^{\pi/2}\tan x\,dx = \lim_{b\to(\pi/2)^-}\int_0^b \tan x\,dx$$

$$= \lim_{b\to(\pi/2)^-}[\ln(\sec x)]_0^b$$

$$= \lim_{b\to(\pi/2)}[\ln(\sec b) - \ln(\sec 0)] = \infty$$

12.

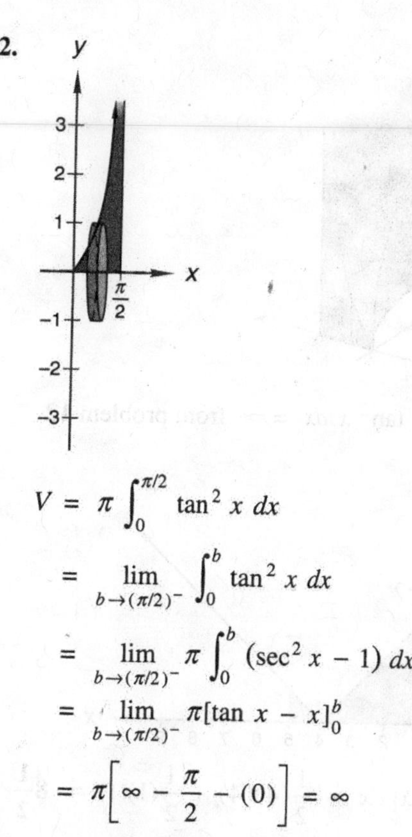

$$V = \pi\int_0^{\pi/2}\tan^2 x\,dx$$

$$= \lim_{b\to(\pi/2)^-}\int_0^b \tan^2 x\,dx$$

$$= \lim_{b\to(\pi/2)^-}\pi\int_0^b(\sec^2 x - 1)\,dx$$

$$= \lim_{b\to(\pi/2)^-}\pi[\tan x - x]_0^b$$

$$= \pi\left[\infty - \frac{\pi}{2} - (0)\right] = \infty$$

13.

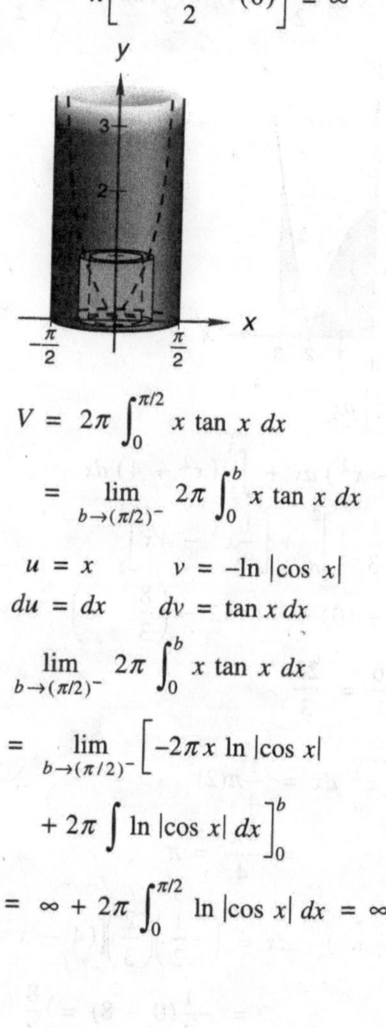

$$V = 2\pi\int_0^{\pi/2}x\tan x\,dx$$

$$= \lim_{b\to(\pi/2)^-}2\pi\int_0^b x\tan x\,dx$$

$u = x \qquad v = -\ln|\cos x|$

$du = dx \qquad dv = \tan x\,dx$

$$\lim_{b\to(\pi/2)^-}2\pi\int_0^b x\tan x\,dx$$

$$= \lim_{b\to(\pi/2)^-}\left[-2\pi x\ln|\cos x| + 2\pi\int\ln|\cos x|\,dx\right]_0^b$$

$$= \infty + 2\pi\int_0^{\pi/2}\ln|\cos x|\,dx = \infty$$

14.

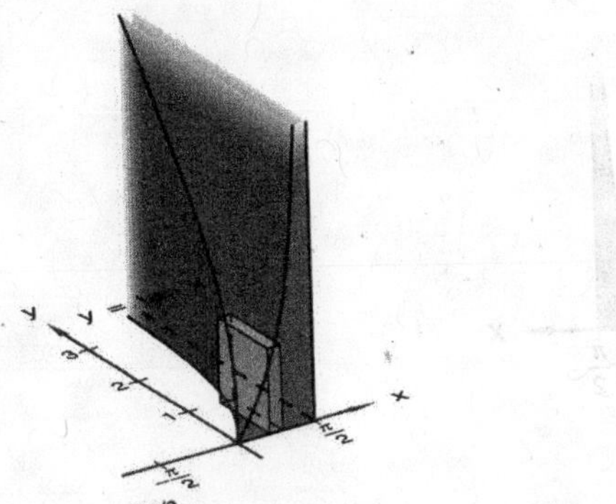

$$V = \int_0^{\pi/2} \tan^2 x\, dx = \infty \text{ from problem 12.}$$

15.

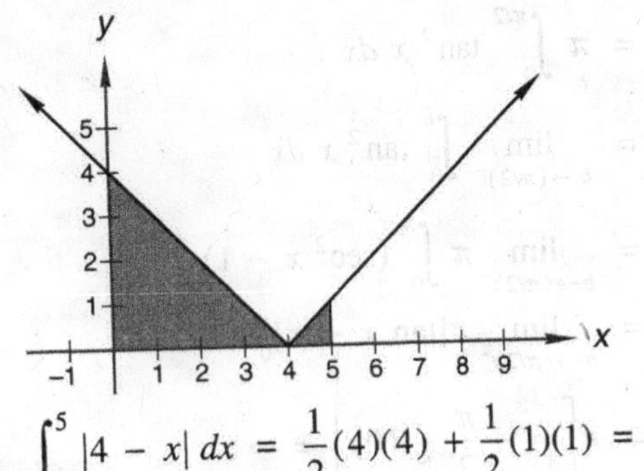

$$\int_0^5 |4 - x|\, dx = \frac{1}{2}(4)(4) + \frac{1}{2}(1)(1) = \mathbf{8\frac{1}{2}}$$

16.

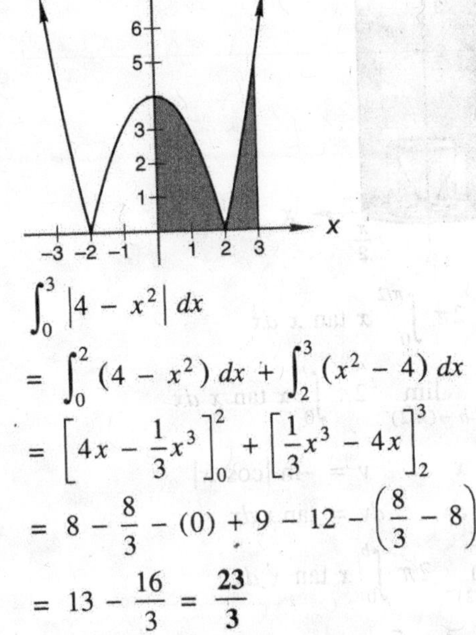

$$\int_0^3 |4 - x^2|\, dx$$
$$= \int_0^2 (4 - x^2)\, dx + \int_2^3 (x^2 - 4)\, dx$$
$$= \left[4x - \frac{1}{3}x^3\right]_0^2 + \left[\frac{1}{3}x^3 - 4x\right]_2^3$$
$$= 8 - \frac{8}{3} - (0) + 9 - 12 - \left(\frac{8}{3} - 8\right)$$
$$= 13 - \frac{16}{3} = \mathbf{\frac{23}{3}}$$

17. $\int_0^2 \sqrt{4 - x^2}\, dx = \frac{1}{4}\pi(2)^2$

$$= \frac{4\pi}{4} = \pi$$

18. $\int_0^2 x(4 - x^2)^{1/2}\, dx = \left(-\frac{1}{2}\right)\left(\frac{2}{3}\right)\left[(4 - x^2)^{3/2}\right]_0^2$

$$= -\frac{1}{3}(0 - 8) = \mathbf{\frac{8}{3}}$$

19. $x^2 = xy + y$

$$2x = x\frac{dy}{dx} + y + \frac{dy}{dx}$$
$$\frac{dy}{dx} = \frac{2x - y}{x + 1}$$
$$\frac{d^2y}{dx^2} = \frac{(x + 1)\left(2 - \frac{dy}{dx}\right) - (2x - y)}{(x + 1)^2}$$
$$\frac{d^2y}{dx^2} = \frac{(x + 1)\left(2 - \frac{2x - y}{x + 1}\right) - (2x - y)}{(x + 1)^2}$$
$$\frac{d^2y}{dx^2} = \frac{2(x + 1) - (2x - y) - (2x - y)}{(x + 1)^2}$$
$$\frac{d^2y}{dx^2} = \frac{-2x + 2y + 2}{(x + 1)^2}$$
$$\frac{d^2y}{dx^2} = \mathbf{\frac{2(y - x + 1)}{(x + 1)^2}}$$

20. $\int \frac{x^3 - x^2 + x - 2}{x^2(x^2 + 1)}\, dx$

$$= \int \left(\frac{A}{x} + \frac{B}{x^2} + \frac{Cx + D}{x^2 + 1}\right) dx$$

$A(x^2 + 1)x + B(x^2 + 1) + (Cx + D)x^2$

$= x^3 - x^2 + x - 2$

$x = 0$: $\quad B = -2$

$x = 1$: $\quad 2A + 2B + C + D = -1$

$\quad 2A + C + D = 3$

$x = -1$: $\quad -2A + 2B - C + D = -5$

$\quad -2A - C + D = -1$

$-2A - C + D + (2A + C + D) = -1 + (3)$

$\quad D = 1$

$2A + C = 2$

$x = 2$: $\quad 10A + 5B + 8C + 4D = 4$

$\quad 10A + 8C = 10$

$\quad 10A + 8C - 5(2A + C) = 10 - 5(2)$

$\quad C = 0$

$2A + C = 2$

$\quad A = 1$

$$\int \left(\frac{A}{x} + \frac{B}{x^2} + \frac{Cx + D}{x^2 + 1}\right) dx$$
$$= \int \left(\frac{1}{x} - \frac{2}{x^2} + \frac{1}{x^2 + 1}\right) dx$$
$$= \mathbf{\ln|x| + \frac{2}{x} + \arctan x + C}$$

21. $(x-1)^2 + y^2 = 1$ becomes $r = 2\cos\theta$
$x^2 + (y-1)^2 = 1$ becomes $r = 2\sin\theta$

$$2\cos\theta = 2\sin\theta$$
$$\tan\theta = 1$$
$$\theta = \frac{\pi}{4}$$

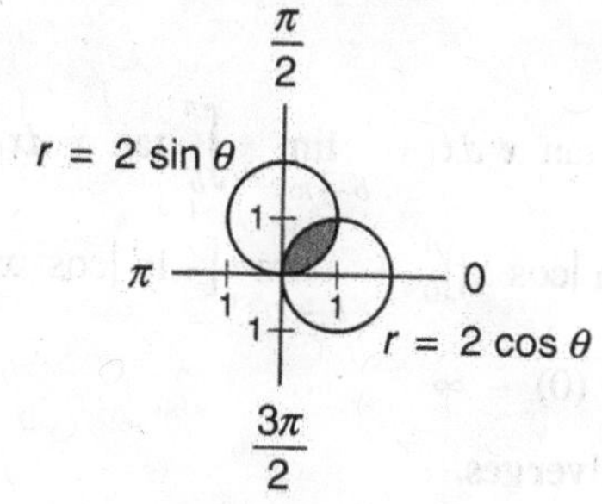

$$A = 2\int_0^{\pi/4} \frac{1}{2}(2\sin\theta)^2\,d\theta$$
$$= \int_0^{\pi/4} (4\sin^2\theta)\,d\theta$$
$$= \int_0^{\pi/4} 4\left[\frac{1}{2} - \frac{1}{2}\cos(2\theta)\right]d\theta$$
$$= \int_0^{\pi/4} [2 - 2\cos(2\theta)]\,d\theta$$
$$= [2\theta - \sin(2\theta)]_0^{\pi/4}$$
$$= \frac{\pi}{2} - 1 - (0) = \mathbf{\frac{\pi - 2}{2}\ units^2}$$

Problem Set 142

1. $\vec{p} = (2\sin t)\hat{i} + (3\cos t)\hat{j}$
$\vec{v} = \mathbf{(2\cos t)\hat{i} - (3\sin t)\hat{j}}$
$\vec{a} = \mathbf{(-2\sin t)\hat{i} - (3\cos t)\hat{j}}$

2. At $t = \frac{\pi}{4}$

$$\vec{v} = \sqrt{2}\hat{i} - \frac{3\sqrt{2}}{2}\hat{j}$$
$$\vec{a} = -\sqrt{2}\hat{i} - \frac{3\sqrt{2}}{2}\hat{j}$$
$$\text{Speed} = \sqrt{\sqrt{2}^2 + \left(-\frac{3\sqrt{2}}{2}\right)^2} = \sqrt{\frac{13}{2}}$$
$$\text{Acceleration} = \sqrt{(-\sqrt{2})^2 + \left(-\frac{3\sqrt{2}}{2}\right)^2} = \sqrt{\frac{13}{2}}$$

3.

n	$f^{(n)}(x)$	$f^{(n)}(1)$
0	$x^4 - 3x^2 - 2$	-4
1	$4x^3 - 6x$	-2
2	$12x^2 - 6$	6
3	$24x$	24
4	24	24
5	0	0

$$f(x) = -4 - 2(x-1) + \frac{6(x-1)^2}{2!} + \frac{24(x-1)^3}{3!} + \frac{24(x-1)^4}{4!}$$
$$= \mathbf{-4 - 2(x-1) + 3(x-1)^2 + 4(x-1)^3 + (x-1)^4}$$

4. $$\cos x = 1 - \frac{x^2}{2!} + \frac{x^4}{4!} - \frac{x^6}{6!} + \cdots = \sum_{n=0}^{\infty} (-1)^n \frac{x^{2n}}{(2n)!}$$

5.

n	$f^{(n)}(x)$	$f^{(n)}\left(\frac{\pi}{6}\right)$
0	$\cos x$	$\frac{\sqrt{3}}{2}$
1	$-\sin x$	$-\frac{1}{2}$
2	$-\cos x$	$-\frac{\sqrt{3}}{2}$
3	$\sin x$	$\frac{1}{2}$
4	$\cos x$	$\frac{\sqrt{3}}{2}$
⋮	⋮	⋮

$$\cos x = \frac{\sqrt{3}}{2} - \frac{x - \frac{\pi}{6}}{2} - \frac{\sqrt{3}\left(x - \frac{\pi}{6}\right)^2}{2(2!)} + \frac{\left(x - \frac{\pi}{6}\right)^3}{2(3!)} + \cdots$$
$$= \mathbf{\frac{\sqrt{3}}{2} - \frac{x - \frac{\pi}{6}}{2} - \frac{\sqrt{3}}{4}\left(x - \frac{\pi}{6}\right)^2 + \frac{\left(x - \frac{\pi}{6}\right)^3}{12} + \cdots}$$

6. $\cos 0.5 \approx S_2 = \dfrac{\sqrt{3}}{2} - \dfrac{0.5 - \dfrac{\pi}{6}}{2} = \mathbf{0.8778247916}$

This is not an alternating series, so there is little that can be said about the error in this S_2 approximation.

7.
$$y = -16t^2 + v_0 t \sin\theta$$
$$-14 = -16t^2 + 15t \sin 20°$$
$$0 = 16t^2 - 15 \sin 20° t - 14$$
$$t \approx 1.1094 \text{ s}$$
$$x = v_0 t \cos\theta$$
$$x \approx 15(1.1094) \cos 20°$$
$$x \approx \mathbf{15.6374\ ft}$$

8. $\displaystyle\lim_{x\to\infty}\left(\frac{x+1}{x}\right)^{7x} = \lim_{x\to\infty}\left[\left(1 + \frac{1}{x}\right)^x\right]^7 = \mathbf{e^7}$

9.
$$|y - 0| < \varepsilon$$
$$|2x + 4 - 0| < \varepsilon$$
$$|2x + 4| < \varepsilon$$
$$|x + 2| < \frac{\varepsilon}{2}$$
$$\delta = \mathbf{\frac{\varepsilon}{2}}$$

10.
$$f(x) = \int_{-3}^{4x^2} \frac{\sin(t^2)}{t^3}\,dt$$
$$f'(x) = \frac{d}{dx}\int_{-3}^{4x^2} \frac{\sin(t^2)}{t^3}\,dt$$
$$= \frac{\sin[(4x^2)^2]}{(4x^2)^3}(8x)$$
$$= \mathbf{\frac{\sin(16x^4)}{8x^5}}$$

11. $\displaystyle\int_0^4 [x]\,dx$

$$= \lim_{a\to1^-}\int_0^a 0\,dx + \lim_{b\to2^-}\int_1^b 1\,dx$$
$$+ \lim_{c\to3^-}\int_2^c 2\,dx + \lim_{d\to4^-}\int_3^d 3\,dx$$
$$= 0 + \lim_{b\to2^-} x|_1^b + \lim_{c\to3^-} 2x|_2^c + \lim_{d\to4^-} 3x|_3^d$$
$$= 0 + 1 + 2 + 3 = \mathbf{6}$$

12.
$$\int_0^\infty e^{-x}\,dx = \lim_{b\to\infty}\int_0^b e^{-x}\,dx$$
$$= \lim_{b\to\infty}[-e^{-x}]_0^b$$
$$= 0 - (-1) = \mathbf{1}$$

13. $\displaystyle\int_0^\pi \tan x\,dx$

$$= \lim_{a\to\pi/2^-}\int_0^a \tan x\,dx + \lim_{b\to\pi/2^+}\int_b^\pi \tan x\,dx$$
$$= \lim_{a\to\pi/2^-}[-\ln|\cos x|]_0^a + \lim_{b\to\pi/2^+}[-\ln|\cos x|]_b^\pi$$
$$= \infty - (0) + (0) - \infty$$

The integral **diverges.**

14.
$$x = e^t \sin t$$
$$\frac{dx}{dt} = e^t\cos t + (\sin t)e^t$$
$$= e^t(\cos t + \sin t)$$
$$\left(\frac{dx}{dt}\right)^2 = e^{2t}(\cos^2 t + 2\sin t\cos t + \sin^2 t)$$
$$= e^{2t}[1 + \sin(2t)]$$
$$y = e^t\cos t$$
$$\frac{dy}{dt} = e^t(-\sin t) + (\cos t)e^t$$
$$= e^t(\cos t - \sin t)$$
$$\left(\frac{dy}{dt}\right)^2 = e^{2t}(\cos^2 t - 2\sin t\cos t + \sin^2 t)$$
$$= e^{2t}[1 - \sin(2t)]$$
$$L_0^\pi = \int_0^\pi \sqrt{2e^{2t}}\,dt$$
$$= \sqrt{2}\int_0^\pi e^t\,dt$$
$$= \sqrt{2}[e^t]_0^\pi$$
$$= \mathbf{\sqrt{2}(e^\pi - 1)\ units}$$

15. $x = 2\tan\theta \qquad dx = 2\sec^2\theta\, d\theta$

$\sqrt{x^2+4} = 2\sec\theta \qquad x^3 = 8\tan^3\theta$

$$\int \frac{x^3}{\sqrt{x^2+4}}\,dx$$

$$= \int \frac{8(\tan^3\theta)2\sec^2\theta}{2\sec\theta}\,d\theta$$

$$= \int 8\tan^3\theta\sec\theta\,d\theta$$

$$= 8\int \tan^2\theta(\tan\theta\sec\theta)\,d\theta$$

$$= 8\int (\sec^2\theta - 1)\tan\theta\sec\theta\,d\theta$$

$$= 8\int [\sec^2\theta(\tan\theta\sec\theta) - \tan\theta\sec\theta]\,d\theta$$

$$= \frac{8}{3}\sec^3\theta - 8\sec\theta + C$$

$$= \frac{8}{3}\left(\frac{\sqrt{x^2+4}}{2}\right)^3 - 8\left(\frac{\sqrt{x^2+4}}{2}\right) + C$$

$$= \frac{(x^2+4)\sqrt{x^2+4}}{3} - 4\sqrt{x^2+4} + C$$

$$= \frac{1}{3}\sqrt{x^2+4}(x^2+4-12) + C$$

$$= \mathbf{\frac{1}{3}\sqrt{x^2+4}(x^2-8) + C}$$

16. $$\int \frac{1}{x^3+x}\,dx = \int \frac{1}{x(x^2+1)}\,dx$$

$$= \int \left(\frac{A}{x} + \frac{Bx+C}{x^2+1}\right)dx$$

$A(x^2+1) + (Bx+C)x = 1$

$x = 0$: $\quad A = 1$

$x = 1$: $\quad 2A + B + C = 1$

$B = -C - 1$

$x = -1$: $\quad 2A + B - C = 1$

$(-C-1) - C = -1$

$C = 0$

$B = -C - 1$

$B = -1$

$$\int \left(\frac{A}{x} + \frac{Bx+C}{x^2+1}\right)dx$$

$$= \int \left(\frac{1}{x} + \frac{-x}{x^2+1}\right)dx$$

$$= \mathbf{\ln|x| - \frac{1}{2}\ln(x^2+1) + C}$$

17. $u = 3x^2 \qquad v = \frac{1}{4}\sin(4x)$

$du = 6x\,dx \qquad dv = \cos(4x)\,dx$

$$\int 3x^2\cos(4x)\,dx$$

$$= \frac{3}{4}x^2\sin(4x) - \int \frac{3}{2}x\sin(4x)\,dx$$

$u = \frac{3}{2}x \qquad v = -\frac{1}{4}\cos(4x)$

$du = \frac{3}{2}\,dx \qquad dv = \sin(4x)\,dx$

$$\int 3x^2\cos(4x)\,dx$$

$$= \frac{3}{4}x^2\sin(4x) - \left[-\frac{3}{8}x\cos(4x) + \int \frac{3}{8}\cos(4x)\,dx\right]$$

$$= \mathbf{\frac{3}{4}x^2\sin(4x) + \frac{3}{8}x\cos(4x) - \frac{3}{32}\sin(4x) + C}$$

18. $$\lim_{n\to\infty} \frac{\frac{3^{n+1}+1}{(n+1)!}}{\frac{3^n+1}{n!}} = \lim_{n\to\infty} \frac{3^{n+1}+1}{(n+1)(3^n+1)} = 0$$

$\sum_{n=1}^{\infty} \frac{3^n+1}{n!}$ **converges** by the **ratio test.**

19. $$\sum_{n=1}^{\infty}\left|(-1)^n\frac{3}{4n+2}\right| = \sum_{n=1}^{\infty}\frac{3}{4n+2}$$

$$\lim_{n\to\infty}\frac{\frac{3}{4n+2}}{\frac{1}{n}} = \lim_{n\to\infty}\frac{3n}{4n+2} = \frac{3}{4}$$

The series is not absolutely convergent by the limit comparison test. However, $\frac{3}{4(n+1)+2} \le \frac{3}{4n+2}$ for all n and $\lim_{n\to\infty}\frac{3}{4n+2} = 0$, so this series is **conditionally convergent** by the **alternating series test.**

20. $$\lim_{n\to\infty}\frac{\frac{n^{2/3}}{n^{6/7}+3}}{\frac{1}{n^{4/21}}} = \lim_{n\to\infty}\frac{n^{18/21}}{n^{6/7}+3} = 1$$

$\sum_{n=1}^{\infty}\frac{n^{2/3}}{n^{6/7}+3}$ **diverges** by the **limit comparison test** with a divergent p-series.

21.

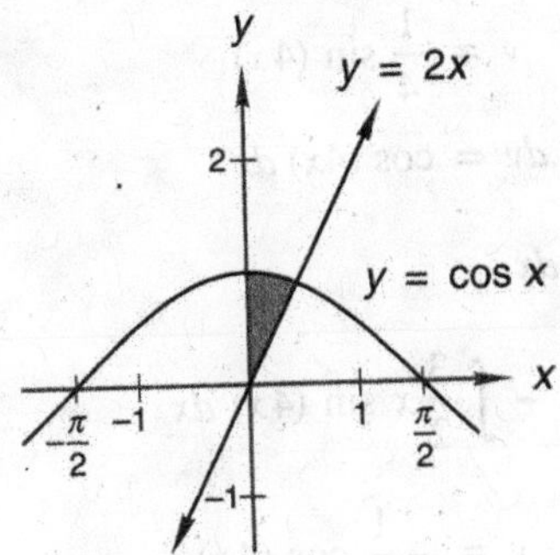

$$\cos x = 2x$$
$$x \approx 0.4502$$

$$A \approx \int_0^{0.4502} (\cos x - 2x)\, dx$$
$$\approx \left[\sin x - x^2\right]_0^{0.4502}$$
$$\approx \mathbf{0.2325\ units^2}$$

22. $T = \frac{2}{8}(1 + \sqrt{5} + 2\sqrt{2} + \sqrt{13} + \sqrt{5})$

$\approx$ **2.976528589**

```
fnInt(√(X²+1),X,
0,2)
          2.957885715
```

$$\int_0^2 \sqrt{x^2 + 1}\, dx \approx 2.957885715$$

The answer using the trapezoidal rule is **larger by 0.0186428739.**

PROBLEM SET 143

1.

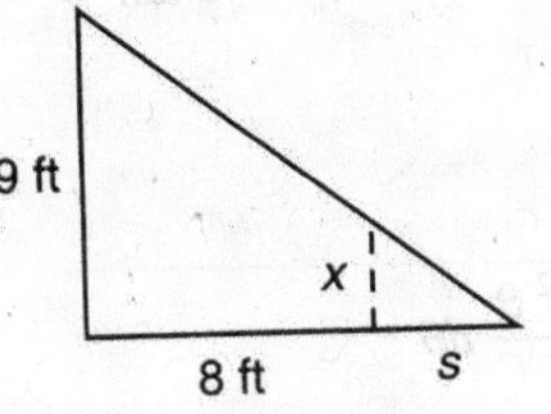

$\frac{dx}{dt} = -1$ ft/s $\qquad x = 3$ ft

$$\frac{3}{9} = \frac{s}{8 + s}$$
$$9s = 24 + 3s$$
$$6s = 24$$
$$s = 4$$

$$\frac{x}{9} = \frac{s}{8 + s}$$
$$9s = x(8 + s)$$
$$9\frac{ds}{dt} = x\frac{ds}{dt} + (8 + s)\frac{dx}{dt}$$
$$9\frac{ds}{dt} = 3\frac{ds}{dt} + (8 + 4)(-1)$$
$$6\frac{ds}{dt} = -12$$
$$\frac{ds}{dt} = -2$$

The shadow is approaching the garage at **2 ft/s.**

2.

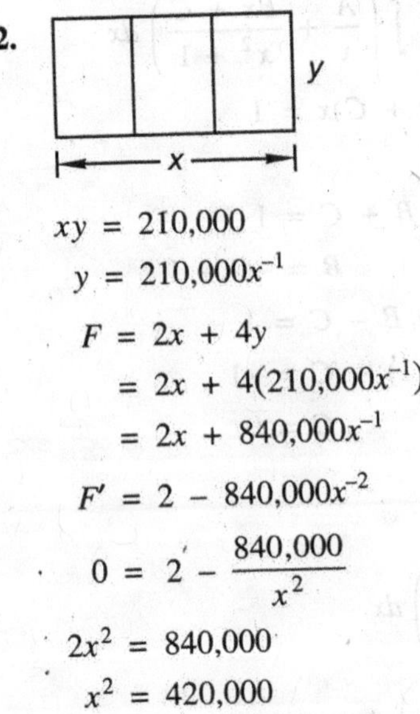

$$xy = 210{,}000$$
$$y = 210{,}000x^{-1}$$
$$F = 2x + 4y$$
$$= 2x + 4(210{,}000x^{-1})$$
$$= 2x + 840{,}000x^{-1}$$
$$F' = 2 - 840{,}000x^{-2}$$
$$0 = 2 - \frac{840{,}000}{x^2}$$
$$2x^2 = 840{,}000$$
$$x^2 = 420{,}000$$
$$x = 100\sqrt{42}$$
$$F(100\sqrt{42}) = 200\sqrt{42} + 200\sqrt{42}$$
$$= \mathbf{400\sqrt{42}\ ft}$$

3. $x = v_0 t\cos\theta$

$$30{,}000 = 500t\cos\theta$$

$$t = \frac{60}{\cos\theta}$$

$$y = -16t^2 + v_0 t\sin\theta$$

$$0 = -16\left(\frac{60}{\cos\theta}\right)^2 + 500\left(\frac{60}{\cos\theta}\right)\sin\theta$$

$$16\left(\frac{60}{\cos\theta}\right) = 500\sin\theta$$

$$1.92 = \sin\theta\cos\theta$$

$$3.84 = 2\sin\theta\cos\theta$$

$$\sin(2\theta) = 3.84$$

The sin (2θ) will never equal 3.84, so **there is no angle** at which the cannon can be fired to strike a target 30,000 ft downrange.

4. $y = (1 + x)^{1/3}$

$$= 1 + \frac{1}{3}x + \frac{1}{3}\left(-\frac{2}{3}\right)\frac{x^2}{2!} + \frac{1}{3}\left(-\frac{2}{3}\right)\left(-\frac{5}{3}\right)\frac{x^3}{3!} + \frac{1}{3}\left(-\frac{2}{3}\right)\left(-\frac{5}{3}\right)\left(-\frac{8}{3}\right)\frac{x^4}{4!} + \cdots$$

$$= \mathbf{1 + \frac{1}{3}x - \frac{1}{9}x^2 + \frac{5}{81}x^3 - \frac{10}{243}x^4 + \cdots}$$

5. To estimate $\sqrt[3]{1.5}$, let $x = 0.5 = \frac{1}{2}$.

$$\sqrt[3]{1.5} = \left(1 + \frac{1}{2}\right)^{1/3}$$

$$\approx 1 + \frac{1}{3}\left(\frac{1}{2}\right) - \frac{1}{9}\left(\frac{1}{2}\right)^2 + \frac{5}{81}\left(\frac{1}{2}\right)^3 - \frac{10}{243}\left(\frac{1}{2}\right)^4$$

$$\approx 1 + \frac{1}{6} - \frac{1}{36} + \frac{5}{648} - \frac{5}{1944}$$

After the first term this is an alternating series, so S_5 produces an approximation with an error less than 0.001 since $a_6 = \frac{11}{11{,}664} \approx 0.0009431$.

$$\sqrt[3]{1.5} \approx S_5 = \mathbf{1.1440}$$

6. $\vec{p} = e^{2t}\hat{i} + e^t\hat{j}$

$$\vec{v} = \mathbf{2e^{2t}\hat{i} + e^t\hat{j}}$$

$$\vec{a} = \mathbf{4e^{2t}\hat{i} + e^t\hat{j}}$$

7. At $t = \ln 2$,

$$\vec{v} = \mathbf{8\hat{i} + 2\hat{j}}$$

$$\vec{a} = \mathbf{16\hat{i} + 2\hat{j}}$$

$$\text{speed} = \sqrt{64 + 4} = \mathbf{2\sqrt{17}}$$

$$\text{acceleration} = \sqrt{256 + 4} = \mathbf{2\sqrt{65}}$$

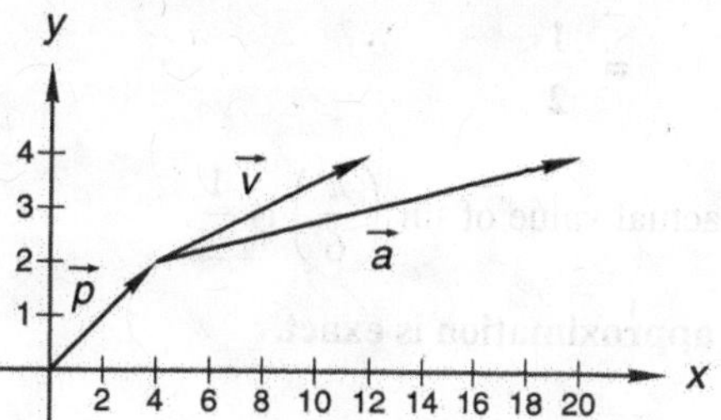

8. This is equivalent to the Maclaurin series for $\sin x$ which is

$$\sin x = \mathbf{x - \frac{x^3}{3!} + \frac{x^5}{5!} - \frac{x^7}{7!} + \cdots}$$

9.

n	$f^{(n)}(x)$	$f^{(n)}\left(\frac{\pi}{6}\right)$
0	$\sin x$	$\frac{1}{2}$
1	$\cos x$	$\frac{\sqrt{3}}{2}$
2	$-\sin x$	$-\frac{1}{2}$
3	$-\cos x$	$-\frac{\sqrt{3}}{2}$
4	$\sin x$	$\frac{1}{2}$
⋮	⋮	⋮

$$\sin x = \frac{1}{2} + \frac{\sqrt{3}}{2}\left(x - \frac{\pi}{6}\right) - \frac{\frac{1}{2}\left(x - \frac{\pi}{6}\right)^2}{2!} - \frac{\frac{\sqrt{3}}{2}\left(x - \frac{\pi}{6}\right)^3}{3!} + \cdots$$

$$= \mathbf{\frac{1}{2} + \frac{\sqrt{3}}{2}\left(x - \frac{\pi}{6}\right) - \frac{1}{4}\left(x - \frac{\pi}{6}\right)^2 - \frac{\sqrt{3}}{12}\left(x - \frac{\pi}{6}\right)^3 + \cdots}$$

10. $\sin\left(\frac{\pi}{6}\right) = \frac{1}{2} + \frac{\sqrt{3}}{2}\left(\frac{\pi}{6} - \frac{\pi}{6}\right) - \frac{1}{4}\left(\frac{\pi}{6} - \frac{\pi}{6}\right)^2 - \frac{\sqrt{3}}{12}\left(\frac{\pi}{6} - \frac{\pi}{6}\right)^3 + \cdots$

$$= \frac{1}{2} + 0 - 0 - 0 + \cdots$$

$$= \frac{1}{2}$$

The actual value of $\sin\left(\frac{\pi}{6}\right)$ is $\frac{1}{2}$.

The approximation is exact.

11. $\lim_{n\to\infty} \frac{\frac{4\sqrt{n} - 1}{n^2 + 2\sqrt{n}}}{\frac{1}{n^{3/2}}} = \lim_{n\to\infty} \frac{4n^2 - n^{3/2}}{n^2 + 2\sqrt{n}} = 4$

$\sum_{n=1}^{\infty} \frac{4\sqrt{n} - 1}{n^2 + 2\sqrt{n}}$ **converges** by the **limit comparison test** with a convergent *p*-series.

12. $\lim_{n\to\infty} \frac{\frac{3}{(4n + 5)^2}}{\frac{1}{n^2}} = \lim_{n\to\infty} \frac{3n^2}{(4n + 5)^2} = \frac{3}{16}$

$\sum_{n=1}^{\infty} \frac{3}{(4n + 5)^2}$ **converges** by the **limit comparison test** with a convergent *p*-series.

13. $\lim_{n\to\infty} \frac{\frac{(n + 1)^3}{2^{n+1}}}{\frac{n^3}{2^n}} = \lim_{n\to\infty} \frac{(n + 1)^3}{2n^3} = \frac{1}{2}$

$\sum_{n=1}^{\infty} \frac{n^3}{2^n}$ **converges** by the **ratio test.**

14. $\lim_{n\to\infty} \frac{\frac{4}{n^{2/3} - 1}}{\frac{1}{n^{2/3}}} = \lim_{n\to\infty} \frac{4n^{2/3}}{n^{2/3} - 1} = 4$

$\sum_{n=2}^{\infty} \frac{4}{\sqrt[3]{n^2} - 1}$ **diverges** by the **limit comparison test** with a divergent *p*-series.

15. $\sum_{n=1}^{\infty} \left|(-1)^{n+1} \frac{1}{\sqrt{n}}\right| = \sum_{n=1}^{\infty} \frac{1}{n^{1/2}}$

This is a divergent *p*-series, so absolute convergence is not attained. However, $\frac{1}{\sqrt{n + 1}} < \frac{1}{\sqrt{n}}$ for all n and $\lim_{n\to\infty} \frac{1}{\sqrt{n}} = 0$ so this series meets the conditions of Leibniz's theorem and **converges conditionally.**

16. $\sum_{n=1}^{\infty} \frac{(-1)^{n+1}}{2^n}$ is a geometric series with $a = \frac{1}{2}$ and $r = -\frac{1}{2}$.

$$S = \frac{\frac{1}{2}}{1 + \frac{1}{2}} = \frac{\frac{1}{2}}{\frac{3}{2}} = \frac{1}{3}$$

This geometric series **converges to $\frac{1}{3}$,** because it is a **geometric series with $|r| < 1$.**

17. $x = \frac{1}{16}y^4 + \frac{1}{2}y^{-2}$

$$\frac{dx}{dy} = \frac{1}{4}y^3 - y^{-3}$$

$$\left(\frac{dx}{dy}\right)^2 = \frac{1}{16}y^6 - \frac{1}{2} + \frac{1}{y^6}$$

$$L_{-4}^{-1} = \int_{-4}^{-1} \sqrt{\frac{1}{16}y^6 - \frac{1}{2} + \frac{1}{y^6} + 1}\, dy$$

$$= \int_{-4}^{-1} \sqrt{\frac{1}{16}y^6 + \frac{1}{2} + \frac{1}{y^6}}\, dy$$

$$= \int_{-4}^{-1} \sqrt{\left(\frac{1}{4}y^3 + \frac{1}{y^3}\right)^2}\, dy$$

$$= \int_{-4}^{-1} \left(\frac{1}{4}y^3 + y^{-3}\right) dy$$

$$= \left[\frac{1}{16}y^4 - \frac{1}{2}y^{-2}\right]_{-4}^{-1}$$

$$= \frac{1}{16} - \frac{1}{2} - \left(16 - \frac{1}{32}\right)$$

$$= -16\frac{13}{32}$$

$$= \mathbf{16\frac{13}{32}\ units}$$

18.

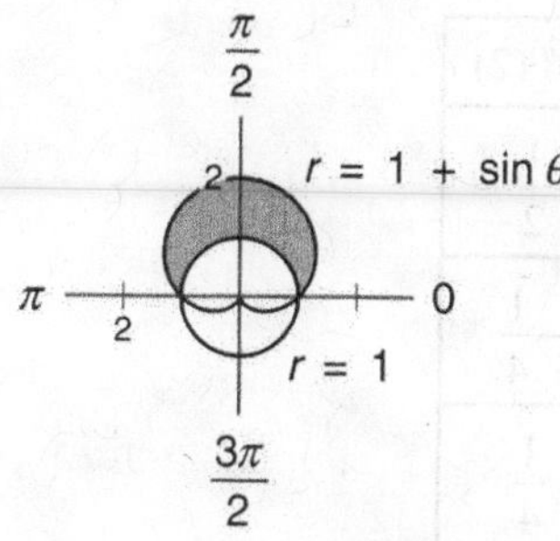

$$A = 2\int_0^{\pi/2} \frac{1}{2}(1 + \sin\theta)^2\, d\theta - \frac{1}{2}\pi(1)^2$$
$$= \int_0^{\pi/2} (1 + 2\sin\theta + \sin^2\theta)\, d\theta - \frac{\pi}{2}$$
$$= \int_0^{\pi/2} \left[\frac{3}{2} + 2\sin\theta - \frac{1}{2}\cos(2\theta)\right] d\theta - \frac{\pi}{2}$$
$$= \left[\frac{3}{2}\theta - 2\cos\theta - \frac{1}{4}\sin(2\theta)\right]_0^{\pi/2} - \frac{\pi}{2}$$
$$= \frac{3\pi}{4} - 0 - 0 - (0 - 2 - 0) - \frac{\pi}{2}$$
$$= \mathbf{\left(\frac{\pi}{4} + 2\right)\ units^2}$$

19.
$$f(x) = \int_{3x^2}^{\sin x} \cos t^2\, dt$$
$$f'(x) = \frac{d}{dx}\int_{3x^2}^{\sin x} \cos t^2\, dt$$
$$f'(x) = \cos(\sin^2 x)\cos x - (6x)\cos(9x^4)$$
$$\text{slope} = f'(2) = \mathbf{\cos(\sin^2 2)\cos 2 - 12\cos 144}$$

20. $f(x) = e^{x^2}$ is an even function.
$$\int_{-b}^{b} e^{x^2}\, dx = 2\int_0^b e^{x^2}\, dx = \mathbf{2L}$$

21. $\lim_{x\to 0} (-x^2 + 2) = \lim_{x\to 0} (x^2 + 2) = 2$

If $-x^2 + 2 \le f(x) \le x^2 + 2$, then $\lim_{x\to 0} f(x) = \mathbf{2}$ by the sandwich theorem.

PROBLEM SET 144

1.

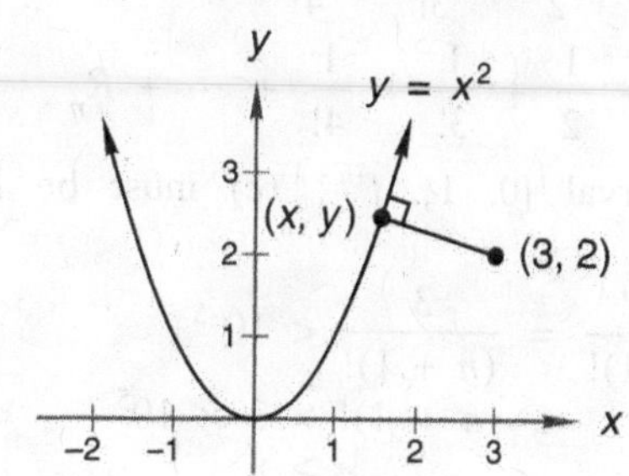

$$d = \sqrt{(x - 3)^2 + (y - 2)^2}$$
$$d = \sqrt{(x - 3)^2 + (x^2 - 2)^2}$$
$$d' = \frac{2(x - 3) + 2(x^2 - 2)(2x)}{2\sqrt{(x - 3)^2 + (x^2 - 2)^2}}$$
$$0 = x - 3 + 2x^3 - 4x$$
$$0 = 2x^3 - 3x - 3$$
$$x \approx 1.5675$$

(1.5675, 2.4571)

2. $a(t) = -32$
$$v(t) = -32t$$
$$h(t) = -16t^2 + 5.5$$
$$0 = -16t^2 + 5.5$$
$$16t^2 = 5.5$$
$$t \approx 0.5863\ \text{s}$$
$$d = rt$$
$$d \approx (500\ \text{ft/s})(0.5863\ \text{s}) = 293.15\ \text{ft}$$

The arrow will hit the ground **0.5863 s** after firing, **293.15 ft** from the bow.

3. $y = -16t^2 + v_0 t \sin\theta$
$$-7 = -16t^2 + 500t\sin 30°$$
$$0 = 16t^2 - 250t - 7$$
$$t \approx 15.6530$$
$$x = v_0 t \cos\theta$$
$$x \approx 500(15.6530)\cos 30°$$
$$= 6777.9478\ \text{ft}$$

This arrow would hit the ground **15.6530 s** after firing, **6777.9478 ft** from the bow. This does not seem reasonable; this is a distance of more than one mile.

4. $e^x = 1 + x + \frac{x^2}{2} + \frac{x^3}{3!} + \frac{x^4}{4!} + \cdots + R_n$

$e = 1 + 1 + \frac{1}{2} + \frac{1}{3!} + \frac{1}{4!} + \cdots + R_n$

On the interval [0, 1], $f^{(n+1)}(c)$ must be less than 3, so

$$R_n < \frac{3 \cdot 1^{n+1}}{(n+1)!} = \frac{3}{(n+1)!} < 10^{-5}$$

$$(n+1)! > 3 \times 10^5$$

$$n \geq 8$$

$$e \approx \mathbf{1 + 1 + \frac{1}{2} + \frac{1}{3!} + \frac{1}{4!} + \frac{1}{5!} + \frac{1}{6!} + \frac{1}{7!} + \frac{1}{8!}} \approx \mathbf{2.718278770}$$

5.

n	$f^{(n)}(x)$	$f^{(n)}\left(\frac{\pi}{6}\right)$
0	$\sin x$	$\frac{1}{2}$
1	$\cos x$	$\frac{\sqrt{3}}{2}$
2	$-\sin x$	$-\frac{1}{2}$
3	$-\cos x$	$-\frac{\sqrt{3}}{2}$

$$\sin x \approx \frac{1}{2} + \frac{\sqrt{3}}{2}\left(x - \frac{\pi}{6}\right) - \frac{1}{2}\frac{\left(x - \frac{\pi}{6}\right)^2}{2}$$

$$\sin 32° = \sin\left(\frac{\pi}{6} + \frac{\pi}{90}\right)$$

$$\approx \frac{1}{2} + \frac{\sqrt{3}}{2}\left(\frac{\pi}{90}\right) - \frac{1}{4}\left(\frac{\pi}{90}\right)^2 + R_2$$

$$R_2 = -\cos(c)\left(\frac{\pi}{90}\right)^3 \frac{1}{3!}$$

$$R_2 \leq \left(\frac{4}{90}\right)^3 \frac{1}{6} = \frac{4}{273{,}375}$$

$$\sin 32° \approx \mathbf{\frac{1}{2} + \frac{\sqrt{3}}{2}\left(\frac{\pi}{90}\right) - \frac{1}{4}\left(\frac{\pi}{90}\right)^2}$$

with an error of less than $\mathbf{\frac{4}{273{,}375}}$

6. $(1 + x)^{2/3}$ can be expanded using a binomial series with $b = \frac{2}{3}$.

$$(1 + x)^{2/3} = 1 + \frac{2}{3}x + \frac{2}{3}\left(-\frac{1}{3}\right)\frac{x^2}{2} + \frac{2}{3}\left(-\frac{1}{3}\right)\left(-\frac{4}{3}\right)\frac{x^3}{3!} + \cdots$$

$$= \mathbf{1 + \frac{2}{3}x - \frac{1}{9}x^2 + \frac{4}{81}x^3 + \cdots}$$

7.

n	$f^{(n)}(x)$	$f^{(n)}(2)$
0	x^{-1}	$\frac{1}{2}$
1	$-x^{-2}$	$-\frac{1}{4}$
2	$2x^{-3}$	$\frac{1}{4}$
3	$-6x^{-4}$	$-\frac{3}{8}$

$$\frac{1}{x} = \frac{1}{2} - \frac{1}{4}(x-2) + \frac{1}{4}\frac{(x-2)^2}{2!} - \frac{3}{8}\frac{(x-2)^3}{3!} + \cdots$$

$$= \mathbf{\frac{1}{2} - \frac{1}{4}(x-2) + \frac{1}{8}(x-2)^2 - \frac{1}{16}(x-2)^3 + \cdots}$$

8. $(1 + x)^{1/3}$

$$= 1 + \frac{1}{3}x + \frac{1}{3}\left(-\frac{2}{3}\right)\frac{x^2}{2!} + \frac{1}{3}\left(-\frac{2}{3}\right)\left(-\frac{5}{3}\right)\frac{x^3}{3!} + \frac{1}{3}\left(-\frac{2}{3}\right)\left(-\frac{5}{3}\right)\left(-\frac{8}{3}\right)\frac{x^4}{4!} + \cdots$$

$$= 1 + \frac{1}{3}x - \frac{1}{9}x^2 + \frac{5}{81}x^3 - \frac{10}{243}x^4 + \cdots$$

$$\sqrt[3]{1.625} = \left(1 + \frac{5}{8}\right)^{1/3}$$

$$= 1 + \frac{1}{3}\left(\frac{5}{8}\right) - \frac{1}{9}\left(\frac{5}{8}\right)^2 + \frac{5}{81}\left(\frac{5}{8}\right)^3 - \frac{10}{243}\left(\frac{5}{8}\right)^4 + \cdots$$

After the first terms this is an alternating series, and since $a_4 = \frac{10}{243}\left(\frac{5}{8}\right)^4 \approx 0.0062793371$, the first four terms can be added to give an error less than 0.01.

$$\sqrt[3]{1.625} \approx \mathbf{1.180000965}$$

9. $\vec{p} = -3(2^t)\hat{i} + 4\cos(2t)\,\hat{j}$

$\vec{v} = -3(2^t)\ln 2\,\hat{i} - 8\sin(2t)\,\hat{j}$

$\vec{a} = -3(2^t)(\ln 2)^2\,\hat{i} - 16\cos(2t)\,\hat{j}$

speed $= \sqrt{[-3(4)\ln 2]^2 + (-8\sin 4)^2}$

speed ≈ 10.2879

$|\vec{a}| = \sqrt{[-3(4)(\ln 2)^2]^2 + (-16\cos 4)^2}$

$|\vec{a}| \approx$ **11.9422**

10. At $t = 2$, $\vec{p} \approx -12\hat{i} - 2.6146\hat{j}$

$\vec{v} \approx -8.3178\hat{i} + 6.0544\hat{j}$

$\vec{a} \approx -5.7654\hat{i} + 10.4583\hat{j}$

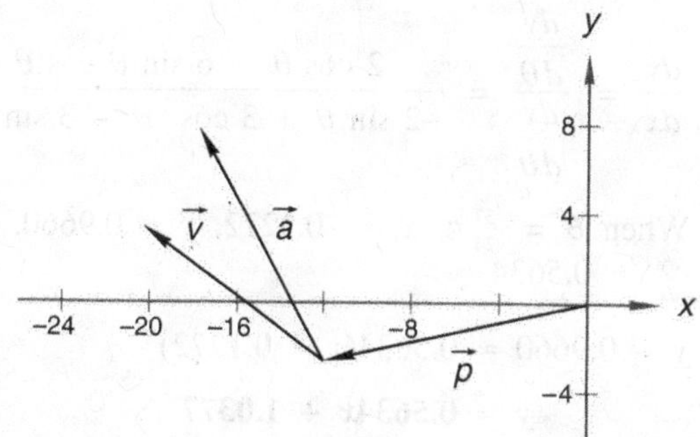

11. $$\lim_{n\to\infty} \frac{\frac{\ln(2n+1)}{n(n+2)}}{\frac{1}{n^{3/2}}} = \lim_{n\to\infty} \frac{n^{3/2}\ln(2n+1)}{n(n+2)}$$

$$= \lim_{n\to\infty} \frac{\ln(2n+1)}{n^{1/2} + 2n^{-1/2}} = \lim_{n\to\infty} \frac{\frac{2}{2n+1}}{\frac{1}{2n^{1/2}} - \frac{1}{n^{3/2}}}$$

$$= \lim_{n\to\infty} \frac{4n^{3/2}}{(2n+1)(n-2)} = 0$$

$\sum_{n=1}^{\infty} \frac{\ln(2n+1)}{n(n+2)}$ **converges** by the **limit comparison test** with a convergent p-series.

12. $$\lim_{n\to\infty} \frac{\frac{(n+4)!}{3!\,(n+1)!\,3^{n+1}}}{\frac{(n+3)!}{3!\,n!\,3^n}} = \lim_{n\to\infty} \frac{(n+4)}{(n+1)3} = \frac{1}{3}$$

$\sum_{n=1}^{\infty} \frac{(n+3)!}{3!\,n!\,3^n}$ **converges** by the **ratio test.**

13. $$\sum_{n=1}^{\infty} \left|(-1)^{n+1}\frac{n}{e^n}\right| = \sum_{n=1}^{\infty} \frac{n}{e^n}$$

$$\lim_{n\to\infty} \sqrt[n]{\frac{n}{e^n}} = \frac{1}{e}$$

This series **converges absolutely** by the **root test.**

14. $$\sum_{n=1}^{\infty} \left|(-1)^n \frac{n+1}{n^{1/2}}\right| = \sum_{n=1}^{\infty} \frac{n+1}{n^{3/2}}$$

$$\lim_{n\to\infty} \frac{\frac{n+1}{n^{3/2}}}{\frac{1}{n^{1/2}}} = \lim_{n\to\infty} \frac{n+1}{n} = \lim_{n\to\infty}\left(1 + \frac{1}{n}\right) = 1$$

This series does not converge absolutely by the limit comparison test with a divergent p-series.

However, the conditions of Leibniz's theorem are met:

$$\frac{n+2}{(n+1)^{3/2}} < \frac{n+1}{n^{3/2}} \text{ for all } n$$

$$\lim_{n\to\infty} \frac{n+1}{n^{3/2}} = \lim_{n\to\infty} \frac{1}{\frac{3}{2}\sqrt{n}} = 0$$

The series **converges conditionally.**

15. $f(x, y) = x^3 + y^2$; $\Delta x = \frac{5.3 - 5}{3} = 0.1$

i	x_i	y_i
0	5	−1
1	5.1	11.6
2	5.2	38.3211
3	5.3	199.2325705

$y(5.3) \approx$ **199.2325705**

16.

$\frac{\pi}{2}$, $r = 2\cos\theta$, π, 0, $r = 1 - \sin\theta$, $\frac{3\pi}{2}$

$1 - \sin\theta = 2\cos\theta$

$\theta = \frac{\pi}{2}$ and $\theta \approx 5.6397$

$$A \approx \int_{\pi/2}^{3\pi/2} \frac{1}{2}(1 - \sin\theta)^2\, d\theta + \int_{3\pi/2}^{5.6397} \frac{1}{2}\left[(1-\sin\theta)^2 - (2\cos\theta)^2\right] d\theta$$

$$= \frac{1}{2}\int_{\pi/2}^{3\pi/2} (1 - 2\sin\theta + \sin^2\theta)\, d\theta + \frac{1}{2}\int_{3\pi/2}^{5.6397} (1 - 2\sin\theta + \sin^2\theta - 4\cos^2\theta)\, d\theta$$

$$= \frac{1}{2}\int_{\pi/2}^{3\pi/2}\left[\frac{3}{2} - 2\sin\theta - \frac{1}{2}\cos(2\theta)\right] d\theta + \frac{1}{2}\int_{3\pi/2}^{5.6397}\left[-\frac{1}{2} - 2\sin\theta - \frac{5}{2}\cos(2\theta)\right] d\theta$$

$$= \frac{1}{2}\left[\frac{3}{2}\theta + 2\cos\theta - \frac{1}{4}\sin(2\theta)\right]_{\pi/2}^{3\pi/2} + \frac{1}{2}\left[-\frac{1}{2}\theta + 2\cos\theta - \frac{5}{4}\sin(2\theta)\right]_{3\pi/2}^{5.6397}$$

$\approx$ **3.5244 units²**

17. $\int_2^{\infty}(x-1)^{-3}\,dx = \lim_{b\to\infty}\int_2^b (x-1)^{-3}\,dx$

$$= \lim_{b\to\infty}\left[-\frac{1}{2}(x-1)^{-2}\right]_2^b$$

$$= \lim_{b\to\infty} -\frac{1}{2}(b-1)^{-2} - \left(-\frac{1}{2}\right)$$

$$= 0 + \frac{1}{2} = \mathbf{\frac{1}{2}}$$

18. $\int_{-2}^{0}(2x+1)^{-2/3}\,dx$

$$= \lim_{a\to -1/2^-}\int_{-2}^{a}(2x+1)^{-2/3}\,dx$$

$$+ \lim_{b\to -1/2^+}\int_{b}^{0}(2x+1)^{-2/3}\,dx$$

$$= \lim_{a\to -1/2^-}\frac{3}{2}\left[(2x+1)^{1/3}\right]_{-2}^{a}$$

$$+ \lim_{b\to -1/2^+}\frac{3}{2}\left[(2x+1)^{1/3}\right]_{b}^{0}$$

$$= \frac{3}{2}(0-\sqrt[3]{-3}) + \frac{3}{2}(1-0)$$

$$= \frac{3}{2}(1-\sqrt[3]{-3}) = \mathbf{\frac{3}{2}(1+\sqrt[3]{3})}$$

19. $x = \frac{3}{2}\sec\theta \quad dx = \frac{3}{2}\sec\theta\tan\theta\,d\theta$

$$\sqrt{4x^2-9} = 3\tan\theta$$

$$(4x^2-9)^{3/2} = 27\tan^3\theta$$

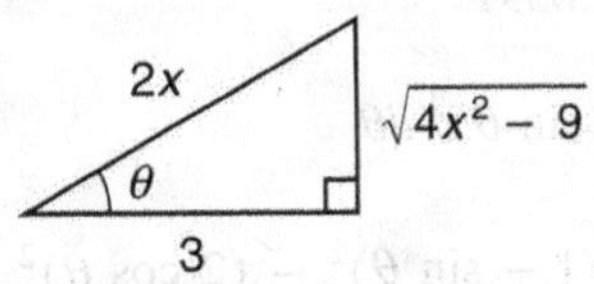

$$\int\frac{1}{(4x^2-9)^{3/2}}\,dx = \int\frac{\frac{3}{2}\sec\theta\tan\theta\,d\theta}{27\tan^3\theta}$$

$$= \frac{1}{18}\int\frac{\sec\theta}{\tan^2\theta}\,d\theta$$

$$= \frac{1}{18}\int\frac{\cos\theta}{\sin^2\theta}\,d\theta$$

$$= -\frac{1}{18}\frac{1}{\sin\theta} + C$$

$$= -\frac{1}{18}\csc\theta + C$$

$$= -\frac{1}{18}\frac{2x}{\sqrt{4x^2-9}} + C$$

$$= \mathbf{\frac{-x}{9\sqrt{4x^2-9}} + C}$$

20. $r = 2 + 3\sin\theta$

$$x = (2+3\sin\theta)\cos\theta = 2\cos\theta + 3\sin\theta\cos\theta$$

$$y = (2+3\sin\theta)\sin\theta = 2\sin\theta + 3\sin^2\theta$$

$$\frac{dy}{dx} = \frac{\frac{dy}{d\theta}}{\frac{dx}{d\theta}} = \frac{2\cos\theta + 6\sin\theta\cos\theta}{-2\sin\theta + 3\cos^2\theta - 3\sin^2\theta}$$

When $\theta = \frac{37}{24}\pi$, $x \approx -0.1272$, $y \approx 0.9660$, and $\frac{dy}{dx} \approx 0.5634$.

$$y - 0.9660 \approx 0.5634(x + 0.1272)$$

$$\mathbf{y \approx 0.5634x + 1.0377}$$

21. $\lim_{h\to 0}\frac{\ln(x+h) - \ln x}{h}$

$$= \lim_{h\to 0}\frac{1}{h}\frac{x}{x}\ln\left(\frac{x+h}{x}\right)$$

$$= \lim_{h\to 0}\frac{1}{x}\frac{x}{h}\ln\left(1+\frac{h}{x}\right)$$

$$= \frac{1}{x}\lim_{h\to 0}\ln\left(1+\frac{h}{x}\right)^{x/h}$$

$$= \frac{1}{x}\ln e = \mathbf{\frac{1}{x}}$$

22. The statement in the question is the epsilon-delta definition of the limit of $f(x)$ as x approaches a, which is correctly expressed by $\lim_{x\to a} f(x) = L$.

The correct choice is **D.**

PROBLEM SET 145

1. $\lim_{n\to\infty}\left|\frac{\frac{x^{n+1}}{(n+1)!}}{\frac{x^n}{n!}}\right| = \lim_{n\to\infty}\frac{|x|}{n+1} = 0$

By the ratio test, $\sum_{n=0}^{\infty}\frac{x^n}{n!}$ converges absolutely for all x. The interval of convergence is **$(-\infty, \infty)$.**

2. $\lim_{n\to\infty}\left|\frac{x^{n+1}}{x^n}\right| = |x|$

By the ratio test, $\sum_{n=0}^{\infty}x^n$ converges absolutely when $|x| < 1$. If $|x| \geq 1$ the series diverges. So the interval of convergence is **$(-1, 1)$.**

3.

n	$f^{(n)}(x)$	$f^{(n)}\left(\frac{\pi}{6}\right)$
0	$\cos x$	$\frac{\sqrt{3}}{2}$
1	$-\sin x$	$-\frac{1}{2}$
2	$-\cos x$	$-\frac{\sqrt{3}}{2}$
3	$\sin x$	$\frac{1}{2}$

$$\cos x \approx \frac{\sqrt{3}}{2} - \frac{1}{2}\left(x - \frac{\pi}{6}\right) - \frac{\sqrt{3}}{2}\frac{\left(x - \frac{\pi}{6}\right)^2}{2!}$$

$$\approx \frac{\sqrt{3}}{2} - \frac{1}{2}\left(x - \frac{\pi}{6}\right) - \frac{\sqrt{3}}{4}\left(x - \frac{\pi}{6}\right)^2$$

$$\cos 35° = \cos\left(\frac{\pi}{6} + \frac{\pi}{36}\right)$$

$$= \frac{\sqrt{3}}{2} - \frac{1}{2}\left(\frac{\pi}{36}\right) - \frac{\sqrt{3}}{4}\left(\frac{\pi}{36}\right)^2 + R_2$$

$$= \frac{\sqrt{3}}{2} - \frac{\pi}{72} - \frac{\sqrt{3}\pi^2}{5184} + R_2$$

$$R_2 = \frac{(\sin c)\left(x - \frac{\pi}{6}\right)^3}{3!} \leq \frac{1\left(\frac{\pi}{36}\right)^3}{6}$$

$$\approx 0.0001107620$$

$\cos 35° \approx$ **0.8190945922** with an error no larger than **0.0001107620.**

4. $(1 + x)^{1/4}$

$$= 1 + \frac{1}{4}x + \frac{1}{4}\left(-\frac{3}{4}\right)\frac{x^2}{2} + \frac{1}{4}\left(-\frac{3}{4}\right)\left(-\frac{7}{4}\right)\frac{x^3}{3!}$$

$$+ \frac{1}{4}\left(-\frac{3}{4}\right)\left(-\frac{7}{4}\right)\left(-\frac{11}{4}\right)\frac{x^4}{4!} + \cdots$$

$$= 1 + \frac{1}{4}x - \frac{3}{32}x^2 + \frac{7}{128}x^3 - \frac{77}{2048}x^4 + \cdots$$

$$\sqrt[4]{1.75} = (1 + 0.75)^{1/4}$$

$$= 1 + \frac{1}{4}(0.75) - \frac{3}{32}(0.75)^2$$

$$+ \frac{7}{128}(0.75)^3 - \frac{77}{2048}(0.75)^4 + \cdots$$

After the first term this is an alternating series. Since $a_5 = \frac{231}{8192}(0.75)^5 \approx 0.0066915751$, the first five terms can be added to give an error less than 0.01.

$\sqrt[4]{1.75} \approx$ **1.145940781**

5.

n	$f^{(n)}(x)$	$f^{(n)}(0)$
0	$(1 - x)^{-1}$	1
1	$(1 - x)^{-2}$	1
2	$2(1 - x)^{-3}$	2
3	$6(1 - x)^{-4}$	6
4	$24(1 - x)^{-5}$	24

$$f(x) = 1 + x + \frac{2x^2}{2} + \frac{6x^3}{3!} + \frac{24x^4}{4!} + \cdots$$

$$= 1 + x + x^2 + x^3 + x^4 + \cdots$$

$$= \sum_{n=0}^{\infty} x^n$$

$$\lim_{n\to\infty} \left|\sqrt[n]{x^n}\right| = |x|$$

By the root test the series converges when $|x| < 1$ and diverges when $|x| \geq 1$. Therefore, the interval of convergence is **(–1, 1).**

6. $y = x^2 + 3x - 4$

$y' = 2x + 3$

When $x = 3$, $m = 9$.

One possible vector with a slope of 9 is $\langle 1, 9\rangle$.

Tangent unit vector: $\left\langle \frac{1}{\sqrt{82}}, \frac{9}{\sqrt{82}} \right\rangle$

Normal unit vector: $\left\langle -\frac{9}{\sqrt{82}}, \frac{1}{\sqrt{82}} \right\rangle$

7. $\int_{-2}^{3} f(x)\,dx$

$$= \lim_{a\to 2^-} \int_{-2}^{a} (x^2 + 1)\,dx + \lim_{b\to 2^+} \int_{b}^{3} (2x + 1)\,dx$$

$$= \lim_{a\to 2^-} \left[\frac{1}{3}x^3 + x\right]_{-2}^{a} + \lim_{b\to 2^+} \left[x^2 + x\right]_b^3$$

$$= \frac{8}{3} + 2 - \left(-\frac{8}{3} - 2\right) + (9 + 3) - (4 + 2)$$

$$= \mathbf{15\frac{1}{3}}$$

8. $f(x) = \int_{\pi}^{\sin x} \sqrt{1 - \cos t}\,dt$

$$f'(x) = \frac{d}{dx}\int_{\pi}^{\sin x} \sqrt{1 - \cos t}\,dt$$

$$f'(x) = \sqrt{1 - \cos(\sin x)}\cos x$$

At $x = \frac{\pi}{2}$,

$$m = \sqrt{1 - \cos\left(\sin\frac{\pi}{2}\right)}\cos\frac{\pi}{2}$$

$$= \sqrt{1 - \cos 1}\,(0) = \mathbf{0}$$

9.

$$|y + 3| < \varepsilon$$
$$|3 - 2x + 3| < \varepsilon$$
$$|-2x + 6| < \varepsilon$$
$$|x - 3| < \frac{\varepsilon}{2}$$
$$\delta = \frac{\varepsilon}{2}$$

10. $3.231231231\ldots = 3 + 0.231231231\ldots$

$$= 3 + \sum_{n=0}^{\infty} 0.231(0.001)^n$$
$$= 3 + \frac{0.231}{1 - 0.001}$$
$$= \mathbf{\frac{1076}{333}}$$

11. $\displaystyle\sum_{n=1}^{\infty} \frac{2^n + 3}{4^n} = \sum_{n=1}^{\infty}\left(\frac{1}{2}\right)^n + \sum_{n=1}^{\infty}\frac{3}{4^n}$

This is the sum of 2 geometric series. The first has $a = \frac{1}{2}$ and $r = \frac{1}{2}$. The second has $a = \frac{3}{4}$ and $r = \frac{1}{4}$.

$$S = \frac{\frac{1}{2}}{1 - \frac{1}{2}} + \frac{\frac{3}{4}}{1 - \frac{1}{4}} = 1 + 1$$

The series converges to **2**.

12. $\displaystyle\int_0^2 \sqrt{1 + x^4}\, dx$

$$T = \frac{2}{8}\left[1 + 2\left(\frac{\sqrt{17}}{4}\right) + 2(\sqrt{2}) + 2\left(\frac{\sqrt{97}}{4}\right) + \sqrt{17}\right]$$
$$= \frac{1}{4}\left(1 + \frac{\sqrt{17}}{2} + 2\sqrt{2} + \frac{\sqrt{97}}{2} + \sqrt{17}\right)$$
$$\approx \mathbf{3.7344}$$

13.

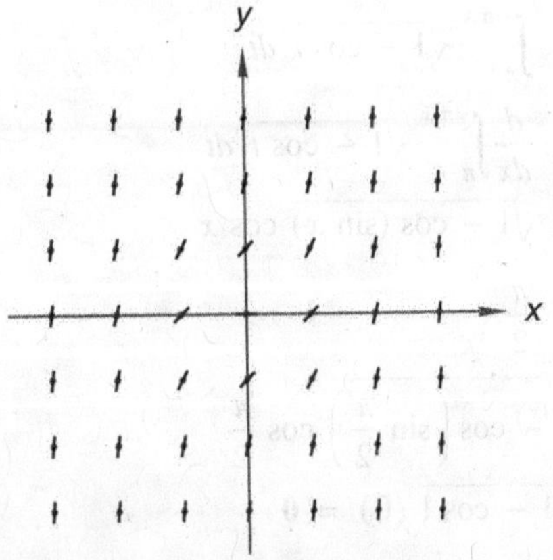

14. With $f(x) = x^3 - 3x + 4$, the value of $f(-3)$ is negative and $f(-2)$ is positive. Newton's method can be used to determine the zero with an initial guess of $x_1 = -2.5$, `Y1=X³-3X+4`, and `Y2=nDeriv(Y1,X,X)`.

```
-2.5→X
                -2.5
X-(Y1/Y2)→X
         -2.238095255
         -2.196814627
          -2.19582391
         -2.195823345
         -2.195823345
```

The approximation of the zero is **−2.195823345.**

15. $u = \sin(3x) \qquad v = \frac{1}{2}e^{2x}$

$du = 3\cos(3x)\,dx \qquad dv = e^{2x}\,dx$

$$\int e^{2x}\sin(3x)\,dx$$
$$= \frac{1}{2}e^{2x}\sin(3x) - \int \frac{3}{2}e^{2x}\cos(3x)\,dx$$

$u = \frac{3}{2}\cos(3x) \qquad v = \frac{1}{2}e^{2x}$

$du = -\frac{9}{2}\sin(3x)\,dx \qquad dv = e^{2x}\,dx$

$$\int e^{2x}\sin(3x)\,dx$$
$$= \frac{1}{2}e^{2x}\sin(3x) - \left[\frac{3}{4}e^{2x}\cos(3x) + \int \frac{9}{4}e^{2x}\sin(3x)\,dx\right]$$
$$\frac{13}{4}\int e^{2x}\sin(3x)\,dx$$
$$= \frac{1}{2}e^{2x}\sin(3x) - \frac{3}{4}e^{2x}\cos(3x) + C$$
$$\int e^{2x}\sin(3x)\,dx$$
$$= \frac{2}{13}e^{2x}\sin(3x) - \frac{3}{13}e^{2x}\cos(3x) + C$$
$$= \mathbf{\frac{1}{13}e^{2x}[2\sin(3x) - 3\cos(3x)] + C}$$

16. $\displaystyle\int \frac{-3x^2 + 2x - 2}{x^2(x - 1)}\,dx$

$\displaystyle= \int \left(\frac{A}{x} + \frac{B}{x^2} + \frac{C}{x - 1}\right) dx$

$A(x - 1)x + B(x - 1) + Cx^2 = -3x^2 + 2x - 2$

$x = 0$: $\quad B = 2$

$x = 1$: $\quad C = -3$

$x = 2$: $\quad 2A + B + 4C = -10$

$A = 0$

$\displaystyle\int \left(\frac{A}{x} + \frac{B}{x^2} + \frac{C}{x - 1}\right) dx$

$\displaystyle= \int \left(\frac{2}{x^2} - \frac{3}{x - 1}\right) dx$

$\displaystyle= \mathbf{-\frac{2}{x} - 3 \ln |x - 1| + C}$

17. $x = 2 \sin (3t) \qquad y = 4 \cos (2t)$

$\displaystyle\frac{dy}{dx} = \frac{-8 \sin (2t)}{6 \cos (3t)} = \frac{-4 \sin (2t)}{3 \cos (3t)}$

$$\frac{d^2y}{dx^2} = \frac{\dfrac{3 \cos (3t)\,[-8 \cos (2t)]}{9 \cos^2 (3t)}}{6 \cos (3t)} - \frac{\dfrac{[-4 \sin (2t)][-9 \sin (3t)]}{9 \cos^2 (3t)}}{6 \cos (3t)}$$

$$= \frac{-24 \cos (3t) \cos (2t) - 36 \sin (2t) \sin (3t)}{54 \cos^3 (3t)}$$

$$= \mathbf{-\frac{4 \cos (2t)}{9 \cos^2 (3t)} - \frac{2 \sin (2t) \sin (3t)}{3 \cos^3 (3t)}}$$

18.

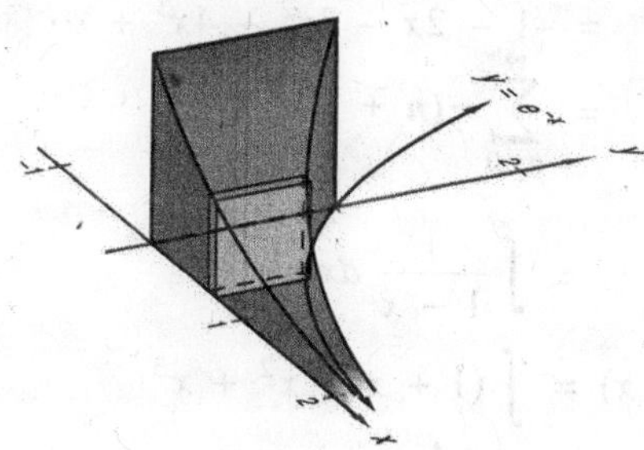

$\displaystyle V = \int_0^{\infty} (e^{-x})^2\,dx$

$\displaystyle= \lim_{b\to\infty} \int_0^b e^{-2x}\,dx$

$\displaystyle= \lim_{b\to\infty} -\frac{1}{2}\left[e^{-2x}\right]_0^b$

$\displaystyle= -\frac{1}{2}(0 - 1) = \mathbf{\frac{1}{2}\ \textbf{unit}^3}$

19. Let Y1=2^X+X³ and adjust the window settings to $x[2.997, 3.003]$ and $y[34.997, 35.003]$. Performing a TRACE results in the following.

x	y
2.9999362	34.997923
3	35
3.0000638	35.002077

If $|x - 3| < 0.0000638$, then $|y - 3| < 0.01$, thus $\delta =$ **0.0000638.** Answers may vary.

20.

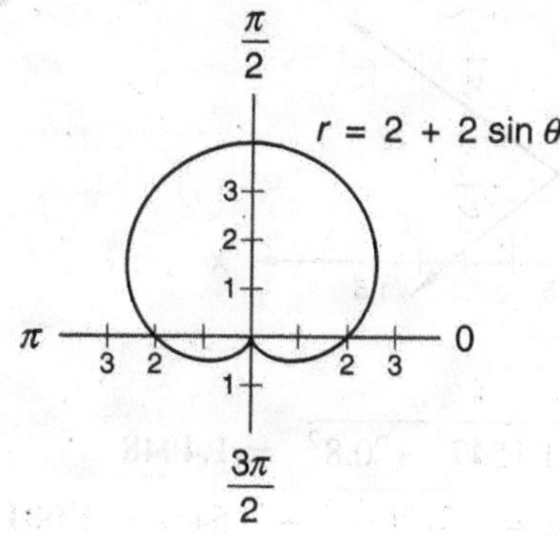

21. $y = xe^{x^2} - \arcsin (x^2)$

$\displaystyle\frac{dy}{dx} = xe^{x^2}2x + e^{x^2} - \frac{2x}{\sqrt{1 - x^4}}$

$\displaystyle\mathbf{\frac{dy}{dx} = e^{x^2}(2x^2 + 1) - \frac{2x}{\sqrt{1 - x^4}}}$

Problem Set 146

1. $x = v_0 t \cos \theta$

$x = 45t \cos 40°$

$\displaystyle t = \frac{x}{45 \cos 40°}$

$y = -16t^2 + v_0 t \sin \theta$

$\displaystyle -7 = -16\left(\frac{x}{45 \cos 40°}\right)^2 + 45\left(\frac{x}{45 \cos 40°}\right) \sin 40°$

$0 = 0.0135x^2 - 0.8391x - 7$

$x \approx$ **69.6050 ft**

2. $\vec{p} = (\arcsin t)\hat{i} + (\arctan t)\hat{j}$

$$\vec{v} = \frac{1}{\sqrt{1-t^2}}\hat{i} + \frac{1}{t^2+1}\hat{j}$$

$$\vec{a} = \frac{t}{(1-t^2)^{3/2}}\hat{i} - \frac{2t}{(t^2+1)^2}\hat{j}$$

At $t = 0.5$, $\vec{p} = 0.5236\hat{i} + 0.4636\hat{j}$

$\vec{v} = 1.1547\hat{i} + 0.8\hat{j}$

$\vec{a} = 0.7698\hat{i} - 0.64\hat{j}$

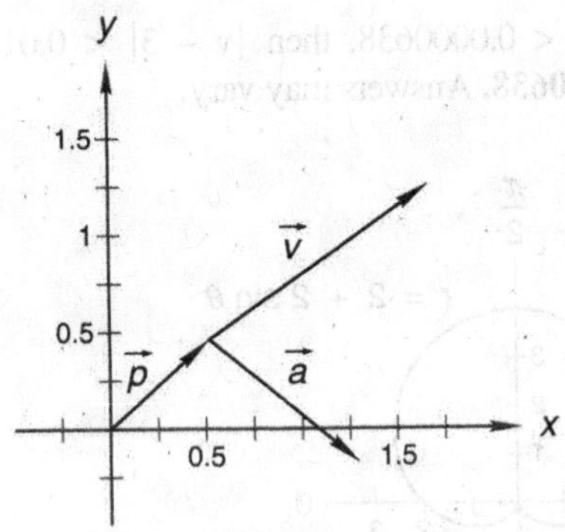

Speed $= \sqrt{1.1547^2 + 0.8^2} =$ **1.4048**

Acceleration $= \sqrt{0.7698^2 + 0.64^2} =$ **1.0011**

3.

n	$f^{(n)}(x)$	$f^{(n)}\left(\frac{\pi}{3}\right)$
0	$\sin x$	$\frac{\sqrt{3}}{2}$
1	$\cos x$	$\frac{1}{2}$
2	$-\sin x$	$-\frac{\sqrt{3}}{2}$
3	$-\cos x$	$-\frac{1}{2}$
⋮	⋮	⋮

$$\sin x = \frac{\sqrt{3}}{2} + \frac{1}{2}\left(x - \frac{\pi}{3}\right) - \frac{\sqrt{3}}{2}\frac{\left(x-\frac{\pi}{3}\right)^2}{2!} - \frac{1}{2}\frac{\left(x-\frac{\pi}{3}\right)^3}{3!} + \cdots$$

$$= \boldsymbol{\frac{\sqrt{3}}{2} + \frac{1}{2}\left(x - \frac{\pi}{3}\right) - \frac{\sqrt{3}}{4}\left(x - \frac{\pi}{3}\right)^2 - \frac{1}{12}\left(x - \frac{\pi}{3}\right)^3 + \cdots}$$

4. $\sin 63° = \sin\left(\frac{\pi}{3} + \frac{\pi}{60}\right)$

$$\approx S_3 = \frac{\sqrt{3}}{2} + \frac{1}{2}\left(\frac{\pi}{60}\right) - \frac{\sqrt{3}}{4}\left(\frac{\pi}{60}\right)^2$$

$= \mathbf{0.8910182137}$

This series is not alternating, so the alternating series estimation theorem cannot be used.

5. $$R_2 = \frac{-\cos c\left(\frac{\pi}{60}\right)^3}{3!}$$

$$R_2 < 1\left(\frac{4}{60}\right)^3\left(\frac{1}{6}\right) = \mathbf{\frac{1}{20{,}250}}$$

6.

n	$f^{(n)}(x)$	$f^{(n)}(0)$
0	$(1-x)^{-1}$	1
1	$(1-x)^{-2}$	1
2	$2(1-x)^{-3}$	2
3	$6(1-x)^{-4}$	6
4	$24(1-x)^{-5}$	24
⋮	⋮	⋮

$$f(x) = 1 + x + \frac{2x^2}{2} + \frac{6x^3}{3!} + \frac{24x^4}{4!} + \cdots$$

$$= 1 + x + x^2 + x^3 + x^4 + \cdots$$

$$= \boldsymbol{\sum_{n=0}^{\infty} x^n}$$

7. $$\frac{-1}{(1-x)^2} = -\frac{d}{dx}(1-x)^{-1}$$

$$= -\frac{d}{dx}(1 + x + x^2 + x^3 + x^4 + \cdots)$$

$$= -1 - 2x - 3x^2 - 4x^3 + \cdots$$

$$= \boldsymbol{\sum_{n=0}^{\infty} -(n+1)x^n}$$

8. $$-\ln(1-x) = \int \frac{1}{1-x}\,dx$$

$$-\ln(1-x) = \int (1 + x + x^2 + x^3 + x^4 + \cdots)\,dx$$

$$-\ln(1-x) = C + x + \frac{x^2}{2} + \frac{x^3}{3} + \frac{x^4}{4} + \cdots$$

$$-\ln(1-0) = C$$

$$0 = C$$

$$-\ln(1-x) = x + \frac{x^2}{2} + \frac{x^3}{3} + \frac{x^4}{4} + \cdots$$

$$= \boldsymbol{\sum_{n=1}^{\infty} \frac{x^n}{n}}$$

9. $\sin x = \sum_{n=1}^{\infty} (-1)^{n+1} \frac{x^{2n-1}}{(2n-1)!}$

$$\lim_{n\to\infty} \left| \frac{x^{2n+1}}{(2n+1)!} \cdot \frac{(2n-1)!}{x^{2n-1}} \right|$$

$$= \lim_{n\to\infty} \left| \frac{x^2}{(2n+1)(2n)} \right| = 0$$

This series converges for all x, and the interval of convergence is **$(-\infty, \infty)$**.

10. $\lim_{n\to\infty} \left| \sqrt[n]{\frac{x^n}{3^n}} \right| = \frac{|x|}{3}$

This series converges when

$$\frac{|x|}{3} < 1$$

$$|x| < 3$$

If $|x| = 3$ the series diverges. The interval of convergence is **$(-3, 3)$**.

11. $(1 + x)^{1/5} = 1 + \frac{1}{5}x + \frac{1}{5}\left(-\frac{4}{5}\right)\frac{x^2}{2}$

$$+ \frac{1}{5}\left(-\frac{4}{5}\right)\left(-\frac{9}{5}\right)\frac{x^3}{3!}$$

$$+ \frac{1}{5}\left(-\frac{4}{5}\right)\left(-\frac{9}{5}\right)\left(-\frac{14}{5}\right)\frac{x^4}{4!} + \cdots$$

$$(1 + x)^{1/5} = 1 + \frac{1}{5}x - \frac{2}{25}x^2 + \frac{6}{125}x^3 - \frac{21}{625}x^4 + \cdots$$

$$\sqrt[5]{1.325} = (1 + 0.325)^{1/5}$$

$$\sqrt[5]{1.325} = 1 + \frac{1}{5}(0.325) - \frac{2}{25}(0.325)^2 + \frac{6}{125}(0.325)^3 - \frac{21}{625}(0.325)^4 + \cdots$$

Without the first term, this is an alternating series. Since $a_5 = -\frac{21}{625}(0.325)^4 = -0.0003748631$, the first 4 terms can be added to give an error less than 0.001.

$\sqrt[5]{1.325} \approx$ **1.05819775**

12. $\sum_{n=1}^{\infty} \left| (-1)^n \frac{2^n}{n!} \right| = \sum_{n=1}^{\infty} \frac{2^n}{n!}$

$$\lim_{n\to\infty} \frac{2^{n+1}}{(n+1)!} \cdot \frac{n!}{2^n} = \lim_{n\to\infty} \frac{2}{n+1} = 0$$

This alternating series **converges absolutely** by the **ratio test.**

13. $\cos^2 n \le 1$ for all n so $\frac{\cos^2 n}{n^2} \le \frac{1}{n^2}$ for all n.

This series **converges** by **comparison with $\sum_{n=1}^{\infty} \frac{1}{n^2}$, a convergent p-series.**

14. $\lim_{n\to\infty} \frac{2^n + 3}{n^2 + 1} = \infty$

$\sum_{n=1}^{\infty} \frac{2^n + 3}{n^2 + 1}$ **diverges** by the **divergence theorem.**

15. $\lim_{n\to\infty} \sqrt[n]{\frac{2^n}{n^n}} = \lim_{n\to\infty} \frac{2}{n} = 0$

$\sum_{n=1}^{\infty} \frac{2^n}{n^n}$ **converges** by the **root test.**

16. $\int_0^4 \frac{1}{x^2 - 4}\,dx$

$$= \int_0^2 \frac{1}{x^2 - 4}\,dx + \int_2^4 \frac{1}{x^2 - 4}\,dx$$

$$\int_0^2 \frac{1}{x^2 - 4}\,dx = \lim_{b\to 2} \int_0^b \left(\frac{-\frac{1}{4}}{x + 2} + \frac{\frac{1}{4}}{x - 2} \right) dx$$

$$= \lim_{b\to 2} \left[-\frac{1}{4}\ln|x + 2| + \frac{1}{4}\ln|x - 2| \right]_0^b$$

$$= -\frac{1}{4}\ln 4 - \infty = -\infty$$

Therefore the entire integral **diverges.**

17. $u = x \quad du = dx \quad v = -e^{-x} \quad dv = e^{-x}\,dx$

$$\int_0^{\infty} xe^{-x}\,dx = \lim_{b\to\infty} \left[-xe^{-x} + \int e^{-x}\,dx \right]_0^b$$

$$= \lim_{b\to\infty} [-xe^{-x} - e^{-x}]_0^b$$

$$= \lim_{b\to\infty} [-be^{-b} - e^{-b} - (0 - 1)]$$

$$= \lim_{b\to\infty} \left(\frac{-b}{e^b} \right) + 1$$

$$= \lim_{b\to\infty} \left(\frac{-1}{e^b} \right) + 1 = \mathbf{1}$$

18. The statement is the epsilon-delta definition of the limit, which is correctly expressed by choice **E.**

19.

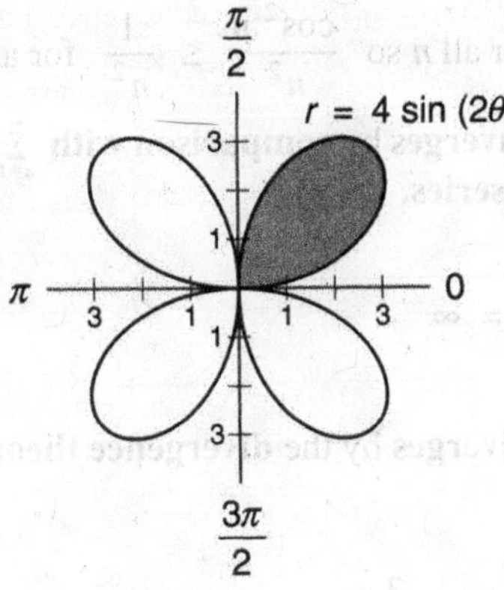

$$A = \int_0^{\pi/2} \frac{1}{2}[4 \sin (2\theta)]^2 \, d\theta$$

$$= 8 \int_0^{\pi/2} \sin^2 (2\theta) \, d\theta$$

$$= 8 \int_0^{\pi/2} \left[\frac{1}{2} - \frac{1}{2} \cos (4\theta)\right] d\theta$$

$$= 8\left[\frac{1}{2}\theta - \frac{1}{8} \sin (4\theta)\right]_0^{\pi/2}$$

$$= 8\left[\frac{\pi}{4} - (0)\right] = \mathbf{2\pi \text{ units}^2}$$

20. $f(x, y) = x^3y^2$; $\Delta x = \dfrac{5 - 2}{5} = \dfrac{3}{5} = 0.6$

i	x_i	y_i
0	2	1
1	2.6	5.8
2	3.2	360.553984
3	3.8	2556248.341
4	4.4	$2.151335444 \times 10^{14}$
5	5	$2.36551412 \times 10^{30}$

$y(5) \approx \mathbf{2.36551412 \times 10^{30}}$

21. $$T = \frac{2}{8}\left[\sin (0) + 2 \sin \left(\frac{1}{4}\right) + 2 \sin (1) + 2 \sin \left(\frac{9}{4}\right) + \sin (4)\right]$$

$$\approx \mathbf{0.7443}$$

PROBLEM SET 147

1. $f(x) = e^x$

$$= 1 + x + \frac{x^2}{2!} + \frac{x^3}{3!} + \frac{x^4}{4!} + \cdots + R_n$$

$$R_n = \frac{f^{(n+1)}(c)(x - a)^{n+1}}{(n + 1)!}$$

$R_n < 5 \times 10^{-9}$ for accuracy to eight decimal places.

To estimate the remainder for e, let $x = 1$, $a = 0$, and $f^{(n+1)}(c) = e^c < 3$ near $c = 1$.

$$R_n < \frac{3(1)}{(n + 1)!} < 5 \times 10^{-9}$$

$$\frac{(n + 1)!}{3} > 0.2 \times 10^9$$

$$(n + 1)! > 6 \times 10^8$$

With $12! = 479{,}001{,}600$ and $13! = 6{,}227{,}020{,}800$, $n = 12$ satisfies the inequality. This means that S_{12} will be accurate to eight decimal places.

$$e \approx 1 + 1 + \frac{1}{2!} + \frac{1}{3!} + \cdots + \frac{1}{11!}$$

$$\approx \mathbf{2.718281826}$$

2. $$\ln (1 + x) = \int \frac{1}{1 + x} \, dx$$

$$= \int (1 - x + x^2 - x^3 + x^4 - \ldots) \, dx$$

$$= C + x - \frac{1}{2}x^2 + \frac{1}{3}x^3 - \frac{1}{4}x^4 + \cdots$$

$$\ln (1 + 0) = C$$

$$0 = C$$

$$\ln (1 + x) = \mathbf{x - \frac{x^2}{2} + \frac{x^3}{3} - \frac{x^4}{4} + \cdots}$$

$$\ln 1.5 = 0.5 - \frac{0.5^2}{2} + \frac{0.5^3}{3} - \frac{0.5^4}{4} + \cdots$$

This is an alternating series, so for the desired accuracy of four decimal places

$$\frac{0.5^n}{n} < 5 \times 10^{-5}$$

$$n = 11$$

S_{10} will produce the desired accuracy.

$$\ln 1.5 \approx S_{10}$$

$$\approx 0.5 - \frac{0.5^2}{2} + \frac{0.5^3}{3} - \frac{0.5^4}{4} + \cdots + \frac{0.5^{10}}{10}$$

$$\approx \mathbf{0.4055}$$

3.

n	$f^{(n)}(x)$	$f^{(n)}\left(\frac{\pi}{6}\right)$
0	$\cos x$	$\frac{\sqrt{3}}{2}$
1	$-\sin x$	$-\frac{1}{2}$
2	$-\cos x$	$-\frac{\sqrt{3}}{2}$
3	$\sin x$	$\frac{1}{2}$
⋮	⋮	⋮

$$\cos x = \frac{\sqrt{3}}{2} - \frac{1}{2}\left(x - \frac{\pi}{6}\right) - \frac{\sqrt{3}}{2}\left(x - \frac{\pi}{6}\right)^2\left(\frac{1}{2!}\right) + \frac{1}{2}\left(x - \frac{\pi}{6}\right)^3\left(\frac{1}{3!}\right) + \cdots$$

$$= \frac{\sqrt{3}}{2} - \frac{1}{2}\left(x - \frac{\pi}{6}\right) - \frac{\sqrt{3}}{4}\left(x - \frac{\pi}{6}\right)^2 + \frac{1}{12}\left(x - \frac{\pi}{6}\right)^3 + \cdots$$

4. $\sqrt{1 + x} = (1 + x)^{1/2}$

$$= 1 + \frac{1}{2}x + \frac{1}{2}\left(-\frac{1}{2}\right)\frac{x^2}{2} + \frac{1}{2}\left(-\frac{1}{2}\right)\left(-\frac{3}{2}\right)\frac{x^3}{3!} + \frac{1}{2}\left(-\frac{1}{2}\right)\left(-\frac{3}{2}\right)\left(-\frac{5}{2}\right)\frac{x^4}{4!} + \cdots$$

$$= 1 + \frac{1}{2}x - \frac{1}{8}x^2 + \frac{1}{16}x^3 - \frac{5}{128}x^4 + \cdots$$

5. $\frac{1}{\sqrt{1 + x}} = 2\frac{d}{dx}\sqrt{1 + x}$

$$= 2\frac{d}{dx}\left(1 + \frac{1}{2}x - \frac{1}{8}x^2 + \frac{1}{16}x^3 - \frac{5}{128}x^4 + \cdots\right)$$

$$= 1 - \frac{1}{2}x + \frac{3}{8}x^2 - \frac{5}{16}x^3 + \cdots$$

6. $\frac{(1 + x)^{3/2}}{3} = \frac{1}{2}\int (1 + x)^{1/2}\,dx$

$$= \frac{1}{2}\int\left(1 + \frac{1}{2}x + \frac{1}{8}x^2 + \frac{1}{16}x^3 + \cdots\right)dx$$

$$= \frac{1}{2}\left(C + x + \frac{1}{4}x^2 + \frac{1}{24}x^3 + \frac{1}{64}x^4 + \cdots\right)$$

$$\frac{(1 + 0)^{3/2}}{3} = \frac{1}{2}(C)$$

$$C = \frac{2}{3}$$

$$\frac{(1 + x)^{3/2}}{3} = \frac{1}{2}\left(\frac{2}{3} + x + \frac{1}{4}x^2 + \frac{1}{24}x^3 + \frac{1}{64}x^4 + \cdots\right)$$

$$= \frac{1}{3} + \frac{1}{2}x + \frac{1}{8}x^2 + \frac{1}{48}x^3 + \frac{1}{128}x^4 + \cdots$$

7. $\sin x = x - \frac{x^3}{3!} + \frac{x^5}{5!} - \frac{x^7}{7!} + \cdots$

$$\sin(x^2) = x^2 - \frac{x^6}{3!} + \frac{x^{10}}{5!} - \frac{x^{14}}{7!} + \cdots$$

$$\sin(x^2) = \sum_{n=1}^{\infty} (-1)^{n+1}\frac{x^{4n-2}}{(2n - 1)!}$$

8. $e^x = 1 + x + \frac{x^2}{2!} + \frac{x^3}{3!} + \frac{x^4}{4!} + \cdots$

$$e^{x^3} = 1 + x^3 + \frac{x^6}{2!} + \frac{x^9}{3!} + \frac{x^{12}}{4!} + \cdots$$

$$e^{x^3} = \sum_{n=0}^{\infty}\frac{x^{3n}}{n!}$$

9. $\lim_{n\to\infty}\left|\frac{(n + 1)!\,x^{n+1}}{n!\,x^n}\right| = \lim_{n\to\infty}|(n + 1)x|$

$$= \infty|x|$$

The interval of convergence for $\sum_{n=0}^{\infty} n!x^n$ consists only of the point $x = 0$.

10. $\lim_{n\to\infty}\left|\frac{(3x)^{n+1}}{(n + 1)!}\cdot\frac{n!}{(3x)^n}\right| = \lim_{n\to\infty}\frac{|3x|}{n + 1} = 0$

By the ratio test, $\sum_{n=0}^{\infty}\frac{(3x)^n}{n!}$ converges for all x. The interval of convergence is $(-\infty, \infty)$.

11.

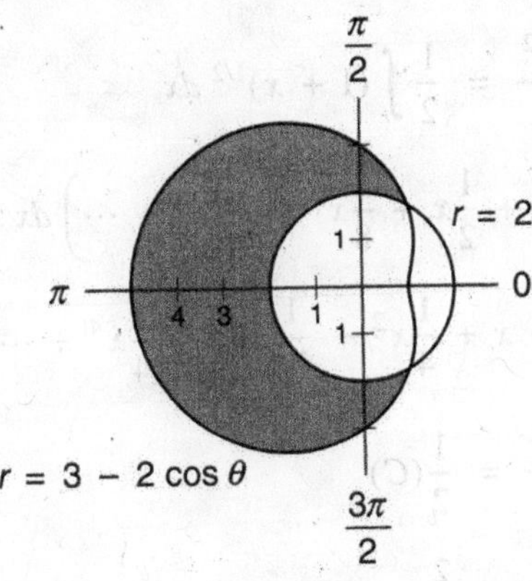

$$2 = 3 - 2\cos\theta$$
$$2\cos\theta = 1$$
$$\cos\theta = \frac{1}{2}$$
$$\theta = \frac{\pi}{3}, \frac{5\pi}{3}$$

$$A = 2\int_{\pi/3}^{\pi} \frac{1}{2}[(3 - 2\cos\theta)^2 - 2^2]\,d\theta$$
$$= \int_{\pi/3}^{\pi} (9 - 12\cos\theta + 4\cos^2\theta - 4)\,d\theta$$
$$= \int_{\pi/3}^{\pi} [5 - 12\cos\theta + 2 + 2\cos(2\theta)]\,d\theta$$
$$= [7\theta - 12\sin\theta + \sin(2\theta)]_{\pi/3}^{\pi}$$
$$= 7\pi - 0 + 0 - \left(\frac{7\pi}{3} - 6\sqrt{3} + \frac{\sqrt{3}}{2}\right)$$
$$= \left(\mathbf{\frac{14\pi}{3} + \frac{11}{2}\sqrt{3}}\right)\textbf{units}^2$$

12. $\vec{p} = (\sin t)\hat{i} + (\cos t)\hat{j} = -\hat{j}$

$\vec{v} = (\cos t)\hat{i} - (\sin t)\hat{j} = -\hat{i}$

$\vec{a} = (-\sin t)\hat{i} - (\cos t)\hat{j} = \hat{j}$

$|\vec{v}| = \mathbf{1}$

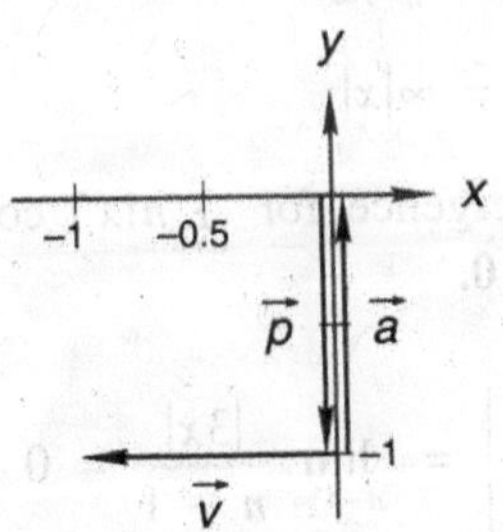

13. $f'(x) = \dfrac{d}{dx}\displaystyle\int_{3x^2}^{\cos x} \sqrt{1 + t^3}\,dt$

$$= \mathbf{\sqrt{1 + \cos^3 x}\,(-\sin x) - \sqrt{1 + 27x^6}\,(6x)}$$

14. $x = 2\tan\theta \qquad dx = 2\sec^2\theta\,d\theta$

$\sqrt{4 + x^2} = 2\sec\theta \qquad x^3 = 8\tan^3\theta$

$$\int \frac{x^3}{\sqrt{4 + x^2}}\,dx$$
$$= \int \frac{8\tan^3\theta\, 2\sec^2\theta\,d\theta}{2\sec\theta}$$
$$= 8\int \tan^3\theta\sec\theta\,d\theta$$
$$= 8\int (\sec^2\theta - 1)\tan\theta\sec\theta\,d\theta$$
$$= 8\int [\sec^2\theta(\sec\theta\tan\theta) - \sec\theta\tan\theta]\,d\theta$$
$$= 8\left(\frac{1}{3}\sec^3\theta - \sec\theta\right) + C$$
$$= \frac{8}{3}\left(\frac{\sqrt{4 + x^2}}{2}\right)^3 - \frac{8\sqrt{4 + x^2}}{2} + C$$
$$= \frac{1}{3}(4 + x^2)^{3/2} - 4\sqrt{4 + x^2} + C$$
$$= \frac{1}{3}(\sqrt{4 + x^2})(4 + x^2 - 12) + C$$
$$= \mathbf{\frac{1}{3}(\sqrt{4 + x^2})(x^2 - 8) + C}$$

15. $\displaystyle\int_0^{\pi} \sec x\,dx = \int_0^{\pi/2} \sec x\,dx + \int_{\pi/2}^{\pi} \sec x\,dx$

$$\int_0^{\pi/2} \sec x\,dx = \lim_{b \to (\pi/2)^-} \ln|\sec x + \tan x|\Big|_0^b$$
$$= \ln|\infty + \infty| - \ln|1 + 0| = \infty$$

Therefore the entire integral **diverges.**

16. $x^3 - 1 = -x^2 + 4$

$0 = x^3 + x^2 - 5$

With $f(x) = x^3 + x^2 - 5$, $f(1) = -3$ and $f(2) = 7$, so the zero lies between $x = 1$ and $x = 2$. Apply Newton's method with $x_1 = 1.5$, `Y1=X³+X²-5`, and `Y2=nDeriv(Y1,X,X)`.

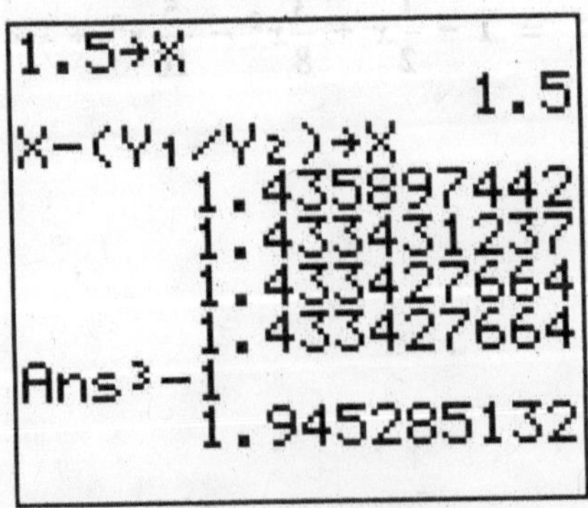

```
1.5→X
                1.5
X-(Y1/Y2)→X
        1.435897442
        1.433431237
        1.433427664
        1.433427664
Ans³-1
        1.945285132
```

(1.433427664, 1.945285132)

17. $T = \frac{2}{8}[1 + 2e^{1/4} + 2e + 2e^{9/4} + e^4]$

$\approx$ **20.6446**

18. Average value $= \frac{1}{2}\int_0^2 e^{x^2}\,dx$

$\approx$ **10.3223**

19. $\sum_{n=1}^{\infty} (-1)^{n+1}\left(\frac{2^n + 10}{5^n}\right)$

$= \sum_{n=1}^{\infty} (-1)^{n+1}\left(\frac{2}{5}\right)^n + \sum_{n=1}^{\infty} (-1)^{n+1}\left(\frac{10}{5^n}\right)$

This is the sum of two geometric series. The first has $a = \frac{2}{5}$ and $r = -\frac{2}{5}$. The second has $a = 2$ and $r = -\frac{1}{5}$.

$$S = \frac{\frac{2}{5}}{1 + \frac{2}{5}} + \frac{2}{1 + \frac{1}{5}} = \frac{2}{7} + \frac{5}{3} = \frac{41}{21}$$

The series **converges to $\frac{41}{21}$**.

20.

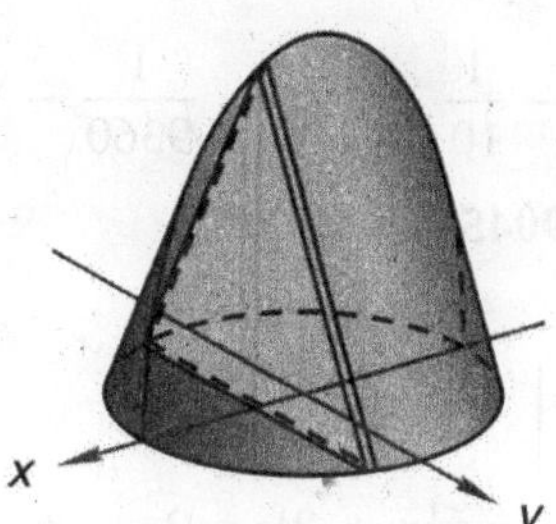

30°
$\sqrt{3}y$
y
60°
2y

$$A(x) = \frac{1}{2}(2y)(\sqrt{3}y) = \sqrt{3}y^2 = \sqrt{3}(4 - x^2)$$

$$V = 2\int_0^2 A(x)\,dx$$

$$= 2\int_0^2 \sqrt{3}(4 - x^2)\,dx$$

$$= 2\sqrt{3}\left[4x - \frac{1}{3}x^3\right]_0^2$$

$$= 2\sqrt{3}\left(8 - \frac{8}{3}\right) = \mathbf{\frac{32}{3}\sqrt{3}\ units^3}$$

21.

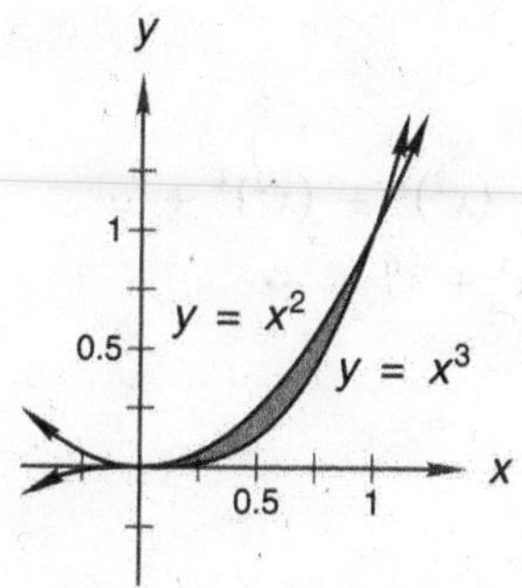

$$A = \int_0^1 (x^2 - x^3)\,dx$$

$$= \left[\frac{1}{3}x^3 - \frac{1}{4}x^4\right]_0^1$$

$$= \frac{1}{3} - \frac{1}{4} = \mathbf{\frac{1}{12}\ unit^2}$$

PROBLEM SET 148

1.
$$x = v_0 t\cos\theta$$
$$320 = 120t\cos\theta$$
$$t = \frac{8}{3\cos\theta}$$
$$y = -16t^2 + v_0 t\sin\theta$$
$$-5.5 = -16\left(\frac{8}{3\cos\theta}\right)^2 + 120\left(\frac{8}{3\cos\theta}\right)\sin\theta$$
$$0 = \frac{1024}{9\cos^2\theta} - \frac{320\sin\theta}{\cos\theta} - 5.5$$
$$0 = \frac{1024}{9}\sec^2\theta - 320\tan\theta - 5.5$$
$$0 = \frac{1024}{9}(\tan^2\theta + 1) - 320\tan\theta - 5.5$$
$$0 = \frac{1024}{9}\tan^2\theta - 320\tan\theta + \frac{1949}{18}$$
$$\tan\theta \approx 2.4191, 0.3934$$
$$\theta \approx 1.1788, 0.3748$$
$$\theta \approx 67.5403°, 21.4745°$$

To reduce the flight time, Aaron should choose the angle of **21.4745°**.

2. $(1 + x)^{-1} = 1 - x + x^2 - x^3 + x^4 + \cdots$

$f(x) = (1 - x)^{-1}$

$= 1 - (-x) + (-x)^2 - (-x)^3 + (-x)^4 + \cdots$

$= 1 + x + x^2 + x^3 + x^4 + \cdots$

$= \sum_{n=0}^{\infty} x^n$

3. $g(x) = \dfrac{1}{1 - x^2}$

$= 1 + (x^2) + (x^2)^2 + (x^2)^3 + \cdots$

$= 1 + x^2 + x^4 + x^6 + \cdots$

$= \displaystyle\sum_{n=0}^{\infty} \mathbf{x^{2n}}$

4. $h(x) = \dfrac{2x}{(1 - x^2)^2}$

$= \dfrac{d}{dx}\left(\dfrac{1}{1 - x^2}\right)$

$= \dfrac{d}{dx}(1 + x^2 + x^4 + x^6 + x^8 + \cdots)$

$= 2x + 4x^3 + 6x^5 + 8x^7 + \cdots$

$= \displaystyle\sum_{n=0}^{\infty} \mathbf{2nx^{2n-1}}$

5. $(1 + x)^{1/2}$

$= 1 + \dfrac{1}{2}x + \dfrac{1}{2}\left(-\dfrac{1}{2}\right)\dfrac{x^2}{2!} + \dfrac{1}{2}\left(-\dfrac{1}{2}\right)\left(-\dfrac{3}{2}\right)\dfrac{x^3}{3!}$

$+ \dfrac{1}{2}\left(-\dfrac{1}{2}\right)\left(-\dfrac{3}{2}\right)\left(-\dfrac{5}{2}\right)\dfrac{x^4}{4!} + \cdots$

$= 1 + \dfrac{1}{2}x - \dfrac{1}{8}x^2 + \dfrac{1}{16}x^3 - \dfrac{5}{128}x^4 + \cdots$

$(1 - x^2)^{1/2}$

$= 1 - \dfrac{1}{2}x^2 - \dfrac{1}{8}x^4 - \dfrac{1}{16}x^6 - \dfrac{5}{128}x^8 + \cdots$

$= \mathbf{1 - \displaystyle\sum_{n=1}^{\infty} \dfrac{x^{2n}}{2^n}}$

6. $\dfrac{x}{\sqrt{1 - x^2}} = -\dfrac{d}{dx}(1 - x^2)^{1/2}$

$= -\dfrac{d}{dx}\left(1 - \dfrac{1}{2}x^2 - \dfrac{1}{8}x^4 - \dfrac{1}{16}x^6 - \dfrac{5}{128}x^8 - \cdots\right)$

$= x + \dfrac{1}{2}x^3 + \dfrac{3}{8}x^5 + \dfrac{5}{16}x^7 + \cdots$

$= \displaystyle\sum_{n=0}^{\infty} \mathbf{\dfrac{|2n - 1|}{2^n}x^{2n+1}}$

7. The integral equals $\frac{1}{4}$ the area of a circle of radius 1.

$\displaystyle\int_0^1 \sqrt{1 - x^2}\, dx = \dfrac{1}{4}\pi(1)^2 = \mathbf{\dfrac{\pi}{4}}$

8. $e^x = 1 + x + \dfrac{x^2}{2!} + \dfrac{x^3}{3!} + \dfrac{x^4}{4!} + \cdots$

$e^{-x^2} = 1 - x^2 + \dfrac{x^4}{2!} - \dfrac{x^6}{3!} + \dfrac{x^8}{4!} + \cdots$

$\displaystyle\int_0^{0.5} e^{-x^2}\, dx = \left[x - \dfrac{1}{3}x^3 + \dfrac{1}{10}x^5 - \dfrac{1}{42}x^7 + \dfrac{1}{216}x^9 + \cdots\right]_0^{0.5}$

$\approx 0.5 - \dfrac{0.5^3}{3} + \dfrac{0.5^5}{10} - \dfrac{0.5^7}{42} + \dfrac{0.5^9}{216} - (0)$

$\approx \mathbf{0.4613}$

9. $\cos x = 1 - \dfrac{x^2}{2!} + \dfrac{x^4}{4!} - \dfrac{x^6}{6!} + \cdots$

$\cos x^2 = 1 - \dfrac{x^4}{2!} + \dfrac{x^8}{4!} - \dfrac{x^{12}}{6!} + \cdots$

$\displaystyle\int_0^1 \cos x^2\, dx = \left[x - \dfrac{1}{10}x^5 + \dfrac{1}{216}x^9 - \dfrac{1}{9360}x^{13} + \cdots\right]_0^1$

$\approx 1 - \dfrac{1}{10} + \dfrac{1}{216} - \dfrac{1}{9360} - (0)$

$\approx \mathbf{0.9045}$

10. $\displaystyle\lim_{n\to\infty}\left|\sqrt[n]{\dfrac{n^2(x + 2)^n}{2^n}}\right| = \dfrac{|x + 2|}{2} < 1$

$|x + 2| < 2$

$-4 < x < 0$

The interval of convergence is **(–4, 0).**

11. $\displaystyle\sum_{n=1}^{\infty}\left|(-1)^{n+1}\dfrac{3^n}{n!}\right| = \sum_{n=1}^{\infty}\dfrac{3^n}{n!}$

$\displaystyle\lim_{n\to\infty}\dfrac{3^{n+1}}{(n + 1)!}\cdot\dfrac{n!}{3^n} = \lim_{n\to\infty}\dfrac{3}{n + 1} = 0$

This alternating series **converges absolutely** by the **ratio test.**

12. $(\sin n + 1) \le 2$ for all n

$\dfrac{\sin n + 1}{n^2} \le \dfrac{2}{n^2}$ for all n.

$\displaystyle\sum_{n=1}^{\infty}\dfrac{\sin n + 1}{n^2}$ **converges by comparison with** $\displaystyle\sum_{n=1}^{\infty}\dfrac{2}{n^2}$**, a multiple of a convergent *p*-series.**

13. $\lim_{n\to\infty} \dfrac{\frac{\ln n}{n^3}}{\frac{1}{n^{5/2}}} = \lim_{n\to\infty} \dfrac{\ln n}{n^{1/2}} = \lim_{n\to\infty} \dfrac{\frac{1}{n}}{\frac{1}{2n^{1/2}}}$

$= \lim_{n\to\infty} \dfrac{2}{n^{1/2}} = 0$

$\sum_{n=1}^{\infty} \frac{\ln n}{n^3}$ **converges** by the **limit comparison test** with a convergent p-series.

14. $\lim_{n\to\infty} \sqrt[n]{\dfrac{n^n}{3^n}} = \lim_{n\to\infty} \dfrac{n}{3} = \infty$

$\sum_{n=1}^{\infty} \dfrac{n^n}{3^n}$ **diverges** by the **root test.**

15. $x = \frac{1}{3}(2t + 3)^{3/2}$

$\dfrac{dx}{dt} = (2t + 3)^{1/2}$

$\left(\dfrac{dx}{dt}\right)^2 = 2t + 3$

$y = \frac{1}{2}t^2 + t$

$\dfrac{dy}{dt} = t + 1$

$\left(\dfrac{dy}{dt}\right)^2 = t^2 + 2t + 1$

$L_0^3 = \int_0^3 \sqrt{2t + 3 + t^2 + 2t + 1}\, dt$

$= \int_0^3 \sqrt{t^2 + 4t + 4}\, dt$

$= \int_0^3 \sqrt{(t + 2)^2}\, dt$

$= \int_0^3 (t + 2)\, dt$

$= \left[\frac{1}{2}t^2 + 2t\right]_0^3 = \frac{9}{2} + 6 = \mathbf{\frac{21}{2}}$ **units**

16. $|3\hat{i} - 6\hat{j}| = \sqrt{9 + 36} = \sqrt{45} = 3\sqrt{5}$

The unit vector with identical direction is $\frac{1}{3\sqrt{5}}(3\hat{i} - 6\hat{j}) = \frac{1}{\sqrt{5}}\hat{i} - \frac{2}{\sqrt{5}}\hat{j}$.

A vector of magnitude 7 is

$7\left(\frac{1}{\sqrt{5}}\hat{i} - \frac{2}{\sqrt{5}}\hat{j}\right) = \mathbf{\frac{7\sqrt{5}}{5}\hat{i} - \frac{14\sqrt{5}}{5}\hat{j}}$

17. `Y1=sin(X)+cos(X)-e^(X)+3X²`, and `Y2=nDeriv(Y1,X,X)` with $x_1 = 3.5$, Newton's method produces

```
3.5→X
                3.5
X-(Y1/Y2)→X
        3.684810955
        3.658408388
        3.657758419
        3.657758032
        3.657758032
```

3.657758032

18.

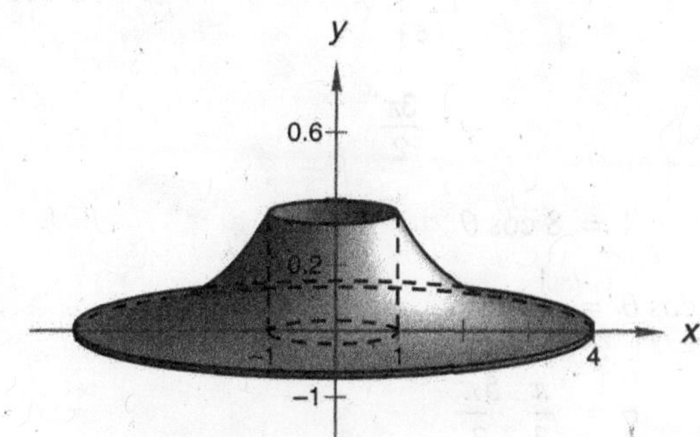

$u = x \quad du = dx \quad v = -e^{-x} \quad dv = e^{-x}\, dx$

$V = 2\pi \int_1^4 xe^{-x}\, dx$

$= 2\pi\left[-xe^{-x} + \int e^{-x}\, dx\right]_1^4$

$= 2\pi[-xe^{-x} - e^{-x}]_1^4 = 2\pi[-e^{-x}(x + 1)]_1^4$

$= \mathbf{2\pi(-5e^{-4} + 2e^{-1})}$ **units**^{3}

19.

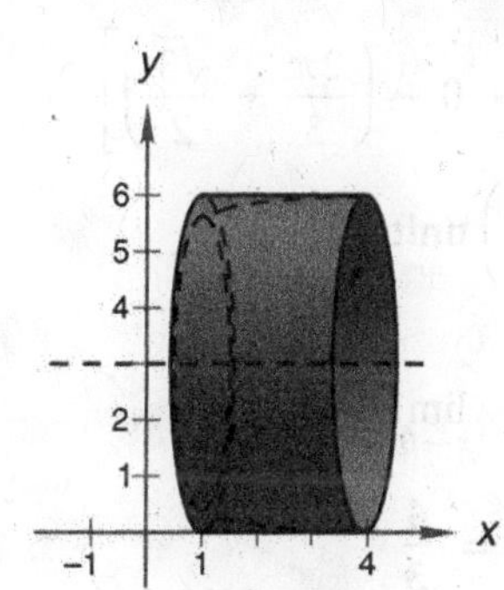

$V = \pi \int_1^4 [(3)^2 - (3 - e^{-x})^2]\, dx$

$= \pi \int_1^4 (6e^{-x} - e^{-2x})\, dx$

$= \pi\left[-6e^{-x} + \frac{1}{2}e^{-2x}\right]_1^4$

$= \pi\left[-6e^{-4} + \frac{1}{2}e^{-8} - \left(-6e^{-1} + \frac{1}{2}e^{-2}\right)\right]$

$= \pi\left(\mathbf{6e^{-1} - \frac{1}{2}e^{-2} - 6e^{-4} + \frac{1}{2}e^{-8}}\right)$ **units**^{3}

20. $x^2 + y^2 = 16$ converts to $r = 4$

$(x-4)^2 + y^2 = 16$ converts to $r = 8\cos\theta$

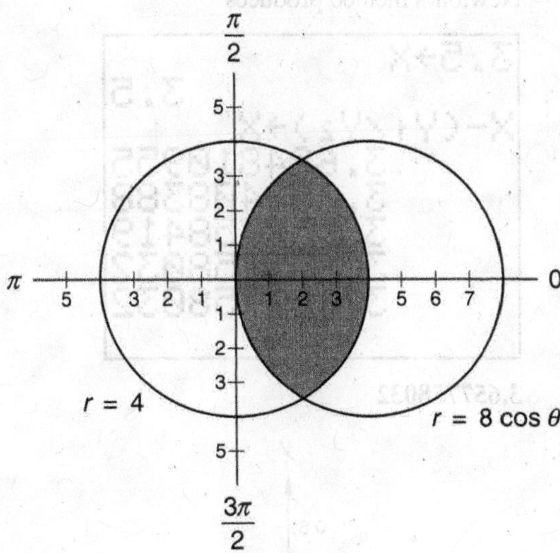

$$4 = 8\cos\theta$$

$$\cos\theta = \frac{1}{2}$$

$$\theta = \frac{\pi}{3}, \frac{5\pi}{3}$$

$$A = 2\left[\int_0^{\pi/3} \frac{1}{2}4^2\,d\theta + \int_{\pi/3}^{\pi/2} \frac{1}{2}(8\cos\theta)^2\,d\theta\right]$$

$$= \int_0^{\pi/3} 16\,d\theta + \int_{\pi/3}^{\pi/2} 64\cos^2\theta\,d\theta$$

$$= \int_0^{\pi/3} 16\,d\theta + 16\int_{\pi/3}^{\pi/2} [2 + 2\cos(2\theta)]\,d\theta$$

$$= [16\theta]_0^{\pi/3} + 16[2\theta + \sin(2\theta)]_{\pi/3}^{\pi/2}$$

$$= \frac{16}{3}\pi + 16\left[\pi + 0 - \left(\frac{2\pi}{3} + \frac{\sqrt{3}}{2}\right)\right]$$

$$= \left(\frac{32}{3}\pi - 8\sqrt{3}\right) \textbf{ units}^2$$

21. $\lim\limits_{x\to 0} [4x\csc(3x)] = \lim\limits_{x\to 0} \dfrac{4x}{\sin(3x)}$

$$= \frac{4}{3}\lim_{3x\to 0} \frac{3x}{\sin(3x)} = \frac{4}{3}$$

22. $\displaystyle\int\left(\frac{5}{1+x^2} - 3^x + \frac{1}{\sqrt{x-1}}\right)dx$

$$= 5\arctan x - \frac{3^x}{\ln 3} + 2\sqrt{x-1} + C$$